ISBN 978-1-5277-7738-5
PIBN 10892613

1 MONTH OF
FREE
READING

at

www.ForgottenBooks.com

By purchasing this book you are eligible for one month membership to ForgottenBooks.com, giving you unlimited access to our entire collection of over 700,000 titles via our web site and mobile apps.

To claim your free month visit:

www.forgottenbooks.com/free892613

English
Français
Deutsche
Italiano
Español
Português

www.forgottenbooks.com

Mythology Photography **Fiction**
Fishing Christianity **Art** Cooking
Essays Buddhism Freemasonry
Medicine **Biology** Music **Ancient
Egypt** Evolution Carpentry Physics
Dance Geology **Mathematics** Fitness
Shakespeare **Folklore** Yoga Marketing
Confidence Immortality Biographies
Poetry **Psychology** Witchcraft
Electronics Chemistry History **Law**
Accounting **Philosophy** Anthropology
Alchemy Drama Quantum Mechanics
Atheism Sexual Health **Ancient History**
Entrepreneurship Languages Sport
Paleontology Needlework Islam
Metaphysics Investment Archaeology
Parenting Statistics Criminology
Motivational

THE

WAR OF THE REBELLION:

A COMPILATION OF THE

OFFICIAL RECORDS

OF THE

UNION AND CONFEDERATE ARMIES.

PREPARED BY

The late Lieut. Col. **ROBERT N. SCOTT**, Third U. S. Artillery.

PUBLISHED UNDER THE DIRECTION OF

The Hon. **REDFIELD PROCTOR**, Secretary of War,

BY

MAJ. GEORGE B. DAVIS, U. S. A.,
MR. LESLIE J. PERRY,
MR. JOSEPH W. KIRKLEY,

Board of Publication.

SERIES I—VOLUME XXXII—IN THREE PARTS.

PART III—CORRESPONDENCE, ETC.

WASHINGTON:
GOVERNMENT PRINTING OFFICE.
1891.

5

CORRESPONDENCE, ORDERS, AND RETURNS RELATING TO OPERATIONS IN KENTUCKY, SOUTHWEST VIRGINIA, TENNESSEE, MISSISSIPPI, ALABAMA, AND NORTH GEORGIA FROM MARCH 1, 1864, TO APRIL 30, 1864.

UNION CORRESPONDENCE ETC.

MORRISTOWN, *March* 1, 1864.

Maj. Gen. U. S. GRANT:

I pushed forward with my advance to this place yesterday. The remainder of my troops will come up to-day. The enemy is still in force in my front. Longstreet has no infantry away unless it may be Ransom's division. I have not been able to learn anything of that division. I am not yet satisfied what the object of his late movement is. It has been raining heavily for two days and the roads are nearly impassable. It will be impossible for me to do much until I get the railroad bridge across the Holston completed.

J. M. SCHOFIELD,
Major-General.

MADISONVILLE, TENN., *March* 1, 1864.

Lieut. Col. J. S. FULLERTON,
Assistant Adjutant-General, Fourth Army Corps:

I have the honor to report that some of my scouts have returned from the vicinity of the junction of the Little Tennessee and Tuckaleechee Rivers. They report a party of the enemy, about 300 strong, with three pieces of artillery, watching the gap. I have sent out an expedition to try and effect their capture. They also report that a portion of Longstreet's force passed through Greenville, S. C.

Very respectfully, your obedient servant,

E. M. McCOOK,
Colonel, Commanding.

LOUDON, *March* 1, 1864.

Major-General THOMAS:

Your dispatch of the 28th has been received by me.* My forces will be concentrated as you direct, as soon as relieved by General Schofield.

GORDON GRANGER,
Major-General.

---

* See Part II, p. 490.

CHATTANOOGA, TENN.,
March 1, 1864.

Maj. Gen. U. S. GRANT,
  Comdg. Mil. Div. of the Mississippi, Nashville, Tenn.:

GENERAL : Some time last winter you mentioned in conversation that you would send General Hovey to report to me, and I think I saw it announced afterward in the papers that he had been placed in command of the District of Indiana. My object in writing this is to propose an exchange of General R. W. Johnson for him, as from what you told me in the conversation alluded to I inferred that General Hovey would prefer duty in the field to such duty as superintending the recruiting service, &c. I think Johnson would like to be placed on such duty. I have also received a proposition from a man (who, from all I can learn of him, is reliable) to burn the bridge over the Etowah for $30,000 in Confederate money. I have but $10,000 and will be obliged if you will send me $20,000 more if you have it. I think it will be well spent if we can get that bridge destroyed.

No further movements of the enemy observed to-day. I have received additional confirmation that the reconnaissance has brought back all the troops which had left Dalton. Mrs. Dr. Gordon, of La Fayette, informs me that she saw two cars of wounded going south.

I am, general, very respectfully, your obedient servant,
GEO. H. THOMAS,
Major-General, Commanding.

, HEADQUARTERS NINTH ARMY CORPS,
Morristown, March 1, 1864.

Brig. Gen. E. FERRERO,
  Commanding First Division, Ninth Army Corps:

GENERAL : You will have your command under arms and ready to move to-morrow morning punctually at 5 o'clock. Your division will follow the command of Brigadier-General Wood.

Your train will be loaded and on the road in readiness to move at 5 o'clock to-morrow morning. The trains will move in the same order as the divisions, following the train of General Wood, under the direction of Capt. P. Hiestand, acting chief quartermaster, who will issue the necessary instructions to division quartermasters.

By order of Major-General Parke :

SAML. WRIGHT,
Assistant Adjutant-General.

BLUE SPRINGS, *March* 1, 1864.

Col. J. S. FULLERTON,
  Assistant Adjutant-General, Fourth Army Corps:

In obedience to order from department headquarters I have sent one regiment, Fourth Ohio, to Calhoun and two regiments, Eighth Kentucky and Twenty-fourth Ohio, to Chattanooga to-day. Have not determined on the veteran regiment as yet.

The casualties of the division on last reconnaissance will not exceed 60. Will send copy of report as soon as completed.

CHARLES CRUFT,
Brigadier-General, Commanding.

HEADQUARTERS DEPARTMENT OF THE CUMBERLAND,
Chattanooga, Tenn., March 1, 1864.

Major-General GRANT :

I will have 400 men at work on the railroad between here and Ringgold to-morrow. The reconnaissance toward Dalton demonstrated that the enemy was still there in force. I have since heard from different sources (all confirmatory) that Johnston had received orders to retire behind the Etowah and send re-enforcements to Selma or Mobile. One informant, Brown, reports that some of the troops had already started, but that our demonstration has brought them back. He is now in Dalton and will report to me immediately any changes Johnston makes. I have signified to General Schofield my willingness to transfer to him all the East Tennessee troops under my command if he will release the Fourth Corps and McCook's division of cavalry. I am entirely crippled for .want of cavalry. I am pushing forward the works for the defenses of the railroad between this and Nashville. When they are completed I am in hopes I can order to the front Howard's entire corps and perhaps a part of Slocum's.

Did you place General Hovey in command of the District of Kentucky ? If so, I think General Johnson would like to exchange duties with him.

GEO. H. THOMAS,
Major-General, U. S. Volunteers, Commanding.

HDQRS. THIRD DIVISION, FOURTEENTH CORPS,
Ringgold, March 1, 1864.

Maj. Gen. G. H. THOMAS :

GENERAL : I am here still with the equipment for a three days' reconnaissance, and of course unable to make such returns, &c., as I otherwise would. I like my post very much, for there are many advantages in being in front, and would like to remain here, but I must represent to you that my position is precarious, provided the enemy should choose to pass around my flanks and cut me off from General Davis. My right, for a distance of 8 miles, is watched by Colonel Harrison, who will give me timely warning, but on my left is Parker's Gap, through which I send a patrol of 10 men daily, the road being as good as the streets of Chattanooga. by which a force could pass to Graysville and thence to the Pea Vine before I would know it. I have not force enough to guard this pass. I have but twelve regiments, and have to put six on guard daily, and will put on a larger force as soon as the One hundred and first Indiana, now at Rossville, arrives. I have asked to have it sent forward, and also the Fourteenth Ohio as soon as it arrives. It is very important that both of these regiments should come up at once. Two days ago General Palmer directed me, in view of a continued occupation of this place, to retain Davis' brigade, but it had already gone back part of the way, so I referred the matter to General Davis. I learn to-day that the brigade is marching toward his camp away from here. I only mention these facts that you may understand exactly how I am situated. I do not think the enemy will attack me, but if he chooses to do so he certainly can with 8,000 or 10,000 men cut me off

from Chattanooga, because I would not be warned of his approach.
If consistent with propriety I would be pleased to know what other
points in my vicinity are occupied by our troops. I only know that
General Johnson is at Tyner's Station, General Davis at McAfee's
Church, and Colonel Harrison with a small cavalry force 8 miles on
my right. Should my left be turned I would not know where to
march in order to receive support. I may mention in the same connection that the only map I have been able to procure of this country
is the Coast Survey map, which gives none of the details of the
country.

I have made repeated application to the engineer department for
maps, but have always been told that none have been completed as
yet. I know that such maps exist, but I have not been able even
to borrow one. My topographical officer is absent with a broken
leg and I can do nothing toward preparing one. Indeed, I have not
the information requisite.

A party of officers arrived here to-day bearing a flag of truce. I
happened to know one of the party, Major Davies, of the Pay Department, and he assured me that the flag was sent out by you, but
as the officer in charge had no pass from u I reminded him that
any party of officers might pass out of the lines on the same pretext.
I felt sure that the party was what it represented itself to be and permitted it to pass. It is now absent. I was informed yesterday that
a rebel division of infantry had taken position half a mile this side
of Tunnel Hill, and last night lights were seen there and drums
heard. Humes' cavalry brigade is between here and there. A good
sup   of forage and rations is arriving, but the roads are becoming
bad rapidly.

Most respectfully, your obedient servant,

A. BAIRD,
Brigadier-General.

HEADQUARTERS DEPARTMENT OF THE CUMBERLAND,
Chattanooga, Tenn., March 1, 1864.

Brig. Gen. A. BAIRD,
Comdg. 3d Division, 14th Army Corps, Ringgold, Ga. :

GENERAL : Your communication of this date addressed to Major-
General Thomas has been received, and he has directed me to reply
to the same.

Brigadier-General Johnson was this morning ordered to send one
brigade to Graysville and observe Parker's Gap.

Colonel Harrison, with the Thirty-ninth Indiana, Twenty-eighth
Kentucky Mounted Infantry, and Second Kentucky Cavalry, is at
Pea Vine Church.

General Davis' division is at McAfee's Church, and General Johnson's division, less the brigade at Graysville, is at Tyner's Station.

Should you be attacked by the enemy in force greater than you
can successfully resist, you will burn your stores and fall back
toward Chattanooga.

The flag of truce you speak of was doubtless one sent from these
headquarters under charge of Col. J. W. Burke, Tenth Ohio Volunteer Infantry, although I do not think permission was given to any
officers to accompany it. Colonel Burke should have been able to

produce an order from these headquarters directing him to take 3 rebel prisoners of war and turn them over to the rebel authorities within their lines.

I will refer that portion of your letter relating to a map to the engineers, that they may furnish you if able.

I am, general, very respectfully, your obedient servant,
WM. D. WHIPPLE,
Assistant Adjutant-General and Chief of Staff.

HDQRS. FIRST DIVISION, FIFTEENTH ARMY CORPS,
Woodville, Ala., March 1, 1864.
Maj. R. R. TOWNES,
Assistant Adjutant-General, Huntsville:

Roddey's command, formerly at Warrenton, near Guntersville, and latterly at Gadsden, has left the latter place in a northerly direction with the intention, as was supposed by the men, of marching to Tunnel Hill, north of Dalton. The citizens on the other side of Tennessee consider the country between that river and Coosa virtually evacuated. There is nobody at Guntersville except two companies of State guards.

P. J. OSTERHAUS,
Brigadier-General, Commanding.

HEADQUARTERS SEVENTEENTH ARMY CORPS,
Judge Rick's Plantation, near Canton, Miss.,
March 1, 1864—11.45 p. m.
Maj. Gen. S. A. HURLBUT,
Commanding, &c. :

GENERAL : Copies of dispatches from Major-General Sherman received. Also letter* from Major-General Butterfield stating that Sooy Smith was in Memphis on Friday last. My advance division encamped at this place, reaching here after dark, and the remainder of the command about 2 miles farther back on the east side of a swamp. The bottom having fallen out, it became necessary to corduroy a portion of it.

Very respectfully, your obedient servant,
JAS. B. McPHERSON,
Major-General.

NASHVILLE, *March* 1, 1864.
Governor T. E. BRAMLETTE,
Frankfort, Ky.:

The memorial of the senators and representatives of the counties of Graves, Hickman, Fulton, McCracken, Ballard, Marshall, and Calloway, to have the State of Kentucky placed in one district or department in order to insure greater uniformity in orders throughout the State, so far as they relate to citizens and the elective franchise, with your indorsement thereon, is received.

---

*See Part II, p. 478.

The Department of the Tennessee was established by order of the War Department, and the limits prescribed by the great natural boundaries of the Tennessee, Ohio, and Mississippi Rivers, with special regard to the best interest of the public service.   There are no reasons stated in said memorial which should induce a change in these boundaries so as to attach that part of the State of Kentucky west of the Tennessee River to the department in which the remainder of the State is comprised.

The placing of territory belonging to different departments into one district, even were it admissible under "regulations" and "orders," would necessarily beget confusion in the commander of such district having to obey the orders of, and report to, several department commanders.   The uniformity of the exercise of the elective franchise throughout the State of Kentucky will not hereafter be interfered with by military orders while the State remains in my command.   It is a matter purely civil and with which the military authorities have nothing to do, except when called on to protect the citizens from violence in the exercise of it under the laws prescribed by the State.

Instructions in accordance herewith will be given to commanders of troops and districts in the State of Kentucky.

U. S. GRANT,
Major-General.

NASHVILLE, TENN., *March* 2, 1864—12.30 p. m.
(Received 2.30 a. m., 3d.)

Maj. Gen. H. W. HALLECK,
General-in-Chief :

News from the south shows that Sherman divided Polk's force and followed south 25 or 30 miles, then went east to Demopolis.   Eight days ago he was back at Meridian, no doubt having destroyed railroad connection with the State of Mississippi completely.

U. S. GRANT,
Major-General.

WASHINGTON, D. C.,
March 2, 1864.

Maj. Gen. U. S. GRANT,
Nashville, Tenn. :

An association for the relief of those citizens of East Tennessee who have been reduced to destitution by the events of the war has been formed in Philadelphia, and a considerable fund has been raised to procure supplies.   The association has appointed as its committee for the distribution of these supplies Messrs. Frederick Collins, Col. N. G. Taylor, and Lloyd P. Smith.   I beg to commend them to your kindness, and to request that you will render them any assistance which may be in your power.   They should have free transportation for themselves, their agents, and the articles which they desire to distribute, upon all Government railroads and chartered vessels.

C. A. DANA,
Assistant Secretary of War.

NASHVILLE, *March 2, 1864.*

Maj. Gen. J. M. SCHOFIELD,
    Knoxville :

If you can possibly dispense with cavalry order them to report by telegraph to General Thomas for orders. General Thomas is very much in want of their services.

U. S. GRANT,
Major-General.

HEADQUARTERS SECOND DIVISION, CAVALRY CORPS,
    Morristown, March 2, 1864.

Major-General STONEMAN :

A citizen who came through from Carter's Station, having left that place last Saturday, reports that the railroad trains are all loaded and crowded with troops en route for Virginia. He reports that the enemy's artillery was unshipped from the cars at Carter's Station. He saw wagon trains going on toward Virginia beyond Greeneville. He saw a force of about 2,000 infantry at Bull's Gap last Sunday. A deserter who has just arrived from Bend of Chucky reports that the enemy at that place yesterday moved from there last night, going beyond Lick Creek. He confirms the report that Martin's cavalry had started to Georgia via Paint Rock.

Very respectfully, your obedient servant,

ISRAEL GARRARD,
Colonel, Commanding Division.

HDQRS. DETACHMENT SECOND DIV., CAVALRY CORPS,
    Morristown, March 2, 1864.

General STONEMAN :

Four deserters from the enemy came in this morning. They report that Johnson's division (to which they belong) fell back 9 miles yesterday from the mouth of Lick Creek, where they were camped. They report that Martin's cavalry had marched in the direction of Newport. General Bushrod Johnson, before leaving Dandridge, told his men in a short speech that the army was not going to fall back farther than Greeneville.

Very respectfully, your obedient servant,

ISRAEL GARRARD,
Colonel, Commanding Second Division, Cavalry Corps.

Two of these deserters are lieutenants from the Seventeenth Tennessee. I send them down to your provost-marshal.

Very respectfully,

ISRAEL GARRARD.

HEADQUARTERS TWENTY-THIRD ARMY CORPS,
    Panther Springs, March 2, 1864—7.45 p. m.

General SCHOFIELD :

GENERAL: I sent you by return orderly Colonel Garrard's dispatches, all the information I possess in regard to the movements of the enemy. The troops under my command will start at once for

New Market, moving slow. A portion of the cavalry will be sent in the direction of Chucky Bend; the rest will stay here until daylight, unless driven away by the enemy. They had a skirmish with the enemy's cavalry about 2 miles from Russellville, driving them off and losing 2 men.

Respectfully, &c.,
GEORGE STONEMAN,
Major-General, Commanding.

HDQRS. SECOND BRIG., THIRD DIV., TWENTY-THIRD CORPS,
Strawberry Plains, March 2, 1864.
Brig. Gen. E. E. POTTER,
Chief of Staff, Strawberry Plains:

GENERAL: From scouting parties and citizens who have come into the lines, I learn that a force of enemy's cavalry entered Dandridge yesterday morning. This force divided, part remaining in Dandridge and part advancing 8 miles this side. The object seems to have been plunder and impressment of citizens. I have had a scouting party out 10 miles to-day, without meeting the enemy. I am inclined to the belief that the party that advanced yesterday has gone back to Dandridge, where I am told there is a considerable force of the enemy, all cavalry. We will be on our guard here, and unless the force is very large, do not apprehend any danger.

Very respectfully, your obedient servant,
DANIEL CAMERON,
Colonel, Commanding.

NEW MARKET, *March 2, 1864—9.45 a. m.*
Major-General GRANGER,
Loudon:

Send one brigade of Colonel McCook's cavalry division to report to Major-General Thomas. Apply to General Thomas by telegraph for orders for the brigade. You must guard the Hiwassee bridge if it is not otherwise guarded.

J. M. SCHOFIELD,
Major-General.

LOUDON, *March 2, 1864.*
Major-General SCHOFIELD:

Some of the cavalry scouts returning report a rebel force of 300 men and three pieces of artillery guarding the pass at the junction of the Little Tennessee and Tuckaleechee Rivers. A force has been sent to capture them. They also report that Longstreet has passed through Greenville, S. C.

G. GRANGER,
Major-General.

NASHVILLE, *March 2, 1864—11 a. m.*
Maj. Gen. G. H. THOMAS,
Commanding Department of the Cumberland:

I have just learned from what I believe to be reliable authority that Johnston has 37,000 infantry at and about Dalton. Your move.

ment no doubt had the effect to hold them there. I have directed General Allen to forward us rapidly horses, mules, and wagons. We must equip the best we can and do without what cannot be got. Reduce the transportation at all depots and railroad stations to the lowest possible standard. Substitute poor animals for their fat ones; dismount quartermaster's employés, orderlies, infantry officers, and all unauthorized persons at every station, and take their horses to mount the cavalry. There is a new strong cavalry regiment here which I will send to Dodge, but which will be left as guard for the road between here and Decatur.

U. S. GRANT.

NASHVILLE, *March* 2, 1864.

Maj. Gen. G. H. THOMAS,
        Chattanooga:

I have directed Schofield to send the cavalry you ask for, if possible. The cavalry with Smith have returned to Memphis and may be looked for in your department soon. I shall recommend the merging of the Department of the Ohio into that of the Cumberland if Schofield is not confirmed. Hovey is not assigned to the command of Kentucky.

U. S. GRANT,
Major-General.

HEADQUARTERS CAVALRY,
Leet's Farm, Ga., March 2, 1864.

General WHIPPLE,
        Chief of Staff, Dept. of the Cumberland, Chattanooga:

GENERAL: All is quiet in front. A few scouting parties in neighborhood of La Fayette, but they are very timid. The infantry did not advance from Dalton when we fell back. There are 1,200 cavalry encamped at a point 1 mile above Tunnel Hill, where the enemy had made a temporary breast-work of rails.

The infantry force is large at Dalton and below. They are building fortifications at every ridge and stream in the direction of Atlanta.

My camp is still at Tyner's Station. If we are to stay here we would like to move it down in this vicinity—to Ringgold at least. If a removal of the camp is approved, I would feel it a favor to have the order sent to my quartermaster at Tyner's Station.

T. J. HARRISON,
Colonel, Commanding.

HEADQUARTERS ELEVENTH CORPS,
March 2, 1864.

Brigadier-General WHIPPLE,
        Assistant Adjutant-General, Dept. of the Cumberland:

GENERAL: A deserter just come into our lines, who left Dalton on February 24, 1864, reports 15,000 troops there at that time. He left at 9 a. m. that day, when the fighting commenced. He states that the intention was to retreat without fighting, as everything was prepared for a retrograde movement to Kingston, all the roads leading to that place having been put in good repair, but our troops pushed on so fast, compelling them to make a stand. Three divisions, except one brigade, left Dalton before Sunday, February 21, for Meridian, Cheatham's, Stewart's, and another. All the artillery nearly has been sent south, it being rumored that they would make a stand at Resaca or Rome. He also heard that Longstreet was retreating toward Virginia. He describes the fortifications at Resaca to be on the north side of the Oostenaula River, the opposite side being entirely controlled by the north shore. Being well acquainted with the country he knows of no good position, south of Resaca, for 15 miles. He represents Rome fortified with three works—two north and one south of the Etowah River. The rebels have a foundry and machine-shop at that place, casting and preparing guns. The Connesauga and Coosawattee Rivers are fordable at several places above Resaca; the trains of the enemy crossing at these fords. The Oostenaula is not fordable, having very high banks. The Coosa River is navigable to Greensport. Three steamers now lying at Rome. Only a small steamer ever runs to Resaca on the Oostenaula. The Etowah is not navigable.

Respectfully, your obedient servant,

O. O. HOWARD,
Major-General.

CHATTANOOGA, TENN.,
March 2, 1864.

Lieut. Col. J. S. FULLERTON,
Assistant Adjutant-General:

The Second and Third Divisions, Fourth Army Corps, are still a part of the Army of the Cumberland. The reports will be furnished this department.

WM. D. WHIPPLE,
Brigadier-General, Chief of Staff.

U. S. FLAG-SHIP HARTFORD,
Off Ship Island, March 2, 1864.

Maj. Gen. N. P. BANKS:

DEAR GENERAL: I received your kind notes, for which I am much obliged.

The time has now passed when you could act to the same advantage in taking the forts at Mobile. The ram Tennessee came down the bay yesterday, and was full in sight to us off Grant's Pass, lying in the middle of the bay. She appeared to me to be very slow. A gale of wind came on from the north, and I am anxious to hear how she stood it.

You will readily understand that she can be in shoal water alongside of the beach inside of the peninsula, and prevent the approach of your troops toward Fort Morgan, and that our ships even after passing the forts will not be able to get at her, at least none but the small vessels who would not be able to make any impression upon her, so that now Mobile will have to be left until the arrival of "iron-clads;" when that will be God only knows.

I only ask for two, and will go in with one. I fear we put off the attack too late, but it is a great consolation to us to know that it was neither our wish nor fault that Mobile was not taken last year or last month.

Very truly,

D. G. FARRAGUT,
Rear-Admiral.

WASHINGTON, *March* 3, 1864—3.30 p. m.

Major-General GRANT,
Nashville, Tenn.:

The Secretary of War directs that you will report in person to the War Department as early as practicable, considering the condition of your command. If necessary you will keep up telegraphic communication with your command while en route to Washington.

H. W. HALLECK,
General-in-Chief.

STRAWBERRY PLAINS, *March* 3, 1864.

Major WHERRY,
Aide-de-Camp:

The pontoon bridge cannot be laid before this evening; it had to be taken up last night to save it. General Whipple telegraphs to me March 1, Chattanooga, that General Thomas is willing that General Schofield shall retain Spears' brigade, provided General Schofield will return the other troops belonging to the Army of the Cumberland, whose services are very much needed.

EDWARD E. POTTER,
Chief of Staff.

KNOXVILLE, *March* 3, 1864.

Major-General SCHOFIELD :

Colonel Crawford has just informed me that he has reliable information that Martin's cavalry, thought to be 4,000, are encamped between Newport and Wilsonville, near Big Pigeon River. I have no fear of their coming here, but think the information may be valuable to you.

DAVIS TILLSON,
Brigadier-General of Volunteers.

CHATTANOOGA, *March* 3, 1864.

General G. GRANGER :

Send a brigade to Calhoun, and telegraph what one you send and who is in command, Further orders will be sent.

WM. D. WHIPPLE,
Brigadier-General, Chief of Staff.

NASHVILLE, *March* 4, 1864.
Brig. Gen. ROBERT ALLEN,
    Chief Quartermaster, Louisville, Ky.:
    The Tennessee is high and rising. I have telegraphed Admiral
Porter to try to run Muscle Shoals with the boats for the upper river.
                                        U. S. GRANT,
                                            Major-General.

_____

KNOXVILLE, *March* 4, 1864.
Maj. Gen. U. S. GRANT:
    I have no additional information of a positive character about
Longstreet's movements. His recent movements, if any, have been
very slow, and do not indicate an intention to abandon East Tennessee. Possibly he may have sent away some of his infantry since the
28th ; I am satisfied that he had not previous to that time. The possession of the crossing at Strawberry Plains removes to a great extent the difficulty of advancing at this season. If I had the necessary
force I could advance as soon as the railroad bridge is completed,
with a fair prospect of ending the campaign in East Tennessee in a
short time. The division you propose to send me would, no doubt,
be sufficient ; if practicable, I think it should be sent at once.
                                        J. M. SCHOFIELD,
                                            Major-General.

_____

NASHVILLE, *March* 4, 1864.
Maj. Gen. J. M. SCHOFIELD,
    Morristown, Tenn.:
    Your force being inferior to that of Longstreet, it will not be ad-
visable to push him so as to bring on an engagement. Take up all
the ground eastward, however, as fast as you can without an unequal
battle. If you should be compelled to fall back, do all the damage
you can to the railroad. Keep Thomas advised of the movements of
the enemy during my absence.
                                        U. S. GRANT,
                                            Major-General.

_____

NASHVILLE, *March* 4, 1864.
Maj. Gen. J. M. SCHOFIELD,
    Knoxville:
    For the better order and efficiency of the troops in the District of
Kentucky you will organize them into two divisions.
    Those at Louisville, and guarding the line of the Louisville and
Nashville Railroad south through the State of Kentucky, and all
west of said road, to constitute one division ; and those east of said
railroad and of Louisville to constitute the other. The former to be
commanded by Brig. Gen. Hugh Ewing, with his headquarters on
the line of said railroad, about midway between Louisville and the
southern boundary of the district ; the commanding officer of the
latter to have his headquarters with his troops.
    The senior officer of the troops garrisoning Louisville to be com-
mander of the post of Louisville, and he will be instructed to furnish
the requisite number of men to Lieut. Col. J. H. Hammond, com-

manding depot for drafted men, to guard said depot, and also to go forward with the men to their regiments.

The commanding officer of the District of Kentucky will make his headquarters at Lexington or Camp Nelson, that he may properly watch our line in that direction.

This change is necessary from the fact that officers in Kentucky heretofore have, many of them. seemed to desire to make a luxury of their position instead of rendering service to the Government.

By order of Major-General Grant :

T. S. BOWERS,
Assistant Adjutant-General.

HEADQUARTERS FIRST CAVALRY DIVISION,
Madisonville, Tenn., March 4, 1864.

Lieut. Col. J. S. FULLERTON,
Assistant Adjutant-General :

I have the honor to report that forage is becoming exceedingly scarce here, and to call the attention of the general commanding to the importance of making some arrangement for procuring forage from the railroad. I have already telegraphed to General Elliott, but as yet have received no answer.

The First Brigade moved to Calhoun at daylight this morning.

Very respectfully, your obedient servant,

EDWARD M. McCOOK,
Colonel, Commanding Division.

[First indorsement.]

HEADQUARTERS FOURTH ARMY CORPS,
Loudon, March 5, 1864.

Respectfully forwarded.

G. GRANGER,
Major-General, Commanding.

[Second indorsement.]

HEADQUARTERS DEPARTMENT OF THE OHIO,
Knoxville, Tenn., March 8, 1864.

Respectfully returned to Major-General Granger, commanding Fourth Army Corps.

The cavalry sent to Loudon to relieve Colonel McCook will have to be foraged by rail. General Granger will have the horses inspected and condemn such as are not worth feeding and have them sold, turned loose, or sent to Kingston to be foraged, as the good of the service may require.

By command of Major-General Schofield :

HENRY CURTIS, JR.,
Assistant Adjutant-General.

LOUDON, *March* 4, 1864.

Major-General THOMAS,
Chattanooga :

From information which I consider reliable, I learn that Longstreet's cavalry is making its way to join Joe Johnston via Marshall, Quallatown, and Murphy, thence to Benton. It was expected at Murphy to-night. Campbell's brigade of cavalry has reached Calhoun.

G. GRANGER,
Major-General.

CALHOUN, *March* 4, 1864—5 p. m.

Lieutenant-Colonel FULLERTON,
Assistant Adjutant-General:

SIR : I have the honor to report that I have just arrived here.
A. P. CAMPBELL,
Colonel, Commanding First Brigade, First Division Cavalry.

HDQRS. SECOND BRIG., SECOND DIV., CAVALRY CORPS,
Wallace's Cross-Roads, March 4, 1864.

Brig. Gen. E. E. POTTER,
Chief of Staff, Knoxville, Tenn.:

GENERAL : Presuming that you are not fully aware of the condition of this brigade, I ask permission to allude to a few facts.

We have been in the saddle almost without cessation for one year. You are familiar with the arduous duties of the cavalry since our arrival in East Tennessee. We have been compelled to subsist, both man and beast, on the country. The same policy which marked our advent into and progress in Tennessee still clings to us. So long as the country afforded us relief, so long as we could secure horses, forage, and commissary supplies, we were content. But the time has arrived when this can no longer be done. We have been eking out a miserable existence for some weeks anxiously awaiting relief. Our stock is unfit for service because of the scarcity of forage. On the march horses are abandoned from sheer exhaustion and men are dismounted.

True, where we now are some forage is secured, but it is at a terrible sacrifice on the part of the citizens. Before we came in here, as elsewhere, all the surplus forage had been taken. The small quantity we now secure is wrung from the people. If you could but hear, general, one-half of the lamentations of good Union men, because their all is taken from them, I feel assured your sympathy would be awakened. Could they by any possible chance secure subsistence, the case would not seem so cruel. If we were of any service here and the stock which we are feeding would rapidly improve, there would seem to be some excuse for grinding the people. To make the stock now on hand serviceable for another campaign would require months of kind care and attention. Aside from animals and forage, commissary supplies for the men are not forthcoming, even at a time when it seems there should be no excuse for their absence. My command is now without bread and meat, and although a division train arrived from Knoxville last evening with small-stores, not one pound of meat or bread was brought with it. The arms of the brigade are also in bad condition, many of them from frequent use having become worthless.

Whether the service performed by the cavalry is or is not appreciated, I know its labor has been great. The men are becoming disheartened and discouraged. Some new recruits have arrived. Being unable to mount them, they (with all others dismounted) are required to move with the command. The result is, many of them have been taken sick from exposure and fatigue. Colonel Capron writes me that he has some 250 new recruits for the Fourteenth Illinois Cavalry, and hopes to forward them to the regiment soon. He also expects to secure new arms for the regiment. Would it not be policy to send the brigade to Camp Nelson or some other point to recruit and refit for the coming campaign? And especially is it not desirable to have the Fourteenth where the new recruits can be properly fitted for service?

Very respectfully, your obedient servant,

F. M. DAVIDSON,
Major, Commanding Brigade.

NASHVILLE, *March* 4, 1864—10 a. m.

Maj. Gen. GEORGE H. THOMAS:

You will have to watch the movements of the enemy closely in front. Should Longstreet join Johnston they will likely attack your advance. At present most of Longstreet's force is up Holston valley. I will direct Schofield to keep you advised of the movements of the enemy.

U. S. GRANT,
Major-General.

NASHVILLE, *March* 4, 1864.

Maj. Gen. J. M. SCHOFIELD,
Morristown, Tenn.:

I shall leave to-morrow morning for Washington, but shall keep up communication with my headquarters here by telegraph. All information of the movements of the enemy, as well as matters affecting the command that require my action, you will telegraph here, that I may get them. Should a movement of the enemy be made in force against any part of our line, and co-operation of troops of different departments be deemed necessary, Maj. Gen. G. H. Thomas will command during such movements.

U. S. GRANT,
Major-General.

(Same to Maj. Gen. G. H. Thomas, Chattanooga; Maj. Gen. J. A. Logan, Huntsville; Maj. R. M. Sawyer, assistant adjutant-general to General Sherman, Huntsville.)

CHATTANOOGA, *March* 4, 1864—12 p. m.

Major-General GRANT,
Nashville, Tenn.:

Your two dispatches of this date are just received. The information that I get from the front to-day is that Johnston's infantry (about 30,000 strong), still remains in Dalton, and, as yet, no changes have been made in his transportation—that is, his transportation being sent to the rear before the reconnaissance from this post was made, has not returned to Dalton. Deserters say it was understood in the army that they would fall back, and that the movements had commenced already, but the troops were all ordered back, Johnston supposing we had advanced against Dalton in full force. Not having brought back his transportation makes me believe he will fall back yet, but I am nevertheless taking every precaution to get the earliest information should he advance against me. None of Longstreet's troops have joined him as yet.

GEO. H. THOMAS,
Major-General, U. S. Volunteers.

NASHVILLE, March 4, 1864.

Brig. Gen. G. M. DODGE,
    Pulaski, Tenn. :

The Tennessee is now up so that an attempt will be made to get steamers above Muscle Shoals. Should they succeed in getting up be prepared to convoy them. One steamer can be retained for your purposes, should they get above.

U. S. GRANT,
Major-General.

PRIVATE.]   NASHVILLE, TENN.,
March 4, 1864.

DEAR SHERMAN : The bill reviving the grade of lieutenant-general in the army has become a law, and my name has been sent to the Senate for the place. I now receive orders to report to Washington immediately in person, which indicates either a confirmation or a likelihood of confirmation.

I start in the morning to comply with the order, but I shall say very distinctly on my arrival there that I accept no appointment which will require me to make that city my headquarters. This, however, is not what I started out to write about.

Whilst I have been eminently successful in this war in at least gaining the confidence of the public, no one feels more than me how much of this success is due to the energy, skill, and the harmonious putting forth of that energy and skill, of those who it has been my good fortune to have occupying a subordinate position under me.

There are many officers to whom these remarks are applicable to a greater or less degree, proportionate to their ability as soldiers, but what I want is to express my thanks to you and McPherson as the men to whom, above all others, I feel indebted for whatever I have had of success. How far your advice and suggestions have been of assistance, you know. How far your execution of whatever has been given you to do entitles you to the reward I am receiving, you cannot know as well as me. I feel all the gratitude this letter would express, giving it the most flattering construction.

The word "*you*" I use in the plural, intending it for McPherson also. I should write to him, and will some day, but starting in the morning I do not know that I will find time just now.

    Your friend,

U. S. GRANT,
Major-General.

NASHVILLE, March 4, 1864.

Maj. Gen. W. T. SHERMAN,
  Commanding Department of the Tennessee:

You will be able better than I to judge how far the damage you have done the railroads about Meridian will disable the enemy from sending an army into Mississippi and West Tennessee with which to operate on the river; also what force will now be required to protect and guard the river. Use the negroes or negro troops more particularly for guarding plantations and for the defense of the west bank of the river. The artillerists among them, of course, you will put in fortifications, but most of the infantry give to Hawkins to be used on the west bank. Add to this element of your forces what you deem an adequate force for the protection of the river from Cairo down as far as your command goes, and extend the command of one army corps to the whole of it. Assemble the balance of your forces at or near Memphis, and have them in readiness to join your columns on this front in their spring campaign. Whether it will be better to have them march, meeting supplies sent up the Tennessee to Eastport, or whether they should be brought around to the latter place by steamers, can be determined hereafter. Add all the forces now under Dodge to the two corps, or to one of the two corps, you take into the field with you. Forces will be transferred from the Chattanooga and Nashville road to guard all the road now protected by your troops. If they are not sufficient, enough will be taken from elsewhere to leave all yours for the field. I am ordered to Washington, but as I am directed to keep up telegraphic communications with this command, I shall expect in the course of ten or twelve days to return to it. Place the Marine Brigade under the command of the corps commander left on the Mississippi River. Give direction that it be habitually used for the protection of leased plantations, and will not pass below Vicksburg nor above Greenville, except by order of the corps commander or higher authority.

U. S. GRANT,
Major-General.

SPECIAL ORDERS, }   HDQRS. MIL. DIV. OF THE MISSISSIPPI,
  No. 59.   }   *Nashville, Tenn., March* 4, 1864.

*   *   *   *   *   *   *

5. Officers of the U. S. Coast Survey within this military division will take the assimilated rank of captain of engineers, and be respected accordingly. When stationed in cities they will be entitled to fuel and quarters in kind.

By order of Maj. Gen. U. S. Grant :

T S. BOWERS,
Assistant Adjutant-General.

SPECIAL ORDERS, }   HDQRS. 2D DIV., 16TH ARMY CORPS,
  No. 50.   }   *Pulaski, Tenn., March* 4, 1864.

I. The Seventh Iowa Veteran Volunteer Infantry will proceed at once with camp and garrison equipage to Prospect, Tenn., and relieve the Twenty-seventh Ohio Infantry Veteran Volunteers. This regiment (Seventh Iowa) will report through its proper brigade at this place.

II. One section of artillery, to be designated by Capt. Fred. Welker, Chief of Artillery, Second Division, Sixteenth Army Corps, will accompany the Seventh Iowa Veteran Volunteers to Prospect, Tenn., and be stationed there until further orders. If possible, the artillery will be moved on the same train with the infantry, but if not, as soon thereafter as practicable.

III. Col. E. W. Rice, Seventh Iowa Infantry Veteran Volunteers, having returned with his regiment, will at once assume command of the First Brigade, Second Division, Sixteenth Army Corps, he being the senior officer present therewith.

By order of Brig. Gen. T. W. Sweeny, commanding:

L. H. EVERTS,
Captain and Assistant Adjutant-General.

KNOXVILLE, *March* 5, 1864.

Maj. Gen. U. S. GRANT:

Since sending my dispatch of yesterday I have learned that Thomas has returned to Chattanooga. If it is now practicable for him to send me the force necessary to drive Longstreet out of East Tennessee, I think it may be done without delay. I will pr   a l have the railroad bridge at Strawberry Plains completed by the time his troops can reach that place. We will then be able to supply our troops without serious difficulty.

J. M. SCHOFIELD,
Major-General.

KNOXVILLE, *March* 5, 1864—12.30 p. m.

Maj. Gen. GEORGE H. THOMAS:

General Carter has just informed me of your return to Chattanooga. Is it not practicable to commence operations against Longstreet? My possession of the railroad bridge at Strawberry Plains removes, to a very great extent, the difficulty of advancing at this season. I hope to have the bridge completed within ten days. My troops have been as far as Russellville and found the road uninjured. Do not think Longstreet has sent any infantry to Georgia. He seems to be moving slowly toward Virginia. If you can help me to drive Longstreet out I will then be able to help you. It does not seem probable that we will have troops enough for both operations at once. Please give me your views on this subject.

J. M. SCHOFIELD,
Major-General.

NEW MARKET, *March* 5, 1864—7.30 p. m.

Brig. Gen. E. E. POTTER,
Chief of Staff at Knoxville, Strawberry Plains:

Your dispatch stating the departure of trains received. No ammunition is wanted at the front at present, beyond the supply on hand.

J. D. COX,
Brigadier-General.

KNOXVILLE, *March* 5, 1864.

Major-General GRANGER,
Loudon:

Let the boats now on the way from Chattanooga with supplies for this place come here instead of unloading at Loudon.

J. M. SCHOFIELD,
Major-General.

HEADQUARTERS NINTH ARMY CORPS,
Mossy Creek, March 5, 1864—5.45 p. m.

Brig. Gen. J. D. COX,
Acting Chief of Staff, &c. :

GENERAL: A force of the enemy's cavalry appeared in our front this evening, following a detachment of the Twenty-third Corps of about 90 men from Panther Springs. The captain of this detachment has come in, and his report will doubtless be sent you from the headquarters of Twenty-third Corps.

They fired on our pickets. Two regiments were sent out to support the line. General Ferrero has just come in and reports seeing about 400 or 500 of the enemy, and that on pressing them they retired. We have 1 prisoner who says that he belongs to Giltner's brigade. No infantry with them; that Longstreet is at Bull's Gap, or from Bull's Gap to Greeneville. We have 1 man wounded slightly.

Very respectfully, your obedient servant,

JNO. G. PARKE,
Major-General.

CAMP ON MOSSY CREEK, TENN.,
March 5, 1864.

General J. D. COX,
Acting Chief of Staff, &c. :

GENERAL: Buckner's division is reported 2 miles this side of Bull's Gap. Two regiments of enemy's cavalry were at Dandridge last night; they have not been heard from to-day. Enemy have pickets on north side of French Broad as far down as Dandridge.

A party of bushwhackers of 8, 2 of whom are known by name and live near Panther Springs, captured 2 men sent by General Judah for a broken-down ambulance, taking their horses from them. One of the men escaped. I sent a party to capture the bushwhackers, but have not as yet heard from them. Two small scouting parties of the enemy were in Morristown yesterday, but left just before our men entered. I suppose General Parke reports everything to you that transpires in his front.

Respectfully, &c.,

GEO. STONEMAN,
Major-General.

Please let me know when General Schofield returns.

G. S.

CHATTANOOGA, *March* 5, 1864.

Brig. Gen. J. A. RAWLINS,
Chief of Staff:

The enemy advanced a brigade of cavalry early this morning on Colonel Harrison's pickets. Thirty-ninth Indiana Mounted Infantry, at Woods' Gap in Taylor's Ridge, and drove them back toward Lee and Gordon's Mills. The enemy then fell back through Gordon's Gap, as reported by General Baird from Ringgold. A scout just from Dalton reports Johnston has been re-enforced by 10,000 men from South Carolina and by Roddey, and he believes he contemplates a forward movement.

GEO. H. THOMAS,
Major-General.

CHATTANOOGA, *March 5*, 1864.

Maj. Gen. JOHN M. SCHOFIELD,
    Knoxville:

It has been reported to Major-General Thomas to-day, and also two days since, that the enemy were heavily re-enforcing at Dalton. General Grant thinks it is not improbable that he may advance against us here. In that case we shall need the Fourth Corps, and wish you to hold it in readiness to send, if it be needed. Cannot send you any assistance while this contingency is hanging over us.

WM. D. WHIPPLE,
Brigadier-General and Chief of Staff.

CHATTANOOGA, *March 5*, 1864—11 p. m.

Major-General SCHOFIELD,
    Knoxville:

I have just received reliable information that Johnston has been re-enforced by 10,000 men from South Carolina and by Roddey, and that he contemplates making an offensive movement in this direction. Can you spare Granger's corps and the cavalry? If so, please direct them to concentrate at Cleveland, leaving a brigade of infantry and battery at Calhoun to guard the railroad at that place.

GEO. H. THOMAS,
Major-General, U. S. Volunteers.

CHATTANOOGA, *March 5*, 1864.

Brig. Gen. CHARLES CRUFT,
    Commanding, Blue Springs:

If General Granger has sent a brigade to Calhoun to relieve Colonel Taylor, order Colonel Taylor to rejoin you.

GEO. H. THOMAS,
Major-General, Commanding.

HEADQUARTERS DEPARTMENT OF THE CUMBERLAND,
Chattanooga, March 5, 1864.

Brig. Gen. CHARLES CRUFT,
    Blue Springs:

The enemy is moving about our front with heavy cavalry force and some infantry. Have you any information of his movements in your region? Answer immediately.

WM. D. WHIPPLE,
Assistant Adjutant-General.

BLUE SPRINGS, *March* 5, 1864.

Brigadier-General WHIPPLE,
  Chief of Staff:

Mr. J. Brown, who is reported to be in the secret service, has sent word verbally by a third party that re-enforcements are arriving at Dalton, reported to be 10,000 infantry from South Carolina and Roddey's cavalry. The report is sent to you just as received; have no means to verify it or to form any opinion upon it.

         CHARLES CRUFT,
           Brigadier-General.

BLUE SPRINGS, *March* 5, 1864.

Brigadier-General WHIPPLE:

Dispatch received; have telegraphed you all I can learn. There was no enemy at Red Clay at 4.30 p. m. Citizens reported the force at Dalton on yesterday, furnished with three days' rations for a movement. Roddey's cavalry reported at Dalton and 10,000 re-enforcements from South Carolina. These are the rumors of to-day, heretofore sent you. I expect a dash here almost any time from the apprehensions of citizens around. How did Baird come out to-day?

         CHARLES CRUFT,
           Brigadier-General.

BLUE SPRINGS, *March* 5, 1864.

Maj. Gen. GEORGE H. THOMAS:

Dispatch received; nothing new in my front that I can learn of. Colonel Long, I am informed, has two scouting parties out; has had regiment of infantry at election precinct 3 miles north of Red Clay to-day. Colonel Enyart just reports cannonading heard by citizens and soldiers from McDaniel's Gap to-day; thought to be a little left of Graysville.

         CHARLES CRUFT.

BLUE SPRINGS, *March* 5, 1864.

Brigadier-General WHIPPLE,
  Chief of Staff:

Cavalry scout just returned from Red Clay, leaving there at 4.30 p. m. Saw nothing of enemy; heard heavy cannonading at or near Ringgold, from, say, 11 a. m. to 1 p. m., and occasional shots till 4 p. m. Citizens represent that forces at Dalton put three days' rations on men yesterday preparatory to a movement. Citizens represented, say, 200 cavalry at Kenyon's.

         CHARLES CRUFT,
           Brigadier-General.

HEADQUARTERS DEPARTMENT OF THE CUMBERLAND,
    Chattanooga, March 5, 1864—9 p. m.

Brigadier-General BAIRD:

Distribute three days' rations to your command and then load up and send your wagons back to Graysville; you will then be prepared for any movement of the enemy. You should send out a reconnoitering party on the La Fayette road to give you timely notice if the enemy attempts to advance on your right or to get in your rear. The Fourteenth and Thirty-eighth Ohio Infantry were sent to you to-day. Report by signal if they have reached you, as well as by courier, reporting at the same time what additional information you may have.

GEO. H. THOMAS,
Major-General, Volunteers.

RINGGOLD, GA.,
March 5, 1864—3.30 p. m.

Major-General PALMER:

Firing has been heard all the morning in direction of Cleveland, and it is reported that our cavalry on right have been driven back to Lee and Gordon's Mills. I am trying to ascertain the truth of latter report.

BAIRD,
Brigadier-General.

HEADQUARTERS FIRST DIVISION, FOURTH ARMY CORPS,
Blue Springs, March 5, 1864.

Lieut. Col. J. S. FULLERTON,
Loudon:

Has a brigade been sent to Calhoun to relieve Colonel Taylor, Fortieth Ohio? If so, I will order him to his command, as authorized from department headquarters.

CHARLES CRUFT,
Brigadier-General.

HEADQUARTERS DEPARTMENT OF THE CUMBERLAND,
Chattanooga, March 5, 1864.

Col. A. P. CAMPBELL,
Calhoun:

If you have not yet started from Calhoun you will not march for Cleveland, but will send a force with provisions and forage to Columbus to watch the road from East Tennessee. It* is reported that Longstreet's cavalry is making its way to join Joe Johnston via Marshall, Quallatown, and Murphy, thence to Benton. He was expected at Murphy last night.

Ascertain what you can regarding it, and report.

WM. D. WHIPPLE,
Chief of Staff.

ATHENS, *March 5, 1864.*

Maj. R. M. SAWYER,   .
Assistant Adjutant-General.

The rebel officers south of Tennessee River say that General Sherman's column is on the return toward Vicksburg. Chattanooga

Rebel of 26th also says he is moving back in two columns, one toward Raymond, one toward Canton. What is your report, if not contraband? Do you credit the report that he is in Selma?

G. M. DODGE,
Major-General.

CAVE CITY, *March 5, 1864.*

Capt. A. C. SEMPLE,
Assistant Adjutant-General:

Richardson, the guerrilla, was killed to-day on the way from Glasgow. He tried to make his escape, and was killed by Captain Stone, of Thirty-seventh Kentucky.

E. H. HOBSON,
Brigadier-General.

HDQRS. 1ST BRIGADE, 3D DIVISION, 17TH ARMY CORPS,
Big Black, Miss., March 5, 1864.

Capt. J. C. DOUGLASS,
Assistant Adjutant-General:

CAPTAIN: I have the honor to state that the rebel patrols are established again on their old beats, just outside our pickets, and burn all cotton coming in and take all goods going out.

I have resumed the rules existing before the late expedition, giving permits to no one to go into Vicksburg except to persons who have taken the oath of allegiance or the amnesty oath, and who intend to remain, and allowing no goods to go outside the lines, except, in rare cases, to well-known persons, of petty articles which cannot be diverted from family use.

The local special agent of the Treasury says General Geiger has permit from General McPherson and the assistant special agent for a trade store at this post, with permission to sell $15,000. I have no other information of this fact, as the Regulations (Rule XV) allow only $3,000 per month. Rule XIV provides that "no supplies shall be allowed to go therefrom except upon permit of the proper special local agent, countersigned by the commander of the post or some person authorized by him for that purpose." The regulations of the Treasury Department seem cautious to provide against supplies going to places under control of the rebels, and General Grant's order prohibits supplies going across the Big Black. I have therefore notified the local special agent that I will not countersign any permit for supplies going outside the lines until I shall be notified by superior headquarters that a new rule is intended.

I am, captain, very respectfully, your obedient servant,

M. F. FORCE,
Brigadier-General, Commanding Post.

CHATTANOOGA, TENN.,
March 5, 1864—11 a. m.

Maj. THOMAS M. VINCENT,
Assistant Adjutant-General:

Twenty-six thousand five hundred veterans enlisted up to 1st instant. Fifteen hundred additional reported unofficially. Am

confident will reach 30,000.   First Cavalry Division not heard from.
Failure of Pay Department to make payments for last three weeks
has had very injurious effect on re-enlistments.

JOHN H. YOUNG,
Captain and Department Commissary of Musters.

SPECIAL FIELD ORDERS, }   HDQRS. DEPT. OF THE TENNESSEE,
No. 23.   }   *Natchez, Miss., March 5,* 1864.

I. The intrenchments now approaching completion at Natchez will
be known as Fort McPherson, and its magazine and armament will
be finished at as early a date as possible.

II. All citizens living within its limits must be removed within a
reasonable time, and all roads leading to and through it will be closed
to the public.

III. The commanding officer at Natchez will assemble a board of
survey, composed of three officers of rank and experience, with a
recorder, which will examine all houses and tenements within the
lines of intrenchments, and such on the outside as should in the judgment of Captain Hains, U. S. Engineers, be destroyed, and assess
their value in gold coin.   A copy of their proceedings will be filed
with the commanding officer at Natchez, another copy sent to the
Quartermaster-General, and a third with the Engineer Department
at Washington, D. C.   A certificate of valuation will be given each
tenant or occupant in possession, regardless of his or her loyalty and
ownership.

IV. The commanding officer at Natchez will give to each party
dispossessed of houses or tenements by this order possession of another house of like value in Natchez which may be vacant, and the
property of some known or suspected rebel.

By order of Maj. Gen. W. T. Sherman:

L. M. DAYTON,
Aide-de-Camp.

WASHINGTON, *March 6,* 1864—11.30 a. m.

Maj. Gen. U. S. GRANT,
Louisville, Ky.:

The Secretary of War directs me to say to you that your commission as lieutenant-general is signed, and will be delivered to you on
your arrival at the War Department.   I sincerely congratulate you
on this recognition of your distinguished and meritorious services.

H. W. HALLECK,
General-in-Chief.

KNOXVILLE, *March 6,* 1864—9 a. m.

Major-General THOMAS,
Commanding:

I have no immediate use for Granger's corps, and will order it to
Cleveland if you so direct.   If Longstreet returns I will be unable
to hold the railroad bridge at Strawberry Plains, and all my work

there will be lost. I could not even hold this place more than a few days without Granger's troops. I must leave it for you to judge whether, under these circumstances, I can spare these troops.

J. M. SCHOFIELD,
Major-General.

CHATTANOOGA, *March* 6, 1864—12 m.

Major-General SCHOFIELD, *Knoxville:*

I do not wish to withdraw Granger's corps unless there be an absolute necessity for it, but there is a great necessity for cavalry in my front. Can you spare McCook's command? It seems to me that there is very little danger to your communications between Calhoun and Loudon if the crossings of the Hiwassee at Calhoun and Columbus are well guarded. Please consider what arrangement you can make with a view of sending me the cavalry, and let me know as soon as possible.

GEO. H. THOMAS,
Major-General, U. S. Volunteers.

KNOXVILLE, *March* 6, 1864—5 p. m.

Maj. Gen. G. H. THOMAS:

I will send you McCook's command at once. I understand he has but six regiments left. The others were ordered to report to you several days ago. I will send a small force of cavalry to take McCook's place. If your cavalry cover the approaches from the southeast very little cavalry will be necessary between the Little Tennessee and the Hiwassee. It will take two or three days for the force I send to reach McCook's position. Meanwhile let him direct his movements so as to protect the railroad from the east and southeast. There is no present danger from the northeast.

J. M. SCHOFIELD,
Major-General.

KNOXVILLE, *March* 6, 1864.

Major-General GRANGER:

Send McCook's entire cavalry command to report to Major-General Thomas; apply to him by telegraph for orders for its movement. I will send you a small force of very poor cavalry to take its place. If you think there is any danger of a raid upon the railroad between Loudon and Charleston detain a portion of McCook's command or so direct its movements as to protect the road until the other arrives, which will be in two or three days. Let the cavalry I send you do as little duty as practicable and have an opportunity to recruit their horses.

J. M. SCHOFIELD,
Major-General.

KNOXVILLE, *March* 6, 1864.

Brigadier-General COX:

Direct the Ninth Corps and Wood's division to be ready to move at a moment's notice. Answer.

J. M. SCHOFIELD,
Major-General.

HEADQUARTERS ARMY OF THE OHIO,
New Market, March 6, 1864.

Brig. Gen. T. J. WOOD,
Commanding Third Division, Fourth Army Corps:

GENERAL: The commanding general directs me to say that no movement of the troops will be made for the present; that all men belonging to the several commands who are at the rear and fit for the field will be sent forward immediately, and that the knapsacks and field baggage for officers may also come forward. Proper officers to take charge of the property will be sent to Knoxville, the details being as small as possible and approved at these headquarters.

Very respectfully, your obedient servant,
J. D. COX,
Brigadier-General, Acting Chief of Staff.

(Copies to Generals Parke and Stoneman.—J. D. C.)

NEW MARKET, *March 6, 1864.*

Major-General SCHOFIELD:

If a movement be made of the Ninth and Fourth Corps, which will necessitate one of the Twenty-third also, they will need about thirty wagons to haul the accumulated stores and ammunition. In the skirmish yesterday the rebels lost 9 killed, including a major; we lost 3 killed, 1 badly wounded, and nearly 20 prisoners. We have 2 rebel prisoners.

No further news from the front.
J. D. COX,
Brigadier-General.

NEW MARKET, *March 6, 1864.*

Capt. J. N. KING,
Commissary of Subsistence, Strawberry Plains:

Do not allow stores to come forward so as to accumulate beyond the capacity of the regimental trains to move them. We do not want depots at the camps which could not be carried away in any movement to front or rear on a moment's notice. Please say the same to Captain Van Ness.

J. D. COX,
Brigadier-General, Acting Chief of Staff in the Field.

NEW MARKET, *March 6, 1864.*

Major-General SCHOFIELD,
Knoxville:

The Twenty-third Corps was, I believe, the only one ordered to send back the officers' horses. I called for the statement of the number before getting your dispatch, and will have it in the morning. Have also given the orders to have no large accumulation of stores at the camps.

J. D. COX,
Brigadier-General, Acting Chief of Staff.

CHATTANOOGA, *March* 6, 1864.

Brig. Gen. CHARLES CRUFT, *Blue Springs:*

General Baird was not disturbed yesterday. Harrison was driven in from Leet's farm to Lee and 'Gordon's Mills. The enemy has disappeared from our front. The last seen of him was by a scouting party sent out by Baird, who skirmished some with his rear guard, going in the direction of Gordon's Gap. Harrison has returned to Pea Vine Church.

WM. D. WHIPPLE,
Assistant Adjutant-General.

CHATTANOOGA, *March* 6, 1864.

Maj. Gen. G. GRANGER:

Have you sent a brigade of infantry to Calhoun; if so, what brigade? It is necessary to know about this, that we may, if possible, draw Colonel Campbell in this direction, where his cavalry is much needed.

WM. D. WHIPPLE,
Brigadier-General, Chief of Staff.

HEADQUARTERS FOURTEENTH ARMY CORPS,
Chattanooga, March 6, 1864.

Brig. Gen. W. D. WHIPPLE,
Assistant Adjutant-General, &c.:

GENERAL: Five deserters just brought in confirm the report that Roddey passed through Rome on his way to Dalton. They say the brigades of Roddey and Patterson came together from Alabama, and that all the troops in that quarter are ordered to Dalton.

I think the reports now in show that there are four cavalry brigades in the neighborhood of Dalton—Davidson's, Humes', Roddey's, and Patterson's. These deserters say the horses are in bad condition. The brigades which came from Alabama are two regiments each.

Respectfully,

JOHN M. PALMER,
Major-General.

HEADQUARTERS DEPARTMENT OF THE CUMBERLAND,
Chattanooga, March 6, 1864.

Col. E. M. McCOOK,
Commanding Cavalry Division:

General Schofield will soon give you orders to move in this direction. Preparatory to that, concentrate your forces, and when you get orders to move you will march to Cleveland and report.

WM. D. WHIPPLE,
Assistant Adjutant-General.

HEADQUARTERS DEPARTMENT OF THE CUMBERLAND,
Chattanooga, March 6, 1864.

Col. ELI LONG, *Cleveland:*

It is expected that Colonel McCook will arrive at Cleveland this week with his division of cavalry. When he arrives you will march with your command for our immediate front, coming this way. You can then transact such business as you may desire at this place. Colonel Campbell has been directed to relieve your company at Columbus and order it to its regiment.

WM. D. WHIPPLE,
Assistant Adjutant-General.

ATHENS, ALA.,
March 6, 1864.

Brig. Gen. J. A. RAWLINS,
        Chief of Staff:
The Tennessee is rising rapidly. A regiment of mounted infantry went to Florence to-day to come up with boats. I think by to-morrow or next day boats can get over the shoals. Troops are passing through Montgomery daily going to Atlanta.

G. M. DODGE,
Brigadier-General.

HEADQUARTERS CAVALRY CORPS,
Mount Sterling, Ky., March 6, 1864.
Brig. Gen. E. E. POTTER,
        Chief of Staff, Knoxville, Tenn. :
SIR : The telegram of General Schofield is just received and answered in general terms.

In my answer I promised to go more into details, by mail, in order that the major-general commanding may be enabled to form an approximate idea of the dilapidated condition of Colonel Wolford's as well as of the other division (still in Tennessee). I would respectfully call his attention to the "inspector's" report of Captain Gouraud, made at my request, and which I presume is on file in your office. It will be there seen that the arms are in a sad condition and of every possible caliber, the equipments are incomplete and worn out, curry-combs and brushes a novelty, &c. ; the demoralization and want of discipline complete.

This was the condition of the cavalry when I took command of it, on the 14th December, 1863. After I took command of it (and before, so far as I know) it was continually on the march and fighting, more or less, almost every day, and subsisting off the country until I left for Kentucky. These circumstances and the march to this place, the general commanding will readily perceive, were not calculated to increase their discipline or general moral tone. Now that they are here, it is necessary to reorganize them, make thorough inspections, make out requisitions for almost every item required by a cavalry soldier, draw horses, drill, and, more than all, discipline them. This will require time, and the general may depend upon my entire energy being devoted toward shortening that as much as possible. I would respectfully repeat my recommendation that the other division be sent in, if possible, so that when the time shall arrive for cavalry to operate according to its legitimate purposes (which I do not think it has been doing for some time) it may start out with some reasonable hopes of accomplishing such expectations as may be entertained of it. As it is, the spring will find us with a portion, and a large portion too, of our cavalry altogether worn out and worthless.

Lest my telegram may miscarry, I will repeat that I believe it will require from six to eight weeks to place this division in anything like condition for successful service, but I will spare no pains to lessen that time.

In regard to driving horses from Kentucky to Knoxville, at this season, for the purpose of remounting cavalry, I consider it in every possible view of the subject altogether impracticable. The roads are in most terrific condition, and will become, if possible, worse as spring advances. A pack-mule cannot, at the outside calculation, carry over 240 pounds, and it will require all of twenty days to make the round trip. Now, a mule will require 12 pounds per day for his own consumption, so that he will require the whole 240 pounds for his own subsistence. But he cannot pack 240 pounds on these roads, and if you had corn in Tennessee to send him back, so that the 120 pounds intended for bringing him back might be devoted to the horses, still I consider that the magnitude of the undertaking, under those circumstances, would render it impracticable and the horses would arrive in Tennessee already broken down, and the resources of Tennessee are not sufficient to bring them up again. Indeed, I would respectfully submit that I cannot see how it will be possible to use cavalry in East Tennessee at all this coming summer. So far as I can see, they will have to operate from some other base than Knoxville, as no large amount of it can subsist there now, and it will be growing worse every day until the fall crop is ready, and I doubt if there will be much of a crop, for in many parts of the country we did not leave, I regret to say, enough for seed. It was to save the country, in this respect, to save the people, and to provide for ourselves for the future, that influenced me to urge upon General Foster the present arrangement, and that contemplated the ultimate withdrawal also of the remaining division.

I am, general, very respectfully, your obedient servant,

S. `D. STURGIS,
Brigadier-General, Commanding.

HDQRS. DISTRICT OF SOUTHERN CENTRAL KENTUCKY,
Cave City, Ky., March 6, 1864.

Col. J. W. WEATHERFORD,
Commanding Thirteenth Kentucky Cavalry:

From information received from Major Martin, I learn that "Richardson's men" have been mistreating and in some instances killing Union men and Federal soldiers. You will send a force to Celina or vicinity, clearing that country, complying with former orders.

By command of Brigadier-General Hobson:

J. S. BUTLER,
Assistant Adjutant-General.

GENERAL ORDERS,) HDQRS. DIST. SOUTHERN CENTRAL KY.,
No. 3.   ∫   *Cave City, March* 6, 1864.

I. Complaints having been filed at these headquarters against certain officers commanding mounted parties for trespassing on citizens, it is ordered that commanding officers, when sending out or accompanying scouts or expeditions of any kind, shall personally attend to having their men supplied with rations for the probable time of absence.

II. The practice of going to houses and ordering food and forage must be discontinued.

III. When it becomes necessary to procure forage it must be receipted for by the commanding officer of the party.

IV. Loyal citizens are requested to report any violation of this order to these headquarters, giving names and dates, and also names of witnesses.

By command of Brig. Gen. E. H. Hobson:

J. S. BUTLER,
Assistant Adjutant-General.

CINCINNATI, *March* 7, 1864.

Maj. Gen. J. M. SCHOFIELD,
    Knoxville, Tenn.:

Lieutenant-General Grant directs me to say that troops cannot be spared from Chattanooga; that you should keep Longstreet as far up the valley as you can, destroying the railroad near him if he advances.

C. B. COMSTOCK,
Lieutenant-Colonel and Assistant Inspector-General.

MADISONVILLE, TENN.,
March 7, 1864.

Lieut. Col. J. S. FULLERTON,
    Assistant Adjutant-General, Fourth Army Corps:

I have the honor to report the following information, obtained by two of my scouts who were inside of the enemy's lines. They are both men of intelligence and their statements can be relied upon. Were at Newport on Wednesday, the 2d instant; took dinner in the town within General Armstrong's lines, whose cavalry is at that place with four pieces of artillery, and is said to be short of artillery ammunition. His (Armstrong's) horses are in middling condition. Were informed by the rebels at that place that General Morgan, with his division and two pieces of artillery, had gone to re-enforce Johnston at Dalton, via Warm Springs and Asheville. From best information they could procure Morgan left about ten days since. General Martin accompanied Morgan's division southward.

Longstreet's headquarters on the 2d instant were at Greeneville, Tenn., at Vance's old hotel. Longstreet was said to be turning over his wagons and mounting his men on train mules and horses, shipping his baggage to Atlanta and Richmond. Rebel soldiers and citizens reported that Longstreet intended retreating to Virginia; others, that he was going to invade Kentucky. Saw two deserters, who informed them that Longstreet's army was between Bull's Gap and Greeneville.

Armstrong sends scouting parties from Newport in the direction of and to Sevierville. Rebels had been informed that three brigades of our cavalry were at Sevierville, and were badly frightened, saddled up, and remained so during the night. They threw away blue overcoats and Yankee clothes in anticipation of being attacked.

I have the honor to be, colonel, your very obedient servant,

E. M. McCOOK,
Colonel, Commanding.

RINGGOLD, *March* 7, 1864.

Major-General THOMAS,
  Chattanooga:

Deserters state that there are six divisions of infantry between Nickajack and Dalton—40,000 men. The cavalry which was on the raid came with one day's rations and no artillery.

Wheeler crossed with 1,500 men at Gordon's Gap; another party closer to the Nickajack, and another 2 miles this side; the object, to turn our right.

A. BAIRD,
Brigadier-General.

LOUDON, *March* 7, 1864.

General THOMAS:

Schofield directs me to send all McCook's cavalry to you. What orders shall I give it?

G. GRANGER,
Major-General.

CHATTANOOGA, *March* 7, 1864.

Major-General GRANGER:

As soon as General Schofield's cavalry get down to relieve McCook, I want him to march to Cleveland.

GEO. H. THOMAS,
Major-General, Commanding.

HEADQUARTERS NINETY-SECOND ILLINOIS VOLUNTEERS,
Triana, March 7, 1864.

Brig. Gen. WILLIAM D. WHIPPLE,
  Asst. Adjt. Gen., Department of the Cumberland:

Under direct orders received from department headquarters, I ordered across the Tennessee River one I. H. Hundley, who was a rebel and had been communicating with the enemy, his brother, a colonel in the rebel army, being in command opposite this place. He refused to take the oath of allegiance. Yesterday he walked into my tent informing me that Col. A. O. Miller had permitted him to come again within our lines, and that he had taken the oath of allegiance at Huntsville. I know him to be a vile rebel. I beg very respectfully to inquire if it be regular, if it be right, when I have acted under orders from department headquarters in sending rebels within the rebel lines, for Colonel Miller to invite them back again?

Hearing that a squad of rebel soldiers were going to cross to this side of the river between here and Whitesburg for the purpose of going to Lincoln County and conscripting, but really, as I think, to act as spies and bushwhackers, I sent out a party and captured them. They were armed to the teeth, crossed with horses and accouterments, and would not have surrendered had they not been fired on by my men. I sent them "as prisoners of war" to Huntsville, and 3 of them were permitted to take the oath of allegiance and returned immediately inside the rebel lines. One of them, A. F. Spain, had captured one of General Mitchel's men at this place in spring of 1862, tied his hands behind him, and taking him to the middle of the river deliberately drowned him. He had taken the oath of allegiance at Columbus, Ohio, once before and went at once to the rebel army. They belonged to Morgan's command and were undoubtedly spies. Again, may I very respectfully inquire, if it be regular, if it be right, for prisoners of war captured in actual battle to be released and returned to the rebel army? I am on an outpost; the enemy has attempted to surprise my pickets, and would have surprised my camp long since if they could. Wide-awake, prompt, vigorous, determined action is expected of me. If notorious rebels are given more privileges in my camp than my own officers have (the most desperate characters of the enemy return to them when captured) possible disaster may come to my command, and I very respectfully forward this letter that my superior officers may know the difficulties I labor under.

Your most respectful and obedient servant,

SMITH D. ATKINS,
Colonel Ninety-second Illinois Volunteers.

HEADQUARTERS DEPARTMENT OF THE TENNESSEE,
Vicksburg, Miss., March 7, 1864.

Major-General McPHERSON,
Commanding District of Vicksburg:

GENERAL: I think it important I should hasten somewhat to my command at Huntsville, Ala. I am therefore compelled again to leave you to the exercise of this most important command, but assure you I do so with absolute confidence. You may rely on my cordial support at all times. You know the plans and purposes of your superiors for some months to come, but to be more certain I will repeat the leading points. The river Mississippi must be held sacred, and any attempt of the enemy to make a lodgment anywhere on its banks must be prevented by any and all means; also its peaceful navigation must be assured. Any firing on boats or molestation of them when engaged in a legitimate and licensed traffic should be punished with terrible severity. I believe that our expedition, in which we destroyed absolutely the Southern Railroad and the Mobile and Ohio at and around Meridian, will prevent the enemy approaching the river with any infantry or heavy artillery, but he will of course reoccupy Mississippi with his marauding cavalry. That can in nowise influence the course of the grand war. I would heed this cavalry but little. Still it may unite and threaten Memphis, in which event I want you to act promptly by embarking as heavy a force as you can spare to ascend the Yazoo as far as Greenwood or Sidon, and strike at Grenada. This would take Forrest in the rear and compel him to fall back on Pontotoc. I cannot believe cavalry will ever trouble you at or near Vicksburg, but may attempt to reach the river at some point above or below. An expedition up the Yazoo is the remedy for the river above, and if we could garrison Harrisonburg and operate up Washita and Tensas it would have a similar effect on that side. But this is not in our command, and we have not the force to spare.

Encourage by all means the packet and through trade on the river as auxiliary to its defense, and also encourage trade with the interior not contraband of war. Such trade will keep the people dependent on the luxuries and conveniences of life, and to that extent shake their love for the impoverished rebel concern. Let the Treasury agents manage this trade and keep your officers aloof from all interest in it. I think the attempt to cultivate plantations premature, and all the protection we can promise is to buy their corn, facilitate their supplies, and give incidental protection ; we cannot try to guard their estates.

The Red River expedition is designed to last but thirty days. Manage your veterans as to furlough so that this detachment of yours may return before all the veterans are spared. Nearly the whole of General Hurlbut's corps will be needed over on the Tennessee River, so that in fact your corps will have to look to the whole river.

The gun-boats and General Ellet's fleet can do all ordinary patroling, and you will only be called on when the enemy attempts some more extended operation than he has hitherto attempted. Make the regular reports to my headquarters, and when you have no special instructions act with the full confidence of a separate commander. I know you want to be in the field, and I will accomplish it if possible, but this command is of vital importance to our cause.

I am, &c.,

W. T. SHERMAN,
Major-General, Commanding.

GERMANTOWN, *March* 7, 1864—9.20 p. m.
Capt. S. L. WOODWARD,
Assistant Adjutant-General, Memphis :
Scout returned from Quinn's Mill. Captured a private of Second Missouri. He says three companies of his regiment were sent up from Oxford on a scout two days ago.. Made their headquarters near Chulahoma. Were to return to-night. Says Forrest is recruiting his horses near Oxford.

L. F. McCRILLIS,
Colonel.

VICKSBURG, MISS., *March* 7, 1864.
Maj. Gen. W. T. SHERMAN,
Commanding Army and Department of Tennessee :
GENERAL : I respectfully request, if consistent with the interest of the public service, to be transferred from the line of the Mississippi River to the field of operations in Southern Tennessee and Northern Georgia and Alabama. Most of the regiments in my command competent to enlist as veterans have done so to the number of twenty-nine, and in accordance with orders and pledges of the Government are entitled to a furlough of thirty days within their own State, transportation to be furnished at the expense of the Government to and from their respective States.

The probabilities are that there will be little else except guerrilla fighting and cavalry raids on the Mississippi River for several months to come, if at all during the war.

Let these regiments, then, have their furloughs at an early day, and when their furloughs expire have them report to me at any point you may designate within the district named for active duty in the field,

In this manner no extra expense will be entailed upon the Government for transporting troops, the integrity of the Seventeenth Army Corps will be preserved, the troops and their commander placed in a position congenial to their wishes.

Very respectfully, your obedient servant,

JAS. B. McPHERSON,
Major-General, Commanding Seventeenth Army Corps.

SPECIAL FIELD ORDERS, }   HDQRS. DEPT. OF THE TENNESSEE,
No. 25.   }   *Vicksburg, March 7, 1864.*

The following disposition is made of the cotton captured and brought to Vicksburg by the Yazoo River expedition, Colonel Coates, Eleventh Illinois Infantry, commanding.

I. One thousand bales will be delivered to the special agent of the Treasury Department, to be by him disposed of as all other abandoned or confiscated personal property, but designed by me to indemnify the owners of the steamer Allen Collier, burned by the rebels near Bolivar Landing, and any other losses sustained by steam-boats navigating the Mississippi between Memphis and Vicksburg engaged in a lawful and licensed commerce.

II. The balance will be held by the post quartermaster of Vicksburg, to be disposed of as follows :

General McPherson will appoint a board of 3 officers, who will hear and adjudicate all claims of loyal citizens residing on the Mississippi River, within the limits of his district, for damages sustained to their property by guerrillas or the public enemy, or our own troops, such as the burning of Dr. Duncan's cotton, in the seed or in bales, and the use for hospitals of Mrs. Grove's cotton. The Board will make an award in kind, viz, in bales of cotton, and their award will be examined by the commanding officer of the District of Vicksburg, and if approved and ordered paid, the quartermaster having it in charge will make the restitution in kind, taking receipts therefor in full satisfaction for all damages sustained.

III. After ninety days from the date of this order, the balance of the cotton, if any, will be turned over to the agent of the Treasury Department as captured property.

IV. Brig. Gen. J. M. Tuttle, U. S. Volunteers, commanding division, Sixteenth Army Corps, is hereby relieved from duty with that corps, and is assigned to duty with the Seventeenth Army Corps, and will report to Major-General McPherson.

*   *   *   *   *

By order of Maj. Gen. W. T. Sherman :

L. M. DAYTON,
Aide-de-Camp.

SPECIAL FIELD ORDERS, }   HDQRS. SIXTEENTH ARMY CORPS,
No. 15.   }   *Vicksburg, Miss., March 7, 1864.*

*   *   *   *   *   *   *

II. The following batteries, with their entire equipage and transportation, will as soon as transportation can be obtained proceed to Memphis, Tenn., there reporting for orders to these headquarters: Ninth Indiana Battery, Fourteenth Indiana Battery, Company E,

First Illinois Light Artillery; Sixth Indiana Battery. The quartermaster's department will furnish necessary transportation.

III. The Ninth Indiana Battery will report to Brig. Gen. A. J. Smith, commanding Red River expedition, for duty and orders.

IV. The Second Iowa Battery is relieved from duty with the Red River expedition, and will proceed to Memphis, Tenn., with entire equipage and transportation. The quartermaster's department will furnish necessary transportation.

By order of Maj. Gen. S. A. Hurlbut:

T. H. HARRIS,
Assistant Adjutant-General.

NEW MARKET, *March* 8, 1864.

Capt. J. N. KING,
Commissary of Subsistence, Strawberry Plains:

The Ninth Corps numbers 3,030 enlisted men and 170 officers; this, with 105 servants, &c., before reported, makes the total 3,305.

J. D. COX,
Brigadier-General, Acting Chief of Staff.

HEADQUARTERS ARMY OF THE OHIO,
New Market, Tenn., March 8, 1864.

Capt. J. N. KING,
Commissary of Subsistence, Strawberry Plains:

SIR: The effective force of the Twenty-third Corps is reported: Judah's division, privates, &c., 3,400; servants and employés not enlisted, 38; corps headquarters, 10; total, 3,448. They will also draw for Garrard's cavalry, 300, making 3,748.a

The Third Division, Fourth Army Corps, General Wood commanding, reports officers and men, 4,525; servants and employés not enlisted, 171; total, 4,696.

The servants and employés Ninth Corps are reported 105. The officers and men I will give this evening.

The issues must be made to correspond within a reasonable margin to these figures, so that the commanding general may know that no fuller rations are issued to one portion of the command than another, and you are specially charged with this duty.

Very respectfully,

J. D. COX,
Brigadier-General, Acting Chief of Staff in the Field.

a NOTE.—This only includes those of Twenty-third Corps drawing rations at post named.

HEADQUARTERS ARMY OF THE OHIO,
New Market, March 8, 1864.

Major-General STONEMAN,
Commanding Twenty-third Army Corps:

I have the honor to inform you that Hascall's Division of your corps has been ordered to move to the front on Friday, reporting to you. A battalion of Third Indiana Cavalry now at Strawberry Plains will report to Colonel Garrard at same time.

Very respectfully, &c.,

J. D. COX,
Brigadier-General and Acting Chief of Staff.

HEADQUARTERS ARMY OF THE OHIO,
New Market, March 8, 1864.
Brig. Gen. T. J. WOOD,
    Comdg. Third Division, Fourth Army Corps :
    SIR : The commanding general directs that "the oldest two veteran
regiments" of your division be sent on Thursday next to Strawberry
Plains, to occupy that place until further orders, relieving Hascall's
division, Twenty-third Army Corps, which will move to this point
on Friday.
    Very respectfully, &c.,
                                    J. D. COX,
            Brigadier-General and Acting Chief of Staff.

NEW MARKET, *March 8, 1864.*
Brig. Gen. E. E. POTTER,
    Chief of Staff, Knoxville :
    General Wood reports it doubtful whether some of the regiments
which offered to re-enlist as veterans would now do so.   He therefore wishes to know more especially whether the prospect is that the
veteran furlough will soon be granted the two regiments ordered to
Strawberry Plains, so that he may be sure that the ones sent there
will certainly re-enlist.   Please answer.
                                    J. D. COX,
        Brigadier-General, Acting Chief of Staff in the Field.

DECATUR, *March 8, 1864.*
Brig. Gen. J. A. RAWLINS :
    We occupied this place at daylight and we hold it.
                                    G. M. DODGE,
                                        Brigadier-General.
(Same to Col. R. M. Sawyer.)

MARCH 8, 1864.
Brig. Gen. MORGAN L. SMITH,
            Larkinsville :
    Mead and Dillon crossed Tennessee River last night with about
15 guerrillas and took the Bellefonte road.   They are now suspected
to be in the neighborhood of Boyd's Switch.   I will try and watch
them from this point, and suggest your doing the same if you think
proper.
                            P. J. OSTERHAUS,
                                Brigadier-General.

HEADQUARTERS SOUTHERN CENTRAL KENTUCKY,
Cave City, March 8, 1864.
Col. J. W. WEATHERFORD,
        Burkesville. Ky. :
    COLONEL : I have ordered all the mounted force of the Thirty-
seventh Kentucky Mounted Infantry to the vicinity of Celina and
Bennett's Ferry.   Colonel Grider, of Fifty-second Kentucky

Mounted Infantry, has been ordered to Scottsville, and will report to me. I have directed commanding officer of Thirty-seventh Kentucky to co-operate with you from Celina and with Colonel Grider at Scottsville, giving you any information they may from time to time obtain as regards rebel movements. I will expect you to give all necessary information relative to the movements of rebels to the commanding officer Thirty-seventh Kentucky, at Celina. You will also keep me fully advised by courier of all important movements. I will expect you to keep scouting parties out at all times to afford protection and gain information. If our army at Knoxville meets with a reverse or are flanked we may expect trouble and plenty of fighting in Kentucky. I notice in papers of recent date that Longstreet is mounting all of his forces, has sent his trains to the rear, &c. If this be true it is his intention evidently to make a raid into Kentucky, and hence the necessity of our being prepared to concentrate and meet any force attempting the invasion of Kentucky. I will expect to hear from you often by courier. It would be well to send all mail matter through by courier to this place, as it requires six or seven days if sent through the usual channels.

Very respectfully,

E. H. HOBSON,
Brigadier-General.

FRANKFORT, KY.,
March 8, 1864.

Lieut. Gen. U. S. GRANT,
Washington, D. C.:

Unless otherwise ordered, General Ammen will take command in Kentucky so soon as relieved from court-martial at Cincinnati. He does not desire the command, and I deem it important to our condition that General .Burbridge be retained in command in Kentucky. I have telegraphed Major-General Schofield, and hope the order may be made to keep General Burbridge in command.

THOS. E. BRAMLETTE,
Governor of Kentucky.

HEADQUARTERS SIXTEENTH ARMY CORPS,
Vicksburg, Miss., March 8. 1864.

Maj. Gen. J. B. McPHERSON,
Commanding Seventeenth Army Corps:

GENERAL: I am informed by Captain Thornton, division quartermaster of General Tuttle's division (First Division, Sixteenth Army Corps), that during the month of February large quantities of cotton, both private property and C. S. A., were hauled in to Big Black Station by order of Brigadier-General Tuttle in army wagons under escort; that for the private cotton so brought in he was to receive and did receive compensation, which General Tuttle personally holds.

All this is in direct violation of orders, and I had therefore ordered General Tuttle to report to me at Memphis that the matter might be examined.

By some means he has obtained a transfer to your corps. I there-

fore forward this statement to you, that, being put in official knowledge of the charges, you may take such course as shall maintain discipline and cause full explanation of the facts.

I have the honor to be, general, your obedient servant,

S. A. HURLBUT,
Major-General.

HEADQUARTERS DEPARTMENT OF THE TENNESSEE,
En Route for Memphis, March 8, 1864.

Brig. Gen. JOHN A. RAWLINS,
Chief of General Grant's Staff, Nashville :

GENERAL : I had the honor to receive, at the hands of General
Butterfield, General Grant's letter of February 18.* I had returned
from Meridian by the time I had appointed, but the condition of
facts concerning the Red River expedition being indefinite, I took
one of the marine boats, the Diana, and went down to New Orleans to
confer with General Banks. En route I saw the admiral and learned
that he was ready, and a large and effective gun-boat fleet would be
at the mouth of Red River ready for action March 5. At New
Orleans I received the general's letter, with inclosures, and was governed by it in my interview with General Banks.

General McClernand had been ingeniously disposed of by being
sent to command in Texas. General Banks is to command in person,
taking with him 17,000 of his chosen troops to move by land from the
end of the Opelousas Railroad, via Franklin, Opelousas, and Alexandria. Steele is to move from Little Rock on Natchitoches, and he
asked of me 10,000 men in boats to ascend Red River, meeting him
at Alexandria the 17th of March. I inclose copies† of General
Banks' letter to me and my answer, which was clear and specific.

I have made up a command of 10,000 men—7,500 of Hurlbut's and
2,500 of McPherson's. General A. J. Smith goes in command of the
whole ; will be at the mouth of Red River by the 10th at farthest, and
at Alexandria on the 17th. These 10,000 men are not to be gone over
thirty days, at the expiration of which time McPherson's quota will
return to Vicksburg and Hurlbut's quota will come to Memphis,
where, if all things remain as now, I can bring them rapidly round
to Savannah, Tenn., and so on to my right flank near Huntsville.
I think this will result as soon as the furloughed men get back.

Inasmuch as General Banks goes in person I could not with delicacy propose that I should command, and the scene of operations
lying wholly in his department, I deemed it wisest to send A. J.
Smith, and to return in time to put my army in the field in shape for
the coming spring campaign.

I have ordered five regiments, under General Veatch, to join Dodge
at once, and I feel sure I can safely draw A. J. Smith's division of
full 5,000 men to the same point in April. McPherson and Hurlbut
are both instructed to furlough their veterans at once and many regiments are already off.

I have inspected Natchez and Vicksburg and feel sure they can
now be held safe with comparatively small garrisons, and the river
is patrolled by gun-boats and the Marine Brigade.

I will inspect Memphis, and in a few days will hasten to Hunts-

---

* See Part II, p. 424.
† See Vol. XXXIV. Part II, pp. —.

ville to put myself in command of my troops in that quarter, and will be ready for work at once, as I am in no manner fatigued. Indeed, the men I took with me to Meridian are better fitted for work now than before we started.

I send by General Butterfield my official report, with copies of orders, letters, &c., giving you full information of all matters up to date.*

I am, with much respect, your obedient servant,

W. T. SHERMAN,
Major-General, Commanding.

GENERAL ORDERS, }   HDQRS. DISTRICT OF KENTUCKY,
    No. 29.   {   *Louisville, Ky., March* 8, 1864.

The following order from the headquarters Military Division of the Mississippi and the acts of the Legislature of Kentucky, referred to therein, are hereby published for the information of whom it may concern:

HEADQUARTERS MILITARY DIVISION OF THE MISSISSIPPI,
Nashville, Tenn., February 27, 1864.

Brig. Gen. S. G. BURBRIDGE,
Commanding District of Kentucky, Louisville, Ky.:

GENERAL: In view of the recent enactments of the Legislature of the State of Kentucky, that State is exempted from the operations of General Orders, No. 4, of date November 5, 1863, from these headquarters. Hereafter the civil law will be exclusively relied on in cases such as were intended to be reached by said General Orders.

By command of Maj. Gen. U. S. Grant:

T. S. BOWERS,
Assistant Adjutant-General.

Acts of the Legislature referred to.

548.—AN ACT to punish disloyal and treasonable practices.

Be it enacted, &c. : SEC. 1. That if any person shall counsel, advise, aid, assist, encourage, or induce any officer or soldier of the so-called Confederate States, or either of them, or any guerrilla, robber, bandit, or armed band, or persons or person engaged, or professing to be engaged in making or levying war upon the Government of the United States or State of Kentucky, or upon any citizen or resident of the State of Kentucky, to destroy or injure any property of this Commonwealth, or shall counsel, encourage, aid, advise, or assist any such person or persons to injure, arrest, kidnap, or otherwise maltreat any citizen or resident of the State of Kentucky, or shall harbor or conceal, or shall voluntarily receive or aid any such persons, knowing them to be such, shall be guilty of a high misdemeanor, and upon conviction thereof shall be fined not less than $100 nor more than $10,000, or confined in the county jail not less than six months nor more than twelve months, and may be both so fined and imprisoned at the discretion of the jury.

SEC. 2. That if any persons or person within this Commonwealth, by speaking or writing against the Government of the United States, or of this State, or in favor of the Government of the so-called Confederate States of America, shall willfully endeavor to excite the people of this State or any of them to insurrection or rebellion against the authority or laws of this State or of the United States, or who shall willfully attempt to terrify or prevent by threats or otherwise the people of this State or any of them from supporting and maintaining the legal and constitutional authority of the Federal Government or of this State, or endeavor to prevent or shall oppose the suppression of the existing rebellion against the authority of the Federal Government, every such person being thereof legally convicted shall be

---

* See Part I, p. 173.

adjudged guilty of a high crime and misdemeanor, and be punished by a fine of not less than $100 nor more than $5,000, or confined in the county jail not less than six months nor more than twelve months, or may be both so fined and imprisoned at the discretion of the jury : *Provided*, That this act shall not be construed as restricting any person in his constitutional right of speaking or writing in reference to the manner of administering the Government, State or national, or against the conduct of any officer of either, when done in good faith with the intent of defending and preserving either of said Governments, or of exposing and correcting the maladministration of either of said Governments, or the misconduct of any officer, civil or military, of either of them.

SEC. 3. That any person who shall fail, if reasonably within his power, to give information to the nearest military authorities or civil officer of the presence in, or raid, or approach of any guerrilla or guerrillas to the vicinity in which he may reside, shall be guilty of a misdemeanor, and upon conviction thereof shall be fined not less than $100 nor more than $1,000, or confined in the county jail not less than three months nor more than twelve months, or may be both so fined and imprisoned, at the discretion of the jury.

SEC. 4. That in any trial as aforesaid it shall be competent to give in evidence to the jury the previous character and reputation of the accused as to loyalty [or] as to disloyalty to the Government of the United States : *Provided*, That in any prosecution under this act the test of loyalty shall be whether the defendant or defendants have adhered to and supported the Constitution of the United States and Kentucky, and have complied with and been obedient to the laws enacted in pursuance thereof.

SEC. 5. Any attorney-at-law in this State who has taken the oath prescribed by the State constitution, and who violates any of the provisions of this act, shall, in addition to the foregoing penalties, if legally convicted, be forever thereafter debarred from practicing law in this State. And the violation of any part of this act by an attorney shall authorize proceedings against him by motion in the circuit court of the county wherein he resides, at the instance of any person or of said court, and if said attorney shall be proven guilty on the trial of said motion, he shall be debarred from again practicing his profession in any court within this Commonwealth.

SEC. 6. This act shall be given in special charge to the grand jury by the circuit judge at each term of the circuit court.

SEC. 7. This act shall take effect after thirty days from its passage.

*   *   *   *   *   *

570.—AN ACT to provide a civil remedy for injuries done by disloyal persons.

Be it enacted, &c. SEC. 1. That if any soldier or body of soldiers, or armed band belonging to, engaged for, acting in the interest of, or professing to act in the interest of, the so-called Confederate States of America, or the so-called provisional government of Kentucky, or any armed band not acting under the authority of the United States or State of Kentucky, or any guerrilla or guerrillas, shall injure or destroy, or take or carry away any property of any person, county, city, corporate body, association, or congregation of this State, or shall arrest, kidnap, imprison, injure, maltreat, wound, or kill any person, the person so arrested, kidnaped, imprisoned, or wounded, if living, shall be entitled to recover such damages as a jury may find ; and if dead, his wife if he should have [one], if no wife, his personal representative or heir at law, shall be entitled to recover damages to the same extent that the person himself might for any of said injuries if death had not ensued ; and for the property injured, destroyed, taken, or carried away as aforesaid, the person, city, corporation, body, association, or congregation so injured shall be entitled to recover double the value thereof in damages, and the damages for any of said injuries may be recovered of any of the persons doing any of said wrongful acts, and of any person or persons who shall aid, advise, abet, encourage, or counsel such acts, or shall harbor, conceal, aid, or encourage such wrongdoing, or shall knowingly permit, when in his power to prevent it, any member of his family living with him under his control so to aid, abet, advise, encourage, or counsel such acts, or harbor, conceal, aid, or encourage such wrong-doers, and may be sued jointly with or without such wrong-doers ; or some or any or all may be sued until the damages sustained as above provided may have been recovered by the party or parties aggrieved. Any disloyal person who has knowledge of the presence within the county of his residence of such guerrilla or guerrillas or predatory band, and fails to give immediate [notice] thereof, if it is reasonably in his power so to do, to either the civil or military authorities in said county, shall be guilty of aiding, harboring, and abetting the wrong-doer under the provisions of this act, and shall be held jointly and severally liable with such wrong-doers for all illegal acts done by such guerrilla or guerrillas, or predatory band, or any one of them, during that incursion in the said county.

SEC. 2. In any action under this act the fact of the loyalty or disloyalty of the defendant may be given in evidence to the court or jury, and person's character for loyalty or disloyalty of the wrong-doers, who are not sued, and who committed said acts, may also be given in evidence to the court or jury : *Provided,* That in any action prosecuted under the provisions of this act the test of loyalty shall be whether the defendant or defendants have adhered to and supported the Constitutions of the United States and of the State of Kentucky, and have complied with and been obedient to the laws enacted in pursuance thereof.

By command of Brigadier-General Burbridge :

JOHN D. BERTOLETTE,
Assistant Adjutant-General.

HEADQUARTERS ARMY OF THE OHIO,
New Market, March 9, 1864.

Maj. Gen. J. G. PARKE,
Commanding Ninth Army Corps:

SIR : The general commanding directs that after issuing three days' rations to the men in haversacks and loading what stores can be carried in regimental wagons, all empty wagons be sent at once to Strawberry Plains. Please report also the name of your acting ordnance officer and what ordnance stores he has at Strawberry Plains.

Very respectfully, your obedient servant,

J. D. COX,
Brigadier-General, Acting Chief of Staff.

(Similar dispatch to General Stoneman, commanding Twenty-third Army Corps.)

NEW MARKET, *March* 9, 1864.

Major-General SCHOFIELD,
Knoxville:

Have just returned from Mossy Creek. Deserters and citizens continue to come in, but their news does not reach beyond Bull's Gap, where Buckner is said to be. Vaughn's brigade is still at Rogersville and does not number over 400 or 500 in all, partly mounted and partly foot. A cavalry outpost at Chucky Bend. One man who came through from Greeneville, on Friday last, reports some troops scattered between Greeneville and Bull's Gap, but cannot say how many. At Greeneville he inquired if an office he saw guarded was Johnson's, and was told, no; it was Longstreet's. Supposed Longstreet was there, but does not know.

A rebel cavalry party, 30 or 40 strong, is reported at Massengale's Mill, on north side of Holston, about 8 miles above Strawberry Plains, yesterday. Colonel Garrard sends a party across to-day to look after them. A regiment goes to Morristown to support a cavalry reconnaissance toward Bull's Gap, and another to Mouth of Chucky for same purpose to-day. I have directed every possible means to be used to get immediately some definite information of the condition of affairs beyond Bay's Mountain. My own belief is that Longstreet is gone, and that Buckner is left in command of whatever force remains. Upon examination it is found that the small trestle bridge at Mossy Creek was partially cut by the rebels with the intent doubtless to make a trap for our first train. I have directed it to be thoroughly examined by General Parke and immediately repaired, if possible. I would suggest the examination of the whole line above the Plains wherever there is a bridge or wooden culvert.

The troops at Mossy Creek have an average of 70 rounds of musket ammunition, and Wood's from 40 to 50. The Ninth Corps and Wood's have some at Strawberry Plains. I telegraphed General Potter this morning the amount of cannon ammunition. General Stoneman reports that some riding animals could be bought at less than common Government rates in the country, and I have directed him to let his corps quartermaster make the purchases and turn the animals over, for the present, to the dismounted officers. Do you approve this? It will somewhat diminish the number to be furnished.

Very respectfully, your obedient servant,

J. D. COX,
Brigadier-General.

NEW MARKET, *March* 9, 1864.
Maj. Gen. J. M. SCHOFIELD,
     Knoxville:
Your dispatch in regard to issuing stores and sending back wagons received, and orders issued. Likewise General Potter's in regard to sending for saddle horses for dismounted officers.

J. D. COX,
Brigadier-General.

NEW MARKET, *March* 9, 1864.
Brig. Gen. E. E. POTTER,
     Chief of Staff, Knoxville:
Wood's division battery has 150 rounds, and the Ninth Corps battery 200 rounds of ammunition, including canister. General Wood thinks he should have an ammunition train for both artillery and small-arms.

J. D. COX,
Brigadier-General.

HEADQUARTERS ARMY OF THE OHIO,
New Market, March 9, 1864.
Maj. Gen. G. STONEMAN,
     Commanding Twenty-third Army Corps:
SIR: The general commanding directs that after issuing three days' rations to the men, and putting in regimental wagons all the commissary stores which can be carried in them (besides necessary baggage), all other empty wagons be sent back at once to Strawberry Plains; also, that Captain Fry proceed to Strawberry Plains to receive to-morrow morning 15 horses and equipments for dismounted

officers of the corps. If, so far from having empty wagons, you have still remaining stores in your commissary of subsistence depot after issuing and loading as above, please report that fact and the number of wagons necessary to move the same. Report also the name of your acting ordnance officer to whom ammunition at Strawberry Plains may be turned over.

Very respectfully, your obedient servant,

J. D. COX,
Brigadier-General, Acting Chief of Staff.

NEW MARKET, *March* 9, 1864.

Capt. JOHN N. KING,
Commissary of Subsistence, Strawberry Plains:

I know of no complaint of the returns of men entitled to rations issued from the Ninth Corps. They now claim 4,274, and you may issue them that number till further orders.

J. D. COX,
Brigadier-General, Acting Chief of Staff.

NEW MARKET, *March* 9, 1864.

Major-General SCHOFIELD,
Knoxville:

General Wood has orders from General Granger to send officers to Loudon to receive and equip recruits arriving for his division. He has sent an ordnance officer, but for the purpose of bringing forward the men desires that General Granger be directed to make details from the division there. He also strongly wishes to have the Thirty-fifth Illinois Infantry, now at work on the bridge at Loudon, relieved by one of Sheridan's and come forward. He has about 450,000 rounds of ammunition at the Plains, and the Ninth Corps has some there also, all of the same caliber. All the troops here have the same caliber musket (.58) except one regiment of Wood's, which has Belgian rifles. Van Ness has called for an ordnance officer to come there and receipt for the ammunition. Would it not be as well to make a train for general use, from which we can issue in the field?

J. D. COX,
Brigadier-General.

RINGGOLD, *March* 9, 1864.

Major-General THOMAS:

I sent the order to Colonel Harrison yesterday afternoon. He has not communicated with me, but we hear cannonading in the direction of Nickajack trail. I hope last week's operations will not be repeated. This morning one of our recruits deserted to the enemy; probably a spy.

A. BAIRD,
Brigadier-General.

RINGGOLD, *March 9, 1864.*

Major-General THOMAS,
    Chattanooga:

Colonel Harrison has arrived here. He reconnoitered Nickajack and the other gaps this morning, and found the rebels in larger force than before since the raid. Whether they will move out again I cannot tell. Harrison's command is 4 miles south of this, picketing beyond.

A. BAIRD,
Brigadier-General.

NASHVILLE, *March 9, 1864.*

Maj. Gen. W. T. SHERMAN,
    Huntsville:

Maj. Gen. U. S. Grant directs by telegraph that you dismount your mounted infantry, armed with cavalry arms, as fast as their horses and arms are required for the purpose of equipping cavalry troops for service. This is rendered necessary from the impossibility of procuring horses and arms for the cavalry arm of the service and the necessity of getting it ready for service without delay.

T. S. BOWERS,
Assistant Adjutant-General.

(Same to Thomas and Schofield.)

HDQRS. FOURTH DIVISION, SIXTEENTH ARMY CORPS,
On board Str. Sir William Wallace, Vicksburg, March 9, 1864.

Colonel HOWE,
    Commanding Second Brigade:

COLONEL: You will, as soon as transportation can be procured for your command, embark on steamers at Vicksburg and report to division headquarters on your arrival at Memphis, Tenn.

Lieutenant Smith, in charge of contrabands, will report to Colonel Howe, commanding Second Brigade, for orders and transportation.

Captain Boren, Twenty-fifth Indiana, will take charge of the transportation for the troops of the division and see that the entire stores, baggage, camp equipage, and animals be shipped to Memphis with the troops, or as speedily thereafter as possible.

Respectfully,

JAMES C. VEATCH,
Brigadier-General.

GENERAL ORDERS, }   HDQRS. FIFTEENTH ARMY CORPS,
. No. 17.   }   *Huntsville, Ala., March 9, 1864.*

Commanding officers will at once institute measures to prevent the destruction of fences and buildings by soldiers of this command, and fix severe penalties for such breaches of discipline. Every facility consistent with the good of the service will be rendered the people to raise subsistence for themselves. No buildings, fences, or other property will be destroyed except upon the written authority of a commanding officer, which authority will not be given except when absolute necessity demands it for the good of the service.

By command of Maj. Gen. John A. Logan :

R. R. TOWNES,
Assistant Adjutant-General.

WASHINGTON, *March* 10, 1864.

Maj. Gen. J. M. SCHOFIELD,
Commanding Department of the Ohio, Knoxville, Tenn. :

Prepare your team mules for pack animals so that you can, when the roads get sufficiently good, drive the enemy out of East Tennessee. It will not be necessary to bring your animals to the front, where feed is hard to procure, until you know you want them.

The troops of which I wrote you will be new Indiana troops.

U. S. GRANT,
Lieutenant-General.

CALHOUN, *March* 10, 1864.

Lieut. Col. J. S. FULLERTON,
Assistant Adjutant-General, Fourth Army Corps :

Division arrived at this point to-day at 12 m. Lieutenant Parsley, Second Indiana Cavalry, is in command of pickets on Murphy road at gap, 6 miles from Tellico Plains. Lieutenant Williams, Fourth Wisconsin Cavalry, is in command of one company 5 miles below gap on Murphy road.

A. P. CAMPBELL,
Colonel, Commanding Division.

HEADQUARTERS DEPARTMENT OF THE OHIO,
New Market, Tenn., March 10, 1864.

Brig. Gen. T. T. GARRARD,
Commanding District of the Clinch:

GENERAL : The major-general commanding the department directs me to inform you that his information leads to the belief that there is no enemy in your front between you and Rogersville, except perhaps scouting parties of cavalry; even at Rogersville not more than a few hundred cavalry, and 200 or 300 infantry; possibly no infantry at all. In view of these facts the general directs that you move immediately upon the enemy, and drive him, if possible, beyond Rogersville. At all events, drive any force you may encounter beyond the Clinch Mountains.

The general desires you to report daily to these headquarters, keeping him informed of all your movements, and giving all information you may be able to gather of the strength and operations of the enemy.

Very respectfully, your obedient servant,

J. A. CAMPBELL,
Major and Assistant Adjutant-General.

HEADQUARTERS ARMY OF THE OHIO,
New Market, March 10, 1864.

Maj. Gen. J. G. PARKE,
Commanding Ninth Army Corps:

GENERAL: The commanding general, who has just arrived from Knoxville, directs me to say that he wishes everything ready for a movement on Saturday morning (12th instant). To this end he wishes the trains brought forward from Strawberry Plains in such shape, if possible, as to start with everything full, so as not to be obliged to send back again to the Plains. He expects the railroad to be in running order to Morristown by the time stated. Please see that the ordnance as well as quartermaster and commissary subsistence departments are fully prepared for the movement. Captain King has been instructed to issue on the estimates for rations which you sent this morning.

Very respectfully, your obedient servant,
J. D. COX,
Brigadier-General, Acting Chief of Staff.

HEADQUARTERS DEPARTMENT OF THE CUMBERLAND,
Chattanooga, March 10, 1864.

Col. T. J. MORGAN,
Commanding Fourteenth U. S. Colored Troops:

You will march with your regiment on Monday morning next on a recruiting expedition. You will march up the Sequatchie Valley to Pikeville, thence to Caney Fork and the Calfkiller Rivers, varying your line of march as you may think best for the accomplishment of the business upon which you set out. You will impress no negroes, but take such as volunteer, and bring them to this place, and add them to the two regiments now being organized at this place. You will take such supplies of provisions as you may think advisable, but encumber yourself with as little transportation as you can make answer. Having finished this duty you will return to your camp at this place.

Very respectfully, your obedient servant,
WM. D. WHIPPLE,
Brigadier-General and Assistant Adjutant-General.

LEXINGTON, KY.,
March 10, 1864.

Brig. Gen. S. D. STURGIS,
Commanding Cavalry Corps, Mount Sterling, Ky.:

The major-general commanding directs me to inform you that he does not wish Wolford's division of cavalry to return to East Tennessee until there is grass enough to furnish feed for the horses.

Respectfully,
J. BATES DICKSON,
Captain and Assistant Adjutant-General.

NEAR MEMPHIS,
                                                           March 10, 1864.
General GRANT:

DEAR GENERAL: I have your more than kind and characteristic letter of the 4th. I will send a copy to General McPherson at once.

You do yourself injustice and us too much honor in assigning to us too large a share of the merits which have led to your high advancements. I know you approve the friendship I have ever professed to you, and will permit me to continue, as heretofore, to manifest it on all proper occasions.

You are now Washington's legitimate successor, and occupy a position of almost dangerous elevation; but if you can continue, as heretofore, to be yourself—simple, honest, and unpretending—you will enjoy through life the respect and love of friends, and the homage of millions of human beings that will award you a large share in securing to them and their descendants a government of law and stability.

I repeat, you do General McPherson and myself too much honor. At Belmont you manifested your traits, neither of us being near; at Donelson also you illustrated your whole character; I was not near, and General McPherson in too subordinate a capacity to influence you.

Until you had won Donelson I confess I was almost cowed by the terrible array of anarchical elements that presented themselves at every point; but that admitted the ray of light which I have followed since.

I believe you are as brave, patriotic, and just as the great prototype, Washington; as unselfish, kind-hearted, and honest as a man should be, but the chief characteristic is the simple faith in success you have always manifested, which I can liken to nothing else than the faith a Christian has in a Savior. This faith gave you victory at Shiloh and Vicksburg. Also, when you have completed your last preparations you go into battle without hesitation, as at Chattanooga, no doubts, no reserves; and I tell you it was this that made us act with confidence. I knew wherever I was that you thought of me, and if I got in a tight place you would come if alive.

My only points of doubt were in your knowledge of grand strategy, and of books of science and history, but I confess your common sense seems to have supplied all these.

Now as to future. Don't stay in Washington. Halleck is better qualified than you to stand the buffets of intrigue and policy. Come West; take to yourself the whole Mississippi Valley. Let us make it dead sure, and I tell you the Atlantic slopes and Pacific shores will follow its destiny as sure as the limbs of a tree live or die with the main trunk. We have done much, but still much remains. Time and time's influences are with us; we could almost afford to sit still and let these influences work. Even in the seceded States your word now would go further than a President's proclamation or an act of Congress. For God's sake and your country's sake come out of Washington. I foretold to General Halleck before he left Corinth the inevitable result, and I now exhort you to come out West. Here lies the seat of the coming empire, and from the West, when our task is done, we will make short work of Charleston and Richmond and the impoverished coast of the Atlantic.

Your sincere friend,

W. T. SHERMAN.

HEADQUARTERS DEPARTMENT OF THE TENNESSEE,
On board Westmoreland, near Memphis, March 10, 1864.
Maj. Gen. U. S. GRANT,
Commanding Division of the Mississippi, Nashville:
GENERAL : Captain Badeau found me yesterday on board this boat and delivered his dispatches.

I had anticipated your orders by ordering Veatch's division of Hurlbut's corps at once to Dodge, via the Tennessee River, and had sent A. J. Smith up Red River with 10,000 men, to be absent not over thirty days, when I designed Smith's division of about 6,000 men also to come round. We must furlough near 10,000 men, and by the time they come back the Red River trip will be made, and I can safely re-enforce my army near Huntsville with 15,000 veterans. I sent you by General Butterfield full details of all past events and dispositions, which will meet your approval.

As to the negroes, of course on arrival at Memphis I will cause your orders to be literally executed. A clamor was raised by lessors by my withdrawal of Osband (400) from Skipwith's and General Hawkins' brigade (2,100) from Goodrich's. I transferred them to Haynes' Bluff to operate up Yazoo, and the effect was instantaneous. Not a shot has been fired on the river since. I also designed to put a similar force at Harrisonburg to operate up the Washita, which would secure the west bank from Red River to Arkansas. Admiral Porter has already driven the enemy from Harrisonburg, so that project is immediately feasible. I assert that 3,000 men at Haynes' Bluff and 3,000 at Harrisonburg would more effectually protect the plantation lessors than 50,000 men scattered along the shores of the Mississippi. You know the geography so well that I need not demonstrate my assertion.

I understand that General Lorenzo Thomas has passed down to Vicksburg, and am sorry I did not see him, but as soon as I reach Memphis to-day I will send orders below and show him how much easier it will be for us to protect the Mississippi by means of the Yazoo and Washita Rivers than by merely guarding the banks of the Mississippi.

After awaiting to observe the effect of recent changes, I will hasten round to Huntsville to prepare for the big fight in Georgia. Fix the time for crossing the Tennessee and I will be there.
Your friend,

W. T. SHERMAN,
Major-General.

————

HEADQUARTERS SEVENTEENTH ARMY CORPS,
Vicksburg, Miss., March 10, 1864.
Capt. J. O. PULLEN,
Provost-Marshal, Seventeenth Army Corps:
CAPTAIN : It being reported that something like 350 bales of cotton brought [was] in from the east side of Big Black within the last four weeks and claimed as private property, though there is very strong presumptive evidence that it was Confederate cotton, the mark C. S. A. on the head of the bales having been removed by changing the end and marked "T. S. Dabney" in stencil on the sides, and this cotton having been shipped to New Orleans to-day, you will proceed down the river by first conveyance, and if possible overhaul the

boat having this cotton on board, and if you find the facts as stated, or that there is evidence of fraud, seize the cotton and have it brought back to this post, or detained until the matter can be investigated.

Very respectfully, your obedient servant,

JAS. B. McPHERSON,
Major-General.

HEADQUARTERS ARMY OF THE OHIO,
New Market, March 11, 1864.

Col. ISRAEL GARRARD,
Commanding Cavalry :

SIR : Klein's battalion of your command will report to Major-General Parke, for an early movement to-morrow morning with Willcox's division toward Mouth of Chucky. The remainder of your force will precede the march of the infantry, which moves at 5 to-morrow morning for Morristown. On reaching Morristown one company will make a reconnaissance toward Chucky Bend and act as outpost for a brigade of Ferrero's division on that road. They will take measures to avoid collision with Klein's men should they return that way. The remainder of the command will reconnoiter toward Bull's Gap and act as outposts for Twenty-third Corps on that road. On the march you will report all information, &c., through the division or corps commander nearest you.

By command of Major-General Schofield :

J. D. COX,
Brigadier-General, Acting Chief of Staff in the Field.

HEADQUARTERS ARMY OF THE OHIO,
New Market, March 11, 1864.

Maj. Gen. J. G. PARKE,
Commanding Ninth Corps :

SIR : Your command will march to-morrow morning at 5 o'clock as follows, viz : Willcox's division will proceed by the road leading to the Mouth of Chucky to the intersection of the Dandridge and Greeneville road. thence up the Dandridge road to the road leading from Mouth of Chucky to Morristown, then, and by the last-mentioned road, to Morristown, or as far in that direction as they can reasonably march with the delays hereinafter mentioned.

Klein's battalion of cavalry will precede this division, and will examine the ford at the Mouth of Chucky. the infantry remaining at the cross-roads, or some proper position in the vicinity, till the reconnaissance by the cavalry is completed. The cavalry will also examine and obtain definite information as to the condition of all the fords on the Chucky from its mouth to the bend. An outpost of the cavalry will be left at the forks of the road from Dandridge to Greeneville and Morristown (at a place called Snoddyville on the maps), and the body of the cavalry will make a reconnaissance as far toward Chucky Bend as possible. If they succeed in reaching the road from Chucky Bend to Morristown they will return to Morristown by that road, taking measures to avoid collision with Colonel Garrard's men, who may be upon it. Ferrero's division will march to Morristown and will encamp upon or near the Chucky

Bend road, throwing forward a brigade 2 or 3 miles on that road as a grand guard and picketing their front and flank, carefully connecting pickets on their left with the Twenty-third Corps.

The trains of both corps will move in rear of the Twenty-third Corps.

General Willcox's division will halt and report for orders when they shall reach a position about 2 miles from Morristown on the Mouth of Chucky road.

By command of Major-General Schofield:

J. D. COX,
Brigadier-General, Acting Chief of Staff in the Field.

HEADQUARTERS ARMY OF THE OHIO,
New Market, Tenn., March 11, 1864.
Maj. Gen. GEORGE STONEMAN,
Commanding Twenty-third Army Corps:

SIR: The general commanding directs that your command march to-morrow morning at 5.30, following Ferrero's division of the Ninth Corps to Morristown. Your train will follow that of the Ninth Corps, and both trains will move in rear of the troops of your command with proper guard. Colonel Garrard's cavalry (excepting Klein's battalion) will precede the column. On reaching Morristown you will encamp in front of the town, astride of the Russellville road, in the first eligible position beyond the place. One company of Garrard's cavalry will report to General Parke for reconnaissance and outpost upon the road from Morristown to the bend of the Nola Chucky, and the rest of the cavalry will, under your direction, make reconnaissance toward Bull's Gap and picket that road. An infantry outpost and picket will be placed by you on the road from Morristown to the Holston River, and your whole front connecting with the Ninth Corps on your right, well covered with pickets.

By command of Major-General Schofield:

J. D. COX,
Brigadier-General, Acting Chief of Staff in the Field.

HEADQUARTERS ARMY OF THE OHIO,
New Market, Tenn., March 11, 1864.
Brig. Gen. T. J. WOOD,
Commanding Third Division, Fourth Army Corps:

SIR: You will move your command to-morrow morning at 6 o'clock, marching to Morristown. If the whole march cannot be made without overworking the men you will encamp at evening at Panther Creek. You will be preceded by the troops now at Mossy Creek and their trains.

On reaching Morristown you will encamp in the position formerly occupied by you, picketing the same roads except the Russellville road, in front of the town, which will now be guarded by the Twenty-third Corps. Willcox's division, Ninth Corps, will make a detour to the right and possibly arrive at Morristown by the Mouth of Chucky road after you get in position. Please give such orders to your command as will avoid any risk of mistaking them for an enemy.

By command of Major-General Schofield:

J. D. COX,
Brigadier-General, Acting Chief of Staff in the Field.

MARCH 11, 1864.

Col. T. S. BOWERS,
  Assistant Adjutant-General, Nashville, Tenn.:

General Sherman arrived in person at Vicksburg, February 27, and left same day for New Orleans to see General Banks. Army arrived March 4 in fine condition; had but little fighting and destroyed railroads generally.

I forwarded General Sherman's dispatch to General Rawlins at Nashville and General Grant at Washington by telegraph last night; also by mail to Nashville.

Your dispatch of the 8th just received.

H. T. REID,
  Brigadier-General.

HUNTSVILLE, ALA.,
  March 11, 1864.

Major-General McPHERSON,
  Vicksburg, Miss.:

The following is received from Major-General Grant, direct by telegraph:

That you dismount your infantry armed with cavalry arms as fast as their horses and arms are required for the purpose of equipping cavalry troops for service. This is rendered necessary from the impossibility of procuring horses and arms for the cavalry arm of the service and the necessity for getting it ready for service without delay.

T. S. BOWERS,
  Assistant Adjutant-General.

You will please comply with the above throughout your command. By order of Major-General Sherman:

R. M. SAWYER,
  Assistant Adjutant-General.

HEADQUARTERS SEVENTEENTH ARMY CORPS,
  Vicksburg, Miss., March 11, 1864.

Capt. WILLIAM FINKLER,
  Depot Quartermaster:

CAPTAIN: On our recent expedition many of the families residing on the plantations within our jurisdiction were completely stripped of everything in the shape of horses, carriages, mules, and wagons, leaving them without the means of hauling provisions or wood for their necessary subsistence. Many of the animals and conveyances cannot be made available for Government service by reason of their size, &c., and I propose to give orders on you in certain cases, when I know the parties are destitute, for these things. In turning over you will be careful to reserve any which are or can be of use to the Government.

Very respectfully, your obedient servant.

JAS. B. McPHERSON,
  Major-General.

CAIRO, ILL., *March* 11, 1864—midnight.
(Received 3.35 a. m., 12th.)

Lieutenant-General GRANT or
General HALLECK :

Left General Sherman yesterday at Memphis. Command all safe.
Our total loss, killed, wounded, and missing, 170 only. General
result of his expedition, including Smith's and the Yazoo River
movement, about as follows :   One hundred and fifty miles railroad,
67 bridges, 7,000 feet trestle, 20 locomotives, 28 cars, 10,000 bales
cotton, several steam-mills, and over 2,000,000 bushels corn were
destroyed. Railroad destruction complete and thorough. Capture
of prisoners exceeds our loss. Upward of 8,000 contrabands and
refugees came in with the various columns. Your dispatches by
Captain Badeau received by General Sherman on the 9th. General
Banks in person commands Red River expedition. Sherman sends
A. J. Smith, with 10,000 men, to co-operate. It is expressly understood that they return in thirty days, by which time McPherson's
furloughed men return. Smith meets Banks' column at Alexandria
on the 17th. I have dispatches from General Sherman. He directs
me to proceed and deliver them to you. Where shall I find you ?
Please answer at Mitchell, if it will reach there by 4 p. m. of the 12th ;
after that, Burnett House, Cincinnati.

DANL. BUTTERFIELD,
Major-General.

HEADQUARTERS DEPARTMENT OF THE TENNESSEE,
Memphis, March 11, 1864.

Hon. S. P. CHASE,
Secretary U. S. Treasury, Washington:

SIR : I venture to address you on a point in which you may be
disposed to differ from me.

Before marching from Vicksburg for Meridian, I detached an expedition up the Yazoo to take advantage of the opportunity to
inflict on that country a punishment merited for the connivance of
its inhabitants in the attacks on the steam-boats navigating the Mississippi River.

I ordered the commanding officer to bring to Vicksburg 1,000
bales of cotton, to be deposited with your special agent at Vicksburg,
coupled with the request that its proceeds should be applied to indemnify owners of steam-boats in whole or in part damaged by the
public enemy.

I had no power over such agent, and I also knew that he had no
right to make such use and distribution, and only used the language
to assure steam-boat owners of my earnest desire to remunerate
them, so far as it lies in my power, for damages sustained when in
pursuit of a lawful commerce, and one which aids us materially in
the exercise of the war power. The 1,000 bales of cotton have been
taken and are now in the hands of your special agents at Vicksburg,
and I ask you to appropriate the proceeds of its sale to the purposes
I have indicated. I know that such prompt indemnification will do
good, more good than to throw the parties on Congress by way of
petition for relief.

I contend that as a military commander I have a right by the
laws of war, in no wise qualified by the acts of Congress, to make

similar acts of restitution in kind, but not in money. Thus, if a good, worthy Union man is robbed of his horse or of his cotton because he is our friend, I contend I have a perfect right to take another horse or equivalent quantity of cotton from a Confederate or accomplice of the robber or enemy and make immediate restitution. I have done so and will continue to do so, for that is war.

. Again, although the orders are that when practicable we shall aid the Treasury agents to collect abandoned or enemy's property, when I find it resorted to to swerve military movements, or to corrupt wagon-masters, steam-boat agents, and even officers, I must check it, for the reason that war is the main object of our army, and anything that tends to corrupt it does more public harm than is compensated by the thing obtained. I make these general points because I know some of your agents regard me as hostile to their office. 'Tis not so; my orders are clear and specific that officers and soldiers must leave all matters of trade to your agents.

I don't want them to exercise a supervising or concurrent action. I want the army to be far above the contaminating influences of trade and gain. Let the merchant count his gain, but the soldier is lost if he dream of a cent beyond his pay.

We are getting along well and fast enough in this quarter. Peace and prosperity exists wherever our foothold is secure and each point is becoming the center of an extending circle. I am willing to use commerce as a means of war to corrupt and demoralize an enemy; to make him dependent on us and to loosen his affections to the impoverished section to which he clings with a love which we should emulate. But our army must keep hands off. No fees, no gain, no association with contaminating trade till war is over and peace supreme.

With great respect,

W. T. SHERMAN,
Major-General.

———

HEADQUARTERS DEPARTMENT OF THE TENNESSEE,
Memphis, March 11, 1864.

Maj. Gen. JAMES B. MCPHERSON,
Commanding, Vicksburg:

GENERAL: I arrived here yesterday. En route I met Captain Badeau, of General Grant's staff, who bore me two letters, copies of which I inclose herewith.*

I answered both fully by General Butterfield, who left in a swift packet last evening, and will find General Grant in Washington or wherever he may be.

I think General Grant is making a mistake in taking all the negro troops and Marine Brigade to cover plantations, or, in other words, that the plan of distributing these troops along the west bank of the river will be less effective than the plan I had initiated of defending the Yazoo and Washita Rivers, which would cover the plantations from the rear. But this will manifest itself in time.

Please order General Hawkins and his brigade of blacks to reoccupy the west bank of the Mississippi in such manner as he deems best to protect the plantations and replace his troops at the bluff, or leave it vacant, as you may judge best.

---

* See pp. 18 and 19.

I suppose Adjutant-General Thomas is with you, and, if so, confer with him and let him have the blacks, namely, all such as are not in actual occupation of the forts at Vicksburg and Natchez.

When the Marine Brigade returns from Red River it also should receive orders as indicated by General Grant. In the meanwhile such of the marine boats as have not gone up Red River can cover the plantations from Vicksburg up as high as Greenville. I inclose herewith a letter for General Thomas, which you can read and cause to be delivered.

I have reflected on the proposition you made me before leaving Vicksburg, and will adopt it substantially. After you have satisfied yourself that no force but Jackson's cavalry followed us back to this side of Pearl River, you may furlough all your veterans, and dispose the remainder as garrisons for Vicksburg and Natchez; place good commanders at each place, then in person come to Memphis and give minute returns of each to General Hurlbut, whom we will leave to command the District of the Mississippi, embracing that of Memphis and Vicksburg; then proceed to Cairo, where you can leave some of your staff to receive and organize your veteran regiments as they return, when you may take a twenty days' leave, getting back to Cairo in time to make two divisions of about 10,000 men, which I will order up the Tennessee and across from Savannah to Pulaski and Huntsville. I will give you four No. 1 divisions, and if times out here justify it I will draw further to embrace General A. J. Smith's division. I will leave Hurlbut here until you come up, and if the garrisons left at Vicksburg and Natchez seem small I will instruct General Hurlbut to stop General Tuttle's division at Vicksburg, and bring General A. J. Smith here, when the Red River trip comes out. I send this by a bearer of dispatches, who will bring me your answers; I await them here. Make the figures as exact as possible. I think General Hurlbut will be required, as commander on the river, to make his headquarters at Vicksburg. I want your opinion on this. I dislike to break up corps, but can't help it.

Truly, your friend,

W. T. SHERMAN,
Major-General, Commanding Department.

[Inclosure.]

HEADQUARTERS DEPARTMENT OF THE TENNESSEE,
Memphis, March 11, 1864.

Brig. Gen. LORENZO THOMAS,
Adjutant-General, U. S. Army, Vicksburg, Miss.:

DEAR GENERAL: I have a letter from General Grant, of date March 4, a copy of which I send by bearer of dispatches to General McPherson, and which is subject to your perusal. I have ordered General McPherson accordingly. I wanted to see you, and am sorry I missed you. I fear you think I do not protect lessees of plantations. I know my action inland and the move up Yazoo more effectually covered the east bank of the Mississippi River above Vicksburg than could have been done by 10,000 troops on its very banks.

I know also a similar disposition up Washita would in like manner cover the west bank from Red River up to the Arkansas. I shall still advise the perfection of the plan. Osband's force at Skipwith's and Hawkins' at Goodrich's may have protected a radius each of, say, 10 or 15 miles, but no more; whereas by putting Hawkins' brigade at Haynes' Bluff with facilities for operating up Yazoo, and a similar brigade at Harrisonburg to maneuver up Washita and Tensas, you can cover the river perfectly.

But I have ordered McPherson to put Hawkins' brigade west of the river, to be disposed according to your wishes, and he can add to Hawkins' command any other black troops not actually employed in the forts at Vicksburg and Natchez. He will also direct such of the Marine Brigade as are not up Red River to protect the river between Vicksburg and Greenville to protect the planters and lessees, and when all the brigade of Ellet's is back, which will be in a month, they also will be devoted to the same end. As a speculation this is a bad one. Every pound of cotton raised will cost the United States $500, and so far as effect is concerned it will not have one particle of effect on the main war.

As a matter of course I dislike to see such a mistake made at this period of the war, when we should at least have learned something by experience of our own. It would be far wiser to pension the lessees of the plantations.

In the end we must defend the Mississippi from the Yazoo and Washita, and if you agree with me I will promise 7,000 men on those rivers to cover and protect the plantations more perfectly than 50,000 could distributed along the banks of the Mississippi.

Since I sent up the Yazoo not a shot has been fired from the east bank of the Mississippi, and now that Admiral Porter has taken Trinity and Harrisonburg, the same could be done west. Transfer the fighting to the Yazoo and Washita, and you have peace on the Mississippi; but leave them uncovered, and 20 guerrillas will break up any plantation you establish.

Nevertheless, I have instructed General McPherson to execute General Grant's orders, and when I meet General Grant I will explain to him what I was about.

I will await the return of this courier, and should like to hear from you. Then I must hasten to Huntsville to resume command of the army in the field. I will leave Hurlbut to command on the river with three full divisions and the local garrisons of Memphis, Vicksburg, and Natchez.

I am, &c.,

W. T. SHERMAN,
Major-General.

SPECIAL ORDERS, }   HDQRS. 2D DIV., 16TH ARMY CORPS,
No. 55.   }   *Pulaski, Tenn., March 11, 1864.*

I. The commanding officer Eighty-first Ohio Volunteer Infantry will proceed without delay with that portion of his regiment now at this place to Lynnville, Tenn., to relieve the troops of the Third Brigade guarding railroad. One company will be dropped at railroad bridge above Reynolds' Station, relieving Captain Dykeman's company of the Thirty-ninth Iowa Infantry Volunteers. The headquarters of the regiment will be established at Lynnville or the station, but the largest force will be stationed at Culleoka, where there is an important trestle, and a competent officer will be sent in the command of the troops to be stationed at that place. Upon relieving the troops at the different bridges, &c., the officers so relieving will be careful to procure all written orders and instructions and such other information possible in reference to his duties. If stockades have not already been constructed they will be put up without delay, and so located as to best protect the bridges, &c.

*   *   *   *   *   *

By order of Brig. Gen. T. W. Sweeny, commanding :
                        L. H. EVERTS,
            Captain and Assistant Adjutant-General.

GENERAL ORDERS, ⎰ WAR DEPT., ADJT. GENERAL'S OFFICE,
    No. 98.   ⎱   *Washington, March* 12, 1864.

The President of the United States orders as follows :

I. Maj. Gen. H. W. Halleck is, at his own request, relieved from duty as General-in-Chief of the Army, and Lieut. Gen. U. S. Grant is assigned to the command of the armies of the United States. The headquarters of the army will be in Washington, and also with Lieutenant-General Grant in the field.

II. Maj. Gen. H. W. Halleck is assigned to duty in Washington as Chief of Staff of the Army, under the direction of the Secretary of War and the lieutenant-general commanding. His orders will be obeyed and respected accordingly.

III. Maj. Gen. W. T. Sherman is assigned to the command of the Military Division of the Mississippi, composed of the Departments of the Ohio, the Cumberland, the Tennessee, and the Arkansas.

IV. Maj. Gen. J. B. McPherson is assigned to the command of the Department and Army of the Tennessee.

V. In relieving Major-General Halleck from duty as General-in-Chief, the President desires to express his approbation and thanks for the able and zealous manner in which the arduous and responsible duties of that position have been performed.

By order of the Secretary of War :

                        E. D. TOWNSEND,
                    Assistant Adjutant-General.

                    PITTSBURG, PA., *March* 12, 1864.
                            (Received 4 p. m.)

Hon. E. M. STANTON,
        Washington, D. C.:

Sherman has sent 10,000 men, under A. J. Smith, up Red River to co-operate with Banks on Shreveport. Banks commands in person. Sherman's expedition was eminently successful. I will be in Nashville on Tuesday.

                        U. S. GRANT,
                        Lieutenant-General.

                    MORRISTOWN, *March* 12, 1864.

Major-General THOMAS and
Brig. Gen. JOHN A. RAWLINS :

I have the bridge at Strawberry Plains completed, and cars run from there to this place. My troops are much improved in condition and effective strength. The enemy occupies Bull's Gap and

Lick Creek in some force. Longstreet has certainly sent a division of cavalry to Georgia and some infantry to Virginia; how much I do not positively know. I do not believe his force is much, if at all, superior to mine. I expect to know soon.

J. M. SCHOFIELD,
Major-General.

HEADQUARTERS ARMY OF THE OHIO,
Morristown, March 12, 1864.

Major-General PARKE,
Commanding Ninth Army Corps:

SIR: The commanding general directs that if possible forage, &c., be sent from your command here to General Willcox for Klein's cavalry, and that they be ordered to remain where they are to-night, watching the Dandridge road. Also that the information contained in General Willcox's dispatch be given in substance to General Ferrero, that he may not expect Klein by the Chucky Bend road to-night.

Very respectfully, your obedient servant,

J. D. COX,
Brigadier-General, Acting Chief of Staff.

PULASKI, *March 12, 1864.*

Col. M. M. BANE,
Lynnville:

The general directs that you halt your brigade at Athens for further instructions.

J. W. BARNES,
Assistant Adjutant-General.

HEADQUARTERS SEVENTEENTH ARMY CORPS,
Vicksburg, Miss., March 12, 1864.

Maj. H. E. EASTMAN,
Comdg. Second Wisconsin Cavalry, Red Bone Church:

MAJOR: Information which I deem reliable places Wirt Adams' brigade of rebel cavalry in the vicinity of Cayuga. Be on the alert and watch well all the fords and ferries across Big Black within your beat.

Very respectfully, your obedient servant,

JAS. B. McPHERSON,
Major-General.

MEMPHIS, *March 12, 1864.*

General HURLBUT:

Push the Twelfth Iowa along as fast as possible. I must have two divisions of veterans back from furlough by April 15. My orders from Grant are imperative; not an hour's delay should be made. This applies to all regiments going home. Let Colonel

Woods go along ; the matter of overstaying his leave can as well be inquired into when he returns. It is time now that we must look to [*sic*].

W. T. SHERMAN.
Major-General, Commanding.

HEADQUARTERS SEVENTEENTH ARMY CORPS,
Vicksburg, Miss., March 12, 1864.

Lieut. Gen. U. S. GRANT,
Comdg. Mil. Div. of the Mississippi, Nashville, Tenn.:

GENERAL : I have the honor to inclose herewith a copy of letter* to Major-General Sherman, commanding the Department of the Tennessee, requesting to be transferred to the field of operations in Southern Tennessee and Northern Alabama and Georgia. Also list of regiments in my command which have enlisted as veterans.

I desire you to have a full and complete understanding of the case, as many of the officers and enlisted men in these regiments are beginning to feel that they are not fairly dealt by. I write this in no spirit of complaint, as I am now, as I always have been, ready and willing to do everything in my power to bring this war to a successful termination and to obey the orders of my superiors.

When the orders and instructions from the War Department relating to the enlistment of veterans were received here the officers and enlisted men of my command entered into the spirit of the matter with commendable zeal, influenced by motives of patriotism, the prospect of getting a furlough, of receiving the liberal bounty offered by the Government, and the chances of getting home to recruit their regiments and thus keep up their organization after their original three years had expired.

About the middle of January instructions were received from the major-general commanding the department that a certain portion of my command would be required about the 1st of February to make a short campaign into the interior of this State. I had then furloughed only two regiments, immediately informed the command that their services would be required in the field, and that I could furlough no more of them at present. Without a dissenting voice they expressed their readiness to go on the expedition, expecting a furlough shortly after their return. Immediately after getting back I furnished 2,500 men for the Red River expedition, and am still, without any additional force being sent me, expected to protect and keep open the Mississippi River and exercise my discretion about furloughing veteran regiments. Without some change many of the regiments will not be able to get their furloughs for months to come. The men will be disappointed in their well-founded expectations and disheartened, and the one great object the officers had in view, viz, getting home to recruit their regiments, defeated.

Already we are beginning to feel the effects, as regiments have been sent home from other commands and are being filled up with recruits, while the regiments of my command, not having the same opportunities, are getting comparatively none.

As there is a prospect of a good deal of hard fighting before the war is over, I think it is of the utmost importance that the strength and esprit of the army be kept up.

Very respectfully, your obedient servant,

JAS. B. McPHERSON.

---

* See p. 35.

MORRISTOWN, *March* 13, 1864.
Col. ISRAEL GARRARD, *Comdg. Cavalry:*
You will be guided by orders from General Stoneman as to the force on Russellville road and report directly to him. I send this note so as to run no risk of misapprehension.
Very respectfully, &c.,
J. D. COX,
Brigadier-General, Acting Chief of Staff.

MORRISTOWN, *March* 13, 1864.
Maj. Gen. J. G. PARKE,
Commanding Ninth Army Corps:
SIR: The commanding general directs that Klein's cavalry be ordered to make a reconnaissance this evening toward the mouth of Burt Creek, to ascertain whether any changes have been made in the enemy's position or force. Colonel Klein is supposed to be at Springvale (or McFarlane's), where he was ordered to take position this morning, and where, after his reconnaissance, he will remain for the night unless otherwise ordered.
Very respectfully, your obedient servant,
J. D. COX,
Brigadier-General, Acting Chief of Staff.

HEADQUARTERS ARMY OF THE OHIO,
Morristown, March 13, 1864.
Maj. Gen. J. G. PARKE, *Comdg. Ninth Corps:*
SIR: Lieutenant-Colonel Klein is ordered to report to and receive orders from you so long as he remains in front of your command. This is explicitly stated to him, to remove some apparent misapprehension as to his relation to Colonel Garrard's command. The company of Colonel Garrard's now in front of General Ferrero will be removed in the morning, and you will please make your arrangements to dispense with its services, relying wholly on Colonel Klein for cavalry in that direction.
By command of Major-General Schofield:
J. D. COX,
Brigadier-General, Acting Chief of Staff.

HEADQUARTERS NINTH ARMY CORPS,
Morristown, March 13, 1864.
Brigadier-General COX,
Chief of Staff, Forces in the Field:
GENERAL: The following dispatch from Willcox was received in absence of General Parke. I was about to forward it when I learned that General Willcox had arrived and was then at department headquarters:

HEADQUARTERS SECOND DIVISION,
Sulphur Springs, March 13, 1864.
CAPTAIN: Two reliable Union men, Johnson and Talley, who were arrested by the rebels in Blount County, taken to Greeneville, and, after some confinement in the jail, were sent to Johnson's division and put in Sixty-third Tennessee, have just come in.

They left Greeneville on Wednesday. Longstreet had his headquarters there at that time. Johnson's division was on Lick Creek, about 2½ miles this side of Midway. It was understood among the rebel soldiers that there was a force at Bull's Gap ; as many there as anywhere. The whole number of Longstreet's force understood to be from 20,000 to 30,000. They had not heard of any being sent out of the State. The transportation had been cut down and surplus wagons sent to Lynchburg. Johnson's men expected to be mounted. The railway trains run as usual. One span of Zollicoffer bridge had been destroyed and repaired. Colonel Klein vouches for the men.

Very respectfully,

O. B. WILLCOX,
Brigadier-General.

I have the honor to be, general, very respectfully, your obedient servant,

SAML. WRIGHT,
Assistant Adjutant-General.

MORRISTOWN, *March* 13, 1864.

Brigadier-General WOOD,
    Comdg. Third Division, Fourth Army Corps:

SIR : On reaching camp at this place please send a messenger to General Willcox, about 4 miles out on Mouth of Chucky road, to inform him of your arrival. He will then move his force in and your grand guard will protect that road.

By command, &c. :

J. D. COX,
Brigadier-General, Acting Chief of Staff.

WOODVILLE, ALA., *March* 13, 1864.

Maj. R. R. TOWNES,
    Assistant Adjutant-General:

Immediately on receipt of General Logan's dispatch yesterday I sent messengers to Claysville with orders to have scouting parties sent out ; one of the parties crossed near Town Creek and found no boats building and no troops there but patrols.

Information, supposed to be reliable, places the garrison at Guntersville at two companies, Colonel Norman commanding post. My party at Claysville could discover no indication of an increase of rebel forces.

P. J. OSTERHAUS,
Brigadier-General, Commanding.

TYNER'S, *March* 13, 1864.

General WHIPPLE,
    Assistant Adjutant-General, Chief of Staff:

A deserter came in to-day ; left Dalton on 3d ; reports 40,000 infantry at and near that place ; three brigades of cavalry at Tunnel Hill. Roddey confronts Harrison. Deserter will be sent down ; name, Farris, Thirty-ninth Georgia ; was paroled at Vicksburg ; belongs to Cumming's brigade, Stevenson's division, Hood's corps. Hood is at Dalton. All quiet near me.

R. W. JOHNSON,
Brigadier-General.

PULASKI, *March* 13, 1864.
HENSAL,
    Chief of Scouts:
Send some of best men south into mountains and make arrangements with Union men living there to go to Rome, Atlanta, Montgomery, and Selma and see what is going on there.
                                        G. M. DODGE,
                                            Brigadier-General.

HEADQUARTERS SEVENTEENTH ARMY CORPS,
                    Vicksburg, Miss., March 13, 1864.
Maj. Gen. W. T. SHERMAN,
    Commanding Army and Department of the Tennessee:
GENERAL : Your letter of the 11th instant,* inclosing copies of letters from Lieutenant-General Grant, is just received. Brig. Gen. L. Thomas stopped here one day and is at present in Natchez, but I am expecting him back soon.

I had some conversation with him in relation to protecting plantation and told him I could place one or two regiments of infantry and a battalion of cavalry (colored) at Goodrich's Landing. This he thought would be amply sufficient for the present on the west side of the river. As soon as he returns I shall have a more full and complete understanding with him and endeavor to harmonize matters.

That portion of the Red River expedition from here got off in time, and when last heard from was at the mouth of Red River. I doubt extremely whether the large transports and first-class gun-boats will be able to ascend very far.

Jackson's cavalry division is back between the Big Black and Pearl Rivers, in nearly the same position as before we went out. A report was brought in yesterday that Lee, with 13,000 infantry, had arrived at Canton, and that they were going to make an attempt to hold that portion of the State at all hazards.

The report also stated that Polk had been relieved; that Loring had been thrown from his horse and killed. I do not credit them, but have sent scouts out to Canton to see if any infantry has followed us back.

I will carry out your instructions in regard to furloughing veterans as fast as possible, having an eye to the safety of the posts on the river and keeping the navigation open. As soon as I can learn something definite in relation to the strength and movements of the enemy I will arrange the garrisons for this place and Natchez, and then proceed to Memphis and see Major-General Hurlbut.

Very respectfully, your obedient servant,
                                    JAS. B. McPHERSON,
                                        Major-General.

HEADQUARTERS SEVENTEENTH ARMY CORPS,
                    Vicksburg, Miss., March 13, 1864.
His Excellency JOHN BROUGH,
    Governor of Ohio:
SIR : I take great pleasure in informing you that every regiment from your State serving in the Seventeenth Army Corps has nobly

* See p. 55.

come forward and enlisted as veteran volunteers, thus giving fresh proofs of their patriotism and of their determination to stand by their country until the last armed rebel has surrendered to the invincible power of our American Government.

The campaign into the heart of secession, from which they have but just returned, required the services of these regiments, and they accordingly have been prevented from availing themselves of their furloughs at an earlier date, while regiments from other commands have been sent home, absorbing the recruits and filling up their organizations.

With this view I earnestly request that every effort be put forth by Your Excellency and the people of Ohio in behalf of these regiments.

The best interests of the service require that men with a record so brilliant as that which they have won for themselves in the Army of the Tennessee should receive every attention at the hands of their friends at home.

The country needs such men; the organization of these regiments should be preserved, and they come home to you with the firm resolve to use every effort to that end.

I sincerely hope that they will not be disappointed, but that they will, at the expiration of their furloughs, return to the Seventeenth Army Corps, their full ranks bearing testimony to the loyalty and patriotism of the people and noble State of Ohio.

Very respectfully, your obedient servant,
JAS. B. McPHERSON,
Major-General.

HEADQUARTERS SEVENTEENTH ARMY CORPS,
Vicksburg, Miss., March 13, 1864.

His Excellency O. P. MORTON,
Governor of Indiana:

SIR: I have the honor to report through you to the superintendent of recruiting service for furlough and reorganization the Twenty-third and Fifty-third Regiments Infantry, the only regiments from your State being in my command.

They come to you with the record brilliant in everything that makes up the reputation of the accomplished and gallant soldier. They have not come home sooner for the reason that the military operations in this portion of the army required their services. I believe, sir, their record in the field, and the necessity of preserving to the Government their organization, will overcome any disadvantage under which they may have to labor by reporting so long after regiments from other commands have been furloughed. Confidently relying on the interest of Your Excellency and the people of Indiana in the welfare of these men. I look forward with hope and exultation to the day when, at the expiration of their furloughs, these regiments will return to the Seventeenth Army Corps, with their numbers filled to the maximum, their organizations preserved, prepared to continue their glorious work until the rebellion is crushed and no traitor's foot pollutes the soil of the United States.

Very respectfully, your obedient servant,
JAS. B. McPHERSON,
Major-General.

HEADQUARTERS SEVENTEENTH ARMY CORPS,
Vicksburg, Miss., March 13, 1864.

His Excellency WILLIAM M. STONE, *Governor of Iowa:*

SIR: I have the honor to call your attention to the fact that three-fourths of the men from Iowa in my command have re-enlisted as veteran volunteers, and that the Fourth Iowa Cavalry, Eleventh, Thirteenth, and Fifteenth Iowa Infantry have already been ordered on furloughs, to report through you to the superintendent of recruiting service for furlough and reorganization. While the veteran regiments from other armies have many of them been sent to your State, thus having the first opportunity to secure recruits, the exigency of the service required the men of the Seventeenth Corps in active campaign in the heart of the enemy's country, from which they have just successfully returned.

In behalf of these men of Iowa, who went without a murmur on the expedition, actuated by the same spirit of self-denial and patriotism which has ever characterized them, and with that gallantry which has won for them on many a bloody battle-field a reputation of which their State and country may be proud, I respectfully bespeak Your Excellency's peculiar interest, unusual exertion being required to preserve the organization of the regiments and to fill their commands up to the maximum.

I trust, sir, that every effort will be made in behalf of these regiments, and that I may be permitted to welcome them back to the Seventeenth Army Corps at the expiration of their furloughs with full ranks, prepared to win fresh laurels on new fields.

Very respectfully, your obedient servant,

JAS. B. McPHERSON,
Major-General.

————

HEADQUARTERS SEVENTEENTH ARMY CORPS,
Vicksburg, Miss., March 13, 1864.

His Excellency RICHARD YATES, *Governor of Illinois:*

SIR: The following regiments from this corps belonging to your State have re-enlisted as veteran volunteers and will be ordered north to report, through you, to the superintendent of recruiting service for reorganization and furlough as fast as the exigencies of the service will permit:

The Eleventh, Twentieth, Twenty-eighth, Twenty-ninth, Thirty-first, Thirty-second, Forty-fifth, and Fifty-third, the Thirtieth and Forty-sixth having already been sent on furlough, the latter regiments returning to this corps with full ranks, bearing evidence of Your Excellency's interest in their behalf and the determination of the people of Illinois to afford at every opportunity proofs of their loyalty and patriotism.

The other regiments of the corps belonging to your State have come nearly up to the prescribed number, and I hope soon to announce them as veterans.

Every officer of every regiment is exceedingly anxious to preserve its organization, and I sincerely hope that Your Excellency will cause every exertion to be put forth to secure them in their wishes.

The State of Illinois and the country can ill afford to lose the services of the Illinois regiments serving in the Seventeenth Army Corps and Army of the Tennessee, with whose history they have become so thoroughly identified and in which they have played so prominent a part.

In view of the fact that regiments from other armies have been furloughed, and have in your State filled up their regiments, while the men of this command have been engaged in active campaign, the most strenuous efforts became necessary to secure to these regiments recruits sufficient to fill up their decimated ranks, and in behalf of these regiments, who were so prompted to re-enlist and whose furloughs have been so long delayed, I bespeak Your Excellency's interest and the earnest attention of the patriotic people of Illinois.

I trust, sir, that no regiment from Illinois belonging to this corps will, from want of men to fill up its ranks, lose its place in the grand army of the Union, but at the expiration of their furloughs I may welcome them again to the proud places which they have won for themselves in the Seventeenth Army Corps, where they have ever stood among the first in everything that makes up a gallant and efficient command.

Very respectfully, your obedient servant,

JAS. B. McPHERSON,
Major-General.

HEADQUARTERS SEVENTEENTH ARMY CORPS,
Vicksburg, Miss., March 13, 1864.

His Excellency J. T. LEWIS, *Governor of Wisconsin:*

SIR: I have the honor to report, through you, to the superintendent of recruiting service for reorganization and furlough every Wisconsin regiment belonging to this command eligible to re-enlist as veteran volunteers. This includes the Twelfth, Fourteenth, Sixteenth, and Seventeenth Wisconsin Infantry and the Second Wisconsin Cavalry. The Fourteenth Wisconsin has already returned, bringing with them the fruits of their labors, assisted by Your Excellency and the patriotic people of Wisconsin.

I sincerely indulge the hope, sir, that the other regiments from this corps reported to you, although delayed by active operations in the field, where they have added fresh laurels to those already won in many a bloody campaign in the Army of the Tennessee, will receive at your hands and the people of your State such care and attention as will secure their return at the expiration of their furloughs to the Seventeenth Army Corps, their organizations complete, prepared in future to add new glory and honor to that already won to their State and country by the gallant sons of Wisconsin.

Very respectfully, your obedient servant,

JAS. B. McPHERSON,
Major-General.

NASHVILLE, TENN., *March* 14, 1864—8 p. m.
(Received 1.30 a. m., 15th.)

Maj. Gen. H. W. HALLECK, *Washington, D. C.:*

All is quiet on this front. Schofield telegraphs from Morristown that he is running cars to that place. The enemy occupies Bull's Gap in some force. They have certainly sent a division of cavalry into Georgia and a division of infantry to Virginia,

U. S. GRANT,
Lieutenant-General.

NASHVILLE, TENN., *March* 14, 1864—8.30 p. m.
(Received 1 a. m., 15th.)
Maj. Gen. H. W. HALLECK,
          Chief of Staff:
I will order what remains in the field of the Ninth Corps to Annapolis, Md., as soon as they can go. Please direct the veterans of that corps to assemble at the expiration of their leave at the same place.
U. S. GRANT,
Lieutenant-General.

NASHVILLE, *March* 14, 1864.
Major-General BURNSIDE:
I have ordered the Ninth Corps from Knoxville to Annapolis and requested the Secretary of War to direct the veterans to rendezvous at that place. Please send this order to all regiments of the corps about to return to the field.
U. S. GRANT,
Lieutenant-General.

NASHVILLE, *March* 14, 1864.
Major-General THOMAS:
Do your troops occupy the same line now they did when you telegraphed me their position last? I shall leave here about the last of the week and should like to be posted as to the present position of both armies before I go.
U. S. GRANT,
Lieutenant-General.

HEADQUARTERS DEPARTMENT OF THE TENNESSEE,
Memphis, March 14, 1864.
Major-General McPHERSON,
          Commanding, &c., Vicksburg, Miss.:
DEAR GENERAL: I wrote you at length on the 11th by a special bearer of dispatches, and now make special orders to cover the movements therein indicated. It was my purpose to await here your answer, but I am summoned by General Grant to be in Nashville on the 17th, and it will keep me moving night and day. I must rely on you. You understand that we must re-enforce the great army at the center as much as possible; at the same time not risk any point on the Mississippi fortified and armed with heavy guns. I want you to push matters as rapidly as possible, and do all you can to put two handsome divisions of your own corps at Cairo, ready to embark up the Tennessee by the 20th or 30th of April at the very furthest. I wish it could be done quicker, but these thirty-days' furloughs in the States of enlistment, though politic, are very unmilitary. It deprives us of our ability to calculate as to time. But do the best you can. Hurlbut can do nothing until Smith returns from Red River and matters settle down, when I will order him to occupy Grenada temporarily, to try to get those locomotives that we need here. I may also order him with cavalry and infantry toward Tuscaloosa at the time we move from the Tennessee.

I don't know as yet the grand strategy, but on arrival at Nashville I will soon catch the points and advise you. Steal a furlough and run to Baltimore *incog.*, but get back and take part in the next move.

Write me fully and frequently of your progress. I have ordered the quartermaster to send as many boats as he can get to facilitate your movements. Mules, wagons, &c., can come up by transient boats.

I am, truly, your friend,

W. T. SHERMAN,
Major-General, Commanding.

NASHVILLE, TENN.,
March 14, 1864—8.30 p. m.

Maj. Gen. J. M. SCHOFIELD,
Knoxville, Tenn.:

Order the Ninth Army Corps to Annapolis, Md., as soon as possible. This will necessarily make your operations defensive, until you can have forces forwarded to you. I have expected 10,000 Indiana troops before this, which will go to your department when they do arrive.

U. S. GRANT,
Lieutenant-General.

NASHVILLE, *March* 14, 1864—9 p. m.

Maj. Gen. J. M. SCHOFIELD,
Knoxville, Tenn.:

General Burbridge seems to be doing so well in Kentucky that I think he had better be retained permanently in the command of the district. General Ammen can be assigned to the command intended for Burbridge.

U. S. GRANT,
Lieutenant-General.

HDQRS. THIRD DIVISION, ELEVENTH ARMY CORPS,
Shellmound, Tenn., March 14, 1864.

ASSISTANT ADJUTANT-GENERAL,
Eleventh Army Corps:

There are three hills running nearly in a north line and nearly parallel to the course of the river some 600 yards above the railroad bridge, the first and third being about 500 yards apart, all of about the same height. The hill nearest the bridge has a small earth-work upon it, constructed by Major Hoffmann last fall.

If a redan were placed upon each of the second and third hills, with the gorges op n to the first, the position would hold the valley toward Hog-Jaw Ridge and the good road leading to those hills from the north, but to hold it would require at least three or four more regiments than are now there.

This I would suggest; but not wishing to work the men more than is necessary, nor knowing the importance which may be attached to the position, I respectfully ask from the major-general commanding the corps whether it would be worth while to construct those works.

Brigadier-General Geary, commanding Second Division, Twelfth Army Corps, came to the First Brigade of this division the other day and told Colonel Robinson, commanding, that Major-Generals Hooker and Howard were very solicitous about the first hill I have named; whereupon Colonel Robinson, without my knowledge, at once commenced the enlargement of the work upon the first hill, and it is now going on. Colonel Robinson did this, of course, for the interest of the service, and the work is an improvement, but I have instructed him to undertake nothing of the kind under either expressed or implied orders from any other than his proper commanders in the future.

The major-general commanding the corps told me that a part of Geary's division might soon occupy that position, in which case would it not be as well for that division to do its own work? Be good enough to instruct me as to the above as early as possible, as the redans named would much strengthen the position if it is to be held.

Very respectfully, your obedient servant,
HECTOR TYNDALE,
Brigadier-General, Commanding Third Division.

HUNTSVILLE, *March* 14, 1864.

Colonel BOWERS :

I have reliable information that all the rebel troops sent in the direction of Sherman and Mobile have returned to Dalton, and all the squads of home guards, &c., except pickets on the river, are ordered there, save three regiments of infantry that are moving in the direction of Granby. The enemy are certainly concentrating for some purpose.

JNO. A. LOGAN,
Major-General.

HDQRS. FIRST DIVISION, FIFTEENTH ARMY CORPS,
Woodville, Ala., March 14, 1864.

[Maj. R. R. TOWNES:]

MAJOR : The extent and nature of the district assigned to me render it almost impossible to guard against a surprise by cavalry without the assistance of some mounted force. I therefore respectfully ask that one or two good companies of cavalry be temporarily assigned to this division.

Very respectfully, your obedient servant,
P. J. OSTERHAUS,
Brigadier-General, Commanding.

WOODVILLE, *March* 14, 1864.

General MORGAN L. SMITH :

Learning that your mounted infantry is in pursuit of the rebel cavalry, I will say that I sent this morning one regiment of infantry, Thirty-first Iowa Infantry, toward Claysville.

P. J. OSTERHAUS,
Brigadier-General, Commanding.

HDQRS. CHIEF OF CAV., MIL. DIV. OF THE MISSISSIPPI,
Nashville, Tenn., March 14, 1864.
Col. WILLIAM B. STOKES,
   Commanding Fifth Tennessee Cavalry:

SIR: Your favor by Lieutenant Carter is received. You have no idea of the demands made upon our Government for horses to re-mount our cavalry. No one Government—not all the Governments of the world—could keep so much cavalry mounted while animals are so recklessly destroyed. You know I will gladly aid you at all times in every way that I can to keep your command in good shape, but horses are absolutely out of the question. You must find and take them in the country you traverse. Horses cannot be bought at the North at any reasonable rate, and but few can be had at any rate whatever. If there are not horses enough where you are, we will have to move you to where they can be obtained. I am informed that there are still many serviceable animals all through White, Van Buren, Jackson, and Overton Counties. These must be taken without exception, until you are fully provided. Endeavor to feed well and insist upon the very best kind of grooming. Our cavalry will share in the coming campaign just in proportion to the nursing they will bestow upon their horses, for it is a question of horses, not men, and none can expect new mounts by purchases made north.

As to arms, I will do my best to secure you the best at the earliest possible moment. I am endeavoring to get a depot of cavalry arms, ammunition, and equipments established here for the prompt supply of all these things.

Galbraith was ordered to join you with all the men he had with him, and I will endeavor as far as possible to keep your whole regiment at all times within your immediate control.

Now "pitch in," colonel, and help yourself to horses; "keep your powder dry" and give the guerrillas "thunder" wherever you can find them.

Yours, always,

WM. SOOY SMITH,
Brig. Gen., Chief of Cavalry, Mil. Div. of the Mississippi.

HEADQUARTERS DEPARTMENT OF THE TENNESSEE,
Memphis, Tenn., March 14, 1864.
Major-General HURLBUT,
        Memphis:

GENERAL: I am somewhat suddenly called by General Grant to Nashville. I must leave at once, and after full reflection on the state of affairs in the department since our Meridian trip, I am sure we can safely spare 15,000 men from the river to re-enforce the army in the field, headquarters Huntsville.

I have therefore ordered General McPherson to assemble two divisions of his corps at Cairo, Ill., ready for embarkation up the Tennessee to join me at Huntsville, and, as you know, the fragment of Veatch's division is also in motion for the same destination. I leave you to command on the river, and without disturbing the corps organization I give you the command of all my troops on the river.

You can make your headquarters anywhere you choose on the river from Memphis to Natchez, but it may be Memphis, for the present, is best on account of its proximity to Cairo, through which point all communication must pass.

I know and you know that the enemy cannot now maintain an army in Mississippi, and we also believe that the movement up Red River, now in progress, will extend our empire to the west.

I want you to make sure the defense of Memphis, Vicksburg, and Natchez against any possible contingency, to encourage and protect the navigation of the river, and, lastly, to encourage the change in feeling toward us and our Government by the citizens of West Tennessee and Mississippi. I don't mean by political combination and conciliation, but by the exercise of that power, strength, and confidence that indicates a permanent change in the affairs in this region.

I see in the future two things to be done :

First. By a combined movement, to secure possession of the remaining locomotives and cars on the railroad below Grenada, to move them north of Yalobusha and use them on the track hence to Grenada ; also to encourage the people in like manner to repair the road hence to Humboldt, and so on to Columbus, Ky.

Second. Should the grand army of the center move in strength across the Tennessee into North Alabama and Georgia in all April and May, Smith's division of infantry, light, and Grierson's cavalry should move straight on Columbus and Tuscaloosa, feigning on Selma and swinging up to the Tennessee River above Decatur, giving prior notice of the time they are likely to appear there.

This would be a self-sustaining move, and might be important, and will likely be referred to by me in some future communication. Study the maps well and provide in advance all things, so that should I order it the movement will be exact on time. You and I have both experienced how foolish such bold moves are if not made concurrent with others of which they form a part. I will see you before starting, and will write you fully from Nashville and Huntsville.

Truly, yours,

W. T. SHERMAN,
Major-General, Commanding.

SPECIAL FIELD ORDERS, ⎱   HDQRS. DEPT. OF THE TENNESSEE,
    No. 28.   ⎰   *Memphis, Tenn., March* 14, 1864.

*   *   *   *   *   *   *

II. Major-General McPherson will organize two good divisions of his corps, the Seventeenth, of about 5,000 men each, embracing in part the re-enlisted veterans of his corps whose furloughs will expire in April, which he will command in person, and will rendezvous at Cairo, Ill., and report by telegraph and letter to the general commanding at department headquarters, wherever it may be. These divisions will be provided with new arms and accouterments and land transportation (wagons and mules) out of the supplies now at Vicksburg, which will be conveyed to Cairo by or before April 15.

III. General McPherson will, out of the troops in the district of Vicksburg not belonging to the two divisions named, organize good garrisons to hold Vicksburg and Natchez, and will order the commanders to make reports and returns to Major-General Hurlbut at Memphis, as also to the corps headquarters in the field.

IV. During the absence of General McPherson from the District of Vicksburg Major-General Hurlbut will exercise command over all the troops in the Department of the Tennessee from Cairo to Natchez, inclusive, and will receive special instructions from department headquarters.

V. The officers of the quartermaster's department, and all others in authority, are hereby commanded to use dispatch in forwarding troops and supplies, that no unnecessary delay may occur, and boats must not be held one hour, night or day, at any military post or wood station except for a military reason. Commanders of troops en route or on furlough may report direct to department headquarters at Huntsville, Ala., any stoppage of their boats for any cause, and if unexplained it will be noticed and punished.

*   *   *   *   *   *

By order of Maj.-Gen. W. T. Sherman :

L. M. DAYTON,
Aide-de-Camp.

PRIVATE.]   EXECUTIVE MANSION,
Washington, D. C., March 15, 1864—6 p. m.

Lieutenant-General GRANT,
Nashville, Tenn. :

General McPherson having been assigned to the command of a department, could not General Frank Blair, without difficulty or detriment to the service, be assigned to command the corps he commanded awhile last autumn ?

A. LINCOLN.

CHATTANOOGA, *March* 15, 1864.

Lieutenant-General U. S. GRANT,
Nashville:

My troops occupy essentially the same position as when I telegraphed last. Information regarding the enemy locates Hardee's corps on the road from Dalton to Cleveland, and Hindman's corps on the railroad between Dalton and Tunnel Hill. His cavalry is at Tunnel Hill and on the La Fayette road. I am still very deficient in the latter arm and artillery horses, notwithstanding all the exertions of myself and Colonel Donaldson. The railroad will be finished to Ringgold by the end of this week.

GEO. H. THOMAS,
Major-General, U. S. Volunteers.

HEADQUARTERS DISTRICT OF THE CLINCH,
Cumberland Gap, Tenn., March 15, 1864.

Brig. Gen. EDWARD E. POTTER,
Chief of Staff to Major-General Schofield:

GENERAL: I have information which I deem reliable that Longstreet's headquarters are at Greeneville and Buckner's at Bull's Gap, and that their troops are along the line of the railroad. Vaughn is at Rogersville, Hodge near Jonesville, and Jones at Long's Mill, 8 miles west of Jonesville, Va. I understand also that every horse within their reach is being pressed into the service ; that every black-smith shop and forge is engaged in shoeing horses ; that there is an expressed determination to invade Kentucky (and probably by several routes) from East Tennessee, and that Lee is determined to co-operate with Longstreet in the movement ; that unless they can go where they can get supplies they are forced to abandon this section of the country and go where they can find subsistence. The above statements, coming from the source which they did, have made, I admit, the impression on me that there is some truth in them, and for that reason I send you the information. The informant thinks that Longstreet's entire force is in East Tennessee and near the lines.

Lieutenant-Colonel Davis, Eleventh Tennessee Cavalry, who was wounded and captured on the 22d ultimo, made his escape and reached our lines to-day. He is still complaining, but fast improving.

On the 9th instant about 500 of the enemy's cavalry crossed Cumberland Mountains, 20 miles above this, for the purpose of capturing our pack trains on the road ; but owing to the high water they were compelled to abandon their plan. They came within 12 miles of the gap on the north side of the mountains, but Cumberland River being unfordable there they returned. It is also probable that they heard of the Ninth New Hampshire Regiment coming up. The Ninth New Hampshire was there on their way from Camp Burnside to this place. From this place to Cumberland Ford is 14 miles. The enemy can come down Cumberland River and go from Cumberland to Loudon, or even to Richmond, and go back by way of Manchester, and not be in the slightest danger.

If a force of 300 or 400 were at Cumberland Ford it would prevent a small force from making a raid in that direction unless they would go through the mountain and strike the road near Flat Lick, and that they would probably fear to do, not knowing but what they might be cut off in the mountain and forced to go back through Owsley, Breathitt, Perry, and Letcher Counties, &c. They being apprised, no doubt, of the presence of our force at Mount Sterling, might not undertake the latter route, and consequently would not make the raid.

Respectfully inviting your attention to my last tri-monthly report, you will perceive that I have no troops to send to Cumberland Ford.

I respectfully make the foregoing suggestions, in compliance with my duty to keep you as well informed as is possible for me to do.

In conclusion, allow me to say that I cannot but believe the statement in regard to the invasion of Kentucky, though it may turn out different.

I am, general, very respectfully, your obedient servant,

T. T. GARRARD,
Brigadier-General.

HEADQUARTERS DISTRICT OF THE CLINCH,
Cumberland Gap, Tenn., March 15, 1864.

Maj. J. A. CAMPBELL,
Assistant Adjutant-General to Major-General Schofield:

MAJOR : I have the honor to acknowledge the receipt of your communication of the 10th instant, which came to hand this day at 1 p. m. Inclosed please find a copy of a letter directed to Brigadier-General Potter, and forwarded this morning.* I beg leave to sug-

*See p. 72.

gest, in reference to the requirements of your communication, that with the force at my command I doubt the practicability of the directed move ; in fact it is extremely doubtful whether it could be made at this time, on account of the difficulty of crossing the streams. Powell's and Clinch Rivers run parallel to each other for some considerable distance above Jonesville, and could not be crossed at this season of the year, except in boats or by wading them at shoals. I am perfectly satisfied from the statement of Lieutenant-Colonel Davis, Eleventh Tennessee Cavalry, who was wounded and captured on the 22d ultimo, but made his escape and reached here yesterday, that Jones' force is not less than 800, and that Hodge's brigade, strength not known, is near Jonesville. Colonel Davis also saw General Ransom, and reports his division not far from Jonesville. He represents, furthermore, that forage and subsistence is getting very scarce in the enemy's districts, which accounts for Jones moving up the valley. In consideration of the aforegoing information, I deem it my duty to mention the available force at my command by respectfully referring to the figures in my last tri-monthly report, which shows that the Ninety-first Indiana Infantry (seven companies) has 387 men for duty ; Thirty-fourth Kentucky Infantry (ten companies) has 207 men for duty. These two regiments (594 effective men) are composed of good material. The other two regiments, the Second North Carolina Mounted Infantry (seven companies), 220 men for duty, and the Eleventh Tennessee Cavalry (ten companies), 252 men for duty (no horses), 472 men total, are without discipline, especially the latter regiment, and with their present organization are of but little value.

The large number of absentees will indicate the state of discipline in the Eleventh Tennessee Cavalry. It will perhaps not be amiss to state that Colonel Davis also informs me that the plan of those 500 cavalry of Jones' command, spoken of in my communication to General Potter and who returned the night Colonel Davis made his escape, was actually as stated in the communication mentioned.

It is very difficult for me to keep up daily communication, as there are only two mounted men in my command. In order to enable me to report daily I would respectfully request that a courier-line be established from the mounted force at your disposal, the courier-line that had been established heretofore between here and Knoxville having been discontinued by department headquarters. Another difficulty is that there are no boats this side of Clinton, a distance of 60 miles from here, which I learn from the couriers who brought your dispatches to-day.

I am, major, very respectfully, your obedient servant,

T. T. GARRARD,
Brigadier-General.

———

NASHVILLE, *March* 15, 1864.

Maj. Gen. A. E. BURNSIDE,
New York City:

Leave the 20-pounder Parrotts of Benjamin's battery at Knoxville, and the horses and harness of the same ; also the horses and harness of all other batteries belonging to the Ninth Corps. They can be replaced at Annapolis.

U. S. GRANT,
Lieutenant-General.

HEADQUARTERS DEPARTMENT OF THE OHIO,
Knoxville, Tenn., March 15, 1864.

Brig. Gen. S. G. BURBRIDGE,
Commanding District of Kentucky:

GENERAL: In accordance with instructions from the headquarters Military Division of the Mississippi, the commanding general directs that the troops in the District of Kentucky be reorganized into two divisions. The troops at Louisville and guarding the line of the Louisville and Nashville Railroad south through the State of Kentucky and all west of said railroad will constitute one division, and those east of said railroad and of Louisville will constitute the other. The former will be commanded by Brig. Gen. Hugh Ewing, with his headquarters on the line of said railroad about midway between Louisville and the southern boundary of the district. The commanding officer of the latter will have his headquarters with his troops. The senior officer of the troops garrisoning Louisville will be commander of the post of Louisville, and will be instructed to furnish the requisite number of men to Lieut. Col. J. H. Hammond, commanding depot for drafted men, to guard said depot and to provide the necessary details to go forward with the drafted men to their regiments. The commanding officer of the District of Kentucky will make his headquarters at Lexington or Camp Nelson, that he may properly watch our line in that direction.

I am, general, very respectfully, your obedient servant,

EDWARD E. POTTER,
Brigadier-General, Chief of Staff.

HEADQUARTERS ARMY OF THE OHIO,
Morristown, March 15, 1864.

Brig. Gen. E. E. POTTER, *Chief of Staff, Knoxville:*

Let the cavalry come by Strawberry Plains. The Thirty-fifth Illinois may stay at the bridge at Loudon.

By command, &c.:

J. D. COX,
Brigadier-General, Acting Chief of Staff in the Field.

HEADQUARTERS ARMY OF THE OHIO,
Morristown, March 15, 1864.

Brig. Gen. E. E. POTTER, *Chief of Staff, Knoxville:*

SIR: The commanding general directs me to acknowledge the receipt of yours of 13th instant, and to say that whilst it is not important that the artillery horses ordered for this department should be forwarded immediately, it is still necessary that they should be procured and kept in readiness awaiting his orders to send them. He desires that Captain Hall should be so instructed, and that a full understanding may be had with Colonel Swords on the subject. There should not be a greater delay than twenty or thirty days in getting the requisite number ready, as the commanding general regards it very important that he should be able to make his calculations upon having the stock at his disposal within that time.

Very respectfully, your obedient servant,

J. D. COX,
Brigadier-General, Acting Chief of Staff in the Field.

NASHVILLE, *March* 15, 1864—11.30 a. m.

Maj. Gen. J. M. SCHOFIELD,
        Knoxville, Tenn.:

Six new regiments of infantry are ready to be sent to you as soon as transportation can be furnished. Will you have them in Tennessee or in Kentucky, and order forward troops from the latter State? There are also five regiments of cavalry all ready, except mounting, which you can have if you require them.

Send the Ninth Corps without its transportation.

.U. S. GRANT,
        Lieutenant-General.

ATHENS, *March* 15, 1864.

Brig. Gen. T. W. SWEENY,
        Pulaski:

The general directs that the Ninth Ohio Cavalry be sent to Athens.

J. W. BARNES,
        Assistant Adjutant-General.

WOODVILLE, ALA.,
        March 15, 1864.

Maj. R. R. TOWNES,
        Assistant Adjutant-General, Fifteenth Army Corps:

Captain House just got in from Claysville. I will send him up by next train to give you all particulars of the attack. The rebels captured not over 30 men and a few carbines; all infantry arms are saved. Our loss is 1 killed and 3 wounded; the enemy's loss 5 killed and 6 wounded. The dead rebels were partly buried by us. Captain Smith, of the rebels, was shot through the abdomen by Captain House.

P. J. OSTERHAUS,
        Brigadier-General, Commanding.

HDQRS. FIRST DIVISION, FIFTEENTH ARMY CORPS,
        Woodville, Ala., March 15, 1864.

Lieut. Col. J. W. JENKINS:

COLONEL: The general directs me to instruct you to remain at Cottonville to-night, if not already past that point, on your return to this place.

Endeavor to learn all particulars about the attack on Claysville, and whether enemy received any aid or information from parties residing on this side of the river. If you find any civilians who have so aided the enemy arrest them and bring them to camp.

You can return to this point from Cottonville to-morrow. Request Captain House to report here in person as soon as possible, as the general is very anxious to see him.

I am, very respectfully, your obedient servant,

W. A. GORDON,
        Assistant Adjutant-General.

HDQRS. MILITARY DIVISION OF THE MISSISSIPPI,
Nashville, Tenn., March 15, 1864.

Brig. Gen. J. A. RAWLINS,
Chief of Staff, Military Division of the Mississippi:

GENERAL : I have the honor to report, in obedience to Special Or. ders, No. 58, Military Division of the Mississippi, March 3, 1864, that I proceeded to Mount Sterling, Ky., where I found the cavalry of the Army of the Ohio, under the command of Brigadier-General Sturgis.

I learn that this command of cavalry, in strength between 6,000 and 7,000, was directed to this point, by order of Major-General Foster, to re-equip, assimilating the arm as much as possible, and remount, which I am told by the commanding officer will take until about 1st May to accomplish. This cavalry command was originally armed with several varieties of carbines and rifles, and one of the purposes of removing it from the front appears to have been to assimilate the arm, condensing the variety of ammunition, which in some cases was different in the same regiment. I should rather infer, from a careful reading of the order, that the intention of the major-general commanding the Department of the Ohio was to concentrate the same kind of arm within the same regiment, and not with the intent of replacing by new arms the old, which from length of service should be but partially worn and in no degree unserviceable. The practice of suggesting to the soldier an indifference to the care of the arm placed in his hands, by holding out a possibility of a new issue, is fraught with damage to the soldier and the service, and therefore should not be allowed without more than ordinary urgency. The same variety of arm will ultimately be received in any new issue from the Ordnance Department, and this command delayed very much in its reorganization. Brigadier-General Sturgis states that requisitions have been forwarded to Washington for this new equipment ; that his horses are now ready for delivery, awaiting the arrival of these ordnance stores. I would respectfully suggest, in view of the immediate necessity of this command in the field, that the arm now in their possession be assimilated by regiments and brigades, that their horses be drawn, and every preparation made for an immediate readiness.

The exposed point in the District of Kentucky is Camp Nelson. The troops are not located either to control or prevent the approach of an enemy through Stone or Pound Gaps, via Whitesburg, Proctor, Irvine, Richmond, to this point, the most direct route and best road, and, in fact, there is not a man stationed along this line, and the enemy could reach Camp Nelson without the least intimation of danger. The disposition of the troops proper of the District of Kentucky is not equal to a successful resistance of a raid ; they are disposed around Louisville, Lexington, and north and south of this latter point along the rail, with but about 300 men at Camp Nelson, where the largest amount of public property is collected. Camp Nelson should be immediately strengthened and an officer sent there in command, with rank to appreciate its importance, as well as to cultivate a possible resistance to any approach of the enemy. The end of foraging and equipping the cavalry under the command of Brigadier-General Sturgis would have been subserved as readily at Camp Nelson, if not better, than at Mount Sterling. Having exhausted the slight amount of forage within hauling distance, this command is now receiving its forage and supplies by rail to Paris and thence by wagon, 22 miles, to Mount Sterling. There is no reason why this command should not have been ordered to Camp Nelson, with an advance at Richmond, 14 miles, and another at Irvine and Proctor, still closer to the mountain, as a protection to Camp Nelson, with the advantage of a better knowledge of the movements of the enemy.

The supplies necessary, with what is already on hand at this post (they have about 600,000 rations of corn), would sustain this command readily while in position of reorganizing. Camp Nelson as a post is an anomaly, an irregularity of very great proportions. Located on the Kentucky River, about 7 miles from Nicholasville, the terminus of the rail, the camp is formed by the Kentucky River on the south and west sides and Hickman Creek on the east, leaving an exposed front on the north side of about 1½ miles, protected by three lunettes for artillery, connected by rifle-pits. The area of the camp is about 4,000 acres, and in my estimation would require 10,000 men to defend it properly. Yet within this very slight defense there is being carried out an expensive outline of making this point a great depot for storing, manufacturing, and repairing, with all the conveniences of shops, stores, houses, &c. They have nearly completed water-works, costing from $15,000 to $20,000, raising the water from the river to a reservoir on the hill, and thence distributing by iron pipes through the camp, and this with the river on two sides of the camp and a large spring about the center.

The garrison at this post, that is, the command, is about 300 undisciplined men. The camps of the different companies intended to man the pieces of artillery in battery are located so far from the batteries that any sudden attack must gain possession of these batteries before the men could possibly gain their posts.

At the present time exposed by this slight defense, there is not less than $5,000,000 of public property there, with a growing expenditure constantly going on. If considered as necessary as an advance post to supply the Army of the Ohio at Cumberland Gap and Knoxville, I must state that all supplies sent from this post are packed on mules, requiring from 5,000 to 6,000 for this end, and that from a careful inquiry I am satisfied that every pound of Government stores sent forward in this manner by this channel costs all of $1 per pound. I do not know the urgency that may have originally suggested this line as a military necessity, but I am confident to continue it is an unwarranted expense; it would be cheaper for the Government to finish the contemplated line of railroad through Danville to Knoxville, and open thereby a direct road to East Tennessee. The present mode is unequal to the necessities and attended by great destruction of property.

So soon as it is possible to supply Cumberland Gap and Knoxville by the Cumberland River via Burnside Point, or by the Tennessee River via Chattanooga, the quartermaster's material at Camp Nelson should be forwarded to Knoxville ; the shops, store-houses, &c., located there, and all the means of transportation at or near Camp Nelson, and between that point and Burnside Point or the gap, gathered up and directed to the front. In the mean time an officer of the Quartermaster's Department should be sent to Camp Nelson with power to draw from thence all cavalry horses, means of transportation, transfer wagons, &c., that may not be directly required for present post purposes and made available for the Army of the Cumberland. All means of transportation between Camp Nelson and

Cumberland Gap, and also Burnside Point, and at that point not required for present use should be ordered back to Camp Nelson, and thence forwarded to this point via Lebanon.

The twelve months' men raised in Kentucky on the call for 20,000 are a disorganized, unavailable band of soldiers strongly in sympathy with a growing class of open and avowed resistants to any enrollment of the colored men. These twelve months' men are partially mounted—that is, one or two or more companies in a regiment, making in the aggregate about 3,000 horses. The nature of the service in connection with their location along the line of the railroad does not require this expensive outfit. The horses are used for pleasure and display, and are fast being destroyed by neglect and bad usage. I would respectfully suggest that these twelve months' men be all dismounted and the horses made available for mounting active cavalry for military purposes.

I have also to state that I spent nearly four days at Camp Nelson examining accounts of Capt. T. E. Hall, assistant quartermaster, at that post. In order more readily to investigate the character of the expenditures and also the integrity with which his duties have been performed, I took with me Captain Grant, acting assistant inspector-general of the District of Kentucky, who had made a report to these headquarters, implying a want of purity in the administration of Captain Hall, giving Captain Grant a full opportunity of bringing before me any person who could make my investigation easy by pointing to facts and directing my research. After a careful and close examination, bringing Captain Hall's accounts down to the 10th March, I can only report that so far as investigation could satisfy me, with my very limited powers of commanding testimony, I could see nothing but exact rectitude. Parties that Captain Grant instanced as knowing circumstances impeaching Captain Hall's honesty were examined by me and sworn, and they were some of the most loyal, influential men in the country, but they all to a man assured me that no man had worked more earnestly for the good and economy of the Government than Captain Hall in the execution of his varied duties.

That expenses unnecessary, outrageous, without judgment, without a military purpose, short-sighted, and without the evidence of experience, have been incurred at Camp Nelson cannot be disguised, but in my judgment they are all traceable to the officer in command, who assumed to direct, and is therefore amenable for the unnecessary outlay at this point.

I am, general, very respectfully, your obedient servant,

JAS. H. STOKES,
Lieut. Col. and Inspector Mil. Div. of the Mississippi.

INDIANAPOLIS, *March* 15, 1864.

Lieutenant-General GRANT:

I transferred six regiments of infantry to General Hovey yesterday, which will leave here the moment transportation can be furnished. I have five regiments of cavalry waiting for horses.

O. P. MORTON,
Governor of Indiana.

NASHVILLE, *March* 16, 1864.

Major-General BURNSIDE:

General Parke is ordered to report to you in person immediately.

U. S. GRANT,
Lieutenant-General.

NASHVILLE, *March* 16, 1864—7 p. m.

Maj. Gen. G. H. THOMAS,
Comdg. Department of the Cumberland, Chattanooga:

From your dispatch of yesterday, and also from one from General Logan, it looks as though the enemy was preparing for a move against our line of communications east of Chattanooga, and it may be west of there also.

You will therefore, if you have not already done so, place heavy guards upon the important railroad bridges both east and west of Chattanooga, so that they cannot, without a severe battle, destroy them. This should be attended to without delay.

U. S. GRANT,
Lieutenant-General.

HEADQUARTERS ARMY OF THE OHIO,
Morristown, March 16, 1864.

Col. [THADDEUS FOOTE],
Commanding Tenth Michigan Cavalry, Mossy Creek:

COLONEL: The commanding general directs that you move from Mossy Creek to-morrow morning at daybreak, by the road to Mouth of Chucky, till you reach the Dandridge and Bull's Gap road. From that point make reconnaissance to the Mouth of Chucky, if possible, then take the Dandridge and Bull's Gap road to Springvale, where you will find Colonel Klein, commanding cavalry in that direction, and after joining Colonel Klein report for further orders. Let your train come to this place.

Very respectfully, &c.,

J. D. COX,
Brigadier-General, Acting Chief of Staff.

CAVE CITY. *March* 16, 1864.

Col. C. S. HANSON,
Glasgow:

Send courier immediately to Colonel Weatherford, at Marrowbone or Burkesville, and give the information about Hamilton's attack, with instruction that sufficient force move immediately in pursuit of rebel force. Send copy of this dispatch to the commanding officer of troops in vicinity of Burkesville, who will obey it immediately. You can send all the information you have in regard   the matter.

E. H. HOBSON,
Brigadier-General.

OFFICE CHIEF ENGINEER DEFENSES
MEMPHIS, VICKSBURG, AND NATCHEZ,
Vicksburg, Miss., March 16, 1864.
Maj. Gen. J. B. McPHERSON:

SIR : In accordance with your directions, I have the honor to make the following report of number of troops necessary for the garrison of this post and of Natchez, Miss. :

The development of the interior crest of the line at Vicksburg is about 10,000 yards in length, and will require for its defenses, at the least calculation, 7,500 men. It may be divided as follows : First, commencing on the right at the bank of the river, and following the line by way of Fort Grant, Castle Fort, Cherry street, and battery on Crawford street to the valley terminating in rear of the jail. This part will require a garrison of 2,000 men, with a reserve of 500, which will be located between Castle Fort and Fort Grant, the key points of that part of the line.

The second division will run from the termination of the first, by way of Fort McPherson and Jackson road, to Fort Sherman on Glass Bayou; this will require a garrison of 2,000 men, with a reserve of 500, the latter to be posted about midway between Forts McPherson and Sherman.

The third division extends from Glass Bayou along the ridge opposite Fort Sherman to the north fort ; thence to the Spanish Fort ; thence to the river. This is the most important part of the line, for if gained by the enemy, it would command the other part of our line, the town, and the river ; it should be garrisoned by at least 2,000 men, with a reserve of 500, the latter to be located in the vicinity of the Spanish Fort, and composed of the best troops in the garrison. This furnishes a complete line around Vicksburg, and I think could be held against any force the enemy can bring to bear upon it with the garrison as estimated.

Fort McPherson, at Natchez, is more as an intrenched camp than for the actual protection of the town. The development of the interior crest is about 10,000 feet in length, and will require a garrison of at least 2,500 men to man the line, and a reserve of 500, the key-points being the work at the hospital and the one on the former site of Susette's house. An interior line has been constructed, to which, in case of disaster, the troops could fall back and hold with 1,000 men.

I would respectfully suggest that in case the garrison is reduced to the minimum, 3,000, that the officers in charge of the quartermaster's, commissary, and ordnance departments be instructed to move their depots inside of the work.

I am, general, very respectfully, your obedient servant,
JOHN M. WILSON,
Captain, Engineers.

———

HEADQUARTERS,
Nashville, March 16, 1864.
Maj. Gen. F. P. BLAIR, *Washington, D. C. :*

Why not the Seventeenth, the command of which is now vacant, instead of the Fifteenth Corps ?

U. S. GRANT,
Lieutenant-General.

HEADQUARTERS SEVENTEENTH ARMY CORPS,
Vicksbury, Miss., March 16, 1864.

Brig. Gen. A. W. ELLET:
Commanding Marine Brigade, Mississippi River:

GENERAL: As soon as the services of your brigade can be spared from the Red River expedition you will return to this point with your boats and cruise between this place and Greenville, assisting to keep the river clear from guerrillas, and extend what protection you can to plantations which are being worked by loyal citizens along its banks. You will report-often to the commanding officer of the district and not go beyond the limits assigned without special orders.

Very respectfully, your obedient servant,

JAS. B. McPHERSON,
Major-General.

PADUCAH, KY.,
March 16, 1864.

General REID:

A gentleman who left Jackson, Tenn., on Monday, says the advance of Faulkner's and Forrest's commands reached that place on that morning.

S. G. HICKS,
Colonel, Commanding.

SPECIAL FIELD ORDERS, }   HDQRS. ARMY OF THE OHIO,
No. 7.   }   *Morristown, Tenn., March 16, 1864.*

I. In obedience to orders from the lieutenant-general commanding the Army, the Ninth Corps, Major-General Parke commanding, is relieved from duty in this department, and will proceed to Annapolis, Md., and report to the Adjutant-General of the Army for orders.

II. Their transportation will all be turned over to the acting chief quartermaster in the field, except what may be necessary to subsist them to Loudon, at which place the remainder will be transferred to the transportation quartermaster at Knoxville, who will make his arrangements to receive the train at the point named. The ambulances will be turned over at Knoxville.

III. The battalion of Sixth Indiana Mounted Infantry (serving dismounted) now with the Ninth Corps will report for duty to Major-General Stoneman, commanding Twenty-third Army Corps. Batteries L and M, Third U. S. Artillery, will turn over their guns, horses, transportation, and material to Captain Shields, Nineteenth Ohio Battery, and the company will be transported by railroad upon being relieved by Captain Shields' company.

The remainder of the Ninth Corps present will march on Thursday morning, taking the road running along the north side of Bay's Mountain, parallel to the Morristown and Knoxville road, and coming into the main road at or near Mossy Creek. Their reserved transportation may be sent by the main road. The officers of the command are enjoined to allow as little as possible to be known of the direction or purpose of their movement.

IV. Brigadier-General Wood, commanding Third Division, Fourth Army Corps, is ordered to relieve Colonel Morrison's brigade, Ninth Corps, on the Chucky Bend road, this (Wednesday) evening, with two regiments of his command. He will move one brigade to-morrow morning, 17th instant, into the line now occupied by the Ninth Corps, keeping the remaining brigade in reserve in vicinity of the present camp.

By command of Major-General Schofield:

J. A. CAMPBELL,
Assistant Adjutant-General.

SPECIAL ORDERS, }   HDQRS. 1ST DIV., U. S. COL. TROOPS,
No. 10.   }   *Vicksburg, Miss., March* 16, 1864.

I. The First Mississippi Infantry, A. D.; Fourth Mississippi, A. D., and one battalion of the First Mississippi Cavalry, A. D., will hold themselves in readiness to proceed with their transportation, camp and garrison equipage, &c., to Goodrich's Landing, La., where they will be assigned, under the direction of Brig. Gen. L. Thomas, Adjutant-General U. S. Army, for the protection of the plantation interests of Milliken's Bend, Goodrich's Landing, La., Lake Providence, and Skipwith's Landing.

The commanding officers of the Fourth Mississippi Infantry, A. D., and the battalion of the First Mississippi Cavalry, A. D., will report to Col. A. W. Webber, First Mississippi Infantry, A. D., for orders.

 *   *   *   *   *

By order of Brig. Gen. J. P. Hawkins:

S. B. FERGUSON,
Assistant Adjutant-General.

GENERAL ORDERS, }   NASHVILLE,
No. 1.   }   *March* 17, 1864.

In pursuance of the following order of the President—

EXECUTIVE MANSION,
Washington, D. C., March, 1864.

Under the authority of an act of Congress to revive the grade of lieutenant-general in the United States Army, approved February 29, 1864, Lieut. Gen. Ulysses S. Grant, U. S. Army, is assigned to the command of the armies of the United States.

ABRAHAM LINCOLN.

I assume command of the armies of the United States, headquarters in the field, and until further orders will be with the Army of the Potomac. There will be an office, headquarters in Washington, to which all communications will be sent except those from the army where headquarters are at the date of their address.

U. S. GRANT,
Lieutenant-General.

NASHVILLE, *March* 17, 1864.

General SCHOFIELD:

I have had an inspection made of Camp Nelson and Mount Sterling. It shows a wasteful extravagance there and also that the points are badly selected. It seems to me that Camp Nelson should be broken up entirely and the public property issued where it will be of service. I would suggest that Brigadier-General Cox or some other intelligent officer be sent into that part of Kentucky, with authority to make such changes as the public good may seem to demand. The troops should watch closely an advance of the enemy from Western Virginia. As soon as I return from the East I will try to get up an expedition from Western Virginia to move onto the railroad to the rear of Breckinridge. I have ordered the new cavalry to Mount Sterling, as you request. Cannot Cumberland Gap be supplied from Knoxville better than as now supplied?

U. S. GRANT,
Lieutenant-General.

MORRISTOWN, *March* 17, 1864—11 p. m.

Lieutenant-General GRANT:

I will send General Cox to Camp Nelson to attend to affairs in that part of Kentucky as you suggest. While compelled to remain on the defensive, I will distribute my force north of the Holston so as to hold the valleys between that river and Cumberland Gap, so as to guard as far as possible against any movement into East Tennessee. I will be able to meet any movement into that State from Western Virginia. Cumberland Gap can, I think, be better supplied from Knoxville, for a time at least. I will so order.

J. M. SCHOFIELD,
Major-General.

MORRISTOWN, *March* 17, 1864.

Brigadier-General POTTER,
Chief of Staff, Knoxville:

General Grant has ordered the Ninth Corps away; they are moving to-day. We send back our surplus wagons to the Plains. Direct Barriger and Ransom to send only such stores as we can at all times issue or carry in one wagon to the regiment.

By command, &c.:

J. D. COX,
Brigadier-General, Acting Chief of Staff in the Field.

NASHVILLE, *March* 17, 1864—10.30 a. m.

Maj. Gen. GEORGE H. THOMAS,
Chattanooga:

Commence moving the surplus troops you have on the line of the Nashville and Chattanooga road to the Columbia and Decatur road, so as to relieve the troops now there to be moved to the front.

There is now on the road a regiment of cavalry, well mounted and over 1,100 strong, and two regiments of colored troops that will be left.

U. S. GRANT,
Lieutenant-General.

NASHVILLE, *March* 17, 1864.

Major-General THOMAS:

Major-General Sherman has been assigned to the command of this military division, and having arrived at Nashville this evening, hereafter all official communications will be addressed to him.

U. S. GRANT,
Lieutenant-General.

(Same to Generals Schofield and Logan.)

CHATTANOOGA, *March* 17, 1864.

Maj. Gen. H. W. SLOCUM,
Tullahoma:

Arrange to send a brigade, in numbers if not in organization, to the defense of the Columbia and Decatur road. The troops on that line are to be sent elsewhere. Do this without reference to Coburn's brigade, which must soon come to the front. Report to-morrow what troops you can send. The troops of the Twelfth Corps will be returned to you eventually, but at present must be used to guard the roads.

WM. D. WHIPPLE,
Assistant Adjutant-General.

HDQRS. FIRST DIVISION, FIFTEENTH ARMY CORPS,
Woodville, Ala., March 17, 1864.

Lieutenant-Colonel KAERCHER,
Twelfth Missouri:

COLONEL: The general has received information that the enemy is crossing the river at Port Deposit. You will use all endeavors to ascertain the truth of the rumor and report facts in the case as soon as possible, using all proper precautions against surprise.

By order of Brig. Gen. P. J. Osterhaus:

W. A. GORDON,
Assistant Adjutant-General.

HEADQUARTERS OF THE POST,
Columbus, Ky., March 17, 1864.

Capt. J. H. ODLIN,
Assistant Adjutant-General, Cairo, Ill.:

CAPTAIN: I have the honor to report that information has been given me to-day by Lieutenant-Colonel Dobozy, of the Second Tennessee Heavy Artillery, as follows:

A contraband reported to him to-day, having just come from Paris, Tenn., that at that town he saw and counted 500 guerrillas; that on the road leading from Paris to this place he counted 216, about 10 miles from Paris, and about 25 miles from there 130 more, making an aggregate of 846; and that as far as he could hear they were making for Mayfield and Paducah. I would again respectfully urge that I be allowed to employ a scout.

I am, sir, very respectfully, your obedient servant.

WM. HUDSON LAWRENCE,
Colonel Thirty-fourth New Jersey Vols., Comdy. Post.

PADUCAH, *March* 17, 1864.

General REID,
    Commanding, Cairo:

Please send me 400 muskets and equipments immediately. If they are not in Cairo please telegraph to Columbus and have them sent up. I have received secret information of a plot to attack this place. I have men enough to use the arms called for. Let me know how soon they will be here.

S. G. HICKS,
Colonel, Commanding.

HEADQUARTERS SEVENTEENTH ARMY CORPS,
Vicksburg, Miss., March 17, 1864.

Col. A. W. WEBBER,
    First Mississippi Infantry, A. D., in command of Forces
        assigned to the protection of Goodrich's Landing:

COLONEL : The following instructions are issued for your guidance in the disposition of the troops of your command in the occupation of the country designed to be protected from the inroads of the enemy : First. You will proceed with your own regiment, the Fourth Mississippi, and Second Louisiana Battery (four guns), to Milliken's Bend, where you will disembark five companies, under command of a competent field officer. Second. Thence you will proceed to Goodrich's Landing, disembark the remainder of your command, and send a strong reconnoitering force out to Bayou Macon to discover if there be any enemy in the vicinity. Third. You will also send a force of at least a regiment up to Lake Providence to reconnoiter the country in that region, with instructions to throw up intrenchments to be occupied by five companies, which you will leave there under a competent field officer. Fourth. While you will afford protection as far as possible to the plantation interests, all your operations will be conducted and dispositions of your forces made with a view to a strictly military occupation of the country. You will see that your troops are not permitted to straggle or small parties placed in positions where they can be successfully attacked by the raids of guerrillas or any scouting force of the enemy.

At the earliest practicable moment you will make a detailed report to these headquarters, showing the results of your reconnoitering parties and disposition of your troops.

Very respectfully, your obedient servant,

JAS. B. McPHERSON,
Major-General.

HEADQUARTERS SIXTEENTH ARMY CORPS,
Memphis, Tenn., March 17, 1864.

Honorable SECRETARY OF WAR,
    Washington, D. C.:

SIR : I have just returned from the Meridian expedition and find a communication for me containing grave charges, signed by one D. Hirsch. I am required to make full report, which will take some time, owing to the absence of Mr. Loop and others. I desire now simply to state that so far as I am charged with official misconduct, or the reception of bribes in any form, the charge is absolutely false, the coinage of a disappointed traitor.

Your obedient servant,

S. A. HURLBUT,
Major-General.

SPECIAL ORDERS, }   HDQRS. SIXTEENTH ARMY CORPS,
No. 62.   }   *Memphis, Tenn., March 17, 1864.*

*   *   *   *   *   *   *

IX. The citizens of the county of Tipton, Tenn., having by a large majority enrolled themselves to preserve life and property and to keep the peace within said county, and pledged themselves in writing so to do against all persons except organized forces of the United States or of the Confederate States, it is ordered that no troops of this command shall enter said county, except under written orders from the commanding officer at Memphis, and that no property of any kind shall be taken by military seizures within said county. This privilege will continue so long as the said citizens shall in good faith perform the said agreement, and the same privilege will be extended to other counties which shall in good faith adopt and carry out this course.

*   *   *   *

By order of Maj. Gen. S. A. Hurlbut:

T. H. HARRIS,
Assistant Adjutant-General.

GENERAL ORDERS, }   HDQRS. MIL. DIV. OF THE MISSISSIPPI,
No. 1.   }   *Nashville, Tenn., March 18, 1864.*

I. The undersigned hereby assumes command of the Military Division of the Mississippi, embracing the Departments of the Ohio, Cumberland, Tennessee, and Arkansas; headquarters in the field, with an office at Nashville, Tenn., where all returns and reports will be addressed.

II. Maj. R. M. Sawyer, assistant adjutant-general, is announced as adjutant-general of the military division, to whom reports will be addressed. The staff for the division will be selected and duly announced in orders.

W. T. SHERMAN,
Major-General, Commanding.

HEADQUARTERS DIVISION OF THE MISSISSIPPI,
Nashville, March 18, 1864.

Major-General SCHOFIELD,
Commanding Department of the Ohio, Knoxville:

GENERAL: I am just arrived and assumed command. General Grant leaves for the East to-morrow. I have had a full conversation with him, and to enable him to fulfill his plans I can merely foreshadow coming events. You will push Longstreet from up the valley as far as you can, and prepare to break up the railroad back toward Knoxville. Hold Knoxville and the gap. Also arrange to have a force of cavalry, infantry, and light artillery on the waters of the Big Sandy in the direction of Prestonburg, which must subsist on the country, and not locate, but act so as to threaten or attack any force coming from the northeast. Your main army should at once be organized for offense, ready at the proper time to drop down to the Hiwassee, to move in concert with the main army. I am aware of the difficulties you have in maintaining your army. Appoint good officers to take charge of this branch of your business, and accumulate stores rather at the Hiwassee than at Knoxville. Your route of advance will be most probably by Spring Place. Keep your own counsel; discourage the presence of all strangers; make the citizens feed themselves, and if they are likely to consume the reserves of the country facilitate their removal to the rear. The necessities of war must have precedence of civilians. Write me fully and frankly always. I will see you in person as soon as I can.

W. T. SHERMAN,
Major-General, Commanding.

NASHVILLE, *March* 18, 1864.

Maj. Gen. J. M. SCHOFIELD,
Knoxville, Tenn.:

Col. Frank Wolford. First Kentucky Cavalry, has this day been ordered to report to you in person in arrest. You will cause your judge-advocate or some other staff officer to prepare charges against him based on his recent speech in Kentucky, and cause, as soon as practicable, a general court-martial to be convened for his trial.

By order of Lieutenant-General Grant:

T. S. BOWERS,
Assistant Adjutant-General.

HEADQUARTERS ARMY OF THE OHIO,
New Market, March 18, 1864.

Major-General STONEMAN,
Commanding Twenty-third Corps:

SIR: The commanding general directs that your command remain for the present at Mossy Creek and hold the position unless threatened by a superior force of the enemy, in which case you will fall back to Strawberry Plains. Two brigades of General Wood's division are ordered to Rutledge, and both portions of the command will make use of all available means to keep constantly informed of the movements of the enemy. Lieutenant-Colonel Klein will remain, with his cavalry, attached to your command until further orders, and Colonel Garrard will cross the Holston with the remainder of the cavalry at Troglan's Ford (a little below mouth of Mossy Creek) and will report to General Wood. The remaining brigade of Wood's division will be at Strawberry Plains. Colonel Crawford, chief of scouts, with his employés, will remain at Mossy Creek, and a telegraph operator will be ordered to report to you there.

The commanding general desires that Crawford's scouts be kept actively at work, and test as thoroughly as possible the truth of the rumored intention of the enemy to make a raid into Kentucky.

Very respectfully, your obedient servant,

J. D. COX,
Brigadier-General, Acting Chief of Staff.

HEADQUARTERS ARMY OF THE OHIO,
New Market, March 18, 1864.

Brigadier-General WOOD,
Commanding Third Division, Fourth Army Corps:

SIR : Your command will march in the morning to Strawberry Plains. From that place you will immediately furlough and send home all veteran regiments re-enlisting. You will then leave the smallest brigade at Strawberry Plains and march with the other two to Rutledge. At that place Colonel Garrard, with his cavalry, will report to you, and you will open communications with General Garrard at Cumberland Gap, and co-operate with him in watching the movements of the enemy on the north side of the Holston, and preventing any movement into Middle Tennessee or Kentucky. You will so dispose your force as best to accomplish this design, taking care to preserve the ability to concentrate your command in time to meet any movement in force on the part of the rebels.

You will communicate promptly to these headquarters all information you may receive, sending a courier at least once a day. Information which ought to be quickly known to General Stoneman at Mossy Creek, you will communicate also to him by courier by way of the fords of Holston.

Very respectfully, your obedient servant,

J. D. COX,
Brigadier-General, Acting Chief of Staff.

KNOXVILLE, *March* 18, 1864.

Major-General GRANGER,
Loudon:

The company of heavy artillery is wanted here. The 3-inch guns, it seems, were sent for Henshaw's battery, and will also be required. General Tillson will send a section of a battery to Loudon with men. Cannot the section which you sent to Hiwassee be returned? I am told there are two batteries now there.

EDWARD E. POTTER,
Brigadier-General, Chief of Staff.

HEADQUARTERS DEPARTMENT OF THE CUMBERLAND,
Chattanooga, Tenn., March 18, 1864.

Maj. Gen. W. T. SHERMAN,
Comdg. Mil. Div. of the Mississippi, Nashville, Tenn.:

GENERAL : I have the honor to report for your information the following as the position of the troops of the Army of the Cumberland :

The Twelfth Corps (Slocum's) at Fort Donelson, Clarksville, Gallatin, Nashville, and on the Nashville and Chattanooga Railroad as far south as Bridgeport..

Two regiments of negro infantry and a regiment of Tennessee cavalry on the Northwestern Railroad.

Stokes' Fifth Tennessee Cavalry at Sparta, operating against the guerrillas, who, under Hamilton, Ferguson, Carter, Murray, and Hughs, have infested that country since the war commenced.

The Eleventh Corps (Howard's) on the railroad, between Bridgeport and this place.

This place is garrisoned by eight regiments of infantry, one regiment of negro troops (Fourteenth U. S. Colored), one company of siege artillery, and six batteries of field artillery, dismounted. The post is commanded by Brig. Gen. James B. Steedman.

Two divisions of the Fourth Corps, under Gordon Granger, and the Tennessee brigade of infantry, are on detached service with the Army of the Ohio in East Tennessee.

One division (Stanley's), Fourth Corps, is stationed at Blue Springs (5 miles in advance of Cleveland, on the railroad between that place and Dalton) and at Ooltewah.

The Fourteenth Corps (Palmer's) is posted as follows : One division (Johnson's) at Graysville, with a strong outpost at Parker's Gap; one division (Baird's) at Ringgold; and one division (Davis') at McAfee's Church, about 8 miles in advance of this place, on the Ringgold wagon road, with a brigade advanced to Gordon's Mills on Chickamauga Creek, at the crossing of the road from this place to La Fayette.

Two brigades of cavalry are at Cleveland, one at Ringgold, and one division at Huntsville, when the regiments taken away by Brigadier-General Smith for the Mississippi expedition return from Memphis.

The troops occupy strong positions, and are favorably placed to guard the railroad to East Tennessee and the Charleston railroad,. so far as occupied.

Signal stations are established in the most favorable positions for observing the roads and the country for 6 or 8 miles in advance of the camps, and the officers on duty have instructions to report immediately all movements of the enemy which they observe. I have telegraph and signal communications with every camp, as well as by courier. I also get information from Dalton every two or three days by two different routes, brought by persons who are unacquainted with each other; so far their reports have been confirmatory. They report the following troops at Dalton : Hardee's corps, composed of Cheatham's, Cleburne's, Walker's, and Bate's divisions; Hood's corps (late Polk's), composed of Stevenson's, Stewart's, and Hindman's divisions; Roddey's cavalry, and two brigades of Wheeler's cavalry.

Johnston commands the army in person. He has about 40,000 infantry, three batteries to each division, and between 10,000 and 11,000 cavalry, with two batteries of artillery. There are very few troops in Rome; about 10,000 State troops at Kingston and Etowah bridge; a small force at Resaca.

I am, general, very respectfully, your obedient servant,
GEO. H. THOMAS,
Major-General, U. S. Volunteers, Commanding.

BRIDGEPORT, *March* 18, 1864.
(Received 5.30 p. m.)
Major-General SLOCUM:

I have just returned from reconnaissance to Trenton and southward. Did not ascertain location of any large bodies of the enemy. Some squads are reported in Will's Valley.

I captured 6 rebel soldiers belonging to Cleburne's division.

JNO. W. GEARY,
Brigadier-General, Commanding.

WOODVILLE, ALA.,
March 18, 1864.
Maj. R. R. TOWNES,
Assistant Adjutant-General, Huntsville, Ala.:

The commanding officer of the Twelfth Missouri Infantry just returned from the river with his regiment and some eighty wagons of forage. He saw the rebel pickets on the south bank of the river, and had information from different parties that they would come across to attack him, but he was not molested in any way. The officer could not find out positively that any rebs had crossed within the last four days. Colonel Gage, with a portion of his regiment, mounted on mules. will be at the river, near, and scout the whole country thoroughly.

P. J. OSTERHAUS,
Brigadier-General, Commanding Division.

MEMPHIS, TENN.,
March 18, 1864—2.30 p. m.
Maj. Gen. W. T. SHERMAN:

Forrest has mounted his whole command; was at Tupelo night before last, bound, I think, for Columbus and Paducah. General Dodge should, I think, be ordered on his flank. My cavalry have not horses enough to mount one-third, but I will have them moving.

S. A. HURLBUT,
Major-General.

HEADQUARTERS SIXTEENTH ARMY CORPS,
Memphis, Tenn., March 18, 1864.
Brig. Gen. B. H. GRIERSON,
Commanding Cavalry Division, Sixteenth Army Corps:

SIR: It is reported that Forrest with about 7,000 men was at Tupelo last night or night before, bound for West Tennessee. Bring your cavalry at once into the best state of efficiency and watch him closely. I think he means Columbus or Paducah. Inform General Buckland fully of all matters you learn. Hire scouts at any price, and if he swings north hang on his rear with such infantry as can be spared. I will see to his reception at Columbus.

Your obedient servant,

S. A. HURLBUT,
Major-General.

PADUCAH, KY.,
March 18, 1864.

Brig. Gen. H. T. REID,
Commanding District of Columbus:

I have received the arms called for ; am quietly distributing them, and have everything in readiness if the contemplated attack should be made. You will hear from me again. I am fully and reliably posted as to their intention and manner of doing it. I am now fully prepared to see them.

Very respectfully, your obedient servant,
S. G. HICKS,
Colonel, Commanding.

WASHINGTON, D. C.,
March 18, 1864—10.55 a. m.

Governor JOHN BROUGH,
Columbus, Ohio :

The Twelfth Regiment Ohio Cavalry will be ordered to Nashville, Tenn., unless otherwise directed by General Grant. Colonel Ratliff will be relieved from court-martial.

H. W. HALLECK,
Major-General, Chief of Staff.

HEADQUARTERS OF THE ARMY,
Washington, March 19, 1864.

General W. T. SHERMAN,
Commanding, &c., Nashville, Tenn.:

MY DEAR GENERAL : I send you herewith your commission as brigadier-general in the Regular Army. My only regret is that it is not for a higher grade, but that I think will not be very long delayed. I have strong hopes that you will be appointed in the vacancy made by General Grant's promotion.

I congratulate you on your new command. It certainly is an important one, and your troops are good. There, however, are some elements in the higher grades that may give you trouble unless you are continually on your guard against their intrigues. Be very cautious in what you say and do, for they will be ever ready to take all possible advantage.

Write to me freely about all your affairs.

Yours, truly,

H. W. HALLECK,
Major-General, Chief of Staff.

KNOXVILLE, *March* 19, 1864.

Maj. Gen. W. T. SHERMAN :

Permit me to urge that the troops intended for this command be forwarded as soon as practicable. Longstreet is making preparations as if for a raid into Kentucky or Middle Tennessee. If this is his design it can be prevented by a successful advance here before he is ready, and I believe in no other way.

J. M. SCHOFIELD,
Major-General.

KNOXVILLE, *March* 19, 1864—11.30 p. m.

Maj. Gen. W. T. SHERMAN:

The Ninth Army Corps is now here waiting for transportation. On account of the difficulty in obtaining transportation by railroad, I propose to send the greater part of the corps via Camp Burnside to Lexington, while the sick and baggage are sent by rail. They can march across in less time than they can go by rail, and the effect on Kentucky may have a beneficial effect, if there is any truth in the reports of impending trouble there. Please inform me whether you approve of the suggestion.

J. M. SCHOFIELD,
Major-General.

HEADQUARTERS ARMY OF THE OHIO,
Strawberry Plains, March 19, 1864.

Major-General STONEMAN,
Commanding Twenty-third Army Corps:

SIR: Your dispatch of this morning is received. The commanding general has supposed that Captains Fry and Treat would provide regularly for the wants of the corps, in addition to the duty required of them here temporarily, and does not desire them relieved of the corps duty. Officers in those departments are few, and he wishes to continue the present arrangement unless the necessities of your command demand their continued personal presence at corps headquarters. In that case he would endeavor in some manner to relieve them here and supply their place. The medical director, as well as Colonel Crawford and the scouts, are ordered to report to you and will be with you to-morrow at furthest.

Very respectfully, your obedient servant,

J. D. COX,
Brigadier-General, Acting Chief of Staff.

HEADQUARTERS OF THE ARMY,
Washington, March 19, 1864.

General G. H. THOMAS,
Commanding, &c., Chattanooga:

MY DEAR GENERAL: I send herewith your commission as brigadier-general in the Regular Army, an appointment long delayed, but most fully earned. In this statement not only the Government and the Army but the whole country will concur.

Yours, truly,

H. W. HALLECK,
Major-General, Chief of Staff.

ATHENS, *March* 19, 1864.

Major-General LOGAN, *Huntsville:*

Phillips has been to Tuscumbia and into Russell Valley up to Mount Hope. No forces only at latter point, where two regiments of re-enlisted infantry and Tenth Alabama Cavalry are stationed. It is understood infantry went there to be furloughed.

G. M. DODGE,
Brigadier-General.

HEADQUARTERS FIFTEENTH ARMY CORPS,
Huntsville, Ala., March 19, 1864.

Brig. Gen. G. M. DODGE,
Athens:

I have just received information this morning of Pensacola troops having arrived at Gadsden. Forrest will be at Somerville to-night, with what force I cannot ascertain. The force on the river in my front is very small. I am inclined to think some movement is on foot, either some of our bridges or Decatur; the latter is the most probable. I will give you from time to time all my information.

JOHN A. LOGAN,
Major-General.

HEADQUARTERS FIFTEENTH ARMY CORPS,
Huntsville, Ala., March 19, 1864.

Brig. Gen. C. L. MATTHIES,
Commanding Third Division:

GENERAL: Forrest with his command got to within 8 miles of the river opposite here last night. Keep a sharp lookout. He evidently intends crossing the river somewhere. Patrol the river well. Send me all information.

R. R. TOWNES,
Assistant Adjutant-General.

(Same to Osterhaus.)

HEADQUARTERS LEFT WING, SIXTEENTH ARMY CORPS,
Athens, Ala., March 19, 1864.

Brig. Gen. JOHN D. STEVENSON,
Commanding Detachment Fourth Division, Decatur:

I inclose an order that no doubt will cause some hardships. When persons desire to go north and are poor people, you can give them transportation by railroad. If you have any unserviceable, worn-out stock, you can let families have a team where they have no other means of moving. Take particular pains that nothing is destroyed, and that all property left is got together and stored with some responsible party.

We desire to cover all movements, and therefore be very strict on your picket-lines and allow no person to come in unless he is a refugee to join our army or a negro whom we can use to advantage, except when in your judgment you can obtain some information. It is to our advantage that all these people should move as far south or north as possible.

I am, very respectfully, your obedient servant,

G. M. DODGE,
Brigadier-General, Commanding.

[Inclosure.]

SPECIAL ORDERS, }   HDQRS. LEFT WING, 16TH ARMY CORPS,
   No. 72.   }   *Athens, Ala., March* 19, 1864.

I. The necessities of the army require the use of every building in Decatur for Government purposes. It is therefore ordered:

First. That all citizens living in Decatur or within 1 mile of the limits of the town on the south side of the Tennessee River shall move outside of the lines within six days from the receipt of this order.

Second. They will be allowed to go north or south, as they deem best, and take with them all their personal and movable property.

Third. As fast as the buildings are vacated the commander of the post will take possession of them and see that they are preserved and no damage done them.

Fourth. No exception to this order will be made except in the case of families of persons in our army or employés of the Government.

Fifth. Brig. Gen. J. D. Stevenson will cause this order to be immediately complied with.

By order of Brig. Gen. G. M. Dodge:

J. W. BARNES,
Assistant Adjutant-General.

ATHENS, ALA.,
March 19, 1864.

Major-General LOGAN,
　　Huntsville:

A scout just in from Somerville reports no force there yet. Nothing this side of mountains of any moment.

G. M. DODGE,
Brigadier-General.

ATHENS, ALA.,
March 19, 1864.

Brig. Gen. J. D. STEVENSON,
　　Decatur:

Will be down in a day or two. Veatch is on way here with rest of division. You will get Logan's dispatch.* Push scouts out toward Somerville and Gadsden. We must be on lookout for that quarter. Keep them to work on fortifications.

G. M. DODGE,
Brigadier-General.

NASHVILLE, *March* 19, 1864.

General WHIPPLE,
　　Assistant Adjutant-General:

There is on hand and to arrive in the next forty-eight hours 14,000 troops for the front. I cannot take off or transport this number unless I cut down subsistence and forage, and this must not be done. I recommend that Brigadier-General Granger be instructed to order these troops to march down by short journeys, and I will transport the rations and baggage in concert with General Granger. We can arrange to subsist the troops at given points, they carrying five days' rations in haversacks.

J. L. DONALDSON,
Senior Quartermaster.

---

* See p. 94.

HEADQUARTERS OF THE ARMY,
Washington, March 19, 1864.
General J. B. McPHERSON,
        Vicksburg:

MY DEAR GENERAL: It gives me great pleasure to send you your commission as brigadier-general in the Regular Army. It has been well earned and is well merited. You have my congratulations and my best wishes that your future career may be as brilliant as the past.
        Yours, truly,

H. W. HALLECK,
Major-General, Chief of Staff.

HEADQUARTERS DEPARTMENT OF THE OHIO,
Knoxville, Tenn., March 20, 1864.   (Received 24th.)
Maj. Gen. W. T. SHERMAN,
        Commanding Division of the Mississippi, Nashville, Tenn.:

GENERAL: I have received your letter of the 18th, giving an outline of the plan of future operations so far as it concerns my command.

I will have, so far as it depends upon me, all preparations made to fulfill the part of the plan assigned me. Indeed, to carry out the first part of it, all I now want is the necessary force. The withdrawal of the Ninth Corps has crippled me very much and renders it impossible for me to do anything until I get more force. It appears to me that time is very important in the plan adopted, for I have a good deal of work to do before I can be ready to join the main army, and it can be done now more easily and with less force than would proba-bly be required a month or more hence. Besides, if Longstreet can be driven out of Tennessee soon the raid into Kentucky, for which he now seems to be preparing, will be prevented. I now have the Twenty-third Corps and two divisions of the Fourth. One of the latter is guarding the railroad from this place to the Hiwassee. I am informed six new regiments are ready to come here and are only waiting for transportation, but have not learned where they are nor when I may expect them. When they arrive my force in the field will be about equal to that of the enemy. I ought to have the other division of the Fourth Corps or an equal force to make success certain and speedy. Longstreet can readily be re-enforced from Virginia unless the Army of the Potomac prevents it. If he receives no re-enforcements I may be strong enough without the other division of the Fourth Corps. My lack of cavalry and inability to support more makes it the more necessary for me to be superior to the enemy in infantry.

My main cavalry force is being remounted and equipped at Mount Sterling, Ky., and will be available for service as soon as it can be used to advantage. I have no infantry force in Kentucky which can be made available for the movement from Northeast Kentucky. General Grant informed me some time since that he expected 10,000 men soon, which he proposed to add to my command. A part of that force might be used for the purpose named if I receive sufficient re-enforcements here from other sources. I have some difficulty in selecting a suitable officer for that command. If my suggestion relative to corps organization in this department be adopted and General Stoneman be assigned to command the Cavalry Corps, General Sturgis will probably be the best available officer for the command on the Big Sandy.

The supplies accumulated here will be little more than sufficient for the campaign in East Tennessee. When I commence to move toward the Hiwassee, supplies can be sent there from Chattanooga as fast as they will be required. I think it would not be wise to accumulate supplies there before that time, since it would require a larger force to guard them and might give the enemy some insight into the plan of operations. I will take care to have supplies there in time.

In considering the plan of operations and the results to be accomplished, the following facts are important, viz : The natural line of defense for East Tennessee and Kentucky is across the Holston Valley near Abingdon. The only point in rear which must be held is the French Broad Gap, and this will require but a small force. There are no other routes by which even cavalry in any considerable force can enter the Holston Valley from the east, while there are several gaps in the Cumberland Mountains through which troops can pass nearly as well as through Cumberland Gap. If the railroad can be destroyed far enough above Abingdon that line can be held with less force than any other, and give much greater security to our communications. To accomplish this the railroad should be destroyed as far as New River, including the bridge across that stream. Then the force you propose to have operate from the Big Sandy would probably be sufficient to hold the Holston Valley, and could be supplied by rail from this place.

It will be difficult to drive the enemy as far back as New River, and may require more time and force than can be spared for the purpose. If so, the plan you propose seems to be the only one left. The road can be destroyed so far up the valley as to prevent any invasion by infantry in considerable force, and we will have to rely upon meeting cavalry raids with cavalry.

In my letter to General Grant, sent by Lieutenant Bartlett, I suggested the preservation rather than destruction of this road, with a view to its use after the rebel army shall have been driven from Virginia. But I have no doubt the General-in-Chief has considered this matter fully in fixing upon his plan of operations; hence I will make all preparations to destroy the road as completely as possible.

I shall hope, general, to see you here soon; meanwhile I will write you fully concerning all matters of importance.

I am, general, very respectfully, your obedient servant,
J. M. SCHOFIELD,
Major-General.

HEADQUARTERS DEPARTMENT OF THE OHIO,
Knoxville, Tenn., March 20, 1864.
Brig. Gen. T. T. GARRARD,
Commanding District of the Clinch, Cumberland Gap:

GENERAL : I have sent a cavalry force, supported by infantry, to occupy the Holston Valley north of the river, and the Clinch Valley in advance of the road leading from Rutledge to Cumberland Gap. Colonel Garrard is in command of the cavalry. Brig. Gen. T. J. Wood, who commands the entire force, will have his headquarters near Rutledge. He is directed to open communication with you and to co-operate with you in observing the movements of the enemy north of the Holston, and in meeting any attempt he may make at a raid into Kentucky or Middle Tennessee. Communicate with General Wood frequently and keep him advised so far as you may learn of the strength, position, and movements of the enemy.

I have received your letter of the 15th to General Potter. Your information agrees nearly with that I have from other sources. No doubt the enemy may attempt a raid into Kentucky or Middle Tennessee, in what force it is difficult to conjecture. We must anticipate and prevent it if possible, and if not, then be prepared to meet it as well as we can. Write me fully and frequently, giving the strength, position, and character of the enemy in your front and vicinity.

I observe in your return of the 10th of March, although you have a regiment of cavalry and one of mounted infantry, you report your entire force as infantry and artillery and report no horses. Is it true that your entire force is dismounted ? I notice also a large number of the Eleventh Tennessee Cavalry "absent without authority." Do you know where they are ? Have any steps been taken to bring them back to duty ?

Your force should not remain on the defensive except when compelled to by the strength of the enemy or other unavoidable circumstances.

Omit no opportunity to strike the enemy when you can do so to advantage. I will increase your force soon if it shall appear to be necessary.

Very respectfully,

J. M. SCHOFIELD,
Major-General.

———

MOSSY CREEK, *March* 20, 1864.

General J. D. COX,
Acting Chief of Staff :

The parties that were at Dandridge, McFarland's Cross-Roads, and Morristown returned last night. No enemy at Dandridge. A small scout had been at McFarland's Cross-Roads. A party of thirty came down yesterday to our outer pickets, but were not afterward seen. The party picked up 13 citizens on the way back, killing one of the citizens. Vaughn's cavalry reported as having gone toward Jonesborough or north. Enemy's force still in Bull's Gap. Armstrong himself gone to Georgia and Buckner to West Virginia. Lieutenant-General Hood gone to D. H. Hill's corps, Field, Johnson, and McLaws each in command of his own division. Great destitution in Longstreet's army and much dissatisfaction.

GEO. STONEMAN,
Major-General.

———

CLEVELAND, *March* 20, 1864.

Brigadier-General WHIPPLE,
Assistant Adjutant-General :

I sent a strong scout on the Dalton road, drove in the enemy's outposts, and found a brigade about 6 miles below Red Clay. The only movement in the rebel lines is that caused by change of camps.

A. P. CAMPBELL,
Colonel, Commanding.

HDQRS. FIFTY-SIXTH REGT. ILLINOIS VOL. INFANTRY,
Whitesburg, Ala., March 20, 1864—4 p. m.
Capt. M. ROCHESTER,
Assistant Adjutant-General, Third Division:

CAPTAIN : I have the honor to inform you that the enemy left the south bank last night, taking their camp and garrison equipage. They broke up three boats and moved toward Somerville. I have had a party over to-day.

Very respectfully, your obedient servant,

JOHN P. HALL,
Lieutenant-Colonel, Commanding.

[Indorsement.]

HDQRS. THIRD DIVISION, FIFTEENTH ARMY CORPS,
Huntsville, Ala., March 20, 1864.

Respectfully forwarded for the information of the major-general commanding Fifteenth Army Corps.

I will hold one section of artillery in readiness to send to Whitesburg, but will not send it till further orders, unless the general commanding deems it desirable to have one there.

C. L. MATTHIES,
Brigadier-General.

———

BLUE SPRINGS, *March 20, 1864.*
General WHIPPLE,
Chief of Staff:

Major Paine, First Wisconsin, commanding, scouted below Red Clay; found rebel pickets at Wade's house. An advance of 3 miles found pickets much stronger than formerly. Rebels say Forrest has joined and is on their right.

D. S. STANLEY,
Major-General.

———

From General G. H. Thomas' journal.

MARCH 20, 1864.

Railroad completed through to Ringgold, Ga. About this time information was received from Dalton confirmatory of the report received from General Gordon Granger on the 5th that a part of Longstreet's cavalry, said to be Martin's division, was re-enforcing Johnston.

———

HEADQUARTERS FIFTEENTH ARMY CORPS,
Huntsville, Ala., March 20, 1864.
Brig. Gen. P. JOSEPH OSTERHAUS,
Woodville, Ala.:

The boats were moored last night from opposite Whitesburg. The pickets are also withdrawn from the opposite bank to-day. They may intend crossing and attacking your force at Vienna. I think this likely. Look out.

JOHN A. LOGAN,
Major-General.

ATHENS, ALA.,
March 20, 1864.

Maj. R. M. SAWYER,
 Assistant Adjutant-General, Nashville:

Scout in from Blount County reports provost guard at Gadsden only; one battalion at Somerville, and all troops in valley had been ordered to Dalton.

G. M. DODGE,
Brigadier-General.

SPECIAL ORDERS, } HDQRS. LEFT WING, 16TH ARMY CORPS,
 No. 73.   }   *Athens, Ala., March* 20, 1864.

 * * * * * * *

V. Mr. Aaron Thomason, living at Athens, Ala., is hereby ordered to move south of the Tennessee River and beyond the Federal lines with his family within three days. If after that time he is found within the Federal lines he will be treated as a spy. He and his family will be allowed to take their wearing apparel and one team; the rest of his property must remain uninjured, as it now stands, and will be seized for the benefit of the United States Government. He is thus ordered beyond the lines of the Federal army from the fact that he has extended aid and comfort to the enemy, knowingly harboring the enemy's spies, and been engaged in contraband traffic since the Federal forces have occupied this country. The provost-marshal-general will see that this order is complied with.

 By order of Brig. Gen. G. M. Dodge:

J. W. BARNES,
Assistant Adjutant-General.

CLEVELAND, TENN.,
March 21, 1864.

Brig. Gen. W. D. WHIPPLE,
 Asst. Adjt. Gen., Department of the Cumberland:

I have the honor to forward the following memoranda of information from deserters direct from Dalton: Linville Sheets, private, Fifty-eighth North Carolina Regiment, belongs to Rennels' [Reynolds'] brigade, of Stevenson's division; left Dalton on Saturday, the 17th instant. Cleburne's division was at Tunnel Hill; Cheatham's division was 2 miles east of Dalton, on the railroad; Stevenson's division 2 miles west of Dalton, toward Tunnel Hill. Walker's and Stewart's divisions were at and a short distance below Dalton. Thinks that there are about 1,500 men in Runnels' [Reynolds'] brigade, to which he belongs, but thinks this brigade smaller than the average in Stevenson's division. A large number of new wagons were received by railroad from Atlanta; also a supply of fresh mules. Says that a great many new wagons were received, and that the talk among the soldiers was that it was intended to fix up the transportation preparatory to a movement up the East Tennessee Valley. Thinks that Johnston has from 40,000 to 50,000 men. He has been re-enforced from Alabama, and he heard that re-enforcements from Charleston, S. C., had arrived. The army gets short rations. Thinks that there is not more than two weeks' supply of short rations on hand at Dalton. Artillery horses are in bad condition. They receive forage from Atlanta. Says Wheeler's headquarters are near Taylor's Bridge, and that most of the cavalry are from Tunnel Hill down via La Fayette in the direction of Rome. About four weeks since a number of cavalry horses were sent to Kingston to forage. There are no fortifications at Dalton. At Resaca, 12 miles south of Dalton, they have some fortifications. Does not know of any troops from Longstreet having joined Johnston, or vice versa. Cars run constantly between Dalton and Atlanta. Seems to be no lack of transportation. In addition to the above information I have the honor to report that Sergeant Creager, Second Michigan Cavalry, returned at 8 p. m. to-day from 1 mile south of Waterhouse's farm; reports everything quiet on that road. Enemy's pickets (about 100) at King's Bridge, on Spring Place road. I also had a scout at Red Clay to-day. All quiet there.

I have the honor to be, very respectfully, your obedient servant,

A. P. CAMPBELL,
Commanding Division.

CLEVELAND, TENN.,
March 21, 1864.

Brig. Gen. WILLIAM D. WHIPPLE,
Asst. Adjt. Gen., Department of the Cumberland:

I have the honor to report that Maj. D. A. Briggs, in command of the Second Indiana Cavalry, returned from the vicinity of Waterhouse's farm at 9.30 p. m. of the 20th instant; reports no enemy on that road excepting scouting parties. Eighty rebels were at that place on the 19th, and remained during the night. One of my scouts left Sumac Creek south of Waterhouse's farm at 12 o'clock last night, and reports having heard drums in a southwest direction from there in the evening. It has also been reported that a cavalry force from Longstreet's command crossed the Hiwassee at Taylor's Ferry, and marched via Ducktown to join Johnston at Dalton. I have also information, which I deem reliable, that a considerable amount of corn and wheat sacked up in sacks marked "C. S. A." has been accumulated at Callaway's Mill, 4 miles from Waterhouse's farm. These stores might be removed to within our lines by sending a considerable force for that purpose. I do not think it would be safe to attempt it without taking all or the greater part of my effective [force] with artillery, but can easily destroy it by burning it. I have communicated this information to General Stanley.

The scouting parties sent out this morning have not yet reported.

I have the honor to be, very respectfully, your obedient servant.

A. P. CAMPBELL,
Colonel, Commanding Division.

CINCINNATI, *March* 21, 1864.

Maj. Gen. JOHN M. SCHOFIELD,
Knoxville:

Your three dispatches received. Send the Ninth Corps by land, letting the sick and baggage come by railroad. I do not apprehend any political trouble in Kentucky. As to Longstreet, as soon as I get the hang of things I will invite him to make a raid into Kentucky. I don't believe Longstreet is in East Tennessee at all. I will return to Nashville to-morrow, and come and see you as soon as possible.

W. T. SHERMAN,
Major-General.

STRAWBERRY PLAINS, *March* 21, 1864.

Major-General SCHOFIELD :

The following from General Stoneman is the only news from the front :

Scouting parties from Rutledge report nothing in that direction, except small parties prowling about the country. Deserters and refugees from Russellville report 300 cavalry at Morristown ; that Longstreet returned from Richmond yesterday, and was to move with his infantry in this direction to-day.

No reports from the Mouth of Chucky or Dandridge road. Three hundred or 400 cavalry, supported by a regiment of infantry, will be sent to Morristown to-day, returning to-morrow.

GEO. STONEMAN,
Major-General.

J. D. COX,
Brigadier-General, Acting Chief of Staff.

HEADQUARTERS ARMY OF THE OHIO,
Strawberry Plains, March 21, 1864.

Major-General STONEMAN,
Commanding Twenty-third Army Corps :

GENERAL : General Wood reports that the cavalry ordered on the 18th instant to cross the Holston, under command of Colonel Garrard, and report to him at Rutledge, has not done so. A small party crossed but did not await his arrival. Please have the omission corrected and report cause of delay.

By command of Major-General Schofield :

J. D. COX,
Brigadier-General, Acting Chief of Staff.

KNOXVILLE, TENN.,
March 21, 1864.

Maj. Gen. A. E. BURNSIDE,
New York :

Transportation from Loudon is so limited that General Schofield decides to send troops over the mountain. I started all men able to march this morning. About 2,000 will go by rail with the baggage. I have gathered up all extra-duty men. There will be nearly 6,000. The head of the column will reach Camp Burnside in six or seven days. I will start to-morrow morning for Cincinnati, and concentrate the corps, and send forward the troops from that point.

O. B. WILLCOX,
Brigadier-General.

HEADQUARTERS ARMY OF THE OHIO,
Strawberry Plains, March 21, 1864.
Brigadier-General WOOD,
Commanding Third Division, Fourth Army Corps:
SIR: Your dispatch of this day is received and forwarded by telegraph to General Schofield at Knoxville. General Stoneman has been directed to have the cavalry report to you at once. The delay is as yet unexplained. Everything is reported quiet in front of Mossy Creek.
Very respectfully, your obedient servant,
J. D. COX,
Brigadier-General, Acting Chief of Staff.

ATHENS, ALA., *March* 21, 1864.
Maj. R. M. SAWYER,
Assistant Adjutant-General, Nashville:
It is reported from pretty reliable sources, but from citizens, that Forrest was at Corinth Wednesday night; that he was to cross the river some point south of Hamburg. I have sent a mounted force toward Florence.
Cypert has a regiment of loyal Tennesseeans at Clifton. My mounted force, you know, is small. What I have is now feeling toward Gadsden, crossed the mountains yesterday, and passed through Somerville; as yet met no force of consequence. The gunboats on Tennessee River should notify us of any movement.
It is very probable they are going where Hurlbut suggests.
G. M. DODGE,
Brigadier-General.

ATHENS, ALA., *March* 21, 1864.
General SWEENY, *Pulaski:*
Reports are current here that General Forrest, with a large force, is crossing the river at or near Eastport. You will send the Seventh Illinois in that direction to ascertain and report the facts. Have them start to-night and report all the news to the nearest point on the railroad, to be telegraphed to headquarters.
One battalion of the Ninth Ohio Cavalry is now in the vicinity of Florence.
By order of General Dodge:
GEO. E. SPENCER,
Colonel and Chief of Staff.

ATHENS, ALA., *March* 21, 1864.
Maj. R. M. SAWYER,
Assistant Adjutant-General, Nashville:
A telegraph operator from rebel lines has come into Decatur and reports that Forrest moved from Columbus, Miss., with a pontoon bridge, and that he is crossing at or near Eastport. I have sent mounted force in that direction. The gun-boats should move up the river and watch it closely. This may be a lie to deceive us. ·
G. M. DODGE,
Brigadier-General.

ATHENS, ALA.,
March 21, 1864.

General J. D. STEVENSON,
Decatur:

General Hurlbut, from Memphis, 18th, telegraphs that General Forrest was at Tupelo on the 16th with large force, ready to move to Columbus and Paducah.

By order of General G. M. Dodge:
GEO. E. SPENCER,
Colonel and Chief of Staff.

HDQRS. SECOND DIVISION, SIXTEENTH ARMY CORPS,
Pulaski, Tenn., March 21, 1864.

Maj. GEORGE H. ESTABROOK,
Commanding Seventh Illinois Infantry:

You will move out immediately with your command, proceeding in the direction of Eastport, on the Tennessee River, at which place it is reported that General Forrest is crossing with a large force of the enemy. Your men will be supplied with five days' rations (two in haversacks and three in wagons) and 60 rounds of ammunition. It is very necessary that you gain all reliable information in your power as regards their strength, designs, of what composed, &c., with as little delay as possible. As fast as you receive important information you will send the same by courier to the nearest point on the railroad where there is a telegraph office, and thence send by wire to headquarters Left Wing, Sixteenth Army Corps, at Athens, Ala., as also to these headquarters.

Be prompt and vigilant in your movements, trying, if possible, to capture prisoners from the enemy of whom you can obtain the desired information. Look well to all roads which may lead to your rear, and keep feelers out in every direction to avoid being surprised, and also to learn of the enemy. One battalion of the Ninth Ohio Cavalry is now in the vicinity of Florence.

By order of Brig. Gen. T. W. Sweeny, commanding:
LOUIS H. EVERTS,
Captain and Assistant Adjutant-General.

HDQRS. FIRST DIVISION, FIFTEENTH ARMY CORPS,
March 21, 1864.

Maj. R. R. TOWNES,
Assistant Adjutant-General, Huntsville, Ala.:

I have just received the following dispatch from Lieutenant-Colonel Gage, Twenty-ninth Missouri, commanding expedition to Tennessee River:

We arrived at Cottonville at 2 p. m., 19th. As I could not learn anything of an enemy there, we visited Deposit. There I saw 2 rebels standing picket at a small earth-work on the south side of the river. From there we marched to Fearns' Landing, where they also have a small guard; we captured 2 prisoners. 1 of them in trying to escape was shot. Shall move up the Tennessee to-morrow. There are only three companies on the other side of the river.

P. J. OSTERHAUS,
Brigadier-General of Volunteers.

NASHVILLE, *March* 21, 1864.

Major-General SHERMAN,
  Burnett House, Cincinnati:
  General Hurlbut telegraphs that he thinks Forrest is intending to go in toward Paducah and Columbus. On advising General Dodge of this he answers that Forrest was at Corinth on the 16th instant, and thinks it highly probable that he (Forrest) intends what Hurlbut suggests, that he was to cross the river near Hamburg. Dodge sent mounted force toward Florence, and there is a regiment of loyal Tennesseeans at Clifton.

R. M. SAWYER,
Assistant Adjutant-General.

NASHVILLE, *March* 21, 1864.

Brigadier-General WHIPPLE,
  Assistant Adjutant-General:
  I have not ceased urging their sending me cavalry and artillery horses and mules. I am disappointed in their coming forward so slow. I have on hand 1,400,000 bushels of grain, and large amounts of other supplies. My receipts now average 30,000 tons a week. The commissary department should hasten their arrangements to drive their beef-cattle down, and I would thereby have ten cars released to me daily for forage.

J. L. DONALDSON,
Senior Quartermaster.

LOUISVILLE, KY., *March* 21, 1864.
(Received 6 p. m.)

His Excellency President LINCOLN :
  The Department of the Cumberland ought to be placed under the command of Major-General Thomas, receiving his instructions and orders directly from Washington.
  I feel satisfied from what I know and hear that placing the command of the department under General Sherman, over Thomas, will produce disappointment in the public mind and impair the public service.
  General Thomas has the confidence of the army and the people, and will discharge his duty, as he has from the commencement of the rebellion. He will, in my opinion, if permitted, be one of the great generals of the war, if not the greatest. I will be in Nashville to-morrow and will dispatch you again.

ANDREW JOHNSON,
Governor of Tennessee.

GENERAL ORDERS, }   HDQRS. DEPARTMENT OF THE OHIO,
  No. 34.   }   *Knoxville, Tenn., March* 21, 1864.
  Brig. Gen. E. E. Potter is, at his own request, relieved from duty as chief of staff of this department, and is granted thirty days' leave of absence, with authority to report by letter to headquarters of the Army for further orders.

Brig. Gen. J. D. Cox is assigned to duty as chief of staff of the Department and Army of the Ohio. His orders as such will be obeyed and respected accordingly.

By command of Major-General Schofield :

J. A. CAMPBELL,
Assistant Adjutant-General.

HEADQUARTERS THIRD DIVISION, FOURTH ARMY CORPS,
Rutledge, March 22, 1864—12 m.

Brig. Gen. J. D. Cox,
    Chief of Staff :

GENERAL : A squad of 10 men of the Seventh Ohio Cavalry has just reported to me.· This is the only cavalry force I have. This squad will be required, and I will so use it, to establish a line of couriers to department headquarters to make the daily communications. Will any more cavalry be sent to me ?

I have had an interview to-day with quite an intelligent woman of Northern birth ; she is a native of Maine, who lives in the vicinity of Rogersville. She left Rogersville last Thursday, and reported that Vaughn's brigade had been stationed there for some time, but crossed the river (Holston) in the early part of last week, anticipating that we would attack Bull's Gap. She further reports that Jones' brigade is at Mulberry Gap (some 20 miles north of Rogersville), some 2,000 strong. The position she seems confident of, but the strength she gives from report. She seems to be very confident, and gives facts to sustain her opinion that Longstreet's force in East Tennessee has suffered no material diminution latterly. She is very well posted in regard to the composition (by division, &c.) of Longstreet's command. She says that Longstreet's command commenced to fall back in the latter part of February to re-enforce Johnston, who had been weakened temporarily by detachments to oppose Sherman, but that the failure of Sherman's expedition relieved the pressure in the south and obviated the necessity for any of Longstreet's command leaving East Tennessee. I will permit her to return to Rogersville.

I have heard nothing from you since leaving Strawberry Plains. Let me have the news.

Respectfully, your obedient servant,

TH. J. WOOD,
Brigadier-General of Volunteers, Commanding.

HEADQUARTERS THIRD DIVISION, FOURTH ARMY CORPS,
Rutledge, March 22, 1864—8.30 p. m.

Brig. Gen. J. D. Cox,
    Chief of Staff :

GENERAL : A very intelligent private soldier, a deserter from the Seventh Georgia, came into our lines this p. m. He left Bull's Gap Saturday afternoon. His regiment is in Hood's old division, now commanded by General Field. He says that no infantry has left Longstreet's command since it fell back from Strawberry Plains four weeks since, but that a portion of the cavalry has gone to Georgia.

He gives the following very intelligent account of the strength of Longstreet's infantry and artillery force:

His division (Field's, late Hood's, Jenkins', &c.) has five brigades; each brigade has five regiments and a battery of four guns, and his brigade is about 1,200 strong. He says the other brigades are about the same strength. This would make his division 6,000 infantry and twenty pieces of artillery.

He says McLaws' old division, now commanded by General Kershaw, has four brigades of five regiments, and he thinks the brigades are about of the same strength as in his division. Each brigade has a battery of four guns. This would give this division 4,800 infantry and sixteen guns. He says these two divisions and Bushrod Johnson's have been formed into a corps, of which General Buckner is the commander, with headquarters at Greeneville. He says Johnson's division is weak, probably not more than 2,000 infantry, and that he does not know how much artillery it has. This statement makes the strength of this corps 12,800 infantry and thirty-six pieces of artillery certain, with pretty certainly more.

He says Ransom's division is a small one. probably 2,000 infantry, but he does not know how much artillery it has. His statement of the strength of this division corresponds with the statement given by the lady with whom I conversed to-day, who said it had passed her house six times, and estimated its strength at 2,200.

The deserter's account gives Longstreet 14,800 infantry and thirty-six pieces of artillery known, with a margin for more. Of the cavalry he says he knows little, but estimates Longstreet's command at between 17,000 and 20,000. His statement of the infantry force, which certainly seems moderate and reasonable, added to the known cavalry force, makes his estimate of the entire strength of Longstreet's command reasonable, and certainly entirely probable. Having examined him closely, I am inclined to think his statement reliable.

He says Longstreet went to Richmond two weeks since, but does not know whether he has returned. He reports his division engaged in fortifying at Bull's Gap, making quite strong fortifications.

I have heard nothing of the cavalry yet.

Respectfully, your obedient servant,

TH. J. WOOD,
Brigadier-General, Commanding.

STRAWBERRY PLAINS,
March 22, 1864.

Major-General SCHOFIELD,
　　Commanding Department:

GENERAL: On inquiring of General Stoneman last evening why the cavalry had not reported to General Wood, I received a dispatch, which I inclose, adding also my reply.

The Forty-first Ohio reported here this morning, and is ordered forward to General Wood.

Respectfully, your obedient servant,

J. D. COX,
Brigadier-General.

P. S.—Since writing the above, I have received General Stoneman's explanation and another dispatch from General Wood, which

I inclose.   I have answered General Wood, saying the question of his occupying the position near Powder Spring Gap is submitted to you, and will be determined by you.   The difficulty he apprehends from the creek in his rear seems to me the only important consideration, as the gap itself is easily occupied by a small detachment, and I should prefer occupying a position in front of the line of communication with Cumberland Gap rather than upon or in rear of it. I know nothing of the creek.

Very respectfully, &c.,

J. D. COX,
Brigadier-General.

[Inclosure No. 1.]

MOSSY CREEK, *March* 21, 1864.

Brigadier-General Cox,
Chief of Staff:

Colonel Garrard was at my tent to-day, and informed me that he had received no orders about going to Rutledge.   He is now on a scout toward Morristown, and will return to-morrow.   Colonel Crawford's scouts are with him, and he is supported by a regiment of infantry.   Understanding Wood's division was still at the Plains, we concluded that the intention of sending cavalry to Rutledge had been abandoned.

GEO. STONEMAN,
Major-General.

[Inclosure No. 2.]

STRAWBERRY PLAINS,
March 21, 1864.

Major-General STONEMAN,
Commanding Twenty-third Army Corps:

GENERAL : Have you not mistaken the purport of orders of the 17th and 18th instant?   Special Field Orders, No. 8, paragraph V, said Colonel Garrard "will receive his orders from Major-General Stoneman, commanding Twenty-third Army Corps," and my note of 18th, directed to you, says, "Colonel Garrard will cross the Holston with the remainder of the cavalry," &c., "and will report to General Wood."   If any portion of the force of cavalry can be sent to General Wood to act as vedettes, &c., till Colonel Garrard's return, please send them at once, and carry out the original plan upon his return from the present expedition.

By command of Major-General Schofield :

J. D. COX,
Brigadier-General, Acting Chief of Staff in the Field.

[Inclosure No. 3.]

MOSSY CREEK, *March* 22, 1864.

Brig. Gen. J. D. COX,
Chief of Staff :

Dispatch received from Colonel Garrard this a. m. reports no enemy at Morristown or Russellville.   Vaughn and his whole force at its old camp on Big Creek, above Rogersville; Dibrell's or Armstrong's cavalry near Parrottsville. No enemy heard of toward Rutledge or Dandridge. Scouting parties seen on the Mouth of Chucky road yesterday morning. All the men left in camp by Colonel Garrard were sent, upon receipt of your last telegram, to report to General Wood. It seems (and I can but regret it) that I was mistaken in regard to your intentions in regard to Colonel Garrard's movements. Colonel Garrard was not receiving his orders from me at Morristown, but received his instructions direct from department headquarters, and it was thought the same course would be pursued in this case. Had I studied carefully previous orders, it might have been inferred that it was the intention for me to issue the order to Colonel Garrard. For fear that you may not be aware of the fact, I consider it my duty to inform you that this command is entirely without forage; also, that the train (railroad) came up yesterday empty, and yet staid at Mossy Creek from 11 a. m. to 3 p. m.

GEO. STONEMAN,
Major-General.

STRAWBERRY PLAINS,
March 22, 1864.

Brig. Gen. T. J. WOOD,
Commanding Third Division, Fourth Army Corps:

SIR: Yours of yesterday, 9 p. m., received at 12 m. to-day, and forwarded to the commanding general for his consideration. General Stoneman says the delay of the cavalry was owing to his mistake as to orders, but that it will be corrected to-day. All quiet in his front, and no advance of enemy beyond former position, none being nearer to you than Rogersville, as far as he can learn.

Very respectfully,

J. D. COX,
Brigadier-General, Acting Chief of Staff.

STRAWBERRY PLAINS,
March 22, 1864.

Major-General SCHOFIELD,
Knoxville:

No enemy found in Morristown by General Stoneman's reconnaissance yesterday. They are reported as remaining in former positions. General Wood objects to Rutledge as a position, and determines to take that of Powder Spring Gap, several miles farther in rear. I send by mail his letter notifying me of the fact, as well as General Stoneman's explanation of the delay in sending the cavalry across Holston.

The Forty-first Ohio passed up this morning on the way to join General Wood. I have heard nothing from him as to the re-enlistment of veterans. If many of his regiments do so, will you consider Colonel Cameron's application in regard to the Sixty-fifth Illinois?

Very respectfully, &c.,

J. D. COX,
Brigadier-General, Acting Chief of Staff.

HEADQUARTERS ARMY OF THE OHIO,
Strawberry Plains, March 22, 1864.

Major-General STONEMAN,
Commanding Twenty-third Army Corps, Mossy Creek:

The commanding general directs that if Colonel Klein has any men dismounted they be mounted by dismounting some of Colonel Garrard's; that the same be done in the case of the Tenth Michigan, so that it also may have all its men mounted; that the Tenth Michigan only be sent to General Wood, Klein's battalion retained by yourself, and that Colonel Garrard, with the remainder of the cavalry, mounted and dismounted, be sent to Knoxville. This includes the battalion of dismounted cavalry received by you from Ninth Corps.

If Garrard has already left you, please notify me at once, so that I can communicate the order to General Wood.

Very respectfully, your obedient servant,
J. D. COX,
Brigadier-General, Acting Chief of Staff.

KNOXVILLE, *March 22, 1864—8.45 p. m.*

Capt. W. L. AVERY,
Acting Assistant Adjutant-General:

The general directs that the troops of the Ninth Corps commence crossing the river at daylight to-morrow morning.
R. O. SELFRIDGE,
Assistant Inspector-General.

STRAWBERRY PLAINS,
March 22, 1864—1.30 p. m.

Major-General SCHOFIELD,
Knoxville:

Your order in regard to cavalry received, and directions issued accordingly. No re-enlistment of veterans from Wood's division reported to me.
J. D. COX,
Brigadier-General, Acting Chief of Staff.

NASHVILLE, *March 22, 1864—11 p. m.*

Major-General THOMAS:

Later intelligence from General Dodge at Athens shows a determination on the part of Forrest to cross the Tennessee River and strike the Tennessee and Alabama Railroad. Will you please direct General Garrard to move his command to act in concert with General Dodge, and order General Elliott to collect all the cavalry available and move immediately with it to oppose Forrest's movement, whatever it may be? Please answer.
W. T. SHERMAN,
Major-General.
By R. M. SAWYER,
Assistant Adjutant-General.

HDQRS. SECOND DIVISION, SIXTEENTH ARMY CORPS,
Pulaski, Tenn., March 22, 1864.
Commanding Officers of Detachments at
    Wales' Station Bridge and Reynolds' Station Bridge:
General Dodge reports that Forrest has a pontoon; will cross the
river and attack railroad above Athens. Watch for the enemy
closely to prevent a surprise, and also to gain information of his
strength and intent. If attacked, move every man into your stockade, fort, or fortification, and defend the bridge or trestle to the last
extremity. Report all important information to these headquarters
immediately.
By order of Brig. Gen. T. W. Sweeny, commanding:
                        LOUIS H. EVERTS,
                Captain and Assistant Adjutant-General.

ATHENS, *March* 22, 1864.
Brig. Gen. T. W. SWEENY, *Pulaski:*
Have two regiments at the depot, ready to go to Decatur as soon
as cars arrive.
By order of General Dodge:
                        J. W. BARNES,
                    Assistant Adjutant-General.

ATHENS, *March* 22, 1864.
Col. G. E. SPENCER, *Decatur:*
Do you consider it reliable that Forrest is crossing? I have noth-
ing from him on this side of river.
                        G. M. DODGE,
                        Brigadier-General.

ATHENS, *March* 22, 1864.
Major-General THOMAS, *Chattanooga:*
Dispatch of 20th just received. Third Alabama Infantry, A. D.,
part of Fourth Alabama Infantry, A. D., just organizing, not
armed; Ninth Ohio Cavalry, two battalions, 800 strong (one battalion in East Tennessee), ordered here. My troops as yet have not
been relieved. Forrest, Clanton, and Roddey in my front.
                        G. M. DODGE,
                        Brigadier-General.

WOODVILLE, ALA.,
March 22, 1864.
Maj. R. R. TOWNES,
    Asst. Adjt. Gen., Fifteenth Army Corps:
Colonel Ferreby, commanding at Vienna, reports that no force of
the enemy can be discovered on the opposite side except the usual
pickets. He has the river well patrolled between the mouth of Paint
Rock and Flint Rivers. An officer of my staff just returned from a

trip down Paint Rock to its mouth, thence descending the Tennessee River to the mouth of Flint River, and concurs in the above statements. He was told by citizens that General Forrest had gone west, toward Decatur.

P. J. OSTERHAUS.

ATHENS, March 22, 1864.

Maj. R. M. SAWYER,
    Assistant Adjutant-General, Nashville:

Scout in from Demopolis; left a week ago last Friday. French's and Loring's divisions were there; they came through Selma; only small force there. The two regiments of infantry at Mount Hope (one from Loring's division) went there for purpose of letting re-enlisted men visit their homes. Says it was currently reported at Demopolis that Forrest, Lee, and Jackson had been ordered north, but did not know to what point.

G. M. DODGE,
Brigadier-General.

ATHENS, ALA., March 22, 1864.

Brig. Gen. J. D. STEVENSON,
    Decatur:

Push mounted force out to-night toward Somerville. Arms and accouterments on to-day's train will be at Junction to-night. Thirty-ninth Ohio on road to you. We must whip them with the force we have got. If fortifications are not complete, work all night.

G. M. DODGE,
Brigadier-General.

ATHENS, March 22, 1864.

Brig. Gen. T. W. SWEENY, *Pulaski:*

Phillips had severe fight near Moulton yesterday. Forrest is between Tuscumbia and Eastport. Considerable force at Moulton and Gadsden. Watch country to west. I suspect they will try to cross below Tuscumbia, or else attack Decatur.

G. M. DODGE,
Brigadier-General.

ATHENS, March 22, 1864.

Maj. R. M. SAWYER,
    Assistant Adjutant-General, Nashville:

Major-General Clanton's advance is at Somerville; his command consists of two brigades. Roddey's advance is at Summit; two brigades. The order from Johnston was for Martin to relieve Roddey. Forrest is trying to cross at Eastport. Garrard's cavalry division should support me. Clanton has two large brigades. I have a man who came up with them. They came from Pollard, Ala. Please order a train of cars to bring forward two regiments. Please answer.

G. M. DODGE,
Brigadier-General.

ATHENS, *March 22*, 1864.

Brig. Gen. T. W. SWEENY,
    Pulaski:

Forrest has a pontoon bridge and will cross and attack north of here, at the same time that Decatur is attacked. Order all forces' on railroad to hold their position under any and all circumstances. If they stick to their stockades, nothing can defeat them. We must be very watchful and hold our works. I will take care of Decatur.

G. M. DODGE,
Brigadier-General.

ATHENS, *March 22*, 1864.

Col. AUGUST MERSY,
    Pulaski:

Phillips yesterday had a running fight for 14 miles with Clanton. He lost 4 men killed and 8 wounded and taken prisoners; Sergeant Hartman, Company B, among the killed. The rebels were too strong for him, and forced him to fall back. He brought in some 20 prisoners.

Respectfully,

J. W. BARNES,
Assistant Adjutant-General.

ATHENS, *March 22*, 1864.

Major-General LOGAN,
    Huntsville:

Major-General Clanton's advance is at Somerville—two brigades, fifteen pieces artillery; General Roddey's, two brigades, advance at Summit. General Forrest trying to cross at or above Eastport. General Jackson, with brigade, on Moulton road. This brigade is part of the force that was at Mount Hope. Scouts with them report to-night that they attack Decatur, while Forrest, if he succeeds in crossing, attacks railroad; they evidently mean mischief.

G. M. DODGE,
Brigadier-General.

ATHENS, *March 22*, 1864.

Brig. Gen. W. SOOY SMITH,
    Chief of Cavalry, Nashville:

I have pushed my mounted force down both sides of the Tennessee River. On south side enemy is very strong. Nothing as yet on north side to stop us. There is no doubt but that they are preparing for some kind of raid. I captured some of Roddey's officers this morning, but they are mum. My mounted force is very small, but will keep it at work. I cannot tell whether Forrest has got all his force in the valley or not. See dispatches to Sawyer for what is south and southeast. If you make any move with cavalry please advise me so far as it will tend to keep me posted, that I may act understandingly.

G. M. DODGE,
Brigadier-General.

ATHENS, ALA.,
March 22, 1864.

Maj. R. M. SAWYER,
Assistant Adjutant-General :

The following is just received :

I have just returned from Pikesville. General Forrest [left] Pikesville on the 17th instant, en route for Eastport. I heard dispatch read from General Forrest to Colonel Johnson, stating that he had his pontoon bridge ready to throw across the river above Eastport, and that his baggage-wagons were loaded with corn, and that his intention is to attack the forces on the railroad somewhere above Athens, and that Roddey and Clanton will attack Decatur at the same time.

The Twenty-seventh, Twenty-first, and Thirty-fifth Alabama Infantry are at Moulton—Twenty-seventh, commanded by Colonel Jackson, 280 rank and file; Twenty-first, commanded by Colonel Pickett [?], 225 for duty; Thirty-fifth, commanded by Colonel Ives, 240 strong. Cavalry at Moulton, 1,200 strong, commanded by Colonel Johnson.

The above is from one of my most reliable scouts. The cavalry should be massed ready to meet Forrest west of us. I will take care of Decatur. There is no doubt that the above is the programme. We have to-day captured soldiers from Roddey's, Clanton's, and Forrest's commands.

G. M. DODGE,
Brigadier-General.

NASHVILLE, *March 22, 1864.*

Maj. Gen. J. B. McPHERSON,
Cairo :

General Sherman is in Cincinnati; he will be back in a day or two. I telegraphed him of your arrival. General Dodge telegraphs this morning that Colonel Phillips, of his command, met the enemy 3 miles south of Moulton, Ala.—two regiments of infantry and 1,000 cavalry. Had a sharp fight and fell back.

Part of Forrest's command is between Tuscumbia and Eastport; some report he intends to strike Decatur, others that he is to cross the river, and that Lee, Forrest, and Jackson are all ordered up toward Tennessee River. I have telegraphed Admiral Porter and asked that the gun-boats keep a good lookout up the river. Will you please give such information as you may deem best in West Tennessee, as it may be that Columbus and Paducah are the points aimed at ?

R. M. SAWYER,
Assistant Adjutant-General.

HDQRS. SECOND DIVISION, SIXTEENTH ARMY CORPS,
Pulaski, Tenn., March 22, 1864.

Maj. GEORGE H. ESTABROOK,
Comdg. 7th Ill. Inf., in Field near Lawrenceburg, Tenn. :

The following dispatch just received from General Dodge at Athens, viz :

Phillips had severe fight near Moulton yesterday. Forrest is between Tuscumbia and Eastport. Considerable force at Moulton and at Gadsden. Watch country to west. I suppose they will try to cross below Tuscumbia or else attack Decatur.

You will keep a part of your force between this place and Lawrenceburg, taking possession and guarding all roads leading to this place from the west and southwest. The map represents a road or bridle-path running from the Lawrenceburg road to the Lamb's Ferry and Lexington roads. If it is practicable you can move a force down on that road to the roads above mentioned. A force must be sent to the junction of the Lamb's Ferry and Lexington roads, or on each. It is impossible to give explicit instructions to govern all of your movements, as circumstances must in a measure control them; but look to all roads leading in from the directions above mentioned, and at the same time feel to the front as far as possible, gaining reliable information and forwarding the same to these headquarters without delay.

This detachment will return, bringing back any information you may have, as their services are needed here.

When you return you will throw out detachments in different directions under commissioned officers, and drive into this place all surplus stock, horned cattle, sheep, and hogs which can be found in the country, as the command here is entirely destitute. Proper receipts will be given by the commanding officers in accordance with existing orders. No family will be entirely stripped, but enough left for their support.

By order of Brig. Gen. T. W. Sweeny, commanding:
LOUIS H. EVERTS,
Captain and Assistant Adjutant-General.

HDQRS. SECOND DIVISION, SIXTEENTH ARMY CORPS,
Pulaski, Tenn., March 22, 1864.
Maj. GEORGE H. ESTABROOK,
Comdg 7th Ill. Inf., in Field near Lawrenceburg:

MAJOR: By direction of Major-General Sherman you will send a detachment to the trading boats on Tennessee River, said to be near Eastport, ordering them to return to Paducah with the utmost dispatch.

The officer sent in command of the detachment will be instructed to ascertain what action the boats take upon receiving the order. It is of the utmost necessity that this order is got to the boats immediately and is promptly obeyed by the same; therefore, select your ablest officer to see it executed. Dispatch from General Dodge at Athens says Forrest has a pontoon bridge, and will cross river and attack railroad north of Athens. Follow instructions received this morning from these headquarters.

By order of Brig. Gen. T. W. Sweeny, commanding:
LOUIS H. EVERTS,
Captain and Assistant Adjutant-General.

HDQRS. SECOND DIVISION, SIXTEENTH ARMY CORPS,
Pulaski, Tenn., March 22, 1864.
Capt. J. D. TOWNER,
Commanding Detachment, Richland, Tenn.:

Keep the strictest watch in your vicinity, as it is reported that Forrest designs an attack on the road somewhere north of Athens.

In case you are attacked draw your entire force into the stockade or fort, and defend the bridge and trestle to the last extremity.

If you have not at least 100 rounds of ammunition per man on hand, you will supply yourself with this amount immediately.

Send by the bearer all the particulars in regard to tunnel trestle, by how strong a force guarded, condition of fortifications, &c. Send any important information you may receive to these headquarters at once. If you are compelled to press horses for bearing dispatches, give proper receipts. Move all your rations, ammunition, &c., to stockade at once.

By order of Brig. Gen. T. W. Sweeny, commanding:

LOUIS H. EVERTS,
Captain and Assistant Adjutant-General.

HDQRS. SECOND DIVISION, SIXTEENTH ARMY CORPS,
Pulaski, Tenn., March 22, 1864.

Col. E. W. RICE,
Commanding First Brigade :

You will send the Fifty-second Illinois Infantry Volunteers to Decatur only. They will report to General Dodge at Athens on their way down. You will remain with the Sixty-sixth Indiana Infantry Volunteers, until further orders, at this place.

By order of Brig. Gen. T. W. Sweeny, commanding.

LOUIS H. EVERTS,
Captain and Assistant Adjutant-General.

MEMPHIS, *March 22, 1864.*

Col. F. HURST,
Germantown :

Prepare the effective force of your command for an immediate and active campaign in West Tennessee. You will go with no transportation, and only such rations, &c., as the men can carry. Take a full supply of ammunition. Make arrangement to send your camp in toward Memphis, probably to White's Station, or the camp of First Brigade. Come in on first train and report for further instructions.

B. H. GRIERSON,
Brigadier-General.

MEMPHIS, TENN.,
March 22, 1864.

Col. L. F. McCRILLIS :

Has the scout from Hurst's command, ordered to proceed eastward, yet returned ? It is reported that Forrest has gone north and is at Bolivar. Have Colonel Hurst send out secret scouts and ascertain the whereabouts of Forrest. Let me know what information you have.

B. H. GRIERSON.

HDQRS. FOURTH DIVISION, SIXTEENTH ARMY CORPS,
Cairo, Ill., March 22, 1864—11.50 p. m.

Brig. Gen. M. BRAYMAN,
　Commanding District of Cairo:

SIR: Your letter stating that Forrest is threatening Columbus is received. The command will immediately be placed in condition to move at any moment.

I have the honor to be, general, very respectfully, your obedient servant,

F. W. FOX,
Assistant Adjutant-General.

HDQRS. DEPT. OF WEST TENN. AND NORTH MISS.,
In the Field, March 22, 1864.

Brigadier-General BUCKLAND or
COMMANDING OFFICER U. S. FORCES,
　Memphis, Tenn.:

GENERAL: I have the honor to transmit the inclosed report, prepared from a thorough investigation of all the facts in the premises:*

I respectfully demand that restitution be made by the U. S. authorities in the sum of $5,139.25 to the citizens of Jackson, Tenn., the amount extorted from them by Col. Fielding Hurst, on or about the 12th day of February, 1864, under threats of burning the town. It appears that within the past two months seven cases of deliberate murder have been committed in this department, most of them known and all believed to have been perpetrated by the command of Colonel Hurst. I therefore demand the surrender of Col. Fielding Hurst and the officers and men of his command guilty of these murders, to be dealt with by the C. S. authorities as their offenses require. It has also come to my knowledge that many citizens of this portion of the State are now held in confinement by the U. S. authorities against whom no charges have been preferred, among them the Rev. G. W. D. Harris, of Dyer County, Tenn., now in confinement at Fort Pillow.

I demand that Mr. Harris be granted a fair trial before a competent tribunal, or else unconditionally and promptly released, or otherwise I shall place in close confinement 5 Federal soldiers, now in my hands, as hostages for his protection, and in case he should die in your hands from ill treatment these men shall be duly executed in retaliation.

Lieut. Col. W. M. Reed, bearer of these dispatches and temporarily attached to my staff, is hereby authorized to examine any communications which may be delivered in reply to the above, and also to conclude such arrangements as may arise from the subjects hereinbefore mentioned, or otherwise to deliver such papers as by me he is authorized in possible contingencies to present.

I am, general, very respectfully, your obedient servant,
N. B. FORREST,
Major-General, Commanding.

---

* See also Forrest to Jack, March 21, *post.*

[Inclosure No. 1.]

HEADQUARTERS FORREST'S COMMAND,
Jackson, Tenn., March 21, 1864.
Maj. J. P. STRANGE,
 Assistant Adjutant-General:

MAJOR : Having been appointed by the major-general commanding to investigate the facts of the recent tax levied by Col. Fielding Hurst upon the citizens of this place to idemnify himself and command against damages assessed by the Federal authorities of Memphis in favor of Mrs. Newman, formerly a citizen of Jackson, whose house had been entered and robbed by the Federal soldiery in the summer of 1863, also the facts available in reference to the murders which have been committed by the enemy upon soldiers and citizens in this part of the State within the past few months, in obedience to instructions I called together a party of citizens, from whom I derived the following facts : About the 7th of February, 1864, Colonel Hurst, with his command, visited Jackson, Tenn., and announced publicly that in consequence of the assessment by the Federal authorities of Memphis, Tenn., against himself and command of damages to the amount of $5,139.25 in favor of Mrs. Newman, formerly a citizen of this place, he was here to demand this amount at once of the citizens, or on refusal or failure promptly to pay said amount into his hands that he would burn the town. Upon application of some of the citizens and the guaranty of 20 of them, five days were granted in which to raise the sum required, to be paid in greenbacks or Kentucky funds. On the 12th of February, 1864, the entire amount, $5,139.25, was paid into the hands of Col. Fielding Hurst by the citizens of Jackson, Tenn.

The murders committed are as follows : Lieut. Willis Dodds, Company F, Colonel Newsom's regiment Tennessee volunteers, Forrest's command, under orders from his commanding officers, collecting his command, was arrested at the residence of his father in Henderson County, Tenn., on or about the 9th of March, 1864, by the command of Colonel Thornburgh, of the Federal army, on their march through this portion of the State eastward, and put to death by torture.

Private Silas Hodges, a scout, acting under orders from Colonel Tansil, states that he saw the body of Lieutenant Dodds very soon after his murder, and that it was most horribly mutilated, the face having been skinned, the nose cut off, the under jaw disjointed, the privates cut off, and the body otherwise barbarously lacerated and most wantonly injured, and that his death was brought about by the most inhuman process of torture.

Private Alex. Vale, Company H, Newsom's regiment Tennessee volunteers, under orders from Colonel Tansil, was arrested and shot to death in Madison County, Tenn., by same command, on or about the 8th March, 1864.

Lieut. Joseph Stewart, Private John Wilson, Private Samuel Osborn, members of Newsom's regiment Tennessee volunteers, while on duty under orders from their commanding officers, were captured by Hurst's command on or about the 15th February, 1864, in McNairy County, Tenn., and about three days thereafter their bodies were found in Haywood County, Tenn., having been shot to death.

On or about the 5th February, 1864, Private Martin, Company —, Wilson's regiment Tennessee volunteers, was captured by same command and was shot to death and the rights of sepulture forbidden while the command remained, some four days. Mr. Lee Doroughty, a citizen of McNairy County, Tenn, a youth about sixteen years of age, deformed and almost helpless, was arrested and wantonly murdered by same command about 1st January, 1864.

I am, major, very respectfully, your obedient servant,

W. M. REED,
Lieutenant-Colonel, Provisional Army, C. S.

[Inclosure No. 2.]

HDQRS. DEPT. OF WEST TENN. AND NORTH MISS.,
In the Field, March 22, 1864.

To whom it may concern :

Whereas it has come to the knowledge of the major-general commanding that Col. Fielding Hurst, commanding [6th] Regiment U. S. [Tennessee Cavalry] Volunteers, has been guilty of wanton extortion upon the citizens of Jackson, Tenn., and other places, guilty of depredations upon private property, guilty of house burning, guilty of murders, both of citizens and soldiers of the Confederate States; and whereas demand has been duly made upon the military authorities of the United States for the surrender of said Col. Fielding Hurst and such officers and men of his command as are guilty of these outrages; and whereas this just demand has been refused by said authorities : I therefore declare the aforesaid Fielding Hurst, and the officers and men of his command, outlaws, and not entitled to be treated as prisoners of war falling into the hands of the forces of the Confederate States.

N. B. FORREST,
Major-General, Commanding.

NOTE.—Lieutenant-Colonel Reed is authorized to deliver this notice in the event an unsatisfactory answer is given to the demands made.

GENERAL ORDERS, }   HDQRS. DISTRICT OF KENTUCKY,
No. 30.   }   *Louisville, Ky., March* 22, 1864.

All churches, court-houses, jails, fair grounds, and all other public buildings now occupied by the military authorities in this district, will at once be vacated and delivered up to the proper authorities. Commanders of districts and posts within the limits of this command will see that this order is immediately complied with. Hereafter no public or private buildings will be taken for the use of troops except in cases of great emergency, and then only with the consent and approval of the sub-district commanders.

By command of Brigadier-General Burbridge:

J. D. BERTOLETTE,
Assistant Adjutant-General.

CHATTANOOGA, *March* 23, 1864.

Maj. Gen. W. T. SHERMAN :

I have already ordered General Garrard to collect his command and report to General Dodge that he has everything in readiness to act in connection with him. General Elliott is now in Nashville.

GEO. H. THOMAS,
Major-General, U. S. Volunteers, Commanding.

NASHVILLE, TENN., *March 23, 1864.*
(Received 11 p. m.)

ADJUTANT-GENERAL U. S. ARMY:

I have just arrived here, and will be here two days before moving to the front.

W. T. SHERMAN,
Major-General.

HEADQUARTERS THIRD DIVISION, FOURTH ARMY CORPS,
Rutledge, March 23, 1864—6 p. m.

Brig. Gen. J. D. COX, *Chief of Staff:*

GENERAL: Nothing has been heard yet of the Tenth Michigan Cavalry or any other cavalry, though as genial a day as this would scarcely be esteemed an impediment to fording the river. Without cavalry I can do nothing toward carrying out General Schofield's instructions, such as opening communication with General Garrard, &c., and hence cannot see the advantage to be gained by keeping me in a position which entails the necessity of wearing out my transportation by dragging my supplies 20 miles from the railroad over a bad road. It is now five days since the order was issued for me to come hither, and for the cavalry to report to me here. From the length of time it has taken for the order not to be obeyed, it is difficult to conjecture how much time may be necessary to obey the order.

Small bands of rebel cavalry have been seen within a few miles of here. To attempt to pursue them with infantry is useless.

I am, general, very respectfully, your obedient servant,

TH. J. WOOD,
Brigadier-General, Commanding.

STRAWBERRY PLAINS,
March 23, 1864.

Brigadier-General COX, *Chief of Staff:*

Negro boy, Jack, left Bull's Gap night before last; was servant for Major Hays, quartermaster of General Field's division; says they have one division at the gap; rest of the corps scattered between there and Bristol. Johnson's division at Midway, General McLaws' division at Greeneville; the rest of cavalry have gone to Georgia. General Gregg commands brigade in Hood's old division. No pickets this side of the mountains. No cavalry at Rogersville, nor between that place and the gap. Camp situated on the right of road, 3 miles above Bull's Gap, on the Kentucky road; one brigade about a mile above the gap. Railroad trains arrive twice each day. The railroad and wagon-road bridge over Lick Creek are in good condition. General Buckner's staff—Captain Galleher, assistant adjutant-general; Major Mastin, assistant inspector-general; Major Hays, quartermaster, of Covington, Ky.; Captain Shelby, commissary of subsistence, Danville, Ky.; Major Gibson, ordnance officer; Dr. Jennings, medical director. Boy belongs to Capt. Jack Lewis, of Knoxville. Hood's new field division at Bull's Gap, 6,000 strong. Each officer is allowed one ration, none furnished servants. Talk of sending all the negroes home. Men have no tents.

GEO. STONEMAN.
Major-General.

STRAWBERRY PLAINS, *March 23*, 1864.
Lieutenant-Colonel RANSOM,
　　Acting Chief Quartermaster, Knoxville :

By some blunder the cars loaded with rations were left here when the train went to Mossy Creek to-day. As General Stoneman telegraphs he is entirely out of subsistence for his command, I shall send the train back to him with these stores. This will account for its not returning at usual time to Knoxville.

　　　　　　　　　　J. D. COX,
　　　　　　　Brigadier-General, Chief of Staff.

STRAWBERRY PLAINS, *March 23*, 1864.
Major-General STONEMAN,
　　Twenty-third Army Corps:

I shall send back the train with the subsistence stores which were left here. Let your commissaries be ready to receive and take charge of them.

By command, &c. :

　　　　　　　　　　J. D. COX,
　　　　　　　Brigadier-General, Chief of Staff.

STRAWBERRY PLAINS, *March 23*, 1864.
Major-General STONEMAN,
　　Commanding Twenty-third Army Corps, Mossy Creek :

I expect to forward orders to-morrow to send the Sixty-fifth Illinois, Colonel Cameron's regiment, home on furlough as veterans. General Wood's men do not report any more regiments re-enlisted and we are only waiting for his official statement on the subject. You may make your arrangements accordingly.

By command, &c. :

　　　　　　　　　　J. D. COX,
　　　　　　　Brigadier-General, Chief of Staff.

CHATTANOOGA, TENN., *March 23*, 1864.
　　　　　　　　(Received 2 p. m., 24th.)
Lieut. Gen. U. S. GRANT,
　　Commander-in-Chief, U. S. Army :

Since telegraphing you regarding the state of my command, I sent General Elliott to Nashville to ascertain the wants and condition of the cavalry. He informs me that there are at that place 4,900 men for duty, exclusive of General Gillem's Tennessee regiments, and only 800 horses there, and the following ordnance stores required in addition to what are there : 2,600 sabers, 3,900 carbines, 3,600 saddles. I spoke to Captain Baylor, my chief of ordnance, concerning this, a few days since, and he showed me an answer to telegram on the subject from Chief of Ordnance, which stated that arms would be furnished as soon as they could be procured, but that they were not to be had.

　　　　　　　　　　GEO. H. THOMAS,
　　　　　Major-General, U. S. Volunteers, Commanding.

STRAWBERRY PLAINS, *March 23, 1864.*

Lieutenant-Colonel RANSOM,
  Acting Chief Quartermaster, Knoxville:

By some blunder the cars loaded with rations were left here when the train went to Mossy Creek to-day. As General Stoneman telegraphs he is entirely out of subsistence for his command, I shall send the train back to him with these stores. This will account for its not returning at usual time to Knoxville.

　　　　　　　　　J. D. COX,
　　　　　　Brigadier-General, Chief of Staff.

———

STRAWBERRY PLAINS, *March 23, 1864.*

Major-General STONEMAN,
  Twenty-third Army Corps:

I shall send back the train with the subsistence stores which were left here. Let your commissaries be ready to receive and take charge of them.

By command, &c. :

　　　　　　　　　J. D. COX,
　　　　　　Brigadier-General, Chief of Staff.

———

STRAWBERRY PLAINS, *March 23, 1864.*

Major-General STONEMAN,
  Commanding Twenty-third Army Corps, Mossy Creek:

I expect to forward orders to-morrow to send the Sixty-fifth Illinois, Colonel Cameron's regiment, home on furlough as veterans. General Wood's men do not report any more regiments re-enlisted and we are only waiting for his official statement on the subject. You may make your arrangements accordingly.

By command, &c. :

　　　　　　　　　J. D. COX,
　　　　　　Brigadier-General, Chief of Staff.

———

CHATTANOOGA, TENN., *March 23, 1864.*
　　　　　　(Received 2 p. m., 24th.)

Lieut. Gen. U. S. GRANT,
  Commander-in-Chief, U. S. Army:

Since telegraphing you regarding the state of my command, I sent General Elliott to Nashville to ascertain the wants and condition of the cavalry. He informs me that there are at that place 4,900 men for duty, exclusive of General Gillem's Tennessee regiments, and only 800 horses there, and the following ordnance stores required in addition to what are there : 2,600 sabers, 3,900 carbines, 3,600 saddles. I spoke to Captain Baylor, my chief of ordnance, concerning this, a few days since, and he showed me an answer to telegram on the subject from Chief of Ordnance, which stated that arms would be furnished as soon as they could be procured, but that they were not to be had.

　　　　　　　　　GEO. H. THOMAS,
　　　　Major-General, U. S. Volunteers, Commanding.

ATHENS, *March* 23, 1864.

General GARRARD,
    Commanding Cavalry Division:
I think Forrest has gone into West Tennessee. I have news of him at Corinth on Wednesday last.

G. M. DODGE,
Brigadier-General.

ATHENS, *March* 23, 1864.

Col. G. E. SPENCER,
    Decatur:
The general intends the Thirty-ninth Ohio to return to this place again. He so instructed Colonel Noyes last evening before starting. The general is quite sick. I know that he wished their camp and garrison equipage to remain here, and the regiment to return when it is ascertained beyond doubt that Decatur is in no danger of attack soon.

J. W. BARNES,
Assistant Adjutant-General.

ATHENS, ALA.,
March 23, 1864.

Brig. Gen. T. W. SWEENY,
    Pulaski:
The Twelfth Illinois leaves Nashville this morning. Have them debark at Pulaski and sent forward to this place by same train [that carried] the regiment now waiting at depot.
    By order of General Dodge:

J. W. BARNES,
Assistant Adjutant-General.

ATHENS, *March* 23, 1864.

Brig. Gen. J. D. STEVENSON :
Order the Thirty-ninth Ohio to return to Athens to-morrow.
    By order of Brigadier-General Dodge:

J. W. BARNES,
Assistant Adjutant-General.

HDQRS. FIRST BRIG., SECOND DIV., 16TH ARMY CORPS,
Pulaski, Tenn., March 23, 1864.

COMMANDING OFFICER,
    Fifty-second Illinois Infantry:
Your command will not move to Decatur as ordered, but will return to camps. The regiment is not needed.
    By order of Col. E. W. Rice:

D. T. BOWLER,
Acting Assistant Adjutant-General.

HDQRS. SECOND DIVISION, SIXTEENTH ARMY CORPS,
Pulaski, Tenn., March 23, 1864.

Col. AUGUST MERSY,
  Commanding Second Brigade:
  I am directed by the general commanding to inform you that the Twelfth Illinois will arrive this evening. Eight companies will rejoin their brigade. Two companies, B and I, will proceed to Richland.
  By order of Brig. Gen. T. W. Sweeny, commanding:
      LOUIS H. EVERTS,
        Captain and Assistant Adjutant-General.

WOODVILLE, ALA., *March 23, 1864.*

Maj. R. R. TOWNES,
  A. A. G., Fifteenth Army Corps, Huntsville, Ala. :
  Colonel Ferreby, commanding at Vienna, reports as follows:

I think the pickets on the opposite side have [been] re-enforced, but as yet no signs of any intentions or preparations for crossing. Sent a man across the river the night before last. My men captured 1 rebel lieutenant and 1 private last night.
      P. J. OSTERHAUS,
        Brigadier-General of Volunteers.

CAIRO, *March 23, 1864.*

Maj. Gen. W. T. SHERMAN :
  I have arrived here in pursuance of your order. Shall I come to Nashville or to any other point to see you personally ?
      JAS. B. McPHERSON,
        Major-General.

NASHVILLE, TENN., *March 23, 1864.*

COMMANDING OFFICER, *Cairo:*
  Has General McPherson started for Nashville? Has General Veatch's command started up the Tennessee ? If not, start them at once. Tell General McPherson I will await him here.
      W. T. SHERMAN,
        Major-General.

NASHVILLE, *March 23, 1864.*

General DODGE, *Athens :*
  If Forrest crosses at Eastport I will want an infantry force to cross at Paducah and move west to Tuscumbia, leaving him to be watched by cavalry on this side.
  Veatch is coming up the Tennessee with over 4,000 infantry that will land at Savannah and march for Pulaski. The moment Forrest detects them he will want to go back. Ascertain the truth as to Forrest and let me know. Have you a train to bring from Huntsville any of Logan's men ?
      W. T. SHERMAN,
        Major-General.

ATHENS, *March* 23, 1864.
Maj. R. M. SAWYER,
  Assistant Adjutant-General, Nashville:

It is probable we may check Forrest's crossing. Will keep General Garrard posted, so he can move, if needed.

G. M. DODGE,
Brigadier-General.

ATHENS, *March* 23, 1864.
Maj. R. M. SAWYER,
  Assistant Adjutant-General, Nashville:

Forrest is undoubtedly crossing the river between Eastport and Tuscumbia. I have a battalion of cavalry in neighborhood of Florence and a regiment of mounted infantry toward Eastport. If Forrest's intention is to strike the railroad, Garrard's division of cavalry should be prepared to meet him before he can reach the road.

G. M. DODGE,
Brigadier-General.

ATHENS, *March* 23, 1864.
Maj. R. M. SAWYER,
  Assistant Adjutant-General, Nashville:

I think that Forrest has gone north into West Tennessee, and his troops that came into the valley were used as a feint. He passed Corinth Wednesday last.

G. M. DODGE,
Brigadier-General.

ATHENS, *March* 23, 1864.
Brig. Gen. T. W. SWEENY,
  Pulaski:

Later advices from Decatur indicate that our force there will be sufficient for the present. You need not send the regiment down. Does the Seventh Illinois send any news of Forrest?

By order of General Dodge:

J. W. BARNES,
Assistant Adjutant-General.

ATHENS, *March* 23, 1864.
Maj. Gen. W. T. SHERMAN,
  Nashville:

I think Forrest has worked north into West Tennessee, sending a few regiments up Tuscumbia Valley to deceive us. My mounted force is on this side of river between Florence and Eastport, with orders to go to Eastport. I have not heard from them in two days, and I judge it is all right. The force at Gadsden, I think, is to relieve cavalry in front of General Thomas. It is under General Clanton, and came from Pollard, Ala. Trains run to Huntsville, stopping here over night.

G. M. DODGE,
Brigadier-General.

HDQRS. SECOND DIVISION, SIXTEENTH ARMY CORPS,
Pulaski, Tenn., March 23, 1864.
Capt. J. D. TOWNER,
    Comdg. Detach. 12th Illinois Infantry, Richland, Tenn. :
Your communication just received, and approved by the general
commanding, who directs that you retain the mounted scouts until
further orders from these headquarters or from General Dodge.
Keep them patrolling the railroad south of you, and particularly to
look out for the roads west of you, and instruct them to bring any
information they receive to these headquarters without delay.
    I remain, captain, with respect, your obedient servant,
                    LOUIS H. EVERTS,
            Captain and Assistant Adjutant-General.

———

HDQRS. SECOND DIVISION, SIXTEENTH ARMY CORPS,
Pulaski, Tenn., March 23, 1864.
Capt. J. W. BARNES,
    Asst. Adjt. Gen., Left Wing, Sixteenth Army Corps:
CAPTAIN : The following is substance of dispatch from Major Esta-
brook, commanding Seventh Illinois Infantry, dated Lawrenceburg,
March 23, just received. His force has been disposed as follows :
Headquarters, with one company, at Lawrenceburg ; one at Waynesborough, patrolling west and south ; one at the factory in vicinity of
Lawrenceburg ; one at or near Lexington ; one in the vicinity of
Lauderdale Mills ; two this side of the forks of the road, 4 or 5 miles
out, patrolling to meet and, if needed, support these last two. A
company left with dispatches and instructions for Eastport at 3 a. m.
to-day, bearing also orders for the detachment at Lauderdale Factory,
to make Florence, to find battalion Ninth Ohio Cavalry, and return
by way of Bainbridge with all information obtained.
    Has ordered the force at Waynesborough to Rawhide, and will
send that at Lexington on to Lamb's Ferry, and move with the
remnant of his command to the cross-roads at Holland's, 2 miles
north of Lauderdale, thus covering all the approaches indicated,
and being with his whole line much nearer the point of observation.
    He sent, under guard of the escort bearing dispatches to us, 8
prisoners, 6 of whom are deserters. One other, W. S. Henderson,
private Company B, Ninth Battalion Tennessee Cavalry, had in his
possession quite a large mail, but unimportant ; also some Confederate scrip. The other represents himself as a citizen.
    Respectfully, your obedient servant,
                    T. W. SWEENY,
    Brig. Gen., Comdg. Second Div., Sixteenth Army Corps.

———

HDQRS. SECOND DIVISION, SIXTEENTH ARMY CORPS,
Pulaski, Tenn., March 23, 1864.
Maj. GEORGE H. ESTABROOK,
    Comdg. 7th Illinois Inf., in the Field near Lawrenceburg :
MAJOR : Your dispatch just received. Your force is very well
disposed of. Bear in mind that it is of the utmost importance that
the roads leading from the west and southwest to this place, Rich-

land and Prospect, are well guarded—Lawrenceburg, Lexington, Lamb's Ferry, Gordonsville, &c.

Some of General Dodge's mounted scouts will operate west of Richland. Instruct your detachment in that direction to communicate with them, in order that a concert of action may be had. Should you fall in with any of Murphy's men send instructions to him to scout the country between Waynesborough and Clifton.

By order of Brig. Gen. T. W. Sweeny, commanding:

LOUIS H. EVERTS,
Captain and Assistant Adjutant-General.

NASHVILLE, *March* 23, 1864.
(Received 24th.)

COMMANDING OFFICER,
Cairo, Ill.:

Have troops at Columbus, Paducah, and Union City warned that Forrest is coming up with his cavalry. I am willing he should be up in that neighborhood. If the people don't manifest friendship, don't divert any troops bound up the Tennessee on that account.

W. T. SHERMAN,
Major-General.

CAIRO, *March* 23, 1864.

Maj. Gen. W. T. SHERMAN:

General McPherson left here for Nashville at noon yesterday, the 22d. General Veatch has not returned from Indiana. His command is here. I will start them and telegraph him.

M. BRAYMAN,
Brigadier-General.

HEADQUARTERS DISTRICT OF CAIRO,
Cairo, Ill., March 23, 1864.

Captain PENNOCK,
Commanding Station:

SIR: I have information which appears reliable that Forrest, with 7,000 cavalry, is approaching Union City. If so, it may be necessary to have a gun-boat in the vicinity of Columbus and Hickman and Paducah in case the river should be approached at either point.

Yours, &c.,

M. BRAYMAN,
Brigadier-General, Commanding.

HEADQUARTERS DISTRICT OF CAIRO,
Cairo, Ill., March 23, 1864.

Capt. F. W. FOX,
Assistant Adjutant-General:

SIR: Forrest, with 7,000 men, is reliably reported to be approaching Columbus, Ky., by way of Union City. I expect to call on your division for 2,000 men to embark for Columbus during the night, depending on information to arrive. Please have them in condition to move at short notice. This trip will not delay your movement up the Tennessee.

Yours, &c.,

M. BRAYMAN,
Brigadier-General, Commanding.

COLUMBUS, KY.,
March 23, 1864.

Brigadier-General BRAYMAN :

Captain Williams' scouts, just arrived, confirm the news. Forrest at Trenton last night, 8,000 strong. Colonel Freeman's [Faulkner's?] regiment has the advance; is 10 miles this side of Trenton, advancing on Union City. This scout confirms Colonel Hawkins' dispatch. Will leave with train immediately.

J. H. ODLIN,
Assistant Adjutant-General.

[MARCH 23, 1864.]

Colonel HAWKINS,
Union City :

Keep a good watch, and give them a fight. Captain Williams' scouts confirm your reports. I leave immediately with train. Have your baggage ready to load on cars.

J. H. ODLIN,
Assistant Adjutant-General.

PADUCAH, *March 23, 1864.*
(Received 8.40 a. m., 24th.)

Brig. Gen. M. BRAYMAN,
Commanding District of Cairo :

I feel from every indication that I would be much safer if I had additional force. I have information outside of your dispatch this day that satisfies me that there is a settled policy to take this place.

Respectfully, your obedient servant,

S. G. HICKS,
Colonel, Commanding Post.

COLUMBUS, KY.,
March 23, 1864.

General BRAYMAN :

Captain Odlin just left on train, 9 p. m. I have sent out all my scouts. It may be possible that Freeman [Faulkner?] has turned to the left and gone to Fort Pillow. Will telegraph you all news of importance promptly.

I. H. WILLIAMS,
Captain and District Provost-Marshal.

UNION CITY, *March* 23, 1864.

Brigadier-General BRAYMAN,
    Commanding District of Cairo:

A troop of 40 rebels at 9 a. m. were within 1 mile of this place, near Gardner's Station. I cannot tell whether they have any connection with the main force or not, but presume they have.

ISAAC R. HAWKINS,
    Colonel, Commanding Seventh Tennessee Cavalry.

UNION CITY, *March* 23, 1864.

Capt. J. H. ODLIN,
    Assistant Adjutant-General:

For fear my three dispatches of this day to the general have not been received, I repeat to you the material points of them:

First. By the arrival of a private scout I learn that General Forrest, with from 6,000 to 7,000 men, was at Jackson on Monday.

Second. That on yesterday the rebels were guarding the public ferries on the Obion and destroying the private ones.

Third. That a company of 40 were at 9 a. m. at Gardner's Station, 12 miles from this place. I have since learned that Colonel Bell's men last evening were 15 miles this side of Trenton, and I have asked that the place be immediately abandoned or largely re-enforced.

I. R. HAWKINS,
    Colonel, Commanding Seventh Tennessee Cavalry.

UNION CITY, *March* 23, 1864.

Capt. J. H. ODLIN,
    Assistant Adjutant-General:

I have nothing later than my dispatches to you at 4.30 p. m. Now have two companies out, who will not return before 12, unless driven in. None of my troops have seen the enemy, but the facts embodied in the dispatches of to-day are as certain as if they had. I shall keep out patrols all night, and report any information received.

ISAAC R. HAWKINS,
    Commanding.

UNION CITY, *March* 23, 1864—4.15 p. m.

Capt. J. H. ODLIN,
    Assistant Adjutant-General:

I am expecting an attack at this place within the next twenty-four hours with five times our numbers, consequently can spare no troops to go into Graves County. I think troops could subsist on that county, but would be better to carry rations. Have my three dispatches to General Brayman been received? If the general is not there, they should be opened immediately. Please answer immediately.

ISAAC R. HAWKINS,
    Colonel, Commanding Post.

MARCH 23, 1864.

Col. I. R. HAWKINS, *Union City, Tenn.:*
Your dispatches are all received. You will receive sufficient aid and definite instructions. Fortify and keep well prepared. Send out scouts and keep me advised.

M. BRAYMAN,
Brigadier-General, Commanding.

MARCH 23, 1864.

Col. S. G. HICKS, *Paducah, Ky.:*
Colonel Hawkins reports a force approaching Union City. Send out scouts and advise me if you need aid.

M. BRAYMAN,
Brigadier-General, Commanding.

COLUMBUS, *March* 23, 1864—9.35 p. m.

General BRAYMAN:
Just arrived, 8 o'clock. Colonel Hawkins is moving telegraph office and troops into the fort. Cannot get dispatch from him until they finish moving. The latest from there is nothing more than you have. Keep Cairo telegraph office open.

J. H. ODLIN,
Assistant Adjutant-General.

MEMPHIS, TENN., *March* 23, 1864.

Colonel McCRILLIS, *Germantown:*
Close your lines and allow no passing in or out. Make arrangements to bring in all the force, &c., to-morrow or next day.

B. H. GRIERSON,
Brigadier-General.

UNION CITY, *March* 23, 1864.

General BRAYMAN,
Commanding District of Cairo:
From all I can learn of the intention of the enemy, I think this post should be evacuated or heavily re-enforced. I have 200 men not mounted. Hope I shall hear from you immediately. I think the enemy will move in two columns, one east of me and the other west.

ISAAC R. HAWKINS,
Colonel, Commanding Post.

UNION CITY, *March* 23, 1864.

Brigadier-General BRAYMAN,
Commanding District of Cairo:
My private scout has just arrived and brings the information that General Forrest is at Jackson with a large force, estimated at from

6,000 to 7,000. On Tuesday they were destroying private ferries on the Obion, doubtless with the view of preventing information from crossing. Detachments had reached Milan. The above is entirely reliable.

ISAAC R. HAWKINS.
Colonel, Commanding.

HEADQUARTERS POST,
Fort Pillow, Tenn., March 23, 1864.
Brigadier-General BRAYMAN,
Commanding District of Cairo:

GENERAL: I have just received reliable information confirming previous information that Forrest, with from 3,000 to 8,000 men, was at Jackson, Tenn., on Monday, 21st instant, and has given orders for the cooking of five days' rations; that Faulkner, with from 600 to 1,200 men, was at Wellwood on Tuesday, 22d instant, 15 miles east of Brownsville, and was also having five days' rations cooked up. The current rumor in their camps was that Forrest intended a raid into Kentucky and was to meet Morgan at some point on the Tennessee River. There was also a report that Faulkner did not have all his men with him, not being able to mount them. The men were not permitted to scatter, but were kept close in camp.

Richardson was reported in the rear with 1,500 men, and would perhaps take Brownsville, Tenn., in his route. They were badly clothed and badly mounted, but seemed to be in buoyant spirits.

I have the honor to be, general, very respectfully, your obedient servant,

W. F. BRADFORD,
Major, Commanding Post.

PADUCAH, KY.,
March 23, 1864.
Brigadier-General BRAYMAN:

Thirty-five guerrillas met railroad train at Mayfield yesterday; killed one negro man and shot several times at a Union man, who escaped. No Union man can go out of this place with safety in that direction. The interior is full of guerrillas. I have no cavalry to send after them.

S. G. HICKS,
Colonel, Commanding Post.

HDQRS. CAVALRY DIVISION, SIXTEENTH ARMY CORPS,
Memphis, Tenn., March 23, 1864.
Lieut. Col. T. H. HARRIS,
Assistant Adjutant-General:

COLONEL: Inclosed please find statement* of scout just returned this a. m. I believe it entirely reliable, as it is corroborated by the statements of citizens from Canton and other points south.

I have consulted with General Buckland, and he does not consider

_____
* Not found.

it best to send infantry from this point. I will send Colonel Hurst, with the effective force of his command, in the morning (800 or 1,000 strong) to proceed via Somerville and Bolivar or Estenaula to hang around, harass, and impede the movements of the enemy. I will instruct him to report as often as possible, by couriers, to our forces at the nearest points. His men are thoroughly acquainted with the country. I have written to General Sherman and sent him a copy of the inclosed communication.

The First Alabama Cavalry will leave here to-morrow for Decatur, as per order. Their horses are in too bad condition to be sent by land, and one-half the regiment is dismounted.

Respectfully, your obedient servant,
B. H. GRIERSON,
Brigadier-General.

HDQRS. CAVALRY DIVISION, SIXTEENTH ARMY CORPS,
Memphis, March 23, 1864.
Maj. Gen. W. T. SHERMAN :

GENERAL : Inclosed please find statement* of scout, who returned this a. m. I consider it entirely reliable, as it is corroborated by statements of citizens from Canton and other points south. The scout, I have reason to believe, is a very reliable man.

All the old cavalry at this point have re-enlisted and are now going home on furlough. What is left is in poor condition and not very reliable. I have consulted with General Buckland and Lieutenant-Colonel Harris, of General Hurlbut's staff, and as General Buckland does not consider it best to send any infantry from this point I have concluded to send Colonel Hurst, with the effective force of his regiment (the Sixth Tennessee), from 800 to 1,000 strong, to hang upon, harass, and watch the movements of the enemy. He will start to-morrow via Somerville and Bolivar or Estenaula. I will instruct him to communicate at every opportunity with the nearest point. His men are thoroughly acquainted with the country, and I have no doubt that he will be able to impede the movements of the enemy.

I will put the rest of my command in the best possible shape with the material at hand, to be used as may be hereafter deemed best.

The First Alabama Cavalry will leave to-morrow for Decatur, as per order. More than half the regiment being dismounted and the horses in bad condition, I send them by river.

Very respectfully, your obedient servant,
B. H. GRIERSON,
Brigadier-General.

HDQRS. DISTRICT OF SOUTHERN CENTRAL KENTUCKY,
Cave City, March 23, 1864.
Capt. A. C. SEMPLE,
Assistant Adjutant-General :

I have the honor to report that I have ordered Colonel Weatherford, Thirteenth Kentucky Cavalry, to move a sufficient force over the river to scout through all the country south of Cumberland River to Livingston, Sparta, and to clear the country of guerrillas.

---
* Not found.

The mounted force of Fifty-second at Scottsville and part of Thirty-seventh Kentucky have been ordered to act in concert with Thirteenth Kentucky Cavalry. I have offered the scattered rebels in that country who have belonged to any regiment the privilege of coming in under the amnesty proclamation or being exchanged.

Very respectfully, your obedient servant,

E. H. HOBSON,
Brigadier-General.

CAVE CITY, *March 23, 1864.*

Capt. A. C. SEMPLE,
Assistant Adjutant-General, Louisville :

Rebel Colonel Hamilton and 12 of his men are here ; will forward them to-morrow. Major Rigney, of Thirteenth Kentucky Cavalry, captured them, and is entitled to the credit, and not Captain Stone, as before stated.

E. H. HOBSON,
Brigadier-General.

GENERAL ORDERS, }   HDQRS. DEPARTMENT OF THE OHIO,
No. 35.   }   *Knoxville, Tenn., March 23, 1864.*

Jeffersonville, in the State of Indiana, having been added to this department by General Orders, No. 49, current series, War Department, Adjutant-General's Office, is annexed to the District of Kentucky.

By command of Major-General Schofield :

J. A. CAMPBELL,
Assistant Adjutant-General.

GENERAL ORDERS, }   HDQRS. DEPARTMENT OF THE OHIO,
No. 36.   }   *Knoxville, Tenn., March 23, 1864.*

I. First Lieut. William J. Twining, Corps of Engineers, is hereby announced as acting chief engineer of the department, and will be obeyed and respected accordingly.

II. The commanding officer of each division and brigade of this army will select from his command a suitable officer, not above the rank of captain, to be attached to his staff as topographical engineer. The names of the officers appointed under this order will be immediately reported to these headquarters.

Division topographical engineers will report for instructions, by letter, to the acting chief engineer of the department.

By command of Major-General Schofield :

J. A. CAMPBELL,
Assistant Adjutant-General.

SPECIAL FIELD ORDERS, }   HDQRS. DEPT. OF THE CUMBERLAND,
No. 83.   }   *Chattanooga, Tenn., March 23, 1864.*

*   *   *   *   *   *   *

X. The garrison of Chattanooga is hereby constituted a separate brigade, and will hereafter be designated as the First Separate Brigade of the Department of the Cumberland. Brig. Gen. J. B. Steedman, commanding, will render his reports and returns direct to these headquarters.

*   *   *   *   *

By command of Major-General Thomas:

WM. D. WHIPPLE,
Assistant Adjutant-General.

SPECIAL ORDERS, } HEADQUARTERS CHIEF OF ARTILLERY,
        DEPARTMENT OF THE CUMBERLAND,
No. 26. }   *Chattanooga, Tenn., March 23, 1864.*

*   *   *   *   *

III. The present organization of the Artillery Reserve is broken up, and the following will be substituted: Batteries F, G, H, M, Fourth U. S. Artillery, and H and K, Fifth Artillery, will constitute the First Division; Batteries A, F, G, and M, First Ohio Artillery, Eighteenth Ohio, and First Kentucky, will constitute the Second Division until further orders. The divisions will be commanded by the senior officer present for duty. Col. James Barnett, First Ohio Artillery, is assigned to the command of the Artillery Reserve, composed of the above divisions, and will give the necessary orders for their immediate equipment for the field.

IV. Company I, Fourth Artillery, and Company D, East Tennessee Artillery, will report to Brig. Gen. R. S. Granger for duty with the artillery of Nashville.

V. Companies D, First Michigan, Eighth Wisconsin, and Twelfth Ohio are assigned to Fortress Rosecrans, at Murfreesborough, for duty as artillerists in the permanent works. They will turn over their guns, horses, harness, &c., under the orders of Colonel Barnett, who will have the property transferred to the batteries of his reserve, if they require it; otherwise it will be turned over to the quartermaster's department and ordnance department in Nashville.

VI. On the removal of the guns at Franklin, the Twenty-first Indiana Battery will take post at Columbia, on Duck River.

VII. Companies E and K, First Ohio Artillery, are assigned to the permanent garrison at Bridgeport, under the command of Maj. W. E. Lawrence, First Ohio Artillery. All the horses of these two companies will be transferred to one company, a field battery, the other company to take charge of the guns in position. Major Lawrence will give the necessary orders and make the selection of the field battery.

VIII. All the guns, carriages, limbers, &c., at Franklin will be disposed of as follows: Two 8-inch howitzers, with implements, to be sent to Columbia, on Duck River; the remainder, viz, one 30-pounder Parrott, two 24-pounders, and two 8-inch howitzers, to Bridgeport, Ala. The commanding officer of the Twenty-first Indiana Battery will see that sufficient ammunition of different kinds is sent to Columbia with the two 8-inch howitzers. The balance of the ammunition and implements will be sent to Bridgeport.

IX. Captain Guenther, Fifth Artillery, will turn over to Lieutenant Nitschelm, Twentieth Ohio Battery, the harness pertaining to Company H, Fifth Artillery, if it is serviceable.

X. The Tenth Indiana Battery is assigned to duty with the artillery garrison of Chattanooga.

XI. The Second Kentucky Battery is transferred from Twelfth Corps, and will remain in its present position and report direct to these headquarters.

By command of Major-General Thomas :

J. M. BRANNAN,
Brigadier-General, Chief of Artillery.

GENERAL ORDERS, ｝　HDQRS. CAV. CORPS, ARMY OF THE OHIO,
　No. 16.　　　｛　　　*Mount Sterling, Ky., March 23, 1864.*

For the information of all concerned, the following are reannounced as staff of the general commanding the corps : Capt. W. C. Rawolle, aide-de-camp and acting assistant adjutant-general; Capt. C. H. Hale, aide-de-camp and commissary of musters ; Capt. H. B. Sturgis, aide-de-camp ; Capt. F. W. Clemons, commissary of subsistence and chief commissary ; Capt. J. F. Coulter, assistant quartermaster and chief quartermaster ; Lieut. Col. J. P. Brownlow, acting assistant inspector-general ; Surg. J. F. Kimbly, medical director ; Maj. H. Tompkins, provost-marshal ; Capt. S. W. Sea, acting ordnance officer ; Capt. H. C. Bacon, judge-advocate, and will be obeyed and respected accordingly.

By order of Brigadier-General Sturgis :

W. C. RAWOLLE,
Capt., Aide-de-Camp, Acting Assistant Adjutant-General.

WASHINGTON, *March 24, 1864—3.45 p. m.*
Lieutenant-General GRANT,
　　　Army of the Potomac :

General Burnside asks to have the Second Ohio Cavalry, now at Cincinnati, and not mounted, ordered to his camp at Annapolis. This is a veteran regiment, which formerly belonged to the Army of the Ohio. Shall they be so ordered ?

H. W. HALLECK,
Major-General, Chief of Staff.

NASHVILLE, TENN., *March 24, 1864.*
(Received 2.30 a. m., 25th.)
ADJUTANT-GENERAL,
　　　Washington :

General Schofield asks for Brig. Gen. Thomas Ewing, now at Saint Louis, Mo. If you will assign him to me I will order him to General Schofield. I find many staff officers curiously situated, as Lieutenant-Colonel Donaldson and Colonel Beckwith proposing to act under special orders of the Secretary of War. I want my own staff under my own sole control, but of course subject to any inspection the Secretary of War or the commanding general may order. I will assign these officers to duty according to their rank, without changing their post at all. I understand that Colonel Swords is not subject to my orders, and therefore shall name General Robert Allen as chief quartermaster. I propose to use the railroad from Nashville to the south exclusively for freight, causing the soldiers to march and prohibiting their use to citizens altogether. In this way we can accumulate stores rapidly on our base of the Tennessee River for future use. All well to the front. Forrest's cavalry has gone up toward Columbus, where he can do us little harm, and it would be folly for me to push him. There are troops enough at Cairo to re-enforce Columbus and Paducah beyond the chance of danger.

W. T. SHERMAN,
Major-General, Commanding.

HDQRS. THIRD DIVISION, FOURTH ARMY CORPS,
Rutledge, March 24, 1864—12 m.

Brig. Gen. J. D. Cox,
Chief of Staff:

GENERAL: The Tenth Michigan Cavalry has just reported. Having remained three days in this position, I will move my camp this afternoon to the vicinity of Powder Spring Gap, for the purpose of keeping on the move, but chiefly to arrange for an excursion into Clinch Valley, opening communication with General Garrard at Cumberland Gap, &c. I will support the movement in that direction with infantry. I will also send some infantry and cavalry up this valley toward Bean's Station. The cavalry, though coming directly from the railroad, is without any rations; says it has had nothing to eat to-day. It has a very provident commissariat.

No news of interest to-day. Thanks for the Commercial of the 17th.

Respectfully, your obedient servant,

TH. J. WOOD,
Brigadier-General of Volunteers, Commanding.

STRAWBERRY PLAINS,
March 24, 1864.

Major-General GRANGER,
Knoxville or Loudon:

Your dispatch of this date received. I have done all I could to get the regiments within the limits of veteranism to re-enlist now, but without success. They say they have been so much disappointed heretofore, buffeted about, and deceived that they will not entertain the proposition. Several of them started once and were ordered back, and they say that there is no assurance that if they were to start again and get as far as Knoxville or Loudon they might not be again ordered back.

TH. J. WOOD,
Brigadier-General.

STRAWBERRY PLAINS,
March 24, 1864.

Major-General SCHOFIELD,
Commanding Department, Knoxville:

On receipt of General Wood's dispatch that his regiments refused to re-enlist as veterans, I telegraphed this morning to General Stoneman that Cameron's regiment could take its veteran furlough at once. By a dispatch from General Granger to General Wood, sent through my hands, I see he regards the question still open. I hope it will not interfere with the Sixty-fifth Illinois, as it would have a bad effect to retract the order regarding their furlough.

J. D. COX,
Brigadier-General, Chief of Staff.

HDQRS. THIRD DIVISION, FOURTH ARMY CORPS,
Powder Spring Gap, March 24, 1864—9 p. m.
Brig. Gen. J. D. COX, *Chief of Staff:*

GENERAL : I changed my camp here this afternoon. I have not more than a day and piece of rations on hand, but trust to get up a train to-morrow, which will give me a supply for three or four days. So soon as this is received I will send an expedition of cavalry and infantry through this gap into the Clinch Valley, with a view to opening communication with General Garrard at Cumberland Gap, and to see what the rebels are doing on the other side of the mountains (Clinch). I will also send an expedition up this valley toward Bean's Station, the fords of the Holston, &c.

No news of interest this evening.

Respectfully, your obedient servant,

TH. J. WOOD,
Brigadier-General Volunteers, Commanding.

HEADQUARTERS CAVALRY CORPS, ARMY OF THE OHIO,
Mount Sterling, March 24, 1864.
General E. E. POTTER,
Chief of Staff, Knoxville, Tenn. :

GENERAL : In compliance with your letter of the 18th instant, I inclose copy of your letter to me of January 31, 1864.

It will hardly be necessary that I point out to you how I am brought down in that letter to a level with an irresponsible scout, and my information, gained in the face of the enemy by fighting him, pitted against the bosh rumors picked up by lying and braggadocio scouts. My letter referred to in that was not a "story," but an official paper, containing the report of an officer of rank and long experience, and was, I think, entitled to somewhat more deference. I trust that the subsequent information received from reconnaissance, &c., will have amply confirmed the "truth" of what I reported at that time.

When you read the inclosed letter, therefore, I feel sure that you will not deem it strange that I felt mortified on receiving it.

I am, general, very respectfully and truly, yours, &c.,

S. D. STURGIS,
Brigadier-General, U. S. Volunteers.

[Inclosure.]

HEADQUARTERS DEPARTMENT OF THE OHIO,
Knoxville, January 31, 1864—9 p. m.
Brig. Gen. S. D. STURGIS:
Commanding Cavalry Corps:

GENERAL : Your dispatch of to-day is received.

The commanding general directs me to say that the information which he has received from scouts does not confirm your report as to strength of the enemy at Sevierville. A reconnaissance will be sent out to-morrow to ascertain the truth of these conflicting stories. After you have rested your horses for a day, and have sent the detachment on the expedition marked out in my last dispatch, you will keep your remaining force in the enemy's front to check him, and discover his strength and intentions.

We have trustworthy information to-day to the effect that all the infantry (rebel) which were over on the French Broad have returned to Morristown. The impression is amongst those who bring the news that Longstreet is satisfied with having checked our movement at Dandridge, and has gone again into winter quarters.

Very respectfully, your obedient servant,

EDWARD E. POTTER,
Chief of Staff.

NASHVILLE. *March 24, 1864.*

General SCHOFIELD,
Commanding, Knoxville:

General Potter is here, and has delivered your dispatches. I will send him to General Allen, at Louisville, to consult with him and determine how much to leave at Camp Nelson and how much to bring away. Your supplies will come via Chattanooga. I have ordered the railroad to be exclusively used for stores, and will make all troops coming forward march from Nashville unless you or Thomas call for haste. The troops can march near the railroad, and have its use to carry the sick and baggage.

General McPherson is now here. I will accompany him to-morrow to Decatur and Huntsville. Then I will come to Chattanooga and Knoxville. I will then make any orders you want, and we can consult on all matters of business.

General Hovey has five full regiments from Indiana, which I have ordered to you, and I will re-enforce you all I can. I must keep the offensive, and I cannot believe that the enemy will attempt any invasion of Kentucky, especially through the mountains of the eastern part of the State.

W. T. SHERMAN,
Major-General.

HEADQUARTERS ARMY OF THE OHIO,
Strawberry Plains, March 24, 1864.

Major-General STONEMAN,
Commanding Twenty-third Army Corps, Mossy Creek:

General Wood complains bitterly that the Tenth Michigan Cavalry does not yet report to him. In explaining the first delay I assured him they would return from Morristown on the 22d and would re- port yesterday. Please report what has still hindered them.

J. D. COX,
Brigadier-General, Chief of Staff.

STRAWBERRY PLAINS,
March 24, 1864.

Major-General STONEMAN,
Commanding Twenty-third Army Corps:

Let the veterans of Sixty-fifth Illinois have their furlough immediately. The men not enlisting will be assigned to other commands or to detached guard duty, &c., till the regiment returns, when they will rejoin it.

By command of Major-General Schofield :

J. D. COX,
Brigadier-General, Chief of Staff.

MOSSY CREEK, *March* 24, 1864.

General SCHOFIELD :

I have the honor to suggest that you allow me to mobilize the Twenty-third Corps and put it in such a condition that as soon as grass comes we can move where and when we please and over any kind of country. I want no wagons or artillery, except a few mountain howitzers, and but 1,000 pack-mules for rations, baggage, and ammunition. Should this meet your views I will communicate more fully with you upon the subject, either verbally or in writing.

GEO. STONEMAN,
Major-General.

HEADQUARTERS DEPARTMENT OF THE CUMBERLAND,
Chattanooga, March 24, 1864.

Maj. Gen. W. T. SHERMAN,
Nashville:

My troops are very much scattered; I should like very much to have them concentrated. It is almost impossible for me to make returns of or find out what are the wants of the troops as things are now.

GEO. H. THOMAS,
Major-General.

NASHVILLE, *March* 24, 1864—noon.

Maj. Gen. GEORGE H. THOMAS:

Your dispatch is received. General McPherson is now here, and we will go to-morrow to Decatur, to Huntsville, Larkinsville, &c. I will then come up to see you, and afterward General Schofield. For the present you may confine your attention to covering your own communications, and from Nashville as far as Columbia. General McPherson will cover from Columbia around to Stevenson. Unless the returning regiments are greatly needed to the front, I will order all troops coming forward to disembark at Nashville and march by easy marches. This will relieve our road, and also do the troops good. We will be pressed for wagons, and I wish you to arrange to strip all troops left to guard roads of their mules, horses, and wagons, to be used in our offensive operations until McPherson's troops arrive on the line of the Decatur road from the Tennessee River. I must move the cavalry division now at Huntsville and here to some point near Duck or Elk Rivers, to our right flank, and I may use it to cross the Tennessee at Decatur to La Fayette, straight to the south.   I shall prohibit all citizens using any of our railroads south of Nashville for passage or use ; and if citizens can't live at the front, they must move to the rear.   We must use our roads exclusively for freight till a supply is in store.

W. T. SHERMAN,
Major-General.

CHATTANOOGA, *March* 24, 1864.
Major-General SLOCUM,
    Tullahoma :
    It will not be necessary to send troops to the Decatur road.   You will therefore prepare to relieve Coburn's brigade, so that it can come to the front.   As soon as the block-houses are finished place them in the garrisons designated by the chief engineer and come to the front with the remainder of your command, except the necessary garrisons at Murfreesborough and Nashville.   The estimate of garrisons for block-houses will be forwarded you by mail.

WM. D. WHIPPLE,
Assistant Adjutant-General.

RINGGOLD, GA.,
March 24, 1864.
Brigadier-General WHIPPLE :
    All is quiet to-day.   The rebels have doubled their pickets in front. A negro from Dalton reports Longstreet's troops there, probably only his cavalry, which was expected.   Artillery arrived there by rail two days ago.   A citizen reports that Polk's corps is expected at Dalton.   Cannot General Elliott visit our cavalry ?

A. BAIRD,
Brigadier-General.

HEADQUARTERS ELEVENTH CORPS,
March 24, 1864.
Brig. Gen. W. T. WARD,
    Commanding First Division :
    GENERAL : A party of 10 men of the First Alabama Cavalry have been cut off and probably captured by a scouting party of the enemy not far beyond Johnson's Crook.   You will send a picked force of 100 mounted men to scout in the vicinity of Johnson's Crook to ascertain the facts, and, if possible, relieve our scouts.   They will take four days' forage in wagons, if necessary, and march as rapidly as possible till they reach Johnson's Crook.   I want the greatest vigilance exercised and all possible information obtained.   Put a perfectly reliable officer in charge.
    By order of Major-General Howard :

F. W. GILBRETH,
Lieutenant and Acting Aide-de-Camp.

ATHENS, *March 24*, 1864.
General SWEENY :

A battalion of the Ninth Ohio Cavalry has just returned from Florence and reports that yesterday two regiments had crossed at Eastport and were still crossing. Order the Seventh Illinois to move forward so as to more closely watch the movements of the enemy and report with all possible dispatch to the nearest points on the railroad.

By order of General Dodge :

GEO. E. SPENCER,
Colonel, Chief of Staff.

————

ATHENS, *March 24*, 1864.
Major-General SHERMAN :

One battalion of cavalry has returned from below Florence and Eastport ; they report that on Sunday about 500 rebels crossed on Donnelly's boat at Eastport. This is a boat trading on Tennessee River, and used to be protected by Roddey, and so they returned to south side of river next day. Yesterday it was reported that they were again crossing, and that two regiments had got over to this side.

G. M. DODGE,
Brigadier-General.

————

ATHENS, *March 24*, 1864.
Col. J. W. FULLER,
        Decatur :

We have no information that Forrest has been repulsed in crossing the river. On Sunday 500 men crossed near Eastport on Donnelly's trading-boat ; made a scout toward Florence and returned to the south side of the river the same day. Yesterday it is reported that two regiments crossed at Eastport, and more were crossing. We have a regiment and battalion watching the movements there, but can learn nothing further.

GEO. E. SPENCER,
Colonel and Chief of Staff.

————

HDQRS. MILITARY DIVISION OF THE MISSISSIPPI,
Nashville, March 24, 1864.
Brig. Gen. ROBERT ALLEN,
        Chief Quartermaster, Louisville :

GENERAL : General Potter comes to me from Knoxville, sent ·by General Schofield, at the instance of General Grant, to inspect the depot at Camp Nelson. General Schofield thinks the depot should not be absolutely discontinued, and it may be well to reduce its dimensions gradually, taking from it such wagons and property as are no longer needed. Knoxville will be naturally supplied from Chattanooga, as its railroad is better than the long road from Camp Nelson. I will go to Knoxville in a few days, and then will consult with General Schofield, whose personal experience may qualify my own opinion. You will therefore confer freely with General Potter, and he can examine the depot, and on his return to Louisville, in concert you will be able on my return to supply me with accurate data and information, which will enable me to act according to my general plan.

Of course, I believe in as few depots as possible, and those on a large scale, well guarded. These depots, I think, should be at Nashville, Chattanooga, Huntsville, and Decatur, the two former of course the principal. I am not yet clear as to the line of operations from East Kentucky, but if anywhere it should not be far from Prestonburg, drawing from the mouth of the Big Sandy.

We are on the offensive, and should not think of any defensive measure. I wish you to use General Potter to examine the question as to East Kentucky, and be prepared for active removal of the depot or diminution of its capacity, according to the facts elicited.

W. T. SHERMAN,
Major-General, Commanding.

COLUMBUS, *March* 24, 1864—4.30 a. m.

General BRAYMAN :

I received the following from Captain Odlin :

The rebels have just driven the pickets on the Dresden and Hickman road. Order the Crawford——

At this point the lines were cut. I supposed it meant to order the Crawford to Hickman for the company, which I have done. I have thrown out my mounted infantry 5 miles, as an advance picket for this post.

WM. HUDSON LAWRENCE,
Colonel Thirty-fourth New Jersey Vols., Commanding.

PADUCAH, *March* 24—9.40 a. m.

Brigadier-General BRAYMAN,
Commanding District:

I have a gun-boat here. I am ready for them.

Respectfully,

S. G. HICKS,
Colonel, Commanding Post.

COLUMBUS, *March* 24—10.15 a. m.

Capt. J. H. ODLIN,
Assistant Adjutant-General:

They have burned the State Line bridge, 6 miles from Union City. We hear nothing from Hawkins.

W. H. LAWRENCE,
Commanding Post.

COLUMBUS, *March* 24, 1864—11.20 a. m.

Captain MUNROE :

Latest information, they are marching on this place. I just saved the train by my boldness. I beat them to the bridge. Send all dispatches to this point, and warn the operator to be careful the line is not tapped and they get the information. Up to this time General Brayman has not arrived.

J. H. ODLIN,
Assistant Adjutant-General.

CAIRO, ILL.,
March 24, 1864—11.45 a. m.

Captain PENNOCK, *Commanding:*

I have just received a dispatch from Columbus stating that the enemy were advancing on Columbus in force. Communication with Colonel Hawkins at Union City has been cut off and nothing heard from him since 3 o'clock this morning. Think it would be advisable to send a gun-boat to Columbus at once, if possible.

Very respectfully, your obedient servant,

J. H. MUNROE,
Assistant Adjutant-General.

CAIRO, *March* 24, 1864.

Brig. Gen. M. BRAYMAN, *Columbus:*

I will try to get a gun-boat to you this evening. Please keep me informed.

A. M. PENNOCK,
Fleet Captain and Commander Station.

CAIRO, *March* 24, 1864.

General BRAYMAN:

Captain Pennock is here and will do all in his power to have a gun-boat sent to Columbus as soon as possible.

J. H. MUNROE,
Assistant Adjutant-General.

CAIRO, *March* 24, 1864.

Capt. J. H. ODLIN,
Assistant Adjutant-General:

Do you want any more troops sent down?

JNO. H. MUNROE,
Assistant Adjutant-General.

COLUMBUS, *March* 24, 1864.

Captain MUNROE:

You need not send any more troops. Have not got boats for what we have. Will return to-night. Colonel Hawkins surrendered at 11 a. m. General directs that you do not allow any reporters to give the stories afloat, but leave the reports for him to sign.

J. H. ODLIN,
Assistant Adjutant-General.

COLUMBUS, KY., *March* 24, 1864.
Maj. Gen. W. T. SHERMAN,
    Nashville, Tenn.:
    Forrest has attacked and probably occupies Union City.   He has
cut the road and wire this side.   I go out with 2,000 men.   Some of
these men belong to General Veatch.   I will return to Cairo and send
them up Tennessee as soon as their boats arrive from Saint Louis.
I will not detain them.
                                            M. BRAYMAN,
                                                Brigadier-General.

HEADQUARTERS OF THE POST,
                                Columbus, Ky., March 24, 1864.
Capt. A. M. PENNOCK,
    Fleet Captain, &c., Cairo, Ill. :
    After capturing Union City, Forrest left northeasterly, perhaps
toward Paducah.   His force not formidable.   Columbus and Paducah in no immediate danger.   Master Commanding Wetmore is on
duty.   I return to-night.
                                            M. BRAYMAN,
                                                Brigadier-General.

COLUMBUS, *March* 24, 1864.
Col. S. G. HICKS,
    Paducah :
    Union City surrendered to Forrest at 11 a. m.   Forrest appears to
intend an attack on you.   His force is much less than supposed, and
you are in no danger.   I go to Cairo to-night.
                                            M. BRAYMAN,
                                                Brigadier-General, Commanding.

CAIRO, ILL., *March* 24, 1864.
Major-General SHERMAN,
    Nashville, Tenn.:
    Your telegram received.   General Brayman, in command, has just
gone to Columbus with two regiments of Veatch's brigade.   Forrest drove in our pickets at Union City this morning at 3 o'clock.
Troops will be sent up the Tennessee as soon as transports can be
procured.   Colonel Hicks, at Paducah, has been informed of all
movements, and telegraphs that he is ready for them.   Your telegram sent to General Brayman at Columbus.
                                            JNO. H. MUNROE,
                                    Captain and Assistant Adjutant-General.

COLUMBUS, KY., *March* 24, 1864.
Capt. A. M. PENNOCK,
    Commanding Station :
    Let the boat report here.   We go out with 2,000 men toward
Union City.   I think the enemy will go toward Paducah.
                                            M. BRAYMAN,
                                                Brigadier-General, Commanding.

NASHVILLE, TENN., *March 24, 1864.*
General HURLBUT, *Cairo:*

General McPherson is here. I will go with him to Decatur and Huntsville to-morrow. If you propose to rejoin, please act at once, as I must know my officers. I know that two divisions of white troops with Grierson's cavalry and the blacks can not only hold the river, but act offensively against the enemy. Forrest is only after horses and conscripts up in West Tennessee.

W. T. SHERMAN,
Major-General, Commanding.

CAIRO, *March 24, 1864.*
Maj. Gen. W. T. SHERMAN:

I am here on my way to Memphis. I think this Forrest movement exaggerated. Grierson is behind him, and will be supported by infantry from Memphis.

S. A. HURLBUT,
Major-General.

PADUCAH, *March 24, 1864.*
Major-General SHERMAN:

Dispatch received. General Veatch left here at noon to-day with his division up the Tennessee River. Will send your dispatch to him by first boat.

S. G. HICKS,
Colonel, Commanding.

HDQRS. CAVALRY DIVISION, SIXTEENTH ARMY CORPS,
Memphis, Tenn., March 24, 1864.
Col. FIELDING HURST,
Commanding Sixth Tennessee Cavalry:

COLONEL: Information having been received that Forrest, with a considerable force of cavalry, had moved to Jackson, Tenn., with the intention either of crossing the Tennessee and operating in the rear of Chattanooga or of striking some point on the Mississippi or Ohio Rivers, you will move with the effective force of your command, with a full supply of ammunition and such rations as can be carried upon the persons of the men, without train or other incumbrance, early on the morning of the 25th of March, via Somerville toward Jackson, crossing the Hatchie River at Estenaula or such other point as the information you obtain may justify. The object of your expedition is to hang upon and harass the enemy, with a view of impeding his movements as much as possible. You will not bring him into a general engagement, but rather cut off and capture his foraging parties, stragglers, &c.

Hold your command well in hand, and do not allow yourself to be drawn into any trap or to be surprised.

Take any forage or provisions you may find which may be necessary to subsist your command.

Extend protection as far as possible to people of known loyalty, and rather forage upon secession sympathizers. You are particularly cautioned against allowing your men to straggle or pillage. Issue and enforce the strictest orders upon this subject, as a deviation from this rule may prove fatal to yourself and command.   Look well with reliable scouts to your flanks and rear, as a portion of the enemy's force is at present south, and will endeavor to form a junction with Forrest.   Communicate as often as possible · by courier or otherwise with the nearest Federal forces, and follow the enemy as long as you may consider it safe and expedient.

With your excellent knowledge of the country I rely upon your ability to inflict serious injury upon the enemy without much loss to your own command.

Yours, truly,

B. H. GRIERSON,
Brigadier-General.

NASHVILLE, *March* 24, 1864.
(Received 11.25 p. m.)

General HURLBUT :

If Veatch's command could be sent rapidly up to Eastport, or even Pittsburg Landing, by a rapid march back to the head of the Hatchie, Forrest would be compelled to scatter to escape.   Dodge thinks Forrest has a steam-boat with which· to cross troops at Eastport.   The gun-boats should be advised. ' I go to Decatur to-morrow.

W. T. SHERMAN,
Major-General.

HEADQUARTERS POST AND DEFENSES,
Vicksburg, Miss,· March 24, 1864.

Captain MCELROY,
Commanding Gun-boat Petrel, &c. :

From information received, and which I consider reliable, General Ross' brigade of cavalry, with three pieces of artillery, have gone from Yazoo City in the direction of Greenville.   I would be pleased to have you proceed with your two vessels up the Sunflower River, making a demonstration to cut him off, destroying his ferries, if he has constructed any, and gathering up such information regarding his movements as will enable me to thwart any designs he may have in obstructing navigation at Greenville or Skipwith's, returning as soon as convenient.   A transport steamer for foraging purposes will accompany you, which you can use in sending any dispatches back, as you see fit.   I would be pleased to have you start to-morrow, if possible.   Let me hear from you at Haynes' Bluff by telegraph when you leave that point.

Your most obedient servant,

J. McARTHUR,
Brigadier-General, Commanding.

GENERAL ORDERS, } WAR DEPT., ADJT. GENERAL'S OFFICE,
No. 117.   { *Washington, March* 24, 1864.

By direction of the President of the United States, Col. Frank Wolford, First Kentucky Cavalry Volunteers, is dishonorably dismissed the service of the United States for violation of the fifth section of the Rules and Articles of War, in using disrespectful words against the President of the United States, for disloyalty, and for conduct unbecoming an officer and a gentleman.

By order of the Secretary of War :

E. D. TOWNSEND,
Assistant Adjutant-General.

GENERAL ORDERS, ⎱ HDQRS. MIL. DIV. OF THE MISSISSIPPI,
No. 3. ⎰ *Nashville, Tenn., March* 24, 1864.

The following officers are named as members of the staff to the Military Division of the Mississippi :

Personal : Maj. J. C. McCoy, aide-de-camp ; Capt. L. M. Dayton, aide-de-camp ; Capt. J. C. Audenried, aide-de-camp.

General : Brig. Gen. J. D. Webster ; Brig. Gen. W. F. Barry, chief of artillery.

They will be respected accordingly.

By order of Maj. Gen. W. T. Sherman :

R. M. SAWYER,
Assistant Adjutant-General.

GENERAL ORDERS, ⎱ HDQRS. SIXTEENTH ARMY CORPS,
No. 31. ⎰ *Memphis, Tenn., March* 24, 1864.

The following orders of the Secretary of War are published for the information of this command :

ORDERS, ⎱ VICKSBURG, MISS.,
No. 7. ⎰ *March* 11, 1864.

All troops of African descent will hereafter be designated by numbers and be reported by the number as regiments of U. S. cavalry, heavy artillery, light artillery, or infantry (colored).

Those in the Department of the Tennessee will be numbered as follows hereinafter.

Those in the Department of the Gulf will be numbered as soon as complete returns of the same have been received.

After the regiments have been designated in accordance with the above, under no circumstances whatever will any other number or denomination be given them.

CAVALRY.

First Mississippi Cavalry (of African descent) as the Third.

HEAVY ARTILLERY.

First Regiment of Tennessee Heavy Artillery (of African descent) as the Second.
Second Regiment of Tennessee Heavy Artillery (of African descent) as the Third.
First Regiment of Mississippi Heavy Artillery (of African descent) as the Fourth.
Second Regiment of Mississippi Heavy Artillery (of African descent) as the Fifth.
First Alabama Siege Artillery (of African descent) to be Sixth.

LIGHT ARTILLERY.

First, Second, and Third Louisiana Batteries (of African descent) as Batteries A, B, and C, Second.
The Memphis Light Battery (of African descent) as Battery D, Second.

INFANTRY.

First Regiment Arkansas Volunteers (of African descent) as the Forty-sixth.
Eighth Regiment Louisiana Volunteers (of African descent) as the Forty-seventh.
Tenth Regiment Louisiana Volunteers (of African descent) as the Forty-eighth.
Eleventh Regiment Louisiana Volunteers (of African descent) as the Forty-ninth.
Twelfth Regiment Louisiana Volunteers (of African descent) as the ₚiftieth.
First Regiment Mississippi Volunteers (of African descent) as the Fifty-first.
Second Regiment Mississippi Volunteers (of African descent) as the Fifty-second.
Third Regiment Mississippi Volunteers (of African descent) as the Fifty-third.
Second Regiment Arkansas Volunteers (of African descent) as the Fifty-fourth.
First Regiment Alabama Volunteers (of African descent) as the Fifty-fifth.
Third Regiment Arkansas Volunteers (of African descent) as the Fifth-sixth.
Fourth Regiment Arkansas Volunteers (of African descent) as the Fifty-seventh.
Sixth Regiment Mississippi Volunteers (of African descent) as the Fifty-eighth.
First Regiment West Tennessee Volunteers (of African descent) as the Fifth-ninth.
First Regiment Iowa Volunteers (of African descent) as the Sixtieth.
Second Regiment West Tennessee Volunteers (of African descent) as the Sixty-first.
First Regiment Missouri Volunteers (of African descent) as the Sixty-second.
Ninth Regiment Louisiana Volunteers (of African descent) as the Sixty-third.
Seventh Regiment Louisiana Volunteers (of African descent) as the Sixty-fourth.
Second Regiment Missouri Volunteers (of African descent) as the Sixty-fifth.
Fourth Regiment Mississippi Volunteers (of African descent) as the Sixty-sixth.
Third Regiment Missouri Volunteers (of African descent) as the Sixty-seventh.
Fourth Regiment Missouri Volunteers (of African descent) as the Sixty-eighth.
By order of the Secretary of War :

L. THOMAS,
Adjutant-General.

By order of Maj. Gen. S. A. Hurlbut :

T. H. HARRIS,
Lieutenant-Colonel and Assistant Adjutant-General.

WAR DEPARTMENT, ADJUTANT-GENERAL'S OFFICE,
Washington, March 25, 1864—3 p. m.

Maj. Gen. W. T. SHERMAN,
Comdg. Mil. Div. of the Miss., Nashville, Tenn.:

SIR : Your telegram of yesterday's date has been submitted to the Secretary of War, who instructs me to reply—

First. That Colonel Donaldson and Colonel Beckwith are assigned to their respective duties at Nashville by the War Department, in accordance with the established rules of the service. They form no part of your staff and are not subject to your assignment.

Second. That neither Colonel Swords nor General Allen are subject to your assignment, but are assigned to their duties by the Quartermaster-General, under the direction of the Secretary of War; and only in case of misconduct, requiring immediate action, they are subject to your orders, other than to answer requisitions for supplies.

Third. If any commissary or quartermaster within the limits of your command, though not under your orders, misbehave or fail to perform their duty, you are authorized to suspend them and report the facts to the War Department, through the chief of the proper bureau, for action, and, if necessary, you are authorized to place the party in arrest until the directions of the Secretary of War can be obtained.

Fourth. These regulations have uniformly prevailed, and their observance by commanders of departments and military divisions is essential to the service, but any suggestion from you will be considered and carried out so far as the service and the proper administration of the War Department will admit.

Fifth. Your proposed use of the railroad is approved, and the Department will contribute every aid and confidence within its power for the success of your operations.

I am, sir, your obedient servant,

E. D. TOWNSEND,
Assistant Adjutant-General.

KNOXVILLE, *March* 25, 1864—4 p. m.

Maj. Gen. W. T. SHERMAN:

Late information, which seems reliable, indicates that the enemy is again falling back toward Virginia, a small force of infantry, cavalry, and artillery being left at Bull's Gap. The cavalry has for some time been preparing for a long march; it may be for a raid into Kentucky, though that seems impossible at this season. Most probably it is going to Virginia or Georgia. Artillery and baggage are being sent back by railroad. I do not believe Longstreet himself has returned from Richmond.

JNO. M. SCHOFIELD,
Major-General.

STRAWBERRY PLAINS,
March 25, 1864.

Major-General SCHOFIELD:

The following message was received this morning:

MOSSY CREEK, *March* 25, 1864.

General COX,
Chief of Staff:

Lieutenant Coutry [?], Sixteenth Battalion Georgia Cavalry, left Bull's Gap night before last, 10 p. m.; reports the infantry encamped about 2 miles beyond the gap, 1 mile to the left of the railroad on the Snapp's Ferry road; does not know where the cavalry are stationed; the cavalry pickets are 1 mile this side of the gap. Giltner's brigade of cavalry are ordered to move this morning for Carter and Johnson Counties. Brigade consists of Tenth Kentucky Cavalry, Tenth Kentucky Mounted Infantry, Fourth Kentucky Cavalry, and Second [First] Tennessee Cavalry (Carter's); also Sixteenth Georgia Battalion Cavalry. Rucker's Legion left for Rogersville last Friday. General Vaughn's cavalry brigade left at same time for Big Creek, about Rogersville. Giltner's brigade ordered to reach Jonesborough to-night; have their horses well shod and carry an extra pair of shoes with them. General Longstreet's headquarters are removed to Jonesborough. They have but one small battery of four guns at the gap; the others were sent up the road on the cars. There is but one regiment of cavalry at the gap—Virginia regiment. Rucker's Legion for some time past have carried a black flag. Joanna Eastef and Cynthia Brockville left Rogersville yesterday morning on the railroad train and came down to Bull's Gap; from there in a wagon to Russellville, and from there on foot; state that nearly all the army of Longstreet's has gone north of Jonesborough. A small force at Bull's Gap. Longstreet has not been this side of Bristol since he went to Richmond. Some troops still at Greeneville, but leaving for the north. Every day baggage being sent north. Conductor said that he thought the railroad train would not come down to Bull's Gap after to-morrow.

STONEMAN,
Major-General, Commanding Corps.

J. D. COX,
Chief of Staff.

(Copy to General Wood.)

MOSSY CREEK, *March* 25, 1864.

General SCHOFIELD:

Scouts just in from Dandridge and Mouth of Chucky. Rebels reported to have gone up toward Greeneville. It is reported by citizens just from Bull's Gap that the infantry has left; none at Blue Springs. A small squad of cavalry at the gap. I have and will send my men out on all of the different roads toward and beyond the gap.

R. A. CRAWFORD,
Colonel and Chief of Scouts.

ATHENS, *March* 25, 1864—9 p. m.

Major SAWYER:

Answer to Burbridge that I will not change General Grant's order till I see General Schofield, in whose department Louisville is. Telegraph General Schofield his dispatch is received by me and that I am on my way to him; in the mean time to feel the enemy to make him develop his plans. I do not believe he intends to invade Kentucky, but that all of Longstreet's army will re-enforce Lee in Virginia. All is well here. I go to Decatur and Huntsville to-morrow.

W. T. SHERMAN,
Major-General, Commanding.

WOODVILLE, ALA.,
March 25, 1864.

Maj. R. R. TOWNES,
Huntsville, Ala.:

Colonel Gage, commanding near Cottonville, reports as follows:

The enemy have a boat at the landing opposite Claysville, and cross and recross every night. I have only 12 men mounted, partly on mules, and no animals to mount more. The mounted force spoken of in one of your dispatches has not yet reported at Claysville. I hear a good deal of chopping in the woods opposite Deposit and think the enemy are putting up a stockade.

P. J. OSTERHAUS,
Brigadier-General, Commanding Division.

ATHENS. *March* 25, 1864.

Maj. Gen. W. T. SHERMAN:

There is something wrong about these trading-boats that run up the Tennessee River. The rebels never take them except when they want to cross a few men, then let them go, and a week or two afterward the boats report the fact at Paducah. If half the stories I hear of them are true they are continually violating the trade regulations, and, whether they do or not, they cannot expect to trade with any one but rebels in that country.

G. M. DODGE,
Brigadier-General.

ATHENS, ALA.,
March 25, 1864.

Maj. Gen. W. T. SHERMAN :

Mr. W. S. Johnson, from La Grange, Tenn., has arrived here. Crossed the Tennessee at Eastport on Tuesday. Two gun-boats and two transports were there. Transports brought cavalry to Clifton. There was heavy cannonading at Hamburg Monday night and gunboats went down. Forrest was reported there with a large force. Met my force near Rawhide, this side of Eastport.

G. M. DODGE,
Brigadier-General.

HDQRS. SECOND DIVISION, SIXTEENTH ARMY CORPS,
Pulaski, Tenn., March 25, 1864.

Maj. FRANK EVANS,
Comdg. Detach. 81st Ohio Inf. Vols., at Nance's Mills:

MAJOR : Lieutenant-Colonel Adams, commanding at Lynnville, reports that small parties of rebels, wearing gray uniforms, are hovering around the lines at Culleoka, well armed and mounted.

Send down your mounted men in that direction, to move cautiously and ascertain what force is there, and all facts possible in reference to the same. Captain De Hews, secret service, with 10 men, goes to Culleoka to-day for the same purpose. Co-operate with him if possible.

Advices from General Dodge at Athens say that two regiments, rebels, have crossed the river at Eastport and are still crossing.

You will be extremely vigilant and use your mounted force to the best advantage in gaining information of the enemy and his movements, reporting the same to these headquarters.

By order of Brig. Gen. T. W. Sweeny, commanding :

LOUIS H. EVERTS,
Captain and Assistant Adjutant-General.

CAIRO, *March 25, 1864.*

Col. S. G. HICKS,
Paducah :

What news from your scouts ? Do you need help ? Lose no time in advising General Brayman of your situation and the whereabouts of the enemy when last heard from.

By command of Brigadier-General Brayman :

C. B. SMITH,
Lieutenant and Aide-de-Camp.

HDQRS. FOURTH DIVISION, SIXTEENTH ARMY CORPS,
Cairo, Ill., March 25, 1864.

Col. JAMES H. HOWE,
Commanding Second Brigade:

The dispatches to-night say that Paducah is attacked and is likely to be overpowered by a rebel force. You will embark one regiment of your command immediately and run up near Paducah, communicating with Captain Shirk, on gun-boat No. 36. If you find that the place can be re-enforced, and that it is expedient for you to land, Captain Shirk will cover your troops with his guns. This move- ment must not delay our voyage up the Tennessee, and you must take everything with you necessary for the march, except your trans- portation, which you will direct to be shipped in the morning.

You must act on your own judgment when you reach Paducah, and be governed by the best information you can obtain.

JAMES C. VEATCH,
Brigadier-General.

GERMANTOWN, TENN.,
March 25, 1864.

Captain WOODWARD:

Lieutenant-Colonel Smith, Sixth Tennessee Cavalry, left Bolivar yesterday morning at 9 a. m. and reports Forrest at Jackson; has 8,000 or 10,000 men, either now with him or on the road to join him.

L. F. McCRILLIS,
Colonel.

HEADQUARTERS POST AND DEFENSES,
Vicksburg, Miss., March 25, 1864.

Brigadier-General SHEPARD,
Commanding at Haynes' Bluff:

GENERAL: From information I have received there is a force of cavalry in the vicinity of Mechanicsburg. Send out Osband's cav- alry on a reconnaissance in that direction and ascertain the truth of the report. He will drive them from there if his force is sufficient; if not, he will engage them sufficiently to ascertain their strength and probable intentions, reporting the facts as early as possible. Should his report warrant it, you will retain the regiment that has been ordered here until further orders from these headquarters. Let them start in the morning early.

Your most obedient servant,

J. McARTHUR,
Brigadier-General, Commanding.

HDQRS. FIRST DIVISION, U. S. COLORED TROOPS,
Vicksburg, Miss., March 25, 1864.

Brig. Gen. I. F. SHEPARD,
Commanding First Brigade:

You will cause the Forty-ninth Regiment U. S. Infantry (col- ored) to move at once with their camp and garrison equipage to this place. Colonel Young will send an officer immediately to select a suitable place for his camp.

By order of Brig. Gen. J. P. Hawkins:

S. B. FERGUSON,
Assistant Adjutant-General.

PADUCAH, *March* 25, 1864—11.20 a. m.

Brig. Gen. M. BRAYMAN,
　　Cairo:

I have scouts out 8 or 10 miles. Have concentrated my force at the fort the three past nights; stand ready at all times. I had a spy arrested this morning. He came in last night; wanted to go out on the train this morning. I have ordered the train stopped until further orders.

S. G. HICKS,
Colonel, Commanding Post.

HEADQUARTERS OF THE POST,
Columbus, Ky., March 25, 1864.

Capt. J. H. ODLIN,
　　Assistant Adjutant-General, Cairo, Ill.:

SIR: I have the honor to inform you that from the latest information received from a Union man, who left Union City last night, the forces which captured Colonel Hawkins and his command at Union City yesterday consisted of about 2,000 men, under the joint command of Forrest and Faulkner, and that their artillery, comprising six pieces, did not come up until Hawkins had surrendered. They then retraced their steps, going back by the way of Jackson. There is a rumor that a column is moving on Fort Pillow. No citizen has come from Union City or Clinton to-day.

I am, sir, very respectfully, your obedient servant,
WM. HUDSON LAWRENCE,
Colonel Thirty-fourth New Jersey Vols., Comdg. Post.

HEADQUARTERS DISTRICT OF CAIRO,
Cairo, Ill., March 25, 1864.

Col. WILLIAM H. LAWRENCE,
　　Commanding Post, Columbus:

COLONEL: Last advices from Paducah state hard fighting. Hicks has repulsed the enemy handsomely several times. Gun-boats are there, and an additional one has reached there by this time. Reenforcements of infantry have gone forward. Hicks cannot be whipped now, as night favors. I advise you to see that vigilance is observed on your lines, and it would be advisable to send scouts out on roads from Columbus. Advise the general of any information you may have. Let the general know your condition for defense.

M. BRAYMAN,
Brigadier-General, Commanding.

METROPOLIS, *March* 25, 1864.

MASON,
　　Manager Cairo Office:

Just this moment returned. Find line O. K. between him and me. When I was about 2 miles from there (Paducah), they were firing about three guns a minute for about thirty minutes. Don't know what to make of it.   Have run my horse all the way from Paducah here.   The citizens on this side the river seemed to be very much alarmed at hearing the reports of the guns.   They were all out on the bank, and asked me what it meant, as I passed.

WALLACE,
Operator.

METROPOLIS, *March 25,* 1864.

MASON,
  Military Operator, Cairo :
  From all appearances Paducah is in flames.   We can see it very distinctly from river bank.   There is fire there sure.   Whether it is a boat on fire or the town I am unable to say.   No circuit from Paducah.   Fire is getting larger.
  Later.—Three men just from Paducah saw fighting in the streets; city on fire; gun-boats and fort firing; assault on fort repulsed; saw rebel officer bearing flag of truce; fighting with rapid discharges of small-arms; great many women and children brought across the river in large wharf-boat; they left in a hurry and know no more.
  Later.—Another arrival of a family from Paducah report all front street in ashes.   Rebel forces charged on fort several times, but failed.   Our forces still hold the fort at 4 p. m.

WALLACE.

CAIRO, *March 25,* 1864.

TELEGRAPH OPERATOR AT METROPOLIS:
  Your dispatches have been received, for which I thank you.   An additional gun-boat has left for Paducah, and re-enforcements are now embarking.   Any information you can get please send here.

M. BRAYMAN,
Brigadier-General, Commanding.
Per SMITH.

NASHVILLE, TENN., *March 25,* 1864.

General M. C. MEIGS, *Washington:*
  DEAR GENERAL : I write you a private note to tell you of the progress of things here.   Sherman has taken command, and this morning General Allen arrived for the purpose of accompanying him to Decatur, Chattanooga, Knoxville, &c.   General Sherman told me Allen must be his chief quartermaster, and I frankly said to him that I had no fancy, after all I had done, to come under General Allen, as I thought I had been treated bad enough already without additional degradation.   He replied that he must have a quartermaster with powers co-ordinate with his own, and that he would urge my promotion, &c.; that General Allen would not interfere with me, but would rather increase my powers, &c.   Now all this is very well, but it is a bitter p l to me to swallow, notwithstanding all the sugar-coating on it, for I am conscious of having earnestly worked for the good of the service.
  The horse and mule question still drags slowly.   There is great want of both in the front, and the prospect is anything but flatter-

ing. I have exhausted all the power I possess to bring both forward, and can do no more. The department is slowly improving. Reports come forward more promptly, and we are beginning to approximate to the true state of things. You can see this in the reports forwarded to your office. I have received and disposed of a vast amount of freight in the last month. I do not believe that the Government ever dealt with such a huge pile at so little cost, both in transportation and demurrage ; and, moreover, I have not lost a pound by sudden risings of the river. The other day it came up 20 feet, but, fearing it, I worked several thousand men all night, and saved everything. Last year they lost 1,000 tons by just such a rise. I am still in want of workmen. I pay $40 a month to laborers, and cannot get enough at that. The want of labor is my great trouble. I have now three railroads out of Nashville, and require an officer for each road, and a disbursing officer for all. The railroads will be an enormous item in our expenses, as rolling-stock, motive power, and materials increase, and employés will be a small army of themselves. I want a first-rate officer to disburse for all of them.

I have Captain Crane in charge of the Nashville and Chattanooga Road, under Colonel McCallum; Captain Ruger in charge of the Northwestern, and think of placing Captain Brown, now at Clarksville, in charge of the Decatur road—Tennessee and Alabama Road. I have instructed Captain Ruger to put up store-houses and prepare a levee at Reynoldsburg, the terminus of the Northwestern Railroad, and shall send a couple of saw-mills there, and the requisite materials. I find I must act in the matter, as the road will be soon completed to the Tennessee River.

Very truly, yours,

J. L. DONALDSON.

CULPEPER, *March* 26, 1864—10 p. m.

Maj. Gen. W. T. SHERMAN, and
COMMANDING OFFICER AT MEMPHIS:

Forrest should not be allowed to get out of the trap he has placed himself in at Paducah. Send Grierson with all your cavalry with orders to find and destroy him wherever found. If General Sherman has sent instructions they will govern.

U. S. GRANT,
Lieutenant-General.

NASHVILLE, *March* 26, 1864.

Major-General SCHOFIELD,
        Knoxville:

Your dispatch to General Sherman was received and forwarded to him at Athens.

He has directed me by telegraph to say to you that he is on his way to see you. In the mean time he desires you to feel the enemy to make him develop his plans. He does not believe the enemy intends to make an invasion of Kentucky, but all of Longstreet's army will re-enforce Lee in Virginia.

Respectfully,

R. M. SAWYER,
Assistant Adjutant-General.

HUNTSVILLE, ALA., *March 26*, 1864.
(Received 3.15 a. m., 27th.)

His Excellency A. LINCOLN,
    President of the United States:

I understand by the papers that it is contemplated to make a change of commanders of the Fifteenth and Seventeenth Army Corps, so as to transfer me to the Seventeenth. I hope this will not be done. I fully understand the organization of the Fifteenth Corps now, which I have labored to complete the organization of this winter, and earnestly hope that the change may not be made.

JOHN A. LOGAN,
Major-General.

NASHVILLE, *March 26*, 1864.

Maj. Gen. W. T. SHERMAN :

GENERAL : General Hovey arrived here last night. A portion of his command will be here to-day and the rest in three or four days. Do you desire him to push forward at once with what troops he has here, or shall he wait until his whole command arrives before leaving Nashville, reporting in advance by letter or telegraph to General Schofield ?

R. M. SAWYER,
Assistant Adjutant-General.

HUNTSVILLE, *March 26*, 1864.

Maj. R. M. SAWYER:

Direct General Hovey to collect his command at Nashville and march from there in a body, reporting in advance by telegraph.

W. T. SHERMAN,
Major-General, Commanding.

NASHVILLE, *March 26*, 1864—9 p. m.

Major-General SHERMAN :

The following telegram was received half an hour since:

FORT DONELSON, *March 26*, 1864.

Major-General ROUSSEAU,
    Commanding, Nashville:

Captain Baker, commanding post at Smithland, telegraphs gun-boat No. 33 arrived at Smithland at 5.20 p. m. to-day from Paducah. · Reports all quiet there. City partly destroyed. Forrest lying in rear of city; attack expected there to-night. Forrest has 4,000 rebels. Brigadier-General Thompson killed. Gun-boat officer apprehends an attack on Fort Donelson.

E. C. BROTT,
Lieutenant-Colonel, Commanding Post.

I have ordered 500 dismounted cavalry and one light battery to be ready to move on steam-boat on river to Fort Donelson at 5 o'clock in the morning. I have ordered cavalry in preference to infantry, as they might be mounted by impressing horses in the neighborhood of Fort Donelson, and if Fort Donelson is not attacked they can join the Sixth Tennessee Cavalry and operate against Forrest.

LOVELL H. ROUSSEAU,
Major-General.

ATHENS, *March* 26, 1864.

Capt. B. P. CHENOWITH.

Acting Assistant Inspector-General, Nashville:

General Veatch has not yet reported, nor has any portion of his division. The latest I heard from him he was landing at Clifton. I expect he is now on the march to Pulaski or this place.

G. M. DODGE,
Brigadier-General.

NASHVILLE, TENN., *March* 26, 1864.

Maj. Gen. W. T. SHERMAN,
Huntsville, Ala.:

The following is received:

BELOW NEW MADRID,
March 25, 1864.

Major-General SHERMAN:

General Grierson's scout just in. General Forrest moved from Tupelo on 14th instant with two brigades of cavalry and six pieces of artillery, about 3,000 strong, by the way of East Davis Bridge and Corinth, arriving at Jackson, Tenn., on 20th; is to be joined at Jackson by Col. Robert McCulloch, with three brigades of cavalry, about 3,500 men, who were ordered to leave Oxford, Miss., on the 20th instant. The command is then to move into Middle Tennessee to unite with Morgan and Wheeler in Major-General Thomas' rear.

Latest information from Johnston is that General Polk had been ordered to join him at Dalton, Ga., and that his right wing is swinging round to support Longstreet, whose headquarters were at Russellville, E. Tenn., on 8th instant, preparatory to movement to the rear of Cumberland Gap by the way of Bull's and Big Creek Gaps. His cavalry is commanded by Morgan; his ordered infantry is commanded by Breckinridge, and comprises Bushrod Johnson's force. General S. D. Lee's force is at Grenada, Canton, and Jackson, Miss., consisting of Wirt Adams' and W. H. Jackson's brigades. Forrest reports that he is moving on Columbus, Ky.

The information from Johnston's army is from a lieutenant, who left Dalton, Ga., on March 10. General Grierson thinks above is reliable.

Hawkins' Seventh Tennessee Cavalry [matched] yesterday at Union City from cowardice of colonel, when 2,000 infantry under Brayman was within 6 miles.

S. A. HURLBUT,
Major-General.

The operator thinks the word "ordered" should not be there, and can make nothing but matched out of the word underlined [in brackets].

R. M. SAWYER,
Assistant Adjutant-General.

HEADQUARTERS SIXTEENTH ARMY CORPS,
Memphis, Tenn., March 26, 1864.

Maj. Gen. W. T. SHERMAN,
Nashville, Tenn.:

Forrest has with him about 2,500 picked men, well armed and mounted. He moves without baggage, and is to be followed by about 2,000 men under McCulloch. These are now on their way from Oxford. I have no doubt he means to cross the Tennessee.

S. A. HURLBUT,
Major-General.

HEADQUARTERS SIXTEENTH ARMY CORPS,
Memphis, Tenn., March 26, 1864.

Maj. Gen. W. T. SHERMAN,
Nashville, Tenn. :

Dispatches of 24th are received. Veatch is ordered up the Tennessee to act as circumstances may require. I believe Forrest proposes to cross the river. I have not asked for any more troops, nor have I proposed to resign. Veatch is delayed at Cairo for want of transportation. The naval officers are informed of Forrest's movement.

S. A. HURLBUT,
Major-General.

———

CAIRO, *March 26, 1864.*

Maj. Gen. W. T. SHERMAN,
Commanding :

My troops are now embarking, and I shall leave at 12 m. to-day. Sent one regiment to Paducah last night to re-enforce that post. Town has been burnt. Hicks still holds the fort. Rebels said to be in possession of the town. The Tennessee is probably obstructed above Paducah. I shall push forward. Dispatch may reach me at Metropolis.

JAMES C. VEATCH,
Brigadier-General.

———

CHATTANOOGA, *March 26, 1864.*

Maj. Gen. G. H. THOMAS,
Commanding :

GENERAL : My operator at Smithland, Ky., informs me that the enemy, 2,500 strong, under Forrest, attacked Paducah yesterday at 1 p. m. and were repulsed, losing 400 killed. Our loss only 2 wounded. He says the city was in flames last night all night. The garrison defended the fort only, and the rebel loss was incurred in several attempts to carry the fort by assault. His information was by boat from Paducah, and up to 10 this a. m. Reports at Smithland say rebels are crossing Tennessee River at or near Chandits [?]; 1,500 are said to be on east side Tennessee River to-day. Line is working to Smithland still, and I have instructed the man to send any and all information he may receive.

Very respectfully,

JOHN C. VAN DUZER,
Captain and Asst. Supt. U. S. Military Telegraph.

———

LOUISVILLE, *March 26, 1864.*

Major-General SCHOFIELD :

The following just received :

LOUISA, KY.,
March 25, 1864.

Brigadier-General BURBRIDGE :

GENERAL : My scouts bring information that three brigades, mounted (Jones', Hodge's, and Colonel Galliger [Giltner ?], commanding General Williams' old brigade), moved up from Lee County to Tazewell, at Cassoll Woods, on the 19th instant.

Colonel Prentice, Captains Cook and Everett, and Major Chenoweth, guerrillas, were ordered to join them, and report says for a move into Kentucky. Detachments of the Second, Eighth, and Sixteenth Virginia (rebel) Cavalry have appeared on my left, in Virginia. I could use the Forty-fifth Kentucky, Col. J. M. Brown, to a great advantage for a few days.

GEO. W. GALLUP,
Colonel Fourteenth Kentucky.

S. G. BURBRIDGE,
Brigadier-General, Commanding.

CAIRO, *March* 26, 1864.

Maj. Gen. W. T. SHERMAN:

The rebel force went from Union City to Paducah and attacked the garrison of about 500 men. Colonel Hicks took the fort. He was aided by two gun-boats. After hard fighting of several hours the enemy were driven off, probably not to return. A considerable portion of Paducah is destroyed. Re-enforcements and supplies have gone up.

M. BRAYMAN,
Brigadier-General, Commanding.

CAIRO, *March* 26, 1864—5.30 p. m.

Maj. Gen. W. T. SHERMAN:

A desperate battle and victory at Paducah. Rebels took the town and we destroyed it from the fort and gun-boats. The enemy lost heavily, including 300 men and General A. P. Thompson killed: Our loss was probably 100 in all. The enemy now making for Columbus; are expected to-night. We shall be ready. I am urging General Veatch, who is at Paducah, to send back three regiments. I think you would send him. Forrest, Faulkner, and Richardson are combined for a desperate effort upon our wire communications and supplies. I do not expect disaster, but the danger is great.

M. BRAYMAN,
Brigadier-General, Commanding.

SMITHLAND, *March* 26, 1864—2 a. m.

Brig. Gen. M. BRAYMAN,
        Commanding:

Have just dispatched a messenger to Colonel Hicks, Paducah, notifying him of your re-enforcements, &c.; also requesting him to send by return messenger any dispatches he wishes to send to you.

WALLACE.

HEADQUARTERS DISTRICT OF CAIRO,
Cairo, Ill., March 26, 1864—3.20 a. m.

Col. W. H. LAWRENCE,
        Columbus, Ky.:

Your dispatches received per steamer Liberty No. 2. Keep a good lookout on your lines, and send scouts on roads east. There may be

some force from that direction. .Don't think there need be any apprehension regarding Fort Pillow. Gather all the information you
can, and keep the general advised by telegraph or boat.

M. BRAYMAN,
Brigadier-General, Commanding.

PADUCAH, *March* 26, 1864.
(Received 1.30 p. m., 26th.)

MASON:
Send White Cloud back to Paducah. Rebels charging on fort
now.

PEEL,
Operator.

CAIRO, ILL., ,
March 26, 1864.

Capt. J. H. ODLIN,
Assistant Adjutant-General, Paducah:
Re-enforcements, ammunition, and rations are on the way.

M. BRAYMAN,
Brigadier-General, Commanding.

CAIRO, *March* 26, 1864.

Captain ODLIN,
Assistant Adjutant-General, Paducah:
A brigade is moving up. I don't think the enemy will trouble you
further.

M. BRAYMAN,
Brigadier-General, Commanding.

MARCH 26, 1864.

Col. W. H. LAWRENCE,
Commanding, Columbus:
Hawkins' men went to Mound City to-night, but I will try to have
them back. Am preparing to assist you, if attacked. Keep me advised of all movements. ·

M. BRAYMAN,
Brigadier-General, Commanding.

MARCH 26, 1864.

Col. W. H. LAWRENCE,
Columbus, Ky.:
Let no boats go below. If any troops are in port going either way
hold them until further orders. Put everything in safe condition,
without confusion or alarm. Have you plenty of ammunition and
arms?

M. BRAYMAN,
Brigadier-General, Commanding.

MARCH 26, 1864.

Capt. A. M. PENNOCK.
　　Commanding, &c., Mound City:

Columbus must be strengthened to-night. I will put all disposable force here on board. Please send the gun-boat.

M. BRAYMAN,
Brigadier-General, Commanding.

MARCH 26, 1864—8 p. m.

Capt. J. H. ODLIN,
　　Assistant Adjutant-General, Paducah:

I shall go to Columbus to-night with a gun-boat, and all troops that can be spared. Be sure and have General Veatch fully advised. I think he will aid us.

M. BRAYMAN,
Brigadier-General, Commanding.

MARCH 26, 1864—8 p. m.

Col. W. H. LAWRENCE,
　　Commanding, Columbus:

The rebels may visit you in force to-night. They are moving toward you. Put your fort and the public property in good condition. I will come down with gun-boat and re-enforcements. They have been beaten at Paducah, and must be again at Columbus.

M. BRAYMAN,
Brigadier-General, Commanding.

MARCH 26, 1864—5 p. m.

Brig. Gen. J. C. VEATCH,
　　On Steamer White Cloud, Metropolis, or,
　　　　　if he has passed, to Paducah:

Please confer with Colonel Hicks. If it is possible, I request that you send back two or three regiments. I am satisfied that Columbus will be next attacked as soon as the enemy can get there.

M. BRAYMAN,
Brigadier-General, Commanding.

PADUCAH, *March* 26, 1864—9.40 p. m.

Major-General SHERMAN:

Reached here at 7.30 o'clock. The enemy had fled, and have taken the direction to Columbus. Force supposed to be 6,500 men, under Forrest. Am now waiting until day for a convoy. Orders will reach me here to-night.

JAS. C. VEATCH,
Brigadier-General.

PADUCAH, *March* 26, 1864—9.40 p. m.

General BRAYMAN :

All quiet here; enemy retreated and report says have gone to Columbus. I can send you no part of my force unless ordered to do so by General Sherman. I shall leave at daylight in the morning. You may be able to reach General Sherman by telegraph to-night and dispatch me before I leave.

JAMES C. VEATCH,
Brigadier-General.

PADUCAH, *March* 26, 1864—10.40 p. m.

Brigadier-General BRAYMAN :

General Veatch refuses to send unless ordered by General Sherman ; his orders are peremptory. I will start on Dispatch as soon as possible. The rebels moved in two columns, one on Columbus road direct, the other on Mayfield road. Enemy took their wounded on train to Mayfield. They lost 300 killed.

J. H. ODLIN,
Assistant Adjutant-General.

HEADQUARTERS DISTRICT OF CAIRO, '
Cairo, Ill., March 26, 1864.

General J. C. VEATCH :

Captain Odlin reports the rebels retreating on the Mayfield road ; the re-enforcements were too much, probably.

He says they acknowledge 300 killed ; wounded unknown. He says they number 6,500, and four pieces of artillery. The line is cut between here and Columbus, and I think an attack in that direction imminent as soon as you are out of reach.

My last return shows 408 men at Paducah, 208 men at Cairo, and 998 at Columbus for duty ; 1,624 in all.

Forrest, Faulkner, Richardson, and Morgan, who is reported across the Tennessee with 300 men, all together will make us trouble.

Grierson is lost ; I know nothing of him ; he ought to be on the heels of Forrest. You will see what I have on my hands. The defeat of a large army would not cripple us as much as a disaster here, the seat of our supplies for army and navy.

I know the urgency of General Sherman's orders as to your movements, and must not advise you what delay you can make, or whether you can leave any of your force for a few days. The supplies for our entire river navy are here and at Mound City. I do not expect to lose any point, but I do consider all in danger while confronted with such a force, mine being inadequate.

I am, general, very respectfully,

M. BRAYMAN,
Brigadier-General, Commanding.

COLUMBUS, KY., *March* 26, 1864.

Capt. J. H. ODLIN, *Assistant Adjutant-General:*

Milburn was entered by 25 of Forrest's men last night. The citizens drove them out, wounding 1 man. One thousand have gone to Hickman, probably for goods. A citizen just in from Pyles', 6 miles from here, reports a force of several hundred stealing horses, &c. I have sent out my mounted infantry to scout there. Can I not have Hawkins' men? They would be invaluable. What do you hear from Paducah?

WM. HUDSON LAWRENCE,
Colonel Thirty-fourth New Jersey Volunteers, Comdg.

CHATTANOOGA, TENN., *March 26, 1864—10 p. m.*
(Received 3.30 a. m., 27th.)

Maj. THOMAS T. ECKERT,
Assistant Manager U. S. Military Telegraph:

A scout just arrived brings following:

Martin's division rebel cavalry had arrived at Cartersville, Ga., from Longstreet's command. Rebels have removed all their heavy artillery from Kingston to Allatoona. Longstreet's force of 26,000 men are to be mounted immediately and sent on raid into Kentucky. Rebel officers say when Longstreet goes to Kentucky Johnston will capture East Tennessee. Forrest is in Southern Kentucky.

SAM. BRUCH.

GENERAL ORDERS, ⎰ HDQRS. DEPT. AND ARMY OF THE TENN.,
No. 1.   ⎱   *Huntsville, Ala., March 26, 1864.*

I. In compliance with General Orders, No. 98, Adjutant-General's Office, of date Washington, D. C., March 12, 1864, the undersigned hereby assumes command of the Department and Army of the Tennessee.

II. Lieut. Col. William T. Clark, assistant adjutant-general, is announced as adjutant-general of the department, to whom reports and returns will be addressed. The staff for the department will be selected and announced in orders.

JAS. B. McPHERSON,
Major-General.

HEADQUARTERS DEPARTMENT OF THE CUMBERLAND,
Chattanooga, Tenn., March 27, 1864.

Maj. Gen. H. W. HALLECK,
Chief of Staff, U. S. Army, Washington, D. C.:

MY DEAR GENERAL: Your letter of the 19th instant, inclosing me my commission as brigadier-general, U. S. Army, was received yesterday.

Please accept my sincere thanks for your kind and complimentary letter, which I can assure you was as acceptable as the commission.

Very respectfully and truly, yours,

GEO. H. THOMAS,
Major-General, U. S. Volunteers.

HEADQUARTERS LEFT WING, SIXTEENTH ARMY CORPS,
Athens, Ala., March 27, 1864.

Maj. Gen. J. B. McPHERSON,
Comdg. Dept. and Army of the Tennessee, Huntsville, Ala.:

GENERAL: When you and General Sherman were here I could not, on account of sickness, give you as good an idea of the roads crossing the mountains as I desired, but will now give in writing a short description of all the important roads leading from the Mississippi line to the Coosa Valley. Commencing on the west I make the initial point of each road where it can be easily, or without material obstacle, reached from any portion of our front.

First. The direct Tuscumbia and Columbus road runs southwest, passes through Russellville, crosses the headwaters of Bear Creek and the westernmost spur of Sand Mountain, avoiding almost entirely any abrupt rise or mountain road. It forks at Millersville, one branch going to Columbus, the other to Pikeville and Fayetteville, crossing the Black Warrior at Tuscaloosa by bridge. Forage, water, &c., are good on almost the entire road, especially after leaving Pikeville.   .

Second. The Tuscumbia and Tuscaloosa road, direct, runs due south from Russellville to Fayetteville, crosses mountains at right angles, is hilly and sparsely populated, lacks forage, and is seldom traveled, although it is passable.

Third. The Byler road leaves the valley at Leighton, runs up Town Creek, crosses mountain in Low Gap, and forks at New London, one branch going toward Columbus, Miss., and one direct to Tuscaloosa. It is an old road, well settled, well watered, fair for forage, crosses the streams high enough up to avoid much difficulty, and is one of the best roads over the mountains.

Fourth. Cheatham's road, the direct Moulton and Tuscaloosa road, runs due south from Courtland to Tuscaloosa, is hilly and mountainous, and forage scarce, but it is not what might be called a bad road. The first mountain is pretty hard to ascend, but the balance of the road is fair.

Fifth. Stout's road runs directly south from Somerville, crossing the headwaters of the Black Warrior. It forks at Elyton, one fork leading southwest down the ridge, between the Black Warrior and the Cahawba, the other fork leading direct to Selma and Montgomery, crossing the Cahawba by ferry. This is an excellent road, well provided with everything, avoids all large water-courses, and is mostly used. It forks near Day's Gap, one branch leading off by way of Blountsville into Coosa Valley, another to Gadsden; crossing of mountains good.

Sixth. Decatur and Gadsden direct road runs through Somerville, rises the Sand Mountain at Summit, where the road from Guntersville comes in, and falls sharply over the mountains into Coosa Valley. This is the nearest road, but two others nearly parallel to it, and known as the Upper and Lower roads, are nearly as good. This road is 10 miles nearer to Gadsden than the one by way of Stout's road, Day's Gap, and Blountsville, but is not so good.

Between the roads mentioned there are by-roads and mountain paths, over which cavalry can travel and probably light trains, but army transportation would stick. On all the roads, except, perhaps, the most westerly one, the rise of Sand Mountain is rather abrupt, but nothing but what a column could overcome in a day or two during good weather. After once crossing the mountains, and as we approach the level lands of Middle and Southern Alabama, roads lead in all directions and are generally very good. The Black Warrior is only bridged at Tuscaloosa, the Cahawba at no point that I know of, the Coosa only at Rome and Wetumpka.

The ferries on the Coosa from Rome to Greensport, head of the rapids, now in use are as follows:

First. Edwards' Ferry, near the mouth of the Chattooga River, 16 miles from Rome.   Between these points Livingston's old ferry used to be in use, but it is now said to be abandoned.

Second. Hampton's Ferry, 22 miles below Rome, on road leading from Will's Valley to Cave Spring.

Third. Garrett's Ferry, on Gadsden and Rome road.

Fourth. Adams' Ferry, at mouth of Terrapin Creek.   From this point south ferries exist every 6 to 10 miles, and over the shoals oftener.   One steamer only now plies from Greensport to Rome; there are more above the rapids, but are said to be disabled.

I am, very respectfully, your obedient servant,

G. M. DODGE,
Brigadier-General Volunteers.

SCOTTSBOROUGH, *March* 27, 1864.
(Received 10.35 p. m.)

Lieutenant-General GRANT :

Your dispatch received.   I had already ordered Veatch with five regiments, who was at Paducah last night, to hurry up the Tennessee and strike inland to intercept Forrest; also that Grierson should follow and attack Forrest, no matter what the odds.

I have with McPherson been examining our bridges at Decatur and Larkin's.   To-night I go to Chattanooga and to-morrow to Knoxville.   I will be at Nashville in three days with a full knowledge of all matters pertaining to this army.

W. T. SHERMAN,
Major-General.

NASHVILLE, *March* 27, 1864.
(Received 30th.)

Major-General HURLBUT, *Memphis:*

General Sherman telegraphs that after being certain that Forrest can not cross the Tennessee and Cumberland Rivers Veatch should push rapidly to Savannah and move to Purdy to cut off his retreat. Grierson should follow Forrest as close as possible all the time.

By order of Major-General Sherman :

R. M. SAWYER,
Assistant Adjutant-General.

NASHVILLE, *March* 27, 1864.
(Received 30th.) .

General HURLBUT, *Memphis:*

Send orders to Grierson to follow Forrest close and attack at all hazards, and follow as long as possible.   General Veatch has orders to move to Purdy and the Hatchie and cut off retreat.

W. T. SHERMAN,
Major-General.

SCOTTSBOROUGH, *March* 27, 1864.

Major SAWYER,
Assistant Adjutant-General, Nashville:

Repeat to General Veatch the order to hasten up the Tennessee, and act in such a manner as to cut off Forrest.   Veatch has plenty of men, and he should aim to get to Purdy and the Hatchie before Forrest. Send orders to him by telegraph to Paducah, also a letter across the country to Savannah ; also get orders to Grierson to follow Forrest close and attack at all hazards, and follow as long as possible. Copies of the orders to be sent to Generals Hurlbut and Brayman. Telegraph Brayman I see no necessity to re-enforce Columbus if Hicks beat off Forrest with his 400 men. I want Veatch to cut off his retreat, as he certainly will.

I have just returned from an inspection of the bridge at Larkin's. Will go to Chattanooga to-night. Telegraph me there.

W. T. SHERMAN,
Major-General.

NASHVILLE, *March* 27, 1864.
Brigadier-General WHIPPLE,
Chief of Staff :
Just received the following :

SMITHLAND, KY.,
March 27, 1864.

Forrest has fallen back to Mayfield with 4,000 men. Scouts from off Tennessee River report the rebels on this side trying to get back ; passed close to them as they lay in ambush : also, they came to farthest bank of river, 30 in number ; the gun-boats cleared them away. All quiet this side of the Tennessee thus far. I have endeavored to communicate with General Veatch, at Fort Henry, and with Generals Hurlbut and Grierson by telegraph.

LOVELL H. ROUSSEAU.

NASHVILLE, *March* 27, 1864.
Brigadier-General WHIPPLE :

We are in receipt of information that gun-boat No. 33 arrived at Smithland at 5.30 p. m. on the 26th instant from Paducah ; reports all quiet there. Forrest lying in or near the city. City partially destroyed. Forrest reported to have 4,000 men with him. Rebel Brigadier-General Thompson killed at 12 m. on 26th instant. Forrest sent flag of truce and demanded of Colonel Hicks the surrender of the fort; Colonel Hicks refused. The gun-boats commenced throwing shells up Broadway. It is supposed Forrest will attack Colonel Hicks. It is stated rebels are crossing Tennessee River. I sent 500 men and one battery to re-enforce Fort Donelson at 11.30 to-day, as it is apprehended Forrest will attack that place.

LOVELL H. ROUSSEAU,
Major-General.

NASHVILLE, *March* 27, 1864.
COMMANDING OFFICER,
Paducah :
Notify General Veatch that after being satisfied that Forrest cannot cross the Tennessee and Cumberland he should push rapidly to Savannah, and move to Purdy to cut off Forrest's retreat. If Veatch has gone up river this morning go after him, if possible.

W. T. SHERMAN,
Major-General.

NASHVILLE, *March* 27, 1864.
COMMANDING OFFICER,
   Pulaski, Tenn., and
General DODGE,
   Athens, Ala.:

General Sherman wishes a message sent to General Veatch, who is now on his way up the Tennessee River, to this effect : To have him land near Savannah and hurry to Purdy and the Hatchie and cut off Forrest's retreat ; that Grierson is following Forrest closely. Send this by a reliable person or party to intercept General Veatch near Savannah. Let the party use all possible dispatch, starting to-night.

By order of Major-General Sherman :
                                          R. M. SAWYER,
                                     Assistant Adjutant-General.

HUNTSVILLE, *March* 27, 1864.
Major SAWYER :
   Assistant Adjutant-General :

Notify General Rousseau that General Veatch is moving up the Tennessee, and to communicate with him if possible at Fort Henry to strengthen Fort Donelson, so that there can be no possibility of Forrest's crossing the Cumberland. Try and get order to the commanding officer at Cairo and Columbus, as also to Generals Veatch and Hurlbut, that after being certain that Forrest cannot cross the Tennessee and Cumberland, Veatch should push rapidly to Savannah and move to Purdy to cut off his retreat. Grierson should follow Forrest as closely as possible all the time.

                                          W. T. SHERMAN,
                                          Major-General.

NASHVILLE, *March* 27, 1864.
General SHERMAN
   (*Care General Thomas, Chattanooga*):

On receipt of your first telegram this afternoon, I telegraphed orders to General Veatch by way of Paducah, with instructions to commanding officer at Paducah to forward this dispatch. General Rousseau sent 500 cavalry and a battery to Fort Donelson this morning, and will communicate with Veatch if possible. I telegraphed order to General Hurlbut relative to Grierson, not knowing how to reach him in any other way. Am I right ? I will again telegraph to Generals Veatch and Brayman as you direct.

                                          R. M. SAWYER,
                                     Assistant Adjutant-General.

PADUCAH, *March* 27, 1864.
Major-General SHERMAN :

Dispatch received. General Veatch left here at noon to-day with his division, up Tennessee River. Will send your dispatch to him by first boat.

                                          S. G. HICKS,
                                       Colonel, Commanding.

NASHVILLE, *March 27*, 1864.
(Received 30th.)
Major-General HURLBUT, *Memphis:*

Re-enforcements by steam-boats left here to-day at 11 o'clock a. m. for Fort Donelson.

General Sherman telegraphs from Huntsville that after you are certain that Forrest cannot cross the Tennessee or Cumberland Rivers you will push rapidly for Savannah and move to Purdy and cut off his retreat, and that General Grierson shall follow Forrest as close as possible all the time.

LOVELL H. ROUSSEAU,
Major-General.

COLUMBUS, KY., *March 27*, 1864.
Col. S. G. HICKS,
    Commanding, &c., Paducah, Ky.:

The enemy is between this place and Mayfield. We are prepared for an attack to-night. I think, however, you have crippled them, and they will not come. Scouts that come in here bring news from them, and I think their loss exceeds your estimate.

M. BRAYMAN,
Brigadier-General, Commanding.

COLUMBUS, KY., *March 27*, 1864.
Capt. A. M. PENNOCK,
    Master of Fleet, &c., Cairo, Ill.:

The enemy is in this neighborhood, and we are ready for attack to-night. They were badly crippled at Paducah and may not come. I will do all that is possible to respond to your wishes concerning Mound City.

M. BRAYMAN,
Brigadier-General, Commanding.

COLUMBUS, KY., *March 27*, 1864.
Captain MUNROE,
    Assistant Adjutant-General, Cairo, Ill.:

Rebels concentrating at Clinton under Forrest and Faulkner; will expect them in the morning; will keep you advised as long as possible. We received 400 men from Madrid this evening under Major Rabb; are in good trim for fighting.

C. B. SMITH,
Lieutenant and Aide-de-Camp.

COLUMBUS, *March 27*, 1864.
Capt. A. M. PENNOCK,
    Commanding Fleet at Cairo:

Last advices from the front show the rebels 4,000 strong at Clinton, under Forrest. We are expecting attack here in the morning early. Received 400 men from Madrid this evening. Are in good trim for fighting.

C. B. SMITH,
Lieutenant and Aide-de-Camp.

HDQRS. CAVALRY DIVISION, SIXTEENTH ARMY CORPS,
Memphis, Tenn., March 27, 1864.

Col. GEORGE E. WARING, Jr.,
Commanding First Cavalry Brigade:

COLONEL: You will organize a force of 300 men from your command, well mounted, armed, and equipped, with five days' light rations and a full supply of ammunition, to proceed northeast of this point with a view of operating on the left of Colonel Hurst, who is now in the vicinity of Somerville. Select a good officer to go in command and let him report here for further instructions.

Major Thompson will start in the morning with such mounted force of the Sixth Tennessee as he can gather up, via Raleigh, with the intention of joining Colonel Hurst above Somerville. Let the officer report here as early as possible in the morning.

By order of Brig. Gen. B. H. Grierson:

S. L. WOODWARD,
Assistant Adjutant-General.

PADUCAH, KY.,
March 27, 1864.

General BRAYMAN:

Home guards just in from the country. Forrest's forces are moving toward Clinton, 12 miles from Columbus. Faulkner's forces are to meet him there.

S. G. HICKS,
Colonel, Commanding.

CAIRO, ILL.,
March 27, 1864.

Captain ODLIN:

Send ammunition for the guns in the fort, if possible, and also an artillerist. Do not think we can mount the gun you spoke of in your dispatch, but will try. Two men came in from Blandville to-day; report about 3,000 to be there to-night. Headquarters of Forrest are in Mayfield.

JNO. H. MUNROE,
Assistant Adjutant-General.

COLUMBUS, KY.,
March 27, 1864.

Captain MUNROE,
Assistant Adjutant-General:

General says the order is imperative; the gun must be mounted. If you have not enough force you will impress the citizens. I have just loaded ammunition for Cairo, Mound City, and Paducah. We have no shells. The enemy are advancing on the Milburn road. Cannot return to-night. The telegraph office must be kept open all night.

J. H. ODLIN,
Assistant Adjutant-General.

NASHVILLE, TENN., *March 27, 1864.*
(Received 8 p. m.)

Brigadier-General BRAYMAN,
Columbus:

The general sees no necessity to re-enforce Columbus if Hicks beat off Forrest with 400 men. He wants General Veatch to cut off his retreat by landing at Savannah and going to Purdy and the Hatchie. I have telegraphed Veatch by way of Paducah. If you can get communication with him please do so, and notify him to this effect. The general also wants Grierson to follow Forrest and attack him at all hazards, and follow him as long as possible. If you can get this word to him please do so.

By order of Major-General Sherman :

R. M. SAWYER,
Assistant Adjutant-General.

HEADQUARTERS POST AND DEFENSES,
Vicksburg, Miss., March 27, 1864—11.30 a. m.

Brigadier-General DENNIS,
Commanding at Big Black :

GENERAL : Have you any answer to the flag of truce ? What is the cavalry at Hebron doing ? I am informed that Lee and Ross are near Mechanicsburg. I fear they contemplate a raid on Haynes' Bluff or General Crocker's camp, most probably the former. I have sent Osband's cavalry out in that direction, to feel of them. Send what cavalry you can spare in the direction of Mechanicsburg, informing them of Osband's movements. Let them act in concert if they come together, and push the enemy sufficiently to develop their strength, and whip them if they can. General Crocker will please send a section of artillery with the cavalry if they have none. Let them start as soon as possible, informing me of their strength.

J. McARTHUR,
Brigadier-General, Commanding.

HEADQUARTERS FRONT,
Big Black Bridge, March 27, 1864.

Lieut. Col. J. H. PETERS,
Commanding Cavalry Forces, Seventeenth Army Corps:

COLONEL : I am directed by the general commanding to say that you will send what cavalry you can spare from your command in the direction of Mechanicsburg for the purpose of discovering the movements of the enemy, who are supposed to be moving for the purpose of an attack either upon Haynes' Bluff or General Crocker's camp, probably the former. Cavalry, under command of Colonel Osband, have been sent in the direction of Haynes' Bluff. You will act in concert with Colonel Osband's cavalry, and push the enemy sufficiently to develop their strength, and whip them if possible. You will report to General Crocker for the purpose of getting section of artillery to accompany your command. You will start as soon as possible, reporting your strength to these headquarters.

I am, colonel, your obedient servant,

W. BEDFORD,
Assistant Adjutant-General.

CULPEPER COURT-HOUSE, VA.,
March 28, 1864.

Maj. Gen. W. T. SHERMAN,
Nashville, Tenn.:

Cannot steamers be used to supply all troops between Bridgeport and Lookout, and again, to supply Knoxville from Chattanooga? If so, it would enable you to accumulate supplies at the latter place.

U. S. GRANT,
Lieutenant-General.

CHATTANOOGA, TENN., *March* 28, 1864—4 p. m.
(Received 29th.)

Lieutenant-General GRANT,
General-in-Chief:

I am here. No change in the attitude of things since you left. I have given orders as to Forrest, which, if executed with rapidity and energy, should result in the dispersion or destruction of his forces.

W. T. SHERMAN,
Major-General.

CHATTANOOGA, *March* 28, 1864—12 p. m.
(Received 6.40 p. m., 29th.)

Lieutenant-General GRANT:

Forrest is reported to have crossed the Tennessee eastward at Eddyville. I do not believe it, but I have ordered him to be pursued from all points, and if done I have no doubt his force will be broken up and destroyed. I wish you would as soon as possible name the generals and staff officers to be assigned to me. I can place them better now than at a later period. General Reynolds [Granger?] has notified me that he has a sixty days' leave from the War Department, of which he proposes to avail himself now, and that he is willing to give up his corps. I would therefore ask that a new corps commander be appointed for the Fourth Corps.

I will go up to Knoxville to-morrow to see General Schofield, after which I can complete the organization and distribution of the whole command.

The enemy to our front and up the Tennessee seems inactive, and I have no apprehension of any movement into East Kentucky. and as soon as our furloughed men are back will be ready to test them on their own ground.

General McPherson and I have inspected the whole line from Decatur to Chattanooga, and have settled down to the conclusion that Decatur and Guntersville are the true offensive points on the Tennessee. General McPherson returns to Huntsville to-night.

W. T. SHERMAN,
Major-General.

HEADQUARTERS DEPARTMENT OF THE CUMBERLAND,
Chattanooga, March 28, 1864.

Brig. Gen. K. GARRARD,
Huntsville, Ala.:

Move your division back to the vicinity of Columbia, and forage your animals on the country round between Columbia and Lynnville, using your dismounted men to occupy the block-houses from Columbia to Lynnville and to guard your depots. Form a depot for forage and subsistence at Columbia for the benefit of your division. Keep the country between the railroad and the Tennessee River south of Duck River thoroughly patrolled, so as to guard the right flank of Major-General McPherson's command as completely as possible, and use all precautions to prevent your men committing any depredations upon the inhabitants.

GEO. H. THOMAS,
Major-General Volunteers, Commanding.

HDQRS. FIRST DIVISION. FIFTEENTH ARMY CORPS,
Woodville, Ala., March 28, 1864.

Major LUBBERS,
Commanding Twenty-sixth Iowa:

MAJOR: It has been ascertained that Mead's company of guerrillas and bushwhackers are in a cave on the mountain where Clear Creek empties into Paint Rock River.

Is Clear Creek near your neighborhood; and, if so, can you make a descent on these rascals? The horses of the gang are said to be kept in the mountain.

Very respectfully, your obedient servant,

W. A. GORDON,
Assistant Adjutant-General.

NASHVILLE, *March* 28, 1864—9 p. m.

Maj. Gen. W. T. SHERMAN
(Care Major-General Thomas, Chattanooga, Tenn.):

It is reported here to-night that a train was captured to-day on the Lebanon Branch road, between Lebanon and the Junction.

This dispatch was received just before telegraphic communication was stopped between here and Louisville. The line is now down between here and Louisville.

Bowling Green reports the line cut between there and Lebanon Junction. The train was captured at New Haven. The force that captured the train consisted of about 80 men.

R. M. SAWYER,
Assistant Adjutant-General.

CAVE CITY, *March* 28, 1864.

Brigadier-General BURBRIDGE,
Louisville:

Couriers left this place this morning with instructions to Colonels Weatherford and Hanson to concentrate their regiments at Columbia. If it becomes necessary, will order them to Glasgow or some other point. If Morgan is advancing in force he has not crossed the Cumberland River between Carthage and Creelsborough, and he could not certainly have crossed above. The guerrilla band that burned the train on Lebanon Branch is much smaller than reported. I will give you all information of importance.

E. H. HOBSON,
Brigadier-General.

CAVE CITY, *March* 28, 1864.
Lieutenant-Colonel SPAULDING,
    Glasgow:
Mount a squad of men and send them immediately in the direction of burnt bridge, on Green River, to try to catch 80 rebels who burnt a train at New Hope this morning. Send a good officer who will pursue them. Send another squad to Brownsville, Edmonson County. Dickerson is in command of rebels.
By order of Brig. Gen. E. H. Hobson:
JOHN S. BUTLER,
Assistant Adjutant-General.

CAVE CITY, KY., *March* 28, 1864.
Brigadier-General BURBRIDGE,
    Louisville:
Rebel squad that burned train to-day numbered 25, if not less. They have been dropping into the State one or two at a time. Information just received from all points on Cumberland River. Expeditions sent to Tennessee report no force of rebels. Colonel Hughs and his men have gone over the mountains. Captain Knight will press a few horses and follow squad from New Haven in direction of Bardstown.

E. H. HOBSON,
Brigadier-General.

LOUISVILLE, *March* 28, 1864.
Major-General SCHOFIELD:
The Eleventh Michigan Cavalry, 900 strong, two companies Second Ohio Heavy Artillery, and two or three small detachments, numbering in all about 1,400 men, is the force at Camp Nelson. The Fourth Kentucky, about 350 strong, is at Lexington, but I will order it at once to camp. I have information to-night, though not reliable, that Forrest with considerable force had captured Paducah, and is now between the Tennessee and Cumberland Rivers, and it is probably his intention to cut the Nashville railroad. I have force enough, however, to protect the railroad. The Sixteenth Kentucky arrived here to-night, and have also three other veteran regiments, which can be used to strengthen the forces on the Nashville railroad or thrown into the eastern portion of the State, as necessity may demand. I will at once concentrate four mounted regiments at some point in supporting distance of Sturgis' force at Mount Sterling. I will keep you informed of Forrest's movements.
S. G. BURBRIDGE,
Brigadier-General, Commanding.

CLEVELAND, TENN.,
March 28, 1864.
Brig. Gen. W. D. WHIPPLE,
    Asst. Adjt. Gen. and Chief of Staff, Dept. of the Cumberland:
I have the honor to report everything quiet. Scouts from my command go to Waterhouse's farm, on Spring Place road, and Red

Clay, on Dalton.   The enemy advanced his picket 2 miles day before yesterday on Dalton road.   His picket is now 3½ miles south of Red Clay and at upper King's Bridge.

I have the honor to be, very respectfully, your obedient servant,

A. P. CAMPBELL,
Colonel, Commanding Division.

MOSSY CREEK, *March* 28, 1864.

General SCHOFIELD:

I have scouts just from Bull's Gap; they report rebel infantry nearly all gone, and are daily leaving the country.   Cavalry at the gap not thought to be many ; also squads of cavalry in all the gaps and roads between Bull's Gap and the bend of the Nola Chucky, 1 mile below the mouth of Lick Creek.   They say the citizens told them the infantry are moving to Virginia, and in few days the cavalry will go to Kentucky.   General Vaughn had pickets stationed 7 miles below Rogersville on Saturday and Sunday ; the cars came to Bull's Gap Friday.   The men are said to be deserting by hundreds and going to North Carolina, the roads being so closely guarded they cannot come this way.

R. A. CRAWFORD,
Chief of Scouts.

STEVENSON, *March* 28, 1864—3 a. m.

Maj. R. M. SAWYER:

I have your dispatch.   Your orders to General Brayman and Veatch all right.

Write a note to superintendent of railroad in Nashville that I have been over all the road, and am of opinion that all loaded trains should make a continuous circuit from Nashville by way of Decatur to Stevenson, and back to Nashville over the old road with empty cars.   A separate set of trains could run from Stevenson up to Chattanooga and beyond.   Not a citizen or pound of private freight should be carried until all the troops are well supplied.

Inform Colonel Donaldson to the same effect, and that General Allen says the mules at Larkinsville, Woodville, &c., should be supplied with oats immediately.

Tell Colonel Donaldson that I find citizens and private freight carried on the cars, and the officers all along the road complain that they cannot get requisitions filled for forage or even clothing.

This must be remedied at once.   I find at least a dozen locomotives here appearing idle, empty cars also, and am satisfied by making the circuit described the present stock of the road could do double the work.

If wood or water is needed on the new road, I will order my troops to provide any quantity necessary.   Tell railroad superintendent he can make his permanent arrangements.

W. T. SHERMAN,
Major-General.

HEADQUARTERS DISTRICT OF CAIRO,
Columbus, Ky., March 28, 1864.

Maj. Gen. S. A. HURLBUT :

The enemy are retreating southward. They left Clinton last night.

I received a dispatch from Major-General Sherman, who orders General Veatch to cut off Forrest's retreat by landing at Savannah and going to Purdy and the Hatchie. I have telegraphed General Veatch by way of Paducah. He also says he wants Grierson to follow Forrest and attack him at all hazards, and follow him up as far as possible, and orders this word to be sent to him.

Please reach him. I return to Cairo this afternoon.

Very respectfully,

M. BRAYMAN,
Brigadier-General, Commanding.

COLUMBUS, KY.,
March 28, 1864.

Lieut. Col. R. M. SAWYER,
Assistant Adjutant-General, Nashville, Tenn. :

Your dispatch is just received. General Veatch was not detained, but passed Paducah at daylight this morning. I know not where Grierson is, but will communicate with him, if possible, as you direct. Forrest and Faulkner are near this place, and I am here expecting attack to-night. I will repeat your order to Captain Pennock to forward by dispatch-boat up the Tennessee.

M. BRAYMAN,
Brigadier-General, Commanding.

COLUMBUS, KY.,
March 28, 1864—11.45 a. m.

Captain PENNOCK,
Cairo or Mound City:

General Sherman instructs me to convey his order to General Veatch to land at Savannah and proceed to Purdy and the Hatchie to cut off the retreat of Forrest. Please convey this to him by dispatch-boat. Also advise General Veatch that Forrest is still within 12 miles of this place, and we are waiting an attack.

M. BRAYMAN,
Brigadier-General, Commanding.

MOUND CITY, *March 28, 1864.*

Brigadier-General BRAYMAN :

As soon as the dispatch-boat arrives, which I sent to Columbus yesterday, I will send her up with General Sherman's order to General Veatch. I have received information from Captain Odlin that a small force of cavalry have crossed the river above this and may attack. I have made all arrangements to meet them.

A. M. PENNOCK,
Fleet Captain, &c.

COLUMBUS, KY.,
March 28, 1864.

Captain MUNROE,
   Assistant Adjutant-General, Cairo, Ill.:

The wives and children of the officers at this post have been placed on board the Crawford instead of the Jewess, as I indicated in my dispatch to Mr. Olds. Anything that you can do or advise to procure them comfort will be appreciated.

Forrest is concentrating at Clinton. Lightest force at Blandville at latest accounts. They will in all probability come in two columns. The men who came from Madrid are disciplined, and will add greatly to the defense of the place; will try to keep you advised of matters here.

C. B. SMITH,
Lieutenant and Aide-de-Camp.

· ————

HEADQUARTERS SIXTEENTH ARMY CORPS,
Memphis, Tenn., March 28, 1864.

Maj. L. F. BOOTH,
   Comdg. First Battalion, First Alabama Siege Artillery:

SIR: You will proceed with your own battalion to Fort Pillow and establish your force in garrison of the works there. As you will be, if I am correct in my memory, the senior officer at that post, you will take command, conferring, however, freely and fully with Major Bradford, Thirteenth Tennessee Cavalry, whom you will find a good officer, though not of much experience.

There are two points of land fortified at Fort Pillow, one of which only is now held by our troops. You will occupy both, either with your own troops alone, or holding one with yours and giving the other in charge to Major Bradford.

The positions are commanding and can be held by a small force against almost any odds.

I shall send you at this time two 12-pounder howitzers, as I hope it will not be necessary to mount heavy guns.

You will, however, immediately examine the ground and the works, and if in your opinion 20-pounder Parrotts can be advantageously used, I will order them to you. My own opinion is that there is not range enough. Major Bradford is well acquainted with the country, and should keep scouts well out and forward all information received direct to me.

I think Forrest's check at Paducah will not dispose him to try the river again, but that he will fall back to Jackson and thence cross the Tennessee. As soon as this is ascertained I shall withdraw your garrison.

Nevertheless, act promptly in putting the work in perfect order and the post into its strongest defense. Allow as little intercourse as possible with the country and cause all supplies which go out to be examined with great strictness. No man whose loyalty is questionable should be allowed to come in or go out while the enemy is in West Tennessee. The post must be held.

Your obedient servant,

S. A. HURLBUT,
Major-General.

HEADQUARTERS SIXTEENTH ARMY CORPS,
Memphis, Tenn., March 28, 1864.
Maj. W. F. BRADFORD,
   Thirteenth Tennessee Cavalry:

MAJOR : I send to Fort Pillow four companies colored artillery, who are also drilled as infantry, and two 12-pounder howitzers.

These are good troops, well tried and commanded by a good officer. Major Booth ranks you and will take command. He has full instructions in writing, which he will show you. I think these troops had better hold the forts, while yours are held for exterior garrison. In case of an attack, you will of course seek refuge in the fortifications.

Keep yourself well posted as to what is going on in the country and keep me advised. I doubt if Forrest will risk himself in the pocket between the Hatchie and Forked Deer, but he may try it. At all events, with 700 good men, your post can be held until assistance arrives.

Your obedient servant,

S. A. HURLBUT,
Major-General.

———

HUNTSVILLE, *March 28, 1864.*
Major SAWYER,
   Assistant Adjutant-General: .

MAJOR : I wrote you on Friday last and sent the same per hands of G. G. Cokeston, in relation to forage and other supplies. Have you ordered Lieutenant-Colonel Donaldson to send forage to this point ? I have exhausted the means in my power to get supplies and am forced to appeal to the commanding general. If forage is not sent to this point my public animals will have to go without eating. This is our true condition and will admit of no delay.

J. CONDIT SMITH,
Chief Quartermaster Fifteenth Army Corps.

———

HDQRS. MILITARY DIVISION OF THE MISSISSIPPI,
Nashville, Tenn., March 28, 1864.
Major-General MCPHERSON,
   Commanding Department of the Tennessee:

GENERAL : Obeying instructions from the Secretary of War, dated War Department, Adjutant-General's Office, Washington, February 14, 1864, I have the honor to inform you that a number of copies of the President's amnesty proclamation, dated December 8, 1863, in small pamphlet form, together with copies of General Orders, No. 64, dated War Department, Adjutant-General's Office, Washington, February 18, 1864, giving instructions as to the disposition to be made of refugees and rebel deserters coming within our lines, have been ordered to be forwarded to you for distribution, as far as possible, among the rebel armies and inhabitants in your front. The Secretary of War directs that upon receiving the proclamation and order, every effort practicable be made for such distribution by cavalry expeditions, scouts, and other means ; and that it be distributed throughout the rebel country in such numbers that it cannot be suppressed. I have the honor to inform you that reports of operations and successes in this distribution will be called for by the Adjutant-General of the Army from time to time.

I have the honor to be, general, most respectfully, your very obedient servant,

R. A. ALGER,
Colonel Fifth Michigan Cavalry, Special Commissioner, &c.

SPRINGFIELD, ILL., *March* 28, 1864.
(Received 11.30 p. m.)

Major-General HEINTZELMAN :

I am informed by telegraph that the Copperheads have killed the surgeon and a private of the Fifty-fourth Illinois Infantry, and wounded the colonel and others at Charleston, Coles County, Ill., to-day. The mayor of Mattoon telegraphs that the Copperheads are rising in Moultrie County, adjoining Coles. I think there is reason to apprehend serious trouble unless promptly checked. The Fifty-fourth Illinois is now at Charleston. There are veteran troops here in camp, say 200, and others can soon be gathered up if necessary. I should be glad to render any service in my power.

JULIUS WHITE,
Brigadier-General, Volunteers.

GENERAL ORDERS, } HDQRS. MIL. DIV. OF THE MISSISSIPPI,
No. 4.   }   *Nashville, Tenn., March* 28, 1864.

Capt. Montgomery Rochester, assistant adjutant-general of volunteers, is assigned to duty in the adjutant-general's department at these headquarters, and will be respected accordingly.

By order of Maj. Gen. W. T. Sherman :

R. M. SAWYER,
Assistant Adjutant-General.

KNOXVILLE, *March* 29, 1864—10 p. m.
(Received 10.40 a. m., 31st.)

Lieutenant-General GRANT,
Culpeper :

Steam-boats run regularly from Bridgeport to Chattanooga and from Chattanooga to Knoxville. Stores are rapidly accumulating at Chattanooga and Knoxville, and I will push them still more rapidly. Longstreet is leaving East Tennessee, and the secessionists are also going away, showing it to be a permanent abandonment.

Schofield has a much smaller command than I supposed, but he will push beyond Bull's Gap and develop the truth of the reports. Shall I order him to take up rails on the railroad, so as to enable me to draw a part of his command to General Thomas when the time comes to move against Johnston. I shall stay here all day to-morrow, and should like to hear from you before I return to Nashville.

W. T. SHERMAN,
Major-General.

CLEVELAND, TENN.,
March 29, 1864.

Brig. Gen. WILLIAM D. WHIPPLE,
　Chief of Staff, Department of the Cumberland :

I have the honor to report that my scouts have just reported from 2½ miles south of Red Clay. Lines of the enemy on that and Spring Place road the same; everything quiet except firing (artillery) in direction of Ringgold or Tunnel Hill. Another scouting party from Spring Place road report Martin's cavalry command moving around on the left of their line to a place called Blue Pond or Blue Mountain.

Eight thousand infantry from Longstreet's command said to have joined Johnston's forces at Dalton.

I have the honor to be, very respectfully, your obedient servant,
A. P. CAMPBELL.

MOSSY CREEK, *March* 29, 1864.
General SCHOFIELD :

Two scouts just in from Falls Branch and Jonesborough. They report rebel infantry are leaving daily, all going to Virginia; also some of their cavalry going to Virginia. Two brigades of cavalry on the 27th instant passed Falls Branch, going to Kingsport. B. R. Johnson's division passed Jonesborough on 25th instant. McLaw's division was leaving Greeneville on the 27th. Some cavalry still in Bull's Gap and Howard's Gap. Three trains of cars come daily to Greeneville and take off troops, artillery wagons, &c. Rebel citizens all leaving the country; a good indication.

R. A. CRAWFORD,
Colonel and Chief of Scouts.

LOUDON, *March* 29, 1864.
Major-General SCHOFIELD :

Colonel Marsh, who is guarding Davis' Ford, on Little Tennessee, reports that quite a large force of rebel cavalry was at Maryville yesterday; also parties at Unitia and Friendsville. General Granger is still absent. Shall I send one of the regiments of cavalry from Madisonville over to drive them out ?

R. O. SELFRIDGE,
Lieutenant-Colonel and Assistant Inspector-General.

LOOKOUT VALLEY,
March 29, 1864—7.30 p. m.

Major-General THOMAS :

General Howard's scouts sent to McLemore's Cove report the gaps of Lookout Mountain guarded by squads of rebel cavalry of about 40 men each. McDonald's, Cooper's, and Stevens' Gaps could not be entered. The inhabitants report a rumor that a regiment of rebel cavalry was on Lookout Mountain.

JOSEPH HOOKER,
Major-General.

LOOKOUT VALLEY, TENN.,
March 29, 1864.

Major-General HOWARD,
  Commanding Eleventh Corps:

  GENERAL: The following telegram has just been received, and in compliance therewith the major-general commanding directs that you detail two regiments of infantry to proceed as early as practicable to-morrow morning to McLemore's Cove:

CHATTANOOGA, *March 29, 1864.*

Major-General HOOKER:

  The major-general commanding directs that you send two regiments of infantry to McLemore's Cove and the gaps of Lookout Mountain for the purpose of ascertaining the strength and position of the rebel cavalry. The regiments will carry three days' rations.

SOUTHARD HOFFMAN,
Major and Assistant Adjutant-General.

  I am, general, very respectfully, your obedient servant,
H. W. PERKINS,
Assistant Adjutant-General.

MARCH 29, 1864.

Brig. Gen. G. M. DODGE,
  Athens:

  General Garrard is ordered by Major-General Thomas to move his cavalry up on the line of the Decatur and Nashville Railroad, occupying Columbia and Lynnville, and guarding that portion of the road. He is at present guarding a portion of the Memphis and Charleston Railroad near Mooresville, and has about 15,000 bushels of corn in that vicinity, which he will turn over to your quartermaster.

  You will make arrangements to relieve his men on Friday, and as soon as he can relieve that portion of your command guarding railroad north of Lynnville you will order them to the front.

JAS. B. McPHERSON,
Major-General.

HUNTSVILLE, *March 29, 1864.*
(Received 30th.)

Brig. Gen. W. D. WHIPPLE:

  Dispatch directing to move my division to vicinity of Columbia received. As soon as General McPherson relieves my troops by arranging for the guard duty they are now performing, and my quartermaster can dispose of the property collected through this section, I will move. My quartermaster is now absent on duty, but should be here day after to-morrow.

K. GARRARD,
Brigadier-General.

KNOXVILLE, *March 29, 1864—10.30 p. m.*

SAWYER, *Nashville:*

  Order the most vigorous pursuit possible of the party that has appeared near Lebanon Junction. Burbridge, at Louisville, should attend to it. There is a force of 2,000 cavalry, under Sturgis, at

Paris, who can prevent escape to the east, and there are several Kentucky regiments of mounted men subject to Burbridge's command. Issue orders assigning to Schofield, Army of the Ohio, General Hovey and the regiments brought by him from Indiana, and order him to conduct them via Murfreesborough, Cowan, Bridgeport, and Chattanooga, to report in advance by letter and telegraph to Schofield at Knoxville. Issue orders that commissaries at the principal stations along the railroad be prepared to issue provisions to troops marching to the front on the return of the officers in command. Commanding officers of regiments on the march should report by telegraph in advance of their progress.

SHERMAN.

NASHVILLE, *March* 29, 1864.

Brigadier-General BURBRIDGE,
  Commanding, Louisville :

The enemy are reported at Eddyville. If Forrest or any portion of the rebel command attempt to cross through Kentucky, Hobson or yourself should collect all the returning veterans and such other troops as you can find and try and cut him off, according to the route he may attempt. The general directs that you impress on all that they must not act on the defensive, but must pursue and do all that is possible to kill, capture, and destroy every man of Forrest's command that has crossed the Tennessee.

The stockade and railroad defenses must be defended if only 50 men have to fight 1,000 men, for Forrest will not have time to stay long in any one place.

Answer what may be your latest information.

By order of Maj. Gen. W. T. Sherman:

R. M. SAWYER,
Assistant Adjutant-General.

ATHENS, *March* 29, 1864.

Maj. R. M. SAWYER,
  Nashville :

Please inform me at what point it is represented that Forrest crossed the Tennessee River, and at what time.

I have no information of Forrest having crossed the river.

G. M. DODGE,
Brigadier-General.

HDQRS. CAVALRY CORPS, DEPARTMENT OF THE OHIO,
Paris, Ky., March 29, 1864.

CHIEF OF STAFF,
  Knoxville, or
Major-General SCHOFIELD :

GENERAL : I regret to have to inform you that the mounting and equipping of my command does not progress as rapidly as I could wish nor as you have probably been expecting.

The circumlocution which is necessary to be gone through with is extremely trying on the nerves of an impatient man, but there is no such thing as avoiding it.

We met with delay everywhere, and I sometimes feel as though the great end the staff departments have in view now-a-days is "how not to do it."

When a requisition goes forward the chances are nine out of ten that it will be sent back for not conforming, in some trifling particular, with some "form" which has probably been gotten up within the last few days, and which is known only to the authors themselves. This is especially and peculiarly the case with the ordnance department, though the others are bad enough.

In one case I was receiving wagons from Camp Nelson, and directed my quartermaster to request the quartermaster at that place, rather than send the wagons empty and thus lose valuable time, to load them with forage; instead of doing so, however, and at once, and thus putting his shoulder to the common wheel, he telegraphed to know "whether we wanted the forage for animals or for men."

Again, I made requisition for seventy-five or one hundred wagons, and was informed that the wagons were at Camp Nelson, but that General Allen had directed that we receive no more. The result was that we could not supply our animals without falling back to this place.

Again, I made an estimate for funds on the chief quartermaster, Cincinnati, sent my quartermaster for them, but instead of getting them and done with it, he was referred to Captain Hall at Camp Nelson, and Captain Hall said he had no funds for this command.

Again, I made a requisition for 3,500 horses to complete the mounting of my men; the requisition goes to the chief quartermaster at Cincinnati (just where it ought to have gone), and in the course of time he (my quartermaster) is informed that by a new arrangement requisition for horses will have to be made on the Cavalry Bureau at Washington.

Then is it possible to accomplish anything in this way? Longstreet will not be apt to wait for all this circumlocution, but will rather be disposed to take advantage of it himself. When the departments knew this force was coming here, had they placed the proper stores at my disposal we should have been ready for service now, and there would have been no trouble at all about getting their receipts.

You are sending two more regiments and a battalion to be equipped. Now, the necessary stores should start for this place when the troops do. Just see what valuable time might be saved. Instead, however, nothing can be done until the troops arrive; then requisitions will be made out and forwarded, and (if some new form should be adopted in the mean time) will probably be returned for informality, &c., and there is no telling when they may be ready for the field. I do not write this with any hope that it will be in your power to remedy these evils, but simply that you may be enabled to appreciate the embarrassments under which I am compelled to labor, and the reason why we are not now ready for effective service. If the enemy enter Kentucky in force (and I fear he has done so already) he will not probably have less than 6,000 or 7,000 infantry, mounted, and artillery. To meet this force I have but about 3,000 mounted men and some 2,000 foot men, all in course of equipping, and not one piece of artillery. To be sure, I am not charged with the defense of Kentucky, and it might be said, therefore, that it is no affair of mine. That would all be true, yet I am anxious about it, and propose to do what I can to keep him out or worst him when he appears.

There is no doubt but Peter M. Everett, with .300 men, is hanging about Owingsville and, I fear, covering the advance of a larger force. Yet I hope it may not be so. Whatever information I may receive from my scouts confirming or contradicting this notion I will communicate to you by telegraph. Forrest is roaming at large in the southwestern portion of the State, probably with the idea of drawing us away from this section.

I am, general, very respectfully, your obedient servant,

S. D. STURGIS,
Brigadier-General.

HDQRS. CAVALRY CORPS, DEPARTMENT OF THE OHIO,
Paris, Ky., March 29, 1864.

CHIEF OF STAFF,
Knoxville, or
Major-General SCHOFIELD,
Commanding Department:

I have removed my headquarters to this place, and am bringing most of the cavalry to within 5 miles of Paris, on the Mount Sterling and Paris pike. By this arrangement I will be able to dispense with a considerable amount of transportation, hasten the equipment of the troops, and guard the country about Mount Sterling equally well. I have thought frequently of writing you on the general condition of affairs for the defense of this part of Kentucky against raids or an invasion, but have been prevented by the idea that as it was not strictly my business it might be better not to trouble you with matters outside my legitimate province. I think, however, it is due to you and to myself that I should at least call your attention to some few facts.

In the first place, my duties here are specific and confined to the limits of my camps, or, in other words, I have no geographical command and am not responsible for the defense of this State. Should an invasion occur I will of course co-operate to the fullest of my power with General Burbridge, as I have already informed him; but as to the forces beyond my own available for defense, I of course have no knowledge of their numbers or location. Being always willing to do my utmost for the common interest, and feeling anxious about the raid from Pound Gap, via Irvine, to Camp Nelson, I some two weeks ago or more telegraphed to inquire of General Burbridge whether or not he had any troops guarding that road, as I wished to send a scout in case he had not. He replied that he had sent the Forty-fifth Kentucky to Irvine. Still feeling uneasy, I some five or six days ago telegraphed again on the subject, and he replied that the Forty-fifth Kentucky had been ordered to Irvine, but whether it had reached that place or not he could not say. Since arriving here to-day, I learn that the Forty-fifth Kentucky is still at Flemingsburg.

Now, I do not refer to these things for the purpose of criticising General Burbridge; his affairs are not mine, and moreover he may have sent some other troops there; yet I do not believe we have a soldier between Camp Nelson and Pound Gap. My own troops are just about in the act of receiving arms, &c., and it is a pity that I should be compelled to scatter them, yet I will have to send something on that road. Again, should a formidable raid be made, I can only act to the best of my judgment, made up from what information I can gather around me, and that you can depend upon my doing.

I have twice applied to your headquarters at Lexington for artillery, but have yet received none.

I was informed that one of my applications had been referred to General Tillson, at Knoxville. If the enemy comes he will certainly have artillery, and it is difficult to get troops without artillery to fight those who have it.

I am, general, very respectfully, your obedient servant,
S. D. STURGIS,
Brigadier-General, Commanding.

HDQRS. DISTRICT SOUTHERN CENTRAL KENTUCKY,
Cave City, Ky., March 29, 1864.
Col. J. W. WEATHERFORD,
Commanding Thirteenth Kentucky Cavalry :

COLONEL : I sent you instructions on yesterday in reference to moving your regiment. I suggested to General Burbridge in dispatch to-day that if all the troops were moved from the Cumberland River that the whole country would be devastated, farming would have to be suspended, and merchants who had laid in stocks of goods would, beyond a doubt, be robbed by the guerrilla bands infesting the country, and to prevent this state of affairs, if he would permit, would so dispose your regiment and afford protection to all the country. He adopted my suggestion. You will therefore station five companies of your regiment at Burkesville, four at Tompkinsville or beyond, and two at Scottsville. To supply your troops at Burkesville and Tompkinsville, supplies can be obtained at this place; for the two companies at Scottsville, supplies can be had at Bowling Green.

As soon as the Thirty-seventh Kentucky Mounted Infantry leaves Glasgow for Columbia it would be well to send one of the companies from Tompkinsville to Glasgow to protect your flank, act as couriers, and afford protection to the country in the interior. You will carry out the instructions contained in this letter without delay. I have worked hard for the interests of the people of the border counties. I hope this arrangement will suit you.

Very respectfully,
E. H. HOBSON,
Brigadier-General.

LOUISVILLE, *March* 29, 1864.
Maj. R. M. SAWYER,
Assistant Adjutant-General, Nashville, Tenn.:

No further news from Forrest. Forces are being arranged to meet him or pursue him. Rebels were reported by my scouts at Emporium Iron-Works yesterday. Indications are that the rebels are trying to enter by way of Pound Gap; their movements are watched.

S. G. BURBRIDGE,
Brigadier-General.

HEADQUARTERS DISTRICT OF KENTUCKY,
Louisville, March 29, 1864—9 a. m.
Maj. R. M. SAWYER,
Assistant Adjutant-General, Nashville, Tenn.:

Scouts just report that only 50 rebels have crossed at Eddyville. but that 50 others crossed below there; they think it a mere raiding party. Mounted men are after them now.

S. G. BURBRIDGE,
Brigadier-General, Commanding.

LOUISVILLE, *March 29, 1864.*
Col. E. A. STARLING, *Hopkinsville:*

General Sherman informs me that Forrest is at Eddyville with his command. Concentrate your regiments immediately at Hopkinsville. Send out numerous scouting parties, particularly in the direction of Eddyville. If the enemy is found, contest every inch of ground, and fall back, if necessary, toward Bowling Green. Omit no precaution; don't be surprised; obey Colonel Maxwell's orders; report by telegraph your movements to him and me. We must act on the offensive, and fight against odds if necessary.

By order of Brigadier-General Burbridge:

THOS. B. FAIRLEIGH,
Lieutenant-Colonel, Actg. Asst. Adjt. Gen.

HEADQUARTERS DISTRICT OF KENTUCKY,
Louisville, March 29, 1864.
Col. C. MAXWELL,
Commanding Southwest Kentucky, Bowling Green:

General Sherman informs me that Forrest and command are at Eddyville. Concentrate the Fifty-second Kentucky and all the mounted men of Forty-eighth Kentucky at Bowling Green immediately. Any outpost in danger will be withdrawn. Colonel Starling is directed to feel the enemy and report to you; if in force he will fall back to Bowling Green, or where you may direct. Attend to Elk Fork bridge; the road north of Bowling Green will be attended to. Act on the offensive, and fight odds if necessary.

By order of Brigadier-General Burbridge:

THOS. B. FAIRLEIGH,
Lieutenant-Colonel and Actg. Asst. Adjt. Gen.

LOUISVILLE, *March 29, 1864.*
Brigadier-General HOBSON,
Cave City:

General Sherman reports Forrest with his command at Eddyville. If possible, have Thirty-seventh Kentucky remain at or near Cave City for the present. Direct Thirteenth Kentucky Cavalry to be ready to move in any direction. It will probably be needed by you. Communicate with Colonel Maxwell at Bowling Green and act in concert. Troops will be sent from here on line of railroad to Cave City. We must act on the offensive, and fight odds if necessary.

By order of Brigadier-General Burbridge:

THOS. B. FAIRLEIGH,
Lieutenant-Colonel and Actg. Asst. Adjt. Gen.

LOUISVILLE, *March* 29, 1864.

Brigadier-General HOBSON, *Cave City :*

Forrest, with a large force, is reported between the Tennessee and Cumberland; was near Rockcastle, Ky. You will order Grider's command from Scottsville to Bowling Green without delay. You will also order Weatherford's and Hanson's regiments to concentrate at Columbia, with a view to throwing them into Eastern Kentucky, in the vicinity of Richmond. There is but little doubt that a large rebel force is about to invade the State by way of Pound Gap. Order Weatherford to make the proper disposition of the stores at Burkesville.

S. G. BURBRIDGE,
Brigadier-General.

LOUISVILLE, *March* 29, 1864.

COMMANDING OFFICER, *Henderson, Ky. :*

Order the troops at Owensborough to join you, and move with the united command to Morganfield, and then toward Princeton. A detachment of Forrest's command is reported across the Cumberland and moving toward Union City ; said to be less than 100 men. You will join Colonel Starling and report to him. A force from Hopkinsville in same direction.

By order of Brigadier-General Burbridge:

THOS. B. FAIRLEIGH,
Lieutenant-Colonel and Actg. Asst. Adjt. Gen.

LOUISVILLE, KY., *March* 29, 1864.

Col. H. G. GIBSON, *Camp Nelson :*

Send two companies of cavalry to scout country in direction of Springfield Bardstown, &c., and let me know the result. A small rebel force, about 30, are in that country, and it is desired to intercept them. They are the same that destroyed the Lebanon train.

By order of Brigadier-General Burbridge:

THOS. B. FAIRLEIGH,
Lieutenant-Colonel and Actg. Asst. Adjt. Gen.

HDQRS. FOURTH DIV., SIXTEENTH ARMY CORPS,
On board Steamer Metropolitan, Clifton, Tenn.,
March 29, 1864—4 a. m.

Major-General SHERMAN, *Nashville :*

I left Paducah at 3.30 p. m. on 27th. Received your dispatch of 27th, about 90 miles above Paducah, at 10.20 a. m. on the 28th. Have made all possible speed to this point. No information about Forrest since I left Paducah. A rumor that he was at Paris and would attempt to cross near the railroad crossing.

Shall push on to Savannah and move to Purdy, as ordered in your dispatch.

Very respectfully,

JAMES C. VEATCH,
Brigadier-General.

ON STEAM-BOAT METROPOLITAN,
Clifton, Tenn., March 29, 1864—4 a. m.
Brigadier-General DODGE,
Athens, Ala. :

I reached here at 3 a. m. No news of Forrest since I left Paducah. Shall go to Savannah, thence to Purdy, as ordered by dispatch from General Sherman.

JAMES C. VEATCH,
Brigadier-General.

NASHVILLE, *March* 29, 1864.
COMMANDING OFFICERS,
Columbia, Pulaski, and Athens :

It is reported that Forrest has crossed the Tennessee River. To be prepared for him in case this be true, the general directs that the veterans marching down the road toward the south be notified, in case Forrest attempts to turn east, south of the Cumberland, to mass in groups of about 2,000 men each and try and ambush him. Impress on all that they must not act on the defensive, but must destroy every man of Forrest's command that has crossed the Tennessee. The stockades and railroad defenses must be defended if only 50 men have to fight 1,000, for Forrest will not have time to stay long in any one place. Answer what your latest information may be, and keep scouts well out toward the river.

By order of Maj. Gen. W. T. Sherman :

R. M. SAWYER,
Assistant Adjutant-General.

NASHVILLE, *March* 29, 1864.
Maj. Gen. L. H. ROUSSEAU,
Commanding District of Nashville :

GENERAL : The following is just received :

CHATTANOOGA. *March* 28, 1864.
Maj. R. M. SAWYER,
Assistant Adjutant-General :

If Forrest be at Eddyville he should be caught. Order all the cavalry near Nashville to be ready to pursue him as soon as his route is understood. Of course he cannot take Fort Donelson, and must turn out by the way of Columbia or cross into Kentucky. Order Rousseau to keep on hand any infantry that may be at Nashville, ready to throw by rail toward a threatened point, but with all the cavalry he can obtain to cause the most energetic pursuit to be made ; not a man should escape. I trust that Veatch is on the track. The probability is that Forrest has divided his command. Veatch should attend to that west of the Tennessee. The veterans marching down the road toward the south should be notified in case Forrest attempts to turn east, south of the Cumberland, to mass in groups of about 2,000 men each and try to ambush him; but if Forrest tries to cross through Kentucky, Burbridge or Hobson should collect all the returning veterans and such other troops as he can find and try and cut him off, according to the route he may attempt. Impress on all that they must not act on the defensive, but must pursue and do all that is possible to kill, capture, and destroy every man of Forrest's command that has crossed the Tennessee. The stockades and railroad defenses must be defended if only 50 men have to fight 1,000, for Forrest will not have time to stay long in a place.

W. T. SHERMAN.
Major-General.

The above is respectfully furnished for your information and guidance. You will please cause such of the instructions contained therein as is within your power to be carried into effect. General Burbridge as also the veteran regiments marching south, will be at once notified from these headquarters of the foregoing, and direction given for their future actions.

R. M. SAWYER,
Assistant Adjutant-General.

NASHVILLE, *March* 29, 1864.

Major-General SHERMAN,
        Knoxville:

No definite news of Forrest has been received to-day. The train which was captured at Lebanon was attacked by a small party of guerrillas. General Burbridge sent in pursuit of them. The force stated to be at Eddyville was, as near as I can learn, but a small party of guerrillas, at least it was not Forrest; in fact, I do not think he has crossed the Tennessee. I have, however, taken every precaution. Your instructions have been fully carried out. Burbridge has been notified in accordance with your telegram, also commanding officers at Columbia, Pulaski, and Athens, relative to notifying veteran troops returning to the front. There is nothing further new.

R. M. SAWYER,
Assistant Adjutant-General.

METROPOLIS, *March* 29, 1864.

Brig. Gen. M. BRAYMAN,
        Commanding:

I am informed by Parson Carrington, from Kentucky side, whom I know to be reliable, that Forrest's headquarters are at Mayfield to-day; that his men are scattered on a furlough until to-morrow morning, and if compelled to leave he intends conscripting the whole country as he goes. This information is from rebel captain in Forrest's command, received this morning from him in Lovelaceville, Ky.

CHAS. WALLACE,
Operator.

PADUCAH, *March* 29, 1864.

Brigadier-General BRAYMAN,
        Commanding:

My scouts have just come in, and report rebels all over the country around Mayfield; headquarters there. They are in gangs of 10 and 20, gathering up all the horses and mules, pressing in wagons and teams, gathering all the bacon, &c. Cavalry force thrown there would do valuable service.

S. G. HICKS,
Colonel, Commanding Post.

CAIRO, ILL., *March* 29, 1864.
Col. S. G. HICKS,
  Commanding, Paducah, Ky. :
  Have just returned from Columbus. Am aware of the presence
of the enemy in the interior, but am informed by General Sherman
that he is indifferent to their presence there. We will protect the
river.
                                      M. BRAYMAN,
                              Brigadier-General, Commanding.

                                      CAIRO, *March* 29, 1864.
Col. S. G. HICKS,
        Paducah :
  The First Alabama and Fortieth Illinois are on their way to you.
                                      M. BRAYMAN,
                              Brigadier-General, Commanding.

                                      CAIRO, *March* 29, 1864.
Col. S. G. HICKS,
        Paducah :
  I will re-enforce you as soon as possible.
                                      M. BRAYMAN,
                              Brigadier-General, Commanding.

                                      CAIRO, *March* 29, 1864.
Capt. A. M. PENNOCK,
        Mound City :
  Colonel Hicks says the enemy are on him again. I am going up
with re-enforcements.
                                      M. BRAYMAN,
                              Brigadier-General, Commanding.

                  HEADQUARTERS SIXTEENTH ARMY CORPS,
                          Memphis, Tenn., March 29, 1864.
Brig. Gen. M. BRAYMAN,
        Commanding District of Cairo, Cairo, Ill. :
  GENERAL: The major-general commanding corps requests that
you will carefully collect the necessary data from which to make a
full and circumstantial report of the late surrender at Union City,
Tenn., as early as practicable.
  The same will apply to the affair at Paducah, in which the general
desires that the part the rebels took in the destruction and plunder-
ing of the town should be clearly shown.
  I have the honor to be, general, very respectfully, your obedient
servant,
                                      T. H. HARRIS,
                              Assistant Adjutant-General.

HEADQUARTERS NORTHERN DEPARTMENT,
Columbus, Ohio, March 29, 1864.
Brig. Gen. JULIUS WHITE,
   Springfield Ill.:
Have you any further information from Charleston or Moultrie County ? How many of the Fifty-fourth Illinois are at Charleston ? Give me full particulars.

S. P. HEINTZELMAN,
Major-General, Commanding.

HEADQUARTERS NORTHERN DEPARTMENT,
Columbus, Ohio, March 29, 1864.
Captain HILL,
   Invalid Corps, Paris, Edgar County, Ill.:
Have you any information of disturbances at Charleston, Coles County, Ill.? If so, let me know at once the facts.

S. P. HEINTZELMAN,
Major-General, Commanding.

GENERAL ORDERS, }   HDQRS. 4TH DIV., 16TH ARMY CORPS,
   No. 6.   }   *Williams' Landing, Tenn., March* 29, 1864.

The troops of this command will march at 5 o'clock a. m. on the 30th instant for Purdy, the First Brigade in advance. Forty rounds of ammunition must be carried by each man and 20 rounds per man must be carried in wagons. Three days' rations will be carried in haversacks. Only one wagon and two ambulances per regiment will be allowed. As much forage must be carried as possible with the limited transportation, as the country is supposed to contain but little.

The troops must march in readiness for battle, as the enemy may be expected at any moment after leaving our present camp.

By order of Brig. Gen. James C. Veatch :

F. W. FOX,
Assistant Adjutant-General.

SPECIAL ORDERS, }   HDQRS. 1ST DIV., U. S. COLORED TROOPS,
   No. 14.   }   *Vicksburg, Miss., March* 29, 1864.

I. The First Brigade, Brig. Gen. I. F. Shepard commanding, will move to Vicksburg, Miss., commencing on the 30th instant, moving one regiment each day until the entire brigade has been transferred, not including the Third U. S. Cavalry (colored) and Battery A, Second U. S. Artillery (colored), which will remain at Haynes' Bluff.

II. The Second Brigade, Col. H. Scofield commanding, will move to Haynes' Bluff in the same order prescribed for the First Brigade, until the brigade has been transferred, commencing on the 30th instant.

III. The headquarters of the respective brigades will be moved as soon as practicable,

IV. Colonel Osband, commanding Third U. S. Cavalry (colored), and the commanding officer of Battery A, Second U. S. Artillery (colored), will make their reports to headquarters Second Brigade.

By order of Brig. Gen. John P. Hawkins:

S. B. FERGUSON,
Assistant Adjutant-General.

CULPEPER, *March* 30, 1864.
(Received 31st.)

Maj. Gen. W. T. SHERMAN,
Nashville:

Maj. Gen. F. P. Blair will be assigned to the Seventeenth Corps, and not the Fifteenth. Assign General Hooker, subject to the approval of the President, to any other corps command you may have, and break up the anomaly of one general commanding two corps.

U. S. GRANT,
Lieutenant-General.

MOSSY CREEK, *March* 30, 1864.

General SCHOFIELD:

A letter from Greeneville of 26th informs me that Longstreet's infantry is certainly leaving East Tennessee, and from the movements and indications it is thought they will go to Lee. The most of the cavalry is said to be moving toward Kingsport, probably looking after forage. They are to guard the salt-works. Raid to Kentucky said to be abandoned for the present.

R. A. CRAWFORD,
Colonel and Chief of Scouts.

LOUISVILLE, *March* 30, 1864.

Brigadier-General POTTER,
Chief of Staff:

It is reported that a portion of Forrest's command has crossed the Cumberland at Eddyville, Ky. It is certain that small numbers have crossed. At present to move headquarters to Lexington would be unadvisable, and I respectfully ask that headquarters remain here until affairs in Southern Kentucky are more settled.

S. G. BURBRIDGE,
Brigadier-General.

LOUISVILLE, *March* 30, 1864.

Maj. R. M. SAWYER,
Assistant Adjutant-General, Nashville:

The rebel squad which captured train on Lebanon road was very small, probably not over 15, and I think were merely returned rebel soldiers organized in the State. They are pursued by several detachments. One of Forrest's men gave himself up to part of my command scouting toward Eddyville. He says Forrest started from

Demopolis on February 28 with 15,000 men ; part went toward Memphis, part into Middle Tennessee, and the balance, about 4,000, went with Forrest to Paducah ; that they were poorly clad and mounted, but well armed ; that those who crossed the Cumberland were furloughed for six days, with orders to report at Mayfield. Reports indicate that the number that crossed will not exceed 100, and my mounted men are hunting them.

S. G. BURBRIDGE,
Brigadier-General.

ATHENS, *March* 30, 1864.
Brig. Gen. T. W. SWEENY, *Pulaski :*
By direction of General Dodge, the Fiftieth Illinois has been ordered to move to Mooresville, relieving General Garrard's command.

J. W. BARNES,
Assistant Adjutant-General.

HDQRS. SECOND DIVISION, SIXTEENTH ARMY CORPS,
Pulaski, 1enn., March 30, 1864.
Col. J. B. WEAVER,
Commanding Post :
You will send Lieutenant Mosely and all of his party of Forrest's scouts to Tullahoma, and turn them over to General Slocum. The guard will number as many as the prisoners, and will be commanded by one of your best lieutenants, who will report at these headquarters for instructions. They will go by railroad to Nashville, and from thence by rail to Tullahoma. Surgeon Marsh reports Mosely able to travel. Send them off to-day if possible.
By order of Brig. Gen. T. W. Sweeny :

JAMES DAVIDSON,
First Lieut. Fifty-second Illinois Vols., Aide-de-Camp.

ATHENS, *March* 30, 1864.
Maj. Gen. JAMES B. McPHERSON, *Huntsville :*
I have ordered Fiftieth Illinois to Mooresville. If General Garrard does not extend his lines south of Lynnville he will only relieve a few companies of mine. If he should guard the road to Pulaski that would allow me to bring forward one brigade. There are more bridges between Pulaski and Lynnville than north of that point.

G. M. DODGE,
Brigadier-General.

ATHENS, *March* 30, 1864.
Maj. R. M. SAWYER,
Assistant Adjutant-General, Nashville :
General Veatch says he arrived at Clinton yesterday, and left for Savannah and Purdy as ordered. Says he has no news of Forrest since he left Paducah.

G. M. DODGE,
Brigadier-General.

HEADQUARTERS LEFT WING, SIXTEENTH ARMY CORPS,
Athens, Ala., March 30, 1864.
Brig. Gen. T. W. SWEENY,
    Commanding Second Division:
    The Second Cavalry Division, Army of the Cumberland, Briga-
dier-General Garrard commanding, has been ordered by General
Thomas to occupy the country and guard the railroad north of
Pulaski, relieving your troops. It will locate at Columbia and
Lynnville and will move from Mooresville Friday. As soon as the
regiments of the Second Brigade are relieved that brigade will be
ordered to the front and will report at Athens for orders. The companies guarding the mills can probably be relieved and the mills
abandoned, as we shall be able hereafter to draw our flour from
Nashville.
    By order of Brig. Gen. G. M. Dodge:
                                        J. W. BARNES,
                                   Assistant Adjutant-General.

WOODVILLE, ALA.,
March 30, 1864.
Maj. R. R. TOWNES,
    Asst. Adjt. Gen., Fifteenth Army Corps, Huntsville, Ala.:
    Colonel Gage, at Cottonville, reports this a. m. as follows: First,
that Sam Henry is stationed at Warrenton with his company of State
troops ; second, that Roddey arrived at Guntersville last night with
his command. If this report be true there must be a mounted force
stationed at Claysville, or we are not safe here at Cottonville.
                                        P. JOS. OSTERHAUS,
                           Brigadier-General, Commanding Division.

HDQRS. DEPARTMENT AND ARMY OF THE TENNESSEE,
Huntsville, Ala., March 30, 1864.
Brig. Gen. M. M. CROCKER,
    Commanding Fourth Division, Vicksburg, Miss.:
    GENERAL: Inclosed please find list* of regiments and batteries to
compose the two divisions of the Seventeenth Army Corps which
are to rendezvous at Cairo, Ill., and to be commanded by yourself
and Leggett, respectively.
    It is all-important that these divisions should be organized and
completely equipped ready for the field at the earliest day possible.
To this end I desire you, assisted by Lieutenant-Colonel Powell and
Captain Conklin, to see that these batteries, the detachments non-
veterans belonging to these regiments, the corps trains, Third and
Fourth Division trains, regimental trains, camp and garrison equipage, and 10,000 new Springfield rifled muskets for the Seventeenth
Corps now in the hands of the ordnance officer at Vicksburg, be
shipped to Cairo and landed there by the 20th of April, or as soon
thereafter as possible.
    Lieutenant Smith, acting assistant quartermaster in charge of the
corps train, will accompany it to Cairo and see that it is properly
taken care of, and the division quartermasters will accompany their

---

* Not found.

respective trains for the same purpose. If Lieutenant-Colonel
Clark has not already detailed the necessary staff officers of the Seventeenth Corps to proceed to Cairo and be ready to meet the troops
as they arrive and escort them to their respective camps, you will
do so immediately. Some of the regiments now on furlough should
be returning by the 20th of April. Two or three of these regiments
on the list are at present in the Red River expedition, but I have the
assurance of General Sherman that they will be back in time. I do
not wish to make the forces around Vicksburg too weak; consequently, do not care to have you send up the Seventy-second Illinois
and the various detachments until the forces return from Red River;
hasten forward, however, the artillery and trains, as these will
require a large amount of transportation. Two or three good-sized
boats will bring up all the troops that are to come from Vicksburg.

Very respectfully, your obedient servant,

JAS. B. McPHERSON,
Major-General, Commanding.

MEMPHIS, TENN.,
March 30, 1864—4 p. m.

Maj. Gen. W. T. SHERMAN :

Grierson has only 2,200 mounted men. Buckland has 2,400 white
infantry and 2,600 colored.

Fifteen hundred men under McCulloch passed through La Grange
yesterday [going] north. Forrest's strength with this is about 4,500,
with some artillery. Grierson has received your orders to follow
and attack, but unless he can reach Veatch and be supported by
him he will not be strong enough to punish him much.

The movement of McCulloch north indicates an intention either to
hold West Tennessee or to cross the river.

I can get no more horses and consequently can arm no more
cavalry.

Have heard nothing from Veatch except that he passed Paducah
Saturday. I do not know whether he received your orders to stop
at Savannah. I sent the order to him as soon as I received it. If
Forrest comes within the reach of infantry I shall try him with what
I can gather.

S. A. HURLBUT,
Major-General.

PADUCAH, *March* 30, 1864—1.30 p. m.

General BRAYMAN and Captain PENNOCK :

I am getting the prisoners together, and will leave as soon as possible for Cairo. The latest reliable information is they are concentrating at Mayfield preparing to go south.

Lieut. M. Knight with 18 men drove in their pickets day before yesterday, but had to fall back in quick time. There were two brigades
advancing yesterday, but have fallen back; they were gathering their
men I think. General Buford sent in a flag of truce for the exchange
of surgeons and to inquire about the rebel wounded and dead, also
about General Thompson. The colonel is fully prepared for any
attack, and there is no chance of their getting this place.

J. H. ODLIN,
Assistant Adjutant-General.

PADUCAH, *March* 30, 1864.
General BRAYMAN :

I have information this evening that Forrest has his headquarters at Mayfield; is conscripting everybody that can serve, and is throwing up breast-works there; that Faulkner has joined him, and he intends another attack on this place. This comes through an apparent reliable source.

S. G. HICKS,
Colonel, Commanding Post.

PADUCAH, *March* 30, 1864.
General BRAYMAN and Captain PENNOCK :

A man just from Mayfield. He left Mayfield last night after dark. Faulkner has just joined Forrest at Mayfield. They have given the Tennessee troops furloughs. He says they are going to stay as long as they please. One Tennessee regiment that was here has gone to Tennessee; the rest of the force is still with him, and say they intend to come here. He reports that Forrest was moving on Columbus yesterday. I just received your dispatch. I have dispatched all the news.

J. H. ODLIN,
Assistant Adjutant-General.

HEADQUARTERS SIXTEENTH ARMY CORPS,
Memphis, Tenn., March 30, 1864.
Brig. Gen. B. H. GRIERSON,
Commanding Cavalry Division, Memphis, Tenn.:

You will take all the available cavalry force at and near Memphis and move as rapidly as possible to attack the force under General Forrest. The march must be active and at the same time cautious. The enemy will be attacked at all hazards wherever met, and be followed closely.

By order of Maj. Gen. S. A. Hurlbut :
T. H. HARRIS,
Assistant Adjutant-General.

HDQRS. CAVALRY DIVISION, SIXTEENTH ARMY CORPS,
Memphis, Tenn., March 30, 1864.
Lieut. Col. THOMAS H. HARRIS,
Assistant Adjutant-General:

Upon the request of the major-general commanding corps, I have the honor to report the following as the condition of this command at the time General Forrest passed north :

The Second Brigade of this division, which was by far the most effective portion of the command, had re-enlisted, and a portion of it had already gone north.

The horses of such as owned their own horses have, by direction of Maj. Gen. W. T. Sherman, been appraised, and such as were serviceable purchased by the Government. These have since been issued to the First Brigade and the non-veterans of the Second Brigade,

Upon hearing of the movement of Forrest I sent Colonel Hurst, with the Sixth Tennessee Cavalry, about 700 strong, toward Jackson, to hang upon and annoy the enemy. I also sent 300 men of the First Brigade northeast, toward Brownsville, to watch the movements of the enemy in that direction. At that time I could mount and equip about 1,500 men, including Colonel Hurst's command and not including the veterans, whose horses were in the hands of the appraisers and have since been issued.

At this time I can mount and equip about 2,200 men, including the command of Colonel Hurst and 300 of the First Brigade; in all, about 1,000 men, which are now out.

Much of this force is new and inexperienced, and not very reliable. This will leave at least 1,000 men in camp, most of whom are effective but for want of horses.

The Seventh Kansas Cavalry are ordered to report to this corps, but have not yet arrived. They are unofficially reported full to the maximum, but I am not advised as to whether or not they are mounted.

Should I not be able to connect with the forces that are now out, I will have with me about 1,200 men.

Very respectfully, your obedient servant,

B. H. GRIERSON,
Brigadier-General.

HDQRS. DISTRICT OF SOUTHERN CENTRAL KENTUCKY,
Cave City, March 30, 1864.
Col. J. W. WEATHERFORD,
Commanding, Burkesville:

COLONEL: I have the honor to acknowledge the receipt of your communication of 29th, and have made report of your success to headquarters, Louisville. I sent you some instructions yesterday, which will be obeyed at proper time. You will, however, for the present, keep your command concentrated at Burkesville, on this side, for the purpose, if B[urbridge] should need you, to assist me in this vicinity. Forrest is reported at Eddyville, and it may be his object to destroy the railroad, hence the necessity of your being in position to act in concert with forces on the line of railroad. I will keep you advised by courier. Will expect also to hear from you. Keep this information strictly private. Accept for yourself, officers, and men my heartfelt thanks and congratulations for your successes and brilliant fights and conduct on the line of the Cumberland River.

Very respectfully,

E. H. HOBSON,
Brigadier-General.

HDQRS. DEPARTMENT AND ARMY OF THE TENNESSEE,
Huntsville, Ala., March 30, 1864.
Maj. Gen. S. A. HURLBUT,
Commanding Sixteenth Army Corps, Memphis:

GENERAL: The programme marked out by Major-General Sherman, while in command of the department, will be substantially carried out, viz: The Districts of Memphis and Vicksburg will be consolidated and called the District of the Mississippi River. Two divisions of the Seventeenth Army Corps will be organized chiefly from veteran regiments, now at home on furlough, and they will rendezvous at Cairo as fast as their furloughs expire.

One division will be commanded by Brigadier-General Leggett, and the other by Brigadier-General Crocker. General McArthur's division will remain in the former District of Vicksburg. The troops remaining under McArthur's command at present, as you will see from the memorandum I left with Brigadier-General Buckland on my way up, are made up of detachments non-veterans and regiments not entitled to enlist as such. Many of these detachments will have to be sent to Cairo in time to join their respective regiments, which are to rendezvous at that place, but the return of the Red River expedition and of veteran regiments belonging to McArthur's division will leave the force under his command quite as strong as at present. Until the veteran regiments return, and also the Red River expedition, it will be impossible to organize the permanent garrisons for Vicksburg and Natchez.

When the Red River expedition returns you can exercise your discretion about stopping Mower's division at Vicksburg or bringing it up to Memphis. Keep it at the point which is most likely to be threatened and where it can be of most service. Brig. Gen. A. J. Smith's division I want stopped at Memphis and put into camp to await orders, the time he remains there to be spent in disciplining, clothing, and arming his men and getting his transportation in order. You are so thoroughly familiar with matters along the Mississippi River that I do not deem it necessary to give any specific instructions, but shall rely largely upon your judgment and discretion.

Very respectfully, your obedient servant,

JAS. B. McPHERSON,
Major-General, Commanding.

HEADQUARTERS NORTHERN DEPARTMENT,
Columbus, Ohio, March 30, 1864.

Brigadier-General CARRINGTON,
Indianapolis, Ind.:

Please let the veteran regiment take the route through Mattoon, Ill., with orders as suggested in your telegram, and please report any information you may have received by telegraph.

Respectfully,

C. H. POTTER,
Assistant Adjutant-General.

HEADQUARTERS NORTHERN DEPARTMENT,
Columbus, Ohio, March 30, 1864.

Maj. Gen. S. P. HEINTZELMAN
(Care of Brigadier-General Terry), Sandusky:

The following has been received. I have telegraphed to General Carrington to send the veteran regiment by way of Mattoon:

INDIANAPOLIS, *March* 30, 1864.

Major-General HEINTZELMAN:

Lieut. Col. James Oakes, Fourth U. S. Cavalry, assistant provost-marshal, telegraphs to send by special train not less than 500 men to Mattoon immediately, with abundant ammunition. A veteran regiment is about starting for Cairo. If it can take that route, unless you order otherwise, I shall take the responsibility of stopping it there. There is not time to communicate with Washington. Please give your opinion.

In haste,

HENRY B. CARRINGTON,
Brigadier-General.

Respectfully,

C. H. POTTER,
Assistant Adjutant-General.

HEADQUARTERS NORTHERN DEPARTMENT,
Columbus, Ohio, March 30, 1864.

Major-General HEINTZELMAN
(*Care of Brigadier-General Terry*), *Sandusky, Ohio:*

The following dispatches have just been received. You will see by General Carrington's dispatches that the veteran regiment is en route:

CHARLESTON, ILL.,
March 30, 1864.

Major-General HEINTZELMAN:

Troubles continue. Forces of insurgents reported increasing. Have just asked for 500 men from Indianapolis. You had better come here in person. Answer me at Mattoon.

JAMES OAKES,
Lieutenant-Colonel, U. S. Army.

MATTOON, *March* 30, 1864.

Major-General HEINTZELMAN:

I arrived here this morning. Proceeded 10 a. m. to Charleston, and have just returned. In affray at Charleston, on 28th, 10 killed and some 15 wounded on both sides; have some 80 prisoners here. Much excitement here, and an attack expected to rescue prisoners; reliable [reports?] state insurgents collecting in large numbers.

JAMES OAKES,
Lieutenant-Colonel, U. S. Army.

INDIANAPOLIS, IND.,
March 30, 1864.

Major-General HEINTZELMAN:

The Forty-seventh Indiana, 560 strong, started within half an hour after the receipt of Colonel Oakes' telegram for Mattoon. Extra ammunition goes on passenger train.

HENRY B. CARRINGTON,
Brigadier-General.

Respectfully,

C. H. POTTER,
Assistant Adjutant-General.

WASHINGTON, *March* 30, 1864—11.37 a. m.

Lieutenant-General GRANT,
Culpeper, Va.:

Governor Bramlette asks to have that part of Kentucky west of the Tennessee River added to the Department of the Ohio. Do you approve the arrangement?

H. W. HALLECK,
Major-General, Chief of Staff.

SPECIAL ORDERS, } WAR DEPT., ADJT. GENERAL'S OFFICE.
    No. 132.   }   *Washington, March* 30, 1864.

*   *   *   *   *   *   *

25. Brig. Gen. N. C. McLean, U. S. Volunteers, is hereby relieved from duty as a member of the general court-martial convened by Special Orders, No. 4, January 4, 1864, from this office, and will report in person, without delay, to Major-General Schofield, U. S. Volunteers, commanding Department of the Ohio, for assignment to duty.

*   *   *   *   *   *   *

By order of the Secretary of War :

E. D. TOWNSEND,
Assistant Adjutant-General.

KNOXVILLE, *March* 31, 1864.
Major-General SHERMAN :

The rebels have all gone from Bull's Gap, and are now beyond Greeneville. They have destroyed the railroad bridge across Lick Creek and the trestle-work near the gap ; they have also broken up the railroad to some extent and carried off the telegraph wire. This is all positive and I take it is conclusive as to Longstreet's designs.

J. M. SCHOFIELD,
Major-General.

LOUDON, *March* 31, 1864.
Major-General SCHOFIELD :

Why don't you send down to this place the pontoon bridge you had at Knoxville ? It could save a vast amount of ferrying and hard work, and would pass your stores rapidly. It will be some time yet before the railroad bridge is done, and I advise you to have the boats and chesses floated down and made at once.

W. T. SHERMAN,
Major-General.

KNOXVILLE, *March* 31, 1864.
Major-General SHERMAN :

My pontoon bridge is not long enough to cross the river at Loudon. I will have it lengthened and put down there without delay.

J. M. SCHOFIELD,
Major-General.

CHATTANOOGA, TENN., *March* 31, 1864—9 p. m.
ADJUTANT-GENERAL U. S. ARMY :

Am just down from Knoxville. Longstreet is doubtless moving out of East Tennessee for Virginia. General Schofield will occupy Bull's Gap with infantry and fill up the valley with cavalry.

Forrest was badly worsted at Paducah, and is still between the Mississippi and Tennessee. I hope to catch him and break him up.

Veatch is near Purdy with infantry, and Grierson's cavalry is operating from Memphis.

I will go to Nashville to-morrow, where I can better direct the movement. All well here.

W. T. SHERMAN,
Major-General.

STRAWBERRY PLAINS, *March* 31, 1864—8 p. m.

Major-General SCHOFIELD, *Knoxville:*

A dispatch from General Wood just received says 3 deserters have come into his lines from Dibrell's (late Armstrong's) division cavalry. They report their division under marching orders, as they believe, for Georgia. They report that it was further understood that the infantry was moving up the railroad. They left on Tuesday. He has information from citizens, which he thinks reliable, that Vaughn's command had left Rogersville on Monday to move up the country and the infantry left Greeneville. Longstreet's headquarters at Bristol, but the reports agree that his army is en route for Virginia. These reports General Wood thinks as reliable as any of the country reports and reports from deserters which he gets.

J. D. COX,
Brigadier-General.

MOSSY CREEK, *March* 31, 1864.

General SCHOFIELD :

I have intelligence from scouts and citizens that rebels are certainly all gone, and now beyond Greeneville. They burnt the railroad bridge and the wagon bridge on Lick Creek ; have torn up the railroad generally, telegraph wire taken off, trestle burned at the gap. This is all reliable. I have men who have seen all I send you.

R. A. CRAWFORD,
Chief of Scouts.

MOSSY CREEK, *March* 31, 1864.

General SCHOFIELD, *Knoxville:*

Hascall's division will leave to-morrow morning accompanied by the cavalry, and unless you prefer I should remain here I shall go myself. We leave with three days' rations for the men and two days' rations for the animals. Will you direct the telegraph operator to follow us as close as possible ? If supplies can be pushed forward we can extend our reconnaissance accordingly.

GEO. STONEMAN,
Major-General.

HDQRS. TWENTY-NINTH MISSOURI VOLUNTEER INFANTRY,
Near Cottonville, Ala., March 31, 1864.

Capt. W. A. GORDON,
Asst. Adjt. Gen., First Div., Fifteenth Army Corps:

CAPTAIN : The enemy have made their appearance in considerable force at the mouth of Paint Rock this afternoon ; they also have been re-enforced at Guntersville.

I have information that a party intends to cross at Mrs. Johnson's wood-yard to-night. This party I shall try and capture.

It would be well to caution the commanding officer at Vienna to be very watchful, for I think they intend crossing there.

Captain, it would be well to send a detachment of infantry from Woodville to the junction of this and the Claysville road to-night so that they cannot interfere with our communication.

Send me all the mounted men you can, for I think there will be something to do soon.

Charlotte Rodden was over to this side last night and returned before daylight this morning.

Very respectfully, your obedient servant,

JOS. S. GAGE,
Lieut. Col. Twenty-ninth Missouri Vol. Inf., Comdg. Regt.

HEADQUARTERS DEPARTMENT OF THE CUMBERLAND,
Chattanooga, March 31, 1864.

General JOSEPH E. JOHNSTON, C. S. Army,
Commanding Army of Tennessee, Dalton, Ga.:

GENERAL: I have the honor herewith to inclose you a list* of the families fed by the U. S. commissary at this post, whose natural supporters are now serving in the armies of the Confederate States, and fighting against the Government which is saving them from starvation.

My object in so doing is to propose that you receive these families and provide for them, as they have no claims upon the United States but those prompted by considerations of humanity. Their friends and their sympathies are all with you and your cause, and I cannot but think that your own sense of justice will agree with me that it is your duty to receive these people within your lines and provide for their necessities.

Very respectfully, your obedient servant,

GEO. H. THOMAS,
Major-General, U. S. Volunteers, Commanding.

LOOKOUT VALLEY, *March 31, 1864—1.15 p. m.*

Brig. Gen. WILLIAM D. WHIPPLE,
Asst. Adjt. Gen., Army of the Cumberland:

General Howard reports that his scouts crossed Lookout Mountain, returning via McLemore's Cove. The squads of rebel cavalry reported in the gaps left Monday. They could hear of only three squads—one 40, one 14, and one 11 men. The two regiments of infantry sent out encamped last night at Paine's farm, south of Trenton.

JOSEPH HOOKER,
Major-General, Commanding.

HOOKER'S HEADQUARTERS, *March 31, 1864.*

Brigadier-General WHIPPLE, *Chief of Staff:*

Report just received from General Howard's scouts just returned from top of Lookout Mountain. Mr. Bateman, Union man, told them

---

* Not found.

that a brother of his wife, who is in Third Confederate Cavalry, was at his house with 50 men ; told her that they were hunting a good road to Bridgeport, and were sent to feel the strength of our forces at Wauhatchie, Whiteside's, and Bridgeport, but could not accomplish their mission, as we have too many cavalry in the valley, some citizens informing them that we had 200 mounted men. Said they would be back again in a few days and try to go farther ; stated they had 60,000 men at Dalton ; that the whole rebel army would probably soon cross Lookout Mountain. Mr. Bateman will be in Chattanooga to-morrow. Nothing further heard from reconnaissance.

JOSEPH HOOKER,
Major-General.

DETROIT, MICH.,
March 31, 1864.
Major-General BURNSIDE
(*Care Adjutant-General*):
Advance expected at Nicholasville to-day. Baggage all arrived at Covington, and odd detachments that came by Louisville have arrived, except 100 men, who are expected to-day. Fifty-first New York and most of the convalescents have left for Annapolis. The batteries have started. The paymaster will go to Annapolis and pay the troops there. Adjutant-General please forward to General Burnside.

O. B. WILLCOX,
Brigadier-General.

HEADQUARTERS DISTRICT OF KENTUCKY,
Louisville, March 31, 1864.
Maj. J. A. CAMPBELL,
Assistant Adjutant-General, Knoxville:
I will furnish General Sturgis with the battery and order four regiments of cavalry and four of infantry to report to him. I will visit Mount Sterling to-morrow or next day. Can concentrate 20,000 men here within twenty-four hours. Forrest crossed 100 men at Eddyville. Have captured a portion of them and think I will get the rest. Gun-boats guarding crossings. No trouble in that direction. In case of emergency I am ordered by General Sherman to use all troops passing through the State and those available in Indiana, Ohio, and Illinois.

S. G. BURBRIDGE,
Brigadier-General, Commanding.

CHATTANOOGA, *March* 31, 1864—9 p. m.
General WEBSTER :
I will come to Nashville to-morrow night. Telegraph to Cairo for General Brayman to give me by telegraph the most reliable news he can of Forrest.
I presume Grierson is after him from the direction of Memphis, and that Veatch has closed the door of escape by the head of the

Hatchie at Purdy. Notify General Brayman to hold on to some veteran regiments and move against Forrest from Columbus if he supposes him to be near Mayfield or Union City; also notify Hurlbut where Veatch is and that he must not let Forrest escape us at this time. Gun-boats should patrol the river well, although, if he does cross the Tennessee and Cumberland into Kentucky, he will have a hard road to travel. But I would prefer to keep him west of the Tennessee and north of the Hatchie.

> W. T. SHERMAN,
> *Major-General.*

NASHVILLE, *March* 31, 1864—12 midnight.
(Received April 3.)
Major-General HURLBUT,
 Memphis:

General Veatch must be now at or near Purdy. Do not let Forrest escape us this time. Is Grierson after him?

> J. D. WEBSTER,
> *Brigadier-General.*

NASHVILLE, *March* 31, 1864.
Brigadier-General WHIPPLE,
 Assistant Adjutant-General:

Following dispatch received:

FORT DONELSON, *March* 30, 1864.
General ROUSSEAU:

The gun-boat (23) has just returned from below Eddyville. I sent 50 men on boat, who scouted the country around, meeting with a party of our troops from Hopkinsville, who had captured 8 of a party of guerrillas. It is certain that Forrest is not on this side of the Tennessee. The rumors regarding his having crossed originated in a party of some 30 men crossing near Eddyville. This party will probably be captured. All is quiet at Smithland, and there is no force threatening any position on the Cumberland. Captain Fitch, of the Navy, reports Forrest near Columbus, on the Mississippi.

> O. L. BALDWIN,
> *Colonel Fifth Kentucky Cavalry, Commanding.*

> L. H. ROUSSEAU,
> *Major-General, Commanding.*

NASHVILLE, *March* 31, 1864.
General BRAYMAN,
 Cairo:

Send to General Sherman by telegraph the most reliable news as to Forrest's movements. Hold on to some veteran regiments and move against Forrest from Columbus if you have reason to believe him to be near Mayfield or Union City. Notify gun-boats to keep a sharp lookout to prevent Forrest crossing the river.

By order of Maj. Gen. W. T. Sherman:

> J. D. WEBSTER.

PADUCAH, *March* 31, 1864.

General BRAYMAN:

A citizen of Mayfield left there at midnight last and came in this evening; reports the enemy in camp, from 3 miles this side of there to Pryorsburg, 6 miles on the other side. Including these, he says, Faulkner has joined the command. They number 12,000, as they say; he thinks about 8,000. He is recommended as a man of truth.

S. G. HICKS,
Colonel, Commanding.

HEADQUARTERS SIXTEENTH ARMY CORPS,
Memphis, Tenn.,·March 31, 1864.

Brig. Gen. B. H. GRIERSON,
Commanding Cavalry Division:

GENERAL: In obedience to the peremptory order of Maj. Gen. W. T. Sherman, you will proceed as soon as practicable to follow and attack the Confederate force in West Tennessee.

Forrest succeeded, as I am just informed, in tapping the wires near Paducah and obtaining General Sherman's orders to General Veatch. He is therefore aware that General Veatch is ordered to land at Savannah and move toward Hatchie via Purdy. In this case he will either push his leading force boldly across the Tennessee or return upon his tracks, picking up his rear guards at Jackson and La Grange.

In the first event, you will meet only this rear guard and are strong enough to break it up and release the prisoners; in the other event, you will have your hands full.

Push your force rapidly toward La Grange and Saulsbury, and if possible in any way open communication with General Veatch.

Your orders from General Sherman are to attack at all hazards and follow the enemy wherever he goes. Large discretion must be given you, but a cavalry officer is rarely found fault with for dash.

Your obedient servant,

S. A. HURLBUT,
Major-General.

HDQRS. CAVALRY DIVISION, SIXTEENTH ARMY CORPS,
Memphis, Tenn., March 31, 1864.

Lieut. Col. T. H. HARRIS,
Assistant Adjutant-General:

COLONEL: In answer to your communication just received I have the honor to report as follows:

In the report of March 20 the Second Brigade, with the addition of the Third Illinois Cavalry, reported an aggregate of 2,264 serviceable horses.

Upon the appraisement of the horses of the Sixth, Seventh, and Third Illinois, there were received by the appraisers only 653 serviceable animals.

Out of nearly 600 horses turned over from the Second Iowa to Captain Eddy, and which were before reported serviceable, only 200 were returned to Capt. O. S. Coffin as serviceable.

The matter seems as follows :

March 20, horses reported serviceable.................................... 4,934
Reported by Second Brigade as serviceable and Third Illinois Cavalry... 2,264
Inspected, appraised, and received as serviceable.................... 853
                                                                    _____
    Difference.. 1,411

Reported by Colonel Hawkins, March 20............................ 295
Reported by First Alabama Cavalry, March 20...................... 270
Reported by Second Illinois Cavalry, now ordered down South....... 138
Reported by Sixth Tennessee Cavalry, March 20............... 1,118
When called upon to march, could only mount................ 600
                                                                    _____
    Difference.. 518

    Total loss... 2,632

    Remaining.. 2,302

The above is as near as possible a correct report of the condition of the command now, as compared with the report of March 20, 1864. Many of the horses reported as serviceable on March 20 were inferior, would have lasted a day or two on the march, and were retained by the regimental commanders in preference to entirely dismounting their commands, but when turned over to the quartermaster's department could not again be issued as serviceable. The only real error in the report was in the report of the Sixth Tennessee, which agreed with their report of that date, and was supposed to be correct until the command was ordered out a few days since, when Colonel Hurst stated that he should be able to take with him over 800 men, but upon coming into line found he had less than 600. This discrepancy I shall expect to be explained by Colonel Hurst. All the above changes have been made since the report of March 20.

In connection with this report I might again state that only about 1,500 horses have been received by this command during the last nine months.

Very respectfully, your obedient servant,
                                        B. H. GRIERSON,
                                          Brigadier-General.

                                SANDUSKY, *March* 31, 1864—9.30 a. m.
Brigadier-General CARRINGTON, *Indianapolis, Ind. :*

Support Colonel Oakes with all the force he may call for. This disturbance must be put down at once. I will be in Columbus in the morning.

                                        S. P. HEINTZELMAN,
                                          Major-General.

                                SANDUSKY, OHIO, *March* 31, 1864.
Lieutenant-Colonel OAKES, *Mattoon, Ill. :*

Send your prisoners under sufficient guard to where there will be no danger of rescue. Call on Springfield and Indianapolis for what force is necessary. I will be back in Columbus by morning.

                                        S. P. HEINTZELMAN,
                                          Major-General, Commanding.

WAR DEPARTMENT, CAVALRY BUREAU,
Washington, D. C., March 31, 1864.

Maj. Gen. W. T. SHERMAN,
   Commanding Military Division of the Mississippi:

GENERAL: The Secretary of War having approved the recommendation of Capt. W. R. Price, an officer of this Bureau sent to the Western armies as a special inspector, to the effect that no more horses be furnished to Tennessee regiments until all other demands are supplied, I have the honor to inform you that orders in accordance with this approval have been issued to the quartermaster's department of this Bureau. If, however, you should deem it necessary to mount any of these regiments, by communicating the fact to the Bureau an arrangement will be made at once to carry out your views.

   Very respectfully, your obedient servant,
                    J. H. WILSON,
             Brigadier-General, in Charge.

SPECIAL ORDERS, }   HDQRS. SIXTEENTH ARMY CORPS,
   No. 79.   }   *Memphis, Tenn., March* 31, 1864.

*   *   *   *   *   *   *

V. In the case of John Hallum, purporting to be an attorney-at-law, he is convicted of surreptitiously procuring passes and exemptions, and disposing of the same for large sums of money. The fact of his belonging to an honorable profession enhances his guilt.

The flimsy pretense that as an attorney-at-law he had a right to "charge his clients" for services is too transparent a subterfuge to avail him. A lawyer has the right to fees for professional services. It is no part of the practice of the law to procure fraudulent passes and make merchandise of them.

It is a disgrace to the profession, and would only be indulged in by an unscrupulous pettifogger regardless of reputation and seeking to make money by any dishonorable trick. It is evident that this man knew that the passes in question were obtained by some underhand practice, probably by his confederate in swindling, Cady. No doubt, too, exists that by reason of these base practices suspicion has been thrown in the public mind upon the officers of the Government as participants in this nefarious traffic.

An example is required in this community, and Mr. Hallum supplies the subject.

It is ordered that John Hallum pay a fine to the United States of $1,000, that he be confined sixty days at Fort Pickering, and that he be forever prohibited from directly or indirectly appearing as attorney in any court organized by military authority, and that at the expiration of the sixty days of imprisonment, if the fine be not paid, he be imprisoned until the same is paid.

It is further ordered that a copy of this order be sent to the clerk of the United States court at Memphis, to be laid before the judge thereof at the next sitting, with the request that the name of said John Hallum be struck from the roll of attorneys.

*   *   *   *   *   *   *

VII. J. W. Sharp, attorney-at-law, has been arraigned and tried for the offense of smuggling.

The proof shows conclusively that he bribed sentinels on duty to pass out contraband goods, among which were found eighteen pairs cavalry boots.

The evidence is irresistible, and to the ordinary guilt of smuggling is added the crime of supplying the enemy with what they most need. The defense sets up the plea that the evidence of colored persons cannot be received. In this the counsel betrays great ignorance. The testimony of negroes has been always received in courts-martial, both in the Army and Navy. Military courts are governed by military law, and there is no distinction as to competency made in such courts by reason of color. The statutes of Tennessee are in abridgment of the common law, civil and military, and not binding upon military courts.

All persons who understand the sanctity of an oath are competent witnesses. The testimony was properly admitted and the guilt is proven.

It is therefore ordered that J. W. Sharp pay a fine of $1,000 to the United States, that he be imprisoned in the military prison at Alton for three years and until the fine is paid. It is further ordered that the wagon and team of the witness Dickerson be restored to him.

    *   *   *   *   *   *   *

By order of Maj. Gen. S. A. Hurlbut :

                              T. H. HARRIS,
                          Assistant Adjutant-General.

Abstract from return of the Department of the Cumberland, Maj. Gen. George H. Thomas, U. S. Army, commanding, for the month of March, 1864.

Command.	Present for duty.		Aggregate present.	Aggregate present and absent.	Pieces of artillery.		Headquarters.
	Officers.	Men.			Heavy.	Field.	
General headquarters.............	71	751	1,004	1,192	....	....	Chattanooga, Tenn.
Fourth Army Corps (Granger) :							
Headquarters.................	6	....	6	8	......	......	Loudon, Tenn.
First Division (Stanley).........	325	6,136	7,566	12,757	....	12	Blue Springs, Tenn.
Second Division (Wagner)	204	3,355	4,157	7,528	....	6	Loudon, Tenn.
Third Division (Wood) ..:......	321	6,218	7,161	15,565	....	6	Powder Spring Gap, Tenn.
Total Fourth Army Corps...	856	15,759	18,890	35,858	....	24	
Hooker's command :							
Headquarters	9	48	57	80	....	......	Lookout Valley, Tenn.
Eleventh Army Corps (Howard):							
Headquarters	9	....	9	10	....	......	Lookout Valley, Tenn.
First Division (Ward).........	176	4,592	5,511	6,474	....	12	Wauhatchie, Tenn.
Second Division (Steinwehr)...	147	2,579	3,548	5,495	....	12	Lookout Valley, Tenn.
Third Division (Tyndale)	151	3,072	3,833	6,440	....	12	Shellmound, Tenn.
Total Eleventh Army Corps.	483	10,243	12,901	18,419	....	36	
Twelfth Army Corps (Slocum) :							
Headquarters	9	....	9	10	....	......	Tullahoma, Tenn.
First Division (Williams)	201	4,505	5,164	7,564	....	14	Do.
Second Division (Geary)......	186	4,469	5,389	7,981	....	10	Bridgeport, Ala,
Total Twelfth Army Corps ..	396	8,974	10,562	15,555	....	24	
Total Hooker's command ...	888	19,265	23,520	34,054	....	60	

Abstract from return of the Department of the Cumberland, &c.—Continued.

Command.	Present for duty.		Aggregate present.	Aggregate present and absent.	Pieces of artillery.		Headquarters.
	Officers.	Men.			Heavy.	Field.	
Fourteenth Army Corps (Palmer):							
Headquarters	4	......	4	4	....	......	Chattanooga, Tenn.
First Division (Johnson).........	218	6,043	7,310	14,120	....	12	Graysville, Ga.
Second Division (Davis)	241	6,180	7,306	11,342	....	12	Near Rossville, Ga.
Third Division (Baird)..........	264	6,494	7,651	13,064	....	12	Ringgold, Ga.
Total Fourteenth Army Corps.	727	18,717	22,271	38,530	....	36	
Cavalry Corps (Elliott):							
Headquarters	7	......	7	8	....	......	Chattanooga, Tenn.
First Division...................	184	3,818	4,708	7,506	....	6	Cleveland, Tenn.
Second Division (K. Garrard)....	343	7,429	8,991	12,414	....	......	Huntsville, Ala.
Detachments..................	89	2,261	2,585	3,584	....	......	
Total Cavalry Corps	623	13,508	16,291	23,602	....	6	
Artillery Reserve (Brannan):							
Headquarters	4	4	8	10	....	......	Chattanooga, Tenn.
Bridgeport, Ala. (Lieutenant-Colonel Lawrence).	5	174	206	310	....	8	
Charleston, Tenn. (Captain Beebe).	3	97	112	154	....	4	
Total Artillery Reserve	12	275	326	474	....	12	
Engineer troops:							
Engineer Brigade (Stanley)	36	1,185	1,496	2,572	.\..	......	Chattanooga, Tenn.
Pioneer Brigade (Buell)	36	928	1,344	2,261	....	......	Do.
Engineer Regiment (Innes)	39	1,184	1,636	1,837	....	......	Bridgeport, Ala.
Total engineer troops.......	111	3,297	4,476	6,670	....	......	
Post of Chattanooga (Steedman)...	112	3,693	4,439	7,176	12	79	
District of Nashville (Rousseau):							
Headquarters	3	......	3	3	....	......	Nashville, Tenn.
Clarksville (A. A. Smith)........	32	669	1,198	1,510	....	6	
Columbia (Major McFall)	2	118	125	141	4	......	
Fort Donelson (Brott)	6	260	469	499	....	4	
Gallatin (Paine).................	18	405	487	1,046	....	6	
Murfreesborough (Van Cleve) ...	99	2,687	3,270	3,758	....	......	
Nashville (Granger)	161	4,051	5,167	6,693	23	54	
Nashville and Northwestern Railroad (Gillem).	93	1,715	2,769	3,239	....	6	
Total District of Nashville ..	414	9,905	13,488	16,889	....	......	
Grand total.................	3,814	85,170	104,705	164,445	39	203	

Abstract from returns of the Department of the Ohio, Maj. Gen. John M. Schofield, U. S. Army, commanding, for the month of March, 1864.

Command.	Present for duty.		Aggregate present.	Aggregate present and absent.	Pieces of artillery.		Headquarters.
	Officers.	Men.			Heavy.	Field.	
General headquarters	16	....	16	16	....	......	In the field.
Ninth Army Corps (Willcox):							
Headquarters	10	39	95	138	....	......	En route to Annapolis, Md.
First Division (Ferrero)	112	2,361	2,748	5,024	....	......	
Second Division (Col. Z. R. Bliss).	86	1,793	2,181	3,530	....	......	
Total Ninth Army Corps......	208	4,233	5,024	8,692	....	......	

Abstract from returns of the Department of the Ohio, &c.—Continued.

Command.	Present for duty. Officers.	Present for duty. Men.	Aggregate present.	Aggregate present and absent.	Pieces of artillery. Heavy.	Pieces of artillery. Field.	Headquarters.
Twenty-third Army Corps (Stoneman):							
Headquarters	7	....	7	7	....	......	Mossy Creek, Tenn.
District of Kentucky (Burbridge): a							
Headquarters	4	....	4	4	....	......	Louisville, Ky.
Eastern Kentucky (Gallup)....	41	1,096	1,338	1,924	...	8	Do.
Northern Central Kentucky (H. G. Gibson).	118	2,309	3,552	4,330	3	28	Camp Nelson, Ky.
Southern Central Kentucky (Hobson).	101	1,966	2,705	3,273	4	33	Cave City, Ky.
Southwestern Kentucky (Maxwell).	110	2,343	2,808	3,102	30	......	Bowling Green, Ky.
Burnside Point, Ky. (Colonel Eve).	25	522	673	1,038	....	6	
Louisville, Ky	14	205	463	739	•	4	
Near Covington, Ky...........	1	79	96	101	....	......	
Total District of Kentucky..	414	8,520	11,639	14,511	37	79	
Second Division (Judah)........	125	3,260	3,954	6,871	....	......	Mossy Creek, Tenn.
Third Division (J. W. Reilly).....	103	2,691	3,136	4,393	....	......	Do.
Detachments....................	12	264	335	616	....	......	Do.
General Manson and staff......	3	....	3	3	....	......	Knoxville, Tenn.
Total Twenty-third Corps.....	664	14,735	19,074	26,401	37	79	
Cavalry Corps (Sturgis)	205	5,306	6,842	10,791	.....	....	Paris, Ky.
District of the Clinch (T. T. Garrard).	81	1,417	1,782	2,478	....	21	Cumberland Gap, Tenn.
Defenses of Knoxville (Tillson)......	123	3,507	4,579	5,613	...	10	
Newport Barracks, Ky. (Sanderson).	3	172	219	224	...	......	
Grand total.....	1,300	29,370	37,536	54,215	37	110	
Grand total according to monthly return of the department.	1,092	25,102	32,602	45,522	....	......	

a Or First Division, Twenty-third Army Corps.

Abstract from returns of the Department of the Tennessee, Maj. Gen. James B. McPherson, U. S. Army, commanding, for the month of March, 1864.

Command.	Present for duty. Officers.	Present for duty. Men.	Aggregate present.	Aggregate present and absent.	Pieces of artillery. Heavy.	Pieces of artillery. Field.	Headquarters.
General headquarters	7	14	21	31	....	......	Huntsville, Ala.
Fifteenth Army Corps (Logan):							
Headquarters	8	16	24	34	....	......	Huntsville, Ala.
First Division (Osterhaus)......	182	3,265	4,384	7,523	....	14	Woodville, Ala.
Second Division (M. L. Smith)....	157	2,995	3,688	7,902	....	16	Larkinsville, Ala.
Third Division (John E. Smith) ..	153	3,161	3,959	6,886	....	14	Huntsville, Ala.
Fourth Division (Harrow)	280	5,504	6,756	8,318	....	14	Scottsborough, Ala.
Cavalry (Col. T. T. Heath)........	22	583	721	961	....	......	Huntsville, Ala.
Total Fifteenth Army Corps.	802	15,524	19,477	31,714	....	58	

Abstract from returns of the Department of the Tennessee, &c.—Continued.

Command.	Present for duty.		Aggregate present.	Aggregate present and absent.	Pieces of artillery.		Headquarters.
	Officers.	Men.			Heavy.	Field.	
Sixteenth Army Corps (Hurlbut):							
Headquarters	9	....	9	9	....	......	Memphis, Tenn.
Left Wing (Dodge):							
Headquarters	13	16		30	....	......	Athens, Ala.
Second Division (Sweeny)	252	6,031	7,	9,631	....	22	Pulaski, Tenn.
Fourth Division (Veatch)......	113	3,045	3, 30	4,666	....	10	Purdy, Tenn.
Colored Troops (Col. W. Camp-bell).	45	1,196	1, 554	1,700	....	......	Pulaski, Tenn.
Cavalry (Lieut. Col. T. P. Cook).	20	640	813	984	....	......	Athens, Ala.
Total Left Wing............	443	10,928	13,787	17,011	....	32	
Detachment Fourth Division (Col. J. H. Howe).	56	1,303	1,536	2,415	....	4	Williams' Landing, Tenn.
Cavalry Division (Grierson)......	135	2,752	5,629	9,166	....	4	Memphis, Tenn.
District of Cairo (Brayman):							
Cairo, Ill......................	26	288	496	744	8	......	
Columbus, Ky. (Colonel Law-rence).	47	1,068	1,499	1,622	....	8	
Island No. 10 (Captain Ekings).	4	170	265	279	7	1	
Paducah, Ky. (Hicks)	23	342	520	555	....	......	
Total District of Cairo......	100	1,868	2,780	3,200	15	9	
District of Memphis (Buckland):							
Fort Pickering (Col. Kappner).	67	2,832	4,062	5,475	71	4	
Fort Pillow (Major Bradford)..	9	262	329	466	....	2	
Memphis	197	4,184	5,373	6,805	....	18	
Total District of Memphis...	273	7,278	9,764	12,746	71	24	
Total Sixteenth Army Corps *a*	1,016	24,129	33,525	44,547	86	73	
Seventeenth Army Corps:							
Headquarters	22	62	124	133	....	......	Vicksburg, Miss.
First Division (Dennis)	103	2,527	3,260	8,561	....	18	In and about Vicksburg.
Third Division (Maltby)	63	2,050	2,592	9,052	....	18	Vicksburg, Miss.
Fourth Division (Crocker)	72	2,488	2,976	8,620	....	20	Near Vicksburg.
Cavalry (Lieut. Col. Peters)	42	1,417	1,812	4,482	....	2	Clear Creek, Miss.
Colored Troops (Hawkins)......	265	4,989	6,755	7,361	....	13	Vicksburg, Miss., and Goodrich's Landing, La.
Mississippi Marine Brigade (Ellet)	34	722	985	1,233	....	......	
Total Seventeenth Army Corps. *b*	601	14,255	18,513	39,442	....	71	
Grand total.................	2,426	53,922	71,536	115,734	86	202	
Grand total according to monthly return of the department.	2,997	63,421	80,352	132,494	72	202	

a Exclusive of First and Third Divisions, absent in the Red River campaign.
b Exclusive of detachment absent in the Red River campaign.

Organization of the artillery of the Army of the Cumberland, April 1, 1864.

Brig. Gen. JOHN M. BRANNAN, Chief of Artillery, Department of the Cumberland.

Maj. JOHN MENDENHALL, Assistant Chief of Artillery, Department of the Cumberland.

Capt. LOUIS J. LAMBERT, Assistant Adjutant-General.
Capt. GEORGE S. ROPER, Commissary of Subsistence.
Surg. PETER J. A. CLEARY, Medical Director.
Lieut. EBEN P. STURGES, Ordnance Officer.
Lieut. WEBSTER J. COLBURN, Acting Assistant Quartermaster.

FOURTH ARMY CORPS.

First Division.

Capt. PETER SIMONSON, Chief of Artillery.

5th Indiana Battery, Capt. Peter Simonson.
B, Independent Pennsylvania, Capt. Samuel M. McDowell.

Second Division.

Capt. WARREN P. EDGARTON, Chief of Artillery.

G, 1st Missouri, First Lieut. Lorenzo D. Immell.
M, 1st Illinois, Capt. George W. Spencer.

Third Division.

Capt. CULLEN BRADLEY, Chief of Artillery.

6th Ohio Battery, Capt. Cullen Bradley.
Bridges' (Illinois) Battery, Capt. Lyman Bridges.

ELEVENTH ARMY CORPS.

Maj. THOMAS W. OSBORN, Chief of Artillery.

First Division.

I, 2d Illinois Artillery, Capt. Charles M. Barnett.
20th Indiana Battery, First Lieut. John I. Morris.

Second Division.

I, 1st New York, Capt. Michael Wiedrich.
C, 1st Ohio, Capt. Marco B. Gary.

Third Division.

13th New York Independent, Capt. William Wheeler.
I, 1st Michigan Artillery, Capt. Luther R. Smith.

TWELFTH ARMY CORPS.

First Division.

9th Ohio Battery, Capt. Harrison B. York.
M, 1st New York Artillery. Capt. John D. Woodbury.

Second Division.

B, 1st Ohio, Capt. Norman A. Baldwin.
E, Independent Pennsylvania, First Lieut. James D. McGill.

FOURTEENTH ARMY CORPS.

Maj. CHARLES HOUGHTALING, Chief of Artillery.

First Division.

Capt. LUCIUS H. DRURY, Chief of Artillery.

A, 1st Michigan Artillery, Capt. Francis E. Hale.
C, 1st Illinois Artillery, Capt. Mark H. Prescott.

Second Division.

Capt. WILLIAM A. HOTCHKISS, Chief of Artillery.

2d Minnesota Battery, Lieut. Richard L. Dawley.
5th Wisconsin Battery, Capt. George Q. Gardner.

Third Division.

Capt. GEORGE R. SWALLOW, Chief of Artillery.

7th Indiana, Lieut. Otho H. Morgan.
19th Indiana, Capt. Samuel J. Harris.

RESERVE ARTILLERY.

Col. JAMES BARNETT, commanding.

First Division.	Second Division.
Capt. EDMUND C. BAINBRIDGE, 5th Artillery, commanding.	Maj. JOHN J. ELY, commanding.
	A, 1st Ohio Volunteer Artillery, Capt. Wilbur F. Goodspeed.
F, 4th U. S. Artillery, First Lieut. Edward D. Muhlenberg.	F, 1st Ohio Volunteer Artillery, Capt. Daniel T. Cockerill.
G, 4th U. S. Artillery, Second Lieut. Christopher F. Merkle.	G, 1st Ohio Volunteer Artillery, Capt. Alexander Marshall.
H, 4th U. S. Artillery, First Lieut. Harry C. Cushing.	M, 1st Ohio Volunteer Artillery, Capt. Frederick Schultz.
M, 4th U. S. Artillery, First Lieut. George W. Dresser.	18th Ohio Battery, Capt. Charles C. Aleshire.
H, 5th U. S. Artillery, Capt. Francis L. Guenther.	1st Kentucky Battery, Capt. Theodore S. Thomasson.
K, 5th U. S. Artillery, First Lieut. David H. Kenzie.	

GARRISON ARTILLERY.

Station and command.	Effective force.		
	Officers.	Men.	Total.
Chattanooga, Tenn. :			
4th Indiana, Lieut. Henry J. Willits................................	2	127	129
8th Indiana, Capt. George Estep a..........................	3	66	69
11th Indiana, Capt. Arnold Sutermeister.......................	2	110	112
3d Wisconsin, Capt. Lucius H. Drury........................	3	97	100
20th Ohio, First Lieut. Charles F. Nitschelm b	3	148	151
I, 1st Ohio, Lieut. William Dammert........................	4	110	114
C, 1st Wisconsin Heavy Artillery, Capt. John R. Davies...............	4	123	127
10th Indiana, Capt. William A. Naylor	3	56	59
K, 1st Michigan, Capt. John C. Schuetz....................	2	119	121
Total	26	956	982
Nashville, Capt. James E. White, chief of artillery :			
12th Indiana, Lieut. James A. Dunwoody	3	92	95
E, 1st Michigan, Capt. John J. Ely b ....:..................	2	76	78
D, 1st Tennessee Artillery, Capt. David R. Young....................	4	90	94
I, 4th U. S. Artillery, Lieut. Frank G. Smith	3	82	85
Total	12	340	352
Fort Donelson :			
C, 2d Illinois, Capt. James P. Flood	1	77	78
Clarksville :			
H, 2d Illinois, Capt. Henry C. Whittemore....................			
Bridgeport, Lieut. Col. Walker E. Lawrence, 1st Ohio Volunteer Artillery, commanding :			
E, 1st Ohio Volunteer Artillery, Lieut. Albert G. Ransom	3	114	117
K, 1st Ohio Volunteer Artillery, Capt. Lewis Heckman	2	71	73
Total	5	185	190
Murfreesborough, Maj. Charles Houghtaling, 1st Illinois Artillery, commanding :	•		
D, 1st Michigan Artillery. Lieut. Henry B. Corbin....................	3	125	128
8th Wisconsin, Capt. Henry E. Stiles.........................	2	91	93
12th Ohio Independent, Capt. Aaron C. Johnson..................	5	122	127
Total	10	338	348

a Temporarily assigned ; does not belong to permanent garrison.
b Mounted.

DETACHED BATTERIES.

Chicago Board of Trade, Lieut. George I. Robinson, commanding.
18th Indiana, Capt. Eli Lilly, commanding.
A, 1st Tennessee, Lieut. Albert F. Beach, La Vergne.
10th Wisconsin, Capt. Yates V. Beebe, Calhoun.
21st Indiana, Capt. William W. Andrew, Columbia.
13th Indiana, Capt. Benjamin S. Nicklin, Gallatin.
2d Kentucky, Capt. John M. Hewett, Elk River.

CHATTANOOGA, *April* 1, 1864.

General SCHOFIELD, *Knoxville, Tenn.* :

The following telegram just received, viz :

MARCH 31, 1864.

I would destroy the railroad as far east of Knoxville as possible. It is a good plan to concentrate all the forces you can when fighting is expected, and make all other preparations necessary to hold defensible for the smallest possible number of troops.

U. S. GRANT,
Lieutenant-General.

Which the general directs me to forward for your information and guidance, but if the enemy has already destroyed the railroad you can defer doing your part until some future time, answering the general's plan better.

L. M. DAYTON,
Aide-de-Camp.

CHATTANOOGA, *April* 1, 1864.

Major-General SCHOFIELD, *Knoxville* :

Occupy Bull's Gap with infantry, and feel the rear of the retiring enemy with cavalry, merely to develop his design. You cannot fight him except at great disadvantage, and I don't want you to be drawn too far up the valley now. With you at Bull's Gap, I do not believe he would venture up either the road by Pound Gap or up the French Broad. I construe your message to mean that Longstreet is moving to Virginia. If so, we cannot prevent it, and must let him go ; only I want to know exactly what kind of a force he leaves to watch you. If on his retrograde he breaks the railroad, you should not, but on the contrary you should seem to be following slowly. In the mean time make all the preliminary arrangements for the plan I indicated. As to the pontoon bridge at Loudon, exercise your own judgment. It is very easy to arrange a draw in a pontoon bridge, and if it be difficult to place the bridge above the stone piers you can put your boats below, where the rebel pontoon bridge was when I first went to Loudon.

Nothing of interest here. I go to Nashville to-morrow.

W. T. SHERMAN,
Major-General.

HDQRS. FIRST DIVISION, FIFTEENTH ARMY CORPS,
Woodville, Ala., April 1, 1864.

Maj. R. R. TOWNES,
Assistant Adjutant-General, Fifteenth Army Corps :

MAJOR : The rebel Lieutenant and Adjutant R. T. Daniel states that he had information that Clanton's brigade arrived at the Tennessee River. The brigade consists of Sixth and Seventh Regiments, one battalion of Alabama cavalry, one battery of field pieces, and they are to re-enforce Lieutenant-Colonel Mead's Alabama rangers and Woodward's battalion of cavalry, who are charged with picketing and guarding the river from Decatur to Guntersville.

My commanders at Vienna and at Cottonville report considerable commotion of the rebel troops on the south side of the river. They made, however, no demonstration toward crossing.

With a view to support Vienna or Cottonville promptly, I stationed a detachment of infantry on the fork of the road, about 11 miles south of here, with orders to co-operate in case of an attack.

Two distinct camps of rebel troops opposite mouth of Paint Rock River, and at Johnson's wood-yard, are in cannon range of our pickets on the river. We ought to give them the benefit of a shelling.

I am, major, very respectfully, your obedient servant,

P. J. OSTERHAUS,
Brigadier-General of Volunteers.

HEADQUARTERS FIFTEENTH ARMY CORPS,
Huntsville, Ala., April 1, 1864.

Brig. Gen. P. J. OSTERHAUS,
Woodville :

Your dispatch received. Enemy withdrawn from opposite Whitesburg yesterday; perhaps have all concentrated at the point mentioned by you. Please take steps at once to prevent their crossing and surprising any forces near the river. If necessary, send such re-enforcements as will be ample for the protection of any parties we may have near the river.

JOHN A. LOGAN,
Major-General.

NASHVILLE, *April* 1, 1864.

Major-General SHERMAN,
On train :

I have just received the following from the commanding officer at Columbia. He states that he has received a communication from Major Murphy, commanding at Clifton, Tenn., dated March 31, 7 p. m., to the effect that he learns from his scouts that Forrest is yet between Jackson and Paducah. He may make a strike at Columbus and perhaps cross the river between Clifton and Reynoldsburg. Five hundred of his men were to be at Jackson last night, the 30th.

The information Murphy has leads him to believe that Forrest will try and get in with Morgan in Kentucky, or in the neighborhood of Nashville; at least, that is what his officers say. There is also another rumor of his making another dash on Paducah. His opinion is he will cross to this side.

This is in substance the dispatch of Major Murphy.

R. M. SAWYER,
Assistant Adjutant-General.

HEADQUARTERS DISTRICT OF KENTUCKY,
Louisville, April 1, 1864.
Major-General SHERMAN,
Nashville, Tenn. :

My last account from Forrest is that he is near Mayfield, Ky. About 100 of his men crossed the Cumberland and were captured or dispersed. General Sturgis dispatches that about 300 rebel cavalry have appeared in his front; he has scouts out looking after them. I will keep you advised.

S. G. BURBRIDGE,
Brigadier-General.

———

NASHVILLE, *April 1, 1864.*
COMMANDING OFFICERS,
Paducah, Cairo, and Columbus:

A rumor reached this place that Forrest, re-enforced by 1,500 men, under McCulloch, who passed through La Grange on the 29th, is somewhere between Paducah and Jackson, meditating another attack on Paducah or dash on Columbus. Another rumor is that he is preparing to cross the Tennessee River. Send word to gun-boats to be on the alert up Tennessee River.

What is your latest information ? Answer.

By order of Major-General Sherman :

R. M. SAWYER,
Assistant Adjutant-General.

———

HEADQUARTERS SIXTEENTH ARMY CORPS,
Memphis, Tenn., April 1, 1864.
Maj. Gen. W. T. SHERMAN,
Comdg. Mil. Div. of the Mississippi, Nashville, Tenn.:

Forrest was in Jackson on the 29th March ; whether with a view to permanent occupation or in retreat for Mississippi, I cannot tell. Grierson is out with his entire effective force. Lee is at Canton, and Loring is reported there. I do not think much impression can be made with the movable force from this place until the return of the Red River expedition. I am satisfied that Forrest was severely crippled in the Paducah affair, and suffered very heavy loss. He tapped the wires and obtained dispatch ordering Veatch to Savannah. His whole movement and the state of the country indicate retreat.

S. A. HURLBUT,
Major-General.

———

CAIRO, *April 1, 1864.*
Col. S. G. HICKS,
Paducah :

Where is the enemy ? Advancing or retreating ? I think their main force is south of Mayfield, and the country above is overrun by their plunderers. Are you in need of help ?

M. BRAYMAN,
Brigadier-General, Commanding.

CAIRO, ILL., *April* 1, 1864.

Brig. Gen. J. D. WEBSTER,
Chief of General Sherman's Staff, Nashville, Tenn. :

Forrest's force is increased, and is vibrating between Paducah and Columbus, threatening both, as well as Mound City and Cairo. His present force at least 8,000. My force is small but active. The Thirty-seventh Illinois is here for New Orleans, and will remain. If Colonel Hicks is not threatened I will go to Columbus and try to find the enemy, if I can with certainty keep between them and the river.

M. BRAYMAN,
Brigadier-General, Commanding.

PADUCAH, KY., *April* 1, 1864.

Brigadier-General BRAYMAN :

I have relieved First Alabama Cavalry from duty here, and ordered them to proceed in accordance with previous order. I have no force here now but my original command. Forrest has a large force at Mayfield. Can you send me more troops ?

S. G. HICKS,
Colonel, Commanding.

PADUCAH, *April* 1, 1864.

General M. BRAYMAN :

I have 665 all told for duty—all worn out by fatigue and loss of sleep. Forrest can come to me in four hours. If possible, I want more men to give these rest and make me more secure.

S. G. HICKS,
Colonel, Commanding.

MOUND CITY, *April* 1, 1864.

Capt. J. H. ODLIN, *Assistant Adjutant-General :*

Went to Johnson County ; captured the commander of the Copperhead regiment ; killed 2 men ; some 30 shots fired. They have 300 men in regiment; all called citizens. A rebel colonel escaped me whom I hoped to capture ; has been engineering raising of regiment to support Forrest if he succeeded in crossing river. Sent a man across river up above Caledonia ; found only 25 of Forrest's men there, engaged in stealing [horses] and mules. No force opposite us.

W. ODLIN,
Captain.

HEADQUARTERS SIXTEENTH ARMY CORPS,
Memphis, Tenn., April 1, 1864.

Maj. R. M. SAWYER,
Asst. Adjt. Gen., Mil. Div. of the Mississippi :

SIR : I have the honor to report, for the information of the major-general commanding, that the whole active force under command of Major-General Forrest, C. S. Army, consisting of about 5,000 to 6,000 men, is now north of the line of the Memphis and Charleston Railroad, Forrest himself having returned to Jackson, Tenn., on the 29th ultimo. This movement on the part of the enemy was unques_ tionably timed on accurate information of the situation of the cavalry force of this corps.

Pursuant to orders from Washington, approved by the major-general commanding, every effort has been made to push forward the re-enlistment of veteran volunteers, and every regiment of cavalry and infantry entitled to re-enlist in this corps has done so. The result is that fragments of non-veterans of the several regiments are left. This result, of course to be expected, limits the efficiency of the cavalry, but even without this a far more stringent difficulty arises from the impossibility of procuring horses. There are, as General Grierson reports, only 2,200 cavalry horses in his command, which of course controls the number of men to be employed in this service. Estimates were sent on from this office to Washington, and to the chief of cavalry of the department, in September, for 5,000 horses, to be furnished beween 1st October and 1st January. None have arrived excepting a few taken up by General W. S. Smith on his late expedition.

The Third Michigan Cavalry is reported at Saint Louis, 1,300, waiting horses and transportation. The Seventh Kansas either is now at Saint Louis or will be in a day or two.

It is utterly useless to follow this marauding force with infantry, as they are all mounted, even if there were disposable infantry here.

The people of West Tennessee and Kentucky are overwhelmingly disloyal, if any clue to men's intentions can be had from their acts ; they readily report all movements of our troops, and rarely furnish any news of the enemy.

I consider the damage done to Paducah as a proper lesson to that place and its vicinity.

General Grierson has orders sent by telegraph from Major-General Sherman to attack, and will do so, but has not, in my judgment, the force to make serious impression. I gather from prisoners and others that the intent of the movement was to seize Paducah and cross, if possible, to destroy Mound City and Cairo. Connected with this was the belief of a rising in Kentucky, in which case Forrest was to cross the Tennessee and operate in Kentucky east of the river. But for the cowardly surrender of Union City by Colonel Hawkins no injury would have been inflicted by this raid upon any part of the country in which the United States have any considerable interest. I was instructed by Major-General Sherman not to attempt anything further than to hold the points on the river until the return of the veterans and of the detached forces now in the field should give a more able force, to be concentrated near Memphis until these events occur. This force is crippled for any active offensive operations, and however much I may chafe under these disabilities, I cannot change the state of affairs.

I have the honor to be, your obedient servant,

S. A. HURLBUT,
Major-General.

———

CHATTANOOGA, *April* 1, 1864.

General McPHERSON, *Huntsville :*

The general desires you to order Corse to report to him at Nashville; also learn from Woods where Warner, Seventy-sixth Ohio Volunteer Infantry, is, and if with his regiment order him to report likewise.

DAYTON.

HEADQUARTERS NORTHERN DEPARTMENT,
Columbus, Ohio, April 1, 1864.   (Received 7 p. m.)

General H. W. HALLECK,
    Chief of Staff, Washington:

All is quiet at Mattoon, Ill. I believe that the disturbances have been suppressed.

S. P. HEINTZELMAN,
Major-General.

HEADQUARTERS NORTHERN DEPARTMENT,
Columbus, Ohio, April 1, 1864.

Maj. Gen. H. W. HALLECK,
    Chief of Staff, Washington:

GENERAL : In compliance with your telegram of the 29th March, I proceeded to Sandusky and made a personal inspection of Johnson's Island with reference to the removal of part or the whole of General Shaler's brigade for return to the Army of the Potomac. I am of the opinion that only the One hundred and twenty-second New York, Lieutenant-Colonel Dwight, Sixty-seventh New York, Colonel Cross, and Sixty-fifth New York, Colonel Hamblin, can be spared to return to the Army of the Potomac.

The heavy artillery furnishes no guards for prisoners, and the Twenty-fourth Indiana Battery is encamped near Sandusky, and has all it can do to care for its horses and the necessary drills. This leaves Colonel Bassett's regiment, Eighty-second Pennsylvania Volunteers, 425 ; Colonel Glenn's regiment, Twenty-third Pennsylvania Volunteers, 474 ; Colonel Hill's regiment, One hundred and twenty-eighth Ohio Volunteers, 735 ; enlisted men present for duty, 1,634.

Out of this force there has to be detailed a daily guard of 306 men for the prisoners and pickets and 100 men for fatigue, as well as the regimental guards and fatigues. The commanding officers are unanimously of the opinion that this is as small a guard as can be relied upon to cover the extensive prison inclosure. In this opinion I fully concur.

An additional objection to any further reduction is that a large portion of Colonel Hill's One hundred and twenty-eighth Ohio is composed of recruits who will not be so reliable as the old soldiers.

This leaves but little provision to repel an attack from without, of which, however, I think there is but little danger.

I have at last been able to settle the question as to the existence of an armed vessel lying in Canadian waters, which has been such a bug-bear in some quarters. The inclosed report of General Terry, dated Sandusky, Ohio, March 29, 1864, will fully explain.

I am satisfied, however, that there is an organized band in Canada watching for an opportunity to do us some damage should a favorable occasion offer. It will probably be turned into burning steamboats and warehouses of stores. This must be guarded against by increased vigilance in the employment of deck-hands on board steamboats, and laborers and watchmen around warehouses.

I have the honor to be, general, very respectfully, your obedient servant,

. S. P. HEINTZELMAN,
Major-General.

[Inclosure.]

HDQRS. U. S. FORCES, SANDUSKY AND JOHNSON'S ISLAND,
AND OF THIRD DIVISION, SIXTH CORPS,
Sandusky, Ohio, March 29, 1864
Capt. CARROLL H. POTTER,
Assistant Adjutant-General:

In obedience to instructions received from headquarters Northern Department, under date of March 12, 1864, to procure all the information in my power as to the truth of a report that a vessel loaded with small-arms and two 12-pounders was lying at Rondeau, Canada, and to report thereon to your headquarters, I have the honor to report that on Tuesday, March 22, 1864, I left Chatham, Upper Canada, with John Mercer, esq., sheriff of Kent County, and proceeded to Rondeau. At the hotel at Raglan, a small village near the head of the bay (Rondeau), I met Colonel Wiley, of the staff of the Governor-General of the Canadas, who had been ordered by the Provincial military authorities from Quebec to investigate as to the character of the vessel in question. He had just returned from on board the suspected vessel, lying about a half mile out, and stated to me there was not the slightest cause of suspicion.

I went on board the vessel with Sheriff Mercer and Capt. Nettleton B. Whitby, the master and owner, and found no arms on board except two fowling-pieces and an old gun of 2½-inch bore, for signal purposes, weighing about 75 pounds. This piece had been on board, I found by inquiry, a long time.

Upon investigation and inquiry I learned that the vessel came to Rondeau in stress of weather, December 18, 1863, and was compelled to stay. Her name, Catarauqui, is on her stern, and she hails from Kingston. The crew, a mate, 4 hands, and a cook were discharged December 18, 1863, except 1 man, who is retained as a servant. The captain, his wife, and this man stay on board the vessel. The captain is á man of more than ordinary ability, and has been engaged in the English merchant service. I examined the vessel thoroughly in every part and found nothing worthy of note. Saw her papers, and found they were in accordance with the captain's statements as to the character and business of the vessel. The collector of customs, with whom I conversed, confirmed all the statements of Captain Whitby. I feel assured that the Catarauqui is a harmless vessel, engaged in the transportation of staves.

But I beg leave to add that there are many rebel refugees in Upper Canada, and that their headquarters are at Windsor, opposite Detroit ; that they have some organization there is no doubt, nor that one of their leaders is a Colonel Snyder, of the Second Missouri (rebel) Cavalry. Mrs. Louisa Phillips now makes her headquarters at Windsor. I saw and conversed with her there.

It is quite clear that they contemplate a raid of some kind, and that in its execution they have nothing to fear except the British authorities.

All of which is respectfully submitted.

HENRY D. TERRY,
Brigadier-General, Commanding.

HDQRS. MILITARY DIVISION OF THE MISSISSIPPI,
Nashville, Tenn., April 2, 1864—11 a. m.   (Rec'd 4.30 p. m.)
Lieut. Gen. U. S. GRANT,
Washington, D. C.:

I am just back, having passed over my whole front and spent a day with all my army commanders, possessing myself of the information necessary to act with intelligence. The problem of supplies is the most difficult. The roads can now supply the daily wants of the army, but do not accumulate a surplus, but I think by stopping the carriage of cattle and men, and by running the cars on the circuit from Nashville to Stevenson and Decatur, it can be done with the present cars and locomotives. The superintendent of railroads here, Mr. Anderson, the quartermaster, Colonel Donaldson, and myself will determine to-night. I find too many citizens and private freights along the road, which are utterly inconsistent with our military necessities at this time. I will aim to accumulate in all April, at Decatur and Chattanooga, a surplus of seventy days' provisions and forage for 100,000 men.

W. T. SHERMAN,
Major-General.

HDQRS. MILITARY DIVISION OF THE MISSISSIPPI,
Nashville, April 2, 1864.   (Received 6 a. m., 3d.)
ADJUTANT-GENERAL,
Washington, D. C.:

Inform the Commander-in-Chief that Schofield's infantry occupies Bull's Gap, and his cavalry is scouting beyond. The enemy is all beyond Jonesborough and probably beyond the Watauga, having burned both railroad and other road bridges, and carried off telegraph wire, but otherwise have not destroyed the railroad. I will not advance the infantry beyond Bull's Gap, as our line is now pretty long and weak.

General Schofield thinks Longstreet is gone to Virginia, leaving about 3,500 cavalry to protect the salt-works.

W. T. SHERMAN,
Major-General, Commanding.

WAR DEPARTMENT,
Washington, April 2. 1864—8.30 p. m.
Major-General SHERMAN,
Nashville:

In the absence of Lieutenant-General Grant, now at Fort Monroe, your telegram of 11 a. m. of this date has been submitted to me. Under the provisions of the act of Congress, you are authorized by the President to take military possession of railroads within your command, to the exclusion of all other business, when in your opinion the service requires such exclusive use. Colonel McCallum has made provision for a large increase of motive power and rolling-stock. General Grant's return is expected to-morrow. Colonel Hatch, of Iowa, and Colonel Edward M. McCook, are nominated for brigadiers.

EDWIN M. STANTON,
Secretary of War.

HDQRS. MILITARY DIVISION OF THE MISSISSIPPI,
Nashville, Tenn., April 2, 1864. (Received 6 p. m.)
Lieut. Gen. U. S. GRANT,
Washington, D. C. :

After a full consultation with all my army commanders, I have settled down to the following conclusions, to which I would like to have the President's consent before I make the orders :

First. Army of the Ohio, three divisions of infantry, to be styled the Twenty-third Corps, Major-General Schofield in command, and one division of cavalry, Major-General Stoneman, to push Longstreet's forces well out of the valley, then fall back, breaking railroad to Knoxville ; to hold Knoxville and Loudon, and be ready by May 1, with 12,000 men, to act as the left of the grand army.

Second. General Thomas to organize his army into three corps, the Eleventh and Twelfth to be united under General Hooker, to be composed of four divisions. The corps to take a new title, viz. one of the series now vacant. General Slocum to be transferred east, or assigned to some small command on the Mississippi. The Fourth Corps, Major-General Granger, to remain unchanged, save to place Major-General Howard in command. The Fourteenth Corps to remain the same. Major-General Palmer is not equal to such a command, and all parties are willing that General Buell or any tried soldier should be assigned. Thomas to guard the lines of communication, and have, by May 1, a command of 45,000 men for active service, to constitute the center.

Third. Major-General McPherson to draw from the Mississippi the divisions of Crocker and Leggett, now en route, mostly of veterans on furlough, and of A. J. Smith, now up Red River, but due on the 10th instant out of that expedition, and to organize a force of 30,000 men to operate from Larkinsville or Guntersville as the right of the grand army; his corps to be commanded by Generals Logan, Blair, and Dodge. Hurlbut will not resign, and I know no better disposition of him than to leave him at Memphis.

I propose to put Major-General Newton, when he arrives, at Vicksburg.

With these changes this army will be a unit in all respects, and I can suggest no better.

Please ask the President's consent, and ask what title we shall give the new corps of Hooker, in lieu of the Eleventh and Twelfth, consolidated. The lowest number of the army corps now vacant will be most appropriate.

I will have the cavalry of the Department of the Ohio reorganize under Stoneman at or near Camp Nelson, and the cavalry of Thomas, at least one good division, under Garrard, at Columbia.

W. T. SHERMAN,
Major-General.

———

HDQRS. MILITARY DIVISION OF THE MISSISSIPPI,
Nashville, Tenn., April 2, 1864.
Major-General HALLECK,
Washington, D. C. :

DEAR GENERAL : I had the pleasure some days ago to receive your letter sending me commission as brigadier-general and to say I have the commission itself.

I have just returned from a visit to all my advanced posts with a view to confer with all commanders and to compare ideas. With a few changes, of which I have telegraphed to-day to General Grant, I believe I can make this grand army a unit in action and feeling. We never have had, and God grant we never may, the dissensions which have so marred the usefulness of our fellows whom a common cause and common interests alone ought to unite as brothers. I wish you to say to the President that I would prefer he should not nominate me or any one to the vacant major-generalship in the Regular Army. I now have all the rank necessary to command, and I believe all here concede to me the ability, yet accidents may happen, and I don't care about increasing the distance of my fall. The moment another appears on the arena better than me, I will cheerfully subside. Indeed, now my preference would be to have my Fifteenth Corps, which was as large a family as I feel willing to provide for, yet I know General Grant has a mammoth load to carry. He wants here some one who will fulfill his plans, whole and entire, and at the time appointed, and he believes I will do it. I hope he is not mistaken. I know my weak points, and thank you from the bottom of my heart for past favors and advice, and will in the future heed all you may offer with the deepest confidence in your ability and sincerity.

I will try and hold my tongue and pen and give my undivided thoughts and attention to the military duties devolving on me, which in all conscience are enough to occupy usefully all my time and thoughts. I hope you noticed that it was my troops that captured Fort De Russy. Now, if the Red River be high, admitting our iron-clads up to Shreveport, I advise that place to be reduced, but if they cannot pass the rapids at Alexandria my part of the joint expedition should go no further at this time. It was necessary to clean out Red River that high to make the Mississippi safe, so as to admit the re-enforcement of this army by that portion of the Army of the Tennessee. I hope to have by May 1 an army on the Tennessee, with a reserve of provisions, forage, and ammunition that will enable me to whip Joe Johnston or drive him back of the Chattahoochee, and leave my right flank clear to sweep down between Georgia and Alabama.

The rumors that the enemy has repaired the damage at Meridian is nonsense; it is an impossibility. Forrest's move up to Paducah will cost the secessionists dear, but will damage us little. I now have a force at Purdy and others advancing from Memphis which should render his escape difficult, if not impossible. With Thomas as my center, McPherson on the right, and Schofield on the left, I will have an army that will do anything within the range of human possibility. I do not much apprehend a raid to my rear, though it is barely possible. My effort shall be to have supplies so accumulated to the front that a raid will hurt the people more than my army. If the people will not suppress guerrillas they must suffer the penalty.

Accept the assurances of my continued friendship and respect.

Believe me, truly, your friend,

W. T. SHERMAN,
Major-General.

HDQRS. MILITARY DIVISION OF THE MISSISSIPPI,
Nashville, April 2, 1864.
Major-General THOMAS,
Chattanooga:
Am at Nashville. Have telegraphed to Washington for authority to make the changes we agreed on. To-night the railroad superintendent (Anderson), Colonel Donaldson, and I will meet and arrange about the railroad management. I will also compel the beef contractor to drive cattle. Unless we devote the railroad solely and exclusively to the use of dead freight, we cannot accumulate the surplus required for our plans. Watch Joe Johnston close. Your weak point is Cleveland. As soon as Schofield can ascertain certain that Longstreet is no longer in force in East Tennessee he will let your troops come below the Hiwassee. I will make the order the moment I hear from Washington.

W. T. SHERMAN,
Major-General.

GRAYSVILLE, *April 2, 1864.*
Brigadier-General WHIPPLE,
Assistant Adjutant-General:
All quiet in our front. Nothing new except the report of a contraband who came into my lines at the gap (Parker's) to-day, leaving Dalton day before yesterday and Tunnel Hill last night. He reports rebels fortifying the special position from which they resisted our advance in the late reconnaissance. The understanding in their camps is that they will fight us there. This "nig" belonged in the Fifth Tennessee. The brigade in which this regiment is left Dalton day before yesterday to go to Alabama to recruit up their horses. It is rumored that Johnston will send large re-enforcements to Richmond. The "nig" thinks it is already commenced.

R. W. JOHNSON,
Brigadier-General of Volunteers.

CLEVELAND, *April 2, 1864.*
General WHIPPLE,
Assistant Adjutant-General:
The enemy is reported hovering around this place. I have detained the trains here until word can be obtained from you whether you deem it prudent for them to proceed.

S. W. PRICE,
Colonel, Commanding.

CLEVELAND, *April 2, 1864.*
Maj. SOUTHARD HOFFMAN,
Assistant Adjutant-General:
I have had a force in the front since early this morning. Have received nothing of importance so far. I will be able to give information this evening.

A. P. CAMPBELL,
Colonel, Commanding.

BLUE SPRINGS, *April 2, 1864.*

Col. A. P. CAMPBELL:

If the rebels have passed north of Benton road. you must follow with all your force and I will support you.

STANLEY,
Major-General, Comdg. First Div., Fourth Army Corps.

BLUE SPRINGS, *April 2, 1864.*

Colonel CAMPBELL:

The rebs at daylight this a. m. were in strong force, cavalry, at least 2,000, 8 miles east of this. on the Dalton and Charleston road. They were advancing north. Have your command ready for action immediately, and send out on Benton road to see what is up.

STANLEY,
Major-General.

CLEVELAND, TENN.,
April 2, 1864.

Brig. Gen. W. D. WHIPPLE,
Assistant Adjutant-General:

The enemy are advancing in force on Charleston road. My picket fell back in the direction of Charleston from cross-roads. I sent out two regiments under Colonel La Grange this a. m. Have not yet heard from him, but think he has checked them at the cross-roads. I am waiting to hear from Colonel La Grange, with my command ready to move at a moment.

A. P. CAMPBELL,
Commanding.

HDQRS. DEPARTMENT OF THE CUMBERLAND,
Chattanooga, Tenn., April 2, 1864.

COMMANDING OFFICER,
Charleston, Tenn. :

Telegram from Cleveland reports 2,000 rebels on the Dalton and Charleston road, 8 miles east of Cleveland. Be on your guard and look out for them.

By order of Major-General Thomas:

SOUTHARD HOFFMAN,
Assistant Adjutant-General.

HDQRS. MILITARY DIVISION OF THE MISSISSIPPI,
Nashville, April 2, 1864.

Major-General SCHOFIELD,
Knoxville :

Am back at Nashville. Telegraph me daily any matters of interest. I have asked the President the necessary authority to announce you as the commander of the Twenty-third Corps. As soon as you can spare Stoneman, order him to go to Kentucky and assemble all the cavalry, mounted and dismounted, of your department at or near Lexington, and to put it in fine order, drawing supplies from Cincinnati and the country. Hovey marches to-morrow, and will report to you his progress. As soon as you can spare Thomas' troops, let them go below the Hiwassee and keep yours above.

W. T. SHERMAN,
Major-General.

BULL'S GAP, *April 2,* 1864.

General SCHOFIELD :

Arrived this 10 a. m. Railroad complete to this point, and will be complete to Lick Creek to-day. Bridge over Lick Creek been destroyed, and all others beyond been destroyed as far as heard from. Have sent parties toward Greeneville and in other directions. Telegraph wire from here on said to be taken down. No rails taken up as far as heard from. Roads very bad, and it will be as much as the teams can do to get up to-day. Have you any orders ?

GEO. STONEMAN,
Major-General.

BULL'S GAP, *April 2,* 1864.

Major-General SCHOFIELD,
Knoxville :

From the best information that can be obtained it appears certain that there are no rebels except roving parties this side of Jonesborough, or within 50 miles of here, and that Longstreet's whole forces have gone beyond the Holston. They took the telegraph wire and insulators with them. All bridges and trestle-work have been destroyed. The bridge across Lick Creek was quite extensive, resting on seventeen stone piers. The long trestle-work this side of Greeneville is completely destroyed. What they have destroyed will take a long time to rebuild. Has any move been made in the direction of Rogersville ?

What do you think of the expediency of organizing the people in this region into home guards and furnishing them with arms ?

GEO. STONEMAN,
Major-General.

KNOXVILLE, *April 2,* 1864.

Maj. Gen. W. T. SHERMAN :

General Stoneman reached Bull's Gap, and his cavalry is scouting beyond that place. The enemy have all gone beyond Jonesborough, and probably beyond the Watauga. Scouts report that Longstreet's main force is moving to East Virginia, only about 3,500 men, mostly cavalry, being left to protect the salt-works. I will know the facts in a few days. Longstreet was with his troops at Bull's Gap while I was at Morristown last week, he having returned from Virginia. Upon learning we were advancing he also brought back a division of infantry, which was then en. route for Virginia. The rebels have destroyed the bridge beyond Bull's Gap and Greeneville, and have carried off the telegraph wire, but have not injured the track as far as learned. I will occupy Bull's Gap with infantry,

15 R R—VOL XXXII, PT III

and scout the country above with cavalry, but will not injure the railroad until I get further instructions from you. I will have all preparations made to carry out your plans.

J. M. SCHOFIELD,
Major-General.

LOUDON, *April 2, 1864.*

Major-General SCHOFIELD:

General Stanley reports that a large force rebel cavalry was seen 8 miles east of Cleveland this morning at sunrise moving in the direction of Charleston. The commanding officer at that post is on the alert.

G. GRANGER,
Major-General.

HEADQUARTERS ARMY OF THE OHIO,
Strawberry Plains, April 2, 1864.

Brig. Gen. T. J. WOOD,
Commanding Third Division, Fourth Army Corps:

GENERAL: General Stoneman went yesterday with a division on a reconnaissance to Morristown. To-day he is at Bull's Gap, and possibly beyond. The result of his movement will determine whether any other force may be required to complete what is to be done on that line. No news from below.

Very respectfully, your obedient servant,

J. D. COX,
Brigadier-General, Chief of Staff.

HDQRS. MILITARY DIVISION OF THE MISSISSIPPI,
Nashville, April 2, 1864.

General SCHOFIELD,
Knoxville:

Your dispatch is received, and is very satisfactory. I will telegraph its substance to Washington.

The Cincinnati papers of the 1st contain dispatches announcing that Buell is to supersede you. There is no truth in this. The report seems to have originated at Chattanooga, and I have telegraphed to Thomas to punish the operator.

The papers also contain a message from Knoxville giving my movements, and gives a message from Parson Brownlow to the effect that the rebels will certainly invade Kentucky by Pound Gap. Tell Parson Brownlow that he must leave military matters to us, and that he must not chronicle my movements or those of any military body. If he confines his efforts to his own sphere of action he will do himself more credit and his country more good.

W. T. SHERMAN,
Major-General.

HDQRS. MILITARY DIVISION OF THE MISSISSIPPI,
Nashville, April 2, 1864.
General MCPHERSON,
    Huntsville:

Am back to Nashville. Telegraph me daily anything of interest. I will give you my personal attention to the question of accumulating of supplies.

Have you made up your mind which is your best point, Huntsville or Decatur? I want to send Corse down the Mississippi to give life to Hurlbut's movements against Forrest. I want the regulars here as a headquarter guard. I will assign Newton to you with a view to his assignment to Vicksburg. I would not give orders about Forrest, who is in your department, only the matter involves Kentucky also.

As soon as he is disposed of I will leave all matters in your department to you. Veatch is posted near Purdy to cut off escape by the head of Hatchie. Hurlbut, with infantry and cavalry, will move toward Bolivar with a view to catch Forrest in flank as he attempts to escape. Brayman will stop a few veteran regiments returning, and will use them out as far as Union City. If you will control the movements I will desist.

I am not satisfied with either Hurlbut or Brayman, and will avail myself of the first chance to change them.

                                        W. T. SHERMAN,
                                            Major-General.

HDQRS. DEPARTMENT AND ARMY OF THE TENNESSEE,
Huntsville, Ala.. April 2, 1864.
Maj. Gen. W. T. SHERMAN,
    Comdg. Mil. Div. of the Mississippi, Nashville, Tenn.:

GENERAL : I inclose herewith the "unofficial" and rather unique report of Brig. Gen. T. Kilby Smith, on the capture of Fort De Russy and the Red River expedition. I have dates from Vicksburg to the 23d ultimo.

Lee's headquarters were at that time at Canton, and Ferguson's, Starke's, and Wirt Adams' brigades of cavalry were occupying the section of country as before our expedition, viz, from Yazoo City to Woodville, below Natchez.

They were putting on rather a bold and defiant air, had a heavier line of pickets along the Big Black than at any time during the winter, and were trying to make the people of Mississippi believe we were driven back to Vicksburg and the State was virtually relieved from Federal occupation. The news also is that Loring's division was in Meridian and that they were bending all their energies to repair the railroad from Mobile to Meridian, having all the soldiers and as many negroes as they can get at work. Brigadier-General Dodge, who has later news, says that Loring's and French's divisions are at Demopolis. I am afraid we will not get our troops back in thirty days; certainly not if they go up to Shreveport.

Our troops reached Alexandria on the 18th instant. No news from General Banks' column to that date. General Banks and staff were to leave New Orleans on the steam-boat Luminary on the 25th. ultimo.

I inclose a communication* from Colonel Potts, commanding one of my veteran regiments, from which you will see that he is apprehensive his regiment may be ordered to the Potomac. His regiment is one that is to make up a part of the two divisions I am to organize at Cairo. If any of the veteran regiments belonging to the Seventeenth Army Corps, now at home on furlough, are ordered east, it will embarrass me very much.

Very respectfully, your obedient servant,

JAS. B. McPHERSON,
Major-General.

HUNTSVILLE, *April* 2, 1864.

Major-General SHERMAN:

Dispatch received. Wrote you by mail this morning giving my views in regard to which is the best point for my depot. Have decided upon Huntsville. I think it best for you to continue to control the movements against Forrest until he is disposed of, as some of the returning veteran regiments Brayman stops may not belong to my command; and furthermore, I feel satisfied Hurlbut will obey your orders with more promptness than mine. If Forrest crosses the Tennessee in this region we will be after him. General Corse starts for Nashville in the morning.

JAS. B. McPHERSON,
Major-General.

HDQRS. MILITARY DIVISION OF THE MISSISSIPPI,
Nashville, April 2, 1864.

Maj. Gen. J. B. McPHERSON,
Huntsville:

According to the best information, Forrest lingered for a few days after his attack on Paducah, near Mayfield, back of Paducah, but has since moved on toward Paris. Small bands of his men have crossed to this side the Tennessee, but got back again. He is supposed to be somewhat bothered to get out, and if Hurlbut acts with energy he will be cooped in above the Hatchie.

Look out for him toward Clifton and Savannah.

W. T. SHERMAN,
Major-General.

HUNTSVILLE, *April* 2, 1864.

Maj. Gen. W. T. SHERMAN,
Commanding:

General Garrard, with two regiments of cavalry, leaves here this morning via Fayetteville, under orders from General Thomas, for Columbia and Lynnville. General Veatch is, I presume, in the vicinity of Purdy, and certainly ought to prevent Forrest from getting across the Tennessee River in the vicinity of Savannah.

JAS. B. McPHERSON,
Major-General, Commanding.

---

* Omitted.

HDQRS. DEPARTMENT AND ARMY OF THE TENNESSEE,
Huntsville, Ala., April 2, 1864.

Maj. Gen. W. T. SHERMAN,
  Military Division of the Mississippi:

GENERAL: Since my return from Chattanooga I have been down to Whitesburg, on the Tennessee River, distance 9 miles from this place, over an excellent macadamized road. I have also been over to Athens to consult with General Dodge in relation to roads on the south side of river.

From all the information I can gather, I am decidedly of the opinion that this is the best point to establish our principal depot.

First. There are plenty of buildings for store-houses.

Second. The road from here to the river is excellent, and will not be materially affected by the weather.

Third. The steam-boat which can be spared from Chattanooga will na   us to transport supplies across the river to any desired pointe   ble .

Fourth. It is one of the places we will have to occupy until our lines are so far advanced as to enable us to change our base of supplies, and, furthermore, we may find it necessary to establish general hospitals. I shall make the necessary arrangements to have this for the principal depot and give directions for having a field-work thrown up on the hill on the east side of town, unless otherwise directed.

Very respectfully, your obedient servant,

JAS. B. McPHERSON,
Major-General, Commanding.

HUNTSVILLE, *April 2, 1864.*

Major-General SHERMAN:

Is it the intention to have a couple of light-draught gun-boats sent up the Tennessee River above the shoals, if the water gets high enough? If so, they should be ready, as the river is rising and a few feet more will enable them to come over.

JAS. B. McPHERSON,
   Major-General.

HDQRS. DEPARTMENT AND ARMY OF THE TENNESSEE,
Huntsville, Ala., April 2, 1864.

Maj. Gen. J. A. LOGAN:

GENERAL: It is of the utmost importance that supplies, ordnance, &c., for this army come forward rapidly. The superintendent of the military railroad informs me that there is a great scarcity of wood along the line, and that it is with the greatest difficulty enough can be procured to run the limited number of trains they are now running on the road. Will you instruct your division commanders to have good details made to cut and haul wood and pile it up along the railroad, especially in the vicinity of Woodville and Madison Stations? The wood to be cut 5 feet long. If there are any refugees about their camps or contrabands out of employment let them be set to work, and reasonable wages will be paid them.

Very respectfully, your obedient servant,

JAS. B. McPHERSON,
Major-General, Commanding.

NASHVILLE, TENN., *April* 2, 1864.
(Received 9.20 p. m.)

Lieutenant-General GRANT, *General-in-Chief:*

Forrest is reported between Paducah and Jackson, Tenn. I have posted Veatch with his five regiments at Purdy, and have ordered Hurlbut to move from Memphis with all his available forces toward the Hatchie. We will watch the Tennessee and Cumberland Rivers and try and collect a force of veterans at Columbus to move against him direct. If I had a good, bold officer at Columbus I would be better satisfied.

W. T. SHERMAN,
Major-General.

HDQRS. MILITARY DIVISION OF THE MISSISSIPPI,
Nashville, April 2, 1864.

Maj. Gen. S. A. HURLBUT, *Memphis:*

Your dispatch is received. Forrest is reported still up about Jackson, Tenn. He will attempt to escape south, with infantry and cavalry. No matter what strength, you should move toward the Hatchie and prevent his escape, more especially with any train or plunder. Communicate if possible with Veatch at or near Purdy. The line of the Hatchie should be watched. It must now be impassable, save above Bolivar. Forrest has had all he wants of attacking fortified places, and the more he attempts it the better we should be satisfied.

W. T. SHERMAN,
Major-General.

HDQRS. MILITARY DIVISION OF THE MISSISSIPPI,
Nashville, April 2, 1864.

Brig. Gen. J. C. VEATCH, *At or near Purdy:*

GENERAL : I want you to remain at or near Purdy. Forrest will soon attempt to escape, and I want you to keep your force well in hand and as he attempts to move south catch him in flank. You can surely prevent his carrying off any train or plunder.

Hurlbut, with infantry and cavalry, will come out from Memphis toward Bolivar, and will try to communicate with you. I will instruct General Brayman, at Cairo, also to feel for Forrest out from Columbus. The Tennessee will be patrolled by gun-boats. If you know for certain that Forrest has crossed into Tennessee or Kentucky, you can also cross and move toward Pulaski.*

W. T. SHERMAN,
Major-General.

HDQRS. MILITARY DIVISION OF THE MISSISSIPPI,
Nashville, April 2, 1864.

General BRAYMAN, *Cairo:*

Read my dispatches to Veatch and Hurlbut.† Forrest will try and carry off plunder. If Hicks could defeat him at Paducah, surely Columbus must not only be safe, but should invite his attack.

---

* See also copy of this dispatch as furnished by General Veatch, Part I, p. 581.
† See two preceding.

If you can collect a couple thousand men of returning veteran regiments, you can go out to Union City and prevent his delaying in that neighborhood; but it would be idle for you to follow him. I depend on Hurlbut and Veatch to catch him or his plunder at the Hatchie.

I observe an article in an Evansville paper that looks as though you had communicated my instructions to private parties for publication. If this be so, it is a high military offense for which you must account. You are an officer of the United States and in no manner of ways accountable to an irresponsible press. I am to judge whether Veatch's command can do better service up the Tennessee behind Forrest, or chasing him about Union City.

If my dispatches to you reach the public and the enemy again you will regret it all the days of your life.

W. T. SHERMAN,
Major-General.

CAIRO, *April 2, 1864.*

Col. S. G. HICKS,
 Paducah, Ky.:

Colonel Slack, Forty-seventh Indiana, will report to you to-night. Let your men rest a little. Colonel Sawyer's dispatch has been sent you, showing that the danger is not yet over. I expect to call on you at 10 to-morrow.

M. BRAYMAN,
Brigadier-General, Commanding.

CAIRO, ILL.,
April 2, 1864.

Col. R. M. SAWYER,
 Assistant Adjutant-General, Nashville, Tenn.:

Yours of this date received. I have sent the Forty-seventh Indiana, 800 strong, to Paducah, and am expecting the Twenty-first Indiana, 600 strong, by rail, and will help Columbus. The enemy are yet near us. We can only protect the river by shifting our small force from point to point of danger. I want more troops, and will stop all that come. An outbreak in Illinois is made in concert with Forrest. Rebel officers are organizing them.

M. BRAYMAN,
Brigadier-General, Commanding.

CAIRO, *April 2. 1864.*

Maj. Gen. W. T. SHERMAN,
 Nashville:

I will stop veteran regiments and chase Forrest out of the neighborhood.. I know nothing of the Evansville paper or its articles. Your dispatches have not been disclosed by me; I know my duty on that point perfectly. I will write you on this subject.

M. BRAYMAN,
Brigadier-General, Commanding.

PADUCAH, *April* 2, 1864.

General BRAYMAN :

I have from my scouts, and what I believe to be reliable news, that Forrest has gone south toward Jackson. His main body of troops has left Mayfield. Straggling parties all over the country back of here.

S. G. HICKS,
Colonel, Commanding.

PADUCAH, *April* 2, 1864.

General M. BRAYMAN,
        Cairo, and
Major-General SHERMAN,
        Nashville:

A scout just in reports Buford's headquarters at Dukedom, 15 miles south of Mayfield, with five or six regiments of cavalry; Faulkner at Clinton, 35 miles west of this place, with 800 men. Forrest at Jackson, with infantry and artillery, amount of force not known; Fitzhugh [S. D. ?] Lee near Memphis, with a division. The messenger is an intelligent man, and is vouched for as a man of veracity. He says he was among them.

S. G. HICKS,
Colonel, Commanding.

HEADQUARTERS DISTRICT OF CAIRO,
Cairo, Ill., April 2, 1864.

Col. S. G. HICKS,
        Commanding, Paducah, Ky.:

SIR : In order to afford your wearied men an opportunity for rest, and to give assurance of entire safety in case of another attack, I send you the Forty-seventh Indiana Infantry Veteran Volunteers, Colonel Slack, who will remain until Monday; longer if necessary. My best information is that Forrest is retreating on Jackson, and that his stay after you defeated him was for purpose of plunder. If the people of Kentucky can stand that we can. Let us take care of our posts and the river.

Yours, &c.,

M. BRAYMAN,
Brigadier-General, Commanding.

HEADQUARTERS DISTRICT OF CAIRO,
Cairo, Ill., April 2, 1864.

Lieut. Col. T. H. HARRIS,
        Asst. Adjt. Gen., 16th Army Corps, Memphis, Tenn.:

SIR : I inclose herewith copies of my orders 15 and 16. Western Kentucky, with the exception of the rivers, is under insurrectionary control. Forrest occupies it with not less than 9,000 men, and his force is increasing.

I have not 1,600 men, and they are divided between Paducah, Cairo, and Columbus, 70 miles. The distance from Columbus to Paducah is less than 40. The enemy lying midway and almost equidistant from each place, each is immediately menaced. Thus far I have kept these places by shifting disposable detachments back and forth, governed by information as to the enemy's movements. For the pa t few months the interior of Western Kentucky has been filled wsith warlike stores and army supplies of every kind. The loose administration of Treasury regulations, the complicity of both Treasury and Army officers, have given free course to this infamous traffic. The large army now threatening is subsisting upon and conveying south these supplies. I may safely say that most of these supplies were intended for them. Without them this force could not well remain and probably would not have come at all.

These are my reasons. added to General Hurlbut's letter of instructions, copy inclosed, for issuing the first-named order No. 15.

Having lately assumed this command, and not being furnished with copies of trade regulations or orders concerning them, it is quite possible that I exceed my authority; but a present necessity forbids the delay requisite to receive instructions, and I shall await with pleasure any orders on the subject.

The provost-marshal of this city, being in Johnson County, 30 miles from here, found a regiment organizing under a colonel from Forrest's command, prepared to co-operate with him. His party were fired upon. He returned the fire, killing 2 Illinois rebels and pursuing, but without overtaking, the rebel officer. This portion of Illinois is infested by domestic traitors and rebels from the South. Our posts and towns are crowded with dangerous persons. They intend mischief. I am satisfied that concert of action exists across the river. Hence the issue of order No. 16.

I respectfully invite the attention of General Hurlbut to these matters, and for information will forward General Sherman a copy of this communication, as it refers to points he may desire to consider at the earliest moment.

Respectfully, yours, &c.,

M. BRAYMAN,
Brigadier-General, Commanding.

[Inclosure No. 1.]

GENERAL ORDERS, }   HEADQUARTERS DISTRICT OF CAIRO,
    No. 15.   }   *Cairo, Ill., April 2, 1864.*

The large quantities of supplies which through permits (too freely granted), as well as by evasion of established regulations, have been carried into the interior of Western Kentucky, now partially under insurrectionary control, are now in the hands of the rebel forces, affording them aid and comfort. Such supplies furnish an inducement to hostile incursions and support the marauders while making them, and it may be presumed that they were shipped and transported to the interior for that very purpose. To prevent the continuance of this abuse, and for the purpose of stopping the enemy's supplies, it is, in accordance with instructions from corps headquarters, ordered:

I. All permits for the landing of goods, supplies, or articles of sale of any description between Paducah (including that point) and Memphis are suspended, and no such goods will be landed until further orders, peremptory seizure and arrest being the penalty for violation.

II. Steamers will not make landings, nor receive or discharge passengers or freight on the Kentucky shore between Paducah and Cairo, nor on either shore between Cairo and Memphis, except at Columbus, Island Ten, and Fort Pillow, except under armed convoy and under orders of a competent military or naval officer.

III. Ferry-boats, trading-boats, skiffs, and other irregular craft are being used for conveyance of spies and traitors and contraband supplies for the enemy's use. No further crossing of the river by such boats, ferries, skiffs, or other craft between Paducah and Memphis will be allowed. The military and naval officers will promptly arrest all persons offending, with their effects, and, in their discretion, hold or destroy all such boats, &c.

IV. The commanding officers at Paducah and Columbus will retain under their control all engines and cars, and permit no running of trains except for military purposes, and under their orders.

V. Officers of the Treasury Department are respectfully advised of the existence of this order and enjoined to cause its due observance.

By order of Brig. Gen. M. Brayman:

J. H. ODLIN,
Assistant Adjutant-General.

[Inclosure No. 2.]

GENERAL ORDERS, }   HEADQUARTERS DISTRICT OF CAIRO,
No. 16.   }   *Cairo, Ill., April 2,* 1864.

The several posts within this district are infested by large numbers of persons who have no honest employment or fixed homes. They move from place to place, eluding the vigilance of both civil and military authorities. They are usually congregated about grog-shops, gambling-houses, and houses of prostitution. Being destitute of a proper sense of moral and social obligations, they are fit material out of which traitors, spies, smugglers, robbers, and house-burners are made. They prowl about our camps, robbing soldiers by dishonest practices. They secure information of the strength and movements of our forces, and inform the enemy. They are ready to burn our boats, destroy our magazines and public property, and interrupt our communications. Their presence at our posts and camps and upon our transports is a scandal to the service. They are more dangerous than organized armies that openly fight. Therefore, for the better security of public property, the safety of the military and naval operations in this district, as well as to make due distinction between good citizens and public enemies, it is ordered:

I. All persons within the limits or vicinity of any post or place occupied by military or naval forces within this district who are not known as loyal and well-disposed persons, having houses, honest employment, or visible and lawful means of support, will be deemed to be persons of the character heretofore specified.

II. All such suspicious persons will be arrested by the provost-marshal and held for examination. They will, if found to be of the class referred to, be forthwith sent out of the district, not to return. or may be held for examination and trial if charged with actual offense against the civil or military laws, or with being spies or disloyal persons.

III. The provost-marshal will utterly prohibit and prevent the sale or gift of intoxicating drinks to soldiers or sailors in the service of the United States; also all gambling, with either officers or soldiers ; also, the keeping of houses of prostitution, to be frequented by either of these establishments, demoralize the army, are the direct cause of the murders, violence, drunkenness, and bad conduct of which good citizens justly complain.   As they take from officers and soldiers the money needed by their families, giving only disease, disgrace, and empty pockets in return, they are to be treated with remorseless severity, the proprietors imprisoned and fined, and if need be their business destroyed.   Officers will be sustained in executing the most rigid measures.

IV. Persons found lurking about public buildings, magazines, boat-yards, and vessels without lawful occasion will be seized, and if detected in the perpetration of mischief, endangering public property, or attempting it, they may be promptly shot.

V. Commanding officers will see that these orders are obeyed, with the use of sufficient force (and no more) to accomplish the object, paying proper respect to the civil authorities, and acting in concert with them when needful, the preservation of public peace under the law being a paramount duty, which end the military must, as far as possible, subserve.

By order of Brig. Gen. M. Brayman :

J. H. ODLIN,
Assistant Adjutant-General.

HDQRS. CAVALRY DIVISION, SIXTEENTH ARMY CORPS,
Memphis, Tenn., April 2, 1864.

Col. FIELDING HURST,
Commanding Sixth Tennessee Cavalry :

COLONEL : Leave 100 mounted men to patrol the Pigeon Roost, Holly Ford, and Hernando roads.   Have the patrols start at different hours by day or night, so as to give information of the movements of any force which may come near the place.   The First Mississippi will also be left here for the purpose of scouting south and southeast.

You will move with the balance of your effective force at 1 o'clock to Raleigh, taking with you one day's forage and all the rations and ammunition the men can carry.   The teams which take out the forage can be sent back to camp to-night.   One regiment of infantry will be at the crossing of the Wolf, near Raleigh.

Instruct the officer left in command of the 100 men to be vigilant and active.

By order of Brig. Gen. B. H. Grierson :

S. L. WOODWARD,
Assistant Adjutant-General.

HDQRS. CAVALRY DIVISION, SIXTEENTH ARMY CORPS,
Memphis, Tenn., April 2, 1864—1 p. m.

Lieut. Col. T. H. HARRIS,
Assistant Adjutant-General :

COLONEL : I am just leaving.   The Fourth Missouri is left behind, with orders to patrol toward La Grange and the crossings of Wolf River.   One hundred men of the Sixth Tennessee are left with orders to patrol all roads running south and southeast.   The First Mississippi will assist in this work. One hundred men, inferiorly mounted, are left under Major Gifford at Fort Pickering, and can be used if needed. With the balance of my force I will scour the country north, northeast, and east from Raleigh, and keep you posted.

Very respectfully, your obedient servant,

B. H. GRIERSON,
Brigadier-General.

HEADQUARTERS NORTHERN DEPARTMENT,
Columbus, Ohio, April 2, 1864. (Received 2.45 p. m.)

Major-General HALLECK,
Chief of Staff :

Lieutenant-Colonel Oakes telegraphs that all is quiet at Charleston and Mattoon. Prisoners will be sent to Springfield to-day. The Forty-first and Fifty-fourth Illinois Veteran Volunteers will be retained at Springfield and Mattoon till after election on Thursday next. No further trouble apprehended after that.

S. P. HEINTZELMAN,
Major-General.

HEADQUARTERS DISTRICT OF KENTUCKY,
Hopkinsville, April 2, 1864.

Brigadier-General BURBRIDGE :

I have no further news of the movements of Forrest. He has disappeared from the vicinity of the rivers. Colonel Woodward, Captains Quains [?] and Swigert swam the Cumberland at daylight, April 1. I have forces after them. I hear nothing of the companies from Henderson. I hold 6 of those who crossed the river at Eddyville here as prisoners. Have not yet received reports of those taken in vicinity of Princeton ; I understand 10 or 15. Would suggest that those coming in and giving themselves up voluntarily be released here on amnesty oath. It would induce others to do the same. They are scattered and have to be hunted up like rabbits. Unless otherwise ordered, I will send them to Louisville, as per your order of March 30. My horses are few and poor.

E. A. STARLING,
Colonel Thirty-fifth Kentucky, Commanding.

HDQRS. MILITARY DIVISION OF THE MISSISSIPPI,
Nashville, Tenn., April 2, 1864.

General BURBRIDGE,
Louisville :

General Schofield reports the enemy leaving East Tennessee for Virginia. He occupies Bull's Gap with his infantry, and his cavalry is scouting beyond. Ask the Louisville Journal to stop alarming the people about an invasion of Kentucky. Such articles are calculated to produce raids—the very thing Kentucky don't want.

There is no real army to threaten Kentucky but Johnston's, and he can't advance. The mountains of East Kentucky are a barrier against anything but a maraud, and you can always collect enough to repel any such. The only force in Southwest Virginia is left to guard their salt-works against a raid by us from the Kanawha or up from Knoxville.

You might push a light cavalry force well up toward Pound Gap. I will give Stoneman command of all the cavalry in the Department of the Ohio, and he will soon come into Kentucky to organize and put it into good shape.

I see the newspapers falling into the bad habit of publishing rumors and nonsense. Check this as much as possible and I will stop them at the front, even if I have to banish all the tribe.

We will need all railroads front of Nashville for pure military freight, so citizens need not come here with the expectation of going beyond Nashville. No private freight or citizens can use the military railroad till the army supplies are complete. All troops also must march from this point. Don't publish this information, but let parties interested find it out.

W. T. SHERMAN,
Major-General.

LOUISVILLE, *April 2, 1864.*

Major-General SHERMAN,
    Nashville, Tenn.:

Colonel Gallup, commanding at Louisa, has just telegraphed me that General Hodge's rebel brigade passed through Pound Gap the 30th of March, and that Lieutenant-Colonel Ferguson drove his advance on the 31st to Prestonburg, but was compelled to fall back upon meeting a superior force. His citizen scouts from Gladesville report that Morgan was at Abingdon on the 27th March with a large force, and was at that time moving toward Kentucky.

S. G. BURBRIDGE,
Brigadier-General.

HEADQUARTERS GENERAL HOVEY'S DIVISION,
Nashville, Tenn., April 2, 1864.

Major-General SCHOFIELD,
    Knoxville, Tenn.:

For want of transportation I am compelled to send all my baggage and sick by rail. To what point shall they be directed? Five regiments march to-morrow morning. The One hundred and twenty-ninth [Indiana] has not yet arrived, but expected to-night.

ALVIN P. HOVEY,
Brigadier-General.

LOOKOUT VALLEY,
April 2, 1864.

Major-General SHERMAN:

I omitted to mention Major-General Butterfield in the reorganization. You will find no cause to regret his assignment to a command corresponding with his rank.

HOOKER,
Major-General.

SPECIAL FIELD ORDERS, } HDQRS. DEPT. OF THE CUMBERLAND,
No. 93.   }   *Chattanooga, April 2, 1864.*

*   *   *   *   *   *   *

VIII. The following is announced as the organization of the cavalry of this department, to take effect April 1, 1864:

First Division, Col. Edward M. McCook, commanding:
First Brigade: Second Michigan Cavalry, First Tennessee Cavalry, Eighth Iowa Cavalry.
Second Brigade: First Wisconsin Cavalry, Second Indiana Cavalry, Fourth Indiana Cavalry.
Third Brigade: Fourth Kentucky Cavalry, Sixth Kentucky Cavalry, Seventh Kentucky Cavalry.
Lilly's Eighteenth Indiana Battery.
Second Division, Brig. Gen. K. Garrard, commanding:
First Brigade: Fourth U. S. Cavalry, Seventh Pennsylvania Cavalry, Fourth Michigan Cavalry.
Second Brigade: First Ohio Cavalry, Third Ohio Cavalry, Fourth Ohio Cavalry.
Third Brigade: Seventeenth Indiana Mounted Infantry, Seventy-second Indiana Mounted Infantry, Ninety-eighth Illinois Mounted Infantry, One hundred and twenty-third Illinois Mounted Infantry.
Chicago Board of Trade Battery.
Third Division: Col. W. W. Lowe, Fifth Iowa Cavalry, commanding:
First Brigade: Fifth Iowa Cavalry, Ninth Pennsylvania Cavalry, Third Indiana Cavalry (battalion).
Second Brigade: Eighth Indiana Cavalry, Second Kentucky Cavalry, Tenth Ohio Cavalry.
Third Brigade: Third Kentucky Cavalry, Fifth Kentucky Cavalry, Ninety-second Illinois Mounted Infantry.
The regiments of Tennessee cavalry, excepting the First Tennessee, will be organized in a division of two or more brigades under the direction of Brig. Gen. A. C. Gillem, U. S. Volunteers.
Division and brigade commanders will organize their staff in accordance with department orders.
All companies and detachments, including clerks and orderlies, at the headquarters of corps, division, brigade, and at depots will be ordered, by the several officers under whose orders they are serving, to join their respective regiments.
Details for escort and orderlies will be made from the troops of the command of the general for whom they are required.
Horses and equipments will be provided by the quartermaster and ordnance departments upon proper requisitions.
The Fifteenth Pennsylvania Cavalry will be subject to the orders of the major-general commanding the department.
The required reports and returns will be made to include March 31, 1864, in accordance with former organizations.
All reports and returns will be forwarded to the chief of cavalry.

*   *   *   *   *   *   *

By command of Major-General Thomas:
WM. McMICHAEL,
Major and Assistant Adjutant-General.

SPECIAL ORDERS, }   HEADQUARTERS FRONT,
   No. 11.   }   *Big Black Bridge, April 2, 1864.*

*   *   *   *   *.   *   *

III. In accordance with instructions from headquarters Post and Defenses, dated Vicksburg, Miss., April 2, 1864, Lieut. Col. N. W. Spicer, commanding First Regiment Kansas Mounted Infantry, will move his command to Powell's plantation, near Haynes' Bluff, taking with them all camp and garrison equipage, for the purpose of occupying that position. They will patrol the road to Oak Ridge, communicating with the cavalry from Clear Creek at that point, until further orders.

IV. Lieut. Col. J. H. Peters, commanding cavalry forces Seventeenth Army Corps, will cause the detachment Fifth Regiment Illinois Volunteer Cavalry of his command to move without delay to Bovina Station, to supply the place and occupy the encampment of the First Regiment Kansas Mounted Infantry (ordered to Powell's plantation, near Haynes' Bluff). They will patrol the road to Baldwin's Ferry, there communicating with the cavalry from Red Bone, until further orders. The cavalry at Clear Creek will patrol the road communicating with the First Kansas Mounted Infantry, at Oak Ridge, and also patrol the road to Messinger's Ferry.

By order of Brig. Gen. E. S. Dennis:

W. BEDFORD,
Assistant Adjutant-General.

CHATTANOOGA, *April 3, 1864—9 p. m.*

Major-General SHERMAN,
   Nashville:

Your dispatch of yesterday received. Will watch Johnston as close as possible, but shall only feel perfectly safe when I can get my troops back from East Tennessee. My outposts report no movements of the enemy, except a reconnaissance on the Spring Place and Cleveland road yesterday, which resulted in nothing.

GEO. H. THOMAS,
Major-General, U. S. Volunteers.

CLEVELAND, TENN.,
April 3, 1864.

Colonel LANE,
   Commanding U. S. Forces, Charleston, Tenn.:

Please forward the following to Major Purdy, commanding cavalry regiment at Columbus: About 800 rebel cavalry are reported east of Benton moving toward Columbus. They have told citizens that they intended to capture the forces at Columbus. If overpowered, retire to Charleston and report their approach to me, so that I may cut them off at Benton. Keep a good lookout and report through post commandant at Charleston.

By command of Col. A. P. Campbell:

ROBT. LE ROY,
Captain and Assistant Adjutant-General.

CLEVELAND, *April* 3, 1864.

Brig. Gen. W. D. WHIPPLE,
    Assistant Adjutant-General.

GENERAL : A scout by the name of Oscar G. Frazier has just come in and reports that he has reliable information that the rebel raid of yesterday was for the purpose of covering the approach of Longstreet from above. Longstreet is re-enforcing Johnston by way of Murphy. The rebs, about 1,500 strong, came up within 8 miles of here, divided into parties, one going out in the direction of Ducktown, through the mountains, the other remaining and falling back toward Dalton.

Very respectfully, your obedient servant,
THOS. E. CHAMPION,
    Colonel, Commanding Post.

HDQRS. ONE HUNDREDTH ILLINOIS VOLUNTEERS,
    Athens, Tenn., April 3, 1864.

General WAGNER :

SIR : Immediately upon the receipt of information of the approach of the enemy, I sent out citizen scouts upon all the roads leading to this place. At 4 a. m. I received from hand of scout sent to Columbus the following message :

HEADQUARTERS FOURTH INDIANA CAVALRY,
    Columbus, Tenn., April 2, 1864.

COMMANDER U. S. FORCES,
    Athens, Tenn.:

SIR : Your scout, F. A. Cameron, has just arrived, and I send the following information : The rebels, some 500 strong, approached to within 12 miles of this place on the Ducktown road, but I am satisfied that they have fallen back, in all probability by the Connesauga River. Colonel La Grange, commanding Second Cavalry Brigade, is on the opposite side of the river with some 1,400 men. All is safe at present.

G. H. PURDY,
    Major, Commanding Regiment.

Scouts reported to me all right, and are reporting now. All pronounced everything quiet.

I impressed yesterday and to-day all the negroes in town and put them at work upon the fortification ; ran a line considerably shorter than the one laid out, and at night had constructed of logs, brush, and dirt a very respectable fortification. The work as now built is smaller than the one planned, but is large enough. The line laid out for me was 1,687 feet in length—a very long line for the force likely to be here. I shall keep at work and will make a strong redoubt.

Respectfully,
ARBA N. WATERMAN,
    Lieutenant-Colonel, Commanding Post.

HDQRS. MILITARY DIVISION OF THE MISSISSIPPI,
    Nashville, April 3, 1864.

General ALLEN,
    Louisville, Ky. :

I have yours of the 2d. The difficulties of transportation to the front are all plain to me. I have made orders to stop all civil business and freight, and the cars to be devoted exclusively to dead freight. If I could prevail on the railroad superintendent to make other modifications I could further increase the work of the railroad. I have no knowledge of McCallum's action, and indeed am more embarrassed than I can well express by the anomalous nature of my authority over this and the staff departments generally. So many independent machines will produce a collision sooner or later, yet I will be as patient as possible.

I want in the next thirty days a surplus of stores to the front, equal to sixty or seventy days' supply, but I see but little chance yet of getting it. It will be too late to wait for the cars and locomotives contracted for by McCallum.

W. T. SHERMAN,
Major-General.

BULL'S GAP, *April 3, 1864.*

Major-General SCHOFIELD,
    Knoxville, Tenn.:

The rebel infantry was at Zollicoffer and the cavalry rear guard at Jonesborough on last Friday. Do you wish either of the bridges over Lick Creek rebuilt? Are the other divisions of the Twenty-third Corps coming up here? Did you receive my telegram of last night?

STONEMAN,
General, Commanding Corps.

KNOXVILLE, *April 3, 1864—*11.30 p. m.

Major-General THOMAS:

Longstreet appears to have gone to Virginia with his main force. I will know the facts in a few days. If he is gone I will at once send you Wood's division, and will send you Sheridan as soon as my troops, now en route from Nashville, arrive.

J. M. SCHOFIELD,
Major-General.

HDQRS. MILITARY DIVISION OF THE MISSISSIPPI,
Nashville, April 3, 1864.

General LEGGETT,
    Zanesville, Ohio:

I must have your division and that of Crocker to rendezvous at Cairo, and come up the Tennessee to join me at the expiration of their furloughs. I am impatient to get you all in hand again, and promise you the most active service. We must all stick together, and if you hear of any of our old regiments being diverted let me know at once. I know Grant would not break up my command.

W. T. SHERMAN,
Major-General.

HDQRS. MILITARY DIVISION OF THE MISSISSIPPI,
Nashville, April 3, 1864.

General BRAYMAN,
 Cairo:

The more men Forrest has, and the longer he stays about Mayfield, the better for us. Don't give rise to such ridiculous nonsense as connecting Forrest's movements with a riot in Illinois.

Forrest must be attacked from below, but you should strike any detachment and should feel him all the time. Where he is he can do us no harm, and he knows it, and will soon escape.

    W. T. SHERMAN,
    Major-General.

CAIRO, *April 3, 1864.*

Brigadier-General BRAYMAN:

Important dispatches from General Sherman for General Veatch and you require your personal attention. I do not deem it prudent to send them on this line to you. You must move.

    J. H. ODLIN,
    Assistant Adjutant-General.

CAIRO, *April 3, 1864.*

Brigadier-General BRAYMAN,
 Paducah:

Captain Pennock thinks you had better come back immediately, and I think the Forty-seventh Indiana will have to go with you.

    J. H. ODLIN,
    Assistant Adjutant-General.

HDQRS. MILITARY DIVISION OF THE MISSISSIPPI,
Nashville, April 3, 1864.

Col. S. G. HICKS,
 Paducah:

Your defense of Paducah was exactly right. Keep cool, and give the enemy a second edition if he comes again. I want Forrest to stay just where he is, and the longer the better. Don't credit any of the foolish and exaggerated reports that are put afloat by design. I know what Forrest has, and will attend to him in time. Whenever you get a chance, strike any small detachments.

    W. T. SHERMAN,
    Major-General.

HDQRS. MILITARY DIVISION OF THE MISSISSIPPI,
Nashville, April 3, 1864.

General A. J. SMITH,
 Comdg. Detachment Army of the Tennessee, up Red River:

GENERAL: By the time you receive this the period for which your forces were loaned to General Banks will have expired, viz, thirty days after you entered Red River.

I have not your official reports, but know beforehand that you have done your full share in the undertaking. General Banks agreed with me to put 17,000 men into Alexandria by March 17. I see by newspapers that he did not start in person from New Orleans till the 22d. I hope this is not true, but will not discuss it.

I want your command right away, and you will, as agreed upon, return to Vicksburg at once, notifying General Banks and General Steele. At Vicksburg replenish your stores according to your judgment, and ascend the Yazoo rapidly to Sidon or Greenwood, and push out to Grenada. Your first object will be to overcome summarily any opposition there, and then to act according to your judgment against any enemy in North Mississippi.

General Corse, who brings this, will explain to you the exact attitude of things and will serve under your orders. When you have struck Forrest or any enemy you may find, destroy railroad south of Grenada and everything connected with the railroad, but spare all locomotives and cars in Grenada, as at a later period I wish to occupy Grenada and use its railroad to Memphis.

After you have done all you can at and about Grenada, strike for Decatur, Ala., doing all the mischief to the enemy and his resources en route you can. You may safely rely on the country to within two days of Decatur for meat, corn, meal, and everything needed but salt, sugar, and coffee, which you should carry.

You will not need much artillery, therefore leave the surplus at Vicksburg, subject to further orders ; and at this end you will find plenty of guns and ammunition, but bring all the animals you have and as many as you gather by the way.

As soon as I hear of your approach I will send out to meet you. Therefore as you leave Grenada send me word round by the river, by a special messenger, the fullest details, especially of the date of your start, the route you propose, and the probable time of your approach to Decatur.

You will have in Generals Corse and Mower two of the finest young officers in any army, and I will endeavor to preserve the most absolute secrecy. Should any combinations now unforeseen arise, you may depend on my reaching you with notice ; therefore act with the confidence that insures success. I want you and the generals I have named to be advanced in rank, and you may rely on all the influence I possess.

Call on Admiral Porter or any naval officer you find for co-operation and assistance and you will find them ever ready. You should have three or five small gun-boats with you up the Yazoo, to escort back to the Mississippi your empty boats. Send to Vicksburg or Memphis all useless men and material, and carry with you nothing but the useful and essential. Send me a special courier from Vicksburg and Grenada, that I may know the exact time and facts.

If the Yalobusha be high, you can ascend as far as you please. I don't limit you, and have named Sidon and Greenwood as the points of disembarkation because I know there are roads thence to Grenada. Don't be deterred by exaggerated reports. Forrest has not to exceed 4,500 men, and Lee still less. Polk, on the Tombigbee near Demopolis, cannot reach you, his force being infantry, as you know.

Yours, truly,

W. T. SHERMAN,
Major-General, Commanding.

HDQRS. MILITARY DIVISION OF THE MISSISSIPPI,
Nashville, April 3, 1864.

Brigadier-General CORSE, *Present:*

GENERAL: I select you for special service, and hereby clothe you with power to use my name to carry out certain plans which I herein describe, and on the exhibition of this letter all commanders subject to my orders will be governed.

You will move with all dispatch to Paducah. Explain to Colonel Hicks my entire satisfaction at his handsome defense of his post, which he may announce to his troops in orders. Deliver him a copy of the inclosed memorandum and one to General Veatch, to be sent up to him by some certain conveyance; then touch at Cairo and explain to General Brayman the same, Columbus and Memphis the same, and then proceed down the Mississippi till you meet the fleet of General A. J. Smith. If you don't meet him this side of Red River you may at your discretion ask for a flat gun-boat or go on in the boat you start with, up Red River, till you find General Smith and deliver to him the orders and instructions for him. Also send to Admiral Porter, General Banks, and General Steele the communications for them.*

After you have had communication with all these report to General Smith and act under his orders. If to carry out my plans you find it necessary, you may make written orders, signing by order of General Sherman, &c.

On your way down, making as little delay as possible, gather all real information you can as to the forces with Forrest, whether any or all of Lee's cavalry be with him, &c., but do not be diverted by idle stories of incredible numbers. We have felt all these forces, and I know General Smith's column is capable of handling all the cavalry in Mississippi, even if re-enforced by a division of infantry. You had better take from Nashville four of our best maps, so that as you approach Decatur you will have the same that we have.

I place at your disposal here at Nashville a fleet steam-boat, guarded by 100 armed and dismounted cavalry, which steam-boat you can take with you all the way or transfer to others, discharging this at your discretion.

At Cairo instruct General Brayman what troops destined for down river should be detained and what not.

I want the furloughed men of Banks not to be detained, nor those for Vicksburg or Memphis, but General Brayman may hold for a short time two or more regiments belonging to Dodge's or McPherson's command, excepting that of Veatch.

. I am, &c.,

W. T. SHERMAN,
Major-General.

[Inclosure.]

CONFIDENTIAL.]   HDQRS. MIL. DIV. OF THE MISSISSIPPI,
Nashville, April 3, 1864.

General memoranda:

1. The posts of Columbus, Cairo, and Paducah to be held in force, and mere excursions sent out to occupy the attention of Forrest.

2. General Veatch to occupy a point near Purdy and to strike Forrest in flank as he attempts to pass out.

3. General Hurlbut to operate from Memphis with his infantry and

---

*See Vol. XXXIV, Part III, pp. 24, 25, 27, respectively.

cavalry, guarding the passes of Big Hatchie and communicating with General Veatch.

4. General A. J. Smith to return from Red River, pause at Vicksburg to replenish supplies, and to push up Yazoo to Greenwood and Sidon, disembark, march rapidly on Grenada, and operate on Forrest's rear. If Forrest is escaped, broken up, or captured, all the troops to resume the statu quo, and General Smith to conduct his force by steady marches across to the Tombigbee and up to Decatur, Ala., whence General Dodge will move out to meet him. General Smith to send word round by Cairo, giving his route of march and indicating the probable time of his arrival. This column to move light as to wagons and artillery, depending for forage, corn, meal, and meat on the country, reckoning for supplies only at Vicksburg and Decatur; General Smith taking with him the two tried generals, Corse and Mower. If General Smith calls for cavalry, General Hurlbut will send as much as he can spare from Memphis, to meet him at some point of the Tallahatchie, and General Smith may call on the commanding general at Vicksburg for enough cavalry to serve as advance guard.

5. General Corse may order in my name any subordinate details to carry out these plans and the instructions of the commanding general.

Copies of this to be sent to Generals McPherson, Veatch, Brayman, Hurlbut, and McArthur, and to the commanding officers at Paducah and Columbus, with express orders of secrecy.

W. T. SHERMAN,
Major-General, Commanding.

SPECIAL ORDERS, ⎱   HDQRS. DEPARTMENT OF THE OHIO,
No. 94.   ⎰   <i>Knoxville, Tenn., April 3,</i> 1864.
*   *   *   *   *   *   *

III. Brig. Gen. J. D. Cox, U. S. Volunteers, is relieved from duty as chief of staff, and is assigned to the command of the Third Division, Twenty-third Army Corps.

IV. Brig. Gen. M. D. Manson will report for duty to Brig. Gen. J. D. Cox, commanding Third Division, Twenty-third Army Corps.

By command of Major-General Schofield:

R. MORROW,
Assistant Adjutant-General.

PRIVATE AND CONFIDENTIAL.]

HEADQUARTERS ARMIES OF THE UNITED STATES,
Washington, D. C., April 4, 1864.

Maj. Gen. W. T. SHERMAN,
Commanding Military Division of the Mississippi:

GENERAL: It is my design, if the enemy keep quiet and allow me to take the initiative in the spring campaign, to work all parts of the army together and somewhat toward a common center. For your information I now write you my programme as at present determined upon.

I have sent orders to Banks by private messenger to finish up his present expedition against Shreveport with all dispatch; to turn over the defense of the Red River to General Steele and the navy, and return your troops to you and his own to New Orleans; to abandon all of Texas except the Rio Grande, and to hold that with not to exceed 4,000 men ; to reduce the number of troops on the Mississippi to the lowest number necessary to hold it, and to collect from his command not less than 25,000 men ; to this I will add 5,000 from Missouri.   With this force he is to commence operations against Mobile as soon as he can.   It will be impossible for him to commence too early.

Gillmore joins Butler with 10,000 men, and the two operate against Richmond from the south side of James River.   This will give Butler 33,000 men to operate with—W. F. Smith commanding the right wing of his forces, and Gillmore the left wing.   I will stay with the Army of the Potomac, increased by Burnside's corps of not less than 25,000 effective men, and operate directly against Lee's army wherever it may be found.

Sigel collects all his available force in two columns—one, under Ord and Averell, to start from Beverly, Va., and the other, under Crook, to start from Charleston, on the Kanawha, to move against the Virginia and Tennessee Railroad.   Crook will have all cavalry, and will endeavor to get in about Saltville and move east from there to join Ord.   His force will be all cavalry, while Ord will have from 10,000 to 12,000 men of all arms.

You I propose to move against Johnston's army, to break it up and to get into the interior of the enemy's country as far as you can, inflicting all the damage you can against their war resources.

I do not propose to lay down for you a plan of campaign, but simply to lay down the work it is desirable to have done, and leave you free to execute in your own way.   Submit to me, however, as early as you can, your plan of operations.

As stated, Banks is ordered to commence operations as soon as he can.   Gillmore is ordered to report at Fortress Monroe by the 18th instant, or as soon thereafter as practicable.   Sigel is concentrating now.   None will move from their places of rendezvous until I direct, except Banks.   I want to be ready to move by the 25th instant if possible ; but all I can now direct is that you get ready as soon as possible.   I know you will have difficulties to encounter getting through the mountains to where supplies are abundant, but I believe you will accomplish it.

From the expedition from the Department of West Virginia I do not calculate on very great results, but it is the only way I can take troops from there.   With the long line of railroad Sigel has to protect he can spare no troops, except to move directly to his front.   In this way he must get through to inflict great damage on the enemy, or the enemy must detach from one of his armies a large force to prevent it.   In other words, if Sigel can't skin himself he can hold a leg whilst some one else skins.

I am, general, very respectfully, your obedient servant,

U. S. GRANT,
Lieutenant-General.

HEADQUARTERS ARMIES OF THE UNITED STATES,
Washington, D. C., April 4, 1864.

ADJUTANT-GENERAL OF THE ARMY :

The President consents to the following changes being made in the Military Division of the Mississippi, to wit:

The Eleventh and Twelfth Army Corps to be consolidated and called the First Army Corps, Maj. Gen. J. Hooker to command.

Maj. Gen. G. Granger to be relieved from command of the Fourth Army Corps, and Major-General Howard appointed to the command.

Major-General Schofield to be appointed to command the Twenty-third Army Corps.

Major-General Slocum will report to General Sherman for assignment, and Major-General Stoneman to General Schofield. General Granger will report by letter to the Adjutant-General of the Army.

Very respectfully, your obedient servant,

U. S. GRANT,
Lieutenant-General.

WASHINGTON, *April* 4, 1864—8 p. m.

Maj. Gen. W. T. SHERMAN:

The Eleventh and Twelfth Corps will be consolidated into the First Corps, Maj. Gen. Joseph Hooker commanding. Major-General Howard will command the Fourth Corps, Major-General Schofield Twenty-third. Relieve Maj. Gen. Gordon Granger. Assign Major-General Slocum to command Vicksburg District, and Newton to a division or wherever else you may think best.

U. S. GRANT,
Lieutenant-General.

HDQRS. MILITARY DIVISION OF THE MISSISSIPPI,
Nashville, Tenn., April 4, 1864.

Brig. Gen. J. A. RAWLINS,
Chief of General Grant's Staff, Washington, D. C.:

GENERAL: Since my return to Nashville I have made the complete circuit, going with McPherson to Decatur, Larkin's Ferry, Chattanooga, and Knoxville. This enabled me to see all my corps and division commanders, and to learn the actual state of affairs.

I have made few or no changes, but have suggested some by telegraph, a copy of which I inclose,* as it is yet unanswered.

I am sending all of Hovey's infantry to Schofield to enable him to return to Thomas Granger's troops that are properly his. I am assembling Garrard's division of cavalry on the right flank, near Columbia, and will give Stoneman all the cavalry of Schofield's department to organize in Kentucky, say near Lexington, to move to the front when there is grass and when I have forage enough at the front. At present the railroads supply bountifully the troops there, but make no surplus.

I am making troops march, cattle ditto, and am cutting down sutlers' and private business so as to gain cars for surplus stores and forage. I am endeavoring to persuade the railroad superintendent to run the cars in a circuit so as to work as an endless chain, but the habit of running by a time-table is so strong that I find him disinclined.

If I could see McCallum I could convince him that his present stock could do double the present work by making the round circuit by Stevenson and Decatur, all the cars running one way loaded and bringing in the empty cars.

I want to have on the line of the Tennessee by May 1 enough stores to enable me to move on, if General Grant so orders it. To

---

*See p. 221.

do this I calculate that Schofield should have 12,000 men, Thomas 45,000, and McPherson 30,000, besides the railroad guards and depot garrisons. I propose that Schofield should be prepared to move from Cleveland, Thomas from Chattanooga, and McPherson from Gunter's Landing on the Rome road. All my plans are subordinate to these general ideas.

Forrest got a severe rebuff by Hicks at Paducah, and still lingers somewhere between the Tennessee and Mississippi and above the Hatchie. I want to keep him there awhile, when I hope to give him a complete thrashing. I order Paducah, Cairo, and Columbus to be held secure. Have placed Veatch with five regiments of infantry at Purdy, and ordered Hurlbut with all of Grierson's cavalry and 2,400 infantry to watch the line of the Hatchie and to catch Forrest in flank as he attempts to pass out.

Last night I sent General Corse down the Cumberland in a steamboat to touch at Paducah, Cairo, and Columbus, with orders and verbal explanations to all these commanders. He is then to push on to Memphis, explain the same to Hurlbut, and then hurry up the Red River to General A. J. Smith, and bring him with all dispatch to Vicksburg and up the Yazoo, and rapidly occupy Grenada. His appearance there with 10,000 men, now hardened by our march to Meridian and recent marching up Red River, will be a big bombshell in Forrest's camp should he, as I fear he will, elude Hurlbut.

At Grenada, Smith will do all the mischief he can and then strike boldly across the country by Aberdeen to Russellville and Decatur, there making his junction with McPherson. This, with Crocker's and Leggett's divisions to rendezvous at Cairo after their furloughs, will make a large decrease of our Mississippi River forces; but I order McPherson to keep one white division at Vicksburg and another at Memphis, which, with the black troops, the Marine Brigade, and the gun-boats, should suffice to protect the river commerce, especially since we have so ruined Meridian that the enemy cannot supply an army near the river with either ammunition or provisions. It is all nonsense about their repairing the break at Meridian; it is a simple impossibility. I would like to have General Grant's opinion as to this move of Smith's across from Grenada. I deem it safe, and its effect will in a measure compensate for the ill effects of William Sooy Smith's repulse and Forrest's recent raid. With 10,000 men and two such dashing officers as Corse and Mower, A. J. Smith can whip all the cavalry and infantry (if any) in North Mississippi. I cannot hope that Hurlbut will ever do any bold act; on the defensive he may do well enough, but I cannot inspire him with offensive ideas.

I want Newton at Vicksburg for safety, and I would like a bold, dashing officer at Memphis, but I will await the assignment of generals, which will, I hope, be made me, before I commit myself to others. Old Hicks has done so well that he should have a life estate at Paducah, but both Hurlbut and Brayman are too easily stampeded to hold the points they now do after their garrisons are reduced, as they must be in a short time.

At present and for some time Cairo will be strong by reason of McPherson's veterans rendezvousing there, en route for his headquarters via the Tennessee River.

I think General Grant never heartily approved the Red River trip. I would not, either, had I not foreseen a necessary delay in operations in Virginia and here, from the time consumed by the furloughs; but since that expedition has developed the fact that the enemy was hard at work to close Red River to us, and the handsome manner in which his works were carried by my troops, I think he will have changed his opinion.

I have yet no official reports, but doubt not those contained in the newspapers are substantially correct, as the names and dates correspond with my orders and instructions.

General Banks positively agreed with me that our troops should form a junction at Alexandria on the 17th of March. Mine were there on time, capturing Fort De Russy en route; and since it is reported they are up at Natchitoches, which is all right, but it seems Banks did not leave New Orleans till March 22; this is not right. This failure in time in conjoint operations is wrong, because it endangers the troops that punctually obey orders. I suppose that Steele is moving on Shreveport with 7,000, and Banks with 17,000. These are enough to co-operate with the gun-boats, and therefore I rightfully claim my 10,000, with General A. J. Smith, at the time agreed on, viz, thirty days after the time they entered Red River, which expires April 10, at which time General Corse should find them at Alexandria and conduct them to their new field of operations. I will move heaven and earth to have my command ready for war as early in May as the furloughed men return, and this you can better expedite from Washington than I can from here.

I will not bother the general at all, but will keep him well advised of all real movements. He must not be disturbed by the foolish rumors that will get into newspapers spite of all precautions.

Write me answers to my inquiries as early as possible, even if they have been answered by telegraph.

I have the honor to be, your obedient servant,

W. T. SHERMAN,
Major-General, Commanding.

NASHVILLE, *April* 4, 1864—12 m.

Major-General THOMAS, *Commanding:*

I will strengthen Schofield as fast as possible, to enable him to send you back your own troops. Should Johnston take the initiative, you can bring forward one of Slocum's divisions; also one or two of Logan's. Now that Schofield has a surplus of provisions a temporary interruption of the railroad would not be serious, but we should hold Ringgold and Cleveland at all hazards.

W. T. SHERMAN,
Major-General.

CHATTANOOGA, *April* 4, 1864—9 a. m.

Maj. Gen. J. M. SCHOFIELD, *Knoxville:*

Dispatch of yesterday evening received. Please instruct General T. J. Wood to march to Cleveland when you relieve him from duty in your department. Send Colonel Klein also, with his battalion of cavalry, as soon as you can spare him. Some of our scouts report that Longstreet is re-enforcing Johnston, but I can hardly credit the report.

GEO. H. THOMAS,
Major-General.

KNOXVILLE, *April* 4, 1864—2 p. m.

Maj. Gen. W. T. SHERMAN :

I have nothing from the front in addition to what I telegraphed you on the 2d. Dispatches from Kentucky say the rebels drove in my advance posts near Prestonburg on the 31st. I cannot believe that it is more than a small cavalry force, certainly not large enough to do any considerable harm in Kentucky. I will send General Thomas' troops to him in a few days. If I am to destroy the road above Bull's Gap, I will have to begin soon in order to be ready to carry out your plans. I believe if a demonstration were made upon the Watauga bridge the rebels would destroy it themselves. If you approve I will try it.

J. M. SCHOFIELD,
Major-General.

HDQRS. MILITARY DIVISION OF THE MISSISSIPPI,
Nashville, Tenn., April 4, 1864.

General SCHOFIELD, *Knoxville:*

Your dispatch received. I don't want your infantry to go beyond Lick Creek. Our line is already too much drawn out, but with cavalry you can demonstrate as far as you please. If you can force the enemy to destroy Watauga bridge, it will be a good thing. Don't destroy the railroad till I give you notice. I will arrange to give you plenty of time. Let Thomas have his troops as soon as you can safely do so, as I regard Cleveland as our weak point.

Hovey is marching to you with 5,000 infantry, and I will put five new regiments of cavalry at Lexington for Stoneman as soon as possible.

W. T. SHERMAN,
Major-General.

HDQRS. MILITARY DIVISION OF THE MISSISSIPPI,
Nashville, April 4, 1864.

Major-General McPHERSON, *Huntsville:*

I will order the balance of Garrard's division of cavalry to rendezvous at Columbia. I wish you would keep scouts and mounted detachments well out to the Tennessee River, toward the mouth of Duck River. I don't care if Forrest does cross to this side, only we should have timely notice. I have sent down General Corse to communicate with Paducah, Cairo, Memphis, and Vicksburg, and then to go on to Red River and bring A. J. Smith's command by a route that will be indicated to you by a confidential messenger. This will divert from Vicksburg a part of your command which you may have designed to form a part of McArthur's command. If this be so, please arrange McArthur's division so that the men now up Red River will belong to Crocker and Leggett. One division of the Sixteenth and one of the Seventeenth Corps, with the black troops, must suffice to protect Memphis and Vicksburg, and the gun-boats must keep the river clear. Forrest is supposed to be at Jackson, Tenn., but I think he will try to get south as soon as possible.

W. T. SHERMAN,
Major-General, Commanding.

HDQRS. TWENTY-NINTH MISSOURI VOLUNTEERS,
Camp Gage, near Cottonville, Ala., April 4, 1864.
Capt. W. A. GORDON,
Assistant Adjutant-General, First Division:

SIR: I have the honor to report that according to the best information I can get Wheeler is at Blue Hills with his command, and one battalion of Roddey's command is at Guntersville. One of the companies that have heretofore been stationed at Guntersville has moved down between Fearns' Landing and opposite the mouth of Paint Rock River. Four companies of State troops are stationed at Warrenton. This I have from, I believe, reliable sources.

Very respectfully, your obedient servant,
JOS. S. GAGE,
Lieutenant-Colonel Twenty-ninth Missouri Vol. Inf.

ATHENS, *April* 4, 1864.
Major WILLARD, *Aide-de-Camp, Huntsville:*

Twenty-seven armed men and 3 captains came in from the rebel force at Mount Hope and gave themselves up at Decatur. They report a squad of 40 more on their way.

G. M. DODGE,
Brigadier-General.

APRIL 4, 1864.
Brig. Gen. G. M. DODGE, *Athens:*

The officer in command of Whitesburg reports that the enemy has increased his force along the river from opposite his position to Triana, and that they are in force (supposed to be 600 strong) at Lacey's Spring, 4 miles from Leeman's Ferry.

It is also reported that Roddey is coming back, and that they have moved to Blue Mountain, 2,500 strong. Have you any force at Triana, and how far up the river from Mooresville do your pickets and patrols extend?

JAS. B. McPHERSON,
Major-General.

ATHENS, ALA., *April* 4, 1864.
Major-General McPHERSON, *Huntsville:*

Roddey was ordered back a long time ago; was waiting to be relieved. The enemy picket all the country reaching from Courtland road to Danville. Their mounted force has increased; two regiments in the west and south; have not heard of any increase to the east. Have scouts in Coosa Valley. I do not picket on the river above Decatur (General Garrard did), but I send patrols up and down, night and day, as far as Triana. I have one regiment picketing the river from Florence to Eastport. General Veatch is still in Purdy. Will send scouts up river on south side in morning.

Blue Mountain is where the cavalry moved back to from the front to recruit. No doubt General Clanton moved up and relieved Roddey.

G. M. DODGE,
Brigadier-General.

APRIL 4, 1864.

Maj. Gen. W. T. SHERMAN,
            Nashville, Tenn. :

General Dodge's scouts report a movement of rebel cavalry along our front, number not stated ; say they are going to join Forrest, and formerly belonged to Wheeler's command. They passed through Tuscaloosa, and General Dodge thinks came out of Coosa Valley.

                        JAS. B. McPHERSON,
                                Major-General.

                        LOUISVILLE, *April* 4, 1864.

Major-General SHERMAN,
            Nashville, Tenn. :

I am concentrating a force at Lexington and have cavalry beyond. I desire to co-operate with General Sturgis in a reconnaissance toward Pound Gap. Our forces now occupy West Liberty, Louisa, Big Hill, and Irvine. I will go up to Mount Sterling on Wednesday. The Seventeenth Indiana is here, mounted. Shall I send it to Nashville by land, and all other mounted regiments ?

                        S. G. BURBRIDGE,
                                Brigadier-General.

HDQRS. MILITARY DIVISION OF THE MISSISSIPPI,
                Nashville, Tenn., April 4, 1864.

General WILSON,
            Chief of Cavalry, Washington, D. C. :

Yours of March 31 is received. We have, as you know, a vast amount of dismounted cavalry. I shall employ a part of it in guarding railroads. As a rule, the newly purchased cavalry horses should go to veterans, with a clear understanding if they fail to take proper care of them they will not again have a remount.

Could not the State troops and militia supply their own horses, receiving the per diem allowed by law ?

                        W. T. SHERMAN,
                                Major-General.

HDQRS. MILITARY DIVISION OF THE MISSISSIPPI,
                Nashville, Tenn., April 4, 1864.

General BRAYMAN,
            Cairo :

General Corse is on his way to Paducah and Cairo in a boat. Will see you and explain all matters. Keep me advised of actual facts, and cause any detachments of Forrest in reach to be punished. Hurlbut reports Forrest down about Jackson, Tenn.

I want communication kept up with Veatch and his force to be strengthened by any regiments arriving for McPherson.

                        W. T. SHERMAN,
                                Major-General.

CAIRO, *April 4, 1864.*

Maj. Gen. W. T. SHERMAN,
    Nashville, Tenn. :

Your communications* to General Hurlbut and General Veatch went forward promptly by dispatch-boat. Gun-boats were sent up the Tennessee yesterday to watch the crossing from Sandy to Duck River.

M. BRAYMAN,
    Brigadier-General, Commanding.

HEADQUARTERS SIXTEENTH ARMY CORPS,
    Memphis, Tenn., April 4, 1864.

Brig. Gen. R. P. BUCKLAND,
    Commanding District of Memphis :

GENERAL : It is necessary that great caution should be exercised in relation to the approaches to Memphis.

The enemy in very considerable force are near Rising Sun. It would be very like their tactics to cross Wolf suddenly near Moscow or at Germantown and move upon the city. To prevent any sudden dashes the picket guards must be strong and the officers cautioned to activity. The mounted men will be thrown well forward and cross patrols from road to road kept up especially at night. It would be well for you to examine the camps personally and ascertain whether or not they can be protected easily from sudden attack by a light intrenchment. I assure you that I consider great vigilance necessary, and I urge upon you that all officers and men be held to strict attention to their duties and to the order enjoining them to be at their posts and in camp.

Your obedient servant,

S. A. HURLBUT,
    Major-General.

HEADQUARTERS SIXTEENTH ARMY CORPS,
    Memphis, Tenn., April 4, 1864.

Brig. Gen. B. H. GRIERSON,
    Commanding Cavalry :

The force in your front must be developed. If it be possible communication should be opened with General Veatch, who should be at Purdy. The intention and purpose of this force must be unmasked. I cannot lay out any special line of action. Keep me advised of whatever may turn up.

Your obedient servant,

S. A. HURLBUT,
    Major-General.

RALEIGH, TENN.,
    April 4, 1864—10 p. m.

Lieut. Col. T. H. HARRIS,
    Assistant Adjutant-General:

Flag of truce which I sent out this morning returned this evening. The enemy has a strong picket, composed of Forrest's old regiment,

---
* See p. 230.

at a point 8 miles from here. There is no travel in this direction and no information can be obtained except from scouts, and that is not very definite. It is evident that there is a considerable force in my front. This is either a demonstration to cover their movement south, or the advance of a large body on Memphis. If this latter is the intention I think the enemy will cross Wolf River at a point above here and attempt to gain Memphis in my rear, as Wolf River can be quickly bridged at any point. In view of this, I have sent a portion of my force to White's Station and scouting parties up Wolf River to watch the crossings.

There are three roads running in an easterly direction between the Wolf and Loosahatchie, and I have not force enough to advance and drive the enemy in my front on all these roads, and it is certainly hazardous to advance upon one of them without strongly guarding the other two. I deem the force at my disposal insufficient, under the circumstances, to communicate with a force supposed to be at Purdy and at the same time cover the approaches to Memphis.

A detachment sent this morning across to the Memphis and Randolph plank road discovered a few scouts. I would suggest that a strong picket be placed on that road at the Wolf River bridge.

Respectfully, your obedient servant,
B. H. GRIERSON,
Brigadier-General.

HDQRS. MILITARY DIVISION OF THE MISSISSIPPI,
Nashville, Tenn., April 4, 1864.

General BURBRIDGE, *Louisville:*

I do not believe the enemy will move far into Kentucky through Pound Gap, unless as a cavalry raid. You should concentrate all your troops at Lexington, with cavalry well out to give notice. Grant designs a move in Southwest Virginia which will check any such move, and by way of East Tennessee we can get to the rear of Pound Gap. Longstreet is reported as going back to Virginia, and would naturally send a small force through the gap to cover the movement. Forrest is now reported at Jackson, Tenn. I have an infantry force at Purdy, and if Hurlbut acts with energy Forrest will have trouble in getting out. You may send that Ohio regiment of cavalry to re-enforce General Sturgis. As soon as certain things are done in East Tennessee, General Stoneman will come to Kentucky. In the mean time you must collect all your detachments at some point near Lexington. In case of any formidable invasion of East Kentucky we can call down from Ohio, Indiana, and Illinois a large force of furloughed veterans, who could reach the threatened points sooner than troops could come from the front, where they are needed.

W. T. SHERMAN,
Major-General. Commanding.

HDQRS. MILITARY DIVISION OF THE MISSISSIPPI,
Nashville, Tenn., April 4, 1864.

General BURBRIDGE, *Louisville:*

Schofield, from Knoxville, reports that there can be nothing threat-ening Kentucky from Pound Gap, but you do right in collecting your troops well in hand at convenient points. I want to give Schofield, at or near Lexington, in addition to his present cavalry, five new regiments. If the Seventeenth Indiana be a new regiment not belonging to Thomas' command you may order it to Lexington by land, reporting by telegraph to General Schofield. But all of the cavalry belonging to Thomas should march to Nashville.

I think it well you should go to East Kentucky and see your troops, allaying all unnecessary fears and encouraging the people.

W. T. SHERMAN,
Major-General.

HDQRS. MILITARY DIVISION OF THE MISSISSIPPI,
Nashville, Tenn., April 4, 1864.

Captain PENNOCK, *Cairo:*

I think we can build gun-boats above the shoals, and I agree with you that it is too late to pass the shoals now. I only repeated a message of General McPherson.

Tell Captain Shirk I send down in the quartermaster's gun-boat Silver Wave General Corse, whom I would like him to see. Ask Captain Shirk to keep up communication good with General Veatch at or near Purdy.

W. T. SHERMAN,
Major-General.

HEADQUARTERS ARMY OF THE OHIO,
Knoxville, April 4, 1864—12.30 p m.

Maj. Gen. GEORGE H. THOMAS,
Comdg. Army of the Cumberland:

I will also send you Colonel Klein's battalion soon. The report that Longstreet is re-enforcing Johnston cannot possibly be true, unless his troops are going around through Virginia by rail. It is certain that none have gone up the French Broad recently.

J. M. SCHOFIELD,
Major-General.

WAR DEPARTMENT, CAVALRY BUREAU,
Washington, April 4, 1864.

Hon. E. M. STANTON,
Secretary of War:

SIR: I have the honor to communicate for your information the following facts, reported by Capt. William R. Price, special inspector of this Bureau:

The mounted force of the Department of the Cumberland consists of twenty-eight regiments of cavalry and seven regiments of mounted infantry.

It is respectfully suggested that the following-named regiments be mounted and equipped and returned to duty before any more new regiments are supplied, viz:

In First Division, First Brigade: the Second Michigan Cavalry, Ninth Pennsylvania Cavalry.

Second Brigade: Second Indiana Cavalry, Fourth Indiana Cavalry, First Wisconsin Cavalry.

Third Brigade : Seventh Kentucky Cavalry, First Tennessee Cavalry.

In the Second Division, First Brigade: Seventh Pennsylvania Cavalry, Fourth Michigan Cavalry, Fourth U. S. Cavalry, Fifth Iowa Cavalry, Third Indiana Cavalry.

Second Brigade : First Ohio Cavalry, Third Ohio Cavalry, Fourth Ohio Cavalry, Tenth Ohio Cavalry, Second Kentucky Cavalry.

Third Brigade: Seventeenth Indiana Mounted Infantry, Seventy-second Indiana Mounted Infantry, Ninety-second Illinois Mounted Infantry, Ninety-eighth Illinois Mounted Infantry, One hundred and twenty-third Illinois Mounted Infantry, Third Kentucky Cavalry, Eighth Iowa Cavalry.

From 6,000 to 9,000 horses are required to properly mount these regiments.

There are several skeleton organizations of Tennessee cavalry regiments, which organization is of the worst description. It is understood that Governor Johnson has gone to Washington to have these regiments mounted, and it is recommended that before mounting them the above mentioned regiments be first mounted ; and also that they are furnished with the Spencer or Sharps carbine.

The Second Michigan, Ninth Pennsylvania, Second Indiana, and First Wisconsin have all signified their willingness to re-enlist if they can be furloughed, but at present they cannot be spared from duty.

At Knoxville and Strawberry Plains, to which points the Army of the Ohio had advanced, the cavalry was almost entirely used up, the horses almost starved to death from the too limited supply of forage.

General Schofield complains of a great want of competent cavalry commanders in his department. Colonel Wolford, in command of a division of cavalry, has but two commands for it—"Scatter l" and "Huddle up !"—about all he uses.

The inspecting officer in his report says :

As the Tennessee regiments now organizing at Nashville are nearly all cavalry, I wish respectfully but earnestly to protest against giving them arms and equipments, as in my opinion it is prejudicial to all the interests of the cavalry service, to the prosecution of the war, and to the best interests of the State of Tennessee, and the dictates of humanity counsel against it.

Regarding the efficiency of these Tennessee regiments there is but one opinion. With the exception of the First Tennessee, they are all worthless. The decision of the Secretary upon this matter, made in March, has been communicated to Governor Johnson and General Sherman.

On the 6th of March nearly all the cavalry of the Department of the Ohio were concentrated at Louisville, Ky. The following plan for the direct communication between the generals commanding and the Cavalry Bureau is respectfully submitted :

First. That the chiefs of cavalry for the different armies be field officers, exercise no command in the field, but perform the duties of a staff officer.

Second. To see that all broken-down horses are turned in and sent to the proper depots for recuperation ; that all branded horses in the hands of the citizens are returned to the Government ; that the proper ration of hay and grain is furnished to the cavalry.

Third. That all surplus ordnance stores are turned over to the proper officers, and the arms kept in good condition.

Fourth. All requisitions to be approved by them, and preference given to those regiments that take the best care of their horses and arms.

If the above suggestions are impracticable, the inspectors of the chiefs of cavalry should be intrusted with the duties.

The experiences of this war, and particularly General Smith's late expedition, have demonstrated that the most successful raids in the enemy's country have been effected by small bodies of troops well armed and equipped. It was with the greatest difficulty that this column was subsisted in the country through which they marched. From 1,500 to 2,500 men, under a skillful commander, could have accomplished much more and effected the junction with General Sherman.

There is nothing more discouraging to brigade or division headquarters than to know that their commands are constantly subject to detail from some chief of cavalry as soon as they have arrived at a proper state of discipline.

On such an extended line of operations as exists in the west a corps organization of cavalry is not deemed expedient. It is seldom that such a large force is called to act together under the command of one officer.

In reach of the Armies of the Cumberland, Tennessee, and Ohio there is now an average of about thirty regiments of mounted troops. This force, organized into three brigades in each army, could at all times prevent any serious damage by raids, and also attend to all the outpost and picket duty that belongs to cavalry.

It is advisable to discourage all mounted infantry regiments. Many of these regiments the Cavalry Bureau have no account of. They deprive the cavalry of their proper allowance of forage, pay no attention to stable duties, have neither curry-combs nor brushes, and General Smith remarks that if these infantry regiments were all dismounted they would furnish enough horses to mount all the cavalry of this department.

The horses forwarded from Saint Louis have begun to arrive at Nashville, and are considered the best lot of horses that have been received for a long time. It is recommended that a quartermaster, under the direction of the Cavalry Bureau, be sent to that place to receive and issue the horses. A plan should also be adopted to care for the broken-down horses. At present very few are taken up or cared for, but turned loose to die of starvation. On the march from Knoxville to Strawberry Plains upward of 200 of the poor animals were seen on the roads starving. These horses should be picked up and corralled.

It is to be feared that the country will be inadequate to supply the horses necessary to keep up the cavalry force in its present condition. Greater care should be taken in the appointment of cavalry commanders. As yet no estimate can be given of the number of horses that will be required for the next six months.

At Mount Sterling, Ky., 36 miles west of Lexington, the inspector found the First Division of Cavalry, of the Department of the Ohio, and the Fifth Indiana Regiment, of the Second Division. They were all in good condition, having received 1,200 horses from the quartermaster, and in expectation of 600 more, all of a very fair quality.

In the Department of the Ohio there were eight one-year mounted infantry regiments, or in process of being mounted, by whose authority no one knows. It is recommended that a depot be established at Louisville, Ky., which would take in Memphis, Nashville, and Knoxville.

The rosters of the Fourth and Sixth Kentucky Cavalry accompany this report. It will be seen that the aggregate force of both does not exceed 700 or 800 men. They should be consolidated if possible. The roster of the Eleventh Michigan Cavalry is also inclosed, it being one of the most efficient regiments in the service. The Tenth Michigan is also a fine organization.

Regarding Colonel Wolford's ability General Sturgis has a better opinion than most other officers; but in the opinion of the inspecting officer the service would be no loser if he were relieved from the service.

The Seventh Pennsylvania has recruited upward of 1,100 men, and horses should be at once furnished them, as it is one of the best regiments in the service. It is essential to have the cavalry of the Department of the Cumberland in an effective condition at once, much more so than that of the Department of the Ohio, as the latter cannot be used for some time. It is thought that horses could be purchased to advantage in Kentucky. The Fifth Indiana, in the Department of the Ohio, is also a fine regiment.

The general desire of the best regiments is to be armed with the Spencer carbine. By arming one or two regiments in each department with them, their old arms turned in will supply the deficiencies in the other regiments.

To the Second and Fourth Michigan, 700 Spencer carbines were furnished; to the Fourth United States, 600. It is proposed to furnish 700 for the Fifth Indiana, and also the Second Iowa, of the Department of the Tennessee.

I am, sir, very respectfully, your obedient servant,

J. H. WILSON,
Brigadier-General, Chief of Cavalry Bureau.

GENERAL ORDERS, }   WAR DEPT., ADJT. GENERAL'S OFFICE,
No. 144.   }   *Washington, April 4, 1864.*

I. By direction of the President of the United States the following changes and assignments are made in army corps commands:

Maj. Gen. P. H. Sheridan is assigned to command the Cavalry Corps, Army of the Potomac.

The Eleventh and Twelfth Army Corps are consolidated, and will be called the Twentieth Army Corps. Maj. Gen. J. Hooker is assigned to the command.

Maj. Gen. G. Granger is relieved from command of the Fourth Army Corps, and Maj. Gen. O. O. Howard is assigned in his stead.

Major-General Schofield is assigned to the command of the Twenty-third Army Corps.

Major-General Slocum will report to Major-General Sherman, commanding Division of the Mississippi, and Major-General Stoneman to Major-General Schofield, commanding Department of the Ohio, for assignment.

Major-General Granger will report by letter to the Adjutant-General of the Army.

II. Capt. Horace Porter, U. S. Ordnance Department, is announced as an aide-de-camp to Lieutenant-General Grant, with the rank of lieutenant-colonel.

By order of the Secretary of War:

E. D. TOWNSEND,
Assistant Adjutant-General.

GENERAL ORDERS, }   HDQRS. TWENTY-THIRD ARMY CORPS,
No. 20.   }   *Bull's Gap, Tenn., April* 4, 1864.

In order to comply with instructions from the headquarters of the Division of the Mississippi, the undersigned hereby relinquishes the command, temporarily, of the Twenty-third Army Corps.

When he assumed command of the corps, he expected and intended to make its headquarters his home during the rebellion, but other duties render this now inexpedient.

In parting with the officers and enlisted men with whom he has been so short a time associated, he takes the occasion to state that in a long and varied service in the army he has never had the honor to command any body of troops which, for bravery, loyalty, and devotion, for intelligence, energy, and zeal, and for all that constitutes the citizen, the soldier, and the patriot, can claim superiority over the corps from which he now relinquishes control, and feels the assurance that your future will not belie the past. And he also takes the occasion to remind you that we have each and all taken upon us the solemn obligation to obey all orders of our superiors, and that we are engaged in a contest for the supremacy of law and the rights of man.

GEORGE STONEMAN,
Major-General.

GENERAL ORDERS, }   HDQRS. TWENTY-THIRD ARMY CORPS,
No. 21.   }   *Bull's Gap, Tenn., April* 4, 1864.

In pursuance of paragraph III, Special Orders, No. 94, current series, from headquarters Department of the Ohio, the undersigned hereby assumes command of the Third Division, Twenty-third Army Corps, and also as senior officer present assumes command of the Twenty-third Army Corps during the absence of Maj. Gen. George Stoneman, who relinquishes the command temporarily in compliance with instructions from headquarters Military Division of the Mississippi.

J. D. COX,
Brigadier-General, U. S. Volunteers.

SPECIAL ORDERS, }   HDQRS. SEVENTEENTH ARMY CORPS,
No. 91.   }   *Vicksburg, Miss., April* 4, 1864.

The following is the organization of the Post and Defenses of Vicksburg, Brig. Gen. J. McArthur commanding:

Garrison proper, to be borne on post returns:

First. The Seventh Missouri Infantry, Seventeenth Illinois Infantry, Eighty-first Illinois Infantry, One hundred and twenty-fourth Illinois Infantry, Eighth Ohio Battery, Twenty-sixth Ohio Battery, will form a brigade, under command of Brig. Gen. J. A. Malt$_{by}$.

Second. The First Division, U. S. Colored Troops, Brig. Gen. J. P. Hawkins commanding; the Second Brigade of the division, Colonel Scofield commanding, will be reported as on detached service at Haynes' Bluff.

Third. The Fourth Regiment U. S. Heavy Artillery (colored), Col. H. Lieb commanding.

Defenses:

First. The First Division, Brig. Gen. E. S. Dennis commanding, composed of the First Brigade, commanded by Col. F. A. Starring, comprising the following regiments, viz: First Kansas Mounted Infantry, Seventy-second Illinois Infantry, Fifty-eighth Ohio Infantry, Thirtieth Missouri Infantry. The Second and Third Brigades, comprising the Fourteenth Wisconsin, Eleventh Illinois, Ninety-fifth Illinois, and regiments to be assigned from the Fourth Division. Artillery: Seventh Ohio Battery; Battery L, Second Illinois Light Artillery; Battery M, First Missouri Light Artillery. Cavalry: Second Regiment Wisconsin Cavalry.

Second. The cavalry forces commanded by Lieut. Col. J. H. Peters will report direct to post headquarters.

    *   *   *   *   *   *   *

VII. Brig. Gen. M. M. Crocker, commanding Fourth Division, will direct the following-named regiments and battalions of his command to proceed forthwith, with their entire camp and garrison equipage, to Big Black River bridge, and report to Brig. Gen. E. S. Dennis, commanding First Division, for orders, viz: Third Iowa Infantry, Forty-first Illinois Infantry, Thirty-third Wisconsin Infantry, Fourteenth Illinois Infantry, Fifteenth Illinois Infantry, Forty-sixth Illinois Infantry, Seventy-sixth Illinois Infantry, Seventh Ohio Battery: Brigadier-General Crocker will then repair to Vicksburg and there proceed to carry out the instructions of the major-general commanding the department.

VIII. Col. R. K. Scott, Sixty-eighth Regiment Ohio Infantry Volunteers, will forthwith proceed with the battalions formed from the veteran regiments of First and Third Divisions, except the Iowa battalion, Major Pomutz commanding, to Cairo, Ill., there to await further orders.

    *   *   *   *   *   *   -

XII. The following-named batteries, with their entire camp and garrison equipage, will forthwith report to Capt. J. T. Conklin, acting chief quartermaster Seventeenth Army Corps, for transportation to Cairo, Ill., at which point they will report to Captain Spear. Fifteenth Ohio Battery, for assignment to camp, and await further orders: First Minnesota Battery; Battery C, First Missouri Light Artillery; Battery H, First Michigan Light Artillery; Battery D, First Illinois Light Artillery; Third Ohio Battery, Tenth Ohio Battery.

Maj. T. D. Maurice, chief of artillery, Third Division, will in person superintend the shipment of the batteries of the Third Division.

    *   *   *   *   *   *   *

By order of Major-General McPherson:

WM. T. CLARK,
Assistant Adjutant-General.

NASHVILLE, TENN., *April 5*, 1864—10 a. m.
(Received 1.20 p. m.)
Lieutenant-General GRANT,
        General-in-Chief:

Dispatch of yesterday received. The change will be made forthwith. Will reconcile all conflicting interests that it is worth while to notice. All well with us. General Schofield is feeling up the valley cautiously, and dispositions are complete to make Forrest pay dear for his foolish dash at Paducah. I wrote very fully yesterday to General Rawlins.

W. T. SHERMAN,
                                Major-General.

CONFIDENTIAL.]   HDQRS. MIL. DIV. OF THE MISSISSIPPI,
                                Nashville, Tenn., April 5, 1864.
Col. C. B. COMSTOCK,
        General Grant's Staff, Washington, D. C.:

DEAR COLONEL: Your letter of March 26 came to me on the 2d instant, and the mail brought me the map yesterday.* The parcel had evidently been opened and the postmaster had marked some additional postage on it. I will cause inquiries to be made lest the map has been seen by some eye intelligent enough to read the meaning of the blue and red lines. We cannot be too careful in these matters.

That map, to me, contains more information and ideas than a volume of printed matter. Keep your retained copies with infinite care, and if you have occasion to send out to other commanders any more I would advise a special courier.

---

*Comstock's letter not found. The map referred to is Colton's New Guide Map of the United States and Canada, edition of 1863, and is marked in pencil as follows:

First. Red line along the Potomac, from its mouth to Williamsport; thence along Baltimore and Ohio Railroad to Oakland; thence via Elizabethtown to Ceredo, Versailles, and Brandenburg, and along the Ohio River to Cairo; thence up the Mississippi to vicinity of Saint Louis, up the Missouri to the Kansas line, and thence in southwesterly direction into Indian Territory.

Second. Red line along the Rappahannock, from its mouth to Rappahannock Station; thence via Madison Court-House and Manassas Gap to Winchester; thence southwest to the headwaters of the Guyandotte, and along the Cumberland Mountains to vicinity of the Tennessee line; thence south to the Smoky Mountains; thence through Tunnel Hill, Guntersville, and Corinth, to Oxford, Miss., and thence along the railroad to Lake Ponchartrain and along the Gulf shore to Pascagoula.

Third. Red line from Vermilion Bay to Bayou Bartholomew, in Drew County, Ark., and thence northwesterly into Indian Territory.

Fourth. Red line about Pensacola and along Santa Rosa Island.

Fifth. Red line about Jacksonville and Fernandino, Fla.

Sixth. Red line along the coast from Savannah to Charleston.

Seventh. Red line from Federal Point, along the coast, to New River Inlet, N. C.; thence via Pollocksville, Washington, Plymouth, and Suffolk, to Saluda, Va., and thence via Gloucester Court-House to the Chesapeake Bay.

Eighth. Blue line from Saluda, Va., via Richmond and the James River to Lynchburg; thence via Liberty to the Blue Ridge, and along there and the Smoky Mountains to connect with red line No. 2.

Ninth. Blue line from New Berne to Raleigh, N. C.

Tenth. Blue line from Tunnel Hill to Atlanta, Ga.

Eleventh. Blue line from Atlanta via Milledgeville to Savannah.

Twelfth. Blue line from Atlanta via Montgomery and Selma to Mobile.

Thirteenth. Blue line from Sabine Pass to Shreveport, La., and thence northwesterly into the Indian Territory.

From that map I see all, and glad am I that there are minds now at Washington able to devise; and for my part, if we can keep our counsels I believe I have the men and ability to march square up to the position assigned me and to hold it. Of course it will cost us many a hard day, but I believe in fighting in a double sense : first, to gain physical results, and next, to inspire respect on which to build up our nation's power.

Of course General Grant will not have time to give me the details of movements east, and the times. Concurrent action is the thing. It would be wise that the general, through you or some educated officer, should give me timely notice of all contemplated movements, with all details that can be foreseen. I now know the results aimed at. I know my base and have a pretty good idea of my lines of operation. No time shall be lost in putting my forces in mobile condition, so that all I ask is notice of time, that all over the grand theater of war there shall be simultaneous action. We saw the beauty of time in the battle of Chattanooga, and there is no reason why the same harmony of action should not pervade a continent.

I am well pleased with Captain Poe, and would not object to half a dozen thoroughly educated young engineer officers.

I am, with respect, your friend,

W. T. SHERMAN,
Major-General, Commanding.

HDQRS. MILITARY DIVISION OF THE MISSISSIPPI,
Nashville, Tenn., April 5, 1864.

General THOMAS,
Chattanooga :

The changes we agreed on are approved. Hooker to command the First Corps, composed of the Eleventh and Twelfth; Howard the Fourth Corps; Schofield the Twenty-third. Slocum goes to Vicksburg. Notify all parties that the orders will come down by the cars to-night.

W. T. SHERMAN,
Major-General, Commanding.

HEADQUARTERS ELEVENTH AND TWELFTH CORPS,
Lookout Valley, Tenn., April 5, 1864.

Brigadier-General GEARY,
Commanding Second Division, Twelfth Corps :

GENERAL : I am directed by the major-general commanding to acknowledge the receipt of the report of Col. C. Candy's very satisfactory reconnaissance on the south side of the Tennessee River.*

It appears that the colonel was upon the route over which the rebels run the mail. If this was the case, will it not be possible to put men in ambush and intercept it? The general desires that you will make inquiries, and if in your judgment it should appear advisable to attempt it, that you will not fail to do so.

Rations should not be issued to citizens living outside our lines,

---

* See Part I, p. 655.

nor should they be permitted to cross them, as many evidences exist of the abuse of this privilege. Important information has been obtained in this way of our condition and communicated to the enemy.

I am, general, very respectfully, your obedient servant,

H. W. PERKINS,
Assistant Adjutant-General.

HEADQUARTERS U. S. FORCES,
Gallatin, Tenn., April 5, 1864.

Capt. B. H. POLK,
Assistant Adjutant-General, Nashville:

SIR: It is my duty again to report matters in and about Lebanon. Lieutenant Burgess, Captain Lustre, and his brother, James Lustre, also two other officers and several non-commissioned officers and privates from the rebel army, are in the neighborhood. I can send 30 men to-morrow evening, perhaps by 8 o'clock p. m., and will meet a force if one can be sent from Nashville, and a small force from La Vergne or Murfreesborough. Have them start so as to arrive at Lebanon about 3 o'clock a. m. the next morning. If the arrangement can be made, I will send word to Colonel Stokes to send 200 men from Chestnut Mound and 100 from Carthage; in that way we can take most of these rebel officers. Their business is to pick up every deserter from their army, and to take back forcibly all of the men who have taken the amnesty oath or parole. I have this from reliable information. Make the arrangement for any day and let me know, and I will go myself. They are threatening everybody with a large rebel force in a short time.

Respectfully submitted.

E. A. PAINE,
Brigadier-General, Commanding.

BULL'S GAP, *April 5, 1864.*

Maj. J. A. CAMPBELL,
Assistant Adjutant-General, Knoxville:

I suppose General Stoneman has given the commanding general the condition of affairs. Both railroad and county bridge over Lick Creek destroyed, and the creek too high to ford at pr nt. No movement beyond the creek can be made without building a bridge or waiting for the stream to fall. A small railroad bridge here was partially destroyed, but could be repaired in half a day when tools come, which are expected. This would enable the cars to go 5 miles farther to Lick Creek. Nothing definite as to the condition of Watauga and Holston bridges, but Colonel Crawford expects positive and reliable information in regard to them in a day or two. No enemy except roving parties of guerrillas heard of south of the Watauga.

J. D. COX,
Brigadier-General, Commanding.

KNOXVILLE, *April 5*, 1864—11.30 a. m.

Maj. Gen. W. T. SHERMAN:

General Stoneman reports that a division of rebel cavalry moved up the French Broad from Greeneville about a week ago on its way to Georgia. This contradicts previous reports. General Stoneman says there is no doubt of its truth. The division was probably about 2,000 strong.

J. M. SCHOFIELD,
Major-General.

———

POWDER SPRING GAP,
April 5, 1864—2 p. m.

Maj. Gen. J. M. SCHOFIELD, *Comdg. Department:*

GENERAL: Dispatch of this date, directing movement of my division by easy marches to Knoxville, is just received. Owing to the lateness of the hour, which would make it late in the afternoon before we could get off, and also that several small streams between this and Strawberry Plains are much swollen by the late rains, but which will run out by to-morrow morning if there is no more rain ad interim, I will delay moving till to-morrow morning, and will reach Knoxville the day after to-morrow, 7th instant. Orders will be carried out in regard to the cavalry.

Respectfully, your obedient servant,

TH. J. WOOD,
Brigadier-General of Volunteers, Commanding.

———

HUNTSVILLE, ALA.,
April 5, 1864.

Maj. Gen. W. T. SHERMAN, *Nashville, Tenn.:*

Scouts in from Columbus, Miss., report passing considerable cavalry force going north. Said they were going to Forrest. They are the same force that crossed Black Water at Tuscaloosa. Stock in good order, and one battery accompanying them. General Veatch was at Florence this morning, on his way to join Dodge: would cross Elk River at Prospect. He landed at Waterloo, and is out of rations. I have not sent him any orders, and did not know that he had left Purdy, and am of the opinion that you did not know it either. The ration matter Dodge will attend to. In view of this concentration of rebel cavalry I am afraid our force in West Tennessee is insufficient.

JAS. B. McPHERSON,
Major-General.

———

HDQRS. DEPARTMENT AND ARMY OF THE TENNESSEE,
Huntsville, Ala., April 5, 1864.

Brig. Gen. M. M. CROCKER,
Fourth Division, Seventeenth Army Corps:

GENERAL: A telegram received from Major-General Sherman last evening renders it necessary to make some change in the organization of the Third and Fourth Divisions from that laid down in my letter to you of March 30.

The entire command of Brig. Gen. A. J. Smith, now up Red River, is to come this way, and that portion of it under Brig. Gen. T. Kilby Smith will be divided between Leggett and yourself.

This will not require any entire regiments now at and in the vicinity of Vicksburg to be transferred to Cairo, Ill., but simply the detachments non-veterans and the recruits belonging to the regiments which are to make up the two divisions. Everything else I desire carried out as indicated in my letter above referred to. I also wish Captain Foster's Fourth Company Ohio Independent Cavalry sent to Cairo in time to join me with the two divisions.

Instruct Colonel Powell, chief of artillery of the corps, to have the batteries which are to accompany the division fully equipped for the field, and with as good horses as can be procured. It will not answer to rely upon better horses at Cairo than are now with the batteries, and more are to be procured here. I inclose with this a statement* giving the organization of the corps under the new state of affairs.

Very respectfully, your obedient servant,

JAS. B. McPHERSON,
Major-General, Commanding.

HDQRS. DEPARTMENT AND ARMY OF THE TENNESSEE,
Huntsville, Ala., April 5, 1864.

Brig. Gen. J. McARTHUR, *Vicksburg:*

GENERAL: Inclosed I send you statement* of the proposed organization of the Seventeenth Corps. These changes are rendered necessary in order that two divisions may be made up at Cairo of veteran regiments as soon as possible. I have left six field batteries in your command for the present, owing to the great difficulty of getting horses and forage for the animals in this section. General Sherman has sent orders to Brig. Gen. A. J. Smith which will result in having that portion of his command under Brig. Gen. T. Kilby Smith go to make up a part of Leggett's and Crocker's divisions.

Keep me advised frequently of the state of affairs, and how you are getting along.

Very respectfully, your obedient servant,

• JAS. B. McPHERSON,
Major-General, Commanding.

ATHENS, *April 5, 1864.*

Major-General McPHERSON, *Huntsville:*

I have just received the following from General Veatch, who was at Florence this morning:

Says he landed at Waterloo and had got that far toward joining me and would cross Elk River at Prospect. Says he was out of rations. Don't think General Sherman knew he had left Purdy; it is the first I knew of it.

G. M. DODGE,
Brigadier-General.

---

* Not found.

ATHENS, *April* 5, 1864.
Brigadier-General SWEENY, *Pulaski:*
There is a cavalry force moving from Coosa Valley toward West Tennessee, by way of Tuscumbia. Instruct Seventh Illinois that they must watch closely the river front from Eastport, or from gun-boat up as far as Bainbridge. Also tell them to ascertain what forces are moving in Tuscumbia Valley opposite them.
G. M. DODGE,
Brigadier-General.

HEADQUARTERS DISTRICT OF CAIRO,
Cairo, Ill., April 5, 1864.
Maj. Gen. S. A. HURLBUT :
SIR : General Corse is going below in a few minutes on business ; he will explain. He brings this.
I was at Paducah on Sunday. Straggling bands in the neighborhood stealing and conscripting, but the main movements were evidently south.
A rumor worth heeding came to me there that the enemy were leaving for the Tennessee to cross near the mouth of Big Sandy. A gun-boat was sent up to guard that point and another to patrol the river between Duck River and Big Sandy. My orders 15 and 16 work well, and I think will cut off supplies of the rebels and lessen the number of incendiaries and spies among us.
Colonel Hicks has not sent his report. His books, &c., were destroyed, embarrassing him somewhat ; he promised it to-day.
Brig. Gen. Sol. Meredith has been ordered to report here. It would seem that he should have come to you first. If he reports and you do not otherwise order I will put him in command at Columbus.
I have the honor to be, general, very respectfully, your obedient servant,
M. BRAYMAN,
Brigadier-General, Commanding.

LOUISVILLE, *April* 5, 1864.
Col. GEORGE W. GALLUP, *Louisa, Ky.:*
The general has this morning started for Paris. He will concentrate a force of cavalry there in a few days and move toward Pound Gap. As a matter of course you are expected to co-operate. He will be at Paris until Monday possibly. Give him all the information you have, and telegraph here also. He will expect to hear from you to-night, and after he moves by courier every day.
THOS. B. FAIRLEIGH,
Lieutenant-Colonel and Acting Assistant Adjutant-General.

HDQRS. FOURTH DIVISION, SIXTEENTH ARMY CORPS,
Camp 1 Mile East of Florence, Ala., April 5, 1864—4 a. m.
Brigadier-General DODGE,
Commanding Left Wing, Sixteenth Army Corps:
GENERAL : I landed at Waterloo and reached this camp last night. I will make my way up Elk River as rapidly as possible to Prospect.

My rations and forage will be consumed before I reach that point. Please send me supplies to some point on the railroad near the Elk River crossing.

Respectfully, your obedient servant,

JAMES C. VEATCH,
Brigadier-General.

HEADQUARTERS SIXTEENTH ARMY CORPS,
Memphis, Tenn., April 5, 1864.

Brig. Gen. B. H. GRIERSON,
Commanding Cavalry Division, Sixteenth Corps:

GENERAL : I send you a copy of last dispatch from Sherman.* I think the movement is south and that every possible effort should be made to reach Veatch. Memphis will take care of itself or go up.

Yours,

S. A. HURLBUT,
Major-General.

HEADQUARTERS SIXTEENTH ARMY CORPS.
Memphis, Tenn., April 5, 1864.

[General GRIERSON :]

GENERAL : I am of opinion that Forrest is moving down south through La Grange and Pocahontas, and is fronting you with his best men to work off his plunder. This, however, is purely guess-work, for I can obtain no information from the country. If this is so the force in your front will disappear to-night. In that case you should turn, cross Wolf River, and proceed toward La Grange.

General Brayman reports Forrest still in the neighborhood of Mayfield with about 9,000 men. I consider this not to be true, although I have no doubt there is a force there. Memphis is strongly picketed and everything ready, and can be sufficiently held by the infantry. I urge you to keep up to these men as closely as possible.

Your obedient servant,

S. A. HURLBUT,
Major-General.

CAIRO, ILL., *April 5, 1864.*

Maj. Gen. W. T. SHERMAN,
Nashville, Tenn.:

Your order to General Veatch to go to Purdy and the Hatchie was delivered to him at Crump's Landing. He went to Purdy, then returned and went to Waterloo on east side, and on Sunday morning marched toward Pulaski, sending back the transports which have arrived. He must have received other orders for that movement. He is probably now beyond reach. Shall I send up the instructions left for him by General Corse, or can you reach him at Pulaski ?

I hear nothing of Grierson's movements.

M. BRAYMAN,
Brigadier-General.

*See p. 230.

NASHVILLE, TENN., *April 5*, 1864.
(Received 2.30 p. m.)

His Excellency A. LINCOLN,
    President of the United States :

The papers state that General Buell is to be sent to Knoxville to take command. I trust in God that General Buell will not be sent to Tennessee. We have been cursed with him here once, and do not desire its repetition.

We had a fine meeting at Shelbyville ; went off well. General Rousseau made a fine speech, taking high ground on the negro question, which will, I think, do great good in Kentucky and Tennessee. If General Rousseau had leave of absence for a short time, which would enable him to visit Kentucky and make some speeches in that State, such as he made at Shelbyville, it would do much good in putting down Copperheads and traitors. If this suggestion was made to General Thomas I have no doubt he would grant him leave of absence for the present. His service would be invaluable in Kentucky.

                                                    ANDREW JOHNSON.

GENERAL ORDERS, }   HDQRS. MIL. DIV. OF THE MISSISSIPPI,
    NO. 5.   }   *Nashville, Tenn., April 5*, 1864.

By and with the approval of the Commander-in-Chief of the Armies of the United States, the following changes are made, which will go into effect at once :

First. The Eleventh and Twelfth Corps are hereby consolidated, and will compose the First* Army Corps, Maj. Gen. Joseph Hooker commanding. Major-General Slocum is relieved from duty in the Department of the Cumberland, and will report in person to Maj. Gen. James B. McPherson, commanding Department of the Tennessee, for assignment to the command of the fortified post and District of Vicksburg.

Second. Maj. Gen. O. O. Howard is assigned to the command of the Fourth Army Corps. Maj. Gen. Gordon Granger is relieved from command of that corps and from duty with the Army of the Cumberland, to enable him to avail himself of a leave of absence heretofore granted him.

Third. Maj. Gen. J. M. Schofield is assigned to the command of the Twenty-third Army Corps, and Maj. Gen. George Stoneman is relieved from the command of that corps, for assignment to the command of a special cavalry force, to be organized under special instructions from these headquarters to the commanding general of the Army of the Ohio.

Fourth. Maj. Gen. John Newton is assigned to duty with the Army of the Cumberland, and will report to Major-General Thomas, at Chattanooga, for assignment to duty according to his rank.

Fifth. Commanding generals of departments will make all rules necessary to carry into effect these orders, and will make such dispositions of the staff officers affected and of corps badges and other insignia as in their judgment will result in the harmony and good of the service.

By order of Maj. Gen. W. T. Sherman :

                                R. M. SAWYER,
                        Assistant Adjutant-General.

---

* Changed to the Twentieth. See Halleck to Sherman, April 6, &c., p. 270.

SPECIAL ORDERS, }   HDQRS. DEPARTMENT OF THE OHIO,
   No. 96.   }   *Knoxville, Tenn., April 5, 1864.*

*   *   *   *   *   *   *

II. In anticipation of an order from the President relieving Maj. Gen. George Stoneman from command of the Twenty-third Army Corps, in order that he may be assigned to command the cavalry of this department, he will without delay repair to Kentucky and assume command of all the cavalry in that State, except that which belongs to the District of Kentucky.

The five new regiments of Indiana cavalry which are ordered to this department will also report to General Stoneman on their arrival in Kentucky. General Stoneman is authorized, if he deem it necessary, to visit Indiana for the purpose of attending to the mounting and equipment of these regiments and bringing them forward, or he may send his staff officers for this purpose.

General Stoneman will assemble all the cavalry assigned to his command at or near Lexington, Ky., and prepare it as quickly and as thoroughly as possible for active service in the field. He will organize his command into brigades and divisions according to his judgment, so as to place the most competent officers in command.

General Stoneman is authorized to organize a pack train for the supply of his command when in the field. Staff officers will honor his requisitions for all things necessary to the complete outfit of his command.

Brig. Gen. S. D. Sturgis is relieved from duty as chief of cavalry of this department, and will report for duty to Major-General Stoneman.

Capt. E. Gay, Sixteenth U. S. Infantry, is assigned to duty as inspector of cavalry.

The assistant inspectors of cavalry of divisions, brigades, and districts will make the periodical reports to Captain Gay, and such special reports as he may require from time to time, and will carry out his instructions relative to the discharge of their duties.

Major-General Stoneman will select competent and reliable officers as assistant inspectors for the brigades and divisions of his command.

*   *   *   *   *   *   *

VI. Brig. Gen. T. J. Wood, commanding Third Division, Fourth Army Corps, will march his division without unnecessary delay, by moderate daily marches, to Cleveland, Tenn., reporting in advance of his arrival at that place to Major-General Thomas, commanding Department of the Cumberland, for further orders.

All transportation and other public property belonging to the division will be returned to General Wood.

The major-general commanding desires to express to Brigadier-General Wood and his command his high appreciation of their cheerful and soldierly discharge of duty while temporarily under his command.

*   *   *   *   *   *   *

IX. All animals which are unserviceable and cannot be recruited in a reasonable time, viz, such as are ordinarily sold by the quartermaster's department, will hereafter be loaned to loyal citizens of East Tennessee, to be fed and used by them until called for by the chief quartermaster of the department. No citizen will be allowed to have a greater number of animals than required for his own use, nor will any be allowed to persons residing where the animals would be exposed to capture. Proper receipts, of a form to be prescribed by the chief quartermaster, will be taken in each case.

Hereafter no animals will be sold by the quartermaster's department in East Tennessee.

*   *   *   *   *

By command of Major-General Schofield:

R. MORROW,
Assistant Adjutant-General.

CULPEPER, *April* 6, 1864.
(Received 12.55 p. m.)

Major-General HALLECK:

The First and Third Corps having been merged into other corps, with the possibility of being filled up hereafter and restored to their corps organization, I would like to have the number of Hooker's corps changed to the Twentieth Corps. If this change is authorized, please notify Sherman by telegraph. It will cause dissatisfaction to give No. 1 to any other but the old corps having that number. To retain either the No. 11 or 12 will probably have the same effect with those losing their number.

U. S. GRANT,
Lieutenant-General.

WASHINGTON, *April* 6, 1864—2.45 p. m.

Maj. Gen. W. T. SHERMAN:

The combined Eleventh and Twelfth Corps under General Hooker is to be called the Twentieth Corps and not the First. Have General Orders, No. 144, so corrected.

H. W. HALLECK,
Major-General, Chief of Staff.

HDQRS. MILITARY DIVISION OF THE MISSISSIPPI,
Nashville, Tenn., April 6, 1864.

General M. C. MEIGS,
Quartermaster-General, Washington, D. C.:

GENERAL: I ought to have an officer of your department with me whose power is co-extensive with my own, whom I can freely converse with, explain plans, figures, reports, and everything. Now I have to deal with four independent departments, besides depot and district supervising quartermasters. Any one you name will be satisfactory to me, especially General Robert Allen. You saw enough out here to know that a general commanding should have such a quartermaster close by him all the time to direct the harmonious working of this vast machinery.

I am, with respect,

W. T. SHERMAN,
Major-General.

HDQRS. MILITARY DIVISION OF THE MISSISSIPPI,
Nashville, Tenn., April 6, 1864.
General J. P. TAYLOR,
Commissary-General, Washington, D. C.:

GENERAL: I ought to have near me an officer of your department clothed with power co-extensive with my own, who could converse with me freely, learn my plans, the strength of my various columns, routes of march, nature of supplies, and everything, and who could direct the harmonious working of the whole machine. Now I have to deal with four distinct commissaries, with no common recognized head. Colonel Kilburn would be perfectly satisfactory to me, or indeed any officer of experience you may name.

I ask the detail of such an officer to be made and to emanate from the highest authority, that his acts would be final.

W. T. SHERMAN,
Major-General.

HDQRS. MILITARY DIVISION OF THE MISSISSIPPI,
Nashville, April 6, 1864.
Maj. Gen. GEO. H. THOMAS,
Comdg. Department of the Cumberland, Chattanooga:

GENERAL: I have heretofore advised you by telegraph that the changes in the organization of your command that we concurred in have been made by the sanction of the Commander-in-Chief, and also that we retain control over our furloughed veterans.

I have ordered, through the State authorities, all absentees to come forward at once, or at furthest at the expiration of their furloughs. I have also sent forward to General Schofield a division of 5,000 infantry (Hovey's), which once at or near Hiwassee will enable you to draw below that river all of the Fourth Corps heretofore detached. These changes simply give you the absolute control of the Army of the Cumberland proper, in a shape that will enable you to handle and control it perfectly.

If you want General Palmer's place to be filled by any officer in my command you have only to ask it, and I think you should have no delicacy, as the general himself must feel that the importance of the occasion demands that you should be entirely satisfied with the ability and experience of your corps commanders.

As to posting the three great corps of which you have the command, I would only say that Chattanooga is your center, Cleveland your left, and Stevenson your right. As a matter of course you should cover your own communications, which I construe to extend back to Nashville and forward to Columbia. At Columbia I want Garrard's division to be composed of as near 4,000 cavalry as you can make it, of the best kind, to move, as it were, on our right flank, and at a certain moment to move against a point that I will probably direct in person. This division will still compose a part of your cavalry command, make all its reports to you, and in due season return to you. In the mean time I may give General Garrard some private and public instructions, of which you shall be duly advised.

Please give all the orders necessary to assemble that division at and in front of Columbia, and you may direct General Garrard, with detachments of his dismounted men, to guard the block-houses at Columbia and along down as far as Lynnville, and to draw oats and corn, as well as supplies generally, from the main depot at Columbia. Please order General Garrard to report to me by letter, when I will shadow to him the special service I expect of him.

This leaves you two other divisions of cavalry, which you can control at your pleasure, looking to the service on your front and the ability to supply and feed. I will do all I can to arm, equip, and mount the cavalry of yours and other commands, but I foresee infinite difficulty, and advise you to mount your best men, and use dismounted cavalry in great part to hold fortified points and guard your communications. This same general reasoning will apply to your artillery.

I would also suggest that the Twentieth Corps (now Hooker's) be organized into four divisions, one of which to be commanded by General Rousseau, who can be left to control the State of Tennessee lying west of the Tennessee River, and as far east as General Schofield's department would naturally cover. This division will necessarily be broken, and might be made to embrace all detachments and fragmentary bodies inconvenient to brigade and handle. The other three divisions should be organized especially for battle.

I understand your other two corps were already well composed of three divisions each, which my experience shows to be the true organization, and in that case depot guards can be made up of details and half sick men naturally left behind.

I have your memorandum before me, and on re-examining it, I think I have done all or nearly all you ask.

Your friend,

W. T. SHERMAN,
Major-General, Commanding.

NASHVILLE, TENN.,
April 6, 1864.

Brig. Gen. W. L. ELLIOTT,
Chief of Cavalry:

General Sherman directs me to say that orders have been sent to the headquarters Department of the Cumberland directing Garrard's entire division to rendezvous at Columbia, Tenn., and the troops now here awaiting their orders to move. Countermand any orders that may have been given that would conflict.

WM. SOOY SMITH,
Brig. Gen., Chief of Cavalry, Mil. Div. of the Mississippi.

BULL'S GAP. *April 6, 1864.*

Maj. J. A. CAMPBELL,
Assistant Adjutant-General, Knoxville:

The party of women and children arrived from Knoxville this evening. Lick Creek continues unfordable, and supposing my report on this subject last night might result in their being detained for a few days I sent back a flag of truce, which came this morning, without mention of our purpose of sending this party through. There is no village here and but one house, and this arrival of 40 women and children is rather embarrassing. I hope, however, to keep them from suffering till to-morrow, and if the creek does not fall, must send them back as far as Russellville. The party is much larger than I expected. Longstreet's mention of his intention to send a train to Lick Creek on the 11th (see his letter sent down to-night) is not consistent with the stories of the destruction of the bridges above, and is puzzling. Colonel Crawford has not yet received the positive reports from Watauga which he is expecting.

J. D. COX,

Brig. Gen., Comdg. Third Div., Twenty-third Army Corps.

NASHVILLE, *April* 6, 1864.

General McPHERSON, *Huntsville*.

Veatch's withdrawal from Purdy was very wrong. Call on him, in my name, for an immediate report.

Have you received any memorandum of movements which General Corse carried down the Mississippi? That will counteract any accumulation of cavalry in Mississippi. I think Johnston wants to feed up his corn on the Tombigbee, which he can't haul away. The cavalry can't do us any more harm, but I am disappointed that Hurlbut and Veatch did not catch Forrest in flank.

W. T. SHERMAN,

Major-General.

HUNTSVILLE, *April* 6, 1864.

Major-General SHERMAN :

I have not received your memorandum of movements which General Corse carried down the Mississippi. In addition to notifying the governors of Ohio, Indiana, Illinois, and Iowa about directing the return of veteran regiments. batteries, &c., you want to notify the governors of Missouri, Wisconsin, Kansas, and Minnesota.

JAS. B. McPHERSON,

Major-General.

HDQRS. MILITARY DIVISION OF THE MISSISSIPPI.

Nashville, Tenn., April 6, 1864.

General McPHERSON, *Huntsville :*

That memorandum taken by General Corse is important and confidential; was sent you by a courier. I will notify the Governors you have named in addition.

W. T. SHERMAN,

Major-General.

ATHENS, *April* 6, 1864.

Brig. Gen. J. D. STEVENSON, *Decatur :*

If you have mounted force enough send it up the river toward Guntersville, and try to catch the force near Triana, Lacey's Spring, &c. Destroy the boats that they cross with.

G. M. DODGE,

·Brigadier-General.

ATHENS, *April* 6, 1864.

Maj. Gen. J. B. McPHERSON,
        Huntsville:

There is no force in the valley around Decatur except some 1,400 near New Mount Hope. This is infantry. There is a cavalry picket line running from Guntersville clear round to Courtland; this is done to catch the deserters and refugees seeking our lines. The mountains are full of them, and they hold the mountain district in spite of all efforts of the rebels to catch them. I know of several companies of at least 100 men, each led by our scouts and members of the First Alabama Cavalry.

The desertions from Johnston's army to the mountains are very large, and a great many come in to us.

G. M. DODGE,
Brigadier-General.

———

ATHENS, *April* 6, 1864.

Brig. Gen. J. D. STEVENSON,
        Decatur:

Send the following to Major Hanna at Mooresville to-night:

General McPherson reports that the rebels have a scow at Triana and cross daily. Send a force there and break up that arrangement. Watch the river close about Triana and catch them.

G. M. DODGE,
Brigadier-General.

———

ATHENS, *April* 6, 1864.
(Received 10 p. m.)

Brigadier-General VEATCH:

I have just received following dispatch:

Major-General Sherman directs me to call upon General Veatch for an immediate report giving the reason for his withdrawal from Purdy, &c. Communicate this to him, and direct him to send his report through these headquarters.

JAS. McPHERSON,
Major-General.

Send the report here. I will forward it.

G. M. DODGE,
Brigadier-General.

———

PULASKI, TENN.,
April 6, 1864.

Lieut. Col. J. C. PARROTT,
        Commanding, Prospect, Tenn.:

COLONEL: The general commanding hereby authorizes you to grant permission to loyal citizens in your vicinity to purchase and keep arms for defense against robbers. You must satisfy yourself fully that the applicants for permission of this kind are men to be trusted, and in no case grant them the favor where a doubt exists. In the permission given make them responsible for the proper use and safety of the arms.

By order of Brig. Gen. T. W. Sweeny, commanding:

JAMES DAVIDSON,
First Lieut. Fifty-second Illinois Vols. and Aide-de-Camp.

HEADQUARTERS SIXTEENTH ARMY CORPS,
Memphis, Tenn., April 6, 1864.
Maj. Gen. F. STEELE,
    Comdg. Department of Arkansas, Little Rock, Ark.:

GENERAL : A considerable body of Confederates, say from 700 to 1,000, under Brigadier-General McRae, infest the country back of Memphis toward Crowley's Ridge.

If it be convenient so to do, it would be well to establish a post of mounted men (one regiment) at Mound City, 4 miles above Memphis. Supplies could be drawn readily from Memphis, and additional force furnished from time to time if required. Either Hopefield or Mound City would do as a post.

    Your obedient servant,

                              S. A. HURLBUT,
                                    Major-General.

                              MEMPHIS, *April 6, 1864.*
Maj. Gen. W. T. SHERMAN :

Arrived 11.30 a. m. Saw General Hurlbut. The cavalry have made several efforts to reach the Hatchie, but failed. General Hurlbut will send them out south of the Memphis and Charleston Railroad to-morrow, with orders to reach Bolivar and open communication with Veatch. The force of the enemy I think is exaggerated, but underrated by yourself. Forrest evidently has Chalmers or some one else south of the Hatchie holding his line of retreat. I leave immediately.

                                JOHN M. CORSE,
                                  Brigadier-General.

HEADQUARTERS SIXTEENTH ARMY CORPS,
Memphis, Tenn., April 6, 1864.
Maj. Gen. W. T. SHERMAN,
    Comdg. Mil. Div. of the Mississippi, Nashville, Tenn.:

GENERAL: Corse brought your orders.* I shall throw Grierson along Coldwater to Pocahontas and Bolivar. He found the enemy too strong on the Raleigh and Somerville route. The Third Michigan and Seventh Kansas Cavalry, now in Saint Louis, should be mounted and forwarded at once. With them Forrest can be successfully attacked ; without them, his force is too strong.

It is not likely that A. J. Smith will get away from Red River before the 20th April. With 10,000 men and a covering regiment of cavalry he can move to Columbus via Grenada, or, which would be better, to Panola, there to be joined by cavalry from here.

The country between Hatchie and La Grange is open for the rebels, and there is talk of Lee coming up. With Lee and Loring both in his way, Smith cannot safely forage on his march. Grierson has orders to force communication with Veatch. Forrest's strength is not less than 6,000. I do not expect to do more then keep him north until proper force comes.

A good regiment should be placed at Cairo, and another at Columbus, so as to cover Government stores.

                              S. A. HURLBUT,
                                  Major-General.

---

                       * Of April 3, p. 244.

HDQRS. MILITARY DIVISION OF THE MISSISSIPPI,
Nashville, April 6, 1864.

Major-General McPHERSON,
Commanding Department of the Tennessee, Huntsville:

GENERAL: The news conveyed by telegraph that General Veatch has come away from Purdy without waiting the development of which he formed an essential part defeats that scheme, and Forrest again escapes us.

I have no faith in Hurlbut as an officer to give impulse to active operations, and I think it would be well for him to be placed at Cairo, whence he can order and direct, at which he is good.

Slocum will be a good commander for Vicksburg and Natchez, and Buckland for Memphis.

I believe the programme I have laid down for A. J. Smith will produce a good effect, and that we must be content this season to confine operations along the Mississippi to defending the river and its immediate neighborhood, in concert with the gun-boats. I deem two white divisions and all the blacks now on the river adequate to that end.

I prefer that, for the sake of time, the entire command of A. J. Smith, already organized for action and afloat, should not be materially changed. I see that this may somewhat embarrass you, and any modification you may order at Vicksburg that will not result in delay you can make. There is yet time, as it will be fully the 15th instant before the Red River command is out. I have little or no official information of it, other than Kilby Smith's informal report, but have no doubt Smith, in concert with the admiral, is above Alexandria. I have seen that there was 7 feet of water on the rapids of Alexandria, which I know to be the only obstruction below Shreveport.

General Banks surely pledged me his word that he would leave New Orleans March 7, and that my troops will not be wanted up the Red River beyond the thirty days after they enter it. That time will expire on the 10th instant, and General Corse will be at the mouth of Red River by that time. He left Cairo with a good boat and two pilots on the 4th instant at 11 a. m.

I have notified you that the War Department authorizes me to control our furloughed veterans. I have already, by telegraph, through the governors of Ohio, Indiana, Illinois, and Iowa, ordered all our veterans to rejoin their respective brigades punctually on the expiration of their furloughs, yours to approach via Cairo.

I want you to arrange your old Seventeenth Corps in divisions, so that the regiments now up Red River be of the two divisions to come to you at Huntsville. Rendezvous the balance of those two divisions at Cairo, sending the regiments thence up the Tennessee as fast as they come to Clifton, whence they can march to where you want them.

Since beginning this letter I have received your letter of April 2. I approve your choice of Huntsville for depot, hospitals, &c. I don't exactly understand that you select Whitesburg or Gunter's as the substitute for Larkin's crossing. I would prefer you in person to see both Whitesburg and Gunter's before we decide. Do you propose to fortify on the east side of the Tennessee at Whitesburg, Gunter's, or Larkin's? The macadamized road to Whitesburg certainly is a strong point in its favor, especially if the bottom is on this side of the river and there be a good hill site on the other.

Give early attention to this matter, and if you can't go in person send some good officer who can give you a good topographical sketch. Gain all possible information as to the roads from Whitesburg and Gunter's across Sand Mountain to Rome and Gadsden.

You will need a good staff or general officer at Cairo till you have put all the furloughed regiments and absentees on the right roads. The commanding officer at Cairo should also have a correct list of the designed station of each of the regiments of the Department of the Tennessee, that he may also answer all proper inquiries.

With great respect,

W. T. SHERMAN,
Major-General, Commanding.

HEADQUARTERS DISTRICT OF KENTUCKY,
Louisville, April 6, 1864.

Brigadier-General POTTER,
Chief of Staff, Knoxville:

Colonel Gallup telegraphs me from Louisa that the rebel general Hodge's brigade has come this side Pound Gap; that Breckinridge is at Tazewell, and Morgan still at Abingdon. I am going to-day to Paris, where I propose concentrating some cavalry, and if Hodge's brigade is really in the State I will hunt him up. Colonel Gallup is rarely mistaken.

S. G. BURBRIDGE,
Brigadier-General.

HEADQUARTERS DISTRICT OF CAIRO,
Cairo, Ill., April 6, 1864.

Lieut. Col. T. H. HARRIS,
Assistant Adjutant-General:

SIR: General Veatch has miscarried. He went to Purdy, returned to the river, went up to Waterloo on the other side, sent back his transports, and marched for Pulaski. I notified General Sherman of this movement, and he instructs all to notify "Hurlbut that Veatch left Purdy without orders," and that it is "too late to correct him." General Hurlbut will by this see that the force he sent out is not supported on the other side.

Yours, &c.,

M. BRAYMAN,
Brigadier-General, Commanding.

CAIRO, ILL., *April 6, 1864.*

Maj. Gen. W. T. SHERMAN,
Nashville, Tenn.:

Your dispatch received.

The following report is from an officer sent up to communicate with General Veatch:

PADUCAH, *April 5, 1864.*

Lieut. Commander J. W. SHIRK,
Mound City:

General Veatch went to Purdy on the 30th ultimo; sent scouts toward Bolivar, Jackson. and Lexington; not hearing anything of Forrest, he returned the following night and proceeded to Waterloo, whence he debarked, and marched the next day, 3d instant, to Athens via Florence.

One of Forrest's regiments (Wisdom's) is stationed at Williams' Landing, 5 miles above Savannah, where they have been some time.

I met the Robb on my return with the convoy yesterday at 11 a. m., about 50 miles below Clifton. There was 4 feet on the shoals when I left Waterloo, and river rising fast. If the Robb can get to Florence General Veatch can be communi-cated with. I sent the Robb to try and get there.

A. F. O'NEIL,
Acting Volunteer Lieutenant, U. S. Navy.

M. BRAYMAN,
Brigadier-General.

NASHVILLE, TENN., *April* 6, 1864.

General BRAYMAN:

Veatch had no business to come away from Purdy, and now it is too late to correct him. Notify Hurlbut that Veatch left Purdy without orders. Hold the communication for him till you have a safe person to send it to me at Nashville.

W. T SHERMAN,
Major-General.

HEADQUARTERS SIXTEENTH ARMY CORPS,
Memphis, Tenn., April 6, 1864.

Brigadier-General GRIERSON:

GENERAL: Send out a strong force to-morrow on the Pigeon Roost and State Line roads.

I sent you word by Lieutenant Woodward of the report as to Forrest's proximity to the city. All the cavalry must be held ready to move at the shortest notice.

Yours, truly,

S. A. HURLBUT,
Major-General.

WASHINGTON, *April* 6, 1864—1 p. m.

Maj. Gen. W. T. SHERMAN,
Commanding Military Division of the Mississippi:

Your telegram of 4th instant received. Any specific recommenda-tion you may make in the matter of mounting militia and short volunteers will meet the approval of the Bureau. Your telegram referred to the General-in-Chief. Every exertion is being made to furnish remounts for your cavalry.

J. H. WILSON,
Brigadier-General.

NASHVILLE, *April* 6, 1864.
(Received 11.25 a. m.)

Hon. E. M. STANTON, *Secretary of War:*

I do hope that General Buell will not be sent to Tennessee; any-body before him. He is not the man to send into Kentucky or Ten-nessee at this time. His influence will be with George D. Prentice and that class of men.

ANDREW JOHNSON,
Military Governor.

GENERAL ORDERS,) HDQRS. MIL. DIV. OF THE MISSISSIPPI,
     No. 6.   (*Nashville, Tenn., April 6,* 1864.

To enable the military railroads running from Nashville to supply more fully the armies in the field, the following regulations will hereafter be observed:

I. No citizen nor any private freight whatever will be transported by the railroads, save as hereinafter provided.

II. Officers traveling under orders or on leave of absence, sick or furloughed soldiers departing from or returning to their regiments, and small detachments of troops will be transported on the orders of post commanders, of Brig. Gen. Andrew Johnson, Military Governor of Tennessee, or of the commanding officer of either of the Departments of the Ohio, the Cumberland, or the Tennessee, or of the Military Division of the Mississippi. Bodies of troops will not be transported by railroads when it is possible for them to march, except upon the order of the commanding officer of some one of the military departments above named. Civil employés of the various staff departments will be transported on the order of the senior and supervising quartermaster Department of the Cumberland, at Nashville, Tenn., or of the commanding officer of either of the military departments above named. Employés of the railroads will be transported on the order of the superintendent or chief engineer of the railroads.

III. No citizens will be allowed to travel on the railroads at all, except on the permit of the commanding officer of one of the three military departments or of the Military Division of the Mississippi, and when their transportation will not prevent that of any army supplies, of which the proper officer of the quartermaster's department will be the judge.

IV. Express companies will be allowed one car per day each way, on each military road, to carry small parcels for soldiers and officers. One car per day more on each road for sutlers' goods and officers' stores may be allowed by the senior and supervising quartermaster at Nashville, at his discretion; these cars to be furnished by the express companies and attached to the passenger trains. When a sufficient surplus of stores has been accumulated at the front, the senior and supervising quartermaster aforesaid may increase this allowance, but not before.

V. Stores exclusively for officers' messes, in very limited quantities, after due inspection by the inspecting officer at Nashville, Tenn., of sutlers' goods, and all private stores, shipped to the front, will be passed free on the several roads, on the order of the senior and supervising quartermaster Department of the Cumberland, at Nashville, Tenn.

VI. Horses, cattle, or other live-stock will not be transported by railroad, except on the written order of the commanding general of the military division or of one of the military departments.

VII. Trains on their return trips will be allowed to bring up private freight, when the shipment thereof does not interfere with the full working of the roads, of which the senior and supervising quartermaster at Nashville will be the judge.

VIII. Provost-marshals have nothing to do with transportation by railroads. Their passes merely mean that the bearer can go from one point to another named in their pass, but not necessarily by rail. The railroads are purely for army purposes.

IX. When the rolling-stock of the railroads is increased, or when a due accumulation of stores has been made at the front, increased facilities may be extended to passengers and private freight, of which due notice will be given. Until that time citizens and sutlers must use wagons.

X. Until the railroad is relieved, all military posts within 35 miles of Nashville and 20 miles of Stevenson, Bridgeport, Chattanooga, Huntsville, and Loudon must haul their stores by wagons.

XI. The general manager of the railroads, and his duly appointed agents and conductors, will control the trains and will be authorized to call on every passenger for his orders for transportation by railroad, that they may be returned to the general manager or superintendent. The military guard will enforce good order, and sustain the agents and conductors of the roads in their rightful authority, but will report any mismanagement or neglect of duty through their officers to these headquarters.

XII. Until other arrangements are perfected, commanding officers, on the request of the railroad managers, will furnish details for providing wood or water at such points as may be necessary to supply the trains.

By command of Maj. Gen. W. T. Sherman:

R. M. SAWYER,
Assistant Adjutant-General.

CULPEPER COURT-HOUSE, VA.,
April 7, 1864—7 p. m.

Maj. Gen. W. T. SHERMAN,
Nashville, Tenn.:

Do you think it will pay to send troops to Grenada at this late day? Unless Smith has already started I think his force had better be got at once where it can operate with one of the main armies.

U. S. GRANT,
Lieutenant-General.

CULPEPER COURT-HOUSE,
April 7, 1864—7.30 p. m.

Maj. Gen. W. T. SHERMAN,
Nashville, Tenn.:

I have ordered all the troops that can be spared from the States west of Ohio to be sent to you. You can send them to Steele or where you think best. Rosecrans reports he can send no troops. I have an inspector there, however, to see. If possible, I will send Steele some from there. I will make provision at Pensacola for supplying a cavalry force.

U. S. GRANT,
Lieutenant-General.

WASHINGTON, *April 7, 1864—2.30 p. m.*

Maj. Gen. W. T. SHERMAN:

GENERAL: I have your dispatch in regard to a chief quartermaster. I appreciate your need, but it is only less difficult to find a senior quartermaster than a commanding general with capacity tor such a command as yours, and the field of selection is smaller. General Robert Allen has powers and duties extending over the military division of the Mississippi Valley. He is of all officers of this department probably most fitted to meet your requirements, but I am in doubt whether he could conduct his immense office business, the distribution of money, and the providing and forwarding supplies to all the Western armies as sufficiently if ordered to your headquarters as he does while stationed on the Ohio River, your base of operations. If he can arrange this difficulty, however, I shall not object to his joining you. I request you to communicate with him on this subject and to advise me of your conclusions. Colonel Donaldson is probably next in ability and efficiency to General Allen. He has not had such an extensive field, but has done all well. But if he is taken from Nashville depot, the immediate base of the army operating from the Tennessee River from Decatur to Knoxville, I do not know how to supply his place. Being at Nashville, you are able to see how important his present duty is and how indispensable to your success is a man of capacity in charge of the depot of Nashville.

I incline to think that were I in your place I should call General Allen to headquarters on all important occasions, keeping constantly with me some confidential officers in good relations with commanding general and senior quartermaster. The latter, during all preparations for a campaign, which is the greater part of the year, is most effective at the base, providing and sending forward supplies. The telegraph, it is to be remembered, affords instant and constant communication, and on important occasions by resorting to the telegraph office conversation can be carried on. When the commanding general takes the field in person the chief quartermaster should be called to his headquarters.

General Allen will be ready to serve wherever most useful, and in this matter I shall be guided by your decision after you have consulted him.

Respectfully, yours,

M. C. MEIGS,
Quartermaster-General.

NASHVILLE, TENN.,
April 7, 1864.

General MEIGS,
Quartermaster-General, Washington, D. C.:

Your dispatch is this moment received, and is fully satisfactory. I have had much conversation with General Allen, and think I can arrange to have him and yet to fill the place I deem necessary. If announced as my chief quartermaster he would not feel the delicacy he now expresses to make orders or give instructions affecting officers now not clearly under him. I will confer with him further and advise you of the result. All is working well now. By marching troops, forbidding all railroad business but pure military freight, we have much enlarged our work.

W. T. SHERMAN,
Major-General.

HDQRS. SECOND BRIGADE, SECOND DIVISION CAVALRY,
Ringgold, Ga., April 7, 1864—7.15 p. m.

Brigadier-General WHIPPLE,
    Chief of Staff, Dept. of the Cumberland, Chattanooga :

SIR : I beg to report the following, which I have learned from a scout this afternoon, for the information of the general commanding : The cavalry force in our immediate front consists of three brigades, viz, two at Tunnel Hill and one at Varnell's Station. McCarter's [?] brigade crossed Coosa River at Cedar Bluffs two days ago, leaving the Sixth Georgia to guard that point, and are now en route for Northern Alabama. The entire cavalry force lately at Carter's Station (or Cartersville) has moved northwest. Northern Alabama is spoken of as their destination, but many believe that they are going to join Forrest in Western Kentucky. I have not received the instructions asked for with regard to Dr. Moss.

I am, respectfully, your obedient servant,
                    ROBT. H. G. MINTY.
                    Colonel, Commanding.

From General G. H. Thomas' journal.

APRIL 7, 1864.

Third Division, Fourteenth Army Corps, Brig. Gen. A. Baird commanding, at Ringgold, Ga., was reviewed ; also Long's brigade of cavalry, stationed at that place. A. B. Thornton, scout, left Atlanta, Ga., about April 2. He discovered the rebels were fortifying to some extent at Chattahoochee bridge. They have also built a wagon-road bridge about 200 yards above the railroad bridge over the Chattahoochee River. First Georgia State troops are guarding both bridges. He understood they had fortified to some extent at Etowah Station (Hightower River), but as he passed there in the night he cannot speak from personal observation. At Resaca there are quite extensive fortifications and quite a number of guns mounted. Brown's brigade stationed 2 miles south of Dalton, and some ten or more pieces of artillery with it. Hood's and Hardee's corps at and around Dalton, numbering about 35,000. The two brigades of cavalry at Tunnel Hill, commanded by General Wheeler. Roddey, with one brigade of cavalry, between Varnell's Station and Spring Place. Martin's cavalry division, said to be 3,000 strong, has gone to North Alabama, via Alpine. The rebels have built formidable defenses at Buzzard Roost. The works are a little northwest of the Slaughter Pen, and across Mill Creek. Still west of the earthworks they have built a dam so as to flow the low-land in the vicinity with water, which makes it quite impossible for troops to pass. The railroad bridge is floored over for the passage of troops. The wagon road is entirely overflowed. It is about 1½ miles from Buzzard Roost to the Slaughter Pen, and about 2 miles from the Slaughter Pen to Dalton. The rebels are preparing to resist an attack from the Federal army in front of Dalton.

BULL'S GAP, *April 7, 1864.*

Maj. J. A. CAMPBELL, *Assistant Adjutant-General :*

Lick Creek being reported fordable at noon, I sent the party for Greeneville with directions to the commandant of the escort to send a detachment farther if necessary, in order to carry the letter I wrote in accordance with General Schofield's telegram.

Parties in from Jonesborough report no large bodies of the rebels south of the Watauga, and there is no evidence that any injury has been done to the railroad except in the vicinity of Lick Creek.

I believe the Watauga and Holston bridges are not injured, though they are said to be slight, temporary structures. Small parties of rebels are heard of in vicinity of Rogersville, and I have sent a detachment to look after them.

J. D. COX,
Brigadier-General.

KNOXVILLE, TENN.,
April 7, 1864.

Brigadier-General BURBRIDGE,
Louisville, Ky.:

Colonel Gallup is certainly mistaken about any considerable force of rebel cavalry having passed Pound Gap; also about Breckinridge being at Tazewell. The rebel cavalry force now in West Virginia is very small. You can easily dispose of any force that can get into Kentucky.

J. M. SCHOFIELD,
Major-General.

HDQRS. TWENTY-NINTH MISSOURI VOL. INFANTRY,
Camp Gage, near Cottonville, Ala., April 7, 1864.

Capt. W. A. GORDON,
Assistant Adjutant-General, First Division:

SIR: I have the honor to report that the Fourth Regiment Alabama Cavalry, 900 men strong, arrived at Warrenton on the night of the 5th instant.

Last night they raised two flat-boats out of the mouth of Shoal Creek; took them up the river opposite Fearns' farm, and repaired them. One of these boats is a large one, capable of crossing 50 men at a time. The enemy have strengthened their pickets along this section of the river. They have eighteen picket posts in a distance of three-quarters of a mile. The enemy also have fourteen families of refugees under guard on the hills opposite Deposit Landing.

The Fourth Alabama Cavalry is a part of Wheeler's command, which has been stationed at Blue Hills.

Very respectfully, your obedient servant,

JOS. S. GAGE,
Lieutenant-Colonel, Twenty-ninth Missouri Volunteers.

HDQRS. LEFT WING, SIXTEENTH ARMY CORPS,
Athens, Ala., April 7, 1864.

Maj. Gen. J. B. McPHERSON,
Commanding Department and Army of the Tennessee:

There is nothing new. Everything is very quiet. The cavalry in Coosa Valley, except a regiment or two at Gadsden, has all gone to the front, and that from the front gone to Blue Mountain or

Oxford. The infantry force still remains at Mount Hope, and a great many deserters come in from it. We get from 20 to 40 daily from the mountains, mostly from Johnston's army. The rebels are doing all they can to catch them, and picket vigilantly every road leading into the mountains, and in fact in every direction from Decatur. Their pickets are 6 to 8 miles away.

The additional force that has gone up to Forrest, I think, is the remnants of regiments left by him and the regiments stationed along the Tombigbee and Alabama Rivers.

We make no headway in getting rations. Lieutenant-Colonel Donaldson, chief quartermaster at Nashville, says he will do what he can, but as it now stands he has all he can do to feed those at the front, let alone accumulating a supply.

I have sent forces up to Triana on this side, and up to Guntersville on the south side; also down the river to clean out the islands, which are full of rebels, negroes, and secesh stock.

Wood-choppers are at work at Mooresville. I pressed 50 negroes near there, and put a good man over them. They will soon get out a good supply of wood. Loring and French were at Demopolis on April 1; Lee and Adams were west of Jackson at the same date; all lying still. Forrest is in and about Jackson. Scouts from that direction say he does not show any signs of moving. They left there four days ago.

General Veatch will be in Prospect to-day.

I am, very respectfully, your obedient servant,

G. M. DODGE,
Brigadier-General.

ATHENS, *April* 7, 1864.

Lieutenant-Colonel PARROTT,
     Prospect:

Has General Veatch, with his command, arrived at Prospect?

J. W. BARNES,
Assistant Adjutant-General.

PADUCAH, *April* 7, 1864.

Captain ODLIN:

General Forrest is at Jackson. General Buford at Trenton, with 3,000 cavalry troops at Dukedom. Faulkner was with Buford on Monday. I presume you know they have Hickman.

S. G. HICKS,
Colonel, Commanding Post.

HEADQUARTERS SIXTEENTH ARMY CORPS,
Memphis, Tenn., April 7, 1864.

Brig. Gen. B. H. GRIERSON,
     Commanding Cavalry Division, Sixteenth Corps:

GENERAL: Under orders from Maj. Gen. W. T. Sherman, you will proceed with your entire available cavalry force skirting the Coldwater and thence by La Grange to Bolivar.

You have seen General Sherman's orders. The line from here to Hatchie via Bolivar is to be held by your cavalry. You will move all disposable cavalry before daylight, sweeping round by La Grange to Bolivar. Let go of Memphis, and give yourself no concern about it. Operate on the flanks and rear of the enemy and open communication with Veatch at and west of Purdy. Rally on them, or here if too strong for you, and press the matter home.

Yours,

S. A. HURLBUT,
Major-General.

APRIL 7, 1864—9.30 p. m.

[General GRIERSON :]

GENERAL : I am just informed that Forrest is crossing Wolf River at the new Raleigh road. This may or may not be true. Your patrols ought to know. Your cavalry should be near the Fair Ground by daylight, so as to meet any sudden dash. I think a portion of his force has crossed Wolf above and will move on the Germantown or Poplar Street road.

It is of paramount importance that strong pickets be kept well out to-night.

Yours,

S. A. HURLBUT,
Major-General.

HDQRS. CAVALRY DIVISION, SIXTEENTH ARMY CORPS,
Memphis, Tenn., April 7, 1864.

Col. GEORGE E. WARING,
Commanding First Brigade :

COLONEL : In pursuance of instructions from Maj. Gen. S. A. Hurlbut, you will prepare your entire available mounted force, including the Fourth Missouri, with all the rations and ammunition that can be carried on the persons of the men, without wagons or ambulances, to march before daylight to-morrow morning. Call in all your patrols, and use the utmost dispatch in your preparations. Report at these headquarters in person at 8 p. m.

By order of Brig. Gen. B. H. Grierson :

S. L. WOODWARD,
Assistant Adjutant-General.

(Similar dispatch to Lieut. Col. W. P. Hepburn, commanding Provisional Cavalry Regiment.)

HEADQUARTERS SIXTEENTH ARMY CORPS,
Memphis, April 7, 1864—9.30 p. m.

Brig. Gen. R. P. BUCKLAND,
Commanding District of Memphis, Tenn. :

GENERAL : It is reported that Forrest has crossed a portion of his force beyond White's Station, and is crossing the rest at the New Raleigh road crossing. If this be true, and it is substantiated by the known fact of a considerable force being north of Wolf to-day, it is of highest importance that the troops be all under arms before day begins to break.   I have ordered Grierson's cavalry to be at the Fair Ground by daylight.

If the attack be made in force, dismounted, the regiments and batteries should have instructions, if they cannot hold their ground, to retire concentrically on the line of the bayou.   We can thus concentrate forces and narrow the front of defense.   The enrolled militia will form on their parade ground and cover the levee and main street. If it is necessary to abandon any buildings containing public stores they will be fired.

It may be that this is not true, but my information is of such a character that I believe it.   The signal for assembling the militia will not be given until the fact of an attack is ascertained.

                                                S. A. HURLBUT,
                                                    Major-General.

                                FORT PICKERING, TENN.,
                                        April 7, 1864.
Capt. C. W. DUSTAN,
    Assistant Adjutant-General, District of Memphis:

CAPTAIN: I have the honor to state that the officers of the day report as follows: That the cavalry encamped on the glacis, east of Fort Pickering and nearly its whole length, are in the habit of being very noisy after tattoo, and in fact at almost any hour; that shots are frequently fired at all times, and not only create alarm but also endanger the lives of the sentinels on the parapet.

I would further respectfully call your attention to the following: The great extent of the camps, the number of men and animals, will render the defense very difficult and problematic, should the enemy decide to attack from the Horn Lake road.   In that event they will certainly dash over our pickets and enter these camps in ten minutes after the first shot is fired.   The panic-stricken crowd will seek safety by running toward the fort, closely followed and mingled with the enemy, and we will have to sacrifice either the lives of our own men outside or the fort.   Should we decide on the former, even then it would be very difficult to save the fort, as of course we could not distinguish the enemy from our men and form no estimate of their number or point of attack.   While writing this it is reported to me that the cavalry broke en masse in the camps of the colored women and are committing all sorts of outrage.   The black is made a man by being trusted with arms, and it is very hard for a man to see his family abused and not to use the arm.   I am afraid it will loosen discipline if not render it impossible.

I respectfully request your careful consideration of the above, and remain, captain, very respectfully, your obedient servant,
                                                I. G. KAPPNER,
    Colonel Second U. S. Heavy Artillery (Colored), Comdg. Fort.

                                        ATHENS, *April 7, 1864.*
Major-General McPHERSON,
                Huntsville:

General Clanton has arrived with his force in the valley; is at Somerville and Whitesburg.   His pickets are now well up the river. The scouts say he is to form a junction with Forrest at Moulton, and they say attack Decatur. The entire force when united, I should think, would amount to 5,000. Do you receive any information from Whitesburg ?

G. M. DODGE,
Brigadier-General.

HEADQUARTERS SIXTEENTH ARMY CORPS,
Memphis, Tenn., April 7, 1864.
Brig. Gen. A. J. SMITH,
Comdg. Expeditionary Forces, Sixteenth Army Corps:

GENERAL : It is of prime importance that you should return as soon as practicable. Sherman's order sent you is impractical. You will live as nearly up to it as circumstances will permit. I do not believe that 10,000 infantry can march across the country he indicates, and prefer that you should move on Panola. In either event I must be notified in advance, so as to support your movement. Keep me advised, so that I can do so.

Accept my congratulations for your success.

Yours, truly,

S. A. HURLBUT,
Major-General.

HDQRS. CHIEF OF CAV., MIL. DIV. OF THE MISSISSIPPI,
Nashville, Tenn., April 7, 1864.
Brig. Gen. J. W. DAVIDSON,
Cavalry Bureau, Saint Louis, Mo.:

SIR : There are now nearly 15,000 cavalry troops at this point awaiting arms, equipments, and horses. The ordnance depot is drained of everything in the nature of supplies for cavalry, and I cannot learn that any considerable shipments are on the way. Extraordinary efforts will have to be made to arm, mount, and equip the cavalry of this military division or it cannot be made available to any useful extent in the coming campaign. The regions of country which we traverse are now so exhausted of horses and mules that very little can be done in the way of raising crops this season, and all our forage will have to be brought from the North. This will render our cavalry movements much more difficult in future, and it would be very unwise and impolitic to take away the few animals that remain. Recent observations have convinced me that I was in error in recommending some time ago that more horses should be obtained in our fields of operation.

What number of horses are now in the possession of those purchasing for the Government at the West, and how soon can they be got to the front?

Yours, truly,

WM. SOOY SMITH,
Brig. Gen., Chief of Cavalry, Mil. Div. of the Mississippi.

HEADQUARTERS DEPARTMENT OF THE CUMBERLAND,
Chattanooga, Tenn., April 7, 1864.
His Excellency Governor JOHN BROUGH,
Columbus, Ohio:

SIR : Your dispatch of to-day has just been received. We are receiving here about 30 deserters from the enemy daily. I do not think it to the interest of the Government that they should remain in Tennessee or Kentucky, as I believe many of them return to the enemy after recruiting their health and strength, because they are rebels by nature; others because of family influence, and others, like the drunkard to his bottle, because they have not sufficient moral firmness to resist the natural depravity of their hearts.

My idea in making the proposition to send them to your State and others in the Northwest was to remove these poor wretches as far from the temptations of secessionism as possible, thinking by so doing some of them at least might be reformed, and by laboring on our Western farms they would in that contribute somewhat in prosecuting the war in our favor. I can send them as far north as Nashville, should the farmers of your State need laborers. I thought by establishing an agency at Nashville they could thereby have an additional source from which they could get them. The expenses of the agency might be defrayed in the usual way of intelligence offices, as I have no doubt that the agent would in a short time have a much larger demand made on him by farmers than he could supply. It is not my idea to form in Nashville a national or State agency, but simply to advise you that the farmers of the Northwest could procure laborers from the rebel deserters, and it occurred to me that an agency similar to that proposed above would be the most efficient and expeditious way of doing so.

I am, sir, very respectfully, your obedient servant,

GEO. H. THOMAS,
Major-General, U. S. Volunteers, Commanding.

CULPEPER, VA.,
April 8, 1864—9.30 p. m.

Maj. Gen. W. T. SHERMAN :

As I notified you before leaving Nashville, I believe the rebels will attempt a raid into Kentucky by the way of Pound Gap or that vicinity as soon as they can travel. From information just received at Washington, Longstreet's force may be added to Breckinridge's to make this so formidable as to upset offensive operations on our part. By vigilance in Southeast Kentucky, which I know you are wide awake to see the necessity of, such a raid can be made disastrous to the rebels and still leave us free to act offensively from Chattanooga. If Forrest succeeds in getting his force out of Kentucky and West Tennessee, do you not think a bolder commander than General Hurlbut will be required for holding the Mississippi firmly?

U. S. GRANT,
Lieutenant-General.

CULPEPER, VA.,
April 8, 1864.

Maj. Gen. W. T. SHERMAN :

I have directed twenty days' forage and provisions to be at Pensacola by 1st of May.

U. S. GRANT,
Lieutenant-General.

Confidential.]   Washington, D. C.,
                                                      April 8, 1864.
Maj. Gen. W. T. Sherman,
          Nashville:

General : Your telegram of yesterday was received this morning.
I have not seen your memoranda sent by General Rawlins, but presume General Grant has, as he alluded to some proposed reorganization of this kind in the West.

We fully agree that the Departments of Arkansas and the Gulf
should be under one commander as soon as the armies come within
communicating distance, but the difficulty is to get a suitable commander. General Banks is not competent, and there are so many
political objections to superseding him by Steele that it would be
useless to ask the President to do it. Moreover, I fear the command
would be too large for Steele. Nevertheless, if the proper man can
be found for the place I shall not hesitate to advise a change now.
No doubt the lines of departments of your command west of the
Mississippi River might also be modified with advantage, but I
would not advise making all three into one, for the reason it would
make you a mere bureau general. You know there is an immense
amount of official business, courts-martial, discharges of soldiers, furloughs, requisitions, &c., which the law and regulations require to
be done by the commander of a department. If you take this it will
either absorb most of y ur time or you must leave it to members of
your staff, a power and œesponsibility which should not be given to
or imposed upon such officers. You ought to be almost entirely free
to direct the movements of your armies. We tried the "three grand
division" system in the Army of the Potomac, and it worked so
badly that everybody was glad to get rid of it. No one here is now
in favor of its renewal. Armies and army corps, divisions, and
brigades are the most proper elements of organization. Center wings
and reserves are organizations for marches and battles, but this is
only a temporary arrangement, corps, divisions, and brigades being
transferred from one to the other as circumstances require.

I fear that General Schofield will be rejected by the Senate. He
is a good officer, and you will find it difficult to supply his place.

If you think the lines of the departments west of the Mississippi
River can be changed with advantage without breaking them up,
please write me your views and I will bring the matter before the
Secretary of War and General Grant.

          Very respectfully, your obedient servant,
                                   H. W. HALLECK,
                              Major-General, Chief of Staff.

                    Nashville, Tenn., *April* 8, 1864—3.30 p. m.
                                        (Received 7.30 p. m.)
Lieutenant-General Grant,
          Culpeper:

It is not too late to bring A. J. Smith's division out of Red River
to join General McPherson by the Mississippi and Tennessee instead
of by Grenada. As soon as I learn what force can be sent to General Steele from the States west of the Ohio I will order them. Have
you ordered General Banks to come away with his troops, or does he

leave any subject to General Steele's orders, and how many? General Steele reported that he had only about 7,000 to take with him from the Arkansas, and that his cavalry and artillery were very bad.

W. T. SHERMAN,
Major-General.

HEADQUARTERS DEPARTMENT OF THE CUMBERLAND,
Chattanooga, April 8, 1864.

Statement of the number of troops necessary to protect the bridges on the Nashville and Chattanooga Railroad, posted in block-houses at the following points, with garrisons at Murfreesborough, Tullahoma, Stevenson, and Bridgeport:

No.	Locality.	Troops.
1	Mill Creek No. 1	30
2	Mill Creek No. 2	30
3	Mill Creek No. 3	30
4	Hurricane Creek (one-half mile north of La Vergne)	30
5	Bridge near Smyrna	30
6	Stewart's Creek	30
7	Overall's Creek	30
8	Stone's River (Fortress Rosecrans)	150
9	Stone's River (3 miles south of Murfreesborough)	40
10	Bell Buckle Creek	20
11	Creek one-half mile north of Wartrace	10
12	Wartrace Creek	30
13	Garrison's Fork	50
14	Duck River	40
15	Norman's Creek (Normandy)	30
16	[Block-house should be erected, I think, between Normandy and Poor Man's Creek, though none is projected by the engineers.]	[30]
17	Poor Man's Creek (one-half mile south of Tullahoma)	30
	[Should be block-house between Poor Man's Creek and Taylor's Creek. The road through a forest. All trains stop for wood, and is the worst place for guerrillas on the whole road, and the distance is too great from Poor Man's Creek to Elk River to admit of patrolling the road with safety.]	[30]
18	[Taylor's Creek (Water Tank) only water between Decherd and Tullahoma. Not projected by engineers.]	[30]
19	Elk River	60
20	Boiling Fork of Elk River (Cowan)	30
21	Trestle (1 mile north of Tantalon)	10
22	Trestle (one-quarter mile north of Tantalon)	10
23	Bridge and station (Tantalon)	20
24	Crow Creek (south of Tantalon)	20
25	......do	20
26	......do	20
27	......do	20
28	Crow Creek (south of Anderson)	20
29	Dry trestle (south of Anderson)	10
30	Crow Creek (south of Anderson)	30
31	......do	30
32	Swamp trestle	20
33	Crow Creek	30
34	Crow Creek (three-quarters of a mile from Stevenson)	20
35	Creek (1 mile east from Stevenson)	20
36	Widow's Creek	20
37	Tennessee River, main bridge, Bridgeport	
38	Tennessee River, east bridge, Bridgeport	100
39	Dry trestle	20
40	Nickajack Creek (one-quarter of a mile west of Shellmound)	30
41	Creek (one-eighth mile east of Shellmound)	30
42	Dry trestle (Narrows)	30
43	Running Water (one-half mile west of Whiteside's)	60
44	Lookout Creek	30
45	Chattanooga Creek	30

Total troops, 1,460, omitting garrison at Bridgeport. The above are projected by the engineers, with the exception of those noted in red ink [inserted in brackets], which are the result of my own observation.

North of General Slocum's old corps the troops stationed as follows:

Fosterville, two companies Twenty-third Missouri.

Between Fosterville and Christiana, one company Twenty-third Missouri.

Christiana, three companies and headquarters Twenty-third Missouri.

Between Christiana and Stone's River, one company Twenty-third Missouri.

Murfreesborough, One hundred and fifteenth Ohio, Thirty-first Wisconsin, 384 convalescents.

At Stone's River, two companies Twenty-third Missouri Volunteers.

Overall's Creek, 5 miles from Murfreesborough, one company Eighty-fifth 'Indiana.

Stewart's Creek, one company Eighty-fifth Indiana.

Smyrna, one company Eighty-fifth Indiana.

Antioch, one company Eighty-fifth Indiana.

La Vergne, five companies Eighty-fifth Indiana. Thirty-third Indiana at present on furlough.

Stockade No. 2, one company Eighty-fifth Indiana.

Stockade No. 1, one company Eighty-fifth Indiana.

The following is the proposed arrangement of troops along the line from Nashville down:

Three batteries in forts at Nashville, already in position. This in addition to the infantry.

The Twenty-third Missouri is to be ordered to McMinnville to relieve the Eighteenth Michigan, which regiment will then join its brigade.

Colonel Coburn's brigade to join its division. Three companies of artillery to be assigned to Murfreesborough. The convalescents to be armed with muskets.

General Rousseau to man the block-houses from Nashville to Murfreesborough.

Two regiments at Murfreesborough, and in block-houses as far as Tullahoma.

Tullahoma, one regiment.

Stevenson, one regiment.

Bridgeport, two regiments proposed, although I should think it requires 3,000 men on both sides of river, and three batteries.

I am, general, very respectfully, your obedient servant,

WM. D. WHIPPLE,
Brigadier-General and Chief of Staff.

NOTE No. 1.—When I passed up on Wednesday, March 20, the timber for these block-houses was prepared and upon the grounds with few exceptions. In the cases of the latter I could not learn that any work had been done upon them as yet. It will probably take until the 16th instant to complete them.

NOTE No. 2.—The block-houses as far south as Anderson are in about the same state of forwardness as those north of that point. Thence to Bridgeport they are probably completed by this time.

———

HEADQUARTERS DEPARTMENT OF THE CUMBERLAND,
Chattanooga, Tenn., April 8, 1864.

Major-General SHERMAN,
Commanding Military Division of the Mississippi:

GENERAL: Your communication of the 6th instant was received to-day. Before receiving it I had determined on organizing the

Twentieth Corps into four divisions, assigning one to Rousseau, who will be called the commander of the District of Tennessee ; his duties, the defense of my communications from here to Nashville and the Louisville and Nashville Railroad to the Kentucky line, and to preserve order in that portion of Tennessee appropriately belonging to my department. The other three divisions to be organized for the field as soon as possible. The only difficulty I see in the way is, that General Hooker is not desirous of having either Schurz or Williams as division commanders. He wishes to give one division to Butterfield, one to Geary, and expresses a willingness to keep Ward as the other. Geary is an excellent officer, but is low in rank ; therefore to retain him in command of a division would necessitate the relieving of Schurz entirely from duty with that corps, and as General Howard is happy to get rid of him I will recommend that he be relieved from duty with this army. I do not think he is worth much from what I have seen of him, and should not regret to have him go. Howard would like to get Newton to command Sheridan's old division. I have said nothing to Palmer, but I do not think he would object to take a division under Buell, and if Buell comes and would be willing to do duty under me I would be very glad to give him the Fourteenth Corps. The three divisions of the Fourteenth Corps are commanded by Davis, Johnson, and Baird, all brigadiers. If you could give Johnson a command in Kentucky, at Louisville, for instance, I think he would be satisfied and Palmer would take his division. Should Buell not come or be willing to take that command, I prefer to have Palmer remain. I have already given orders to General Garrard to concentrate his command at Columbia, and will telegraph him to-night to report to you by letter. I expect he has reached Columbia already with a portion of his command. His brigade commanders are Wilder, Minty, and Long—all three active and intelligent. Wilder is in Indiana with his regiment, but it is time for him to come back. Please telegraph to Governor Morton about his return. I am using every exertion to get ready, but our animals are coming to the front very slow. I send you some rebel papers of the latest date. Johnston does not seem inclined to attack.

  Yours, truly,

            GEO. H. THOMAS.

        CHATTANOOGA, *April* 8, 1864—12 midnight.

Major-General SHERMAN :

 Does General Butterfield return to this department ? If he does I can give him a division in General Hooker's corps. If you have sufficient major-generals to dispense with Schurz, I would recommend he be relieved from duty with this army. He is neither agreeable to General Hooker nor General Howard. If Buell is willing to take the Fourteenth Corps, I do not think General Palmer will object to taking a division under him. General Howard would like to get Newton if he is willing to serve under him. I will then have in the Fourth Corps, Stanley, Newton, and Wood as division commanders ; in the Fourteenth Corps (should Buell take it), Generals Palmer, Davis, and Johnson, or Baird, as division commanders ; in the Twentieth Corps, Rousseau, Geary, Williams (A. S.), and Stein-wehr, division commanders.

I have directed Garrard to report to you by letter. I presume he is already in Columbia.

GEO. H. THOMAS,
Major-General.

HDQRS. MILITARY DIVISION OF THE MISSISSIPPI,
Nashville, Tenn., April 8, 1864.
General SCHOFIELD, *Knoxville:*

I have no four regiments subject to assignment at this time, and I know of none to come. Stoneman passed up into Kentucky to-day. He, too, will ask for cavalry, but horses and mounted men are scarce. Do the best you can.

W. T. SHERMAN,
Major-General.

LEXINGTON, KY.,
April 8, 1864.
Major-General SCHOFIELD :

The Twelfth Kentucky Volunteers is at Burnside Point. The Forty-fifth Ohio, One hundred and twelfth Illinois, and Sixteenth Kentucky are at Camp Nelson, all with orders to proceed at once to Knoxville. The Eleventh Kentucky Infantry gives me some trouble ; it is not as loyal as I wish. I would like for it to be ordered out of the State and some other regiment in the stead. The influence of the First, Eleventh, and Twelfth Kentucky Cavalry is very danger-ous in Kentucky at this time. The quiet of the State demands that they be removed as soon as possible.

S. G. BURBRIDGE,
Brigadier-General.

HUNTSVILLE, *April* 8, 1864.
Major-General SHERMAN :

The following just received from General Dodge :

General Clanton is on Flint River. We skirmished with him last night and this morning. Scouts in from all points south. Johnston is evidently getting ready for a move. Morgan left Decatur, Ga., on 27th, and went to Longstreet's army. East Tennessee ; said to be going on a big raid. Polk at Demopolis. Mobile and Ohio Railroad finished to Tibbee Creek bridge : say they will finish to Corinth.

Cannot Garrard relieve a portion of Dodge's command from Co-lumbia and Pulaski, and let the troops thus relieved come to the front ? General Veatch's command will join Dodge to-day.

JAS. B. McPHERSON,
Major-General.

NASHVILLE, *April* 8, 1864.
General McPHERSON, *Huntsville:*

Garrard's dismounted cavalry will guard the railroad from Co-lumbia down to Lynnville. I don't understand General Dodge's message. The only Flint River that I know of is the one east of Huntsville. Thomas reports all quiet on his front. There are no signs of raid from the east into Kentucky. Johnston will hardly attack Thomas' fortified line, nor do I see what the enemy gain by working the Mobile and Ohio Road. At this stage of water the Tennessee is impassable to Athens, and all the troops in Mississippi will be scattered and harmless to us. I have sent orders to-day at Grant's suggestion for A. J. Smith to come around by water instead of overland by Grenada.

W. T. SHERMAN,
Major-General.

HUNTSVILLE, April 8, 1864.

Major-General SHERMAN :

General Dodge refers to Flint Creek, which empties into the Tennessee on the south side between Somerville and Decatur.

JAS. B. McPHERSON,
Major-General.

HDQRS. DEPARTMENT AND ARMY OF THE TENNESSEE,
Huntsville, Ala., April 8, 1864.

Maj. Gen. J. A. LOGAN,
  Comdg. Fifteenth Army Corps, Huntsville, Ala. :

GENERAL : The indication and evidence of scouts go to show that the enemy has increased his force on the opposite side of the river within a day or two past. Notify the commanders of outposts along the river and detachments on the railroad to be on the alert and guard against any surprise, and to communicate promptly anything of importance which may come to their knowledge.

Very respectfully, your obedient servant,
JAS. B. McPHERSON,
Major-General.

HEADQUARTERS LEFT WING, SIXTEENTH ARMY CORPS,
Athens, Ala., April 8, 1864.

Maj. Gen. J. B. McPHERSON,
  Comdg. Dept. and Army of the Tennessee, Huntsville, Ala. :

GENERAL : I send report of scout, who arrived this morning. I did not telegraph, it being too long.

Left Rienzi, Miss., March 15, 1864. Met Forrest at Tupelo. He had rations issued to 4,800 horses. Buford's division was with him. His troops are all Tennesseeans and Kentuckians.

Left General Polk's headquarters, at Demopolis, March 26. Cars can run to Tibbee bridge on Mobile and Ohio Railroad. Cars not running from Meridian to Selma, but men are at work on it. Polk was to move to Meridian as soon as the road was finished ; he has 10,000 troops (French's and Loring's), besides some 3,000 Vicksburg prisoners in camp not armed. No troops have gone from Polk to Johnston since Sherman was there. Nothing at Columbus, Miss. Lee and Adams are toward Vicksburg.

Left Selma March 26 ; nothing there. A good deal of army work going on there.

Left Montgomery March 27 ; nothing there.

Left Atlanta March 28 ; considerable number of troops there, all State troops. General Morgan, with his command, left on the 26th, going northeast ; was going up to Longstreet's army ; said to have 6,000 men, all mounted.

Left Atlanta March 28 ; went to Rome, Ga. General Brown's brigade at Rome ; very small force, not to exceed 1,500 ; men are at work on battery, covering the crossing of the Oostenaula. Passed twenty-one cars loaded with pontoon bridges at Kingston, going to Dalton. They also had a large amount of pontoons at Atlanta, and were building them there and at Selma and Demopolis. Johnston has about 45,000 men all told, infantry, cavalry, and artillery ; most of his army, say 35,000, is at and about Dalton. It is the general impression that Johnston is getting ready to move. He has a considerable stock of provisions on hand ready. Johnston keeps his lines closed; allows no persons in or out. It is the general talk that Grant has taken a large force from our front to Washington.

The movement on our right at Decatur, &c., they are watching closely; have a courier line to Rome, and do not know what to make of it. Went back from Rome to West Point, Ga. Left there April 2 ; came up across the Blue Mountains ; left there April 3. At that point Martin's division of cavalry had just arrived to recruit, and moved 15 miles south ; also three batteries that had been stationed there to recruit had gone to the front. Few cavalry left at Gadsden.

Clanton left Saturday ; crossed the mountains at Summit, thence Oleander, thence to Whitesburg, thence to Flint River, where he was this morning. Our mounted forces were skirmishing with him at Flint River.

Johnston's army is in good spirits, and at all other points despondent. They do not increase the army by the conscript act very much. It is the general belief that Sherman intends to turn their left by way of Coosa Valley, but it is the general rumor that Johnston intends to turn our left. They believe Thomas has only a small force ; that Grant is accumulating some 250,000 men in front of Richmond, and has weakened Sherman to do it.

At Rome the scout saw an assistant quartermaster who was collecting 1,000 artillery horses, and he said Johnston was about ready ; that he had 1,000 wagons loaded with commissary stores. The scout also says that it was talked generally that Forrest was to cross on our right, Morgan on our left, and break our communications. Morgan, Forrest, and S. D. Lee were in consultation at Columbus, Miss., just before Forrest moved north ; this was from March 12 to 15.

So far as what the scout saw the report is reliable, and he is a shrewd observer and one of my best men. He gives the rumors as he heard them. All the talk of officers was that Johnston intends to take the initiative. All furloughs have been stopped ; no troops since March 11 of any account have moved either east or west. Johnston's army is fed almost entirely from Southern Alabama, and a large amount of produce goes from Southwest Georgia to Lee's army. Stores in considerable quantities are accumulated at Atlanta and Marietta, and a good deal of corn is brought from South Alabama to Blue Mountain over Selma and Rome Railroad. The scout says everything north of Atlanta is virtually skinned, and the road he traveled from West Point to Blue Mountains is very poor, and the first good country he struck was around Jacksonville, Benton County. Columbus, Ga., is being extensively fortified.

Forrest left all his trains at Tupelo, and they are engaged hauling corn to that point. Two soldiers belonging to General Smith's command, wounded in the fight at Okolona, were killed in the hospital at Aberdeen by some of Forrest's men. It created considerable excitement and indignation among the citizens. The railroad from Demopolis to Selma is lined with corn-cribs.

Lieutenant-General Polk said if Smith had reached Sherman he would have gone to Selma, and they could not have stopped him. He (Polk) said he estimated Sherman's forces at about 20,000 men. Scout had orders from General Forrest, General Polk, Atlanta, Rome, &c. He says they all say their army is to-day at its maximum, and that they cannot increase it. Every point he was at he saw gangs of deserters at work in chains, and met them on all trains; the slave exemptions creating a good deal of bitter feeling. I send a number of Southern papers of dates up to April 6.

I am, general, very respectfully, your obedient servant,

G. M. DODGE,
Brigadier-General.

HUNTSVILLE, *April* 8, 1864.
Brig. Gen. G. M. DODGE,
    Athens :

No news from Whitesburg except indications that the enemy has increased his force on the opposite side of the river. The bridges on the Memphis and Charleston Railroad at Beaver Dam and Limestone are not very strongly guarded. Will you have an eye to them ?

The force at this point is not strong, in consequence of the absence of veterans. You have force enough, have you not, to attend to Decatur and other points on your line, even though Forrest and Clanton should unite ? Veatch ought to be with you shortly, which will enable you to strengthen the garrison at Decatur. As soon as General Garrard can get his cavalry division together, I will apply to Major-General Sherman to have him guard the line of the railroad as far down as Pulaski.

.JAS. B. McPHERSON,
Major-General.

ATHENS, *April* 8, 1864.
Major-General McPHERSON,
    Huntsville :

I can take care of everything in my command. Don't believe they dare attack Decatur. Will have another regiment at Limestone bridge to-morrow.

General Veatch's command will be here to-day. Forwarded a report to-day that will give a pr   good idea of all enemy's forces up to April 2 or 3. General Garrard has a large force at Columbia, but has not relieved any of my troops yet.

G. M. DODGE,
Brigadier-General.

HDQRS. MILITARY DIVISION OF THE MISSISSIPPI,
Nashville, Tenn., April 8, 1864.

General BRAYMAN,
Cairo :

Send word to General A. J. Smith, at Vicksburg, to reach him before he attempts the Yazoo expedition, that he will not attempt to come across by Grenada and Decatur, but that he will come to Huntsville, Ala., as expeditiously as possible, by Cairo and Paducah, up Tennessee River to Clifton, and march to Huntsville. Written orders will come by to-morrow's mail, but you can send this by a special courier to General Hurlbut and commanding officer at Vicksburg.

W. T. SHERMAN,
Major-General.

HDQRS. MILITARY DIVISION OF THE MISSISSIPPI,
Nashville, Tenn., April 8, 1864.

General A. J. SMITH,
Comdg. Red River Expedition, Vicksburg, en route :

GENERAL : Changes in circumstances render it better that your entire division and command should come by water via Cairo, Paducah, and up the Tennessee via Clifton. You need not therefore attempt the march to Grenada and across by land, but come in your boats by the route via Cairo. Copies of this will be sent to Generals McPherson, Hurlbut, and commanding officers at Cairo and Paducah.

One cause of this change is that General Veatch, instead of occupying Purdy, came away, and I had no notice of his coming till we heard of his troops at Florence.

I am, &c.,

W. T. SHERMAN,
Major-General, Commanding.

HDQRS. DEPARTMENT AND ARMY OF THE TENNESSEE,
Huntsville, Ala., April 8, 1864.

Maj. Gen. W. T. SHERMAN,
Comdg. Mil. Div. of the Mississippi, Nashville, Tenn. :

GENERAL : I am just in receipt of General Orders, No. 5, from your headquarters, and your letter of the 6th instant.

I think the assignment of Major-General Slocum to the command of the District of Vicksburg an excellent arrangement, but how is it going to affect General Hurlbut ? Slocum ranks him, although General H. commands the Sixteenth Corps by order of the President. The troops in the District of Vicksburg, however, belong to the Seventeenth Army Corps. I thought as soon as A. J. Smith's command arrived here, and the army for the field was thoroughly organized, that I would make some transfers, so as to have the Fifteenth and Seventeenth Corps here and the Sixteenth on the Mississippi River, and let the Sixteenth embrace all the troops from Cairo down to the Department of the Gulf. It is not absolutely necessary, but will simplify matters very much in the way of making out returns, reports, &c.

By sending Slocum to Vicksburg and bringing Dodge and A. J. Smith's command here we are virtually taking the greater part of the Sixteenth Army Corps out from under General Hurlbut's control. If you deem it advisable to send him to Cairo I prefer having you issue the order, as his actions since my assignment to the command of the department show that he bears me no good will.

Who is to command the Seventeenth Army Corps ? Whoever it is, I hope will arrive in time to go to Cairo and assist in reorganizing the two divisions which are to start from that point up the Tennessee River.

In my communication to you giving the reasons in favor of selecting Huntsville as the point for the main depot, I did not intend to express an opinion as to the best point for crossing the river in force when we make a forward movement.

My information in relation to the character of the road on the other side of the river was not sufficient to enable me to judge correctly. But by using the steam-boat, which can be spared from Chattanooga, supplies can be transported from Whitesburg to any desired point, and they can be very easily taken from here to Whitesburg.

I have been to Whitesburg and will go to Guntersville soon, and in the mean time am gaining all the information I can in relation to roads, &c., which I will communicate to you.

Very respectfully, your obedient servant,
JAS. B. McPHERSON,
Major-General.

NASHVILLE, *April* 8, 1864.

Major-General McPHERSON,
Huntsville :

Would you be willing to give Butterfield your Fourth Division, Fifteenth Army Corps, General Logan ? Butterfield is young, zealous, and full of knowledge.

W. T. SHERMAN,
Major-General.

HUNTSVILLE, *April* 8, 1864.

Major-General SHERMAN :

I have seen General Logan in relation to Butterfield. He does not wish any change made in his division commanders if it can be avoided. If officers are assigned to us the only way will be to place them on duty as near as may be according to rank without consulting any one, all other things being equal.

JAS. B. McPHERSON,
Major-General.

ATHENS, *April* 8, 1864.

Brig. Gen. J. D. STEVENSON,
Decatur :

General Veatch's command is here. Will be in Decatur to-morrow about noon.

G. M. DODGE,
Brigadier-General.

PADUCAH, *April* 8, 1864.
Brigadier-General BRAYMAN,
    Commanding, Cairo:
    Reports confirmed that Forrest is at or in the neighborhood of
Jackson in force. General Buford at Trenton day before yesterday.
Forces at Dukedom and Perryville on the stand-still. Cannot tell
where they intend to strike. If you have the force to spare I would
be pleased to have additional forces.
    All quiet here, except the feverish excitement among the citizens.
                                        S. G. HICKS,
                                        Colonel, Commanding.

                            ———

                                        PADUCAH, *April* 8, 1864.
Brigadier-General BRAYMAN:
    I have just seen U. S. mail agent on railroad from here to Union
City. He was at Mayfield yesterday evening. Small force of enemy there then. He reports, from best information he could get,
Forrest re-enforced by McCulloch at Jackson and Trenton. Buford
and Faulkner were at Trenton. He says Forrest has under him
now between 10,000 and 15,000 men moving in this direction.
    He has charge of mails here with instructions from you. Could
he not detain all mail matter suspected, and which might be of value
to you?
    Colonel Hicks is very vigilant; you may depend he is ready to
fight at all times. Captain Talmadge and self leave on boat Anderson this p. m.
                                        C. B. SMITH,
                                        Lieutenant and Aide-de-Camp.

                            ———

            HEADQUARTERS SIXTEENTH ARMY CORPS,
                        Memphis, Tenn., April 8, 1864.
Maj. Gen. W. T. SHERMAN,
    Comdg. Mil. Div. of the Mississippi, Nashville, Tenn.
    Dispatch from Brayman received. Grierson has been recalled.
The bulk of Lee's cavalry is with Forrest. Lee himself is reported
at Canton. Three regiments infantry at Okolona waiting for horses.
It is believed that Forrest proposes to cross the Tennessee as soon as
he can mount his force.
    The showing of force toward Memphis is, I think, to cover the
march of trains south. These trains I will try and reach. The city
militia turn out pretty well.
                                        S. A. HURLBUT,
                                        Major-General.

                            ———

            HEADQUARTERS POST AND DEFENSES,·
                        Vicksburg, Miss., April 8, 1864.
Maj. Gen. W. T. SHERMAN,
    Nashville, Tenn.:
    Arrived about 8 a. m. Will coal and leave at 11 a. m. Will make
mouth of Red River to-morrow at about 7 a. m. Gave General Mc-
Arthur the memoranda, and informed him of the projected plan. He

can give us 500 cavalry and will mount the 100 you gave me for an escort, which I will retain and bring back overland. General Mc-Arthur says that the enemy has strengthened his lines along this front and prohibited ingress or egress, which he thinks indicates a movement north, covered by this additional picketing. He says the railroad from Meridian to Jackson is about half finished, and that it will be completed in three weeks; that they are working on the Mobile and Ohio Railroad. Hurlbut informed me that a construction train was at Okolona, running south some week or ten days since. Loring's forces are at work on the railroad between Jackson and Meridian. Lee is still at Canton in person. I directed scouts to be sent out immediately, so as to have all information possible by my return. Also a cavalry force thrown out to see whether two brigades of cavalry that were at Mechanicsburg are still there or not. The tendency is to overestimate the enemy wherever I go, but I think that if we can find a crossing on the Tombigbee we can whip anything they have got. From information I can gather I am induced to believe our best route is from Grenada to Columbus, thence to Decatur, on the ridge between the Tombigbee and Black Warrior. However, we will see.

Very respectfully, your obedient servant,

JNO. M. CORSE,
Brigadier-General, Commanding.

WASHINGTON, *April* 8, 1864—3.30 p. m.

Lieutenant-General GRANT:

I have to-day ordered 40,000 bushels of grain and 700 tons of hay from eastern ports to Pensacola under sealed orders. First shipment to be made by steam, to arrive by the 1st of May; all by the 10th. Also sent by Mississippi and Atlantic orders to Colonel Holabird. chief quartermaster New Orleans, to send a cargo of forage from New Orleans to Pensacola, to be there by the 1st of May to meet any contingency.

M. C. MEIGS,
Quartermaster-General.

HDQRS. CHIEF OF CAV., MIL. DIV. OF THE MISSISSIPPI,
Nashville, Tenn., April 8, 1864.

Brig. Gen. J. H. WILSON,
Chief of Cavalry Bureau, Washington, D. C.:

SIR : I have thus far found it impossible to procure estimates from department chiefs of cavalry for the horses, arms, and equipments that they require, and I have recently sent an officer into each department of this military division to inspect the cavalry and bring back the reports, returns, and estimates required by the orders issued from time to time from these headquarters.

In the absence of all estimates I cannot furnish you even an approximation to the number of horses required for the cavalry of this division, but to supply the dismounted troops now awaiting mounts in this city will require 10,000 horses. As many more will be needed to fit up the cavalry commands belonging to the Department of the Ohio and now in process of reorganization in Kentucky. Ten thousand more will be needed at Memphis and below to meet the wants of Grierson's command and to supply the cavalry now stationed at and near Vicksburg. These wants are all immediate and pressing. Eight thousand enlisted men are now idle in this neighborhood alone for want of horses, arms, and equipments.

The ordnance depot here is kept constantly drained of everything in the nature of cavalry arms and equipments. No advices have been received of any considerable shipments on the way, and really we have reason to fear that we shall fail utterly in getting our cavalry forces mounted, armed, and equipped in time to make them effective in the coming campaign.

I think those engaged in purchasing horses confine themselves too much to large cities that have already been pretty well exhausted of their surplus horses and mules, and I fear that they content themselves with "sitting down" in soft places and waiting for stock to come to them. Extraordinary efforts will have to be made at once or a failure is near at hand that will be rung throughout the country. The system of paying in vouchers is very objectionable. Those who receive them are subjected to such inconveniences and discounts as prevent any particular desire on the part of others to make sales.

Let us have horses, arms, and equipments as fast as they can be possibly crowded forward.

Yours, truly,

WM. SOOY SMITH,
Brig. Gen., Chief of Cavalry, Mil. Div. of the Mississippi.

(Same to Brig. Gen. J. W. Davidson, chief of cavalry bureau, Saint Louis, Mo.)

HDQRS. MILITARY DIVISION OF THE MISSISSIPPI,
Nashville, April 8, 1864.

General ROBERT ALLEN,
        Louisville:

DEAR GENERAL: Draw me up a programme whereby orders may issue from the War Department enabling you to act as my chief, with power to visit by yourself or inspectors every part of my command, to direct the course and accumulation of supplies, the distribution of the means of transportation, and all details purely pertaining to your department. I must have some quartermaster whose sphere is co-ordinate with my own, and the Quartermaster-General seems to recognize the necessity.

I suppose you can remain at Louisville, though I would prefer you to be near me, especially if we advance beyond the Tennessee.

I inclose you a copy of my General Orders, No. 6, which will give us daily some thirty and odd cars, and instead of yielding to the pressure of civilians I am inclined to be more rigid. I will have down on me all the Christian charities who are perambulating our camps, more to satisfy their curiosity than to minister to the wants of the poor soldier. My universal answer is that 200 pounds of powder or oats are more important to us than that weight of bottled piety. As to sanitary goods, they can come here where they can be distributed as other stores, according to the known wants of the troops. I want

you to back me in this, as I know the President and Secretary of War, yielding to *ex parte* clamor, will fail to see my reasons, nor will I explain them till asked for ; you might do so.   I must accumulate to the front at once as large a surplus as the capacity of the road will accomplish.
Yours, truly,

W. T. SHERMAN,
Major-General.

———

WASHINGTON, *April* 8, 1864—2.45 p. m.
Major-General HEINTZELMAN,
    Columbus, Ohio:
Lieutenant-General Grant directs that you cause a thorough examination to be made in your department, so as to get every available man into the field as early as possible.   All delays, irregularities, and neglects to forward the men should be reported to the Adjutant-General of the Army, that the necessary orders may be issued.   All recruits and new organizations, and all the old troops that can possibly be spared from Ohio and Michigan, are to rendezvous at Washington, and all in Indiana and Illinois at Louisville.   This order does not apply to veterans, who will return to the commands to which they belong unless otherwise specially ordered ; nor does it apply to recruits for particular corps.   The lieutenant-general wishes the old troops in your department reduced to the lowest number of men necessary for the duty to be performed.
H. W. HALLECK,
Major-General, Chief of Staff.

———

HEADQUARTERS DISTRICT OF KENTUCKY,
        Louisa, April 8, 1864.
Lieutenant-Colonel FAIRLEIGH,
    Acting Assistant Adjutant-General:
No force except Hodge's in Kentucky, except a battalion of Virginia rebels above on my left.   My advance outposts are at Prestonburg.   I have received but 300 horses yet, and of course my mounted force cannot act independent.   If I had the Forty-fifth Kentucky I could drive the rebels "now in" out of the State and leave this point safe.   Could I not order the company I have at Greenup to join me ?
Yours, &c.,

G. W. GALLUP,
Colonel Fourteenth Kentucky, Commanding.

———

GENERAL ORDERS, }   HDQRS. CAV. CORPS, ARMY OF THE OHIO,
    No. 21.   }   *Paris, Ky., April* 8, 1864.
The withdrawal of the mounted infantry regiments from this command making it necessary to change the organization of the corps, it is hereby reorganized as follows :
First Division, Col. Israel Garrard, Seventh Ohio Volunteer Cavalry, commanding :
First Brigade : Seventh Regiment Ohio Volunteer Cavalry, Ninth Regiment Michigan Cavalry. First Regiment Kentucky Cavalry.

Second Brigade, Colonel Capron commanding: Fourteenth Illinois Volunteer Cavalry, Fifth Indiana Volunteer Cavalry, Eighth Michigan Cavalry.

Second Division, Col. James Biddle, Sixth Indiana Cavalry, commanding:

First Brigade, Colonel Crittenden commanding: Twelfth Regiment Kentucky Cavalry, Sixteenth Regiment Illinois Cavalry.

Second Brigade, Colonel Holeman commanding: Sixth Indiana Cavalry, Eleventh Kentucky Volunteer Cavalry.

To this organization other regiments will be attached as they arrive.

Commanders of divisions and brigades will make such changes in the present location of the troops as may be rendered by this order.

By command of Brigadier-General Sturgis:

WM. C. RAWOLLE,
Capt., Aide-de-Camp, U. S. Army, and Actg. Asst. Adjt. Gen.

GENERAL ORDERS, }   HEADQUARTERS ELEVENTH CORPS,
No. 8.   }   *April* 8, 1864.

In accordance with an order just received from headquarters Military Division of the Mississippi, I am assigned to a new command. Our intimate relations for the past year in sunshine and sorrow have knit us together in close ties of friendship. To me you are known and tried and beloved, so that it is needless to say that there is much that is painful in the change. We have met reverse together, and borne it. We have won victory together, and claim the honor. If by my example and effort I have succeeded in preserving unity, and therefore strength, and have thus been instrumental in enabling you to make a noble record in behalf of your country, I am satisfied. I take leave of you perfectly assured from the past brief though eventful history of the Eleventh Corps that you will give to the new organization of which you will form a part, and to our common leader at the head of it, tried and honored in so many battles of this war, the same obedient, cheerful, and energetic spirit that has carried you through every description of danger.

By a continued devotion to duty, under the Divine blessing, a reward hardly as yet anticipated is in store for each of you, as for every soldier of the Union, at the hands of free and grateful people.

O. O. HOWARD,
Major-General, Volunteers.

GENERAL ORDERS, }   HDQRS. SECOND DIV., 16TH ARMY CORPS,
No. 7.   }   *Pulaski, Tenn., April* 8, 1864.

The general commanding regrets that the state of discipline in this command has become so loose as to compel him to publish a general order on the subject. No officer having the good of the service at heart can fail to see the pernicious effect of a too free social intercourse between officers and men. All officers are therefore strictly forbidden to associate on terms of equality with enlisted men. This applies especially to officers messing, playing at games of any description, or visiting with their men, as also permitting them to visit their quarters except upon business, which is to be done in the proper manner. In a general sense this order will make it the duty of officers to require respectful and courteous treatment from enlisted men on all occasions. Whenever company officers or officers connected with regiments or batteries are guilty of violating this order it shall be the duty of regimental commanders to place such officer or officers in arrest, and prefer the proper charges against the same without delay, and any regimental commander neglecting to do this will be placed in arrest by his brigade commander and the charge of neglect of duty preferred against him.

This order applies to staff officers who may have enlisted men directly under their charge, and any violation of this order will subject them to the same penalty as above prescribed, the general commanding division and commanders of brigades being the proper officers to execute the same.

Officers of the inspector-general's department are charged with the responsibility of seeing this order properly executed, and will report without favor any officer who violates its requirements.

This order will be read to each regiment and battery composing this command at the evening parade following its receipt.

By order of Brig. Gen. T. W. Sweeny, commanding:

LOUIS H. EVERTS,
Captain and Assistant Adjutant-General.

SPECIAL ORDERS, }   HDQRS. LEFT WING, 16TH ARMY CORPS,
    No. 90.   }   *Athens, Ala., April 8, 1864.*

I. Brig. Gen. J. C. Veatch, commanding Fourth Division, Sixteenth Army Corps, will proceed with his command to Decatur, posting one regiment at Mooresville and a sufficient force at the junction to secure the safety of stores and trains at that point. He will have command of all troops at Mooresville Junction and Decatur.

*   *   *   *

By order of Brig. Gen. G. M. Dodge:

J. W. BARNES,
Assistant Adjutant-General.

CULPEPER COURT-HOUSE, VA..
April 9, 1864—10 p. m.   (Received 3 p. m., 10th.)

Maj. Gen. H. W. HALLECK:

Will you please ascertain if General F. P. Blair is to be sent to General Sherman? If not, an army corps commander will have to be named for the Fifteenth Corps.

I would much sooner have General Hunter or Buell at Memphis than Hurlbut, and General Sherman is not willing to try Hurlbut in the field again.

U. S. GRANT,
Lieutenant-General.

CULPEPER, VA., *April 9*, 1864—10.30 p. m.
(Received 3 p. m., 10th.)

Maj. Gen. H. W. HALLECK:

General Sherman thinks Hurlbut not bold enough to retain at Memphis. I will think over the matter and suggest some one to take his place, but in the mean time do not know where to send Hurlbut. How would he do to command at Charleston during Gillmore's absence ?

U. S. GRANT,
Lieutenant-General.

NASHVILLE, TENN., *April* 9, 1864.
(Received 6 p. m.)
Lieutenant-General GRANT,
Culpeper:

Your dispatch of yesterday is received. I have Stoneman now in East Kentucky with all the cavalry of the Army of the Ohio. General Schofield's troops are at Bull's Gap, and I have no indications of an invasion of Kentucky from Pound Gap. That road is very long and very bad. Forrest will escape us. Veatch went to Waverly and came away without orders, because he could hear nothing of Forrest.

We will want a bolder man than Hurlbut at Memphis. Why not send Buell ?

Should any force come into East Kentucky could it not be checkmated by a comparatively small force sent to the mouth of Big Sandy to march by Louisa and Prestonburg ? In the mean time I am collecting everything with General Schofield, Generals Thomas and McPherson to act offensive south of the Tennessee.

I will continue to draw here all detachments and furloughed men. I am also endeavoring to accumulate surplus stores to the front, which would enable me to move troops rapidly by railroad.

McPherson's two divisions will soon begin to arrive at Cairo from their furloughs.

W. T. SHERMAN,
Major-General.

CULPEPER, VA.,
April 9, 1864—10.30 p. m.
Major-General SHERMAN:

I have no objection to your proposed march of A. J. Smith across from Grenada. All I want is all the troops in the field that can be got in for the spring campaign. I do not think any more generals will be sent to you unless you want Milroy, McCook, or Crittenden.

U. S. GRANT,
Lieutenant-General.

NASHVILLE, TENN., *April* 9, 1864—10.30 p. m.
(Received 12.50 p. m., 10th.)
Lieutenant-General GRANT,
Culpeper:

Your letters of April 4 are this moment received, and suit me exactly. I will write fully. All is well with me, and I will be on time, anyhow.

W. T. SHERMAN,
Major-General.

CULPEPER, *April 9, 1864*—12.30 noon.
Maj. Gen. W. T. SHERMAN:
General Banks is ordered to take all his troops with him, and to turn over the defense of Red River to General Steele and the Navy. One regiment and a part have been ordered to General Steele at Little Rock, and the Thirty-fifth Wisconsin Regiment is subject to your orders.

U. S. GRANT,
Lieutenant-General.

WASHINGTON, *April 9*, 1864—4.20 p. m.
Major-General SHERMAN, *Nashville, Tenn.*:
The Thirty-fifth Wisconsin Regiment will be placed under your command, and the Adjutant-General will order it where you wish. General Grant thinks you will wish to send it to Steele. Please answer where you want it.

H. W. HALLECK,
Major-General, Chief of Staff.

NASHVILLE, *April 9*, 1864.
Maj. Gen. G. H. THOMAS, *Commanding:*
Dispatches of the 8th received. I wish you would give Butterfield a division.
If Hooker will address you a letter, and you indorse it, I will make other disposition of Schurz. Newton is still at Cincinnati with sore eyes, but he is subject to your assignment. There appears some trouble about Buell. I offered to take him, but General Grant does not answer my dispatch.
Make up your command to suit yourself exactly, and I will try and maintain it without change during the campaign. Butterfield is doubtless with Hooker now. Assign him at once, for he belongs to Hooker's command yet.

W. T. SHERMAN,
Major-General, Commanding.

HEADQUARTERS DEPARTMENT OF THE CUMBERLAND,
Chattanooga, April 9, 1864.
Major-General MCPHERSON, *Huntsville, Ala.*:
I think of sending a small command down the Tennessee from Bridgeport to Decatur to destroy all boats and canoes on the river. Will any of your plans be interfered with by so doing, or will you have them destroyed from Larkinsville down?

GEO. H. THOMAS,
Major-General, U. S. Volunteers.

HUNTSVILLE, ALA., *April 9*, 1864.
Maj. Gen. G. H. THOMAS, *Chattanooga:*
None of my plans will be interfered with by your sending a force down the Tennessee River to destroy all boats and canoes.
A temporary draw can easily be fixed in the pontoon bridge at

Larkin's Ferry to let the boat or boats pass in down to Decatur. I have no boats except what are in use in the pontoon bridges, and would like very much to have the force you send continue on down to Decatur.

It is reported that there is a force of the enemy about 400 strong, opposite Whitesburg ; they have as yet displayed no artillery.

JAS. B. McPHERSON,
Major-General.

CHATTANOOGA, *April 9, 1864.*

Major-General SHERMAN :

General Garrard has reached Columbia. Orders were sent him last night to report to you by letter. Orders were given by General Elliott when in Nashville that Garrard's division should be mounted and equipped first of any of my cavalry, and he reports to me that when equipped the division will muster over 6,000 men.

GEO. H. THOMAS,
Major-General, U. S. Volunteers, Commanding.

BULL'S GAP, *April 9, 1864.*

Maj. J. A. CAMPBELL,
Assistant Adjutant-General, Knoxville :

Flag-of-truce party not back yet, and Lick Creek again unfordable from the heavy rain of the past twenty-four hours. No bridging tools have been sent up yet. If we had them the county bridge over Lick Creek and the small trestle here could be repaired in a day. Our wagons will not be able to recross on their way back from Greeneville till the stream falls. I have placed Klein's cavalry at the creek to protect them. No enemy anywhere near us in force. Reports show none below the Watauga, and probably none south of Bristol.

J. D. COX,
Brig. Gen., Comdg. Third Division, 23d Army Corps.

HDQRS. 1ST CAV. DIV., DEPT. OF THE CUMBERLAND,
Cleveland, Tenn., April 9, 1864.

Brig. Gen. WILLIAM D. WHIPPLE,
Chief of Staff, Department of the Cumberland :

I have the honor to report all quiet. My scouting parties are sent out daily on all the roads leading from this point. They find the enemy's pickets at the same positions as previously reported. I have inaugurated a system of patrolling at all hours of the day and night, by which I am persuaded a band of spies and mail carriers from the enemy will be either captured or broken up. I would respectfully suggest that the post commander be instructed to exercise more strictness in granting passes to citizens, as I am induced to believe that information is obtained by the enemy through persons who pass through here.

I have the honor to be, general, very respectfully, your obedient servant,

EDWARD M. McCOOK,
Colonel, Commanding Division.

[First indorsement.]

HEADQUARTERS DEPARTMENT OF THE CUMBERLAND,
Chattanooga, April 19, 1864.

Respectfully referred to General J. B. Steedman, commanding post of Chattanooga, for his information and guidance.

By command of Major-General Thomas :

WM. McMICHAEL,
Major and Assistant Adjutant-General.

[Second indorsement.]

HEADQUARTERS POST,
Chattanooga, April 20, 1864.

Respectfully returned to department headquarters.

No passes are given to citizens by the post provost-marshal except to those who come in to draw rations and are known to be loyal.

JAMES B. STEEDMAN,
Brigadier-General, U. S. Army, Commanding.

HDQRS. MILITARY DIVISION OF THE MISSISSIPPI,
Nashville, Tenn., April 9, 1864.

General CORSE,
Vicksburg:

After consultation with General Grant it is determined not to make the march from Grenada. Smith's forces will therefore come up the Mississippi to Cairo, and thence up the Tennessee, there to join McPherson. I have sent orders to that effect. After Smith is out of Red River you may therefore rejoin me, wherever I may be, via Nashville.

W. T. SHERMAN,
Major-General, Commanding.

ATHENS, *April 9, 1864.*

Brig. Gen. J. D. STEVENSON,
Decatur:

No news from Huntsville. Let mounted force push up river as you proposed.

G. M. DODGE,
Brigadier-General.

ATHENS, *April 9, 1864.*

Maj. Gen. J. B. McPHERSON,
Huntsville:

Scouts in from south. Left Gadsden April 6. The day before the sick of Loring's division came up from Selma to Shelby Spring Hospital. They all stated that Loring's division was ordered to North Alabama, and left Demopolis on Monday. They were moving over-land.

Yesterday passed through Clanton's camp at Woodall's Bridge

over Flint, and also passed about 1,000 of his men on road going to Moulton ; part of his men at Whitesburg and Somerville. Martin's division of cavalry was near Blue Mountain. No force of any amount at Gadsden.

> G. M. DODGE,
> *Brigadier-General.*

HUNTSVILLE, *April* 9, 1864.

Brig. Gen. G. M. DODGE, *Athens:*

Nothing special from Whitesburg ; a few men seen on the other side of the river. Reports place the enemy's force near Whitesburg at about 400 men, and that they have collected some boats above and intend to cross and surprise some of our outposts. If they come over I do not think many of them will get back.

> JAS. B. McPHERSON,
> *Major-General.*

ATHENS, *April* 9, 1864.

Brig. Gen. J. D. STEVENSON, *Decatur:*

The company of Seventh Illinois picketing river from Elk River to Eastport, on this side, reports to-day the appearance of considerable force of rebels at Bainbridge and Florence. General McPherson says they report about 400 rebels opposite Whitesburg, and some above and below that point.

> G. M. DODGE,
> *Brigadier-General.*

ATHENS, *April* 9, 1864.

Maj. Gen. J. B. McPHERSON, *Huntsville:*

Most of Clanton's force has gone to Moulton. I have ordered mounted force to push up to Whitesburg if possible. Have you any news from that direction?

> G. M. DODGE,
> *Brigadier-General.*

HUNTSVILLE, *April* 9, 1864.

Major-General SHERMAN,
  Commanding, &c.:

General Veatch in his report,* which I send by mail of to-day, incloses copy of order from General Hurlbut which leads me to believe that General Hurlbut is before this advised of his withdrawal from Purdy. I do not see that we can do anything from here to relieve Grierson if he is in any danger, not knowing where he is. The rebel cavalry seem to be making around toward Eastport, possibly with the intention of joining Forrest and trying to get across the Tennessee and interrupt communication in our rear. We will give them a warm reception.

> JAS. B. McPHERSON,
> *Major-General.*

---

* See Part I, p. 574.

NASHVILLE, *April* 9, 1864.

General McPHERSON,
        Huntsville :
    I have no doubt of the truth of the report by General Dodge's scouts, and I am glad of it. I would rather have Loring to our front than their bothering Hurlbut. I am afraid Veatch's coming away will endanger Grierson, who is not hunting for him.
                    W. T. SHERMAN,
                Major-General, Commanding.

NASHVILLE, TENN., *April* 9, 1864—4.30 p. m.
                (Received 12th.)
Maj. Gen. S. A. HURLBUT,
        Memphis :
    General Dodge's scout reports that Loring's division is marching from Demopolis for North Alabama. This is more probable than that he will remain in Mississippi.
                    W. T. SHERMAN,
                    Major-General.

MEMPHIS, TENN.,
                April 9, 1864.
Maj. Gen. W. T. SHERMAN,
        Comdg. Mil. Div. of the Mississippi, Nashville, Tenn.:
    On yesterday I destroyed a bridge erected by the rebels to cross Wolf 5 miles from town. They have abandoned the idea of coming in here. Forrest's train and artillery are reported moving up via Saulsbury. He means to cross Tennessee in force and should be looked for about Big Sandy.
    Cairo should have a full regiment and another for Columbus. S. D. Lee is reported to have chief command of expedition in your rear.
                    S. A. HURLBUT,
                    Major-General.

HDQRS. MILITARY DIVISION OF THE MISSISSIPPI,
            Nashville, Tenn., April 9, 1864.
General HURLBUT,
        Memphis :
    Your dispatch of the 6th is received. I have sent orders that Smith's command will not come by Grenada as proposed.
    Veatch went to Purdy as ordered and came right away, and I did not hear of his coming till he had got to Florence. I fear that Grierson in trying to communicate with him will get in a scrape, but I ordered General Brayman to advise you of the fact as quickly as possible.
    The object of Forrest's move is to prevent our concentration as against Johnston, but we must not permit it. Until McPherson's veteran volunteers assemble at Cairo I cannot make my plans to attack Forrest where he is. You have force enough to defend Memphis, and Forrest does us little harm where he is.
    There are gun-boats at Eastport, and we have a large force at

Decatur. Should Grierson be cut off from Memphis by Veatch's blunder, I hope he can reach one or the other of these places, but I suppose Forrest is scattered. Lee and Loring cannot feed their commands in that part of Tennessee.

W. T. SHERMAN,
Major-General.

LOUISVILLE, *April* 9, 1864.
(Received 10.40 p. m.)

General M. C. MEIGS, *Quartermaster-General:*

Have shipped since the 1st of November to the 25th of March 138,000 bushels corn, 572,000 bushels oats, and 16,000 tons of hay. This does not include shipments made the depots at Memphis, Vicksburg, and Natchez, of which I have no returns. Can ship from Saint Louis in April and May 200,000 bushels of grain each month, and 2,000 tons of hay. It will be useful for me to know how much forage will be required at New Orleans. I get no return from there.

R. ALLEN,
Brigadier-General and Quartermaster.

HDQRS. MILITARY DIVISION OF THE MISSISSIPPI,
Nashville, Tenn., April 9, 1864.

M. C. MEIGS,
Quartermaster-General, Washington, D. C.:

GENERAL : I take the liberty to inclose you copies of my General Orders, No. 6.* They were submitted to and modified by Colonel Donaldson and Mr. Anderson. We act in perfect concert and have in view exactly the same end, viz, the transportation of army supplies. I want two more changes—that the collecting a cent by way of passage money by a railroad hand or conductor be a death matter ; and that the cars should run on a circuit, carrying the heavy cars down to Stevenson via Decatur and bringing back over the old and bad road the empty cars. This would make collisions unlikely, but these railroad men are so accustomed to time-tables that I believe they would run on a single track if a double one lay side by side, and if a conductor can collect pocket-money by the way the cars will be gradually used to that end instead of carrying munitions of war and provisions.

Yet I have begun, and as soon as Mr. McCallum comes I will let him work out the balance of the problem. I am convinced by making all these changes we can supply, with the use of the boats completed and in progress, 100,000 men operating from our base, viz, Chattanooga to Decatur.

McCallum can't get his increased stock of cars here in time to contribute to our operations this spring. We should have an accumulation of stores at the front rather than an increased means of transportation, for I take it for granted, as we collect our troops for action, our roads will be frequently interrupted.

I want accumulations at Chattanooga, Bridgeport, and Huntsville by May 1.

I am, with respect,

W. T. SHERMAN,
Major-General.

---

* See p. 279.

SPECIAL FIELD ORDERS, ⎰ HDQRS. DEPT. OF THE CUMBERLAND,
No. 100.   ⎱   Chattanooga, Tenn., February 9, 1864.

*   *   *   *   *   *   *

V. The Second Minnesota Battery, Capt. W. A. Hotchkiss commanding, is hereby detached from the Second Division, Fourteenth Army Corps, and assigned to the permanent garrison of Chattanooga, and will report accordingly.

*   *   *   *   *

By command of Major-General Thomas:

WM. D. WHIPPLE,
Assistant Adjutant-General.

GENERAL ORDERS, ⎰   HDQRS. DEPARTMENT OF THE OHIO,
No. 45.   ⎱   Knoxville, Tenn., April 9, 1864.

I. By direction of the President, Maj. Gen. George Stoneman is relieved from the command of the Twenty-third Army Corps, and the major-general commanding the department assumes immediate command of that corps. Major-General Stoneman is assigned to command the Cavalry Corps of this department.

II. Lieut. Col. G. W. Schofield, Second Missouri Artillery, is assigned to duty as chief of artillery and ordnance, and will relieve Brig. Gen. Davis Tillson, U. S. Volunteers, and Capt. W. H. Harris, U. S. Ordnance Corps, from the duties of chief of artillery and chief of ordnance, respectively.

III. Lieut. Col. F. M. Keith, First Ohio Heavy Artillery, is assigned to duty as judge-advocate of the Twenty-third Army Corps.

By command of Major-General Schofield :

J. A. CAMPBELL,
Assistant Adjutant-General.

SPECIAL ORDERS, ⎰ HDQRS. LEFT WING, 16TH ARMY CORPS,
No. 91.   ⎱   Athens, Ala., April 9, 1864.

*   *   *   *   *   *   *

II. The Fiftieth Regiment Illinois Infantry Volunteers, after turning over such stock as the First Regiment Alabama Cavalry Volunteers may need, and upon being relieved by troops from the Fourth Division, Sixteenth Army Corps, will march to Athens, Ala., and report to its brigade commander. The Thirty-ninth Regiment Ohio Infantry Volunteers, after the arrival at Athens, Ala., of the Fiftieth Regiment Illinois Infantry Volunteers, will march to Decatur, Ala., and report to its brigade.

By order of Brig. Gen. G. M. Dodge :

J. W. BARNES,
Assistant Adjutant-General.

PRIVATE AND ⎰   HDQRS. MIL. DIV. OF THE MISSISSIPPI,
CONFIDENTIAL. ⎱   Nashville, Tenn., April 10, 1864.

Lieut. Gen. U. S. GRANT,
    Commander-in-Chief, Washington, D. C.:

DEAR GENERAL : Your two letters of April 4 are now before me, and afford me infinite satisfaction. That we are now all to act in a common plan, converging on a common center, looks like enlightened war.

Like yourself you take the biggest load, and from me you shall have thorough and hearty co-operation. I will not let side issues draw me off from your main plan, in which I am to knock Joe Johnston, and do as much damage to the resources of the enemy as possible. I have heretofore written to General Rawlins and Colonel Babcock, of your staff, somewhat of the method in which I propose to act. I have seen all my army corps and division commanders, and have signified only to the former, viz, Schofield, Thomas, and McPherson, our general plans, which I inferred from the purport of our conversation here and at Cincinnati.

First, I am pushing stores to the front with all possible dispatch, and am completing the organization according to the orders from Washington, which are ample and perfectly satisfactory. I did not wish to displace Palmer, but asked George Thomas to tell me in all frankness exactly what he wanted. All he asked is granted, and all he said was that Palmer felt unequal to so large a command, and would be willing to take a division, provided Buell or some tried and experienced soldier were given the corps. But on the whole Thomas is now well content with his command; so are Schofield and McPherson.

It will take us all of April to get in our furloughed veterans, to bring up A. J. Smith's command, and to collect provisions and cattle to the line of the Tennessee. Each of the three armies will guard by detachments of its own their rear communications. At the signal to be given by you, Schofield will leave a select garrison at Knoxville and Loudon, and with 12,000 men drop down to Hiwassee and march on Johnston's right by the old Federal road. Stoneman, now in Kentucky organizing the cavalry forces of the Army of the Ohio, will operate with Schofield on his left front; it may be, pushing a select body of about 2,000 cavalry by Ducktown on Ellijay and toward Athens.

Thomas will aim to have 45,000 men of all arms and move straight on Johnston wherever he may be, fighting him cautiously, persistently, and to the best of advantage. He will have two divisions of cavalry to take advantage of any offering.

McPherson will have nine divisions of the Army of the Tennessee if A. J. Smith gets in, in which case he will have full 30,000 of the best men in America. He will cross the Tennessee at Decatur and Whitesburg, march toward Rome and feel for Thomas. If Johnston fall behind the Coosa, then McPherson will push for Rome, and if Johnston then fall behind the Chattahoochee, as I believe he will, then McPherson will cross and join with Thomas. McPherson has no cavalry, but I have taken one of Thomas' divisions, viz, Garrard's, 6,000 strong, which I now have at Columbia, mounting, equipping, and preparing. I design this division to operate on McPherson's right rear or front, according as the enemy appears; but the moment I detect Johnston falling behind the Chattahoochee, I propose to cast off the effective part of this cavalry division, after crossing Coosa, straight for Opelika, West Point, Columbus, or Wetumpka, to break up the road between Montgomery and Georgia. If Garrard can do this work good, he can return to the main army; but should a superior force interpose, then he will seek safety at Pensacola, and join Banks, or after rest act against any force that he can find on the east of Mobile, till such time as he can reach me.

Should Johnston fall behind Chattahoochee I would feign to the right, but pass to the left, and act on Atlanta, or on its eastern communications, according to developed facts.

This is about as far ahead as I feel disposed to look, but I would ever bear in mind that Johnston is at all times to be kept so busy that he cannot, in any event, send any part of his command against you or Banks.

If Banks can at the same time carry Mobile and open up the Alabama River he will in a measure solve the most difficult part of my problem—provisions. But in that I must venture. Georgia has a million of inhabitants. If they can live, we should not starve. If the enemy interrupt my communications, I will be absolved from all obligations to subsist on our own resources, but will feel perfectly justified in taking whatever and whenever I can find. I will inspire my command, if successful, with my feeling that beef and salt are all that is absolutely necessary to life, and parched corn fed General Jackson's army once on that very ground.

As ever, your friend and servant,

W. T. SHERMAN,
Major-General.

NASHVILLE, TENN., *April* 10, 1864.
(Received 5 p. m.)

Major-General HALLECK,
Washington, D. C.:

Order the Thirty-fifth Wisconsin to General Steele, up Red River. The regiment should embark in boats, direct for Alexandria, La.

W. T. SHERMAN,
Major-General.

NASHVILLE, *April* 10, 1864.

Maj. Gen. G. H. THOMAS,
Commanding:

Order your commissaries to have by May 1 a proper supply of beeves collected near your base. They must not lose a minute of time, as the cattle must be driven. If present contracts don't come up to requirements, they must buy in Tennessee and Kentucky and Nashville, rather than be behind time.

W. T. SHERMAN,
Major-General.

LOUDON, TENN.,
April 10, 1864.

Major-General THOMAS:

I have assumed command of the Fourth Army Corps. Headquarters will be moved to Cleveland to-morrow. I wish to remain over until Tuesday morning to review General Wagner's division, with your permission. General Wood's division is here; is now crossing the river.

O. O. HOWARD,
Major-General.

HEADQUARTERS DEPARTMENT OF THE CUMBERLAND,
Chattanooga, April 10, 1864.
Brig. Gen. J. W. GEARY,
Commanding Division, Twelfth Army Corps:

The major-general commanding the department directs that you take the steamer Chickamauga, upon her arrival at Bridgeport, place upon her two of your regiments, with plenty of ammunition and ten days' rations, and one piece of artillery to guard the boat, and proceed with the same down the Tennessee River as far as Decatur, examining carefully the south bank and all streams emptying into the Tennessee upon the south side, and destroying all boats of whatever kind you may find. You will also notify the inhabitants that no more boats will be permitted to be built or used, except with permission of the major-general commanding the department.

Upon returning you will examine, in the same manner, the north side of the river, and destroy what boats you may find, with the exceptions hereinafter mentioned, unless Major-General McPherson shall need them for some purpose, in which case you will turn them over to him. You will not destroy the boats at Decatur or Larkin's Landing, which will be the only points at which communications across the river will be permitted.

You will give the same notice to the inhabitants living on the north side of the river as upon the south.

Having completed the work assigned you, you will return to your station.

Very respectfully, your obedient servant,
WM. D. WHIPPLE,
Brigadier-General and Chief of Staff.

BULL'S GAP, *April 10, 1864.*
Maj. J. A. CAMPBELL, *Asst. Adjt. Gen., Knoxville:*

The order organizing the division transfers the Sixty-third Indiana from the Second Brigade, where it now is, to the First Brigade, and will leave only two regiments present in the Second Brigade, with a lieutenant-colonel as senior officer, one regiment having no field officers present on duty. Is the general commanding aware of this? The flag-of-truce party sent to Greeneville has got back to Lick Creek, and will be here to-night. The rebel families which came up to-day will have to wait till to-morrow, as my ambulances all went with the other party. The party stopped at Greeneville for the smaller detachment to go forward to Jonesborough with the letter for General Ransom and return. This was contrary to my intention, and has caused two days' delay.

J. D. COX,
Brigadier-General, Commanding Third Division.

APRIL 10, 1864.
Major-General McPHERSON, *Huntsville:*

Force that went to Triana and Whitesburg on south side of river have returned. Met small force of enemy at each place. All there, except three squads, moved to Moulton and Danville with Clanton's brigade.

G. M. DODGE,
Brigadier-General.

MADISON STATION, ALA.,
April 10, 1864.

Maj. R. R. TOWNES,
Assistant Adjutant-General, Huntsville, Ala. :

·SIR : I have to report that upon information I deemed reliable I sent a small party, under command of Lieut. William H. Birtwhistle, after 2 or 3 men whom I had heard of as having crossed the Tennessee River on Friday night, which resulted in the capture of Maj. J. E. Mason, of Confederate army, whom I have this morning forwarded to provost-marshal at Huntsville.

Rebels still continue to cross and recross at Triana, and distrust all negroes and Union citizens in the vicinity.

I am, very respectfully, your obedient servant,

WM. OWENS,
Captain Fifth Ohio Cavalry, Commanding Detachment.

HUNTSVILLE, ALA.,
April 10, 1864.

Maj. Gen. W. T. SHERMAN, *Nashville:*

Do you think there is a sufficient force in Memphis? I have not been able to get any returns from there, and do not know how many veterans are absent on furlough. If Forrest gets re-enforcements he may try and make a dash on that city. Though I have no fears of his taking and holding the place, still he might cause us immense destruction of property.

JAS. B. McPHERSON,
Major-General.

HDQRS. MILITARY DIVISION OF THE MISSISSIPPI,
Nashville, Tenn., April 10, 1864.

General McPHERSON,
Huntsville:

Hurlbut has at Memphis Buckland's brigade, 2,000; Grierson's cavalry, mounted, 2,400; dismounted, 3,000; in the fort 1,200 blacks, and outside of the fort full 2,000 blacks; in all 10,600, which are amply sufficient, besides three full regiments of armed citizens. The fort has sixty heavy guns mounted. I feel no apprehension whatever for the safety of Memphis, but only that Hurlbut may exhibit timidity and alarm.

W. T. SHERMAN,
Major-General, Commanding.

HDQRS. MILITARY DIVISION OF THE MISSISSIPPI,
Nashville, April 10, 1864.

General McPHERSON,
Huntsville:

The more of the enemy's cavalry that keep over toward the Mississippi the better, as our object is to disperse them. They cannot make a lodgment on the river, anyhow, and only wander about consuming the resources of their own people.

Look well to getting your troops from Cairo and below for the movement from the Tennessee River as soon as possible. Tell Macfeely he should have 2,000 or 3,000 good beeves from Cairo up the Tennessee, and across to you from Clifton with the troops. I will start on time, if necessary, with only beef, bread, and salt. I will write you again. I have full and explicit letters from Grant.

W. T. SHERMAN,
Major-General.

HEADQUARTERS SIXTEENTH ARMY CORPS,
Memphis, April 10, 1864.
Brig. Gen. N. B. BUFORD,
Commanding Northeast Arkansas:

GENERAL : Your communication of 8th April has been received. I regret that it is impossible now to furnish the cavalry you ask for. I have but 2,200 horses. The Third Michigan, 1,280 strong, and the Seventh Kansas, 1,100 strong, are detained in Saint Louis for want of horses. The country around me is held by the rebels in force. I would recommend direct application to Major-General Sherman, at Nashville.

Your obedient servant,

S. A. HURLBUT,
Major-General.

HEADQUARTERS SIXTEENTH ARMY CORPS,
Memphis, Tenn., April 10, 1864.
Maj. Gen. J. B. McPHERSON,
Commanding Department of the Tennessee:

GENERAL : Not having yet received your orders assuming command and designating your staff, I address this communication to you.

I suggest that to consolidate Memphis and Vicksburg into the District of the Mississippi River will create confusion, as the Military Division of the Mississippi is so similar in title. I have therefore simply directed troops of the Seventeenth Army Corps on the Mississippi to report to me, and assume command until the Seventeenth Corps shall be reorganized.

If it is intended that I should remain in charge of the river and its garrisons merely, it would certainly conduce to the interest of the service that the two divisions of the Sixteenth Corps, now in Middle Tennessee (Dodge's and Veatch's), and the two divisions of the Seventeenth Corps, now on their way, be combined and reorganized into the Seventeenth Corps, leaving such troops of the Sixteenth and Seventeenth Corps on the river, and such others as may be attached, to constitute the Sixteenth Corps.

This will of course remove from my command officers and troops whom I value highly, but I am satisfied will simplify returns and put the active force in the field into more compact and manageable form. I have no feeling about the matter, further than to facilitate the progress of our arms.

At present the force about Memphis and at posts above is not more than adequate for defense, and will so continue until the return to this post of the veteran cavalry.   If, however, I am to judge by the reports I receive, my cavalry regiments will remain dismounted for a long time.   The Third Michigan, 1,300 strong, and Seventh Kansas, 1,100 strong, have been three weeks at Saint Louis, waiting horses. I have here but 2,200 horses.

I further suggest that the colored troops in this command should be fully under the control of the commanding general, and that the system by which Brigadier-General Thomas is authorized to issue independent orders direct to them, without passing through my headquarters, is injurious in every respect.

My view of the best mode of covering that wretched speculation, Government-leased plantations, is to occupy Yazoo City with one regiment white troops, two of colored infantry, and Osband's colored cavalry, with a good battery under a good officer.   Osband's negro cavalry are good, and if properly armed they will handle Ross' brigade.   They now require 700 carbines, which I have not to give them.   With this force at Yazoo City Grenada would not be tenable, except by heavy force, which cannot be spared.

The cotton of the Yazoo, for which article the war seems to be carried on, would be brought out and Memphis would be covered by a threat from that base of operations.

A similar occupation of Harrisonburg would cover the west bank if our movement up Red River proves a success.   The Marine Brigade could then be employed, not on regular and known beats, but suddenly and at unexpected times and places, to advantage, and my cavalry division, when recruited and mounted, keep West Tennessee and Northern Mississippi in order.

Memphis and Vicksburg should be able at any time to throw out a full division in any direction required as a movable column without reducing the necessary garrison, and by joining the two columns be enabled to send a force of 10,000 effective men to the Tombigbee or the Coosa as you move down.   This, however, cannot be done if the colored troops are to be scattered up and down the river as plantation guards.

If my requisitions for horses are met with any promptness, I can move 7,000 good and well-armed cavalry by the 15th of May.   It is the absence of veterans and the lack of horses that has caused the Forrest raid.

I am, general, your obedient servant,

S. A. HURLBUT,
Major-General.

WOODVILLE, ALA.,
April 10, 1864.

Brig. Gen. M. L. SMITH,
Larkinsville, Ala.:

Thanks for your notice.   I received the same information yesterday and sent out patrols as strong as I could.   If you have any mounted force at all, I would suggest that you have them patrol the river down to opposite the head of Pine Island.   They can then co-operate with my forces.   This will secure our front and give us timely information of any movements.

P. J. OSTERHAUS,
Brigadier-General, Commanding.

HEADQUARTERS SIXTEENTH ARMY CORPS,
Memphis, Tenn., April 10, 1864.

Brig. Gen. A. J. SMITH,

    Comdg. Expeditionary Column, 16th Corps, on Red River:

GENERAL: I forward you with this a copy of dispatch* from General Sherman. In obedience to this, you will move up the river as soon as practicable, picking up all fragments at Vicksburg. At this place you will receive your batteries, and move on the route designated by General Sherman.

Send forward in advance by an officer requisitions for supplies, &c.

        S. A. HURLBUT,
           Major-General.

HEADQUARTERS OF THE POST,
Columbus, Ky., April 10, 1864.

Capt. J. H. ODLIN,

    Assistant Adjutant-General, Cairo, Ill.:

CAPTAIN: From information this day received from refugees, I learn that Faulkner, with 800 men, is intrenching Union City. Forrest is reported to be concentrating at Murray, from which place he will try to cross the Tennessee. The rumor is that he has been driven back by our forces, and found this the only means of escape.

There are small bands all sides of us. They have been in Clinton, Milburn, Blandville, and Hickman, in squads of 20 to 40 men, conscripting all and taking everything in the shape of a horse. I will have a scout with a full report in a day or two.

I am, sir, respectfully, your obedient servant,

        WM. HUDSON LAWRENCE,
           Colonel, Commanding Post.

HEADQUARTERS SIXTEENTH ARMY CORPS,
Memphis, Tenn., April 10, 1864.

Maj. Gen. W. T. SHERMAN,

    Comdg. Mil. Div. of the Mississippi, Nashville, Tenn.:

Forrest's force in West Tennessee is about 8,000 effective men: Bell's brigade, five regiments cavalry; Buford's brigade, three regiments mounted infantry; Faulkner's brigade, three regiments cavalry; Neely's brigade, two regiments cavalry; Chalmers' brigade, three regiments cavalry; McCulloch's brigade, two regiments cavalry; Duckworth's brigade, two regiments cavalry. He has four 3-inch rifled guns, captured at Chickamauga, and eight howitzers.

His artillery and wagon train were moving up from Pontotoc two days since. I am satisfied, from all information, that he proposes to cross at Clifton, at mouth of Big Sandy, and operate in Kentucky and Middle Tennessee.

        S. A. HURLBUT,
           Major-General.

HDQRS. MILITARY DIVISION OF THE MISSISSIPPI,
Nashville, Tenn., April 10, 1864.

Col. JAMES B. FRY, *Washington, D. C.:*

DEAR COLONEL: Yours of April 5 received. I have, by letter and telegraph, stated my entire willingness to have General Buell as-

* See p. 297,

signed to duty with me, and I indicated two commands for him, either of which would be highly honorable, but I don't think it would be just for me to advise Schofield to be displaced as commander of the Department of the Ohio. He enjoys the confidence of General Grant and of his command, and were I to give preference to General Buell I would do an act of injustice by adding what little weight I possess to that of a clamor raised because General Schofield did not allow himself to be used by a political faction.

General Buell's true interest is to get on duty, and then rise to his proper station by the ordinary progress of events.

If General Buell's friends put in circulation the reports that gained publicity that he was to supersede Schofield for the purpose of producing that result, I would be compelled, as an honest man, to counteract it ; but I think I know the general too well to believe he would resort to such measures to injure a brother officer, who, though younger than himself, seems to have devoted his best energies and services to the common cause.

The damned newspaper mongrels seem determined to sow dissensions wherever their influence is felt.

With great respect,

W. T. SHERMAN,
Major-General.

SPECIAL ORDERS, }   HDQRS. DEPARTMENT OF THE OHIO,
    No. 101.   {   *Knoxville, Tenn., April* 10, 1864.

I. The Twenty-third Army Corps will be reorganized as follows, to take effect on the 11th instant :

First Division, Twenty-third Army Corps, Brig. Gen. A. P. Hovey commanding:

First Brigade, Col. R. F. Barter commanding : One hundred and twentieth Indiana Volunteer Infantry, One hundred and twenty-fourth Indiana Volunteer Infantry, One hundred and twenty-eighth Indiana Volunteer Infantry.

Second Brigade, Col. J. C. McQuiston commanding : One hundred and twenty-third Indiana Volunteer Infantry, One hundred and twenty-ninth Indiana Volunteer Infantry, One hundred and thirtieth Indiana Volunteer Infantry.

Artillery attached to First Division: Twenty-third Indiana Battery, Capt. James H. Myers ; Twenty-fourth Indiana Battery, Lieut. Henry W. Shafer commanding.

Second Division, Twenty-third Army Corps, Brig. Gen. H. M. Judah commanding:

First Brigade, Brig. Gen. M. S. Hascall commanding : Twenty-fifth Michigan Volunteer Infantry, Eightieth Indiana Volunteer Infantry, Thirteenth Kentucky Volunteer Infantry, Third East Tennessee Volunteer Infantry, Sixth East Tennessee Volunteer Infantry.

Second Brigade, Col. M. W. Chapin, Twenty-third Michigan, commanding: Twenty-third Michigan Volunteer Infantry, One hundred and eighteenth Ohio Volunteer Infantry, One hundred and eleventh Ohio Volunteer Infantry, Forty-fifth Ohio Volunteer Infantry, One hundred and seventh Illinois Volunteer Infantry.

Artillery attached to Second Division: Battery F, First Michigan,

Captain Paddock; Nineteenth Ohio Battery, Capt. J. C. Shields commanding.

Third Division, Twenty-third Army Corps, Brig. Gen. J. D. Cox commanding:

First Brigade, Brig. Gen. M. D. Manson commanding: One hundredth Ohio Volunteer Infantry, Sixty-third Indiana Volunteer Infantry, One hundred and fourth Ohio Volunteer Infantry, Sixteenth Kentucky Volunteer Infantry, Eighth Tennessee Volunteer Infantry.

Second Brigade: Twenty-fourth Kentucky Volunteer Infantry, One hundred and twelfth Illinois Volunteer Infantry, One hundred and third Ohio Volunteer Infantry, Sixty-fifth Indiana Volunteer Infantry, Fifth Tennessee Volunteer Infantry, Sixty-fifth Illinois Volunteer Infantry.

Artillery attached to Third Division: Fifteenth Indiana Battery, Lieut. A. D. Harvey; Battery D, First Ohio Artillery, Captain Cockerill.

Fourth Division, Twenty-third Army Corps, Brig. Gen. Jacob Ammen commanding:

First Brigade, Brig. Gen. T. T. Garrard commanding: Ninety-first Indiana Volunteer Infantry, Thirty-fourth Kentucky Volunteer Infantry, Second North Carolina Mounted Infantry, Eleventh Tennessee Volunteer Cavalry, Battery L, First Michigan Artillery; Battery F, First Tennessee Artillery; Battery M, First Michigan Artillery; Twenty-second Ohio Battery.

Second Brigade (Reserve Artillery), Brig. Gen. Davis Tillson commanding: Second Tennessee Volunteer Infantry, First Ohio Heavy Artillery, First U. S. Colored Heavy Artillery, Battery A, First Ohio Artillery; section Wilder Battery, Twenty-first Ohio Battery, Tenth Michigan Volunteer Cavalry.

Third Brigade, Col. S. A. Strickland commanding: Fiftieth Ohio Volunteer Infantry, Twenty-seventh Kentucky Volunteer Infantry, First Tennessee Volunteer Infantry, Fourth Tennessee Volunteer Infantry, Henshaw's Independent Illinois Battery, Fourteenth Illinois Volunteer Cavalry.

Fifth Division, Twenty-third Army Corps, Brig. Gen. S. G. Burbridge commanding:

All troops belonging to the District of Kentucky. They will be organized by their commander into sub-divisions or brigades, and brigade commanders assigned as directed in instructions from these headquarters dated March 15, 1864.

II. The District of East Tennessee will consist of that portion of East Tennessee occupied by the Fourth Division, Twenty-third Army Corps, including the present District of the Clinch.

III. Maj. H. W. Wells, First Tennessee Artillery, is relieved from duty as chief of artillery of the Twenty-third Army Corps, and will report to Brig. Gen. Davis Tillson for duty as inspector of his brigade.

IV. District commanders will make their reports and returns to department headquarters at Knoxville, Tenn. Division commanders in the field will report to corps headquarters in the field. Where brigade commanders are not assigned in this order the senior officers present for duty will be assigned by the division commanders.

By command of Major-General Schofield:

R. MORROW,
Assistant Adjutant-General.

GENERAL ORDERS, }   HDQRS. SIXTEENTH ARMY CORPS,
No. 35.   }   *Memphis, Tenn., April 10, 1864.*

Under instructions from Maj. Gen. W. T. Sherman, commanding Military Division of the Mississippi, and Maj. Gen. J. B. McPherson, commanding Department and Army of the Tennessee, the undersigned assumes command of all troops heretofore attached to the Seventeenth Army Corps now on the Mississippi River.

Until the reorganization of the Seventeenth Army Corps shall be effected, all troops on the Mississippi River heretofore reporting to the commanding general of the Seventeenth Army Corps will report through brigade and division commanders to these headquarters, commencing with the tri-monthly for this date.

Officers assigned to specific commands by orders from headquarters Seventeenth Army Corps will continue to act under such assignment until further orders.

A full roster of commanders and staff officers for each headquarters, and of the commanding officers of each regiment, battery, or detachment, and a consolidated morning report of each regiment, battery, or detachment, in the portion of this command above referred to, full and complete in all the details prescribed by the notes and headings, will be made up immediately upon the receipt of this order, and forwarded to these headquarters by messenger.

The headquarters of the command will be at Memphis, Tenn., and the staff of the Sixteenth Army Corps, announced below, will be obeyed and recognized throughout the command.

Lieut. Col. T. H. Harris, assistant adjutant-general.
Col. W. L. Lothrop, chief of artillery and ordnance.
Lieut. Col. W. H. Thurston, assistant inspector-general.
Lieut. Col. Elias Nigh, chief quartermaster.
Lieut. Col. C. B. Hinsdill, chief commissary.
Surg. A. B. Campbell, U. S. Volunteers, medical director.
Capt. J. H. Burdick, acting ordnance officer.
Maj. J. O. Pierce, assistant adjutant-general, acting judge-advocate.

S. A. HURLBUT,
Major-General, Comdg. Sixteenth Army Corps.

WASHINGTON, D. C.,
April 11, 1864—2.30 p. m.

Lieutenant-General GRANT:

The Secretary of War has no information in regard to General Blair's case.

General Hurlbut has not sufficient military experience for so important a command as the Department of the South. I will write you in regard to this matter, and also in regard to Generals Buell and Hunter.

H. W. HALLECK,
Major-General, Chief of Staff.

HEADQUARTERS OF THE ARMY,
Washington, April 11, 1864.

Lieutenant-General GRANT, *Culpeper, Va.:*

GENERAL: I regard our establishments at Morris Island, Hilton Head, and on the sea islands of immense importance. As soon as Gillmore leaves the rebels will probably attack one or more of these places. To defend them properly we want a general there with experience and military education. My own opinion of General Hurlbut has been favorable, but I do not deem him equal to the command of the Department of the South, with its diminished forces. General Hatch is hardly the man for the place, but probably he is the best that can now be spared from the field.

I would like very much to see Buell restored to a command and have several times proposed him to the War Department, but there has been such a pressure against him from the West that I do not think the Secretary will give him any at present.

I think General Hunter would not accept any command under McPherson, or if he did trouble would follow. He is even worse than McClernand in creating difficulties. If you had him in the field under your immediate command perhaps things would go smoothly. Before acting on General Hunter's case, it would be well for you to see his correspondence while in command of a department.

Very respectfully, your obedient servant,

H. W. HALLECK,
Major-General, Chief of Staff.

HDQRS. MILITARY DIVISION OF THE MISSISSIPPI,
Nashville, Tenn., April 11, 1864.

General GEORGE H. THOMAS, *Comdg. Dept. of the Cumberland:*

GENERAL : Since my interview with you I have a letter from Grant, full, clear, and explicit, which I well understand but cannot now impart, but will in due time. The arrangements we began and the organizations are in exact accordance with the part assigned us, only the general fixes the time a little earlier than I did ; yet I will risk my judgment that the time I named to you will be as soon as others will be ready. Get your three corps well in hand, and the means of transportation as ready as possible.

When we move we will take no tents or baggage, but one change of clothing on our horses, or to be carried by the men and on pack-animals by company officers ; five days' bacon, twenty days' bread, and thirty days' salt, sugar, and coffee ; nothing else but arms and ammunition, in quantity proportioned to our ability. Even this will be a heavy incumbrance, but is rather the limit of our aim than what we can really accomplish.

Draw your forces down from the direction of Knoxville so as not to attract attention. I read the reports of your scouts with interest. I usually prefer to make my estimate of the enemy from general reasoning than from the words of spies or deserters.

We will go prepared for the maximum force possible of the enemy. We must not be led aside by any raids. We will be much aided by a diversion in a different quarter, of which I prefer not to write but may communicate by the first confidential opportunity.

Look well to our supply of beef-cattle on the hoof, and salt in large excess of the rations. Encourage drills by brigades and divisions, and let the recruits practice at the target all the time.

Newton is still detained by sore eyes. Keep a division for him, but in all else make up your organization to suit yourself and corps commanders. R. S. Granger wants a leave. Do you object? I suppose Rousseau could do district and post duty both.

Your friend,

W. T. SHERMAN,
Major-General, Commanding.

HEADQUARTERS DEPARTMENT OF THE CUMBERLAND,
Chattanooga, April 11, 1864.
Brig. Gen. A. BAIRD,
Commanding Third Division, Fourteenth Army Corps :
GENERAL : The Fifteenth Pennsylvania Cavalry being unable to furnish the detail necessary to make a scout into Broomtown Valley, the major-general commanding directs that you detail a force of from 100 to 150 mounted men to proceed, under the guidance of Dick Turpin, to Broomtown Valley, for the purpose of capturing 46 men and 100 horses of the rebel Captain Davenport's company, left in the valley for the purpose of assisting the enrolling officers. The party will take three days' rations.

Very respectfully, your obedient servant,
HENRY STONE,
Captain and Assistant Adjutant-General.

———

From General G. H. Thomas' journal.

APRIL 11, 1864.
The cavalry command of the Army of the Cumberland was reorganized, forming four divisions, commanded by Col. Edward M. McCook, Brig. Gen. Kenner Garrard, Brig. Gen. Judson Kilpatrick, and Brig. Gen. A. C. Gillem, each division containing three brigades, averaging three regiments to a brigade. First Brigade, First Division, Fourth Army Corps, was reviewed at Ooltewah.

———

KNOXVILLE, TENN.,
April 11, 1864.
Maj. R. M. SAWYER,
Asst. Adjt. Gen., Hdqrs. Division of the Mississippi :
In compliance with orders just received, I have the honor to report as follows, viz : Twenty-third Army Corps, First Division, Brigadier-General Hovey commanding, en route from Nashville, 4,500 ; Second Division, Brigadier-General Judah commanding, at Mossy Creek, 4,200 ; Third Division, Brigadier-General Cox commanding, at Bull's Gap, 3,900 ; Fourth Division, Brigadier-General Ammen commanding, in East Tennessee, 4,700 ; Fifth Division, Brigadier-General Burbridge commanding, in Kentucky, 9,500 ; total effective for service in the field, 12,600 ; total effective for district duty, 14,200. Cavalry corps, Major-General Stoneman commanding, effective strength not known ; in Kentucky remounting.
J. M. SCHOFIELD,
Major-General.

———

BULL'S GAP, *April* 11, 1864.
Maj. J. A. CAMPBELL,
Assistant Adjutant-General, Knoxville :
The foreman of the bridge-builders, who came up this afternoon, reports that it will take a week to get out the timber and repair the small railroad bridge here and the county bridge at Lick Creek so

as to be available. Please inform me whether this report will make it unadvisable in the opinion of the commanding general to begin the work.

J. D. COX,
Brigadier-General, Commanding Third Division.

———

HDQRS. MILITARY DIVISION OF THE MISSISSIPPI,
Nashville, Tenn., April 11, 1864.
Maj. Gen. J. B. McPHERSON,
Comdg. Department of the Tennessee, Huntsville, Ala.:

GENERAL : Yours of April 8 is received. Slocum's assignment to Vicksburg was made at Grant's suggestion. I did name Newton, having in mind his engineering qualities, but General Grant feared Newton might entertain a natural prejudice against the negro element which will hereafter enter so largely into the means of defense to the river. I wish we had a bold, dashing officer to put at Memphis; and as it is, if you say so, I will make an order for you to hold Vicksburg district with one division of white troops and the negroes organized in that region, and Memphis with a brigade of white infantry (Buckland's), division of cavalry (Grierson's), and such negro organizations and white detachments as now belong there or may afterward be assigned ; headquarters of the river defenses at Cairo. I want Smith's entire command to come to your right flank for a special reason. I want Mower and his command. He is the boldest young soldier we have. He and Corse, with 5,000 men each, would break through any line you encounter. In your operations in the campaign you will need two such officers as Mower and Corse. Now, though we take substantially the Sixteenth Corps, I know Hurlbut cannot manage them in the field, but he is generally willing to order • movements, but personally don't direct them. Therefore, though lawfully the commander of the Sixteenth Corps, we do not need his personal services. I know that you feel embarrassed by him, and I will draft a letter to send you with this, which, if you like, we will send him before making any positive orders.

Veatch's withdrawal from Purdy makes Forrest's escape from the trap in which he caught himself easy and certain, but if you have at Cairo anything that could go up the Tennessee and move inland on Jackson or Paris even, it would disturb Forrest more than anything Hurlbut will do from Memphis. I take it Forrest is now scattered ; some of his men on furlough and at mischief stealing horses and recuperating. He may cross over the Tennessee into Kentucky or Tennessee, but I don't care if he does. Should he break the railroad between this and Louisville it would not bother us, for we have vast supplies here, and if he comes over to the neighborhood of Pulaski or Columbia we will give him more than he expects.

As our great problem is to whip Joe Johnston, we want a surplus of our best troops on the line of the Tennessee. When that is done we can give more attention to the Mississippi as against the small bands that threaten it. Surely there is now nothing there that can touch Memphis, Vicksburg, and Natchez, and it will not be long till Banks will turn against Mobile, when the Confederates must look to the safety of their own lines of the Alabama.

Give your chief thoughts to the making up your Army of the Tennessee and gathering everything necessary to make the move from your present line on Rome and the Coosa. You will have the longest marches, and it may be the hardest knocks, but you have the elements of the best army. You will have nine divisions, averaging from 4,000 to 5,000 men, viz: Harrow's, Smith's (Morgan L.), Osterhaus' (in which is Charles R. Woods, a magnificent officer), and John E. Smith's, composing the Fifteenth Corps; Logan's, Veatch's, Sweeny's, and A. J. Smith's, under Dodge, and Crocker's and Leggett's, under Frank Blair. I am told Blair will soon leave Washington. I wrote him he would be wanted by April 20 at Cairo; you may telegraph him.

You had better begin moving up to Clifton your regiments and wagons as fast as they accumulate at Cairo. You can get steamers plenty at Cairo and Saint Louis.

Grant says he will be all ready April 25, and when he moves we must. Thomas and Schofield are progressing well in their preparations.

Your friend,

W. T. SHERMAN,
Major-General, Commanding.

PRIVATE.]   HDQRS. MIL. DIV. OF THE MISSISSIPPI,
                            Nashville, Tenn., April 11, 1864.
Maj. Gen. S. A. HURLBUT,
        Commanding District of Mississippi, Memphis, Tenn.:

DEAR GENERAL : The withdrawal of Veatch from Purdy without orders makes it easy for Forrest to escape with his plunder and stolen horses, and I doubt not he will escape Grierson. It is too late to remedy so fatal a mistake.

Two divisions of McPherson's will soon be at Cairo, but we are so intent now on the preparations of the grand operations soon to open that we cannot divert troops for minor things. These two divisions and A. J. Smith's command must hasten to join onto McPherson's right via the Tennessee River and Clifton. Not one hour must be lost. In taking A. J. Smith's division I feel that I strip you pretty close, but it can't be helped. We will need all the effective force we can gather to fulfill the part assigned us from this quarter.

Joe Johnston must be attacked in his chosen position, and at the same time other grand movements will occur on other distant fields, but all subordinate to one grand plan. The Mississippi must, in the mean time, be left on the defensive. Gun-boats and transports now patrol it in its whole length, and the enemy cannot reach it save with muskets and small field pieces. We hold Natchez, Vicksburg, Memphis, and Columbus with heavy artillery, and I think the troops now there ample for defense, and I would be glad if the enemy continues to keep Forrest's and Lee's cavalry there, as also Polk's infantry, but I am sure these or nearly all will soon swing over to the line of the Alabama.

General Slocum has been selected by General Grant as commander of the District of Vicksburg, which incloses Natchez and the Yazoo and ought to be extended also to embrace the Washita. I think you could safely leave Buckland at Memphis, and the garrisons as now at Columbus and Paducah, and yourself take post at Cairo, with a good regiment in reserve, which you can take out of A. J. Smith's division. Then from Cairo you can direct all movements looking to the safety of the Mississippi and Tennessee Rivers as lines of operation and communication. General McPherson can also detach one of Smith's regiments to remain at Clifton, where there is now a mounted Tennessee regiment, and where others can easily be thrown by a railroad now under construction from here to Reynoldsburg. This occurs to me to be the best arrangement, and I will suggest it to General McPherson and order it if he thinks my orders will give more satisfaction than his own. I see fully the points of delicacy involved in the questions of rank and seniority as between you, McPherson, and Slocum, but surely in times like these patriotism should induce us all to do anything and everything to make union and harmony prevail everywhere. So help me God, I will cheerfully subside, and if required will take command of a company post if ordered or even suggested by those who from success, merit, or even chance, have the lawful control. I know you must regard me as your personal friend; I am so, and will continue to be, and will manifest it by frankness. You have a high order of professional knowledge, but I do not think you naturally inclined to the rough contact of field service. Your orders and instructions are all good, but your execution not so good; as in case of the non-destruction of that bridge above Canton and your declining the Red River command. Of this no one knows but myself. Grant thinks you cling too close to Memphis from a love of ease, or other reason, and if Dodge were a major-general I think he would have taken away your command of the corps, as he has of Gordon Granger, for other similar reasons. We must now have men of action. I would like to hear from you in all confidence, and hope you will appreciate mine.

Truly, your friend,

W. T. SHERMAN,
Major-General, Commanding.

HDQRS. SECOND DIVISION, TWELFTH ARMY CORPS,
Bridgeport, Ala., April 11, 1864.

Major-General McPHERSON,
Comdg. Department of the Tennessee, Huntsville, Ala.:

Under instructions from Major-General Thomas I start with troops on the Chickamauga down the Tennessee to Larkin's Landing and Decatur to-morrow morning. My orders require me to burn all boats except those at these two places, and those you require to be saved.

You will oblige me by having your men on the river communicate with me as to your wishes. Please answer.

JNO. W. GEARY,
Brigadier-General, Commanding.

APRIL 11, 1864.

Major-General McPHERSON,
Huntsville:

I was over to Decatur yesterday. The enemy's cavalry appeared to be working around to our right. Clanton's force is all at Moulton and Danville, with a considerable force stretched along the river from Town Creek down. Only one company yesterday in Whitesburg.

G. M. DODGE,
Brigadier-General.

HEADQUARTERS SIXTEENTH ARMY CORPS,
Memphis, Tenn., April 11, 1864.

Maj. Gen. W. T. SHERMAN,
Comdg. Mil. Div. of the Mississippi, Nashville, Tenn. :

In dispatch of 8th April, 1864, to A. J. Smith, you direct his whole command to move up river. Do you include Mower's brigade? You promised furlough to three regiments of Mower's command. Again, you direct movement to be made via Fort Valley. I do not know any such place. Do you mean Fort Henry? I will have Smith's batteries and transportation ready as he comes up.

S. A. HURLBUT,
Major-General.

HDQRS. DEPARTMENT AND ARMY OF THE TENNESSEE,
Huntsville, Ala., April 11, 1864.

Maj. Gen. W. T. SHERMAN,
Comdg. Mil. Div. of the Mississippi, Nashville, Tenn.:

GENERAL: In pursurance to Special Orders, No. 24, paragraph V, dated April 11, 1864, from headquarters Military Division of the Mississippi, I have the honor to make the following report:

The effective force of the department is 67,505, distributed as follows:

The Fifteenth Army Corps, Maj. Gen. John A. Logan commanding, 17,763, situated on the line of the Memphis and Charleston Railroad. between Stevenson and Huntsville.

The Sixteenth Army Corps, Maj. Gen. S. A. Hurlbut commanding, 32,605, stationed as follows: Left Wing, Brig. Gen. G. M. Dodge commanding, 10,944 strong, stationed between Decatur and Pulaski, Tenn. Cavalry Division, Brigadier-General Grierson commanding, 5,153 strong, in the vicinity of Memphis. The District of Memphis, Brigadier-General Buckland commanding, 7,208 strong. The balance of the corps are at Cairo, Columbus, Paducah, and on the Red River expedition.

The Seventeenth Army Corps, —— —— commanding, 10,104 strong, stationed at Vicksburg and Natchez, under command of Brig. Gen. J. McArthur. The remainder of the Seventeenth Army Corps are at home on veteran furlough, and will rendezvous at Cairo, under command of Generals M. M. Crocker and M. D. Leggett. Corps D'Afrique, Brig. Gen. J. P. Hawkins commanding, 7,017 strong, stationed at Vicksburg and Natchez.

Very respectfully, your obedient servant,

JAS. B. McPHERSON,
Major-General.

HDQRS. FOURTH DIVISION, SIXTEENTH ARMY CORPS,
Decatur, Ala., April 11, 1864.

Captain JOHNSON,
Acting Commissary of Subsistence, Decatur, Ala. :

CAPTAIN: In reply to your note of inquiry of yesterday I am directed by Brigadier-General Veatch to say that the troops which arrived at this place in his command consist as follows: Officers, 119; enlisted men, 2,500; aggregate, 2,619.

I am, captain, very respectfully, your obedient servant,

F. W. FOX,
Assistant Adjutant-General

PADUCAH, KY.,
April 11, 1864.

General BRAYMAN:

The enemy is all around me. It takes all my men to do duty. They are worn out and broken down. I stand in need of more forces. If you can spare them, please send.

I sent for 30,000 rounds of .58-caliber ammunition some days since. Captain Odlin said it should be sent; it has not come yet; I stand in need of it. I also sent for artillery ammunition, the amount and character I wanted; it has not come. I may need it before it gets here.

S. G. HICKS,
Colonel, Commanding Post.

PADUCAH, KY.,
April 11, 1864.

Brigadier-General BRAYMAN:

None of the ammunition I sent for has come yet; please send it as soon as possible. Five companies of Faulkner's command came into Mayfield last night, and 180 rebels within 6 miles of this place this morning, hovering around us.

S. G. HICKS,
Colonel, Commanding.

PADUCAH, *April* 11, 1864.

General BRAYMAN:

God bless you for your prompt attention to my request in relation to ammunition. I am looking and waiting for Messrs. Forrest & Co. There is an awful shaking among the timid, but the righteous are bold as a lion.

S. G. HICKS,
Colonel, Commanding.

GENERAL ORDERS, }　　HDQRS. DEPARTMENT OF THE OHIO,
No. 47.　　　　 }　　　*Knoxville, Tenn., April* 11, 1864.

The loyal citizens of East Tennessee will be encouraged to cultivate their farms, and will be protected by the troops as far as practicable. Unserviceable horses and mules will be loaned to the loyal farmers, in accordance with instructions heretofore given to the chief quartermaster, to be recruited and used until they shall be required for the military service. All destruction of buildings, fences, or other property of loyal citizens, is strictly prohibited.

Hereafter, until further orders, forage and provisions will not be taken from the loyal citizens of East Tennessee except by purchase, with the free consent of the owners. Public animals will not be foraged upon inclosed fields, except in cases of necessity, when just compensation will be made for the forage consumed.

Commanding officers will be held responsible for any violation of this order by the officers or men under their command. When unauthorized seizures or unnecessary damage to private property shall be reported to these headquarters, the pay of the officers and men implicated will be stopped until full restitution shall be made and the guilty parties brought to justice.

By command of Major-General Schofield:

J. A. CAMPBELL,
Assistant Adjutant-General.

GENERAL ORDERS, }   HDQRS. FIRST DIV., CAV. CORPS,
No. 1.   }   ARMY OF THE OHIO, *Paris, Ky.*, *April* 11, 1864.

I. In accordance to General Orders, No. 21, dated headquarters Cavalry Corps, Army of the Ohio, April 8, 1864, the undersigned hereby assumes command of the First Division, Cavalry Corps, Army of the Ohio.

II. The following-named officers serving on staff of the First Division, Cavalry Corps, Army of the Ohio, are hereby relieved from duty in their respective departments and will report for duty at once to their regimental commanders:

Lieut. Watson B. Smith, acting assistant adjutant-general.
Capt. Thomas Rowland, acting assistant inspector-general.
Lieut. E. F. Smith, acting ordnance officer.
Lieut. R. H. Humphrey, acting assistant quartermaster.
Lieut. W. C. Root, acting assistant commissary of subsistence.

ISRAEL GARRARD,
Colonel, Commanding Division.

OFFICE OF THE CHIEF QUARTERMASTER,
Louisville, April 12, 1864.

General M. C. MEIGS,
Quartermaster-General, U. S. Army, Washington, D. C.:

GENERAL: I will leave to-morrow morning to confer personally with General Sherman. The sovereign difficulty that General Sherman has to contend with is in getting supplies forward to the advanced depots. Up to the present moment the rolling-stock on the roads leading out of Nashville has only been sufficient to transport the daily want. All the engines and cars to carry forward the surplus have yet to arrive from the East; they are coming at the rate of about 15 per day; from 1,500 to 2,000 are required to do the work. The depots at Nashville are overstocked with provisions and forage.

Very respectfully, your obedient servant,

R. ALLEN,
Brigadier-General and Quartermaster.

HEADQUARTERS DISTRICT OF NASHVILLE,
Nashville, Tenn., April 12, 1864.

Brigadier-General GARRARD,
Comdg. Cavalry Division, near Columbia, Tenn. :

GENERAL: Col. S. K. N. Patton, commanding Eighth Tennessee Cavalry, has telegraphed to these headquarters that you have assumed command of the post of Columbia and its vicinity. I suppose your action has been taken without knowledge of the fact that Columbia is a post within my district, and by order of Major-General Thomas placed under my control.   I hope you will refrain after this information from further interference with the officer placed in command by me, under direction of Major-General Thomas.

I shall be pleased to serve Brigadier-General Garrard and advance the interests of the service in any way in my power.

I am, general, very respectfully, your obedient servant,

LOVELL H. ROUSSEAU.

[Indorsement.]

HEADQUARTERS SECOND CAVALRY DIVISION,
Columbia, April 12, 1864.

This communication from General Rousseau is respectfully referred to department headquarters.

Under orders from Generals Thomas and Sherman I am at this place.   It is necessary for me to have the store-houses and shops for my use in this town; it is necessary for me to have my own provost guard and regulate the police in town.   The troops of the Eighth Tennessee Cavalry are new and not fit for duty.   I have no use for them, and notwithstanding the communication I will retain control of this place and order the Eighth Tennessee out of the town.   As I neither wish nor have time at present for a correspondence with General Rousseau, I have the honor to request that the major-general commanding department may direct that General Rousseau be instructed that orders required me to guard the railroad from Duck River to Lynnville, and that I am in no way subject to the order from District of Nashville.

K. GARRARD,
Brigadier-General, Commanding Division.

HEADQUARTERS DISTRICT OF NASHVILLE,
OFFICE OF INSPECTOR OF FORTIFICATIONS,
Nashville, Tenn., April 12, 1864.

Captain WILLIAMS,
Acting Assistant Adjutant-General:

CAPTAIN : Pursuant to order received from Major-General Rousseau, I visited Columbia, Tenn., to examine the fortifications at that place.   They consist of two small circular, or nearly so, breastworks thrown up, one within the other, on the top of a steep, conical hill, which overlooked the town and country for miles ; they are small affairs, and would be of little avail against a spirited attack.   Moreover, they do not protect the town, though they might 'prevent the enemy from holding it.   In the work there is a small magazine, entirely too small to hold the ammunition kept on hand.   I saw a considerable quantity of ammunition piled up on the ground and covered with tarpaulins, the magazine being entirely filled, on which account I was unable to examine thoroughly, but it appeared to be dry. There were.four howitzers in the works.   There is no water to be had inside the works, nor are there any tanks or other means of keeping it on hand.   If it is deemed advisable to construct any fortifications at Columbia I think it would be best to build a small redoubt on the hill already occupied and to put the main work on the hill close to the railroad depot, which affords a place to build store-houses and to cover them from attack, besides being close to the railroad depot.

I am having a plan of the works at Franklin, Tenn., made out by an assistant engineer ; when finished I shall send you a copy. I visited Franklin, and found the principal work, Fort Granger, in a dilapidated condition ; no attempt appears to have been made to keep it in proper order or repair. The magazines are very damp and entirely unfit to store ammunition. I noticed green mold on the ceiling. All the heavy guns are being remounted, and I understand it is the intention to keep two field pieces in the fort. I rode on the locomotive during my trip for the purpose of observing what work had been done on the block-houses now being built on the Nashville and Decatur Railroad. They were in an unfinished condition, and I should judge they were three-fourths done ; the most of the work remaining to be done is to put on the roofs. I have sent a copy of this report to Capt. William E. Merrill, chief engineer Department of the Cumberland, so that he may give his opinion and instructions relative to putting up works at Columbia, should General Rousseau desire it to be done. I expect to visit McMinnville, Tenn., this week, if I find I can do so without detriment to the engineer department at Nashville, Tenn.

I have the honor to be, your obedient servant,

JAMES R. WILLETT,
First Lieutenant Thirty-eighth Illinois Infantry,
Inspector Fortifications District of Nashville.

KNOXVILLE, TENN.,
April 12, 1864.

Maj. Gen. W. T. SHERMAN :

It is stated that the Senate committee has reported against my confirmation as major-general. I have good reason to believe that this report is made upon the assumption that I have not done all that I ought to have done in East Tennessee. If you can with propriety make the facts known to your brother or some other Senator you will do me a great service.

J. M. SCHOFIELD,
Major-General.

KNOXVILLE, *April* 12, 1864.

Maj. Gen. GEORGE H. THOMAS :

The troops of the Fourth Corps now at Loudon will march for Charleston in a few days. I will have to detain those on the railroad between Loudon and Charleston a few days longer, and will also have to depend upon your troops to hold the Hiwassee until Hovey arrives. I will stop him at Charleston.

J. M. SCHOFIELD,
Major-General.

KNOXVILLE, *April* 12, 1864.

Brigadier-General COX, *Bull's Gap :*

I think it advisable to rebuild the trestle-work this side of Bull's Gap, so that the cars can run to Lick Creek. By the time this is done

I will be able to decide about the wagon bridge across Lick Creek. What information did the flag-of-truce party gain about the condition of the road above Greeneville?

J. M. SCHOFIELD,
Major-General.

BULL'S GAP, *April* 12, 1864.

Major-General SCHOFIELD,
Knoxville:

The evidence is conclusive that the railroad is uninjured, except near Lick Creek. The rebels ran their cars down from Bristol yesterday, but the bridges at Watauga and Holston are reported to be such light affairs that it is doubtful if they stand the ordinary spring freshets. The wagon roads are reported in horrible condition.

J. D. COX,
Brigadier-General.

KNOXVILLE, TENN.,
April 12, 1864.

Major-General SHERMAN,
Nashville, Tenn. :

The rebels have not injured the railroad above Greeneville. The Watauga and Holston bridges are still standing. I have not yet learned definitely what force remains in the vicinity of Bristol. The wagon roads are nearly impassable. It rains almost continually. I have sent one division of the Fourth Corps to General Thomas, and will send the other in a few days.

J. M. SCHOFIELD,
Major-General.

LEXINGTON, KY.,
April 12, 1864.

Colonel GALLUP :

You will at once send sufficient force in direction of Preston to watch the movements of the enemy, and report all developments to these headquarters. If you have any news report at once.

By command of Brigadier-General Hobson :
J. S. BUTLER,
Assistant Adjutant-General.

HUNTSVILLE, ALA.,
April 12, 1864.

Maj. Gen. W. T. SHERMAN,
Nashville :

Dodge's mounted force came up day before yesterday on the south side of the Tennessee to opposite Whitesburg and met only small scouting parties of rebels. Clanton's brigade of rebel cavalry has gone to Moulton and Danville.

Brigadier-General Geary is coming down the river from Bridgeport to-day in the Chickamauga with a force to destroy all enemy's boats as low down as Decatur. Do you not think we will have to take a pontoon train along when we advance ?

The Coosa, from the best information I can get, is from 300 to 400 feet in width.

JAS. B. McPHERSON,
Major-General.

HDQRS. MILITARY DIVISION OF THE MISSISSIPPI,
Nashville, Tenn., April 12, 1864.

General McPHERSON,
 Huntsville :

I have a fine pontoon train all ready for you here, under good engineer officers. I will send it forward with all its equipment in time. It is large enough to bridge the Coosa twice. Thomas has a similar one. There is no enemy to your front but one of observation. Forrest acts as though he wanted to threaten our rear from the direction of West Tennessee, but your two divisions at Cairo will change his mind.

W. T. SHERMAN,
Major-General.

APRIL 12, 1864.

Major-General McPHERSON,
 Huntsville :

Reports this morning from Whitesburg, Triana, and Somerville show no force there. The regiments of infantry that were at Mount Hope have moved to Tuscaloosa ; went down the Byler road.

General Clanton has moved round to Tennessee River, to west of us. A letter from one of Roddey's men, dated April 1, in front of Dalton, says they are ordered to East Tennessee ; also says there is to be a general move of the enemy.

G. M. DODGE,
Brigadier-General.

HUNTSVILLE, <i>April</i> 12, 1864.

Brig. Gen. G. M. DODGE,
 Athens :

General Geary started this morning from Bridgeport down the Tennessee River in the Chickamauga with a force for the purpose of destroying all enemy's boats. He will run down as far as Decatur.

JAS. B. McPHERSON,
Major-General, Commanding.

HEADQUARTERS SIXTEENTH ARMY CORPS,
Memphis, Tenn., April 12, 1864.

Hon. GIDEON WELLES,
 Secretary of the Navy, Washington, D. C. :

I am informed, and I believe credibly, that a submerged torpedo-boat is in course of preparation for attack upon the fleet at Mobile,

The craft is described to me as a propeller, about 30 feet long, with engines of great power for her size, and boiler so constructed as to raise steam with great rapidity. She shows above the surface only a small smoke outlet and pilot-house, both of which can be lowered and covered. The plan is to drop down within a short distance of the ship, put out the fires, cover the smoke-pipe and pilot-house, and sink the craft to a proper depth, then work the propeller by hand, drop beneath the ship, ascertaining her position by a magnet suspended in the propeller, rise against her bottom, attach to it by screws, drop their boat away, pass off a sufficient distance, rise to the surface, light their fires, and work off. The torpedo to contain 40 pounds of powder and work by clock-work.

As near as my informant can give the plan I send you a rude sketch.* One of the party has gone north for a magnet and air-pump. I expect to catch him as he comes back. The boat is to be ready by 10th May.

Your obedient servant,

S. A. HURLBUT,
Major-General.

APRIL 12, 1864.

Major-General McPHERSON,
Huntsville:

General Veatch and command reached there three days ago.

Is General Garrard to relieve any of my troops? As yet I guard the railroad to Columbia.

G. M. DODGE,
Brigadier-General.

HUNTSVILLE, *April* 12, 1864.

Brig. Gen. G. M. DODGE,
Athens:

I shall not transfer Colonel Morgan's regiment from General Veatch's division. I have telegraphed twice to Major-General Sherman in regard to having General Garrard relieve a portion of your men now guarding railroad, and presume he will do so very soon. Hurlbut telegraphs from Memphis that Forrest is evidently making preparations to cross the Tennessee River in force, about the mouth of Big Sandy, and that S. D. Lee has joined him. Do you know whether forage for horses, mules, and cattle can be obtained along the road from Clifton to Pulaski?

JAS. B. McPHERSON,
Major-General, Commanding.

APRIL 12, 1864.

Major-General McPHERSON,
Huntsville:

Forage plenty on that road or near it. I am going to Mooresville to-day, and if I have time will go to Huntsville on the train to-night.

G. M. DODGE,
Brigadier-General.

---

* Not found.

PADUCAH, KY.,
April 12, 1864.

Capt. A. M. PENNOCK:

The rebels are in force around us. The colonel and the gun-boats are waiting for an attack. I can hardly believe that they will make the effort to take the place with four gun-boats. We do not allow any transports to go down the river, nor will we until we can give convoy. The Peosta, Moose, Brilliant, and Fair Play are here. The Key West went up the river this morning with an army convoy. The Silver Lake is patrolling the river below.

Beware of rebel strategy and lookout for Cairo and Columbus. I think the rebels want to cross the Ohio.

JAMES W..SHIRK,
Lieutenant-Commander, Comdg. Seventh District.

PADUCAH, KY.,
April 12, 1864.

General BRAYMAN:

A confidential messenger just in reports the enemy in heavy force this side Lovelaceville, coming this way.

S. G. HICKS,
Colonel, Commanding.

HEADQUARTERS OF THE POST,
Columbus, Ky., April 12, 1864.

Capt. J. H. ODLIN,
Assistant Adjutant-General:

CAPTAIN: I have the honor to report that the day has passed quietly. A report was brought in that Forrest, 20,000 strong, was at Mayfield last night. I have the news from my scouts, who will not return until they have positive information.

I am, captain, very respectfully, your obedient servant,
WM. HUDSON LAWRENCE,
Colonel, Commanding Post.

HEADQUARTERS SIXTEENTH ARMY CORPS,
Memphis, Tenn., April 12, 1864—7 p. m.

Brig. Gen. R. P. BUCKLAND,
Comdg. District of Memphis, Memphis, Tenn.:

GENERAL: You will send with all possible dispatch a good regiment, with four days' rations and full supply of ammunition, to re-enforce Fort Pillow. They will embark at the earliest moment on the steamer Glendale, or such other boat as may be furnished by the quartermaster's department.

Promptness is all important.

S. A. HURLBUT,
Major-General,

HEADQUARTERS DISTRICT OF MEMPHIS,
Memphis, Tenn., April 12, 1864.
Col. I. G. KAPPNER:

SIR: You will send with all possible dispatch the Fifty-fifth United States (colored), with four days' rations, or as much as they can carry in their haversacks, to re-enforce Fort Pillow. The men will take 40 rounds of ammunition in cartridge-boxes, and you will send 100 rounds extra on wagons to the boat. They will embark at the earliest moment on the steamer Glendale, or such other boat as may be furnished by quartermaster's department. Promptness is all important.

By order of Brigadier-General Buckland:

ALF. G. TUTHER,
Captain and Acting Assistant Adjutant-General.

HEADQUARTERS SIXTEENTH ARMY CORPS,
Memphis, Tenn., April 12, 1864.
OFFICER COMMANDING FORCE FOR FORT PILLOW
(*Through Brig. Gen. R. P. Buckland*):

COLONEL: You will proceed as rapidly as possible by steamer to Fort Pillow and re-enforce the garrison there. With this addition, and the great natural strength of the place, you should be able to hold it. Two gun-boats will be there, with whom you will communicate before landing. Immediately upon landing ascertain as nearly as you can from Major Booth the precise state of affairs, and send report to Cairo and here.

If you find on approaching Fort Pillow that it has unfortunately been taken, you will request the officer of the gun-boat to reconnoiter as closely as possible, and develop some accurate idea of the strength of the enemy, and return. If you succeed in re-enforcing the fort in time it must be held at all hazards and to the last man. Report immediately and by every boat that passes.

Your obedient servant,

S. A. HURLBUT,
Major-General.

[APRIL 12, 1864.—For Grant to Rosecrans, about sending transportation to Sherman's army, see Vol. XXXIV, Part III, p. 145.]

SPECIAL FIELD ORDERS, } HDQRS. DEPT. OF THE CUMBERLAND,
No. 103.   } *Chattanooga, April* 12, 1864.

*   *   *   *   *   *   *

XII. Maj. Gen. L. H. Rousseau, commanding District of Nashville, will, without delay, relieve the Twenty-third Regiment Missouri Volunteers, the Eighty-fifth Indiana Volunteers, and the detachment of the Thirty-third Indiana, along the line of the Nashville and Chattanooga Railroad, by troops from the garrison at Nashville as far as Murfreesborough, and by the troops from the garrison of Murfreesborough as far as the place known as Kelley's Camp, 2½ miles north of Bell Buckle, placing detachments at the points and of the strength named in the inclosed list.*

Upon being relieved, the Twenty-third Missouri will proceed to

---
* Not found; but see Whipple's statement, p. 290.

McMinnville and relieve the Nineteenth Michigan at that place, which regiment, upon being relieved, will join its brigade (Coburn's). Coburn's brigade will march to the front and report for duty to Maj. Gen. Joseph Hooker, commanding Twentieth Army Corps.

*   *   *   *   *   *

By command of Major-General Thomas :

WM. D. WHIPPLE,
Assistant Adjutant-General.

SPECIAL ORDERS, ⎱   HDQRS. DEPARTMENT OF THE OHIO,
No. 103.   ⎰   *Knoxville, Tenn., April* 12, 1864.

*   *   *   *   *   *

VII. The One hundred and twelfth Illinois Infantry is hereby transferred from the First to the Second Brigade, Third Division, Twenty-third Army Corps, and the Sixty-third Indiana Infantry is transferred from the Second to the First Brigade, Third Division, Twenty-third Army Corps.

*   *   *   *   *   *

IX. The Fiftieth Ohio Infantry and Fourth Tennessee Infantry will move, without unnecessary delay, to Loudon, Tenn., and take post at that place under the direction of Brigadier-General Ammen, commanding Fourth Division, Twenty-third Army Corps. On the arrival of the Fiftieth Ohio at Loudon, the troops of the Fourth Army Corps now at that place and between that place and Knoxville will be relieved from further duty in this department. They will march to Charleston, on the Hiwassee, and report for further orders to Major-General Thomas, commanding Army of the Cumberland.

The troops now stationed on the railroad between Loudon and Charleston will remain in their present positions until further orders.

*   *   *   *   *   *

XI. The Fourth Division, Twenty-third Army Corps, Brigadier-General Ammen commanding, will be distributed as follows, viz :

1. The First Brigade, Brigadier-General Garrard commanding, will occupy Cumberland Gap, and keep open its line of communication with its depot of supplies in Kentucky. The Eleventh Tennessee Cavalry and Second North Carolina Mounted Infantry (now dismounted) will be remounted as soon as the horses can be obtained and forage becomes sufficient for their support. They will then protect the communication with Knoxville, and scout as far as practicable in front of Cumberland Gap, keeping inferior forces of the enemy at a distance and gaining early and accurate information of the movements of any superior force.

Cumberland Gap must be held obstinately, and raids into Kentucky or Middle Tennessee prevented as far as possible with the troops of the First Brigade.

2. The Second Brigade (Reserve Artillery), Brigadier-General Tillson commanding, will occupy the defenses of Knoxville, and, if practicable, protect the railroad bridge at Strawberry Plains and the railroad to Loudon. The regiment of cavalry attached will be employed under the direction of the brigade or division commander in scouting the surrounding country for the purpose of gaining early and accurate information of any movement of the enemy. Special care must be taken to keep the horses in serviceable condition.

Knoxville must be held at all hazards and against any force, however large. Its defenses will be completed under the immediate direction and superintendence of Brigadier-General Tillson, and will be made as formidable as practicable. Store-houses for the arms and commissary of subsistence depots will be erected at suitable places within the defenses, large enough to contain four months' supplies for the garrison.

Brigadier-General Tillson is assigned to the immediate command of the Reserve Artillery and of the defenses of Knoxville, with his headquarters at Knoxville. He will equip and keep prepared for the field such reserve light artillery as may from time to time be ordered, and will re-equip and refit such batteries as may be sent to the rear for that purpose. He is also charged with the care of the reserve supplies of artillery and ordnance stores, and will attend to the filling of all requisitions for such supplies for troops in the field.

Brigadier-General Tillson will continue the organization of colored troops in the District of East Tennessee and the care of the contrabands at Knoxville, in accordance with orders which he has heretofore received.

The Second Tennessee Infantry will furnish such details as may be required by the provost-marshal-general of East Tennessee for the execution of his orders.

3. The Third Brigade, Colonel Strickland commanding, will be distributed under the direction of the division commander in such manner as to hold the railroad bridge at Loudon, protect the railroad between that point and the Hiwassee as far as practicable, and hold the railroad bridge and supply depot at the Hiwassee as long as may be necessary.

The regiment now at Kingston may be left at that place and vicinity for protection of quartermaster's property and for such other duty as may be required.

Brigadier-General Ammen, commanding Fourth Division, will give his special attention to the drill, discipline, and efficiency of the Third Brigade, and to the erection of defenses at Loudon and the Hiwassee, and spend at those points as much of his time as can be spared from other duties. He will make his headquarters at any point in his district where his presence may at any time be most needed.

The disposition herein ordered for the Fourth Division is subject to such modifications as circumstances may, in the opinion of the general commanding the division, require from time to time, having in view the importance of holding the four points—Knoxville, Cumberland Gap, Loudon, and Hiwassee.

*   *   *   *   *

By command of Major-General Schofield:

R. MORROW,
Assistant Adjutant-General.

GENERAL ORDERS, }   HDQRS. DEPT. AND ARMY OF THE TENN.,
    No. 3.   }   *Huntsville, Ala., April 12, 1864.*

Maj. Gen. H. W. Slocum, having reported for duty in accordance with General Orders, No. 5, headquarters Military Division of the Mississippi, is hereby assigned to the command of the District of Vicksburg, extending from the mouth of the Arkansas River on the west side of the Mississippi and the Tallahatchie River on the east side down to the Department of the Gulf, headquarters at Vicksburg, Miss.

By order of Maj. Gen. James B. McPherson :

L. S. WILLARD,
Major and Acting Assistant Adjutant-General.

SPECIAL ORDERS, }   HDQRS. SIXTEENTH ARMY CORPS,
  No. 93.   }   *Memphis, Tenn., April 12, 1864.*

*   *   *   *   *   *   *

IX. The four companies Sixteenth Kentucky Cavalry serving in the District of Cairo will immediately proceed to Louisville, Ky., there to report to Brig. Gen. S. G. Burbridge, commanding District of Kentucky. The quartermaster's department will furnish necessary transportation.

*   *   *   *

By order of Maj. Gen. S. A. Hurlbut :

T. H. HARRIS,
Assistant Adjutant-General.

APRIL 13, 1864.

Maj. Gen. W. T. SHERMAN,
  Comdg. Division of the Mississippi, Nashville, Tenn. :

Yours of the 6th instant has been presented to the Secretary of War, who has directed that Col. A. Beckwith, aide-de-camp and commissary of subsistence, shall be ordered to report to you.

J. P. TAYLOR,
Commissary-General of Subsistence.

HDQRS. MILITARY DIVISION OF THE MISSISSIPPI,
Nashville, Tenn., April 13, 1864.

General THOMAS,
  Chattanooga :

Continue to send me reports of scouts and rebel newspapers. Yours are most interesting. Two of mine are in from Memphis, having come from Holly Springs, Pontotoc, Aberdeen, Columbus, Selma, Montgomery. West Point, back to Selma, up to Talladega and Blue Mountain. The enemy is collecting a cavalry force at Blue Mountain, which is about 25 miles from Gadsden, on account of forage which comes up the railroad from Selma and Talladega ; and it is believed that Loring's division is ordered to the same point from Demopolis. Johnston doubtless is trying to make up a force to watch that flank, which he must observe is being threatened by McPherson. Forrest is reported again to be attacking Columbus, Ky., and also trying to cross the Tennessee near Hamburg. He seems to be omnipresent, but I think his cavalry is scattered over between the Mississippi and the Tennessee stealing horses and feeding them. I would as lief have him there as anywhere else now. Newton is here and will come forward to-morrow. Keep a good division for him.

Keep on collecting your command, as we arranged, and unload your cars as fast as possible. I will push forward stores as fast as possible.

W. T. SHERMAN,
Major-General.

HEADQUARTERS DEPARTMENT OF THE CUMBERLAND,
Chattanooga, Tenn., April 13, 1864.
Maj. Gen. W. T. SHERMAN,
Comdg. Mil. Div. of the Mississippi, Nashville, Tenn.:

GENERAL : I am this moment in receipt of your letter of the 11th. Affairs are working quietly, but so far satisfactorily. I am gradually moving my troops down from East Tennessee, but have to watch the newspaper men closely to prevent them from exposing everything. I also find great difficulty in preventing my division commanders as well as subordinates from publishing to the world everything they see, hear, or conjecture. However, I will not complain, but have merely mentioned this to remind you of the difficulties we are laboring under.

My signal men at Ringgold discovered the rebel signal cipher, and have been reading their messages for some days. The officer foolishly informed Baird that he could do so and Baird let it get out all over camp, thus carelessly throwing away a most important advantage.

All your suggestions in regard to drills, &c., are executed daily, and I hope and believe you will find this army ready. I am willing to risk Granger on leave, if he desires to go. I should think Rousseau could give personal attention to both for a time. Newton will get a division in either the Fourth or Fourteenth. Palmer has told me that he would be perfectly willing to serve under Buell. If I could get a good place for Steinwehr there would be no difficulty in organizing Hooker's command very efficiently. Hooker, I am gratified to see, seems pleased.

I have no especial news from the front to-day.
Yours, truly,

GEO. H. THOMAS,
Major-General.

CLEVELAND, TENN.,
April 13, 1864.
Brig. Gen. W. D. WHIPPLE,
Chief of Staff, Department of the Cumberland:

I have the honor to forward papers, memoranda, maps, &c., captured on the person of Capt. F. R. R. Smith, attached to the rebel General Johnston's corps of engineers. I would call your attention especially to the map of Atlanta and vicinity, and the order requiring him to make a topographical survey of it. I hope it may prove valuable, as also the maps of the vicinity where he was captured. My scouts came near capturing Captain Herman of the enemy's engineers on yesterday, but his horse was too fast. From the inquiries he made and his operations, he was evidently making a survey of the country south of the Connesauga River, west of the Federal road, north of Sumac Creek. Captain Smith says he was ordered to make a survey of the country south of Sumac Creek, west of the Federal road, east of Connesauga Creek, and north of Spring Place. I will send him to you to-morrow. The capture of the outpost this morning was not the result of carelessness or inefficiency on the part of either officers or men, so far as I can learn. The country where they were stationed is full of small roads coming in from all points, and, according to the report of Captain Comstock, the commanding officer, they were attacked in front, flank, and rear at the same time. They fought, but were overpowered. A deserter who came in to General Howard reports the force at 2,500, sent out to capture an infantry regiment supposed to be occupying the same isolated position this post did. They are now encamped at Barnett's Mills, 26 miles from this place. If the general commanding sees proper to give me permission, I will give them so much work defending their own camp and outposts that they will have neither time nor opportunity to annoy us.

Very respectfully, your obedient servant,

E. M. McCOOK,
Colonel, Commanding.

HDQRS. SECOND BRIGADE, FIRST CAVALRY DIVISION,
DEPARTMENT OF THE CUMBERLAND,
Cleveland, Tenn., April 13, 1864.

Capt. ROBERT LE ROY,
Assistant Adjutant-General:

CAPTAIN: I respectfully report that the Second Brigade moved at 9 a. m. on the Benton road, turning toward the right about a mile from town, and following a by-road to the house of Mr. Webb, 9 miles from Cleveland, where several hundred of the enemy had passed before midnight. A short time before reaching this point the order to strike the Spring Place road was received, and passing down a road parallel with the Federal road, the main column proceeded as far as King's Bridge, and a battalion was sent to the left down the Federal road, and, crossing the Connesauga River at Waterhouse's Mill, proceeded a mile beyond that point. At the mill 3 of our scouts killed a horse and captured his rider with the loss of a horse. No more of the enemy were seen. General Wheeler commanded the rebel forces, as nearly as could be ascertained about 1,000 strong. We were two hours behind, and the retreat was rapid and orderly. He had no cannon.

A considerable cavalry force of the enemy is now camped at Barrett's Mills, about 26 miles from Cleveland.

Very respectfully,

O. H. LA GRANGE,
Colonel, Commanding.

CLEVELAND, TENN.,
April 13, 1864.

Brigadier-General WHIPPLE,
Chief of Staff:

A deserter from Wheeler's cavalry says the raid was made this morning for the purpose of capturing an infantry regiment which was reported to be beyond support and near the State line; that the number of our cavalry taken by them was 26 ; that his command was about 2,500 strong, and that it left the vicinity of Tunnel Hill yesterday at 10 a. m.

O. O. HOWARD,
Major-General, Commanding.

BULL'S GAP, *April* 13, 1864.
Major-General SCHOFIELD, *Knoxville :*

The inspection of the regiments at Loudon will be made at once. Do you intend that the Tenth Michigan Cavalry shall report here ? I have not heard where they are. The small bridge on railroad will be completed to-morrow evening, and the workmen will be ready for your decision as to repair of Lick Creek wagon bridge. No news of interest except rumor that Vaughn's cavalry brigade is ordered back to Rogersville. It was not there yesterday.

J. D. COX,
Brigadier-General, Commanding Third Division.

HDQRS. MILITARY DIVISION OF THE MISSISSIPPI,
Nashville, Tenn., April 13, 1864.
General SCHOFIELD, *Knoxville, Tenn. :*

You can get rid of all citizens in your department by ordering them to enlist or go away. All passes are made void by fraud or crime. You can apply these principles without my using names. I will write to John Sherman on the matter you ask. Try and get rid of those newspaper reporters ; they will detect and publish our movements in time for Joe Johnston to guess at our plans.

W. T. SHERMAN,
Major-General.

KNOXVILLE, *April* 13, 1864—3.30 p. m.
Maj. Gen. W. T. SHERMAN :

My latest reports indicate that Longstreet's main force is still in the vicinity of Abingdon and Bristol. It is reported that the rebels have been strengthening the railroad bridges across the Watauga and Holston, both before and since they fell back. These reports come from very reliable Union men.

General Burbridge reports Morgan having passed Pound Gap with 3,000 cavalry supported by infantry. I do not get any such information from this direction.

J. M. SCHOFIELD,
Major-General.

HDQRS. MILITARY DIVISION OF THE MISSISSIPPI,
Nashville, Tenn., April 13, 1864.
General SCHOFIELD, *Knoxville :*

We are perfectly willing that Longstreet should remain up at Abingdon, and I would not object to his sending a force through Pound

Gap. I am pushing forward stores and waiting for the balance of McPherson's command, which ought to be at Cairo by the 20th of this month.

W. T. SHERMAN,
Major-General.

KNOXVILLE, TENN.,
April 13, 1864.
Colonel CRAWFORD,
Chief of Scouts, Bull's Gap:
Have you no information relative to movement of rebels through Pound Gap?

J. M. SCHOFIELD,
Major-General, Commanding.

BULL'S GAP, *April* 13, 1864.
Major-General SCHOFIELD :
I have merely rumor ; it is by no means certain there are any movements in that direction. The main force is still at Abingdon, Va., Bristol, Zollicoffer. and Kingsport.

R. A. CRAWFORD,
Colonel, Chief of Scouts.

BULL'S GAP, *April* 13, 1864.
General SCHOFIELD :
The force at Kingsport are 400, under Vaughn ; 250 at Zollicoffer, 150 at Carter's Depot, 400 near Blountsville ; no force below Jonesborough. A few scouts between here and Jonesborough, not over 50 men. I have scouts just in since my last dispatch ; they hear of no movement toward Pound Gap, but hear that the rebels say they intend to go there soon. My scouts are from near Kingsport and Jonesborough.

R. A. CRAWFORD,
Colonel, Chief of Scouts.

APRIL 13, 1864.
Maj. Gen. J. B. McPHERSON, *Huntsville:*
Colonel Rowett, commanding Seventh Illinois, stationed near Florence, reports that on yesterday Forrest was crossing near Hamburg. His force was represented to be 6,000. Only 100 had got across when Rowett received his information.

G. M. DODGE,
Brigadier-General.

ATHENS, ALA., *April* 13, 1864.
Brig. Gen. J. C. VEATCH. *Decatur:*
General Geary is on his way down the Tennessee River from Bridgeport to Decatur, with steamers and troops, and will destroy all boats in the river and creeks that the enemy can use. Give him such aid as he may request when he arrives at Decatur. There are three companies of General Logan's command guarding bridges at

Mooresville.   Colonel Montgomery has also sent companies to secure bridges.   Instruct him he can camp his regiment together as long as Logan's companies guard the bridges.   This will give him a chance to drill.   Also instruct him to keep the wood parties at work getting out wood for railroad use.

G. M. DODGE,
Brigadier-General.

LEXINGTON, KY.,
April 13, 1864.

Major-General SCHOFIELD :

General Sturgis reports that the enemy has appeared at Proctor. I have also information from parties just from Abingdon that Morgan has passed through Pound Gap with 3,000 cavalry, supported by infantry.   General Stoneman and myself think it best to detain the troops ordered to Knoxville until the enemy's movements are developed.   I will keep you advised.

S. G. BURBRIDGE,
Brigadier-General.

KNOXVILLE, TENN.,
April 13, 1864.

Brigadier-General BURBRIDGE,
Lexington, Ky.:

If it is true that Morgan has the force reported, Camp Burnside is more exposed than any other important point which he can reach. Consider this in determining whether to detain the infantry which is ordered to Knoxville, and in making your other dispositions.

J. M. SCHOFIELD,
Major-General, Commanding.

LOUISVILLE, *April* 13, 1864.

Col. GEORGE W. GALLUP,
Paintsville :

Dispatch received.   As a matter of course you will hold your position or secure a better one.   A force is ordered from West Liberty, on Salyersville road, to attempt the rear of the party attacking you and to co-operate with you.   Give any other information you may have.

By order of General Burbridge :

THOS. B. FAIRLEIGH,
Lieutenant-Colonel, Acting Assistant Adjutant-General.

HEADQUARTERS SIXTEENTH ARMY CORPS,
Memphis, Tenn., April 13, 1864.

Brig. Gen. B. H. GRIERSON,
Commanding Cavalry Division, Sixteenth Corps :

GENERAL : You have probably heard that Fort Pillow has been captured.   I also apprehend that Jackson's brigade of cavalry crossed above Panola on Sunday.

The cavalry patrols on all roads must be kept strong and well out, and a strong detachment should sweep up on the north side of Loosahatchie and in the space between Loosahatchie and Wolf.   The construction of bridges should be watched, and every precaution taken against surprise.

Your cavalry must be kept up to its full strength by the use of all horses fit for service.   Officers must be kept with their men, and men must not be allowed to race their horses in the manner they are now doing.   If no other way can be devised, men will not be allowed to leave the camp on horseback to visit the city except on duty and in charge of an officer.

S. A. HURLBUT,
Major-General.

HDQRS. CAVALRY DIVISION, SIXTEENTH ARMY CORPS,
Memphis, Tenn., April 13, 1864.

Col. GEORGE E. WARING,
Commanding First Brigade Cavalry:

COLONEL: Information has been received that there are several hundred of the enemy on this side of Wolf River, at what point is not known.

The general commanding directs that you send out about 200 men to scour the country well between this point and the Wolf, and to examine closely the river at all points to see that the enemy are not preparing crossings.   They should look well on toward the crossing on the Macon and Memphis road.

Respectfully, your obedient servant,
S. L. WOODWARD,
Assistant Adjutant-General.

HDQRS. CAVALRY DIVISION, SIXTEENTH ARMY CORPS,
Memphis, Tenn., April 13, 1864.

Col. G. E. WARING, *Commanding First Brigade:*

COLONEL: You have probably heard that Fort Pillow has been captured.   I am also apprised that Jackson's brigade of cavalry crossed the river above Panola on Sunday.   The cavalry patrols on all the roads must be kept well out and moving.

You will send two expeditions of 150 men each, well mounted and armed, one to sweep north of the Loosahatchie and the other between Loosahatchie and Wolf.   The men will carry two days' rations, and the commanding officer of each expedition will report here for further information and instruction.   Your patrols will be notified to report promptly to these headquarters any information they may obtain.

By order of Brig. Gen. B. H. Grierson:
S. L. WOODWARD,
Assistant Adjutant-General.

HDQRS. CAVALRY DIVISION, SIXTEENTH ARMY CORPS,
Memphis, Tenn., April 13, 1864.

Lieut. Col. W. P. HEPBURN,
Commanding Provisional Cavalry Regiment:

COLONEL: You have probably heard that Fort Pillow has been captured.   I am also assured that Jackson's brigade of cavalry crossed above Panola on Sunday. The patrols must be kept moving and well out on the different roads. They will be instructed to report promptly any information to these headquarters.

Your men will be required to take the best possible care of their horses, and none will be allowed to come into the city on horseback unless on duty or in charge of an officer. The shoeing will be pushed forward rapidly.

By order of Brig. Gen. B. H. Grierson :

S. L. WOODWARD,
Assistant Adjutant-General.

NASHVILLE, *April* 13, 1864.

General BRAYMAN :

Give me all the information you have relative to the attack on Columbus

W. T. SHERMAN,
• Major-General.

CAIRO, ILL., *April* 13, 1864.

Col. S. G. HICKS :

Demonstrations are made on Columbus, but may mean Paducah. Keep your forces ready. Captain Shirk will stay with you. Let no boats come down.

M. BRAYMAN,
Brigadier-General, Commanding.

CAIRO, ILL., *April* 13, 1864.

Col. S. G. HICKS,
Paducah :

Captain Pennock will telegraph you about the shell. Your ammunition went up ; I fear it was carried by. All safe at Columbus. Fort Pillow said to have been taken.

M. BRAYMAN,
Brigadier-General, Commanding.

CAIRO, *April* 13, 1864—8.30 p. m.

Maj. Gen. W. T. SHERMAN,
Nashville :

The surrender of Columbus was demanded and refused at 6 this morning. Women and children brought away. Heavy artillery firing this forenoon. I have sent re-enforcements. Paducah also threatened. No danger of either, but I think that Fort Pillow, in the Memphis district, is captured. General Shepley passed yesterday and saw the flag go down, and thinks it a surrender. I have enough troops now from below and will go down if necessary to that point. Captain Pennock will send gun-boats. If lost, it will be retaken immediately.

M. BRAYMAN,
Brigadier-General.

HDQRS. MILITARY DIVISION OF THE MISSISSIPPI,
Nashville, Tenn., April 13, 1864.
General BRAYMAN, *Cairo:*

Rumor says Forrest is attacking Columbus. I hope it is true, and will catch a second edition of Paducah. I hope Forrest will prolong his visit in that neighborhood till Smith comes up, or till McPherson's two divisions come to Cairo.

W. T. SHERMAN,
Major-General.

HEADQUARTERS SIXTEENTH ARMY CORPS,
Memphis, Tenn., April 13, 1864.
Brig. Gen. J. MCARTHUR, *Comdg. at Vicksburg, Miss.:*

GENERAL : Fort Pillow is reported captured yesterday about noon. This closes the river temporarily.

The Third Division, Seventeenth Army Corps, already under orders, must be 'hurried forward as fast as possible, as it will be necessary to retake the fort from the land side, and it is doubtful whether General Sherman will furnish any force from above.

Forward the inclosed to Brig. Gen. A. J. Smith by first and quickest dispatch.

As the gun-boats are engaged in Red River, you will order two of the Marine Brigade boats to report at Memphis for duty.

I am pretty sure that Loring's infantry is moving on North Alabama, and that most of Lee's cavalry is also above Grenada on the march north. Under these circumstances you can, if you judge it expedient, occupy Yazoo City. The proper force for this would be one regiment white infantry, two of colored, a battery, and the whole or part of Osband's cavalry.

I have no return of forces, and cannot therefore judge what can be spared. The negro troops should not be scattered. The occupation of Yazoo City is the best protection for the Mississippi River up to Greenville.

Your obedient servant,

S. A. HURLBUT,
Major-General.

[Inclosure.]

HEADQUARTERS SIXTEENTH ARMY CORPS,
Memphis, Tenn., April 13, 1864.
Brig. Gen. A. J. SMITH,
Comdg. Expdy. Column, 16th Army Corps, in Red River:

GENERAL : Fort Pillow has been taken by the rebels. Loring's division of infantry is reported east of Corinth. Forrest occupies West Tennessee.

It is of prime importance that the orders sent you by General W. T. Sherman to return be promptly carried out. With your forces here I can rapidly clear West Tennessee and reopen the river; without it, we in Memphis are practically in a state of siege. You will therefore move with your entire command as rapidly as possible to Memphis, reporting to me, as previously advised.

I am, general, your obedient servant,

S. A. HURLBUT,
Major-General.

HDQRS. MILITARY DIVISION OF THE MISSISSIPPI,
Nashville, Tenn., April 13, 1864.
General HURLBUT,
  Memphis :
  In my dispatch of the 8th the mistake is with the telegraph operator, who will correct.
  Let the command come round by Cairo and the Tennessee River. I want Mower's command, because of Mower in person. The three regiments can have their furloughs from Cairo. I write fully by mail through General McPherson.
W. T. SHERMAN,
Major-General, Commanding.

APRIL 13, 1864.
Maj. Gen. W. T. SHERMAN,
  Nashville:
  It is reported that Forrest was crossing the Tennessee River yesterday near Hamburg. The information came from Colonel Rowett, Seventh Illinois, stationed near Florence. Forrest is reported to have 6,000 men ; only 100 had got across when he received his information. The Seventh Illinois, mounted, and Ninth Ohio Cavalry have been ordered to push rapidly over in that direction to ascertain the facts and watch the movements.
  General Garrard, at Columbia, and the regiment of State troops at Clifton should be notified.
JAS. B. McPHERSON,
Major-General.

HDQRS. MILITARY DIVISION OF THE MISSISSIPPI,
Nashville, Tenn., April 13, 1864.
General McPHERSON,
  Huntsville :
  Forrest can hardly attack Columbus and cross the Tennessee at Hamburg the same day. Let him develop his design. I want him to stay up in that pocket till your two divisions get together at Cairo. Go on getting your command ready for the big move.
W. T. SHERMAN,
Major-General.

HUNTSVILLE, *April* 13, 1864.
Major-General SHERMAN :
  I presume General Brayman has made use of all the available forces at Cairo. There must have been 700 or 800 men, composed of detachments of the Seventeenth Army Corps, at Cairo, and possibly one or two regiments going or returning from furlough. If the commanding officer exercised proper vigilance and did not allow himself to be surprised, I do not think Forrest can take the place.
JAS. B. McPHERSON,
Major-General.

[APRIL 13, 1864.—For Rosecrans to Grant, about sending transportation to Sherman's army, see Vol. XXXIV, Part III, p. 145.]

SPECIAL ORDERS, }   HDQRS. DEPARTMENT OF THE OHIO,
    No. 104.   }   *Knoxville, Tenn., April* 13, 1864.

*   *   *   *   *   *   *

VI. Paragraph VII, Special Orders, No. 103, current series, from these headquarters, is hereby amended to read as follows :

The One hundred and twelfth Illinois Infantry is hereby transferred from the Second to the First Brigade, Third Division, Twenty-third Army Corps, and the Sixty-third Indiana Infantry is transferred from the First to the Second Brigade, Third Division, Twenty-third Army Corps.

*   *   *   *   *

By command of Major-General Schofield :

R. MORROW,
Assistant Adjutant-General.

SPECIAL ORDERS, }   HDQRS. SIXTEENTH ARMY CORPS,
    No. 94.   }   *Memphis, Tenn., April* 13, 1864.

*   *   *   *   *   *   *

II. The Tenth Ohio Battery, Capt. F. Seaman commanding, on steamer Hope, will disembark at Memphis, Tenn., and await further orders.

III. Brig. Gen. B. H. Grierson, commanding Cavalry Division, will send 200 men of the Sixth Tennessee Cavalry Volunteers, with arms, accouterments, and horse equipments complete, without horses, to Helena, Ark., there to report for duty temporarily to Brig. Gen. N. B. Buford, commanding District of Eastern Arkansas.

The quartermaster's department will furnish necessary transportation.

*   *   *   *

By order of Maj. Gen. S. A. Hurlbut :

T. H. HARRIS,
Assistant Adjutant-General.

HDQRS. MILITARY DIVISION OF THE MISSISSIPPI,
Nashville, Tenn., April 14, 1864.

General RAWLINS,
    Chief of Staff, Washington :

DEAR GENERAL : I send you a parcel of papers of the latest dates from the South. You will find them interesting.

One set of my former scouts is just in from Memphis, having come from Holly Springs, Pontotoc, Aberdeen, Columbus, Miss., Selma, Montgomery, Opelika, West Point, and Columbus, Ga., thence back to Selma and up the railroad to Talladega, Jacksonville, and Blue Mountain.

The enemy is collecting at a place near Centreville, a camp to which Loring's division is to come from Demopolis. This force will be behind the Coosa, and is clearly designed by Johnston to watch McPherson as he advances against Rome.

Forrest still is up between the Tennessee and Mississippi, and is reported to-day crossing the Tennessee at Hamburg ; also attacking

Columbus. I admire his great skill, but he can't do that. I am willing he should continue to attack our posts ; and he may also cross the Tennessee. We have plenty of stores here ; also pushing them to the front fast as possible. I will not let Forrest draw off my mind from the concentration going on.

Longstreet is represented still up about Bristol and Abingdon, but I do not believe he will move into Kentucky by Pound Gap. Road too bad and long. He may send some cavalry in, but he don't probably know that he can't interrupt our communications ; because if the Louisville road is reached by a dash we are not disturbed, and then to get out would be a question.

All well with us. I await McPherson's two divisions on furlough and A. J. Smith from Red River.

W. T. SHERMAN,
Major-General.

[Inclosure No. 1.]

OFFICE PRO. MAR. GEN., DEPT. OF THE CUMBERLAND,
Chattanooga, April 11, 1864.

Statement of J. C. Moore, scout :

I left this place on the 6th instant, and proceeded to Dalton, where I remained till the night of the 8th instant.

Four miles from Round Pond, on Taylor's Ridge, and 10 miles this side of Dalton, at Shipp's Gap, there is a force of 20 men guarding the gap. Their next picket line is about 3 miles this side of Dalton.

There are two corps at Dalton, commanded by Generals Hood and Hardee. Hood's corps is composed of the following divisions, viz : Stevenson's, Hindman's, Stewart's, and Johnson's. The following divisions are in Hardee's corps, viz : Cleburne's, Walker's, Bate's, and Cheatham's, and, I think, one other division. There are four brigades in each of the divisions except one, which has but three. No brigade has more than four regiments in it, and a good many of them have but three. I think their regiments will not average more than 250 men each.

General Stewart's division is now in front, but it will be relieved before long, and some other division will take its place. Stewart's headquarters are at Tunnel Hill. General Wheeler and two of his brigadier-generals, Kelly and Allen, are there also. I could not find out how large a force Wheeler has. General Martin is at Blue Mountain, in North Alabama, with ten regiments of cavalry ; is said to be there for the purpose of resisting an attack on Rome. I learned from a lieutenant of artillery that they had forty batteries at Dalton ; could not learn how many guns in a battery.

General Johnston has not received any re-enforcements, nor has he sent any troops away from his army. The general opinion seems to be that there will be a fight at Richmond before there is one here, and that Lee will be able to hold Richmond against Grant. I consider General Johnston's army in as good condition to-day as Bragg's army ever was.

Col. B. J. Hill, provost-marshal-general, gave me particular instructions to find out if the Federals were making any preparations to move, and to let him know at least three days before they did move, if possible. He also asked if General McPherson would bring his troops from Mississippi to this place.

There are no fortifications at Tunnel Hill or Dalton. I brought with me three rebel newspapers of date April 6, 1864.

[Indorsement.]

HEADQUARTERS DEPARTMENT OF THE CUMBERLAND,
Chattanooga, April 12, 1864.

Respectfully forwarded to Major-General Sherman, commanding Military Division of the Mississippi, for his information.

GEO. H. THOMAS,
Major-General, U. S. Volunteers, Commanding.

[Inclosure No. 2.]

OFFICE PRO. MAR. GEN., DEPT. OF THE CUMBERLAND,
Chattanooga, April 12, 1864.

Statement of O. G. Frazier, scout (by letter):

On Sunday, April 10, I went out 10 miles southeast of Cleveland. All night, on the night of the 10th, the rebels were prowling about through the country stealing horses. Their picket-lines have been drawn in a few miles. On last Saturday seventeen car-loads of soldiers left Dalton for South Carolina.

[Indorsement.]

HEADQUARTERS DEPARTMENT OF THE CUMBERLAND,
Chattanooga, Tenn., April 12, 1864.

Respectfully forwarded for information of the major-general commanding Military Division of the Mississippi.

I have heard from several of my scouts that Martin had taken position at Blue Mountain, about 6 or 8 miles west and northwest of Rome. One of my scouts reported yesterday that Roddey was preparing to leave the vicinity of Varnell's Station or Deep Spring, Judy Kenyon's place, and that Martin was to relieve him.

Wheeler still remains at Tunnel Hill, supported by infantry (either a division or brigade, the scouts cannot say which), between Tunnel Hill and Buzzard Roost. A dam has been built across the gap at Buzzard Roost, so that the wagon road can be flooded. I think this will prove advantageous to us and to their disadvantage, if we succeed in routing their forces this side of Tunnel Hill.

GEO. H. THOMAS,
Major-General, U. S. Volunteers, Commanding.

NASHVILLE, *April 14, 1864.*
(Received 9 p. m.)

Lieutenant-General GRANT, *Culpeper:*

General Hazen is here. Says W. F. Smith was promised a division. Of course if Hazen is to be advanced I will heartily agree, but not otherwise. Without orders, he will have his old brigade in Howard's corps.

W. T. SHERMAN,
Major-General.

HEADQUARTERS ELEVENTH AND TWELFTH CORPS,
Lookout Valley, Tenn., April 14, 1864.

Brigadier-General WHIPPLE,
Chief of Staff, Chattanooga:

I think it would be more for the interests of the service to have the consolidated corps under my command known as the Twelfth

Corps, instead of the Twentieth. Should it meet General Thomas' approval, I would like him to telegraph to General Sherman requesting, through him, the War Department to make the change. I have no personal interest in it, but think it very desirable for the troops. It would gratify the pride and wishes of the Twelfth Corps; the greater portion, in fact nearly all, of the Eleventh Corps unite with the Twelfth in the wish. To the new division it is of course immaterial.

I am, general, very respectfully, your obedient servant,

JOSEPH HOOKER,
Major-General.

HDQRS. THIRD DIVISION, TWENTY-THIRD ARMY CORPS,
Bull's Gap, Tenn., April 14, 1864.

Capt. G. F. HERRIOTT,
Commanding Left Wing, Third Indiana Cavalry:

SIR: You will send out a scouting party of about 100 men, under the guidance of Colonel Fry and Captain Reynolds, for the purpose of thoroughly scouting the upper end of Greene County, and, if it be possible, to capture the rebel desperadoes under Reynolds, who infest that county. The party of guides will be at your camp at 2 o'clock this afternoon, and your detachment will leave on their arrival. Should you prefer doing so, you can take the detachment yourself, in which case you will notify these headquarters who is left in command of your camp.

By command of Brigadier-General Cox:

ED. D. SAUNDERS,
Captain and Assistant Adjutant-General.

TOM'S CREEK, JOHNSON COUNTY, KY.,
April 14, 1864.

General BURBRIDGE:

The enemy in full retreat. I hope to be able to punish them severely.

Yours,

GEO. W. GALLUP,
Colonel, Commanding.

DECATUR, *April* 14, 1864.

Major-General McPHERSON, *Huntsville:*

Nothing new here. Scouts in from all points report forces back. Only one company on river, one battalion at Somerville, rest on Flint and southwest of us.

G. M. DODGE,
Brigadier-General.

ATHENS, *April* 14, 1864.

Brig. Gen. J. C. VEATCH, *Decatur:*

Order reconnoitering party from First Alabama Cavalry to move up river on this side until we ascertain truth of these reports.

G. M. DODGE,
Brigadier-General.

ATHENS, *April* 14, 1864.
Brig. Gen. J. D. STEVENSON,
  Decatur:
 Have you heard any news from Tuscumbia, Moulton, or Russellville within a day or two ?
        G. M. DODGE,
         Brigadier-General.

APRIL 14, 1864.
Brig. Gen. G. M. DODGE,
  Athens:
 General Geary returned about 5 o'clock p. m. yesterday. Found the rebels in considerable force near Triana, with one piece of artillery. One regiment of enemy's infantry on this side of river, above Triana, and below the mouth of Indian Creek, and two regiments on the south side.
      JAS. B. McPHERSON,
       Major-General, Commanding.

HDQRS. FOURTH DIVISION, SIXTEENTH ARMY CORPS,
    Decatur, Ala., April 14, 1864—10.40 a. m.
Colonel MONTGOMERY,
  Mooresville:
 Send out strong scouting party up the river toward Triana and report when they return.
      JAMES C. VEATCH,
       Brigadier-General.

ATHENS, *April* 14, 1864.
JAMES HENSAL,
  Chief of Scouts, Decatur:
 Do you hear anything from Somerville, Russellville, or Tuscumbia ? You must get men out to the rear of Tuscumbia, and see what force is down there. Report fully.
      G. M. DODGE,
       Brigadier-General.

HDQRS. SECOND DIVISION, SIXTEENTH ARMY CORPS.
    Pulaski, Tenn., April 14, 1864.
Col. RICHARD ROWETT,
  Commanding Seventh Illinois Infantry:
 Reports are coming in daily of small parties of the enemy in different sections of the country, well armed and equipped. You will keep a sharp lookout for all such detached and broken forces and cut off and capture them whenever it may be possible, as they will doubtless annoy us very much if left alone. They must be chased away at all events, and the fords so closely watched as to prevent their crossing or recrossing, if possible.
 By order of Brig. Gen. T. W. Sweeny, commanding:
      LOUIS H. EVERTS,
    Captain and Assistant Adjutant-General.

ATHENS, *April* 14, 1864—9.30 a. m.
Maj. Gen. J. B. McPHERSON,
    Huntsville:
    Just received your dispatch. General Veatch reports all quiet
this morning. Think our patrols should have struck that force.
Colonel Rowett reports heavy force on opposite side of river, but
thinks that they have as yet only crossed in squads. They captured
one company of Ninth Ohio Cavalry yesterday morning before daylight, and got them across without firing a shot. This is the first
expedition of that regiment. They are evidently green. All sorts
of rumors down in that country. Rowett says they are building
boats at Pride's, 12 miles below Tuscumbia, and hauling them to
six different points on the river. The rest of the Ninth Ohio Cavalry is with Rowett before this, and he will watch close. I have
ordered cavalry up the river on both sides.
                                    G. M. DODGE,
                                        Brigadier-General.

HDQRS. FOURTH DIVISION, SIXTEENTH ARMY CORPS,
                Decatur, Ala., April 14, 1864—11.12 a. m.
Brigadier-General DODGE,
    Athens:
    I have ordered Major Kuhn toward Somerville and Triana. Sent
dispatch to Colonel Montgomery at Mooresville to send out a strong
party toward Triana. Major Kuhn's scouts report the roads strongly
picketed by the enemy, so that they cannot penetrate the country
toward Florence. I have no news from that quarter.
                                    JAMES C. VEATCH,
                                        Brigadier-General.

APRIL 14, 1864.
Major-General McPHERSON,
    Huntsville, Ala.:
    The scouting parties sent toward Tuscumbia could not make much
headway. The enemy evidently hold the roads with pretty strong
detachments; yet I do not believe their force is much increased, but
knowing about our mounted force they dispose theirs to meet us.
Major Kuhn has not returned from Triana. A scout in from there
reports a large force at Whitesburg or Guntersville, and scouts sent
up on this side, as well as regular patrols, report nothing unusual.
Nothing yet from detachment sent from Mooresville. Scout from
Whitesburg says it was reported by soldiers that General [Colonel]
Patterson with a cavalry force was on the way to this front.
                                    G. M. DODGE,
                                        Brigadier-General.

HDQRS. THIRD DIVISION, FIFTEENTH ARMY CORPS,
                Huntsville, Ala., April 14, 1864—2 a. m.
Col. GREEN B. RAUM,
    Commanding Second Brigade:
    COLONEL: You will move at once with all your available force in
camp at Whitesburg, with one day's rations in haversacks and 60

rounds of ammunition in cartridge-boxes.   You will move as rapidly as p   , and join Lieut. Col. John P. Hall, as it is feared an attack will dssemblede upon him at daylight by a force estimated of at least 1,000 men.   You will take the usual precaution to prevent surprise while marching down.

By order of Brig. Gen. John E. Smith:

C. L. WHITE,
Acting Assistant Adjutant-General.

HDQRS. LEFT WING, SIXTEENTH ARMY CORPS,
Athens, Ala., April 14, 1864.

Col. RICHARD ROWETT,
Comdg. 7th Illinois and 9th Ohio Cavalry Volunteers:

I am sorry to hear of the capture of that company. The regiment is now with you, and you must be very vigilant. Employ men to go over the river; I will pay them. Keep the country covered with scouts. Let us know what is really over there. Morgan is in East Tennessee.

Roddey is at Dalton, so they cannot be where that negro says; citizens certainly can get across. Our troops should not camp on the river bank or in sight, but should be on the move constantly, as the enemy could cross a force in the night that would take them. Headquarters of the regiment should be some distance from the river, with patrols on the river all the time.

Say to Colonel Hamilton, if any of his officers have disobeyed my instructions, or are at fault in the capture of that company, to put them under arrest.   It is disgraceful to be captured without making any resistance.

If you find the enemy crossing at any point, or several points, get your command together and pitch into them.   Annoy them and retard all you can.   Do not fail to keep me fully posted.

I am, very respectfully, your obedient servant,

G. M. DODGE,
Brigadier-General.

APRIL 14, 1864.

Major-General McPHERSON, *Huntsville:*

General Stevenson reports that forces sent out day before yesterday could not get through the enemy's pickets on Flint.   Major Kuhn started out yesterday with the Ninth Illinois Mounted Infantry, but we have had no report from him.   The enemy yesterday were picketing Flint and a line covering Moulton, Courtland, and the river.   I think we will ascertain their strength to-day.

G. M. DODGE,
Brigadier-General.

LOOKOUT VALLEY, *April 14, 1864.*

Brig. Gen. WILLIAM D. WHIPPLE,
Assistant Adjutant-General, Army of the Cumberland:

Scouts just in report two regiments rebel cavalry in vicinity of Valley Head on the 12th.

.JOSEPH HOOKER,
Major-General, Commanding.

HDQRS. FOURTH DIVISION, SIXTEENTH ARMY CORPS,
Decatur, Ala., April 14, 1864—6 p. m.
Brig. Gen. G. M. DODGE,
Commanding Left Wing, Sixteenth Army Corps, Athens:

Major Kuhn states that his scouts find no large body of the enemy near, but squads or companies on all the roads, forming a chain of pickets at an average distance of 6 miles from here. He has sent a strong detachment toward Triana, and parties on all the roads leading south and west.

I ordered a detachment from Mooresville to go up the river. Will send dispatch as soon as I get report.

JAMES C. VEATCH,
Brigadier-General.

ATHENS, *April* 14, 1864.
Brig. Gen. J. C. VEATCH, *Decatur :*

Send Ninth Illinois, mounted, out toward Somerville and Triana.

General Geary returned ; reports a force of enemy three regiments strong, and artillery [near Triana], and one regiment on this side of river. Have them ascertain what is in the valley. Troops at Florence report heavy force opposite them. Do you get any news from that quarter?

G. M. DODGE,
Brigadier-General.

APRIL 14, 1864.
Brig. Gen. G. M. DODGE, *Athens :*

Feel out strongly from Decatur toward Somerville and opposite Triana. It is reported there are three regiments rebel infantry, with some artillery, in that vicinity.

JAS. B. McPHERSON,
Major-General, Commanding.

LEXINGTON, KY.,
April 14, 1864.
Colonel TRUE,
Commanding Fortieth Kentucky, Mount Sterling :

Information just received from Colonel Gallup. Rebels in full retreat from Paintsville. Lose no time in uniting with Colonel Gallup, and if possible get in rear of rebels. Colonel Brown, Eleventh Michigan, will be in Mount Sterling by 10 a. m. to-morrow.

E. H. HOBSON,
Brigadier-General.

LEXINGTON, KY.,
April 14, 1864.
Major-General STONEMAN, *Paris :*

Colonel True, Fortieth Kentucky, will leave Mount Sterling tomorrow morning for Paintsville to assist Colonel Gallup. I have ordered him to support troops at West Liberty in their advance.

Will you order the troops from West Liberty through Colonel True at Mount Sterling. Eleventh Michigan Cavalry have left this place for Mount Sterling ; no rebel force in vicinity of Booneville, Proctor, or Irvine. Forty-fifth Kentucky scouting in that region.

E. H. HOBSON,
Brigadier-General.

LEXINGTON, April 14, 1864.

Lieut. Col. T. B. FAIRLEIGH,
 Assistant Adjutant-General, Louisville, Ky. :
 Information just received. No rebels in the direction of Proctor or Booneville ; the country has been thoroughly scouted.

E. H. HOBSON,
Brigadier-General.

HDQRS. FIRST DIVISION, DISTRICT OF KENTUCKY,
Lexington, Ky., April 14, 1864.

Col. JOHN M. BROWN,
 Commanding Forty-fifth Kentucky Mounted Infantry :
 COLONEL : I have the honor to acknowledge the receipt of your letter of this date. You can, as suggested, halt your command at the point designated, 10 miles this side of Irvine, and await further orders from these headquarters, unless circumstances should compel you to move. In that event you will be governed by verbal instructions given you yesterday.
 Colonel Gallup was attacked by 1,000 rebels at Paintsville yesterday. He has a strong position. I am endeavoring to re-enforce him by sending troops via Mount Sterling. Keep me advised.
 Very respectfully,

E. H. HOBSON, ·
Brigadier-General.

MOUNT STERLING, April 14, 1864—9.45 p. m.

Brig. Gen. E. H. HOBSON :
 Can get no information here in relation to the enemy. Can you not let me have the Twelfth Ohio, instead of the Eleventh Michigan ? Will push on early to-morrow morning and get in rear of the enemy if possible.

C. J. TRUE,
Colonel Fortieth Kentucky.

LEXINGTON, April 14, 1864—4.12 p. m.

General STONEMAN :
 Colonel Gallup reports that he was attacked at Paintsville yesterday by 1,000 rebels. General Burbridge wishes the Fifteenth Kentucky, at West Liberty, to move on Salyersville road to co-operate with Gallup. I will send Eleventh Michigan Cavalry in supporting distance and hold any other forces with me in readiness to assist. Gallup has good position and will hold it until Fifteenth Kentucky co-operate. Please communicate with me.

E. H. HOBSON,
Brigadier-General, Commanding.

LEXINGTON, KY., *April* 14, 1864.

Col. C. J. TRUE, *Mount Sterling, Ky.* :

Colonel Gallup was attacked yesterday at Paintsville. He is in strong position in that vicinity. Move your regiment via Salyersville and support the troops at West Liberty, who have instructions to move in direction of Pound Gap to co-operate with Colonel Gallup. Eleventh Michigan Cavalry leaves this place for Mount Sterling this evening, with instructions to support you. Do not delay your movement. If you are attacked on the route by large force, skirmish your way back, holding rebel advance in check ; if possible, go through to Gallup.

E. H. HOBSON,
Brigadier-General.

HEADQUARTERS DISTRICT OF KENTUCKY,
Louisville, Ky., April 14, 1864.

Brigadier-General HOBSON:

Colonel Gallup telegraphs that he was attacked yesterday at Paintsville, by about 1,000 rebels; his force is 750, and having secured a good position he would hold it. Direct the force now at West Liberty to move rapidly on the Salyersville road toward Pound Gap and co-operate with Gallup at Paintsville ; by this means we may get in their rear. Order the Eleventh Michigan to move with all possible speed and by nearest route to support the force moving from West Liberty.

If it can be done the Eleventh Michigan should join that force; if not, it can move in supporting distance. Hold balance of your command ready to move in any direction. Inform General Stoneman of this dispatch, and procure his consent to use the detachment of First Kentucky now at West Liberty.

By order of General Burbridge :

THOS. B. FAIRLEIGH,
Lieutenant-Colonel and Acting Assistant Adjutant-General.

LEXINGTON, KY., *April* 14, 1864.

Colonel FAIRLEIGH, *Actg. Asst. Adjt. Gen., Louisville, Ky.:*

Colonel True, Fortieth Kentucky, will arrive at Mount Sterling to-night ; have ordered him to support troops at West Liberty and move in direction of Pound Gap. Eleventh Michigan leave for Mount Sterling this evening to support Colonel True. Col. J. M. Brown, Forty-fifth Kentucky, is making reconnaissance in vicinity of Proctor and Irvine. Will give you all information of importance.

E. H. HOBSON,
Brigadier-General.

LEXINGTON, KY., *April* 14, 1864.

Lieutenant-Colonel FAIRLEIGH,
Acting Assistant Adjutant-General, Louisville:

Dispatch just received from Colonel Gallup. Enemy in full retreat. Colonel True will push in from Mount Sterling in direction of Pound Gap.

E. H. HOBSON,
Brigadier-General.

LEXINGTON, KY.,
April 14, 1864.

Colonel GALLUP,
    Louisa or Paintsville, via Catlettsburg:
    General Burbridge is not at this place. Your dispatch received stating that rebels were in full retreat. Colonel True is moving to your support, is beyond Mount Sterling. Eleventh Michigan Cavalry will be at Mount Sterling to-morrow 10 a. m. Have instructions to move toward Pound Gap and co-operate with you. Report to me direct all information.
                                            E. H. HOBSON,
        Brigadier-General, Comdg. First Div., Dist. of Kentucky.

HDQRS. FIRST DIVISION, DISTRICT OF KENTUCKY,
Lexington, Ky., April 14, 1864.

Col. S. B. BROWN,
    Eleventh Michigan Cavalry:
    COLONEL: Move with your command without delay to Mount Sterling, Ky., and co-operate with Colonel True, Fortieth Kentucky, who has instructions to support the troops at West Liberty in their advance toward Paintsville, Ky., and to co-operate with Colonel Gallup at that place. Colonel True has been instructed to send me information of rebel movements, and if he is attacked by superior force to skirmish his way back to this place. I will telegraph you all the information, from time to time, received from Colonel True, and direct your movements if it becomes necessary for you to go beyond Mount Sterling. Immediately upon your arrival at Mount Sterling, give me all the information you may obtain as to rebel movements. If Colonel True is beaten back to Mount Sterling you will co-operate with each other and fall back to this place, holding in check as long as possible the enemy's advance.
                                            E. H. HOBSON,
                                                Brigadier-General.

BURKESVILLE, *April* 14, 1864.

General E. H. HOBSON:
    Have just received a letter from Lieutenant Gubber, commanding a company under Colonel Hughs, wanting to surrender them if I would parole or allow them to take the oath here. He says he can get up all the stragglers in that country, and all want to come in. Give me authority, if possible, to administer the oath and release those that have not been connected with murdering raids. I cannot get them any other way, only by catching one at a time. I think it would be an advantage to do so. I have promised our answer to-morrow.
                                            J. W. WEATHERFORD,
                                        Colonel Thirteenth Kentucky Cavalry.

LEXINGTON, *April* 14, 1864.

Col. J. W. WEATHERFORD,
        Burkesville, Ky.:
    Inform Lieutenant Gubber, of rebel Colonel Hughs' command, that if he will surrender his command that they will be sent to

Louisville and treated as prisoners of war, and all that wish to abandon the rebel service I will use my influence in securing their pardon or release upon their taking the oath.

E. H. HOBSON,
Brigadier-General.

HDQRS. CAVALRY COMMAND, DEPT. OF THE OHIO,
Paris, Ky., April 14, 1864.

Maj. Gen. J. M. SCHOFIELD,
Comdg. Department of the Ohio, Knoxville, Tenn.:

GENERAL: The day after my arrival here, General Sturgis and myself reviewed this cavalry, and upon inspection I find their condition as follows:

The effective strength is 5,466, of which there are mounted 2,720, leaving dismounted 2,746. A portion of those mounted are still without arms, and a large portion of those dismounted are entirely unarmed. I find that requisitions have been made by General Sturgis for everything necessary to complete the mounting, arming, and equipping of the whole command, and that in all probability the whole will soon be armed and equipped, as stores are arriving almost daily in small lots.

But 150 horses have been received during the past ten days, and Colonel Swords, at Cincinnati, informed General Sturgis that no more would be sent here, as all cavalry horses were ordered to be sent to Nashville. Many of those we have require shoeing, which is being done as rapidly as the means will allow. I have telegraphed to General Davidson, chief of cavalry bureau in the West, to ascertain how soon we can calculate upon more horses, and informing him how many we want to mount the men now here and to arrive.

I have also telegraphed to the Governor of Indiana in regard to the cavalry regiments now being raised by him. No reply as yet from either. One division moved to-day for Nicholasville, and the other will follow to-morrow.

The command will be held in readiness, as heretofore, to co-operate with the forces under General Burbridge whenever the exigencies may require.

I am, very respectfully, your obedient servant,

GEORGE STONEMAN,
Major-General, Commanding.

CAIRO, *April* 14, 1864.

Maj. Gen. W. T. SHERMAN:

Fort Pillow was taken by storm at 3 p. m. on the 12th, with six guns. The negroes, about 300, murdered, after surrendering with their officers. Of the 200 white men, 57 have just arrived, and sent to Mound City; about 100 are prisoners, and the rest killed. The whole affair was a scene of murder. The gun-boats not returned. Forrest reported wounded and gone to Brownsville with prisoners, taking all the artillery. Nothing from below Pillow. Scouts bring rumor that Morgan is approaching Nashville.

M. BRAYMAN,
Brigadier-General.

HEADQUARTERS SIXTEENTH ARMY CORPS,
Memphis, Tenn., April 14, 1864.
Lieutenant-Commander PATTISON, U. S. N.,
    Commanding Naval Station, Memphis, Tenn.:

DEAR SIR : It is important that the actual state of affairs at Fort Pillow should be ascertained. The best means for doing this is by reconnaissance made by the gun-boats.

I am of opinion that the enemy will not remain long, and will be much obliged if you will direct such movements on the part of the gun-boats as will ascertain the fact of occupation or abandonment.

Very truly, your obedient servant,

S. A. HURLBUT,
Major-General.

HDQRS. MILITARY DIVISION OF THE MISSISSIPPI,
Nashville, Tenn., April 14, 1864.
General BRAYMAN,
    Cairo:

What news from Columbus ? Don't send men from Cairo to Fort Pillow; let Hurlbut take care of that quarter. The Cairo troops may temporarily re-enforce at Paducah or Columbus, but should be held ready to come up the Tennessee.

One object that Forrest has is to induce us to make these detachments and prevent our concentration in this quarter.

W. T. SHERMAN,
Major-General.

HDQRS. MILITARY DIVISION OF THE MISSISSIPPI,
Nashville, Tenn., April 14, 1864.
General BRAYMAN,
    Cairo:

Fort Pillow has no guns or garrison. It was evacuated before I went out to Meridian. Hurlbut has plenty of force if he will use it. What force have you from below ? As soon as enough of McPherson's troops come to Cairo I will repeat the Purdy move, but hope that some officer will manage to catch some of Forrest's men that are now scattered from Paducah down to Memphis.

W. T. SHERMAN,
Major-General.

CAIRO, ILL.,
April 14, 1864.
Maj. Gen. W. T. SHERMAN,
    Nashville:

Enemy left Columbus and are now attacking Paducah. I sent up a regiment last night. No danger. Nothing further from Pillow. No boats up. A gun-boat has gone down to see. No regiments, but only fragments belonging to Seventeenth Corps have yet arrived. I will only use them as directed in your last dispatch, just received. I have nothing from Hurlbut or Grierson.

M. BRAYMAN,
Brigadier-General.

PADUCAH, *April* 14, 1864.
Brigadier-General BRAYMAN :
Arrived at 8.30 p. m. Enemy has retreated. They stole the horses belonging to the quartermaster, while the flag of truce was at fort. Ammunition has arrived. Please forward the artillery ammunition we sent the Crawford after. The 32-pounder ammunition on hand is of no account. Please telegraph to Saint Louis for ammunition for the 32-pounder. We have none in the district, and the communication to Memphis is cut off.
J. H. ODLIN,
Assistant Adjutant-General.

PADUCAH, *April* 14, 1864.
Brigadier-General BRAYMAN :
What is the news from below ? All quiet.
J. H. ODLIN,
Assistant Adjutant-General.

PADUCAH, *April* 14, 1864.
General BRAYMAN and Captain PENNOCK :
Hostilities have ceased for a few moments. Enemy supposed to be retreating on Mayfield road. They took all Government horses out of rolling mill. The fort has been shelling them as they retreat. They have not fired again.
OPERATOR.

CAIRO, ILL.,
April 14, 1864—11 p. m.
Capt. J. H. ODLIN,
Assistant Adjutant-General, Paducah, Ky.:
Fort Pillow is taken and more than half its defenders murdered after surrender. You will have no trouble at Paducah.
M. BRAYMAN,
Brigadier-General, Commanding.

HEADQUARTERS OF THE POST,
Columbus, Ky., April 14, 1864—12.30 p. m.
CAPTAIN : I have a scout just in from Mayfield. The enemy have not been there in force for two weeks, neither could he hear of any large bodies near there.
General Buford marched from Clinton to Milburn, and from Milburn to Blandville, where he was to be last night. From what the scout could gather, he hopes to cross the Ohio at Copeland's Landing, Tapman's Ferry, to Illinois. He could not gather much information, as he was conscripted at Mayfield and confined, but this is reliable. They expect John H. Morgan to attack Nashville.
I am, captain, very respectfully, your obedient servant,
WM. HUDSON LAWRENCE,
Colonel Thirty-fourth New Jersey Vols., Comdg. Post.

HDQRS. U. S. COLORED TROOPS IN TENNESSEE,
Memphis, Tenn., April 14, 1864.

Hon. E. B. WASHBURNE,
Washington, D. C.:

MY DEAR SIR : Before this letter reaches you you will have learned of the capture of Fort Pillow and of the slaughter of our troops after the place was captured.   This is the most infernal outrage that has been committed since the war began.   Three weeks ago I sent up four companies of colored troops to that place under Major Booth, a most brave and efficient [officer], who took command of the post.   Forrest and Chalmers, with about 3,000 devils, attacked the place on the 12th at 9 a. m. and succeeded after three assaults, and when both Major Booth and Major Bradford, of the Thirteenth Tennessee Cavalry, had been killed, in capturing the place at 4 p. m. We had, in all, less than 500 effective men, and one-third of whom were colored.

The colored troops fought with desperation throughout.   After the capture our colored men were literally butchered.   Chalmers was present and saw it all.   Out of over 300 colored men, not 25 were taken prisoners, and they may have been killed long before this.

There is a great deal of excitement in town in consequence of this affair, especially among our colored troops.   If this is to be the game of the enemy they will soon learn that it is one at which two can play.

The Government will no doubt take cognizance of this matter immediately and take such measures as will prevent a recurrence.

It is reported that Forrest will move on this place in a few days. I do not believe it.   I am hurried and can write no more to-day.   I am feeling dreadfully over the fate of my brave officers and men. Like all others, I feel that the blood of these heroes must be avenged.

Forrest will probably try to get out of West Tennessee as soon as he can.   We have re-enforcements coming in, and we shall soon be on his track.

In haste, sincerely, your friend,

CHETLAIN,
Brigadier-General.

SPECIAL FIELD ORDERS, }   HDQRS. DEPT. OF THE CUMBERLAND,
No. 105.   }   *Chattanooga, Tenn., April* 14, 1864.
*   *   *   *   *   *   *

IV. It having been ordered that the Eleventh and Twelfth Army Corps be consolidated to form the Twentieth Army Corps, the following is announced as the organization of the latter, Maj. Gen. Joseph Hooker commanding :

The Third Division, Twentieth Army Corps, Maj. Gen. Daniel Butterfield commanding :

First Brigade, Brig. Gen. W. T. Ward commanding : Seventieth Indiana Infantry, Seventy-ninth Ohio Infantry, One hundred and second Illinois Infantry, One hundred and fifth Illinois Infantry, One hundred and twenty-ninth Illinois Infantry.

Second Brigade : Twenty-second Wisconsin Infantry, Nineteenth Michigan Infantry, Thirty-third Indiana Infantry, Eighty-fifth Indiana Infantry, Fifth Connecticut Infantry.

Third Brigade : One hundred and thirty-sixth New York Infantry, Fifty-fifth Ohio Infantry, Seventy-third Ohio Infantry, Thirty-third Massachusetts Infantry, Twenty-sixth Wisconsin Infantry.

First Division, Twentieth Army Corps, Brig. Gen. A. S. Williams commanding:

First Brigade, Brig. Gen. Joseph F. Knipe commanding: One hundred and forty-first New York Infantry, Twentieth Connecticut Infantry, One hundred and twenty-third New York Infantry, Third Maryland Infantry, Forty-sixth Pennsylvania Infantry.

Second Brigade, Brig. Gen. Thomas H. Ruger commanding: Second Massachusetts Infantry, Third Wisconsin Infantry, Thirteenth New Jersey Infantry, Twenty-seventh Indiana Infantry, One hundred and seventh New York Infantry, One hundred and fiftieth New York Infantry.

Third Brigade, Brig. Gen. H. Tyndale commanding: Eighty-second Ohio Infantry, Sixty-first Ohio Infantry, Forty-fifth New York Infantry, One hundred and forty-third New York Infantry, Eighty-second Illinois Infantry, One hundred and first Illinois Infantry.

Second Division, Twentieth Army Corps, Brig. Gen. John W. Geary commanding:

First Brigade: Fifth Ohio Infantry, Seventh Ohio Infantry, Twenty-ninth Ohio Infantry, Sixty-sixth Ohio Infantry, Twenty-eighth Pennsylvania Infantry, One hundred and forty-seventh Pennsylvania Infantry.

Second Brigade : Twenty-seventh Pennsylvania Infantry, Seventy-third Pennsylvania Infantry, Thirty-third New Jersey Infantry, One hundred and nineteenth New York Infantry, One hundred and thirty-fourth New York Infantry, One hundred and fifty-fourth New York Infantry, One hundred and ninth Pennsylvania Infantry.

Third Brigade : Sixtieth New York Infantry, Seventy-eighth New York Infantry, One hundred and second New York Infantry, One hundred and thirty-seventh New York Infantry, One hundred and forty-ninth New York Infantry, Twenty-ninth Pennsylvania Infantry, One hundred and eleventh Pennsylvania Infantry.

Fourth Division, Twentieth Army Corps, Maj. Gen. L. H. Rousseau commanding:

First Brigade, Brig. Gen. R. S. Granger commanding : Thirteenth Wisconsin Infantry, Eighteenth Michigan Infantry, Seventy-third Indiana Infantry, One hundred and second Ohio Infantry, Tenth Tennessee Infantry.

The following-named regiments of the Fourth Division, Twentieth Army Corps, are not assigned to brigades: Fifty-eighth New York Infantry, Sixty-eighth New York Infantry, Seventy-fifth Pennsylvania Infantry, One hundred and fifteenth Ohio Infantry, Twenty-third Missouri Infantry, Eighty-third Illinois Infantry, Seventy-first Ohio Infantry, One hundred and sixth Ohio Infantry, Thirty-first Wisconsin Infantry.

Officers assigned to the command of divisions will report immediately to the corps commander. Officers assigned to the command of brigades will report immediately to the division commanders. Commanding officers of the several regiments enumerated will report to their respective brigade commanders herein designated. Commanding officers of the several regiments enumerated will report direct to their respective division commanders herein designated.

The following assignment of staff officers is hereby made, to take effect upon the completion of the business connected with their late positions :

Lieut. Col. C. W. Asmussen, assistant inspector-general Eleventh Army Corps, assigned to the Twentieth Army Corps as assistant inspector-general.

Lieut. Col. George W. Balloch, commissary of subsistence Eleventh Army Corps, assigned to the Twentieth Army Corps as commissary of subsistence.

Lieut. Col. Hiram Hayes, quartermaster Eleventh Army Corps, transferred to the Fourth Army Corps, vice Ransom, detached.

Lieut. Col. T. A. Meysenburg, assistant adjutant-general Eleventh Army Corps, is relieved from duty in this department, and will report by letter for orders to the Adjutant-General U. S. Army.

Brig. Gen. A. von Steinwehr is hereby relieved from duty with the Twentieth Army Corps and assigned to command of the Third Brigade, First Division, Fourteenth Army Corps.

*   *   *   *   *

By command of Major-General Thomas :
WM. D. WHIPPLE,
Assistant Adjutant-General.

CULPEPER, VA.,
April 15, 1864—8 p. m.

Major-General SHERMAN :

Forrest must be driven out, but with a proper commander in West Tennessee there is force enough now. Your preparations for the coming campaign must go on, but if it is necessary to detach a portion of the troops intended for it, detach them and make your campaign with that much fewer men.

Relieve Maj. Gen. S. A. Hurlbut. I can send General Washburn, a sober and energetic officer, to take his place. I can also send you General L. C. Hunt to command District of Columbus. Shall I send Washburn ? Does General Hurlbut think if he moves a part of his force after the only enemy within 200 miles of him that the post will run off with the balance of his force ?

If our men have been murdered after capture, retaliation must be resorted to promptly.

U. S. GRANT,
Lieutenant-General.

WAR DEPARTMENT,
April 15, 1864—10.30 p. m.

Lieutenant-General GRANT :

I have seen General Sherman's dispatch, which arrived after my telegram to you. Another has reached here from Admiral Pennock, which I have directed to be forwarded to you. The substance is the same as Sherman's, but with fuller particulars. I will give Colonel Kautz the brigadier's commission, and send him to Fortress Monroe immediately. General Brooks left Pittsburg for Fortress Monroe yesterday.

EDWIN M. STANTON.

WAR DEPARTMENT,
April 15, 1864—3.40 p. m.

Lieutenant-General GRANT,
Culpeper:

The rebels have captured Fort Pillow, sacked Paducah again, and have demanded surrender of Columbus, which has not yet been given up. The slaughter at Fort Pillow is great. The news came first by way of Cairo, but I telegraphed Nashville and the operator confirms the news.

EDWIN M. STANTON,
Secretary of War..

HDQRS. MILITARY DIVISION OF THE MISSISSIPPI,
Nashville, Tenn., April 15, 1864. (Received 2.30 p. m.)

Lieutenant-General GRANT,
Culpeper, Va.:

General Brayman reports from Cairo the arrival of 50 wounded white soldiers from Fort Pillow, and that the place was attacked on the 12th, 50 white soldiers killed and 100 taken prisoners, and 300 blacks murdered after surrender. I don't know what these men were doing at Fort Pillow. I ordered it to be abandoned before I went to Meridian, and it was so abandoned. General Hurlbut must have sent this garrison up recently from Memphis. So many men are on furlough that Grierson and Hurlbut seem to fear going out of Memphis to attack Forrest. I have no apprehension for the safety of Paducah, Columbus, or Memphis, but without drawing from Dodge, I have no force to send over there, and don't want to interrupt my plans of preparation for the great object of the spring campaign. I expect McPherson's two divisions from Vicksburg to rendezvous at Cairo from furlough about the 20th, and I look for A. J. Smith up daily from Red River. Whenever either of these commands arrive I can pen Forrest up, but it will take some time to run him down. Do you want me to delay for such a purpose, but shall I go on to concentrate on Chattanooga? I don't know what to do with Hurlbut. I know that Forrest could pen him up in Memphis with 2,500 men, although Hurlbut has all of Grierson's cavalry and 2,500 white infantry, 4,000 blacks, and the citizen militia, 3,000. If you think I have time I will send a division from Dodge to Purdy, and order A. J. Smith as he comes up to strike inland to Bolivar, Jackson, &c., and come across by land to the Tennessee. This may consume an extra two weeks. Corse was at Vicksburg ready to start up the Red River the 8th.

W. T. SHERMAN,
Major-General.

NASHVILLE, TENN.,
April 15, 1864—12 m.

General J. P. TAYLOR,
Commissary-General:

No commissary has yet reported to me. Colonel Beckwith is not here. I must have by May 1 near Chattanooga a large amount of beef-cattle on the hoof, and each commissary is making separate contracts utterly useless. We cannot supply transportation for cattle.

They must travel by land, and I may be forced to seize even breeding cattle in Tennessee to supply meat, for we can't wait our movement for such matters of economy.

W. T. SHERMAN,
Major-General.

———

BULL'S GAP, *April* 15, 1864.

Major-General SCHOFIELD:

I have information, which seems reliable, that most of the rebel cavalry remaining above crossed the Holston last night at ferries near Kingsport. They are reported from 1,000 to 1,500 strong. I send a party to warn our men in front, and will take all proper precautions against surprise.

Reports brought back from the rebel lines show that they are all informed as to our numbers and the kind, &c., of our force, but the best evidence still is that the bulk of Longstreet's command has continued its eastward movement.

J. D. COX,
Brigadier-General, Commanding Third Division.

———

KNOXVILLE, *April* 15, 1864.

Brigadier-General COX,
Bull's Gap:

There is a possibility of the rebels attempting to get in your rear by way of Rogersville. If Longstreet still remains at Bristol he will most likely attempt something of the kind ; watch him closely.

J. M. SCHOFIELD,
Major-General.

———

BULL'S GAP, *April* 15, 1864.

Major-General SCHOFIELD,
Knoxville:

I am watching our left closely. The Holston is not fordable at present. I have a part of cavalry reconnoitering to-day beyond Greeneville.

J. D. COX,
Brigadier-General, Commanding Third Division.

———

BULL'S GAP, *April* 15, 1864.

Lieutenant-Colonel BOYD,
Chief Quartermaster, Knoxville:

To complete the wagon bridge at Lick Creek we shall need plank for flooring, which it seems impossible to get here. Can it be furnished from the mill at Knoxville, and, if so, how soon ? It will take about 3,500 feet of 2-inch stuff. I would like to have part of it by to-morrow's train.

J. D. COX,
Brigadier-General, Commanding Third Division.

HDQRS. THIRD DIV., TWENTY-THIRD ARMY CORPS,
Bull's Gap, April 15, 1864.
Captain QUALMAN,
Commanding Third Indiana Cavalry:

I have information which leads me to suspect that a cavalry force of the enemy may make an effort to surprise you or the One hundred and fourth Ohio to-morrow or the next day. It is reported that perhaps 1,000 of their cavalry have crossed the Holston near Kingsport, and will push in probably by the Snapp's Ferry road. This may not be reliable, but should put you on your guard, and you should have everything safe. Send a small party to communicate with Captain Herriott to-night if possible, so that he may be upon his guard and take precautions against being cut off or led into a snare. If he finds a force between him and camp he should take some other route which his guides may advise. Send an intelligent officer with the party, who will communicate this verbally. The information may be false, and there should be no alarm, but every road, especially at your left, should be carefully watched and the infantry kept informed of all you may learn. Report promptly to me any news you may get.

*J. D. COX,
Brigadier-General, Commanding.*

HDQRS. FOURTH DIVISION, SIXTEENTH ARMY CORPS,
Decatur, Ala., April 15, 1864.
Brigadier-General DODGE,
Commanding Left Wing, Sixteenth Army Corps, Athens:

GENERAL : Major Kuhn's forces returned last night. They were unable to cross Flint in the direction of Triana or Somerville. All the crossings are picketed by the enemy too strongly for him to get through. He reports from 600 to 800 men encamped between the bridge and Danville. His command had skirmishes on the Danville and Triana roads. losing 1 man. Clanton is at Danville covering all the roads. A force of two regiments of infantry and some cavalry is reported still at Moulton. All the roads in that direction are strongly held. The force of 1,500 cavalry reported at Lebanon as moving this way must be the same reported by General Geary. We have not sufficient mounted force to penetrate beyond Flint.

JAMES C. VEATCH,
Brigadier-General.

CHATTANOOGA, *April 15, 1864.*
Major-General SHERMAN :

Eleventh and Twelfth Corps unite in the request that the new corps be designated the Twelfth Corps instead of the Twentieth. As it would meet the wishes of all concerned, I would recommend that the designation of the new corps be changed from the Twentieth to the Twelfth.

GEO. H. THOMAS.
Major-General, Commanding.

HDQRS. FOURTH DIVISION, SIXTEENTH ARMY CORPS,
Decatur, Ala., April 15, 1864.
Colonel MONTGOMERY,
Twenty-fifth Wisconsin, Commanding at Mooresville :

A force of the enemy was reported to be on the river above Triana, and rumor said that one regiment had crossed over to the north side. I think this improbable. I sent dispatch yesterday and this morning to you, but get no answer.

I wish you to keep the First Alabama Cavalry on active duty, scouting the country along the river up to Triana, and send me daily reports in writing.

General Dodge directs that you look after the parties who are cutting wood for the railroad and see that the work is pushed on. Get all the information about forage that you can. You will not be required to use the Twenty-fifth Wisconsin guarding bridges. Put their camp in a convenient place, and see that orders in relation to drills are strictly carried out. Have the camps of all the troops carefully policed. Detail from the First Alabama Cavalry couriers to bring your dispatches.

JAMES C. VEATCH,
Brigadier-General.

APRIL 15, 1864.
Major-General McPHERSON,
Huntsville, Ala. :

Major Kuhn was unable to get beyond Flint. The enemy hold all the crossings. He skirmished pretty sharply with about 1,800 men on the Danville and Triana roads. We lost a few men. Clanton is still at Danville, covering all the roads. The new force that has arrived on Flint is Patterson's, estimated at 2,000. I do not see how they can subsist all this cavalry. I have men in their rear, who will report to-day or to-morrow. I think that the force Geary struck is the same force that moved right on to Flint. They now have at least 5,000 men surrounding Decatur ; too large for our cavalry to penetrate. What do you hear from opposite Whitesburg ?

G. M. DODGE,
Brigadier-General.

HDQRS. DEPARTMENT AND ARMY OF THE TENNESSEE,
Huntsville, Ala., April 15, 1864.
Maj. Gen. JOHN A. LOGAN,
Comdg. Fifteenth Army Corps, Huntsville, Ala. :

GENERAL : A telegram just received from General Dodge states that there are about 5,000 rebel cavalry under Clanton and Patterson on the opposite side of the river, extending from below Whitesburg along Flint Creek and around to Danville and Moulton, holding and picketing all the roads leading out from Decatur.

Direct your scouting parties, patrols, and detachments on the river from Larkinsville down to Triana to be particularly active and on the alert, and to communicate promptly any information they may obtain. If the enemy should make any attempt to cross the river to make a raid on the railroad or capture any of our detachments we ought to have early notice of it.

Very respectfully, your obedient servant,

JAS. B. McPHERSON,
Major-General.

HEADQUARTERS DISTRICT OF KENTUCKY,
Lexington, Ky., April 15, 1864.

Brig. Gen. E. H. HOBSON,
Comdg. First Division, District of Kentucky, Lexington:

GENERAL: I am directed by the general commanding to inform you that instructions have been issued to Brigadier-General Ewing, commanding Second Division, to use in cases of necessity all troops of your division lying between the railroad and a line passing from Lebanon through Burkesville to the Tennessee line.

The troops will not be ordered by General Ewing unless in cases of emergency. They will make all the reports to you that are required, and be regarded for all other purposes as part of your command. You will issue the necessary orders to those troops.

I am, very respectfully, your obedient servant,

THOMAS B. FAIRLEIGH,
Lieutenant-Colonel and Acting Assistant Adjutant-General.

FRANKFORT, *April* 15, 1864.

Brigadier-General HOBSON:

I send you dispatch from Mount Sterling:

The troops have all evacuated this place. The town and vicinity I believe in great danger. If I have authority from you, I will call out first battalion of my regiment, which is organized, and protect the place.

ROBERT THOMAS,
Lieutenant-Colonel Seventy-fifth Regiment Kentucky Militia.

I have referred him to you to keep you posted and not call out the militia.

RICHD. T. JACOB,
Lieutenant and Acting Governor.

LEXINGTON, *April* 15, 1864.

RICHARD T. JACOB,
Lieutenant-Governor:

Infantry was withdrawn from Mount Sterling on yesterday. I have two regiments cavalry beyond that point, having passed through yesterday and to-day. One company ordered to remain in the place.

E. H. HOBSON,
Brigadier-General.

LEXINGTON, KY., *April* 15, 1864.

General BURBRIDGE, *Louisville, Ky.*:

Just received the following dispatch:

General HOBSON:

Mr. Salyer, said to be a rebel by Union citizens, says he came through Pound Gap seven days ago with Hodge, who had 3,000 men; says he saw General Breckinridge, who went back to Abingdon to bring up more men. Says John Morgan was at Abingdon, and that the officers and men seemed certain that they were merely the advance of a heavy force.

C. J. TRUE,
Colonel.

Two of my regiments are beyond Mount Sterling.

E. H. HOBSON,
Brigadier-General.

BURKESVILLE, *April* 15, 1864.

General E. H. HOBSON:

Had I best send another company to Glasgow? I do not think one is sufficient there.

J. W. WEATHERFORD,
Colonel Thirteenth Kentucky Cavalry.

MOUNT STERLING, *April* 15, 1864.

Brigadier-General HOBSON:

Colonel Brown has arrived. I do not believe there are any rebels this side of West Liberty, from best information. My regiment has moved to Mud Lick. Will move as rapidly as possible to West Liberty, or best point to get enemy's rear. Will Colonel Brown move forward to support me or not?

C. J. TRUE,
Colonel.

LEXINGTON, KY., *April* 15, 1864.

Col. C. J. TRUE,
    Mount Sterling:

Colonel Brown will move forward and co-operate with your regiment, leaving one company at Mount Sterling. If you should meet large force advancing, be guided by verbal instructions in possession of Colonel Brown. Send often by courier to Mount Sterling all information to be telegraphed from that point.

E. H. HOBSON,
Brigadier-General.

LEXINGTON, *April* 15, 1864.

Col. J. W. WEATHERFORD,
    Burkesville:

Send another company to Glasgow, if you deem it important.

E. H. HOBSON,
Brigadier-General.

LEXINGTON, *April* 15, 1864.

Colonel TRUE,
    Fortieth Kentucky, Mount Sterling :

By direction of Major-General Stoneman, the detachment First Kentucky Cavalry at West Liberty will co-operate with you.

E. H. HOBSON,
Brigadier-General.

Operator at Mount Sterling will send this dispatch to Colonel True by courier.

. E. H. HOBSON,
Brigadier-General.

HDQRS. MILITARY DIVISION OF THE MISSISSIPPI,
Nashville. Tenn., April 15, 1864.

General McPHERSON, *Huntsville :*

Your two dispatches received. Estimate for 250 to 300 cartridges in the boxes, wagons, and at Huntsville depot.

Forrest took Fort Pillow. killing 50 whites and taking 100 prisoners; also 300 negroes were murdered after capture. I don't understand it as the place was long since abandoned by my order. I think Forrest is trying to draw us off and to prevent our concentration; same of the cavalry to which Dodge alludes.

Tell Dodge to find some other name for Flint River south of the Tennessee, which misleads me in his reports. Of course I don't suppose the enemy has anything like 5,000 men about Decatur. It is a force to observe and watch your movements.

W. T. SHERMAN,
Major-General.

WOODVILLE, ALA., *April* 15, 1864.

Maj. R. R. TOWNES,
    Assistant Adjutant-General, Huntsville, Ala. :

Effective strength of infantry at Woodville and Paint Rock is 213 commissioned officers and 3,617 enlisted men; effective strength of infantry at Vienna is 16 commissioned officers and 263 enlisted men; effective strength of infantry at Cottonville is 16 commissioned officers and 251 enlisted men; effective strength of artillery is 10 commissioned officers and 297 enlisted men; aggregate present, all arms, including sick, is 5,246; aggregate present and absent, 7,741. One thousand veterans are on their way to this command.

P. JOS. OSTERHAUS,
Brigadier-General, Commanding Division.

PADUCAH, *April* 15, 1864.

General BRAYMAN :

A reliable gentleman has just come in from Mayfield; says Buford is there; that 2,000 rebels came from the south and met him there last night; that they say Forrest is at Obion, bridging to get his guns over; that they say they intend to take this place. Let them come; I am ready.

S. G. HICKS,
Colonel, Commanding Post.

METROPOLIS, *April* 15, 1864.

General BRAYMAN:

A fisherman from this place crossed the river this morning in a skiff; 8 of rebel cavalry captured him; threatened his life if he did not take 3 of their friends over the river to escape conscript. Captain Lovelace has his headquarters at Lovelaceville; the 3 men are here in town; they say rebels are conscripting every man they get hold of in Kentucky.

CHAS. WALLACE,
Operator.

HEADQUARTERS OF THE POST,
Columbus, Ky., April 15, 1864.

Capt. J. H. ODLIN,
Assistant Adjutant-General, Cairo, Ill.:

CAPTAIN: I have a scout just in from Jackson, Dresden, and that line, and I have every reason to believe his reports reliable. He was employed by General Smith and Colonel Waring. He reports as follows: General Forrest has two divisions—First Division, 3,400 strong, which is concentrated at Jackson, Tenn.; Second Division, 2,000 strong, concentrated at Dresden; 1,000 under Duckworth, from Jackson's command. Forrest said that a large force of our troops had landed at Pittsburg Landing, and that he was going to drive them back and across into North Alabama. The Second Division is said to be about to cross at the mouth of the Big Sandy into Middle Tennessee. My scout thinks their object is to get behind Chattanooga, somewhere about Winchester. Col. Aaron Forrest, brother of the general, died at Jackson on Thursday night last. Generals Fitzhugh [Stephen D.?] Lee and Jackson, with 9,000 men, are reported near Memphis. I shall try and rebuild the telegraph between us to-morrow. All the small squads are ordered to join their commands immediately at Dresden, under General Buford, who is on his march there.

I am, captain, very respectfully, your obedient servant,
WM. HUDSON LAWRENCE,
Colonel, Commanding Post.

CAIRO, ILL., *April* 15, 1864—3 p. m.
(Received 9.30 p. m.)

Hon. GIDEON WELLES,
Secretary of the Navy:

On the 13th instant the rebels demanded the surrender of Columbus, Ky., which was refused by Colonel Lawrence. Troops and two gun-boats were sent from here, but the enemy had retired before they reached Columbus. Hearing that Fort Pillow had been attacked I directed Lieutenant-Commander Fitch, if he could be spared from Columbus, to proceed to Fort Pillow with gun-boats Hastings and Moose. Last night I learned that Fort Pillow had been captured, after a desperate resistance by the garrison. The gun-boat New Era assisted in the defense. Lieutenant-Commander Fitch will, on his arrival, endeavor to shell the rebels from the fort, and to keep the river open at all hazards. The greater part of the rebel force is said to have left in the direction of Memphis.

On the 14th a flag of truce was sent by the rebels to Paducah. One hour was given by them to move the women and children. At the expiration of the hour no attack was made. Lieutenant-Commander Shirk reports that the gun-boats shelled the upper part of the town, and drove the rebels out, and I am informed that the troops in the fort also shelled them and killed several. Paducah has been re-enforced by troops sent to General Brayman, and we have four gun-boats there. Information has reached me that the rebels are in force at Blandville, Ky., and will cross the Ohio into Illinois, if they can, about 20 miles above Mound City. I have had all the ferries and skiffs between this place and Paducah destroyed, and will keep the river closely watched with all the force we have at our disposal. A part of the rebel programme is, I believe, to destroy the large amount of ordnance stores we have at Mound City, and other Government property at that place. We have taken every precaution in our power to guard against it. We have constantly to be on the lookout for incendiaries. Admiral Porter has left me ample instructions for guidance during his absence, which I shall carry out to the extent of my ability. I will telegraph you when I hear from Lieutenant-Commander Fitch.

A. M. PENNOCK,
Fleet Captain and Commander of Station.

SPECIAL ORDERS, ⎱ HDQRS. ARMIES OF THE UNITED STATES,
No. 12.   ⎰   *In the Field, Culpeper C. H., April* 15. 1864.

I. Brig. Gen. J. Kilpatrick, U. S. Volunteers, is hereby relieved from duty in the Army of the Potomac, and will report in person without delay to Maj. Gen. W. T. Sherman, commanding Military Division of the Mississippi, for orders.

*   *   *   *   *

By command of Lieutenant-General Grant:

T. S. BOWERS,
Assistant Adjutant-General.

CONFIDENTIAL.]   HDQRS. MIL. DIV. OF THE MISSISSIPPI,
Nashville, April 16, 1864.

Maj. Gen. H. W. HALLECK,
Washington, D. C.:

DEAR GENERAL: Yours of April 8 is received. I see the points you make and admit their full force.

The division of a large command into departments, coupled with the fact that the law confers on the department commanders the power of discharge, furloughs, &c., is a good and sufficient reason for the present plan. All I can then ask is that you keep in mind that the territory lying so remote as Arkansas is more naturally belonging to a division west of the Mississippi than this, more especially as soon I will be in immediate command of an army that will engross all my thoughts and action. I dislike even to attempt to name a commander west of the Mississippi that could reconcile the discordant claims of Curtis, Rosecrans, Steele, and Banks. Of them I would prefer Steele, because he will fight, but his movements are too slow for this stage of the war.   Banks is entirely too much engrossed in schemes of civil experiments.   These ought to be deferred till all large armies of the Confederacy are broken up and destroyed.   Our efforts heretofore to cover trading schemes, local interests, and matters of civil reconstruction has almost paralyzed large armies by dividing them up into little squads easy of surprise and capture.   The recent garrison of Pillow was not a part of our army, but a nondescript body, in process of formation and posted there to cover a trading post for the convenience of families supposed to be friendly to us, or at least not hostile.

But all these things are well known to you, and I should not refer to them.   Though Steele is subject to my orders I must naturally leave him to act on his own judgment, confining my attention to the concentration of force now rapidly being made on the Tennessee from Chattanooga to Decatur.

I am, with respect, yours, truly,

W. T. SHERMAN,
Major-General, Commanding.

HDQRS. MILITARY DIVISION OF THE MISSISSIPPI,
Nashville, Tenn., April 16, 1864.

General THOMAS,
Chattanooga:

Movements such as Geary's will always do good.   They should be repeated from time to time in concert with land excursions of McPherson's men.   They will serve to distract the enemy.

I will telegraph to Washington about the title of Hooker's corps, but want him to go on with his organization regardless of the mere number, which is an immaterial title.   It will be better known as Hooker's corps than by its numerical designation.

W. T. SHERMAN,
Major-General.

CINCINNATI, *April 16, 1864.*

General W. T. SHERMAN :

I learn that 8,000 cattle, large size, were bought on hoof at Nashville about 10th instant.   I think they will be enough for number of men mentioned.   I leave here to-morrow to join you.

C. L. KILBURN,
Lieutenant-Colonel and Assistant Commissary-General.

CLEVELAND, *April 16, 1864.*

Brigadier-General WHIPPLE,
Assistant Adjutant-General:

General Wood has arrived, and has gone into camp as directed ; Cruft's brigade will be relieved on Tuesday morning ; Wagner has been relieved by General Schofield, and will start Monday morning.

O. O. HOWARD,
Major-General.

BULL'S GAP, *April* 16, 1864.
Major-General SCHOFIELD. *Knoxville:*

The rebel families and surgeons last sent beyond our lines are still at Blue Springs, and do not get any transportation from the enemy. They apply for rations, and also to be sent to Greeneville. The roads are bad, and the former trips were hard on our teams, but I think they should either go back to Knoxville or farther to the front. Have you any instructions?

> J. D. COX,
> *Brigadier-General, Commanding.*

KNOXVILLE, TENN., *April* 16, 1864.
Brigadier-General COX, *Bull's Gap:*

The enemy should furnish transportation for persons sent through the lines from the point where the railroad cannot be used; at all events do not send them to Greeneville until the roads are in better condition. You will have to feed them while they remain with you.

> J. M. SCHOFIELD,
> *Major-General.*

BULL'S GAP, *April* 16, 1864.
General SCHOFIELD:

I have intelligence more reliable this evening from Kingsport that Vaughn and his cavalry went toward Blountsville, going to North Carolina, as they said, instead of crossing the Holston. Jones is at Estillville, 7 miles from Kingsport, with 700 men. Day, with 200 men, did not cross the river last evening.

> R. A. CRAWFORD,
> *Chief of Scouts.*

LOUDON, *April* 16, 1864.
Lieut. Col. J. S. FULLERTON,
　　Assistant Adjutant-General, Fourth Army Corps:

General Ammen has arrived, relieving me of command of this post. I will leave here with my command on Monday morning and arrive at Charleston on Wednesday.

> G. D. WAGNER,
> *Brigadier-General, Commanding.*

BULL'S GAP, *April* 16, 1864.
Major-General SCHOFIELD:

I strongly suspect that the cavalry under Vaughn, which crossed near Kingsport, is making for North Carolina to break up the regiment Kirk was organizing. Kirk was in Knoxville in arrest a few days ago, but on a partial investigation of the complaint I advised its withdrawal. I think it important that he should rally his command as soon as possible.

> J. D. COX,
> *Brigadier-General.*

HDQRS. DEPARTMENT AND ARMY OF THE TENNESSEE,
Huntsville, Ala., April 16, 1864.

Maj. Gen. W. T. SHERMAN,
  Military Division of the Mississippi:

GENERAL : In pursuance to Special Orders, No. 24, paragraph 5, from headquarters Military Division of the Mississippi, dated April 11, 1864, I have the honor to submit the following report of the effective force of the department:

The Fifteenth Army Corps, Maj. Gen. John A. Logan commanding, 16,338 strong, stationed on the Memphis and Charleston Railroad, between Stevenson and Huntsville, Ala.

I have no changes to notice in the Sixteenth and Seventeenth Army Corps, with the exception of Brig. Gen. G. M. Dodge's command, as no reports have been received from these corps at these headquarters since last report was forwarded.

The Left Wing, Sixteenth Army Corps, Brig. Gen. G. M. Dodge commanding, numbers 10,222, stationed along the railroad from Columbia, Tenn., to Decatur, Ala., and Mooresville, Ala. Two regiments of cavalry are patrolling the Tennessee River from Florence to Eastport and Hamburg.

I am, general, very respectfully, your obedient servant,
JAS. B. McPHERSON,
Major-General, Commanding.
By L. S. WILLARD,
Major and Acting Assistant Adjutant-General.

HDQRS. FOURTH DIVISION, SIXTEENTH ARMY CORPS,
Decatur, Ala., April 16, 1864—9.45 p. m.

Brigadier-General DODGE, *Athens:*

Patterson was on the Danville road, 12 miles from here, at 10 o'clock a. m. I have no means of estimating their force. Scouts say that Roddey's force alone is 4,000. This, if true, would give them over 6,000 in all. I have ordered the Twenty-fifth Wisconsin from Mooresville to-night. Have directed the operator to keep open all night.
JAMES C. VEATCH,
Brigadier-General.

APRIL 16, 1864.

Brig. Gen. J. C. VEATCH, *Decatur:*

How far from Decatur is Patterson's force, and what news, if any, from toward Danville and Courtland ? Unless their commands have greatly increased, Roddey, Patterson (who is a colonel), Clanton, and Johnson, all told, are not equal to us.
G. M. DODGE,
Brigadier-General.

APRIL 16, 1864.

Maj. Gen. J. B. McPHERSON, *Huntsville :*

To-day at 10 o'clock a. m., Patterson was on the Danville road. Scouts and citizens from Somerville report that Roddey camped at

Sulphur Springs, 9 miles from that place, last night. They tell citizens that they are going to attack Decatur. The move is to a country destitute of forage ; must have some object, but I cannot think they have any serious intentions on Decatur.

> G. M. DODGE,
> *Brigadier-General.*

HDQRS. FOURTH DIVISION, SIXTEENTH ARMY CORPS,
Decatur, Ala., April 16, 1864—7.50 p. m.

Brigadier-General DODGE,
Comdg. Left Wing, Sixteenth Army Corps, Athens :

The scout Rose, just in, reports Patterson in the valley on this side of Flint, moving on this place. A citizen, Wiles, just in from Somerville, reports Roddey with his force camped at Sulphur Springs, 9 miles beyond Somerville, last night. These reports are confirmed by Major Kuhn's scouts. They report an intention to attack this place. I regard this as quite probable. I need ammunition for the four regiments lately arrived here. Send me to-night 200,000 rounds of ammunition, caliber .58, and artillery ammunition for James and Greenwood rifled 6-pounders. We have only 80 rounds for this battery, and it is in a damaged state.

> JAMES C. VEATCH,
> *Brigadier-General.*

APRIL 16, 1864.

Brig. Gen. G. M. DODGE,
Decatur :

Dispatch from Colonel Rowett just received. He reports no great force of enemy near the river ; that they are building boats near Yellow Creek and Clifton. Refugees report 2,000 Confederate troops near Jackson, from Alabama, to join Forrest, who report that Forrest was to attack Memphis. Others report that he intends crossing the river near Clifton. Rowett sent scouts over river, who have not yet returned.

> J. W. BARNES,
> *Assistant Adjutant-General.*

APRIL 16, 1864—10.30 p. m.

Brig. Gen. J. C. VEATCH,
Decatur :

Reports from Clifton, Eastport, Florence, &c.. to-night do not show any large force opposite any of those places. I will send a scouting party to Brown's Ferry to-night, and thence down to Lamb's Ferry, to see if we can discover anything. They have some project on hand ; we must try to find out what it is. A letter from a conscript officer from Fayette Court-House, near Tuscaloosa, says Polk's staff officers have been north to examine roads in North Alabama, and that he is about to move, &c.

> G. M. DODGE,
> *Brigadier-General.*

HDQRS. FOURTH DIVISION, SIXTEENTH ARMY CORPS,
Decatur, Ala., April 16, 1864—9 p. m.

Colonel MONTGOMERY,
Commanding Twenty-fifth Wisconsin, Mooresville:

You will move with your regiment immediately for this place. Leave your camp equipage and bring your ammunition. You must move with all dispatch, as the place is threatened.

JAMES C. VEATCH,
Brigadier-General.

MOUNT STERLING, KY.,
April 16, 1864.

Brigadier-General HOBSON :

Rumors are rife that a rebel force are to attack this town to-night. I have thirty "Spencers," with good men behind them to defend it. Taking all things into consideration, with the movement of the sympathizers, the rumor has some foundation.

EDWIN C. MILES,
Captain, Commanding.

LEXINGTON, *April 16, 1864.*

Col. C. J. TRUE
(Care of Captain Miles), Mount Sterling:

I learn you are only at Olympian Springs as yet. Move on and ascertain fully if there are any rebels in that country.

By command of Brig. Gen. E. H. Hobson:

J. S. BUTLER,
Assistant Adjutant-General.

HDQRS. FIRST DIVISION, DISTRICT OF KENTUCKY,
Lexington, Ky., April 16, 1864.

Col. J. W. WEATHERFORD,
Commanding Thirteenth Kentucky Cavalry:

COLONEL : Inclosed find copy of letter of instructions* from General Burbridge, which you will be governed by, if it should become necessary for General Ewing to use your regiment. Please give me notice of the duty, &c. You will make your regular reports to these headquarters. We have had some little excitement in the eastern part of the State. I think and believe that there will be no formidable invasion. Let me hear from your command often.

Very respectfully,

E. H. HOBSON,
Brigadier-General, Commanding.

---

*See p. 371.

WAR DEPARTMENT,
Washington, April 16, 1864—11.45 a. m.

Major-General SHERMAN, *Nashville :*

You will please direct a competent officer to investigate and report minutely, and as early as possible, the facts in relation to the alleged butchery of our troops at Fort Pillow.

EDWIN M. STANTON,
Secretary of War.

NASHVILLE, *April 16, 1864.*

Brigadier-General BRAYMAN :

Order a good officer to examine witnesses at the Mound City hospital, and afterward, if necessary, to proceed to Fort Pillow and Memphis, and make a minute and full report of all the circumstances attending the capture by the enemy of Fort Pillow, more especially as to the perpetration of unusual cruelties to prisoners of war, whether white or black. Copy of report to be made to me and another direct to the Secretary of War. Answer.

W. T. SHERMAN,
Major-General.

CAIRO, *April 16, 1864.*

Maj. Gen. W. T. SHERMAN, *Nashville, Tenn. :*

Fort Pillow is destroyed and evacuated. The river is clear, and the fleet of transports are leaving here. A gun-boat lies at that point to guard the way. A gun-boat was fired upon above Mound City last night. I have sent up above Mound City a battery and 200 mounted infantry. Paducah and Columbus annoyed, but in no danger. I will have the investigation as you direct. News from Memphis reports all quiet. Fragments only of Seventeenth Corps yet here.

M. BRAYMAN,
Brigadier-General, Commanding.

PADUCAH, *April 16, 1864.*

General BRAYMAN :

I have received yours in relation to Colonel Mitchell, and will act accordingly. The enemy are all around me ; we were under arms all night. Great excitement in the city ; many citizens leaving. I am able and will keep all right, general.

S. G. HICKS,
Colonel, Commanding.

HDQRS. MILITARY DIVISION OF THE MISSISSIPPI,
Nashville, Tenn., April 16, 1864·

General S. A. HURLBUT, *Memphis :*

There has been marked timidity in the management of affairs since Forrest passed north of Memphis. General Grant orders me to relieve you. You will proceed to Cairo and take command there.

Leave for the present Buckland to defend Memphis and district. His brigade, with Grierson's cavalry, can and should hunt up Forrest and whip him.

W. T. SHERMAN,
Major-General.

CULPEPER, *April* 16, 1864—7 p. m.

Major-General SHERMAN :
General Washburn is ordered to Memphis. General Hurlbut relieved. I will order Hunt or Prince to command over Brayman. Washburn will obey your instructions and establish no posts, except wherever you order them.

U. S. GRANT,
Lieutenant-General.

HDQRS. MILITARY DIVISION OF THE MISSISSIPPI,
Nashville, Tenn., April 16, 1864—10.30 a. m.

Lieutenant-General GRANT, *Culpeper, Va.:*
Send Washburn to Memphis, and I would be glad to have Hunt at Columbus. In making up our fighting force we have left inferior officers on the river. General Hurlbut has full 10,000 men at Memphis, but if he had a million he would be on the defensive.

The force captured and butchered at Fort Pillow was not on my returns at all. It is the first fruits of the system of trading posts designed to assist the loyal people of the interior. All these stations are a weakness, and offer tempting chances for plunder.

In a day or so there ought to be enough of McPherson's troops at Cairo to clean out Forrest without materially delaying our concentrating along the front.

W. T. SHERMAN,
Major-General.

HDQRS. MILITARY DIVISION OF THE MISSISSIPPI,
Nashville, Tenn., April 16, 1864.

General BRAYMAN, *Cairo:*
General Grant is properly offended at the timidity displayed at and about Memphis, and has ordered General Hurlbut to be relieved. I have instructed General McPherson as soon as possible to transport his wagons, mules, &c., up to Clifton and to make up a force to strike inland from the Tennessee at Forrest. Make your dispositions to that end.

W. T. SHERMAN,
Major-General.

HDQRS. MILITARY DIVISION OF THE MISSISSIPPI,
Nashville, Tenn., April 16, 1864.

General McPHERSON, *Huntsville:*
General Grant is properly offended at Hurlbut's timidity, and has ordered me to relieve him. I have ordered him up to Cairo. General Washburn will be ordered by General Grant to Cairo, and General Hunt to Columbus.

Give orders that the wagons, mules, and detachments of your two divisions be carried up to Clifton, and make up a force out of these detachments and the first regiments to arrive at Cairo to ascend the Tennessee and strike at Forrest inland. Were Veatch now at Purdy this would be certain of success.

It may also be necessary for you to send a force across from Pulaski to Savannah and Purdy to cure that mistake. Notify General Slocum to hasten to Vicksburg and put in active motion the troops there to occupy the full attention of Lee's cavalry and prevent their going north to Forrest. I have good information that Loring's infantry is moving eastward; they were at Montgomery on Monday last. It is all humbug about their repairing the railroad, though the railroad companies are working to that end for supplies to the city of Mobile.

I expect to hear of A. J. Smith in a day or so, but he had better hurry round to the Tennessee River. Steele is moving too slow. He had stopped on the 6th at Camden to await provisions from Pine Bluff, but I have reason to believe that Generals Smith and Banks, with gun-boats, were well up toward Shreveport.

W. T. SHERMAN,
Major-General.

HDQRS. CHIEF OF CAV., MIL. DIV. OF THE MISSISSIPPI,
Nashville, Tenn., April 16, 1864.
Brig. Gen. J. W. DAVIDSON,
Chief of West Div., Cav. Bureau, Saint Louis, Mo.:

SIR: Your favor of the 11th instant is just received, and, together with the inclosures, will be submitted to General Sherman, as you request. The paragraph to which you refer in my letter of the 8th instant was in no wise intended nor calculated to reflect upon you. I have every reason and disposition to believe that you are doing all that is in your power to supply the enormous demands made upon the cavalry bureau for horses, arms, and equipments. The points of purchase should in my opinion be the centers of districts which contain the most horses. These will not always coincide with the large cities, especially where agents have been purchasing in those cities ever since the commencement of the war. You do not personally make purchases, and if those who do remain in our largest cities, awaiting stock, instead of penetrating the region in which it is to be found speedily, I do not believe that the inducement of vouchers discounted at from 2 to 5 per cent. will draw together horses in sufficient numbers to supply us as soon as they will be required to enable us to perform our proper part in the coming campaign. If certificates of indebtedness could be given, instead of vouchers, or in payment of them promptly, or, better still, if funds could be supplied to those making purchases, I feel sure that stock would come in much more freely.

These things were barely hinted at in my letter of the 8th, with a desire to assist you simply. The inspectors you have had occasion to relieve were not of my suggestion. Mathews, Hoblitzell, and Beaton were nominated by me. I would suggest that you relieve O'Connell and Rendlebrock, of the Fourth U. S. Cavalry, as soon as they can possibly be spared, as their regiment is almost stripped of its commissioned officers.

Please keep me advised of the number of horses shipped and on the way to this military division. I will gladly co-operate with you and aid you in every way possible in your efforts to supply our cavalry at the West.

Yours, truly,

WM. SOOY SMITH,
Brig. Gen., Chief of Cavalry, Mil. Div. of the Mississippi.

[APRIL 16, 1864.—For Grant and Sherman to Rosecrans, about sending troops to Cairo, Ill., see Vol. XXXIV, Part III, p. 184.]

WAR DEPARTMENT,
April 16, 1864—1.15 p. m.

Lieutenant-General GRANT,
        Culpeper :

Governor Bramlette is extremely anxious to have the western counties of Kentucky included in the same command as the remainder of the State, so that the whole State may be under command of General Burbridge. Is there any objection to the change being made?

EDWIN M. STANTON,
Secretary of War.

CULPEPER COURT-HOUSE, *April* 16, 1864.
(Received 3.40 p. m.)

Hon. E. M. STANTON :

The only objection to West Kentucky being placed under General Burbridge is that it belongs to a different department from the balance of the State. One officer cannot well make returns and reports to two departments, and it would not be advisable to add that part of Kentucky to the Department of the Ohio. In consequence of the weakness exhibited by the commander of West Kentucky, I expect to send another general there, and the one I have selected ranks above Burbridge. The latter has now as much as he can attend to well.

U. S. GRANT,
Lieutenant-General.

SPECIAL FIELD ORDERS, ⎱ HDQRS. DEPT. OF THE CUMBERLAND,
        No. 107.   ⎰   *Chattanooga, Tenn., April* 16, 1864.

*   *   *   *   *   *   *

IV. Maj. Gen. John Newton, U. S. Volunteers, having reported at these headquarters, is assigned to the command of the Second Division of the Fourth Army Corps, and will report in person to Maj. Gen. O. O. Howard, commanding the corps.

*   *   *   *   *   *   *

XXIII. The following transfers are hereby made in the Twentieth Army Corps :

The Twentieth Connecticut Infantry is transferred from the First Brigade, First Division, Twentieth Army Corps, to the Second Brigade, Third Division, Twentieth Army Corps;

The Fifth Connecticut Infantry is transferred from the Second Brigade, Third Division, Twentieth Army Corps, to the First Brigade, First Division, Twentieth Army Corps.

* * * * *

By command of Major-General Thomas:

WM. D. WHIPPLE,
Assistant Adjutant-General.

CULPEPER COURT-HOUSE, '
April 17, 1864—10.30 p. m.

Major-General SHERMAN :

I have ordered General Rosecrans to send to Cairo all the forces he can, specifying three regiments that must be sent. You can have them used against Forrest.

U. S. GRANT,
Lieutenant-General.

HDQRS. MILITARY DIVISION OF THE MISSISSIPPI,
Nashville, Tenn., April 17, 1864.

Colonel KILBURN,
Commissary of Subsistence, Cincinnati, Ohio :

I want on the Tennessee River, at or near Bridgeport, beef-cattle on the hoof to be driven along with the army about May 1, enough for a month's supply for 75,000 men. Inquire what has been done to that end, and order what is necessary in my name.

I wish you to come down.

W. T. SHERMAN,
Major-General.

KNOXVILLE, TENN.,
April 17, 1864.

Brigadier-General JUDAH,
Mossy Creek :

I have ordered two squadrons of cavalry from Strawberry Plains to report to you for temporary duty. Later reports do not indicate any probable movement of the rebels toward your position. Do not use the cavalry unnecessarily. It is important that the horses keep in good condition. I think it better not to make the transfer referred to in your dispatch for the present.

J. M. SCHOFIELD,
Major-General.

HDQRS. MILITARY DIVISION OF THE MISSISSIPPI,
Nashville, Tenn., April 17, 1864.

Maj. Gen. JAMES B. McPHERSON,
Comdg. Dept. of the Tennessee, Huntsville, Ala. :

GENERAL : Captain Poe, U. S. Engineers, has here a fine pontoon train of 600 feet, complete in all respects. It is subject to your control. I wish you to think well over the matter. You will have to cross the Coosa, but to reach it will have near 75 miles to march, over two mountains—the Sand Mountain and Raccoon. Each wagon, of which there are about twenty, will require about 8 mules, and these are scarce and have to be fed.

Now we know that we can always safely count on lumber of old houses. We can make balks of trees, and can make abutments and piers of logs, as well as trestles of such timber as we can count on at the banks of Coosa.

You can take the whole or part of this pontoon train, and I leave it somewhat to your judgment and experience. The labor for such a train for the distance named will almost, if not entirely, equal that of construction when we get there. We will need boats, and I am willing you should have them, and spikes, nails, ropes, and everything likely to be needed, but I do doubt the necessity of carrying along the whole train.

After you have thought the matter all over, you can send an officer here to Nashville to take down just what you want.

The pontoons consist of two side frames, with cross-pieces all ready tenoned and morticed, with canvas to cover all the balks and chesses, with anchors, ropes, and everything complete, are here ready to march off as soon as mules are hitched on. But you and I know the labor and trouble of hauling such heavy loads, but I leave it to you to determine.

I am, &c.,

W. T. SHERMAN,
Major-General.

HDQRS. DEPARTMENT AND ARMY OF THE TENNESSEE,
Huntsville, Ala., April 17, 1864.

Maj. Gen. W. T. SHERMAN.

    Comdg. Mil. Div. of the Mississippi, Nashville, Tenn.:

GENERAL : I have just returned from a trip to Guntersville Landing, Cottonville, Port Deposit, and Claysville, sometimes called Vienna, and as soon as I get some sketches made and ascertain something more definite about roads opposite Port Deposit, will give you my views as to the best point for crossing the Tennessee River.

I have just received a telegram from Dodge, who is now at Decatur. The enemy are hovering around him in considerable force. Three brigades of cavalry—Roddey's, Patterson's, and Clanton's—and three regiments of Alabama infantry are at Moulton, and they have given out that they intend to attack Decatur. Dodge has sent a force out once or twice. and they invariably fall back before the infantry, but stop our cavalry. I do not think they have any serious intentions of attacking Decatur, but are covering some other movement. We will endeavor to watch them closely.

It is reported the enemy are building boats to cross the Tennessee on Yellow Creek, above Hamburg. The gun-boat should watch the river closely from Clifton to Chickasaw.

I inclose herewith a letter* which I have just received from a friend of mine in Canton, Miss., whose information has heretofore been considered reliable, and whose facilities for knowing what he writes about are good. I believe him sincere and anxious to do everything in his power to aid our cause.

---

* Not found.

Major-General Hurlbut writes me that he can only mount 2,200 cavalry, and that the Third Michigan, 1,300 strong, and the Seventh Kansas, 1,100 strong, have been three weeks in Saint Louis waiting horses. His letter is dated the 10th instant. I inclose herewith your letter * to him.

Very respectfully, your obedient servant,

JAS. B. McPHERSON,
Major-General.

HUNTSVILLE, *April* 17, 1864—12 midnight.
(Received 18th.)

Major-General SHERMAN :

General Slocum left Tullahoma yesterday for Nashville. Will undoubtedly see you. Have telegraphed General Gresham to proceed immediately to Cairo and assume command of detachments. There are 3,700 men, belonging to twenty-six different regiments and eight batteries. Four hundred and fifty are now at Columbus and 400 at Paducah. There are a good many recruits in these detachments and very few officers, the most of them being absent with their regiments on furlough. Do you wish these detachments sent up to Clifton before any veteran regiments return ?

JAS. B. McPHERSON,
Major-General.

APRIL 17, 1864.

Major-General McPHERSON,
Huntsville :

General Veatch reports the enemy 5 miles out on Moulton road this morning, and says everything indicates they intend to attack. They may be trying to cover some move. From what we get from their lines, they are evidently posted on our strength at that point.

G. M. DODGE,
Brigadier-General.

HUNTSVILLE, *April* 17, 1864.

Brig. Gen. G. M. DODGE,
Athens :

I have just arrived from Woodville and received your dispatch. Can you learn of any infantry force threatening you ? It seems to me that they would hardly give out publicly that they were going to attack Decatur if such was really their intention. General Sherman says Loring was in Montgomery last Monday. If so, he has most probably gone to Johnston. If you think that Decatur is to be attacked, and that you may need re-enforcements, telegraph to the superintendent of the railroad and have a train sent to Athens, to be subject to your orders.

JAS. B. McPHERSON,
Major-General, Commanding.

---

* See p. 326.

HUNTSVILLE, *April* 17, 1864.

Maj. Gen. H. W. SLOCUM,
  Cairo, Ill.:

GENERAL: I am directed by Major-General McPherson to say that you will hasten to Vicksburg and put in active motion the troops there, to occupy the full attention of Lee's cavalry and prevent their going north to Forrest.

L. S. WILLARD,
  Major and Acting Assistant Adjutant-General.

DECATUR, *April* 17, 1864.

Major-General McPHERSON,
  Huntsville:

A scout in from Tuscaloosa. Left 14th instant. Brings papers of 13th. Says Polk's forces are at Demopolis and Meridian. Polk issues an order from that place against guerrillas in paper of 13th. Saw no forces from Tuscaloosa until he reached Moulton; there saw Roddey; says he came up ahead of him. Tuscaloosa papers of 13th speak of his being in town; he went there to see his wife. This side of Moulton, on direct road to this place, passed through Clanton's and Patterson's brigades bivouacked.

G. M. DODGE,
  Brigadier-General.

DECATUR, *April* 17. 1864.

Major-General McPHERSON,
  Huntsville:

I am here to-day. The enemy made their appearance this a. m. in considerable force, and, as far as I can ascertain, they have got considerable re-enforcements. All reports agree in Roddey's coming up last night.

I moved out with a small force on Courtland road to make them develop. and struck them about 5 miles out. I think the demonstration is to cover some other move. They give out all over the country that they are going to attack this place. All the artillery I can discover is eight pieces. They still show a bold front, but move off when we go after them with infantry; they fall back, but stop our mounted force every time.

G. M. DODGE,
  Brigadier-General.

APRIL 17, 1864.

Brig. Gen. G. M. DODGE,
  Decatur:

Scouting parties from Ninth Ohio Cavalry have started direct for Brown's Ferry, Elk River, and Lamb's Ferry, with written instructions to patrol the river, closely watch these three points and all places where a crossing can be effected, and to ascertain all possible information of the enemy.

J. W. BARNES,
  Assistant Adjutant-General.

HDQRS. LEFT WING, SIXTEENTH ARMY CORPS,
Athens, Ala., April 17, 1864.

Maj. Gen. J. B. McPHERSON,
   Comdg. Dept. and Army of the Tennessee, Huntsville, Ala.:

GENERAL : I returned from Decatur yesterday by way of Moores-ville. I think General Geary must have made some mistake ; there certainly was not the force he reported.

The enemy in the valley has closed in on us, and this morning their advance is 5½ miles out. Roddey is reported by scouts and citizens to have camped 9 miles from Somerville, at Sulphur Springs, night before last. Citizens from Somerville report this.

This addition to their force in the valley is all we know of since the arrival of Patterson except three regiments of infantry at Moulton. Deserters come in from there direct ; they are the Twenty-seventh, Thirty-first, and Fifty-fourth Alabama.

The scout in from Pikeville reports no movements, but says Polk's staff officers passed up examining the roads, and says that his army is about to move. I inclose a letter* from the conscript officer at Fay-ette Court-House, Ala.; it is addressed to one of our men, although he is not aware who he is writing to. Our mail arrangements to Montgomery will be completed in a week or so, and we will get the papers regularly as well as the reports.

Colonel Rowett reports a few regiments opposite him ; also that they are building boats in Yellow Creek and opposite Clifton. Last heard of Forrest he was in Jackson. Last Sunday refugees from McNairy County, Tenn., made two reports—one was that a con-siderable force had gone to join him from the south, and that he was to attack Memphis ; the other, that he was sending his trains. con-scripts, &c., south preparatory to crossing the Tennessee River. We are in communication with the force at Clifton. Major Murphy, commanding that force, says Forrest is going to cross, but he can-not tell at what point. We have the river so closely watched that they cannot get over without our having due notice of it.

I am, very respectfully, your obedient servant,

G. M. DODGE,
Brigadier-General, Commanding.

HDQRS. NINTH OHIO VOLUNTEER CAVALRY,
Martin's Mills, April 17, 1864.

[General G. M. DODGE:]

GENERAL : I have sent Major Williamson to take command of the men sent to the mouth of Elk River, giving him your orders. He will connect with the Seventh Illinois, who patrol down to the mouth of Cypress Creek, joining my patrols, who patrol as far as Eastport. The enemy are sometimes seen patrolling opposite Florence, Cheat-ham's Ferry, and along the river. A reliable man whom I saw to-day says that they talk of crossing and trying to capture our patrols. I have sent Mr. Harris over to-day, who will learn what is to be known as to their movements. I think there is no heavy force near here ; Johnson's and Jackson's regiments, I think, are all ; they probably do not exceed 400 or 500 men. From letters capt-ured, dated March 17, it seems that a forward movement into Ten-

---

*Not found.

nessee is in preparation, and Decatur probably the point of attack. I think their patrols are watching their own deserters more than anything else. One came over yesterday, and I have made arrangements with a man on the other side to send them over as fast as they come. He says the woods are full of them, but they are afraid to venture. I learn that there are some boats and a flat-boat on the other side in some of the inlets. I have directed Mr. Harris to ascertain and get the deserters to bail them out and bring them over if possible ; also to learn where Jackson is encamped. If practicable, I intend visiting him some night. The neighborhood has sent a delegation to wait upon you in relation to the protection of their property. I find many of them in rather a destitute condition, some of them quite so. I think our men have not used proper discrimination in their levies. The officers are not sufficiently explicit in their instructions to the men, or the men are not sufficiently careful to follow the instructions received. I think generally the greatest evils arise from the latter cause. Since my arrival I have returned a number of animals taken by my men before I came, and a number of others I would return if they had not been sent off. I will see you further in relation to this expedition when I return.

I have the honor to be, general, your obedient servant,

W. D. HAMILTON,
Colonel, Commanding Ninth Ohio Volunteer Cavalry.

DECATUR, *April* 17, 1864.

Major-General McPHERSON,
Huntsville :

Unless I relieve Sweeny's forces by forces from here he could not take over four regiments and what artillery he wants. The Seventh Illinois, mounted, could be added if you think his move would make the right secure.

G. M. DODGE,
Brigadier-General.

DECATUR. *April* 17, 1864.

Capt. J. W. BARNES,
Assistant Adjutant-General, Athens :

Send scouting parties to Brown's Ferry, direct to Elk River, and Lamb's Ferry, and have them to watch the river closely.

G. M. DODGE,
Brigadier-General.

APRIL 17, 1864.

Brig. Gen. J. C. VEATCH,
Decatur :

That ammunition left here at midnight on trains. Do you consider it reliable that Roddey is in the valley ? He is reported to be in front of Dalton. A few men sent to the rear of Flint River would settle the question.

G. M. DODGE,
Brigadier-General.

APRIL 17, 1864.

Brig. Gen. G. M. DODGE,
        Decatur :

The scouting party sent to Brown's Ferry last night has returned. Reports no boats found between ferry and Elk, nor on Elk below Florence road ; also reports that no news of enemy on opposite side of river could be obtained.   I do not think the officer in charge of the scout is a very sharp or thoroughgoing man.

J. W. BARNES,
Assistant Adjutant-General.

APRIL 17, 1864.

Brig. Gen. G. M. DODGE,
        Decatur :

Colonel Rowett reports that all is quiet on the Tennessee River from Lamb's Ferry to Eastport ; that the enemy has no pickets between Rogersville and Bainbridge at present.   He has sent a scouting party along the river as far as Clifton to destroy all boats.

J. W. BARNES,
Assistant Adjutant-General.

HDQRS. LEFT WING, SIXTEENTH ARMY CORPS,
        Athens, Ala., April 17, 1864.

Col. R. ROWETT,
        Bailey's Springs :

I desire you to send in no more negro women and children than is absolutely necessary.   They are only a burden upon us.   We need all able-bodied men you can get.   The women and children should stay on the plantations and aid in working them.   It is better for them and us both.

The enemy are increasing their force in front of Decatur and moving heavy bodies of cavalry to the south of us.   I am disposed to think the movement has some connection with Forrest and Polk. You should make every endeavor to gain all information of the enemy possible.   Question closely every citizen who crosses, send spies over, &c.

Reports show that Forrest was in the neighborhood of Columbus and Fort Pillow three days ago.

I am, very respectfully, your obedient servant,

G. M. DODGE,
Brigadier-General, Commanding.

HDQRS. FOURTH DIVISION, SIXTEENTH ARMY CORPS,
        Decatur, Ala., April 17, 1864.

Col. GEORGE E. SPENCER,
        First Alabama Cavalry, Mooresville :

Send six companies of your command here immediately.

JAMES C. VEATCH,
Brigadier-General.

HDQRS. FOURTH DIVISION, SIXTEENTH ARMY CORPS,
Decatur, April 17, 1864.

Colonel SPRAGUE, Decatur Junction:

Return here immediately.

JAMES C. VEATCH,
Brigadier-General.

HDQRS. FOURTH DIVISION, SIXTEENTH ARMY CORPS,
Decatur, Ala., April 17, 1864—7.30 a. m.

Brigadier-General DODGE,
Comdg. Left Wing, Sixteenth Army Corps, Athens:

All quiet during the night. The advance of the enemy was last night 5½ miles out on the Moulton road. All the indications show that they are gathering their forces for an attack. No ammunition has yet arrived.

JAMES C. VEATCH,
Brigadier-General.

HDQRS. FOURTH DIVISION, SIXTEENTH ARMY CORPS.
Decatur, Ala., April 17, 1864—10 a. m.

Brigadier-General DODGE, Athens:

The pickets report the enemy advancing in line of battle on the Courtland road. Ammunition has arrived. I think it certain that Roddey is in the valley.

JAMES C. VEATCH,
Brigadier-General.

LEXINGTON, April 17, 1864.

Captain MILES, Mount Sterling:

There is no immediate danger at Mount Sterling, but of course you must look out for anything that may happen. A force of 25 men under a captain will be at Mount Sterling to-night.

J. S. BUTLER,
Assistant Adjutant-General.

GILL'S MILLS, VIA MOUNT STERLING, KY.,
April 17, 1864.

Brigadier-General HOBSON:

From best information the rebel force does not exceed 700 men; 600 reported to have been at Salyersville Wednesday night. A small detachment of Fourteenth Kentucky were in Salyersville Tuesday. Scouts have just returned from direction of West Liberty and Salyersville; report no rebels this side either place. I shall be in Salyersville to-morrow by 4 p. m. if possible, and will endeavor to ascertain facts. It is impossible to get any reliable information here. The roads are very bad; horses stand it very well. The rebels are a part of Hodge's brigade, and are commanded by Zeke Clay. This is the only rebel force I can hear of in any direction.

C. J. TRUE,
Colonel.

· MOUNT STERLING, KY., *April 17, 1864.*
J. S. BUTLER,
    Assistant Adjutant-General:
Do not receive any news from Colonel True. All quiet at this place, Mount Sterling. I made preparation to receive any guerrilla force that might wish to encroach upon this place, stretching wires across the streets and making barricades on pavements for protection of men.

EDWIN C. MILES,
Captain, Commanding.

HDQRS. FIRST DIVISION, DISTRICT OF KENTUCKY,
    Lexington, April 17, 1864.
Col. J. M. BROWN,
    Commanding at Irvine, Ky.:
COLONEL : I have the honor to acknowledge the receipt of your communication of 16th instant. I have been fully satisfied for several days that no formidable invasion could be made through the eastern part of the State ; a great deal of alarm on the part of citizens brought about by rumors of an invasion, put in circulation by the friends of the rebellion. I am confident that the plan proposed by Capt. Seldon F. Bowman, if carried out, will effectually rid the eastern border counties of marauders and guerrilla bands. Let the captain make application to the Governor in proper form, with your indorsement, and forward to these headquarters, and I will give it full approval and urge its adoption. Colonel Gallup fought the enemy on the 14th instant ; drove them to Salyersville ; killed and wounded 24, among them Col. E. F. Clay ; captured 50, 100 horses, 200 stand of arms. Colonel True, with Fortieth Kentucky and Eleventh Michigan, should have been at Salyersville last night. True captured 6 rebels beyond Mount Sterling. I have full confidence in your ability, and will leave to your own discretion and judgment the disposition of your regiment.
Very respectfully,

E. H. HOBSON,
Brigadier-General.

HEADQUARTERS SIXTEENTH ARMY CORPS,
    Memphis, Tenn., April 17, 1864.
Maj. Gen. W. T. SHERMAN,
    Comdg. Mil. Div. of the Mississippi, Nashville, Tenn.:
The Mobile and Ohio Railroad is now in running order from Mobile to Okolona, and will be to Corinth in a week. All damage done to it has been repaired. No news from A. J. Smith.

S. A. HURLBUT,
Major-General.

HEADQUARTERS SIXTEENTH ARMY CORPS,
    Memphis, Tenn., April 17, 1864.
Maj. Gen. J. B. McPHERSON, *Huntsville. Ala.:*
GENERAL : I have heard indirectly from Brig. Gen. A. J. Smith above Natchitoches. General Corse, conveying dispatches, had

reached as high as Alexandria. My best impression is that it will be impossible for him to get up as far as this point before 1st of May.

I am exceedingly desirous, in case the enemy continue to occupy West Tennessee, to push a column of about 5,000 men out from this place into the country. They can march to the Tennessee at any given point as rapidly as they can be transported, with their wagons, &c., by river. I do not, however, feel myself at liberty to deviate from General Sherman's orders as to their line of march. The trains for the command are here, and can be shipped at any time when deemed advisable.

The city is full of all kinds of flying reports. Many persons believe that infantry of Polk's army are at Corinth, and some say at La Grange. I have sent out many messengers, who do not return as yet. Lee unquestionably left Grenada on Sunday last, and went east. My informant saw them go.

There is no doubt but that the Mobile and Ohio Railroad has been fully repaired and is now running, or will be in a day or two, to Corinth. This gives them a new base on your flank, and exposes the Tennessee equally with West Tennessee.

There is no force of any consequence between here and Vicksburg, and I expect a concentration of all their spare strength, with Corinth for [a] base. Of these things you are no doubt advised from other sources.

I have considered it necessary to order up the remnant of the Third Division of your corps to this place as soon as it can be spared. You are aware that Memphis itself, if attacked by a competent force, is not a defensible point. My instructions, in such an event, are to draw in the outside camp within Gayoso Bayou, destroy the bridges, and hold that line as long as it may be tenable, keeping always communications open with the fort as matter of last resort. This, of course, implies attack by a very serious force. Nothing but infantry, with competent artillery, can induce such action.

Unless, therefore, some union shall be made of infantry arriving via Corinth with the force now in West Tennessee, so as to very largely outnumber the present garrison, I have no expectation of attack upon the city, and the less so as it is very generally and properly understood that as a last resort I will destroy the city before it shall be held by the enemy. Still, I consider the situation in West Tennessee very precarious and one that calls for the early concentration of troops to drive the enemy from their location.

Very respectfully, your obedient servant,

S. A. HURLBUT,
Major-General.

HEADQUARTERS POST AND DEFENSES,
Vicksburg, Miss., April 17, 1864.

Col. H. SCOFIELD,
Comdg. Second Brig., First Div., U. S. Colored Troops:

COLONEL: You will proceed with two regiments of your command and Osband's cavalry, together with the Seventeenth Illinois Infantry and one battalion of Tenth Missouri Cavalry, with one section of artillery (that have been ordered to report to you), to Yazoo City, reaching there by land, taking five days' rations and 100 rounds of ammunition per man and 200 rounds artillery ammunition per gun; one tent per company, and one hospital tent for each regiment. You will occupy Yazoo City and defenses, and give such protection and assistance as may be in your power to the parties sent by the quartermaster's department for the raising of the machinery of steamboats sunk in Yazoo River. You will clean the country as you march up of any forces of the enemy. The occupation of Yazoo City it is expected will clear the country between you and the Mississippi River as far north as Greenville. Your operations will have that object in view. You will allow the citizens of the country to bring forward and sell their products as freely as your military duties will allow; arresting all steam-boats that are not properly cleared from this post, approved by me, sending them back under guard to this place. All Treasury permits to purchase cotton will be required to be approved at these headquarters. Allow no supplies to pass your lines to disloyal persons, granting privileges only to those who attest their loyalty by voluntarily taking the oath of allegiance. Your commissary of subsistence will take thirty days' supply by steamboat. Forage for animals will be drawn from the country and such stock as you can procure for cavalry purposes. One regiment with the First Kansas Mounted Infantry will guard your present encampment until your return, the time for which will be determined hereafter. The expedition will start on Tuesday, 19th instant, at as early an hour as possible, reporting as frequently as circumstances will permit to these headquarters.

Very respectfully,

J. McARTHUR,
Brigadier-General, Commanding.

HEADQUARTERS DISTRICT OF CAIRO,
Cairo, Ill., April 17, 1864.

Lieut. Col. T. H. HARRIS,
Assistant Adjutant-General, Sixteenth Army Corps:

COLONEL: For the further information of the general commanding, I write this note by a boat about leaving.

A gun-boat up from Fort Pillow during last night brought up 10 more wounded and some 20 others, all of whom were sent to Mound City. The proof of horrid barbarities in ways without example accumulates daily. I am securing testimony of eye-witnesses, by affidavit and otherwise, and shall report fully at the earliest possible day.

My reports concerning Union City and Paducah, which ought to have reached you ere this, have been delayed by the pressure of imperative duties growing out of the disturbances here. I shall endeavor during this week to bring up all my returns as to all operations here.

The gun-boat on her way up found guerrillas at different points, and at one wooding station shelled a party of them with effect. On Friday night a gun-boat was fired upon by about 100 guerrillas opposite Mound City, without effect. Last night a trading-boat near Metropolis, on the Illinois side, was found to have on board Confederate uniforms, new, and, according to best information, the boat was a rebel recruiting station for receiving volunteers from the Illinois side. The keeper of the boat ran away.

At Paducah, Columbus, and Fort Pillow the numerous flags of truce sent in by the enemy have been dishonored in every case, by movements, attacks, murders, horse-stealing, &c., while negotiating, being used to cover these acts. I have kept Paducah and Columbus supplied with means of defense, and afforded to each sufficient re-enforcements from transient detachments, having very few men attached to my local commands.

Last night I sent a battery and 200 infantry to take position on Illinois shore, above Mound City. The naval authorities have co-operated most efficiently.

In haste, yours, &c.,

M. BRAYMAN,
Brigadier-General, Commanding.

PADUCAH, *April* 17, 1864.

General BRAYMAN:

Report, believed to be perfectly reliable, has just come in that Buford and Faulkner, strongly re-enforced, are at Lovelaceville, believed to be coming here. I have everything in readiness for them. The cavalry has arrived.

S. G. HICKS,
Colonel, Commanding.

CAIRO, ILL., *April* 17, 1864.

Maj. Gen. W. T. SHERMAN,
Nashville, Tenn.:

Major Barnes, now on duty at Paducah with his battalion of Sixteenth Kentucky Cavalry, 400 strong, not mounted, has been ordered to Louisville. This leaves Colonel Hicks with about 120 white troops; the rest black. If they must go, I request a regiment from some other source. I dare not leave Colonel Hicks in so feeble a condition. The remnants of Hawkins' command, about 60, which have gathered here, are ordered to Memphis, leaving me with not a mounted man.

M. BRAYMAN,
Brigadier-General, Commanding.

SAINT LOUIS, MO., *April* 17, 1864—5.30 p. m.
(Received 9.30 p. m.)

Lieut. Gen. U. S. GRANT,
Culpeper, Va.:

The Ninth Iowa will be sent as ordered. The Twelfth Missouri and Thirteenth Illinois Cavalry can follow, but they are not mounted, nor have we any other mounted troops within 120 miles of Saint Louis. Judging from the last news of the rebels going south from Fort Pillow, and the tenor of your dispatches, I shall await your orders before sending forward foot troops.

W. S. ROSECRANS,
Major-General.

SPECIAL ORDERS, } HDQRS. ARMIES OF THE UNITED STATES,
No. 14.   } In Field, Culpeper C. H., Va., April 17, 1864.

I. Brig. Gen. Henry Prince, U. S. Volunteers, is hereby relieved from duty with the Army of the Potomac, and will report in person without delay to Maj. Gen. W. T. Sherman, commanding Military Division of the Mississippi, for orders. The quartermaster's department will furnish transportation for horses.

*   *   *   *   *   *   *

III. Maj. Gen. David Hunter, U. S. Volunteers, will proceed with dispatches and instructions from the lieutenant-general commanding to Maj. Gen. N. P. Banks, commanding Department of the Gulf, at New Orleans, or wherever it may be necessary to enable him to deliver the same to General Banks in person. Upon the delivery of his dispatches and the execution of his orders he will report in person to these headquarters.

By command of Lieutenant-General Grant :

T. S. BOWERS,
Assistant Adjutant-General.

SPECIAL ORDERS, } WAR DEPT., ADJT. GENERAL'S OFFICE,
No. 150.   } Washington, April 17, 1864.

*   *   *   *   *   *   *

III. Maj. Gen. C. C. Washburn, U. S. Volunteers, will proceed at once to Memphis and relieve Major-General Hurlbut, U. S. Volunteers, in command of the District of West Tennessee.

IV. Major-General Hurlbut will report from Cairo by letter to the Adjutant-General at what point orders will reach him.

By order of the Secretary of War :

E. D. TOWNSEND,
Assistant Adjutant-General.

SPECIAL FIELD ORDERS, } HDQRS. DEPT. OF THE CUMBERLAND,
No. 108.   } Chattanooga, Tenn., April 17, 1864.

*   *   *   *   *   *   *

VI. Maj. Gen. Carl Schurz is hereby relieved from duty with this department and will report in person to Maj. Gen. W. T. Sherman, commanding Military Division of the Mississippi, for assignment.

*   *   *   *   *   *   *

By command of Major-General Thomas :

WM. D. WHIPPLE,
Assistant Adjutant-General.

CULPEPER, *April* 18, 1864—7 p. m.

Major-General SHERMAN,
    Nashville, Tenn. :

Have you any information of movements of troops from Johnston's army to Lee's ?

U. S. GRANT,
Lieutenant-General.

CULPEPER, *April* 18, 1864—7 p. m.

Major-General SHERMAN, *Nashville, Tenn.*:

General Smith has made requisition for 30,000 cavalry horses. It will be impossible to supply half the number. Use dismounted cavalry to guard depots and stations, and relieve infantry to go to the front. I have sent General Prince to command West Kentucky. He will report to you.

U. S. GRANT,
Lieutenant-General.

NASHVILLE, TENN., *April* 18, 1864—11.30 p. m.
(Received 3 a. m., 19th.)

Lieutenant-General GRANT, *Culpeper, Va.*:

General Sooy Smith made his requisition for horses without consultation with me. I did not expect half the number you name, and indeed had already ordered the dismounted cavalry to be used as you suggest. I have full accounts from General Thomas up to date. None of Johnston's army have gone east. There was a talk in Johnston's camp about Hardee's corps going east. Mere camp talk and nothing more.

W. T. SHERMAN,
Major-General.

SAINT LOUIS, *April* 18, 1864.

Maj. Gen. W. T. SHERMAN:

Will the 3,000 head of cattle you require at Cairo be wanted to start with the expedition? The number is so large that I fear I shall have to pay a very high price if I purchase at once. They can be procured, but at not less than 7 cents gross, delivered here. If necessary to have them at once, I will furnish them.

T. J. HAINES,
Colonel and Commissary of Subsistence.

HDQRS. MILITARY DIVISION OF THE MISSISSIPPI,
Nashville, Tenn., April 18, 1864.

Colonel HAINES,
Chief Commissary, Saint Louis:

The price is nothing. I want the Army of the Tennessee to have beef-cattle on the hoof at or near Huntsville by May 1. The easiest way is to send them up to Clifton, on the Tennessee, and drive across. They should come up the Tennessee at the same time with the troops from Cairo.

W. T. SHERMAN,
Major-General.

LOUISVILLE, *April* 18, 1864.

General W. T. SHERMAN:

Telegraphed you on the 16th, directed to Moscow. Am using prompt, and I hope successful, means to get the cattle to Bridgeport by first proximo. I do not intend the commissary department shall be behind in furnishing your supplies. The contractor is here. Am urging him to be up to time. Have seen General Allen. Have his promise that the contractor has cars from Chicago and here for his cattle. Colonel Beckwith and myself leave here for Nashville on first train. Have ordered Major Symonds to buy at once cattle and ship by boat or drive. Have ordered Major Du Barry to buy at once and ship by boat. Have ordered the 1,200 cattle which we had in reserve at Danville, Ky., to be driven at once to Nashville.

C. L. KILBURN,
Lieutenant-Colonel.

LEXINGTON, *April* 18, 1864.

General SHERMAN :

I have about 3,000 men now mounted. General Schofield has called for 1,000 of them. Can I not get the Third Iowa, now in Saint Louis. to in part replace those taken by General Schofield ? I am trying in every direction to get horses. The whole force I now have, 6,000 strong, will be armed and equipped by the 1st of May. Please have the Third Iowa Cavalry sent to me.

GEORGE STONEMAN,
Major-General.

HDQRS. MILITARY DIVISION OF THE MISSISSIPPI,
Nashville, Tenn., April 18, 1864.

General McPHERSON,
    Huntsville :

I don't want the detachments now at Cairo to go up to Savannah till a few good regiments get there to serve as a nucleus. Colonel Potts reports his regiment will be at Cincinnati to-night, and I will order it to Cairo. My programme of this morning shows that the force up the Tennessee is only to scout as far out as the head of the Hatchie.

W. T. SHERMAN,
Major-General.

HUNTSVILLE, ALA.,
April 18, 1864.

Maj. Gen. W. T. SHERMAN,
    Nashville :

I telegraphed General Dodge to know what troops he could send from Pulaski under General Sweeny to West Tennessee, to operate against Forrest and still guard his portion of the railroad.

He says, without drawing forces from Decatur, he can only send four regiments. In view of the threatening demonstrations against Decatur, I do not deem it safe to withdraw any troops from there, and four regiments will be too small a force to send against Forrest across the Tennessee, unless united with some force from Cairo.

JAS. B. McPHERSON,
Major-General, Commanding.

HDQRS. MILITARY DIVISION OF THE MISSISSIPPI,
Nashville, April 18, 1864.

General McPHERSON,
Huntsville:

Dispatch of 17th from Woodville is received. General Slocum started this morning for Vicksburg. I have sent Sturgis down to Memphis to give life to that command, and want to put some of your furloughed men down to the neighborhood of Purdy as soon as possible. I will telegraph to Indiana for Gresham.

W. T. SHERMAN,
Major-General, Commanding.

HDQRS. DEPARTMENT AND ARMY OF THE TENNESSEE,
Huntsville, Ala., April 18, 1864.

Brig. Gen. W. Q. GRESHAM,
Comdg. Fourth Division, 17th Army Corps, Cairo, Ill. :

GENERAL : You will proceed immediately to organize the detachments of regiments belonging to the Fourth Division (a list of which is herewith inclosed*), which may be at Cairo and vicinity, into an effective force, to which you will add any veteran regiments belonging to the Third or Fourth Divisions, Leggett's and Crocker's, of the Seventeenth Army Corps, which may be returning from furlough, in order to bring your command up to 3,000 or upward.

Select from the artillery of the Fourth Division one 6-gun battery, or at the rate of four guns for a thousand men, to accompany you. Embark with this force on transports as soon as possible and proceed up the Tennessee River to Savannah or Crump's Landing, where you will disembark and push out to Purdy and the Hatchie to operate against Forrest and cut off his retreat if possible.

You should come up provided with 100 rounds of infantry ammunition to the man, besides that in cartridge-boxes, and 200 rounds of artillery ammunition per piece; fifteen days' rations of hard bread and small-stores, and ten days' rations of meat, and without camp and garrison equipage. Bring along transportation enough to carry your supplies and ammunition, cooking utensils for the men, and the minimum amount of baggage for the officers. The pioneer corps of the Fourth Division should accompany you.

On your arrival at Purdy you will have to be governed very much by your own judgment and discretion, the great object being to whip Forrest and prevent him from getting away with his plunder. Forrest's style of fighting is bold and dashing, and he will maneuver to attack you in front and on both flanks at the same time. In this case dash through him in force, and then sweep around him on the detached parties. Try and open communication with Memphis so as to act in conjunction with the force operating from there.

Should you learn that Forrest has crossed the Tennessee River, and be certain of the fact, you will move to Pulaski via Savannah or Clifton. Communicate with me as often as possible via Clifton.

Very respectfully, your obedient servant,

JAS. B. McPHERSON,
Major-General.

---

* Not found.

                                                    APRIL 18, 1864.
Brig. Gen. G. M. DODGE,
          Decatur:
    Harris has returned from Brown's Ferry. Reports a regiment of
cavalry about 4 miles from Brown's Ferry and 8 miles from Decatur,
at a point where the Decatur road crosses the Brown's Ferry and
Hillsborough road. Their pickets were seen on other side of river
near the ferry last night. A refugee from the neighborhood of
Moulton some days since reported the enemy in front of Decatur,
some 5,000 strong, almost entirely mounted, with eight pieces of
artillery. A scout has started from the ferry to go in rear of enemy
over the mountains; will probably not return till the last of this
week. Is there anything of interest at Decatur this a. m.? A detail
from the Ninth Ohio Cavalry is watching the river in neighborhood
of Brown's Ferry and to the west.
                                            J. W. BARNES,
                                    Assistant Adjutant-General.

                                           DECATUR, *April* 18, 1864.
Major-General McPHERSON,
          Huntsville:
    I cannot believe that the enemy will attack this place; they may
have had it in view, but knowing our strength they give it up; if
they should we have force enough. I have watched more closely for
a move to our right, either with a view of joining Forrest or crossing the river. To-day they show themselves on the front, but in no
large force. Colonel Rowett sends dispatch that he can hear of no
force of any amount opposite him from Elk River to Savannah. I
only know of three regiments of infantry in the valley, except their
mounted infantry. Clanton, Roddey, Patterson, and Colonel Johnson are no doubt in the valley. This is a large mounted force, and
it appears to me must have something in view besides watching
Decatur. I will endeavor to watch their movements, and should
they go to Forrest or cross get timely notice of it.
                                            G. M. DODGE.

                HDQRS. DEPARTMENT AND ARMY OF THE TENNESSEE,
                            Huntsville, Ala., April 18, 1864.
Maj. Gen. JOHN A. LOGAN,
          Commanding Fifteenth Army Corps:
    GENERAL: The following instructions relative to transportation
for the army in the field will at once be communicated to your command:
    First. Each regiment, battery, or detachment will be allowed two
wagons and no more; one for the cooking utensils of the men, the
other for the baggage and mess of the officers.
    Second. Each brigade headquarters will be allowed two wagons
and no more.
    Third. Each division headquarters will be allowed three wagons
and no more.
    Fourth. The remaining teams of the command will be organized
into an ordnance and supply train—the ordnance train under the

direct supervision of the ordnance officer of the division, who will be assisted by a competent quartermaster detailed for that purpose; the supply train of the division under the immediate control of the division quartermaster, assisted by the quartermaster of the command, who must not lose sight of their teams. Quartermasters must be present to superintend the moving of their trains in the morning, and will see them parked for the night. This must not be left for the wagon-masters.

Fifth. Not a tent will be taken with the army, and officers will govern themselves accordingly.

All surplus baggage must be thrown out and disposed of at once, and the army placed in a condition to move.

By order of Major-General McPherson :

WM. T. CLARK,
Assistant Adjutant-General.

(Same to Hurlbut, Dodge, Leggett, and Crocker.)

NASHVILLE. *April* 18, 1864.

COMMANDING OFFICER,
  Memphis:

Lieutenant-General Grant has made the following order : He has ordered three regiments from Saint Louis to Cairo with which to reenforce Paducah, Cairo, and Columbus, and to feel out to Union City. Union City must not be garrisoned, but simply visited by scouts and patrols. As soon as possible a division or strong brigade of General McPherson's command (due from furlough about the 20th instant), General Gresham, if possible, will hasten up the Tennessee River, leave its wagons and incumbrances at Clifton, but proceed to Savannah and scout across by Purdy to the head of the Hatchie. Maj. Gen. H. W. Slocum has gone to Vicksburg to assume command there, and General Sturgis has started this morning to assume command of all the cavalry at and near Memphis, with which he will sally out and attack Forrest wherever he may be. General Grierson may seize all the horses and mules in Memphis to mount his men and be ready for the arrival of General Sturgis, and General Buckland's brigade of infantry should be ready to move out with the cavalry. General Mower's division, now up Red River, will be detained at Memphis on its way up river, and A. J. Smith will come, as ordered, up the Tennessee River. General C. C. Washburn is ordered to Memphis and General Hunt to Columbus. General Hurlbut will take post for the present at Cairo, and Hicks remain in command at Paducah.

All the troops along the Mississippi River must act with vigor against any portion of the enemy within reach. Paducah, Cairo, Columbus, Memphis, Vicksburg, and Natchez must be held, and all minor points exposed should be evacuated.

The troops at Memphis should act by land ; those at Vicksburg should operate up Yazoo at Yazoo City, and threaten Grenada. All former orders will be modified to suit this general plan.

W. T. SHERMAN,
Major-General.

(Same to McPherson, Brayman, and Slocum.)

MEMPHIS, TENN.,
April 18, 1864.

Brig. Gen. B. H. GRIERSON,
Comdg. Cavalry Division, Sixteenth Corps:

GENERAL : In a dispatch received yesterday from Maj. Gen. W. T. Sherman occurs the following passage : "Buckland's brigade and Grierson's cavalry can and should hunt up Forrest and whip him." You will furnish me in writing your official opinion whether or not this opinion of the major-general can be carried out.

Your obedient servant,
S. A. HURLBUT,
Major-General.

(Same to Buckland.)

HEADQUARTERS SIXTEENTH ARMY CORPS,
Memphis, Tenn., April 18, 1864.

Brig. Gen. B. H. GRIERSON,
Commanding Cavalry:

GENERAL : Chalmers and McCulloch passed through La Grange on Saturday night, and report Forrest following them on his route down to meet the Federals in Alabama.

Take your disposable cavalry and push out. Their artillery is below La Grange.

Your obedient servant,
S. A. HURLBUT,
Major-General.

HDQRS. CAVALRY DIVISION, SIXTEENTH ARMY CORPS,
Memphis, Tenn., April 18, 1864.

Col. GEORGE E. WARING,
Commanding First Brigade Cavalry :

COLONEL : In pursuance with instructions from Maj. Gen. S. A. Hurlbut you will prepare your whole effective force, with as much rations and ammunition as can be carried on the persons of the men, to move before daylight to-morrow morning. The artillery will not be taken. Report in person to these headquarters this afternoon.

By order of Brig. Gen. B. H. Grierson :
S. L. WOODWARD,
Assistant Adjutant-General.

HEADQUARTERS SIXTEENTH ARMY CORPS,
Memphis, Tenn., April 18, 1864—2 p. m.

Maj. Gen. W. T. SHERMAN,
Comdg. Mil. Div. of the Mississippi, Nashville, Tenn. :

Chalmers and McCulloch, with artillery, passed south of La Grange on Saturday night. They report themselves moving to Alabama to meet the Federals. Forrest is reported behind them on same route. Grierson is ordered out. Report just arrived.

S. A. HURLBUT,
Major-General.

HEADQUARTERS SIXTEENTH ARMY CORPS,
Memphis, Tenn., April 18, 1864.

Maj. L. S. WILLARD,
Actg. Asst. Adjt. Gen., Hdqrs. Army of the Tennessee:

SIR: In obedience to Circular Orders, dated headquarters Department of the Tennessee, Huntsville, Ala., April 11, 1864, received this day, I have the honor to report the effective strength of this corps, where posted, and by whom commanded:

Five regiments of the First Division, ten regiments of the Third Division, and two batteries, now up Red River, under command of Brig. Gen. A. J. Smith, on an expedition. Total present for duty, equipped, by last return, 7,770.

The Second and Fourth Divisions, Brig. Gen. G. M. Dodge commanding, headquarters at Athens. Ala., occupying Pulaski, Tenn., Athens and Decatur, Ala.; total present for duty, equipped, by last return, 11,827.

The garrison of Memphis. Brig. Gen. R. P. Buckland commanding. 6,325 total present for duty, equipped.

The District of Cairo, Brig. Gen. M. Brayman commanding, comprising post of Paducah, Col. S. G. Hicks, Fortieth Illinois Volunteers, commanding, 332; post of Cairo, Col. J. I. Rinaker, One hundred and twenty-second Illinois Volunteers, commanding, 237; post of Columbus, Col. W. H. Lawrence, Thirty-fourth New Jersey Volunteers, commanding, 1,138; post of Island 10, Capt. R. M. Ekings, Thirty-fourth New Jersey Volunteers, commanding, 214; totals present for duty, equipped, by last returns.

The Cavalry Division, Brig. Gen. B. H. Grierson commanding, at and near Memphis, Tenn., 2,001 present for duty, equipped, by last returns; comprised in part of the fragments of regiments at home on furlough, but poorly mounted, and chiefly useful for scouting and picket duty.

No returns or reports received from the troops at Vicksburg and Natchez.

I have the honor to be, sir, very respectfully, your obedient servant,

S. A. HURLBUT.
Major-General, Commanding Sixteenth Corps.

P. S.—The garrison of Memphis consists of: White infantry, 2,159; white artillery, 606; colored infantry, 2,312; colored artillery, 1,257.

HEADQUARTERS SIXTEENTH ARMY CORPS,
Memphis, Tenn., April 18, 1864.

Maj. Gen. W. T. SHERMAN,
Comdg. Mil. Div. of the Mississippi, Nashville, Tenn.:

Dispatch of 16th is received. I shall go to Cairo with my personal staff Tuesday or Wednesday. I shall leave corps headquarters here until you designate the commander of the Sixteenth Corps. I shall expect specific orders at Cairo. You will hear more fully from me by mail.

S. A. HURLBUT,
Major-General.

HEADQUARTERS SIXTEENTH ARMY CORPS,
Memphis, Tenn., April 18, 1864.
Maj. Gen. W. T. SHERMAN,
   Commanding Military Division of the Mississippi:
   GENERAL: Your telegram of the 16th instant was received last night. I shall of course obey the orders contained, although they are exceedingly vague. I am ready to turn over the command of the Sixteenth Army Corps whenever you will oblige me by designating the officer to whom it shall be turned over.
   As I command only the Sixteenth Army Corps I cannot consider that Lieutenant-General Grant means by "relieving me" anything else than relieving me of that command. Duty, however, to the public service requires that in the order relieving me some other officer be designated to take the command.
   I shall proceed to Cairo, as ordered, as soon as I can sign off the official records and papers of the corps, and shall go to-morrow or Wednesday. As I already command the troops at Cairo I am somewhat at a loss to understand your directions "to take command there," but expect to find full instructions from you on my arrival.
   Portions of your telegram are of such a nature as justify and, in fact, require that I should demand a court of inquiry, where all the facts and circumstances may be developed, and your charge of "marked timidity" be proven or disproven. When that shall have been done, and the responsibility of the late disasters fixed upon the proper parties. I shall do myself the justice of tendering to the President of the United States my resignation of a commission which cannot be advantageously held by me in subordination to officers who entertain and express the opinions contained in your dispatch.
   I have the honor to be, general, your obedient servant,
                              S. A. HURLBUT,
                                    Major-General.

———

HEADQUARTERS MILITARY DIVISION OF THE MISSISSIPPI,
Nashville, Tenn., April 18, 1864.
General BRAYMAN,
      Cairo:
   Don't diminish the garrison at Paducah for the present. General Grant notifies me he has ordered three regiments from Saint Louis to Cairo. When they reach Cairo you can with them re-enforce Paducah and Columbus, and then the battalion of the Sixteenth Kentucky can go to Louisville as ordered.
                              W. T. SHERMAN,
                                    Major-General.

———

HEADQUARTERS SIXTEENTH ARMY CORPS,
Memphis, Tenn., April 18, 1864.
The honorable SECRETARY OF WAR:
   Having received the following dispatch from Maj. Gen. W. T. Sherman, commanding Military Division of the Mississippi, I am compelled in justice to myself and the Government to ask that a court of inquiry may be ordered at the earliest possible moment, to ascertain and report upon my administration of military affairs in connection with the recent incursion of Forrest into Tennessee and

Kentucky, and to determine whether with the force under my command and under the orders received from my superiors the disasters which have occurred could have been prevented.

I am not willing to rest under the imputation of "marked timidity," and request what I believe is assured me by the Regulations—an inquiry by competent and disinterested officers.

The telegram referred to is subjoined.*

I have the honor to be, your obedient servant,

S. A. HURLBUT,
Major-General of Volunteers.

[First indorsement.]

HDQRS. MILITARY DIVISION OF THE MISSISSIPPI,
Nashville, Tenn., April 23, 1864.

Respectfully forwarded.

If General Hurlbut wants an inquiry there is no objection.

W. T. SHERMAN,
Major-General, Commanding.

[Second indorsement.]

APRIL 30, 1864.

Respectfully forwarded to Lieutenant-General Grant for his orders.

H. W. HALLECK,
Major-General, Chief of Staff.

[Third indorsement.]

HEADQUARTERS ARMIES OF THE UNITED STATES,
In Field, Culpeper Court-House, Va., May 2, 1864.

Respectfully returned.

It is not consistent with the interests of the public service to convene the court of inquiry demanded by Maj. Gen. S. A. Hurlbut. Whether his course was "timid" or not, it has been unsatisfactory. The propriety of relieving a subordinate officer when it is believed that some other officer can act more efficiently is beyond question, and it is not necessary or proper to assign specific reasons for such a change or to convene a court to determine whether injustice has been done the officer so relieved.

U. S. GRANT,
Lieutenant-General.

HDQRS. CAVALRY DIVISION, SIXTEENTH ARMY CORPS,
Memphis, Tenn., April 18, 1864.

Brig. Gen. L. THOMAS,
Adjutant-General, U. S. Army:

GENERAL: I beg leave through you to invite the attention of the War Department to the condition of the cavalry under my command.

First. Eight regiments, the oldest and most experienced in the command, have re-enlisted as veterans, and been sent home on furlough. Two of these, the Third Michigan and Seventh Kansas, were

---

* See Sherman to Hurlbut, April 16, p. 381.

sent away in January, and should have returned four weeks since. I am unofficially informed that they are in Saint Louis awaiting horses, and that the Seventh Kansas has been ordered to report to Department of the Missouri.

The term of furlough of the other six regiments will expire from the 1st to the 10th of May. This leaves me an aggregate effective force of about 3,500 effective men, composed mostly of three new and inexperienced regiments, and the remnants of the regiments which have been sent home on furlough. Of this force less than 2,000 are available as cavalry in consequence of the lack of horses, only about 1,500 horses having been furnished to this command during the past ten months. Many of these horses are not effective for a long expedition in consequence of the exceeding lack of forage.

Second. But for the lack of horses and the non-return of the Third Michigan and Seventh Kansas Cavalry, I should be able to put into the field a mounted force of at least 5,000 men.

I would most respectfully suggest that measures be taken to procure horses for the purpose of mounting this command ; or that the command be entirely dismounted and schooled in infantry tactics ; as in its present condition it is of more expense to the Government than its efficiency would justify.

As a measure for mounting the command, I would respectfully suggest that a price be set by the Government at which horses will be bought, and that the people of the North be required to furnish the requisite number of horses at such prices ; and to this end that means be used to impress horses, unless voluntarily furnished at the prices offered.

I would further suggest that corps commanders be empowered to authorize the purchase of horses for their respective commands.

Very respectfully, your obedient servant,

B. H. GRIERSON.

WASHINGTON, *April* 18, 1864—2.30 p. m.

Brigadier-General BRAYMAN,
　　Commanding :

What is the date of the latest news you have from General Banks' expedition up the Red River ? What is its purport ? Answer in cipher.

EDWIN M. STANTON,
　　Secretary of War.

CAIRO, ILL., *April* 18, 1864.
(Received 10.40 p. m.)

Hon. E. M. STANTON,
　　Secretary of War, Washington, D. C. :

General A. J. Smith, of the Sixteenth Army Corps, was within 30 miles of Shreveport at last accounts. General Banks' expedition had not overtaken Smith.

General Sherman has sent for Smith to return immediately and go up the Tennessee. I presume he is overtaken by the messenger. I will report as soon as I hear about General Banks' force.

M. BRAYMAN,
　　Brigadier-General, Commanding.

GENERAL ORDERS, } HDQRS. MIL. DIV. OF THE MISSISSIPPI,
No. 7.   }   *Nashville, Tenn., April* 18, 1864.

I. When troops serving in this military division are transferred from one post to another, or from one department to another department, the orders will embrace transportation for all the wagons, mules, horses, tents, clothing, and camp equipage properly pertaining to such troops.

II. When troops are ordered to march for action, or to be in condition for action, all incumbrances must be left in store at the most safe and convenient point. Mounted officers (general, regimental, or cavalry) will be expected to carry on their own or led horses the necessary bedding and changes of clothing, with forage and provisions for themselves for three days, which must last five days. Infantry officers and soldiers must carry on their persons or on led horses or mules the same ; to which end will be allowed to each company, when praticable, one led horse or pack-mule. Artillery can carry the same on their caissons, so that all troops must be in readiness for motion without wagons for a five days' operation.

III. For longer periods of service, the generals in command of armies, divisions, or brigades will indicate in orders beforehand the number of wagons to each headquarters and subdivision of command. In no event will tents be carried, or chests, or boxes, or trunks. Wagons must be reserved for ammunition proper, for cooking utensils, for provisions consisting exclusively of bread or flour, salt, sugar, coffee, and bacon or pork, in the proportion of thirty days' sugar and coffee, double of salt, twenty days' of bread or flour, and six of pork or bacon. The meat ration must be gathered in the country or driven on the hoof. Officers must be restricted to the same food as soldiers, and the general commanding knows that our soldiers will submit to any deprivation, provided life and health can be sustained and they are satisfied of the necessity.

IV. One or two ambulances and one wagon should follow each regiment. All other wheeled vehicles should be made up into trains of convenient size, always under command of some quartermaster with a proper escort ; and minute instructions should be imparted to the officers in charge of trains as to keeping closed up, doubling up on the roads when they are wide enough, or parking in side fields when there is any cause of delay ahead, so that the long periods of standing in a road, which fatigue the troops so much, may be avoided.

These orders are preliminary.

By order of Maj. Gen. W. T. Sherman :

R. M. SAWYER,
Assistant Adjutant-General.

SPECIAL FIELD ORDERS, } HDQRS. DEPT. OF THE CUMBERLAND,
No. 109.   }   *Chattanooga, Tenn., April* 18, 1864.

*   *   *   *   *

VIII. The Twenty-second Regiment Indiana Volunteers is hereby transferred from the First Brigade, Second Division, Fourth Army Corps, to the Third Brigade, Second Division, Fourteenth Army

Corps, and the Twenty-eighth Kentucky is transferred from the Second Division, Fourteenth Army Corps, to First Brigade, Second Division, Fourth Army Corps.

****

By command of Major-General Thomas:

WM. D. WHIPPLE,
Assistant Adjutant-General.

HEADQUARTERS ARMIES IN THE FIELD,
Culpeper Court-House, Va., April 19, 1864.

Maj. Gen. W. T. SHERMAN,
Commanding Military Division of the Mississippi:

GENERAL : Since my letter to you I have seen no reason to change any portion of the general plan of campaign, if the enemy remain still and allow us to take the initiative. Rain has continued so uninterruptedly until the last day or two that it will be impossible to move, however, before the 27th, even if no more should fall in the mean time. I think Saturday, the 30th, will probably be the day for our general move.

Colonel Comstock, who will take this, can spend a day with you, and fill up many a little gap of information not given in any of my letters.

What I now want more particularly to say is, that if the two main attacks, yours and the one from here, should promise great success, the enemy may, in a fit of desperation, abandon one part of their line of defense and throw their whole strength upon a single army, believing that a defeat with one victory to sustain them is better than a defeat all along their line; and hoping, too, at the same time, that the army meeting with no resistance will rest perfectly satisfied with their laurels, having penetrated to a given point south, thereby enabling them to throw their force first upon one and then on the other.

With the majority of military commanders they might do this. But you have had too much experience in traveling light and subsisting upon the country to be caught by any such ruse. I hope my experience has not been thrown away. My directions, then, would be, if the enemy in your front show signs of joining Lee, follow him up to the full extent of your ability. I will prevent the concentration of Lee upon your front if it is in the power of this army to do it.

The Army of the Potomac looks well, and, so far as I can judge, officers and men feel well.

Yours, truly,

U. S. GRANT,
Lieutenant-General.

HDQRS. MILITARY DIVISION OF THE MISSISSIPPI,
Nashville, Tenn., April 19, 1864.

General THOMAS,
Chattanooga:

I taxed the telegraph for publishing the fact that Hardee's corps was ordered from Johnston to Richmond. This dispatch has led to inquiries of me by General Grant and others as to its truth. Tell the officer who receives the dispatches to be more careful, and I will also make a check here. We must not let Johnston re-enforce Lee. but I understand your later news from the enemy says nothing of this.

W. T. SHERMAN,
Major-General.

NASHVILLE, TENN., *April* 19, 1864—12 midnight.
(Received 2.40 a. m., 20th.)
Lieutenant-General GRANT,
Culpeper, Va.:

Thomas reports by telegraph to-night that he has satisfactory intelligence that no troops have left Dalton for Richmond. His dates from Johnston's camp are as late as the 18th.

W. T. SHERMAN,
Major-General.

HDQRS. MILITARY DIVISION OF THE MISSISSIPPI,
Nashville, Tenn., April 19, 1864.
General JOHN A. RAWLINS,
Chief of General Grant's Staff, Washington, D. C.:

GENERAL: I received a dispatch from General Grant asking me if the report that Johnston was sending off Hardee's corps was true. I have answered that Thomas thinks not. You know how easy such reports get currency. I have read every official report from all quarters very carefully, and the only one which even hints at such a thing is one from Thomas—the words of a deserter, taken down by the usual provost-marshal, under date of April 15, that there was a camp rumor in Johnston's camp when he left that Hardee's corps was to be sent to Virginia ; but subsequent reports describe minutely the position and strength of the rebel army as unchanged since you left, save that a heavy cavalry force is being collected near the Coosa, abreast of Guntersville, evidently for the purpose of watching McPherson. Although I have daily the reports of thousands and tens of thousands marching and raiding all round the compass, yet I have now scouts in from Memphis, who bring in passes and papers from Selma, Montgomery, West Point, Opelika. and Talladega, and from them I learn that things remain as I describe above.

Thomas is gradually drawing down his command to a common focus—Chattanooga.

Schofield has infantry force at Bull's Gap and a small cavalry force beyond, but is preparing to have about 12,000 infantry near Hiwassee at the time appointed—May 1—with his cavalry, under Stoneman, remounting and refitting as fast as possible near Lexington, Ky., whence at the right time I will move them to the Hiwassee. McPherson has Decatur well fortified, and is examining the river carefully to ascertain the best point to cross over. He still is in doubt whether Guntersville or Whitesburg be the place, but one or the other is, and our bridge at Larkin's can, on a short notice, drop down.

This will give him two good points of invasion. I am doing all I can to get forward the necessary stores, and more still to diminish the useless mouths that eat up our substance.

I inclose you two orders,* which are preliminary, but I am resolved when General Grant gives the word to attack Johnston in the manner I have heretofore described, if our men have to live on beef and salt; they will do it if necessary, we know.

As long as cavalry officers can let their horses run down and get a remount by a mere requisition they will bankrupt any Government. Grierson had 7,000 horses when I made up the Meridian count, and Smith and he reported the capture of some 4,000 animals, and yet now the excuse for not attacking Forrest is that he can mount only 2,400 men. Even with that he should have attacked the enemy at Somerville, as it was then known Forrest was up about Paducah with a considerable force, and what was at Somerville was of course only a part and should have been fought at all odds.

At Memphis are Buckland's full brigade of splendid troops, 2,000. Three other white regiments, one of black artillery, in Fort Pickering, 1,200 strong, about 1,000 men floating, who are camped in the fort, near 4,000 black troops; 3,000 enrolled and armed militia, and all of Grierson's cavalry, 10,983, according to my last returns, of which surely not over 3,000 are on furlough. Out of this a splendid force of about 2,500 well-mounted cavalry and 4,000 infantry could have been made up, and by moving to Bolivar could have made Forrest come there to fight or get out.

I have sent Sturgis down to take command of that cavalry and whip Forrest, and, if necessary, to mount enough men to seize any and all the horses of Memphis, or wherever he may go.

The forces of Fort Pillow are not on my returns. I broke it up, and the garrison was composed of a regiment of Tennesseeans enlisting, and four companies of blacks, of which I have no satisfactory report as yet, but have sent for full details. It does seem as though Forrest has our men down there in cow, but I will try new leaders, for I believe our men will fight if led.

I think everything hereabouts is working as well as I can promise, and if A. J. Smith is coming and McPherson's two furloughed divisions reach us I will be ready at the drop of a hat to cross the Tennessee and pitch in.

I sent for the Governor of Kentucky and he is well satisfied with all the steps taken, and undertakes by his militia and the troops now controlled by Burbridge to catch the wandering guerrillas and keep peace in his State.

But we are now independent of Kentucky, for there are here now all the essentials for an army of 80,000 men for six months. Railroad accidents are still happening, but as seldom as we could expect.

I am, &c.,

W. T. SHERMAN,
Major-General, Commanding.

CHATTANOOGA, *April* 19, 1864.

Major-General SHERMAN:

There is no foundation for the report that Johnston is re-enforcing Lee. One of my most reliable men reports as follows: Dalton, April 12.—No change at Dalton. Resaca, April 15.—No change at Resaca or Dalton. Trains full of soldiers going and coming on fur-

---

* The only order found is that of April 18 to commanding officer at Memphis, &c., p. 402. The other inclosure is Thomas to Sherman, April 13, p. 341.

lough. Resaca, April 18.—No change in Dalton. Wash. Johnson and command left here for Dalton at 10 this morning; 400 Florida troops took their places. A large number of wagons, loaded with crackers at Calhoun, have been waiting orders some few days.

Besides the above-mentioned man, I have by the way of others who visit Dalton at least once a week each. They all confirm what he says regarding the position of the enemy there.

GEO. H. THOMAS,
Major-General.

(Copy to Grant from Sherman, April 20.)

HDQRS. MILITARY DIVISION OF THE MISSISSIPPI,
Nashville, Tenn., April 19, 1864.

Major-General THOMAS,
Commanding Department of the Cumberland, Chattanooga:

GENERAL: I have read with interest General Geary's report and your indorsements.* With all the facts before me, especially the complete details of the facts given by your scouts, I have no doubt that Johnston's main army is on the railroad at or near Dalton ; that it is about 40,000 strong, well commanded and in good order, but it cannot move many days' march, except along the line of that road, front and rear ; that he has a good force of cavalry, one part of which is kept to his right rear for food, and that another part, say 4,000 men, are on his left, over about the Blue Mountain Depot, for the same purpose, and to watch the assemblage of the Army of the Tennessee, which he knows threatens his left flank, and which has two good bridges with which to pass the Tennessee at pleasure. This cavalry, with some infantry supports, are seen often at Larkin's and at Decatur, and some skirmishing has been carried on with them, but we want to mask our force by the Tennessee till the right time. Of course, then, McPherson can sweep them from his front as a cobweb.

At Blue Mountain Depot this cavalry gets corn, which is sent up from the line of the railroad and Selma, and this point is the present terminus of that railroad.

It is 10 miles south of Jacksonville, which is 22 miles east by south of Gadsden, which is full 45 miles from Guntersville, the nearest point of the Tennessee. I have no apprehension of a raid on our right, for the reason that the enemy cannot pass the Tennessee, save at isolated points, and then only in small parties ; besides, the stream of troops soon to come up the Tennessee from Cairo, and across to Huntsville, from Savannah and Clifton, will serve to cover that flank. Still we must push our measures to accumulate a surpius of all essentials to the front, so that a temporary interruption will not cripple us or delay our general plans, which remain unchanged.

The only real move I see for Joe Johnston is to strike your line at his nearest point, about Cleveland or Ooltewah, but this he cannot reach without first fighting the Ringgold force. I advise you to group your commands so as to admit of easy and rapid concentration at such point as your judgment approves, and be careful not to accumulate stores anywhere but inside of Chattanooga.

---

*See Part I, p. 663.

The season is now mild, and even surplus tents and all useless baggage should thus be placed, that the troops in camp could pack up and move at the shortest notice. Study all means to save wagons and transportation, at all events till our advance passes the Coosa.

Please continue as heretofore the scout reports. I have two smart girls who have just come in from Memphis via Okolona, Columbus, Selma, Montgomery, West Point, back to Selma, up the railroad to Talladega and Blue Mountain, whence they crossed on foot by way of Gadsden, Black River, Will's Creek, Town Creek, and Larkin's. They saw little or no infantry, and the only cavalry they saw was at the Blue Mountain and close up to the Tennessee River.

I am, &c.,

W. T. SHERMAN,
Major-General, Commanding.

HDQRS. 1ST CAV. DIV., DEPT. OF THE CUMBERLAND,
Cleveland, April 19, 1864.

Brigadier-General WHIPPLE,
Chief of Staff, Department of the Cumberland:

GENERAL : I have the honor to report all quiet in our front. One party of scouts went down to Waterhouse's this morning. The rebel scouts had been there last night. The report in the neighborhood is that it is the intention of the rebels to encamp a regiment of cavalry at King's Bridge. Three of our scouts, who went out dismounted, brought in 2 prisoners, who gave their names as A. D. Gamble, of the Twenty-second Georgia, and A. J. Reagan, of the Sixtieth Georgia Regiment. They were taken about 20 miles from here, in that State, near their homes, where they claim to have been sent to recover from wounds. I sent them to Major-General Howard.

Another party of scouts went about 5 miles below Red Clay. They saw nothing of the enemy, but stopped at the house of a woman who had been visited on Sunday by her husband and son, both of the rebel army. She says that they told her that the rebels were evacuating Dalton ; that there were only 5,000 or 6,000 troops there, and that their army was moving in the direction of Richmond.

I am, general, very respectfully, your obedient servant,

EDWARD M. McCOOK,
Colonel, Commanding.

KNOXVILLE, TENN., *April 19, 1864.*
(Received April 20.)

Major-General SHERMAN :

I have information this evening that Longstreet's three divisions of infantry have gone east as far as Lynchburg ; the last left Bristol on Wednesday, the 13th instant. My informant is a man who was employed on the railroad, and went from Bristol to Lynchburg on the 13th and returned on the 14th. He is believed to be loyal and truthful. Reports from other sources also corroborate this statement. Vaughn's cavalry brigade, from 800 to 1,500 strong, moved, at about the same time, from Kingsport toward North Carolina, by the road leading up the Watauga. This leaves the force in South-west Virginia little more than that which was recently driven through Pound Gap by Colonel Gallup. From all the information obtained while in command here, I estimate the effective strength of Longstreet's three divisions at 12,500. General Foster's estimate was somewhat larger. I state this, as it may be of importance to General Grant in Virginia at this time.

J. M. SCHOFIELD,
Major-General.

(Copy to Grant from Sherman, April 20.)

———

BULL'S GAP, *April 19, 1864.*
Major-General SCHOFIELD,
Commanding:
Reports from the front are that the rebel infantry is near Wythe-ville; their cavalry between Abingdon and Zollicoffer. Two regiments, under Vaughn, said to have gone to North Carolina. The wagon bridge at Lick Creek is completed. Roads get no better, on account of the continuous rain.

J. D. COX,
Brigadier-General.

———

HDQRS. FOURTH DIVISION, SIXTEENTH ARMY CORPS,
Decatur, Ala., April 19, 1864—9 a. m.
Brigadier-General DODGE,
Comdg. Left Wing, Sixteenth Army Corps, Athens:
Scout from Triana reports all quiet. Rebel picket of 4 men has again appeared opposite Triana. No new movement at this point. Our pickets were fired upon at 7 this morning on the Danville road, but no large force in that direction as far as ascertained.

Strong rebel parties in the direction of Somerville. Have sent one company down the river bank on the north side to go as far as the roads will allow.

Lieut. J. J. Calkins, First Michigan Artillery, will go up on train this morning.

JAMES C. VEATCH,
Brigadier-General.

———

HDQRS. MILITARY DIVISION OF THE MISSISSIPPI,
Nashville, Tenn., April 19, 1864.
General McPHERSON,
Huntsville:
I saw General Slocum and had a conversation with him. It would be well for you to write him general instructions as to his district and its resources, its strong points and weak points, and urge him at all times to keep the enemy busy by threats towards Clinton or Yazoo City. Same of the Natchez. That force should not be idle, but send parties inland on both sides of the river.

W. T. SHERMAN,
Major-General.

HDQRS. FOURTH DIVISION, SIXTEENTH ARMY CORPS,
Decatur, Ala., April 19, 1864—8 p. m.
Brigadier-General DODGE,
Athens:

All quiet. Scouting party went down the river bank on north side to Brown's Ferry. Saw nothing, and no signs of crossing. Strong rebel pickets are still kept on the Courtland road. This evening they have advanced a picket on the Somerville road, this side of Flint. Information from scouts indefinite and unsatisfactory. If their statements are reliable a large force is collecting near us.

JAMES C. VEATCH,
Brigadier-General.

———

HUNTSVILLE, *April* 19, 1864.
Maj. Gen. WILLIAM T. SHERMAN,
Nashville:

I think it will be best to order Major-General Hurlbut around with his corps. As soon as A. J. Smith arrives, there will be three divisions of it here, and I am pretty certain he will be better satisfied and do better in the field than at Cairo.

Does not Brigadier-General Ewing command the District of West Kentucky in the Department of the Cumberland, and will we not have to give some other name to General Prince's command? Will New Madrid come within his jurisdiction? His district, I think, should embrace that portion of Kentucky and Tennessee west of the Tennessee River, and north of a line from Big Sandy through Paris to the Obion River, and along this to the Mississippi.

JAS. B. McPHERSON,
Major-General, Commanding.

———

HDQRS. DEPARTMENT AND ARMY OF THE TENNESSEE,
Huntsville, Ala., April 19, 1864.
Maj. Gen. S. A. HURLBUT,
Comdg. Sixteenth Army Corps, Memphis, Tenn.:

GENERAL: Lieut. Gen. U. S. Grant has ordered three regiments from Saint Louis to Cairo, with which to re-enforce Paducah, Cairo, and Columbus, and to feel out to Union City. Union City is not to be garrisoned, but visited frequently by patrols and scouting parties.

Brig. Gen. S. D. Sturgis is en route for Memphis to assume command of all the cavalry in that vicinity, and to move out and attack Forrest wherever he can be found. Direct Brigadier-General Grierson to seize all the horses and mules, or as many as may be necessary, in Memphis to mount your cavalry and have them ready for service when General Sturgis arrives, and have Brigadier-General Buckland's brigade of infantry ready to move out with cavalry.

As soon as it can be done, a force will be organized at Cairo, composed of detachments and veteran regiments belonging to the Seventeenth Army Corps, under Brigadier-General Gresham, and proceed up the Tennessee River, and co-operate with the force from Memphis from the vicinity of Purdy.

Major-General Slocum is en route for Vicksburg and will immediately organize a force and strike at the enemy from Yazoo City and threaten Grenada.

On the return of the Red River expedition, Brigadier-General Mower's division will stop at Memphis and be subject to your orders. The remainder of the force under Brig. Gen. A. J. Smith will move, as heretofore directed, up the Tennessee River via Cairo. Maj. Gen. C. C. Washburn is ordered to Memphis to assume command of the forces in that vicinity. and Brigadier-General Prince to Columbus, Ky. Colonel Hicks remains in command at Paducah.

You will for the present take post at Cairo and assume general control of the movements against Forrest.

All the troops along the Mississippi River must act with vigor against any force of the enemy within striking distance.

Paducah, Cairo, Columbus, Memphis, Vicksburg, and Natchez should be held at all hazards, and all minor points which are exposed should be evacuated.

The colored troops within your jurisdiction are under your control and cannot be moved or their station changed without your orders. There are two regiments of colored troops organized under authority of Brig. Gen. L. Thomas, Adjutant-General, from men in contraband camps not physically qualified for active service, which have never been borne on our returns, but have been employed guarding these camps, under the direction of Colonel Eaton, general superintendent of freedmen.

Very respectfully, your obedient servant,

JAS. B. McPHERSON,
Major-General.

HDQRS. DEPT. AND ARMY OF THE TENNESSEE,
Huntsville, Ala.. April 19, 1864.
Maj. Gen. H. W. SLOCUM,
Comdg. District of Vicksburg. Vicksburg, Miss.:

GENERAL : In pursuance of orders from Lieut. Gen. U. S. Grant, you will immediately make up as large a force as you can from the troops at and in the vicinity of Vicksburg, leaving a sufficient garrison for the place to make it secure against any contingency.

With this force you will operate up the Yazoo River, and push out from Yazoo City to threaten Grenada, in order to prevent any more of Lee's cavalry from being sent to North Mississippi and Tennessee. Strike at the enemy wherever you can. so as to keep him occupied and engage his attention in that quarter.

Frequent demonstrations should be made in the direction of Clinton and Raymond, and the commanding officer at Natchez should be instructed to operate inland from Natchez on both sides of the river very often.

The line of the Big Black from its mouth up to Birdsong's Ferry and thence across to Haynes' Bluff should be held, and the latter point especially, which gives us control of the Yazoo River, should not be given up except in an emergency. Consult with the officers in command of the gun-boats up the Yazoo River, who will co-operate with you.

. It is not expected that you will with your present force occupy Yazoo City or any point in the interior permanently, but make expeditions to them, when it can be done advantageously.

Vicksburg and Natchez must be held at all hazards, and the enemy prevented from obtaining a lodgment on the river to prevent the passage of boats.

The Government having adopted the policy of leasing out the abandoned plantations and giving employment to the freedmen, you will of course extend to them such protection as you can; but you will have to look at the matter from a military point of view and keep your force well in hand for defensive as well as offensive purposes; the holding of Vicksburg and Natchez and keeping the navigation of the river unobstructed being paramount to every other consideration. The plan of establishing small isolated posts along the river is bad, and should not be carried out to any extent.

A few posts well located, with strong defensive works to enable the garrison to hold out against a greatly superior force until re-enforcements can be sent them, with active scouting parties and patrols, is all that can be done by the land forces, and the gun-boats and Marine Brigade must do the balance by patrolling the river.

When your force is increased by the return of veteran regiments and recruits so that the circumstances of the case will warrant it, a post at Yazoo City will most effectually cover the country between the Yazoo River and the Mississippi. The force sent up there must be strong and amply sufficient to take care of itself. Of this you must be the judge.

We have now held Vicksburg ten months, and there are many people in the city doing business under the protection of the military authorities. It is but right and proper that they should be ready and willing to assist in defending their property in case of emergency. To this end you will cause all the men capable of bearing arms to be enrolled and organized into home guard companies. To these companies, when organized, you can direct the issue of arms, accouterments, caps, and blouses, in order to give them a uniform appearance, and they should be required to drill at least twice a week. Select a building or buildings conveniently located for armories and drill-rooms for them, and notify all concerned that unless they enter into this matter promptly and willingly they will be required to close their business and leave the district.

Very respectfully, your obedient servant,

JAS. B. McPHERSON,
Major-General.

HDQRS. DEPARTMENT AND ARMY OF THE TENNESSEE,
Huntsville, Ala., April 19, 1864. (Received 21st.)

Major-General SHERMAN,
Comdg. Military Division of the Mississippi, Nashville:

GENERAL: I send by Lieutenant-Colonel Macfeely letters of instruction to Major-General Hurlbut, Major-General Slocum, and Brigadier-General Brayman, based on the telegraph letter of instructions from Lieutenant-General Grant.

Will you please read and forward them if they do not contravene any orders you may have issued. They were written before the receipt of your telegram suggesting the propriety of ordering Major-General Hurlbut to the field, headquarters at Decatur. I have been a good deal in the dark in relation to the orders and instructions which have been issued to General Hurlbut and General Brayman.

I did not know that Fort Pillow was garrisoned, and the last return in this office gives no such post. I knew that it was garrisoned by our troops at one time (the Fifty-second Indiana being stationed there), but I supposed it was evacuated when that regiment was ordered away. It is a deplorable affair, but will in the end I am certain be most damaging to the rebels.

Very respectfully, your obedient servant,

JAS. B. McPHERSON,
Major-General.

HDQRS. FIRST DIVISION, DISTRICT OF KENTUCKY,
Lexington, Ky., April 19, 1864.

Lieutenant-Colonel FAIRLEIGH,
Acting Assistant Adjutant-General, Louisville, Ky.:

COLONEL: Letters received from Colonels True and Brown state that they hear of no rebels in large force in the eastern part of the State. Small commands are prowling through the country depredating and foraging on the citizens. Would it not be best to send one of my brigades to the vicinity of Irvine and one to Mount Sterling, leaving one at this place? They can be supplied with forage and subsistence from this point. If this arrangement is indorsed by the general commanding it will enable me to protect the citizens in counties beyond the above-named points; also rid the country of rebel bands.

Respectfully, your obedient servant,

E. H. HOBSON,
Brigadier-General.

HDQRS. FIRST DIVISION, DISTRICT OF KENTUCKY,
Lexington, Ky., April 19, 1864.

Col. JOHN M. BROWN,
Commanding at Irvine, Ky.:

COLONEL: Your communication of 18th instant was received to-day. You are at liberty to move a force through Hayward, and if possible intercept any force in that vicinity retreating from Colonel Gallup.

Your rations will leave to-day. I design in a few days sending Colonel Hanson, with the Thirty-seventh and Fifty-second Kentucky, in the vicinity of Irvine, making that place the headquarters of the Third Brigade. Forage and subsistence will be sent from this place. This arrangement will enable me to scout the country in every direction; also give protection to Irvine, Richmond, and Winchester.

The Second Brigade will be sent to Mount Sterling or Glenn's Mills, and will co-operate with First Brigade, Colonel Gallup, and Third Brigade, Colonel Hanson.

Respectfully,

E. H. HOBSON,
Brigadier-General.

FRANKFORT, KY.,
April 19, 1864.

General E. H. HOBSON:

John D. Hall, commanding recruits at Harrodsburg, with a squad of armed men, forcibly rescued John Patterson, a recruit, on trial before the judge for felony. The court cannot progress without pro-

tection. Send a mounted company or two to-morrow to Harrodsburg to protect the court, with orders to arrest Patterson and Hall
and deliver them to the civil authorities. Answer.

THOS. E. BRAMLETTE,
Governor.

SALYERSVILLE, *April* 19, 1864.

Brig. Gen. E. H. HOBSON:
Colonel Gallup is at Paintsville. I have communicated with him.
The enemy have retired. They passed through Pound Gap on Friday. There is nothing to fight in this section. In my opinion no
troops are needed in this vicinity at present. The Eleventh Michigan marches for Mount Sterling immediately, via Hazel Green; will
reach Mount Sterling by noon on the 20th. I will be at Gill's Mills
to-morrow, and will await orders from you. Please send two days'
rations for 900 men to Mount Sterling at once.

C. J. TRUE,
Colonel.

LEXINGTON, *April* 19, 1864.

Lieut. Col. THOMAS B. FAIRLEIGH,
Acting Assistant Adjutant-General, Louisville, Ky.:
No rebels this side of Pound Gap. They retreated through gap
Friday last. Colonels True and Gallup both heard from. Eleventh
Michigan returning to this place. Colonel True will remain at Gill's
Mills until further orders.

E. H. HOBSON,
Brigadier-General.

HEADQUARTERS SIXTEENTH ARMY CORPS,
Memphis. Tenn., April 19, 1864.

Maj. Gen. J. B. MCPHERSON,
Huntsville, Ala.:
I am credibly informed that Polk's force, 17,000 strong, including
Lee's and Jackson's cavalry, passed Starkville on 11th April for
Huntsville. Forrest's force is returning south, via La Grange and
Saulsbury.

S. A. HURLBUT,
Major-General.

HDQRS. MILITARY DIVISION OF THE MISSISSIPPI,
Nashville, Tenn., April 19, 1864—4.30 p. m.

Lieutenant-General GRANT,
Washington:
General Hurlbut reports the Mobile and Ohio Railroad done from
Mobile to Okolona, and that it will be finished to Corinth in a week.
I don't believe it, but, even if true, when Banks strikes it near Mobile
it will be worse than useless to the enemy.

W. T. SHERMAN,
Major-General.

CAIRO, *April* 19, 1864.

Maj. Gen. W. T. SHERMAN,
Nashville, Tenn. :

Your plan of operations received. I think Forrest will be south of the Hatchie before the movements can be made. He is moving off with his plunder. Do you wish me to forward copy to General Hurlbut at Memphis? I have some information of an attempt upon communications by the rivers and the Nashville road.

M. BRAYMAN,
Brigadier-General.

CAIRO, ILL., *April* 19, 1864.
(Received 20th.)

Maj. Gen. W. T. SHERMAN :

Captain Pennock has unofficial letter from Red River, from which it appears that Banks and Smith had a severe battle with heavy loss near Mansfield, below Shreveport, receiving a check, but beating off the enemy. This may delay the return of Smith. We expect more authentic accounts to-morrow. Particulars are given, but not entirely reliable.

M. BRAYMAN,
Brigadier-General.

GENERAL ORDERS, }   HDQRS. MIL. DIV. OF THE MISSISSIPPI,
No. 8.   }   *Nashville, Tenn., April* 19, 1864.

I. Provisions will no longer be issued to citizens at military posts south of Nashville. When citizens cannot procure provisions in the country there is no alternative but they must remove to the rear.

II. Provisions must not be sold to any persons save officers in the service of the United States, and the hired men employed by the quartermaster's or other departments of the Government, at a rate not to exceed one ration per day. Commanding officers will give their personal attention to this matter, as it is of vital importance. It is idle for us to be pushing forward subsistence stores if they are lavished and expended on any persons except they belong to the army proper.

By order of Maj. Gen. W. T. Sherman :

R. M. SAWYER,
Assistant Adjutant-General.

GENERAL ORDERS, }   HDQRS. MIL. DIV. OF THE MISSISSIPPI,
No. 9.   }   *Nashville, Tenn., April* 19, 1864.

Col. Amos Beckwith, additional aide-de-camp and commissary of subsistence, U. S. Army, having reported at these headquarters, in compliance with Special Orders, No. 146, War Department, Adjutant-General's Office, current series, is announced as chief commissary of the M tar Division of the Mississippi, and will be respected accordingly.ili y

By order of Maj. Gen. W. T. Sherman :

R. M. SAWYER,
Assistant Adjutant-General.

GENERAL ORDERS, | HDQRS. DEPT. AND ARMY OF THE TENN.,
No. 4. }   *Huntsville, Ala., April* 19, 1864.

I. The provost-marshal's department of the Army and Department of the Tennessee will be composed of one provost-marshal-general, one provost-marshal for each corps, and one assistant provost-marshal for each division of a corps.

II. The provost-marshal and assistants will be appointed by respective corps and division commanders, and will be considered as part of the staff. They will receive instructions from the provost-marshal-general of the department as to their general duties and will make such reports as he may require, but will be subject to orders from their immediate commanders, as in the case of quartermasters, commissaries, &c.

III. Commanding officers of corps will at once report to these headquarters the name, rank, and regiment of all officers now appointed as provost-marshals and assistants, and will notify the provost-marshal-general of all changes that may be made hereafter.

IV. District and local provost-marshals will be appointed by the provost-marshal-general ; will receive their orders and instructions from him, and may be removed by his order, whenever he may deem it necessary for the good of the service. Commanders of posts may, however, when the exigencies of the service require it, appoint local provost-marshals, subject to the approval of the provost-marshal-general, but will notify him immediately of such appointments ; they will also report to him at once the name and rank of such now on duty at their several posts.

V. The existing rules and regulations for the guidance of district and local provost-marshals will remain in force until otherwise ordered by the provost-marshal-general.

VI. Moneys properly receivable by provost-marshals of districts and posts are such as are usually collected by the municipal authorities of cities, viz : Fines for disorderly conduct, for the violation of orders, for licenses for hacks, drays, barbers, theaters, markets, &c., and for all trade not properly under control of the Treasury Department. All such will be reported to the provost-marshal-general and will be disposed of as he may direct, and must not be confounded with the funds arising from the flour savings of post bakeries, and from such other sources as a post commander is authorized or may find it necessary to draw from, for the creation of a post fund.

By order of Maj. Gen. James B. McPherson :

W. T. CLARK,
Assistant Adjutant-General.

SPECIAL FIELD ORDERS, | HDQRS. DEPT. OF THE CUMBERLAND,
No. 110. }   *Chattanooga, Tenn., April* 19, 1864.

* * * * * *

VIII. The following assignment of batteries is hereby made :

To be assigned to the Twentieth Army Corps : First Division, Twentieth Army Corps—Battery M, First Regiment New York Volunteer Artillery ; Battery I, First Regiment New York Volunteer Artillery. Second Division, Twentieth Army Corps—Battery E, Pennsylvania Independent Artillery ; Thirteenth Independent Battery New York Volunteer Artillery. Third Division, Twentieth Army Corps—Battery C, First Regiment Ohio Volunteer Artillery ;

Battery L, First Regiment Michigan Volunteer Artillery. Fourth Division, Twentieth Army Corps—Ninth Ohio Battery, Twentieth Indiana Battery.

*   *   *   *   *   *   *

XVI. The following changes and assignments of batteries are hereby ordered :

Battery B, First Regiment Ohio Volunteer Artillery, is assigned to duty in the garrison of Bridgeport, Ala., to report to Maj. W. P. Edgarton, First Ohio Volunteer Artillery, commanding garrison artillery. Battery K, First Ohio Volunteer Artillery, Capt. Lewis Heckman, is relieved from further duty at Bridgeport, Ala., and is assigned to duty at Stevenson, Ala., to form the permanent garrison of that post.

The Ninth Ohio Battery, Fourth Division, Twentieth Army Corps, will proceed to Bridgeport, Ala., forthwith, reporting to the chief of artillery, Twentieth Army Corps. The Second Kentucky Battery is relieved from further duty at Decherd and Elk River, and will relieve the Ninth Ohio Battery at Tullahoma, Tenn.

*   *   *   *   *   ◄

By command of Major-General Thomas :

WM. D. WHIPPLE,
Assistant Adjutant-General.

HDQRS. MILITARY DIVISION OF THE MISSISSIPPI,
Nashville, April 20, 1864—7 p. m.

Lieut. Gen. U. S. GRANT,
Comdg. U. S. Armies, Washington, D. C. :

General Schofield reports positive information that Longstreet has gone to Virginia, and has not destroyed the railroad. I have ordered him to feel up as far as Watauga and expect the enemy will break that bridge. If they do not, I will order it done. Hovey can occupy the road above Hiwassee, and Thomas will now collect his whole command from Cleveland to Bridgeport, ready to unite at Chattanooga on a day's notice and be all ready to advance. Schofield only awaits my orders to drop down with his complement to Hiwassee.

Guntersville will, in my judgment, be the place of concentration for McPherson, but his two furloughed divisions have not yet rendezvoused at Cairo, though all his transportation is there ready to come up the Tennessee as soon as the regiments come in.

No authentic news from Red River, although it seems the enemy will have had time to make a concentration at Shreveport. I have the rumor of a check at Mansfield, which must be partial, for Mansfield is back from Red River on the Texas road.

If Banks, Smith, Steele, and the gun-boats all reach Shreveport in concert, they ought to make short work. Still I have nothing satisfactory from that quarter.

Hurlbut reports from Memphis that Forrest has escaped south by way of La Grange. It does seem as though he has not made the least effort to stop him or molest him. He is on his way to Cairo, and I will bring him round to his corps at Decatur. I have not yet heard of Washburn or Prince. If Forrest is below Memphis, ought we not to disturb him by way of the Yazoo and Grenada ?

W. T. SHERMAN,
Major-General, Commanding.

HDQRS. MILITARY DIVISION OF THE MISSISSIPPI,
Nashville, Tenn., April 20, 1864.
General THOMAS, *Chattanooga:*

General Schofield reports positively that Longstreet has retired to Virginia. He will send his cavalry as far as Watauga. He cannot longer have any need of your troops, and you may draw them down quietly to Cleveland. I suppose by this time Hovey's division is up, and can replace yours above the Hiwassee. We hear of fighting up Red River, and our troops are delayed there beyond the time of our calculation.

W. T. SHERMAN,
Major-General.

———

CHATTANOOGA, *April 20, 1864.*
Major-General SHERMAN,
Comdg. Mil. Div. of the Mississippi, Nashville, Tenn.:

Nearly the whole of Howard's corps is already at Cleveland. Hovey passed here to-day. He will be at Charleston, on Hiwassee, day after to-morrow. I have taken measures to repair the railroad from Cleveland to Red Clay at once, and for further repairs as we advance. The enemy remains quiet. A deserter reports to-day some of Roddey's cavalry going from Gadsden toward Guntersville last Thursday, and another reports Johnston's army concentrated on my front, and that he has neither received re-enforcements nor sent any of his troops away.

GEO. H. THOMAS,
Major-General.

———

QUARTERMASTER-GENERAL'S OFFICE,
Washington, D. C., April 20, 1864.
Maj. Gen. GEORGE H. THOMAS,
Comdg. Dept. of the Cumberland, Chattanooga, Tenn.:

GENERAL : Exertions have been made to supply your army with animals. Operations last fall and winter destroyed or broke down in Tennessee and Georgia not less than 30,000 draft animals and an unknown number of cavalry horses. The destruction of cavalry horses in Virginia was also very great, and the country feels the loss. We are short both East and West. Heretofore there have been more animals at Chattanooga and in East Tennessee than it was possible to feed. The animals sent to the rear from East Tennessee and Chattanooga are not yet fit for service. The Quartermaster's Department will do its best, but I think you must move with smaller trains than last year, when, as I was informed at Chattanooga, twenty to thirty days' supplies moved with the army.

General Grant, I understand, has ordered General Rosecrans to send five hundred teams now in Missouri to you. One thousand mules were to reach Nashville from Camp Nelson on the 12th instant. How many mules has the Army of the Cumberland received since 1st November? How many does it now need? In fitting out a marching column of 35,000 troops here, General Grant has decided on giving them 600 wagons only. You have at Nashville 24,000,000 rations and grain for 50,000 animals to 1st January.

I am, very respectfully, your obedient servant,
M. C. MEIGS,
Quartermaster-General.

HEADQUARTERS DEPARTMENT OF THE CUMBERLAND,
Chattanooga, April 26, 1864.

Respectfully referred to Lieut. Col. L. C. Easton, chief quartermaster, Department of the Cumberland, for the information requested by Brig. Gen. M. C. Meigs, Quartermaster-General.

This paper to be returned.

By command of Major-General Thomas :

WM. McMICHAEL,
Major and Assistant Adjutant-General.

[Second indorsement.]

HDQRS. DEPT. OF THE CUMBERLAND, OFFICE CHIEF Q. M.,
Sugar Valley, Ga., May 13, 1864.

Respectfully returned to Brig. Gen. W. D. Whipple, chief of staff.

The Army of the Cumberland has received from the 1st of November, 1863, to this date, 7,502 mules, and now require about 3,000 mules.

L. C. EASTON,
Lieutenant-Colonel and Chief Quartermaster.

LOUISVILLE, *April 20, 1864.*

Maj. Gen. W. T. SHERMAN :

Seven days ago I telegraphed the chief quartermaster at Saint Louis, by authority from Lieutenant-General Grant, to withdraw from the frontier transportation of the Missouri department 3,000 mules for your use. These mules will now be coming in and will be shipped to Nashville as fast as they arrive. I will strip the city teams here of all the good stock, and will derive some 250 good mules and draft horses from this source. Every resource is brought in requisition to add to your transportation. If time were allowed it would be complete.

ROBT. ALLEN,
Brigadier-General.

NASHVILLE, *April 20, 1864.*

General SCHOFIELD,
Knoxville :

I wish you would be certain as to Longstreet's withdrawal, and in what state he has left the railroad from Bull's Gap to Abingdon. I don't intend to operate in that direction, and only want to be sure of the actual state of the railroad, bridges, &c., on our flank and rear when we do move.

W. T. SHERMAN,
Major-General.

KNOXVILLE, *April 20, 1864.*

Major-General SHERMAN :

My information is positive as to condition of the railroad. It is not injured above Greeneville as far as Abingdon. I will send all my cavalry as far up as practicable and ascertain positively as to Longstreet's withdrawal. I think it probable the enemy will destroy the Watauga and Holston bridges on our approach. If he does not, shall we destroy them?

J. M. SCHOFIELD,
Major-General.

CLEVELAND, *April* 20, 1864.

Major-General SCHOFIELD:

General Thomas wished me to ask you how soon you will be able to relieve the troops at Charleston and Columbus. He thinks Columbus ought always to be held by at least a regiment, to prevent raids upon the lines of communication.

O. O. HOWARD,
Major-General, Commanding.

GRAYSVILLE, *April* 20, 1864.

Brigadier-General WHIPPLE,
Assistant Adjutant-General:

A scout sent out last night fell in with some of the faithful in my vicinity. They are ostensibly Union, but gave him in his assumed character of rebel spy all the information they possessed as to my troops, position, &c., as to which they were well informed.

He found where one of Johnston's spies, Taylor by name, had passed the previous night, who had gone on to Chattanooga, Tenn. This spy told the citizen that Johnston was concentrating all his troops in this front. Taylor is now in the neighborhood of Mission Ridge, where there is a citizen who visits town and brings news and papers to him. The spies have a regular trail between Rossville and this place. Nothing new in front.

R. W. JOHNSON,
Brigadier-General.

MOSSY CREEK, *April* 20, 1864.

Major-General SCHOFIELD:

Two companies of cavalry reported to me. One left this morning with the reconnaissance to Dandridge, which will be pushed from here toward Sevierville as far as safety and rations will permit. From all the information I can gather, no ford of Holston between Strawberry Plains and Morristown is practicable.

H. M. JUDAH,
Brigadier-General, Commanding Division.

HEADQUARTERS,
Clifton, Tenn., April 20, 1864.

Col. R. ROWETT,
Bailey's Springs, Ala.:

COLONEL: Yours of the 16th I received last night. Forrest was in Jackson Thursday night. I learn that he received four flesh wounds at Fort Pillow. He is concentrating all his force at Jackson, and has ordered them to be provided with ten days' rations; they are trying to make the impression that they are going to Memphis. One of my scouts assures me that he will cross the river. I think he will, and is watching his opportunity.

Very respectfully, your obedient servant,

J. MURPHY,
Major Fifth Tennessee Cavalry, Commanding Post.

HDQRS. MILITARY DIVISION OF THE MISSISSIPPI,
Nashville, April 20, 1864.

General SCHOFIELD,
Knoxville:

I want to defer the destruction of that railroad or the bridges till the last moment, as it will clearly reveal our plans not to operate up toward Virginia. But if your cavalry reach the Watauga bridge it is useless longer to defer it, and you may order its destruction.

We are waiting for our troops from Red River before acting offensively on the main lines.

W. T. SHERMAN,
Major-General.

MOSSY CREEK, *April 20, 1864.*

Major-General SCHOFIELD:

A Mr. J. W. Thornburgh, who lives on Buffalo Creek, and whose reputation for reliability is good, sends word to Capt. T. D. Edington, captain and acting assistant adjutant-general, at Strawberry Plains, that he (Thornburgh) has from reliable authority that in a few days a raid is to be made on the East Tennessee and Virginia Railroad between the Plains and Morristown. General Vaughn will come down north of Holston and cross at Tanlow's Ford. Another force is to come from North Carolina via Dandridge and form a junction east of the Plains. It is thought that if attempted it will be in considerable force.

I have increased the escort to a forage train for Dandridge this morning to a regiment, for reconnoitering purposes.

Where is Tanlow's Ford?

H. M. JUDAH,
Brigadier-General, Commanding.

HEADQUARTERS ARMY OF THE OHIO,
Knoxville, Tenn., April 20, 1864.

Brigadier-General JUDAH,
Mossy Creek:

I have never heard of Tanlow's Ford. It may be Turley's Ford that is meant; that is nearly on a straight line from Dandridge to Bean's Station, and about 12 miles above the mouth of Mossy Creek. I had reports of a similar character to that of Mr. Thornburgh's several days ago, but they are contradicted by later ones. It will of course be well to be on your guard. The rebels can do but very little damage to the railroad. The only way they can injure us is by capturing some of our detachments. Look out for that. Correspond with General Cox, so as to get what information he may have without unnecessary delay. Have the two squadrons of the Tenth Michigan Cavalry reported to you?

J. M. SCHOFIELD,
Major-General.

———

KNOXVILLE, *April* 20, 1864.
Major-General HOWARD:

General Hovey's division arrived at Chattanooga this morning, and is ordered to Charleston. As soon as he arrives there your troops at Charleston and Columbus can be relieved.

J. M. SCHOFIELD,
Major-General.

———

HDQRS. FIRST DIVISION, DISTRICT OF KENTUCKY,
Lexington, April 20, 1864.
Judge NEWMAN:

DEAR SIR: I received dispatch last night from Governor Bramlette requesting me to send one or two companies of Federal soldiers to Harrodsburg for the protection of circuit court, now in session at that place; also to arrest recruiting officer John D. Hall and recruit John Patterson.

One company left this place this morning under command of Captain White, Thirty-seventh Kentucky Mounted Infantry, with instructions to arrest John Patterson and turn him over to the civil authorities; also to arrest John D. Hall and send him to these headquarters under arrest. The commanding officer of company has instructions not to permit his men to remain about the court-house or court grounds when court is in session. If, however, there should be any interference with the business of the court, you are at liberty to call on the captain commanding for protection. Will you have the kindness to forward a full statement of the facts and conduct of John D. Hall and John Patterson in relation to the recent interference with the business of circuit court in Mercer County? Send statement to my headquarters.

Very respectfully, your obedient servant,

E. H. HOBSON,
Brigadier-General.

———

HDQRS. DEPARTMENT AND ARMY OF THE TENNESSEE,
Huntsville, Ala., April 20, 1864.
Maj. Gen. W. T. SHERMAN,
Comdg. Military Division of the Mississippi, Nashville:

GENERAL: I inclose herewith report from Brigadier-General Dodge in relation to the movements of the enemy in his immediate front, and of Forrest's force in West Tennessee.

I have been in the habit of sending all reports of scouts, &c., to you which have a semblance of reliability, in order that you may compare them with reports from other quarters and thus be more certain of getting at something like the facts in the case.

If Forrest's force is as large as reported, I am of opinion that nothing less than a division under Gresham, or Crocker and Gresham, should be sent up the Tennessee River to Purdy. This force will be isolated and have to rely upon itself, and the morale of Forrest's command no doubt is good and his men will fight determinedly.

If Gresham could be certain of co-operation from Memphis, a less force than a division would answer ; but though he may expect co-operation, and he ought to have it, it will not answer to count upon it too strongly. It will, I am aware, require more time to get a division together, but will not the facts warrant the delay ? I can send three regiments from Pulaski to Clifton to be ready to join him when he comes up.

Gresham received my telegram yesterday and would start for Cairo by first train. The detachments belonging to the Seventeenth Corps which came up from Vicksburg are somewhat scattered, and it will take a little time to get them together.

Major-General Hurlbut stopped one battery at Memphis ; the guns of another were taken off at Columbus and the troops divided up between Columbus, Cairo, Mound City, and Paducah by General Brayman.

Please answer as to whether I shall direct General Gresham to remain in Cairo until he can get a division or its equivalent together, or come up the Tennessee River as soon as he can get about 3,000 men and be joined at Clifton by three regiments of infantry from Pulaski.

Very respectfully, your obedient servant,

JAS. B. McPHERSON,
Major-General.

[Inclosure.]

HDQRS. LEFT WING, SIXTEENTH ARMY CORPS,
Athens, Ala., April 19, 1864.

Maj. Gen. JAMES B. McPHERSON,
Comdg. Dept. and Army of the Tennessee, Huntsville, Ala.:

GENERAL : The enemy south of the river remain as before ; all close up to Decatur. I inclose Colonel Rowett's last dispatch. We have been to their rear in all directions, and they appear to be pretty well closed up.

Reports from West Tennessee indicate that Forrest is making out of the country. I have followed him enough to satisfy me that infantry cannot even get a shot at him, unless it is so weak a force that he is satisfied he can whip it. He watches this country very closely, especially the river from Eastport north, and no doubt anticipates a movement from this direction ; at least this is what the citizens and scouts all say, and so far as I can judge from all reports he has about 6,000 effective men in West Tennessee. It is possible that he may have added 1,000 or 2,000 to it since he went there.

He takes everything without regard to former principles of the owners, and that entire country is feasting him and his officers. I know of a large number who have professed great "love" for our flag who have outdone themselves in toadying to Forrest. It would be a just judgment on West Tennessee if the troops sent there were given orders to burn the entire country, take everything that can walk, and destroy any and every thing a rebel can eat or drink or be of any benefit whatever to them.

I am, general, your obedient servant,

G. M. DODGE,
Brigadier-General.

[Sub-inclosure.]

BAILEY'S SPRINGS, ALA.,
April 18, 1864—5.30 p. m.

Capt. J. W. BARNES,
Assistant Adjutant-General:

SIR: I have this moment received a communication from you, dated April 17, which the courier informs me left your office this morning at 7 o'clock.

The citizen (Thompson) whom I sent to the south of the river a few days since has just returned. He went from Tuscumbia to La Grange, Ala.; he reports that Jackson's command (Twenty-seventh and Thirty-fifth Alabama Mounted Infantry), with Moreland's and Wines' [Warren's?] battalions of cavalry, in all about 1,200 men, moved from Russellville, Ala., on Saturday morning. They reported that they were going to bring on an engagement at Decatur. Everything has left the Valley of Tuscumbia but Colonel Williams' [?] battalion (cavalry), who are stationed at Tuscumbia and patrolling the river, assisted by a great many citizens. He could not hear anything of Forrest, but refugees reported him near Memphis on Thursday last. My scouts have not yet returned from Clifton.

I have the honor to remain, sir, your obedient servant,

RICHARD ROWETT,
Colonel.

HEADQUARTERS LEFT WING, SIXTEENTH ARMY CORPS,
Athens, Ala., April 20, 1864.

Lieut. Col. WILLIAM T. CLARK,
Assistant Adjutant-General, Huntsville, Ala.:

COLONEL: I send you the reports from Florence and Decatur to-day, which will give you a pretty good idea of matters. I am not afraid of any attack by the force they have in our front as yet. It appears to me that they mean something else. I watch the river very closely and try to keep posted on all additional forces that arrive in our front. It is possible that they may concentrate on this flank when Johnston moves, if he does, so as to prevent any movement from this quarter. Dispatches received this noon show that part of their forces, say two regiments, are encamped on west side of Flint. All the force they have this side of the mountains is in and around Decatur, covering all approaches. I think I will connect our works with regular intrenchments with basket or gabion revetments. If this meets the approval of the general please let me know. The works as laid out around Decatur have some grave faults. They were thrown up by green hands while I was on my back. In putting up intrenchments I will try to rectify these mistakes as much as possible. The angles of rifle-pits are all salient now. I will change that and other errors.

I am, very respectfully, your obedient servant,

G. M. DODGE,
Brigadier-General, Commanding.

HDQRS. DEPARTMENT AND ARMY OF THE TENNESSEE,
Huntsville, Ala., April 20, 1864.
Maj. Gen. W. T. SHERMAN,
  Comdg. Military Division of the Mississippi, Nashville:

GENERAL : In answer to your letter of the 17th instant with regard to the pontoon train now at Nashville, I have thought the matter over carefully, and although I know and appreciate fully the labor and difficulty of transporting a train of this kind, still the advantages which we may reasonably expect to derive from having one along I think sufficient to warrant us in taking it or at least a portion of it. If the only question involved was that of constructing a bridge across the Coosa I should most certainly decide not to take it, as we are deficient in transportation and it is very difficult to obtain forage for the animals. But we may reasonably expect a determined resistance to our advance on the line of the Coosa, if not before, and it may be all-important to us to have the means at hand of crossing that river quickly and of deceiving the enemy as to the points of crossing. If we have to rely upon getting the materials to construct a bridge of the length required from buildings or from the woods the time required to do this and the noise attending it would develop our plans, and might render our crossing a matter of serious difficulty.

Four hundred feet of the bridge, however, is all we will require. I will send up an officer to bring this much of it down.

Very respectfully, your obedient servant,
JAS. B. McPHERSON,
Major-General, Commanding.

HDQRS. DEPARTMENT AND ARMY OF THE TENNESSEE,
Huntsville, Ala., April 20, 1864.
Maj. Gen. C. C. WASHBURN,
  Memphis, Tenn.:

GENERAL : In accordance with instructions from Lieut. Gen. U. S. Grant, you are hereby assigned to the command of all the U. S. forces at and in the vicinity of Memphis.

Brig. Gen. S. D. Sturgis is ordered down to take command of the cavalry and to move out and attack Forrest wherever he can be found. Direct Brigadier-General Grierson to seize as many horses and mules as may be necessary to mount the cavalry, and to assist in organizing and getting them ready by the time General Sturgis arrives.

Brigadier-General Buckland's brigade of infantry should be ordered to hold itself in readiness to move out with the cavalry.

On the return of the Red River expedition Brigadier-General Mower's division will be stopped at Memphis, and you will make such disposition of it as circumstances require. The remainder of the command, under Brig. Gen. A. J. Smith, will move as heretofore directed.

As soon as it can possibly be done, a force under Brigadier-General Gresham will be sent up the Tennessee River and will endeavor to co-operate with the force to be sent out from Memphis against Forrest. The great object is to defeat him, if possible, and prevent him from getting off with his plunder. All the force along the Mississippi River must strike at the enemy wherever they can do so to advantage and occupy his attention and keep him busy in that quarter.

Paducah, Cairo, Columbus, Memphis, Vicksburg, and Natchez must be held at all hazards. All weak, isolated points which are exposed must be evacuated. The plan of establishing small posts on the river is bad, and must not be carried out to any extent. The navigation of the river must be kept open by means of the permanent posts above named, a thorough system of scouting parties and patrols, and the assistance of the gun-boats and Marine Brigade. Brig. Gen. Henry Prince is assigned to the command of the Defenses and District of Columbus (a sub-district of Memphis), which embraces all that portion of Kentucky and Tennessee west of the Tennessee River and north of a line running from the Big Sandy west through Paris to the Obion River, and thence along this to the Mississippi River, and is directed to make his regular reports and returns to your headquarters in Memphis.

Maj. Gen. H. W. Slocum is assigned to the command of the District of Vicksburg, which extends from the mouth of Arkansas River, on the west side of the Mississippi, and the Tallahatchie River, on the east side, to the Department of the Gulf. He is instructed to keep the attention of the enemy occupied in his district and prevent him from sending any more forces to North Mississippi and Tennessee. You must not understand, however, that you are expressly limited to district lines. If the enemy makes his appearance and you can strike him to advantage do so, and follow him as long as you can make it pay.

You will make your regular reports and returns to the headquarters Sixteenth Army Corps, Major-General Hurlbut commanding.

Very respectfully, your obedient servant,
JAS. B. McPHERSON,
Major-General, Commanding.

WOODVILLE, ALA.,
April 20, 1864.

Maj. R. R. TOWNES,
Assistant Adjutant-General, Huntsville, Ala.:

Effective strength of infantry at Woodville and Paint Rock is 209 commissioned officers and 3,704 enlisted men. Effective strength of infantry at Vienna, 17 commissioned officers and 274 enlisted men. Effective strength of infantry at Cottonville is 14 commissioned officers and 262 enlisted men. Effective strength of artillery is 7 commissioned officers and 192 enlisted men. Aggregate present, all arms, including sick, is 5,155. Aggregate present and absent is 7,621.

The First Iowa Battery, aggregate 152, has been transferred to the Fourth Division since last report.

P. JOS. OSTERHAUS,
Brigadier-General, Commanding Division.

HDQRS. FOURTH DIVISION, SIXTEENTH ARMY CORPS,
Decatur, April 20, 1864.

Brigadier-General DODGE,
Comdg. Left Wing, Sixteenth Corps, Athens:

GENERAL: A scout sent out last night reports a strong picket force all along Flint toward Somerville, and indications of a new force having arrived in that vicinity. Report of citizens is that

Martin's command has joined Roddey, but any accurate information of their strength I have not been able to get. All the indications would show an intention to attack this place. My opinion of their movements on the Somerville road and the Courtland road at the same time is to induce us to send out a part of our force to attack them at one of these points while they will attempt to strike us with the other.

Everything is quiet on the river above and below as far as I can hear, and no movement except in this vicinity.

Respectfully,

JAMES C. VEATCH,
Brigadier-General.

HDQRS. FOURTH DIVISION, SIXTEENTH ARMY CORPS,
Decatur, April 20, 1864—4.20 p. m.

Major-General McPHERSON, *Huntsville :*

No news. All quiet here. A considerable rebel force near us.

JAMES C. VEATCH,
Brigadier-General.

HDQRS. MILITARY DIVISION OF THE MISSISSIPPI,
Nashville, Tenn., April 20. 1864.

General BRAYMAN, *Cairo:*

Your dispatch of yesterday just received. Telegraph me the earliest authentic news from Red River. McPherson has sent the necessary orders for Washburn to command at Memphis, Prince at Columbus, and Hurlbut to join his corps at Decatur. A. J. Smith's division will follow by river, and Mower remain at Memphis for the present.

W. T. SHERMAN,
Major-General, Commanding.

HDQRS. MILITARY DIVISION OF THE MISSISSIPPI,
Nashville, Tenn., April 20, 1864.

General McPHERSON, *Huntsville :*

Let Hurlbut come around with his corps. Ewing has a district in Kentucky lying wholly east of the Tennessee River. Prince's district would be defined as you say, but he should not stop as against any enemy at any line. Any commander of troops on the Mississippi should act against any enemy he can reach.

Colonel Wilson passed in the night, and I approve your instructions to Gresham. Make similar ones for General Washburn at Memphis.

W. T. SHERMAN,
Major-General.

HDQRS. MILITARY DIVISION OF THE MISSISSIPPI,
Nashville, April 20, 1864.

General HURLBUT, *Cairo:*

You are not relieved of the command of the Sixteenth Corps, but were relieved of the command on the river by General Washburn. You will join your corps at Decatur, via Nashville.

I would like you to give orders for A. J. Smith's division to follow by the Tennessee River, and that of Mower to remain at Memphis. Bring your corps staff along.

W. T. SHERMAN,
Major-General.

HEADQUARTERS DISTRICT OF CAIRO,
Cairo, Ill., April 20, 1864.
Maj. Gen. W. T. SHERMAN,
Commanding Military Division of the Mississippi:
SIR: Captain Shirk, of the gun-boat Peosta, a cool and intelligent officer, whose judgment is valuable, and whose trips up the Tennessee give him means of obtaining information, writes me as follows:

U. S. S. PEOSTA,
Paducah, Ky., April 19, 1864.

GENERAL: I have just been informed of a solution of the movements of the rebels in West Tennessee and Kentucky, which, if true, ought to be known to Major-General Sherman.
It is this: That Forrest is to hold this portion of these two States between Memphis and Paducah, while General Polk moves north and has secured a place upon the Tennessee River to cross, when he is to be joined by Forrest, and the combined force is then to cross and cut off the supplies of the army near Chattanooga. I am told it is a fact that General Polk is moving north. Colonel Hicks tells me that he has information that there is an infantry force of rebels now at Paris, Tenn. These two reports would seem to corroborate each other.
I am, very respectfully, &c.,
JAMES W. SHIRK,
Lieut. Commander, U. S. Navy, Comdg. 7th Dist., Mississippi Squadron.

Very respectfully,

M. BRAYMAN,
Brigadier-General, Commanding.

P. S.—I am securing affidavits in relation to the Fort Pillow affair, and find the facts as stated in press substantiated.

LEXINGTON, *April* 20, 1864.
Lieutenant-Colonel FAIRLEIGH,
Acting Assistant Adjutant-General, Louisville:
Rebels Gay and Bradshaw, with 80 men, left Quicksand Creek, in Breathitt County, Tuesday last, pursued by detachments Forty-fifth Kentucky Mounted Infantry. Rebels retreated through Pound Gap. No rebel force in my district.

E. H. HOBSON,
Brigadier-General.

CAIRO, ILL., *April* 20, 1864.
(Received 11.20 p. m.)
Hon. E. M. STANTON, *Secretary of War:*
I am collecting from the survivors sworn testimony concerning the tragedy at Fort Pillow, and find all the published accounts substantiated. Fort Pillow is not within my command, but survivors were brought here. A full report will reach you as soon as possible.
M. BRAYMAN,
Brigadier-General.

QUARTERMASTER-GENERAL'S OFFICE,
Washington, D. C., April 20, 1864.

Maj. Gen. W. T. SHERMAN,
  Comdg. Mil. Div. of the Mississippi, Nashville, Tenn.:

GENERAL : I have received your letter of 9th with copies of Orders, No. 6. Colonel McCallum has been sick, but is now on his way to Nashville.

By use of all the steam-boats from Bridgeport to Chattanooga, and by running the heavy trains over the easier grades and better rails of the Decatur route, I doubt not you can accelerate the accumulation of stores at the front. Mr. Anderson will do what is possible to further your views, and Colonel McCallum, on his arrival, you will find possessed of great capacity.

Resist the pressure of civilians and private donations and supplies, march your troops, and devote the cars solely to transportation of military necessities, and you will accomplish much. Many civilians can give charitable, patriotic, benevolent, and religious reasons to be allowed to go to the front ; the reasons are so good that nothing but an absolute and unchangeable prohibition of all such travel will do any good.

I understand that one engine per day is being sent forward to Nashville, and that fifteen cars per day are also added to the stock. We have had to quietly but firmly impress the locomotive manufactories ; that is, notify them that the engines must be made and delivered for the United States in bar of all other customers or contractors. You have grain for 50,000 animals to 1st January next at Nashville, your base, and rations for 200,000 men for four months. All the energy heretofore directed to forwarding supplies to Nashville should now be devoted to getting them in advance of that point, and the purchase and forwarding to Nashville should be stopped. Will you see to this ? Money is needed for all purposes and should not be spent upon accumulating a surplus in Nashville.

You will be obliged, I think, to move with smaller trains than Rosecrans had last year. The broken-down animals of the last campaign in East Tennessee and Georgia have not recovered yet ; the dead cannot be replaced. We are short of mules east and west, and I find great difficulty in procuring cavalry horses needed here. The Cavalry Bureau, charged specially with mounting the cavalry, is also in difficulties. They find the supply of horses deficient.

To a marching column of 35,000 men here General Grant has assigned 600 wagons for all purposes.

Captain Poe, in charge of your engineer depot at Nashville, has, I am told, charge of the photographic establishment. Some very interesting p t grap of the scenery about Nashville and Knoxville, I am told have been taken. I have seen a set of Chattanooga views, which are interesting and beautiful. Can you not send me two sets of each, one for my office and one for myself ? I should prefer them sent on thin paper, to be mounted here. They are less injured in the mail.

  I am, very truly, yours,

  M. C. MEIGS,
  Quartermaster-General.

General Smith (W. S.), chief of cavalry, has, I learn, called for 30,000 horses for the cavalry of your military division. These cannot be obtained in time for the opening of the campaign. I learn unofficially that an order has issued to dismount mounted infantry and transfer their horses to cavalry. The nominal cavalry force is too large.

QUARTERMASTER-GENERAL'S OFFICE,
Washington, D. C., April 20, 1864.

Maj. Gen. W. T. SHERMAN,
    Comdg. Military Division of the Mississippi, Nashville:

GENERAL: I have your letter, and agreeing with you entirely I have requested the Adjutant-General to issue an order nearly in the words you suggest.

I hope that General Allen will be able, by the large control he will have of the resources of the Quartermaster's Department, to aid you materially in your operations.

I have applied to the Secretary, having some time since consulted General Grant, for orders to accompany the headquarters of the lieutenant-general commanding during the approaching campaign, believing that during the active operations I can be more useful there than in this Bureau. During the time of preparations this was undoubtedly my place, but our preparations are completed.

To one thing let me call your attention—the burdensome tentage of your armies. Requisitions are still referred here, asking, in violation of general orders, for Sibley tents, wall-tents, A-tents, &c. We make no more Sibley tents. The eastern armies are fitted out with shelter-tents entirely.

Burnside's command turned in the other day a complete outfit of A-tents, which they had received while encamped at Annapolis, and yesterday they marched through Washington, every man with a shelter-tent rolled up on his knapsack, all contented. I rode out to meet them on Sunday evening, and I saw a division go into camp. In half an hour after stacking arms, without waiting for wagons, every man had his shelter-tent up and all were housed. The shelter-tent is more healthy than the A, or wall, or Sibley, and the difference in mobility of an army thus sheltered and an army with the other tents is enormous.

To Burnside's column, intended to be 35,000 strong (infantry, cavalry, and artillery), were assigned, on the estimates for his outfit, 600 wagons and 180 ambulances. If any difference in strength is made the outfit will be changed. Of these wagons, five go to 1,000 men for ammunition, three only for baggage; provisions and forage take up the rest.

Wishing you all success, I am, very truly, your friend,
M. C. MEIGS,
Quartermaster-General.

There is a difference between the Eastern and Western columns, which excites dissensions and should be corrected. I inclose a copy of General Orders, No. —, from Headquarters of the Army, which is the rule and should be enforced.*

---

* Order not found as an inclosure.

Report of effective strength of Third Division, Twenty-third Army Corps, commanded by Brig. Gen. J. D. Cox, April 20, 1864.

Command.	Present for duty.		
	Officers.	Men.	Aggregate.
Division staff and escort, Brig. Gen. J. D. Cox commanding	8	11	19
Detachment, 65th Illinois (provost guard), Lieut. S. G. Lewis, 24th Kentucky	1	52	53
1st Brigade, Col. James W. Reilly, 104th Ohio Volunteer Infantry, commanding	6	7	13
8th Tennessee Volunteer Infantry, Col. Felix A. Reeve	27	369	396
100th Ohio Volunteer Infantry, Col. P. S. Slevin	9	381	390
104th Ohio Volunteer Infantry, Lieut. Col. O. W. Sterl	12	583	595
16th Kentucky Volunteer Infantry a			
112th Illinois Volunteer Infantry a			
Total 1st Brigade	54	1,340	1,394
2d Brigade, Brig. Gen. M. D. Manson commanding	7	15	22
63d Indiana Volunteer Infantry, Col. I. N. Stiles	21	644	665
24th Kentucky Volunteer Infantry, Col. [John S. Hurt]	19	300	319
103d Ohio Volunteer Infantry, Capt. W. W. Hutchinson	8	383	391
5th Tennessee Volunteer Infantry a			
65th Indiana Volunteer Infantry a			
65th Illinois Volunteer Infantry a			
Total 2d Brigade	55	1,342	1,397
15th Indiana Battery a			
Battery D, 1st Ohio Volunteer Light Artillery a			
Left Wing, 3d Iowa Cavalry, Capt. George F. Herriott	13	293	306
Total present for duty	131	3,048	3,169

a Not yet reported.

HDQRS. THIRD DIVISION, TWENTY-THIRD ARMY CORPS,
  Bull's Gap, Tenn., April 20, 1864.

J. D. COX,
Brigadier-General, Commanding.

ED. D. SAUNDERS,
  Captain and Assistant Adjutant-General.

NASHVILLE, *April 21, 1864.*

ADJUTANT GENERAL:

Maj. Gen. Carl Schurz is thrown out by the combination of the Eleventh and Twelfth Corps. I cannot assign him to a division in any of my armies without displeasing some one who has long been identified with their command.

General Schurz would like the command in West Kentucky, but that is given by General Grant to General Prince. Do you know of any command to which he may be properly assigned, as he is very anxious to remain on duty ?

W. T. SHERMAN,
Commanding.

(Copy sent General Grant April 22, 1864, by General Halleck, Chief of Staff.)

NASHVILLE, TENN.,
April 21, 1864—7.40 p. m.

Lieutenant-General GRANT,
    Culpeper Court-House:

I send the following dispatch, just received:

KNOXVILLE, *April* 21, 1864.
Major-General SHERMAN,
    Nashville:

Later reports confirm what I sent you on the 19th of the movements of Longstreet's main force, but indicate that Hoyle's [?] division, about 2,500 strong, still remains near Bristol. The two divisions which have gone are Field's (formerly commanded by Hood) and McLaws'. They amount to about 10,000 men. Railroad employés say these troops took the cars from Lynchburg for Orange Court-House. They also report it as generally understood among the officers of Longstreet's command that Lee is receiving re-enforcements from Beauregard and Johnston.

I go to Bull's Gap to-morrow.

J. M. SCHOFIELD,
Major-General.

W. T. SHERMAN,
Major-General.

___

HDQRS. MILITARY DIVISION OF THE MISSISSIPPI,
Nashville, Tenn., April 21, 1864.

Lieutenant-General GRANT,
    Washington:

I have just received the following dispatch from General Corse, whom I sent to bring up my Red River command:

CAIRO, *April* 21, 1864—2.30 p. m.
Major-General SHERMAN :

Banks was attacked by Kirby Smith near Mansfield, La., on the 8th instant, and retreated to Grand Ecore *a la* Bull Run. He refused to let Smith go, for obvious reasons, stating, however, that he had authority from both Generals Grant and Halleck to retain your troops longer. The admiral's iron-clads are caught by low water, some above the bars at Grand Ecore, the rest above the falls, and he not only refuses to consent to the removal of Smith, but refused to allow him a transport to take him out of the river, stating that to take Smith away would occasion the loss of his fleet, the utter destruction of General Banks' demoralized command, and enable the enemy to crush General Steele. I have communications from General Banks and Admiral Porter, and will be with you as speedily as possible.

JOHN M. CORSE,
Brigadier-General.

W. T. SHERMAN,
Major-General.

___

CULPEPER, *April* 21, 1864—5 p. m.
Major-General SHERMAN,
    Nashville, Tenn.:

Washburn has gone to relieve Hurlbut; the latter to report from Cairo, where orders will reach him. I would not trust him with any further command. Prince has gone to West Kentucky. I would recommend leaving that portion of the Sixteenth Corps in the field to the command of Dodge, and Washburn to command from Cairo to Memphis. I would not spare infantry intended for your main column to go after Forrest, but if you can make the cavalry force strong enough to cope with him it would be well. I have ordered

Rosecrans to send troops to Cairo, intended to drive Forrest out of Tennessee, and then go to Steele. They have been so slow coming that they will be of no use for the first part of the purpose intended. Order them where you think best.

U. S. GRANT,
Lieutenant-General.

NASHVILLE, *April* 21, 1864.

Maj. Gen. G. H. THOMAS:

Dispatch of yesterday received. All accounts concur in your statement of the position and strength of our enemy. His cavalry is patrolling from Gadsden to Guntersville and Decatur, watching McPherson. Wilder is supposed to be marching from Louisville toward Columbia at this time. I will make further inquiries, and see that all of Garrard's division is assembled there. Allen is moving heaven and earth to get mules for you, but I would undertake to reach Coosa with our present means.

W. T. SHERMAN,
Major-General.

CHATTANOOGA, *April* 21, 1864—10.30 p. m.

Major-General SHERMAN:

As affairs seem to be quiet I would like to visit you for a day, unless you can spare the time to come down here.

GEO. H. THOMAS,
Major-General.

HUNTSVILLE, ALA.,
April 21, 1864.

Brig. Gen. G. M. DODGE,
Athens:

Major-General Hurlbut telegraphs from Memphis, under date of April 19, that he is credibly informed that Polk's force, 17,000 strong, including Hoffy's and Jackson's cavalry, passed Starkville on the 11th of April for Huntsville. Forrest's force, he also stated, is returning south through La Grange and Saulsbury.

Have you any confirmation of this report, and where is Starkville? I cannot find it on any map I have got. Who is Hoffy? Is it not Roddey?

JAS. B. McPHERSON,
Major-General, Commanding.

MOSSY CREEK, *April* 21, 1864.

Major-General SCHOFIELD:

I should like to send out the company of cavalry now here with an infantry force to-morrow toward Trogdon's Ford, said to be the best over the Holston, some 10 miles from here, to return on 23d. If permitted, I will send word to Colonel Bond, One hundred and eleventh, on a reconnaissance, with Dandridge as a base, not to return with the other cavalry company until 23d; otherwise that company now out will be back to-morrow evening.

I have rumors from two different sources, but which I cannot deem reliable, to the effect that General Jones is on north side of Holston with a brigade, two regiments of infantry and three of cavalry. I wish to ascertain the condition of the most practicable ford (Trogdon's) and collect other information if possible.

H. M. JUDAH,
Brigadier-General, Commanding Division.

HDQRS. MILITARY DIVISION OF THE MISSISSIPPI,
Nashville, Tenn., April 21, 1864.

Maj. Gen. J. B. McPHERSON,
Comdg. Dept. and Army of the Tennessee, Huntsville, Ala.:

GENERAL : I am directed by the major-general commanding to acknowledge the receipt, by the hands of Lieutenant-Colonel Macfeely, of your communications to Major-General Hurlbut, Memphis; Major-General Slocum, Vicksburg, and Brigadier-General Brayman, Cairo, and to state that they have been forwarded to their destination, with the following indorsement upon the one addressed to Major-General Hurlbut :

If Forrest has moved south of Coldwater there will be no necessity for Gresham's command going to Purdy, but it will go up to Clifton. land there, and act across to the west of the Tennessee, if information then received make it useful.

W. T. SHERMAN,
Major-General, Commanding.

And also the following indorsement upon that of Major-General Slocum :

Approved. No distant expeditions will be expected till you have reason to believe the main armies are in motion. Then all the forces of the United States should occupy the detachments of the enemy as much as possible.

W. T. SHERMAN,
Major-General, Commanding.

I have the honor to be, general, very respectfully, your obedient servant,

M. ROCHESTER,
Assistant Adjutant-General.

HDQRS. MILITARY DIVISION OF THE MISSISSIPPI,
Nashville, Tenn., April 21, 1864.

General McPHERSON,
Huntsville:

Dispatches by Macfeely received. Nor did I know there was a garrison at Pillow till I heard it was captured. I broke it up by an order at the same time as Corinth, and now await Hurlbut's reasons for reoccupying it. I knew a regiment of Tennesseeans was forming in the country back, but had no idea that any guns or black troops were there. Hurlbut reports Forrest passed south by La Grange. He seems to have made no efforts to prevent it. Grierson's cavalry ought to be near 7,000, and Smith reports the capture of enough horses and mules to mount all of these at the time he went to Okolona; yet Hurlbut says he could only mount 2,400 men. He has also Buckland's brigade, four other white regiments, and near 4,000 black troops.

The assignment of Slocum, Washburn, and Prince is made by orders of General Grant. I will indorse your instructions to all these, and add for Hurlbut to join his corps here, as he will be one too many at Cairo.

You may order your two divisions to come up to Clifton with their wagons and mules, and from that point to act against Forrest according to the strength present and the information received. If Forrest has escaped, we can only reach him by an independent expedition up the Yazoo to Grenada, such as I contemplated ; but before we make any orders we must wait till the Red River trip is out, and until we have one good division at Vicksburg and another at Memphis.

The cavalry now in front of Dodge is from Johnston's army, watching you. It might be well to keep them uneasy by occasional sallies in force from Decatur and Larkin's.

W. T. SHERMAN,
Major-General.

HDQRS. MILITARY DIVISION OF THE MISSISSIPPI,
Nashville, Tenn., April 21, 1864.

General BRAYMAN,
  Cairo:

Can you tell me anything certain of the fate of the Major Bradford who was at Fort Pillow at the time of its destruction by Forrest? Give me the name of the officer who is making the official inquiry into the history of that affair.

Facilitate all you can the movement of McPherson's troops and wagons up the Tennessee. I have notified Colonel Parsons of the movement. Time is getting precious and must be used.

W. T. SHERMAN,
Major-General.

CAIRO, April 21, 1864.

Major-General SHERMAN,
  Nashville, Tenn.:

On arriving here to-day I found your telegram inquiring if I could use General Schurz. I replied that I could not tell until I arrived at Memphis and ascertained what troops there were there. Since then I have seen one of General Hurlbut's aides, who is just up from Memphis, and he informs me that there are now there only about 2,000 white troops and four regiments of colored and about 1,100 cavalry. If this is the case I do not see how I can do anything for General Schurz. Whether the force at Memphis is sufficient to resist any probable attack you can judge. With the cavalry there certainly but little can be done toward intercepting raids of the enemy. I hear that there are 1,000 cavalrymen without horses at Memphis, and I shall endeavor to procure horses for them at the earliest moment.

The disaster upon Red River I suppose may delay the return of General Mower. A large amount of cavalry belonging to Memphis I hear is at home on furlough and will soon be back, but as they will be horseless it will take some time to mount them. I telegraphed you to-day inquiring if you had any orders or instructions, but have received no answer.

The disclosures in regard to the Fort Pillow massacre make out a much worse case than any of the published accounts. The Sioux Indians after this will be regarded as models of humanity.

I am, general, your obedient servant,

C. C. WASHBURN,
Major-General.

HDQRS. MILITARY DIVISION OF THE MISSISSIPPI,
Nashville, Tenn., April 21, 1864.

General WASHBURN, *Cairo:*

General McPherson will give full instructions by letter. In the mean time hasten to Memphis, get all the cavalry you can, and infantry, and punish Forrest if you can possibly reach him. I fear it is too late, but do all that is possible. You will find Sturgis there and Slocum at Vicksburg. McPherson will need troops up to the neighborhood of Purdy as fast as they assemble at Cairo. I fear we are too late, but I know there are troops enough at Memphis to whale Forrest if you can reach him.

W. T. SHERMAN,
Major-General.

HDQRS. LEFT WING, SIXTEENTH ARMY CORPS,
Athens, Ala., April 21, 1864.

Lieut. Col. WILLIAM T. CLARK,
Asst. Adjt. Gen., Dept. and Army of Tenn., Huntsville, Ala.:

COLONEL: Capt. J. K. Wing, on his return from Huntsville, informed me that it was expected that I should accumulate forage and stores for troops of the Seventeenth Army Corps, expected here. Please inform me at what point on my line the commissary stores will be needed, and where they will be most likely to require forage. I now have about thirty days' rations on hand for my own command, and am accumulating as fast as possible.

The disposition of the enemy on the south side of the river this morning is as follows:

Roddey camped on Flint River, forces extending to Danville bridge; General Clanton's headquarters at Oakville; his troops extend to Blue Banks, 6 miles north of Moulton.

Colonel Johnson, Colonel Jackson, and Colonel Nash [?] extend their commands around to the river on the west. Their entire force ranges from 5,000 to 7,000 men; not less than 5,000 nor more than 7,000. They have three batteries and three regiments of infantry. General Veatch's division arrived here without any trains except regimental. I have got together for him a very poor train, the stock being such as I could pick up. I am satisfied I shall not be able to obtain any from Nashville. Could not some of the good transportation left on the Mississippi River be ordered around ? The general is aware that my transportation is very light for the number of troops I will have to supply, in comparison with other commands. I now have about six wagons to a regiment, and 120 in the Second Division and seventy-nine in the Fourth Division. This includes ordnance trains and all, and will haul fifteen days' rations of bread, sugar, coffee, and salt, together with the ammunition.

I am, very respectfully, your obedient servant,

G. M. DODGE,
Brigadier-General.

HUNTSVILLE, *April* 21, 1864.
Brig. Gen. W. Q. GRESHAM,
          Cairo, Ill. :

General Hurlbut reports Forrest passing south through La Grange. He has probably made his escape. You will come up the Tennessee River to Clifton and disembark your command and await further orders. Telegraph me when you start from Cairo.

JAS. B. McPHERSON,
Major-General, Commanding.

ATHENS, ALA.,
April 21, 1864.
Lieut. Col. C. S. SHELDON,
          Eighteenth Missouri Volunteers :

March to Decatur, Ala,. reporting to Brig. Gen. J. C. Veatch. By order of Brig. Gen. G. M. Dodge:

J. W. BARNES,
Assistant Adjutant-General.

ATHENS, *April* 21, 1864.
General SWEENY:

Reports are current here that General Forrest with a large force is crossing the river at or near Eastport. You will send the Seventh Illinois in that direction to ascertain and report the facts. Have them start to-night, and report all the news to the nearest point on the railroad, to be telegraphed to headquarters. One battalion of the Ninth Ohio Cavalry is now in the vicinity of Florence.

By order of General Dodge :

GEO. E. SPENCER,
Colonel, &c.

CAIRO, *April* 21, 1864—7 p. m.
(Received 11 p. m.)
SECRETARY OF WAR:

General Corse, who was sent by General Sherman to recall General A. J. Smith's command from Red River, has returned. Our loss is 4,000 men, 16 guns, and over 200 wagons. Banks returned to Grand Ecore badly injured. He refused to return Smith's command. The naval force is caught in low water with shoals above and below.

M. BRAYMAN,
Brigadier-General, Commanding.

HEADQUARTERS SIXTEENTH ARMY CORPS,
Memphis, Tenn., April 21, 1864.
Col. I. G. KAPPNER,
     2d U. S. Heavy Artillery (Colored), Comdg. Fort Pickering :

SIR: I have been directed to inform you that a committee appointed by the Congress of the United States to investigate the facts attending the late massacre at Fort Pillow will probably visit Memphis in a few days, and it is the desire of the major-general commanding corps that the necessary effort be made to have all the evidence obtainable reduced to writing; that all officers conversant with the facts be required to at once make up full and circumstantial reports, and forward them to these headquarters.

The only report as yet received at these headquarters is that of Lieutenant Van Horn. No correct information has yet been furnished of the strength of the battalion Sixth U. S. Artillery (colored), when it embarked for Fort Pillow, nor of the number who escaped.

You will therefore proceed to get all the data on the subject which can be obtained in a shape to present to the committee on its arrival, as clear and precise in detail as possible.

I have the honor to be, sir, very respectfully, your obedient servant,

T. H. HARRIS,
Assistant Adjutant-General.

GENERAL ORDERS, }   HDQRS. SIXTEENTH ARMY CORPS,
No. 41.   }   *Memphis, Tenn., April* 21, 1864.

In obedience to orders from Maj. Gen. W. T. Sherman, commanding Military Division of the Mississippi, the undersigned removes his personal headquarters to Cairo, Ill.

The army corps headquarters will remain at Memphis until further orders from competent authority.

*   *   *   *   *   *   *

S. A. HURLBUT,
Major-General.

CULPEPER, *April* 22, 1864—noon.

Maj. Gen. SHERMAN,
Nashville, Tenn.:

Dispatch just received from General Brayman satisfies me of what I always believed, that forces sent to Banks would be lost for our spring campaign.

You will have to make your calculations now leaving A. J. Smith out. Do not let this delay or embarrass, however. Leave for him, if he should return, such directions as you deem most advisable. He may return in time to be thrown in somewhere, very opportunely.

U. S. GRANT,
Lieutenant-General.

HDQRS. MILITARY DIVISION OF THE MISSISSIPPI,
Nashville, Tenn., April 22, 1864. (Received 23d.)

Lieutenant-General GRANT,
Culpeper:

I will calculate to leave Smith's command out. My chief trouble will be supplies, but I am hurrying forward beef-cattle.

W. T. SHERMAN,
Major-General.

CHATTANOOGA, *April* 22, 1864.
Major-General SHERMAN,
        Nashville:
    A rebel chaplain came in to Baird's division to-day. He left Dalton day before yesterday, and reports Hardee's, Hood's, and part of Polk's corps there; that Johnston is making no preparations for moving, but expects us to march on him. He estimates Johnston's army at 60,000. I also have Atlanta papers of the 20th. They state that the remainder of Wheeler's cavalry has arrived at Atlanta, en route for Dalton. Colonel La Grange returned to Cleveland to-day from a scout toward Spring Place, near which place he surprised an outpost of the enemy, capturing 2 commissioned officers, 12 men, 6 horses, 8 saddles, and 15 rifles.
                    GEO. H. THOMAS,
                Major-General, U. S. Volunteers.

NASHVILLE, *April* 22, 1864.
Maj. Gen. G. H. THOMAS,
        Chattanooga:
    Give full instructions to General Hooker. Notify Generals Howard and Schofield of your temporary absence, and come up for a day. If you feel the least doubt, however, I will come down.
                    W. T. SHERMAN,
                        Major-General.

HEADQUARTERS TWENTIETH CORPS,
    Lookout Valley, Tenn., April 22, 1864.
Brig. Gen. A. S. WILLIAMS,
        Commanding First Division, Twentieth Corps:
    GENERAL: I have the honor to acknowledge the receipt of your communication of the 21st instant, and am directed by the major-general commanding the corps to instruct you to withdraw the troops of your division at Shelbyville, Fayetteville, and Tracy City, and have them take post at some convenient point, with a view to your march to the front.
    The indigent inhabitants at Fayetteville will be sent to Nashville, and until further orders the two companies of Tennessee Cavalry will take post at Tracy City and the senior officer be instructed to report by letter to Major-General Rousseau, at Nashville, for further orders.
    I am, general, very respectfully, your obedient servant,
                    H. W. PERKINS,
        Lieutenant-Colonel and Assistant Adjutant-General.

HDQRS. FIRST CAV. DIV., DEPT. OF THE CUMBERLAND,
        Cleveland, April 22, 1864.
Brig. Gen. W. D. WHIPPLE,
        Chief of Staff, Chattanooga:
    GENERAL: I have the honor to report all quiet in our front. There are rumors that the enemy in small parties have been seen near the

railroad in the neighborhood of Charleston and Athens. Colonel La Grange has returned with a scouting party of 300 men sent out yesterday, having captured 1 captain, 1 lieutenant, and 12 men, forming part of one of the enemy's outposts, without loss. This occurred at a point 29 miles distant from Cleveland, half way between Spring Place and Boiling Spring. Colonel La Grange reports from information obtained by the way that the enemy's cavalry force, now small, but soon to be considerably augmented, is at Tunnel Hill.

I am, general, very respectfully, your obedient servant,
EDWARD M. McCOOK,
Colonel, Commanding.

/ ———

CLEVELAND, TENN.,
April 22, 1864.
Col. J. B. DORR,
Commanding First Brigade:

The colonel commanding directs me to say that from information received at these headquarters it is evident that the enemy are making a reconnaissance in the direction of Cleveland, caused probably by the reconnaissance of Colonel La Grange. He directs that you cause the pickets on the Spring Place road, with the posts thrown out therefrom, to be strengthened by an additional detail of 40 men, to be relieved or ordered in in the morning, should nothing occur to make it necessary to continue the re-enforcement. They will be instructed to exercise the utmost vigilance, and at 3 a. m. they will start patrols out on the Spring Place road and also on the Dalton road so as to prevent the possibility of surprise.

I am, colonel, very respectfully, your obedient servant,
ROBERT LE ROY,
Captain and Assistant Adjutant-General.

———

HEADQUARTERS DEPARTMENT OF THE OHIO,
Knoxville, April 22, 1864.
Major-General SCHOFIELD,
Bull's Gap:

The following dispatch has just been received:

CHATTANOOGA, *April 22, 1864.*

Major-General SCHOFIELD:

I am advised by steam-boat captain that two guerrilla parties, 12 to 15 men each, crossed from north to south side of Tennessee River last night, are at mouth of Hiwassee and above.

GEO. H. THOMAS,
Major-General.

I have informed commanding officers at Madisonville and Sweet Water, and authorized them, if necessary to capture the parties, to press horses belonging to citizens. Have you any further instructions?

J. A. CAMPBELL,
Major and Assistant Adjutant-General.

HEADQUARTERS DEPARTMENT OF THE OHIO,
Knoxville, April 22, 1864.
Brig. Gen. W. F. BARRY,
        Chief of Art., Mil. Div. of the Miss., Nashville, Tenn.:

GENERAL: I have the honor to present the following facts in regard to the reorganization of light batteries for active field service in this department, and respectfully request your opinion or instructions in the matter:

The only smooth-bore guns now here in a serviceable condition are 12-pounder light guns; of these, two batteries of four guns each have been organized and equipped for the field, and two more are in process of being refitted.

It is feared that with the somewhat inferior quality of horses now being furnished us these batteries will not be able to continue the march any length of time, with but 6 horses to a carriage. In your letter of instructions, dated Nashville, April 6, 1864, you limit the number of horses for a four-gun battery to 80, which will confine them to 6 horses for each carriage.

I would deem this allowance entirely sufficient were the horses all or on an average what artillery horses ought to be, but those received here so far have been on an average much below the standard for good artillery horses, and I respectfully ask whether these batteries cannot be allowed 8 horses to each carriage.

I am, general, very respectfully, your obedient servant,
G. W. SCHOFIELD,
Lieutenant-Colonel and Chief of Artillery and Ordnance.

NICHOLASVILLE, *April 22, 1864.*
Major-General SCHOFIELD:

I have made such arrangements with Captain Hall, assistant quartermaster, to-day, as I think will insure the fitting out of a pack train by the 1st. I believe I will have 5,000 completely fitted out by that time, and that everything has been done in my power. We are now getting plenty of forage at this post.

GEO. STONEMAN,
Major-General.

ATHENS, *April 22, 1864.*
Maj. Gen. J. B. McPHERSON, *Huntsville:*

Do you get any news from about Larkin's Ferry of any movement of cavalry west, and does General Thomas report my leaving his front? Yesterday and to-day's reports are conflicting. I would like to satisfy myself. Man in from Itawamba County, Miss.; heard nothing of Polk. He says Forrest was at Jackson, Tenn.

G. M. DODGE,
Brigadier-General.

DECATUR, *April 22, 1864.*
Major-General McPHERSON, *Huntsville:*

Scouts in from southeast say Martin's division of cavalry is moving into the valley. I think there is no doubt of a part of it at least coming this way.

G. M. DODGE,
Brigadier-General.

HUNTSVILLE, *April 22, 1864.*
Brig. Gen. G. M. DODGE,
　　　Athens:
In view of the concentration of rebel forces in the valley and in the vicinity of Decatur, you had better have your troops along the railroad in readiness to move to the front. If you think the force at Decatur not sufficient, you might send a portion of the troops from Athens, and replace them from General Sweeny's division. I have telegraphed General Sherman to have General Garrard relieve your troops on the line of the railroad down to and including Pulaski.
　　　　　　　　　　　　JAS. B. McPHERSON,
　　　　　　　　　　　　　Major-General, Commanding.

APRIL 22, 1864.
Maj. Gen. J. B. McPHERSON,
　　　Huntsville:
I do not think they have got force enough yet to hurt me. So far it is all cavalry except three regiments, all close around us. Not to exceed a regiment between Courtland and Corinth, put all together. I can move everything I have got to spare on the railroad in an hour's notice. I have taken the infantry regiment at Mooresville and sent it to Decatur, leaving the cavalry there. Scout in from Colonel Rowett says that Lee was reported to be at Okolona. Don't put much dependence in the report. The Eighteenth Missouri Infantry, 600 strong, left Nashville yesterday. I will push it right through to Veatch.

　　　　　　　　　　　　G. M. DODGE,
　　　　　　　　　　　　　Brigadier-General.

HDQRS. DEPARTMENT AND ARMY OF THE TENNESSEE,
　　　　　　　Huntsville, Ala., April 22, 1864.
Brig. Gen. G. M. DODGE,
　　　Commanding Left Wing, Sixteenth Army Corps:
GENERAL: In answer to your communication of yesterday, I will state that the supplies which are to be accumulated for the Seventeenth Army Corps will be collected at Pulaski. Two divisions of this corps, aggregate about 12,000 men, will come up the Tennessee River to Clifton, disembark there, and march across the country to Pulaski, and thence to the front. There will be about 3,500 in the two divisions.

Five days' provisions and forage is all that you need accumulate, as the troops will come up amply provided, and these supplies are directed to be there in case of emergency. I have ordered up the whole corps train, the division trains, and regimental wagons belonging to the two divisions, and think with a proper distribution of the transportation we will be able to take along everything we require.

From a recent order from Major-General Sherman you will see that no camp and garrison equipage, trunks, chests, boxes, &c., can be taken along, everything in the way of officers' baggage being cut down to a minimum.

　　　Very respectfully, your obedient servant,
　　　　　　　　　　　　JAS. B. McPHERSON,
　　　　　　　　　　　　　Major-General.

HDQRS. DEPARTMENT AND ARMY OF THE TENNESSEE,
Huntsville, Ala., April 22, 1864.

Brig. Gen. G. M. DODGE,
  Comdg. Left Wing, Sixteenth Army Corps, Athens, Ala.:

GENERAL: I sent you yesterday by telegraph a communication which I received from Major-General Hurlbut, dated Memphis, April 19, to the effect that he had reliable information that Polk's force, 17,000 strong, including Hoffy's and Jackson's cavalry, passed through Starkville on the 11th of April for Huntsville, and that Forrest was going south through Saulsbury and La Grange. The telegraph not being in working order between this place and Athens, I presume you did not receive it.

I asked the questions, Have you had any confirmation of this report or any news bearing upon the matter? Where is Starkville? supposing that he referred to a town of this name in Alabama; and who is Hoffy? I have since learned by having the message repeated that Lee's cavalry is what was meant, and that Starkville, in Oktibbeha County, Miss., is probably the place referred to.

If the infantry under Polk have gone from Demopolis to Starkville it looks as though they had design on some point on the Mississippi River, or else intend to concentrate heavily upon our right flank. Should the latter be the case, it may be necessary to concentrate nearly the whole of your available force at and in the vicinity of Decatur. It will be at least ten days before we can count upon the arrival of any troops belonging to the Seventeenth Army Corps at Pulaski.

Very respectfully, your obedient servant,
JAS. B. McPHERSON,
Major-General.

DECATUR, *April 22, 1864.*

Major-General McPHERSON,
  Huntsville:

Starkville is on line of Mobile and Ohio Railroad, south of Okolona. I have no reports from there, though I have men in Columbus, Miss. All reports sent you from that quarter indicated a move north by Polk. Will send men out to-night to go there.
G. M. DODGE,
Brigadier-General.

DECATUR, *April 22, 1864.*

Major-General McPHERSON,
  Huntsville:

No doubt "Hoffy" means Roddey, as he came north through Tuscaloosa on the 14th instant, but had no troops with him. His troops came by way of Day's Gap and Somerville, and he joined them at Moulton. I am well satisfied that Polk had made no general move up to the 13th. The letters I sent to you, written to Meddens, at Pikeville, evidently foreshadowed a move north by Polk. I also think that none of Polk's forces have gone toward Johnston. Loring himself may have been in Montgomery, but none of his troops were with him. Four Texas regiments have been ordered to Roddey's command, and yesterday, when we were practicing artillery, the forces 5 miles out were all drawn up in line of battle in plain view of our mounted men.

G. M. DODGE,
Brigadier-General.

ATHENS, *April 22, 1864.*

Brigadier-General SWEENY:

Phillips had severe fight near Moulton yesterday. Forrest is between Tuscumbia and Eastport. Considerable force at Moulton and at Gadsden. Watch country to west. I suspect they will try to cross below Tuscumbia or else attack Decatur.

G. M. DODGE,
Brigadier-General.

HDQRS. LEFT WING, SIXTEENTH ARMY CORPS,
Athens, Ala., April 22, 1864.

Brig. Gen. T. W. SWEENY,
Comdg. Second Div., Sixteenth Army Corps, Pulaski:

Two divisions of the Seventeenth Army Corps will land at Clifton, march to Pulaski, thence to the front. There will be 12,000 men and 4,000 animals. You will instruct your commissary of subsistence to prepare to supply them with five days' rations, and your acting assistant quartermaster the same amount of forage. They will arrive in about ten days.

I am, very respectfully, your obedient servant,

G. M. DODGE,
Brigadier-General, Commanding.

HUNTSVILLE, *April 22, 1864.*

Maj. Gen. W. T. SHERMAN, *Nashville:*

Major-General Hurlbut telegraphs from Memphis, under date 19th April:

I have reliable information that Polk's force, 17,000 strong, including Lee's and Jackson's cavalry, passed through Starkville April 11 for Huntsville. Forrest is going south through Saulsbury and La Grange.

I have no confirmation of this movement here. If Polk's force has gone from Demopolis up through Starkville, it looks as though some point on the Mississippi River was aimed at and the retiring of Forrest a mere feint, or else they propose to concentrate a large force on our right flank. In the latter event Dodge will find it necessary to concentrate the whole of his available force at and near Decatur. Cannot Garrard's cavalry relieve Dodge's force on the railroad down to and including Pulaski? I have directed Brigadier-General Gresham with his command to come up the Tennessee River to Clifton and await orders.

I am afraid we will not get that force back from the Red River in a month, if at all.

Everything quiet opposite here. The force around Decatur, around Flint Creek, through Danville, Oakville, and around to the Tennessee River, west of Tuscumbia, General Dodge estimates at between 5,000 and 7,000 strong.

I have sent Captain Reese, engineer, over to Decatur to arrange and lay out the defensive lines, and directed General Dodge to have them made as strong and perfect as time and circumstances will admit.

JAS. B. McPHERSON.
Major-General Commanding.

HDQRS. FOURTH DIVISION, SIXTEENTH ARMY CORPS,
Decatur, Ala., April 22, 1864—9.15 p. m.

Brigadier-General DODGE, *Athens:*

Two of Major Kuhn's men, captured on Sunday, escaped from Danville last night and came in since dark. Roddey was at Danville on Monday and left there on Tuesday. They knew nothing of his forces. The Sixth Alabama is the only regiment they saw. It left Danville yesterday with three days' rations and went toward Woodall's Bridge. The roads and crossings are strongly picketed for miles. The scout at Triana was fired on by rebels from the opposite side to-day. Hall's regiment is reported 5 miles back. This is a new command, or at least a new name. All quiet on Courtland road.

JAMES C. VEATCH,
Brigadier-General.

HEADQUARTERS,
Florence, Ala., April 22, 1864.

Capt. J. W. BARNES,
Asst. Adjt. Gen., Hdqrs. Left Wing, 16th Army Corps:

SIR : I have to report the following rumor : Citizens who crossed at Eastport yesterday morning report Forrest's advance moving up on the south side of the river. I have sent scouts to ascertain, if possible, the correctness of the rumor. I merely send this as a rumor until I hear further.

I have discovered in the woods near Rice's iron-works four iron, old pattern, 6-pounder guns, with a quantity of spherical case and grape-shot. What shall I do with them?

I have the honor to be, very respectfully, your obedient servant,

R. ROWETT,
Commanding Seventh Illinois.

DECATUR, *April 22, 1864.*

Col. GEORGE E. SPENCER, *Mooresville:*

General Hurlbut telegraphs that Polk is moving north by way of Starkville, Miss. Have Forney and Meddens go through as soon as possible, and get facts in relation to Polk's movements.

G. M. DODGE,
Brigadier-General.

HDQRS. LEFT WING, SIXTEENTH ARMY CORPS,
Athens, Ala., April 22, 1864.

Col. R. ROWETT, *Seventh Illinois:*

The general directs that the Ninth Ohio Cavalry be sent to Athens on the 25th instant. The regiment will be returned in a few days,

During their absence the general desires you to keep as close watch as possible at all the principal points now covered by them. We have conflicting reports in relation to Polk's forces, Lee's cavalry, &c. They are said to be moving up the Mobile and Ohio Railroad. If possible, ascertain the facts. It is also reported that Forrest is moving south.

I am, very respectfully, your obedient servant,

J. W. BARNES,
Assistant Adjutant-General.

HDQRS. SEVENTY-FOURTH ILLINOIS VOLUNTEERS,
Columbus, Tenn., April 22, 1864.

Brigadier-General WAGNER:

GENERAL: I have the honor to report "all quiet" on the Hiwassee, except some little excitement caused by rather bold and frequent stealing of mules by persons supposed to be connected with guerrillas from below. I learn also from refugees in to-day that in the vicinity of Ducktown the people were expecting a raid to-day or to-morrow by a force of about 100, under command of a certain notorious Dr. Young. I don't get reliable information of any particular evidence of the movement further than the expectations of the people there. Among the refugees in to-day was a gentleman of more than ordinary intelligence and shrewdness, and apparently better posted up in matters pertaining to the rebel army than any one I have before met with. His statement is that the nominal force of Johnston's army, as shown by the muster-rolls last month, was 42,000 all told, but constantly diminishing by desertion, sickness, &c. I desire instructions whether to continue my report direct to you, and where. I have reported daily, but get no answer whether my dispatches reach you.

Your obedient servant,

JASON MARSH,
Colonel, Commanding Seventy-fourth Illinois Volunteers.

8 O'CLOCK A. M.

P. S.—I am just in receipt of reliable information that a squad of rebel cavalry, 50 or 60, are dashing through 5 miles above me, making for my picket station at Savannah. I have dispatched two companies in pursuit.

J. M.

HDQRS. SEVENTY-FOURTH ILLINOIS VOLUNTEERS,
Columbus, Tenn., April 22, 1864.

Brigadier-General WAGNER:

GENERAL: As I stated in my dispatch of this morning, I sent two companies in the quickest possible time to the point where the rebel cavalry seemed, by their inquiries, to be making for the purpose of crossing the Hiwassee. On arriving there it was ascertained that they proceeded in that direction as far as Goley's Mill, about 3¼ miles from this point, and about the same distance from Savannah, and then struck for the trail over the mountain; judging from their inquiries at different points, I concluded they would make for the crossing called Broad Shoals, about 12 miles, and might not get there before night. As soon as I learned their apparent course, I dispatched 30 men to Broad Shoals, in the hope of intercepting them during the night. As yet (midnight) I have not heard from the expedition. From entirely reliable information, they consisted of 64, divided into two squads, thoroughly armed, but very much jaded out. The most correct account I can get of their companies is that they come from the direction and within about 4 miles of Riceville; beyond that I have not been able to trace them. The boldness and success of the affair demonstrates the necessity of having more force, and particularly some cavalry, in this vicinity, if it is important to prevent such raids or to have the present command here at all safe. It was their declared intention, before they got to Goley's Mill, to pounce upon my force at Savannah and capture them. I can't think why they changed their purpose, as I can see no reason why they should not have succeeeded and got off before I could have rallied any force to stop them. I am satisfied that Goley aided them all he could. What shall I do with such men, when I have good reason to suspect them?

I have the honor to be, your obedient servant,

JASON MARSH,
Colonel, Commanding Seventy-fourth Illinois Volunteers.

P. S.—I desire instructions whether furloughs are still granted under the order giving 5 per cent. I am told that order has been suspended, but I can find no official notice of it among my papers.

J. M.

———

CAIRO, ILL., *April 22, 1864.*

Captain SHIRK, *U. S. Navy:*

CAPTAIN: In compliance with instructions just received from Major-General McPherson, commanding Department of the Tennessee, I have the honor to request of you a convoy to accompany an expedition in my charge up the Tennessee River.

My command will consist of at least 3,000 infantry and one six-gun battery, and I will leave here as soon as I can get transportation. Be good enough to inform me at once whether you can furnish the convoy, and, if so, how soon.

I am, captain, very respectfully, your obedient servant,

W. Q. GRESHAM,
Brigadier-General.

———

CAIRO, *April 22, 1864.*

Maj. Gen. W. T. SHERMAN :

General McPherson's orders have arrived. Generals Washburn and Hunter went down last light. General Hurlbut not arrived. Generals Leggett, Crocker, and Gresham are here, but their troops come slowly. Forrest is doubtless out of reach beyond the Hatchie. The Congressional committee are at work. I am ahead of them in securing proof. My report to you will be sent as quick as possible. I am aiding them also. I notice in your dispatch that General Prince goes to Columbus. I am commanding the District of Cairo, and Columbus is a part. He is my senior in rank. Is there not a mistake, or does he relieve me?

M. BRAYMAN,
Brigadier-General, Commanding.

HDQRS. MILITARY DIVISION OF THE MISSISSIPPI,
Nashville, Tenn., April 22, 1864.
General BRAYMAN, *Cairo:*

Your dispatch received. I think all orders have been given by McPherson which are necessary. Washburn goes to Memphis and exercises command over all the troops from Cairo down, and Slocum commands the Vicksburg district. You remain at Cairo; General Hurlbut also for the present. As soon as possible send me the report of the officers inquiring into the Pillow affair, as I must soon go forward.

W. T. SHERMAN,
Major-General.

HDQRS. MILITARY DIVISION OF THE MISSISSIPPI,
Nashville, Tenn., April 22, 1864.
General HURLBUT, *Cairo:*

A dispatch to me from General Grant, at Culpeper, shows that he wishes Dodge to command that part of your corps now at and near Decatur. Therefore, remain at Cairo until we can arrange matters. Washburn will command from Cairo down below Memphis, and Slocum on down to Banks' department. Steele will command on Red River. McPherson's troops will come up the Tennessee and join him at Huntsville, unless it turns out that Forrest is still above Memphis.

W. T. SHERMAN,
Major-General.

HDQRS. MILITARY DIVISION OF THE MISSISSIPPI,
Nashville, Tenn., April 22, 1864.
Major-General HURLBUT, *Cairo:*

GENERAL: I have your letter of April 18. My dispatch to you is not vague, but very clear.

The fact that Forrest's and Chalmers' forces, as well as that of McCulloch, passed by the flank within 50 miles of Memphis unattacked does show timidity somewhere. I didn't fix it in my dispatch to you. My dispatch was based on one from General Grant, since which time I have received the printed Orders, No. 150, which are explicit enough. I believe you had at Memphis force enough to have insured the safety of the place and left at least 4,000 infantry and as much cavalry with which to have attacked Forrest in flank going north or returning south.

I did intend to have you come to command your corps here, but orders from headquarters are that you report by letter to the Adjutant-General from Cairo.

I am, &c.,

W. T. SHERMAN,
Major-General, Commanding.

HEADQUARTERS POST AND DEFENSES,
Vicksburg, Miss., April 22, 1864.
Col. H. SCOFIELD, *Commanding Expedition:*

SIR: Your communication dated April 21, 1864, has been received, and while it is regretted that you have not entered Yazoo City, still you can better determine from your knowledge of the enemy's force in your front what is best, and it is intended that your own best judgment shall guide you in all your movements in carrying out the instructions you have received from these headquarters. If in your judgment you think it advantageous for carrying out the object of the expedition to enter Yazoo City, without endangering too much your command, do so; if not, you will occupy a tenable position, such as in your judgment the circumstances and necessity require. If you do not enter Yazoo City, and can with security hold some position near there until you can send dispatches here reporting your position, do so. Keep the transports that report to you, subject to your orders, for the use of the expedition. Medical supplies have been ordered to be sent to you on the boat going up to-day, and all the troops belonging to the expedition that have been left behind, and are able for duty, will be ordered to you on this boat.

By command of Brig. Gen. J. McArthur:

W. H. F. RANDALL,
Assistant Adjutant-General.

CAIRO, ILL., *April 22, 1864.*
(Received 4.15 p. m.. 23d.)

Hon. E. M. STANTON,
    Secretary of War:

We find the atrocities at Fort Pillow to exceed the representations in the papers.

D. W. GOOCH.

HEADQUARTERS NORTHERN DEPARTMENT,
Columbus, Ohio, April 22, 1864. (Received 2.50 p. m.)

Hon. E. M. STANTON,
    Secretary of War, Washington:

From letter of War Department, March 8, Gallipolis is not in this department. Special Orders, War Department, April 5, transfers the general hospital at that place to Western Virginia.

In reply to a communication I addressed Brigadier-General Crook in relation to the exposed situation at Gallipolis, he writes under date of Charleston, W. Va., February 26, 1864, that his forces are disposed to prevent any rebel raid being made on that place. Should there be there would be ample time to concentrate forces for its protection. There is one company, Trumbull Guards, at Gallipolis.

S. P. HEINTZELMAN,
Major-General.

GENERAL ORDERS, }   HDQRS. DEPT. OF THE CUMBERLAND,
    No. 60.   }   *Chattanooga, Tenn., April 22, 1864.*

The Army of the Cumberland is notified that it will be required to move, during the approaching campaign, with the smallest possible allowance of baggage, as the wagons will be required to transport provisions, forage, and ammunition. The allowance of camp and garrison equipage will be that authorized by paragraph 65, page

517, Appendix B, Revised Army Regulations, edition of 1863, and will not be exceeded. The enlisted men will be required to carry their shelter-tents and all their baggage upon their persons.

Attention is called to General Orders, No. 7, from headquarters Military Division of the Mississippi, dated Nashville, Tenn., April 18, 1864.

   By command of Major-General Thomas:

WM. D. WHIPPLE,
Assistant Adjutant-General.

SPECIAL FIELD ORDERS,)   HDQRS. DEPT. OF THE CUMBERLAND,
    No. 113.   )   *Chattanooga, Tenn., April 22, 1864.*

*   *   *   *   *   *   *

V. The Fifty-eighth Indiana Volunteer Infantry, Col. G. P. Buell, is hereby transferred from the Second Brigade, Second Division, Fourth Army Corps, to the Pioneer Brigade, and will report accordingly.

*   *   *   *   *

   By command of Major-General Thomas:

WM. D. WHIPPLE,
Assistant Adjutant-General.

NASHVILLE, *April 23, 1864*—midnight.

Maj. Gen. G. H. THOMAS:

   Colonel Comstock is here from General Grant, and I expect orders to move quite as early as May 1. I know all the difficulties, but want you to draw in your forces and make every possible preliminary preparation. Cannot one of the gun-boats be got ready to patrol the river from Bridgeport to Guntersville? When McPherson moves on down, all the cavalry to his front will disappear. McPherson's force will be less than we estimated, for A. J. Smith is still at Red River, and his two furloughed divisions are not yet up; therefore, increase your forces as much as possible as far out as the Coosa, whence the surplus will be sent back. Can you start with 50,000, counting Garrard as 5,000? Answer.

W. T. SHERMAN,
Major-General.

HEADQUARTERS DEPARTMENT OF THE CUMBERLAND,
Chattanooga, Tenn., April 23, 1864.

Major-General SHERMAN,
   Comdg. Military Division of the Mississippi, Nashville:

   GENERAL: Since my telegram to you about going to Nashville I have felt some uncertainty about the propriety of leaving this place for a longer period than one day, for fear something might occur to produce disorder. I wished to see you so as to have a full understanding about our movements, but if you cannot conveniently come down, I can send one of my aides to receive a copy of General Grant's letter to you, if you think it will be prudent to send me one. My

.. only object is to have a clear understanding of what is to be done. Another object for wishing to see you was to have an understanding about the travel on the railroad. By my arrangements only such persons traveled by rail as seemed to have legitimate business here, and they were required to leave as soon as their business was finished, and all refugees and deserters were sent to the rear without any trouble. All persons who got permission to travel had to pay their fare, unless they traveled under orders from proper authority (military division or some department headquarters). Now persons come on every train, permitted by papers signed by your provost-marshal-general and indorsed by Captain Crane, the transportation quartermaster for railroads at Nashville. My military conductors have orders to see that no one gets on the cars unless he has proper authority. The railroad conductors were required to collect tickets from passengers, and if the passenger had no ticket to collect the regular fare and report daily. The military conductors took up the passes and reported daily to my provost-marshal-general, thus acting as a check on the railroad conductors to prevent them from extorting money from passengers, or permitting improper persons from traveling; for the railroad superintendent, by comparing the checks taken up by his conductors with the papers taken by the military conductors each day, could easily discover if anything improper was done by his conductors. I frequently find also that persons who have been refused permission to come here by me, go to your provost-marshal-general, get papers, and come down in defiance of my authority. I think after reading my telegrams with this explanation you will understand my idea about the travel on the railroad, which I really believe the best for the interests of the service.

Very respectfully and truly, yours,

GEO. H. THOMAS,

Major-General, U. S. Volunteers, Commanding.

HDQRS. FIRST DIVISION, FOURTH ARMY CORPS,
Blue Springs, April 23, 1864.

Colonel FULLERTON,
Assistant Adjutant-General:

Scout toward Red Clay returned. Went 1 mile below there; found no enemy. Everything quiet there at 3 this a. m.

D. S. STANLEY,

Major-General.

CLEVELAND, *April 23, 1864.*

Brigadier-General WHIPPLE,
Chief of Staff:

General Stanley reports that his scouts have returned. They went as far as Claus' Chapel, 5½ miles from King's Bridge. No rebels have crossed. Saw no signs of movement. Went on to Spring Place road and no movement there. He cannot account for the rockets.

O. O. HOWARD,

Major-General, Commanding.

CHATTANOOGA, *April* 23, 1864.
Major-General HOWARD :
  What the pickets saw was a signal that the enemy was sending a strong reconnaissance across upper King's Bridge. They are out to see what Colonel La Grange's expedition meant. Send McCook out to meet them with a force sufficiently strong to whip them.
                                   GEO. H. THOMAS,
                                   Major-General, U. S. Volunteers.

HEADQUARTERS FOURTH ARMY CORPS,
                        Cleveland, Tenn., April 23, 1864—8.30 a. m.
Colonel McCOOK,
        Commanding Cavalry Division:
  COLONEL : Herewith inclosed* I send you, for your information, a dispatch just received at these headquarters from Major-General Thomas.
  You will comply with the instructions contained in the latter part of the dispatch. You had better send out a force to discover the intention of the enemy, and hold the rest of your force in readiness to make a dash or move at once.
  By order of Major-General Howard :
                                   J. S. FULLERTON,
                                   Assistant Adjutant-General.

CHATTANOOGA, *April* 23, 1864.
Col. E. M. McCOOK :
  General Thomas has expressed to me his being satisfied with Colonel La Grange's success of yesterday, and says keep the rebels stirred up, with caution, however.
                                   W. L. ELLIOTT,
                                   Brigadier-General and Chief of Cavalry.

BLUE SPRINGS, *April* 23, 1864.
Colonel FULLERTON,
        Assistant Adjutant-General, Fourth Army Corps:
  Scouts returned. Went to Claus' Chapel, 5½ miles from King's Bridge. No rebels have crossed. Saw no signs of movement. Went on to Spring Place road. Nothing moving there. Any movement must be east of Connesauga. I cannot account for the rockets.
                                   D. S. STANLEY,
                                   Major-General.

HEADQUARTERS TWENTIETH CORPS,
                        Lookout Valley, Tenn., April 23, 1864.
Brig. Gen. W. D. WHIPPLE,
        Assistant Adjutant-General, Army of the Cumberland:
  GENERAL : Major-General Rousseau reports that of his division he has at Nashville the Thirteenth Wisconsin, Eighteenth Michi-

―――――――――――――――――
  * See dispatch immediately preceding.

gan, and One hundred and second Ohio, aggregate for duty, 1,414; at Gallatin, and on railroad between Nashville and Kentucky border, the One hundred and sixth and Seventy-first Ohio, effective strength 571, and the Eighty-third Illinois at Fort Donelson and Clarksville, strength 483; total, 2,468. By his return of April 15 this officer reports in his division present for duty 4,189. Add to this the number recently transferred to him from the Eleventh and Twelfth Corps, 706, will make his whole effective force 4,895. Deduct from this number the troops in position at and beyond Nashville, 2,468, it will leave General Rousseau 2,409 officers and men to establish along the line of communications between Lookout Mountain and Nashville, or a few more than is required, as per the statement of Brigadier-General Whipple (1,460), to occupy the block-houses, omitting the garrisons at Murfreesborough, Tullahoma, Stevenson, and Bridgeport.

I desire that the attention of the major-general commanding the department may be called to the foregoing figures, and should like to be informed if, in his judgment, so large a force should be retained at Nashville and at the points beyond, now held by General Rousseau's forces. Cannot two regiments be with safety removed from Nashville?

I am informed that there are an unusual number of convalescents, contrabands, and, for aught I know, other troops not fitted for field service at that place. Please reply at your earliest convenience.

Very respectfully, your obedient servant,

JOSEPH HOOKER,
Major-General, Commanding.

HDQRS. MILITARY DIVISION OF THE MISSISSIPPI,
Nashville, April 23, 1864.

General SCHOFIELD,
Knoxville:

Colonel Comstock is here from General Grant. We may have to begin quite as soon as I first estimated, May 1. You will commence at once to break up railroad above Bull's Gap, and either bend and twist the bars or carry them to Knoxville, and move down the infantry force about the Hiwassee. Stoneman will be able to overhaul us before we will need the flanking force.

W. T. SHERMAN,
Major-General.

KNOXVILLE, *April 23, 1864.*

Major-General SHERMAN,
Nashville:

I have just returned from Bull's Gap. Nothing new of importance. All my cavalry, about 500, supported by a brigade of infantry, will start on a reconnaissance to the Watauga to-morrow.

J. M. SCHOFIELD,
Major-General.

BULL'S GAP, *April 23, 1864.*
Lieut. Col. J. W. BARRIGER,
Commissary of Subsistence, Knoxville:

It is very important that I should have here to-night 10,000 rations to enable me to carry out orders of General Schofield. Can they be sent up by extra train so as to reach here during the night? Please answer.

J. D. COX,
Brigadier-General, Commanding Third Division.

HDQRS. MILITARY DIVISION OF THE MISSISSIPPI,
Nashville, April 23, 1864.
General MCPHERSON, *Huntsville:*

We must make calculations, leaving A. J. Smith out. Banks cannot spare him, as I feared. Hurry up the two divisions from Cairo, and get ready as soon as possible, for I think Grant is pushing matters. I have news from Dalton to the 20th. A part of Polk's troops have arrived there. We must not allow our chief attention to be drawn toward Mississippi, as that is what the enemy wants.

W. T. SHERMAN,
Major-General.

HDQRS. MILITARY DIVISION OF THE MISSISSIPPI,
Nashville, April 23, 1864.
General MCPHERSON, *Huntsville:*

Colonel Comstock is here from General Grant, and we may have to move sooner than we are ready, but we can go as far as the Coosa. I will throw forward provisions enough to load your wagons, and they can be replenished at Ringgold.

If we move before Crocker gets up I will require you to move by Lebanon and Chattooga, to communicate with Thomas at La Fayette and Villanow. But I will write at length. If we move by May 1, the divisions at Scottsborough, Larkin's, and Woodville should cross at Larkin's. Dodge's force and Garrard should cross at Decatur and move to Guntersville, and a junction made at Lebanon. I do not propose to cross the Coosa till all are up, but we will gain time by a move in concert with Grant.

W. T. SHERMAN,
Major-General.

HDQRS. LEFT WING, SIXTEENTH ARMY CORPS,
Athens, Ala., April 23, 1864.
Maj. Gen. JAMES B. MCPHERSON,
Comdg. Dept. and Army of the Tennessee, Huntsville, Ala.:

GENERAL: Rumors over the river are very conflicting, but up to this time I am not satisfied that the force has been greatly increased. I think a small force of cavalry in addition has joined Roddey.

Two of the Ninth Illinois Infantry, who have been prisoners at Danville, escaped last night; they report a pretty large force, all mounted.

Day before yesterday, when we commenced artillery practice at Decatur, the force west of there, on the Courtland road, came out in plain view of our cavalry pickets in line of battle and advanced toward the place a short distance. The officer in command of the picket judged there were about 1,500 in all.

The scouts that go to the rear report no scattering troops; that all are closed around Decatur, and we do not have much trouble in getting men around their entire command. From reports brought from Gadsden I am satisfied more cavalry are on their way toward us; whether it comes to Decatur or not we have not fully ascertained. General Veatch reports Hall's regiment picketing this morning within 5 miles of town; this is a new regiment and used to belong to Davidson's brigade, Martin's division. I inclose Colonel Rowett's report that came in this morning; if true, we will soon know it, as we have a number of men in the valley. It also seems impossible for Polk to move without my getting good notice, as I have men posted on the Mobile and Ohio Railroad about Columbus, Miss., Tuscaloosa, Selma, Fayetteville, &c., and all watching for his move. I do not believe the enemy contemplates an attack on Decatur right away; they have a lookout on the mountain 10 miles out, from which they can see every house in the town, our troops, &c., and they certainly would not attack with their and our present forces.

The officers at Decatur set their entire force at 7,000 men. I have figured closely on it and think it nearer 5,000 or 6,000; but this does not include any that may have reached the valley since day before yesterday.

Do the troops at Larkin's Ferry hear from the country south of them? All this cavalry must pass their front.

Orders in relation to transportation, reports, &c., received, and will be promptly carried out.

I am, general, very respectfully, your obedient servant,

G. M. DODGE,
Brigadier-General.

[Inclosure.]

HEADQUARTERS,
Florence, Ala.. April 23, 1864.

Capt. J. W. BARNES,
Asst. Adjt. Gen., Hdqrs. Left Wing, 16*th Army Corps* ·

SIR: I have the honor to report as follows:

I have reliable information that Wisdom, with Forrest's old regiment, is at Tuscumbia; three regiments moving through Iuka. Forrest was ordered to Okolona, but the order was countermanded on the 19th. Corn was being hauled from Okolona to Corinth for distribution to Forrest's command. Forrest is reported moving east with his entire command. I think his destination is Decatur, Ala.

I had a long interview with Calvin Goodloe, who came over by flag of truce this morning.

Received communication from Major Murphy complaining that Thrasher with his men are committing many depredations, and asking that Thrasher be ordered to report to him. Citizens make frequent complaints of the depredations committed by Thrasher's men.

I have the honor to be, very respectfully, your obedient servant,

R. ROWETT,
Commanding Seventh Illinois and Ninth Ohio.

April 23, 1864.

Hensal, *Chief of Scouts, Decatur :*

Try to get a man out east of Flint to work around in the rear toward Day's Gap, and see what is coming into the valley from that direction.

G. M. DODGE,
Brigadier-General.

HDQRS. FOURTH DIVISION, SIXTEENTH ARMY CORPS,
Decatur, Ala., April 23, 1864—9 a. m.

Brigadier-General DODGE,
Athens :

A large force was found encamped on the Danville road last night at the foot of the mountains, 5½ miles out. This morning scouts report the trail of a heavy force had crossed last night toward the Moulton road. Patterson sends a flag of truce on the Moulton road, dated at Oakville, 22d, asking to exchange 7 prisoners for a like number in our hands. I direct Captain Pollock to say that we have no prisoners, but will receive our men, if he chooses to release them, and send him an equal number when we have them. I think the flag of truce is a trick. Their forces are certainly growing larger.

JAMES C. VEATCH,
Brigadier-General.

April 23, 1864.

Brig. Gen. J. C. VEATCH, *Decatur :*

I have sent some men out on east side of Flint to try to get to the rear of those men. We must watch closely. The Eighteenth Missouri Infantry will be here in a day or two.

G. M. DODGE,
Brigadier-General.

HDQRS. FOURTH DIVISION, SIXTEENTH ARMY CORPS,
Decatur, Ala., April 23, 1864—9 p. m.

Brigadier-General DODGE,
Comdg. Left Wing, Sixteenth Army Corps, Athens :

The force on the Danville road passed westward during last night, or very early this morning. Heavy pickets have been found on the Moulton and Courtland roads, but no force on the Danville or Somerville road within 6 miles. No signs of the enemy at Triana.

JAMES C. VEATCH,
Brigadier-General.

HUNTSVILLE, ALA.,
April 23, 1864.

Brig. Gen. G. M. DODGE, *Athens :*

General Smith reports from Larkinsville a considerable force of rebel cavalry moving westward ; say they are going to join Forrest. It is probably a part of Martin's division.

JAS. B. McPHERSON,
Major-General, Commanding.

HEADQUARTERS DISTRICT OF WEST TENNESSEE,
Memphis, Tenn., April 23, 1864.
Hon. E. M. STANTON,
     Secretary of War, Washington, D. C.:
     SIR : I report that I arrived here to-day and assumed command. Nothing special to report, except that a reconnaissance made by General Grierson, which returned last night, reports that Forrest, after running his prisoners and plunder down into Mississippi, had returned with his whole force, about 8,000 strong, and was near Jackson. Tenn.
     I have only 1,800 mounted cavalry here, and that very poor, 2,000 infantry, and 3,500 colored troops, entirely too weak, as you see, to move far aggressively, without leaving Memphis at his mercy. I have advised General Grant and General Sherman fully of the situation here. The rebels have repaired the Mobile and Ohio Railroad north as far as Corinth.
     I have the honor to be, your obedient servant,
C. C. WASHBURN,
Major-General.

HEADQUARTERS DISTRICT OF WEST TENNESSEE,
Memphis, Tenn., April 23, 1864.
Brig. Gen. JOHN A. RAWLINS,
     Chief of Staff:
     SIR : I report that I arrived here and assumed command to-day. All quiet in town, but Brigadier-General Grierson, who returned from a scout last night, reports that Forrest, after sending his prisoners and plunder down into Mississippi, had returned with his whole force and was in the neighborhood of Jackson, Tenn. He is reported to have seven brigades, under the following-named brigade commanders, viz : General Bell, Colonel Faulkner, Colonel Duckworth, Colonel Neely, General Chalmers. Colonel Forrest, and General Buford, the last named commanding a division. Forrest's total force is said to be about 8,000 men, all well mounted. In returning into West Tennessee he, of course, means mischief somewhere. I regret that my force here is not sufficient to enable me to move out and assail him. I have only 1,800 very poor cavalry mounted, made up of odds and ends, and about 1,000 dismounted cavalry. The rest of the cavalry force of the Sixteenth Army Corps are at home on furlough ; two regiments filled to the maximum, the Third Michigan and Seventh Kansas, reached Saint Louis a month ago on their return, and detained there for horses and arms. My whole troops consist of only 2,000 infantry, white, 600 white artillery, and 3,500 colored troops. You will readily see that this force will allow me to do little but act on the defensive.
     Information deemed entirely reliable by Major-General Hurlbut represents that the rebels have repaired the railroad north to Corinth. The road is also said to be in good repair from Corinth west to La Grange. If this is the case, there can be no difficulty in their massing a large force of infantry in a short time at Corinth or La Grange. The brigade of Brigadier-General Mower, which was ordered by General Sherman up here, is likely to be detained by General Banks for an indefinite period.
     The massacre at Fort Pillow turns out to be worse than the newspapers have reported. I am taking measures to ascertain the names of officers in command and the regiments engaged in that affair,

hoping that the President will issue a proclamation of outlawry against them. Of one thing you may be certain, that I shall not issue any orders requiring the troops of this command to spare the monsters engaging in a transaction that renders the Sepoy a humane being and Nana-Sahib a clever gentleman. I send up by the same boat that takes this a duplicate to be telegraphed to General Sherman, in regard to the continued presence of Forrest in Tennessee, and of the repair of the railroad to Corinth. While with the force I have here I feel perfectly secure against any mounted force they may bring, I do not feel that I could venture to go in pursuit of Forrest without hazarding the city, unless I have more force.

As soon as I learn more about matters, I shall again write you.

I am, general, your obedient servant,

C. C. WASHBURN,
Major-General.

HDQRS. MILITARY DIVISION OF THE MISSISSIPPI,
Nashville, Tenn., April 23, 1864.

General BURBRIDGE,
Commanding, Louisville, Ky. :

GENERAL : I have a series of papers from General Halleck which go to show a conspiracy on the part of mischievous men residing in Kentucky, Indiana, Ohio, and Canada for the purpose of destroying steam-boats and even cities. We cannot operate by military force against such devils, but we can shelter and protect steam-boat captains who resort to extraordinary measures to guard the property and lives in their charge against such villains. You may notify them that if they detect among their passengers or crew one or more whom they know to be engaged in such a scheme that they should be disposed of summarily, viz, drowned or killed on the spot. The only question is of proof, which should be as clear as possible. It is not war for individuals to burn steam-boats or supply them with coal or wood charged with gunpowder, and the laws of war do not apply to such people ; therefore, I don't care to have our military prisons or courts encumbered with such cases.

The information on which this plot is inferred comes from the provost-marshal of Louisville and others, viz, Lieut. Col. J. R. Smith, commanding at Detroit. Two of the principal men engaged in the plot are named McRay and Jones, residing at Windsor, Canada West, who have recently passed through Louisville.

I think if the captains of the steam-boats are notified and sustained, they will more effectually counteract such a plot than we can do by any direct military interference.

I am, &c.,

W. T. SHERMAN,
Major-General, Commanding.

HDQRS. MILITARY DIVISION OF THE MISSISSIPPI,
Nashville, Tenn., April 23, 1864.

Major-General ROSECRANS,
Commanding Department of the Missouri.

GENERAL : I have from General Halleck a series of papers going to show a combination and conspiracy pervading the mischievous "to burn steam-boats and even cities in our country."

Of course it is difficult, if not impossible, for any military system to be devised which will counteract such plots, but it is well to be warned and authorize the necessary remedies.

I would have no hesitation in authorizing steam-boat captains who find among their crews one or more such mischievous characters to drop them overboard and let them find the bottom in their own way. Self-preservation, being a law of nature, will justify any means of prevention, and our prisons and courts should not be embarrassed by men who would resort to such means of carrying on war. It is not war, and the rules of war do not apply to such criminals, and the only question is to the proof necessary to establish a case.

I will justify any steam-boat captain that finds on board as crew or passenger a man found attempting to fire his boat or in supplying it with powder-charged coal or wood who kills him on the spot in his own way.

I am, &c.,

W. T. SHERMAN,
Major-General, Commanding.

HDQRS. MILITARY DIVISION OF THE MISSISSIPPI,
Nashville, Tenn., April 23, 1864.

Hon. E. M. STANTON,
Secretary of War, Washington:

SIR: Pursuant to your orders two officers are now engaged in taking affidavits and collecting testimony as to the Fort Pillow affair. They are ordered to send you direct a copy of their report and one to me.

I know well the animus of the Southern soldiery, and the truth is they cannot be restrained. The effect will be of course to make the negroes desperate, and when in turn they commit horrid acts of retaliation we will be relieved of the responsibility. Thus far negroes have been comparatively well behaved, and have not committed the horrid excesses and barbarities which the Southern papers so much dreaded.

I send you herewith my latest newspapers from Atlanta, of the 18th and 19th instant. In them you will find articles of interest and their own accounts of the Fort Pillow affair.

The enemy will contend that a place taken by assault is not entitled to quarter, but this rule would have justified us in an indiscriminate slaughter at Arkansas Post, Fort De Russy, and other places taken by assault. I doubt the wisdom of any fixed rule by our Government, but let soldiers affected make their rules as we progress. We will use their own logic against them, as we have from the beginning of the war.

The Southern army, which is the Southern people, cares no more for our clamor than the idle wind, but they will heed the slaughter that will follow as the natural consequence of their own inhuman acts.

I am, &c.,

W. T. SHERMAN,
Major-General, Commanding.

CAIRO, *April* 23, 1864. (Received 25th.)
General SHERMAN :

Grierson on the 21st was between Olive Branch and La Grange. Reports three brigades of Forrest's command returning north. He was reported at Coldwater Station ; not credited. Grierson was to move there to ascertain.

S. A. HURLBUT,
Major-General.

GENERAL ORDERS, }   WAR DEPT., ADJT. GENERAL'S OFFICE,
No. 178.   }   *Washington, April* 23, 1864.

I. Maj. Gen. F. P. Blair, jr., is assigned to the command of the Seventeenth Army Corps.

II. Capt. Andrew J. Alexander, Third Regiment U. S. Cavalry, is assigned as assistant adjutant-general of the Seventeenth Army Corps, with the rank of lieutenant-colonel, under the 10th section of the act approved July 17, 1862.

By order of the President of the United States :

E. D. TOWNSEND,
Assistant Adjutant-General.

SPECIAL ORDERS, }   HDQRS. MIL. DIV. OF THE MISSISSIPPI,
No. 33.   }   *Nashville, Tenn., April* 23, 1864.

I. Brig. Gen. J. Kilpatrick, U. S. Volunteers, having reported in person at these headquarters pursuant to Special Orders, No. 12, dated headquarters Armies of the United States in the field, Culpeper Court-House, Va., April 15, 1864, is assigned to duty with the Army of the Cumberland, and will report in person to Maj. Gen. George H. Thomas, commanding, for assignment to a cavalry command.

*   *   *   *   *   *   *

By order of Maj. Gen. W. T. Sherman :

R. M. SAWYER,
Assistant Adjutant-General.

SPECIAL FIELD ORDERS, }   HDQRS. DEPT. OF THE CUMBERLAND,
No. 114.   }   *Chattanooga, Tenn., April* 23, 1864.

*   *   *   *   *   *   *

X. Battery A, First Regiment Ohio Artillery, Capt. Wilbur F. Goodspeed, now in the Artillery Reserve, Nashville, is hereby transferred to the Second Division, Fourth Army Corps, and Battery G, First Regiment Missouri Volunteer Artillery, is transferred to the permanent garrison of Chattanooga.

By command of Major-General Thomas :

WM. D. WHIPPLE,
Assistant Adjutant-General.

CONFIDENTIAL.]   HDQRS. MIL. DIV. OF THE MISSISSIPPI,
Nashville, Tenn., April 24, 1864.

Lieut. Gen. U. S. GRANT,
Commanding Armies of the United States, Culpeper, Va.:

GENERAL : I now have, at the hands of Colonel Comstock, of your staff, the letter of April 19, and am as far prepared to assume the

30 R R—VOL XXXII PT III

offensive as possible; I only ask as much time as you think proper to enable me to get up McPherson's two divisions from Cairo. Their furloughs all expire about this time, and some of them should now be in motion for Clifton, whence they march to Decatur and join on to Dodge.

McPherson is ordered to assemble the Fifteenth Corps near Larkin's, and to get Dodge and Blair at Decatur at the earliest possible moment, and from those two points he will direct his forces on Lebanon, Summerville, and La Fayette, where he will act against Johnston if he accepts battle at Dalton. or move in the direction of Rome if he gives up Dalton and falls behind the Oostcnaula or Etowah. I see there is some risk in dividing our forces, but Thomas and Schofield will have forces enough to cover all the valley as far as Dalton, and should Johnston turn his whole force against McPherson, the latter will have his bridge at Larkin's and the route to Chattanooga via Will's Valley and the Chattanooga, and if Johnston attempts to leave Dalton, Thomas will have force enough to push on through Dalton to Kingston, which would checkmate him.

My own opinion is Johnston will be compelled to hang to his railroad, the only possible avenue of supply to his army, estimated from 45,000 to 60,000 men.

At La Fayette all our armies will be together, and if Johnston stands at Dalton we must attack him in position. Thomas feels certain that he has no material increase of force, and that he has not sent away Hardee or any part of his army.

Supplies are the great question. I have materially increased the number of cars daily. When I got here they ran from 65 to 80 per day. Yesterday the report was 193, to-day 134, and my estimate is 145 per day will give us daily a days' accumulation.

McPherson is ordered to carry in wagons twenty days' supplies, and rely on the depot at Ringgold for the renewal of his bread ration. Beeves are now being driven to the front, and my commissary, Colonel Beckwith, seems fully alive to the importance of the whole matter.

Our weakest point will be from the direction of Decatur, and I will be forced to risk something from that quarter, depending on the fact that the enemy has no force available with which to threaten our communications from that direction.

Colonel Comstock will explain much that I cannot commit to paper.

I am, with great respect,

W. T. SHERMAN,
Major-General.

[Inclosure.]

HDQRS. MILITARY DIVISION OF THE MISSISSIPPI,
Nashville, Tenn., April 24, 1864.

REPORT OF EFFECTIVE STRENGTH AND STATIONS.

Department of the Cumberland.

Chattanooga and headquarters Department of the Cumberland 4,992
Fourth Army Corps (Major-General Howard commanding) 17,619
Fourteenth Army Corps (Major-General Palmer commanding) 21,330
Twentieth Army Corps (Major-General Hooker commanding) 27,038

Cavalry command (Brigadier-General Elliott, chief) 11,930
Engineer troops 3,334
Unassigned artillery (twenty-seven guns) 1,072
Post troops: Nashville, Tenn.; Fort Donelson, Tenn.; Clarksville, Tenn.;
Gallatin, Tenn.; Murfreesborough, Tenn.; Nashville and Northwestern
Railroad 5,405

Total 92,720

FOURTH CORPS.

Headquarters, Cleveland, Tenn.
First Division (Major-General Stanley), Cleveland, Blue Springs, and Ooltewah, Tenn.
Second Division (Brigadier-General Wagner), Loudon, Charleston; one regiment, Lenoir's Station; one regiment, Athens, Tenn.; one regiment. Sweet Water, Tenn.
Third Division (Brig. Gen. T. J. Wood), on march to Cleveland, Tenn.

FOURTEENTH CORPS.

Headquarters, Chattanooga, Tenn.
First Division (Brig. Gen. R. W. Johnson), Graysville; one regiment, Tyner's Station; one regiment, Parker's Gap; one regiment, Chattanooga; two regiments, Lookout Mountain.
Second Division (Brig. Gen. J. C. Davis), Rossville, Lee and Gordon's Mills; one regiment, Nashville.
Third Division (Brig. Gen. A. Baird), Ringgold, Ga.

TWENTIETH CORPS.

Headquarters, Lookout Valley.
First Division (Brig. Gen. A. S. Williams), headquarters, Tullahoma; on Nashville and Chattanooga Railroad from Wartrace to Stevenson; Bridgeport; one regiment, Shelbyville; one regiment, Fayetteville; one regiment. Shellmound; one regiment, Whiteside's.
Second Division (Brig. Gen. J. W. Geary), Bridgeport, Stevenson, Shellmound, Lookout Valley.
Third Division (Major-General Butterfield), Lookout Valley; one regiment, Decherd; one regiment. Whiteside's.
Fourth Division (Maj. Gen. L. H. Rousseau), Nashville; one regiment. Whiteside's; two regiments, Murfreesborough; two regiments, Shellmound; one regiment, Christiana; two regiments, Gallatin and railroad; one regiment, Fort Donelson and Clarksville.

CAVALRY.

First Division (Col. E. M. McCook), Cleveland, Tenn.
Second Division (Brig. Gen. K. Garrard), Columbia, Tenn.
Third Division (Col. W. W. Lowe), Ringgold, Bull's Gap, Nashville. (Four regiments on furlough.)

ENGINEER TROOPS.

Chattanooga, Bridgeport, and Nashville and Northwestern Railroad.

Department of the Tennessee.

FIFTEENTH CORPS (MAJ. GEN. JOHN A. LOGAN).

On line of Memphis and Charleston Railroad, Ala.—14,341 *a* men.
First Division (Brigadier-General Osterhaus), Woodville.
Second Division (Brig. Gen. M. L. Smith), Larkinsville.
Third Division (Brig. Gen. John E. Smith), Huntsville.
Fourth Division (Brig. Gen. William Harrow), Scottsborough.

SIXTEENTH CORPS.

Left Wing (Brigadier-General Dodge), stationed along railroad from Columbia, Tenn., to Decatur and Mooresville, Ala., with two regiments cavalry patrolling river from Decatur to Hamburg, 12,453 *a*. Balance of Sixteenth Corps (Memphis, Columbus, Cairo, Paducah, and up Red River), 19,624.

SEVENTEENTH CORPS.

District of Vicksburg (Major-General Slocum), Vicksburg, Natchez, &c.; white, 6,461 ; colored, 7,775 ; total, 14,236.
Third Division (Brigadier-General Leggett), now rendezvousing at Cairo, Ill., 6,000.
Fourth Division (Brigadier-General Crocker), now rendezvousing at Cairo, Ill., 6,000.

Department of the Ohio.

TWENTY-THIRD CORPS.

First Division (Brig. Gen. A. P. Hovey), en route to Charleston, 4,500 *b*.
Second Division (Brigadier-General Judah), Mossy Creek (ordered to Charleston), 4,200 *b*.
Third Division (Brig. Gen. J. D. Cox), Bull's Gap (ordered to Charleston), 3,900 *b*.
Fourth Division (Brigadier-General Ammen), Cumberland Gap, Knoxville, Loudon. &c., 4,700.
Fifth Division (Brigadier-General Burbridge), Louisville, District of Kentucky, 9,500.
Cavalry (Major-General Stoneman), Nicholasville. No report of effective strength. In Kentucky, remounting, about 5,000 *b*.

Army of Invasion of Georgia.

Left, Major-General Schofield commanding :

Hovey, 4,500 ; Judah, 4,200 ; Cox, 3,900	12,600
Stoneman's cavalry	5,000
Total	**17,600**

Center, Maj. Gen. G. H. Thomas commanding :

Howard, 15,000 ; Palmer, 20,000 ; Hooker, 20,000	55,000
Kilpatrick's cavalry	5,000
Total	**60,000**

a 10,000 for action.   *b* For action.

Right. Maj. Gen. J. B. McPherson commanding:

Logan, 10,000 ; Dodge, 10,000 ; Blair, 10,000........................ 30,000
Garrard's cavalry 5,000

Total... 35,000

Grand aggregate... 112,600

This exceeds the probable force for duty, but is based on my official reports. If I can put in motion 100,000 it will make as large an army as we can possibly supply.

HDQRS. MILITARY DIVISION OF THE MISSISSIPPI,
Nashville, Tenn., April 24, 1864.

Maj. Gen. H. W. HALLECK,
Washington, D. C.:

DEAR GENERAL: I now send you two more newspapers, my latest from Atlanta. I don't know if you have a quicker mail from that foreign port. I sent dates of the 18th and 19th by Colonel Comstock, and these are of the 20th.

Of course, in spite of all secrecy, Lee and Johnston are well apprised of the concentration going on to their front and are preparing for the conflict which they know to be inevitable. My greatest difficulty arises from the question of supplies, but when Grant moves I will, and then stand from under.

I see a mischievous paragraph that you are dissatisfied, and will resign ; of course I don't believe it. If I did I would enter my protest. You possess a knowledge of law and of the principles of war far beyond that of any other officer in our service. You remember that I regretted your going to Washington for your own sake, but now that you are there you should not leave.

Stability is what we lack in our Government, and changes are always bad. Stand by us and encourage us by your counsels and advice. I know Grant esteems you, and I assure you I do.

I will go forward and command in person the moment I get the word start. I am now moving all my men into position and am drawing forward everything I can by way of reserve and road guards.

As ever, your friend,

W. T. SHERMAN.

HDQRS. MILITARY DIVISION OF THE MISSISSIPPI,
Nashville, April 24, 1864.

General THOMAS,
Chattanooga:

You may be as severe as possible with citizens who smuggle themselves into the cars. All are prohibited from going. I have more than doubled the number of cars per day. Yesterday we got off one hundred and ninety-three cars.

If you send a staff officer I will send you copies of General Grant's letters. They embrace the points of mine. Time is nearly up, and you cannot have your preparations too far advanced. For the first week out we will need but few wagons.

As McPherson will not have A. J. Smith's division, and some of his furloughed regiments will be late, you had better make ready with every man you can take along, and as McPherson's detachments come up your surplus forces can be sent back. I will come down as soon as possible.

W. T. SHERMAN,
Major-General.

CHATTANOOGA, *April* 24, 1864—10.30 p. m.
(Received 25th.)
Major-General SHERMAN :

I will send Captain Kellogg, my aide, to-morrow to report to you. Orders were given early this morning to concentrate General Hooker's command. I will put in motion as many as I can. General Howard's corps is now concentrated near Cleveland. One of the gun-boats is now on its way to this place from Bridgeport; another will be finished next week.

GEO. H. THOMAS,
Major-General.

CHATTANOOGA, *April* 24, 1864—10 a. m.
Major-General SHERMAN,
Nashville:

I have given orders for the distribution of General Rousseau's troops along the railroad from Nashville to this place, General Hooker being at the same time directed to concentrate his command in Lookout Valley. These dispositions can be completed, I hope, by the end of the month. One of the gun-boats is now ready to receive her armament and crew. Admiral Porter agreed with General Grant to furnish both if desired. I should prefer it, but willingly leave the choice to you. I can take into the field between 45,000 and 50,000 men. I shall lose from 5,000 to 8,000 men by the middle of June, by reason of expiration of service.

GEO. H. THOMAS,
Major-General U. S. Volunteers.

HEADQUARTERS DEPARTMENT OF THE CUMBERLAND,
Chattanooga, April 24, 1864.
Brigadier-General BAIRD :

Your dispatch.* reporting the attack on the outpost at Nickajack Gap, received. I am well aware that extreme outposts are always exposed, and for that reason they should be sleeplessly vigilant. If we do not run risks we never shall know anything of the enemy. I am afraid the outpost, although ready for an attack, had not kept up its connection with the next toward Ringgold by patrols, nor did the commanding officer keep himself informed of the situation of affairs in his neighborhood, but contented himself with thinking he was safe as long as his vedettes in the pass in his front were not dis-

---

* See Part I, p. 678.

turbed. All outposts, pickets, and vedettes should be ceaseless in their vigilance; otherwise, no matter how strong or how little advanced they may be, they are in danger of being overwhelmed. The outrages committed by the enemy on the prisoners will be attended to.

GEO. H. THOMAS,
Major-General, U. S. Volunteers, Commanding.

HDQRS. SECOND BRIG., FIRST DIV., 20TH ARMY CORPS,
Tullahoma, Tenn., April 24, 1864.
Capt. S. E. PITTMAN,
Asst. Adjt. Gen., First Div., Twentieth Army Corps:

SIR: I have the honor to submit the following report of condition of defenses on line of Nashville and Chattanooga Railroad from Bell Buckle bridge to Poor Man's Creek bridge, inclusive, so far as any changes have been made since last report:

Bell Buckle bridge (1 mile south of Bell Buckle): One small redoubt completed and one block-house nearly completed. Number of days' rations on hand, 7; number of days' wood and water, 7.

Wartrace bridge (1 mile north of Wartrace): One small fort and one stockade completed and one block-house nearly completed. Number of days' rations on hand, 7; number of days' wood and water, 7.

Wartrace: No change since last report. Number of days' rations on hand, 7; number of days' wood and water, 7.

Garrison's Fork bridge (1 mile south of Wartrace): No change since last report. Number of days' rations on hand, 7; number of days' wood and water, 7.

Duck River bridge: No change since last report. Number of days' rations on hand, 10; number of days' wood and water, 10.

Normandy: Since last report the men at this post have been engaged in banking up and covering the block-house recently constructed by the Michigan Engineers. It will require about five days to complete it. Number of days' rations on hand, 7; number of days' wood and water, 7.

Tullahoma: No change since last report. Number of days' rations on hand, 7; number of days' wood and water, 7.

Poor Man's Creek bridge (1 mile south of Tullahoma): A block-house is being erected at this post. Number of days' rations on hand, 7; number of days' wood and water, 7.

Very respectfully, your obedient servant,

THOS. H. RUGER,
Brigadier-General, Commanding.

HEADQUARTERS DEPARTMENT OF THE CUMBERLAND,
Chattanooga, April 24, 1864.
Maj. Gen. JOSEPH HOOKER,
Commanding Twentieth Army Corps:

GENERAL: Inclosed I send you copies of telegrams just received from Major-General Rousseau, which show that he has sufficient force to guard the railroad from Nashville to Chattanooga, leaving garrisons at Tullahoma, Stevenson, and Bridgeport, in addition to the one at Murfreesborough, which is already fixed.   One regiment is to be stationed at Tullahoma, one at Stevenson, and two at Bridgeport.   The major-general commanding directs that you put him in position as quickly as possible, and relieve and bring to the front those of the other division now on the line of the route in accordance with the schedule sent you.   In addition to that list there has been added a block-house at Estill Springs, 20 men, and one at the wood-yard between there and Tullahoma of 20 men, making a force of 1,400 men required to man the block-houses from Nashville to Chattanooga.   One regiment can be withdrawn from the garrison of Nashville and placed farther down the road.

I am, general, very respectfully, your obedient servant,

HENRY STONE,
Assistant Adjutant-General.

[Inclosure No. 1.]

NASHVILLE, *April 23, 1864.*

Brig. Gen. W. D. WHIPPLE,
Chief of Staff:

Coburn's brigade left here for the front on Tuesday morning last, Colonel Utley commanding.   It is now on the march between this and General Hooker's headquarters.   The effective-force report of the regiments in my division was sent on the 18th, just the date of your previous dispatch.   Another was sent to Major-General Hooker this day.   I have not any report from the Fifty-eighth New York nor the Seventy-fifth Pennsylvania Regiments, transferred from the Eleventh Corps to my division.

The following is the strength of regiments :

18th Michigan	625
102d Ohio Volunteer Infantry	293
13th Wisconsin	498
73d Indiana	206
10th Tennessee	755

This includes Granger's brigade.   The unassigned regiments are—

115th Ohio Volunteer Infantry	589
31st Wisconsin	570
23d Wisconsin	647
71st Ohio	334
106th Ohio	237
83d Illinois	483
68th New York	334

These are the aggregate, and as soon as I hear from the Fifty-eighth New York and Seventy-fifth Pennsylvania I will telegraph you.

LOVELL H. ROUSSEAU,
Major-General.

[Inclosure No. 2.]

NASHVILLE. *April 24, 1864.*

Brigadier-General WHIPPLE,
Chief of Staff:

Effective strength of the Seventy-fifth Pennsylvania, commissioned officers, 14 ; enlisted men, 229.

LOVELL H. ROUSSEAU,
Major-General.

HEADQUARTERS TWENTIETH CORPS,
Lookout Valley, Tenn., April 24, 1864.

Maj. Gen. L. H. ROUSSEAU,
    Commanding Fourth Division, &c.:

GENERAL : I am directed by the major-general commanding the
Twentieth Corps to transmit for your information and government
a copy of a letter dated headquarters of the department, Chattanooga, April 24, 1864.*

From this letter it appears that two additional block-houses have
been added to the list already furnished, which will require to be
held by your troops. It appears further that in the opinion of the
commander of the department two regiments only will be necessary
to hold Nashville. This will leave you an additional force to dispose of on the line of communications, and the general suggests that
so many as are not required to fulfill the other conditions of your
orders be instructed to take post on the south side of theTennessee
River opposite to Bridgeport. This point is deemed one of great
importance, where all troops not required at other points should be
sent.

I am further instructed by the major-general commanding to call
your attention to the necessity of having your troops dispatched to
their destinations at the earliest practicable moment, as his orders
for assembling the troops relieved at the end of the month are imperative.

Very respectfully, your obedient servant,
                                   H. W. PERKINS,
                            Assistant Adjutant-General.

LOOKOUT VALLEY, *April 24, 1864.*

Brig. Gen. JOHN W. GEARY, *Bridgeport :*

The general commanding directs that upon being relieved you
concentrate your troops at Bridgeport, and report by telegram for
orders.
                                   H. W. PERKINS,
                            Assistant Adjutant-General.

LOOKOUT VALLEY, *April 24, 1864.*

Brig. Gen. ALPHEUS S. WILLIAMS, *Tullahoma :*

The general commanding directs that you march your division to
the front as soon as it is relieved by General Rousseau's troops.
                                   H. W. PERKINS,
                            Assistant Adjutant-General.

HEADQUARTERS TWENTIETH CORPS,
Lookout Valley, Tenn., April 24, 1864.

Brig. Gen. A. S. WILLIAMS,
    Commanding First Division, Twentieth Army Corps:

GENERAL : General Rousseau has been ordered to relieve the whole
of your command, and it will be done as soon as possible.

I am, general, very respectfully, your obedient servant,
                                   H. W. PERKINS,
                Lieutenant-Colonel and Assistant Adjutant-General.

* See p. 471.

KNOXVILLE. *April* 24, 1864.
Major-General SHERMAN :
    Your dispatch of yesterday directing me to destroy the railroad
and move down to the Hiwassee is just received. I have ordered the
cavalry which left Bull's Gap this morning to push forward and
destroy the Watauga and Holston bridges, and the brigade of infantry, which also started this morning, to break up the same. and
to destroy the bridges above Greeneville. My other troops will destroy the road from Lick Creek toward Greeneville. I will push the
work rapidly, and move down to the Hiwassee as soon as possible :
think it will take me until the 1st of May to reach there if I take
time to destroy the roads thoroughly. Will that be soon enough, or
must I be there sooner ?
                                    J. M. SCHOFIELD,
                                         Major-General.

                                    NASHVILLE. TENN.,
                                         April 24, 1864.
General SCHOFIELD :
    May 1 will be soon enough for you to be at the Hiwassee.   Colonel
Comstock has just started for Washington and will keep me well
advised of the progress there.   We must move in concert with General Grant.   I have written you fully by courier to-day.
                                    W. T. SHERMAN,
                                         Major-General.

            HDQRS. MILITARY DIVISION OF THE MISSISSIPPI,
                        Nashville, April 24, 1864.
General SCHOFIELD,
            Knoxville :
    Your dispatch is received.   I telegraphed you last night to begin
your movement toward the Hiwassee in preparation for the advance
into Georgia.   Let the brigade of infantry sent beyond Bull's Gap
make the break in the railroad, and begin to move your command
for active service down to Charleston.   I write you fully to-day.
                                    W. T. SHERMAN,
                                         Major-General.

CONFIDENTIAL.]   HDQRS. MIL. DIV. OF THE MISSISSIPPI,
                        Nashville, Tenn., April 24, 1864.
Maj. Gen. J. M. SCHOFIELD,
        Commanding Department of the Ohio, Knoxville :
    GENERAL : I now have a messenger out from General Grant, which
convinces me that the Army of the Potomac, from its shorter lines
and superabundant supplies, will be ready sooner than we ; but let
come what may we must attack Joe Johnston in position, or force
him back of Coosa, at the moment the initiative is made in the East.
I prefer that Johnston should not move at all, but receive us on his
present ground.   But I do not propose rushing on him rashly until
I have in hand all the available strength of your, Thomas', and Mc-
Pherson's armies.

Supplies are the chief trouble; but if the worst comes to the worst, we can live on beef and salt, with such bread as our road ought to carry for us to Ringgold.

Of course there remains now in East Tennessee no rebel force that can come down on our flank that could seriously endanger us moving forward from Chattanooga; but I wish you to dispose your command to guard against that chance. Destroy a considerable section of the railroad above Bull's Gap, bending and twisting the rails or carrying them to Knoxville.

Leave Knoxville and Loudon well guarded, and assemble your effective force near Charleston, on the Hiwassee, prepared by May 1, if possible, to move in concert with Thomas down by way of Varnell's Station direct on Dalton.

Order Stoneman to move by the best route available to him so as to report to you. If Johnston refuses us battle, this cavalry will be sent by way of Spring Place, or it may be higher up by the copper mines, to threaten the enemy's right rear.

Order all your forces in Kentucky to be most active, even to feel out through Pound Gap into the valley beyond. I have no apprehension of the enemy interfering with our lines of communication in Kentucky, because we have here in Nashville the essential supplies for six months. Those in the western part of Kentucky ought to watch well the line, and to arrest all suspicious men hanging about who have no honest employment. Precaution may save us temporary annoyance. Such men are not prisoners of war, but simply men held by us rather than incur the risks of their mischievous acts.

It is useless for us to expect the new cavalry from Indiana. We cannot mount even the veteran cavalry, which should, of course, have precedence. I will be at Chattanooga about May 1.

Truly, yours,

W. T. SHERMAN,
Major-General, Commanding.

———

KNOXVILLE, *April* 24, 1864.

Major-General HOWARD.

I have ordered your troops between the Hiwassee and Loudon to be relieved according to your request.

J. M. SCHOFIELD,
Major-General.

———

KNOXVILLE, TENN., *April* 24, 1864.

Brigadier-General COX, *Bull's Gap:*

General Sherman directs me to destroy the railroad above Bull's Gap immediately and proceed to carry out his plans. Order General Manson to destroy at once all the bridges above Greeneville and break up and destroy the rails as far as possible, working back this way from the bridges. Let the cavalry push on and destroy the Watauga and Holston bridges, if possible. Commence yourself to-morrow to destroy the road from Lick Creek toward Greeneville. I will send up tools to-night. I have ordered General Hascall's brigade to Bull's Gap to support you. Let the work be pushed forward as rapidly as possible; time is important.

J. M. SCHOFIELD,
Major-General.

BULL'S GAP, *April* 24, 1864.

Major-General SCHOFIELD,
        Knoxville:

Manson got off promptly at daybreak this morning. The cavalry are ordered to make 30 miles a day, and the infantry 20. All have five days' rations and forage. The instructions for their guidance in different contingencies I made out fully as you directed. The news brought in by scouts makes me confident of success for the expedition, there being no rebel force sufficient to meet them this side of Holston.

J. D. COX,
Brigadier-General, Commanding.

KNOXVILLE, TENN.,
        April 24, 1864.

Brigadier-General COX:

Your dispatch is received. As indicated in my second dispatch, Reilly's brigade will have to finish its work to-morrow. Manson's may be able to remain longer, but not much. Hascall's will not go as far as Bull's Gap unless he learns that you need his assistance.

If you have reason to apprehend an attack send for him; he was ordered to march to Morristown this evening.

J. M. SCHOFIELD,
Major-General.

BULL'S GAP, *April* 24, 1864.

Major-General SCHOFIELD,
        Knoxville:

Yours of this day received. Please let me know how much time ought to be used on the work ordered, so that if it cannot be done continuously through the whole distance we can scatter it at proper intervals. Shall I leave here before Hascall arrives, or wait for him?

J. D. COX,
Brigadier-General, Commanding.

KNOXVILLE, TENN.,
        April 24, 1864.

Brigadier-General COX,
        Bull's Gap:

Later orders from General Sherman require greater expedition than I at first supposed. Do all you can on the railroad to-morrow, and be prepared to march the next day. Let the cavalry go on as before ordered. Let Manson's brigade do its work to-morrow, and return the next day, unless the cavalry shall need its support. Send your sick and baggage to Knoxville by rail as far as practicable. Tools will be sent up to-night. Do not forget the Lick Creek bridge.

J. M. SCHOFIELD,
Major-General.

BULL'S GAP, *April* 24, 1864.

Major-General SCHOFIELD,
Knoxville :

Your second dispatch received, and orders given accordingly. Manson cannot get back here before Wednesday and do any work. By getting rid of the sick and of the baggage, I will answer for moving the whole division together faster than it could go divided.

J. D. COX,
Brigadier-General, Commanding Third Division.

HDQRS. THIRD DIVISION, TWENTY-THIRD ARMY CORPS,
Bull's Gap, Tenn., April 24, 1864.

Brig. Gen. M. D. MANSON,
Commanding Second Brigade, Greeneville :

GENERAL : Since you left this morning I have received a dispatch from General Schofield, directing that after destroying the Watauga bridge the cavalry join you, destroying all others, and as much of the track as possible by bending the rails and burning the ties, &c. From Jonesborough you may commence working this way, putting your men systematically at it, and doing the business thoroughly. I will myself begin at Lick Creek and work toward you. Communicate by sure messenger with Lieutenant-Colonel Trowbridge, and inform him that his instructions are modified as above. Time is important, and we will not delay to see what the enemy may do, but do the work ourselves. Let your officers and men use their ingenuity to discover rapid means of rendering the rails useless, as this is the most important thing. Leave no bridges, but if you have not time to destroy all the rails continuously it will be better to do it at intervals rather than all at one point. In this event begin at a bridge or trestle, and destroy this way as far as time will permit, and then pass to the next. Keep an accurate account of what is done, so that an exact report may be made.

While this is going on let small parties watch your flanks so that you may not be surprised. The Tenth Michigan Cavalry will remain with you, but send back the Third Indiana, as soon as they report to you after destroying Watauga bridge. Order these last to report to me at First Brigade headquarters on the road.

Very respectfully, your obedient servant,

J. D. COX,
Brigadier-General, Commanding.

MOSSY CREEK, *April* 24, 1864.

Major-General SCHOFIELD :

Your dispatch ordering me to move my brigade to Bull's Gap as soon as possible I have just received. I judge it was started this morning, as you thought I might reach Morristown to-day. By some neglect somewhere I have only just received it. My transportation is out on a foraging expedition to Dandridge and will return to-morrow. If there is any emergency I will march the men at the earliest moment ; if not, would prefer to have my transportation along. Please answer.

MILO S. HASCALL,
Brigadier-General, Commanding Brigade.

KNOXVILLE. TENN..
April 24, 1864.

Brigadier-General HASCALL,
Mossy Creek:

The order to move to Bull's Gap was sent this morning. It is now too late to do any good, hence the order is countermanded. The fault was in the operator at Mossy Creek. Investigate and inform me the cause of it.

J. M. SCHOFIELD,
Major-General, Commanding.

HDQRS. MILITARY DIVISION OF THE MISSISSIPPI,
Nashville, Tenn., April 24, 1864.

Maj. Gen. W. T. SHERMAN :

Three veteran regiments, Thirty-second Ohio, Thirtieth Illinois, and Sixteenth Wisconsin, with an aggregate of 1,705 men, have reached Cairo. Brigadier-General Leggett has arrived there and reported for duty. The Twentieth, Sixty-eighth, and Seventy-eighth Ohio Regiments, which should have been ready to return to Cairo before the end of this month, will not leave Ohio before the 6th or 7th of May, their furloughs not being up until that date, as they were detained several days to be paid off before their furloughs were given them. I am afraid the same thing may have occurred in some of the other States. It is going to be a difficult matter to bring the two divisions up to 5,000 men each, leaving out Brig. Gen. T. Kilby Smith's command up Red River, but I suppose it cannot be helped now. Have you anything definite from Forrest? The accounts I get here are very conflicting. Some reports state that he is still in Jackson, Tenn., others that he is moving south.

JAS. B. McPHERSON,
Major-General.

HDQRS. MILITARY DIVISION OF THE MISSISSIPPI,
Nashville, April 24, 1864.

General McPHERSON.
Huntsville:

Let the regiments at Cairo, the detachments, and transportation come up to Clifton at once, and some general officer left there to forward the others as fast they come. To save time I will order the Twentieth, Sixty-eighth, and Seventy-eighth Ohio Regiments to come to you all the way by railroad via Nashville, and try and get them started by May 1. Nothing from Forrest. Hurlbut reports him positively south of La Grange. Washburn will soon find out. Make up the best force you can for your projected advance, and I will try and get some detachments to protect your roads until all your troops reach you. Get as near 30,000 as you can. I will send the pontoons down by the cars, but they need not start across the Tennessee till we know we will want them.

W. T. SHERMAN,
Major-General,

CONFIDENTIAL.] ·　　HDQRS. MIL. DIV. OF THE MISSISSIPPI,
Nashville, Tenn., April 24, 1864.

Maj. Gen. J. B. MCPHERSON,
　Commanding Department of the Tennessee, Huntsville:

GENERAL : I telegraphed you last night that Colonel Comstock had come from General Grant with a letter ; that he (General Grant) would be ready by the 27th to take the initiative, if in the mean time Lee did not, and of course he wants me to act at the same time, but Colonel Comstock tells me he does not think General Grant can do anything till May 2.

Of course the movement in Virginia is the principal and ours is secondary, and must conform. We must be as far ready as possible.

First. Give General Slocum and Washburn orders to seem most active : to hold there all the enemy possible, even at a small risk to the river, for if we whip Joe Johnston good, everything lying west will feel the blow.

Second. Do all that is within the power of mortal to get up your two divisions from Cairo, with wagons, beef-cattle, &c. I will write to Lieutenant-Commander Shirk, U. S. Navy, to watch the Tennessee all that is possible to prevent any damage to our roads from that quarter.

Third. You should at once move your effective force of the Fifteenth Corps to the neighborhood of Larkin's, or wherever you propose to cross, ready to move on Lebanon. Dodge's command should cross at Decatur and brush away that cavalry, and move on Guntersville and Lebanon. From Lebanon your army should move, as light as possible, by Summerville or other good route toward La Fayette or Villanow to communicate with Thomas. From La Fayette you can renew your supply of bread, salt, sugar, and coffee from Ringgold, to which point we have cars. We are accumulating stores as fast as possible at Chattanooga. If you can start with twenty days' supply it is all that I now expect. I will explain to Comstock and send word to General Grant how important it is we should have the two divisions now at Cairo and on furlough, and have him correspond by telegraph with them at Cairo, and judge when they can reach your right flank via Clifton.

You should have a force of about 30,000, exclusive of Garrard's cavalry, which will remain with your extreme right till we are beyond the Coosa, when it must strike for the Montgomery and Atlanta road.

I think I understand the cavalry force in front of Dodge. It is a detachment from Johnston sent there to watch your operations, but the moment you cross the Tennessee in force it will hasten to cover Rome, and watch Johnston's left flank and rear.

The worst we have to apprehend is that Forrest may come across to act against our right flank, but this would be prevented if Washburn and Slocum threaten Grenada.

I take it for granted that unless Banks gets out of Red River and attacks Mobile, which is a material part of General Grant's plan, that we will have to fight Polk's army as well as Johnston's. General Corse has returned. Banks would not spare Smith. Indeed, it appears that Smith's force is the real substance of his army. He was whipped near Mansfield and retreated to Grand Ecore, 40 miles, though Banks claims a victory ; but from what General Corse tells me, he might have made it a victory by going ahead, but by retreating he left the enemy in possession of wounded, dead, artillery, and trains, and, worst of all, leaves Steele in danger. General Banks writes me that all is well there, but facts do not sustain him.

General Prince will go to Columbus, and you had better give Washburn command of all the river from Cairo down, to include the Memphis district. Grant thinks him a man of action. I will send your pontoon train down, and I think you had better have it at Scottsborough with orders to follow as soon as facts demonstrate that Johnston will not fight us this side of the Coosa. Until that fact is demonstrated we should be as little encumbered as possible.

Yours, &c.,

W. T. SHERMAN,
Major-General, Commanding.

HDQRS. DEPARTMENT AND ARMY OF THE TENNESSEE,
Huntsville, Ala., April 24. 1864.

Brig. Gen. P. J. OSTERHAUS,
Comdg. First Div., 15th Army Corps, Woodville, Ala.:

GENERAL: Yours of 22d instant received. In relation to the class of people you speak of within your lines, if they are acting in bad faith and secretly giving assistance to the enemy, you can send them across the line. You need not wait for positive proof of the facts. When this can be obtained the parties will be arrested and tried before a military commission for harboring guerrillas. The fact that the parties are strong rebel sympathizers, and that their conduct is suspicious, will be sufficient to warrant you in sending them across the river.

Very respectfully, your obedient servant,

JAS. B. McPHERSON,
Major-General.

OFFICE OF CHIEF SIGNAL OFFICER,
DEPARTMENT AND ARMY OF THE TENNESSEE,
Huntsville, Ala., April 24, 1864.

Lieut. Col. W. T. CLARK,
Assistant Adjutant-General:

COLONEL: I have the honor to state for the information of the major-general commanding that a reconnaissance of the country bordering on the Tennessee River between the mouth of Paint Rock Creek, 16 miles above Whitesburg, and Triana, 14 miles below that point, has been made by Lieut. Sam. S. Sample, acting signal officer. He states in a report made last evening that a line of stations may be established between those two above-mentioned points, which shall be in communication by signals. These stations may be occupied as stations of observation, and will be situated upon elevated points along the river and commanding a view of the enemy's country bordering on the river and of the enemy's movements. This line may be extended to Decatur, and may be done, Lieutenant Sample thinks, with the signal force at my disposal in this vicinity. He says:

To select the locations will occupy five days, and to build the stations will take 50 men of the pioneer corps five days more. As soon as the pioneer work is done the line should be in working order. In my opinion, this line could be depended upon in all weather, at least during the day for observations, and during the night for signaling. I consider no guard necessary unless movements of the enemy become so threatening that the general commanding will place strong guards at the river crossings or abandon the proposed line.

The field telegraph line hence to Whitesburg, in connection with the proposed line, will place the general in direct communication with any station on the river and with Decatur. Should the general commanding deem it advisable, the work upon this line may be commenced immediately.

I have the honor to be, colonel, very respectfully, your obedient servant,

O. H. HOWARD,
Captain and Chief Signal Officer.

APRIL 24, 1864.

Major-General McPHERSON,
Huntsville:

Colonel Rowett reports this morning as follows :

I have reliable information that Wisdom's regiment, of Forrest's command, has arrived at Tuscumbia; three more moving through Iuka. Forrest was ordered south to Okolona, and on the 19th it was countermanded and he was ordered east. He is reported moving east with his entire command. Corn was being hauled to Corinth to feed him. General Veatch reported last night that enemy was moving around to his right.

G. M. DODGE,
Brigadier-General.

APRIL 24, 1864.

Brig. Gen. J. C. VEATCH,
Decatur:

Colonel Rowett reports this morning that Wisdom's regiment, of Forrest's command, has arrived at Tuscumbia ; that three more regiments had passed through Iuka, and that a great portion of his command was moving cast. If the enemy have left the line of Flint and Danville, scouting parties better be sent out in that direction and ascertain what facts they can. The movement to your right may have something to do with Forrest's move, if true.

G. M. DODGE,
Brigadier-General.

HDQRS. LEFT WING, SIXTEENTH ARMY CORPS,
Athens, Ala., April 24, 1864.

Lieut. Col. R. ROWETT,
Seventh Illinois, Florence:

I am in receipt of your report of 23d instant. It is very probable that Forrest may be making this way, but reports from Memphis indicate that he is moving south through La Grange and Saulsbury, crossing the Tallahatchie. He may have sent part of his force through Iuka, thence south. It is very important that we should know if he is advancing toward Decatur, and you must use every endeavor to get reliable news from the south side of the river. The man Thrasher you speak of I know nothing about. He is not in my command, nor ever has been. You better inform Major Murphy. He must belong to the State troops. Any of his men committing unauthorized depredations will be arrested if they come within your jurisdiction.

As I before informed you, there is a heavy force near Decatur, and they appear to be working to our right.

I am, very respectfully, your obedient servant,

G. M. DODGE,
Brigadier-General, Commanding.

HDQRS. LEFT WING, SIXTEENTH ARMY CORPS,
Athens, Ala., April 24, 1864.

Lieut. Col. WILLIAM T. CLARK,
Assistant Adjutant-General, Huntsville, Ala. :

I inclose Colonel Rowett's dispatch* of 23d instant and make the following explanation : Wisdom's regiment is Colonel Forrest's old regiment. Colonel Forrest was killed near Okolona by General Smith's cavalry. The regiments passing through Iuka are on one of the most direct and feasible routes from Jackson south to Okolona, and they may be moving south instead of east.

The man Colonel Rowett speaks of meeting under flag of truce is one of the best posted on the south side of the river and a good friend to us. Anything he should report I should place great confidence in. In conversation with a citizen of Jackson, Tenn., who left there a few days ago, I learned that he heard Forrest say that it was about played out trying to get us to send a force to West Tennessee after him. He supposed that if we did not come he would have to go to us, and he did not want to get where they could pit him or any of his force against Wheeler again, as his men had no confidence in him. He also says Forrest took many men out of West Tennessee, but not near as many as reported ; that he sent south about 500 men of ours as prisoners. Everything indicated that he was about leaving West Tennessee for good. I have had no report from General Veatch to-day.

So far as taking forage to Corinth from Okolona, it has been going on for a month or more. They have the road so repaired that they haul it up in bunk and hand cars, hitching mules to them.

The man Thrasher Colonel Rowett complains of is not in my command, and I do not know who he is.

I am, very respectfully, your obedient servant,

G. M. DODGE,
Brigadier-General.

HDQRS. CAVALRY DIVISION, SIXTEENTH ARMY CORPS,
Memphis, Tenn., April 24, 1864.

Lieut. Col. T. H. HARRIS,
Assistant Adjutant-General:

COLONEL : In obedience to the request of Major-General Hurlbut I beg leave to state that at the time of the recent entrance of the

---
*See p. 460.

enemy under General Forrest into West Tennessee I had under my control about 1,700 mounted men.

The cause of the reduction of the cavalry force in this corps since February 29 has been abundantly explained in all tri-monthly and special reports since March 10, 1864.

Upon a consultation at the time with General Buckland as to the propriety of sending infantry to operate in conjunction with the small force of cavalry against the enemy, he considered it hazardous to weaken the garrison at Memphis by sending any portion of the infantry force in search of the enemy.

By information obtained from scouts, spies, and by reconnaissances and engagements, I do not hesitate to say that the force of the enemy under General Forrest, north of the railroad, was at least 7,000 mounted men, while at the same time the force of General S. D. Lee, at least 6,000 strong, had been hovering along Coldwater within striking distance of Memphis and supporting distance of General Forrest.

Unusual exertions have been made recently by the enemy to mount troops, and several brigades of infantry have recently been mounted and placed under the disposal of Generals Forrest and Lee. In my opinion, the small and not reliable cavalry force at my disposal, with the addition of General Buckland's brigade of infantry, about 1,200 men, could not have moved out from Memphis and attacked the enemy with any certainty of success.

Very respectfully, your obedient servant,

B. H. GRIERSON,
Brigadier-General.

HDQRS. MILITARY DIVISION OF THE MISSISSIPPI,
Nashville, Tenn., April 24, 1864.

General R. ALLEN,
Louisville

Telegraph to Colonel Myers to hold at Memphis all cavalry horses not shipped, and enough teams for Mower's division when it comes to Memphis from Red River, and what he needs for the post; all else could come to Cairo and thence up to Clifton and across to Huntsville along with McPherson's troops, which are to come that way. We want at Memphis enough wagons for one division of, say, 6,000 men; all others can come to Huntsville. If Colonel Myers has sent up to Cairo all his teams by a mistake, those for one division should return.

W. T. SHERMAN,
Major-General.

ATHENS, *April 24, 1864.*

Brig. Gen. T. W. SWEENY:

Major Plessner reports from Florence that some 500 of the enemy crossed at Eastport on the 22d. There is said to be a larger force still to cross, how large not stated. If this is so, Major Estabrook should have known it before this and sent you word.

By order:

J. W. BARNES,
Assistant Adjutant-General.

MEMPHIS, *April* 24, 1864.
(Received 27th.)

Major-General SHERMAN:

A large amount of cavalry belonging here is at Saint Louis waiting for horses. They had better be sent here at once to assist in garrisoning this place while other troops are after Forrest.

C. C. WASHBURN,
Major-General.

HEADQUARTERS DISTRICT OF WEST TENNESSEE,
Memphis, Tenn., April 24, 1864.

Maj. Gen. W. T. SHERMAN,
Comdg. Mil. Div. of the Mississippi, Nashville, Tenn.:

GENERAL: Since I arrived here yesterday morning I have written and telegraphed to you the condition of affairs and what I propose to do. With the very limited means I have it is difficult to do what ought to be done, but I shall do my best with the means I have.

I have sent three steamers to-day to Vicksburg to bring cavalry from there, and as soon as they arrive I shall move in pursuit of Forrest. They can hardly get here before Friday, and the horses should rest a few hours on shore before starting on a march. Colonel Winslow, with 550 men and 800 horses, has just arrived, the men without arms, and the horses are all to be shod. They will be armed with muskets at once and the horses put in marching order.

The cars can be run as far as Moscow, and I propose to run 2,000 infantry to that point on Saturday morning, from which they will march to support the cavalry in the pursuit of Forrest, who is still at or near Jackson. I regret that there should be any delay in moving, but I see no help for it. I intend that my force shall reach Bolivar Sunday night, and shall expect to meet an infantry force there, sent by you from the Tennessee River.

A spy returned last night who was at Bolivar, and went to within a few miles of Corinth. He says that Forrest, with all his force, is at and near Jackson. He also says that the railroad is not repaired to Corinth, but that the cars are running to Tupelo, and they are repairing the road as fast as they can.

General Sturgis reported to-day. I have examined the lines thoroughly to-day. I do not feel much apprehension of an attack here, but I think they mean to menace us to disturb your equanimity. If we should be attacked by a very large force we might have to retire to the fort. On account of the large amount of Government supplies in the city and the prestige which its capture would give the rebs it is very desirable to hold the city, and I shall only in case of attack retire to the fort as a last resort. I have every confidence that we can take care of ourselves here, but as caution is the parent of safety, it is well to look at all the chances.

Suppose I send a column of 5,000 as far as Jackson, 100 miles from here. That will leave me a very small force here. Forrest, being able to move more rapidly than our infantry which I send after him, might swoop down upon us here with his whole force. If you could manage to send 1,000 or 2,000 men from Cairo to arrive about Sunday morning to remain until Sturgis returns it might be a proper measure of prudence. Of that you can judge. There are one or two regiments at Cairo on their way to the Department of the Gulf, which I would detain for a few days as they pass here but for the miserable fiasco on Red River. They are probably wanted there worse than I want them.

I am, general, your obedient servant,

C. C. WASHBURN,
Major-General.

CONFIDENTIAL.] HDQRS. MIL. DIV. OF THE MISSISSIPPI,
Nashville, Tenn., April 24, 1864.

General C. C. WASHBURN,
Commanding District of Memphis:

GENERAL: Yours of April 21 from Cairo is this moment received. I answered your dispatch the minute it came, in hopes it would catch you at Cairo, but am glad you hurried down.

There should be at Memphis—

Buckland's brigade, entire	2,000
Three white regiments (103d Illinois one)	1,500
Kappner's negro regiment, Fort Pickering	1,200
Chetlain's black brigade	2,000
Grierson's division of cavalry, at least	4,000
Total	10,700

We have never taken any of Grierson's cavalry from Memphis, and it amounted to nearly 10,000, with over 7,000 horses, before the Smith expedition. What has become of them? Please make close inquiry.

I know our troops fall off fearfully, but I cannot imagine how such discrepancies occur. Smith reported bringing in from his Okolona trip 4,000 animals. None have been brought away save 600 recently sent to General Allen.

I cannot understand General Hurlbut's reports. He took a short leave of absence when I first came to Nashville, and hearing that Forrest had passed above Memphis, wrote me that Grierson was after him, supported by infantry. Every report since, the strength of the cavalry has fallen off more and more, until now you report it down to 1,100. Please examine into it and let me know as early as possible the exact truth. My opinion is by a close examination you will find at Memphis full 7,000 good men, beside the garrison of Fort Pickering and the militia.

I know that the furloughed veterans have reduced our armies terribly. Mine and Grant's are far less than the world suppose, and we have to keep the truth to ourselves. I expect that I will have to advance against Joe Johnston with one, and it may be three, divisions less than we calculated.

Do the best you can, but try and not exaggerate the forces of the enemy or your own weakness, but use your force to the best advantage. Don't let Forrest insult you by passing in sight almost of your command. At the time I had Memphis in 1862, I had but one division and one regiment, 600 cavalry (Grierson's), and Van Dorn was at Holly Springs with a division of cavalry and near 8,000 infantry.

More than one-half my cavalry here is dismounted and it is almost impossible to procure horses. I don't see how our cavalry destroy so

many horses.   When I left Memphis Grierson had full 5,000 horses. Not one has been drawn away, and I want to know what has become of them.
    Truly, your friend,
                                                W. T. SHERMAN,
                                        Major-General, Commanding.

                HDQRS. MILITARY DIVISION OF THE MISSISSIPPI,
                                Nashville, Tenn., April 24, 1864.
ADJUTANT-GENERAL OF OHIO,
            Columbus:
    General McPherson tells me that the furloughs of the Twentieth, Sixty-eighth, and Seventy-eighth Ohio will not expire till May 6, owing to a delay occurring before they got their furloughs in the State.   It is all-important that they should reach their command at as early a date as possible.   If they could be got ready by May 1, I would order them transported all the way by cars via Nashville.
                                                W. T. SHERMAN,
                                                Major-General.

CONFIDENTIAL.]   HDQRS. MIL. DIV. OF THE MISSISSIPPI,
                                Nashville, Tenn., April 24, 1864.
Brig. Gen. A. J. SMITH,
        Commanding Detachment on Red River:
    DEAR GENERAL : General Corse has returned.   He brought no letter from you but gave good accounts of you and your troops.   I had hoped, from the rapid work you did up to Alexandria, that the whole expedition would go on in like manner.   I want your command, but of course you could not leave under the circumstances by which you were surrounded on the 14th of April.   General Corse says that in the second day's fight at Pleasant Hill the enemy were beaten and were retreating.   I cannot understand why our army retraced its steps to Grand Ecore, when it was so important in time, in distance, more especially as Steele was known to be approaching from the north. But all will be explained in time.   I have simply ordered that when you do come out of Red River, that Mower's division remain at Memphis, and yours come round by Cairo, and up the Tennessee to Clifton, and thence across to Decatur ; but as time and circumstances may change, I will have orders meet you at Memphis.   General McPherson now commands the department, and all our attention is engaged in the awful responsibilities that rest on us here. General Grant has ordered that Steele command on Red River, and he must order things according to the result of your expedition.   I was in hopes it would have been made more rapidly, so that those troops could have taken part with us in the events soon to transpire.
    You will, as soon as you can possibly be spared, come to Memphis, where orders will meet you.
    I am, with respect, your obedient servant,
                                                W. T. SHERMAN,
                                        Major-General, Commanding.

CAIRO, ILL., *April* 24, 1864.
Maj. Gen. JAMES B. MCPHERSON,
  Comdg. Department of the Tennessee, Huntsville, Ala.:

Have my force organized, and will leave as soon as Captain Duncan returns from Saint Louis with accouterments and ammunition and transports all procured. Captain Conklin will have transports by to-morrow evening. Will not delay a moment.

W. Q. GRESHAM,
Brigadier-General.

HDQRS. CAVALRY DIVISION, SIXTEENTH ARMY CORPS,
Memphis, Tenn., April 24, 1864.
Lieut. Col. W. P. HEPBURN,
  Commanding Provisional Cavalry Regiment:

COLONEL: Citizens report a force of the enemy under Lee between this point and Holly Springs, moving in this direction.

You will organize a force of 100 men to proceed as far as Olive Branch, and beyond if practicable.

They will look well in all directions with patrols, and gain all possible information, reporting to these headquarters as soon as possible.

By order of Brig. Gen. B. H. Grierson :
S. L. WOODWARD,
Assistant Adjutant-General.

SPECIAL ORDERS, }   HDQRS. SEVENTEENTH ARMY CORPS,
  No. 102.   }   *Cairo, Ill., April 24, 1864.*

*   *   *   *   *   *   *

IV. The following is announced as the organization for the expedition ordered by the major-general commanding the Department and Army of the Tennessee, under command of Brig. Gen. W. Q. Gresham, viz :

First. Seventeenth Wisconsin Infantry, Thirteenth Iowa, Fourteenth Wisconsin Infantry, detachment First Battalion, Fourth Division, will form the First Brigade, under command of Col. A. G. Malloy, Seventeenth Wisconsin Infantry.

Second. The Thirty-second Ohio Infantry, Thirtieth Illinois Infantry, Fourteenth Illinois Infantry, Second Battalion, Fourth Division, will form the Second Brigade, under command of Col. B. F. Potts, Thirty-second Ohio Infantry.

Third. The First Minnesota Battery.

Fourth. The pioneer corps, Fourth Division.

Colonels Malloy and Potts will at once organize their brigades into an effective force, and see that their men are properly armed and equipped and ready to move at a moment's notice, and will report to Brigadier-General Gresham for specific instructions.

*   *   *   *   *   *   '

By order of Maj. Gen. James B. McPherson :
SAM. L. TAGGART.
Assistant Adjutant-General.

CULPEPER, *April 25*, 1864.

Major-General SHERMAN,
        Nashville, Tenn. :
    The following dispatch has been received from Cairo :

CAIRO, *April 23*, 1864—noon.

Col. ANSON STAGER,
        Washington:
    Captain Bush, commanding at Smithland, Ky., reports rebels commenced crossing Tennessee River at Birmingham and above at 8 p. m. yesterday, and were still crossing when his informant left Chandet's early this morning. Wire is cut between Smithland and Fort Donelson.

.   W. J. MASON,
                                                                        Cipher Operator.

Have you received the information and taken measures to attend to them ?

                                                U. S. GRANT,
                                                    Lieutenant-General.

NASHVILLE, *April 25*, 1864.
(Received at Washington 9.50 p. m.)

General GRANT,
        Culpeper :
    I have no account of any force crossing the Tennessee. The officer commanding at Fort Donelson reports about 100 men committing depredations between the Cumberland and Tennessee. Boats are constantly ascending and descending, and the Tennessee is closely watched.

                                                W. T. SHERMAN,
                                                    Major-General.

CULPEPER, *April 25*, 1864—11.30 a. m.

Major-General SHERMAN :
    Will your veterans be back to enable you to start on the 2d of May ? I do not want to delay later.

                                                U. S. GRANT,
                                                    Lieutenant-General.

NASHVILLE, TENN., *April 25*, 1864—11.30 a. m.
(Received 12.40 p. m.)

Maj. Gen. H. W. HALLECK,
        Chief of Staff :
    All unassigned troops in Illinois and the Northwest should at once be sent to Cairo in reserve, for they will be needed down the Mississippi or up the Tennessee when, by an advance, we weaken our lines of communication. At Cairo they could be consolidated and organized.

                                                W. T. SHERMAN,
                                                    Major-General.

WASHINGTON, *April 25*, 1864—3 p. m.
Lieutenant-General GRANT,
          Culpeper, Va.:

General Sherman requests that all unassigned troops in Illinois and the Northwest rendezvous at Cairo. Your orders sent to those States were to rendezvous at Louisville. Shall I change the order as Sherman requests? Dispatches just received from Generals Butler and Peck state that the garrison at Plymouth, after a small loss, surrendered to the rebels on Wednesday, the 20th. No particulars. General Butler says nothing about what he intends to do. I have just seen Admiral Porter's dispatch, dated Grand Ecore, April 14, to the Navy Department. He says, whatever may be said, the army there has met with a great defeat and is much demoralized. He speaks in strong terms of Banks' mismanagement, and of the good conduct of A. J. Smith and his corps.

He fears that if Smith is withdrawn Banks will retreat still farther, and Steele's command and the gun-boats above the rapids (which, from fall of water, cannot be withdrawn) will be greatly periled, if not lost. He says Banks' army was ten days behind the appointed time. He protests against the withdrawal of Smith at this time, as it would be fatal to us.

The Navy Department asks to know this, in order to telegraph instructions to Cairo for Admiral Porter. What shall I reply?
                    H. W. HALLECK,
                    Major-General, Chief of Staff.

NASHVILLE, TENN., *April 25*, 1864—3.30 p. m.
                    (Received 6.20 p. m.)
Lieut. Gen. U. S. GRANT,
          Culpeper, Va.:

The veteran divisions cannot be up by May 2, but I am willing to move with what I have. Colonel Comstock left for you last night and has facts and figures. As soon as you see them make your orders. I am now getting all in hand ready, but every day adds to my animals and men. If you can, give me till May 5.
                    W. T. SHERMAN,
                    Major-General, Commanding.

HDQRS. MILITARY DIVISION OF THE MISSISSIPPI,
                    Nashville, April 25, 1864.
Maj. Gen. GEORGE H. THOMAS,
          Comdg. Department of the Cumberland, Chattanooga:

GENERAL: I have received your several dispatches and letters touching the check on railroad travel. I have ordered the quartermaster to check the tendency of our military railroads sliding into a public convenience, but to keep it just as he would a train of army wagons. Nobody should travel in the cars save officers and soldiers under orders entitling them to transportation. I left him to ease off by sending only such as were caught away from home by the change. I think it will in time come out all right. If we allow conductors to collect money we know they will little by little pick up way-travelers for their own profit. We have not the system of checks that would enable us to detect peculation and fraud. The officers of the Army of the Tennessee have complained bitterly that in all matters pertaining to the railroad they were slighted, and there were some grounds, not intentional on your part, but calculated to raise a prejudice, that after they had come to the relief of the Army of the Cumberland they were denied bread or any facilities from the road. Some even thought you shared this feeling, and had refused them even a passage to or from Nashville.

This resulted from the fact that the conductors and your guards were familiar with your passes, and were not with those of Logan or other commanders of that wing. This made my transportation order manifestly just, putting all department commanders on a just equality.

We have increased the daily cars from about 80 to from 130 to 190. If I can get the average to 150 the road will supply us, and make an accumulation. I wish you to increase the facilities for throwing stores forward to Ringgold, as McPherson, Schofield, and you will have to draw from that common depot. All I can now hope for is to get McPherson to La Fayette, or thereabouts, with twenty days' bread, salt, &c., from Guntersville.

McPherson's two divisions are not yet at Cairo, and in many cases the furloughs were dated after a long delay in the State waiting for payment, so that I can't even tell when they will be up to Clifton ; but we are pushing as hard as possible. I want McPherson to have 30,000 men, independent of Garrard's cavalry ; but if we can't get these two divisions in time, his force will fall far short. As he and Schofield cover your flanks, I want to make your force as heavy as possible as far out as Dalton, Resaca, and Kingston. By that time we will have a better knowledge of what we will need, and can trim down and send back such as should remain to guard your rear. The only danger I apprehend is from resident guerrillas, and from Forrest coming from the direction of Florence. I did want A. J. Smith on the Tennessee, about Florence, to guard against that danger, but Banks cannot spare him, and Grant orders me to calculate without him. General Corse is here from Red River. The battle up Red River resulted thuswise : The advance cavalry, encumbered with wagons, met the enemy in position 4 miles from Mansfield, where the road forks to Texas. Lee, who commanded the cavalry, sent back for supports. A brigade of infantry was sent, but both cavalry and infantry were driven back in disorder. Another brigade sent forward shared the same fate, and the enemy pursuing struck Franklin, who held them till night. Next day A. J. Smith got up, and a hard fight ensued on the 9th, extending into night. Our troops had the advantage, but in the night both armies retired—ours 40 miles back to Grand Ecore ; and the enemy discovering first our retrograde, took advantage of it. So they have the victory. They took all the wagons of the cavalry, over 200, and some eighteen guns, two of which were recovered.

Banks was refitting on the 14th at Grand Ecore, preparing to advance. Nothing from Steele, who, at that date, should have been near Shreveport, on the north and east bank of the river.

I am quite uneasy about Steele, as the movement up Red River has been so slow that all the Texas and Louisiana forces are assembled, and having defeated Banks, may turn against Steele ; but still I hope Banks will not pause, but resume his march, and prevent

Kirby Smith from crossing to the north side of Red River. Our joint forces are far superior to those of the enemy, and we have also the gun-boats and transports in Red River.

The best fighting was evidently done by my troops, and Admiral Porter writes me that A. J. Smith's command saved Banks' army from utter rout. Banks should have 17,000, Steele 7,000 to 9,000, and Smith 10,000.

The joint force of the enemy is reckoned at 25,000. Grand Ecore is the river town of Natchitoches, a little back from Red River, but on one of the roads leading to Shreveport, and about 40 miles from Natchitoches.

I will be with you by May 1.

Truly, yours,

W. T. SHERMAN,
Major-General.

NASHVILLE, *April 25, 1864.*

Maj. Gen. G. H. THOMAS:

General Grant telegraphs me to be ready May 2. Make dispositions accordingly. McPherson is least ready.

W. T. SHERMAN,
Major-General.

HEADQUARTERS DEPARTMENT OF THE CUMBERLAND,
Chattanooga, April 25, 1864.

Brigadier-General BAIRD,
Ringgold:

General Johnson reports as follows :

Scouts just in report that directly in front of Parker's Gap, and only 1½ or 2 miles from it, they found last night a strong picket-line of mounted men, which they claim to have followed for 2 miles to the south of the gap, where it ran up the ridge. Large camp-fires are seen at Red Clay.

General Johnson has been directed to send out a strong reconnoitering party, under a judicious officer, to investigate the report. The party is directed to ascend White Oak Ridge from the side opposite the point where the scouts report the rebel cavalry touched the ridge, by which it is hoped some of the rebs may be captured. The major-general commanding directs that you also send a party to your right and rear upon the ridge and along it for the same purpose.

WM. D. WHIPPLE,
Assistant Adjutant-General.

RINGGOLD, *April 25, 1864.*

Brigadier-General WHIPPLE,
Assistant Adjutant-General:

My infantry patrol went within 1½ miles of Parker's Gap, thence east 5 miles to Salem Church, and back, Catoosa Springs, and Stone Church. Saw only 3 rebels. No large bodies have been there. Cavalry scouts met Johnson's party near Parker's Gap. Moved out thence on Cleveland road and returned, seeing no signs of enemy. Our party beyond Nickajack attempted to capture pickets, but found them withdrawn. The indications are that enemy is watching more toward Cleveland.

A. BAIRD,
Brigadier-General.

HEADQUARTERS DISTRICT OF NASHVILLE,
Nashville, Tenn., April 25, 1864.
Lieut. Col. H. W. PERKINS,
Assistant Adjutant-General, Twentieth Army Corps:

COLONEL : Pursuant to your instructions to relieve Brigadier-General Williams as soon as may be, I have ordered the One hundred and second Ohio Volunteer Infantry and Thirteenth Wisconsin Infantry, together about 1,278 strong, to Tullahoma and Stevenson to occupy those two posts and the defenses of the Nashville and Chattanooga Railroad between Normandy and Bridgeport. They are ordered to start to-morrow morning at daybreak.

Colonel West, commanding Thirty-first Wisconsin, who was ordered to relieve the troops of Brigadier-General Williams as far as Normandy, informs me by telegraph that General Williams' troops still remain at those points under orders from Major-General Hooker. I have instructed Colonel West to remain at the points where his command has been posted until further orders.

I am, colonel, very respectfully, your obedient servant,
LOVELL H. ROUSSEAU,
Major-General.

HDQRS. MILITARY DIVISION OF THE MISSISSIPPI,
Nashville, April 25, 1864.
General SCHOFIELD, *Knoxville:*

General Grant telegraphs me to be ready by May 2. Make preparations accordingly. Order Stoneman forward with all the cavalry that is ready ; the rest can follow.

W. T. SHERMAN,
Major-General.

BULL'S GAP, *April 25, 1864.*
Major-General SCHOFIELD, *Knoxville:*

Have just returned from Midway Station, 8 miles above here. I expect Reilly's brigade to work a mile farther to-night. The work is very thoroughly done as far as we have gone, and I feel confident the enemy will not repair it this season. Reilly will push ahead in the morning. As there was some risk of a dash at this post by way of Rogersville, I ordered back the Eighth Tennessee and left Reilly the remainder. Manson camped last night 2 miles beyond Greeneville. He was to reach Jonesborough and the cavalry the Watauga to-day. There is no evidence of any considerable force this side of Bristol. Some 200 cavalry, reported at Watauga bridge, are all I can hear of.

J. D. COX,
Brigadier-General, Commanding.

KNOXVILLE, TENN.,
April 25, 1864.
Brigadier-General COX,
    Bull's Gap:
    I have just received your dispatch of this evening, and Captain
Bartlett has explained to me the difficulty about your moving before
Manson returns. As I dispatched you this afternoon, I deem it quite
desirable for you to march on the 27th. Yet, if Manson has gone to
Jonesborough to-day, he cannot get back in time; but your work
will be done the more promptly and you will probably yet be in
time. Hascall's brigade did not move as at first ordered. Judah's
division will move this way to-morrow.
                                    J. M. SCHOFIELD,
                                        Major-General.

KNOXVILLE, TENN.,
April 25, 1864.
Brigadier-General COX,
    Bull's Gap:
    You may continue the work of destruction above Lick Creek
until Manson returns; then move your whole division together.
Meanwhile send to Knoxville everything which would impede your
march. If Manson can destroy the bridges above Greeneville to-
day. and get back to the gap by to-morrow night, and the other
brigade work all of to-day and to-morrow on the road above the
creek, I think the result will be satisfactory, both in point of time
and of work done.
                                    J. M. SCHOFIELD,
                                        Major-General.

HDQRS. MILITARY DIVISION OF THE MISSISSIPPI,
Nashville, April 25, 1864.
General MCPHERSON,
    Huntsville:
    General Grant telegraphs me to be ready by May 2. We cannot
wait for the veterans. It may be well for your whole column to
move from Scottsborough. They could be moved to that point by
rail. The two divisions expected up from Cairo would cover that
flank and guard the roads, or join you via Chattanooga. Make
every possible preparation.
                                    W. T. SHERMAN,
                                        Major-General.

WOODVILLE, ALA.,
April 25, 1864.
Maj. R. R. TOWNES,
    Assistant Adjutant-General, Huntsville, Ala.:
    Effective strength of infantry at Woodville, 179 commissioned
officers and 3,044 enlisted men. Effective strength of infantry at
Cottonville, 15 commissioned officers and 263 enlisted men. Effect-
ive strength of infantry at Vienna, 19 commissioned officers and 266

enlisted men. Effective strength of infantry at Triana, 46 commissioned officers and 677 enlisted men. Effective strength of artillery is 7 commissioned officers and 191 enlisted men. Aggregate present all arms, including sick, is 5,172. Aggregate present and absent, 7,612.

P. JOS. OSTERHAUS,
Brigadier-General of Volunteers, Commanding Division.

HDQRS. FOURTH DIVISION, SIXTEENTH ARMY CORPS,
Decatur, Ala., April 25, 1864—1.40 p. m.

Brigadier-General DODGE,
Comdg. Left Wing, Sixteenth Army Corps, Athens:

Major Kuhn has just returned from a scout on Somerville road. Stewart's battalion is picketing Flint; had sharp skirmishing with them, getting 1 man severely wounded. Learned from citizens the rebels lost 2 killed and 2 wounded in the dash on us last evening. Major Kuhn found their parties so arranged that he could not go beyond the foot of the mountains without getting them on his rear. No other news from that quarter. Scout from Triana reports Twenty-third and Thirtieth Indiana at Triana.

JAMES C. VEATCH,
Brigadier-General.

NASHVILLE, *April 25, 1864.*

General HURLBUT,
Cairo:

The orders for you to go to Cairo and report to the Adjutant-General were made by General Grant. They are not yet received by mail. I will refer your dispatches to General McPherson. I construe you to be still in command of the corps.

W. T. SHERMAN,
Major-General.

HUNTSVILLE, ALA., *April 25, 1864.*

Brig. Gen. W. Q. GRESHAM,
Cairo, Ill.:

You will come up to Clifton on the Tennessee River and disembark your command. Orders will be sent you at that point. Did you receive my former dispatch to this effect?

JAS. B. McPHERSON,
Major-General, Commanding.

LOUISVILLE, *April 25, 1864.*

General J. D. WEBSTER:

Four thousand mules will have been shipped from Saint Louis by the 1st of May; several hundred are being sent from Bowling Green and other points, now arriving, I presume, daily; 400 are on the river from Memphis, and will arrive in a day or two; in all, between 5,000 and 6,000, at an early day. I think General Sherman will be satisfied with this.

ROBT. ALLEN,
Brigadier-General and Quartermaster.

NASHVILLE, TENN., *April* 25, 1864—7 p. m.
(Received 10 p. m.)
Hon. EDWIN M. STANTON,
Secretary of War:

There are five regiments of Indiana cavalry in Indiana. We cannot, of course, mount or equip them, and Governor Morton thinks it a breach of good faith to make them serve on foot. I want them at Nashville in a camp of instruction as a reserve. Will you use your influence to produce this end at once? I must go to the front in a day or two, and want to know if this is to be done.

W. T. SHERMAN,
Major-General.

HDQRS. MILITARY DIVISION OF THE MISSISSIPPI,
Nashville, Tenn., April 25, 1864.
Governor O. P. MORTON,
Indianapolis:

DEAR SIR: I have telegraphed you my opinion that we cannot possibly arm and equip the five regiments of cavalry which I learn are mustered in and are now in the State of Indiana. Still these men might do good service. They could be armed as infantry and be held in reserve here at Nashville, to which point horses could come as easily as at Indianapolis. I will be compelled to take the initiative with 10,000 men less than I calculated, on account of the check sustained by Banks at Mansfield. He borrowed of me 10,000 men, with a clear understanding that he would reach Shreveport and be able to send them back by the time named, which would have enabled them to come by water up the Tennessee and either joined me or guarded that exposed flank of our great field of operations. With our railroad in perfect order, it is all we can do to supply our armies along the line of the Tennessee.

I have reason to suppose that Forrest, who has taken the advantage of this absence up Red River of that force, and also of our furloughed veterans, who return slowly, will endeavor to make a lodgment at some point of the Tennessee River, when by his bold and rapid move he will strike our railroad somewhere about Columbia or Pulaski. I should have a reserve force here where they can easily be supplied without taxing our roads, ready to move rapidly to any point threatened. I don't know where to look for such a reserve, unless it be in Indiana.

Ohio is taxed to its uttermost by the calls East, West Virginia, and Kentucky. Illinois reserves should be at Cairo and yours here. I can keep a general officer here, with orders to establish a camp of instruction, which will serve a double purpose. Men enlisted as cavalry should be paid as such, and when we can we should mount them, but you have already seen that horses sent to the Tennessee all perish. A horse needs 20 pounds of food daily, whereas a man can get along with only 2. I dislike to tell you how much dismounted cavalry we now have, and we must employ them as railroad guards. What I want the new Indiana cavalry here for is a reserve.

East Kentucky is not threatened now. Please answer immediately, as I want to go to the front. You could start the regiments at once, and I will give the necessary orders to put them into camp here.

W. T. SHERMAN,

CONFIDENTIAL.]   HDQRS. MIL. DIV. OF THE MISSISSIPPI,
Nashville, Tenn., April 25, 1864.

Captain PENNOCK,
    U. S. Navy, Cairo, Ill.:

DEAR CAPTAIN : I send you some letters for Red River, which I beg you will send to the admiral by your next regular boat.   There is no necessity of unusual expedition.

I wish you would notify Captain Shirk that we will in May be actively engaged beyond the Tennessee, and I have no doubt the enemy will work up along the Mobile and Ohio Railroad and try and cross the Tennessee to attack my lines of communication.   What we want is the earliest possible notice of such movement sent to Nashville, and also keep my headquarters here advised where a gun-boat could be found with which to throw men across to the west bank of the Tennessee when necessary.

For some time McPherson's command will be running up the Tennessee as far as Clifton, which is the shortest line of march to Pulaski and Decatur.   Please facilitate this movement all you can.

I am, with respect, your friend and servant,
W. T. SHERMAN,
Major-General, Commanding.

SPECIAL ORDERS, }   HDQRS. MIL. DIV. OF THE MISSISSIPPI,
    No. 35.   }   *Nashville, Tenn., April 25, 1864.*

I. The armies now on the line of the Tennessee for the purpose of war will constitute one army, under the personal direction of the major-general commanding the division, but for the purpose of administration will retain the separate department organizations. All department commanders will exercise as heretofore full control of all matters pertaining to the troops properly belonging to them, and of the local districts which compose the field of their respective departments.

II. The effective Army of the Cumberland will be the center, that of the Ohio the left wing, and that of the Tennessee the right wing.   Each commander of these armies will give all needful supervision of the supplies for his command, and keep near his person a complete staff to regulate the receipt and distribution of supplies of kind.   The commander-in-chief will be habitually with the center, but may shift from time to time to either flank, leaving a staff officer near the center to receive reports and make orders.   May 1, the center will be at Chattanooga.

III. In all movements each army will be kept well in hand with no detachments except scout and skirmish, and risking as little as possible in side issues or small affairs.   The wings will confine their movements to those of the center habitually.   Should the routes to be indicated in future orders bring either army in contact with the enemy he should be engaged vigorously, after proper reconnaissance, and all attacks of the enemy in position should be preceded by a good line of skirmishers to develop the position of the enemy's artillery and masses.   Great care should be taken not to use artillery or volleys of musketry unnecessarily, as the sound is calculated to mislead the neighboring army.

IV. General Stoneman, under Major-General Schofield, will command the cavalry of the left, and General Garrard, of the Army of the Cumberland, is temporarily attached to the right, and will receive orders from Major-General McPherson until he is relieved by the commanding general. Major-General Thomas will organize out of his remaining cavalry force a division to act on his front and to keep up communications. The habit of general officers taking cavalry for escorts and orderlies is very ruinous to the cavalry arm of the service, and should be discontinued as far as possible. Commanders of brigades and divisions and of corps, when acting compactly, should as far as possible mount a few infantry as orderlies and escorts, leaving the cavalry arm entire to fulfill its most important part of clearing the front and flank. Cavalry is most effective when appearing suddenly on the flank or rear of the enemy, as it usually is the advance of a column of infantry, and thus appearing it causes that idea, but if it hesitates in acting the effect is lost.

V. Army commanders will give great attention to their lines of communication. A small force in a block-house, disencumbered of baggage and stores not needed, can hold their ground and protect their point against any cavalry force until relief comes. They should be instructed to fight with desperation to the last, as they thereby save the time necessary for concentration. Small reserves capable of being shifted to a way-point by a train of cars should be placed judiciously and instructed. The main reserves will be at Nashville, Murfreesborough, Columbia, Decatur, and Stevenson, from which places they can be rapidly transported to the point of danger. Danger to our line of communication is most to be apprehended from the west, and most care must be observed in that direction. The Tennessee River will be patrolled by gun-boats, both above and below the Shoals. General Schofield will, as heretofore, look to his left and rear, General Thomas to his immediate rear, including Duck River and Columbia, and General McPherson to his right rear, especially Decatur and from the direction of Florence. On notice of danger the commanding general of the reserve at Nashville will promptly provide for the emergency, and see that damages, if done, are quickly repaired, but all officers are cautioned against the mischievous and criminal practice of reporting mere vague rumors, often sent into our lines by the enemy for his own purposes. Actual facts should be reported to the headquarters at Nashville and in the field, that they may be judged in connection with other known facts. An army of a million men could not guard against the fabulous stories that are sent to headquarters. Officers must scrutinize and see with their own eyes or those of some cool, experienced staff officer before making reports that may call off troops from another quarter, where there may be more need of them. When troops are intrenched or well covered by block-houses, a surrender will entail disgrace, for we have all seen examples when a few determined men have held thousands in check until relief came or the necessities of the enemy forced him to withdraw.

VI. Army commanders will make such orders and instructions to their respective commands as will carry out these orders.

*　　*　　*　　*　　*　　*

By order of Maj. Gen. W. T. Sherman:

R. M. SAWYER,
Assistant Adjutant-General.

SPECIAL FIELD ORDERS, ⎰ HDQRS. DEPT. OF THE CUMBERLAND,
No. 116.   ⎱   *Chattanooga, Tenn., April 25, 1864.*
*   *   *   *   *   *   ·   *

IV. Brig. Gen. J. Kilpatrick, U. S. Volunteers, having reported to the major-general commanding, pursuant to orders from headquarters Military Division of the Mississippi, is assigned to the command of the Third Cavalry Division.
*   *   *   *   *

By command of Major-General Thomas:
WM. D. WHIPPLE,
Assistant Adjutant-General.

WASHINGTON, D. C.,
April 26, 1864—3 p. m.
Maj. Gen. W. T. SHERMAN,
Nashville, Tenn.:
The Third Iowa Cavalry can be mounted at Saint Louis. Its last orders were for Vicksburg. Where shall it go?
H. W. HALLECK,
Major-General, Chief of Staff.

NASHVILLE, TENN., *April 26, 1864.*
(Received 9.36 p. m.)
Major-General HALLECK:
The Third Iowa should stop at Memphis. I will be at Chattanooga May 1, but will leave General Webster and other staff officers at Nashville. All well here.
W. T. SHERMAN,
Major-General.

LOUISVILLE, *April 26, 1864.*
Major-General SHERMAN:
I have not lost a moment's time in the shipment of mules. The Missouri trains had to come into Saint Louis from the frontier posts, and if boats are not detained at Harpeth Shoals a large number will arrive by the first of the month. From other points they should be arriving daily. Wherever it was possible to obtain a mule it has been procured. I have no orders yet from Washington to join you here. Have telegraphed several times.
ROBT. ALLEN.

HEADQUARTERS DEPARTMENT OF THE CUMBERLAND,
Chattanooga, April 26, 1864.
Maj. Gen. W. T. SHERMAN,
Nashville:
Do you desire me to move on the 2d May, or to concentrate my troops in readiness to move on that date?
GEO. H. THOMAS,
Major-General, Commanding.

NASHVILLE, *April 26, 1864.*

Maj. Gen. GEORGE H. THOMAS :

Don't move, only get ready. I will be down Thursday or Friday.

W. T. SHERMAN,
Major-General, Commanding.

HDQRS. FIRST CAV. DIV., DEPT. OF THE CUMBERLAND,
Cleveland, April 26, 1864.

Brig. Gen. W. D. WHIPPLE, *Chief of Staff, &c.:*

GENERAL : Everything has been quiet in our front to-day. Smith and Chandler, two of my scouts, went yesterday, between Spring Place and Red Clay, on main Dalton road, within 4½ or 5 miles of Dalton. The rebel cavalry pickets are on this side of the Connesauga River at Kenyon's. They have a very strong line of infantry pickets 4 miles from town. Elijah Tucker, a Union citizen, left Dalton the day before yesterday. He says that there are very few troops there, not more. he thinks, than 500. Most of their troops are between Buzzard Roost and Tunnel Hill, and their number is given by rumor at from 30,000 to 40,000. Harrison's and Dibrell's brigades, with six pieces of artillery, are at the water-tank, 1½ miles below Dalton. The rest of Wheeler's cavalry is between Tunnel Hill and Kenyon's place.

No citizens are permitted to pass the lines. There are no fortifications at Dalton, but it is reported that the enemy is fortified at Buzzard Roost.

I am, general, very respectfully, your obedient servant,

EDWARD M. McCOOK,
Colonel, Commanding.

KNOXVILLE, *April 26, 1864.*

Maj. Gen. G. H. THOMAS, *Chattanooga:*

If we move as soon as General Sherman expects I will probably be short of transportation. My mules are on the way from Kentucky, but will probably not reach here in time. In that event, can you lend me some teams until mine arrive ?

J. M. SCHOFIELD,
Major-General.

CHATTANOOGA, *April 26, 1864.*

Major-General SCHOFIELD :

We are very short of transportation, like yourself, and cannot assist you in that respect.

GEO. H. THOMAS,
Major-General.

LOOKOUT VALLEY, *April 26, 1864.*

Brig. Gen. WILLIAM D. WHIPPLE, *Chattanooga:*

The orders have been given for the movement of General Rousseau's troops. He reports that General Williams' command will be relieved by Thursday night. The latter is ordered to move to the front as soon as relieved.

JOSEPH HOOKER,
Major-General, Commanding.

KNOXVILLE, *April* 26, 1864.
Brigadier-General COX,
       Bull's Gap:
   I hope you will hear to-night or in the morning the result of the expedition above. Manson will, of course, have to remain where he can support the cavalry until he knows it is safe. Cars will go up to-night. I will give you the number and all details soon.
                         J. M. SCHOFIELD,
                                   Major-General.

BULL'S GAP, *April* 26, 1864.
Major-General SCHOFIELD,
       Knoxville:
   Yours of this morning received. I will have Reilly quit work at noon and reach here this evening. We will do our best to carry out the programme. Manson was last night 100 miles from Knoxville, and Reilly 70. As soon as it is settled what number of cars can be put at my disposal please have Ransom inform me. There is a possibility that the enemy may run down a force to meet our cavalry, and so involve Manson in some delay. I shall not feel that we are free from contingencies till I know he is at Greeneville.
                         J. D. COX,
                              Brigadier-General, Commanding.

BULL'S GAP, *April* 26, 1864.
Major-General SCHOFIELD,
       Knoxville:
   A train of seven cars has arrived, on which I send down part of Eighth Tennessee. They have four days' rations. The telegraph line was not working this afternoon, and I had no notice of the coming of the train. One regiment will march at daylight, the other I shall have to keep till I hear from Manson, who has sent me no news as yet. I have ordered the Eighth Tennessee to march from Knoxville at daylight unless otherwise ordered by you, and to draw two wagons to carry their cooking utensils and extra rations. As wagons and animals cannot go by rail we shall have to supply the regiments with new transportation, or let them wait at some point where they can be supplied by rail till their wagons arrive. Which mode shall we take?
                         J. D. COX,
                         Brigadier-General, Commanding Third Division.

KNOXVILLE, *April* 26, 1864.
Maj. Gen. GEORGE STONEMAN,
       Nicholasville, Ky.:
   General Sherman directs that you come forward at once with all the cavalry which is now ready, and let the rest follow as soon as practicable. What force can you start now?
                         J. M. SCHOFIELD,
                                   Major-General.

KNOXVILLE, TENN.,
April 26, 1864.

Brigadier-General COX,
    Bull's Gap:

Your division must be at its destination by the 1st of May. This can be accomplished by the use of such cars as can be spared for the purpose. I will place one or more trains at your disposal. Let each detachment be carried only so far that it can march the remainder of the distance by the time specified.

J. M. SCHOFIELD,
Major-General.

———

KNOXVILLE, TENN.,
April 26, 1864.

Brigadier-General JUDAH,
    Strawberry Plains:

I desire, if practicable, to regulate your march so as to reach Charleston the 30th. This will require that you march some distance beyond Knoxville to-morrow. Provision has been made for storing the overcoats of your men and issuing the required shoes. I think you will be able to arrange all of your business here and make the desired march.

J. M. SCHOFIELD,
Major-General.

———

CAIRO, *April 26, 1864.*

Maj. Gen. J. B. McPHERSON,
    Huntsville, Ala.:

Received both your dispatches to go to Clifton and disembark. Am only waiting for transportation and ammunition, which ought to have been here yesterday from Saint Louis. Will not delay a moment.

W. Q. GRESHAM,
Brigadier-General.

———

CAIRO, *April 26, 1864—9 a. m.*
(Received 27th.)

Major-General SHERMAN :

Nothing yet started for Clifton. Generals Crocker, Leggett, and Gresham are here. They have your orders in full. I will show them your telegram, and continue to give all the aid in my power. I will ask them to report progress to you. Maj. Gen. S. A. Hurlbut here.

M. BRAYMAN,
Brigadier-General.

———

PADUCAH, *April 26, 1864.*

Brigadier-General BRAYMAN :

My scouts have just got in from Columbus ; report the enemy in force at Clinton, Lovelaceville, and Mayfield, moving this way.

They are all around me.   While I feel satisfied I can repel them, if you have spare force that is bound up the river I would be pleased to have them come up and stop here awhile.

S. G. HICKS.

FORT DONELSON, TENN.,
April 26, 1864.

Major-General ROUSSEAU,
   Nashville, Tenn.:
   No news of importance from between the rivers.   From 500 to 1,000 rebels passed up on the west side Tennessee River yesterday; were seen at mouth of Sandy.

E. C. BROTT,
Lieutenant-Colonel, Commanding Post.

HDQRS. CAVALRY DIVISION, SIXTEENTH ARMY CORPS,
Memphis, Tenn., April 26, 1864.
Capt. W. C. RAWOLLE,
   Acting Assistant Adjutant-General:
   CAPTAIN: I have the honor to report that the mounted portion of my command, about 2,000 strong, is now ready for the field.   Of this force about 300 horses will not sustain over three days' march.
   I have the honor to be, captain, very respectfully, your obedient servant,

B. H. GRIERSON,
Brigadier-General.

HDQRS. CAVALRY DIVISION, SIXTEENTH ARMY CORPS,
Memphis, Tenn., April 26, 1864.
Maj. R. M. SAWYER,
   Assistant Adjutant-General:
   MAJOR: I respectfully report to the major-general commanding that there are eight regiments of my command now absent as veterans, while there are only five small regiments remaining here, they not being eligible to re-enlistment.
   Brig. Gen. S. D. Sturgis having assumed command of the cavalry in West Tennessee, I respectfully ask to be relieved from duty with the cavalry at this point; and ordered to Illinois and Iowa, for the purpose of reorganizing, arming, mounting, and equipping the regiments of my old division, now absent on furlough.
   I feel confident of being able to thus render more efficient service, and regain the largest and best portion of my command for active service at an earlier period than by remaining on duty with the small command now at Memphis, with which there is already another brigadier-general.
   With no other than the most earnest wishes to serve our country where I can render the most efficient service, I am, major, most respectfully, your most obedient servant,

B. H. GRIERSON,
Brigadier-General.

HEADQUARTERS POST AND DEFENSES,
Vicksburg, Miss., April 26, 1864.

Maj. Gen. C. C. WASHBURN,
Commanding District of West Tennessee:

GENERAL : Your dispatch by the hand of Major Morgan is received and being acted on as far as practicable. I send you 575 men, mounted and equipped, leaving me about 400 for this post, and these rather poorly mounted. I send also the dismounted men of the Fourth Iowa, numbering about 230 more. I am sorry your information was such as to lead you to expect so many men from here, but such is the condition of affairs. The last raid of General Sherman to Meridian has told severely on the horses of this command. I do not deem it safe, with my extended line, to reduce my cavalry force any more, as I will now be scarcely able to do more than picket the several roads leading to the city. I require about 2,500 horses and carbines to equip this command. I would be obliged to you if you can assist in procuring them. Your old regiment has only 125 serviceable horses. I am extremely desirous to assist Colonel Stephens in his efforts in refitting his regiment. I inclose to you the nearest information I have as to the strength and condition of the enemy's cavalry, together with some other information that I consider reliable, which may be of some service to you.*

Accept my congratulations in having you so near a neighbor.

Most respectfully, your obedient servant,
J. McARTHUR,
Brigadier-General

———

NASHVILLE, TENN.,
April 26, 1864.

General M. C. MEIGS,
Quartermaster-General, Washington:

DEAR GENERAL : Yours of April 20 is at hand. General Allen, Colonel Donaldson, and Mr. Anderson are doing all that men can. I think we all comprehend the problem. Nashville is abundantly supplied, and our business is now to feed our men and animals on the front line and accumulate a surplus to warrant our departure. I have already doubled the daily supply of cars out, and have made their loads more in accordance with our wants. Our reports show in Thomas' department 230,000 rations issued to citizens in a month. Now, those citizens are of doubtful use to us in war, and, laying aside the humanities, I would rather have those rations in our warehouses at Chattanooga and Ringgold. Cattle, too, are being driven, and troops marching.

If I only could count on a few more days, I would have a thirty days' start, but I may have to move on the 2d of May, with barely enough to warrant the move, and beef-cattle and salt, on which we may have to live, come forward too slowly.

Commissaries are too apt to think their work done when the vouchers of purchase are in due form and the price in Chicago or the moon is cheap. But all are laboring now to the one end, and I am content.

Colonel McCallum has not yet come. General Thomas reports one gun-boat done and two others approaching completion on the Ten-

———

* Inclosures not found.

nessee. I will order them temporarily equipped, and let the navy officers, when they come, change the armament and crew. One naval officer has gone to the front. I don't believe any treasury can stand the load ours has, and we may in self-preservation be forced to resort to the same means our enemy has already done—take the one-tenth as tax and the nine-tenths as impressment. It is now going to be a grand scramble who will get the horses, Forrest or ourselves. I think Forrest can beat us in the horse-stealing business, but we must learn. As I advance into Georgia, Forrest will surely manage somehow to gather the horses in Tennessee and Kentucky, and if we could make our minds up to it, we might take them first. But it has ever been that the Confederates take as a matter of course what would be an awful vandal outrage on our part.

By our returns we have 52,000 cavalry, but if I can get up three divisions of 5,000 each by May 2 I will deem myself lucky. As to teams I will use what we have. I inclose you copies of my orders* on this subject, which are as moderate as you could ask. For myself and staff I will take but one wagon, and other commanders ought to follow my example, which I will endeavor to impress.

I have sent word to Captain Poe, who will send you two copies of his photograph sketches, which are very beautiful.

You must make up your mind to heavy losses of stores this year, as our best troops are at the front, and the enemy, being superior to us in cavalry at all points, and having a cheap appreciation of horse-flesh, will make heavy swoops at our lines of communication. I will take all the precautions I can.

With much respect, &c.,

W. T. SHERMAN,
Major-General.

WAR DEPARTMENT,
Washington, April 26, 1864—11.40 a. m.

Major-General SHERMAN,
Nashville:

There is no breach of faith to the Indiana cavalry, and I have so informed Governor Morton, and instructed him that the men must be sent forward, mounted or dismounted. He acquiesced, and it is only needed that you send a good officer to bring them out of the State. The Governor has had every facility and is more than three months behind time with these troops. Please let me know whether you send an officer for them, and who he is, and this Department will see that you get them.

EDWIN M. STANTON,
Secretary of War.

NASHVILLE, TENN., *April 26, 1864.*
(Received 5.20 p. m.)

Hon. E. M. STANTON,
Secretary of War:

Am glad you claim the right to control cavalry dismounted. The true rule is, when troops are mustered and paid by the United States

---

* See General Orders, No. 7, p. 408.

we are to judge how and where they shall be employed. I have organized a camp of instruction for them here, under General Carl Schurz. I will look around for a good officer to send to Indianapolis to expedite the mount, and will give you the name in the course of the day.

W. T. SHERMAN,
Major-General.

GENERAL ORDERS, } HDQRS. MIL. DIV. OF THE MISSISSIPPI,
No. 10.   }   *Nashville, Tenn., April 26, 1864.*

I. There will be established, at or near Nashville, one or more camps of instruction, in which will be collected all regiments arriving from the rear which are not assigned to any one of the departments or armies in the field, all detachments or individuals who have got astray from their commands, and all convalescents discharged from hospitals. These camps will be under the general supervision of the commanding officer of the District of Nashville, who will assign to each a general officer, who will be instructed to organize and equip for service all such regiments and detachments and subject them to a thorough system of instruction in the drill and guard duties.

II. All officers, regiments, and detachments belonging to any of the established departments will, without further orders, be sent with dispatch to their proper posts; but such as are not thus provided for will be held in reserve at Nashville to re-enforce any part of the lines of communication to the front, and subject to orders from these headquarters.

III. Soldiers' homes are merely designed for the accommodation of men in transitu; and when delayed from any cause, the men will be sent to the camp of instruction. Officers and men also in and about Nashville awaiting orders will be sent to the camp of instruction.

IV. Maj. Gen. Carl Schurz is assigned to the command of one of these camps, and will report to Major-General Rousseau for further instructions.

V. Patrols will, from time to time, be sent to collect men and officers who are in Nashville without proper authority. All who are not in possession of written orders that warrant their presence in Nashville will be arrested and taken to the camp of instruction, where they will be put on duty till forwarded, under guard or otherwise, to their proper posts.

VI. In time of war leaves of absence can only be granted, and that for limited periods, by commanders of separate armies or departments. Subordinate commanders cannot send officers or men away without such sanction; and therefore the numerous shifts of that kind will be treated as void.

VII. Staff departments, on proper requisitions approved by General Rousseau, will issue the provisions, camp and garrison equipage, arms, and accouterments necessary to carry into effect these orders.

By order of Maj. Gen. W. T. Sherman:

R. M. SAWYER,
Assistant Adjutant-General.

GENERAL ORDERS, }   HDQRS. DEPT. OF THE CUMBERLAND,
No. 62.   }   *Chattanooga, Tenn., April 26,* 1864.

I. General Orders, No. 91, series of 1863, is hereby rescinded. The flags hereinafter described will be used to designate the headquarters of the department, corps, divisions, and brigades named in this order.

Headquarters of the department: The national flag, 5 feet square, embroidered spread eagle in the field, lower part of the eagle resting upon the lower edge of the field, with the stars of the Union arranged above.

Headquarters Fourth Army Corps: Silk with yellow fringe, or bunting, red with blue field; size of field 2 feet square, same size as for department headquarters, with gilt or embroidered eagle in the field.

First Division, Fourth Army Corps: The flag of the corps, without fringe or the eagle in the field; size of field the same as the flag of the corps; of bunting with white bar, 3 inches wide, running from right-hand upper corner of field to left-hand lower corner.

Second Division, Fourth Army Corps: The same as for the First Division, with the addition of a white bar, 3 inches wide, running from left-hand upper corner to right-hand lower corner, forming cross with the first.

Third Division, Fourth Army Corps: Same as for Second Division, with addition of a third white bar, 3 inches wide, running parallel to staff through center of field.

All brigade flags to be forked; distance from staff to angle of the fork, 3 feet; size of flag otherwise, same as for divisions, with same colors, with division bars in the field.

First Brigade, First Division, Fourth Army Corps, with addition of one white star, midway between center of lower edge of field and lower edge of flag.

Second Brigade, First Division, Fourth Army Corps: The same as for the First Brigade, except that there will be two white stars, arranged equidistant from each other and center of lower edge of field and lower edge of flag, on a line parallel to the staff.

Third Brigade, First Division, Fourth Army Corps: The same as for the First Brigade, except that there will be three white stars, arranged as described for the Second Brigade.

Flags for headquarters of the brigades of the Second and Third Divisions: Same as for the first, with the exception of the distinguishing bars of the divisions in the field.

Headquarters Fourteenth Army Corps: Silk with yellow fringe, or bunting; same size as for department headquarters; blue with red field; size of field, 2 feet square; gilt or embroidered eagle in field.

Headquarters First, Second, and Third Divisions, Fourteenth Army Corps: Blue flags, with red field, with same distinguishing marks as the corresponding divisions of the Fourth Corps.

Flags for the headquarters of the brigades of the Fourteenth Army Corps: Same as for the corresponding brigades of the Fourth Corps, with the exception of the colors, which will be those described for the Fourteenth Army Corps.

Headquarters Twentieth Army Corps: Blue swallow-tailed flag, white Tunic cross in center, with the numerals "20" in red in center of the cross.

The division flags of this corps will be 6 feet square.

First Division: Red star on white flag.

Second Division: White star on blue flag.

Third Division : Blue star on white flag.

Fourth Division : Green star on red flag.

The flags for the brigades of the respective divisions will be in the shape of an equilateral triangle (each side 6 feet in length), similar in color and device to the division flags.

The flag of the First Brigade will be without border.

That of the Second Brigade have border same color as star, 6 inches wide, down the staff.

That of the Third Brigade a border 6 inches wide all around the flag.

Headquarters cavalry command : Red, white, and blue flag, 6 feet by 4; stripes vertical, red outermost, with cross sabers yellow, the hilt and point of sabers extending over one-half of red and blue stripes. Staff portable, 14 feet long, and in two joints. Yellow silk fringe around the flag, 4 inches wide.

First Division : White flag, 6 feet by 4, with cross sabers red, figure (1) blue.

First Brigade : White triangle, cross sabers red, figure (1) blue.

Second Brigade : White triangle; blue border on staff, 6 inches wide; cross sabers red; figure (2) blue.

Third Brigade : White triangle; blue border around flag, 4 inches wide; cross sabers red; figure (3) blue.

Second Division : Blue flag, 6 feet by 4; cross sabers white; figure (2) red.

First Brigade : Blue triangle; cross sabers white; figure (1) red.

Second Brigade : Blue triangle; cross sabers white; red border on staff, 6 inches wide; figure (2) red.

Third Brigade : Blue triangle; cross sabers white; red border, 4 inches wide around flag; figure (3) red.

Third Division : White flag, 6 feet by 4; cross sabers blue; figure (3) red.

First Brigade : White triangle; cross sabers blue; figure (1) red.

Second Brigade : White triangle; cross sabers blue; red border on staff, 6 inches wide ; figure (2) red.

Third Brigade : White triangle; cross sabers blue; red border, 4 inches wide, around flag; figure (3) red.

Fourth Division : White flag, 6 feet by 4; cross sabers blue; figure (4) red ; yellow border around flag, 9 inches wide.

First Brigade : White triangle ; cross sabers red ; figure (1) blue ; yellow border around flag, width 4 inches.

Second Brigade : Blue triangle; cross sabers white; figure (2) red ; yellow border around flag, width 4 inches.

Third Brigade : White triangle ; cross sabers blue ; figure (3) red ; yellow border around flag, width 4 inches.

Figures in center of sabers ; points of sabers up.

Cross sabers in corps and division flags, 4½ feet long, 3 inches wide; in brigade flags, 2½ feet long, 1¼ inches wide.

Cavalry headquarters flag will be made of silk; division and brigade, of bunting.

Brigade flags will be 4 feet on staff and 6 feet on sides.

Engineer Brigade : A white and blue flag, blue uppermost and running horizontally, 6 feet by 4.

Pioneer Brigade : A blue, white, and blue flag, running vertically; crossed axes in engineer wreath on one side and spread eagle on the other.

Hospital and ambulance flags: Same as prescribed by General Orders, No. 9, current series, War Department.

Subsistence depots and store-houses: A plain light-green flag, 3 feet square.

Quartermaster depots and store-houses: Same flag, with letters "Q. M. D." in white, 1 foot long.

Ordnance department, general headquarters: A bright-green flag, 3 feet square, with two crossed cannon in white, set diagonally in a square of 3 feet, with a circular ribbon of 6 inches wide and 3 feet greatest diameter (or diameter of inner circle 2 feet), with the letters " U. S. Ordnance Department " in black, 4 inches long. on ribbon, and a streamer above flag, 1 foot on staff by 4 feet long, crimson color, with words "Chief of Ordnance " in black, 6 inches long.

Division ordnance: Same flag, with cannon and ribbon, but no streamer.

II. For the purpose of ready recognition of the members of the corps and divisions of this army, and to prevent injustice by reports of straggling and misconduct through mistakes as to organizations, the following-described badges will be worn by the officers and enlisted men of all the regiments of the corps mentioned. They will be made either of cloth or metal, after the patterns deposited in the office of the assistant adjutant-general, at department headquarters, and will be securely fastened upon the center of the top of the cap, or upon the left-hand side of the hat when that is worn:

For the Fourth Corps: An equilateral triangle, red for First Division, white for Second Division, blue for Third Division.

For the Fourteenth Corps: An acorn, red for First Division, white for Second Division, and blue for Third Division.

For the Twentieth Corps: A star, as heretofore worn by the Twelfth Corps.

Pioneer Brigade: Crossed hatchets, as prescribed by paragraph 1585, Revised Army Regulations, edition of 1863.

The chief quartermaster of the department will furnish the cloth from which to make the badges, upon proper requisitions, and officers of the inspector-general's department of this army will see that they are worn as directed.

By command of Major-General Thomas:

WM. D. WHIPPLE,
Assistant Adjutant-General.

SPECIAL FIELD ORDERS, } HDQRS. DEPT. OF THE CUMBERLAND,
No. 117.   }   *Chattanooga, Tenn., April 26, 1864.*

*   *   *   *   *   *   *

V. Battery I, First Ohio Volunteer Artillery (Capt. H. Dilger), of the garrison of Chattanooga, is assigned to the First Division, Fourteenth Army Corps, relieving Battery A, First Michigan Volunteer Artillery. Battery A, First Michigan Artillery (Capt. F. E. Hale), on being relieved, is assigned to the permanent garrison, Chattanooga.

*   *   *   *   *

By command of Major-General Thomas:

WM. D. WHIPPLE,
Assistant Adjutant-General.

General Orders,)   Hdqrs. Dept. and Army of the Tenn.,
No. 5.   {   *Huntsville, Ala., April 26, 1864.*

The following officers are announced as the staff of the major-general commanding, on duty at these headquarters. They will be respected and obeyed accordingly:

Lieut. Col. William T. Clark, assistant adjutant-general and chief of staff.

Lieut. Col. J. D. Bingham, chief quartermaster.

Lieut. Col. Robert Macfeely, chief commissary.

Lieut. Col. William E. Strong, assistant inspector-general.

Capt. A. Hickenlooper, judge-advocate.

Maj. L. S. Willard, aide-de-camp.

Capt. D. H. Gile, aide-de-camp.

Capt. G. R. Steele, aide-de-camp.

Col. Ezra Taylor, chief of artillery.

Lieut. Col. James Wilson, provost-marshal-general.

Surg. John Moore, U. S. Army, medical director.

Asst. Surg. D. L. Huntington, U. S. Army, assistant medical director.

Capt. C. B. Reese, U. S. Army, chief engineer.

Capt. D. H. Buel, U. S. Army, chief of ordnance.

Capt. John H. Munroe, assistant adjutant-general.

Capt. Rowland Cox, assistant adjutant-general.

Lieut. Kilburn Knox, Thirteenth U. S. Infantry, commissary of musters.

Lieut. A. C. Blizzard, acting assistant quartermaster.

E. A. Duncan, acting assistant surgeon, U. S. Army, in charge of staff and escort.

By order of Maj. Gen. James B. McPherson :

W. T. CLARK,
Assistant Adjutant-General.

Circular.]   Hdqrs. Department of the Ohio,
Office Chief of Artillery and Ordnance,
Knoxville, April 26, 1864.

In organizing the ordnance trains for the army in the field, as directed by Major-General Schofield, commanding department, the following general rules will be observed :

First. The corps ordnance train will carry 100 rounds per piece of ammunition for all small-arms and a supply of artillery ammunition equal to that carried in the ammunition chests of all the batteries.

Second. Each division ordnance train will carry sixty rounds per piece of ammunition for all small-arms in its division, and it will habitually march immediately in rear of the division baggage train. The division ordnance officers will be responsible for the ammunition carried in the division ordnance train, and will issue direct to regiments.

Third. No other stores, baggage, or articles of any kind, excepting forage for mules and drivers' necessary baggage, will be allowed in any of the wagons composing the ordnance train.

Fourth. On the march the wagons composing the ordnance trains will not be allowed to scatter or to be separated by allowing other wagons to get between them, and in camp, when practicable, will be parked in a body and separate from other trains.

Fifth. It will be the duty of each division ordnance officer to know the particular kind and caliber of ammunition in each wagon of his train, so that there may be no delay when called on to issue.

In pursuance of these instructions you will immediately ascertain the quantity of ammunition required in your respective divisions to supply each man with 100 rounds (40 rounds in cartridge-boxes and 60 in wagons), and will at once make requisition for the quantity deficient.

Very respectfully, your obedient servant,

G. W. SCHOFIELD,
Lieutenant-Colonel, Chief of Artillery and Ordnance.

SPECIAL ORDERS, }   HDQRS. DEPARTMENT OF THE OHIO,
No. 117.   }   *Knoxville, Tenn., April 26, 1864.*

*   *   *   *   *   *   *

XIV. Brig. Gen. S. S. Fry, U. S. Volunteers, is relieved from command of the forces at Burnside Point, and will await further orders at Louisville, Ky.

Brig. Gen. S. G. Burbridge, commanding District of Kentucky, will designate an officer to command at Burnside Point.

*   *   *   *   *   *

By command of Major-General Schofield:

R. MORROW,
Assistant Adjutant-General.

HDQRS. MILITARY DIVISION OF THE MISSISSIPPI,
Nashville, April 27, 1864.

Lieutenant-General GRANT,
        Culpeper:

In view of the fact that I will have to take the initiative with 20,000 less men in McPherson's army than I estimated, I intend to order all McPherson's disposable force (20,000) and Garrard's cavalry (5,000) to Chattanooga, to start from a common center. I go forward to-morrow.

W. T. SHERMAN,
Major-General.

NASHVILLE, *April 27, 1864.*

Maj. Gen. G. H. THOMAS,
        Chattanooga:

It will be impossible to get up McPherson's two veteran divisions in time, and instead of putting his force (20,000) with Garrard's cavalry, by way of Lebanon and Summerville, I will order all to Chattanooga, so we may start from a common center.

W. T. SHERMAN,
Major-General.

HEADQUARTERS DEPARTMENT OF THE CUMBERLAND,
Chattanooga, April 27, 1864.
Major-General HOOKER,
Lookout Valley:
Major-General Sherman telegraphs in cipher that he wants—

A gun-boat manned to patrol the river below Bridgeport to Decatur to cover Mc-Pherson's movements. It could be done by using field guns and dismounted artillery, till such time as the Navy can complete the proper crew and armament. General Sherman wishes to move the bridge at Larkinsville, so as to save that garrison.

The major-general commanding directs that General Geary move the gun-boat and place the field guns thereon, the men to return to Bridgeport and rejoin their division as soon as possible.
Very respectfully, your obedient servant,
WM. D. WHIPPLE,
Assistant Adjutant-General.

LOOKOUT VALLEY, *April 27, 1864.*
Brig. Gen. WILLIAM D. WHIPPLE,
Chattanooga:
Please inform the general that Williams reports that his division will be at Bridgeport Saturday night.
JOSEPH HOOKER,
Major-General, Commanding.

HDQRS. FIRST CAV. DIV., DEPT. OF THE CUMBERLAND,
Cleveland, April 27, 1864.
Brigadier-General WHIPPLE,
Chief of Staff:
GENERAL: I have the honor to report all quiet in my front. The scouting party which left here yesterday under command of Colonel Dorr, hearing that the picket post which it was intended to surprise had been moved, pushed for Spring Place, which town it entered at 3 o'clock this morning. The enemy left so rapidly that it was impossible to make but 3 prisoners. Colonel Dorr states in his report that the scouting party has developed the fact that the enemy have no forces of any kind east of the Connesauga and north of the Coosawattee, and that, if desirable, his lines of communication from Dalton to Atlanta might be interrupted. They have infantry with their cavalry on the other side of the Connesauga.
I am, general, very respectfully, your obedient servant,
EDWARD M. McCOOK,
Colonel, Commanding.

NASHVILLE, *April 27, 1864.*
Brigadier-General WHIPPLE :
Wilder joined his brigade this morning. His regiment was to reach Columbia to-day. Horses have been pressed. Garrard will have over 5,000 ; has over 3,000 now. Looks fine. I will leave for Chattanooga to-morrow.
W. L. ELLIOTT,
Brigadier-General.

KNOXVILLE, *April 27*, 1864.
Major-General SHERMAN :

I have received your letter of instructions of April 24, and Special Orders, No. 35, of April 25. The main body of my troops will be at Charleston on the 30th. Those sent to destroy the railroad will be somewhat later. I will bring them down by railroad as rapidly as possible. The troops coming from Kentucky have not arrived, but must be here in a few days. I have not learned the result of the expedition to the Watauga. The infantry has done its work thoroughly. I have no fears of the rebels ever attempting to rebuild road.

J. M. SCHOFIELD,
Major-General.

BULL'S GAP, *April 27*, 1864.
General SCHOFIELD :

General Manson was 8 miles above Greeneville last night ; says he will reach Lick Creek to-night. The enemy were strongly posted at Watauga, but partially destroyed the bridge themselves. River too high to ford. Our troops skirmished across the river but could not accomplish the entire destruction of the bridge. We lost 3 killed and 18 wounded. Manson has destroyed all bridges from Jonesborough to where he is, and fully one-third of the track, as he reports. I send remainder of the Tennessee regiment and part of the One hundred and fourth Ohio by this train, and remainder of the last by next train if the cavalry get here to make some guard for to-night. The One hundredth Ohio is marching.

J. D. COX,
Brigadier-General.

BULL'S GAP, *April 27*, 1864.
Major-General SCHOFIELD :

Manson is at Lick Creek and will be in at his old camp, which he left standing, in the morning. How far his men can go to-morrow is doubtful ; they are very weary and footsore. I would like to have a train as early as possible to-morrow for the dismounted cavalry and lame infantry. The sick and wounded, with rest of the One hundred and fourth Ohio, go down on the train now here. I will march with Manson's men in the morning, and have the telegraph operator connect with the wire where we halt.

J. D. COX,
Brigadier-General.

NICHOLASVILLE, *April 27*, 1864.
Major-General SCHOFIELD :

I leave here day after to-morrow with 2,000 men fitted for the field. Of those I leave behind 2,300 are mounted and equipped and partly armed. The rest have nothing. Of those left behind some have pistols without cases and carbines without slings. My ordnance officer is now in Cincinnati trying to hurry up things, and a thousand may possibly be got ready by the 1st of May. Horses are not coming in as fast as they were promised us, and the pack-mules have mostly been sent to Knoxville.

GEO. STONEMAN,
Major-General.

HDQRS. FIRST DIVISION, DISTRICT OF KENTUCKY,
Lexington, Ky., April 27, 1864.

Col. S. B. BROWN,
Commanding Eleventh Michigan Cavalry:

Messrs. McAllister and Crockett represent that you have in your camp a number of negroes belonging to them and their neighbors. You will afford these gentlemen any and every facility for procuring their negroes. These negroes are enrolled and must be delivered up.

By command of Brigadier-General Hobson:

W. W. WOODWARD,
Captain and Pro. Mar. Gen., 1st Div., Dist. of Kentucky.

LEXINGTON, KY.,
April 27, 1864.

Col. C. J. TRUE,
Comdg. Second Brig., First Div., Dist. of Kentucky:

COLONEL: Mr. P. Swaggart represents that he has a negro boy in the Twelfth Ohio Cavalry, the servant of one of the majors. You are directed to at once investigate the case. If the boy named "Jim Finney" is in any of your camps he will be arrested and sent under guard to these headquarters. The negro is enrolled and no person other than the enrolling officer has any right to him whatever. Inclosed find his letter.*

By order of Brigadier-General Hobson:

W. W. WOODWARD,
Captain and Pro. Mar. Gen., 1st Div., Dist. of Kentucky.

NASHVILLE, TENN.,
April 27, 1864.

General GARRARD,
Columbia:

You will move your effective cavalry division to Decatur and act in concert with General Dodge, who will move from Decatur to Guntersville and Lebanon. We are pressing all the horses possible and send them forward at once.

I want you to have 5,000. The rest can be left in depot at and near Columbia. I want you at Decatur as early as May 2. As few wagons as possible. Surplus wagons can be sent to Chattanooga to join you from there.

W. T. SHERMAN,
Major-General, Commanding.

---

* Not found.

COLUMBIA, *April 27*, 1864.

Major-General SHERMAN :

GENERAL : Your telegram of this date received. I have about 3,000 effective men ; no pack-saddles. Can move as I am and be at Decatur at the time mentioned. Would it not be well for me to see you ?

K. GARRARD,
Brigadier-General.

HDQRS. MILITARY DIVISION OF THE MISSISSIPPI,
Nashville, April 27, 1864.

Brigadier-General GARRARD,
Commanding Second Division Cavalry, Right Wing:

GENERAL : General McPherson is now here, and on consultation, taking into consideration all the facts known to me of the strength and position of the enemy, we have concluded that McPherson's troops can reach their position at and near La Fayette more expeditiously by Chattanooga than by the contemplated road by Decatur, Gunter's, and Lebanon.

It is very desirable that the whole army should be at and in front of Chattanooga by May 5. You may therefore put in motion your cavalry that is mounted and equipped, with the wagons needed for efficient action, and the rest as fast as horses are received, leaving, as heretofore arranged, your dismounted men at Columbia and along the road.

General Rousseau will send a regiment to hold the road down as far as Pulaski. Enough horses are now on hand to increase your mounted force to 5,000. With these I want you at Chattanooga about the 5th of May, and as there is no necessity of your moving with Dodge, you can select your own route, and move by brigades and regiments, as you please. On arrival at Chattanooga take position near the extreme right of the whole army.

General McPherson will see you to-morrow. These orders may seem to you a little sudden, but are made necessary by orders from General Grant.

I am, &c.,

W. T. SHERMAN,
Major-General.

APRIL 27, 1864.

Maj. Gen. J. B. McPHERSON
(Care of Major-General Sherman), Nashville:

Reports show Forrest at Jackson with most of his force ; Martin at Blue Mountain ; Clanton gone to Kingston, Ga., with part of his force ; the force in the valley same as before ; Polk still at Meridian or thereabouts ; Lee is said to be this side of Okolona, but nothing certain. This is up to the 24th. Forrest has heavy pickets at Bear and Yellow Creeks and several boats in each, but so far as I can learn no part of his force proper is there yet.

G. M. DODGE,
Brigadier-General.

HDQRS. LEFT WING, SIXTEENTH ARMY CORPS,
Athens, Ala., April 27, 1864.
Brig. Gen. T. W. SWEENY,
Commanding Second Division,
Brig. Gen. J. C. VEATCH,
Commanding Fourth Division:

I desire to impress upon you the importance of strict vigilance in guarding our trains. After we cross the Tennessee River we will have on our flanks a large cavalry force, who will annoy and, unless we are prepared and on the alert, delay us.   •

The move I have to make requires celerity on our part, and we must not give this cavalry, which has been placed in our front for the purpose, an opportunity to retard us. Trains must be kept closed up, infantry distributed through them, and such orders given as will make them at all times and under all circumstances safe. The loss of any part would cripple us so as to force a halt, which at this time would be ruinous to us.

I know that I have only to call your attention to this to have your active and constant attention to it.

I am, very respectfully, your obedient servant,
G. M. DODGE,
Brigadier-General, Commanding.

DECATUR, ALA.,
April 27, 1864.
Brigadier-General DODGE,
Commanding Left Wing, Sixteenth Army Corps, Athens:

Scout Looney came in last night, bringing 14 deserters from Winston County. He says that Roddey is at Sims' Mill, on Moulton and Danville road. Patterson on Decatur and Moulton road at Shoal Creek. Heard nothing of Polk's forces and nothing of any rebel force coming this way from West Tennessee.

JAMES C. VEATCH,
Brigadier-General.

NASHVILLE, *April 27, 1864.*
Brigadier-General LEGGETT,
Cairo:

General Gresham is ordered to disembark at Clifton, and remain there watching the operations of Forrest, and endeavor to counteract them should he attempt to cross the Tennessee River to threaten our communications until the arrival of another brigade, when he is to push forward and join me via Pulaski and Huntsville.

The brigade which relieves Gresham will remain at Clifton until relieved by another, when it will follow Gresham, and so on successively until the whole of the Second Division is brought forward to the front. The last brigade will come right on through. Hurry up the troops as fast as possible by brigades, or what is equivalent to a brigade, at a time.

JAS. B. McPHERSON,
Major-General.

CAIRO, *April* 27, 1864.
Major-General SHERMAN :
  Have seen your dispatch of yesterday to General Brayman. Am
waiting for transports and ammunition, which should have been
here from Saint Louis yesterday. Think I can get off in the morning. Will not delay a moment.
                                    W. Q. GRESHAM,
                                            Brigadier-General.

CAIRO, *April* 27, 1864.
Maj. Gen. W. T. SHERMAN :
  Does your dispatch of yesterday to General Brayman include more
than the command of General Gresham ? The Twentieth, Thirty-
first, and Forty-fifth Illinois, and Twentieth, Sixty-eighth, and
Seventy-eighth Ohio have not yet returned. The Eighty-first,
Ninety-fifth Illinois, and Fourteenth Wisconsin are on Red River
expedition. I am doing all in my power to hasten the organization
of division. Crocker's division in same condition as mine. Gresham
expects to get off to-night. He has been delayed by quartermaster
and ordnance officers at Saint Louis.
                                    M. D. LEGGETT,
                                            Brigadier-General.

HEADQUARTERS DISTRICT OF WEST TENNESSEE,
                          Memphis, Tenn., April 27, 1864.
Maj. Gen. J. B. MCPHERSON,
        Commanding Department of the Tennessee:
  GENERAL : I avail myself of the opportunity offered by one of
your staff to say that I arrived here and took command five days
ago. I found the condition of matters here most deplorable, and the
troops in wretched condition. The cavalry was all broken down,
and less than 2,000 could be mounted. I have worked night and
day since I came here to get the troops into some kind of shape to
enable me to move after Forrest. He is still hovering round, 7,000
or 8,000 strong. I have sent to Vicksburg for cavalry, and the
moment they arrive I shall send out a force that I am certain will
whip him and drive him from the State. I have seized all the horses
here, with which I shall mount the dismounted cavalry, and by this
means and by the help from Vicksburg I hope to make a satisfactory campaign. I have only about 2,500 white infantry here, 2,000
of which I shall send out to support the cavalry. I shall move early
Saturday morning. Brigadier-General Sturgis has arrived and will
command the expedition.
  I am, general, your obedient servant,
                                    C. C. WASHBURN,
                                            Major-General.

  P. S.—What am I to understand my command to consist of ? Are
the troops at Cairo, Paducah, and Columbus under my orders, and,
if not, what are the limits of the District of West Tennessee ?

HEADQUARTERS SIXTEENTH ARMY CORPS,
Cairo, Ill., April 27, 1864.
Lieut. Col. W. T. CLARK,
    Asst. Adjt. Gen., Department and Army of the Tennessee:

SIR : I beg leave to report to the major-general commanding that I have received copies of instructions to Major-General Washburn, Maj. Gen. H. W. Slocum, and Brigadier-General Prince, for which I am indebted.

As there is visible contradiction between these orders and Special Orders, No. 150, Adjutant-General's Office, which latter order is, to say the least, ill-advised, I propose to state for the information of the major-general my views of my rights and duties.

There is no such district as West Tennessee, nor has there been for more than a year. It was abolished when General Grant took command of the department and has never been reinstated. I never commanded any such district, and therefore cannot be relieved from it. I do command the Sixteenth Army Corps, and intend to until properly removed. The troops within the old District of West Tennessee are part of that corps and subject to my command.

The order of Major-General McPherson is correct as I understand it, and places Major-General Washburn in command of the District of Memphis, including therein all of the District of Columbus except Cairo, with orders to report to me.

Personally, it is a matter of indifference to me what disposition the authorities make of me, but I intend that that disposition shall be made openly, fairly, and distinctly, and that neither the rights of the Sixteenth Army Corps nor my own shall be evaded by any such orders as Special Orders, No. 150.

Lieutenant-General Grant, acting under mistaken information, has done me an injustice which can only be rectified by a court of inquiry, which has already been demanded.

You will no doubt have heard from Memphis that General Washburn has stopped the Fourth Iowa Cavalry, en route for Vicksburg, and has sent Major Morgan to Vicksburg with orders to stop and turn back all boats he meets, and to bring up from Vicksburg all the cavalry there. This, of course, General Slocum, under your orders, is not likely to permit, nor is it desirable that an officer of such large experience in the field and success as General Washburn, sent to Memphis expressly to punish Forrest, with a force that I considered inadequate, should be re-enforced to the extent contemplated. He was sent there to do that which "marked timidity" on my part prevented from being done, and should use only the material which I left there. He also, as I understand, wants more infantry, which I presume he will find somewhere.

The truth is that the enemy are running the Mobile and Ohio Railroad to Tupelo, and are working a heavy force toward Corinth so as to complete that part. Until that is done, Corinth will be headquarters for Forrest, who is now withdrawing his forage and supplies from Jackson. Detached bands may be held in West Tennessee, but I think the main force will concentrate around Corinth. If they do, and Washburn moves out on Saturday, he will have his hands full.

The cavalry of Grierson, now at Memphis, is of little value. Horses are run down, what there are of them. All the dash and energy they ever had was taken out by Sooy Smith's misfortune. The Fourth Missouri, Second New Jersey, Nineteenth Pennsylvania,

Sixth Tennessee, and Seventh Indiana are the only organized regiments remaining, of which the Fourth Missouri is the only one reliable for serious action. The rest of the command is of detachments of non-veterans, and not near enough horses to mount these. I have sent heretofore statements of the infantry.

If General Washburn attempts the movement he contemplates with the force I left in Memphis, and conducts it as he has conducted his previous commands, he will probably lose Memphis. If he is sufficiently re-enforced and the command led by an officer of experience and knowledge, it may do something that will be creditable. It is my plain duty to notify you, from my knowledge of that country, that any serious disaster to the covering force at Memphis will result in the loss of the city, and that a movement of infantry from the garrison 60 or 70 miles into the country will expose them to the danger of a move by the enemy's mounted men, under cover of the Wolf, or Hatchie, or Coldwater, upon the reduced garrison. I may overestimate the danger, but my personal record leads me to feel sure that I shall not be charged with personal timidity. I therefore affirm as my deliberate opinion that no movement should be made to bring Forrest to action with less than 5,000 good men, and that it is infinitely better and safer to wait the return of the veteran cavalry, now past due. I do not believe that Banks can or will permit A. J. Smith's command to return without imperiling his expedition, for they are the life of his force.

I shall remain here and wait events with philosophic resignation, and in order to carry on the business of the corps have ordered my headquarters here, "possessing my soul" with patience until the Government make up their minds whether they want my services or not.

I am, colonel, your obedient servant.

S. A. HURLBUT,
Major-General, Comdg. Sixteenth Army Corps.

ON BOARD THE DISPATCH-BOAT FOR COLUMBUS,
April 27, 1864. (Received 30th.)

[Major-General WASHBURN:]

GENERAL: I mailed a letter to you this morning, and have not a copy with me, having left my baggage at Cairo. Being on my way down to inspect Columbus I find Colonel —— on board going immediately to Memphis, and I will endeavor to give the substance of my letter by him because you will get it sooner, I suppose.

I have the honor to report to you per orders in pursuance of Special Orders, No. 35, of Major-General Sherman.

On arriving at Cairo yesterday I found a letter from Major-Gen. eral McPherson, dated 20th, which does not in describing my district mention Cairo as in it, and hence, to my surprise, it is thought by the present commander of the district that a new district has been made. This is the opinion of Major-General Hurlbut also, who is on duty here. General Brayman doubted if I was entitled to any of the books of the district headquarters, on account of my district being, in their opinion, different from [what] it has been up to this time, but he has, I believe, concluded to let me have some of them. The department staff in the district I perceive it is his intention to refuse.

I purpose, unless I discover reasons to change my intention, to visit and inspect Columbus and Paducah, and then assume command. By that time, about three days, I shall probably hear from you. Unless objected to by you, my course seems to be to assume command and direct the department staff officers of the district to report to me. The district, without any change in itself, has changed its name on the records, being sometimes called that of Cairo and sometimes that of Columbus. In the general-order book General Asboth assumes command of the District of Columbus, and in the same order names the posts included in it. commencing with Cairo. At present, on the papers of the office, it is called the District of Cairo.

In conversation with General Grant he said to me that I would have the selection of the place for my headquarters between Columbus and Cairo, and I had no suspicion of any change in the district till General Brayman and General Hurlbut mentioned it.

Deeming it possible you may not have a copy of the orders of General McPherson, I inclose the original,* which please return. You will perceive that I am assigned to the command of the Defenses and District of Columbus, which includes Paducah, &c. It is also said that I am not confined to this named boundary, and, when afterward speaking of the forces within my jurisdiction, it is said that certain troops are to rendezvous at Cairo—Seventeenth Army Corps—and "three regiments of infantry have been ordered from Saint Louis to re-enforce Paducah, Cairo, and Columbus." Cairo is, I think, the base of the defenses of the district.

In want of information regarding your staff I address you directly.

I am, general, with great respect, your obedient servant,

HENRY PRINCE,
Brigadier-General.

GENERAL ORDERS, }   HDQRS. DEPT. OF THE CUMBERLAND,
      No. 63.   }   *Chattanooga, Tenn., April 27, 1864.*

The defenses of Chattanooga will hereafter be known by the names given to them in this order.

1. The detached work on the high hill east of the town, as Fort Creighton, in honor of Colonel Creighton. Seventh Regiment Ohio Volunteers, commanding First Brigade, Second Division, Twelfth Army Corps. who was killed in the assault upon the enemy's lines on Taylor's Ridge, near Ringgold, Ga., November 26, 1863.

2. The detached work on the plain near the Rossville road, southeast from the main railroad depot, Fort Phelps, in honor of Col. E. H. Phelps, Thirty-eighth Regiment Ohio Volunteer Infantry, commanding Second Brigade, Third Division, Fourteenth Army Corps, who was killed in the assault upon Missionary Ridge, November 25, 1863.

3. The main interior line of the eastern side of the town, running from the old reservoir to the hill near department headquarters, known as Signal Hill, Fort Sherman, in honor of Maj. Gen. W. T. Sherman, commanding the Military Division of the Mississippi.

4. The battery of Fort Sherman, near the old reservoir, will be known as Battery Bushnell, in honor of Major Bushnell. Thirteenth Illinois Volunteers, who was killed in the battle of Chattanooga, November 25, 1863.

---

*See Part I, p. 516.

5. The lunette in the main line of Fort Sherman, about midway between the extremities and in front of the topographical engineer office, will be known as Lunette O'Meara, in honor of Lieutenant-Colonel O'Meara, Ninetieth Regiment Illinois Volunteers, who was killed at the battle of Chattanooga, November 25, 1863.

6. The redoubt of Fort Sherman, on Signal Hill, will be known as Redoubt Putnam, in honor of Colonel Putnam, Ninety-third Regiment Illinois Volunteers, who was killed at the battle of Chattanooga, November 25, 1863.

7. The advanced battery in front of Battery Bushnell, on the spur overlooking the low lands near the mouth of Citico Creek, will be known as Battery McAloon, in honor of Lieut. Col. P. A. Mc-Aloon, Twenty-seventh Regiment Pennsylvania Volunteers, who was killed at the battle of Chattanooga, November 25, 1863.

8. The Star fort, on the spur southwest of the railroad depot, will be known as Fort Lytle, in honor of Brig. Gen. William H. Lytle, who was killed at the battle of Chickamauga, September 20, 1863.

9. The redoubt and indented line due west of Fort Lytle will be called Redoubt Crutchfield.

10. The fort on the spur of Cameron Hill, immediately south of the gap and of the summit of the hill, will be called Fort Mihalotzy, in honor of Col. Geza Mihalotzy, Twenty-fourth Regiment Illinois Volunteers, who was killed in the affair before Dalton, February 25, 1864.

11. The battery on a lower projection of this spur, on the same side of the road, through the gap and west of Fort Mihalotzy, will be called Battery Coolidge, in honor of Maj. Sidney Coolidge, Sixteenth U. S. Infantry, who was killed at the battle of Chickamauga, September 19, 1863.

12. The citadel on Cameron Hill will be known as Fort Cameron.

13. The redoubt on the northeast spur of Cameron Hill will be known as Redoubt Carpenter, in honor of Maj. Stephen D. Carpenter, who was killed at the battle of Stone's River, December 31, 1862.

14. The redoubt on the rocky knob east of the railroad depot to be known as Redoubt Jones, in honor of Capt. William G. Jones, Tenth U. S. Infantry, colonel of the Thirty-sixth Regiment Ohio Volunteers, who was killed at the battle of Chickamauga, September 19, 1863.

15. The first embrasure battery for field guns in the line of parapet running from Lunette O'Meara to Redoubt Jones will be known as Battery Taft, in honor of Lieut. Col. J. B. Taft, Seventy-third Regiment Pennsylvania Volunteers,* who was killed at the battle of Chattanooga, November 25, 1863.

16. The second embrasure battery for field guns in the same line, south of Battery Taft, and occupying the highest part of the line, will be known as Battery Erwin, in honor of Maj. S. C. Erwin, Sixth Regiment Ohio Volunteer Infantry, who was killed at the battle of Chattanooga, November 25, 1863.

By command of Major-General Thomas :

WM. D. WHIPPLE,
Assistant Adjutant-General.

---

* Lieutenant-Colonel Taft belonged to the One hundred and forty-third New York, but was in temporary command of the Seventy-third Pennsylvania.

SPECIAL FIELD ORDERS, } HDQRS. DEPT. OF THE CUMBERLAND,
No. 118.   }   *Chattanooga, Tenn., April 27, 1864.*

*   *   *   *   *   *   *

XII. The Wilder Indiana Battery, now at this place, will proceed without delay to Charleston, Tenn., and report for duty to Brigadier-General Hovey, commanding at that place. The quartermaster's department will furnish the necessary transportation.

*   *   *   *   *   *   *

By command of Major-General Thomas :

WM. D. WHIPPLE,
Assistant Adjutant-General.

CULPEPER, VA., *April 28, 1864*—11 p. m.
(Received 1.40 a. m., 29th.)

Major-General SHERMAN :

Get your forces up so as to move by the 5th of May.

U. S. GRANT,
Lieutenant-General.

NASHVILLE, TENN., *April 28, 1864*—11 a. m.
(Received 1.40 p. m.)

Maj. Gen. H. W. HALLECK,
    Chief of Staff:

The following dispatch is just received, and sent for the information of General Grant :

All my troops are now moving toward the one objective point. In consequence of the detention down Red River of A. J. Smith, and the delay attending the collection of McPherson's furloughed regiments, I will be short three divisions of my right, in consequence of which I will not attempt to move on Johnston's rear at the start, but collect the entire army in front of Chattanooga, and make no detachments till the first issue at Dalton is determined. By May 5 all my infantry will be within one day's march of the enemy, but my cavalry, as usual, may be late, because of the difficulty of getting horses. I must imitate Forrest's example, and help myself. I began here yesterday, and at once have got here 1,000 good horses. I start for Chattanooga at noon to-day.

W. T. SHERMAN,
Major-General.

NOTE.—The dispatch above spoken of did not accompany the message from General Sherman, which was not discovered until after he had left for Chattanooga.

CIPHER OPERATOR.

HEADQUARTERS DEPARTMENT OF THE CUMBERLAND,
Chattanooga, April 28, 1864.

Maj. Gen. JOHN A. LOGAN,
    Comdg. Fifteenth Army Corps, Huntsville, Ala. :

GENERAL : I yesterday understood that the officers of the Army of the Tennessee have complained that in all matters pertaining to the railroad they were slighted, and after they had come to the relief of the Army of the Cumberland they were denied bread or any facilities from the road, some even thinking that I had refused them passage to and from Nashville, this resulting from the fact that the conductors and my guards were familar with my passes, and not with those of yourself or other commanders of the left wing.

I was very much astonished to hear of such complaints coming from you, as this was the first intimation I had received that any grounds existed for them, and I assure you that any such slight was entirely unintentional on my part, and had I known that such was the feeling on the part of your officers I would have spared no pains to have removed it. I had in fact given orders that your passes should receive the same consideration as my own in all respects, and had I known that such was not accorded them I would have taken measures to have enforced my orders in this respect.

I regret very much that you did not communicate with me on this subject before reporting it to the major-general commanding the Military Division of Mississippi.

As to the Army of the Tennessee coming to the relief of the Army of the Cumberland, it came in obedience to orders from the War Department. I am nevertheless very thankful to those troops for the excellent service they rendered in co-operation with the Army of the Cumberland, and I have never failed when opportunity offered to make due acknowledgments of such services, both privately and officially.

Hoping that this explanation may prove satisfactory and tend to the removal of any ill feeling on the part of your officers and restore that cordiality and good will which should govern all who are engaged in the great work which we have before us,

I remain, very respectfully, your obedient servant,

GEO. H. THOMAS,
Major-General, U. S. Volunteers, Commanding.

NASHVILLE, *April* 28, 1864.
General STONEMAN,
 Nicholasville:

Send forward your regiments by divisions as they are ready and reach the neighborhood of Chattanooga by the 5th of May, with your horses in good condition as possible.

W. T. SHERMAN,
Major-General.

NICHOLASVILLE, *April* 28, 186?

Major-General SCHOFIELD :

One regiment moves to-day, two to-morrow, two the day aft . and one the day following. I have allowed regiments eight days to reach Kingston, where we expect and hope to find forage provided for us, and where I expect to be on the 5th of May. I shall push the horses through as fast as possible consistent with their newness and future usefulness. Please notify me if you have provided forage for us at Kingston, or if not, at what points, and give me any specific instructions you may have regulating our movements.

GEO. STONEMAN,
Major-General.

CAMP 1 MILE NORTH OF LOUDON,
April 28, 1864.

Major-General SCHOFIELD :

It is impossible to get my command across the river to-night. The heat, long marches at first, and new shoes have broken down a great many men. Can I rely upon railroad for transportation for 200 men from Loudon in the morning? Please reply, and if affirmatively I will leave the men.

H. M. JUDAH,
Brigadier-General, Commanding Division.

LEXINGTON, KY.,
April 28, 1864.

Capt. S. E. JONES,
Provost-Marshal District of Kentucky :

CAPTAIN : The general commanding the district directs me to transmit to you a copy of a letter* received from Major-General Sherman, commanding Military Division of the Mississippi, referring to a plot to burn steam-boats and cities on the Ohio and Mississippi Rivers ; that you notify the captains of steam-boats of the contemplated plot, rendering them all the assistance in your power to prevent its consummation and to punish the conspirators. Should troops be needed you will call upon the military commandant of Louisville, who will furnish you the required number, and in case we cannot furnish them they will be furnished on application from these headquarters.

Every exertion must be made to fully carry out General Sherman's suggestions.

I am, very respectfully, your obedient servant,
N. S. ANDREWS,
Lieut. Sixth Michigan Battery and Actg. Chief of Artillery.

HDQRS. DEPARTMENT AND ARMY OF THE TENNESSEE,
Huntsville, Ala., April 28, 1864.

Brig. Gen. W. Q. GRESHAM,
Commanding Forces :

GENERAL : Disembark your command at Clifton, Tenn., and remain there, watching the operations of Forrest, and endeavor to counteract him should he attempt to cross the Tennessee River and interfere with our communications.

Brig. Gen. John D. Stevenson will remain in command of the forces at and in the vicinity of Decatur and along the line of the railroad north to Pulaski. Colonels Rowett and Murphy will patrol the river around from Decatur via Florence to Clifton and below. You will endeavor to keep in communication with General Stevenson, and advise him of everything important in relation to the movements of the enemy which may come to your knowledge.

As soon as you are relieved by another brigade you will push forward and join me via Pulaski and Huntsville. Bring along the cattle if any of them arrive at Huntsville before you leave.

Yours, respectfully,
JAS. B. McPHERSON,
Major-General.

*See p. 463.

HUNTSVILLE, ALA., *April 28, 1864.*

Maj. Gen. W. T. SHERMAN, *Nashville:*

The enemy still hang around Decatur in considerable force. As the object of leaving a force there is to protect our right flank and railroad communications, would it not be better to withdraw the force we proposed leaving at Decatur to this side of the river and station it on the high ground near the junction? Take up the pontoon bridge and bring the boats up Limestone Creek to near the railroad, where they can be guarded and sent to any desired point.

The force stationed at the point I suggest will be more securely located and in a position where it can better operate to repel any attack on the railroad.

JAS. B. McPHERSON,
Major-General, Commanding.

HDQRS. DEPARTMENT AND ARMY OF THE TENNESSEE,
Huntsville, Ala., April 28, 1864.

Maj. Gen. JOHN A. LOGAN,
Comdg. Fifteenth Army Corps, Huntsville, Ala.:

GENERAL: You will immediately put three divisions of your command in motion for Chattanooga by the dirt road, which follows substantially the line of the railroad. The remaining division will, in connection with the force left by Brigadier-General Dodge, guard our lines of communication via Athens, Decatur, Huntsville, and Stevenson. One brigade of the division which is left will be sent immediately to Decatur to strengthen temporarily the garrison at that post, and will report to Brig. Gen. John D. Stevenson. The term of service of the Thirteenth Illinois Volunteer Infantry expiring in May, will remain back and report to the commanding officer of the division left to pr e the roads, whose headquarters, until otherwise directed, will be at Huntsville. The sick and convalescents of the division which are to move will be brought to Huntsville, and a convalescent camp established, under thoroughly competent officers, who will see that the men are forwarded to their respective commands as fast as they become fit for duty. The two regiments of Brig. Gen. Morgan L. Smith's division, at present guarding pontoon bridge at Larkin's Ferry, will remain there until the bridge is removed, when they will push on and join their division as rapidly as possible.

The troops in moving will take their camp and garrison equipage, 140 rounds small-arm ammunition per man, and 200 rounds artillery ammunition per gun, ten days' provisions, including three in haversacks, and forage to last them from one depot to another. Depots for forage will be at Huntsville, Stevenson, and Chattanooga. It is all-important that these troops be at Chattanooga about the 5th of May.

The guards at the different bridges must be strong enough to protect them against local guerrillas and small detachments of the enemy's cavalry, and must be cautioned to be particularly vigilant, and to defend their positions at all hazard.

The Fifth Ohio Cavalry will remain and report to the commanding officer at Huntsville for patrol and picket duty.

Very respectfully, your obedient servant,

JAS. B. McPHERSON,
Major-General, Commanding.

ATHENS, *April 28*, 1864—6 p. m.

Brig. Gen. T. W. SWEENY,
    Pulaski:

Move with your command direct to Huntsville via Elkton. Send the Seventh Illinois wagons and detachment to this place. I will order Bane to move from here day after to-morrow to join you there. You will find forage at Huntsville and will not have to haul much. Teams can be loaded so they can move right along. I will send orders to Rowett. When you get to Huntsville report by telegraph and move right on to Stevenson, taking forage there to take you to that point, where I will have forage for you. Acknowledge the receipt of this. I have received no answer to my dispatch in relation to what was left at different bridges.

G. M. DODGE,
Brigadier-General.

___

APRIL 28, 1864.

Brig. Gen. J. C. VEATCH, *Decatur:*

You will move at daylight, May 1, and not take much forage; one or two days' is sufficient. Load commissary train so it will go right along. Have your train parked on this side of river at the junction this side of swamp on evening April 30. The brigade spoken of in my letter, that was to move April 30, will move with you May 1. Answer.

G. M. DODGE,
Brigadier-General.

___

HDQRS. LEFT WING, SIXTEENTH ARMY CORPS,
Athens, Ala., April 28, 1864.

Brig. Gen. J. C. VEATCH,
    Commanding Fourth Division, Decatur, Ala.:

GENERAL: I desire you to be ready with the command designated in my dispatch to move May 2, at daylight. One brigade will be ready to move at noon, May 1, to Flint River, to cover Captain Armstrong's pioneers, who will bridge Flint during that night. The Ninth Illinois Infantry and First Alabama Cavalry should move with them. You will have to make the proper disposition of troops left behind. Detail acting staff officers, &c.

I think I shall place General Stevenson in command of all troops left of this command, extending from Lynnville down to and including Decatur.

If Captain Armstrong thinks it will take more time to bridge Flint, we will have to move on the morning of May 1; at least, part of your command will. I will try to be there on the 30th day of April, and you better have everything loaded and ready to go May 1, should my troops coming up get close enough. I desire that the movement should not be known outside of Decatur until it is made. The Ninth Ohio Cavalry will be added to the garrison of Decatur, as well as convalescents, or part of them, of the Second Division, and we should get the new fortifications as far advanced as possible.

I have written Captain Armstrong to-day. Give your pioneer corps as many teams as Captain Armstrong thinks necessary, but they must not carry anything only what we will need in the field.

A good supply of intrenching tools must be taken. The mounted force will load all wagons but three with forage alone.

I have been informed since writing the above that Flint is fordable at Somerville crossing. If this is so for artillery and teams, we will only need a foot-bridge.

I am, general, very respectfully, your obedient servant,

G. M. DODGE,
Brigadier-General.

HDQRS. LEFT WING, SIXTEENTH ARMY CORPS,
Athens, Ala., April 28, 1864.

Brig. Gen. J. C. VEATCH,
Commanding Fourth Division:

Since writing you, my orders have been changed in such a manner as will make it unnecessary for us to change our line of march. As telegraphed you, you will move with First and Second Brigades, Ninth Illinois, and First Alabama on May 1 on direct road to Huntsville, thence to Stevenson. Forage will be at Huntsville, Stevenson, and other points where we may need it. Order one company of First Alabama Cavalry to report here on evening of April 30.

Inform Captain Armstrong that he need not make any preparations to bridge Flint.

One brigade from Logan's command will join the force at Decatur, and the Seventh Illinois (mounted) will be left on this side of the river to watch from Elk River down.

Orders will be issued from these headquarters putting General Stevenson in command of all troops left on the line of the railroad from Lynnville to and including Decatur, &c.

I am, very respectfully, your obedient servant,

G. M. DODGE,
Brigadier-General, Commanding.

HDQRS. LEFT WING, SIXTEENTH ARMY CORPS,
Athens, Ala., April 28, 1864.

Col. R. ROWETT,
Commanding Seventh Illinois:

You have before this will reach you undoubtedly received orders to move to this place. Orders since received render it necessary for you to remain on the river. Watch the river from Elk River closely as before. After May 1 you will make your reports to Brigadier-General Stevenson, whose headquarters will be at Decatur. Your train and dismounted men will be ordered to this place.

I am, very respectfully, your obedient servant,

G. M. DODGE,
Brigadier-General, Commanding.

NASHVILLE, TENN.,
April 28, 1864.

General McPHERSON, *Huntsville:*

The following dispatch is just from General Washburn. Please give him general instructions before starting that we want him to hold Forrest and as many of the enemy near him as he can, rather than to risk too much in his attack. I have answered that he should not count on a co-operating force from the direction of the Tennessee, because your troops are now in motion toward Dalton:

HEADQUARTERS DISTRICT OF WEST TENNESSEE,
Memphis, April 24, 1864.

Major-General SHERMAN, *Nashville:*

I send two boats to-day to bring cavalry from Vicksburg. As soon as they return I shall send all the cavalry I can raise, with 2,000 infantry, in pursuit of Forrest. He is still at Jackson, 8,000 strong. The cavalry from Vicksburg will not be here so that I can move before the 30th. In sending this force away I leave this city somewhat exposed, and if 1,000 or 2.000 men could be sent here from Cairo for a week it would insure our safety. On the same day I move from here an infantry force should move from Tennessee River toward Purdy and Bolivar. Your infantry, in the absence of further advice, should leave the Tennessee River Saturday morning and should arrive at Bolivar Sunday night. My troops will reach Bolivar at the same time. I believe it is not true that the railroad is in operation to Corinth, but is to Tupelo, and is being repaired as fast as possible.

C. C. WASHBURN,
Major-General.

W. T. SHERMAN,
Major-General, Commanding.

NASHVILLE, TENN., *April 28, 1864.*

General C. C. WASHBURN, *Memphis:*

I have sent orders to Saint Louis for all men belonging to you not to be detained for horses on any account. We are now all in motion for Georgia. I fear we cannot at this time divert men to Purdy. The two divisions of McPherson, collecting at Cairo, will have to follow us via Clifton and Pulaski.

Don't hesitate to take horses and everything in the country that will strengthen you. It is only a question whether you or Forrest shall have them. I sent your dispatch to McPherson at Huntsville, but he, too, will soon be in motion for Chattanooga and Dalton.

We want you to hold Forrest and as much of the enemy as you can over there, until we strike Johnston. This is quite as important as to whip him. You should have a good force of infantry of about 4,000 men as a solid column, against which Forrest could make no impression by his bold dashes. Don't calculate on a force moving inland from the Tennessee River now, as we cannot spare it, but rely on your own command, which make as strong as possible. We cannot judge at this distance as well as you can, but don't let Forrest move about in that country as he has done.

We have information, deemed reliable, that part of Polk's command is with Johnston and the balance near Demopolis.

The calculation is, next to strike the Mobile and Ohio Railroad near Mobile from the direction of New Orleans. I sent by telegraph your dispatch of the 24th to McPherson, who will give you more specific instructions, based on the present position of his troops.

W. T. SHERMAN,
Major-General.

HDQRS. CAVALRY DIVISION, SIXTEENTH ARMY CORPS,
Memphis, Tenn., April 28, 1864.

Capt. M. M. LATTIMER,
Commanding Provisional Cavalry Regiment:

CAPTAIN: In pursuance of the inclosed order* of General Washburn, you will send out a party of a commissioned officer and 25 men

---

*Omitted; instructions herein repeated.

on each of the following roads : Horn Lake, Hernando, and Holly Ford. They will start at precisely 3 o'clock to-morrow morning. Those on the Horn Lake and Hernando roads will go about 10 miles. The party on the Holly Ford road will go to the crossing of the Nonconnah. These parties will all remain out until 3 o'clock in the afternoon. They will allow all persons coming in to pass without interruption ; but will arrest and detain all persons going out, keeping them out of sight of the road, so that parties coming in will not see them, and their operations will not be reported in Memphis. At 3 o'clock p. m. they will return, and will bring with them to the city all parties whom they have arrested.

The First Brigade is instructed to send out similar parties on each of the other roads running from Memphis.

At 3 o'clock to-morrow you will send other parties of 20 men each on the following roads : The Randolph, New and Old Raleigh, Germantown, New State Line, Pigeon Roost, Holly Ford, Hernando, and Horn Lake.

They will go out a distance of 5 or 6 miles on each road, and keep themselves well concealed, allowing every one to pass in, but detaining all who attempt to pass out. These last parties will remain out until relieved. These last scouts must be made up of the detachments of the Third, Seventh, and Ninth Illinois, Seventh Kansas, and Third Michigan. The detachments of the Second Iowa and Sixth Illinois will await orders in camp. Be very explicit in the instructions of your officers, and be sure that they understand their instructions.

By order of Col. G. E. Waring, jr., Fourth Missouri Cavalry, commanding division :

S. L. WOODWARD,
Assistant Adjutant-General.

HDQRS. CAVALRY DIVISION, SIXTEENTH ARMY CORPS,
Memphis, Tenn., April 28, 1864.

Col. JOSEPH KARGÉ,
    Commanding First Cavalry Brigade :

COLONEL : In pursuance of the inclosed order* of Major-General Washburn, you will send out at 3 o'clock to-morrow morning a scout of 25 men and 1 commissioned officer upon each of the following roads : Randolph, New Raleigh, Old Raleigh, Germantown, New State Line, and Pigeon Roost.

They will allow all persons to come into Memphis unmolested, but will arrest and detain all who are passing out, keeping them concealed off the road, so that persons coming in shall not bring information of the transaction to Memphis. At 3 o'clock in the afternoon these parties will return, bringing with them all intercepted persons. They will be relieved by a similar scout from the Provisional Regiment about 3 o'clock in the afternoon.

Be very explicit in your instructions to the several officers, and be sure that they understand these instructions.

By order of Col. George E. Waring, jr., Fourth Missouri Cavalry, commanding division :

S. L. WOODWARD,
Assistant Adjutant-General.

---

* Omitted ; instructions herein repeated.

HEADQUARTERS DISTRICT OF WEST TENNESSEE,
Memphis, April 28, 1864.

Major-General McPHERSON, *Huntsville:*

Your letter of 20th just received. Forrest is still around, with headquarters at Jackson. I shall move against him on the 30th with all the cavalry I can raise and 2,000 infantry. Could only raise 550 mounted men at Vicksburg, who will be here to-night. I intend to thoroughly scour and clear out West Tennessee before the troops return. Have pr   all the horses I could find, and hope to have 3,500. General Sturgis is here.

C. C. WASHBURN,
Major-General.

CAIRO, *April 28, 1864.*

Major-General WASHBURN:

GENERAL: In visiting Columbus yesterday I found that there was so much to be done there that I assumed command and gave the post commander written instructions resulting from my inspection of the place. I proceed to Cairo to-day on my way to Paducah for an examination similar to the one I have made at Columbus, and have concluded that I must promulgate the orders, of which I inclose a copy,* at once.

A party of mounted infantry sent from Columbus to Paducah— about 70 men—has arrived there and reported to me this morning that it will not be safe for them to return by land, in which, from other sources of information, I concur. Parties of the enemy's mounted forces are distributed about my district occupied in obtaining men and horses. No apprehension is entertained of their attempting to do anything else at present.

I am, general, very respectfully, your obedient servant,

HENRY PRINCE,
Brigadier-General of Volunteers.

CAIRO, *April 28, 1864.*

Maj. Gen. W. T. SHERMAN, *Nashville, Tenn.:*

Would have got off last night but the boats assigned me could not carry my command and the cattle—900 head. Have supplied another boat, and will be off in two hours.

W. Q. GRESHAM,
Brigadier-General.

CAIRO, *April 28, 1864—noon.*

Maj. Gen. W. T. SHERMAN, *Nashville:*

The First Illinois Cavalry en route for Vicksburg; the Ninth Illinois Cavalry, for Memphis, are here without horses, and go to-day; the Eighth Iowa Infantry, of Mower's division, is here for Memphis, and the Twelfth will be here to-morrow. Five thousand Springfield muskets with accouterments should be sent to arm returning troops.

S. A. HURLBUT,
Major-General.

---

*See Part I, p. 516.

NASHVILLE, *April 28*, 1864—11.30 a. m.

Brigadier-General LEGGETT,
        Cairo:

Do the best you can. General McPherson has started for Huntsville, and I start for Chattanooga at 12 m. The Army of the Tennessee is now moving for position, and will have three divisions less for action than we estimated. You must do your best to overtake us, but you know when we start it is not easy to overhaul us. General McPherson has sent you full instructions on all points foreseen.

W. T. SHERMAN,
Major-General.

GENERAL ORDERS, }   HDQRS. CAV. CORPS, ARMY OF THE OHIO,
        No. 5.   }   *Nicholasville, Ky.*, *April 28*, 1864.

That portion of this command now ready to take the field will move as follows : One regiment of Colonel Biddle's brigade, to be selected by the brigade commander, will move to-day, and reach Point Burnside on the 1st of May. From thence it will proceed to Kingston, Tenn., reaching that point on the 5th of May. The other two regiments of this brigade will follow to-morrow, April 29, reaching Point Burnside on the 2d of May, and joining the other regiment of this brigade at Kingston on the 6th of May.

Colonel Holeman's brigade will move on the 30th, and regulate its march by Biddle's brigade, keeping not more than one day's march behind it.

The Fifth Indiana will move on the 1st of May, regulating its march by Holeman's brigade, and keeping not more than one day's march behind this brigade. Supplies of forage for animals and subsistence for troops will be procured at Camp Nelson, Point Burnside, and Kingston. Lieutenant Smith, in charge of pack train, will furnish each regiment on its arrival at Camp Nelson with such pack-animals, &c., as are authorized by existing orders, but the movements of no regiment will be delayed on account of the pack-mules not being on hand or ready to be turned over, as their places will be supplied temporarily by wagons as far as Point Burnside, where pack-mules will be obtained. After leaving Point Burnside the movement of every regiment of the command will not be delayed by its transportation, but each will make its march, and if the transportation cannot keep up it will be left behind to follow after. All the men of Colonels Biddle and Holeman who are left behind will be turned over to Colonel Capron, who will see that they are fitted out and forwarded to their regiments as soon as possible.

By command of Major-General Stoneman :

C. H. HALE,
Captain and Acting Assistant Adjutant-General.

CIRCULAR.]   HDQRS. CAV. COMMAND, DEPT. OF THE OHIO,
        Nicholasville, Ky., *April 28*, 1864.

First. The commanding general is aware of the active and valuable service, fatigue, and hardships which the cavalry of this command has passed through during the past year, and the report it has written for itself, worthy of a page in the history of warfare, by its rapid marches, in its more than brilliant achievements in the many hard-earned victories in skirmishes and battles against the enemy of our country. All has been borne alike by the officers and soldiers of the entire command; and while he feels proud of the achievements and of such patriots and soldiers, he would enjoin upon them, now that we are about to enter on an active campaign, even to the crushing of the gigantic rebellion, the necessity of the most strict discipline for the good of the soldiers and the efficiency of this command. He would call the attention of officers to fully provide their men for the field, and upon the soldiers strict attention to duty, that all may share the fatigue, services, and honors alike.

Second. A commissioned officer will march in the rear of each company, and allow no one to leave the ranks unless absolutely necessary, and when such a necessity arises a pass will be given by the officer in command.

Third. Each regiment will have a rear guard, permitting none to fall behind without leaving a guard to bring them forward.'

Fourth. No soldier will be permitted to straggle or enter a private dwelling-house unless on account of sickness, after getting a certificate from the surgeon and approved by the medical director of this command.

Fifth. Excuses are often made to fall out of ranks to procure water. There can be no necessity for this. Men must fill their canteens before marching.

Sixth. Private property must be respected. No individual foraging will be permitted.

Seventh. Each brigade will detail 1 commissioned officer, 4 sergeants, and 16 privates as provost guard.

Eighth. As there is an opinion prevailing ·that an officer's duty ceases with his own command, which is incorrect, it will be enjoined upon all to arrest for and correct all violations of orders or conduct tending to the prejudice of good order and military discipline coming under his observation within this command.

Commanding officers will have this order read to their respective companies. No excuse will be received for neglect of duty or ignorance of orders. All offenses committed, punishable under General Orders, No. 18, must be promptly punished as therein stated.

By command of Maj. Gen. George Stoneman:

C. H. HALE,
Captain, Aide-de-Camp, and Actg. Asst. Adjt. Gen.

HDQRS. MILITARY DIVISION OF THE MISSISSIPPI,
Chattanooga, Tenn., April 29, 1864—11 a. m.
(Received 1.40 p. m.)

General GRANT,
  Culpeper, Va.:

I am here. Thomas is already in position; Schofield will be by May 2, and McPherson is marching for La Fayette via this place. All my effective cavalry is heading for Dalton, and I will be all ready by May 5. I will write you fully to-night.

W. T. SHERMAN,
Major-General.

NASHVILLE, *April* 29, 1864.

Major-General SHERMAN :
    The following just received :

WASHINGTON, *April* 29, 1864—1.45 p. m.

Major-General SHERMAN :
    The Secretary of War is of opinion that it would be injurious to remove General Allen from the immediate supervision of the vast business transacted by the quartermaster's department at Louisville, and therefore disapproves the order which I had requested as suggested by you.

M. C. MEIGS,
Quartermaster-General.

Respectfully,

M. ROCHESTER,
Assistant Adjutant-General.

HDQRS. MILITARY DIVISION OF THE MISSISSIPPI,
In the Field, Chattanooga, April 29, 1864.

General WEBSTER,
    Nashville, Tenn. :
    I am here all right. Tell Rousseau the road appears thinly guarded about Wartrace ; he had better send 100 men there for a short while till people get used to the diminution of the road guard. I have received several dispatches by the way, which I will answer as soon as I get a locality.

W. T. SHERMAN,
Major-General, Commanding.

HDQRS. MILITARY DIVISION OF THE MISSISSIPPI,
In the Field, Chattanooga, April 29, 1864.

General ROUSSEAU,
    Nashville, Tenn. :
    Order General Paine and the regiment now at Gallatin to Tullahoma, and give him charge of the defense of the road, embracing Duck and Elk River bridges. Replace Paine's troops by some guard at the bridges. The road north of Nashville is not important to us, but that south is vital. Remember to place gun-racks and muskets in all the forts and strong buildings, so that citizens may, if necessary, assist in the defense of Nashville. But there is no danger there now and cannot be for a month to come.

W. T. SHERMAN,
Major-General, Commanding.

LOOKOUT VALLEY, *April* 29, 1864.

Brigadier-General WHIPPLE :
    The gun-boat will be ready to leave Bridgeport to go down the river early to-morrow morning.

JOSEPH HOOKER,
Major-General.

NASHVILLE, TENN, *April* 29, 1864.
(Received 2.10 p. m.)

Maj. Gen. H. W. HALLECK, *Chief of Staff:*

This is the message referred to in cipher of yesterday :

KNOXVILLE, TENN.,
April 27, 1864—11.30 a. m.

General W. T. SHERMAN :

I have intelligence from the Watauga expedition. As was anticipated, the rebels destroyed the bridge after being driven across it by our cavalry. The river was too high to be forded. Our loss in the fight was 3 killed and 18 wounded ; that of the enemy not yet reported. The troops will reach Lick Creek to-night. They have destroyed all the bridges from Bull's Gap to the Watauga, and about 20 miles of the track. Considering the time allowed them, think they have done remarkably well, and all that could be desired.

J. M. SCHOFIELD,
Major-General.

W. T. SHERMAN,
Major-General.

HDQRS. MILITARY DIVISION OF THE MISSISSIPPI,
In the Field, Chattanooga, April 29, 1864.

General SCHOFIELD, *Knoxville, Tenn. :*

General Grant gives me to the 5th to be ready. I will expect your quota at or near Charleston by May 2, where I will come to see you or get you to come here in person. Keep your movements from the press as much as possible. Let the enemy find out our movements through their own spies, not ours. Thomas is all right and McPherson is coming.

W. T. SHERMAN,
Major-General, Commanding.

KNOXVILLE, *April* 29, 1864.

Col. R. M. SAWYER, *Assistant Adjutant-General:*

My effective force to be concentrated on the 2d of May is as follows :

First Division, Brigadier-General Hovey commanding....................... 4,370
Second Division, Brigadier-General Judah commanding.................. 3,850
Third Division, Brigadier-General Cox commanding...................... 4,020
Engineer battalion 160

Total infantry 12,400

Artillery, twenty-four pieces.

J. M. SCHOFIELD,
Major-General.

HDQRS. MILITARY DIVISION OF THE MISSISSIPPI,
In the Field, Chattanooga, April 29, 1864.

General McPHERSON, *Huntsville, Ala. :*

General Grant wants me to be all ready by the 5th of May. To accomplish this the Fifteenth Corps could march here by that date, but we would have to push up Dodge's command in cars, leaving the

wagons to follow and overtake them at some point to be hereafter
fixed ; therefore, order Dodge's march by roads that will carry them
near the railroad.   The cavalry must, of course, come all the way
by the common road.

W. T. SHERMAN,
Major-General, Commanding.

HDQRS. MILITARY DIVISION OF THE MISSISSIPPI.
In the Field, Chattanooga, April 29, 1864.

General McPHERSON.
Huntsville, Ala. :

Put everybody in motion at once for Chattanooga by roads north
of the Tennessee, according to the figures we agreed on, viz, 10,000
of the Fifteenth Corps and 10,000 of the Sixteenth Corps and Garrard's cavalry.   I have a dispatch from General Grant wanting me
to be all ready by May 5.   You know how I like to be on time.   A
steam-boat has gone to Larkin's for the bridges.   Make your orders
for the two divisions at Cairo and Clifton as full as possible, and
when all things are working well come up.

W. T. SHERMAN,
Major-General, Commanding.

HUNTSVILLE, *April 29, 1864.*

Maj. Gen. W. T. SHERMAN :

The enemy still hang around Decatur in considerable force.   As
the object in leaving a force there is to protect our right flank and
railroad communication, would it not be better to withdraw the force
we proposed leaving at Decatur to this side of the river and station
it on the high ground near the junction, take up the pontoon bridge,
and bring the boats up Limestone Creek to near the railroad where
they can be guarded and sent to the desired points?   The force
stationed at the points I suggest will be more securely located and
in a position where it can better operate to repel attacks on railroad.

JAS. B. McPHERSON,
Major-General.

HDQRS. MILITARY DIVISION OF THE MISSISSIPPI,
In the Field, Chattanooga, April 29, 1864.

General McPHERSON,
Huntsville, Ala.:

I approve your suggestion as to the evacuation of Decatur, but it
should only be as an alternative at the last moment.   If it be possible
to get any of the Clifton force I would prefer to hold Decatur, as it
is a constant threat to North Alabama.   It is desirable to keep the
rebel cavalry there as long as possible, and I would risk something.
It is there merely to watch you.

W. T. SHERMAN,
Major-General.

HDQRS. MILITARY DIVISION OF THE MISSISSIPPI,
In the Field, Chattanooga, April 29, 1864.

General McPHERSON, *Huntsville, Ala. :*

I have notified the manager of the railroads that I may have to use all his cars and the road exclusively from Huntsville to Chattanooga to bring forward Dodge's command on Wednesday next.

W. T. SHERMAN,
Major-General.

ATHENS, ALA., *April 29, 1864.*

Brig. Gen. T. W. SWEENY,
Commanding Second Division :

From the dispatch you received last night you will perceive that our line of march has been changed, and we will not for the present be troubled with any enemy. You can therefore march your brigades separately, with parts of train accompanying each, &c.

I want to make as quick a march as the roads will admit of; therefore take every advantage in camping, starting column, &c. Lieutenant-Colonel Bingham, chief quartermaster of Department and Army of the Tennessee, will have forage for you at Huntsville; take enough to last you to Stevenson, where I will have more ready to take us to our destination. We can get rations also at either place should we need them.

The pioneer corps will join you at Huntsville; Colonel Bane's brigade also, and I shall want a report of the force you have in the field at that point. Should I not overtake you there, leave it with General McPherson and push right on, taking the best and most feasible road you can find. General Veatch will move May 1, and this will keep him one or two days behind you.

The Seventh Illinois, for the present, will be kept guarding the river, and I believe the Seventh Iowa have some 15 or 20 mounted men that you can use for your inspectors, in accordance with General Orders, No. 44. I have given such instructions as will cause our mail to follow us. I fear you will have trouble to-day at Tunnel Hill, but hope not.

Communicate with me by messenger or telegraph, if possible, of your daily progress.

I am, general, very respectfully, your obedient servant,

G. M. DODGE,
Brigadier-General.

ATHENS, *April 29, 1864.*

Maj. Gen. J. B. McPHERSON, *Huntsville :*

General Sweeny moved this morning with his train all loaded, as before ordered. General Veatch moves to-morrow. His trains are all loaded. All camp and garrison equipage has been ordered to Huntsville for storage. It is too late now to change the route. My trains, I think, will go through. We will lighten daily. They have taken 250 rounds of artillery and 200 of infantry ammunition. I can order General Veatch to reduce his ammunition, if you think best. Please answer to-night.

G. M. DODGE,
Brigadier-General.

ATHENS, *April 29, 1864.*

Brig. Gen. J. C. VEATCH, *Decatur*.

General McPherson says we must load light, so as to move fast. You can reduce ordnance to 140 rounds to a man and 200 to a gun, and the supply train so you know it will move right along. The road beyond Huntsville is rough, and we can get supplies along the line of railroad at any time. I think the supply train is not very heavily loaded; if any wagons are, take off enough to make them sure. We must move fast. Be sure to get everything at junction to-morrow night.

G. M. DODGE,
Brigadier-General.

HDQRS. DEPARTMENT AND ARMY OF THE TENNESSEE,
Huntsville, Ala., April 29, 1864.

Maj. Gen. C. C. WASHBURN,
Comdg. District of West Tennessee, Memphis, Tenn.:

GENERAL: Your dispatch of April 24 to Major-General Sherman just received, and General Sherman sends me word that he has telegraphed you not to count upon any co-operating force moving up the Tennessee River, and thence out to Purdy and in the direction of Bolivar.

Under orders from him, Leggett's and Crocker's divisions of the Seventeenth Army Corps, now rendezvousing at Cairo, are to get ready for the field as rapidly as possible, and urged to hasten forward to the grand army in Northern Georgia. All my available troops here are moving in the same direction. This will necessarily leave you to rely upon your own resources and such troops as you may be able to draw temporarily and with safety from the District of Vicksburg. You may not be able with the troops at your disposal to assume the offensive with as much boldness as is desirable against an enemy like Forrest, and force him to fight or be driven out of West Tennessee. It is of the utmost importance, however, to keep his forces occupied, and prevent him from forming plans and combinations to cross the Tennessee River and break up the railroad communications in our rear.

By assuming the offensive-defensive—watching him closely and striking a blow whenever it can be put in to advantage—he will be compelled to be on his guard, and will not, I hope, be able to inflict upon us any serious damage.

You can direct Brig. Gen. Henry Prince, commanding District of Columbus, to remove the garrison and guns from Island No. 10 and break up the post, in accordance with Lieutenant-General Grant's instructions that all weak, isolated posts must be abandoned.

Very respectfully, your obedient servant,

JAS. B. McPHERSON,
Major-General.

HDQRS. MILITARY DIVISION OF THE MISSISSIPPI,
In the Field, Chattanooga, April 29, 1864.

General HURLBUT, *Cairo, Ill.:*

The intention is that one of McPherson's divisions remain at Vicksburg and one of yours (Mower's) at Memphis. Allen is ordered to keep at Memphis enough wagons to move 6,000 men (infantry) at any time. If too many wagons and mules have been brought from Memphis they should be sent back. All of Grierson's cavalry should go to Memphis, and not wait at Saint Louis for horses. Horses can be sent them, and in the mean time they can do garrison duty. McPherson has at Cairo enough new muskets for his two divisions, and I understand you have some at Memphis. Troops destined for Memphis can be armed there, but if you need more at Cairo, by telegraphing to the Chief of Ordnance at Washington he will order them sent from Saint Louis. You had better have your corps staff with you. Give all orders necessary to expedite the movement of troops to their proper divisions. I will be near here for five days.

W. T. SHERMAN,
Major-General, Commanding.

SAINT LOUIS, *April* 29, 1864.

Major-General SHERMAN :

I have mounted the Third Iowa, 800 strong, and sent it to Memphis by General Halleck's order. General Rosecrans has taken possession of the Third Michigan Cavalry here at Saint Louis.

J. W. DAVIDSON,
Brigadier-General.

CIRCULAR, } HDQRS. DEPT. AND ARMY OF THE TENNESSEE,
          } OFFICE PROVOST-MARSHAL-GENERAL,
No. 3.   } *Huntsville, Ala., April* 29, 1864.

In accordance with General Orders, No. 4, headquarters Department and Army of the Tennessee, April, 1864, the following instructions are published for the guidance of provost-marshals :

Provost-marshals in this department will be divided into two classes : First, those serving with troops in the field as provost-marshals of corps and divisions; second, those serving at posts or in geographical districts.

The first class are staff officers of the generals commanding their corps and divisions, and accompany the movement of the troops of the several commands to which they belong. When in the field their duties are confined principally to the custody and disposition of prisoners of war and citizens suspected of giving information to the enemy or of other crimes, and to the enforcing of order in such towns as the troops may pass through or be encamped near during the march.

Any property seized by a provost-marshal while on the march, and needed for the use of the army, will at once be turned over to the proper officer entitled to receive the same, as the quartermaster, commissary, ordnance officer, &c., and all other property not belonging to any military department, and which circumstances render it impracticable to turn over to the Treasury agent, will be destroyed or disposed of as the commanding general may direct.

When permanently in camp they are required to enforce the military laws, maintain order in and around their camps, and to perform such other duties of a kindred nature as their commanding officer may direct.

The second class are appointed by the provost-marshal-general, with the approval of the general commanding the department, and will not be considered as upon the staff of the post or district commanders. Their position will not be affected by any change that may occur in such commanders. They will attend to such duties as are usually performed by the magistrates and civil officers of towns, as far as consistent with the military occupation of a place ; grant licenses for carrying on such trades and occupations as the post or district commander may decide to establish ; maintain order, quiet, and cleanliness ; punish those guilty of vice and crime ; try all citizens guilty of violation of orders ; inflict fines or order imprisonment as the nature of the case may require ; decide all cases of dispute as to personal property or question of right arising among citizens ; arrest and punish all parties engaged in giving information to the enemy, in smuggling or carrying on illicit trade of any kind ; seize and confiscate all goods belonging to such parties ; receive and forward to the proper camps prisoners of war ; hold in custody other prisoners awaiting trial ; dispose of deserters and refugees in accordance with existing orders ; give permits to soldiers and citizens to pass from the post, under such restrictions as the post commander or superior headquarters may impose, and enforce such orders as the post or district commander may find it necessary to issue. When prisoners are arrested whose crimes are punishable by long imprisonment or death their cases will be referred to a military commission for trial.

Provost-marshals will make application to post or district commanders for the necessary officers and men to enable them to perform the duties required of them.

By order of Maj. Gen. James B. McPherson :

JAMES WILSON,
Lieutenant-Colonel and Provost-Marshal-General.

Instructions.

Reports will be made on the 15th and last day of each month.

PRISONERS.

Provost-marshals of corps will cause the assistants in their several divisions to make to them true and correct reports of all prisoners of war captured, and to furnish rolls properly made out in alphabetical order, due succession of rank, with company, regiment, when, where, and by whom captured, and in the last column such remarks as may be necessary, stating the disposition made of the prisoners.

These rolls will be made out on the blanks furnished by the Commissary-General of Prisoners. If there are no blanks on hand, then foolscap sheets will be used, opened out and ruled to cover the entire sheets when opened.

When it is not practicable to forward the prisoners North, directly to a camp established for rebel prisoners, they will be sent to the nearest p   and placed in charge of the local provost-marshal there, who will consolidate all rolls of prisoners and forward the prisoners to the proper camps under charge of a sufficient guard. The officer placed in charge of the prisoners in transitu to such camps will be furnished with two rolls, one of which will be turned over with his prisoners, and the other, when receipted by the officer in command of the camp, will be returned to the provost-marshal who forwarded the prisoners. A full record will be kept of the prisoners thus turned over, and the receipted roll will then be forwarded direct to the Commissary-General of Prisoners at Washington, D. C., with a letter of transmittal, a copy of which will be kept on file.

Officers in charge of prisoners en route to the camps in the North will receive written instructions as to what is required of them, and they must be particularly directed to note all changes that may occur among their prisoners until they are turned over; if any die, are left sick in hospital, or escape, the fact must be noted in the column of remarks opposite their names.

When prisoners of war are forwarded from one post to another, a note will be made on the rolls that accompany them that " no copy has been sent to the Commissary-General of Prisoners," and it shall be the duty of the provost-marshal having them in charge last, previous to sending them to the camp for rebel prisoners, to forward the rolls to Washington, and he will be held accountable for any omission. A copy of the roll of prisoners as forwarded to the Commissary-General of Prisoners, with the alterations noted on it, will be sent to this office. No other rolls of prisoners will be required here, but in the letter of transmittal accompanying the semi-monthly reports the number of prisoners passing through their offices will be stated.

DESERTERS.

The oath of allegiance will be administered to all deserters from the rebel army as soon as they have been examined by the commander of the division or detached brigade nearest to place of surrender. They will not be permitted to run at large near the lines, but when practicable will be forwarded North, or may be employed in the rear of our lines in the quartermaster or engineer departments as provided for by General Orders, No. 10, headquarters Military Division of the Mississippi, December 12, 1863. Particular attention is called to this order and to General Orders, No. 64, War Department, present series, as covering the whole subject of the disposition to be made of deserters.

Rolls of deserters will be forwarded to this office with the usual semi-monthly reports; in the column of remarks must be .stated what disposition was made of the men.

PROPERTY.

A correct report must be made of all property seized, which will be headed, "Semi-monthly report of property seized by —— ——, provost-marshal of ——, from the —— day of —— to the —— day of ——," and columns as follows : Date, number or quantity, articles, number or marks, weight, from whom seized, why seized, condition, disposition ; and the report must be dated at the time of making out the same and signed officially.

All property abandoned, captured, confiscated as belonging to disloyal persons, or seized under military orders, which shall come into possession of any provost-marshal, shall be turned over to the agent of the Treasury Department, excepting arms, munitions of war, forage, horses, mules, wagons, beef-cattle, and supplies which are necessary in military operations, which shall be turned over to the proper officers of the ordnance, or of the quartermaster, or of the commissary departments, respectively, for the use of the army.

When the property is turned over it will be invoiced to the officer receiving it and receipts taken in duplicate, one of which will accompany the report as a voucher.

The attention of provost-marshals is especially called to the Treasury regulations and to General Orders, No. 88, War Department, March 31, 1863, with the requirements of which they will strictly comply.

FUNDS.

Money received by local provost-marshals for fines, licenses, &c., will be accounted for semi-monthly. The report will be headed, "Report of cash received by ——— ———, provost-marshal of ———, from the —— day of ——— to the —— day of ———," and will contain columns headed as follows: Date, from whom received, for what, by whose order, remarks; and in addition a regular cash account will be forwarded. The balance on hand from last accounts will be brought forward. All payments will be accounted for particularly, and duplicated receipts taken for all expenditures, one of which will be forwarded with the account as a voucher. A balance will be struck showing the amount on hand at the date of the report. These balances, when exceeding $100, will be forwarded by local provost-marshals to the district provost-marshal, who will, after making up his accounts and reports, forward the balance on hand to the provost-marshal-general Department of the Tennessee by express. When there is no district provost-marshal the reports and balances will be forwarded directly to this office.

All Confederate money captured will be reported and forwarded separately, and a statement will be made of all the circumstances connected with the seizure, and if any has been paid out state why or by whose order. Confederate money seized is ordered to be reported and sent to the Adjutant-General of the Army, and provost-marshals will be particular to forward all information referring to such seizure, so the order can be fully complied with at this office.

The necessary expenses of local and district offices will be paid out of the funds collected. Whatever is required for the full and complete working of the office will be obtained, but no unnecessary or lavish expenditure will be allowed.

Provost-marshals will use great caution in the employment of detectives. Many abuses have crept into the provost-marshal's department from the employment of worthless and dishonest men. When any such can be convicted of improper conduct, of compromising with persons guilty of violating orders, or concealing or withholding information that may come in their possession, of accepting bribes, or of any other offense, they will be at once arrested and punished by the provost-marshal, or their cases will be brought before a military commission for trial, and they must not be merely sent out of the department, as is too frequently the case.

Citizens must not be employed as clerks when it is possible to obtain enlisted men. If it is absolutely necessary to hire clerks, preference will be given to soldiers honorably discharged from the service.

General Orders, No. 4, headquarters Department of the Tennessee, April 19, 1864, designate what moneys properly belong to the provost-marshal fund.

OATHS.

In administering the oath of allegiance (as embodied in the President's proclamation of March 26, 1864) to refugees and others, the blanks that have been distributed for that purpose will be used whenever practicable; when such blanks are not on hand, the oath will be written out on the top of a sheet of foolscap, commencing, "We, the undersigned, do solemnly swear," &c., and columns will be ruled, headed date, name, residence; this will be signed by the persons taking the oath, and when the sheet is filled the officer will certify on it that the oath was administered to the parties by him on the date opposite to their names. These lists will be forwarded directly to tie Department of State, Washington, with a letter of transmittal.

Persons taking the oath will be furnished with a certificate, and a record will be kept in the office.

A statement of the number of oaths administered will be made to this office at the time of making the usual reports and for the time covered by the reports.

JAMES WILSON,
Lieut. Col. and Provost-Marshal-General.

SPECIAL ORDERS, } HDQRS. DEPARTMENT OF THE OHIO,
No. 120.   }   *Knoxville, Tenn., April 29, 1864.*

I. Until further orders, no sutlers will be allowed with the troops in the field. Division commanders will see that all sutlers with the army in the field are sent to the rear at once.

*   *   *   *   *

By command of Major-General Schofield:

R. MORROW,
Assistant Adjutant-General.

HDQRS. MILITARY DIVISION OF THE MISSISSIPPI,
In the Field, Chattanooga, April 30, 1864—6.30 p. m.
(Received 7.50 p. m.)

General GRANT,
Culpeper:

I have news from Atlanta 24th and Dalton 27th. Some of Polk's troops have arrived. By the 5th all of Thomas' and Schofield's troops will be within one march of Dalton, and I doubt not McPherson will be on time. All things working as smoothly as I could expect.

Rosecrans holds some of the Memphis dismounted cavalry to guard against some secret plot in Saint Louis. I think the city police and militia could attend to all such machinations and leave us all our troops at this critical time.

W. T. SHERMAN,
Major-General.

HDQRS. MILITARY DIVISION OF THE MISSISSIPPI,
In the Field, Chattanooga, April 30, 1864.
Lieutenant-Colonel SAWYER,
Nashville, Tenn.:

Announce Corse, Warner, and Ewing as acting inspectors-general. Notify Colonel Donaldson and Colonel McCallum on Monday and Tuesday to bring forward on the cars all the detachments of troops they can, and on Wednesday to move from Huntsville to Chattanooga Dodge's command of 10,000 men. I give this early notice, as I want everybody here possible on the 5th of May.

W. T. SHERMAN,
Major-General.

RINGGOLD, *April* 30, 1864.
Brigadier-General WHIPPLE:

There are indications that the enemy are gathering in force on my right flank. The cavalry near Nickajack trail has largely increased, and our pickets in that vicinity have heard drums beating in the valley east of Taylor's Ridge. A scout also reports tents there, which he thinks belong to infantry. I shall probably learn nothing more until morning. If you think best Davis and Johnson might be notified in case you should want to send them here.

A. BAIRD,
Brigadier-General.

HDQRS. THIRD DIVISION, FOURTEENTH ARMY CORPS,
Ringgold, Ga., April 30, 1864.   (Received May 1.)
Brigadier-General WHIPPLE,
Chief of Staff, Hdqrs. Department of the Cumberland:

GENERAL: I send you herewith a communication just received from General Kilpatrick.

During the day of yesterday and to-day parties of dismounted men have passed up onto our advanced vedettes on the Houston Valley road, leading south on Taylor's Ridge and intersecting the Nickajack trace. The increase of force about the outlet of the trail on this side, and the indications of an infantry force there, make it necessary to be on the lookout. This is my weak flank, and the one on which I will be attacked if at all. The enemy will have the advantage of ground in some respects approaching along the ridge, and may use artillery, while I cannot. Should the enemy choose to begin the campaign by a general attack here, I might be much damaged before the rest of the army could come up.

The trouble of the position is that, in order to make as stubborn a fight as I would wish to, I must involve my men so much in the mountains that in case of necessity I could not withdraw without great loss. If it is not designed to fight a battle here, there are fine defensive positions all the way to Graysville.

I think I can whip a large force here, but perhaps not the whole rebel army. My men are in fine spirits.

Most respectfully, your obedient servant,

A. BAIRD,
Brigadier-General, Commanding.

[Inclosure.]

HEADQUARTERS THIRD CAVALRY DIVISION,
Ringgold, Ga., April 30, 1864.
ASSISTANT ADJUTANT-GENERAL,
Headquarters U. S. Forces:
Captain Stratton, field officer of the day, has just come in from Nickajack. He reports that there is every indication that the enemy has moved up and encamped in considerable force in the second valley beyond and to right of Nickajack trace. This has been done within the last forty-eight hours. The enemy's picket-line has been advanced and strengthened to-day. His vedettes are now within speaking distance of each other along the entire ridge beyond Taylor's Ridge.

One of my scouts just come in confirms this report, and adds that a considerable number of tents and other indications of a considerable force, and he thinks, too, of infantry, can be seen in valley mentioned above. Drums were distinctly heard late this evening by my outposts on the old Alabama road, next to Nickajack trace.

Very respectfully, your obedient servant,
J. KILPATRICK,
Brig. Gen. of Volunteers, Comdg. Third Cavalry Division.

BRIDGEPORT, *April* 30, 1864.
Brigadier-General WHIPPLE,
Assistant Adjutant-General:
The gun-boat is not quite ready to start. She will certainly leave to-morrow. The pontoon bridge west of the island will be taken up on Monday. The work on the bridges and fortifications will continue to be pressed.
JNO. W. GEARY,
Brigadier-General.

BRIDGEPORT, *April* 30, 1864.
Brig. Gen. W. D. WHIPPLE:
My division can move on Monday or Tuesday if I wait the arrival of my Third Brigade. The pontoon at Larkinsville has not to my knowledge been taken up.
JNO. W. GEARY,
Brigadier-General.

NASHVILLE, *April* 30, 1864.
Colonel McCALLUM,
General Superintendent U. S. Military Railroads:
COLONEL: By a telegram just received from Major-General Sherman at Chattanooga I am directed to advise you as follows:
He desires arrangements to be made to carry forward to Chattanooga on Monday and Tuesday next by cars all detachments of troops the trains can possibly transport. On Wednesday he desires the

command of General Dodge (10,000) to be moved by cars from Huntsville to Chattanooga. He desires all the force possible concentrated at Chattanooga on the 3d of May.

I have the honor to be, very respectfully, your obedient servant,

R. M. SAWYER,
Lieutenant-Colonel and Assistant Adjutant-General.

CHARLESTON, *April* 30, 1864.

Maj. Gen. W. T. SHERMAN,
Commanding Military Division of the Mississippi:

I am here with the main body of my troops. The remainder of the old command will be here to-morrow and the troops from Kentucky by the 4th. Mules for my general supply train will arrive at Knoxville on the 2d from Kentucky. I will have here on the 5th teams enough for an eight days' march, and will be able to get up the supply train by the end of that time. Will spare no effort to be fully ready and am confident of success.

J. M. SCHOFIELD,
Major-General.

HDQRS. MILITARY DIVISION OF THE MISSISSIPPI,
In the Field, Chattanooga, April 30, 1864.

General McPHERSON,
Huntsville, Ala.:

Have the Fifteenth Corps (10,000) march at once so as to be here the 5th May. I will order the cars to bring forward Dodge's 10,000 on Wednesday from Huntsville or this side. Wagons should follow as soon as possible. If there be any citizens about that you mistrust send them to the rear at once. As soon as all matters are arranged come to Chattanooga. I want your command at Rossville on the 5th May.

W. T. SHERMAN,
Major-General, Commanding.

HDQRS. LEFT WING, SIXTEENTH ARMY CORPS,
Athens, Ala., April 30, 1864.

Brig. Gen. JOHN D. STEVENSON,
Decatur, Ala.:

GENERAL: From the inclosed dispatch* you will see that there is some intention of evacuating Decatur. When all our forces get to the front the intention is to put the force on this side of the river and run the bridge up Limestone at or near the railroad crossing. I think with the force you have you can hold the place without any doubt, and I know from experience that it is the best protection to this line of railroad we can get with same number of men. As soon as we evacuate the enemy will cross into the road near Florence and hold that country, giving a direct communication with Forrest, and

---

* Not found as an inclosure.

effectually covering his movements. I judge [from] the tenor of the dispatch that the move will not be made for some time y , and you will have an opportunity to fully judge of the effect themove will have.

I am, general, very respectfully, your obedient servant,

G. M. DODGE,
Brigadier-General.

HEADQUARTERS U. S. FORCES,
Clifton, Tenn., April 30, 1864.

Maj. Gen. JAMES B. MCPHERSON,
Comdg. Dept. and Army of the Tenn., Huntsville, Ala.:

GENERAL: I arrived here with my command at 4 p. m. to-day. The Gladiator and Ed. Walsh reported to me at Cairo with 900 head of cattle aboard, and I have got them here, but there is no officer in charge of them and I have no orders what to do with them. There is forage aboard the boats for the cattle for two days. Please send me orders immediately what to do with them. I thought of sending them to Pulaski in charge of the Tennessee regiment at this place, but on reflection concluded it would be better to wait for orders.

Am disembarking, and will send the transports back to Cairo in the morning. Saw quite a number of guerrillas on the right bank of the river, and 30 miles above Paducah some eight or ten shots were fired at the fleet.

Forrest is at Jackson, and Major Murphy, commanding at this place, says part of his force is at Corinth, La Grange, and Bolivar.

I am, general, very respectfully, your obedient servant,

W. Q. GRESHAM,
Brigadier-General.

HEADQUARTERS DISTRICT OF WEST TENNESSEE,
Memphis, April 30, 1864.

Maj. Gen. W. T. SHERMAN:

Forrest is still in West Tennessee, 8,000 strong, scattered in the neighborhood of Jackson, Brownsville, Covington, and Bolivar. He has issued orders for all his force to rendezvous at Jackson May 4. I sent out my expedition to-day, 3,500 cavalry and 2,000 infantry, and I am confident that they will whip him and drive him from the State. I think your communications are in no danger. My orders are to follow him wherever he may go, and not be stopped unless Forrest shall be re-enforced by a largely superior force.

C. C. WASHBURN,
Major-General.

HEADQUARTERS SIXTEENTH ARMY CORPS,
Cairo, Ill., April 30, 1864.

Maj. Gen. C. C. WASHBURN,
Commanding District of Memphis:

GENERAL: I expected before this to have received reports from you, but I am informed by Colonel Harris that you had not received General McPherson's orders. I am instructed by Major-General

McPherson to exercise general supervision of all movements against Forrest. Hence it was of prime necessity that I should hear from you. I am in the dark as to your movements and plans, except as I hear of them through third persons.

In stopping the Fourth Iowa Cavalry, en route for Vicksburg, you have exceeded your authority and probably crippled General Slocum. Nothing but the most extreme necessity will justify this course. So I am informed you have sent for the cavalry from Vicksburg. This, unless you have private orders authorizing such jurisdiction, is an usurpation, and that, too, upon an officer very much your senior. Every effort is being made to send down to you the troops of your command and the returning veterans of Mower's division.

I shall continue to urge the horses and material forward as fast as can be done, so that the cavalry now disorganized may be fitted up for the campaign. I would advise you not to put too much confidence in the cavalry at present about Memphis. From the breaking up of regimental organizations, the Smith retreat, and the carelessness of officers, they are far from being in good condition for an active campaign. As soon as the veterans return I wish the best regiments supplied with the Spencer carbine, which has been promised and I suppose will be there.

You will send me as soon as you possibly can a detailed statement of your acts since taking command, and your plans for action; also your present effective force of all arms. Advise me constantly day by day of movements and of what you learn from scouts, and hereafter send no telegrams direct to any superior officers. Send your information here and I will have it telegraphed if advisable to be done.

I shall be pleased to give you at all times every assistance practicable, and I will sustain you frankly in all energetic measures for the public good.

Do not move against Forrest at any distance from Memphis without sufficient force to beat him if you bring him to action. Of the amount of that force I will not assume to determine, as my opinion on that question has been called in question. If you do go or have gone when this reaches Memphis, the officer whom you leave in charge must look with special care to the south approaches to Fort Pickering.

I am, general, with great respect, your obedient servant,

S. A. HURLBUT,
Major-General, Commanding

HEADQUARTERS SIXTEENTH ARMY CORPS,
Memphis, Tenn., April 30, 1864.

Maj. Gen. C. C. WASHBURN,
Comdg. District of West Tennessee, Memphis, Tenn.:

GENERAL: In reply to your inquiry of yesterday evening if Maj. L. F. Booth, late commander of Fort Pillow, had made any request or requisition on Maj. Gen. S. A. Hurlbut, commanding Sixteenth Army Corps, for re-enforcements, I have the honor to state that no information, verbal or written, was received at these headquarters that re-enforcements were desired at Fort Pillow, and the intelligence of the attack on the fort was not received until the evening of the 12th instant, some hours after the capture of the fort by assault. The last communication of any kind received at these headquarters from Fort Pillow was a report from Major Booth, commanding, dated 3d instant, in which the major states: " Everthing seems to be very quiet within a radius of from 30 to 40 miles around, and I do not think any apprehensions need be felt or fears entertained in reference to this place being attacked or even threatened. I think it is perfectly safe."

General Hurlbut's written instructions to Major Booth were full and explicit. He was ordered to " act promptly in putting the work into perfect order and the post into its strongest defense. All information received send direct to me."

On 7th instant General Hurlbut sent two additional guns (10-pounder Parrotts) to Major Booth at Fort Pillow, with 300 rounds of ammunition.

It was the impression of every commanding officer that Forrest was aiming to cross the Tennessee River, either north into Kentucky or east into Middle Tennessee.

Very respectfully, your obedient servant,

T. H. HARRIS,
Lieutenant-Colonel and Assistant Adjutant-General.

HEADQUARTERS SIXTEENTH ARMY CORPS,
Cairo, Ill., April 30, 1864.

Lieut. Col. W. T. CLARK,
Asst. Adjt. Gen., Army and Department of the Tennessee:

SIR: I have the honor to acknowledge receipt this day of personal letter of instructions to me from Maj. Gen. J. B. McPherson, of date of April 19. Where it has been delayed I do not know. I forwarded to Major-General Washburn official copy of instructions from Major-General McPherson to him, which he states never before reached him. I have ordered him to report to me, but have not yet received any reply. If Major-General Washburn reports so that I can exercise supervision over movements against Forrest I will do so, but I rather imagine that he considers himself just now in a sort of independent command. I learn indirectly that he proposes to move to-day from Memphis. What force he takes or in what direction I am not advised.

I have placed the Fifty-second Indiana and Twenty-first Missouri, returned veterans of A. J. Smith's division, at Columbus.

General Prince in a day or two will be strong enough for offensive operations as far as it can be done by infantry.

The Eighth and Twelfth Iowa, returned veterans of Mower's division, go to Memphis to-day, and I have, in pursuance of orders from General Sherman, directed all my cavalry at Saint Louis to be forwarded to Memphis, horses to follow.

I am, colonel, very respectfully,

S. A. HURLBUT,
Major-General.

HDQRS. MILITARY DIVISION OF THE MISSISSIPPI,
In the Field, Chattanooga, April 30, 1864.

Captain PENNOCK,
U. S. Navy, Cairo, Ill.:

One gun-boat is now done, and three more are nearly ready. If the admiral can send us commanders, petty officers, and engineers we can undertake to supply here the crews. We also can supply provisions and all material ; also guns and ammunition of army pattern. I want the river above Muscle Shoals patrolled as soon as possible, as it will set free one local garrison.

W. T. SHERMAN,
Major-General, Commanding.

HDQRS. FIRST DIVISION, DISTRICT OF KENTUCKY,
Lexington, Ky., April 30, 1864.

Col. C. J. TRUE,
Comdg. Second Brigade, Mount Sterling, Ky.:

The general directs that you send an expedition consisting of three companies in direction of Prestonburg and beyond, with instructions to kill and capture all rebel bands found on the route. Let the men carry sufficient rations on pack-horses and in haversacks; also forage on pack mules or horses. The commanding officer will be instructed not to interfere with property belonging to citizens. You will also send scouting parties through Bath, Fleming, and Rowan Counties with same instructions. You will report the success and operations as soon as these expeditions return, and all information that you may receive before they return.

Very respectfully, your obedient servant,

J. S. BUTLER,
Assistant Adjutant-General.

HDQRS. MILITARY DIVISION OF THE MISSISSIPPI,
In the Field, Chattanooga, April 30, 1864.

General ALLEN,
Chief Quartermaster, Louisville:

At last, after I have started to open a desperate campaign, the Secretary of War denies me the services of a chief quartermaster. Well, I must do the best I can with you at Louisville. Donaldson at Nashville, and Easton here. The confusion in the wagons of Memphis illustrates how important it is I should have a chief near me. One division of white troops will remain at Vicksburg, one division at Memphis; all others will come to this quarter. All wagons, mules, and horses should take the same general course. Wagons, mules, and horses can best reach us here via Clifton and the Tennessee River, as long as the two divisions rendezvousing at Cairo are coming that way as escort.

All the furloughs are out, and these troops should now be all en route. After they have come the way will be safest from Louisville to Nashville, &c. Events won't wait for me to be all ready, but I must act when others are ready.

W. T. SHERMAN,
Major-General.

GENERAL ORDERS, }   HDQRS. MIL. DIV. OF THE MISSISSIPPI,
  No. 11.   }   *Nashville, Tenn., April 30, 1864.*

The following-named officers are announced as acting inspectors-general of this army, and will be respected accordingly:

Brig. Gen. John M. Corse, U. S. Volunteers.

Lieut. Col. Charles Ewing, assistant inspector-general, Fifteenth Corps.

Lieut. Col. Willard Warner, Seventy-sixth Ohio Volunteer Infantry.

They will report in person to the major-general commanding in the field.

By order of Maj. Gen. W. T. Sherman:

R. M. SAWYER,
Assistant Adjutant-General.

CIRCULAR.]   HDQRS. DEPARTMENT OF THE CUMBERLAND,
Chattanooga, Tenn., April 30, 1864.

I. The following instructions are published for the information of the Army of the Cumberland, to be observed during the approaching campaign:

Should the routes to be indicated in future orders bring the army in contact with the enemy, he should be engaged vigorously, after proper reconnaissances, and all attacks of the enemy in position should be preceded by a good line of skirmishers to develop the position of the enemy's artillery and masses. Great care should be taken not to use artillery or volleys of musketry unnecessarily, as the sound is calculated to mislead the neighboring army.

The habit of general officers taking cavalry for escorts and orderlies is very ruinous to the cavalry arm of the service, and should be discontinued as far as possible. Commanders of brigades and divisions and of corps, when acting compactly, should, as far as possible, mount a few infantry as orderlies and scouts, leaving the cavalry arm entire to fulfill its most important part of clearing the front and flanks.

A small force in a block-house, disencumbered of baggage and stores not needed, can hold their ground and protect their point against any cavalry force until relief comes. They should be instructed to fight with desperation to the last, as they thereby save the time necessary for concentration.

All officers are cautioned against the mischievous and criminal practice of reporting mere vague rumors, often sent into our lines by the enemy for his own purposes. Actual facts should be reported to the headquarters in the field, that they may be judged in connection with other known facts. An army of a million men could not guard against the fabulous stories that are sent to headquarters. Officers must scrutinize and see with their own eyes, or those of some cool, experienced staff officer, before making reports that may call off troops from another quarter where there may be more need of them. When troops are intrenched, or well covered by block-houses, a surrender will entail disgrace, for we have all seen examples where a few determined men have held thousands in check till relief came, or the necessities of the enemy forced him to withdraw.

II. All surplus baggage in the hands of the troops will be stored without delay at Bridgeport, where the quartermaster has been directed to provide storage.

III. In consequence of the large amount of unserviceable property on hand requiring inspection, and the inability of division inspectors to attend to this duty as promptly as desired, brigade inspectors are hereby authorized to inspect such property with a view to condemnation within their respective brigades until June 1, 1864.

By command of Major-General Thomas:

WM. D. WHIPPLE,
Assistant Adjutant-General.

Abstract from returns of the Department of the Cumberland, Maj. Gen. George H. Thomas, U. S. Army, commanding, for the month of April, 1864.

Command.	Present for duty. Officers.	Men.	Aggregate present.	Aggregate present and absent.	Pieces of artillery. Heavy.	Field.	Headquarters.
General headquarters	71	777	1,035	1,208			Chattanooga, Tenn.
Fourth Army Corps (Howard):							
Headquarters	7	......	7	10			Cleveland, Tenn.
First Division (Stanley)	399	7,339	9,058	13,714		12	Blue Springs, Tenn.
Second Division (Newton)	295	4,632	5,651	9,107		6	Cleveland, Tenn.
Third Division (Wood)	413	8,053	9,688	14,842		12	McDonald's Station, Tenn.
Total Fourth Army Corps	1,114	20,024	24,404	37,673		30	
Fourteenth Army Corps (Palmer):							
Headquarters	5	......	5	5			Chattanooga, Tenn.
First Division (Johnson)	294	7,796	9,355	15,068		12	Graysville, Ga.
Second Division (Davis)	313	7,354	8,605	12,165		12	Near Ringgold, Ga.
Third Division (Baird)	364	7,678	9,160	13,082		12	Ringgold, Ga.
Total Fourteenth Army Corps	976	22,828	27,125	40,340		36	
Twentieth Army Corps (Hooker): a							
Headquarters	14	57	75	82			Lookout Valley, Tenn.
First Division (Williams)	342	6,909	8,208	11,136		12	In the field.
Second Division (Geary)	290	6,758	8,284	11,305		12	Bridgeport, Ala.
Third Division (Butterfield)	325	7,264	8,626	11,054		12	Lookout Valley, Tenn.
Total Twentieth Army Corps b	971	21,048	25,193	33,577		36	
Cavalry Corps (Elliott):							
Headquarters	7	......	7	8			Chattanooga, Tenn.
First Division (McCook)	169	3,820	4,660	7,422		6	Cleveland, Tenn.
Second Division (K. Garrard)	212	6,466	7,514	10,203		6	Columbia, Tenn.
Third Division (Kilpatrick)	181	3,428	4,247	6,851			Ringgold, Ga.
Fourth Division (Gillem)	230	4,973	6,103	7,341		6	Nashville, Tenn.
Detached (Palmer)	19	364	431	670			Rossville, Ga.
Total Cavalry Corps	818	19,051	22,962	32,485		18	
Artillery Reserve (Barnett)	32	999	1,080	1,287		50	Nashville, Tenn.
Engineer troops:							
Engineer Brigade (McCreery)	74	1,486	2,026	2,940			Chattanooga, Tenn.
Pioneer Brigade (Buell)	36	742	1,082	2,229			Do.
First Michigan Engineers (Innes)	37	1,002	1,684	1,835			Bridgeport, Ala.
Total engineer troops	147	3,230	4,792	7,004			
Post of Chattanooga, Tenn. (Steedman)	147	3,246	3,860	5,605		74	
Unassigned troops:							
Infantry	93	2,260	2,682	3,264			Chattanooga, Tenn.
Artillery c	17	572	622	695	3	23	
Total unassigned	110	2,832	3,304	3,959	3	23	
District of Nashville (Rousseau):							
Headquarters	3	......	3	3			Nashville, Tenn.
Clarksville (Smith)	3	85	96	100		6	
Columbia (Funkhouser)	3	124	135	150	4	2	
Fort Donelson (Brott)	......	61	64	98		4	
Gallatin (Paine)	8	130	157	159		6	
Murfreesborough (Van Cleve)	16	414	461	520	28	26	
Nashville (Granger)	339	7,562	10,052	12,322	19	26	
Nashville and Northwestern Railroad (Gillem)	89	1,732	2,705	3,208		6	
Total District of Nashville	461	10,099	13,673	16,555	51	76	
Grand total	4,847	104,134	127,428	179,088	54	343	
Grand total according to monthly return of the department.	4,813	103,458	126,446	178,018	54	343	

a Formed by consolidation of Eleventh and Twelfth Army Corps.
b The Fourth Division reported at Nashville, Tenn.
c At Bridgeport, Cleveland, Stevenson, and Tullahoma.

Troops in the Department of the Cumberland, Maj. Gen. George H. Thomas, U. S. Army, commanding, April 30, 1864.

GENERAL HEADQUARTERS.

10th Ohio, Col. Joseph W. Burke.
1st Battalion Ohio Sharpshooters, Capt. Gershom M. Barber.
Signal Corps, Capt. Paul Babcock, jr.

FOURTH ARMY CORPS.

Maj. Gen. OLIVER O. HOWARD.

FIRST DIVISION. *

Maj. Gen. DAVID S. STANLEY.

First Brigade.	*Third Brigade.*
Brig. Gen. CHARLES CRUFT.	Col. WILLIAM GROSE.
21st Illinois, Maj. James E. Calloway. 38th Illinois, Capt. William C. Harris. 31st Indiana, Lieut. Col. Francis L. Neff. 81st Indiana, Lieut. Col. William C. Wheeler. 1st Kentucky, Col. David A. Enyart. 2d Kentucky, Lieut. Col. John R. Hurd. 90th Ohio, Lieut. Col. Samuel N. Yeoman. 101st Ohio, Col. Isaac M. Kirby.	59th Illinois, Col. P. Sidney Post. 75th Illinois, Col. John E. Bennett. 80th Illinois, Lieut. Col. William M. Kilgour. 84th Illinois, Capt. John P. Higgins. 9th Indiana, Col. Isaac C. B. Suman. 30th Indiana, Capt. William Dawson. 36th Indiana, Lieut. Col. Oliver H. P. Carey. 77th Pennsylvania, Capt. Joseph J. Lawson.
Second Brigade.	*Artillery.*
Brig. Gen. WALTER C. WHITAKER.	Capt. PETER SIMONSON.
96th Illinois, Col. Thomas E. Champion. 115th Illinois, Col. Jesse H. Moore. 35th Indiana, Maj. John P. Dufficy. 84th Indiana, Lieut. Col. Andrew J. Neff. 21st Kentucky, Col. Samuel W. Price. 40th Ohio, Col. Jacob E. Taylor. 51st Ohio, Lieut. Col. Charles H. Wood. 99th Ohio, Lieut. Col. John E. Cummins.	Indiana Light, 5th Battery, Lieut. Alfred Morrison. Pennsylvania Light, Battery B, Capt. Samuel M. McDowell.

SECOND DIVISION.†

Brig. Gen. JOHN NEWTON.

First Brigade.	*Second Brigade.*
Col. FRANCIS T. SHERMAN.	Brig. Gen. GEORGE D. WAGNER.
36th Illinois,‡ Col. Silas Miller. 44th Illinois,§ Capt. Alonzo W. Clark. 73d Illinois, Capt. Ezekiel J. Ingersoll. 74th Illinois, Col. Jason Marsh. 88th Illinois, Lieut. Col. George W. Chandler. 2d Missouri, Lieut. Col. Arnold Beck. 15th Missouri,§ Col. Joseph Conrad.	100th Illinois, Maj. Charles M. Hammond. 40th Indiana, Col. John W. Blake. 57th Indiana,§ Lieut. Col. George W. Lennard. 58th Indiana, Lieut. Col. Joseph Moore. 26th Ohio, Lieut. Col. William H. Squires. 97th Ohio, Col. John Q. Lane.

---

* Headquarters Second and Third Brigades and artillery at Blue Springs, the First Brigade at Cleveland.
† At Cleveland, Tenn.
‡ Returned from veteran furlough.
§ Absent on veteran furlough.

Third Brigade.

Brig. Gen. CHARLES G. HARKER.

22d   Illinois, Lieut. Col. Francis Swanwick.
27th Illinois, Lieut. Col. William A. Schmitt.
42d   Illinois, Lieut. Col. Edgar D. Swain.
51st Illinois,* Col. Luther P. Bradley.
79th Illinois, Col. Allen Buckner.
3d   Kentucky, Col. Henry C. Dunlap.
64th Ohio,* Col. Alexander McIlvain.
65th Ohio,† Maj. Orlow Smith.
125th Ohio, Col. Emerson Opdycke.

Artillery.

1st Illinois Light, Battery M, Capt. George W. Spencer.
1st Ohio Light, Battery A.‡

Unattached.

24th Wisconsin, Lieut. Col. Theodore S. West.

THIRD DIVISION.§

Brig. Gen. THOMAS J. WOOD.

First Brigade.

Col. WILLIAM H. GIBSON.

25th Illinois, Maj. Samuel Houston.
35th Illinois, Lieut. Col. William P. Chandler.
89th Illinois, Col. Charles T. Hotchkiss.
32d   Indiana, Col. Frank Erdelmeyer.
8th   Kansas,† Col. John A. Martin.
15th Ohio,* Col. William Wallace.
49th Ohio,* Lieut. Col. Samuel F. Gray.
15th Wisconsin, Maj. George Wilson.

Second Brigade.

Brig. Gen. WILLIAM B. HAZEN.

6th   Indiana, Maj. Calvin D. Campbell.
5th   Kentucky, Col. William W. Berry.
6th   Kentucky, Maj. Richard T. Whitaker.
23d   Kentucky,† Maj. James C. Foy.
1st   Ohio, Maj. Joab A. Stafford.
6th   Ohio, Col. Nicholas L. Anderson.
41st Ohio, Lieut. Col. Robert L. Kimberly.
93d   Ohio, Lieut. Col. Daniel Bowman.
124th Ohio, Lieut. Col. James Pickands.

Third Brigade.

Brig. Gen. SAMUEL BEATTY.

79th Indiana, Col. Frederick Knefler.
86th Indiana, Col. George F. Dick.
9th   Kentucky, Lieut. Col. Chesley D. Bailey.
17th Kentucky, Col. Alexander M. Stout.
13th Ohio,* Col. Dwight Jarvis, jr.
19th Ohio. Col. Charles F. Manderson.
59th Ohio, Lieut. Col. Granville A. Frambes.

Artillery.

Capt. CULLEN BRADLEY.

Illinois Light. Bridges' Battery, Capt. Lyman Bridges.
Ohio Light. 6th Battery, Lieut. Oliver H. P. Ayres.

---

* Returned from veteran furlough.
†Absent on veteran furlough.
‡ Also reported as at Chattanooga.
§At McDonald's Station, Tenn.

FOURTEENTH ARMY CORPS.

Maj. Gen. JOHN M. PALMER.

FIRST DIVISION.*

Brig. Gen. RICHARD W. JOHNSON.

First Brigade.	Second Brigade.
Brig. Gen. WILLIAM P. CARLIN.	Brig. Gen. JOHN H. KING.
104th Illinois, Lieut. Col. Douglas Hapeman.	19th Illinois, Maj. James V. Guthrie.
38th Indiana, Col. Benjamin F. Scribner.	11th Michigan, Capt. Patrick H. Keegan.
42d Indiana, Lieut. Col. William T. B. McIntire.	69th Ohio,† Lieut. Col. Joseph H. Brigham.
88th Indiana, Lieut. Col. Cyrus E. Briant.	15th United States, 1st Battalion, Maj. Albert Tracy.
2d Ohio, Col. Anson G. McCook.	15th United States, 2d Battalion, Maj. John R. Edie.
33d Ohio, Lieut. Col. James H. M. Montgomery.	16th United States, 1st Battalion, Capt. Robert P. Barry.
94th Ohio, Lieut. Col. Rue P. Hutchins.	16th United States, 2d Battalion, Capt. Solomon S. Robinson.
10th Wisconsin, Capt. Jacob W. Roby.	18th United States, 1st Battalion, Capt. George W. Smith.
15th Kentucky, Lieut. Col. William G. Halpin.	18th United States, 2d Battalion, Capt. William J. Fetterman.
	19th United States, 1st Battalion, Capt. James Mooney.

Third Brigade.

Col. JAMES M. NEIBLING.

24th Illinois, Capt. August Mauff.
37th Indiana, Lieut. Col. William D. Ward.
21st Ohio, Capt. Samuel F. Cheney.
74th Ohio, Col. Josiah Given.
78th Pennsylvania, Col. William Sirwell.
79th Pennsylvania, Col. Henry A. Hambright.
1st Wisconsin, Capt. Thomas H. Green.
21st Wisconsin, Lieut. Col. Harrison C. Hobart.

Artillery.

Capt. LUCIUS H. DRURY.

1st Illinois Light, Battery C, Capt. Mark H. Prescott.
1st Ohio Light, Battery I, Capt. Hubert Dilger.

SECOND DIVISION.‡

Brig. Gen. JEFFERSON C. DAVIS.

First Brigade.	Second Brigade.
Brig. Gen. JAMES D. MORGAN.	Col. JOHN G. MITCHELL.
10th Illinois, Col. John Tillson.	34th Illinois, Lieut. Col. Oscar Van Tassell.
16th Illinois, Col. Robert F. Smith.	78th Illinois, Col. Carter Van Vleck.
60th Illinois, Col. William B. Anderson.	98th Ohio, Lieut. Col. John S. Pearce.
10th Michigan,† Col. Charles M. Lum.	108th Ohio, Lieut. Col. Joseph Good.
14th Michigan,† Col. Henry R. Mizner.	113th Ohio, Lieut. Col. Darius B. Warner.
	121st Ohio, Col. Henry B. Banning.

---

* At Graysville.
† On veteran furlough.
‡ Near Rossville.

Third Brigade.

Col. Daniel McCook.

85th Illinois, Col. Caleb J. Dilworth.
86th Illinois, Lieut. Col. Allen L. Fahnestock.
110th Illinois, Lieut. Col. E. HibbardTopping.
125th Illinois, Col. Oscar F. Harmon.
22d Indiana, Lieut. Col. William M. Wiles.
52d Ohio Light, Lieut. Col. Charles W. Clancy.

*Artillery.**

Capt. Charles M. Barnett.

2d Illinois Light, Battery I, Lieut. Alonzo W. Coe.
Wisconsin Light, 5th Battery, Capt. George Q. Gardner.

THIRD DIVISION.†

Brig. Gen. Absalom Baird.

First Brigade.

Brig. Gen. John B. Turchin.

82d Indiana, Col. Morton C. Hunter.
11th Ohio, Lieut. Col. Ogden Street.
17th Ohio, Col. Durbin Ward.
31st Ohio, Col. Moses B. Walker.
89th Ohio, Maj. John H. Jolly.
92d Ohio, Col. Benjamin D. Fearing.

Second Brigade.

Col. Ferdinand Van Derveer.

75th Indiana, Lieut. Col. William O'Brien.
87th Indiana, Col. Newell Gleason.
101st Indiana, Lieut. Col. Thomas Doan.
2d Minnesota, Col. James George.
9th Ohio, Col. Gustave Kammerling.
35th Ohio, Maj. Joseph L. Budd.
105th Ohio, Lieut. Col. George T. Perkins.

Third Brigade.

Col. George P. Este.

10th Indiana, Lieut. Col. Marsh B. Taylor.
74th Indiana, Lieut. Col. Myron Baker.
4th Kentucky,‡ Col. John T. Croxton.
10th Kentucky, Col. William H. Hays.
18th Kentucky, Lieut. Col. Hubbard K. Milward.
14th Ohio, Maj. John W. Wilson.
38th Ohio, Col. William A. Choate.

Artillery.

Capt. George R. Swallow.

Indiana Light, 7th Battery, Lieut. Otho H. Morgan.
Indiana Light, 19th Battery, Lieut. William P. Stackhouse.

---

*The Second Minnesota Battery reported as transferred to post of Chattanooga April 27, but not accounted for on return of that command.
†At Ringgold, Ga.
‡On veteran furlough.

TWENTIETH ARMY CORPS.*

Maj. Gen. JOSEPH HOOKER.

ESCORT.

15th Illinois Cavalry, Company K, Capt. William Duncan.

FIRST DIVISION.

Brig. Gen. ALPHEUS S. WILLIAMS.

First Brigade.

Brig. Gen. JOSEPH F. KNIPE.

5th Connecticut, Col. Warren W. Packer.
3d Maryland,† Col. Joseph M. Sudsburg.
123d New York, Col. Archibald L. McDougall.
141st New York, Col. William K. Logie.
46th Pennsylvania, Col. James L. Selfridge.

Second Brigade.

Brig. Gen. THOMAS H. RUGER.

27th Indiana, Col. Silas Colgrove.
2d Massachusetts, Col. William Cogswell.
13th New Jersey, Col. Ezra A. Carman.
107th New York, Col. Nirom M. Crane.
150th New York, Col. John H. Ketcham.
3d Wisconsin, Col. William Hawley.

Third Brigade.

Brig. Gen. HECTOR TYNDALE. ‡

82d Illinois, Maj. Ferdinand H. Rolshausen.
101st Illinois, Lieut. Col. John B. Le Sage.
45th New York, Col. Adolphus Dobke.
143d New York, Col. Horace Boughton.
61st Ohio,§ Col. Stephen J. McGroarty.
82d Ohio, Col. James S. Robinson.

Artillery.

Capt. JOHN D. WOODBURY.

1st New York Light, Battery I, Lieut. Christian Stock.
1st New York Light. Battery M, Capt. John D. Woodbury.

SECOND DIVISION.

Brig. Gen. JOHN W. GEARY.

First Brigade.

Col. CHARLES CANDY.

5th Ohio, Col. John H. Patrick.
7th Ohio, Lieut. Col. Samuel McClelland.
29th Ohio, Col. William T. Fitch.
66th Ohio, Lieut. Col. Eugene Powell.
28th Pennsylvania, Lieut. Col. John Flynn.
147th Pennsylvania, Col. Ario Pardee, jr.

Second Brigade.

Col. ADOLPHUS BUSCHBECK.

33d New Jersey, Lieut. Col. Enos Fourat.
119th New York, Lieut. Col. Isaac P. Lockman.
134th New York, Lieut. Col. Allan H. Jackson.
154th New York, Col. Patrick H. Jones.
27th Pennsylvania, Lieut. Col. August Riedt.
73d Pennsylvania, Maj. Lewis D. Warner.
109th Pennsylvania (detachment).‖

---

*Reorganized April 14, 1864, under General Orders. No. 144, Adjutant-General's Office, and Special Field Orders, No. 105, headquarters Department of the Cumberland.

† Only 1 officer and 79 men reported present; the remainder on veteran furlough.

‡ Division return reports Col. James S. Robinson commanding, and that officer so signs the brigade return, but reports Tyndale as commanding since April 13, 1864. Corps return as above.

§ On veteran furlough.

‖ Commander not of record.

Third Brigade.

Col. DAVID IRELAND.

60th New York, Col. Abel Godard.
78th New York, Col. Herbert von Hammerstein.
102d New York, Col. James C. Lane.
137th New York, Lieut. Col. Koert S. Van Voorhis.
149th New York, Lieut. Col. Charles B. Randall.
29th Pennsylvania, Col. William Rickards, jr.
111th Pennsylvania, Lieut. Col. Thomas M. Walker.

Artillery.

Capt. WILLIAM WHEELER.

New York Light, 13th Battery, Capt. William Wheeler.
Pennsylvania Light, Battery E, Capt. James D. McGill.

THIRD DIVISION.

Maj. Gen. DANIEL BUTTERFIELD.

First Brigade.	*Second Brigade.*
Brig. Gen. WILLIAM T. WARD.	Col. SAMUEL ROSS.
102d Illinois, Lieut. Col. James M. Mannon.	20th Connecticut, Col. Samuel Ross.
105th Illinois, Col. Daniel Dustin.	85th Indiana, Col. John P. Baird.
129th Illinois, Col. Henry Case.	19th Michigan, Col. Henry C. Gilbert.
70th Indiana, Col. Benjamin Harrison.	22d Wisconsin, Col. William L. Utley.
79th Ohio, Col. Henry G. Kennett.	

Third Brigade.

Col. JAMES WOOD, jr.

33d Massachusetts, Lieut. Col. Godfrey Rider, jr.
136th New York, Lieut. Col. Lester B. Faulkner.
55th Ohio, Col. Charles B. Gambee.
73d Ohio, Lieut. Col. Richard Long.
26th Wisconsin, Maj. Frederick C. Winkler.

Artillery.

Capt. MARCO B. GARY.

1st Michigan Light, Battery I, Capt. Luther R. Smith.
1st Ohio Light, Battery C, Capt. Marco B. Gary.

FOURTH DIVISION.*

(Organization incomplete.)

---

* For composition of the First (Granger's) Brigade, see post of Nashville, p. 560;
and for the artillery and unassigned infantry, see posts of Bridgeport, Clarksville,
Fort Donelson, and Gallatin, District of Nashville, p. 560.

CAVALRY CORPS.*
Brig. Gen. WASHINGTON L. ELLIOTT.
FIRST DIVISION.†
Col. EDWARD M. McCOOK.

First Brigade.

Col. JOSEPH B. DORR.

8th Iowa, Lieut. Col. Horatio G. Barner.
2d Michigan, Maj. Leonidas S. Scranton.
9th Pennsylvania,‡ Maj. Edward G. Savage.
1st Tennessee, Lieut. Col. James P. Brownlow.

Second Brigade.

Col. OSCAR H. LA GRANGE.

2d Indiana, Lieut. Col. James W. Stewart.
4th Indiana, Lieut. Col. Horace P. Lamson.
1st Wisconsin, Lieut. Col. William H. Torrey.

Third Brigade.

Col. LOUIS D. WATKINS.

4th Kentucky, Col. Wickliffe Cooper.
6th Kentucky, Maj. William H. Fidler.
7th Kentucky, Capt. Charles C. McNeely.

Artillery.

Indiana Light, 18th Battery, Lieut. William B. Rippetoe.

SECOND DIVISION.
Brig. Gen. KENNER GARRARD.

First Brigade.

Col. ROBERT H. G. MINTY.

4th Michigan, Lieut. Col. Josiah B. Park.
7th Pennsylvania, Col. William B. Sipes.
4th United States, Capt. James B. McIntyre.

Second Brigade.

Col. ELI LONG.

1st Ohio, Col. Beroth B. Eggleston.
3d Ohio, Lieut. Col. Horace N. Howland.
4th Ohio, Lieut. Col. Oliver P. Robie.

Third Brigade.

(Mounted infantry.)

Col. JOHN T. WILDER.

98th Illinois,§ Lieut. Col. Edward Kitchell.
123d Illinois, Lieut. Col. Jonathan Biggs.
17th Indiana, Lieut. Col. Henry Jordan.
72d Indiana, Col. Abram O. Miller.

Artillery.

Chicago Board of Trade Battery, Lieut. George I. Robinson.

THIRD DIVISION.‖
Brig. Gen. JUDSON KILPATRICK.

First Brigade.¶

Col. WILLIAM W. LOWE.

3d Indiana, Lieut. Col. Robert Klein.
5th Iowa, Lieut. Col. Matthewson T. Patrick.
9th Pennsylvania, Col. Thomas J. Jordan.

Second Brigade.

Col. CHARLES C. SMITH.

8th Indiana, Col. Thomas J. Harrison.
2d Kentucky, Lieut. Col. Elijah S. Watts.
10th Ohio, Maj. Thomas W. Sanderson.

* Reorganized under Special Field Orders, No. 93, headquarters Department of the Cumberland, of April 2.
† The Third Brigade opposite Chattanooga : remainder of division at Cleveland.
‡ Reported also as in First Brigade, Third Division, Colonel Jordan commanding, and as absent on veteran furlough.
§ Also reported at post of Columbia. See p. 560.
‖ Organized April 2, Colonel Minty commanding till April 17 : Colonel Murray, April 17 to 26, and Kilpatrick since that date.
¶ But according to another return the Third Indiana and Fifth Iowa were in First Brigade, Second Division, and the Ninth Pennsylvania in First Brigade, First Division.

Third Brigade.

Col. ELI H. MURRAY.

92d Illinois (mounted Infantry), Col. Smith D. Atkins.
3d Kentucky, Maj. Lewis Wolfley.
5th Kentucky,* Lieut. Col. Oliver L. Baldwin.

FOURTH DIVISION.

Brig. Gen. ALVAN C. GILLEM.†

First Brigade.

Lieut. Col. DUFF G. THORNBURGH.

2d Tennessee, Lieut. Col. William F.
    Prosser.
3d Tennessee, Maj. John B. Minnis.
4th Tennessee, Lieut. Col. Jacob M.
    Thornburgh.
1st Tennessee Light Artillery, Battery
    A, Capt. Albert F. Beach.

Second Brigade.

Lieut. Col. GEORGE SPALDING.

5th Tennessee, Maj. William J. Clift.
10th Tennessee, Lieut. Col. George W.
    Bridges.
12th Tennessee, Maj. John S. Kirwan.
1st Kansas Battery, Capt. Marcus D.
    Tenney.

Third Brigade.

Col. JOHN K. MILLER.

8th Tennessee, Col. Samuel K. N. Patton.
9th Tennessee, Maj. Etheldred W. Armstrong.
13th Tennessee, Maj. George W. Doughty.

UNATTACHED.

15th Pennsylvania, Col. William J. Palmer.

ARTILLERY.‡

Brig. Gen. JOHN M. BRANNAN, Chief.

ARTILLERY RESERVE.

Col. JAMES BARNETT.

First Division.

Capt. EDMUND C. BAINBRIDGE.

4th United States, Battery F, Lieut.
    Edward D. Muhlenberg.
4th United States, Battery G, Lieut.
    Eugene A. Bancroft.
4th United States, Battery H, Lieut.
    George B. Rodney.
4th United States, Battery M, Lieut.
    Samuel Canby.
5th United States, Battery H, Capt.
    Francis L. Guenther.
5th United States, Battery M, Capt. Edmund C. Bainbridge.

Second Division.

Maj. JOHN J. ELY.

Kentucky Light, 1st Battery, Capt. Theodore S. Thomasson.
1st Ohio Light, Battery F, Capt. Daniel T. Cockerill.
1st Ohio Light, Battery G, Capt. Alexander Marshall.
1st Ohio Light, Battery M, Capt. Frederick Schultz.
Ohio Light, 18th Battery, Capt. Charles C. Aleshire.

Unassigned.

2d Kentucky Battery, Lieut. George W. Nell, Tullahoma, Tenn.
1st Ohio Light Artillery, Battery K, Capt. Lewis Heckman, Stevenson, Ala.
10th Wisconsin Battery, Capt. Yates V. Beebe, Cleveland, Tenn.

---

* According to another return was in Third Brigade, First Division.
† Also commanding troops along Nashville and Northwestern Railroad.
‡ See also the artillery attached to divisions, &c.

ENGINEER TROOPS.

Engineer Brigade.

Col. WILLIAM B. MCCREERY.

13th Michigan, Col. Joshua B. Culver.
21st Michigan, Lieut. Col. Loomis K. Bishop.
22d Michigan, Maj. Henry S. Dean.
18th Ohio, Lieut. Col. Charles H. Grosvenor.

Pioneer Brigade.

Col. George P. BUELL.

1st Battalion, Capt. Milton Kemper.
2d Battalion, Capt. Joseph W. R. Stambaugh.
Pontoon Battalion, Capt. Patrick O'Connell.

Unattached.

1st Michigan Engineers, Col. William P. Innes.

POST OF CHATTANOOGA, TENN.

Brig. Gen. JAMES B. STEEDMAN.

First Separate Brigade.

15th Indiana, Col. Gustavus A. Wood.
29th Indiana, Lieut. Col. David M. Dunn.
44th Indiana, Lieut. Col. Simeon C. Aldrich.
51st Indiana, Lieut. Col. John M. Comparet.
68th Indiana, Lieut. Col. Harvey J. Espy.
8th Kentucky (five companies), Capt. John Wilson.
3d Ohio, Capt. Leroy S. Bell.
24th Ohio, Lieut. Col. Armstead T. M. Cockerill.

Artillery.

Maj. CHARLES S. COTTER.

Indiana Light, 4th Battery, Lieut. Henry J. Willits.
Indiana Light, 8th Battery, Capt. George Estep.
Indiana Light, 10th Battery, Capt. William A. Naylor.
Indiana Light, 11th Battery, Capt. Arnold Sutermeister.
1st Michigan Light, Battery K, Capt. John C. Schuetz.
1st Missouri Light, Battery G, Lieut. Lorenzo D. Immell.
Ohio Light, 20th Battery, Lieut. William Backus.
1st Wisconsin Heavy, Company C, Capt. John R. Davies.
Wisconsin Light, 3d Battery, Lieut. Hiram P. Hubbard.

Unattached.

58th Indiana, Lieut. Col. Joseph Moore.
9th Michigan, Lieut. Col. William Wilkinson.
14th U. S. Colored Troops, Lieut. Col. Henry C. Corbin.
16th U. S. Colored Troops, Col. William B. Gaw,

DISTRICT OF NASHVILLE.

Maj. Gen. LOVELL H. ROUSSEAU.

ARTILLERY.

Col. CYRUS O. LOOMIS, Chief.

Bridgeport, Ala.

Lieut. Col. ALBERT VON STEINHAUSEN.

58th New York,* Capt. Michael Esembaux.
68th New York,* Lieut. Col. Albert von Steinhausen.
75th Pennsylvania,* Lieut. Col. Alvin V. Matzdorff.
20th Indiana Battery,* Lieut. George F. Armstrong.
1st Ohio Light Artillery. Batteries B and E, Maj. Warren P. Edgarton.
9th Ohio Battery, Capt. Harrison B. York.

Christiana, Tenn.

31st Wisconsin (six companies), Col. Francis H. West.

Clarksville, Tenn.

Col. ARTHUR A. SMITH.

83d Illinois* (five companies). Capt. Joshua M. Snyder.
2d Illinois Light Artillery, Battery H. Capt. Henry C. Whittemore

Columbia, Tenn.

Col. JOHN J. FUNKHOUSER.

98th Illinois, Lieut. Col. Edward Kitchell.

Fort Donelson, Tenn.

Lieut. Col. ELIJAH C. BROTT.

83d Illinois* (five companies), Capt. John G. Hamrick.
2d Illinois Light Artillery, Battery C, Sergt. Jesse Robertson.

Gallatin, Tenn.

Brig. Gen. ELEAZER A. PAINE.

71st Ohio,* Maj. James W. Carlin.
106th Ohio,* Maj. Lauritz Barentzen.
13th Indiana Battery. Capt. Benjamin S. Nicklin.

McMinnville, Tenn.

23d Missouri, Col. William P. Robinson.

Murfreesborough, Tenn.

Brig. Gen. HORATIO P. VAN CLEVE.

115th Ohio, Col. Jackson A. Lucy.
31st Wisconsin (four companies). Maj. Robert B. Stephenson.
1st Michigan Light Artillery. Battery D, Lieut. Henry B. Corbin.

12th Ohio Battery. Capt. Aaron C. Johnson.
8th Wisconsin Battery, Capt. Henry E. Stiles.

Post of Nashville, Tenn.

Brig. Gen. ROBERT S. GRANGER.

Infantry.†

73d Indiana, Maj. Alfred B. Wade.
18th Michigan, Col. Charles C. Doolittle.
102d Ohio, Col. William Given.
10th Tennessee, Lieut. Col. James W. Scully.
15th U. S. Colored Troops, Col. Thomas J. Downey.
17th U. S. Colored Troops, Col. William R. Shafter.
13th Wisconsin, Col. William P. Lyon.

Artillery.

Maj. JOSIAH W. CHURCH.

12th Indiana Battery, Lieut. James A. Dunwoody.
1st Michigan, Battery E, Capt. Peter De Vries.
1st Tennessee, Battery D, Lieut. Solomon Strombaugh.
1st Tennessee, Battery G, Capt. Henry C. Kelly.
4th United States, Battery I, Lieut. Frank G. Smith.

Nashville and Northwestern Railroad.

Brig. Gen. ALVAN C. GILLEM.

1st Missouri Engineers, Col. Henry Flad.
12th U. S. Colored Troops, Col. Charles R. Thompson.
13th U. S. Colored Troops, Col. John A. Hottenstein.

---

*Assigned to Fourth Division, Twentieth Army Corps.
†The white regiments, constituting the First Brigade, Fourth Division, Twentieth Army Corps, Brigadier-General Granger commanding.

Abstract from returns of the Department of the Tennessee, Maj. Gen. James B. McPherson, U. S. Army, commanding, for the month of April, 1864.

Command.	Present for duty.		Aggregate present.	Aggregate present and absent.	Pieces of artillery.		Headquarters.
	Officers.	Men.			Heavy.	Field.	
General headquarters..............	19	15	34	51	....	......	Huntsville, Ala.
Fifteenth Army Corps (Logan):							
Headquarters	7	12	19	21	....	......	Huntsville, Ala.
First Division.................	213	3,538	4,776	7,016	....	10	Woodville, Ala.
Second Division	178	3,441	4,202	7,697	....	12	Larkinsville, Ala.
Third Division	134	2,989	3,921	6,890	....	8	Huntsville, Ala.
Fourth Division	287	5,659	6,972	8,250	....	8	Scottsborough, Ala.
Cavalry........	22	583	721	961	....	......	Huntsville, Ala.
Total Fifteenth Army Corps.	841	16,172	20,611	30,825	....	38	
Sixteenth Army Corps:							
Headquarters	10	....	10	10	....	......	Memphis, Tenn.
District of West Tennessee (Washburn):							
Headquarters	3	....	3	3	....	......	Memphis, Tenn.
District of Cairo (Prince):							
Headquarters	12	....	12	12	....	......	Cairo, Ill
Cairo, Ill. (Colonel Rinaker) ...	17	417	614	741	....	....	
Columbus, Ky. (Colonel Lawrence).	50	1,431	1,959	2,428	....	....	
Island No. 10 (Captain Ekings).	2	88	111	130	7	1	
Paducah, Ky. (Colonel Hicks) .	18	850	1,054	1,309	....	....	
Total District of Cairo	99	2,786	3,750	4,620	7	1	
District of Memphis (Buckland).	278	6,106	8,052	9,815	71	30	Memphis.
Cavalry division (Grierson)......	145	4,462	5,784	8,002	....	9	Do.
Total District of West Tennessee.	525	13,354	17,589	23,040	78	40	
Left Wing (Dodge):							
Headquarters	9	15	23	26	....	....	In the field.
Second Division (Sweeny)	261	6,358	7,764	9,605	....	14	Do.
Fourth Division (Veatch)	246	5,997	7,685	9,720	....	16	Decatur, Ala.
Total Left Wing.............	516	12,370	15,424	19,351	....	30	
Total Sixteenth Army Corps.	1,051	25,724	33,028	42,401	78	70	
Seventeenth Army Corps:							
Headquarters	12	62	114	122	....	......	Cairo, Ill.
Third Division (Leggett)	28	1,332	1,678	6,448	....	18	Do.
Fourth Division (Crocker)*a*	127	2,361	2,768	5,960	....	24	Do.
District of Vicksburg (Slocum)..							
Headquarters	9	....	9	9	....	....	Vicksburg, Miss.
First Division (Dennis)	147	3,475	4,207	5,848	....	12	Do.
Maltby's brigade	56	1,015	1,418	2,685	....	12	Do.
Colored troops (Hawkins)	320	5,854	7,813	8,351	....	13	Do.
Cavalry (Mumford)............	16	802	1,081	3,446	....	......	Do.
Defenses of Natchez, Miss. (Tuttle).	115	2,978	3,897	4,530	....	......	
Mississippi Marine Brigade (Ellet).	32	805	1,037	1,309	....	......	
Total District of Vicksburg .	695	14,929	19,462	26,238	....	37	
Total Seventeenth Army Corps.	862	18,684	24,022	38,768	....	79	
Grand total Department of the Tennessee *b*.	2,773	60,595	77,690	112,055	78	187	
Grand total, according to monthly return of the department.	3,004	63,423	80,360	132,508	72	202	

a The Second Brigade reported in the District of Vicksburg with First Division, Seventeenth Army Corps.

b According to the most accurate returns and omitting troops absent in the Red River campaign.

Organization of the Department and Army of the Tennessee, commanded by Maj. Gen. James B. McPherson, U. S. Army, April 30, 1864.

FIFTEENTH ARMY CORPS.

Maj. Gen. JOHN A. LOGAN.

FIRST DIVISION.

Brig. Gen. PETER J. OSTERHAUS.

First Brigade.

Brig. Gen. CHARLES R. WOODS.

26th Iowa, Col. Milo Smith.
30th Iowa, Lieut. Col. Aurelius Roberts.
27th Missouri, Col. Thomas Curly.
76th Ohio, Col. William B. Woods.

Second Brigade.

Col. DAVID CARSKADDON.

4th Iowa,* Col. James A. Williamson.
9th Iowa, Capt. Paul McSweeney.
25th Iowa, Col. George A. Stone.
31st Iowa, Col. William Smyth.
25th Missouri, Lieut. Col. Joseph S. Gage.
31st Missouri, Col. Thomas C. Fletcher.

Third Brigade.

Col. HUGO WANGELIN.

3d Missouri, Col. Theodore Meumann.
12th Missouri, Lieut. Col. Jacob Kaercier.
17th Missouri, Col. John F. Cramer.
32d Missouri, Capt. Charles C. Bland.

Artillery.

Maj. CLEMENS LANDGRAEBER.

2d Missouri Light, Battery F, Capt. Louis Voelkner.
Ohio Light, 4th Battery, Capt. George Froehlich.

SECOND DIVISION.

Brig. Gen. MORGAN L. SMITH.

First Brigade.

Brig. Gen. GILES A. SMITH.

55th Illinois, Col. Oscar Malmborg.
111th Illinois, Col. James S. Martin.
116th Illinois, Lieut. Col. Anderson Froman.
127th Illinois, Lieut. Col. Frank S. Curtiss.
6th Missouri, Lieut. Col. Delos Van Deusen.
8th Missouri, Lieut. Col. David C. Coleman.
57th Ohio, Col. Americus V. Rice.

Second Brigade.

Brig. Gen. JOSEPH A. J. LIGHTBURN.

83d Indiana, Col. Benjamin J. Spooner.
30th Ohio, Col. Theodore Jones.
37th Ohio, Lieut. Col. Louis von Blessingh.
47th Ohio, Col. Augustus C. Parry.
54th Ohio, Lieut. Col. Robert Williams, jr.
4th West Virginia, Col. James H. Dayton.

Artillery.

Capt. PETER P. WOOD.

1st Illinois Light, Battery A, Capt. Peter P. Wood.
1st Illinois Light, Battery B, Capt. Israel P. Rumsey.
1st Illinois Light, Battery H, Capt. Francis De Gress.

---

*On veteran furlough.

THIRD DIVISION.

Brig. Gen. JOHN E. SMITH.

First Brigade.

Col. JESSE I. ALEXANDER.

63d Illinois, Col. Joseph B. McCown.
48th Indiana, Lieut. Col. Edward J. Wood.
59th Indiana, Lieut. Col. Jefferson K. Scott.
4th Minnesota, Lieut.Col. John E. Tourtellotte.
18th Wisconsin, Lieut. Col. Charles H. Jackson.

Second Brigade.

Col. GREEN B. RAUM.

56th Illinois, Lieut. Col. John P. Hall.
17th Iowa, Capt. Thomas Ping.
10th Missouri, Col. Francis C. Deimling.
24th Missouri, Company E, Lieut. Daniel Driscoll.
80th Ohio, Lieut. Col. Pren Metham.

Third Brigade.

Brig. Gen. CHARLES L. MATTHIES.

93d Illinois, Lieut. Col. Nicholas C. Buswell.
5th Iowa, Col. Jabez Banbury.
10th Iowa, Lieut. Col. Paris P. Henderson.
26th Missouri, Col. Benjamin D. Dean.

Artillery.

Capt. HENRY DILLON.

Wisconsin Light, 6th Battery, Lieut. Samuel F. Clark.
Wisconsin Light, 12th Battery, Capt. William Zickerick.

Cavalry.

4th Missouri, Company F, Lieut. Alexander Mueller.

FOURTH DIVISION.

Brig. Gen. WILLIAM HARROW.

First Brigade.

Col. REUBEN WILLIAMS.

26th Illinois, Maj. John B. Harris.
90th Illinois, Maj. Patrick Flynn.
12th Indiana, Lieut. Col. James Goodnow.
100th Indiana, Lieut.Col. Albert Heath.

Second Brigade.

Col. CHARLES C. WALCUTT.

40th Illinois, Lieut.Col Rigdon S. Barnhill.
103d Illinois, Maj. Asias Willison.
6th Iowa, Lieut. Col. Alexander J. Miller.
46th Ohio, Maj. Henry H. Giesy.

Third Brigade.

Col. WELLS S. JONES.

48th Illinois, Col. Lucien Greathouse.
97th Indiana, Col. Robert F. Catterson.
99th Indiana, Col. Alexander Fowler.
53d Ohio, Lieut.Col. Robert A. Fulton.
70th Ohio, Lieut. Col. De Witt C. Loudon.

Artillery.

Capt. HENRY H. GRIFFITHS.

1st Illinois Light, Battery F, Capt. Josiah H. Burton.
Iowa Light, 1st Battery Lieut. William H. Gay.

UNATTACHED.

15th Michigan Infantry, Col. John M. Oliver.
5th Ohio Cavalry, Col. Thomas T. Heath.

SIXTEENTH ARMY CORPS.

Maj. Gen. STEPHEN A. HURLBUT.

LEFT WING.

Brig. Gen. GRENVILLE M. DODGE.

SECOND DIVISION.

Brig. Gen. THOMAS W. SWEENY.

First Brigade.

Col. ELLIOTT W. RICE.

52d Illinois. Lieut. Col. Edwin A. Bowen.
66th Indiana, Capt. Felix C. Bivin.
2d Iowa, Maj. Noel B. Howard.
7th Iowa, Lieut. Col. James C. Parrott.

Second Brigade.

Col. PATRICK E. BURKE.

9th Illinois, Maj. John H. Kuhn.
12th Illinois, Maj. James R. Hugunin.
66th Illinois. Capt. William S. Boyd.
81st Ohio, Lieut. Col. Robert N. Adams.

Third Brigade.

Col. MOSES M. BANE.

7th Illinois (mounted), Col. Richard Rowett.
50th Illinois, Maj. William Hanna.
57th Illinois, Lieut. Col. Frederick J. Hurlbut.
39th Iowa, Lieut. Col. James Redfield.

Artillery.

Capt. FREDERICK WELKER.

1st Michigan Light. Battery B, Capt. Albert F. R. Arndt.
1st Missouri Light. Battery H, Capt. Frederick Welker.
1st Missouri Light, Battery I, Lieut. John F. Brunner.

FOURTH DIVISION.

Brig. Gen. JAMES C. VEATCH.

First Brigade.

Col. JOHN W. FULLER.

64th Illinois, Col. John Morrill.
18th Missouri (detachment), Lieut. Frederick Partenheimer.
27th Ohio, Lieut. Col. Mendal Churchill.
39th Ohio, Col. Edward F. Noyes.

Second Brigade.

Col. JOHN W. SPRAGUE.

35th New Jersey, Capt. Charles A. Angel.
43d Ohio, Col. Wager Swayne.
63d Ohio, Lieut. Col. Charles E. Brown.
25th Wisconsin, Col. Milton Montgomery.

Third Brigade.

Col. JAMES H. HOWE.

25th Indiana, Lieut. Col. John Rheinlander.
17th New York, Col. William T. C. Grower.
32d Wisconsin, Maj. Charles H. De Groat.

Artillery.

Maj. WILLIAM H. ROSS.

2d Illinois Light, Battery D, Lieut. Joseph Hockman.
1st Michigan Light, Battery C, Capt. George Robinson.
Ohio Light, 4th Battery, Capt. Jerome B. Burrows.
2d United States, Battery F, Lieut. Albert M. Murray,

Cavalry.

1st Alabama, Maj. George L. Godfrey.

FIRST AND THIRD DIVISIONS. *

Brig. Gen. JOSEPH A. MOWER.

FIRST DIVISION.

First Brigade.†

Col. WILLIAM L. MCMILLEN.

114th Illinois. Lieut. Col. John F. King.
93d Indiana, Col. DeWitt C. Thomas.
72d Ohio, Lieut. Col. Charles G. Eaton.
95th Ohio, Lieut. Col. Jefferson Brumback.
1st Illinois Light Artillery, Battery E, Capt. John A. Fitch.
2d Illinois Light Artillery, Battery B, Capt. Fletcher H. Chapman.

Second Brigade.

Col. LUCIUS F. HUBBARD.

47th Illinois, Col. John D. McClure.
5th Minnesota, Maj. John C. Becht.
11th Missouri,‡ Lieut. Col. William L. Barnum.
8th Wisconsin. Lieut. Col. John W. Jefferson.
2d Iowa Battery,§ Lieut. Joseph R. Reed.

Third Brigade.

Col. SYLVESTER G. HILL.

8th Iowa,‡ Col. James L. Geddes.
12th Iowa,‡ Lieut. Col. John H. Stibbs.
35th Iowa, Lieut. Col. William B. Keeler.
33d Missouri, Maj. George W. Van Beek.
6th Indiana Battery,§ Lieut. Louis Kern.

THIRD DIVISION.

First Brigade.

Col. WILLIAM F. LYNCH.

58th Illinois, Maj. Thomas Newlan.
119th Illinois, Col. Thomas J. Kinney.
89th Indiana, Col. Charles D. Murray.
21st Missouri,‖ Lieut. Col. Edwin Moore.
9th Indiana Battery. Capt. George R. Brown.

Second Brigade.

Col. WILLIAM T. SHAW.

14th Iowa, Capt. Warren C. Jones.
27th Iowa, Col. James I. Gilbert.
32d Iowa. Col. John Scott.
24th Missouri, Maj. Robert W. Fyan.
3d Indiana Battery, Capt. James M. Cockefair.

Third Brigade.

Col. RISDON M. MOORE.

49th Illinois, Capt. Jacob E. Gauen.
117th Illinois. Lieut. Col. Jonathan Merriam.
52d Indiana,‖ Col. Edward H. Wolfe.
178th New York, Col. Edward Wehler.
14th Indiana Battery,† Lieut. Francis W. Morse.

----

* Serving (with exceptions noted) in the Red River campaign under Brig. Gen. Andrew J. Smith. See Vol. XXXIV.
† Detached at Memphis, Tenn.
‡ On veteran furlough.
§ Detached at Vicksburg. Miss.
‖ Detached at Columbus, Ky.

CAVALRY DIVISION.

Col. GEORGE E. WARING, JR.*

First Brigade.	Second Brigade.
Col. JOSEPH KARGÉ.	Col. EDWARD F. WINSLOW.
7th Indiana, Col. John P. C. Shanks.	4th Iowa, Lieut. Col. John H. Peters.
4th Missouri, Maj. Gustav Heinrichs.	Provisional Regiment, Lieut. Col. William P. Hepburn.
2d New Jersey, Maj. P. Jones Yorke.	
19th Pennsylvania, Lieut. Col. Joseph C. Hess.	
6th Tennessee, Col. Fielding Hurst.	

DISTRICT OF WEST TENNESSEE.

Maj. Gen. CADWALLADER C. WASHBURN.

DISTRICT OF MEMPHIS.

Brig. Gen. RALPH P. BUCKLAND.

First Brigade.	Fort Pickering.
Col. EDWARD BOUTON.	Col. IGNATZ G. KAPPNER.
59th U. S. Colored Troops, Maj. Robert Cowden.	55th U. S. Colored Troops, Lieut. Col. James M. Irvin.
61st U. S. Colored Troops, Col. Frank A. Kendrick.	1st Illinois Light Artillery, Company G, Capt. Raphael G. Rombauer.
2d U. S. Colored Light Artillery. Battery D. Capt. Carl A. Lamberg.	3d U. S. Colored Heavy Artillery, Lieut. Col. James P. Harper.
	6th U. S. Colored Heavy Artillery, Col. William D. Turner.

Second Brigade.	Memphis.
Col. GEORGE B. HOGE.	7th Wisconsin Battery. Capt. Henry S. Lee.
108th Illinois. Maj. William R. Lackland.	63d U. S. Colored Troops (two companies), Capt. Henry S. Hay.
113th Illinois, Lieut. Col. George R. Clarke.	
120th Illinois, Col. George W. McKeaig.	

DISTRICT OF CAIRO.

Brig. Gen. HENRY PRINCE.

Cairo, Ill.	Columbus, Ky.
Col. JOHN I. RINAKER.	Col. WILLIAM H. LAWRENCE.
122d Illinois, Lieut. Col. James F. Drish.	10th Minnesota, Lieut. Col. Samuel P. Jennison.
	34th New Jersey (eight companies), Lieut. Col. Timothy C. Moore.
	2d Illinois Light Artillery. Battery G, Capt. John W. Lowell.

Island No. 10.	Paducah, Ky.
Capt. ROBERT M. EKINGS.	Col. STEPHEN G. HICKS.
34th New Jersey, Company B, Capt. Jesse W. Cogswell.	1st Kentucky Heavy Artillery, A. D., Companies A, B. C. and D, Lieut. Richard D. Cunningham.
34th New Jersey, Company C, Lieut. Augustus W. Grobler.	7th Minnesota, Col. William R. Marshall.

---

*Commanding division during temporary absence of General Benjamin H. Grierson.

SEVENTEENTH ARMY CORPS.

Maj. Gen. FRANK P. BLAIR, Jr.

ESCORT.

4th Company Ohio Cavalry, Capt. John S. Foster.

DISTRICT OF VICKSBURG.

Maj. Gen. HENRY W. SLOCUM.

FIRST DIVISION.

Brig. Gen. ELIAS S. DENNIS.

First Brigade.

Col. FREDERICK A. STARRING.

72d Illinois, Lieut. Col. Joseph Stockton.
1st Kansas (mounted), Lieut. Col. Newell W. Spicer.
30th Missouri, Capt. William T. Wilkinson.
58th Ohio, Lieut. Col. Ezra P. Jackson.

Second Brigade.

Col. JAMES H. COATES.

11th Illinois, Maj. George C. McKee.
95th Illinois,* Col. Thomas W. Humphrey.
14th Wisconsin,* Col. Lyman M. Ward.

Artillery.

Capt. WILLIAM H. BOLTON.

2d Illinois Light, Battery L, Capt. William H. Bolton.
1st Missouri Light, Battery M, Lieut. John H. Tiemeyer.
Ohio Light, 7th Battery, Lieut. Harlow P. McNaughton.

Second Brigade, Fourth Division.

Col. BENJAMIN DORNBLASER.

46th Illinois, Lieut. Col. John J. Jones.
76th Illinois, Lieut. Col. Charles C. Jones.

Mississippi Marine Brigade.

Brig. Gen. ALFRED W. ELLET.

1st Mounted, Col. George E. Currie.
1st Cavalry Battalion, Capt. John R. Crandall.
Segebarth's (Pennsylvania) battery, Capt. Daniel P. Walling.
Ram Fleet, Lieut. Col. John A. Ellet.

Maltby's Brigade.

Brig. Gen. JASPER A. MALTBY.

17th Illinois, Maj. Frank F. Peats.
81st Illinois,* Lieut. Col. Andrew W. Rogers.
124th Illinois, Lieut. Col. John H. Howe.
7th Missouri, Maj. William B. Collins.
8th Ohio Battery, Capt. James F. Putnam.
26th Ohio Battery, Capt. Theobold D. Yost.

Cavalry.

2d Wisconsin, Col. Thomas Stephens.

CAVALRY BRIGADE.

Maj. HORACE P. MUMFORD.

5th Illinois, Capt. Alexander S. Jessup.
11th Illinois, Capt. Thomas O'Hara.
10th Missouri, Capt. Jeremiah F. Young.

* On Red River campaign.

FIRST DIVISION COLORED TROOPS.

Brig. Gen. John P. Hawkins.

First Brigade.

Brig. Gen. Isaac F. Shepard.

46th U. S. Colored Troops, Col. William F. Wood.
48th U. S. Colored Troops. Col. Frederick M. Crandal.
49th U. S. Colored Troops, Col. Van E. Young.
53d U. S. Colored Troops, Col. Orlando C. Risdon.

Second Brigade.

Col. Hiram Scofield.

47th U. S. Colored Troops, Capt. De Witt C. Wilson.
50th U. S. Colored Troops, Col. Charles A. Gilcrist.
52d U. S. Colored Troops, Col. George M. Ziegler.

Forces at Vicksburg.

3d U. S. Colored Cavalry, Col. Embury D. Osband.
2d U. S. Colored Artillery, Battery A, Capt. Robert Ranney.
4th U. S. Colored Heavy Artillery, Col. Herman Lieb.

U. S. Forces Goodrich's Landing, &c.

Col. A. Watson Webber.

51st U. S. Colored Troops, Lieut. Col. Julian E. Bryant.
66th U. S. Colored Troops, Col. William T. Frohock.
2d U. S. Colored Lig Artillery, Battery B, Capt. William M. Pratt.

DEFENSES AND POST OF NATCHEZ. MISS.

Brig. Gen. James M. Tuttle.

28th Illinois, Maj. Hinman Rhodes.
29th Illinois, Lieut. Col. John A. Callicott.
58th U. S. Colored Troops, Col. Simon M. Preston.
4th Illinois Cavalry. Lieut. Col. Martin M. R. Wallace.
2d Illinois Light Artillery, Battery K. Capt. Benjamin F. Rodgers.
5th U. S. Colored Heavy Artillery, Col. Bernard G. Farrar.

THIRD DIVISION.

Brig. Gen. Mortimer D. Leggett.

First Brigade.

Brig. Gen. Manning F. Force.

20th Illinois, Lieut. Col. Daniel Bradley.
31st Illinois. Lt. Col. Robert N. Pearson.
45th Illinois, Maj. John O. Duer.

Second Brigade.

Col. Robert K. Scott.

20th Ohio. Lieut. Col. John C. Fry.
32d Ohio. Col. Benjamin F. Potts.
68th Ohio, Lieut. Col. George E. Welles.
78th Ohio. Lieut. Col. Greenberry F. Wiles.

Third Brigade (Maltby's).*

Brig. Gen. Jasper A. Maltby.

(Reported as garrison of Vicksburg.)

Artillery.

Maj. Thomas D. Maurice.

1st Illinois Light, Battery D, Lieut. George P. Cunningham.
1st Michigan Light, Battery H, Lieut. William Justin.
1st Missouri Light, Battery C, Capt. John L. Matthaei.
Ohio Light, 3d Battery, Lieut. John Sullivan.

*See District of Vicksburg, p. 567.

Cavalry.

2d Wisconsin, Company H. Lieut. Charles Doerflinger.

FOURTH DIVISION.*

Brig. Gen. MARCELLUS M. CROCKER.

First Brigade.†	*Third Brigade.*
Brig. Gen. THOMAS KILBY SMITH.	Brig. Gen. WALTER Q. GRESHAM.
41st Illinois. Lieut. Col. John H. Nale.	32d Illinois, Col. John Logan.
53d Illinois.‡ Lieut. Col. John W. Mc-	23d Indiana. Col. William L. Sanderson.
Clanahan.	53d Indiana, Lieut. Col. William Jones.
3d Iowa, Lieut. Col. James Tullis.	12th Wisconsin. Col. George E. Bryant.
33d Wisconsin. Col. Jonathan B. Moore.	

Artillery.

Capt. EDMUND SPEAR.

2d Illinois Light. Battery F, Lieut. Richard Osborne.
Minnesota Light, 1st Battery, Capt. William Z. Clayton.
Ohio Light, 10th Battery, Lieut. William J. Mong.
Ohio Light, 15th Battery, Lieut. James Burdick.

Cavalry.

11th Illinois, Company G, Lieut. James M. Gregory.

Abstract from returns of the Department of the Ohio, Maj. Gen. John M. Schofield, U. S. Army, commanding, for the month of April, 1864.

Command.	Present for duty.		Aggregate present.	Aggregate present and absent.	Pieces of artillery.		Headquarters.
	Officers.	Men.			Heavy.	Field.	
General headquarters	47	....	47	47	....	....	In the field.
Twenty-third Army Corps (Scho- field):							
Headquarters	7	....	7	7	....	....	In the field.
First Division (Hovey).............	192	4,282	4,816	5,770	....	8	Charleston, Tenn.
Second Division (Judah).........	161	3,429	4,113	6,342	....	....	Do.
Third Division (Cox).....	158	3,640	4,440	6,052	....	....	Near Charleston, Tenn.
Fourth Division (Ammen).......	258	5,620	7,156	9,629	....	53	Knoxville, Tenn.
Fifth Division *a* (Burbridge).....	445	9,054	11,728	15,121	34	35	Lexington, Ky.
Cavalry Corps.	139	3,549	4,615	6,453	....	....	
Engineer troops (McAlester) ...	4	167	210	265	....	....	
Total Twenty-third Corps.....	1,364	29,741	37,085	49,639	34	96	
Newport Barracks, Ky., (C. C. Smith)	2	83	95	95	....	....	
Grand total	1,413	29,824	37,227	49,781	34	96	
Grand total according to monthly return of the de- partment.*b*	1,392	30,211	37,762	50,558	...	....	

a Or District of Kentucky.   *b* Pieces of artillery not accounted for.

*For Second Brigade see District of Vicksburg, p. 567.
†On Red River campaign.
‡On veteran furlough.

Abstract from returns of the District of Kentucky (or Fifth Division, Twenty-third Army Corps), Brig. Gen. Stephen G. Burbridge, U. S. Army, commanding, for the month of April, 1864.

Command.	Present for duty.		Aggregate present.	Aggregate present and absent.	Pieces of artillery.		Headquarters.
	Officers.	Men.			Heavy.	Field.	
General headquarters..............	4	....	4	4	....	......	Lexington, Ky.
First Division (Hobson):							
Headquarters	4	....	4	4	....	......	Do.
First Brigade (Gallup)....... ...	53	1,391	1,025	1,929	....	8	Louisa, Ky.
Second Brigade (True)	77	1,521	1,832	2,356	....	......	Mount Sterling, Ky.
Third Brigade (Hanson)........	48	1,084	1,291	1,536	....	......	Irvine, Ky.
Fourth Brigade (J. M. Brown)...	87	1,711	2,107	3,361	....	......	Lexington, Ky.
Second Division (Ewing):							
Headquarters	5	....	5	5	....	......	Munfordville, Ky.
First Brigade (S. D. Bruce)......	93	1,652	2,708	3,711	4	27	Louisville, Ky.
Second Brigade (C. Maxwell)	74	1,695	2,062	2,215	30	......	Bowling Green, Ky.
Total *..............	445	9,054	11,728	15,121	34	35	

Troops in the Department of the Ohio, Maj. Gen. John M. Schofield, U. S. Army, commanding, April 30, 1864.

TWENTY-THIRD ARMY CORPS.†

Maj. Gen. JOHN M. SCHOFIELD.

HEADQUARTERS.

Engineer Battalion, Capt. Charles E. McAlester.

FIRST DIVISION.

Brig. Gen. ALVIN P. HOVEY.

First Brigade.

Col. RICHARD F. BARTER.

120th Indiana, Lieut. Col. Allen W. Pratler.
124th Indiana, Col. James Burgess.
128th Indiana, Col. Richard P. De Hart.

Second Brigade.

Col. JOHN C. McQUISTON.

123d Indiana, Lieut. Col. William A. Cullen.
129th Indiana, Col. Charles Case.
130th Indiana, Col. Charles S. Parrish.

Artillery.‡

23d Indiana Battery, Lieut. Luther S. Houghton.
24th Indiana Battery, Lieut. Henry W. Shafer.

_____

* Included in strength of the department, p. 569.
† Reorganized under Special Orders, No. 101, headquarters Department of the Ohio, April 11, 1864.
‡ Lieut. Col. George W. Schofield, chief of corps artillery.

SECOND DIVISION.

Brig. Gen. HENRY M. JUDAH.

First Brigade.

Col. JOSEPH A. COOPER.

80th Indiana, Lieut. Col. Alfred D. Owen.
13th Kentucky, Col. William E. Hobson.
25th Michigan, Lieut. Col. Benjamin F. Orcutt.
3d Tennessee, Col. William Cross.
6th Tennessee, Lieut. Col. Edward Maynard.

Second Brigade.

Brig. Gen. MILO S. HASCALL.

107th Illinois, Maj. Uriah M. Laurance.
23d Michigan, Lieut. Col. Oliver L. Spaulding.
45th Ohio.*
111th Ohio, Col. John R. Bond.
118th Ohio, Lieut. Col. Thomas L. Young.

Artillery.

1st Michigan Light, Battery F, Capt. Byron D. Paddock.
19th Ohio Battery, Capt. Joseph C. Shields.

THIRD DIVISION.

Brig. Gen. JACOB D. COX.

First Brigade.

Col. JAMES W. REILLY.

100th Ohio, Col. Patrick S. Slevin.
104th Ohio, Lieut. Col Oscar W. Sterl.
8th Tennessee, Col. Felix A. Reeve.

Second Brigade.

Brig. Gen. MAHLON D. MANSON.

63d Indiana, Col. Israel N. Stiles.
65th Indiana, Lieut. Col. Thomas Johnson.
24th Kentucky, Col. John S. Hurt.
103d Ohio, Capt. Philip C. Hayes.
5th Tennessee, Col. James T. Shelley.

FOURTH DIVISION.

Brig. Gen. JACOB AMMEN.

First Brigade.

Col. JOHN MEHRINGER.

91st Indiana, Maj. James M. Carson.
34th Kentucky, Col. William Y. Dillard.
2d North Carolina,† Lieut. Col. J. Albert Smith.
1st Michigan Light Artillery, Battery L, Lieut. Thomas Gallagher.
1st Michigan Light Artillery, Battery M, Lieut. Augustus H. Emery.
22d Ohio Battery, Lieut. Peter Cornell.
1st Tennessee Light Artillery, Battery B, Capt. William O. Beebe.
11th Tennessee Cavalry, Lieut. Col. Reuben A. Davis.

Second Brigade.

Brig. Gen. DAVIS TILLSON.,

1st Ohio Heavy Artillery, Col. Chauncey G. Hawley.
2d Tennessee, Col. James P. T. Carter.
1st U. S. Heavy Artillery (colored), Maj. John E. McGowan.
Colvin's (Illinois) Battery, Capt. John H. Colvin.
Elgin (Illinois) Battery, Capt. Andrew M. Wood.
Wilder (Indiana) Battery (one section), Lieut. John S. White.
21st Ohio Battery, Lieut. James H. Walley.
10th Michigan Cavalry, Col. Thaddeus Foote.

---

* Borne on division return as " not reported ; " not accounted for on brigade returns, and probably en route from Cumberland Gap to Knoxville.
† Mounted.

Third Brigade.

Col. SILAS A. STRICKLAND.

27th Kentucky, Lieut. Col. John H. Ward.
50th Ohio, Lieut. Col. George R. Elstner.
1st Tennessee, Lieut. Col. John Ellis.
4th Tennessee, Lieut. Col. Michael L. Patterson.
Henshaw's Illinois Battery, Lieut. Azro C. Putnam.
14th Illinois Cavalry,* Lieut. Col. David P. Jenkins.

DISTRICT OF KENTUCKY.†

Brig. Gen. STEPHEN G. BURBRIDGE.

FIRST DIVISION.

Brig. Gen. EDWARD H. HOBSON.

First Brigade.	*Third Brigade.*
Col. GEORGE W. GALLUP.	Col. CHARLES S. HANSON.
14th Kentucky,‡ Lieut. Col. Orlando Brown, jr.	37th Kentucky.‡ Maj. Samuel Martin.
39th Kentucky,‡ Col. David A. Mims.	52d Kentucky,‡ Col. John H. Grider.
11th Michigan Cavalry. Col. Simeon B. Brown.	
Battery.§ Capt. Drew J. Burchett.	
Second Brigade.	*Fourth Brigade.*
Col. CLINTON J. TRUE.	Col. JOHN M. BROWN.
40th Kentucky,‡ Lieut. Col. Mathew Mullins.	30th Kentucky.‡ Lieut. Col. William B. Craddock.
13th Kentucky Cavalry, Col. James W. Weatherford.	45th Kentucky,‡ Lieut. Col. Lewis M. Clark.
12th Ohio Cavalry, Lieut. Col. Robert H. Bentley.	47th Kentucky, Maj. Thomas H. Barnes.
	49th Kentucky, Capt. Stephen Golden.
	1st Wisconsin Heavy Artillery. Company B, Capt. Walter S. Babcock.

SECOND DIVISION.

Brig. Gen. HUGH EWING.

First Brigade.	*Second Brigade.*
Col. SANDERS D. BRUCE.	Col. CICERO MAXWELL.
20th Kentucky. Lieut. Col. Thomas B. Waller.	26th Kentucky, Maj. Cyrus J. Wilson.
48th Kentucky, Col. Hartwell T. Burge.	35th Kentucky, Col. Edmund A. Starling.
23d V. R. C., Company D, Capt. Charles W. Chase.	2d Ohio Heavy Artillery (six companies), Lieut. Col. Martin B. Ewing.
2d Battalion. Veteran Reserve Corps:	
40th Company, Capt. Patrick Dwyer.	
56th Company, Capt. Charles Armstrong.	
77th Company, Lieut. Joseph H. Davis.	

---

* One battalion ordered. April 27, on duty at corps headquarters.
† Or Fifth Division. Twenty-third Army Corps.
‡ Mounted.
§ Manned by Company K, 14th Kentucky.

CAVALRY CORPS.*

Maj. Gen. GEORGE STONEMAN.

FIRST DIVISION.

Col. CHARLES D. PENNEBAKER.

First Brigade. '

1st Kentucky, Lieut. Col. Silas Adams.
11th Kentucky. Col. Alexander W. Holeman.

Second Brigade.

6th Indiana, Lieut. Col. Courtland C. Matson.
8th Michigan, Maj. Elisha Mix.

Third Brigade.

16th Illinois. Maj. Christian Thielemann.
12th Kentucky, Col. Eugene W. Crittenden.

SECOND DIVISION.

Col. ISRAEL GARRARD.

First Brigade.†

Col. ISRAEL GARRARD.

9th Michigan, Maj. Solomon P. Brockway.
7th Ohio, Capt. Solomon L. Green.

Second Brigade.

5th Indiana, Col. Thomas H. Butler.
16th Kentucky,‡ Maj. George F. Barnes.

MISCELLANEOUS.

CAMP BURNSIDE, KY.

Brig. Gen. SPEED S. FRY.

12th Kentucky, Lieut. Col. Laurence H. Rousseau.
30th Kentucky (four companies), Col. Francis N. Alexander.
49th Kentucky, Lieut. Col. Philos Stratton.
22d Indiana Battery, Capt. Benjamin F. Denning.

MUNFORDVILLE, KY.

Col. HORATIO G. GIBSON.

48th Kentucky (six companies), Lieut. Col. William W. Hester.
2d Ohio Heavy Artillery (six companies), Maj. Daniel W. Hoffman.

---

*According to tri-monthly return, Department of the Ohio, for April 30, when not otherwise indicated. That return reports all the cavalry as at Kingston, Ga. The regimental commanders are taken from the regimental returns.
†According to brigade return.
‡Reported on monthly return of the department. Not accounted for on tri-monthly.

CONFEDERATE CORRESPONDENCE, ETC.

DALTON, *March* 1, 1864.

Brig. Gen. J. H. MORGAN :

The orders in regard both to yourself and your troops are from Richmond. I regret them very much, but have no power to modify them.

J. E. JOHNSTON.

HEADQUARTERS,
Demopolis, Ala., March 1, 1864.

Hon. JAMES A. SEDDON,
Secretary of War, Richmond, Va.:

SIR : I have the honor to call to your attention the importance of a change in the administration of the Conscript Bureau within my department, and to request that the management and control of the affairs of that bureau be intrusted to me.

The present arrangement I find exceedingly inconvenient and embarrassing. Officers have been assigned temporarily to duties connected with the Conscript Bureau taken from the army which I command. Their services are now required by their commands, yet it would seem to be incompetent for me to withdraw them from their present assignment and order them to the field. So with the troops of that department (most of them belong to my army) that were ordered to report to General Pillow for temporary duty as a supporting force. Under the operation of the present system they are now beyond my control, not to be recalled by me even in an emergency. I respectfully submit that this should not be so, but that the officers and men of this bureau should report to me and be subject to my authority.

There is a large amount of conscript material within my department. By an energetic and judicious prosecution of the work our army here may be largely increased and strengthened within the next sixty days. An officer remote from the field cannot control the machinery of such a system, whatever his abilities, as one immediately at hand, with a full knowledge of all the facts and familiar with the condition of the people and the wants of the service. It is a most delicate and at the same time a most important task. Upon its faithful and successful execution hang in a great measure the destinies of the country. We must have more fighting men.

Should you see proper to confide to me, as I think should be done, the management and control of the Bureau of Conscription within my department, I feel satisfied that it will be so administered as to secure the happiest results within the shortest practicable period.

I have the honor to be, sir, your most obedient servant,

L. POLK,
Lieutenant-General, Commanding.

GENERAL ORDERS, }   HDQRS. ARMY OF TENNESSEE,
No. 27.   }   *Dalton, Ga., March* 1, 1864.

General Johnston brings to the notice of the army the gallant conduct and fidelity to his trust of Private Charles Renig, Fifteenth Tennessee Regiment. Posted as a sentinel on the 29th instant [ultimo] at the depot in Dalton, he was surrounded by 200 disorderly soldiers, who threatened to force his guard and seize the stores. Finding that they could not persuade him or intimidate, they prepared to force the door, when Renig cocked his gun, took the position of ready, and notified them that he would shoot the first man who attempted it. This defiance was met by threats of instant death if he fired, but he coolly answered that he would kill as many as they could. By his heroic firmness he kept them at bay until a guard sent to disperse the crowd arrived and drove them off. Private Renig has set an example worthy of imitation by his comrades, and entitled himself to this public acknowledgment from his general.

By command of General Johnston :

KINLOCH FALCONER,
Assistant Adjutant-General.

GENERAL ORDERS, }   HEADQUARTERS HOOD'S CORPS,
    No. 31.   }   *Dalton, Ga., March* 1, 1864.

The lieutenant-general commanding desires to say to the officers and men of this corps that though he comes among them a stranger he trusts they will not be strangers long. He has come to share their hardships and their dangers, their pleasures and their triumphs. The welfare of the command will be the object of his most anxious solicitude. To fight it successfully in the day of action is his highest ambition, but the history of war teaches that two-thirds of the elements of success in battle consist in preparation for it. He will therefore expect from all prompt and cheerful compliance with orders and the requirements of discipline, and a cordial co-operation with him in his efforts to carry this corps to the highest point of military efficiency.

A short period will perhaps elapse before the opening of the campaign. Let us employ each day with singleness of purpose in perfecting our drill, our organization, and our discipline, and we may confidently await the trial of arms.

By command of Lieutenant-General Hood :

ARCHER ANDERSON,
Assistant Adjutant-General.

GENERAL ORDERS, }   HEADQUARTERS HOOD'S CORPS,
    No. 32.   }   *Dalton, Ga., March* 1, 1864.

I. The following officers of the general staff are attached to these headquarters :

Lieut. Col. W. H. Sellers, assistant adjutant-general, chief of staff.

Lieut. Col. Archer Anderson, assistant adjutant-general, chief of the adjutant-general's department.

Maj. J. P. Wilson, assistant adjutant-general (on temporary duty).

Lieut. Col. E. H. Cunningham, assistant adjutant-general, chief of the inspector-general's department.

Maj. A. C. Avery, assistant inspector-general.

Maj. J. W. Ratchford, assistant inspector-general.

Maj. M. B. George, chief quartermaster.

Maj. E. H. Ewing, quartermaster.

Capt. Charles Vidmer, assistant quartermaster.
Capt. J. W. Bradford, paymaster.
Maj. S. A. Jones, chief commissary.
Maj. Isaac Scherck, commissary of subsistence.
Surgeon J. H. Erskine, medical director.
Assistant Surgeon J. F. Young, medical purveyor.
Capt. T. Coleman, chief engineer.
First Lieut. George M. Helm, engineer.
Capt. W. C. Duxbury, chief ordnance officer.
Capt. D. L. Sublett, assistant ordnance officer.
II. Col. R. F. Beckham is announced as chief of artillery.
III. Maj. James Hamilton and First Lieuts. B. H. Blanton, F. H. Wigfall, and E. B. Wade, aides-de-camp, compose the personal staff of the lieutenant-general commanding.
By command of Lieutenant-General Hood :

> J. P. WILSON,
> *Assistant Adjutant-General.*

HEADQUARTERS DEPARTMENT OF EAST TENNESSEE,
Greeneville, March 2, 1864.

Maj. Gen. S. B. BUCKNER,
    Commanding Division, Bull's Gap :

General Longstreet desires you to send out and ascertain whether there is any truth in the report of General Johnson's pickets. Send scouts both to the front and rear of the enemy. Prepare to move forward if there is any truth in the report.

> O. LATROBE,
> *Assistant Adjutant-General.*

HEADQUARTERS DEPARTMENT OF EAST TENNESSEE,
Greeneville, March 2, 1864.

Brig. Gen. W. E. JONES,
    Commanding Brigade Cavalry :

The lieutenant-general commanding has information through Colonel Rucker that one corps of the enemy is at Morristown and another corps at Dandridge, the latter advancing. General Vaughn has been instructed to find out the truth of these reports, and in case of an advance of the enemy to notify you. On such notification you will, with your own and Hodge's brigades, move down to Rogersville, join Vaughn, and await further orders. Keep in readiness to make this move promptly as soon as advised by Vaughn.

Very respectfully, your obedient servant,

> OSMAN LATROBE,
> *Assistant Adjutant-General.*

HEADQUARTERS DEPARTMENT OF EAST TENNESSEE,
Greeneville, March 2, 1864.

Brig. Gen. J. C. VAUGHN,
    Comdg. Brigade, Big Creek, 4 miles east of Rogersville :

Colonel Rucker reports that his pickets were driven in at Morristown on the evening of the 29th ultimo ; that the Twenty-third Army Corps occupy that place ; that the Ninth Army Corps are at Dandridge, and advancing.

The lieutenant-general commanding desires you at once to find out, if possible, what truth there is in this. If you get accurate information of a general advance of the enemy notify General W. E. Jones, who is ordered on such notification to concentrate with his own and Hodge's brigades on you at Rogersville, and there await further orders.

Send such information as you may get at once to these head-quarters.

Respectfully, your obedient servant,

OSMAN LATROBE,
Assistant Adjutant-General.

———

DEMOPOLIS, *March 2*, 1864.

General S. COOPER,
Adjutant and Inspector General:

Following from one of my staff officers, dated Hillsborough, 26th :

Sixteenth Army Corps commenced crossing Pearl River at Ratliff's Ferry 17th ; at Grant's Ferry, en route to Canton, 27th ; enemy finished crossing to-day ; head of column are passing through Canton.

L. POLK,
Lieutenant-General.

———

ENGINEER OFFICE,
Mobile, March 2, 1864.

Capt. L. J. FRÉMAUX,
Engineer, Fort Gaines:

CAPTAIN : Captain Howard, of the Engineer Corps, proceeds with 100 negroes and the necessary overseers to Cedar Point for the purpose of constructing the small work in lunette shape ordered by Major-General Gilmer. He will take charge of the works at Cedar Point and Fort Powell, with Mr. Biberon as assistant.

From this morning's report I see that your force consists of 311 negroes. Sand-bags. gabions, wheel-barrows, and axes have been forwarded to you by yesterday's boat. Please push the work at the extreme point of Dauphin Island as vigorously as possible. Its right flank. according to instructions received from Major-General Gilmer, is to be traced so that a well and a newly dug grave will come nearly in front of the right-hand gun-chamber. Its left flank is to extend far enough toward the house on the point to give the requisite space for the four guns.

The cedars have to be left standing. even should it be necessary to build the parapet around them. Only timber enough will be cleared away to give your guns a sufficient field of fire.

The two 32-pounder rifled and banded guns will be mounted at the two salients right and left ; the two guns on siege carriages between them with traverses for their protection. Platforms are being sent to-day ; also 3,000 [feet] of 3-inch plank for the construction of temporary magazines.

Fifty ax-men will be sufficient to proceed at once to the construction of the much-desired sawyer obstructions, and you will please carry out the instructions contained in the letter which Mr. Biberon will have handed you.

Four coils of rope, a quantity of chain, and a number of mushroom anchors have been sent to Fort Morgan, sufficient to justify you in pushing on the work with all possible energy. So soon as some progress will have been made in the preparation of these saw-yers the necessary teams and forage will be sent to you.

You will please intrust Captain Gallimard with the construction of the work on Dauphin Island, and superintend in person the con-struction of the channel obstructions. Sixty Singer torpedoes will be transferred back from Cedar Point to Fort Morgan, and will be placed in the main channel between that point and the west bank. For Fort Powell sixteen torpedoes of this class and a number of General Rains' torpedoes are deemed sufficient.

Very respectfully, your obedient servant,
V. SHELIHA,
Lieutenant-Colonel and Chief Engineer.

SPECIAL ORDERS, }   HEADQUARTERS,
No. 62.   }   *Demopolis, Ala., March 2, 1864.*

I. Brig. Gen. A. Buford is relieved from duty with Major-General Loring's division, and will report to Major-General Forrest for as-signment.

    *   *   *   *   *

By command of Lieutenant-General Polk :
THOS. M. JACK,
Assistant Adjutant-General.

HEADQUARTERS,
Demopolis, March 3, 1864.
General JOSEPH E. JOHNSTON :

GENERAL : I am just in receipt of your letter of the 17th January, which by some means has been detained in the mails or elsewhere until now. As I find in it you advert to a matter which I regard of great importance to the public interests, to wit, the transfer to this department of Cheatham's division of Tennesseeans, and as I perceive, too, in that connection you think, with me, that "Northern Missis-sippi offers us the best base of offensive operations," I take the lib-erty of sending you a copy of a letter* I addressed some days ago to His Excellency the President, in which I ask him to let me have that division, and indicate why I deem it expedient and the uses to be made of it. The plan of campaign indicated I think might be car-ried out and with good results. Hoping you might find it conven-ient to let me have the troops asked for,

I remain, general, respectfully, your obedient servant,
L. POLK,
Lieutenant-General.

EXECUTIVE DEPARTMENT,
Richmond, Va., March 3, 1864.
General S. COOPER,
Adjutant and Inspector General:

GENERAL : I have the honor, by the direction of the President, to forward the following copy of a telegram from General L. Polk,

---

*See Part II, p. 813.

dated Demopolis, March 2, 1864, and to inform you that the President has approved General Polk's order:

His Excellency President DAVIS :

I have ordered the Kentucky regiments under my command to report to General Forrest for duty, and to be mounted immediately.

L. POLK,
Lieutenant-General.

Very respectfully, your obedient servant,
BURTON N. HARRISON,
Private Secretary.

DEMOPOLIS, ALA.,
March 3, 1864.
Lieut. Col. T. F. SEVIER,
Assistant Inspector-General:

COLONEL : I have the honor to make the following report of the reconnaissance which I made in obedience to orders from department headquarters dated February 23 :

I proceeded down the Mobile and Ohio Railroad as far as Enterprise, having struck the road at Meridian, and I found that the enemy had torn up the road in spots from Lauderdale Springs to the bridge over the Chickasawha, which is a short distance below Quitman. The damage done to the road extends over a distance of 48 miles, but not more than about 30 miles of the road is actually damaged. The damage to the road consists in the bridges being burned and the cross-ties burned, and the rails bent for the distance which I have named. The damage done to the Southern road was very much the same as that done to the Mobile and Ohio. The tunnel was damaged very little, the masonry at each end being simply knocked in. The Mississippi and Alabama River road was destroyed in the same way as the other roads for 9 miles. The telegraph wires on the Mississippi and Alabama River road were destroyed for 9 miles, the wire in some places having been burned, a good many of the posts cut down, and a good many of the glasses broken. Upon the Mobile and Ohio road the damage to the wires was very much the same as upon the Mississippi and Alabama River road.

When I left Cuba Station, 21 miles this side of Meridian, last Wednesday morning, the wires were up from Mobile to Meridian, or within a short distance of it. Nothing, however, had been done toward repairing the lines from this place to Meridian. At Meridian I found that the enemy had burned and destroyed all of the Government houses except one house, in which a family was living. They also burned a good deal of private property, consisting of two hotels and all the stores in the place, as well as the Clarion office. In Enterprise all of the Government houses were burned, as well as a good deal of private property. The bridge across the river was also burned. All the cotton along the road was burned.

I beg leave also to say something in regard to tories and deserters who infest Jones County and a portion of Lauderdale. The tories in Jones County made a raid upon Paulding not many days ago, about 200 strong, and carried off a good deal of corn as well as other property. They are becoming very troublesome, as well as dangerous, to the country around. In regard to the tories and deserters in Lauderdale County, I have to say that a citizen of the county, Mr.

W. W. Hall, who was at one time a member of the Legislature, informed me that in the western portion of Lauderdale County, where
he was just from when I saw him, there was being formed a company
of men who intend joining the Federal army as soon as possible.
This organization was headed by a Dr. Longmire, who lives in Gar-
landville, Miss. The company met while Mr. Hall was in the neighborhood at the house of a man named Joe Mayberry. The enemy
wherever they went stripped the people of provisions, and I am
afraid that some of them will suffer.

   I am, respectfully, your obedient servant,
                                        A. H. POLK,
                  First Lieutenant and Actg. Asst. Insp. Gen.

                                    MONTGOMERY, *March* 3, 1864.
Lieut. Col. T. M. JACK,
         Demopolis:
   Nothing from Pensacola but a dispatch from Colonel Murphey,
commanding at Greeneville, that the enemy are advancing toward
Pollard. If anything comes in will keep you informed.
                                        J. M. WITHERS,
                                            Major-General.

                                            HEADQUARTERS,
                          Demopolis, Ala., March 3, 1864.
General S. COOPER,
         Adjutant and Inspector General:
   The weakness and inefficiency exhibited by the agents of the Bureau
of Conscription and absentee volunteers in this department are producing the most serious evils. Conscripts and deserters have banded
together in Jones County, and others contiguous, to the number of
several hundred; have killed the officer in charge of the work of conscription and dispersed and captured his supporting force. They are
increasing in numbers and boldness; have destroyed the houses of
many loyal men by fire, plundered others, and have within a few days
made a raid into Paulding with a wagon train and helped themselves
largely to Government and other stores. The arrest of these men
and the suppression of such excesses has been and is intrusted to the
Bureau of Conscription. The administration demanded for such
work is far more vigorous than can be exercised by a bureau having its seat at Richmond.
   The forces I have in the field will have to be turned aside to put
down this combination, which is fast attaining formidable proportions, greatly to my inconvenience and the interference with permanent duties elsewhere. I am satisfied that the duty of collecting
and conscribing these men and arresting these deserters should be
placed directly in the hands of the general commanding the department.
   One set of troops then could do the work of conscription, arrest deserters and paroled prisoners, and maintain a proper military police,
and they would be where they ought to be, under the direct order
of the commander of the department. As it is, I have to detail a
force for the conscription officers and another to arrest deserters,

absentees, and paroled men, and keep down such rebellions as that above. It is a great inconvenience and annoyance to have troops in the department who are not acting under the orders of the department commander. It interferes with discipline very greatly, and brings many evils, of which the affairs in Jones and other counties are the proof. I cannot be held responsible for the proper administration of the department when the power to control its affairs is divided between me and another officer, and I again ask that the whole of the military operations of my department be placed in my hands.

I remain, general, respectfully, your obedient servant,

L. POLK,
Lieutenant-General.

[Indorsement.]

To comply with the suggestions in this letter would but add to the military responsibilities of General Polk, and would not lessen the evil complained of, inasmuch as it would require the same amount of force to enforce conscription and apprehend deserters, to which the general here objects.

S. C.

HEADQUARTERS STATE OF MISSISSIPPI,
Macon, March 3, 1864.

Brigadier-General CHALMERS,
Commanding Cavalry near Starkville, Miss.:

GENERAL: I am directed by His Excellency the Commander-in-Chief to forward to you the inclosed order for Col. John McGuirk, commanding the Third Regiment Mississippi State Cavalry, and to request that the regiment be dispatched with all convenient speed. It is destined for a special and important service, which brooks no delay; otherwise, the Governor instructs me to say he would await the return of Major-Generals Lee and Forrest before issuing the inclosed order.

I have the honor to be, general, very respectfully, your obedient servant,

W. H. McCARDLE,
Colonel and Adjutant-General.

[Inclosure.]

SPECIAL ORDERS, }   HEADQUARTERS STATE OF MISSISSIPPI,
No. 83.   }   *Macon, March 3, 1864.*

Col. John McGuirk will move forthwith with his regiment to this point, and on his arrival report at these headquarters for orders.

By order of Charles Clark, Governor and Commander-in-Chief:

W. H. McCARDLE,
Adjutant-General.

ATLANTA, GA., *March 3, 1864.*

Brig. Gen. W. W. MACKALL,
Chief of Staff, Army of Tennessee, Dalton, Ga.:

GENERAL: Special Orders, No. 57, dated February 28, 1864, headquarters Army of Tennessee, assigned Brig. Gen. M. J. Wright to the command of this post. I beg to be informed if the order is to be interpreted as relieving me from duty, inasmuch as nothing of the kind appears on the face of the order. I was assigned to duty in command of the troops and defenses of Atlanta by the honorable Secretary of War in July, 1863. I have been anxious to be relieved for some time and have so expressed myself, but the order assigning General Wright does not do it, except by implication, he being superior in rank, though I was never assigned to duty in command of the post. An early reply will greatly oblige me, as I will then know whether I am to turn over public property, &c., to General Wright or not. I would greatly prefer being relieved in due form than simply by an implied order.

I am, general, &c.,

M. H. WRIGHT,
Colonel, Commanding, &c.

CONFIDENTIAL.]   HDQRS. DEPT. OF EAST TENNESSEE,
March 4, 1864.

General R. E. LEE,
Commanding Army of Northern Virginia:

GENERAL: My letter in reply to yours of the 17th ultimo failed to notice your suggestion in regard to co-operation between General Johnston and myself. My move upon Knoxville last month was made with the view of getting co-operation on the part of General Johnston, and after we had driven the enemy into his works around Knoxville I telegraphed General Johnston of our situation, asking him to cut the enemy's line of communication in order to prevent his re-enforcing at Knoxville with great odds against me. General Johnston, in reply, said that he had detached so strong a force that he could not aid me. Under these circumstances it seemed to me hardly worth the time and trouble that would be necessary for me to lay siege to Knoxville again.

Soldiers just in from Middle Tennessee report the enemy moving back to Kentucky in great force to meet a move expected in that State by this army. If this is true, the plan that I have proposed becomes the more important, if not essential, and it seems to me that it will be necessary in order to feed this army, if not for food for yours. By great exertions it is feasible and gives promise of great results. I feel confident, too, of doing more in it than meets the eye.

There is another way of making the move, but I think it more difficult than the one that I have previously proposed; that is, to move your army, or a part of it, with mine. By yielding for a time your present position you could join me with part of your army and move on into Kentucky, keeping in Virginia enough force to hold Richmond until Johnston's army could be transported there. In that way Johnston would be able to remain in position until he could draw the enemy off from his front, and he would also have time to get to Richmond before any serious injury could be inflicted in that quarter.

It is in our power to place matters in such a position as to secure peace upon such terms as we wish within the year or year and a half, if we use the energy, caution, and perseverance that we owe to our people who have yielded to our care their all ; but to do this we must have our own plans and not allow ourselves to be diverted from them by any effort of the enemy.

I hoped to be able to visit you soon, but I fear that I may not be able to do so. If, however, you feel at liberty to go to Richmond, and will telegraph me, I will try and meet you, unless the enemy becomes more enterprising than he has been recently.

I remain, general, very respectfully, your obedient servant,

J. LONGSTREET,
Lieutenant-General.

N. B.—Please send me the 1,500 saddles and bridles that you say that you can spare. Spurs with them if possible.

RICHMOND, VA.,
March 4, 1864.

General J. LONGSTREET,
Greeneville, Tenn. :

Your letter of 25th February received. Your assignment of General Buckner to Hood's old division not approved. The order from this office assigning General Field to that division will be carried into effect.

S. COOPER,
Adjutant and Inspector General.

GREENEVILLE, *March* 4, 1864.

General S. COOPER :

Would it meet the views of the Department to assign Major-General Field to the division formerly commanded by Major-General McLaws?

J. LONGSTREET.

RICHMOND, VA.,
March 4, 1864.

Lieutenant-General LONGSTREET :

It does not suit the views of the President to assign Major-General Field to the division lately commanded by Major-General McLaws. He is to take the division to which he was assigned in orders from this office.

S. COOPER,
Adjutant and Inspector-General.

HEADQUARTERS DEPARTMENT OF EAST TENNESSEE,
March 4, 1864.

General J. E. JOHNSTON,
Dalton, Ga. :

Soldiers just returned from Middle Tennessee report that troops have gone back in great force from your front into Kentucky to meet an expected advance of mine into that State. Have you any information corroborative of this?

J. LONGSTREET.

DALTON, *March* 4, 1864.

Lieutenant-General LONGSTREET,
   Greeneville, Tenn.:

At the date you give General Thomas was in front of me with all his troops. Our scouts report no movements of Federal troops to the rear, but state that recruits have been arriving at Chattanooga in large numbers.

          J. E. JOHNSTON.

        ATLANTA, GA.,
         March 4, 1864.

Maj. A. P. MASON,
  Assistant Adjutant-General, Dalton, Ga.:

Effective strength of garrison at this place, two companies of artillery and 13 men of another; in all, 135 men. Local troops from our shops, &c., about 500 strong when called out. Many of the local troops failed to re-enlist in February. The troops from the convalescent camps cannot be relied upon, all able for duty having been sent to front. All dismounted men of cavalry sent here have been turned over to General Morgan, as belonging to his command. Forces entirely inadequate to defense of place.

         M. H. WRIGHT,
           Colonel, Commanding.

  HEADQUARTERS ARMIES CONFEDERATE STATES,
      Richmond, March 4, 1864.

General JOSEPH E. JOHNSTON,
  Commanding Army of Tennessee:

GENERAL : In reply to yours of the 27th ultimo,* just received, I hasten to inform you that your inference from the letters of the President and Secretary of War is correct, and you are desired to have all things in readiness at the earliest practicable moment for the movement indicated. It is hoped but little time will be required to prepare the force now under your command, as the season is at hand and the time seems propitious.

Such additional forces will be ordered to you as the exigencies of the service elsewhere will permit, and it is hoped your own efforts will secure many absentees and extra-duty men to the ranks.

The deficiency you report in artillery horses seems very large, and is so different from the account given by General Hardee on turning over the command that hopes are entertained there must be some error on your part. Prompt measures should be taken by you, however, to supply the real want, whatever it may be. The part of your letter relating to this and field transportation will be referred to the Quartermaster-General.

Any defect which may exist in the organization of your artillery should be speedily corrected. Whatever action may be necessary here will be promptly taken on your report in detail.

Colonel Alexander, applied for by you as chief of artillery, is deemed necessary by General Lee in his present position. Brig. Gen. W. N. Pendleton, an experienced officer of artillery, has been

---

     *See Part II, p. 808.

ordered to your headquarters to inspect that part of your command and report on its condition. Should his services be acceptable to you, I am authorized to say you can retain him. I am exceedingly anxious to gratify you on this point, for I know the deficiency now existing. It is more than probable that such a junction may soon be made as to place Colonel Alexander under your command.

Very respectfully, general, your obedient servant,

BRAXTON BRAGG,
General.

HEADQUARTERS,
Demopolis, Ala., March 4, 1864—7 p. m.

Maj. Gen. S. D. LEE,
Commanding, &c., Gainesville, Ala.:

GENERAL : I am informed that a number of boats (transports and trading-boats) have gone up the Yazoo and that the force accompanying them is made up chiefly of negroes, a small number only of white soldiers being with the expedition. It will be seen by the dispatch from Macon (sent you by courier) that Ross is on that river with his brigade. I think if you would send at least one brigade more on the river with Ross you might capture or destroy those boats and a large amount of property and probably many prisoners. Your presence, also, to direct the operations would be of great importance at such a juncture. I hope, therefore, you will press to the front as soon as you can dispose of the necessary matters that have detained you. The report of the operations of your troops makes me hope for the best results. General Forrest's troops will cut them off from above Grenada should they attempt to leave their boats and retreat in the direction of Memphis.

Most respectfully,

THOS. M. JACK,
Assistant Adjutant-General.

DEMOPOLIS, *March* 4, 1864.

Major-General WITHERS,
Montgomery:

General Pillow dispatches that you cannot give him any orders without orders from me. I know not what orders are required for you other than those you already have. Colonel Preston has ordered that the companies in North Alabama shall not be taken by me away from that region, but that they shall remain for the conscript service. I cannot control them, therefore. General Pillow says eight of them have joined Roddey ; inquire into this. I will send you a list of the companies which Major Denis says are within your reach to-morrow.

L. POLK,
Lieutenant-General.

SPECIAL ORDERS, }
No. 64.   }

HEADQUARTERS,
Demopolis, Ala., March 4, 1864.

I. Major-General Lee will, as far as practicable, reoccupy the line held by his command prior to the late movements of the enemy, changing his position to the right or left as in his discretion it may appear expedient. He will keep the enemy's force in front of him in observation, refit his batteries, and put his command in condition for an active spring campaign.

II. Major-General Forrest will take such portion of his command as he may think necessary and make a short campaign in West Tennessee. He will leave his artillery at or near Columbus to be refitted, as also his wagon train. The rest of his command he will order to take such a position in North Mississippi as he may deem most suitable to hold the enemy in check during his campaign. He will keep these headquarters constantly advised of his movements by way of the Mobile and Ohio Railroad.

* * * * *

By command of Lieutenant-General Polk:

THOS. M. JACK,
Assistant Adjutant-General.

RICHMOND, VA.,
March 5, 1864.

Maj. Gen. D. H. MAURY,
Commanding Mobile, Ala.:

GENERAL: The attention of the Adjutant and Inspector General has been called to your monthly return. in which your command is designated as "the Department of the Gulf." I am directed by him to inform you that as you command a district of country in the Department of Alabama, Mississippi, and East Louisiana, the name is incorrect. There is no order constituting such a department. The error probably arose from the incautious language of the telegram sent to you April 27, 1863, when at Knoxville, Tenn.. in which you are directed "to proceed to Mobile and take command of that department." Prior to that time the State of Alabama was a portion of General Bragg's command and subsequently of General Johnston's. Please see copies of a letter to General Johnston August 12, 1863, and Special Orders, No. 23. 1864. from this office, herein inclosed.* Strictly speaking, you command Mobile and its defenses, within such limits as may be prescribed by Lieutenant-General Polk, commanding, and with authority to communicate directly to the Adjutant and Inspector General upon all matters which demand the prompt attention of the War Department.

I am, general, very respectfully, your obedient servant,

H. L. CLAY,
Assistant Adjutant-General.

HEADQUARTERS,
Greeneville, East Tenn., March 5, 1864.

General G. W. C. LEE,
Aide-de-Camp to the President:

GENERAL: General Alexander has just arrived, and has given me a partial idea of a combined movement of General Johnston's army and my own. The most serious difficulty in my way is the scarcity of supplies. but I think that I can get through as far as Madisonville if the weather is favorable. There are two routes from this to Madi-

---

*See of January 28. Part II, p. 627.

sonville ; one by passing some 15 miles south of Knoxville, the other by passing down north of Knoxville. I shall send out to-morrow to gather information about them both. In the mean time may I ask that you will give me the more detailed views of His Excellency; for instance, in making the move it would be well that S. D. Lee and Forrest should cross the Tennessee River and strike the enemy's line of communication between Chattanooga and Nashville, if they can be spared for that purpose, and then unite them with General Johnston's army.

I am, general, very respectfully, your most obedient servant,
J. LONGSTREET,
Lieutenant-General.

HEADQUARTERS,
Greeneville, East Tenn., March 5, 1864.

General J. E. JOHNSTON,
Commanding Army of Tennessee:

GENERAL: I have received a verbal message from the President, through General Alexander, to confer with you upon the propriety and practicability of uniting our armies at or near Madisonville, East Tenn., with a view to a move into Middle Tennessee upon the enemy's line of communication. There are two routes from this to the point mentioned—one by passing south of Knoxville and the Holston River, the other by passing Knoxville on the north side, about 90 miles by either route. On the former I should cross six rivers; the first has a bridge, however. The road is a single dirt road, through a mountainous country, and the road passes within 15 miles of Knoxville, where the enemy has a stronger force than I, but it is very much demoralized, and I feel quite confident that I can make the march if you can meet me promptly at Madisonville with subsistence stores and forage for my army. My transportation is so limited that I cannot take more than enough to supply us on the road. There is nothing in the country through which I would pass, or so little that we could place no reliance upon the country for supplies. The other route north of Knoxville would throw my column still nearer the enemy's stronghold, Knoxville, and I should be obliged to cross the Holston and the Tennessee Rivers. The latter stream would require a bridge, which I cannot haul ; but if you can meet me there, so as to prevent forces from Chattanooga molesting my march. I can make a bridge and unite my forces with yours. I shall be obliged to depend upon you for food and forage when we are united.

From here your difficulties look to me greater than mine, except that you will have the railroad to depend upon for supplies, and yet I cannot see that you can count upon that, unless your army is much stronger than I have supposed it to be, and the enemy's much weaker. I had estimated his forces at 40,000 available men.

Please give the matter that mature deliberation which it merits, and give me your views at as early a moment as may be convenient.

I remain, general, very respectfully, your most obedient servant,
J. LONGSTREET,
Lieutenant-General.

P. S.—I take the liberty to address you directly, in order that the matter may not be known by more parties than necessary.

J. L.

HEADQUARTERS,
Greeneville, East Tenn., March 5, 1864.

General A. R. LAWTON,
   Quartermaster-General, Richmond, Va.:

GENERAL : Can't you make arrangements for supplying us abun-
dautly with corn, &c., by stopping the use of the railroad for any
other than army purposes for forty days ? It seems to me that it is
almost essential to our safety. If we can make a telling campaign
early in the spring we may be able to get an honorable peace in a
short time ; if we do not, the war will in all probability be prolonged,
and no one can tell what may be the result. It will require extra
exertions on your part, but I hope that it may not be impossible.

An effective campaign, early in the season, will have greater effect
upon our people and upon our cause than anything that may happen at a later day. If we can break up the enemy's arrangements
early, and throw him back, he will not be able to recover his position
nor his morale until the Presidential election is over, and we shall
then have a new President to treat with. If Lincoln has any success
early he will be able to get more men and may be able to secure his
own re-election. In that event the war must go on for four years
longer. Do let us all exert ourselves to the utmost of our resources
to finish the war in this year. I know that you are working hard
and to great advantage now, but I have an idea that men are seldom worked to the utmost of their capacity, and if you are not I
desire to urge you up to that point.

I remain, very respectfully and truly, your most obedient servant,
J. LONGSTREET,
Lieutenant-General.

HEADQUARTERS,
Artesia, Miss., March 5, 1864.

General CHALMERS,
   Starkville:

You will move your entire command to the vicinity of Tibbee and
Mayhew Stations and report to me in person at Columbus to-morrow.
Send my escort and headquarters wagons with Morton's battery
direct to Columbus.
N. B. FORREST,
Major-General.

SPECIAL ORDERS, } ADJT. AND INSPECTOR GENERAL'S OFFICE,
   No. 54.   }   *Richmond, Va., March 5, 1864.*
*   *   *   *   *   *   *

VII. Brig. Gen. Francis C. Armstrong, Provisional Army, C. S.
(cavalry), is relieved from duty with the Army of Tennessee, and will
proceed without delay to Demopolis, Ala., and report to Lieut. Gen.
L. Polk, commanding, &c., for assignment.
*   *   *   *   *

By command of the Secretary of War :
JNO. WITHERS,
Assistant Adjutant-General.

GENERAL ORDERS, } HDQRS. DEPT. OF ALA., MISS., AND E. LA.,
No. 41. } Demopolis, Ala., March 5, 1864.

Information having reached the lieutenant-general commanding that there is a large class of officers and men in this department who, by wounds received in battle and other causes, are disabled for active field service but capable of other and lighter duty, it is ordered that all such officers and men, whether belonging properly to this department or not, report without delay at the rendezvous to be established at Demopolis, Ala.

Their services should not be lost to the country. They will be encamped at Demopolis and assigned to useful and appropriate duty, as the requirements of the Government may demand.

Commanding officers throughout the department, in the field as well as at posts, will see to the execution of this order, which is not intended, however, to apply to such as may have been heretofore assigned to duty on surgeons' certificates.

By command of Lieutenant-General Polk:

THOS. M. JACK,
Assistant Adjutant-General.

SPECIAL ORDERS, } HEADQUARTERS,
No. 65. } Demopolis, Ala., March 5, 1864.

*   *   *   *   *   *

IX. Brig. Gen. T. H. Taylor will proceed to the District of South Mississippi and East Louisiana, relieve Colonel Dillon of the command of that district, and report to Major-General Lee.

*   *   *   *   *   *

By command of Lieutenant-General Polk :

THOS. M. JACK,
Assistant Adjutant-General.

SPECIAL ORDERS, } HDQRS. NORTHERN DISTRICT OF ALABAMA,
No. 11. } Montgomery, Ala., March 5, 1864.

I. Brigadier-General Pillow is assigned to the command of the cavalry of this district. He will organize it into regiments and brigades with the least possible delay.

Field transportation and field batteries required will be furnished from these headquarters as rapidly as the completions of the organizations may require.

II. By order of the Secretary of War, he is directed to organize also all the supporting companies of the volunteer and conscript bureau in Alabama and Mississippi not retained by Colonel Preston. He will also, under the same authority, include the two companies of Captain Bibb, and under authority of Lieutenant-General Polk he will embrace in the organization Captain Lewis' squadron.

By command of Major-General Withers :

D. E. HUGER,
Major and Assistant Adjutant-General.

DALTON, GA.,
March 6, 1864.

General WHEELER,
  Tunnel Hill:
  Colonel Harrison has been ordered to return to East Tennessee.
He takes with him the men of his brigade on duty in the vicinity of
Rome. General Johnston wishes you to take all steps necessary in
the premises.
                          KINLOCH FALCONER,
                            Assistant Adjutant-General.

CONFIDENTIAL.]   HDQRS. GREENEVILLE, EAST TENN.,
                                  March 7, 1864.

General G. T. BEAUREGARD,
  Commanding South Carolina, Georgia, and Florida:
  GENERAL: It seems to be very necessary that we should advance
into Kentucky with the armies in the West, and it is a most difficult
problem to ascertain the practical means of doing so. The most
serious difficulty is the scarcity of forage and subsistence stores
throughout the State of Tennessee, and particularly the portion
through which our armies must pass.
  General Johnston can hardly get around the enemy by passing to
the west of Chattanooga, for the reason that the distance to be overcome by his army before he can get supplies is too great. He cannot pass it by the east and north for the same reason, and in addition
his flank and rear would be exposed from the moment that he left
Dalton.
  The trouble on his route is that the railroad cannot supply General
Lee's army and the small force that I now have here. This force of
itself in its present organization cannot make the move without great
danger of being met and overcome by accumulated numbers.
  The only means left us, in my judgment, is to mount my command
and throw it upon the railroad between Nashville and Louisville.
We could contend against any mounted force that the enemy could
bring against us, and in all probability destroy it. If the enemy's
army is withdrawn to operate against us we can avoid anything like
battle and probably break him up by destroying his trains, &c.
  This proposition has one very serious objection, which is the difficulty of getting animals to mount our men. I write this to ask if
you cannot, by reducing your transportation to the lowest practical
point, furnish us with 2,000 horses and mules. I think that I would
prefer mules for mounted infantry.
  I can see no other practical way by which we can move at all, and
if the enemy continues to hold his present lines we will soon be
obliged to abandon ours for want of supplies. Besides, the Northern
people will gain more confidence and the authorities more power as
long as they maintain their positions as they now do.
  Our troops are in fine condition and in fine spirits and eager for a
reasonable opportunity, but if they are allowed to remain in their
present positions and are brought down to half rations, as they soon
must be if we remain idle, I fear that we may become seriously demoralized, and of course the enemy, now demoralized, will gain
morale, courage, and confidence.

I am very anxious to make my move about the 1st of April, if I can get the number of animals that I require. I regret that I have not advised you of this sooner so as to give you more time for consideration, but the matter has been before the Government some time without approval or disapproval. I was in hopes that a decision would have been made long ago, so as to enable me to advise you in time to allow you more time to help me in.

I am, general, very respectfully and truly, your obedient servant,

J. LONGSTREET,
Lieutenant-General, Commanding.

HEADQUARTERS DEPARTMENT OF EAST TENNESSEE,
Greeneville, March 7, 1864.

Mr. W. H. BATES AND OTHERS,
Jonesborough :

GENTLEMEN : Your letter of the 4th instant to Lieutenant-General Longstreet has been received.

He directs me in reply to assure you of the regret with which he learns of the unlawful and improper conduct of any of the troops of his army, and you are right in believing that it is his desire that such license as you refer to should be effectually checked and the guilty parties punished. Such disposition will be made of the information given by you as may best apply a remedy for the evils set forth.

I am, gentlemen, very respectfully, your obedient servant,

G. M. SORREL,
Lieutenant-Colonel and Assistant Adjutant-General.

HEADQUARTERS DEPARTMENT OF EAST TENNESSEE,
Greeneville, March 7, 1864.

Col. H. L. GILTNER,
Comdg. Cav. Brigade (through Maj. Gen. S. B. Buckner) :

The commanding general desires you to send out scouts to the flank and rear of the enemy, to ascertain what force he has at Mossy Creek and what there is at Strawberry Plains. The information should be as complete and accurate as possible, and is desired as soon as possible.

I am, colonel, very respectfully, your most obedient servant,

G. M. SORREL,
Lieutenant-Colonel, Assistant Adjutant-General.

(A similar copy of same date was sent to General Vaughn.)

DALTON, *March 7, 1864.*

Lieutenant-General LONGSTREET,
Greeneville, Tenn. :

Yes is the answer to your cipher. The enemy's forces occupy the Ringgold Gap.

J. E. JOHNSTON.

DALTON, *March 7*, 1864.

General WHEELER :

Have you any information as to the passes in Taylor's Ridge, north and east of Cleveland, and whether the enemy are holding or observing these. I congratulate you on your late success.

Respectfully, your obedient servant,

W. W. MACKALL,
Brigadier-General.

———

HEADQUARTERS ARMIES CONFEDERATE STATES,
Richmond, March 7, 1864.

General JOSEPH E. JOHNSTON,
Commanding Army of Tennessee:

GENERAL : Since my letter of the 4th instant I have seen the returns from your command and find your artillery organization is entirely changed from what I left it.

My tabular report, with recommendation for the appointment of field officers, I am told at the Adjutant-General's Office, was sent to you after I left the army for your approval and has not since been returned. Let me suggest that you attend to this matter immediately. It will be as well, too, for you to take measures to secure horses as soon as possible, and without waiting for action here, as I am confident but little can be done.

Should General Pendleton not remain with you I hardly know who to suggest. Lovell was one of the best artillery officers in the old service, a good judge and fond of good horses, which is a qualification Alexander is specially deficient in. J. G. Martin, now a brigadier in North Carolina, was a good artillery officer in the old service. So was Lieutenant-Colonel De Lagnel, now on ordnance duty here.

All diligence should be used by your staff department in getting forward supplies and in preparing your transportation and bridge train. The enemy is not prepared for us, and if we can strike him a blow before he recovers success is almost certain. The plan which is proposed has long been my favorite, and I trust our efforts may give you the means to accomplish what I have ardently desired but never had the ability to undertake.

Communicate your wants to me freely, and I will do all I can to give you strength and efficiency. We must necessarily encounter privations and hardships and run some risk, but the end will justify the means.

Very respectfully, general, your obedient servant,

BRAXTON BRAGG,
General.

———

GENERAL ORDERS, }   HEADQUARTERS HOOD'S CORPS,
     No. 36. }   *Dalton, March 7*, 1864.

I. The attention of division and brigade commanders is called to the evil results that may follow from their officers and men having wrong impressions in regard to being flanked by the enemy ; much care should be taken to instruct them in this matter.

II. A division commander occupying the extreme flank of a line of battle should, if attacked on the extreme flank, change front of such portion of his line as may be necessary to repel it and promptly notify the corps commander, that assistance may be sent him. In like manner a brigade commander, if thus attacked, should change the front of one or more of his regiments, promptly notifying the division commander, that he may make the necessary dispositions and communicate the facts to the corps commander.

III. The importance of holding all ground taken from the enemy cannot be overestimated, as to relinquish it invariably demoralizes not only the troops immediately engaged but all others cognizant of the fact, and hence troops should never retire from the field for any purpose whatever, even to replenish ammunition (much of which can be obtained from our own and the enemy's wounded and dead), without authority from the corps and division commanders; as to do so would be second only to withdrawing without having fired a shot.

IV. Firing on the enemy at long range should never be permitted, since its lack of effectiveness often gives encouragement instead of causing demoralization, as a well-directed fire at short range is certain to do. In receiving an attack the enemy should be permitted to come close enough to enable our men to select the man they fire at, and in making an attack our fire should be held until it can be delivered with deadly effect, and, if practicable, should be followed by a determined charge, as it is all-important to break the enemy's line, not merely for the encouragement it gives our men but the demoralization and confusion that it forces upon him. Every officer and man should understand that in long-range fighting the Yankees are our equals, but at close quarters we are vastly superior to them. The history of the war abundantly proves that they have never repulsed a determined and well-sustained charge.

V. Another point to be observed in making an attack is that the troops when advancing in line of battle should not be moved at the double-quick or in any way be fatigued before engaging the enemy, that they may be in the best possible condition for pressing him and improving any advantages which may be gained.

By command of Lieutenant-General Hood:

ARCHER ANDERSON,
Assistant Adjutant-General.

RICHMOND, VA., *March 7*, 1864.

Lieut. Gen. L. POLK, *Demopolis:*

It is of the first importance that we should have additional cavalry for the protection of Richmond. The President relies on you to send here promptly seven independent companies of Mississippi cavalry to add to the Mississippi Jeff Davis Legion, and as many independent Alabama companies as you can spare. I urge your exertions on this subject.

S. COOPER,
Adjutant and Inspector General.

GENERAL ORDERS, }　　HEADQUARTERS FORREST'S CAVALRY,
　No. 12.　　　 }　　　　*Columbus, Miss., March* 7, 1864.

The troops of this command will be organized as follows :*

First Brigade, Brig. Gen. R. V. Richardson commanding: Seventh

---

* Artillery not accounted for.

Tennessee Regiment, Colonel Duckworth ; Twelfth Tennessee Regiment, Colonel Green ; Thirteenth Tennessee Regiment, Colonel Neely ; Fourteenth Tennessee Regiment, Colonel Stewart.

Second Brigade, Col. R. McCulloch commanding : Second Missouri Regiment ; Willis' battalion ; First Mississippi Partisans ; Fifth Mississippi Regiment ; Eighteenth Mississippi Battalion ; Nineteenth Mississippi Battalion ; McDonald's battalion.

Third Brigade, Colonel Thompson commanding : Third Kentucky Regiment ; Seventh Kentucky Regiment ; Eighth Kentucky Regiment ; Faulkner's Kentucky regiment ; Forrest's Alabama regiment.

Fourth Brigade, Col. T. H. Bell commanding : Second Tennessee [Barteau's] Regiment ; Fifteenth Tennessee Regiment, Colonel Russell ; Sixteenth Tennessee Regiment, Colonel Wilson commanding.

II. The First and Second Brigades will be organized into a division, and will be known and designated as First Division of Forrest's cavalry, Brig. Gen. J. R. Chalmers commanding.

III. The Third and Fourth Brigades will be organized into a division, and will be known and designated as Second Division, Forrest's cavalry, Brig. Gen. A. Buford commanding.

By command of Major-General Forrest :

. J. P. STRANGE,
Assistant Adjutant-General.

DEMOPOLIS, *March* 8, 1864.

General COOPER :

Your dispatch of yesterday regarding cavalry received. There are no such detailed (detached) companies in Mississippi and Alabama that can be relied on for the purpose indicated. I suggest that you allow me to send instead a brigade of two full regiments with their brigade commander, General Clanton. He is an experienced cavalry officer, very efficient and enterprising. One regiment is well organized and officered, the other just formed and without field officers. If this substitution is agreeable to the President I will nominate as field officers Major Thomas and Major Huger, of General Withers' staff, as colonel and lieutenant-colonel, and Major Ball, of General Forney's staff, as major.

Those are all officers of high promise—the first and last graduates of West Point, the other from one of the State military academies. Such a brigade could be relied upon. It is in the northeastern part of Alabama, and ten days nearer than any force I have ; they could march to Atlanta and go thence by rail.

They have with them a field battery of four guns. The men and horses might and should be sent with the brigade ; the guns and harness might be supplied elsewhere if necessary. I could add another regiment to follow them ; two in a few days if necessary.

L. POLK,
Lieutenant-General.

CONFIDENTIAL.]   HDQRS. ARMY OF NORTHERN VIRGINIA,
March 8, 1864.

Lieut. Gen. JAMES LONGSTREET.
Commanding, &c., Greeneville, Tenn. :

GENERAL : I was in Richmond when your letter arrived, and have been so much occupied by the recent movements of the enemy that it is only to-day that I can reply. I think the enemy's great effort will be in the West, and we must concentrate our strength there to meet them. I see no possibility of mounting your command without stripping all others of animals and rendering them immovable. If horses could be obtained for you, where are the forage and equipments to be procured? The former is not to be had nearer than Georgia. It could not be furnished by the railroad, and I do not think equipments could be impressed through the country. If you and Johnston could unite and move into Middle Tennessee, where I am told provisions and forage can be had, it would cut the armies at Chattanooga and Knoxville in two and draw them from those points where either portion could be struck at in succession as opportunity offered. This appears to me at this distance the most feasible plan. Can it be accomplished? By covering your fronts well with your cavalry, Johnston could move quietly and rapidly through Benton, across the Hiwassee, and then push forward in the direction of Kingston, while you, taking such a route as to be safe from a flank attack, would join him at or after his crossing the Tennessee River. The two commands upon reaching Sparta would be in position to select their future course; would necessitate the evacuation of Chattanooga and Knoxville, and by rapidity and skill unite on either army. I am not sufficiently acquainted with the country to do more than indicate the general plan. The particular routes, passages of rivers, &c., you and Johnston must ascertain and choose. The condition of roads, &c., may oblige you to pass through the western portion of North Carolina, but this you can soon ascertain, if you do not already know, as well as the distances each column would have to traverse before uniting, their point of junction, time of marching, &c. The agents of the commissary department tell me there is an abundance of provisions and forage in Middle Tennessee, which is corroborated by individuals professing to know that country. But this should be investigated, too. It is also believed by those acquainted with the people that upon the entrance of the army into that country that its ranks will be recruited by the men from Tennessee and Kentucky who have left it. A victory gained there will open the country to you to the Ohio.

Study the subject, communicate with Johnston, and endeavor to accomplish it, or something better. We cannot now pause. I will endeavor to do something here to occupy them if I cannot do more. I hope Alexander has joined you with his new commission. The promotion of the other officers of artillery was ordered, as proposed during my last visit to Richmond. Walton retains his former position in the Washington Battalion.

Wishing you all success and happiness, I am, ver truly,

R. E. LEE,
General.

———

RICHMOND, VA.,
March 8, 1864.

Brig. Gen. J. A. SMITH,
Comdg. Brig. Texas Vols., Cleburne's Div., Army of Tenn.:

GENERAL: In response to a memorial of the officers of the Texas brigade under your command, praying to be returned to their commands in the Trans-Mississippi Department, submitted by the Texas delegation, the Secretary of War directs me, through you, to communicate the views of the Government respecting these troops.

The difficulty of assembling the commands where their services were most needed has heretofore prevented it, and the necessities for their service in Tennessee at this time are not less urgent than heretofore.

The Government sympathizes deeply with the wish expressed on the part of these gallant troops, whose invariable good conduct, courage, and self-sacrificing spirit entitle them to the warmest commendations and gratitude of the Government and the country; and it is not doubted that they will appreciate and yield to the public need for their continuance in their present positions, where they have already rendered inestimable service.

If the exigencies of the service permitted, the wishes of the memorialists would be cheerfully complied with, but their own sense of duty, as well as the immeasurable injury which the cause must suffer by acceding to their petition, will, it is confidently believed, furnish sufficient inducement to these troops to cheerfully acquiesce in the wishes of the Government.

I am, general, very respectfully, your obedient servant,
SAMUEL W. MELTON,
Major and Assistant Adjutant-General.

HEADQUARTERS DEPARTMENT OF WESTERN VIRGINIA,
Dublin, March 8, 1864.

Lieutenant-General LONGSTREET,
Commanding Department of East Tennessee:

GENERAL: Under the orders of the honorable Secretary of War, I am charged with guarding the salt-works just on the border of Washington and Smyth Counties and within the limits of my department. A glance at the map will, however, show you that the main approaches to this point are through the three gaps in the mountain ridge dividing the counties of Russell and Washington, and within your command. I therefore respectfully ask that you will inform me whether you have made any arrangements for picketing these roads and obtaining early information of the approach of the enemy upon these roads, and, if so, what they are. The importance of the salt-works at this juncture will be readily perceived, and I shall be very glad to receive any information that you may deem useful, and to have your co-operation in guarding that point from raids of the enemy.

Very respectfully, general, your obedient servant,
JOHN C. BRECKINRIDGE,
Major-General.

P. S.—I have only one regiment of infantry (600 effectives) and some artillery at Saltville.

OFFICE CHIEF COMMISSARY,
Savannah, March 8, 1864.

Col. L. B. NORTHROP,
Commissary-General, Richmond, Va.:

COLONEL: Under date March 2, Major Cummings informed me that the requirements of General Johnston's army are 70,000 rations daily, besides 15,000 rations more for posts, hospitals, &c., making in all a daily call for 85,000 rations. According to General Hardee's information to me personally, and that of other officers just down from that army, there were but 40,000 men present the other day with their standards. There have been so many abuses in over-drawing, through incorrect returns, that I desire these conflicting statements to be laid before the Secretary of War, in order that a special report may be furnished me by the adjutant and inspector general of General Johnston's army, so that we may have some check against overissues. We have no surplus on hand to waste.

Yours, most respectfully,

J. L. LOCKE,
Major and Chief Commissary.

[Indorsements.]

OFFICE COMMISSARY-GENERAL,
March 16. 1864.

Respectfully referred to the Adjutant-General for investigation as to the correctness of this.

L. B. NORTHROP,
Commissary-General.

ADJUTANT AND INSPECTOR GENERAL'S OFFICE,
March 29. 1864.

Respectfully referred to General J. E. Johnston, who is requested to cause this matter to be investigated and to report the result.

The returns of the Army of Tennessee show that 85.000 rations daily are more than necessary for the subsistence of that army.

By order of Adjutant and Inspector General :

H. L. CLAY,
Assistant Adjutant-General.

DALTON, *April* 8, 1864.

Respectfully referred to Lieutenant-General Hardee, who will please inform General Johnston whether his name has been properly used for this report.

W. W. MACKALL,
Brigadier-General.

CIRCULAR.]   HDQRS. DEPARTMENT OF EAST TENNESSEE,
Greeneville, March 8, 1864.

I am directed to notify you in the temporary absence of the lieutenant-general commanding the command of the Department devolves upon Maj. Gen. S. B. Buckner.

I am, general, very respectfully, your obedient servant,

G. M. SORREL,
Lieutenant-Colonel and Assistant Adjutant-General.

GENERAL ORDERS, }   HEADQUARTERS,
    No. 42.   {   *Demopolis, Ala., March* 8, 1864.

All officers and men in this department who have been assigned to duty on surgeon's certificate of disability for field service are ordered to report in writing to these headquarters without delay, giving their names, commands, and the nature of the service to which they are assigned, and stating the date of their assignment and by whose authority made.

By command of Lieutenant-General Polk :

.THOS. M. JACK,
Assistant Adjutant-General.

GREENEVILLE, *March 9,* 1864.

General S. COOPER,
Adjutant and Inspector General :

There is not corn enough here to feed the transportation animals of the Hampton Legion from this to Asheville, and nothing on the road. Please send us corn and meat enough to take us somewhere, unless we can be supplied to make a campaign from here.

J. LONGSTREET,
Lieutenant-General.

RICHMOND, *March* 9, 1864.

Lieutenant-General LONGSTREET,
Commanding, &c., Greeneville, Tenn.:

GENERAL : I have had the honor to receive your note of the 5th instant, and reply without delay. Fully realizing the importance of. and sympathizing with, the views you entertain as to the importance of the campaign soon to open, it is painful to me to feel conscious that this Department cannot accumulate such supplies as will place our armies in the field under the most favored circumstances. I am willing to be stimulated to the discharge of my duties to the full extent, and especially, general, by one who has so much at heart the true interests of the country as yourself. As our objects are the same, I trust our conclusions will not differ when they are based upon the facts of the case. I confess that I was not a little disconcerted when I first learned that it was necessary to ship corn to your command. This corn practically comes from Georgia whether sent from a depot in Virginia or not, for Virginia is out of corn except to a limited extent. Last year at this time no corn was brought to Virginia from any point beyond North Carolina, and the army was subsisted on wheat flour. Now nearly all the corn used for horses is brought from Georgia, and the Subsistence Department has consumed all the flour and relies upon corn to be ground up into meal for the bread of the army. To supply all this will require all the available rolling-stock of all the roads between this and Georgia, without allowing for the frequent disturbance caused by the movement of troops and raids of the enemy, &c.

You perceive, therefore, what a task there is before us, and how impossible it is to accumulate supplies at points so distant (by circuitous railroads) from the point of production. Supplies of forage to a limited extent are now going forward to you, but I replied to your dispatch in such plain terms because I feared you might be deceived as to our ability to accomplish what you desire.

If the passenger trains are all stopped what becomes of the furloughed soldiers, conscripts, &c., coming into the army every day by hundreds ? I thank you, general, for writing to me freely. I will always be pleased to hear from you, and will respond to your calls whenever it is possible.

A. R. LAWTON,
Quartermaster-General.

———

HDQRS. DEPARTMENT OF WESTERN VIRGINIA,
March 9, 1864.

General S. COOPER,
Adjutant and Inspector General, C. S. Army:

GENERAL: I have this morning been informed by Colonel Browne, commanding the Forty-fifth Virginia Regiment at Saltville, that his regiment and the few remaining troops at that point are claimed by Lieutenant-General Longstreet as belonging to his command. I presume the claim is founded on the fact that Saltville is just on the line between the counties of Smyth and Washington, of which the latter has been assigned to the Department of East Tennessee.

I am informed by my assistant adjutant-general, Major Stringfellow, who has been on duty here since December, 1862, that in the special order of the Department assigning Major-General Jones to this department, issued 25th November, 1862 (a copy of which cannot now be found), that the line of the Virginia and Tennessee Railroad and the salt-works were specially mentioned as objects of his particular care and attention. He further informs me that although the six southwestern counties of Virginia, including Washington, were cut off from this department long before General Jones left it, up to this time no claim has been made by commanding officers of the Department of East Tennessee that Saltville was regarded as under their command; that Generals Jones and Buckner, impressed with the inconvenience arising from having so important a point directly on the dividing line of their respective commands, entered into a correspondence with each other and with Richmond for the purpose of having it distinctly decided who should be held responsible for its safety, with the understanding that the officer to whom this point should be particularly intrusted should ask for a strong local force for its defense. Major Stringfellow says that he has no knowledge of the distinct settlement of this question by the Department on that occasion, but that General Jones always continued to regard himself as mainly responsible for the safety of Saltville, and was strengthened in this opinion by a telegram from the honorable Secretary of War, in reply to one from General Jones, asking whether he should assist General Buckner with troops from Saltville, in which the Secretary directed General Jones to be governed by his own judgment, adding, however, that the protection of the salt-works was his special care.

Under these circumstances I respectfully submit the question for your decision, with the request that it may be forwarded at an early day.

Respectfully, your obedient servant,

JOHN C. BRECKINRIDGE,
Major-General.

P. S.—In case Saltville shall be placed under the control of the commander of the Department of East Tennessee, I respectfully request that the troops now there who belong to this department may report to me here. Their services will be much needed. Many of the troops belonging to this department are beyond its limits, and those within it are hardly adequate for its defense.

I again respectfully request that the boundaries of this department to the east and south may be defined.

. Respectfully, your obedient servant,
                    JOHN C. BRECKINRIDGE,
                                Major-General.

[Indorsement.]

General COOPER:

Saltville is placed on the map in Washington County, which, under the last order defining the Department of East Tennessee, would bring it within General Longstreet's command.

The order assigning General Jones does not mention Saltville but does the railroad, a copy of which was furnished General Breckinridge.
                    JNO. WITHERS,
                    Assistant Adjutant-General.

                    DALTON, *March* 9, 1864.
General BRAGG, *Richmond:*

Our intelligence from Mississippi is to the effect that Sherman's troops have gone to Vicksburg and transports have been sent down the river to that point. Are they destined for Mobile or Chattanooga? I think the latter.
                    J. E. JOHNSTON.

                    RICHMOND, VA., *March* 9, 1864.
Lieut. Gen. L. POLK, *Demopolis, Ala.:*

Maj. Gen. M. L. Smith has been assigned to duty as Chief of the Engineer Bureau at Richmond during the absence of Major-General Gilmer. You will order him to report in person immediately.
                    S. COOPER,
                    Adjutant and Inspector General.

                    DEMOPOLIS, *March* 9, 1864.
His Excellency President DAVIS :

I call your attention to a communication from headquarters to General Cooper, of the 3d instant,* also to another to the Secretary of War, of the 29th ultimo,† and urge the suggestions contained in these as indispensable to the order, security, and efficient administration of this department. I have been in command now long enough to comprehend and appreciate its wants and to perceive its weakness, and to be held responsible for its management I should be clothed with all the power necessary to success.
                    L. POLK,
                    Lieutenant-General.

---

*See p. 580.   †See Part II, p. 814.

HDQRS. FIRST DIV., FORREST'S CAVALRY DEPARTMENT,
Mayhew Station, March 9, 1864.
Lieutenant-Colonel WILLIS,
    Commanding Second Brigade:

COLONEL : The brigadier-general commanding directs that your command be supplied with 40 rounds of ammunition to each effective man and four days' rations, with as little delay as possible, and that it be held in readiness to move at a moment's notice as soon as these supplies are obtained.

When a movement is made no wagons will be taken except those belonging to brigade and regimental headquarters and a sufficient number to transport the cooking utensils of the command. The ordnance wagons will be sent to Columbus to be put in complete repair, and the others will be parked near this place in charge of a proper officer. The Eighteenth Mississippi Battalion will be sent forward to-morrow to Panola to collect forage and build a pontoon bridge across the Tallahatchie. The Second Arkansas Regiment will be detached from the brigade, and will report at these headquarters as provost guard. The dismounted men and those with disabled horses will be encamped near this place but a distance from the wagon train, under the charge of an efficient officer, who will enforce a strict discipline among them.

The order in regard to roll-calls and drills will be strictly carried out, and a proportion of the cooking utensils will be left with these men.

I am, colonel, your obedient servant,

W. A. GOODMAN,
Assistant Adjutant-General.

MOBILE, ALA., *March 9, 1864.*
Hon. JAMES A. SEDDON,
    Secretary of War, Richmond, Va.:

SIR : I have devoted the past sixteen days to the inspection, supervision, and direction of the defenses of this city. I have also prepared in great detail precise instructions for the government of the engineer officers in the further construction of works designed to give greater security to Mobile.

Having completed this labor, I start this morning, with the consent and approval of Major-General Maury, commanding Department of the Gulf, on my return to Savannah, Ga., to give by personal control a proper direction to the defenses of that city, as they are far from being as complete as they ought to be.

From the most reliable information we can obtain here it is not probable that the enemy can attack this place with land forces at any early day. Every effort is being made to give additional strength to the outer line of harbor defenses, which can be made, in my opinion, strong enough by the batteries under construction, aided by sawyers, torpedoes, and ropes, to keep the enemy's fleet outside the lower bay. If at the same time a show of naval strength be made on our part, I will feel the greater confidence that the enemy will not attempt to force the passage. General Maury hopes to have such support from Admiral Buchanan, commanding the naval forces on this station.

I am, sir, very respectfully, your obedient servant,

J. F. GILMER,
Major-General and Chief Engineer Bureau.

SPECIAL ORDERS, }   HEADQUARTERS,
     No. 69.   }   Demopolis, Ala., March 9, 1864.

*   *   *   *   *   *   *

XIII. Brigadier-General Cockrell, commanding French's division, will report for duty with his command, until further orders, to Major-General Loring.

XIV. Major-General Withers will order the Fifty-fourth Alabama Regiment to Montgomery, Ala.

By command of Lieutenant-General Polk:

THOS. M. JACK,
Assistant Adjutant-General.

SPECIAL ORDERS, }   HEADQUARTERS FORREST'S CAVALRY,
     No. 29.   }   Columbus, Miss., March 9, 1864.

*   *   *   *   *   *   *

VI. Brigadier-General Chalmers, commanding division, will order Colonel Duckworth and Lieutenant-Colonel Crews to prepare their commands without delay with five days' rations of hard bread and bacon and two days' rations of corn bread, with 60 rounds of ammunition to the man, 40 to be carried in cartridge-boxes, and 20 rounds each to the man to be taken on pack-mules. The pack-saddles can be procured from Major Severson, chief quartermaster; the mules to be taken from the wagons of their commands. All dismounted men and disabled horses will be left to move with the division train. They will move to Okolona, crossing Chuckatouchee at Ellis' Bridge, and will report to these headquarters at what time they will be in readiness to move.

VII. Brig. Gen. J. R. Chalmers is relieved from duty with this command, and will report to Lieutenant-General Polk for orders.

By order of Major-General Forrest:

J. P. STRANGE,
Assistant Adjutant-General.

Abstract from return of the Army of Tennessee, General Joseph E. Johnston, C. S. Army, commanding, March 10, 1864; headquarters Dalton, Ga.

Command.	Present for duty.		Effective total present.	Aggregate present.	Aggregate present and absent.	Pieces of artillery.
	Officers.	Men.				
General staff...................................	16	....	....	16	16	......
Hardee's corps:						
Staff......................................	13	....	....	13	14	......
Cheatham's division a .... ·	547	4,170	4,013	5,604	8,597	......
Cleburne's division......................	493	5,374	5,241	6,785	9,932	......
Walker's division	368	4,824	4,742	6,006	9,299	......
Bate's division	384	3,538	3,410	4,437	7,132	......
Total...	1,805	17,906	17,406	22,845	34,974	......

a Cheatham's division, which was ordered to Lieutenant-General Polk, has returned to this army, since last report.

Abstract from return of the Army of Tennessee, &c.—Continued.

Command.	Present for duty.		Effective total present.	Aggregate present.	Aggregate present and absent.	Pieces of artillery.
	Officers.	Men.				
Hood's corps:						
Staff..	21	....	....	21	23	......
Hindman's division..............................	498	5,704	5,565	6,963	12,038	......
Stewart's division..	438	5,184	5,054	6,448	11,646	......
Stevenson's division............................	486	6,196	6,054	7,538	10,951	......
Total...	1,433	17,084	16,673	20,970	34,658	....
Battalion Engineer troops.....	17	417	414	494	615	......
1st Louisiana Infantry (Regulars)	6	111	107	129	255	......
Total infantry	3,277	35,518	34,600	44,454	70,518	......
Cavalry :						
Wheeler's cavalry corps	434	4,604	4,512	6,247	11,007	......
Escort army headquarters	7	152	152	171	240	......
Escorts Hardee's corps..........................	15	195	194	250	366	......
Escorts Hood's corps	5	106	104	183	287	......
1st Louisiana Cavalry *b*........................	....	....	....	....	....	......
Total cavalry	461	5,057	4,962	6,851	11,900	....
Artillery :						
Hardee's corps.................................	52	1,061	1,085	1,269	1,680	45
Hood's corps...................................	38	889	857	1,060	1,277	36
Wheeler's corps	7	189	185	215	282	10
Reserve regiment...............................	44	803	769	957	1,206	36
Total artillery	141	2,942	2,846	3,501	4,395	127
Grand total Army of Tennessee................	3,879	43,517	42,408	54,806	86,813	127

b First Louisiana Cavalry ordered to the Mississippi Department.

Abstract from return of the Army, Department Alabama, Mississippi, and East Louisiana, Lieut. Gen. Leonidas Polk, C. S. Army, commanding, March 10, 1864 ; headquarters Demopolis, Ala.

Command.	Present for duty.		Effective total.	Aggregate present.	Aggregate present and absent.
	Officers.	Men.			
General staff....................................	10	....	....	10	11
Loring's division :					
Infantry.......................................	420	4,335	4,284	5,510	9,465
Artillery......................................	24	423	405	493	829
Total..	444	4,758	4,689	6,003	10,294
French's division :					
Infantry.......................................	236	2,315	2,286	2,959	4,938
Artillery......................................	11	177	168	201	271
Total..	247	2,492	2,454	3,160	5,209
Post of Demopolis	38	335	335	386	426
Post of Selma...................................	22	174	174	216	262
Post of Cahaba..................................	37	254	254	351	501
Engineer troops.................................	16	84	84	118	156
Paroled and exchanged prisoners *a*.............	36	289	278	878	637
Lee's division of cavalry and escort *b*...	656	7,729	7,655	10,040	16,734
Artillery in Ruggles' command...................	11	74	73	110	137
Grand total *c*.................................	1,517	16,189	15,996	20,772	34,367

a No report from General Withers.   *b* No report from General Forrest.   *c* Artillery, 26 field pieces.

Organization of troops in the Department of Alabama, Mississippi, and East Louisiana, commanded by Lieut. Gen. Leonidas Polk, C. S. Army, March 10, 1864.

LORING'S DIVISION.

Maj. Gen. WILLIAM W. LORING.

Adams' Brigade.

Brig. Gen. JOHN ADAMS.

6th Mississippi, Col. Robert Lowry.
14th Mississippi, Col. George W. Abert.
15th Mississippi, Col. M. Farrell.
20th Mississippi, Col. William N. Brown.
23d Mississippi, Col. Joseph M. Wells.
26th Mississippi, Col. Arthur E. Reynolds.
1st Confederate Battalion, Lieut. Col. George H. Forney.

Featherston's Brigade.

Brig. Gen. WINFIELD S. FEATHERSTON.

3d Mississippi, Col. T. A. Mellon.
22d Mississippi, Col. Frank Schaller.
31st Mississippi, Col. J. A. Orr.
33d Mississippi, Lieut. Col. J. L. Drake.
1st Mississippi Battalion Sharpshooters, Maj. J. M. Stigler.

Scott's Brigade.

Col. THOMAS M. SCOTT.

55th Alabama, Col. John Snodgrass.
57th Alabama, Col. C. J. L. Cunningham.
9th Arkansas, Col. Isaac L. Dunlop.
12th Louisiana, Lieut. Col. N. L. Nelson.

Division Artillery.

Charpentier's (Alabama) battery, Capt. Stephen Charpentier.
Lookout (Tennessee) Battery, Capt. Robert L. Barry.
Pointe Coupée (Louisiana) Battery, Capt. Alcide Bouanchaud.
Reserve (Mississippi) Battery, Capt. James J. Cowan.
Withers' (Mississippi) Artillery, Company A, Capt. William T. Ratliff.

FRENCH'S DIVISION.

Ector's Brigade.

Brig. Gen. MATTHEW D. ECTOR.

29th North Carolina, Lieut. Col. Bacchus S. Proffitt.
9th Texas, Maj. J. H. McReynolds.
10th Texas Cavalry (dismounted), Col. C. R. Earp.
14th Texas Cavalry (dismounted). Col. John L. Camp.
32d Texas Cavalry (dismounted), Lieut. Col. James A. Weaver.

Cockrell's Brigade

Brig. Gen. FRANCIS M. COCKRELL.

1st and 3d Missouri Cavalry (dismounted), Lieut. Col. D. Todd Samuels.
1st and 4th Missouri Infantry, Col. A. C. Riley.
2d and 6th Missouri Infantry, Col. P. C. Flournoy.
3d and 5th Missouri Infantry, Col. James McCown.

Division Artillery.

Hoskins' (Mississippi) battery, Capt. James A. Hoskins.
1st Missouri Battery, Capt. Henry Guibor.

RUGGLES' COMMAND.

Rice's (Tennessee) battery, Capt. T. W. Rice.

CAVALRY CORPS.

Maj. Gen. STEPHEN D. LEE.

JACKSON'S DIVISION.

Brig. Gen. WILLIAM H. JACKSON.

First Brigade.

Col. PETER B. STARKE.

1st Mississippi, Col. R. A. Pinson.
28th Mississippi, Col. Peter B. Starke.
Ballentine's (Mississippi) Regiment, Col. John G. Ballentine.
Escort (Louisiana) Company, Capt. Junius Y. Webb.
Georgia Battery, Capt. Edward Croft.

Adams' Brigade.

Brig. Gen. WIRT ADAMS.

11th Arkansas Mounted Infantry, Col. John Griffith.
14th Confederate, Capt. Josephus R. Quin.
9th Louisiana, Capt. E. A. Scott.
4th (2d) Mississippi, Maj. J. L. Harris.
4th Mississippi, Maj. Thomas R. Stockdale.
Wood's (Mississippi) Regiment, Col. Robert C. Wood, jr.
9th Tennessee Battalion, Maj. James H. Akin.
Mississippi Battery, Capt. Calvit Roberts.

Second Brigade.

Col. LAWRENCE S. ROSS.

1st Texas Legion, Col. E. R. Hawkins.
3d Texas, Col. Hinchie P. Mabry.
6th Texas, Col. Jack Wharton.
9th Texas, Col. Dud. W. Jones.
Escort (Texas) Company, Lieut. Rush L. Elkin.
Missouri Battery, Capt. Houston King.

Ferguson's Brigade.

Brig. Gen. SAMUEL W. FERGUSON.

2d Alabama, Col. R. G. Earle.
56th Alabama, Col. William Boyles.
12th Mississippi, Col. W. M. Inge.
2d Tennessee (Barteau's regiment), Lieut. Col. George H. Morton.
South Carolina Battery, Capt. John Waties.

CHALMERS' COMMAND.

Brig. Gen. JAMES R. CHALMERS.

First Brigade.

Col. W. F. SLEMONS.

2d Arkansas, Col. W. F. Slemons.
3d Mississippi (State), Col. John McGuirk.
5th Mississippi, Col. James Z. George.
7th Tennessee, Col. William L. Duckworth.
Mississippi Battery, Capt. J. M. McLendon.

Second Brigade.

Col. ROBERT McCULLOCH.

1st Mississippi Partisan Rangers, Lieut. Col. L. B. Hovis.
18th Mississippi Battalion, Lieut. Col. Alexander H. Chalmers.
19th Mississippi Battalion, Lieut. Col. William L. Duff.
Willis' Texas Battalion, Lieut. Col. Leonidas Willis.
2d Missouri Regiment, Lieut. Col. R. A. McCulloch.
Mississippi Battery, Lieut. H. C. Holt.

General Polk's escort (Louisiana company), Capt. Leeds Greenleaf.
General Lee's escort (Georgia company), Capt. Thomas M. Nelson.

DALTON, *March* 10, 1864.

Lieutenant-General POLK,
Demopolis:

Information of Sherman's movements is important to me. You will oblige me greatly by giving it as it comes to you.

J. E. JOHNSTON.

DEMOPOLIS, *March* 10, 1864.

General J. E. JOHNSTON,
Dalton, Ga.:

At last accounts Sherman had reached Vicksburg with his army, having retreated in haste and suffered loss in transportation and troops from the vigorous blows of Lee's cavalry. He suffered at Yazoo City from an attack upon that place also by the joint forces of Ross and Richardson. I hear that empty transports came down Mississippi River a few days ago, supposed to take Sherman's army up stream. I will keep you advised of his movements as they reach me.

L. POLK,
Lieutenant-General.

DALTON, GA.,
March 10, 1864.

Hon. JAMES A. SEDDON,
Secretary of War:

MY DEAR SIR: I inclose to you two letters, one sent to the President and one to General Bragg. You well know how often I have expressed my views to you, and I inclose to you the within so as to get your assistance, provided you think it best. I believe you feel that I have the interest of my country at heart, and I know you are confident that I have written these letters in thorough friendship and good feeling. I am an earnest friend to the President and am ever willing to express to him my ideas in regard to the approaching campaign. There is more depending upon our coming campaign than ever before, and I want the troops concentrated. General Grant's great point is to overpower by numbers. We should be prepared to meet him. He will never move upon us until he has an overwhelming force. I am very much pleased with the condition of our army, as I expressed to the President. After the enemy concentrates his forces our chance of success will be in having an opportunity to strike him in case he should divide his forces. But we have a sufficient number of troops, if thrown together, to defeat his entire army, and I think it all-important that we should make certain of it. I hope you will think of this matter, and I shall be delighted to hear from you.

Believe me, most sincerely, your friend,

J. B. HOOD.

[Inclosure No. 1.]

DALTON, GA., *March* 7, 1864.

His Excellency President JEFFERSON DAVIS:

MY DEAR SIR: I have delayed writing to you so as to allow myself time to see the condition of this army. On my arrival I found the enemy threatening our position. I was, however, delighted to find our troops anxious for battle. He withdrew after taking a look, and is now resting with his advance at Ringgold. I am exceedingly anxious, as I expressed to you before leaving Richmond, to have this army strengthened so as to enable us to move to the rear of the enemy and with a certainty of success. An addition of 10,000 or

15,000 men will allow us to advance. We can do so, anyhow, by uniting with Longstreet, but so much depends upon the success of our arms on this line I thoroughly appreciate the importance of collecting together all the forces we possibly can in order to destroy the army under Grant. We should march to the front as soon as possible, so as not to allow the enemy to concentrate and advance upon us. The addition of a few horses for our artillery will place this army in fine condition. It is well clothed, well fed, and the transportation is excellent and the greatest possible quantity required.

I feel that a move from this position, in sufficient force, will relieve our entire country. The troops under Generals Polk and Loring united with the forces here, and a junction being made with General Longstreet, will give us an army of 60,000 or 70,000 men, which, I think, should be sufficient to defeat and destroy all the Federals on this side of the Ohio River. I sincerely hope and trust that this opportunity may be given to drive the enemy beyond the limits of the Confederacy. I never before felt that we had it so thoroughly in our power. He is at present weak, and we are strong. His armies are far within our country, and the roads open to his rear, where we have a vast quantity of supplies. Our position in Virginia can be securely held by our brave troops under General Lee, which will allow us to march in force from our center, the vital point of every nation.

You find, Mr. President, that I speak with my whole heart, as I do upon all things in which I am so deeply interested. God knows I have the interest of my country at heart, and I feel in speaking to you that I am so doing to one who thoroughly appreciates and understands my feelings. I am eager for us to take the initiative, but fear we will not do so unless our army is increased.

I am happy to inform you that my health was never so good.

The divisions of Stewart, Stevenson, and Hindman make up my corps. You perceive I have all the untried troops of this army ; I hope, however, to do good work.

My prayer is that you may be spared to our country, and that we may be successful in the coming campaign.

Please present my kindest regards to Mrs. Davis and Miss Maggie, and believe me, with great respect, your friend and obedient servant,

J. B. HOOD.

[Inclosure No. 2.]

DALTON, GA.,
March 10, 1864.

General BRAXTON BRAGG,
Richmond, Va. :

MY DEAR GENERAL: Knowing the deep interest you feel in this army and in our success, I am prompted to call your attention to a few important facts. We have here about 40,000 men of all arms of the service. The enemy in our front, I presume, has about 50,000. He will not offer to give battle till he is largely re-enforced, and I don't think many days will pass before Sherman will make a junction with him, as I see quite a large number of empty transports have passed down to Vicksburg.

It is all-important that we should know whether this army is to be strengthened or not. If not, I fear more of our territory will be given up to the enemy.   We shall be compelled to concentrate here sooner or later.   We can never relieve our country by crossing the Potomac, as my experience has taught me that whenever the attempt is made we will be defeated.

If we can get the troops now under Polk and Loring. and it is known that General Longstreet would be allowed to go with us to the rear of the enemy, I think we might feel certain of success.

I think the question is naturally divided into two parts : First, if we can concentrate and fall upon the enemy before he is ready we shall beat him badly and regain our lost territory ; second, if he masses his forces and we fail to do so we shall finally be forced back from our present position. After we are defeated I fear it will be too late for us to attempt to bring together our scattered forces, as there would not be a sufficient number to give new life to this army after another defeat.

.I take this to be our true condition, and I hope you will give it your earnest thought.   I have written this letter after observing matters here and much thought upon it.

I am, general, yours, most truly and sincerely,
J. B. HOOD.

DEMOPOLIS, *March* 10, 1864.
General COOPER,
Adjutant and Inspector General, Richmond :
I telegraphed you on the 8th in reply to yours of the 7th in regard to a force of cavalry for the special service you indicated.   As I have received no further instructions I fear my telegram may not have reached you.
L. POLK,
Lieutenant-General.

RICHMOND, VA.,
March 10, 1864.
Maj. Gen. JOHN H. FORNEY *(through General Polk):*
GENERAL : I am directed by the Adjutant and Inspector General to inform you, in response to your communication of February 27, 1864, requesting assignment to duty. that your gallantry and efficiency are highly estimated by the Department, but that there are at this time no less than 15 general officers unassigned, some of whom have long been waiting for orders and for whom there are no commands vacant suitable to their rank.

Under these circumstances the Department cannot assign you to a command at this time, but will take pleasure in doing so whenever the state of the service will admit of it.

Very respectfully, general, your obedient servant,
H. L. CLAY,
Assistant Adjutant-General.

DEMOPOLIS, *March* 10, 1864.
General FORREST,
Columbus. Miss. :
General Armstrong has orders to report to me.   Left La Grange to-day.   I will order him to report to you immediately on his arrival.

I have repeated my nominations of Bell and McCulloch and Russell for brigadiers. I will add Thompson. Keep me advised of your movements. Write me the reasons for relieving the officers named in your dispatch of to-day.

L. POLK,
Lieutenant-General.

HEADQUARTERS FORREST'S CAVALRY DEPARTMENT,
Columbus, March 10, 1864.

Col. T. M. JACK,
　　Assistant Adjutant-General:

COLONEL : If nothing occurs to prevent, will leave here on Monday next with General Buford's division and four small pieces of artillery. Will get from the First and Forty-third Mississippi Infantry about 100 horses. Will need 150 horses to complete the four batteries, and 150 more for mounting the three Kentucky regiments under Colonel Thompson. I have also about 200 men of Chalmers' and Buford's divisions without horses, most of whom lost their horses in the recent engagements with the enemy.

My scouts report six regiments of Federal cavalry moving from Memphis to Nashville, and that there are no Federals on the Memphis and Charleston Railroad east of Germantown. Scouting parties, however, are sent out daily.

Hurst is still reported in West Tennessee, and a portion of Jackson and Brownsville have been burned by his men.

Will order six companies of Colonel Forrest's regiment, under Captain Warren, to Marion County, Ala., to protect the foundries. &c., against tories and deserters. Will also send Colonel McCulloch, commanding Chalmers' division, with the brigade now here with orders to divide his command and breast the country from this toward Memphis and Panola, arresting all stragglers and deserters.

I am, very respectfully, your obedient servant,

N. B. FORREST,
Major-General.

HEADQUARTERS FORREST'S CAVALRY DEPARTMENT,
Columbus, March 10, 1864.

Col. T. M. JACK,
　　Assistant Adjutant-General:

COLONEL : I have the honor respectfully to forward you a copy of letter received from Brig. Gen. James R. Chalmers, and to state that I have relieved him from duty with my command and ordered him to report to the lieutenant-general commanding for assignment. I am satisfied that I have not and shall not receive the co-operation of Brigadier-General Chalmers, and that matters of the smallest moment will continue, as they have heretofore done, to be a source of annoyance to myself and detrimental to the service, and, holding myself responsible to the proper authority for all orders I have or may hereafter issue, I deem it both necessary and beneficial that we should separate.

Hoping that the lieutenant-general commanding may be able to place Brigadier-General Chalmers in a position more congenial to his taste and wishes than the one he now occupies, I am, very respectfully, your obedient servant,

N. B. FORREST,
Major-General.

MAYHEW, MISS.,
March 10, 1864.
Col. T. M. JACK:

General Forrest took my only tent from me and gave it to his brother. I wrote him a letter which he considered disrespectful, and he has relieved me from my command and ordered me to report to you. I have asked for a court of inquiry and to be restored to my command. I ask permission to remain in North Mississippi until my application is answered.

JAS. R. CHALMERS,
Brigadier-General.

HEADQUARTERS FIRST DIVISION, FORREST'S CAVALRY,
Mayhew Station, March 10, 1864.
General S. COOPER,
Adjutant and Inspector General, Richmond, Va.:

GENERAL: On the 8th instant I was deprived of the tent which I was then using, and the only one in my possession, by order of Major-General Forrest, commanding this cavalry department. I therefore addressed a note to him, a copy* of which is inclosed. To-day I have been relieved from my command and ordered to report to Lieutenant-General Polk, which order I shall obey under protest. I respectfully ask for a court of inquiry upon my conduct in the matter, and that I may be restored to my command.

I am, sir, very respectfully, your obedient servant.

JAS. R. CHALMERS,
Brigadier-General.

HDQRS. FIRST DIV., FORREST'S CAVALRY DEPARTMENT,
Mayhew Station, March 10, 1864.
Brig. Gen. R. V. RICHARDSON,
Commanding Brigade Cavalry:

GENERAL: The brigadier-general commanding directs me to say to you that General Forrest orders that you remove from Grenada to the Tallahatchie River, near Abbeville, as many of the boats or pontoons now at Grenada as may be necessary to construct a bridge across that river. The bridge will be constructed near the railroad bridge, and will be completed as rapidly as possible. The pontoons will be transported from Grenada to the river by railroad.

Your obedient servant,

W. A. GOODMAN,
Assistant Adjutant-General.

---

* Not found.

GENERAL ORDERS, }   HEADQUARTERS,
    No. 43.   }   *Demopolis, Ala., March* 10, 1864.

I. All authority heretofore granted for the impressment of slaves is hereby revoked, except that delegated to F. S. Blount, chief agent of impressment, which is still in force.

Slaves will hereafter be impressed only by authority given at these headquarters on requisition. Without such direct authority no impressments whatever will be permitted.

II. With the view of promoting the efficiency of the military police of this department, it is divided into districts as follows :

First. The State of Mississippi is divided into four districts, to wit:

First District will comprise all that portion of the State west of the Mississippi Central road and north of the Southern Railroad, with a chief provost-marshal, whose headquarters will be at Grenada.

Second District will comprise all that portion of the State west of the New Orleans, Jackson and Great Northern Railroad and south of the Southern Railroad, with a chief provost-marshal, whose headquarters will be at Jackson.

Third District will comprise all that portion of the State east of the Mississippi Central Railroad and north of the Southern Railroad, with a chief provost-marshal, whose headquarters will be at Columbus.

Fourth District will comprise all that portion of the State east of the New Orleans, Jackson and Georgia Northern Railroad and south of the Southern Railroad, excluding the counties of Hancock, Harrison, and Jackson, which are attached to the Fourth District of the State of Alabama, with a chief provost-marshal, whose headquarters will be at Meridian.

Second. The State of Alabama is divided into four districts:

First District will comprise the counties of Lauderdale, Limestone, Madison, Jackson, Franklin, Lawrence, Morgan, Marshall, De Kalb, Cherokee, Blount, Winston, and Marion, with a chief provost-marshal, whose headquarters will be at Blountsville.

Second District will comprise the counties of Fayette, Walker, Jefferson, Saint Clair, Benton, Randolph, Talledega, Shelby, Bibb, Tuscaloosa, and Pickens, with a chief provost-marshal, whose headquarters will be at Tuscaloosa.

Third District will comprise the counties of Sumter, Green, Perry, Antanga, Coosa, Tallapoosa, Chambers, Marengo, Dallas, Lowndes, Montgomery, Macon, Russell, and Wilcox, with a chief provost-marshal, whose headquarters will be at Montgomery.

Fourth District will comprise the counties of Choctaw, Clarke, Washington, Mobile, Baldwin, Monroe, Conecuh, Butler, Pike, Barbour, Henry, Dale, Coffee, and Covington, with a provost-marshal, whose headquarters will be at Mobile.

The three southern counties of Mississippi, viz, Hancock, Harrison, and Jackson, are attached to this district.

III. That portion of the State of Louisiana lying east of the Mississippi River will form a district by itself, with a chief provost-marshal, whose headquarters will be at Clinton, La.

IV. Maj. J. C. Denis, provost-marshal-general, is authorized to assign provost-marshals to the several districts above enumerated, as the exigencies of the service may require.

By command of Lieutenant-General Polk:

                              THOS. M. JACK,
                            Assistant Adjutant-General.

CIRCULAR.]   HDQRS. DEPT. OF ALA., MISS., AND E. LA.,
Demopolis, March 10, 1864.

All commanding officers in the field and commandants of posts will furnish Maj. J. C. Denis, provost-marshal-general, and his subordinate officers such military aid as may be required in the discharge of the duties of his department.

By command of Lieutenant-General Polk:

THOS. M. JACK,
Assistant Adjutant-General.

RICHMOND, VA.,
March 11, 1864.

Lieutenant-General POLK,
Demopolis, Ala.:

I have submitted to the President your dispatch of the 8th. He does not desire the force you suggest, but limits his wish to that communicated in my former dispatch.

S. COOPER.
Adjutant and Inspector General.

DEMOPOLIS, *March* 11, 1864.

Brigadier-General CHALMERS,
Mayhew Station:

Remain in North Mississippi until your application is answered.

THOS. M. JACK,
Assistant Adjutant-General.

CIRCULAR.]   HEADQUARTERS,
Demopolis, Ala., March 11, 1864.

Missourians are relieved from the operation of circular dated February 29, 1864, from these headquarters, ordering all unattached men in this department belonging to the Trans-Mississippi Department to report to Lieut. Col. H. C. Davis, Cahaba, Ala.

All Missourians not engaged in actual service east of the Mississippi River will report to the commanding general of the First Missouri Brigade at Demopolis, Ala., in accordance with Special Orders, No. 247, Adjutant and Inspector General's Office, dated Richmond, Va., October 17, 1863.

By command of Lieutenant-General Polk:

THOS. M. JACK,
Assistant Adjutant-General.

GENERAL ORDERS, }   HEADQUARTERS HOOD'S CORPS,
No. 38.   }   *Dalton, Ga., March* 11, 1864.

To avoid dangerous confusion in action, each regiment and battery will be required to bear the Confederate battle-flag.

The chief quartermaster is instructed to take immediate steps to provide the command with these colors.

The lieutenant-general commanding can well understand the pride many regiments of the corps feel in other flags which they have gloriously borne in battle. but the interests of the service are imperative. He would therefore suggest that such standards be sent for safe keeping to the capitol of the States to which the troops belong, as it will be found inconvenient to have more than one flag in a regiment.

By command of Lieutenant-General Hood :

ARCHER ANDERSON,
Assistant Adjutant-General.

HEADQUARTERS DEPARTMENT OF EAST TENNESSEE,
Greeneville, March 11, 1864.

Brig. Gen. W. E. JONES,
Commanding Cavalry :
(Through Major-General Ransom.)

The disposition of the troops of this department at present is such as to leave greatly exposed the important point of Abingdon and the salt-works. This becomes more serious and excites greater concern from the supposed presence of Wolford's cavalry at Mount Sterling, Ky., from which point he could readily make a movement across the mountains and by a sudden raid on the points above mentioned cause great loss and damage. Under these circumstances, the major-general commanding the department desires you to throw your brigade into such a position as may best serve to cover the approaches to Abingdon and the salt-works, and protect those points from any movement that may be undertaken against them.

I am. general, very respectfully, your obedient servant,

G. M. SORREL,
Lieutenant-Colonel, Assistant Adjutant-General.

DALTON, *March* 12, 1864.

General BRAXTON BRAGG :

GENERAL : I have had the honor to receive your letter of the 4th instant. in which I am desired to "have all things in readiness, at the earliest practicable moment, for the movement indicated."

The last two words quoted give me the impression that some particular plan of operations is referred to; if so, it has not been communicated to me. A knowledge of it and of the forces to be provided for is necessary to enable me to make proper requisitions. Permit me, in that connection, to remind you that the regulations of the War Department do not leave the preparations referred to to me, but to officers who receive their orders from Richmond, not from my headquarters.

The defects in the organization of the artillery cannot be remedied without competent superior officers. for whom we must depend upon the Government. I respectfully beg leave to refer to my letter to the President. dated January 2,* for my opinions on the subject of our operations on this line.

Is it probable that the enemy's forces will increase during the spring, or will they diminish in May and June by expiration of terms

---

*See Part II. p. 510.

of service? It seems to me that our policy depends on the answers to these questions. If that to the first is affirmative we should act promptly; if that to the second is so we should not, but, on the contrary, put off action, if possible, until after the discharge of many of his old soldiers, if any considerable number is to be discharged.

Most respectfully, your obedient servant,

J. E. JOHNSTON,
General.

P. S.—Should Sherman join Thomas this army would require reenforcement to enable it to hold its ground. Our army. which takes the offensive, should be our strongest in relation to its enemy.

J. E. J.

CONFIDENTIAL.]   HDQRS. ARMIES CONFEDERATE STATES,
Richmond, March 12. 1864.

General J. E. JOHNSTON,
Commanding Army of Tennessee, Dalton:

GENERAL : In previous communications it has been intimated to you that the President desired a forward movement by the forces under your command, and it was suggested that such preparations as were practicable and necessary should be commenced immediately. I now desire to lay before you more in detail the views of the Department in regard to the proposed operations, and to inform you of the means intended to be placed at your disposal. Of course, but a general outline is necessary, as matters of detail must be left to your judgment and discretion.

It is not deemed advisable to attempt the capture of the enemy's fortified position by direct attack, but to draw him out and then, if practicable, force him to battle in the open field. To accomplish this object we should so move as to concentrate our means between the scattered forces of the enemy, and failing to draw him out for battle, to move upon his lines of communication.

The force in Knoxville depends in a great measure on its connection with Chattanooga for support, and both are entirely dependent upon regular and rapid communication with Nashville. To separate these two by interposing our main force, and then strike and destroy the railroad from Nashville to Chattanooga, fulfills both conditions. To accomplish this it is proposed that you move as soon as your means and force can be collected so as to reach the Tennessee River near Kingston, where a crossing can be effected ; that Lieutenant-General Longstreet move simultaneously by a route east and south of Knoxville, so as to form a junction with you near this crossing. As soon as you come within supporting distance Knoxville is isolated and Chattanooga threatened, with barely a possibility for the enemy to unite. Should he not then offer you battle outside of his intrenched lines, a rapid move across the mountains from Kingston to Sparta (a very practicable and easy route) would place you with a formidable army in a country full of resources, where it is supposed, with a good supply of ammunition, you may be entirely self-sustaining, and it is confidently believed that such a move would necessitate the withdrawal of the enemy to the line of the Cumberland.

At the same time, when this move is made it is proposed to throw a heavy column of cavalry as a diversion into West Tennessee, and thence, if practicable, into Middle Tennessee, to operate on the enemy's lines of communication and distract his attention.

If by a rapid movement, after crossing the mountains, you can precipitate your main force upon Nashville, and capture that place before the enemy can fall back for its defense, you place him in a precarious position. But in any event, by a movement in rear of Nashville while the Cumberland is low, similar to the one in passing Chattanooga, you isolate that position and compel a retrograde movement of the enemy's main force.

It is needless, general, for me to impress upon you the great importance, not to say necessity, of reclaiming the provision country of Tennessee and Kentucky, and, from my knowledge of the country and people, I believe that other great advantages may accrue, especially in obtaining men to fill your ranks.

The following forces it is believed will be available if nothing shall occur to divert them, viz:

	Infantry.	Artillery.	Cavalry.	Total.
Your own command	33,000	3,000	5,000	41,000
General Martin's cavalry, now en route to join			3,000	3,000
From General Polk	5,000			5,000
From General Beauregard	10,000			10,000
General Longstreet's command	12,000	2,000	2,000	16,000
Total	60,000	5,000	10,000	75,000

It is proposed to hold the re-enforcements ready, and to put them in motion just as soon as you may be able to use them. To throw them to the front now would only impede the accumulation of supplies necessary for your march. Measures have been taken to aid in supplying you with artillery horses. Additional means of transportation will be furnished as soon as practicable. The efficient organization of engineer troops in your command will supply every want in that department.

Ammunition in abundance is on hand, subject to your call, and it is believed the means of subsistence are ample in your immediate rear if efficient measures are inaugurated to get them forward. On this point you are desired to act at once in your own behalf, as the Department here could do no more than refer you to its resources within your reach and control.

It will give me much pleasure, general, to have your views in full on this subject in all its bearings, and no effort will be spared in bringing to your assistance the resources of the Government not essential at other points. Communicate fully at once, and afterward in detail, as points may arise requiring action.

I have the honor to be, general, very respectfully, your obedient servant,

BRAXTON BRAGG,
General, &c.

DEMOPOLIS. *March* 12, 1864.

General COOPER,
Adjutant and Inspector General, Richmond:

The whole of Loring's division has, with great enthusiasm, re-enlisted for the war, and the best feeling prevails throughout the command.

L. POLK,
Lieutenant-General.

DEMOPOLIS, *March* 12, 1864.
General RUGGLES,
    Columbus, Miss.:
    General Cooper replies: "I know of no assignment that can be made of General Ruggles; have many general officers off duty waiting assignment, but there are no places for them." To disembarrass you of the annoyance of your present position, I have directed you to be relieved and ordered to await orders. You will turn over the command to the commander of the post, or if there be no commander, then to Col. Richard Harrison, of the Forty-third Mississippi.

L. POLK,
Lieutenant-General.

HEADQUARTERS FORREST'S CAVALRY COMMAND,
Columbus, March 12, 1864.
Lieut. Gen. L. POLK,
    Commanding:
    GENERAL: I have the honor to acknowledge the receipt of yours yesterday; am glad to know that Brigadier-General Armstrong will report to me.
    I regretted the necessity of relieving Brigadier-General Chalmers, but his letter addressed to me, a copy of which I have forwarded you, speaks for itself. He has never been satisfied since I came here, and being satisfied that I have not had and will not receive his support and co-operation, deemed it necessary that we should separate. I must have the cordial support of my subordinate officers in order to succeed and make my command effective, and holding myself responsible for all my acts and orders to the proper authority, have forwarded his letter, also his application for a court of inquiry. I hope you may be able to place him where he will be better satisfied than with me.
    Brigadier-General Richardson is relieved on account of charges preferred against him by Colonel Green, and is ordered to report to you at Demopolis.
    I am, general, very respectfully, your obedient servant,
N. B. FORREST,
Major-General.

CONFIDENTIAL.]   HEADQUARTERS FORREST'S CAVALRY,
Columbus, March 12, 1864.
Col. R. McCULLOCH,
    Commanding Division:
    COLONEL: You will send the First Mississippi Partisans up the railroad as far as Corinth, with orders to breast the country from thence to Holly Springs, south of the Memphis and Charleston Railroad, and from thence to Oxford. You will send also another battalion or regiment as far up as Tupelo, with orders to move west and south of the Tallahatchie River to Oxford; you will also send another command from Starkville through Choctaw, Chickasaw, Yalobusha, Panola, and La Fayette Counties. You will order the officers in

command of the above troops to breast the country, and arrest all men found absent without proper leave ; also all men subject to conscription. They will also collect all squads and unattached companies of cavalry, and report with them to your headquarters. You will take your wagon train with you, also your dismounted men, to Oxford, also the wagons belonging to Colonel Duckworth and McDonald's battalion, leaving ten of your best wagons in charge of a competent wagon-master to be repaired and fitted up as an ordnance train. They will report to Maj. C. S. Severson, assistant quartermaster, at this place. You will leave a detail of 20 picked men to remain with and guard the ordnance wagons from this place to Oxford, directing your ordnance officer, so soon as the wagons are ready and loaded with the ammunition, say 40 rounds to the man, for your division, to move with them to Oxford. You will instruct your ordnance officer to make requisition for 40 rounds of ammunition for your division. Leave one squadron under a competent officer two days behind you, for the purpose of gathering all stragglers and men who may be left behind of your command. All the stragglers and conscripts that may be arrested in Tippah, Tishomingo, Itawamba, and Pontotoc Counties you will send to this place ; the others order taken to Oxford. All absentees and deserters from other commands you will have forwarded to the provost-marshal at this place, to be sent to their respective commands.

Impress upon the officers commanding the regiments sent out to scour and breast the country to do the work thoroughly and catch, if possible, the men who are going through the country and impressing and stealing horses without authority. You will send out and scout thoroughly in the direction of Memphis. Should the enemy move after me you will follow in his rear, and communicate with me. Establish a courier-line from Waterford to Saulsbury, and one from Oxford to Pontotoc, to connect with a line established by General Gholson from Tupelo to Pontotoc. You will re-open the telegraph office at Waterford, so that dispatches can be sent you at Oxford ; also to Panola via Grenada.

In the absence of any move of the enemy on me, use your discretion as to any operations in your front. You will order one commissioned officer from each regiment of General Richardson's brigade to report to my headquarters at Jackson, Tenn., or wherever they may be, with complete lists of all absentees from their respective regiments.

By order of Major-General Forrest :

J. P. STRANGE,
Assistant Adjutant-General.

RICHMOND, VA.,
March 12, 1864.

Lieut. Gen. J. LONGSTREET,
Greeneville, Tenn.:

Has General Law been arrested by you ? If so, send the charges immediately to this office for action.

S. COOPER,
Adjutant and Inspector General.

GREENEVILLE, *March* 12, 1864.

General S. COOPER:

General Longstreet is temporarily absent. Your dispatch relative to General Law will be laid before him on his return, as it is a matter on which I am incompetent to act in his absence.

S. B. BUCKNER,
Major-General, Commanding.

ATLANTA, *March* 13, 1864.

Lieutenant-General LONGSTREET:

GENERAL: I met your courier here, where I am on a tour of inspection.

I will obey any orders of the President zealously and execute any plan of campaign of his to the best of my ability. It seems to me, however, that the one suggested to you is impracticable to us, at least at any early day.

In the first place, the enemy could prevent our junction at Madisonville. If I attempt to march directly to that point they can unite all their forces against me. If to avoid that I diverge into North Carolina, they can unite those forces upon you. If we unite for such an object it should be by your moving into Northwestern Georgia to some point in rear of Dalton.

In the second place, we must have the means of moving from Madisonville with food for man and beast for at least ten days, for the march thence into the productive part of Middle Tennessee and getting the first supplies there would require at least as long. To enable us to do that the Quartermaster's Department must increase the supply train of this army, as well as yours, very much, and the Commissary Department furnish the means of loading them. It is a greater undertaking, I think, than anything yet accomplished by those Departments, and if they succeed it will not be very soon.

I have had orders to prepare for a forward movement, but its precise object has not been imparted to me. It seems to me that we shall be compelled to wait for the grass of May, as we did on the prairies, and besides we ought to let the enemy advance if he will, that we may fight him as far as possible from his base and near to ours. If he will not advance, we must.

In writing to the President on this subject, I expressed the opinion that the only practicable mode of assuming the offensive here seemed to me to be to wait for the enemy's advance, and if we beat him, follow into Middle Tennessee, it being much easier to beat him in Georgia than beyond the Cumberland Mountains and the results of victory much greater. If, as seems probable, Sherman's troops should be brought to Chattanooga, we may have an opportunity to practice this theory. If they come, the union of your army with mine would be necessary.

I regret very much we cannot confer personally. You know how much I value your military opinions.

Most respectfully, your obedient servant,

J. E. JOHNSTON,
General.

HEADQUARTERS DEPARTMENT OF EAST TENNESSEE,
Greeneville. Tenn., March 13, 1864—4.30 p. m.
Brig. Gen. J. B. KERSHAW,
Commanding Division :

Developments made in the front yesterday and to-day indicate a probable advance on the part of the enemy. To meet any movement that may be undertaken, the commanding general desires that you will hold your command in readiness to move down at an early hour to-morrow morning in the direction of Midway to give the necessary support to our forces in the front. If you move, Colonel King's battalion of artillery will move with you. Please give him the necessary notification.

I am, general, very respectfully, your obedient servant,
G. M. SORREL,
Lieutenant-Colonel and Assistant Adjutant-General.

HEADQUARTERS DEPARTMENT OF EAST TENNESSEE,
Greeneville, Tenn., March 13, 1864.
Brig. Gen. E. P. ALEXANDER,
Chief of Artillery :

There is reason to think that the enemy is contemplating an advance. Kershaw's division is under orders to be in readiness to move down early in the morning. I have asked General Kershaw to give Colonel King the necessary notification. I would like to know by the returning courier what batteries you have with General Field and what with General Johnson.

I am, general, very respectfully. your obedient servant.
G. M. SORREL.
Lieutenant-Colonel and Assistant Adjutant-General.

HEADQUARTERS DEPARTMENT OF EAST TENNESSEE.
Greeneville, Tenn., March 13, 1864—7.30 p. m.
Brig. Gen. B. R. JOHNSON,
Commanding Division:

I am in receipt of the information sent by you, in relation to the recent movements of the enemy, together with your inquiry thereon; and in reply am directed to say that in the event of Rucker's command being attacked, it will not be necessary for you to move your infantry to the gap. In the event of Colonel Rucker's being too strongly attacked to hold them. he must fall back on you to cover your front and the left flank of General Field. He must, however, hold the enemy in check long enough to give you timely notice. Your own position, the commanding general desires, should be such as to defend the crossings of Lick Creek, and to enable you to move to the support of General Field by the railroad bridge, and also the bridge on the Midway road, and he desires that you will hold yourself in readiness to make the movement to General Field's support whenever it may become necessary.

I am, general, very respectfully, your obedient servant,
G. M. SORREL,
Lieutenant-Colonel and Assistant Adjutant-General.

DEMOPOLIS, *March* 13, 1864.

General PILLOW, *Montgomery, Ala.:*

I find the President prefers the proposition first made by General Cooper. General Clanton, therefore, will not go. You will prepare three companies from Alabama to join those from Mississippi, which will move as soon as practicable. Telegraph me their names, strength, and where they are now, and how soon they can move. Colonel Lockhart asks me so earnestly for Lewis' squadron that you must let him have it and take something else in its place. Telegraph him that you will do so.

L. POLK,
Lieutenant-General.

HEADQUARTERS LEE'S CAVALRY DEPARTMENT,
Canton, Miss., March 13, 1864.

Lieut. Col. T. M. JACK,
   Assistant Adjutant-General, Demopolis, Ala.:

COLONEL: I arrived here two days since; have nothing special to report. The enemy committed many ravages in this country; on their line of march they took or destroyed everything; they carried off every animal and some 8,000 negroes (men, women, and children); they burnt every vacant house and destroyed furniture, &c. The destruction is really frightful. General Jackson got here in time to stop their pillaging, or rather confining it to the road on which they marched. The people are badly whipped and much depressed. Large amounts of cotton were run into Vicksburg during our absence from this country and the enemy got much Government cotton. Many of the citizens sold the Government cotton; have arrested several engaged in it.

The enemy have disposed of their forces as follows:

The disposable force, excepting the garrison of Vicksburg and the regiments sent on furlough, have gone on an expedition up Red River. I do not think a move on Mobile is contemplated at present. My command is now recruiting; it is much jaded and broken down. Ross is opposite Yazoo City, Starke near Livingston, Ferguson near Madison Station, Adams near Crystal Springs.

There is no enemy on the Yazoo. I ask to be informed as early as practicable as to the contemplated spring campaign, so I can commence to operate on the river as early as practicable should it not interfere; it will take several weeks to recruit my command.

I inclose, general, the indorsements relative to the seizure and confiscation of wagons, &c., engaged in trade with the enemy.

In the particular case referred to. Mr. Day applied to me and to General Johnston for his wagons. It was positively refused; in retaining the wagons I obeyed General Johnston's telegraphic and verbal orders, as is shown by the copies. The indorsement of the Secretary of War reflects on me. I consider this rather harsh, when as a soldier I was obeying orders.

Please send me written orders relative to the trade, confiscation, &c., as the order now in force is the telegram of General Johnston, and it is my duty as my pleasure as a soldier to obey all orders and carry out the policy of my superiors.

I am, colonel, yours, respectfully,

S. D. LEE,
Major-General.

[Inclosure No. 1.]

GRENADA, *November* 23, 1863.

General JOSEPH E. JOHNSTON,
Meridian, Miss.:

The civil authorities in North Mississippi are issuing writs to recover wagons and teams captured trading with the enemy. Am I to regard these writs? Trading is being carried on largely; urgent and prompt measures are necessary to stop it. I advise that all captures be confiscated to the Government at once. Will hold property till I hear from you.

S. D. LEE,
Major-General.

[Inclosure No. 2.]

MERIDIAN, *November* 23, 1863.

Maj. Gen. S. D. LEE,
Grenada, Miss.:

The Secretary of War decides that wagons and teams employed in trade with the enemy are subject to confiscation; therefore maintain such confiscations.

JOS. E. JOHNSTON

[Inclosure No. 3.]

FEBRUARY 18, 1864

ADJUTANT-GENERAL:

Refer to Lieutenant-General Polk. At the date of this seizure there was no law nor any orders for the seizure of the articles mentioned. The orders of Major-General Lee were without any authority for their support. The Constitution of the Confederate States forbids the confiscation of property by any such officer or by any such summary proceeding. If this man has done anything worthy of death or bonds, he must be tried and punished according to law by a judicial tribunal.

Restore the property unless some judicial proceeding is taken to hold it.

By order:

J. A. CAMPBELL,
Assistant Secretary of War.

SPECIAL ORDERS, } HEADQUARTERS FORREST'S CAVALRY,
No. 33.   *Columbus, March* 13, 1864.

Col. R. McCulloch, commanding division, will order one battalion to move to Bankston (10 miles south of Greensborough), and report to J. M. Wesson, president of manufacturing company, for the purpose of arresting some detailed men (as shoemakers) that have been disturbing the citizens and producing disorganization, and will send them to this place.

He will also order the distillery at Springfield to be destroyed, and all others from that place to Bankston. On leaving Bankston you will order the officer commanding the battalion to proceed, in returning by way of Grenada, to destroy all distilleries and arrest all men found absent from their commands without proper authority.

By order of Major-General Forrest:

J. P. STRANGE,
Assistant Adjutant-General.

HEADQUARTERS DEPARTMENT OF EAST TENNESSEE,
Greeneville, Tenn., March 14, 1864—5.30 a. m.

Brig. Gen. J. B. KERSHAW, *Commanding Division:*

The commanding general desires you to put your division in motion at once and march to the vicinity of Midway, where you will camp to-night. You may select any point in its vicinity that you may deem best for a temporary camp and for the purpose of giving to the troops in front all the support that may be required. Colonel King's battalion of artillery will not at present move with you. If the reports from below become more threatening it will be sent down to rejoin you.

The commanding general will be to-night at Blue Springs, some 2 or 3 miles from Midway. Please let him know there the point you select for your halt.

I am, general, very respectfully, your most obedient servant,

G. M. SORREL,
Lieutenant-Colonel and Assistant Adjutant-General.

HEADQUARTERS DEPARTMENT OF EAST TENNESSEE,
March 14, 1864.

Lieutenant-General LONGSTREET
(*Care of General Cooper, Richmond, Va.*):

The enemy moved up from Mossy Creek to Morristown on the 12th, and their main infantry force is reported as now lying 2 miles east of Morristown. They are reported to have had an accession of 1,200 fresh cavalry from Kentucky. Their pickets have been advanced and strengthened. The pontoon bridges at Strawberry Plains and the railroad bridges at Strawberry Plains and Loudon are reported completed. The intentions of the enemy are not fully developed. Kershaw has been moved to Midway.

G. M. SORREL,
Lieutenant-Colonel and Assistant Adjutant-General.

DEMOPOLIS, *March* 14, 1864.

General COOPER,
Adjutant and Inspector General, Richmond:

General Forrest relieves General Chalmers for alleged cause, and orders him to report to department headquarters. The latter obeys under protest. My decision is that the former has exceeded his authority, notwithstanding precedents quoted. It is referred to the War Department. Please answer.

L. POLK.
Lieutenant-General.

DEMOPOLIS, *March* 14, 1864.

General J. E. JOHNSTON, *Dalton, Ga.:*

The following dispatch received from General Lee, dated—

CANTON, *March* 13, 1864.

From the 2d to 6th instant twenty-two boats passed up Mississippi River to Vicksburg. Opposite Port Gibson, on night of the 6th, thirteen boats, supposed to be loaded with troops, went down Mississippi River from Vicksburg. Sherman is reported in

New Orleans. Sherman is not in Vicksburg. Indications are his force is moving down river. Rumor has it that an expedition is fitting out at Natchez, either for Mobile or up Red River. The enemy have all left Yazoo River. The above is from scouts' reports just received. A citizen just out of Vicksburg, who was carried in a prisoner, reports that most of Sherman's army have gone up Red River. The troops which have gone up the Mississippi are mostly furloughed regiments. This is, I consider, reliable.

L. POLK,
Lieutenant-General.

DEMOPOLIS, *March* 14, 1864.

General S. D. LEE, *Canton, Miss.:*

Your dispatch of the 13th, reporting what you regarded as reliable information concerning enemy's movements, received. All indications lead to the belief that he is now moving from Tennessee River down on Middle Alabama; also that he proposes to repeat his movement from West Tennessee on the prairies in Mississippi. You will therefore leave such force as you may think necessary on the western front, and move promptly with the rest of your command so as to strike Columbus [Pickensville or Warsaw *]. Answer immediately.

L. POLK,
Lieutenant-General.

DEMOPOLIS, *March* 14, 1864.

General FORREST, *Okolona:*

The Twenty-fourth and Twenty-seventh Regiments of Infantry in North Alabama not being under your orders, you will revoke your orders to them, and allow them to do the duty on which they were sent. Order an officer over to Decatur to make a close reconnaissance and send me his report. Have wires extended up to Tupelo or higher up. Establish a post there and a line of couriers from that post to the infantry command in North Alabama.

L. POLK,
Lieutenant-General.

DEMOPOLIS, *March* 14, 1864.

General S. COOPER,
Adjutant and Inspector General:

Maj. Gen. M. L. Smith will be ordered to report to you in person as soon as orders can be made to reach him.

L. POLK,
Lieutenant-General.

MOBILE, *March* 14, 1864.

General S. COOPER,
Adjutant and Inspector General:

Mr. Helm informs me from Havana, 7th, the mail steamer just in from New York; from reliable source stated enemy sending supplies to Hilton Head for 20,000 men, intending land attack on Charleston.

*As corrected, same date. by General Polk.

General S. D. Lee reports, Canton, March 13, rumored that expedition is fitting out at Natchez for Red River. Most of Sherman's force gone up Red River; furloughed regiments gone up Mississippi.

DABNEY H. MAURY,
Major-General.

MOBILE, *March* 14, 1864.

General S. COOPER :

Spies report many troops sent in sea steamers from New Orleans for Florida; about 15,000 in all. Saturday, 5th, he saw 2,000 embark on steamer Mississippi, drawing 18 feet of water. Sherman in New Orleans on 4th; crazy.

DABNEY H. MAURY,
Major-General.

HEADQUARTERS CAVALRY BRIGADE.
Near Madison Station, March 14, 1864.

Maj. WILLIAM ELLIOTT,
Assistant Adjutant and Inspector General:

MAJOR : I received the order directing me to move my command below Raymond at 6 o'clock this evening, and shall march at an early hour to-morrow morning.

I sent report of recent operations of my brigade to Captain Moorman this afternoon and hope it has reached you.

I inclose you herewith two letters* received to-day from William Haley, sheriff of Copiah County, one giving information of the shipment of corn down Pearl River, as he supposes for sale to the enemy, and the other giving information of a notice or handbill posted in Bahala by deserters or other disloyal parties. Bahala is on the railroad, 10 miles below Gallatin.

I have received information to-night that disloyal men living on the Yazoo River 10 to 20 miles above Yazoo City are engaged in ginning the cotton on Colonel Field's and other plantations for the purpose of selling it to the enemy. I have instructed Lieutenant Moore, whom I send to-morrow morning with a small detail after some deserters from Captain Yerger's company, to arrest or shoot the scoundrels engaged in this business.

A gentleman direct from Port Gibson informs me that Ellet's marine brigade returned to Rodney on Saturday last. They have been engaged for some time past, during the absence of General Lee's command, in hauling off Government cotton from the interior, of which they have secured a large supply. They doubtless intend resuming this lucrative business. From 500 to 1,000 bales were also taken from the lower part of Hinds and upper part of Claiborne Counties by small parties of Yankees during the absence of our cavalry.

This gentleman reports that Sherman with a number of transports filled with troops passed down the river last week.

I am, major, very respectfully, your obedient servant,

WIRT ADAMS,
Brigadier-General.

---

* Not found.

HEADQUARTERS CAVALRY BRIGADE,
Near Madison Station, Miss., March 14, 1864.

Maj. WILLIAM ELLIOTT,
Assistant Adjutant and Inspector General :

MAJOR : I would respectfully call the attention of the major-general commanding to the recent occurrences constituting subjects of grave complaint on the part of those who suffered by them and of the universal condemnation on the part of the citizens of the country, and calculated seriously to injure the character of his command.

On the night of the 4th instant a party of 5 men belonging to Lieutenant Baker's scouts seized a wagon while passing through Clinton, filled with hospital stores sent by the Federal authorities at Vicksburg to the Federal wounded at Jackson. This was done notwithstanding the earnest protest of Col. John Duncan, in charge, who made an explanation of all the circumstances of the case. The wagon also contained dry goods and other articles of considerable value, purchased by ladies residing within the Federal lines and sent to their friends in Jackson. All these supplies, both public and private, were taken by the parties seizing them to Raymond and appropriated to their own use. In this act of highway robbery the following-named men belonging to Lieutenant Baker's command are said to have been engaged : Tucker. Allen, Cobb, Williamson, and Smith.

On hearing of this lawless proceeding, I immediately sent Lieutenant O'Callahan and 10 men to arrest the parties engaged in it, and recover, if possible, and return the articles stolen to the parties to whom they were consigned. This order Lieutenant Baker refused to respect, and still holds both the stores and the goods, or has appropriated the latter to the use of his command.

Two or three days subsequent to this occurrence Tucker and Allen were sent with two ladies, Mrs. Askew and Miss Askew, to headquarters at Canton. They detained these ladies all night in a camp on the road, offered them every indignity, and are supposed to have violated one or both of them. The ladies themselves complained that every indignity was offered them.

I am, major, very respectfully, your obedient servant,

WIRT ADAMS,
Brigadier-General.

EDINBURG, LEAKE COUNTY, MISS.,
March 14, 1864.

JEFFERSON DAVIS,
President, &c. :

DEAR SIR : At the risk of being adjudged presumptuous, I have resolved to offer you some facts and suggestions. I do so because I know that you cannot know the status of the public feeling and mind in every locality, and the extent to which they are drifting. Mississippi is in a most deplorable condition, and is rapidly tending to the most deplorable disgrace. Very many of the middle class, a large number of the more intelligent, and nearly all of the lower class of her people are drifting to the Yankees. The more they are abused by the Yankees, the more they strive to go with them. These are facts that can be proved beyond all question. Desertion from the army, trading with the enemy, and the removal of deserters and their families into the lines and supposed lines of the enemy is now the order of the day, and the citizen who opposes these things stands almost alone and in great personal danger.

Many of the men not liable to military service and nearly all the women are openly at work to weaken our army, procure desertion, and assail the Confederacy. Unless this thing is speedily arrested, the army and people of Mississippi will soon be so demoralized that no remedy can be found ; no temporizing policy will answer. The most radical and severe treatment is required. The women and non-combatants must be handled speedily and roughly. Deserters must be put to death or in service most remote from their homes. I know many deserters now in desertion for the fourth, fifth, and sixth times who have never been punished. I am glad to see that the writ of habeas corpus is suspended in certain cases, and hope the offenders will be promptly arrested.

Our only salvation is in the most rigid and energetic efforts. Let those who trade with the enemy, those who desert the army, those who give aid and comfort to deserters, those who assail the Confederacy, early feel the hospitalities of the prisons and short rations. The State is now under the tacit rule of deserters, thieves, and disloyal men and women. The lower and middle tier of counties are vastly rotten. Confederate muskets, rifles, and cartridges are in every disloyal house, and defiance bid to the powers that be.

Many of our soldiers who remain in or along with the service are as destructive to property as the Yankees ; they steal, destroy, and appropriate without restraint ; everything useful or valuable to the citizen that can be reached by them is grasped. Open-day and midnight robbery is practiced every day and night in every neighborhood by deserters, pretended soldiers, and soldiers with their commands. Officers in command are much to blame for this, and they alone can correct it, yet they often in effect encourage it. Privates steal, and officers refuse to give up the property when identified by the citizens, and even punish the citizens for making claim to it. The discipline is awfully bad. These things tend to dishearten and disaffect our best citizens, and are swelling the tide against us.

I have admired your mercy and the broad liberty allowed to all, but it has ceased to be appreciated or improved. It is now simply casting pearls before swine, and is used to sap the Government and outrage the families of the good and true. I now hope to see an iron rule enforced with iron hand and hearts of stone. Mississippi is almost a Sodom and Gomorrah ; the purifying element is with you, and the day of our salvation, if neglected for a day, is forever gone. I am no alarmist, but tremble in view of a just comprehension and full knowledge of the extent, depth, and magnitude of these evils.

The cavalry sent among us to arrest conscripts and deserters have been a nuisance to the cause and country in a large degree. They spend a large part of their time in gaming parties, drunkenness, marrying, horse-racing, and stealing.

Capt. Jonathan Davis, of Twentieth Mississippi Regiment, Walthall's brigade, now with his company, was the only recruiting officer in my knowledge who did his duty, and when here, did rid the country of conscripts and deserters when all others had signally failed because they were failures anyway.

I trust, amid our gloom, that a better day will soon dawn upon us. Accept my highest confidence in your integrity, firmness, and ability, and best wishes for you and our cause.

Truly, &c.,

R. S. HUDSON,
Judge Fifth District of Mississippi.

[Indorsement.]

Respectfully referred by direction of the President to Lieut. Gen. L. Polk for perusal, &c.

BURTON N. HARRISON,
Private Secretary.

———

HEADQUARTERS,
Petersburg, Va., en route to East Tenn., March 15, 1864.

General G. T. BEAUREGARD :

GENERAL : Since writing you of the move proposed into Kentucky by mounting a large force of infantry, the prospects for getting the animals have fallen far short of what I had thought reasonable at the time of writing. I have therefore proposed instead a junction of your forces and mine at Abingdon, Va., via Greenville, S. C., to march through Pound Gap upon Louisville. By that route you would have but little over 300 miles to march to reach Louisville. I would march a little over 150, and our forces together could hold Kentucky and the enemy's line of communication long enough to force him to withdraw his forces from Georgia and Tennessee, when General Johnston could advance into Kentucky, and we could effect a junction, and with our combined forces meet and overcome any army that the enemy could bring against us.

This move seemed to me to have amongst other advantages that of enabling us to prepare for it and get our columns in motion before the enemy could have any idea of our real intention, for you could send your transportation to Greenville, S. C., and your quartermaster and commissary of subsistence could accumulate supplies at that point under the pretext that they were there for my army, which could be given out as about to start down to join General Johnston. Your transportation ready, and your supplies, you could throw your troops up by rail and have them on the march before the move could be suspected. It would be better if you could start out from Morganton, N. C., as you would thus save about 60 miles march ; but to make the work on the railroads easier, I proposed that you should set out from Greenville. To make this move as strong as it should be, I suggested that a great portion of the troops in Mississippi should be sent to South Carolina to relieve your command. Neither the one or the other of my propositions have been positively rejected, but I fear that both will be, or that they will be held under consideration until it is too late to accomplish what either would, if acted upon with that promptness and energy which should characterize all military operations.

The enemy in Tennessee, as elsewhere, is much discouraged, not to say demoralized, and any effective move against his rear must have a powerful effect upon his troops and upon his political affairs, which would in all probability result in a settlement of our troubles by negotiation and treaties of peace.

The general feeling at the Department seems to be in favor of my joining General Johnston, in order that the armies should move together, which would be better if it were possible for us to make a junction in time to take the initiative, and if, when united, the resources of the country through which we would advance were such as to enable the united forces to subsist and forage. The proposition is that the forces united should advance via Kingston and Sparta into Middle Tennessee.

At Sparta it is supposed we may get forage and subsistence for our army. The information that I have in regard to the resources of that part of the State are not such as would warrant me to take my little army there with the hope of living there. About Sparta is the point at which we should expect the enemy to concentrate his entire force to resist our advance. If the nature of the country is such as to enable the enemy to get a strong position, and it is more or less mountainous, we might be obliged to fight them under very disadvantageous circumstances. If we should then meet with reverse we would probably be destroyed, as we could not have enough of supplies to take us to Sparta and back. The condition of the enemy is such, however, that we can count with almost certainty upon victory, if we fight upon anything like equal ground, and if we are in time to take the initiative. I fear that I cannot join General Johnston under a march of 300 miles. Being united with him I should be 150 miles farther from Louisville than I am in East Tennessee at this moment, with several formidable rivers on the route between Dalton and Louisville.

We are all equally interested in the successful issue of this year's operations, as by success we shall surely win a speedy and happy termination of the war. If, on the other hand, we are unfortunate we shall almost as surely have a continuation of the war for the next four years.

Please give the whole matter that mature consideration which the situation so earnestly demands, and let us all go to work with a will and determination which may soon relieve our oppressed country.

The information that I have in regard to the route through Pound Gap into Kentucky is that we may get supplies of subsistence and forage about 100 miles from Abingdon, and in abundance thence on to Louisville, with but one stream of any consequence to cross. General Bragg, who ought to know definitely the resources of Middle Tennessee, seems to be quite confident that our combined forces can get an abundance of supplies there.

I am, general, very respectfully, your obedient servant,

J. LONGSTREET,
Lieutenant-General.

P. S.—I do not think that the enemy will be in condition to commence active operations before the 1st of May. I presume that the Department will communicate with you very soon upon the subject that I have presented, and I hope that I may have been able to present the matter in such a light as to enable you to prepare yourself for an early answer to any points that may be laid before you.

J. L.

ATLANTA, GA., *March* 15, 1864.

Brig. Gen. M. J. WRIGHT, *Commanding at Atlanta:*

SIR : The clause of the late order from army headquarters prohibiting non-combatants from visiting Dalton is, until further instructions are received, revoked. You are requested to allow all persons whom you think, in the exercise of a sound discretion, ought to have passports, to go. This is not intended to affect any orders heretofore issued prohibiting doubtful characters of either sex from going to the army.

By command of General Johnston.

Very respectfully, your obedient servant,

BENJ. S. EWELL,
Assistant Adjutant-General.

ATLANTA, GA.,
March 15, 1864.

Brig. Gen. M. J. WRIGHT,
Commanding at Atlanta:

SIR : It has been reported that there are upward of 300 prisoners confined at this post, against a large number of whom no charges have been preferred. Where it is impracticable to bring the parties to trial, by reason of want of witnesses or other good cause, you are respectfully requested to send them to their commands ; also, when the witnesses are with the commands of the accused, or when the interests of the service seem to demand their trial there ; also in all cases in which charges have not been preferred, a sufficient time for this since the arrests having elapsed. Those intended for trial here ought to have their cases speedily disposed of. The object of all this is to have a general prison delivery.

It has been reported that the condition of the prisons allow communication between the Confederate and Federal prisoners. This ought to be corrected.

By command of General Johnston.

Very respectfully, your obedient servant,

BENJ. S. EWELL,
Assistant Adjutant-General.

ATLANTA, GA.,
March 15, 1864.

Brig. Gen. MARCUS J. WRIGHT,
Commanding Post:

GENERAL : In compliance with your instructions of this date, I have the honor to submit the following report of the number of men belonging to the local troops at this place who are effective, and who could be relied upon in defense of the city :

Arsenal battalion, Maj. J. K. McCall commanding........................... 150
Artillery company, Captain Hudson.. 99
Captain Baird's company of infantry (detailed men, with Major Cunningham). 100
Confederate States Naval Works company..................................... 80
Capt. T. C. Jackson's company of infantry.................................. 20
Capt. J. F. Alexander's company of cavalry 40
Capt. G. G. Hull's company of infantry, Atlanta and West Point Railroad 20
Capt. J. H. Porter's company of infantry, Georgia railroad 20
Capt. H. H. Witt's company of infantry, Southern Express Company 20

Total 549

The Confederate States Naval Works company has never been organized and mustered as the other local troops, but can be relied upon when needed. The companies composed of the employés on the railroads and in Southern Express Company have quite a small effective force at all times ready, in comparison with the numbers shown on their muster-rolls, owing to the nature of their employment, which keeps them constantly traveling to and from this place. The strength of the commands as shown above can be relied upon at all times.

I am, general, very respectfully, your obedient servant,

M. H. WRIGHT,
Colonel, Commanding.

DEMOPOLIS, *March* 15, 1864.

Maj. Gen. S. D. LEE,
Canton, Miss. :

Later intelligence and the reported condition of certain affairs with you warrants the suspension of the movement ordered for the present. Answer.

L. POLK,
Lieutenant-General.

DEMOPOLIS, *March* 15, 1864.

General MAURY,
Mobile :

Sherman has given out he is to make an expedition up Red River ; I do not believe it. He and Hurlbut have gone down the river from Vicksburg with about one-half or two-thirds of his army ; I think we shall hear of him on the Gulf coast ; many of his troops have been furloughed and gone up the river. Keep a special lookout along the coast, especially on Pensacola.

L. POLK,
Lieutenant-General.

DEMOPOLIS, *March* 15, 1864.

Major-General FORREST,
Okolona :

General Lee reports a number of Sherman's troops gone off up river on furlough ; McPherson at Vicksburg ; Sherman and Hurlbut gone down river with rest of army in forty-two steamers, said to be going up Red River as far as Shreveport. McPherson reports the spring campaign inaugurated by Sherman, Thomas, and Smith a failure. Chalmers is here. Your action on his case referred to War Department. I have no other orders for you besides those given when you were here. Keep me advised through the telegraph on the Mobile and Ohio Railroad.

L. POLK,
Lieutenant-General.

DEMOPOLIS, *March* 15, 1864.

General COOPER,

Adjutant and Inspector General :

General Lee, from Canton, reports a considerable number of Sherman's troops gone up river on furlough from Vicksburg. McPherson left in command at Vicksburg. Sherman and Hurlbut gone down river with large part of army on forty-two boats ; said to be going up Red River as far as Shreveport. McPherson reports the spring campaign inaugurated by Sherman, Banks, Thomas, and Smith a failure. General Forrest states that seven-eighths of Smith's cavalry have gone to Nashville. General Maury's scouts report many troops sent in sea steamers to Florida.

L. POLK,
Lieutenant-General.

Send this dispatch also to General Johnston.

L. POLK,
Lieutenant-General.

WAR DEPARTMENT, C. S. A.,
Richmond, Va., March 15, 1864.

Lieut. Gen. L. POLK.

Commanding, &c. :

GENERAL : Your letter of February 29* was received a few days since by the hands of the officer intrusted with its delivery, but my engagements were at the time so pressing I was unable to reply before his return.

I regret to be unable to accord with you in the views you entertain and the changes you propose in the control of the commissary arrangements of your department. You are scarcely aware, perhaps, of the many embarrassments and difficulties which existed, before the present system was adopted, in collecting supplies for the general commissariat, and their equitable distribution among the various armies of the respective departments. So long as the control vested with the commander of each department over the operations of the quartermaster and commissary bureaus within his military command, there always was, as there naturally would be, a decided predominance given to the supply and provision by each commander of his special command ; not until stores deemed ample by each, not only for present use, but possible contingencies, were supplied to his own department, was there aid or even permission given to the officers of the bureau to obtain and remove supplies for other armies. It not unfrequently happened, indeed, that commanders of adjoining departments, instead of aiding, were zealously operating against each other to prevent any resources from being withdrawn from their respective departments. This course of action, while always injurious, could yet be borne so long as the resources of each department sufficed in the main for the needs of the special command ; but when. as more recently has become the case, it is absolutely necessary for the maintenance of the armies in some of the departments that supplies should be largely drawn from others, it becomes absolutely necessary to correct the evil and adopt a more general system.

---

* See Part II, p. 814.

With this view the plan now in operation was devised. Under it the officers of the Commissary and Quartermaster's Bureaus, acting independently, are required to collect and accumulate stores of supplies from all portions of the Confederacy, and to hold them in convenient depots within the various departments, subject to equitable distribution, and prepared to meet requisitions from the armies in the field. My conviction of the necessity of this system is strong, and carried out efficiently and equitably it ought to secure more general satisfaction than has heretofore been attained. There may be irregularities or imperfection in the working which it is desirable should be disclosed and corrected, but the system is right in itself, and may, I feel assured, be made to work well. The officers of the Commissary and Quartermaster's Bureaus are intended to be directly responsible to the respective heads, but at the same time they are always to be subject to the inspection of the commander of the department, and to any call for information or returns, and may be required, as they ought to do, to give information of the depots and accumulations, so that proper provision may, in case of necessity, be made for the defense or removal of supplies.

Most of the difficulties, I think, which are suggested by you must have resulted from some omissions or irregularities in the conduct of the officers. They certainly should have made reports, and may be called on for such to you, whenever you deem it important, for their p n s of depot and the amount of accumulated supplies, and I should die pleased at all times to receive from you any suggestions as to the difficulties existing under the present arrangements and the best mode of remedying them. I trust, however, that reflection will induce you to concur in the superiority of the general plan, and that you will address your attention to making it as regular and efficient in its execution as possible.

Very respectfully,

JAMES A. SEDDON,
Secretary of War.

HEADQUARTERS DEPARTMENT OF THE GULF,
Mobile, Ala., March 15, 1864.

Col. T. M. JACK,
Assistant Adjutant-General:

COLONEL: On the — instant I sent Colonel Maury with 200 cavalry of his regiment, a battalion of sharpshooters, and a section of horse artillery, by rail as far as Shubuta, to move at once into Jones County and break up the organized deserters who were threatening to interfere with the repairs of the Mobile and Ohio Railroad. He appears to have discharged the duty assigned him with his accustomed vigor and success. I have received no detailed report from him yet, but have learned from him that he has long ago broken them up and driven them out of Jones County; caused them to cease their depredations and break up their organizations in the neighboring counties of Covington and Perry.

In several instances he inflicted summary punishment upon those captured. I have ordered him to withdraw his forces, and have taken measures to cause the deserters to come in and report to their regiments. Among others I permitted the Rev. Mr. Collins, a man of intelligence and high respectability, to go into Jones County and use his personal influence to induce the men to return to their colors. Of course I charged him to make no pledges or promises for me. I inclose Colonel Maury's last dispatch.

I am, colonel. very respectfully, your obedient servant,

DABNEY H. MAURY,
Major-General, Commanding Department of the Gulf.

[Inclosure.]

ELLISVILLE, *March* 12, 1864.

MY DEAR GENERAL: Yesterday we moved on Leaf River, 10 miles west of this place, and I am satisfied that there no longer remains any organization of deserters in this county, although some few scattered outlaws are still lurking about in the swamps and will have to be hunted out with dogs. They have scattered in every direction; some west, but most for Honey Island and the coast. They brag that they will get Yankee aid and return. They are panic-stricken, and although their leaders twice got them in position to ambush me they fled both times to the swamps on my approach. They don't mind being taken prisoners and sent off, but they won't face the hanging.

There has never been at any time more than 150 resident deserters in this county, although some more have been over from Perry and Covington to help to whip the cavalry. This is positive, and there are not 20 men lying out in Jones at this time.

If I were sure you would not want us I would scout on Pearl River, but I hear nothing from you lately. I got a dispatch from Garner last night: " Don't leave a company in Jones County," which I don't understand, but presume refers to some previous order which I have missed. We have moved about very rapidly. and there is no part of the county unexplored by us. I shall send Moreland to report to you and the other companies to Conoley, as I have no further need of infantry.

We have supplied ourselves from Jasper County, and have drawn nothing from Mobile since we left, which I suppose you are glad of. Send to Bob Cottrell for a bear's skin, if you have not already received it.

Most sincerely and affectionately, yours,

H. MAURY,
Colonel, &c.

P. S.—The state of affairs which has prevailed here is on account of the want of protection to property afforded by the presence of even a small number of troops. The adjoining counties, Perry, Green, and Covington, are in just as bad a condition, and all the southern counties in Mississippi will follow if they are not intimidated by what has been done in Jones. The women are frightened and are working hard to get the men to come in. and are doing some good. They no longer encourage them to take the woods, which is a favorable change.

H. M.

———

DEPARTMENT OF LIEUTENANT-GENERAL POLK,
March 15, 1864.

Maj. J. C. DENIS. *Provost-Marshal-General, Mobile, Ala.:*

MAJOR : I have the honor to report that in compliance with instructions received from your office, I proceeded as near the enemy's lines as was necessary and completed such arrangements as will secure to the general commanding information from time to time of the forces. designs, and movements of the enemy, as well as other information of general use to the Confederacy. I have also placed within the lines a person who will within the next few weeks traverse a large part of the West and North, gathering all the general movements of the enemy, their strength, and future plans as far as an individual can. This person is a highly intelligent and observant lady, and one who from her connections has access to influential and popular leaders of different political parties. She proposes to be in Richmond during the month of April. Letters by flag of truce, chemically prepared. will be sent me at Fort Valley, Ga.. as that was the best point I could arrange for the present, and I respectfully suggest that I be sent there for a time at least. These agents will be named to the department commander or yourself if deemed prudent.

I trust the letters forwarded you on my route from time to time have been received and were useful. I regret to say that the condition of affairs in Northwestern Mississippi exhibits much demoralization, and the tone of feeling toward the South is much weakened. This is attributable to the association with Yankees in Memphis, the want of protection afforded against robbers, and a depreciated currency of no value in procuring such supplies as the necessities of the people demand.

Immediately upon the withdrawal of the forces of General Forrest from the line of the Tallahatchie a general movement of cotton took place toward Memphis, and not less than 2,000 bales were carried in. The excuse for this traffic with the enemy was the necessity for procuring food and clothing for family use and for relatives in the Confederate army, and in some instances it was true, but in very many cases it was for the purposes of speculation and extortion, and to carry into Memphis such information as would be of use to the Yankees in their future raids.

This traffic is encouraged by the Federals for many reasons—for the cotton, for the purpose of obtaining from the citizens of the South an oath of allegiance to the United States, thus giving foundation to the reports of a returning Union sentiment throughout the country, and by this means encouragement to the Federal administration.

No one can buy or sell produce or supplies without taking the oath, and the practice is dangerous in its effects and pernicious in its influence. and whether regarded as binding or not by those who take it creates them in law, if not in fact, alien enemies, and I have found that those who associate much with Yankees adopt very many of their opinions.

I find that of late some very influential and wealthy citizens of Memphis have gone back and taken the oath to secure their property, collect their rents, &c., and those, too, who were loudest in their professions of attachment to the South, telling of their sacrifices for her welfare and the sons given to sustain her in her hour of trial, but no word has been said of their increased wealth by speculation and extortion. Some of these persons have large property among us. The following persons are among the number: W. B. Greenlaw owns a large amount of cotton in the South, has taken oath ; Newton Ford ; —— Flarrity owns property in Selma ; a brother of W. K. Brinkley collects his rents in Memphis. Such men as these influence others.

I find also in other instances persons from the South going through the country proclaiming the Southern Confederacy as played out; was nothing but a military despotism ; that Bragg's men would not fight without they were paid in greenbacks.   These were the disloyal expressions of one G. W. Hunt, a brother of Maj. W. R. Hunt, C. S. Army, who was purchasing hogs, he said, for the use of troops at Selma at 25 cents per pound.   This from a person of his standing and connections is of great injury to our cause.

It is reported to me that a Major Pleasants has been engaged in sending cotton to Memphis as the property of the Confederate States and speculating upon its returns, and that a Colonel Dickins, who claims to be in the C. S. Army, has also been engaged in the contraband trade.

The evidences of these reports can be obtained at Panola, and the names of all who have been or are engaged in trade with the enemy may be procured at the different ferries upon the Coldwater River. The counties west and north of Columbus are filled with deserters and robbers, who are devastating the country of horses and mules. Many claim to be impressing officers, but are with few exceptions irresponsible persons ; and around the country from the Tallahatchie to Memphis are organized bands of men acting, they say, under authority of the War Department, but having no such authority, who are living upon the people upon the plea of being soldiers and then stealing every available horse, mule. or hog they can lay hands upon.

A Captain Bobo has a company of this description, and Colonels Price and Collins have been depredating upon the people in like manner. and, as they report, under the same authority. In many cases these men of Bobo's have taken the cotton and supplies of people, and themselves sold it upon the lines for their own use and benefit. and in one instance levied a contribution of $900 upon one Houghton. This was done by a party under a Sergeant English, but most of the depredations have been upon the unprotected families of soldiers, whose natural guardians are battling for their country's cause while these deserters are preying upon their families.

Mr. M. F. Davis, of Calhoun County, can point out the whereabouts of the deserters of that county. He lives near Bond's hat manufactory. Col. Ben. Bedford, of Panola County, can give the localities of those in that county. He lives 5 miles south of Senatobia. I herewith append a list of Federal spies who are frequently in the South and within our lines : Miss Dora Slaughter, lives in Shanghai.   Boyt, lives in Nonconnah Bottom, on west side, and on Hernando plank road. John Hunt, deserter from C. S. Army, lives 1 mile north of Horn Lake road, on old plank road. Whitney, lives 1½ miles north of Shanghai and one-half mile west of Hernando plank road. Hunter, lives near Whitney, on railroad. Ordam, deserter from C. S. Army, in a company commanded by Cartwright, a notorious robber and spy, and lives near same place. Widow Calhoun and mother, lives in Shanghai. Widow Kinsley, from Vicksburg, at large. Steel, lives on edge of Nonconnah Bottom, 1 mile east of Hernando plank road. William Alman, deserter from C. S. Army— says he escaped from Mobile after stabbing the guard—lives on Ben. Bedford, jr.'s, place. near Horn Lake. Mrs. Ferris and Black, frequently in the South, live in Memphis. Joe and John Payne, live near Fort Pickering. Tom and Joe Sellers, live near same place. A list of these names has been given by me to General Forrest.

The limited means placed in my hands have prevented me from remaining longer in that part or visiting other parts of the country in Northwest Mississippi, or from employing other agents than those who act gratuitously. I would in conclusion respectfully suggest to the general commanding a plan for the suppression of most, if not all, the lawlessness prevalent in that part of the country, and that is the employment of one or more companies of cavalry as a permanent provost guard, patrolling the country in all directions and destroying all ferries and roads except those absolutely necessary for travel; thus breaking up the mode of egress and ingress to Memphis as much as possible. These guards will answer the double purpose of scouts, couriers, and are ready for service against small raiding parties from the enemy's lines. They could scatter through the country so as not to attract the attention of a large force, and can be easily consolidated when necessary. These, under the command of a deputy provost-marshal-general for the northern part of Mississippi and West Tennessee, would do much to prevent these disorders.

Respectfully, your obedient servant,

H. WINSLOW.

DALTON, March 16, 1864.

General BRAGG :

GENERAL : I have had the honor to receive your letter of the 7th instant.

The organization of the artillery which I found in this army had been made by Lieutenant-General Hardee, with a corresponding tabular report and recommendations for the appointment of field officers. I postponed action in the matter from day to day, hoping for the assistance of a general officer of artillery. You speak of Major-General Lovell in connection with that position ; might he not be assigned to it ? It is no more inadequate to the grade of major-general than are most of our divisions of infantry.

You direct me to take measures to procure artillery horses as soon as possible. I have been doing so since January, but I beg that it may be considered that I am confined to my small limits in the northwestern part of Georgia and the mountains of Alabama, long since stripped of everything necessary to an army. I shall therefore be dependent on the Department in Richmond for all the supplies enumerated in my letter to you of February 27. My "staff departments" can get forward only such supplies as may be furnished by officers who owe obedience neither to them nor to me, and whose purchases are necessarily made outside of my department. In connection with this subject I beg leave to say that the plan of campaign to which you have twice referred has not been communicated to me, and that the scale on which preparations are to be made must depend on a knowledge of it and of the forces to be used.

Lieutenant-General Longstreet has written to me that he is directed to confer with me in relation to a junction of our forces at Madisonville, East Tenn., for a movement thence into Middle Tennessee. It seems to me that the point of junction is too near the enemy and that his armies, being much nearer to each other than ours are, might easily unite against either of ours before the junction. It seems to me that such a junction should be by routes on which our troops would not be exposed to such a chance. I respectfully suggest, too, for consideration the magnitude of the outfit required for such a march, in order that the proper departments in Richmond may be urged to great exertion. Everything required must be taken from this point—ordnance stores for a campaign and food for man and beast for our army—to Madisonville, and for both thence until we can gather provision in Middle Tennessee ; in all, eighteen or twenty days. A great additional quantity of field transportation will be required.

Most respectfully, your obedient servant,

J. E. JOHNSTON,
General.

HEADQUARTERS,
En route for East Tennessee, March 16, 1864.

General J. E. JOHNSTON,
Commanding, &c. :

MY DEAR GENERAL : I send you a copy of a letter just finished to the President. As it expresses my ideas more fully than I expect to be able to do, I send it that you may give it such consideration as it may merit. I do not know what is most likely to be done. The President and General Bragg seem bent upon a campaign into Middle Tennessee. They may adopt my proposition, however, and move Beauregard and myself into Kentucky by Pound Gap. I think it the strongest effort that has been attempted during the war and have confidence in its resulting in a speedy peace.

General Lee came down to assist me in having it adopted, but we do not know yet what will be done. All agree in the idea that we should take the initiative. If I were with you I am satisfied that we could work out great results, but it would be by a slower and much more tedious and difficult process. The result I have no doubt of, however, if there is anything in Middle Tennessee to feed our troops upon.

The President is expecting to hear from you soon, and I believe that this is his reason for inaction at present.

I remain, general, very respectfully, your obedient servant,

J. LONGSTREET,
Lieutenant-General.

[Inclosure.]

HEADQUARTERS,
En route for East Tennessee, March 16, 1864.

His Excellency President DAVIS :

SIR : I have the honor to acknowledge your favor of the 7th instant.

The army now occupying a portion of East Tennessee has been obliged to depend entirely upon the resources of the country for subsistence stores and for forage, and in some measure for clothing. To hold a part of the State which could supply the wants of the army we were obliged to occupy a line very near the enemy.

The line from Dandridge, on the French Broad, across the Holston near Mossy Creek, was selected as necessary to our subsistence. The enemy occupying Cumberland Gap to our right and rear, it was necessary that we should have a considerable cavalry force to watch any movements from that quarter, and to break up any foraging parties that the enemy might send out upon the east side of the mountains. The general disposition of the troops was made more with a view to gathering supplies than for active military operations. In December last I reported to the Department that Rogersville was the nearest to the enemy that I could occupy without General Martin's cavalry, as the enemy's cavalry was strong and we entirely dependent upon foraging for our existence. Under the hope that the Department had advised you of these facts I was in hopes that I might retain the cavalry as long as it was intended that we should hold East Tennessee. The enemy re-enforced his cavalry force to a considerable extent from Middle Tennessee, and made an effort about the middle of January to get possession of the country that we were occupying for forage, &c., but we were fortunate enough to retain the country occupied by us and to drive the enemy entirely back to his fortifications. In his retreat the enemy gave such evidence of demoralization that I determined to advance our entire force as soon as our railroad was repaired and our men shod. Early in February the railroad was finished and all of our men were tolerably comfortable with their winter clothing; the army was therefore advanced as far as Strawberry Plains. General Martin's cavalry was advanced on the south side of French Broad, and his pickets were posted so as to keep the enemy under the protection of his fortifications. Our pickets on the north side of the Holston were also advanced and the enemy's stronghold reconnoitered from both sides of the river. The strength of the fortifications was greatly increased since the last siege, and many other works and improvements had been added to the general system of defenses. But the enemy had no provisions on hand, and I determined to ask for 10,000 men to aid me against any succoring army in the reduction of the garrison at Knoxville. I telegraphed General Johnston at the same time, asking him to cut the communication between Chattanooga and Knoxville, so as to keep back any succoring force.

Failing to get the re-enforcements and co-operation both, it seemed to be useless to lay siege to Knoxville again with an almost certainty of being obliged to raise it again before the enemy could be starved out. As we could not expect to capture the enemy's force at Knoxville unassisted, there was no particular reason for holding my lines so near the enemy's.

The order for the removal of General Martin's cavalry to General Johnston came, therefore, at the very moment that we were in want of some reason for withdrawing our lines to a point where we could give our men and animals some rest and time to prepare for the summer's campaign. Our present position is probably more secure than the line indicated in your letter, as the topographical features of the country are stronger. It also gives a little advantage over the other line, which we had entirely exhausted of forage and other supplies. It also gives us a little more room for maneuvers in case the enemy should come out from his works.

The advantage in taking Knoxville would have been very considerable, I think, inasmuch as we should have captured an army of 12,000 or 15,000 men and our loss would have been small, as we should have taken it by starving the enemy out. He was much demoralized and had no supplies in depot except meal. It would have given us a very strong point, too, for future operations against the enemy's line of communication in Middle Tennessee.

My proposition to mount my infantry for the purpose of throwing it upon the enemy's line of communication in Kentucky would be attended with much difficulty, but I am inclined to believe that it might be accomplished. Three-fourths of our men claim to be able to mount themselves. I presume that nearly half of them could. I could mount a third in case of emergency, and I thought it probable that I might get animals from elsewhere for the balance by reducing transportation to the lowest possible limit.

This force mounted and in Kentucky could destroy any mounted force that the enemy could bring against us. and it could avoid any infantry force that might be too strong for us. If obliged to avoid one point of the enemy's railroad it could move around and occupy others, and finally force the enemy to retreat from Tennessee, and probably to the northern part of Kentucky. In this position mounted we could hardly be farther from the other armies than we are at present, inasmuch as the greater rapidity of our movements would enable us to co-operate as readily as we now can.

The proposition to unite the army of General Johnston with my forces at Maryville, East Tenn., for the purpose of moving into Middle Tennessee, via Sparta, would have the effect to force the enemy to withdraw his forces and concentrate near Nashville, for the purpose of giving battle. If he did not fight we could force him still farther back by moving into Kentucky. If he should fight, our forces ought to be able to win a glorious victory. I apprehend some difficulty, however, in making the move so as to effect a junction of the forces in good time.

The two armies are about 200 miles apart, with the enemy holding all the country between us. As soon as either army starts to move, the enemy must get advised of it. He occupying the railroad will have great facilities for concentrating his forces against one or the other of these armies, and he would cripple the one that he might encounter so badly as to prevent the further progress of the campaign. This we must assume that he will do at all hazards, as there are no supplies in the country through which our armies would pass. The enemy might depend upon delaying us by occupying the mountain passes until our supplies are consumed and force us to retreat in that way. Both armies would be compelled to have everything in the way of forage, subsistence, ammunition, &c., from the moment of starting out, and in such quantities as to last them until they reached Sparta, without then the certainty of reaching these articles in any considerable quantities. My information leads me to fear that at Sparta we would find a great scarcity of supplies—that is, for any large army.

It occurs to me that a better plan for making a campaign into Middle Tennessee would be to re-enforce General Johnston in his present position by throwing the Mississippi troops and those from General Beauregard's department and my own to that point.

The shortest practicable route by which I could join him must be a little over 200 miles, and this through a very rough, mountainous country, and at a season of the year when we may expect some delays from the mountain streams. It would probably be better, therefore, to take a quicker route and march from my present position to Greenville, S. C., and take the railroad thence to Atlanta and march up from Atlanta.

As there are two routes of railway to Atlanta I have supposed that one can be used for the speedy transportation of troops while the other is occupied in transporting provisions, &c. This move may be made, if it is begun very soon, in time to enable us to take the initiative in the approaching campaign.

Our strongest and most effective move, however, is to concentrate an army near Abingdon, Va., and throw it into Kentucky upon the enemy's lines of communication. This can be done best by moving General Beauregard up via Greenville, S. C., to unite with my troops and march through Pound Gap.

General Beauregard could collect his transportation and supplies at Greenville, S. C., for the purpose ostensibly of supplying my army, which could be advertised as about to march by that route for General Johnston's army. Having his supplies and transportation ready, he could throw his troops up by rail and put them on the march as rapidly as they could arrive. We could thus mask the move so completely that our own people would not suspect it before the troops were well on the march for Kentucky.

If General Beauregard could start on his march from Morganton. N. C., he would have some 60 miles less than if he sets out from Greenville or Spartanburg, S. C. The move itself would not surprise the enemy, of course, but the strength of it would, and we should in all probability encounter a force of his which could not stand before us.

If the enemy is obliged to abandon his present line he must give up nearly. if not all, of Tennessee south of the Cumberland. This of itself will be equal to a great victory for us. If he moves his entire force to the rear for the purpose of attacking General Beauregard with his concentrated forces, General B., if he sees fit, can avoid him, and our armies, Johnston's and Beauregard's, can unite in Tennessee and then advance into Kentucky. or if we only hold Tennessee without a fight we shall have accomplished great moral advantages.

But there can scarcely be a doubt but we can advance into Kentucky and hold that State if we are once united. I presume that nearly all of General Beauregard's troops could be spared from his department by drawing off General Loring's division from Mississippi and General Maury's at Mobile, and replacing the troops drawn from General Beauregard's department by one of these commands, and placing one at Atlanta to re-enforce Charleston. Savannah, Mobile. or Dalton.

This last position would only be necessary as a temporary precaution, of course, as the enemy will be entirely occupied by the move into Kentucky as soon as he begins to feel us upon his rear. This move would leave our own positions as securely covered as they now are, at the same time gives us the opportunity to strike a vital blow at the enemy. It can be made much sooner than any other; promises much greater results than any other without such difficult and complicated maneuvers as the move into Middle Tennessee; it gives us the certain means of getting provisions for our troops, and if entirely successful will put an end to the war.

It has the objection that there may be some difficulty in joining the armies of General Johnston and General Beauregard. but it is more probable that these two armies would be able to unite without serious trouble. After the enemy has been thrown back into Kentucky, and whilst in the confusion and trouble attending his speedy retreat [sic]. than that two armies starting from the two ends of the enemy's lines to effect a junction at an intermediate point would be able to join and have an opportunity to get a blow at the enemy.

There would be no necessity that General Johnston should pursue the enemy rapidly, so as to expose himself to the enemy.

He could throw the cavalry under Generals Lee (S. D.), Forrest, Roddey, and Wheeler upon the enemy's rear, and damage him so much during the retreat that he would hardly be prepared to give us battle in Kentucky when he reached there. If we should fight him in Kentucky with General Beauregard's army alone, there can be no great doubt but we can greatly cripple him without any great injury to ourselves, and then move back and join General Johnston at our leisure.

My troops can start out upon this or any other move in three days. General Beauregard could not prepare, however, sooner than the 1st of April. If we can get the troops in motion by that time we shall be able to take the initiative, as the enemy will not be prepared to move before the 1st of May. He may, and probably will, make a diversion in Virginia before that time for the purpose of trying to draw my troops from the West, and thus put a stop to this campaign. He seems already in some concern about our position and movements.

These ideas are given under the supposition that, if they are thought worthy to be adopted, it will be done with a determination to execute the movements with such undivided vigor as to insure great results. In order that there may be as little delay as possible, I have hurriedly given my views. In my hurry I fear that I may not have made myself as well understood as I would like, and I may have failed to make the suggestions as much in detail as you would like.

I remain, sir, with great respect, your most obedient servant,

> J. LONGSTREET,
> *Lieutenant-General.*

HEADQUARTERS,
Petersburg, Va., March 16, 1864.

General R. E. LEE,
  Commanding, &c.:

DEAR GENERAL: I have delayed at this place to answer the letter of the President, which you read to me in his presence on Monday. I send you a copy of the letter as the readiest means of explaining my appreciation of our position.* I fear that my views may not be regarded by the President and General Bragg as worthy of much attention; as I have better hope of calm consideration from you, I send them to you. The move of Beauregard's and my forces will, if as strong as it should be made, say even 40,000 men (infantry and artillery), be the beginning of the end of this war. It can be made, and therefore should be made, even if it costs us some little inconvenience elsewhere. It can be made an entire success. Your influence with the President, and your prestige as a great leader, will enable you to cause its adoption and successful execution. You can remain with your present army until the head of our column reaches Cumberland Mountains.

It is quite probable that the enemy will be too much occupied for his safety in the event to attempt anything in Virginia. If he should, your successor could fight him well enough to prevent any serious trouble, or he could retire slowly, and depend upon the fortifications. All of the preparations for our move into Kentucky I

---

* See p. 637.

can arrange before General Beauregard reaches me, and we can do without you until we get near. The enemy's unnecessary delay and want of decision may prolong the war another four years, and may possibly result in our entire destruction. My great hope is in you, and I know that this is the feeling of the army, and I believe it to be of the country.

You complain of my excess of confidence, but I think that it is based upon good judgment and a proper appreciation of our difficulties. I have entire confidence if our affairs are properly managed, but I have none if they are not well managed. Hence my great anxiety and concern at our present inaction.

You spoke in one of your letters of some 1,500 saddles which you could let me have, and bridles. Please send them to me, that I may use them in mounting some infantry, temporarily, for the purpose of sending parties into Kentucky for the purpose of getting out beef-cattle. If we remain quiet much longer our provisions will give out, and as the commissary-general will send us nothing, I must begin to prepare to supply ourselves.

I remain, general, most respectfully, your obedient servant,

J. LONGSTREET,
Lieutenant-General.

DALTON, *March* 16, 1864.

His Excellency the PRESIDENT:
Richmond:

Scouts report rumors of the transfer of the Eleventh and Twelfth Corps. In consequence all measures in my power are taken to ascertain the fact. Observation will be continued. Scouts report troops coming from Knoxville to Chattanooga. Lieutenant-General Polk reports most of Mississippi troops gone with Sherman to Shreveport. Scouts report, on 13th, troops passing Bridgeport to Chattanooga for the last three days.

J. E. JOHNSTON.

ATLANTA, GA.,
March 16, 1864.

General MACKALL,
Chief of Staff:

GENERAL: It is my conviction from what I've seen since I have been here that at least a regiment of average strength is necessary for the proper preservation of order at this post and for preventing officers and soldiers belonging to the army from remaining here without proper authority, even in larger numbers than the guard asked for by General Wright. There are so many facilities for escaping observation by those inclined to do so that great vigilance, with a sufficient guard, is, in my opinion, absolutely essential. There has been a marked change for the better since the troops now here arrived.

Very respectfully, &c.,

BENJ. S. EWELL,
Assistant Adjutant-General.

TUNNEL HILL, GA.,
March 16, 1864.

General J. E. JOHNSTON:

DEAR GENERAL: On the receipt of your letter I sent a note to 3 officers who were in General Wharton's division at the time the false order was written by him or by his sanction, and to which you referred. I called the attention of these officers to the forged order and required them to state what they recollected regarding the circumstances and facts connected with the matter. These officers each made their statements, neither of them knowing that another statement was being made, as they were in different parts of the command. Their statements differ on minor points, but all go to show that the order was written and that it had a bad effect. The facts, as they came to me at the time, were as follows: On the 9th of December last, with the sanction of General Hardee, I ordered General Wharton to move to a point south of Coosa River to recruit, rest, and instruct his command. General Wharton delayed starting with his command for two days. On the receipt of my order to move to the rear an order was written and laid upon the table of his adjutant's office, which order purported to come from me, and directed that Wharton's command should commence picketing on the left of our army and run a line of pickets over Lookout Mountain to the Tennessee River.

Such a disposition would of course have destroyed the horses of the command, as it would have been impossible for them to have been fed.

The command was of course dissatisfied, and abused me as the author of the order, at the same time severely criticising my judgment in disposing of cavalry. General Wharton came to me and in a laughing way remarked that he got up a joke by having an order published ordering his command to picket on the mountain in order to see how the command would take it.

I fear, however, that he did not mention it to me until he had become convinced that the matter was so public that I would hear of it by other means.

The truth is. General Wharton allowed his ambition to completely turn his head, as his friend in Congress had assured him that he should command the cavalry of this army, he being one of those politicians (not statesman) who looked upon things we would consider dishonorable as legitimate tricks, and he forgot that he was an officer instead of a frontier political trickster. This state of things has been going on for some time, the object appearing to be to convince his command that he was their friend, while I was not, and also that he was superior as an officer, &c. I regret to state that such things are very contagious and spread to the officers, who sought to cover their own delinquencies by reflecting falsely upon their superiors. I have taken hold of the matter very firmly, and am holding all such officers to a strict account for their conduct, both as officers and honorable men, and it is already having a good effect. I am determined to root out the last vesture of such dealing in this command or fall in the attempt to accomplish this object. I am getting the command to understand the matter, and everything is going on smoothly. I am pleased to state that my efforts to improve and instruct my command are appreciated by both privates and officers, and notwithstanding the misrepresentation made by the disorganizers, they have failed to deprive me of the esteem of my soldiers, which is so essential to success. It is true a few soldiers have by their efforts been induced to believe their false representations, and thus allow themselves to be prejudiced, but I am happy to state they are very few.

Very respectfully,

JOS. WHEELER,
Major-General.

GENERAL ORDERS, }   HEADQUARTERS HOOD'S CORPS,
No. 40.   }   *Dalton, Ga., March 16, 1864.*

I. Guns and colors captured from the enemy in time of battle, being the most valuable trophies of war, as establishing the valor of the troops capturing them, the following instructions are given for the guidance of divisions, brigades, and regimental commanders:

II. When guns are captured one or more slightly wounded men should be detailed to remain with them to prevent their being claimed by troops not engaged in their capture.

III. When colors are captured and the troops are still pressing forward they should be torn from the staff and tied around the waist of one of the men, or sent to the rear by a wounded man.

IV. Commanding officers should see that captured colors are not lost or mislaid, but that they are placed in the capital of the Confederate States, or the capital of the State to which the captors belong, as a proud memorial to future generations of their heroic achievements.

By command of Lieutenant-General Hood:

J. P. WILSON,
Assistant Adjutant-General.

RICHMOND, VA.,
March 16, 1864.

Lieut. Gen. L. POLK.
Demopolis, Ala.:

General Forrest has no power to relieve an officer and order him to report in person to the department commander. The officer should remain with the command and be tried if amenable to charges.

S. COOPER,
Adjutant and Inspector General.

WAR DEPARTMENT, C. S. A.,
Richmond, Va., March 16, 1864.

Lieut. Gen. L. POLK.
Commanding, &c.:

GENERAL: I have the honor to acknowledge your letter of the 1st instant, and have to express regret at my inability to give it an earlier reply. I can well understand that serious embarrassments must exist in the regular administration of the conscript law in your department; but they result, in my judgment, mainly from the irregular action which was established under the authority given to General Johnston, similar to that which you now propose should be intrusted to you.

During the emergency of the Mississippi campaign, when it was hoped the people might be turned out almost in mass, the power of administering the law was granted to General Johnston at his request. He soon turned the whole matter over to General Pillow. That officer, with characteristic energy and zeal, with numbers of supernumerary officers and in an irregular manner, proceeded to change the old system of administration previously adopted by the Conscript Bureau, and to enforce a sort of general impressment of all the conscript classes in some way into the service. Numberless complaints of irregularities, of disregard of the exemptions and restrictions of law, and of the employment only of military coercion besieged the Department. The whole proceeding was a departure from what had been, on deliberation, adopted as the system of administering the law. The idea of the Department has been, as it believes was the contemplation of Congress, that the conscription should be enforced by the regular agencies of law, and chiefly under the influence and prestige the law commands, steadily and impartially, but with due regard to all the exceptions and limitations contained in its provisions. The idea of the law and that the claim of service was made under its authority was to be kept ever distinct and paramount.

The substitution in lieu of mere military authority and the employment of coercion, when there was really no resistance, was believed to be, as it has proved, mischievous and productive of great discontent. In consequence it was found necessary to revoke General Pillow's authority and again inaugurate the regular administration of the Conscript Bureau.

Of course, the critical period of transition must be one of imperfect execution; but the attention of Colonel Preston, the present efficient head of the Conscript Bureau, is being earnestly directed to the removal of irregularities, and the withdrawal of the supernumeraries called for by General Pillow's plan, and the substitution of the more regular and simpler administration of the law. I am sanguine that the result will soon be manifested of less dissatisfaction, and yet more thorough enforcement of conscription. Instead, therefore, of seeking a remedy in another change and the substitution of a new direction I would earnestly invoke your aid and co-operation, as the commander of the department, to the operations of the Conscript Bureau. Colonel Preston will be happy at all times to profit by your suggestions, and will exact from all his officers and agents due deference to your counsels and wishes.

On the subject of deserters and stragglers within your department, on which you have likewise written. I am very reluctant to oppose any objection to the authority you ask for their recruitment into new organizations. That plan of tempting deserters and stragglers to resume their duty as defenders of the country has been frequently urged on the attention of the Department, and it is not to be denied that, with reference to special localities, it is probable more men could be recruited in that way than by enforcing the previous obligation to service. It must be recollected, however, that the question has a wider scope, and that such mode of proceeding, besides being subversive of discipline. may result most mischievously to the general service by producing dissatisfaction and tempting to desertion.

It has been the deliberate judgment of most of the officers in command, among whom may be specially named Generals Lee and Johnston, that all authority to raise new organizations, and much more those in districts where deserters abound, are mischievous and demoralizing on the soldiers generally. They have consequently written me, urging earnestly that no such authorities should be granted by the Department.

Finding, from my limited experience, not only the pernicious effects described, but likewise that such authorities were often abused and rarely successfully exercised, I have accorded with their request, and for the last month or more have issued no authorities whatever. This has been done, too, by the advice and with the approval of the President himself. Under these circumstances, while I do not say that if on reflection the authority you request is still thought advisable it will not be granted, I prefer, for the present at least, to request your serious reconsideration of the matter, with the hope that fuller information may convince your judgment of the inexpediency of such power.

Very respectfully,

JAMES A. SEDDON,
Secretary of War.

RICHMOND, VA.,
March 17, 1864.

General J. LONGSTREET,
Greeneville, Tenn.:

Send the Hampton Legion, Colonel Gary, with his transportation, overland via Asheville to Greenville, S. C., where they will receive further orders. Let it move at once.

S. COOPER,
Adjutant and Inspector General.

DALTON, *March* 17, 1864.

General BRAGG,
Richmond:

Scouts report enemy's main force at Ringgold, and that re-enforcements have come from Knoxville. Please decide in regard to artillery officers. Railroad repaired nearly to Ringgold.

J. E. JOHNSTON.

ATLANTA, GA.,
March 17, 1864.

Brigadier-General MACKALL,
Chief of Staff:

GENERAL: The following is an extract from a letter received from Maj. E. Taliaferro, ordnance officer at the Confederate States arsenal at Macon, Ga.:

I wish to ask if you cannot assist us at this arsenal by giving us from the army some good workmen who are disabled from field service. We have been much weakened here from time to time by the withdrawal of our operatives, and if that process continues it will eventually cripple our energies to a degree that cannot easily be remedied. We are all the time engaged on work for your army—artillery ammunition, harness accouterments, &c.—and the reports of the last several months will show a large amount of issues to Colonel Oladowski, chief of ordnance. Recently Colonel Walter, assistant adjutant-general, was here, and on looking over our lists of detailed soldiers took from us several of our very best mechanics back to their commands. To-day Lieutenant-Colonel Hays, of General Johnston's staff, came to this office on the same business and looked over the lists, but as only two or three men now remain with us from the Army of Tennessee, and those in bad health, he did not withdraw them. He informed me, however, that there were now with you a large number of men reported as unfit for field service, and whom it is intended to send to Government works. He suggests that we should make requisitions for their services, and I write to you to inquire and to request that if it be possible to send us any good machinists, molders, or blacksmiths, you will get them detailed for that purpose and ordered to report to us. Had I a list I would make formal application by name and regiment, but in lieu thereof write to you to request this favor at your hands. We have many facilities here that cannot be fully turned to account whilst we are so short of operatives skilled in their trades.

The foregoing is respectfully submitted for such action as you may deem necessary. Major Taliaferro is an officer of high merit and his statements are worthy of confidence.

Very respectfully, your obedient servant,

BENJ. S. EWELL,
Assistant Adjutant-General.

GENERAL ORDERS, } HEADQUARTERS HOOD'S CORPS,
No. 41. } *Dalton, Ga., March* 17, 1864.

I. Colors will never be used by sharpshooters when employed as such, nor by skirmishers, as they are too much exposed to capture to be thus risked ; besides, it is often important that our sharpshooters and skirmishers should approach the enemy without attracting unnecessary attention.

II. The attention of division, brigade, and regimental commanders is called to the fact that in attacking an enemy it is all-important to break his front line promptly, as the confusion to which he is thereby subjected renders it comparatively easy to break his second and even third line, which should always be done by our first line if possible. To insure this it is absolutely necessary that our men do not become broken or scattered, which should be fully impressed upon them.

After breaking the enemy's first line, and before attacking his second, brigade commanders will invariably correct the formation and alignment of their commands, if necessary making a temporary halt for this purpose, that such an attack may be made with an unbroken front, thereby avoiding the great risk of failure to which a broken line or disorganized mass is subjected. Such attention should, however, be given to the alignment of the troops while in motion as to avoid the necessity of a halt, as a line of battle once engaged should, if possible, press on until relieved by other troops.

III. The second line should be kept well in hand by division commanders, and when it engages the enemy the first line will halt, reform, and then follow it in support.

IV. Coolness in time of battle on the part of both officers and men is essential to success, as by its exercise officers are better enabled to comprehend and perform their duties, and the men to understand orders and deliver their fire with deadly effect.

V. Official reports of wounded will be based upon the reports of the medical officers, for by including such as are so slightly wounded as to be able to remain on duty false impressions result to ourselves and much encouragement is given the enemy, both of which should be avoided.

By command of Lieutenant-General Hood :

J. P. WILSON,
Assistant Adjutant-General.

SPECIAL ORDERS, (HDQRS. DEPT. OF ALA., MISS., AND E. LA.,
No. 77. $ Demopolis, Ala., March 17, 1864.
*   *   *   *   *   *   *

IV. Brig. Gen. James R. Chalmers will resume command of his division and report to Maj. Gen. N. B. Forrest, commanding, &c.

*   *   *   *   *   *   *

By command of Lieutenant-General Polk :

THOS. M. JACK,
Assistant Adjutant-General.

DEMOPOLIS, *March* 17, 1864.

Capt. W. A. GOODMAN,
     Oxford :

Have the pontoons at Panola and Abbeville constructed at once, and everything ready for immediate movement. If necessary, let McCulloch act promptly in my absence.

JAS. R. CHALMERS,
Brigadier-General.

HEADQUARTERS, *March* 18, 1864.

Maj. Gen. S. B. BUCKNER,
     Midway :

General Longstreet has just arrived. He wishes you to send him all the information of the enemy you have. Send out also scouts to the rear of the enemy to gain quickly all the information they can get.

G. M. SORREL,
Lieutenant-Colonel and Assistant Adjutant-General.

GREENEVILLE, *March* 18, 1864.

General S. COOPER,
     Adjutant and Inspector General, Richmond, Va.:

The enemy is near enough for us to strike him, if we could move. We have no forage for our transportation animals, and our cavalry is only foraged by being far out on our flanks. Please send us supplies or orders to go where we may get them. We will, in any event, require forage for ten or twelve days to take us to some point where we may receive more.

J. LONGSTREET,
Lieutenant-General.

HEADQUARTERS DEPARTMENT OF EAST TENNESSEE,
Greeneville, Tenn., March 18, 1864.

Col. A. FORSBERG,
     Commanding Wharton's Brigade :
     (Through Brig. Gen. B. R. Johnson, commanding division.)

The lieutenant-general commanding directs that you move your brigade to-morrow morning at daylight for this point, and desires that you will lose no time in reaching here.

I am, colonel, very respectfully, your obedient servant,

G. M. SORREL,
Lieutenant-Colonel and Assistant Adjutant-General.

HEADQUARTERS DEPARTMENT OF EAST TENNESSEE,
Greeneville, Tenn., March 18, 1864.

Maj. Gen. C. W. FIELD,
Commanding Division:

Wharton's brigade is ordered to move from Harris' Gap (its vicinity) at daylight to-morrow morning for this point, and the lieutenant-general commanding desires that you will have a brigade of your division in its place in full time to allow it to get off at the hour indicated.

I am, general, very respectfully, your obedient servant,

G. M. SORREL,
Lieutenant-Colonel and Assistant Adjutant-General.

HEADQUARTERS IN THE FIELD,
Camp Milton, McGirt's Creek, Fla., March 18, 1864.

Lieut. Gen. JAMES LONGSTREET,
Greeneville, Tenn.:

I regret I cannot assist you. My wagons, horses, and serviceable saddles are totally insufficient for present wants. If your plans were carried out and enemy should take possession of Cumberland Mountain gaps how could you get supplies of ammunition, &c.?

The true maxims of war require us never to abandon our communications, but act on those of the enemy without exposing our own.

G. T. BEAUREGARD.

DALTON, *March* 18, 1864.

General BRAGG,
Richmond:

The enemy have concentrated at Ringgold, drawing troops from Knoxville, as permitted by Longstreet's withdrawal. They are repairing the railroad. Does not this indicate advance? General Polk's infantry (too few to be of use in Mississippi) would greatly strengthen us. I suggest the immediate temporary transfer. Hindman's division has been without a commander for months. Do give it the one I recommend. The senior brigadier, Deas, has resigned.

J. E. JOHNSTON.

DALTON, *March* 18, 1864.

General B. BRAGG,
Richmond:

Your letter, by Colonel Sale, received. Grant is at Nashville. Sherman by last accounts at Memphis. Where Grant is we must expect the great Federal effort. We ought therefore to be prepared to beat him here. He has not come back to Tennessee to stand on the defensive. His advance, should we be ready for it, will be advantageous to us. To be ready we must have the troops you name immediately; otherwise we might be beaten, which would decide events. Give us those troops, and if we beat him we follow. Should he not advance we will thus be ready for the offensive. The troops can be fed as easily here as where they now are.

J. E. JOHNSTON.

DEMOPOLIS, *March* 18, 1864.
General COOPER,
   Adjutant and Inspector General, Richmond :
General Lee telegraphs as follows from Canton:

Sherman and Hurlbut are in Memphis.   Hurlbut has taken command in Memphis.
Six regiments of cavalry camped at Memphis fixing for a tramp.   The expedition
by Red River said to consist of eight gun-boats and twenty-two transports.   Part
of Hurlbut's corps has returned to Memphis.

L. POLK,
Lieutenant-General.

(Sent also to General Johnston at Dalton and General Maury at
Mobile.)

HEADQUARTERS,
Tupelo, March 18, 1864.
Lieutenant-General POLK,
   Demopolis:
Dispatches received ; orders to Colonel Jackson revoked.   Will
leave this morning for West Tennessee.   All important reports from
North Alabama and elsewhere will be sent you through General
Gholson at this place.   Scouts at Austin report five large transports
passed up the river with 3,500 troops from 7th to 11th instant.
Sherman and staff at Memphis on the 11th.   Memphis scout reports expedition fitting out for Red River. ' Cavalry at Memphis
reported as ordered to East Tennessee.   Governor Clark has con-
sented to transfer the State cavalry to Confederate service, to be
formed into a Mississippi brigade and be kept, if not required elsewhere.   I recommend that enough of the unattached companies of
this portion of the State be ordered to General Gholson to fill up his
three regiments.
N. B. FORREST,
Major-General.

EXECUTIVE OFFICE,
Macon, Miss., March 18, 1864.
Lieut. Gen. L. POLK,
   Commanding, &c., Demopolis, Ala.:
GENERAL: I inclose you copies of letters from Major-Generals
Forrest and Gholson in relation to transfer of State forces (cavalry)
to Confederate States.   General Gholson states the command at
1,968 ; effective aggregate, 1,172.
I have no doubt that from the men absent 200 or 300 can be obtained, so as to raise the effective force to 1,300 or 1,400.   If you
have authority to accept them, and will do so, I will propose to the
Legislature, which meets here next week, to authorize the transfer,
and will also ask that the horses (some 300), the property of the
State, be donated to the regiment, to mount men not able to mount
themselves.   I think they should be turned over without waiting to
recruit, as under the late act of Congress they cannot recruit as State
troops.   They may, by your order, afterward be recruited to the
desired number, as all subject to duty under late act will desire to
join old organizations.

I send this by courier, and request an answer by him. I hope you will make it as favorable as possible, as you are well aware of the difficulties always to be expected in such changes of the status of the troops. I have offered a bounty of $50 to all who volunteer for the war, and I hope you may be able to promise them efficient arms, &c. Their arms are indifferent.

McGuirk's regiment has some five months' pay due it; also for some 40 horses killed in action. You will much aid the transfer of that regiment by sending a paymaster to pay them for the time and loss while in Confederate service.

These troops are all good, and nearly all have served long, and are in as good state of discipline and as effective as those of the Confederacy. As State troops they cannot now be recruited, and it would be wrong to discharge them at the present conjunction. I hope, therefore, that the arrangement proposed can be effected.

I hope also that you will, at the proper time, find it consistent with your sense of propriety to join in the recommendation of General Gholson as brigadier-general, as I shall most cordially do; but of course this is no part of the proposition of transfer.

I have the honor to be, with high respect, your obedient servant,

CHAS. CLARK,
Governor of Mississippi.

P. S.—I send Colonel McGuirk's regiment to General Gholson to-morrow to Buena Vista, and thence they will probably move, as General Forrest suggests, to Tupelo. Please to send the paymaster to them as soon as possible.

[Inclosure No. 1.]

HEADQUARTERS FORREST'S CAVALRY,
Aberdeen, March 15, 1864.

His Excellency Governor CHARLES CLARK,
Governor of Mississippi:

GOVERNOR : I have the honor to say that General Gholson has returned here, and states that you are willing to turn over the State troops under his command to the Confederate States. I have promised, if possible, to make him a brigade of 1,800 men, and recommend him to be appointed its brigade commander.

I respectfully suggest, therefore, that General Gholson be ordered and authorized to reorganize the State cavalry and fill up and consolidate the commands into full regiments, and then to turn them over.

I desire to give, or that by this arrangement General Gholson shall have, a large Mississippi brigade, for which I desire to fit him up a battery, &c., but consider it of the first importance that the regiments shall be full and well officered and organized, and that it be done as early as practicable. I desire the brigade to defend this portion of the country, and will keep it in this section unless ordered away by the lieutenant-general commanding this department.

I am, very respectfully, your obedient servant,
N. B. FORREST,
Major-General.

[Inclosure No. 2.]

HEADQUARTERS MISSISSIPPI STATE TROOPS,
Near Buena Vista, Miss., March 17, 1864.

His Excellency CHARLES CLARK,
Governor, &c., Macon, Miss. :

GOVERNOR : Since the interview between you and myself relative to the transfer of the State troops to the Confederate service I have seen Major-General Forrest, and herein inclose his letter to you expressing his views and wishes on the subject. My command at present consists of Colonel McGuirk's regiment, aggregate, 325 ; Lieutenant-Colonel Lowry's regiment, aggregate, 350 ; Major Ham's battalion, aggregate, 320 ; Major Harris' battalion, aggregate, 177 ; grand total effective, 1,172.

This is the number of effective men, but the muster-rolls show 1,968, and perhaps the effective force can be raised to 1,300. I think it can. There are also several companies organized under your late call, but have not officially reported, and are not included.

I am, very respectfully, your obedient servant,
S. J. GHOLSON,
Major-General, Commanding State Forces.

GREENEVILLE, *March* 18, 1864.

General S. COOPER :

Your dispatch of 12th is received. General Law is in arrest by my order. The charges will be forwarded as early as possible.
J. LONGSTREET,
Lieutenant-General.

CIRCULAR.]   HEADQUARTERS,
Demopolis, Ala., March 18, 1864.

To the Citizens of Alabama, Mississippi, and East Louisiana :

The commanding general of the Department of Alabama, Mississippi, and East Louisiana, in order to the more effectual organization of a system for the procurement of labor, orders as follows :

First. All power of impressment of slave labor heretofore granted is hereby revoked.

Second. Impressments hereafter made will be under direct authority issuing from these headquarters.

Third. The system will be carried out by one chief agent, and to insure an intelligent and just exercise of this power his orders will be executed through sub-agents, recommended by the governors of the respective States in which impressments are ordered.

Fourth. All applications for labor must be made to these headquarters, and must specify the number of slaves, the length of time, and the purpose for which required.

Fifth. Impressments will be made with a due regard to the amount of labor hitherto furnished, and the burden to be borne in future will be equalized. No impressment of labor will be made for a longer period than sixty days, unless under stringent necessity ; otherwise the laborers will be returned at the end of that period.

Sixth. All orders of exemption heretofore granted are hereby revoked. Applications for exemptions and discharge must be made to the chief agent of impressment, who alone is empowered to grant such exemptions and discharge, and who will report the same to department headquarters.

Seventh. Contracts with the Government form no ground for exemptions except in cases contained in orders from the Adjutant and Inspector General's Office at Richmond.

Eighth. Impressments now being made by the orders of the chief agents of impressment are not revoked by this order.

The citizens of Alabama, Mississippi, and East Louisiana, in which impressments of labor for public service may be required, are cordially and earnestly solicited to furnish such labor as the necessities of the country at this time imperatively demand. Their co-operation with the military authorities in the defense of our common country is confidently relied on from their known patriotism and loyalty.

By command of Lieutenant-General Polk:

T. M. JACK,
Assistant Adjutant-General.

DALTON, *March* 19, 1864.

General BRAGG:

GENERAL: I had the honor to receive your letter of the 12th from Colonel Sale yesterday, and to make a suggestion by telegraph on the subject to which it relates.

Permit me to suggest that the troops intended for the operations you explain should be assembled in this vicinity. The enemy could, without particular effort, prevent their junction near Kingston by attacking one of our armies with his united forces. His interior positions make it easy. There is another reason. Grant's return to Tennessee indicates that he will retain that command for the present at least. He certainly will not do so to stand on the defensive. I therefore believe that he will advance as soon as he can with the greatest force he can raise. We cannot estimate the time he may require for preparation, and should consequently put ourselves in condition for successful resistance as soon as possible by assembling here the troops you enumerate. I am doing all I can in other preparations, and do not doubt that abundance of ammunition, food, and forage will be collected long before we can be supplied with field transportation. My department is destitute of mules. I must therefore depend on the Quartermaster's Department for them.

It strikes me that we cannot isolate Knoxville in the manner you propose, because we cannot hope to be able to take with us such supplies as would enable us to remain on the line of communication long enough to incommode the forces there. We cannot do so unless we can occupy a position from which we can maintain our own communications and interrupt those of Knoxville. Such a position can only be found near Chattanooga.

The march into Middle Tennessee via Kingston would require all the stores we should be able to transport from Dalton, so that we could not reduce Knoxville en route. Would it not be easier to move into Middle Tennessee through North Alabama? I believe fully, however, that Grant will be ready to act before we can be, and that if we are ready to fight him on our own ground we shall have a very plain course, with every chance of success. For that we should make exactly such preparations as you indicate for the forward movement, except that I would have the troops assembled here without delay, to repulse Grant's attack and then make our own, or should the enemy not take the initiative, do it ourselves. Our first object, then, should be your proposition to bring on a battle on this side of the Tennessee.

Should not the movement from Mississippi precede any advance from this point, so much as to enable those troops to cross the Tennessee before we move? Lieutenant-General Polk thought at the end of February that he could send 15,000 cavalry on such an expedition. Even two-thirds of that force might injure the railroads enough to compel the evacuation of Chattanooga; certainly it could make a powerful diversion.

I apprehend no difficulty in procuring food (except meat) and forage. This department can furnish nothing. Its officers receive supplies from those of the subsistence and quartermaster's departments at and beyond Atlanta. The efficient head of the ordnance department has never permitted us to wait for anything that could reasonably be expected from him. I am afraid that the collection of the additional field transportation will require a good deal of time. None can be obtained within the limits of my authority.

There has been an unnecessary accumulation of breadstuffs and corn at Mobile, a six months' supply for a much larger force than Major-General Maury's. Half of it will spoil during the summer if left in Mobile. It would be economical, therefore, as well as convenient, to transfer that portion of it to this army.

Lieutenant-Colonel Cole, at Augusta, informs me that the artillery horses required will be furnished by the 1st of April.

Most respectfully, your obedient servant,

J. E. JOHNSTON,
General.

RICHMOND, VA., *March* 19, 1864.

General LONGSTREET,
        Greeneville, Tenn.:

Send at once to General Johnston the other cavalry division referred to in your dispatch to the President of 26th February, which was previously ordered from here.

S. COOPER,
Adjutant and Inspector General.

RICHMOND, VA., *March* 19, 1864.

General LONGSTREET,
        Grecneville, Tenn.:

Orders have been issued to you to send Martin's command to General Johnston. This includes more than Martin's division, and was intended to embrace the two additional brigades now under Col. G. G. Dibrell. The last-named brigades will follow Martin's division at once.

S. COOPER,
Adjutant and Inspector General.

GREENEVILLE, EAST TENN., *March* 19, 1864.

General BRAXTON BRAGG, *Richmond, Va.:*

There are three army corps at Morristown. Upon my arrival I gave preparatory orders to go out and try to cut them off from Knoxville. I found afterwards that we had no corn and was obliged to abandon the idea. I fear that our animals will soon be so reduced that we cannot move in any direction, and it is not improbable that they may starve. Please send us corn and meal.

J. LONGSTREET,
Lieutenant-General.

HEADQUARTERS,
Greeneville, East Tenn., March 19, 1864.

General S. COOPER,
Adjutant and Inspector General, Richmond, Va.:

GENERAL: The supply of corn promised us from Virginia comes in so slowly that we shall not be able to keep our animals alive more than a week or two, unless some improvement may be made in forwarding supplies. Our rations, too, are getting short, so that we will hardly be able to march to any point at which we may be needed unless we can receive orders inside of a week, and then we must receive corn by railroad in order that our animals may make a march.

We have suffered more or less since we have been here in this department for want of proper supplies, but have been able to get along very poorly clad through the winter months, and could, now that the weather is becoming more mild, do very well if we could get food and forage. Without either of these our army must soon become entirely helpless.

The enemy is in front of us at Morristown, with three army corps, and could be struck to great advantage were it possible for us to move. The greater part of his force could probably be captured, but animals cannot work without food. The only corn in this country is far out upon our flanks, and is barely sufficient for the cavalry there, and the cavalry is necessary there to prevent its falling into the hands of the enemy.

I beg that you will send us supplies at once, in sufficient quantity at least to enable us to march to some point where our troops can be partially supplied and where they may be useful. These are perhaps the best troops in the Confederate armies, and should not be left where they must starve, and at the same time be of no service to the country.

The enemy is in much poorer fighting condition than he has been since the beginning of the war, and we should have but little difficulty in breaking him up if we can be furnished the means of getting at him. I respectfully urge, therefore, that no more time may be lost in making the necessary arrangements for active operations. If our armies can take the initiative in the spring campaign they can march into Kentucky with but little trouble and finish the war in this year. If we delay and give the enemy his full time the war will, in all probability, be prolonged for another four years.

I remain, sir, very respectfully, your most obedient servant,

J. LONGSTREET,
Lieutenant-General, Commanding.

HEADQUARTERS DEPARTMENT OF EAST TENNESSEE,
Greeneville, Tenn., March 19, 1864.

Maj. Gen. C. W. FIELD, *Commanding Division:*

The lieutenant-general commanding desires you to send the Hampton Legion, Col. M. W. Gary commanding, to this point at once. Send its transportation with it. The movement of the regiment may be considered permanent, and its baggage and equipments should be brought up.

I am, general, very respectfully, your obedient servant,

G. M. SORREL,
Lieutenant-Colonel and Assistant Adjutant-General.

GREENEVILLE, TENN.,
March 19, 1864.

Brig. Gen. J. B. KERSHAW, *Commanding Division:*

The commanding general directs that you move your division and King's battalion artillery back to your camp near this point.

I am, general, very respectfully, your obedient servant,

G. M. SORREL,
Lieutenant-Colonel and Assistant Adjutant-General.

HDQRS. DEPT. OF S. C., GA., AND FLA.,
Charleston, S. C., March 19, 1864.

General JAMES LONGSTREET:

GENERAL: Your letter of March 15, 1864, received in the absence of General Beauregard, will be forwarded to him by a special courier. Since it was received, however, a dispatch from him has reached me to be communicated to you in connection with the subject-matter of your previous communication, handed him by Lieutenant G., to the following effect:

That he regrets he cannot assist you with animals or saddles, which are now totally insufficient for present wants of the service in this department; that if your plans were carried out and the enemy should seize and occupy Cumberland Mountain gaps how would you get supplies of ammunition, &c.? That, in his opinion, the maxims of war require us never to abandon our communications, but to act on those of the enemy without exposing our own.

In a plan he proposed in December last it was urged that all the forces available in the Confederacy should be assembled in your quarter, if practicable; if not, then at or about Rome or Dalton, and thrown thence into Middle Tennessee. He thought this could be most effectively done from your direction, because from it the line of march would conduct an army most directly on the enemy's flank or rear, and that there would in that case be no exposure of our communications. Without all the advantages possessed by East Tennessee as the of departure or "breaking out," yet Dalton, being now favorably situated for purposes of concentration, he regarded that as a suitable point or base of operations. His plan was founded, however, on a combined movement in our army of all our forces, to the extent of about 100,000 men, who were to be moved in light marching order, and a renunciation of the evil system of keeping in the field separate armies, acting without concert on distant and divergent lines of operation, and thus enabling our enemy to concentrate at convenience his masses against our fragments. But, as I understand your plan, it was simply to strike a blow at the enemy's communications and depots with a movable column of mounted infantry, and looking to the results to the enemy, if successful, as disastrous for the season, in view of his remoteness from his base and sources of supply.

About the same time your letter from Petersburg was handed me a dispatch came from General Cooper directing us to send to Virginia four full regiments of cavalry and eight companies, in addition to four companies ordered there some weeks ago—that is, taking from the department fifty-two companies of cavalry at a sweep of the pen. This looks very much like another advance from Virginia, I fear across our northern border. However, these troops are to be held in readiness to be moved to Virginia under General Hampton, and it may be meant to divert them at the proper moment before marching to you across the mountains, which I hope may be the case.

Respectfully, general, your obedient servant,

THOS. JORDAN,
Chief of Staff.

SPECIAL ORDERS, } ADJT. AND INSP. GENERAL'S OFFICE,
No. 66. } *Richmond, Va., March* 19, 1864.

* * * * * * *

IX. Saltville, **Va.**, will hereafter be considered as in the Department of Southwestern Virginia.

* * * * * * *

XXXI. Brig. Gen. F. A. Shoup is relieved from present duty and will report to General Joseph E. Johnston, commanding, &c., at Dalton, Ga., for assignment to artillery duty.

* * * * *

By command of the Secretary of War:

JNO. WITHERS,
Assistant Adjutant-General.

Abstract from return of the Army of Tennessee, General Joseph E. Johnston, C. S. Army, commanding, March 20, 1864; *headquarters Dalton, Ga.*

Command.	Present for duty.		Effective total present.	Aggregate present.	Aggregate present and absent.	Pieces of artillery.
	Officers.	Men.				
General staff................................	15	....	....	15	16	......
Hardee's corps:						
Staff	12	....	....	12	14	......
Cheatham's division *a*....................	469	3,749	8,616	4,941	8,624	......
Cleburne's division........................	466	5,197	5,059	6,646	9,815	......
Walker's division..........................	341	4,635	4,552	5,903	9,252	......
Bate's division	376	3,489	3,360	4,373	6,934	......
Total..................................	1,664	17,070	16,587	21,875	34,639	......
Hood's corps:						
Staff	21	....	....	21	23	......
Hindman's division	490	5,700	5,555	7,003	11,990	......
Stewart's division..........................	410	5,155	5,028	6,502	11,061	......
Stevenson's division	479	6,225	6,078	7,623	10,964	......
Total..................................	1,400	17,080	16,661	21,149	34,638	......

a Eighth and Twenty-eighth Tennessee Regiments on detached duty at Atlanta, Ga.

Abstract from return of the Army of Tennessee, &c.—Continued.

Command.	Present for duty. Officers.	Present for duty. Men.	Effective total present.	Aggregate present.	Aggregate present and absent.	Pieces of artillery.
Battalion engineer troops	19	412	409	487	606	......
1st Louisiana Infantry (Regulars)	9	110	107	129	255	......
Total infantry.................................	3,107	34,672	33,764	43,655	70 154	......
Cavalry :						
Wheeler's cavalry corps *b*........................	461	4,634	4,531	6,271	10,925	......
Escort army headquarters......................	7	161	131	181	239	......
Escorts Hardee's corps........................	15	214	213	272	397	......
Escorts Hood's corps	4	80	80	163	227	......
Total cavalry	487	5,089	4,985	6,887	11,788	......
Artillery :						
Hardee's corps	49	989	971	1,220	1,640	45
Hood's corps................................	46	851	819	1,044	1,285	36
Wheeler's corps	9	203	200	243	283	10
Reserve regiment............................	46	796	764	964	1,218	36
Total artillery.................................	150	2,839	2,754	3,471	4,426	127
Grand total Army of Tennessee	3,744	42,600	41,503	54,013	86,368	127

b Ninth Tennessee Battalion (aggregate present and absent, 295) assigned to Davidson's brigade.

Abstract from return of the army in the Department of Alabama, Mississippi, and East Louisiana. Lieut. Gen. Leonidas Polk, C. S. Army, commanding, March 20, 1864 ; headquarters Demopolis, Ala.

Command.	Present for duty. Officers.	Present for duty. Men.	Effective total.	Aggregate present.	Aggregate present and absent.	Pieces of field artillery.
Commanding general and staff	10	....	....	10	11	......
Loring's division :						
Infantry	447	4,678	4,619	5,857	10,158	......
Artillery	24	440	424	512	854	18
Total...	471	5,118	5,043	6,369	11,012	18
French's division :						
Infantry	230	2,172	2,151	2,821	4,935	......
Artillery	11	169	159	189	272	8
Total...	241	2,341	2,310	3,010	5,207	8
Post of Demopolis...................................	38	335	335	386	426	......
Post of Selma.....................................	22	174	174	216	262	......
Post of Cahaba	37	254	254	351	501	......
Engineer troops....................	16	81	81	118	158	......
Paroled and exchanged prisoners	37	232	224	284	575	......
Lee's cavalry corps :						
Cavalry division	652	7,685	7,611	9,981	16,640	......
Escort company	4	45	45	60	95	......
Total .... ,....................	656	7,730	7,656	10,041	16,735	......
Grand total *a*...........................	1,528	16,265	16,677	20,775	34,887	26

a No report from General Withers.

Organization of troops in the Department of Alabama, Mississippi, and East Louisiana, commanded by Lieut. Gen. Leonidas Polk, C. S. Army, March 20, 1864.

LORING'S DIVISION.

Maj. Gen. WILLIAM W. LORING.

Featherston's Brigade.

Brig. Gen. WINFIELD S. FEATHERSTON.

3d Mississippi, Col. T. A. Mellon.
22d Mississippi, Col. Frank Schaller.
31st Mississippi, Col. J. A. Orr.
33d Mississippi, Lieut. Col. J. L. Drake.
40th Mississippi, Col. W. Bruce Colbert.
1st Mississippi Battalion Sharpshooters, Maj. J. M. Stigler.

Scott's Brigade.

Col. THOMAS M. SCOTT.

55th Alabama, Col. John Snodgrass.
57th Alabama, Col. C. J. L. Cunningham.
9th Arkansas, Col. Isaac L. Dunlop.
12th Louisiana, Lieut. Col. N. L. Nelson.

Adams' Brigade.

Brig. Gen. JOHN ADAMS.

6th Mississippi, Col. Robert Lowry.
14th Mississippi, Lieut. Col. W. L. Doss.
15th Mississippi, Col. M. Farrell.
20th Mississippi, Col. William N. Brown.
23d Mississippi, Col. Joseph M. Wells.
26th Mississippi, Col. Arthur E. Reynolds.
1st Confederate Battalion, Lieut. Col. George H. Forney.

Artillery.

Charpentier's (Alabama) battery, Capt. Stephen Charpentier.
Cowan's (Mississippi) battery, Capt. James J. Cowan.
Lookout (Tennessee) Battery, Capt. Robert L. Barry.
Pointe Coupée (Louisiana) Battery, Capt. Alcide Bouanchaud.
Ratliff's (Mississippi) battery, Capt. William T. Ratliff.

FRENCH'S DIVISION.

Maj. Gen. SAMUEL G. FRENCH.

Ector's Brigade.

Brig. Gen. MATTHEW D. ECTOR.

29th North Carolina, Lieut. Col. Bacchus S. Proffitt.
9th Texas, Col. William H. Young.
10th Texas Cavalry (dismounted), Col. C. R. Earp.
14th Texas Cavalry (dismounted), Col. John L. Camp.
32d Texas Cavalry (dismounted), Lieut. Col. James A. Weaver.

Cockrell's Brigade.

Brig. Gen. FRANCIS M. COCKRELL.

1st and 3d Missouri Cavalry (dismounted), Col. Elijah Gates.
1st and 4th Missouri, Col. A. C. Riley.
2d and 6th Missouri, Col. P. C. Flournoy.
3d and 5th Missouri, Col. James McCown.

Artillery.

Hoskins' (Mississippi) battery, Capt. James A. Hoskins,
1st Missouri Battery, Capt. Henry Guibor,

CAVALRY CORPS.

Maj. Gen. STEPHEN D. LEE.

JACKSON'S DIVISION.

Brig. Gen. WILLIAM H. JACKSON.

First Brigade.

Col. PETER B. STARKE.

1st Mississippi, Col. R. A. Pinson.
28th Mississippi, Col. Peter B. Starke.
Ballentine's (Mississippi) Regiment, Col. John G. Ballentine.
Escort (Louisiana) Company, Capt. Junius Y. Webb.
Georgia Battery, Capt. Edward Croft.

Adams' Brigade.

Brig. Gen. WIRT ADAMS.

11th Arkansas Mounted Infantry, Col. John Griffith.
14th Confederate, Capt. Josephus R. Quin.
9th Louisiana Battalion, Capt. E. A. Scott.
4th Mississippi, Maj. Thomas R. Stockdale.
4th (2d) Mississippi, Maj. J. L. Harris.
Wood's (Mississippi) Regiment, Col. Robert C. Wood, jr.
9th Tennessee Battalion, Maj. James H. Akin.
Mississippi Battery, Capt. Calvit Roberts.

Second Brigade.

Col. LAWRENCE S. ROSS.

1st Texas Legion, Col. E. R. Hawkins.
3d Texas, Col. Hinchie P. Mabry.
6th Texas, Col. Jack Wharton.
9th Texas, Col. Dud. W. Jones.
Escort (Texas) Company, Lieut. Rush L. Elkin.
Missouri Battery, Capt. Houston King.

Ferguson's Brigade.

Brig. Gen. SAMUEL W. FERGUSON.

2d Alabama, Col. R. G. Earle.
56th Alabama Partisan Rangers, Col. William Boyles.
12th Mississippi, Col. W. M. Inge.
2d Tennessee (Barteau's regiment), Lieut. Col. George H. Morton.
South Carolina Battery, Capt. John Waties.

CHALMERS' DIVISION—FORREST'S COMMAND.*

First Brigade.

Col. WILLIAM L. DUCKWORTH.

7th Tennessee, Col. William L. Duckworth.
12th Tennessee, Col. John U. Green.
13th Tennessee, Col. James J. Neely.
14th Tennessee, Col. Francis M. Stewart.

Third Brigade.

Col. A. P. THOMPSON.

3d Kentucky Mounted Infantry, Lieut. Col. G. A. C. Holt.
7th Kentucky Mounted Infantry, Col. Ed. Crossland.
8th Kentucky Mounted Infantry, Lieut. Col. A. R. Shacklett.
12th Kentucky, Col. W. W. Faulkner.
Forrest's (Alabama) Regiment, Lieut. Col. D. M. Wisdom.

Second Brigade.

Col. ROBERT McCULLOCH.

2d Missouri, Lieut. Col. R. A. McCulloch.
Texas Battalion, Lieut. Col. Leonidas Willis.
1st Mississippi Partisan Rangers, Maj. J. M. Park.
5th Mississippi Battalion.
18th Mississippi Battalion, Lieut. Col. Alexander H. Chalmers.
19th Mississippi Battalion, Lieut. Col. William L. Duff.
McDonald's (Tennessee) Battalion, Lieut. Col. J. M. Crews.

Fourth Brigade.

Col. TYREE H. BELL.

2d Tennessee, Col. C. R. Barteau.
15th Tennessee, Col. R. M. Russell.
16th Tennessee, Col. A. N. Wilson.

---

*But see organization March 7, p. 593.

GREENEVILLE, TENN.,
March 20, 1864.

General S. COOPER,
Richmond, Va.:

The removal of the two brigades of cavalry will uncover the road to Greenville, S. C. It will be necessary to keep them until the Hampton Legion passes on that road.

J. LONGSTREET,
Lieutenant-General.

HEADQUARTERS DEPARTMENT OF EAST TENNESSEE,
Greeneville, Tenn., March 20, 1864.

Maj. Gen. C. W. FIELD,
Commanding Division:

The commanding general desires that you will start the Hampton Legion for Greenville, S. C., as ordered by the War Department on Tuesday morning, provided you do not receive authority from the Department before then to retain it. The Legion will take with it its transportation, and you will please order your quartermaster to issue to it an additional wagon and team.

I am, general, very respectfully, your obedient servant,

G. M. SORREL,
Lieutenant-Colonel and Assistant Adjutant-General.

DEMOPOLIS, ALA.,
March 20, 1864.

General S. COOPER,
Adjutant and Inspector General, Richmond, Va.:

My Memphis scout reports, 18th instant, General Sherman gone to Grant's department; Veatch to Cairo. Troops still going up river, supposed to Nashville. Transportation steamers at Memphis. Cavalry still camped at South Race-Track.

L. POLK,
Lieutenant-General.

(Same to General J. E. Johnston.)

HEADQUARTERS,
Demopolis, Ala., March 20, 1864.

Maj. Gen. D. H. MAURY:

GENERAL: Information from other sources confirms the statement in the dispatch of Colonel Maury as to the extent of the defection in the southern counties of Mississippi. The lieutenant-general commanding is of opinion that an infantry force is indispensable so far as Smith County is concerned. He has accordingly organized such a force, which will leave here to-morrow for Meridian, under Colonel Lowry, one of the oldest colonels in this army, and an officer of vigor and decision. He will go to Smith County to commence operations. The lieutenant-general commanding desires you to direct Colonel

Maury to report and co-operate with Colonel Lowry until the work is thoroughly accomplished, reporting by wire at Meridian, whence he may receive a reply from Colonel Lowry.

Most respectfully, your obedient servant,

T. M. JACK,
Assistant Adjutant-General.

SPECIAL ORDERS, }   HEADQUARTERS,
No. 80.   }   *Demopolis, Ala., March 20, 1864.*

I. Colonel Lowry, Sixth Mississippi Regiment, will take charge of the expedition against deserters and disloyal men between Pearl River and Tombigbee, south of the Southern Railroad. ·He will proceed without delay by cars to Meridian, with the command organized for that purpose, and execute with vigor the verbal instructions already received from the lieutenant-general commanding.

*   *   *   *   *   *

By command of Lieutenant-General Polk:

T. M. JACK,
Assistant Adjutant-General.

HEADQUARTERS,
Demopolis, March 21, 1864.

His Excellency President DAVIS,
Richmond:

Colonel Ives has spent several days at these headquarters, and having seen my army will speak to you of its condition. I have also given him such information as was necessary to put him in possession of the history of the late campaign, its facts and incidents. .

I have also spoken to him of certain things which I regard as of great importance in the successful management of this department. Of these I have requested him to speak to you, and inclose copies of two communications* regarding them, addressed by me to the War Department. To them I beg leave to call your particular attention. The resources of this department in food are abundant, as also in quartermaster's stores, but under the present system they are not brought out, and the dependence to which it subjects the commanding general is fraught with damaging delays and great dangers. ·I can see no good objection to the change proposed. In regard to the inefficiency and mischiefs of the conscription system now in operation it is sufficient to refer to this state of things in the southern counties of Mississippi. If the whole of the executive part of all military operations in the department were placed in the hands of the department commander these evils could not arise, and many lives sacrificed in suppressing them would be saved to their families and the country.

In regard to the condition of affairs in the counties alluded to, I have to report that Col. Harry Maury, under my orders, through the commander of the District of the Gulf, made a campaign against the deserters and traitors in Jones, Perry, &c., about a week ago. He found them, as reported, in open rebellion, defiant at the outset, pro-

---

* Not found as inclosures; probably those of February 29, Part II, p. 814, and March 1, p. 574.

claiming themselves " Southern Yankees," and resolved to resist by force of arms all efforts to capture them. My orders were very stringent, and very summary measures were taken with such as were captured, and with marked benefit to many of the rest. Some escaped to the bottoms on Pearl River, swearing they would return with Yankee re-enforcements; others were brought to reason and loyalty, and have come in and surrendered themselves. I have to-day dispatched another expedition from this place to the counties of Smith and others lying on Pearl River, to break up an organization which has been formed there, and which has held three public meetings. I shall not stop until these outbreaks are suppressed and their authors punished, but it would be far better for the Government to dispose of its military resources in such a way as to prevent them.

I remain, respectfully, your obedient servant,

L. POLK,
Lieutenant-General.

[First indorsement.]

APRIL 22, 1864.

Referred to General Bragg for consideration and remarks.

J. D.

[Second indorsement.]

APRIL 26, 1864.

No doubt many abuses exist in the administration of the department to which this communication refers; but the remedy I conceive to be in their correction, not the inauguration of a new and less perfect system. Such was my effort in Tennessee, which the general seems to have misapprehended.

BRAXTON BRAGG,
General.

HEADQUARTERS FORREST'S CAVALRY,
Jackson, Tenn., March 21, 1864.
Col. THOMAS M. JACK,
Asst. Adjt. Gen., Dept. of Ala., Miss., and East La.:

COLONEL : I forward, for the information of the lieutenant-general commanding, the inclosed statement of outrages committed by the commands of Col. Fielding Hurst and others of the Federal Army.* I desire, if it meets with the approval of the lieutenant-general commanding, that this report may be sent to some newspaper for publication. Such conduct should be made known to the world.

Very respectfully, colonel, your obedient servant,

N. B. FORREST,
Major-General, Commanding.

HDQRS. CAV. DEPT. OF WEST TENN. AND NORTH MISS.,
Jackson, March 21, 1864.
Lieut. Col. T. M. JACK,
Assistant Adjutant-General :

COLONEL : I have the honor to report the arrival of my advance at this place on yesterday morning at 11 o'clock, and deem it proper

---

*See Forrest to Buckland, March 22, p. 117.

to give the lieutenant-general commanding a report of the condition of the country through which I have passed, also the state of affairs. as they exist, with such suggestions as would naturally arise from observations made and a personal knowledge of facts as they exist. From Tupelo to Purdy the country has been laid waste, and unless some effort is made either by the Mobile and Ohio Railroad Company or the Government the people are bound to suffer for food. They have been by the enemy and by roving bands of deserters and tories stripped of everything; have neither negroes nor stock with which to raise a crop or make a support. What provisions they had have been consumed or taken from them, and the majority of families are bound to suffer. They are now hauling corn in ox wagons and by hand-cars from Okolona and below to Corinth, and as far north as Purdy, also east and west of Corinth, on the Memphis and Charleston Railroad, but their limited means of transportation will not enable them to subsist their families, and my opinion is that the railroad can be easily and speedily repaired, and that any deficiency in iron from Meridian north can be supplied from the Memphis and Charleston Railroad, and that a brigade of cavalry with a regiment or two of infantry placed at Corinth would afford protection to that section, and would be the means of driving out of the country or placing in our army the deserters and tories infesting that region, whose lawless appropriation of provisions, horses, and other property is starving out the defenseless and unprotected citizens of a large scope of country. Repairing and running the railroad would enable the inhabitants to procure provisions from the prairies and would prove an invaluable acquisition in the transportation of supplies and troops from this section. But little can be done in returning the deserters from our army now in West Tennessee, and collecting and sending out all persons subject to military duty, unless the railroad is rebuilt or repaired, as they will have to be marched through a country already, for want of labor and supplies, insufficient for the subsistence of its own inhabitants. With a conscript post or an established military post at Corinth and the railroad from thence south they could be rapidly forwarded to the army. The wires can also be extended and a telegraph office established. The whole of West Tennessee is overrun by bands and squads of robbers, horse thieves, and deserters, whose depredations and unlawful appropriations of private property are rapidly and effectually depleting the country. The Federal forces at Paducah, Columbus, and Union City are small. There is also a small force at Fort Heiman, on the Tennessee, and Fort Pillow, on the Mississippi River. About 2,000 men of Smith's forces, composed of parts of many regiments, have crossed the Tennessee River at Clifton and Fort Heiman, and returned to Nashville; four regiments of Illinois cavalry have re-enlisted and have gone home on furlough. The cavalry force at Memphis is therefore small.

Numerous reports having reached me of the wanton destruction of property by Col. Fielding Hurst and his regiment of renegade Tennesseeans, I ordered Lieut. Col. W. M. Reed to investigate and report upon the same, and herewith transmit you a copy of his report.* Have thought it both just and proper to bring these transactions to the notice of the Federal commander at Memphis, and by flag of truce will demand of him the restitution of the money taken

---

* See Forrest to Buckland, March 22, p. 117.

from the citizens of Jackson, under a threat from Hurst to burn the town unless the money was forthcoming at an appointed time. Have also demanded that the murderers be delivered up to Confederate authority for punishment, and reply from that officer as to the demand, &c., will be forwarded you as soon as received. Should the Federal commander refuse to accede to the just demands made, I have instructed the officer in charge of the flag to deliver the notice inclosed* outlawing Hurst and his command.

I am, general, very respectfully, your obedient servant,

N. B. FORREST,
Major-General.

HEADQUARTERS FORREST'S CAVALRY DEPARTMENT,
Jackson, Tenn., March 21, 1864.

Col. R. McCULLOCH,
Commanding Division, Oxford, Miss.:

COLONEL: I am directed by the major-general commanding to say that he will move on Union City and Paducah, and has forwarded you orders to send Richardson's brigade to Brownsville. He directs also that you move the remaining brigade of your division up as near to Germantown as possible, keeping on hand five days' rations ready to be cooked at a moment's notice. The general commanding thinks you can move over to Waterford; at any rate, move as far over as you can subsist your command, and be ready for a forward movement should the enemy move after me from Memphis, or further orders be sent you. Should it become necessary, or you be ordered to move, you will leave one regiment to guard the country and your wagon train, and bring with you only such wagons as may be necessary to carry your extra ammunition and as few cooking utensils as will do your command. He directs me also to say that the force of the enemy at Paducah, Columbus, and Union City is reported as small, and that he will move on Union City at once.

Respectfully, your obedient servant,

CHAS. W. ANDERSON,
Aide-de-Camp to Major-General Forrest.

HDQRS. DEPT. OF WEST TENN. AND NORTH MISS.,
Jackson, Tenn., March 21, 1864.

Col. ROBERT McCULLOCH,
Commanding Division:

COLONEL: You will order Richardson's brigade to move via Hudsonville and La Grange or Moscow, direct to•Brownsville. They will move five days' cooked rations, and 60 rounds of ammunition to the man, if possible to get it; not less than 40 rounds in cartridge-boxes, bringing no more wagons than will be necessary to bring the extra ammunition, if any. The commanding officer of the brigade will dispatch a courier to these headquarters at Jackson, stating the time, &c., that the command will reach Brownsville, starting the courier as soon as the command passes La Grange or Moscow.

By command of Major-General Forrest:

W. N. MERCER OTEY,
Acting Assistant Adjutant-General.

---

* See Forrest to Buckland, March 22, p. 117.

CIRCULAR.]   HEADQUARTERS ARMY OF TENNESSEE,
                        Dalton, Ga., March 21, 1864.

The infirmary corps of the army will be formed by selecting 3 good men for each 100 effectives, including in the selection all musicians suitable for the purpose.

A non-commissioned officer will be put in charge of the detail of each regiment and a commissioned officer will be placed in command of that of each brigade. The officers and non-commissioned officers will act under the instructions of the surgeon of the brigade and the surgeon of the regiment. The officers and non-commissioned officers will only be armed.

By command of General Johnston :
                                    A. P. MASON,
                            Assistant Adjutant-General.

                        RICHMOND, VA., *March* 22, 1864.
General J. E. JOHNSTON,
        Commanding &c. :

GENERAL: To man efficiently and at once the vessels of the navy it has become necessary to transfer 1,200 men from the armies. To this end the Secretary of the Navy has detailed officers with instructions to proceed to the headquarters of each army for the purpose of selecting and designating the men so to be transferred. From the Army of Tennessee 170 men will be designated, whom you are requested to transfer to the navy upon the written request of the naval officer sent to your command, and under his direction to send 150 to Savannah, Ga., and 20 to Saint Marks, Fla.

You will please forward a list of the men so transferred to this office without delay.

By command of the Secretary of War :
                                    S. COOPER,
                        Adjutant and Inspector General.

(The same *mutatis mutandis* to Longstreet, Maury, and Polk. Army of East Tennessee, 80 men to go to Kinston, N. C. ; District of the Gulf, 55 men to Columbus, Ga., and Army of Alabama, Mississippi, and East Louisiana, 55 men to Columbus, Ga.)

                        DALTON, *March* 22, 1864.
General BRAXTON BRAGG, *Richmond:*

In my dispatch of 19th I expressly accept taking offensive, only differ with you as to details. I assume that the enemy will be prepared for advance before we are and will make it to our advantage ; therefore, I propose as necessary both for offensive and defensive to assemble our troops here immediately. Other preparations for advance are going on.

                                    J. E. JOHNSTON.

        HEADQUARTERS DEPARTMENT OF EAST TENNESSEE,
                        Greeneville, Tenn., March 22, 1864.
Col. IRA R. FOSTER,
        Quartermaster-General of Georgia :

COLONEL : Your letter to Lieutenant-General Longstreet, by Mr. C. A. King, agent, was presented simultaneously with the 3,000 suits of clothing, which the liberality and forethought of the State of Georgia had provided for her destitute sons in the field.

General Longstreet has intrusted to me the pleasing duty of thanking you for the promptness and extent of the effort made by you in clothing and sheltering the brave Georgians in his army. The privations uncomplainingly borne by them during the last campaign, and their gallant and distinguished services throughout the war, render them fully worthy of the grateful attention and fostering care of their noble State, which in no way more exhibits her greatness than in the bountiful manner in which she provides for her faithful soldiers.

With the assurance of the high admiration of the lieutenant-general commanding for the efficiency of the department which has been able to accomplish such results, I have the honor to be, colonel, very respectfully, your obedient servant,

G. M. SORREL,
Lieutenant-Colonel and Assistant Adjutant-General.

CIRCULAR.]   HEADQUARTERS ARMY OF TENNESSEE,
Dalton, Ga., March 22, 1864.

Corps commanders will forward lists of all such molders, machinists, and blacksmiths of their commands as may be disqualified for field service.

By command of General Johnston :

A. P. MASON,
Assistant Adjutant-General.

GREENEVILLE, TENN.,
March 22, 1864.
General S. COOPER,
Adjutant and Inspector General :
The Hampton Legion is on the march, but the troops will be obliged to lay by for two or three days on account of a very heavy snow-storm. They can hardly be expected to pass the mountains until the snow melts.

J. LONGSTREET,
Lieutenant-General.

GREENEVILLE, *March 22, 1864.*
General S. COOPER :
The enemy is retreating again toward Knoxville.

J. LONGSTREET,
Lieutenant-General.

GREENEVILLE, *March 22, 1864.*
General B. BRAGG,
Richmond, Va. :
We have not the means of foraging our horses one day, if concentrated to strike the enemy. If we should be four days in getting at

him our horses would perish. Let me assure you that I shall never lose any opportunity to do all that can be done. The enemy fled the day before I could get my troops disposed so as to advance, but if he had not the want of supplies would have prevented my intended attack.

J. LONGSTREET,
Lieutenant-General.

SPECIAL ORDERS, }   HEADQUARTERS,
  No. 82.   }   *Demopolis, Ala., March 22, 1864.*
  *   *   *   *   *   *   *

IV. Brig. Gen. F. C. Armstrong will report to Maj. Gen. S. D. Lee for assignment to duty.
  *   *   *   *   *

By command of Lieutenant-General Polk :

T. M. JACK,
Assistant Adjutant-General.

WAR DEPT., C. S. A., ADJT. AND INSP. GEN.'S OFFICE,
Richmond, Va., March 23, 1864.
Lieutenant-General POLK,
  Commanding Army of Mississippi:

GENERAL : The Secretary of War directs me to call your attention to the law repealing the act to organize bands of partisan rangers, published in General Orders, No. 29, current series. It is the policy of the Department to use this law to place, as early as the circumstances of special commands and the interest of the service will allow, the partisan organizations on the same footing with those of the Provisional Army. Your co-operation in this respect is sought and relied on. If there are any companies of partisan rangers within your command, serving within the lines of the enemy, whose discipline, gallantry, and good conduct would make it expedient they should be retained as partisans, you are desired to recommend them for retention. Should, in such cases, you deem it advisable that other or different conditions should be prescribed for their continuance and control, you will please suggest them, with the reasons therefor, for the consideration of the Department.

Very respectfully, general, your obedient servant,

H. L. CLAY,
Assistant Adjutant-General.

HEADQUARTERS THIRTY-FIFTH ALABAMA REGIMENT,
Mount Hope, Ala., March 23, 1864.
Lieutenant-Colonel JACK,
  Assistant Adjutant-General:

SIR : I have the honor to report the arrival of my command at this point on the 14th instant, since which time I have arrested a number of deserters from my own as well as other commands. The field is a good one, and I am satisfied that I shall be able to recruit my command greatly in a short time, as well as return to duty many deserters belonging elsewhere. I found the enemy in possession of a portion of the Tennessee Valley. On the 21st instant they were engaged at Moulton by Colonel Johnson's cavalry, supported by the Twenty-seventh Alabama Regiment and my own. They were put to flight and driven to Decatur, to which place I am satisfied they will in future confine themselves, if they do not recross the Tennessee. I shall on to-morrow move my regiment to Russellville, 15 miles west of this. I have kept my command well together, and shall continue to do so. I have never been absent myself, and assure you that I shall spare no effort to accomplish faithfully the objects of my mission here, and to return my command in safety and greatly augmented in numbers. I have transmitted to General Withers a duplicate of this. I shall continue to report promptly each week my progress and whereabouts.

Very respectfully, your obedient servant,

S. S. IVES,
Colonel, Commanding Thirty-fifth Alabama Regiment.

GREENEVILLE, TENN.,
March 23, 1864.

General S. COOPER,
Adjutant and Inspector General:

The great reduction of my cavalry force recently ordered makes it necessary that I should withdraw my troops to a position where I can occupy a much shorter line than I now hold.

J. LONGSTREET,
Lieutenant-General, Commanding.

HEADQUARTERS DEPARTMENT OF EAST TENNESSEE,
Greeneville, Tenn., March 23, 1864.

Major-General FIELD,
Commanding Division:

Your note of yesterday is received. Your directions as to the issue of rations are approved. I regret very much that there is any occasion for a reduction of the usual ration, but the great scarcity of breadstuffs, as well as meat, renders it absolutely necessary. I am not yet advised of any arrangement on the part of the Government to send us supplies by rail. The arrangement of five brigades in your division was never a permanent organization, but an accident, the original and permanent organization being four brigades. The other brigade was put in the division when one of the old brigades was absent and supposed to be permanently so.

You will see the manifest impropriety of retaining this irregular organization of five brigades in one division, when there is another division of this army of but two brigades. I regret very much the loss of the Hampton Legion to one of your finest brigades, but it is the order of the War Department, and we must hope that it will be for the best interests of the service.

I remain, very respectfully and truly, yours,
J. LONGSTREET,
Lieutenant-General, Commanding.

P. S.—The reduction of our cavalry force just ordered by the War Department will make it necessary to withdraw our line to the vicinity of Bristol. Please make your arrangements to march on Sunday for the north side of the Holston. Your division will be in

rear of the infantry column, and will, in case of any threatening
move on the part of the enemy, co-operate in resisting his advance
until other troops may have time to aid you.

J. LONGSTREET,
Lieutenant-General.

GREENEVILLE, *March 23, 1864.*

Maj. Gen. JOHN C. BRECKINRIDGE :

Lieutenant-Colonel Prentice, just from the border of Kentucky,
reports indications of a raid by the enemy into Virginia, expected
to be from Louisa and Mount Sterling very shortly. Enemy shoeing their horses and preparing to send supplies up the Sandy River
as far as Piketon. The force at Mount Sterling under Wolford is
variously reported from 5,000 to 10,000.

J. LONGSTREET,
Lieutenant-General.

HEADQUARTERS DEPARTMENT OF EAST TENNESSEE,
Greeneville, Tenn., March 23, 1864.

Brig. Gen. A. E. JACKSON,
Commanding Brigade, Carter's Station :

In reply to your communication of the 21st instant, asking the
policy to be pursued toward deserters from or members of the Federal armies residents of this section of country, I am directed to say
that you will have all of that class arrested and sent to Richmond,
except such as may be employed by competent authority in the niter
and mining operations. The names of such parties you will please
report to the Niter and Mining Bureau in Richmond, with a statement of the facts against them and the circumstances of their presence here.

The great importance and utility of the niter operations, and the
proper watchfulness of the bureau against any interference with its
operations, makes necessary this modified course.

I am, general, very respectfully, your most obedient servant,

G. M. SORREL,
Lieutenant-Colonel and Assistant Adjutant-General.

Report of troops "In for the War," March 23, 1864.

Divisions.	Total present and absent.	Re-enlisted.	Total present March 10, 1864.
Cheatham's	7,791	4,304	4,980
Cleburne's	8,715	5,282	6,247
Walker's	8,648	4,404	5,578
Bate's	6,268	2,365	3,997
Artillery regiments	1,562	1,026	1,210
Grand total	32,984	17,471	22,012

T. B. ROY,
Assistant Adjutant-General,

DALTON, GA., *March 23, 1864.*

RICHMOND, *March* 24, 1864.

General J. E. JOHNSTON :

MY DEAR GENERAL : Your several dispatches recommending the appointment and promotion of artillery officers have been submitted to the President. He has deferred action, except to send General Shoup, an educated and disciplined soldier, senior now and heretofore to those artillery officers who have served so long with the Army of Tennessee.

It is desired that a complete organization be made, and field officers be appointed for all your artillery, and the Department therefore awaits General Pendleton's report of his inspection and your own recommendations in full.

A tabular report of organization, accompanied by a recommendation for promotions, was made to the Adjutant-General last November, but, I learn on inquiry, was returned to you for your action. It was based on two years' acquaintance with the artillery officers of your army. The Adjutant-General informs me it has not been again received at his office.

Recently some complaints, I learn privately, have been heard from your artillery officers that they were being overslaughed by their juniors from the Army of Northern Virginia. Lieutenant-Colonel Dearing was junior, for instance, to all the field officers with you until recently promoted in the organization of General Lee's artillery. I should very much fear the effect of such transfer, unless there was some transcendent or overshadowing ability or achievements to silence all complaints.

These are merely friendly suggestions thrown out, which I hope may aid you in the important and delicate work.

I am, general, most respectfully and truly, yours,

BRAXTON BRAGG.

<hr>

HEADQUARTERS,
Greeneville, East Tenn., March 24, 1864.

General S. COOPER,
Adjutant and Inspector General:

GENERAL : The order received a few days ago directing that the other two brigades of General Martin's cavalry should return to Georgia so reduces my cavalry force that it becomes necessary that I should withdraw my forces to a shorter line than the one we now occupy. The great scarcity of corn for the last ten days has so reduced the horses of the cavalry that will be left that it becomes necessary that they should have rest as well as food. Our present line is so long that the cavalry force that will remain with us could not supply it with the necessary vedettes, and we could not expect to have any cavalry for active work against cavalry. I have selected the line of the Holston as our new line. Our move will be made on the 27th. The cavalry to return to Georgia will start for General Johnston's army on the same day. I have detained these brigades, as their position covers the road to Asheville, N. C., and Greenville, S. C., by which the Hampton Legion is marching.

I remain, sir, very respectfully, your obedient servant.

J. LONGSTREET,
Lieutenant-General.

RICHMOND, VA., *March* 24, 1864.

Lieut. Gen. L. POLK, *Demopolis, Ala.:*

The President desires that Twenty-sixth Mississippi Regiment, Col. A. E. Reynolds, and the First Confederate Battalion, Lieut. Col. G. H. Forney, both of Adams' brigade, be transferred to the Army of Northern Virginia and assigned to Brig. Gen. Joe Davis' brigade.

S. COOPER,
Adjutant and Inspector General.

SPECIAL ORDERS, }   HEADQUARTERS,
No. 84.   }   *Demopolis, Ala., March* 24, 1864.

*   *   *   *   *   *

XI. Maj. R. C. McCay, Thirty-eighth Mississippi Regiment, will operate with his command in the section of country below the Southern Railroad and between Pearl River and the Mississippi, collecting all stragglers and deserters and placing them, when necessary, in jails of the different counties.

*   *   *   *   *   *

XIV. Captain Estelle, commanding detachment Thirty-eighth Mississippi Regiment, will report with his command to Maj. R. C. McCay at Jackson, Miss., for orders.

*   *   *   *   *

By command of Lieutenant-General Polk:

T. M. JACK,
Assistant Adjutant-General.

RICHMOND, VA., *March* 24, 1864.

Hon. J. A. SEDDON, *Secretary of War:*

SIR : I append herewith an order or circular issued by Lieut. Gen. L. Polk, which conflicts with Special Orders, No. 247, of October 17, 1863, issued by yourself in regard to Missourians, and attaching all east of the Mississippi River, and not in active service at that time, to the First Missouri Brigade, General Cockrell. Fearing this circular of Lieutenant-General Polk might produce a conflict of interests, and be considered to attach to Missourians who come through by the exchange and are sent on to Cockrell's brigade by me to be temporarily attached, although belonging to organizations in the Trans-Mississippi Department, I therefore respectfully ask that General Polk's circular, as far as it applies to Missourians, may be suspended, as conflicting with the said Special Orders, No. 247.

Very respectfully, your obedient servant,

R. S. BEVIER,
Lieut. Col. and Recruiting Officer, Cockrell's Mo. Brig.

[First indorsement.]

MARCH 28, 1864.

ADJUTANT-GENERAL :

Call General Polk's attention to the order respecting Missourians to be attached temporarily to General Cockrell's brigade, and request that his order be so modified as not to conflict with it.

J. A. S.

[Second indorsement.]

ADJUTANT AND INSPECTOR GENERAL'S OFFICE,
March 28, 1864.

Respectfully referred to Lieutenant-General Polk, with attention invited to the indorsement of the Secretary of War, and to Special Orders, No. 247, last series, from this office, a copy of which is inclosed.

By order of Adjutant and Inspector General :

H. L. CLAY,
Assistant Adjutant-General.

[Inclosure No. 1.]

CIRCULAR.]   HEADQUARTERS,
Demopolis, February 29, 1864.

All unattached men in this department belonging to the regiments in the Trans-Mississippi Department are ordered to report to Lieut. Col. H. C. Davis, Cahaba, Ala., for the purpose of being organized into a trans-Mississippi battalion.

By command of Lieutenant-General Polk :

THOS. M. JACK,
Assistant Adjutant-General.

The above circular is published for the information of all men on this side of the Mississippi River whose regiments may be in the Trans-Mississippi Department. It is important that they should report without delay. As all the Federal prisoners captured in this department are confined at this post, it is necessary that a strong guard be immediately organized.

By order of Lieut Col. H. C. Davis, commanding :

H. A. M. HENDERSON,
Assistant Adjutant-General.

[Inclosure No. 2.]

SPECIAL ORDERS,)   ADJT. AND INSP. GENERAL'S OFFICE,
No. 247.   )   *Richmond, October* 17, 1863.
  *   *   *   *   *   *   *

IX. All Missouri soldiers not engaged in actual service east of the Mississippi River will report to the commanding general of the First Missouri Brigade at Demopolis, Ala.

The men belonging to military organizations west of the Mississippi River will be temporarily attached to the above-mentioned brigade. The remainder will be permanently attached.

The chief of the Conscription Bureau will order all Missourians east side of the Mississippi liable to conscription to the same brigade.
  *   *   *   *

By command of the Secretary of War :

JNO. WITHERS,
Assistant Adjutant-General.

SPECIAL ORDERS,)   ADJT. AND INSP. GENERAL'S OFFICE,
No. 71.   )   *Richmond, Va., March* 25, 1864.
  *   *   *   .   *   *   *

XVI. In order to define more particularly the boundary between the geographical department of Tennessee, under General Joseph E.

Johnston, and the department of Alabama, Mississippi, and East Louisiana, under Lieut. Gen. L. Polk, the following will govern, viz: From Gunter's Landing, on the Tennessee River, in a direct line to Gadsden, on the Coosa River; thence down that river to its junction with the Tallapoosa River; thence in a direct line to the intersection of the northern boundary of Florida with the Chattahoochee River, and down that river and bay to the Gulf. All west of said line will be considered in the Department of Alabama, Mississippi, and East Louisiana, and east of the line from the northern boundary of Florida at its intersection by the Chattahoochee River in the Department of Tennessee.

*   *   *   *   *   *   *

XVIII. Col. A. E. Reynolds, of the Twenty-sixth Regiment Mississippi Volunteers, and Lieut. Col. G. H. Forney, of the First Confederate States Battalion, Adams' brigade, Department of Alabama, Mississippi, and East Louisiana, will immediately proceed with their commands to headquarters Army of Northern Virginia and report to General R. E. Lee, commanding, &c., for assignment to Brig. Gen. J. R. Davis' brigade.

*   *   *   *

By command of the Secretary of War:

JNO. WITHERS,
Assistant Adjutant-General.

DALTON, *March* 25, 1864.

General BRAXTON BRAGG, *Richmond:*

The enemy is rapidly receiving re-enforcements at Ringgold. A scout, an officer, reported last night that he saw four trains of troops arrive there night before, and citizens told him they had been arriving so for five days, agreeing with Louisville papers. For a battle they can also draw troops from Knoxville, so collecting a larger force than that of last campaign. Ours is less. We should be re-enforced immediately. Troops can be spared from Mobile. Those at Demopolis are useless there or in Mississippi. Further delay will be dangerous. I don't know what General Beauregard can spare.

J. E. JOHNSTON.

DALTON, GA., *March* 25, 1864.

General WHEELER, *Tunnel Hill:*

General Johnston desires you to use every means in your power to gain further information in regard to the movements of large bodies of infantry toward Nashville by rail.

KINLOCH FALCONER,
Assistant Adjutant-General.

RICHMOND, VA., *March* 25, 1864.

Lieut. Gen. JAMES LONGSTREET,
Greeneville, East Tenn.:

GENERAL: Your letter of March 15 [16th] has been received. Although a discussion of past events was not invited by me, yet as they are introduced by you in connection with your future operations I reply in regard to them.

Your reasons for your recent withdrawal from before Knoxville are conclusive. You inform me that the strength of its fortifications, heretofore tested by you, has been increased, and that that portion of Tennessee has been devastated. With your dependence upon the railroad for supplies, which were to be brought from here, you could hardly hope to starve out the enemy at Knoxville, or, if you took it, to use it as a base for future operations. These difficulties would have been increased by adding to the number of your troops, and your plans for the capture of Knoxville required a re-enforcement of 10,000 men. This force was not available for your suggested purpose. In view of these considerations, your retreat seemed expedient.

The line indicated in your former letter was suggested as preferable to falling back to Bristol, as you proposed in your telegram of February 20, and was not designated as an exact position to be occupied. Subsistence and topographical features must, in connection with the disposition of the enemy's forces, mainly be considered in settling that question, and the decision could not be definitely made here.

In your telegram of January 29 to General Cooper you complain that one-half of General Martin's command is detained at Dalton, and suggest that unless these men can be sent to you that General Martin's command be sent back to General Wheeler. In view of the co-operation you required from Colonel Johnston, and the disintegration of Wheeler's command by the absence of General Martin's force, and its scattered condition, as represented by you, it seemed best to send it to Dalton.

You have received the brigade of General Hodge since that order, which, as reported to me, should restore your cavalry to about three-fourths the number it had before General Martin was ordered away, and General Morgan's force, when fully assembled, must remove any numerical deficiency which may, until then, exist. The plan of mounting your whole force, if desirable, was impracticable. In your letter of February 22 to the Secretary of War you proposed that 6,000 or 8,000 horses should be procured from the armies of Generals Lee, Beauregard, and Johnston.

An embarrassing scarcity of horses is complained of by the first and last named generals, and there is great difficulty in supplying their ascertained wants. But, could the horses be sent to you, the forage could not be forwarded from here, and, as appears from your telegrams and letters, it is to this point you look for the means of feeding the horses of your command.

In suggesting the junction at Maryville it was contemplated that the movement should be so masked as not to be known until well advanced, and this might be effected by passing to the south of the Smoky range of mountains, which would then cover the flank of your column.

In your proposed plan to re-enforce General Johnston by using the railroad from Greenville, S. C., you will perceive the troops must be transported from Kingsville on a railroad which forms part of the route over which the corn is brought from Georgia to feed the Army of Virginia. It cannot move troops and adequately bring forward supplies at the same time. To furnish you the troops you require, in your proposed plan, from General Beauregard, and to re-enforce General Johnston from Mobile and the West, would expose all of our productive country and the principal cities of the South, the reserve proposed to be retained at Atlanta being too small, as well as too remote from Mobile and Charleston, to afford them the requisite assistance in the probable event of attack. Furthermore, General Beauregard has not indicated that the troops in his department can now be withdrawn to any considerable extent. The difficulties of making the junction of your corps with the army of General Johnston are admitted, but if, as you suppose, the enemy cannot be prepared to move before May, he ought not to be able to interfere seriously with the proposed movement to unite the two wings of the Army of Tennessee.

Very respectfully and truly, yours,

JEFFERSON DAVIS.

CIRCULAR.]   HEADQUARTERS HARDEE'S CORPS,
                          Dalton, Ga., March 25, 1864.

The infirmary corps will not be included in the "effective total." Privates will be reported on "extra duty;" musicians as heretofore.

By command of Lieutenant-General Hardee:

T. B. ROY,
Assistant Adjutant-General.

GENERAL ORDERS, }   HEADQUARTERS HOOD'S CORPS,
    No. 44.   }   Dalton, Ga., March 25, 1864.

Lieut. Col. Archer Anderson, assistant adjutant-general, having been relieved from duty with this corps, pursuant to orders from the War Department, all communications for the lieutenant-general commanding will be addressed to Maj. J. P. Wilson, assistant adjutant-general.

By command of Lieutenant-General Hood:

J. P. WILSON,
Assistant Adjutant-General.

SPECIAL ORDERS, }   HEADQUARTERS,
    No. 85.   }   Demopolis, Ala., March 25, 1864.

*   *   *   *   *   *   *

V. Col. A. E. Reynolds, Twenty-sixth Mississippi Regiment, will proceed with his command to the Army of Northern Virginia for assignment to the brigade of Brig. Gen. Joe Davis. He will leave an officer behind charged with the duty of collecting and carrying forward the absentees of his regiment.

VI. Lieut. Col. G. H. Forney will rejoin his command, First Confederate Battalion, at Cahaba, Ala., and proceed with it to the Army of Northern Virginia for assignment to Brig. Gen. Joe Davis' brigade.

*   *   *   *   *

By command of Lieutenant-General Polk:

T. M. JACK,
Assistant Adjutant-General.

GENERAL ORDERS, ⎱ HDQRS. 1ST DIV., FORREST'S CAV. DEPT.,
      No. 8.   ⎰   Oxford, March 25, 1864.
In obedience to orders from the lieutenant-general commanding department, the undersigned resumes command of this division.

                        JAMES R. CHALMERS,
                              Brigadier-General.

———

                                          MOBILE, March 26, 1864.
General S. COOPER:
News from New Orleans 18th instant. Yankees met with severe reverse near New Iberia. Two regiments reported captured. All gun-boats except eight have left for Red River. 'Tis reported that Fort De Russy was taken by assault on 14th instant. Not credited. On 18th instant Colonel Holland, Thirty-seventh Mississippi, attacked the enemy on Choctawhatchie Bay, and entire boat crew, about 25, killed and drowned. No loss on our side. He captured over 500 head of cattle and some 20 horses.

                        DABNEY H. MAURY,
                              Major-General.

———

                                       GREENEVILLE, TENN.,
                                          March 26, 1864.
Maj. Gen. R. RANSOM, Jr.,
      Midway:
Is there any truth in the report that the enemy is at Morristown? If he is there the commanding general desires the movement suspended, and wishes you to notify Generals Field and Johnson of it. Please advise us to-night by telegraph, in order that the troops here may be stopped if the report is correct.

                        G. M. SORREL,
          Lieutenant-Colonel and Assistant Adjutant-General.

———

                                       GREENEVILLE, TENN.,
                                          March 26, 1864.
Col. J. B. PALMER,
      Commanding District of Western North Carolina:
In reply to your communication of the 16th instant, which has been under consideration by the lieutenant-general commanding, I am directed to say that your views are concurred in by him, and you are authorized to take the steps that you propose to augment the forces for the protection of your district.
I send you inclosed herewith an order* for the object in view. The operations of the man Kirk, of whom you write, should be checked. Could you not capture or disperse his party by attacking him simultaneously on both sides? It would be useless to attack only on one side and leave the other open.
The detachment of a large force of our cavalry makes it necessary for the army to occupy a shorter line. The line of the Holston has

———

* Not found.

been selected and the movement will begin on Sunday, as indicated in General Orders, No. 33, which I have sent you.

The headquarters of the commanding general will be established at Bristol.

I am, very respectfully, your obedient servant,

G. M. SORREL,
Lieutenant-Colonel and Assistant Adjutant-General.

I would like to be informed of who will remain in command of your district.

HEADQUARTERS DEPARTMENT OF EAST TENNESSEE,
Greeneville, Tenn., March 26, 1864—8 p. m.

Maj. Gen. R. RANSOM, Jr.,
      Commanding Cavalry:

I am directed to say that the movement of the army to the north side of the Holston, as indicated in General Orders, No. 33, from these headquarters, is suspended until Monday, the 28th instant. The reported presence of the enemy at Morristown make this necessary. If the reports of the enemy's advance should prove correct we will not be able to move on Monday, as now contemplated. Meantime the commanding general desires you to retain Colonel Dibrell until more is known, and he also wishes you to send, so soon as you shall learn that the enemy has advanced toward Morristown, scouts down to the flank and rear of his force, to get between him and the river, and learn by observation and from citizens reliably and accurately what is the enemy's position and force. You had better send these scouts out at night after you find the enemy near Morristown, and endeavor to receive their information as quickly as possible, to enable the commanding general to make his dispositions.

If an apportunity offers we will seize it to strike the enemy a blow.

I remain, general, very respectfully, your obedient servant,

G. M. SORREL,
Lieutenant-Colonel and Assistant Adjutant-General.

GREENEVILLE, *March 27, 1864.*

General S. COOPER,
      Adjutant and Inspector General, Richmond, Va.:

The main force of the enemy's cavalry is at Mount Sterling, under General Sturgis. It would be better to keep the brigades left by General Martin here. They are under orders to move on Tuesday.

J. LONGSTREET,
Lieutenant-General.

HEADQUARTERS DEPARTMENT OF EAST TENNESSEE,
Greeneville, Tenn., March 27, 1864.

Major-General RANSOM,
      Commanding Cavalry:

I have the honor to inclose you herewith a communication* received this afternoon from Colonel Dibrell. I inclose also a letter* from a

---

* Not found.

number of citizens of Rogersville for your attention.   I am directed to say on this subject that you may leave a force there of 100 mounted men under a good officer.   The point will constitute a good outpost and the remainder of Vaughn's force may move back toward Kingsport.

I am, general, very respectfully, your obedient servant,
G. M. SORREL,
Lieutenant-Colonel and Assistant Adjutant-General.

HEADQUARTERS DEPARTMENT OF EAST TENNESSEE,
Greeneville, Tenn., March 27, 1864.

Brig. Gen. G. C. WHARTON,
Commanding Brigade:

The commanding general desires that your brigade should not halt at Jonesborough, as directed in my note of last night.   You will continue your march, as indicated in General Orders, No. 33, from these headquarters.

I am, general, very respectfully, your obedient servant,
G. M. SORREL,
Lieutenant-Colonel and Assistant Adjutant-General.

HEADQUARTERS,
Greeneville, East Tenn., March 27, 1864.

Brig. Gen. T. JORDAN,
Chief of Staff, Dept. of S. C., Ga., and Fla.:

GENERAL: Your letter of the 19th and the general's telegram were received yesterday.   I send a copy of my letter to the President,* which will explain my proposition for the spring campaign in the West.

The troops in this department are living on half rations of meat and bread, without any good reason to hope for better prospects.   Our animals are in the same condition, with the hope of getting grass in a month more.   Supplies seem to be about as scarce all over the Confederacy.   It seems a necessity, therefore, that we should advance, and this route seems to offer more ready and complete relief than any other.   If we had an abundance of supplies it seems to me that we should go into Kentucky as a political move.

If we retain our present positions the enemy will, in the course of a few months, be able to raise large additional forces, and when entirely ready he will again concentrate his forces upon some point, and will eventually get possession, and he will continue to proceed in the same way to the close of the chapter.   If we go into Kentucky, and can there unite with General Johnston's army, we shall have force enough to hold it.   The enemy will be more or less demoralized and disheartened by the great loss of territory which he will sustain, and he will find great difficulty in getting men enough to operate with before the elections in the fall, when in all probability Lincoln will be defeated and peace will follow in the spring.

The political opponents of Mr. Lincoln can furnish no reason at this late day against the war so long as it is successful with him, and

---

*See inclosure of Longstreet to Johnston, March 16, p. 637.

thus far it has certainly been as successful as any one could reasonably expect. If, however, his opponents were to find at the end of three years that we held Kentucky and were as well to do as at the beginning of the war, it would be a powerful argument against Lincoln and against the war. Lincoln's re-election seems to depend upon the result of our efforts during the present year. If he is re-elected, the war must continue, and I see no way of defeating his re-election except by military success.

I was under the impression that General Beauregard could bring into the field at least 20,000 men. These, with what we have here, could go into Kentucky and force the Yankee army out of Tennessee as far back as the borders of Kentucky. If the enemy should attack us before Johnston joins us, he would be obliged to do so in some haste, and we ought, therefore, to be able to beat him. If he uses caution we could maneuver so as to avoid battle and make a junction with Johnston, when we could advance to the Ohio.

This, though, should be done without delay and before the enemy can have time to begin his plans. If he begins to operate I fear that we shall adopt our usual policy of concentrating our troops just where he wants them. Dalton, as you say, would be a more easy point of concentration, but I should have to travel a thousand miles to get there, and should then be twice as far from Louisville as I am at present. His troops (the general's) would be farther from Louisville at Dalton than they would be at Morganton, N. C., and they would be quite as far from Louisville at Dalton as they would be at Greenville or Spartanburg, S. C. From Dalton we should be obliged to march through a country that may not be able to supply the army. My chief objection to Dalton, however, is the time that will be occupied in getting there and getting away from there. One or the other I regard as essential.

You speak of the enemy getting behind us to fortify the Cumberland Mountain passes. This I regard as next to an impossibility. He will be obliged to seek a base before he can do anything else, and whilst he is doing this Johnston can open ours, and we shall have the mountain passes besides.

I remain, general, very respectfully, your obedient servant,

J. LONGSTREET,
Lieutenant-General, Commanding.

MONTGOMERY, *March* 28, 1864.

Col. THOMAS M. JACK,
    Assistant Adjutant-General:

I inclose for General Polk's information, and such action as he may deem proper, copies of important communications from General Johnston's headquarters. I inclose also copies of my instructions to Brigadier-General Clanton,* and of my communication in reply to that from General Johnston. I have received several important and urgent appeals from citizens for force in that region of the State. The people up in that section have a strong conviction that the force now stationed at Decatur of the enemy is designed to make a dash on Central Alabama. I give the general all the facts, embodying important information from that section. I think

---

* Not found.

the safety of the great interior interests make it absolutely necessary to strengthen the force in the front and without loss of time.
Clanton's force, sixteen companies, is not capable of presenting any
serious resistance to an advancing column of 4,000 cavalry. I have
to-day given orders for four more companies to join him, but the
companies turned over to me are scattered and so remote that it will
require several weeks to get them in hand and [use?] them. Lockhart has not turned me over any others, though I have applied to
him to do so.
Respectfully,
GID. J. PILLOW,
Brigadier-General, C. S. Army.

P. S.—General Johnston sent these dispatches by an officer of his
staff.
G. J. P.

[Inclosure No. 1.]

HEADQUARTERS ARMY OF TENNESSEE,
Dalton, Ga., March 26, 1864.
General GIDEON J. PILLOW,
Comdg., &c., Headquarters Montgomery, Ala.:
GENERAL: I am instructed by General Johnston to inclose to you
the accompanying letter from Col. B. J. Hill, provost-marshal-general of this army, with the earnest request that you will give the
matter to which it relates the consideration it merits. He desires me
simply to inclose you the letter for such action as to you may seem
best.
A copy of Colonel Hill's letter has been sent to General Wheeler
with the information that you would be written to on the subject.
It is probable that he will send General Morgan, of Martin's cavalry
division, with the necessary command, for temporary duty in Northern Alabama.
I am, general, with high respect, your obedient servant,
E. J. HARVIE,
Colonel and Assistant Inspector-General.

[Sub-inclosure.]

HEADQUARTERS ARMY OF TENNESSEE,
PROVOST-MARSHAL-GENERAL'S DEPARTMENT,
Dalton, March 25, 1864.
Col. E. J. HARVIE,
Assistant Inspector-General:
COLONEL: Private E. D. Meroney, Company D, Third Confederate
Cavalry, was captured at Philadelphia, East Tenn., on the 20th
October, 1863, and put in prison at Knoxville, and remained there
about two weeks, when he made his escape and went to his home
in Blount County, North Ala. He got an intimation while in
prison that there was a secret society organized between the Northern and Southern armies, the object of which is to deplete our ranks
by desertion. He mentioned to one of the guards that he would give
anything to get out of prison. The guard replied: "If you were all
right, Jack, and had plenty of money you could get out." On his
arrival in North Alabama he found the whole country disloyal and
full of deserters. He was sick for some time ; as soon as he was able
to go about he went to work to find out how he could become a member of this secret society. He found out, took the oath, and became

a member, and makes the following divulgement of their proceedings, signs, pass-words, and oaths. They swear not to give any aid or comfort to a Confederate soldier, nor give any enrolling officer, or any one engaged in the Conscript Bureau, any satisfaction, aid, or comfort, nor to write any of the secrets or signs of the society upon paper, earth, or earthenware.

The sign : When you meet a man walking salute him with your right hand closed, the thumb pointing back behind the shoulder. If he is all right he grasps his own left hand with his right, the knuckles of the right up, those of the left down. They then look one another in the eye and tap the right foot with a small stick or other article ; after this is done, one party picks up a small stick, breaks it in pieces with his right hand, and throws them over his left arm. This gives the other party to understand that he can speak of any secret matter whatever connected with the order. When in a crowd three slaps carelessly on the right leg will signify to the other party that you are all right. If on horseback, the sign is giving the bridle-reins (holding them in your left hand) three slaps toward the right hand.

Pass-words : If in prison or in the guard-house, repeat the word "Washington" four times, and you will be released within twenty-four hours. When approaching a Yankee guard-post, after being halted and challenged, you say "Jack;" the sentinel replies, "All right, Jack, pass on with your goose-qnills." In line of battle the sign is to place the gun against the right hip at about an angle of 45 degrees, holding in this position long enough to be distinguished, then carry the piece to the left shoulder in position of Scott's "shoulder arms."

Mr. Meroney reports that the enemy have a secret line of spies from Tennessee to Tallapoosa County, Ala., through the instrumentality of the secrecy of this society.

The following enrolling officers and members of Conscript Bureau are members of this society, viz : Lieut. John F. Musgrove, conscripting officer, lives 5 miles from Blountsville, Ala. He gives passes to deserters good for twelve months. Lieutenant Wilkerson, commanding rendezvous at Blountsville, gave Meroney three passes at pleasure. Clark Livingston, enrolling officer, lives in Winston County, Ala. ; James Ooten, enrolling officer, lives in Winston County, Ala. There are other enrolling and conscripting officers who belong to this league in North Alabama whose names are forgotten.

The following citizens and deserters from our army are members of the society, viz : Allen Reive (citizen), lives in Walker County, Ala.; J. Martin (deserter), lives in Blount County, Ala.; William Chamble (deserter), postmaster at Sapp's Cross-Roads, Walker County, Ala.; K. Gambol (deserter), Yankee spy, Blount County, Ala.; John Gambol (deserter), Yankee spy, Blonnt County, Ala.; Wesley Prentice (deserter), Yankee spy, Blount County, Ala.; Joe Crutcher (conscript), Blount County, Ala.; Polk Hillman (deserter), Winston County, Ala.; George Baker (deserter), Winston County, Ala.; Mrs. Murphy (Yankee rendezvous), Winston County, Ala.

Mr. Meroney states that with a regiment of cavalry the entire society could be captured in North Alabama. He knows the country, and would like to accompany the party as a guide.

Respectfully submitted.

B. J. HILL,
Colonel and Provost-Marshal-General.

[Inclosure No. 2.]

MONTGOMERY, ALA.,
March 28, 1864.

Colonel HARVIE,
   Assistant Inspector-General:

The communications accompanying the dispatch by Lieutenant Safley are received. I have given the names of the enrolling officers mentioned as concerned to Lieutenant-Colonel Lockhart, commandant of conscripts, with the advice to order them to his headquarters, and when they arrive to have them placed in arrest and confinement. I have also given (sent by special courier) copies of the papers to Brigadier-General Clanton, who is at Blue Mountain on the railroad, with instructions secretly and promptly to arrest all the parties whose names are mentioned and have them sent under strict guard to this place. If possible to get the necessary papers prepared in time, courier will leave on boat for Selma to-night for Clanton's headquarters. I have information to-day from the river, and am advised that an officer called Major May has withdrawn the pickets from the river, leaving us without the means of knowing anything that is being done or any movements of the enemy. I thought this measure, if ordered by General Johnston, must have been done under some misapprehension as to other forces taking their places, but I have as yet no command, General Polk having failed to give me any command as yet, except a small force, less than two regiments (Clanton's and an unarmed regiment). I now suspect treason in that officer, and suspect he is one of the "order." If I had a command I could not have the river picketed for the reason that General Johnston's department runs clear across this State, and includes all of the river that lies in Alabama. Under these circumstances I think nothing can be done except for General Johnston to keep a watchful eye, a vigilant picket force all along on the river, and communicate with General Polk, urging him to increase the force on that front, and grant authority for this force to advance to the river, and renew his application to the Government to change the boundaries of the department so that the force which may be ordered to protect the interior of Alabama may be charged with the duty of picketing the river.

I will communicate a copy of these papers and of this order to General Polk.

Respectfully,

GID. J. PILLOW,
Brigadier-General, C. S. Army.

HEADQUARTERS THIRTY-FIFTH ALABAMA REGIMENT,
Russellville, Ala., March 28, 1864.

Lieut. Col. T. M. JACK,
   Assistant Adjutant-General:

COLONEL: On the day following my last report I changed the headquarters of my command from Mount Hope to this point. The enemy in small force occupy Decatur, 45 miles in distance from this place. As yet, on account of their close proximity, I have been unable to do much, but I am satisfied that before the lapse of many days the field will be open. In the mean time I shall work in my rear very industriously and am confident that my labors will inure to the good of the service.   There is a circuit of country some 20 miles in extent in my rear in which I propose to labor for the present. It is a poor, hilly section and I have reliable information which induces me to believe that it is filled with disaffected deserters and those liable to conscription.   Loyal citizens propose to furnish me with a sufficient number of horses to mount men enough to hunt down and arrest men of the above description.   I have availed myself of this offer to mount a portion of my command for that purpose. If in the opinion of General Polk it would be to the interest of the public service to mount my whole command I could easily accomplish it in a few days without expense to the Government.

I assure you that I shall spare no effort to accomplish faithfully the purposes of my mission here.

Very respectfully, yours, &c.,

S. S. IVES,
Colonel, Commanding Thirty-fifth Alabama Regiment.

DALTON, *March* 29, 1864.

General BRAGG:

GENERAL: I respectfully report that Major-General Martin, on reaching Kingston, stated that his division was unfit for service on account of the condition of the horses.   Major-General Wheeler, who visited the troops, expressed the same opinion.   The division has been ordered, therefore, to the district southwest of Rome, to put the horses in better condition.

Major-General Martin reported his effective force to be 1,500 instead of 3,000, as you supposed it, and they require 600 arms.

I have seen a copy of a letter from Lieutenant-General Longstreet to the President, proposing an expedition into Kentucky by an army to be formed of his own and General Beauregard's troops.   As you have given me permission to express my views in regard to such operations, I take the liberty of suggesting the importance of collecting into one army all the troops to be employed in Tennessee and Kentucky.   It is very unlikely that the Federal troops in those States will form more than one.   It would therefore put us at great disadvantage to divide ours into two.

Most respectfully, your obedient servant,

J. E. JOHNSTON,
General.

RICHMOND, *March* 29, 1864.

General S. COOPER,
Adjutant and Inspector General. C. S. Army:

GENERAL: Having in obedience to instructions visited General Johnston's army for the purpose of inspecting its artillery, and contributing under conference with the general all that might lie in my power toward remedying any evils found existing and promoting its best efficiency, I have the honor to submit the following report of duty discharged, facts observed, and arrangements made:

Leaving Richmond on the morning of March 8, and traveling uninterruptedly, I reached Dalton on the morning of the 12th, and proceeded at once to report to General Johnston. Through his kind attention I was enabled immediately to enter upon the work of inspection, and examined that day the batteries grouped in reserve. The day following was devoted to a general review of the artillery serving with the two army corps. Special inspections were continued on subsequent days until every battery had been carefully examined as to its material, management, and condition. The performance of the artillery was also repeatedly witnessed in drills and reviews.

In addition to these personal observations, I sought from the commanding general and other officers likely to know such information as they could give, and especially called for and received from the artillery commanders detailed statements of the service seen by the several batteries, of the defects, in their judgment, needing remedy and wants requiring supply, with an expression in every case of what they deemed their own condition. An acquaintance tolerably accurate with the entire condition of the artillery of that army was thus in a few days obtained, so that defects could be pointed out and remedies applied as far as means existed.

General Johnston and the corps commanders evinced great concern that the artillery might be rendered as efficient as possible at an early day. Its condition they deemed unsatisfactory on account of defective armament, insufficient strength in animals, and want alike of adequate chiefs and of suitable organization. The armament I found less strong than is desirable; with other particulars it will be seen in the tabular report (A). The 6-pounders, of which there were fifteen, are, in the present state of fire-arms, nearly useless, if not indeed worse, employing and exposing as they do a number of men and animals, while they can scarcely ever accomplish anything against the more powerful guns or even the long-range muskets of the enemy. The 12-pounder howitzers, of which there were twenty-seven, are scarcely more valuable; a few batteries of these for special service in that broken and wooded country may be useful, but the proportion is obviously too large. As rapidly as possible these deficiencies will be remedied; perhaps by 10th April nearly all the 6-pounders will be substituted by the more efficient 12-pounder Napoleon, and within a few weeks, the Chief of Ordnance assures me, several rifle batteries will be furnished in place of so many howitzers.

The animals were, for the most part, certainly thin; some had died from hard usage and disease not uncommon in our artillery service, and others were worn down below the standard for use. This I regard not as peculiar or as matter for blame, but as chiefly unavoidable and incident to the nature of the case. Extreme care will not always keep artillery horses in good condition, necessarily subject as they are at times to excessive draft, injurious exposure, and long fasting. The end of the fall campaign generally leaves them seriously reduced; the vicissitudes of winter and the difficulties in the way of supplies of forage sufficient in quantity and suitable in quality scarcely allow of their being adequately recruited by spring. In the mean time diseases will more or less prevail, and the animals are therefore often found still below a satisfactory standard in numbers and in flesh when a new campaign is about to open.

This state of things did not strike me as existing to a greater extent in the Army of Tennessee than in other commands at all similarly situated. The prevalent condition of the forces is nearly, if not quite, up to the average seen at this season in most of our artillery animals on the fronts, where hard service and hard fare occur together. With the addition of about 500, soon to be furnished, I was assured by the chief quartermaster, they will be capable at an early day, I am satisfied, of effective service. With the exception of a few instances of ignorance or neglect in their treatment, evidences are decisive that reasonable care for them has been exercised. In good health, as in the main they appear to be, inured to hardship, they may be more confidently relied upon than many better-looking animals not thus seasoned. No serious anxiety need be felt, I believe, respecting them. Arrangements are also in progress for keeping up a supply to meet casualties in battle and in marching. The main wants which I observed were a good chief to superintend the whole artillery service of the army, one or two sub-chiefs to direct the several groups of battalions, and an adequate system to maintain the arm in its full power, as well as to bring it thoroughly to bear in battle.

A battalion arrangement, designed to remedy some of the evils long observed as incident to the plan of segregating batteries with brigades, had already been introdueed, but it needed important additions and the presence of some superior officers to render it fully effective. Such complete system of administration I deemed it incumbent on me, after careful consideration, to recommend to General Johnston in the form of a memorandum of an order, a copy of which (marked B) is herewith furnished. On intimate personal knowledge of their eminent capacity, services, and merit in this branch, I also recommended to General Johnston Col. Thomas H. Carter, of the artillery in the Army of Northern Virginia, to be his general chief of artillery, with the rank of brigadier, and Lieut. Col. James Dearing to command one of the corps groups, with the rank of colonel, Colonel Beckham having been already appointed to command the other. Brigadier-General Shoup, said to be an excellent officer, was subsequently assigned by the Department, instead of Colonel Carter, to be General Johnston's chief of artillery, and his arrival at Dalton was daily expected when, having completed my work, I left there on the evening of the 21st. Of Colonel Dearing nothing has been heard. His services there, in the capacity indicated, would, if not more needed elsewhere, undoubtedly prove of great value.

Besides repeated conferences with the chief officers, and especially with General Johnston, and in addition to the documents (A and B) already referred to, I submitted to him a brief supplementary statement of my views, a copy of which (marked C) is also herewith given. In connection with those documents, and with what has been said herein, it leaves little more to be added.

It therefore only remains for me to express the decided conviction which I received that, with the improvements indicated as speedily to be accomplished, the artillery of the Army of Tennessee will prove satisfactorily efficient, and capable of contributing, with due power, to the great results for which, under the Divine blessing, we may justly hope.

I have the honor to be, general, respectfully, your obedient servant,

W. N. PENDLETON,
Brig. Gen. and Chief of Arty., Army of Northern Virginia.

[Inclosures.]

A.

Organization of the artillery of the Army of Tennessee, March 29, 1864.

Command.	Their date.	Captains' date.	6-pounders.	12-pounder howitzers.	Napoleons.	3-inch rifles.	10-pounder Parrotts.	Men present for duty.	Horses needed.
Hardee's (Melancthon Smith, chief ; major August 26, 1862) :									
Hoxton's battalion (major April 6, 1863):									
McCants' (Florida) battery	Dec. 12, '61	Apr. 2, '63	2	2				86	12
Turner's (Mississippi) battery	July 1, '61	May 2, '63			4			80	12
Phelan's (Alabama) battery	May 1, '61	Jan. —, '62			4			116	20
Hotchkiss' battalion (major May 3, 1863):									
Swett's (Mississippi) battery	May 1, '61	May 9, '61			3			103	5
Semple's (Alabama) battery	Mar. 1, '62	May 7, '62			4			109	7
Key's (Arkansas) battery	May 1, '61	Oct. 22, '63		4				61	4
Martin's battalion (major August 29, 1863):									
Bledsoe's (Missouri) battery	June —, '61	June 11, '61			4			80	20
Ferguson's (South Carolina) battery	Apr. —, '61	Dec. —, '61	2		2			95	20
Howell's (Georgia) battery	May —, '62	Aug. —, '63		4				101	10
Palmer's battalion (major October 13, 1862):									
Corput's (Georgia) battery	Aug. —, '61	July 11, '62			4			115	25
Rowan's (Georgia) battery *a*	Sept. —, '61	June 30, '63			4			140	62
Marshall's (Tennessee) battery	June —, '61	Jan. 6, '64			4			95	24
Total			4	10	33				
Hood's (R. F. Beckham, chief ; colonel March 1, 1864. Lieut. Col. J. W. Bondurant, March 2):									
Courtney's battalion (major January 14, 1862):									
Douglas' (Texas) battery	July 2, '61	May —, '62	2	2				92	13
Garrity's (Alabama) battery	Mar. 4, '61	Jan. 1, '63				2	2	94	24
Dent's (Alabama) battery	Dec. 21, '61	June 1, '63	2		2			110	20
Eldridge's battalion (major January 7, 1863):									
Stanford's (Mississippi) battery	May 17, '61	May 17, '61			4			96	....
Oliver's (Alabama) battery	Feb. 26, '62	Feb. 26, '62					4	117	....
Fenner's (New Orleans) battery	Apr. 15, '62	Apr. 15, '62	2	2				151	....
Cobb's battalion (captain September 1, 1861):									
Gracey's (Kentucky) battery	Sept. 20, '61	Sept. —, '61			4			138	18
Slocomb's (New Orleans) battery	May 26, '61	May 26, '61	2	2				140	30
Mebane's (Tennessee) battery	Oct. 15, '61	May 28, '61			4			103	20
Total			8	10	10	6	2		
Reserve (J. H. Hallonquist, commander; lieutenant-colonel April 2, 1862):									
Robertson's battalion (major June 29, 1863):									
Lumsden's (Alabama) battery	Nov. 29, '61	Nov. 29, '61			4			117	9
Barret's (Missouri) battery	Apr. 1, '62	Apr. 1, '62		4				108	....
Havis' (Georgia) battery	Apr. 1, '62	Apr. 1, '62	1	1	2			117	25
Anderson's (Georgia) battery	Apr. 1, '62	Apr. 1, '62					4	133	23
Williams' battalion (major December, 1862):									
Jeffress' (Virginia) battery	June 26, '61	June 26, '61					4	80	31
Kolb's (Alabama) Battery	Apr. —, '62	Feb. 9, '61	2	2				115	17
Darden's (Mississippi) battery	May —, '61	Apr. 3, '61			4			68	25
Waddell's battalion (major April, 1863):									
Emery's (Alabama) battery	May —, '61	May 6, '61						84	....
Bellamy's (Alabama) battery	May —, '61	May 15, '61							
Total			3	7	10		8		
Grand total			15	27	53	6	10		

a Formerly Third Maryland Battery.

[Sub-inclosure.]

A list of the field officers of the Corps of Artillery, Provisional Army, C. S., on duty in the Army of Tennessee [March 29, 1864].

Field officers.	State.	Date of appointment.	Remarks.
Col. R. F. Beckham.........	Va	Feb. 24, 1864	Commanding regiment Hood's corps.
Lieut. Col. J. H. Hallonquist.	S. C......	Apr. 7, 1862	Commanding regiment Reserve Artillery.
Lieut. Col. J. W. Bondurant.	Va......	July 11, 1863	Hood's corps.
Maj. W. C. Preston.........	S. C......	Apr. 2, 1862	Inspector of artillery Army of Tennessee.
Maj. M. Smith..............	Ala	Aug. 26, 1862	Commanding regiment of artillery Hardee's corps.
Maj. A. R. Courtney.........	Va........	July 14, 1862	Commanding battalion of artillery Hood's corps.
Maj. J. Palmer.............	S. C.......	Oct. 13, 1862	Commanding battalion of artillery Hardee's corps.
Maj. J. W. Eldridge.........	Tenn	Jan. 7, 1863	Commanding battalion of artillery Hood's corps.
Maj. S. C. Williams.........	Ga......	Feb. —, 1863	Commanding battalion Reserve Artillery.
Maj. J. F. Waddell	Ala......	Apr. 1, 1863	Do.
Maj. L. Hoxton...........	Va......	Apr. —, 1863	Commanding battalion Hardee's corps.
Maj. T. R. Hotchkiss	Miss	May —, 1863	Do.
Maj. John Rawle...	La........	June 3, 1863	On duty with Major-General Wheeler.
Maj. F. H. Robertson........	Tex.......	June 29, 1863	Commanding battalion Reserve Artillery.
Maj. R. Martin	S. C.......	Aug. —, 1863	Commanding battalion Hardee's corps.

B.

GENERAL ORDERS,   HEADQUARTERS ARMY OF TENNESSEE.
    No. —.

Toward securing alike the efficiency of the artillery and its thorough co-operation with other arms, it will in this army be regulated as follows:

I. As a distinct arm of service, with its own proper organization, it will be administered through the general chief of artillery, who represents for this arm the commanding general. All reports, requisitions, &c., will be made through him. On the field he will also have a general supervision of the artillery service, and special command wherever the commanding general may direct. He will be assisted in his duties by an appropriate staff.

II. The battalions, to consist of three batteries each, will be grouped in three commands, each of which will have two commanders, a senior and junior, and a staff consisting of a quartermaster, a commissary, and an adjutant, and as a surgeon the senior medical officer serving with the command. Two of these commands will serve respectively with the two army corps, and will consist of as many battalions as there are divisions in the corps. The third will constitute a general reserve; not to remain in the rear for service remotely contingent, but to be always at hand and ready for the most active operations on any part of the front as exigency may require.

III. The artillery commands operating with the army corps will also, at any time, make to the corps commanders such reports as they may require, and receive from them such orders, not conflicting with the views of the commanding general, as they may deem necessary. This will especially be the case on the march and in action.

IV. Battalions marching or operating with certain divisions will draw rations from the trains of those divisions. The reserve, or any artillery not thus attached, must have its own supply wagons or draw from the general train.

V. Beside the general reserve ordnance train for the army, the artillery ordnance will be collected in three trains, one for each command, each to have its own ordnance officer and its own quartermaster. The movements of these trains to be regulated by the chief of ordnance, and in special cases by the corps and artillery commanders.

VI. There will be with the general chief of artillery an ordnance officer, as chief of ordnance for the artillery, through whom, under the chief of artillery, the artillery ordnance service will be conducted, and with each of the senior sub-commanders, also, an ordnance officer having charge of the ordnance service for that command.

[Sub-inclosure.]

Report of Maj. M. Smith, commanding artillery, Hardee's corps.

I.—RESPECTING OFFICERS.

Commanders.	Entered the Confederate service.			In battles of—
	When.	Whence.	With what rank.	
Maj. Melancthon Smith	July 1, '61	Ala *a*	Captain of light artillery.	Belmont, Shiloh, Perryville, Chickamauga, Missionary Ridge.
Maj. Joseph Palmer...	Mar. —, '61	Ga..	First lieutenant of infantry.	Carrick's Ford, Greenbrier, Perryville, Elizabethtown, Muldraugh's Hill (Nos. 1 and 2), Noland's Ferry, Rolling Fork, and Chickamauga.
Capt. Max Van Den Corput.	Aug. —, '61	Ga..	Sergeant of artillery.	Cumberland Gap, Tazewell, Warrenton (gun-boat fleet), Baker's Creek, Vicksburg, Lookout Mountain, Missionary Ridge.
First Lieut. Meshack L. McWhorter.	Aug. —, '61	Ga..	Private of artillery.	Cumberland Gap, Tazewell, Vicksburg, Missionary Ridge.
Second Lieut. William S. Hoge	Aug. —, '61	Ga..	...do	Cumberland Gap, Warrenton, Baker's Creek, Vicksburg, Missionary Ridge.
Second Lieut. John E. Stillwell.	Aug. —, '61	Ga..	Sergeant of artillery.	Cumberland Gap, Warrenton, Tazewell, Baker's Creek, Vicksburg, Lookout Mountain, Missionary Ridge.
Second Lieut. William A. Russell.	Aug. —, '61	Ga..	....do	Cumberland Gap, Warrenton, Tazewell.
Capt. John B. Rowan..	....	......	... .	
First Lieut. William L. Ritter.	....	......	... .	
Second Lieut. Thomas D. Giles.	....	....		
Second Lieut. James W. Doncaster.	....	......		
Capt. L. G. Marshall...	June —, '61	Tenn	Private of artillery.	Belmont, Perryville, Murfreesborough, Lookout Mountain, Chickamauga.
First Lieut. James M. Cockrill.	May —, '61	Tenn	Private of infantry.	Belmont, Perryville, Murfreesborough, Chickamauga. Cheat Mountain.
Second Lieut. A. T. Watson.	Aug. —, '61	Tenn	Private of artillery.	Shiloh, Perryville, Murfreesborough, Chickamauga, Missionary Ridge.
Second Lieut. Finis E. White.	June —, '61	Tenn	Private of infantry.	Belmont, Perryville, Murfreesborough, Lookout Mountain, Chickamauga.
Maj. Lewellyn Hoxton.	June —, '61	Va..	First lieutenant, C. S. Army.	Farmington, Corinth (skirmish), Perryville, Murfreesborough, Missionary Ridge.
Capt. Robert P. Mc-Cants.	Jan. —, '62	Fla..	First lieutenant, P. A. C. S.	Chickamauga.
First Lieut. Thomas J. Perry.	Jan. —, '62	Fla..	Sergeant of artillery.	Richmond, Ky., Chickamauga, Missionary Ridge.
First Lieut. Andrew J. Neal.	Mar. — '61	Fla..	Private of infantry.	Do.
Second Lieut. James C. Davis.	May 14, '62	Fla..	Private of artillery.	Richmond, Ky.
Capt. William B. Turner.	Apr. 24, '61	Miss.	Private of infantry.	Belmont, Shiloh, Perryville, Murfreesborough, Chickamauga, Missionary Ridge.
First Lieut. Chandler S. Smith.	Apr. 23, '61	Ala.	Second lieutenant of infantry.	Belmont, Shiloh, Perryville, Murfreesborough, Chickamauga.
Second Lieut. W. W. Henry.	Apr. 24, '61	Miss.	Sergeant of infantry.	Belmont, Shiloh, Perryville, Chickamauga, Missionary Ridge.
Second Lieut. B. T. Harman.	Apr. 24, '61	Miss.	....do	Shiloh, Perryville, Murfreesborough, and Leesburg (as private).

a State service.

Report of Maj. M. Smith, commanding artillery, Hardee's corps—Continued.

I.—RESPECTING OFFICERS—Continued.

Commanders.	Entered the Confederate service.			In battles of—
	When.	Whence.	With what rank.	
First Lieut. John Phelan.	May —, '61	Ala..	Sergeant of infantry.	Chickamauga and Missionary Ridge.
First Lieut. Robert Perrin.	June —, '61	Ala..	Private of infantry.	Do.
Second Lieut. N. Venable.	May —, '61	Ala..	Sergeant of infantry.	
Second Lieut. William Dailey.	May —, '61	Ala..	Private of infantry.	Do.
Maj. T. R. Hotchkiss ...	July —, '61	Miss.	Private of artillery.	Farmington, Perryville, Murfreesborough, Chickamauga, skirmish Liberty Gap.
Capt. Charles Swett ...	Aug. —, '61	Miss.	Captain of artillery.	Woodsonville, Shiloh, Farmington, Perryville, skirmish Liberty Gap, Chickamauga,
First Lieut. H. Shannon.	Aug. —, '61	Miss.	First lieutenant of artillery.	Woodsonville, Shiloh, Farmington, Perryville, skirmish Liberty Gap, Chickamauga, and Tunnel Hill.
Second Lieut. H. N. Steele.	Aug. —, '61	Miss.	Private of artillery.	Do.
Second Lieut. F. M. Williams.	Aug. —, '61	Miss.	....do	Do.
First Lieut. John Doscher.	Apr. —, '61	Ga	....do	Shiloh, Chickamauga, Missionary Ridge.
Capt. Henry C. Semple.	Mar. —, '62	Ala..	Captain of artillery.	Perryville, Murfreesborough, Chickamauga, Tunnel Hill.
First Lieut. Richard W. Goldthwaite.	Mar. —, '62	Ala..	Second lieutenant of artillery.	Perryville, Murfreesborough, Chickamauga, Tunnel Hill, and Ringgold Gap.
First Lieut. E. G. McLelland.	Mar. —, '62	Ala..	Sergeant of artillery.	Perryville, Murfreesborough, Tunnel Hill.
Second Lieut. C. M. Dowd.	Mar. —, '62	Ala..	Private of artillery.	Perryville, Murfreesborough, Tunnel Hill, and Chickamauga.
Capt. Thomas J. Key..	Apr. —, '62	Ark	Private of infantry.	In battles of this army from November, 1862, to February, 1864.
First Lieut. Robert Fitzpatrick.	Dec. —, '61	Ark	First lieutenant of artillery.	Shiloh, Perryville, Murfreesborough.
First Lieut. W. M. Hopwood.	July —, '61	Tenn	Private of artillery.	Shiloh, Perryville,. Murfreesborough, Chickamauga.
Second Lieut. James G. Marshall.	Dec. —, '61	Ark	....do	Do.
Maj. Robert Martin....		S. C	Captain of infantry.	Fall of Sumter, Fort McAllister, Jackson, Miss., Missionary Ridge.
Capt. Hiram M. Bledsoe.	Apr. 21, '62	Miss.	Captain of artillery.	In the battles of the Missouri campaign, first and second siege of Corinth, Vicksburg, Port Hudson, and Jackson, Miss.
First Lieut. R. L. Wood.	Apr. —, '62	Miss.	First lieutenant of artillery.	Do.
First Lieut. Charles W. Higgins.	Apr. —, '62	Mo .	....do	Do.
Second Lieut. H. W. Anderson.	Apr. —, '62	Mo ..	Second lieutenant of artillery.	Do.
Second Lieut. L. L.? Maughas.	Apr. —, '62	Mo .,	....do	Do.
Second Lieut. John S. Wheatley.	Apr. —, '62	Mo..	Second lieutenant of artillery.	In the battles of the Missouri campaign, first and second siege of Corinth, Vicksburg, Port Hudson, and Jackson, Miss.
Capt. Thomas B. Ferguson.	Apr. —, '62	S. C.	Captain of artillery.	Jackson, Miss.
First Lieut. R. T. Beauregard.	Apr. —, '62	S. C.	First lieutenant of artillery.	Jackson and Missionary Ridge.
First Lieut. H. D. Calhoun.	Apr. —, '62	S. C.	....do	Do.
Second Lieut. John A. Alston.	Apr. —, '62	S. C	Second lieutenant of artillery.	Do.
Capt. Evan P. Howell..	May —, '62	Ga..	First lieutenant of artillery.	Fort McAllister, Jackson (Miss.), Missionary Ridge, Lookout Mountain.
First Lieut. W. G. Robson.	May —, '62	Ga..	Second lieutenant of artillery.	Fort McAllister, Jackson (Miss.), Missionary Ridge, Lookout Mountain, Chickamauga.
Second Lieut. T. J. Gilmore.	May —, '62	Ga..	....do	Do.
Second Lieut. R. T. Gibson.	May —, '62	Ga..	Sergeant of artillery.	Do.

Report of Maj. M. Smith, commanding artillery, Hardee's corps—Continued.

I.—RESPECTING OFFICERS—Continued.

Commanders.	Experience in artillery service.	Occasion of promotion.	Date of present rank.	Remarks.
Maj. M. Smith	Acquired at U. S. Military Academy and in this war.	Appointed by President on recommendation of his generals.	Aug. 26, '62	
Maj. J. Palmer	From Apr., 1862, to date.	Recommendation of superior officers.	Oct. 13, '62	Formerly commanded battery in John H. Morgan's cavalry.
Capt. M. V. D. Corput	From Aug., 1861, to date.	Promotion of captain.	July 11, '62	
First Lieut. M. L. McWhorter.	....do	Election	Apr. 1, '62	
Second Lieut. W. S. Hoge.	....do	...do	Apr. 1, '62	
Second Lieut. J. E. Stillwell.	....do	...do	Aug. 21, '62	
Second Lieut. W. A. Russell.	....do	...do	Aug. 21, '62	
Capt. J. B. Rowan			June 30, '63	This battery is at Kingston without horses.
First Lieut. W. L. Ritter.			June 30, '63	
Second Lieut. T. D. Giles.	•		Mar. 21, '63	
Second Lieut. J. W. Doncaster.			June 30, '63	
Capt. L. G. Marshall.	From June, 1861, to date.	Resignation of captain.	Jan. 6, '64	
First Lieut. J. M. Cockrill.	From Apr., 1861, to date.	Promotion of first lieutenant.	Jan. 6, '64	
Second Lieut. A. T. Watson.	From Aug., 1861, to date.	Election	Aug. 18, '62	
Second Lieut. F. E. White.	From Sept., 1861, to date.	...do	Dec. 4, '63	
Maj. L. Hoxton	Acquired at West Point and since war.	Recommendation of General Hardee.	Apr. 0, '63	
Capt. R. P. McCants	From Jan., 1862, to date.	Resignation of captain.	Apr. 2, '63	
First Lieut. T. J. Parry.	....do	Election	Apr. 2, '63	
First Lieut. A. J. Neal	From May, 1862, to date.	...do	Apr. 14, '63	
Second Lieut. J. C. Davis.	....do	...do	Apr. 15, '63	
Capt. W. B. Turner	From July, 1861. to date.	Appointed by President for skill and valor.	May 2, '63	
First Lieut. C. S. Smith. a	From Oct., 1861, to date.	Appointed by Lieutenant-General Polk.	May 14, '62	
Second Lieut. W. W. Henry.	From July, 1861, to date.	...do	May 14, '62	
Second Lieut. B. T. Harman.	From Mar., 1862, to date.	Election	Nov. 16, '63	
First Lieut. John Phelan.	From Dec., 1861, to date.	...do	Jan. 27, '62	Passed board of examiners and assigned to duty as captain Mar. 16, 1864.
First Lieut. R. Perrin.	....do	...do	Jan. 27, '62	
Second Lieut. N. Venable.	....do	...do	Jan. 27, '62	
Second Lieut. William Dailey.	....do	...do	Mar. 1, '62	
Maj. T. R. Hotchkiss	From May, 1862, to date.	Recommended by General A. S. Johnston.	May 31, '63	
Capt. C. Swett	From May, 1861, to date.	Election	May 9, '61	State service.
First Lieut. H. Shannon.	....do	...do	May 9, '61	Major Hotchkiss mentions Lieutenant Shannon as conspicuous at Murfreesborough and Tunnel Hill.
Second Lieut. H. N. Steele.	From Dec., 1863, to date.	...do	Dec. 17, '63	Lieutenant Steele reported inefficient.
Second Lieut. F. M. Williams.	... do	...do	Jan. 1, '64	

a Detailed as regimental adjutant. He was examined by a board for the captaincy. The then senior first (Turner) having failed to pass, Lieutenant Smith passed and was recommended by the Board for the captaincy. The recommendation was forwarded, but never since heard from. Severely wounded at Chickamauga. I think him entitled to the promotion for which the board recommended him.

Report of Maj. M. Smith, commanding artillery, Hardec's corps—Continued.

I.—RESPECTING OFFICERS—Continued.

Commanders.	Experience in artillery service.	Occasion of promotion.	Date of present rank.	Remarks.
First Lieut. J. Doscher.	From Apr., 1862, to date.	Election	Aug. 25, '62	Adjutant Hotchkiss' battalion ; belongs to Pritchard's battery ; reported as very inefficient.
Capt. H. C. Semple...	From Mar., 1862, to date.	... do	Mar. 7, '62	
First Lieut. R. W. Goldthwaite.	...do	...do	Mar. 6, '63	Major Hotchkiss mentions Lieutenant Goldthwaite as conspicuous at Chickamauga and Ringgold Gap.
First Lieut. E. G. McLelland.	....do	....do	June 13, '63	
Second Lieut. C. M. Dowd.	From July, 1863, to date.	...do	July 21, '63	
Capt. T. J. Key........	From Apr., 1862, to date.	Appointed by General Bragg.	Oct. 22, '63	
First Lieut. R. Fitzpatrick.	From Dec., 1861, to date.	Election	July 1, '62	
First Lieut. W. M. Hopwood.	From July, 1861, to date.	.. do	Jan. 25, '63	
Second Lieut. J. G. Marshall.	From Apr., 1862, to date	....do	June 25, '63	Major Hotchkiss mentions Lieutenant Marshall as conspicuous at Chickamauga and Tunnel Hill.
Maj. R. Martin...... .	From Feb., 1861, to date.	Appointed by Secretary of War.	Aug. 29, '63	
Capt. H. M. Bledsoe..	From June, 1861, to date.	Election	June 11, '61	State service.
First Lieut. R. L. Wood.	From Apr., 1862, to date.	.. do	Apr. —, '62	
First Lieut. C. W. Higgins.	....do	...do	June —, '61	
Second Lieut. H. W. Anderson.	...do	...do	June —, '61	
Second Lieut. L. L. Maughas.	....do	...do	June —, '61	On detached service.
Second Lieut. J. S. Wheatley.	....do	...do	June —, '61	On detached service ; never will be fit for the field on account of wounds.
Capt. T. B. Ferguson.	...do	... do	Dec. --, '61	
First Lieut. R. T. Beauregard.	....do	...do	Dec. --, '61	
First Lieut. H. D. Calhoun.	....do	...do	Dec. --, '61	
Second Lieut. J. A. Alston.	....do	...do	Jan. 1, '62	
Capt. E. P. Howell ...	From May, 1862, to date.	Promotion of captain.	Aug. --, '63	
First Lieut. W. G. Robson.	....do	Promotion of first lieutenant.	May --, '62	
Second Lieut. T. J. Gilmore.	....do	Promotion of second lieutenant.	June —, '63	
Second Lieut. R. T. Gibson.	....do	....do	June —, '63	

II.—RESPECTING BATTERIES.

Batteries.	Raised.			Service seen.	Losses.	
	When.	Where.	By whom.		Men.	Horses.
Corput's ..	1861..... .	Ga...	Capt. Marcellus A. Stovall	Active service from 1861 to date.	7 killed at Baker's Creek, Vicksburg, and Jackson.	64 killed and captured at Vicksburg and Baker's Creek.
Marshall's.	1861..... .	Tenn .	Capt. W. H. Jackson.	From Belmont to date.	2 killed at Perryville, 2 at Murfreesborough, and 7 at Chickamauga.	7 killed at Perryville, 7 at Murfreesborough, and 49 at Chickamauga.
Rowan's ..	....	Ga..a.	. . . .	....	....	....

a Formerly Third M——

Report of Maj. M. Smith, commanding artillery, Hardee's corps—Continued.

II.—RESPECTING BATTERIES –Continued.

Batteries.	Raised.			Service seen.	Losses.	
	When.	Where.	By whom.		Men.	Horses.
McCants' ..	Dec. 12, '61	Fla ...	Capt. John M. Martin.	Active service to date.	1 lieutenant and 1 private killed at Richmond, Ky.	6 at Richmond, Ky., 10 at Missionary Ridge, and 1 at Chickamauga.
Turner's. {	Apr. 24, '61	....	Capt. James S. Terrall, as infantry.	} Active service from August, 1861, to date.	2 at Shiloh, 1 at Murfreesborough, 1 lieutenant and 1 private at Chickamauga.	40 disabled at Shiloh, 1 at Perryville, and 8 at Chickamauga.
	July 1, '61	Miss ..	Capt. M.Smith, as artillery.			
Fowler's...	May —, '61	Ala ...	Capt. Robert E. Rodes, as infantry.	From April. 186 ', to date	7 at Chickamauga	23 at Chickamauga.
Swett's	May —, '61	Miss ..	Captain Swett.	From August, 1861, to date.	5 killed at Shiloh, 2 at Farmington, 2 at Perryville, 1 at Murfreesborough, 1 lieutenant and 4 men at Chickamauga, and 1 lieutenant and 6 men at Tunnel Hill.	11 at Shiloh, 3 at Perryville, 10 at Murfreesborough, 5 at Chickamauga, and 4 at Tunnel Hill.
Semple's...	Mar.—, '62	Ala ...	Captain Semple.	From August, 1862, to date.	2 at Perryville, 4 at Murfreesborough, 2 at Chickamauga, and 1 at Ringgold Gap.	31 killed.
Key's	May —, '61	Ark...	Capt. A. W. Clarkson.	From 1861 to date.	7 killed in battle ..	22 killed and disabled.
Bledsoe's ..	June —, '61	Mo....	Captain Bledsoe.	Active service in Missouri campaign and to date.	70 lost in all from different causes.	Cannot tell.
Ferguson's.	Apr. —. '62	S. C ...	Captain Ferguson.	Served in South Carolina and to date.	21 captured on retreat from Missionary Ridge.	50.
Howell's...	May —, '62	Ga....	Capt. R. Martin.	Active service since to date.	2 killed at Jackson and 3 at Chickamauga.	3 at Jackson and 6 at Chickamauga.

Batteries.	Losses.			Re-equipments received.	Armament.	Strength.		
	Guns.	Transportation.				Total present.	Aggregate present.	Aggregate present and absent.
Corput's a ...	Four captured at Baker's Creek.	Four wagons at Vicksburg.		Re-equipped since the capture of Vicksburg.	Four 12-pounder Napoleon guns.	115	120	139
Marshall's a .	None	Four wagons near Chattanooga captured foraging.		Re-equipped in horses and small articles and different guns.	....do	95	100	140
Rowan's a ..	....	....		....	....do	140	145	165
McCants' a ..	Two 6-pounders at Missionary Ridge captured.	One 2-mule wagon belonging to battalion headquarters lost in retreat from Missionary Ridge.		Received two 6-pounders from Scogin's battery, it being broken up.	Two 6-pounder guns and two 12-pounder howitzers.	86	88	104

a Equipment and condition good.

Report of Maj. M. Smith, commanding artillery, Hardee's corps—Continued.

II.—RESPECTING BATTERIES—Continued.

Batteries.	Losses.				Strength.		
	Guns.	Transportation.	Re-equipmcts received.	Armament.	Total present.	Aggregate present.	Aggregate present and absent.
Turner's *a* ...	Three at Shiloh; the teams being sent after Yankee guns by General Polk, brought off ten guns from the field.	None	Exchanged two 0-pounders for two Yankee guns at Perryville, and obtained other two Napoleons at Murfreesborough.	Four 12-pounder Napoleons.	89	93	129
Fowler's *a* ...	None	....do	....	....do	116	119	155
Swett's *a*	One disabled at Rocky Ford.	....do	Guns exchanged for Napoleons.	Three 12-pounder Napoleons.	103	107	130
Semple's *a* ...	One captured at Murfreesborough.	Three wagons captured and lost on retreat.	New harness received and caissons.	Four 12-pounder Napoleons.	109	114	143
Key's *b*	None	None	At times parts of harness.	Four 12-pounder howitzers.	61	63	81
Bledsoe's *c* ...	One abandoned at Elk Horn.	....do	Re-equipped at different times with different articles.	Four 12-pounder Napoleons.	80	84	111
Ferguson's *d*.	Four guns and three caissons.	....	Re-equipped since Missionary Ridge.	Two 12-pounder Napoleons and two 6-pounder guns.	95	100	195
Howell's *a* ...	Two 6-pounders lost at Lookout Mountain.	None	Received two howitzers since Missionary Ridge.	Four 12-pounder howitzers.	101	105	125

a Equipment and condition good.
b Equipment good. but knapsacks and haversacks needed ; condition good.
c Equipment incomplete, otherwise good.
d Need some few equipments; condition good.

III.—RESPECTING EVILS TO BE REMEDIED.

The only disease at present among the animals is "scratches" and a few cases of "scours," and some of the horses have vermin. For scratches, wash clean and apply soft soap and grease; also, bluestone, copperas, white-lead, poke-root, and red-oak bark have been used. For vermin a strong decoction of tobacco has proved efficacious, with sulphur given in the food. The horses the past winter have been severely affected with a severe and fatal distemper (now not prevalent) strongly resembling glanders. Various remedies were tried without success. The horses on exhibition of first symptoms were removed from the other horses, as the disease was very contagious. Steps have been taken to procure a veterinary surgeon, the want of whom is much felt. Failure of supplies were at times reported up to February 12 (time about the present organization); since then none have been reported. No officers are reported for neglecting stable-calls, watering, or grooming. No improper use of animals. A stringent order is in force in this regiment that Government horses are not to be used only on Government business.

Report of Maj. M. Smith, commanding artillery, Hardee's corps—Continued.

IV.—RESPECTING WANTS TO BE SUPPLIED TO COMPLETE ORGANIZATION.

Batteries.	Horses.	Harness.	Suitable guns.	Equipments and ammunition.
Corput's.................	25	....	....	
Marshall's...............	24	One double set.	....	
Rowan's..................		......		
McCants' *a*	12	....	Two howitzers to replace two 6-pounders.	
Turner's..................	12		....	Needs two new gun carriages in place of two 24-pounder howitzer carriages.
Fowler's *b*	20	Twenty-five new collars.	....	Need good friction primers.
Swett's..................	5	....	One gun required in place of one disabled in late skirmish.	Do .
Semple's	7	....	....	Forty-five knapsacks. Need good friction primers.
Key's *c*	4	....	....	
Bledsoe's	20			
Ferguson's..............	20	....	Two 12-pounder Napoleons instead of two 6-pounder guns.	
Howell's................ .	10	......	....	

a Captain McCants has sent in his resignation ; not yet heard from.
b Lieutenant Perrin forwarded his resignation ; not yet heard from.
c Lieutenant Fitzpatrick on post duty—lost a hand ; Lieutenant Hopwood unheard of since November, 1863. Their places should be filled.

Under this head I will mention that the construction forges which each battalion now have (one to each) are to be taken away. I consider them indispensable, as with them the battalion quartermaster is enabled to keep the transportation in repair, to shoe the mules, and to weld the tires when they break. It is impossible to get sufficient heat on the battery forges.

I need an inspector on my staff, and have recommended Sergt. George O. Jordon, of Turner's battery. He has been a sergeant in that (formerly Smith's) battery since the beginning of the war. He received a military education at Lexington, Va.; he is intelligent, temperate, vigilant, and brave, and I have noticed him on the field and in the camp, and think him deserving of promotion. His recommendation has been forwarded.

Respectfully submitted.

MELANCTHON SMITH,
Major, Comdg. Art. Regt., Hardee's Corps, Army of Tenn.

C.

HEADQUARTERS ARMY OF TENNESSEE,
March 21, 1864.

General J. E. JOHNSTON,
Commanding:

GENERAL : Having, under instructions from Richmond, visited this army for the purpose of inspecting its artillery, conferring with yourself in relation thereto, and presenting such views toward its full efficiency as my experience may suggest, and having devoted to the facts ten days' careful examination and reflection, I have now the honor to submit for your consideration the results to which my judgment is brought.

These are systematically presented in the tabular report (A) and in the memorandum of an order respectfully suggested (B). Beside these synopses, a few brief statements in addition may also be useful and therefore proper.

I. The transportation of your artillery is, I think, in a better than average condition; the wagons for the most part strong, and the animals quite serviceable.

II. With arrival of better guns, expected soon, the armament will be much improved and quite efficient, if not all that might be desired.

III. The horses, as is generally the case in our artillery service at the end of winter, owing to several depressing causes, are for the most part comparatively thin ; but they have been in the main obviously well cared for, are in promisingly good health, and being inured to hard service, may, with the additions indicated and expected at an early day, the Chief Quartermaster now assures me, be relied upon, I think, for efficient performance, however early it may be demanded.

IV. The officers, so far as brief acquaintance and limited inquiry authorize me to judge, are earnest, capable, experienced, and generally efficient, and the organization already arranged, with certain additions indicated, may be expected to bring out their best energies and to give the arm its full force. My own preference would have been for battalions of four batteries, authorizing two field officers to each ; but as they had been already formed with three batteries, it appears best to retain them in that form and adapt the other elements of organization to that feature.

V. The promotions or assignments needed ought, it appears to me, to be made as soon as practicable. Incompleteness in provision for command may be a serious hinderance to thorough efficiency. It has not been practicable for me to acquire the exact personal knowledge to justify any special recommendation. Majors Courtney, Williams, Hoxton, and Robertson are recommended by their immediate superiors ; Captain Cobb should undoubtedly be made major ; Captains Stanford, Slocomb, Darden, Dent, Lumsden, Garrity, and Barret are also commended by their commanders; there may besides be others equally deserving. The general chief of artillery will, on arriving, find this a point entitled to his early attention.

VI. In conclusion, my belief is decided that your artillery, thus adjusted and well commanded, will prove greatly efficient and powerfully contribute to the great victory which this army is, by the blessing of Providence, destined, I trust, to achieve at no distant day.

I have the honor to be, general, respectfully, your obedient servant,

W. N. PENDLETON,
Brigadier-General Artillery, C. S. Army.

[Sub-inclosure No. 1.]

HEADQUARTERS ARMY OF TENNESSEE,
March 12, 1864.

Colonel HALLONQUIST :

COLONEL : Will you be so good as to furnish me for your command brief replies to the following inquiries :

I. Respecting officers.

1. Regimental and battalion commanders, when, whence, and with what rank they entered the Confederate service; in what battles they have been; what experience had of artillery service; occasion of promotion.

2. Battery officers, similar particulars.

3. Any of whatever grade inefficient or conspicuously deserving promotion.

II. Respecting batteries.

1. Name, where, when, by whom raised; what service seen.

2. Any losses experienced in men, horses, guns, transportation, equipments; when, where, how.

3. Re-equipments received.

4. Present armament, strength, equipment, and condition.

III. Respecting evils to be remedied.

1. Any disease or vermin among animals; what steps taken.

2. Any failure of supplies, extra hard service, neglect by officers of stable-calls, feeding, watering, and grooming; improper use of animals.

IV. Respecting wants to be supplied.

1. Of officers to complete organization.

2. Of horses to make each battery efficient.

3. Of guns sufficiently powerful.

4. Of harness and other equipments.

5. Of good ammunition.

Respectfully, your obedient servant,

W. N. PENDLETON,
Brigadier-General, C. S. Artillery.

[Sub-inclosure No. 2.]

Report of Maj. Alfred R. Courtney* respecting his battalion of artillery, in response to General W. N. Pendleton's interrogatories.

I.—RESPECTING OFFICERS.

Batteries.	Names of officers.	When entered service.	Whence.	Rank entered	Names of battles in which engaged.	What experience had of artillery.	Occasion of promotion.
Douglas'.	Capt. James P. Douglas.	July 2, '61	Tex.	First lieutenant.	Elk Horn, Ark., Richmond, Ky., Murfreesborough, Chickamauga, Missionary Ridge, and Ringgold Gap.	In the service since July, 1861, as an artillery officer.	Promoted by election May, 1862.
	First Lieut. John H. Bingham.	July 2, '61	Tex.	Private..	Same battles, except Ringgold Gap.	....do	Do.
	First Lieut. Benjamin Hardin.	July 2, '61	Tex.	Sergeant major.	Richmond, Murfreesborough, Chickamauga, and Missionary Ridge.	....do	Promoted by election August, 1863.
	Second Lieut. M. L. Fleishl.	July 2, '61	Tex.	Private..	Same as Douglas' except Ringgold.	..do	Promoted by election September 5, 1862.

* Maj. A. R. Courtney entered the Confederate States service May 11, 1861, from Henrico County, Va., as second lieutenant of artillery. Has been in the battles of Cross Keys, Port Republic, Cold Harbor, Malvern Hill, Cedar Run, Second Manassas, Harper's Ferry, Sharpsburg, Chickamauga, and Missionary Ridge. Served in light artillery since May 11, 1861. Promoted July 14, 1862, for meritorious conduct at Cross Keys and before Richmond, Va.

Report of Maj. Alfred R. Courtney, &c.—Continued.

I.—RESPECTING OFFICERS—Continued.

Batteries.	Names of officers.	When entered service.	Whence.	Rank entered.	Names of battles in which engaged.	What experience had of artillery.	Occasion of promotion.
Douglas'.	Second Lieut. W. J. Sanders.	July 2, '61	Tex.	Private.	In all of the above except Murfreesborough and Ringgold.	In the service since July, 1861, as an artillery officer.	Promoted by election September 5, 1862.
Garrity's	Capt. James Garrity.	May 4, '61	Ala.a	Sergeant major.	Shiloh, Farmington, Munford ville, Murfreesborough, Chickamauga, and Missionary Ridge.	In artillery service since May, 1861.	For gallantry at Murfreesborough, January 1, 1863.
	First Lieut. Philip Bond.	May 4, '61	Ala.	Corporal	In all of last above except Farmington.	....do	Do.
	First Lieut. Maynard A. Hassell.	May 4, '61	Ala..	Private..	In same as Captain Garrity except Shiloh and Missionary Ridge.	....do	Do.
	Second Lieut. J. Lyons.	May 4, '61	Ala..	...do	In same as Captain Garrity except Missionary Ridge.	....do	Elected February, 1864.
Dent's ...	Capt. S. H. Dent.	Feb. 28, '61	Ala.b	First lieutenant infantry.	Pensacola, Shiloh, Farmington, Chickamauga, and Missionary Ridge.	In artillery service since December, 1861.	Assigned as first lieutenant and promoted as captain, June 1, 1863.
	First Lieut. H. H. Richardson.	Feb. 8, '61	Miss.c	Private.	Pensacola, Shiloh, Farmington, and Murfreesborough	In artillery service since February, 1861.	Appointed first lieutenant May 5, 1862.
	First Lieut. W. T. Stockton.	Apr. 4, '61	Fla.d	Sergeant	Shiloh, Farmington, Murfreesborough, and Chickamauga.	In artillery since December, 1861.	Appointed first lieutenant June, 1862.
	Second Lieut. D. L. Southwick.e	Feb. 28, '61	Ala.b	Private.	Pensacola, Shiloh, Farmington, Murfreesborough, Chickamauga, Missionary Ridge.	In artillery service since February, 1861.	Appointed second lieutenant August, 1863.
	Second Lieut. G. B. Zeigler.	Apr. 4, '61	Fla.d	..do	....do	In artillery service since December, 1861.	Do.

a Mobile.
b Eufaula.
c Natchez.
d Quincy.
e Captured at Missionary Ridge, and is now a prisoner on Johnson's Island.

II.—RESPECTING BATTERIES.

Batteries.	Where from.	By whom raised.	When.	What service seen.	Losses—when, where, and how.
Douglas'	Tex.	Capt. J. J. Good.	July 2, '61	From Elk Horn.	Elk Horn—1 man killed, 15 wounded, 22 horses killed, and 1 caisson lost ; Richmond, Ky.—1 officer and 2 men killed and same number wounded, and 2 horses killed ; Murfreesborough—1 man wounded ; Chickamauga—1 horse killed ; Missionary Ridge—1 man wounded and 1 prisoner.

Report of Maj. Alfred R. Courtney, &c.—Continued.

II.—RESPECTING BATTERIES—Continued.

Batteries.	Where from.	By whom raised.	When.	What service seen.	Losses—when, where, and how.
A l a b a m a State Artillery.	Ala.*a*	Capt. W. H. Ketchum.	May 4,'61	From May 4, 1861.	Shiloh—15 killed and wounded and 1 gun lost ; Murfreesborough—23 killed and wounded ; Chickamauga—3 men wounded ; Missionary Ridge—2 wounded and 10 captured, 1 gun and 1 wagon lost. Lost horses in all the actions except Chickamauga, but do not remember number.
Dent's	Ala.	Capt. F. H. Robertson	Dec.21,'61	Since Dec. 21, 1861.	Shiloh—2 men killed and 17 wounded, and 23 horses killed ; Farmington—1 man wounded and 3 horses lost ; Murfreesborough—2 men killed, 23 wounded, and 26 horses lost, and 1 caisson ; Chickamauga—3 men killed, 19 wounded, 1 officer wounded, and 20 horses lost ; Missionary Ridge—7 men killed, 1 officer and 20 men wounded and captured, 5 guns lost, 2 caissons and 35 horses lost.

Batteries.	Re-equipments received.				Present armament.					Strength.			Condition.
	3-inch rifles.	12-pounder Napoleon.	6-pounders.	Caissons.	10-pounder Parrotts.	3-inch rifles.	12-pounder Napoleons.	12-pounder howitzers.	6-pounders.	Caissons.	Total effective.	Aggregate present.	Aggregate present and absent.	
Douglas' *b* . . .	. . .	. . .	. . .	. . .	. . .	. . .	. . .	. . .	2	2	4	76	92	102	Good, except carriages, which are bad.
A l a b a m a State Artillery.*c*	2	. . .	. . .	4	2	2	. . .	. . .	. . .	. . .	4	79	04	123	Two carriages unserviceable.
Dent's *d*	. . .	1	2	. . .	. . .	. . .	2	. . .	2	4	82	110	136	Good, except harness, which is old and much worn.

a Mobile.
b The re-equipments put down only include those recently received. Equipments complete.
c The guns named were old guns taken from the companies which were broken up after Missionary Ridge losses on account of inability to re-equip them. Equipments complete.
d Equipments complete.

III.—RESPECTING EVILS TO BE REMEDIED.

1. No disease and but little vermin among the animals of this battalion, and sulphur, grease, and tobacco have been used to eradicate these so far as has been possible to procure the medicines.

2. Forage has been generally plentiful, as also other supplies from the quartermaster's department. Most of the essential supplies from the ordnance department have been recently promptly furnished, but have found it impossible to get some articles, such as guns, harness-oil, leather, tarpaulins. All officers attend stable-calls, feeding, and grooming, and there is no improper use of animals, except that the officers of Douglas' battery are mounted on Government horses. They have, however, asked permission to purchase horses from the Government, being unable otherwise to get them.

Report of Maj. Alfred R. Courtney, &c.—Continued.

IV.—WANTS TO BE SUPPLIED.

Batteries.	Officers to complete organization.	Horses to make battery efficient.	Suitable guns.		Harness or other equipments.	Of good ammunition.
			10-pounder Parrotts.	12-pounder Napoleons.		
Douglas'	None needed	a13		4	None needed as yet.	None needed.
Garrity's	...do	24	b2			Do.
Dent's	...do	20		c2	None needed immediately.	Do.

a Of the horses required 35 have been condemned as unserviceable.
b The guns required are such as I would prefer if at liberty to fill out the command to my choice.
c But six Napoleons would make the armament very good. There would then be two Napoleon and one rifle battery, the rifle battery consisting of two Parrotts and two Confederate States 3-inch rifles.

The horses are carried to water twice a day in column of twos at a walk, under command of a sergeant. In the morning pass the officer of the day, who inspects each animal closely and reports condition.

A. R. COURTNEY,

Major, Comdg. Artillery Battalion, Beckham's Regiment,
Hood's Corps, Army of Tennessee.

[Sub-inclosure No. 3.]

Report of Maj. J. Wesley Eldridge* respecting his battalion of artillery, in reply to General W. N. Pendleton's interrogatories.

I.—RESPECTING OFFICERS.

Batteries.	Names of officers.	When entered service.	Whence.	Rank entered.
Stanford's	Capt. Thomas J. Stanford	May 17, 1861	Grenada, Miss	Captain.
	First Lieut. Hugh R. McSwine	May 17, 1861	...do	First lieutenant.
	Second Lieut. James S. McCall	May 17, 1861	....do	Private.
	Junior Second Lieut. William A. Brown.	Nov. 6, 1861	....do	Do.
Eufaula	Capt. McDonald Oliver	Feb. 26, 1862	Eufaula, Ala	Junior first lieutenant.
	First Lieut. William J. McKenzie.	Feb. 26, 1862	....do	Junior second lieutenant.
	Second Lieut. William H. Woods.	Feb. 26, 1862	....do	Sergeant.
	Junior Second Lieut. Francis M. Caldwell.	Mar. 1, 1861	...do	Private.
Fenner's	Capt. Charles E. Fenner	Apr. 15, 1861	New Orleans	First lieutenant of infantry.
	First Lieut. T. J. Duggan	May 16, 1862	Jackson, Miss	First lieutenant.
	Junior First Lieut. W. T. Cluverius.	May 16, 1862	New Orleans	Sergeant.
	Second Lieut. E. Montgomery	May 16, 1862	....do	Do.
	Junior Second Lieut. C. J. Howell.	May 16, 1862	....do	Private.

* Maj. J. W. Eldridge entered Tennessee State service April 1, 1861, as a private from Memphis, Tenn.; was promoted to the rank of major in May, 1861, and transferred to Confederate service July 1, 1861; raised a light battery by authority of the Secretary of War; was captain of same October 15, 1861; reported to General A. S. Johnston, Bowling Green, Ky.; engaged in the battle of Corinth, and complimented on the field by General Donelson for gallantry and valuable services. Appointed major of artillery January 7, 1863, by recommendation of Generals Braxton Bragg and Breckinridge; assigned to duty with Maj. Gen. A. P. Stewart as chief of artillery; had command of his batteries at Hoover's Gap and Chickamauga; mentioned in official report of battle of Chickamauga by General Stewart for gallantry and effective use of artillery at right time and place.

Report of Maj. J. Wesley Eldridge, &c.—Continued.

I.—RESPECTING OFFICERS—Continued.

Batteries.	Names of officers.	Names of battles in which engaged.	What experience had of artillery.	Occasion of promotion.
Stanford's.	Capt. Thomas J. Stanford	Shiloh, Perryville, Murfreesborough, Chickamauga, Missionary Ridge.	In active service since May 17, 1861.	No promotion.
	First Lieut. Hugh R. McSwine.	Shiloh, Perryville, Murfreesborough.	Since May 17, 1861.	Has not been promoted.
	Second Lieut. James S. McCall.	Same as Stanford.............	...do.........	Promotion by election.
	Junior Second Lieut. William A. Brown.	.....do.....................	Active service since November 6, 1861.	Do.
Eufaula ...	Capt. McDonald Oliver ...	Tazewell and Chickamauga..	Active service since May, 1862.	Promotion by resignation.
	First Lieut. William J. McKenzie.	Tazewell, Murfreesborough, Hoover's Gap, Missionary Ridge.	...do.........	Promotion by death.
	Second Lieut. William H. Woods.	Tazewell, Hoover's Gap, Chickamauga, Missionary Ridge.	...do.........	Promotion by election.
	Junior Second Lieut. Francis M. Caldwell.	Same as Lieutenant McKenzie.	...do.........	Do.
Fenner's ..	Capt. Charles E. Fenner ..	Jackson, Miss	Active service until September, 1863; sent to Mobile.	Do.
	First Lieut. T. J. Duggan ..	......do.............	...do.........	No promotion.
	Junior First Lieut. W. T. Cluverius.	......do.............	...do.........	Promotion by election.
	Second Lieut. E. Montgomery.	......do..........	...do.........	Do.
	Junior Second Lieut. C. J. Howell.	......do.............	...do.........	Do.

II.—RESPECTING BATTERIES.

Batteries.	Where from.	By whom raised.	When.	What service seen.	Losses—when, where, and how.
Stanford's.	Grenada, Miss ..	Capt. T. J. Stanford.	May 17, '61	Active service from battle of Shiloh.	At Shiloh, Perryville, Chickamauga, and Missionary Ridge —39 men and 11 horses.
Eufaula Artillery.	Eufaula, Ala ...	Capt. John W. Clark.	Feb. 26, '62	Active service since May, 1862.	5 men and 35 horses at Murfreesborough, Chickamauga, and Missionary Ridge ; 1 gun at Missionary Ridge, horses being killed.
Fenner's ..	New Orleans ...	Capt. Chas. E. Fenner.	Apr. 15, '62	Engaged in one battle and several skirmishes.	2 men killed at Jackson, Miss. ; no horses, guns, or transportation lost.

Batteries.	Re-equipments received—3-inch rifle.	3-inch rifles.	12-pounder Napoleons.	12-pounder howitzers.	6-pounders.	Caissons.	Total effective.	Aggregate present.	Aggregate present and absent.
			Present armament.					Strength.	
Stanford's *a*....			4				91	96	125
Eufaula Artillery........	1	4					115	117	154
Fenner's........				2	2	....	147	151	196

a Requisition made upon ordnance department to fill deficiency in equipments. Condition of battery good. By reference to this table it will be seen that Capt. T. J. Stanford is one of the eldest captains of artillery in this army ; that he has seen much service, and been in all the important battles fought. He is therefore respectfully recommended for promotion.

Report of Maj. J. Wesley Eldridge, &c.—Continued.

III.—RESPECTING EVILS TO BE REMEDIED.

Ordnance department slow in furnishing supplies, and have ever been so, so far as my wants extended. Some scratches and vermin among the horses. Means are used to eradicate this. Officers attend punctually all calls. No improper use of animals, and with one exception (myself) all officers ride their own horses.

IV.—RESPECTING WANTS TO BE SUPPLIED.

Batteries.	Officers to complete organization.	Horses to make battery efficient.	Suitable guns.	Harness or other equipments.	Of good ammunition.
Stanford's	None needed.	Full number on hand.	None needed...	Good condition; none needed.	None needed; full supply.
Eufaula Artillery.	....do	...do	One 8-inch rifle *a*	Complete and in good condition.	Ammunition good.
Fenner's *b*	....do	...do	Four Napoleons.	....do	Ammunition good; full supply.

a One of the rifle pieces is much worn ; if possible, a new rifle gun should be furnished instead.
b A very strong company ; has an 8-pounder battery; it could be made much more useful if furnished with Napoleons.

All of which is respectfully submitted.

J. W. ELDRIDGE,
Major, Comdg. Bat. Light Arty., Hood's Corps, Army of Tenn.

[Sub-inclosure No. 4.]

Statistical report of the battalion of artillery, of Hood's corps, commanded by Capt. Robert Cobb.

Batteries.	Names of officers.	When enlisted.	Whence.	With what rank.
Cobb's	Capt. Robert Cobb	July 16, 1861	Lyon County, Ky.	First lieutenant.
	First Lieut. Frank P. Gracey	July 16, 1861	....do	Second lieutenant.
	First Lieut. R. B. Matthews	July 16, 1861	....do	Private.
	Second Lieut. B. A. James	July 16, 1861	....do	Orderly sergeant.
Slocomb's	Capt. C. H. Slocomb	May 26, 1861	New Orleans	Second lieutenant.
	First Lieut. W. C. D. Vaught	Mar. 6, 1862	...do	First lieutenant.
	First Lieut. J. A. Chalaron	Mar. 6, 1862	...do	Second lieutenant.
	Second Lieut. A. J. Leverich	Mar. 6, 1862	.. do	Sergeant.
	Second Lieut. C. J. Johnson	Mar. 6, 1862	.. do	Private.
Mebane's	Capt. John W. Mebane	May 28, 1861	Fayette County, Tenn.	Second lieutenant.
	First Lieut. J. W. Phillips	Oct. 15, 1861	Tennessee	Orderly sergeant.
	Second Lieut. J. C. Grant	Nov. 25, 1861	....do	Private.
	Second Lieut. L. E. Wright	June 3, 1861	....do	Do.

Batteries.	Names of officers.	What battles in.	What experience in artillery.	Occasion of promotion.
Cobb's	Capt. Robert Cobb	See under head of losses.	From September, 1861, to present time.	Vice Captain Lyon, promoted.
	First Lieut. Frank P. Gracey	See losses, excepting Baton Rouge and Murfreesborough.	...do	Elected.
	First Lieut. R. B. Matthews	Excepting Baton Rouge.	...do	Do.
	Second Lieut. B. A. James	Excepting Baton Rouge and Chickamauga.	...do	Do.

Statistical report of the battalion of artillery, &c.—Continued.

Batteries.	Names of officers.	What battles in.	What experience in artillery.	Occasion of promotion.
Slocomb's	Capt. C. H. Slocomb	See under head of losses.	....	Vice Captain Hodgson, promoted.
	First Lieut. W. C. D. Vaught.	See under head of losses ; was at Manassas, Munson's Hill, and Lewinsville.	March 6, 1862	Elected.
	First Lieut. J. A. Chalaron ..	See under head of losses.	....do	Do.
	Second Lieut. A. J. Leverich.	....do................	...do............	Do.
	Second Lieut. C. J. Johnson.	....do....	...do......	Do.
Mebane's	Capt. John W. Mebane......	....do................	September 20, 1861, to present time.	Vice Captain Wright, promoted.
	First Lieut. J. W. Phillips ...	....do.....	From October 15, 1861, to present.	Vice J. W. Mebane, promoted.
	Second Lieut. J. C. Grant....	....do.....	From November 25, 1861, to present.	Elected.
	Second Lieut. L. E. Wright..	.... do................	From December 8, 1861, to present.	Promoted for gallantry at Murfreesborough.

ORGANIZED.

Name.	Where.	When.	By whom.	What service seen.
Cobb's First Kentucky Battery.	Bowling Green, Ky ..	Sept. 20, 1861	Capt. H. B. Lyon......	Day of organization to present time.
Slocomb's Fifth Company, Washington Artillery.	New Orleans, La......	Feb. 22, 1832	....	
Mebane's (Tennessee) battery.	Fayette County, Jackson, Tenn.	Oct. 15, 1861	Capt. J. W. Eldridge .	Do.

LOSSES.

Batteries.		Shiloh.	Farmington.	Vicksburg.	Perryville.	Corinth.	Baton Rouge.	Murfreesborough.	Jackson.	Chickahauga.	Hartsville.	Missionary Ridge.	Picket.	Total.
Cobb's *a*	Men killed	12	....	....	....	....	2	2	3	3	1	....	23	
	Men wounded.	29	....	1	....	....	2	9	7	10	11	7	....	76
	Men missing .	....	....	....	....	....	....	....	....	....	....	3	....	3
	Total....	41	....	1	....	....	2	11	9	13	14	11	....	102
	Pieces.........	2	....	....	....	....	....	....	....	....	4	....	6	
	Caissons	6	....	....	....	....	....	....	....	....	4	....	10	
	Horses killed.	68	....	....	....	....	6	....	3	6	3	....	86	
	Horses wounded.	10	....	....	....	2	7	....	5	5	....	....	29	
	Total....	78	....	....	....	2	13	....	8	11	3	....	115	
	Ammunition expended (rounds).	487	....	1,125	....	51	1,125	195	400	385	482	....	4,252	

a A correct statement cannot be made of the various re-equipments received. The following batteries have been consolidated into one, with such of their equipments as was required to make the battery effective: Byrne's [Mississippi] battery, at Corinth, May, 1862 ; Graves' [Mississippi] battery, at Murfreesborough, November, 1862 ; fragments of Green's [Kentucky] battery, Hart's [Arkansas] battery, and Waters' [Alabama] battery in January, 1864.

Statistical report of the battalion of artillery, &c.—Continued.

LOSSES—Continued.

Batteries.		Shiloh.	Farmington.	Vicksburg.	Perryville.	Corinth.	Baton Rouge.	Murfreesborough.	Jackson.	Chickamauga.	Hartsville.	Missionary Ridge.	Picket.	Total.
Slocomb's a..	Men killed....	6	....	......	1	....	....	3	....	13	....	7	....	23
	Men wounded.	20	1	......	5	....	....	3	1	20	....	7	....	57
	Men missing ..	....	....	......	....	....	....	....	....	....	....	3	....	3
	Total.....	26	1	......	6	....	....	6	1	33	....	10	....	83
	Horses killed..	30	1	......	10	....	....	8	3	20	....	21	....	93
	Horses wounded.	....	....	......	....	....	....	....	....	....	....	....	....	......
	Total.....	30	1	......	10	....	....	8	3	20	....	21	....	93
	Pieces and caissons.	....	....	......	....	....	....	....	....	....	....	6	....	6
	Ammunition expended (rounds).	723	80	......	758	....	....	638	211	682	....	675	209	3,876
Mebane's b ..	Men killed...	....	....	......	....	....	....	6	....	....	....	....	....	6
	Men wounded.	....	....	......	....	....	....	14	2	3	....	2	....	21
	Men missing .	....	....	......	....	....	....	2	1	....	....	1	....	4
	Total....	....	....	......	....	....	....	22	3	3	....	3	....	31
	Pieces.......	....	....	......	....	....	....	2	....	....	....	....	....	2
	Ammunition chests.	....	....	......	....	....	....	....	....	....	....	1	....	1
	Horses killed.	....	....	......	....	....	....	12	2	....	....	....	....	14
	Horses wounded.	....	....	......	....	....	1	12	5	....	....	2	....	20
	Total....	....	....	......	....	....	1	24	7	....	....	2	....	34
	Ammunition expended (rounds).	....	....	......	....	....	30	475	....	175	....	543	....	1,223

a A correct statement cannot be made of the re-equipments received as the books of the company are at the rear.

b A correct statement cannot be made, books being at the rear.

Batteries.	Present armament.								Strength of batteries.	Equipment.	Condition.	Disease among the animals and steps taken.
	12-pounder Napoleons.	12-pounder howitzers.	6-pounder smooth-bores.	Solid shot.	Shell.	Spherical case shot.	Canister.	Total.				
Cobb's	4	....	....	128	256	64	64	512	138	Complete	Good	Scratches, distemper. The cases of distemper in my battery have been so vile that I have found nothing that will cure it. Scratches by exercise and washing with soft soap.
Slocomb's .	....	2	2	183	140	237	156	716	177	Incomplete.	Bad.	Scours, scratches, and vermin. A strong decoction of tobacco applied to animals will kill the vermin ; soft soap and blue-stone for scratches.
Mebane's .	....	....	4	171	293	67	....	531	103	Complete	Fair .	Scours, scratches, and vermin. Sage tea for scours, decoction of tobacco for vermin, and soft soap for scratches.

Statistical report of the battalion of artillery, &c.—Continued.

LOSSES—Continued.

Batteries.	Failure of supplies.	Negligence of officers.				Improper use of animals.
		Stable-calls.	Feeding.	Watering.	Grooming.	
Cobb's.....	During month of January forage was scarce and inferior.	Regularly attended to.	Attended to.	Regularly attended to.	Not as much attention to length of time and kind of grooming as should be given, but more than is generally given as far as my knowledge goes in the Army.	None.
Slocomb's .	Supplies very irregular. During December very scarce and bad.	...do	Regularly attended to.	... do	Regularly attended to.	Do.
Mebane's ..	During last month quantity of forage good, though quality bad.	...do	...do	...do	...do	Do.

WANTS TO BE SUPPLIED.

Cobb's battery : Eighteen horses are requisite to make the battery efficient. Some 10 and 15 second fuse are also wanted, as none longer than five seconds are on hand.

Slocomb's battery: On hand, 30 serviceable horses. Wanted, four Napoleon and two rifled guns with equipments complete. Harness complete; ammunition complete.

Mebane's battery : Twenty horses required to fill deficiency.

Respectfully submitted.

R. COBB,
Captain, Commanding Battalion.

[Sub-inclosure No. 5.]

Report of regiment Reserve Artillery, Lieut. Col. J. H. Hallonquist commanding.

I.—RESPECTING OFFICERS.

Names of officers.	When entered C. S. service.	Whence.	Rank entered.
Lieut. Col. James H. Hallonquist..	Mar. —, 1861	South Carolina ...	Lieutenant, Confederate States Artillery.
Maj. Felix H. Robertson..........	Mar. —, 1861	Texas	Second lieutenant, Confederate States Artillery.
Maj. Samuel C. Williams	Mar. —, 1861	Georgia..........	Lieutenant, Confederate States Artillery.
Maj. James F. Waddell...........	May 12, 1861	Alabama	Captain, Sixth Alabama Volunteers.
Robertson's battalion :			
Capt. Charles L. Lumsden	Nov. 29, 1861	Alabama	Captain, Lumsden's battery.
Lieut. Ebenezer H. Hargrove..	Nov. 29, 1861	Alabama	Second lieutenant, Lumsden's battery.
Second Lieut. A. C. Hargrove..	Nov. 29, 1861	Alabama	Sergeant, Lumsden's battery.
Capt. Overton W. Barret.	Apr. 1, 1862	Missouri	Captain, Barret's battery.
Lieut. William Brown	Apr. 1, 1862	Missouri	Sergeant, Barret's battery.
Second Lieut. Isaiah Lightner.	Apr. 1, 1862	Missouri	Do.
Second Lieut. G. W. Orear	Apr. 1, 1862	Missouri	Do.
Capt. M. W. Havis	Apr. 1, 1862	Georgia..........	Lieutenant, Palmer's battery.
Lieut. James R. Duncan	Apr. 1, 1862	Georgia..........	Do.
Lieut. Hamblin R. Felder	Apr. 1, 1862	Georgia..........	Second lieutenant, Dawson's battery.
Second Lieut. C. H. Smith	Apr. 1, 1862	Georgia..........	Second lieutenant, Palmer's battery.

Report of regiment Reserve Artillery, Lieut. Col. J. H. Hallonquist, &c.—Cont'd.

I.—RESPECTING OFFICERS—Continued.

Names of officers.	When entered C. S. service.	Whence.	Rank entered.
Robertson's battalion—Cont'd.			
Second Lieut. James R. Rice ..	Apr. 1, 1862	Georgia..........	Sergeant, Palmer's battery.
Capt. R. W. Anderson..........	Apr. 1, 1862	Georgia..........	Lieutenant, Dawson's battery.
Lieut. Henry S. Greaves	Apr. 1, 1862	Georgia..........	Private, Dawson's battery.
Second Lieut. R. H. Brown	Apr. 1, 1862	Georgia..........	Do.
Second Lieut. Willis G. Allen ..	Apr. 1, 1862	Georgia....... ...	Do.
Williams' battalion :			
Capt. William C. Jeffress	June 22, 1861	Virginia	Captain, Jeffress' battery.
Lieut. Bernard H. Todd	June 22, 1861	Virginia	Lieutenant, Jeffress' battery.
Lieut. Edwin W. Jones	June 22, 1861	Virginia	Private, Jeffress' battery.
Second Lieut. Atwell W. Robertson.	June 22, 1862	Virginia	Sergeant, Jeffress' battery.
Second Lieut. Samuel B. Wingo	June 22, 1862	Virginia	Do.
Capt. Reuben F. Kolb	Feb. 9, 1861	Alabama	Sergeant, battery.
Lieut. Robert Cherry	Feb. 9, 1861	Alabama	Do.
Lieut. F. P. Powers	Feb. 9, 1861	Alabama	Do.
Second Lieut. Robert Flournoy	Feb. 9, 1861	Alabama	Second lieutenant, battery.
Second Lieut. W. Y. Johnston.	Feb. 9, 1861	Alabama	Private, battery.
Capt. Put. Darden............	Apr. 3, 1861	Mississippi.......	Do.
Lieut. H. W. Bullen..........	Apr. 3, 1861	Mississippi.......	Do.
Second Lieut. F. W. Coleman.	July —, 1861	Mississippi.......	Do.
Second Lieut. C. B. Richardson.	Apr. 13, 1861	Mississippi.......	Do.
Waddell's battalion :			
Capt. Winslow D. Emery.... .	May 6, 1861	Alabama	Private, Sixth Alabama Volunteers.
Lieut. Thomas J. Bates........	May 15, 1861	Alabama	Sergeant, Sixth Alabama Volunteers.
Lieut. Archibald H. Burch	May 15, 1861	Alabama	Private, Sixth Alabama Volunteers.
Second Lieut. M. M. Allen......	May 15, 1861	Alabama	Do.
Second Lieut. Robert H. Boykin	May 15, 1861	Alabama	Do.
Capt. Richard H. Bellamy.....	May 15, 1861	Alabama	Do.
Lieut. Francis A. O'Neal......	May 15, 1861	Alabama	Do.
Lieut. R. M. Harvey..........	May 15, 1861	Alabama	Do.
Second Lieut. J. T. Holland....	Feb. 26, 1862	Alabama	Do.
Second Lieut. Thomas W. Crowder.	Aug. 15, 1861	Alabama	Do.

Names of officers.	Names of battles in which engaged.	What experience had of artillery.	Occasion of promotion.
Lieut. Col. James H. Hallonquist.	First bombardment of Sumter and Vicksburg, Shiloh, Perryville, Murfreesborough, Chickamauga, Missionary Ridge.	Graduate U. S. Military Academy ; artillery duty since.	Appointed major ; promoted April 7, 1862.
Maj. Felix H. Robertson ..	First bombardment of Sumter and Fort Pickens; Shiloh, Farmington, Murfreesborough, Chickamauga, Missionary Ridge.	Since the beginning of the war on arty. duty.	Appointed June 29, 1863.
Maj. Samuel C. Williams ..	First bombardment of Sumter, Kernstown, Perryville, Chickamauga.	Graduate U. S. Military Academy ; artillery duty since.	Appointed December, 1862.
Maj. James F. Waddell....	Richmond Ky., Baker's Creek, siege of Vicksburg.	Captain of artillery January 7, 1862.	Appointed April, 1863.
Robertson's battalion :			
Capt. Charles L. Lumsden.	Farmington, Perryville, Chickamauga, and retreat from Missionary Ridge.	Since entrance into service.	Raised a battery..
Lieut. Ebenezer H. Hargrove.	Perryville, Chickamauga, and retreat from Missionary Ridge.	...do	Election.
Second Lieut. A. C. Hargrove.	Farmington, Perryville, Murfreesborough, Chickamauga. and retreat from Missionary Ridge.	....do	Skill and gallantry at Perryville and Chickamauga.
Capt. Overton W. Barret.	Elk Horn, Murfreesborough, and Chickamauga.	... do	Raised a battery.
Lieut. William Brown .	Elk Horn, Perryville, Chickamauga, and Missionary Ridge.	Since entrance into C. S. service.	Election.
Second Lieut. Isaiah Lightner.	Carthage, Dry Wood, Lexington, Oak Hill, Perryville, Murfreesborough, Chickamauga, and Missionary Ridge.	....do	Do.
Second Lieut. G. W. Orear.	......do	...do	Skill and gallantry at Murfreesborough, Perryville.

Report of regiment Reserve Artillery, Lieut. Col. J. H. Hallonquist, &c.—Cont'd.

I.--RESPECTING OFFICERS—Continued.

Names of officers.	Names of battles in which engaged.	What experience had of artillery.	Occasion of promotion.
Robertson's battalion—C'd.			
Capt. M. W. Havis.....	Perryville, Chickamauga, Morgan's winter campaign in Kentucky.	Since entrance into service.	Seniority.
Lieut. James R. Duncan.	.....do	....do	Do.
Lieut. Hamblin R. Felder.	Murfreesborough, Hoover's Gap, Chickamauga, and Missionary Ridge.	....do	Do.
Second Lieut. C. H. Smith.	Perryville, Chickamauga, Morgan's winter campaign in Kentucky.	... do	Election.
Second Lieut. James R. Rice.	.....do	....do	Do.
Capt. R. W. Anderson..	Murfreesborough, Hoover's Gap, Chickamauga, Missionary Ridge	....do	Seniority.
Lieut. Henry S. Greaves	Wharton's cavalry fight in 1862...	....do	Do.
Second Lieut. R. H. Brown.	....	....	Election.
Second Lieut. W. G. Allen.	Murfreesborough, Hoover's Gap, Chickamauga, Missionary Ridge	....do	Do.
Williams' battalion :			
Capt. Wm. C. Jeffress .	Prestonburg, Princeton, Chickamauga.	....do	Do.
Lieut. Bernard H. Todd	.....do	....do	Do.
Lieut. Edwin W. Jones	......do	....do	Do.
Second·Lieut. Atwell W. Robertson.	......do	....do	Do.
Second Lieut. Samuel B. Wingo.	......do .'.............. ....do	....do	Do.
Capt. R. F. Kolb	Chickamauga, Missionary Ridge .	....do	Do.
Lieut. Robert Cherry ..	......do	...do	Do.
Lieut. F. P. Powers	......do	...do	Do.
Second Lieut. Robert Flournoy.	......do	...do	Do.
Second Lieut. W. Y. Johnston.	......do	...do	Do.
Capt. Put. Darden	Triune, Hoover's Gap, Shiloh, Perryville, Chickamauga, Murfreesborough.	....do	Do.
Lieut. H. W. Bullen	......do	....do	Do.
Second Lieut. F. W. Coleman.	......do	....do	Do.
Second Lieut. C. B. Richardson.	......do	....do	Do.
Waddell's battalion :			
Capt. Winslow D. Emery.	Richmond, Ky., Baker's Creek, and siege of Vicksburg.	Since February 2, 1862.	Appointed by Major Waddell in organizing battalion.
Lieut. Thomas J. Bates	......do	Since April 20, 1862.	Do.
Lieut. Archibald H. Burch.	.....do	....do	Do.
Second Lieut. M. M. Allen.	Baker's Creek	Since February 1, 1862.	Do.
Second Lieut. Robert H. Boykin.	Baker's Creek and siege of Vicksburg.	....do	Do.
Capt. Richard H. Bellamy.	Richmond, Ky., Baker's Creek, and siege of Vicksburg.	....do	Do.
Lieut. Francis A. O'Neal.	Richmond, Ky., and siege of Vicksburg	... do	Do.
Lieut. R. M. Harvey....	Siege of Vicksburg..............	Since April 1, 1862.	Do.
Second Lieut. J. T. Holland.	Baker's Creek and siege of Vicksburg.	....do	Do.
Second Lieut. Thomas W. Crowder.	Baker's Creek	Since May 16, 1863.	Do.

The officers of the command are efficient. Majors S. C. Williams and Robertson conspicuously deserve promotion. Capts. P. Darden, C. L. Lumsden, and O. W. Barret are in like manner deserving of it.

Report of regiment Reserve Artillery, Lieut. Col. J. H. Hallonquist, &c.—Cont'd.

II.—RESPECTING BATTERIES.

* Batteries.	Where raised.	When raised.	By whom raised.	Service seen.
Lumsden's.	Ala ...	Nov. —,'61	Captain Lumsden.	Corinth, Miss., Kentucky campaign, campaign of Middle Tennessee and North Georgia.
Barret's ...	Mo ...	Apr. —,'62	Captain Barret.	Do.
Havis'	Ga	Apr. —,'62	Major Palmer.	Bragg's Kentucky campaign, Morgan's Kentucky campaign, Middle Tennessee, and North Georgia.
Anderson's	Ga	Apr. —,'62	Captain Dawson.	Campaign Middle Tennessee and North Georgia.
Jeffress' ...	Va. ..	June--,'61	Captain Jeffress.	In Southwestern Virginia, Kentucky, and Army of Tennessee.
Kolb's . ..	Ala ..	Apr. —,'62	Captain Reeves.	In Army of Tennessee.
Darden's ..	Miss ..	May —,'61	Captain Harper.	All engagements from Shiloh to Chickamauga.
Emery's ...	Ala...	Oct. —,'63	Major Waddell	These two batteries formerly constituted Waddell's battalion, and served in Kentucky campaign and in Mississippi previous to and during siege of Vicksburg.
Waddell's .	Ala...	Oct. —,'63	....do	

LOSSES, ETC.

Lumsden's battery lost men and horses May, 1862, at the battle of Farmington, killed by the enemy. In October, 1862, he lost men and horses killed at Perryville. On December 31, 1862, lost horses killed at Murfreesborough. No guns or transportation lost.

Barret's battery lost men and horses December 31, 1862, at Murfreesborough, and the same loss on September 19 and 20, 1863, at battle of Chickamauga, and the same loss November 25 at Missionary Ridge. No transportation or guns lost.

Havis' battery lost men and horses October, 1862, at Perryville, killed by enemy ; the same loss September 19 and 20, 1863, at Chickamauga, killed by enemy. At Missionary Ridge this battery lost men and horses and two Napoleon guns captured ; no blame attached, the battery fighting to the last. No transportation lost. Rear parts of caissons lost in January, 1863, Morgan's campaign in Kentucky ; forced to be abandoned on the retreat, the horses giving out.

Anderson's battery lost horses on December 31, 1862, at Murfreesborough, killed by enemy ; the same loss in June, 1863, at Hoover's Gap, from same cause. It lost men and horses September 19 and 20, 1863, at Chickamauga, same cause; also men November 25, 1863, at Missionary Ridge. The battery lost nearly all of its horses in January by the breaking out of a fatal epidemic. No transportation lost.

Jeffress' battery has met with no losses.

Kolb's battery lost men and horses September, 1863, at Chickamauga in action. No transportation lost.

Darden's battery lost men and horses on April 6 and 7, October, and December 31, 1862, and September 19 and 20, 1863, at Shiloh, Perryville, Murfreesborough, and Chickamauga, in action. No t. .nsportation lost.

Emery's and Bellamy's batteries, recently organized, were, as Waddell's battalion, surrendered at Vicksburg.

Report of regiment Reserve Artillery, Lieut. Col. J. H. Hallonquist, &c.—Cont'd.

Batteries.	Re-equipments received.			Armament.						Strength.				Condition.
	Guns.	Horses.	Equipment.	12-pounder howitzers.	6-pounders.	Napoleons.	10-pounder Parrotts.	6-pounder Blakelys.	12-pounder Blakelys.	Total effective.	Aggregate present.	Aggregate present and absent.	Equipment.	
Lumsden's	4	....	Harness	...	....	4				96	117	121	Good	Good ; horses fair.
Barret's	4			4						85	103	108	..do .	Do.
Havis'	2		Harness	1	1	2	...			102	117	122	..do .	Do.
Anderson's	4	50					4			118	133	137	..do .	Good ; horses good.
Jeffress'							4			69	80	8?	..do .	Good ; horses bad.
Kolb's				2	2					100	115	118	..do .	Do.
Darden's	4	...	Harness			4				55	68	71	..do .	Do.
Emery's	4	76	Complete.					4		69	84	88	..do .	Good ; horses very good.
Bellamy's	4	61	..do					2	2	68	80	83	..do .	Do.

The batteries have received at various times partial equipments in horses and ordnance stores generally. There has been no entire equipment except what is noted.

III.—RESPECTING EVILS TO BE REMEDIED.

Vermin among the horses of Williams' and Robertson's battalions. Remedies used—wash with tobacco-juice and sassafras tea, sulphur internally in good weather. A few cases of scratches—wash with soap and blue-stone. Supplies furnished—except for two days' short rations of corn and long forage. The officers attend promptly and willingly to stable-calls, feeding, watering, and grooming. No improper use of horses, except that in Waddell's battalion—the cannoneers were allowed to ride on boxes. This has been stopped.

IV.—RESPECTING WANTS TO BE SUPPLIED.

Batteries.	Guns.			Remarks.
	Horses.	12-pounder howitzers.	Napoleons.	
Lumsden's	9			No harness required ; all in excellent order. Ammunition for smooth-bore guns and howitzers good. For 10-pounder Parrotts some little defective, but invoice of a supply to fully fill up the chests has been received, and the ammunition will be here on the 14th. Blakely ammunition defective. Shells imperfect in casting. The 12-pounder shell is too heavy, weighing 16 pounds.
Barret's				
Havis'	25		2	
Anderson's	23			
Jeffress'	31			
Kolb's	17	2		
Darden's	25			
Emery's				
Bellamy's				

It would be desirable that the commanders of regiments be allowed an adjutant, to be selected elsewhere than from the subalterns of his command. A regimental quartermaster should also be allowed.

Respectfully submitted.

J. H. HALLONQUIST.
Lieutenant-Colonel, Commanding Reserve Artillery.

HEADQUARTERS FORREST'S CAVALRY,
Jackson, Tenn., March 29, 1864.

Brig. Gen. J. R. CHALMERS, *Commanding Division:*

GENERAL: The major-general commanding directs me to say that he desires you to assume command of your division, and to move with the same to Brownsville, Tenn., via La Grange, keeping in communication with him by courier-line to Saulsbury. You will report to him the time that you will reach La Grange. You will bring only such wagons with you as may be necessary to transport your ammunition and cooking utensils. You will leave the Fifth Mississippi Regiment and Nineteenth Mississippi Battalion to scout the country in the direction of Memphis, and any movement of the enemy will be reported at the earliest moment.

Captain Rodgers will be allowed to proceed with the organization of his company, and when completed will report to Lieutenant-Colonel Crews. Six hundred prisoners are now in transitu for Corinth, and you will keep an eye that no move of the enemy is made to recapture them; and in case of any such movement, you will use every exertion to prevent its accomplishment, and communicate the fact to me at this place, and to officers in command of the guard from this point to Corinth, or from Corinth to Tupelo.

I am, general, very respectfully, your obedient servant,
W. N. MERCER OTEY,
Acting Assistant Adjutant-General.

———

COLUMBUS, MISS, *March 29, 1864.*

Maj. J. C. DENIS, *Provost-Marshal-General:*

Information obtained from Lieutenant-Colonel Patrick, of One hundred and fifty-fourth Tennessee, recently commandant of post at Grenada, Miss.:

Blockade-running to and from Memphis and the northwestern and north central counties of Mississippi is carried on extensively and openly, no one, officer or citizen, interfering with it. The route taken generally is through Graysport and Coffeeville, on Mississippi Central Railroad, between Grenada and Oxford, and across to Mississippi River, where cotton is shipped, or by way of Panola and Hernando to Memphis. Colonel Patrick was informed by one person that he saw 250 bales of cotton pass through Panola. Colonel Chalmers was heard to say at Panola that he had no particular orders about the matter. A doctor from Memphis, who was recently in Grenada, told Colonel Patrick that he never before saw so much cotton on the bluffs at Memphis.

Respectfully submitted.

JOS. HANLON,
Lieut. Col. and Chief Provost-Marshal Third Dist. of Miss.

———

OFFICE MISSISSIPPI CENTRAL RAILROAD COMPANY,
Grenada, March 29, 1864.

Lieut. Gen. LEONIDAS POLK, *C. S. Army, Demopolis:*

DEAR SIR: I find the engines and other equipments on this road are fast wearing out, and probably before many months transpire they will become almost, if not entirely, useless, unless I can obtain materials for repairs. The business of this road is now almost entirely confined to government transportation, and the income but little, if any, more than sufficient to pay expenses. The cost of subsistence is so great that I am frequently compelled to increase the wages of employés to enable them to pay their daily expenses for board. I find it almost impossible to hire blacks to keep our track in safe condition. It is quite probable I could obtain a limited supply of materials for repairs from within the Federal lines if permitted to send out cotton in payment for them. I have no other means of paying for them if obtained outside of the Confederate lines. Will you grant such permission? If granted it is quite probable I could obtain some army supplies also and make the effort if you will enter into a contract with me to that effect on the same terms and conditions that contracts have been granted to others. I received notice about a week since through Colonel Tate that you wished this road repaired into Canton and desired me to commence the work at once. I immediately commenced making such preparations as I could to facilitate repairs, and informed Colonel Tate that it would be impossible for me to hire labor, and if obtained it must be done through the military authorities. Since then I have no further instructions, and nothing has been yet done.

Yours, respectfully,

W. GOODMAN,
President.

CAMP TWENTY-FOURTH MISSISSIPPI REGIMENT,
Dalton, Ga., March 29, 1864.

Hon. JAMES A. SEDDON,
Secretary of War, C. S. Army:

SIR: I would most respectfully submit for your consideration the following statement of facts, and for the relief of the loyal citizens of Southeastern Mississippi earnestly solicit the attention of the War Department to the condition of affairs now existing in that section of the State. I have just returned to the army from a short leave of absence, which I spent in Greene County, Miss., and I therefore make my statements from a personal knowledge of their truth. Previous to starting to Mississippi I was aware of the presence of large numbers of deserters and conscripts in that section of the State, but until I arrived in the country I did not know that they were in organized bodies and committing depredations and deeds of violence, bloodshed, and outlawry, and that there was no force in the country to contend against them or to defend the loyal portion of the citizens from their savage caprices and brutal whims. But such I found to be the case, and the whole southern and southeastern section of Mississippi is in a most deplorable condition, and unless succor is sent speedily the country is utterly ruined, and every loyal citizen will be driven from it or meet a tragic and untimely fate at the hands of those who are aiding and abetting our enemies. Several of the most prominent citizens have already been driven from their homes, and some have been slaughtered in their own homes because they refused to obey the mandates of the outlaws and abandon the country. Numbers have been ordered away and are now living under threats and in fear of their lives. It is a matter of great personal danger and risk for an officer or soldier of the Confederate army to make his appearance in the country, and so perfect are these organizations and systems of dispatching that in a few hours large bodies of them can be collected at any given point prepared to attempt almost anything. On the 24th of February Capt. John J. Bradford, of Company B, Third Mississippi Regiment, who had previously been commanding conscript rendezvous at Augusta, Perry County, was captured by them and barely escaped with his life by accepting a parole, the conditions of which were that he would never again enter the county as a Confederate officer under orders or authority, or in any way aid or assist in molesting them. The house in which he was sleeping was surrounded at daylight, and he was called out, and after some discussion and persuasion on the part of the gentleman with whom he was staying, they agreed to take a vote of the crowd as to whether he should be hanged or be permitted to accept the parole, and by a majority of one vote he was granted the parole. There were in that company 21 men, well armed and equipped, and on the same day they took forcible possession of the depot containing the tax in kind and compelled one of the citizens to issue it out to families in the neighborhood.

Every officer or soldier who enters the county is compelled, if they can catch him, to submit to one of the following requirements : First, desert the army and join them ; second, take a parole not to molest them or give information in regard to their acts and localities of rendezvous, or to pilot Confederate cavalry into the country ; or, third, to leave the country immediately. Through the instrumentality and assistance of loyal friends, and my own influence with certain citizens whom I knew to be vedettes and spies for these outlaws, I remained in the country several days without being troubled, but was compelled to be very guarded in my actions and words. The citizens are afraid to speak of them in their own houses for fear of spies. Government depots filled with supplies have been either robbed or burned. Gin-houses, dwelling-houses, and barns, and the court-house of Greene County have been destroyed by fire. Bridges have been burned and ferry-boats sunk on almost every stream and at almost every ferry to obstruct the passage of troops ; their pickets and vedettes lie concealed in swamps and thickets on the roadside; spies watch the citizens and eavesdrop their houses at night, and a tory despotism of the most oppressive description governs the country ; citizens' horses, wagons, guns, &c., are pressed at the option of any outlaw who may desire them, and if the citizen makes any remonstrance he is treated to a caning, a rope, or is driven from the country. Deserters from every army and from every State are among them. They have colonels, majors, captains, and lieutenants ; boast themselves to be not less than a thousand strong in organized bodies, besides what others are outsiders and disloyal citizens (of whom I regret to say there are many). They have frequent and uninterrupted communication with the enemy on Ship Island and other points; have a sufficiency of arms and ammunition of the latest Northern and European manufacture in abundance, and I was told that they boast of fighting for the Union.

Gentlemen of undoubted veracity informed me that the Federal flag had been raised by them over the court-house in Jones County, and in the same county they are said to have fortified rendezvous, and that Yankees are frequently among them. Companies of 40 or 50 men go together to each other's fields, stack arms, place out a picket guard, and then cut and roll logs, repair fences, &c., and in this way they swear they intend to raise crops and defend themselves from cavalry this season. The country is entirely at their mercy.

Colonel Maury with a regiment of cavalry had been sent from Mobile into Jones County and had encountered and captured some of them, but cavalry, unaided by well-drilled infantry troops in large forces, will never be able to dislodge them and relieve the country. The loyal citizens are sorely oppressed and are looking to the Government for relief, and unless they get such relief soon the country will be utterly and irretrievably ruined. It is a serious matter, one that calls loudly for prompt and immediate attention on the part of the Government, and as a Confederate officer, as a citizen of that portion of Mississippi, whose friends and family are exposed to this growing evil, I have felt it my duty to lay the matter before the proper authorities and in behalf of the oppressed to solicit the consideration and succor of the Government. I give it as my honest opinion, based upon what I saw and learned, that not less than a brigade of well-drilled infantry troops, a force sufficient to sweep the country at once, will be able to exterminate them from the country. Cavalry can never do it, and as yet only cavalry has been sent, and only in small bodies. These they have heretofore driven out of the country, and have grown the more daring after each success.

Trusting that this may meet the serious consideration of those into whose hands is committed the destinies of our struggling young country, and with the assurance that I can substantiate by as much evidence as may be desired all and even more than has been stated in the foregoing,

I am, very respectfully, your obedient servant,

W. WIRT THOMSON,
Captain Company A, Twenty-fourth Mississippi Regiment.

[Indorsement No. 1.]

APRIL 5, 1864.

ADJUTANT-GENERAL:

Forward to General Polk, with request that prompt and decisive measures be taken to arrest and punish these marauding bands of deserters.

J. A. S.

[Indorsement No. 2.]

ADJUTANT AND INSPECTOR GENERAL'S OFFICE,
April 19, 1864.

Respectfully referred to Lieutenant-General Polk, whose attention is requested to indorsement of the Secretary of War.

By order of Adjutant and Inspector General:

H. L. CLAY,
Assistant Adjutant-General.

SPECIAL ORDERS, } HDQRS. DEPT. ALA., MISS., AND E. LA.,
No. 89.   } *Demopolis, Ala., March 29, 1864.*

*   *   *   *   *   *   *

V. Major-General French will proceed with his command by easy marches to Lauderdale Springs, Miss., and there halt and await further orders.

*   *   *   *   *

By command of Lieutenant-General Polk:

DOUGLAS WEST,
Assistant Adjutant-General.

DALTON, *March* 30, 1864.

General BRAGG:

GENERAL: I have just had the honor to receive your letter of the 24th instant.

On joining this army I determined to organize its artillery without delay. It was then divided into bodies of three companies each; each one assigned to a division, except two, constituting the reserve. I united the two latter under Lieutenant-Colonel Hallonquist, and formed the others into two bodies, one for each corps, under the senior officer, intending to recommend such promotion as the law allows. Lieutenant-General Hardee thought none of the officers who had belonged to his corps competent for higher grades. He has since recommended his senior major, M. Smith, for lieutenant-colonelcy, in which I have joined. I have also recommended for that grade W. C. Preston, the senior major of the army, an excellent officer. It was because of this opinion of one who had served with the officers in question long that I applied for the transfer of Colonel Carter and Lieutenant-Colonel Dearing. In the skirmishing which we had in the latter part of February I was not favorably impressed by the little I saw of our officers (artillery). They exhibited a childish eagerness to discharge their pieces. The only complaint that has reached me came from an officer from the Virginia army, who, after his arrival here, had been promoted to lieutenant-colonelcy over several seniors. Lieutenant-General Hood having brought with him a colonel of artillery, this officer thought himself ill-used.

We may expect active operations at any time. General Shoup has not been heard of, and we have no officer who has ever commanded more than twelve guns; I mean, of course, artillery officers. I beg, therefore, that should His Excellency the President promote the two officers recommended, you will do me the kindness to inform me by telegraph.

Most respectfully, your obedient servant,

J. E. JOHNSTON,
General.

DALTON, *March* 30, 1864.

General BRAGG:

GENERAL: Maj. W. E. Moore has shown me a letter from the office of the Commissary-General, of which the inclosed is a copy. I respectfully ask if the instructions it contains, especially in the last paragraph and indorsement, are authorized by the Department. You have repeatedly urged me to prepare to advance. Let me again remind you that the country over which my limited authority extends can furnish neither draft animals nor food. The officers of the quartermaster's and subsistence departments, upon whom we depend for food and forage and the means of transporting them, receive their orders from Richmond. We must, therefore, depend on the chiefs of those two departments for the means of crossing the Tennessee and marching to a productive country. We have now field transportation for about 100 rounds of ammunition for small-arms, and food and forage for five days. One hundred and thirty-five wagons have been prepared for the bridge equipage, and 1,000 mules (about 800 of them are for those wagons) are reported on the way from Mississippi. We also expect 300 of our own that have been restored to condition since December. I believe that large numbers might be purchased in Alabama and Mississippi, and respectfully suggest that orders to collect them immediately be given to the proper officers.

Most respectfully, your obedient servant,

J. E. JOHNSTON,
General.

[First indorsement.]

APRIL 5, 1864.

Respectfully referred to the honorable Secretary of War, through Adjutant and Inspector General's Office.

. The paragraph in the letter from Commissary-General of Subsistence Office is unfortunate; can do no good, and may do harm.

BRAXTON BRAGG,
General.

[Second indorsement.]

APRIL 10, 1864.

COMMISSARY-GENERAL:

For consideration, giving special attention to the sentence most complained of, and for remarks.

J. A. S.,
Secretary.

[Third indorsement.]

APRIL 13, 1864.

QUARTERMASTER-GENERAL:

For report as to that portion of General Johnston's letter that refers to his limited means of transportation.

J. A. S.,
Secretary.

[Fourth indorsement.]

QUARTERMASTER-GENERAL'S OFFICE,
April 15, 1864.

Respectfully referred to Inspector-General of Field Transportation for a report of the number of animals that have been called for by General Johnston's chief quartermaster, and the number furnished.

By order of Quartermaster-General:

. W. F. ALEXANDER,
Major and Assistant to the Quartermaster-General.

[Inclosure.]

SUBSISTENCE DEPARTMENT, C. S. A.,
Richmond, Va., March 4, 1864.

The Commissary-General of Subsistence directs me to give you the following extracts from a letter written by him to the Adjutant and Inspector General, for your information and guidance:

The duties of a chief commissary of an army in the field (not the chief purchasing commissary of a State) are:

First. To organize with the chief quartermaster the brigade and division trains, which are assigned to carry supplies, the former for immediate use, the latter for replenishing the first and hurrying forward supplies from points selected on conference with the Commissary-General of Subsistence for furnishing the train for hospital supplies needed for sick and wounded.

Second. He must see that strict adherence is observed by the army commissary to the necessities of his supplying or reducing the rations, when there is well-grounded probability of not getting sufficient to last until more can be obtained.

Third. He must see that provision returns are made out on principles of proper adjustment, so that troops going off or coming in may not cause more or less rations to be issued than are appropriate to the whole number of men to consume them.

Fourth. He must, in harmony with the purchasing commissaries of this Bureau, obtain from the commanding general such information as may enable these officers to prepare for any movement for getting or securing supplies.

Fifth. He must have funds to place in the hands of brigade commissaries when detached, and give them instructions to buy in conformity with the rates of purchases in the different districts, under circumstances when they can buy, and the State (commissary purchasing) agents are not operating so as not to dissatisfy the people by unequal rates. He must familiarize himself with the laws of impressment and be ready to impress under instructions of the general commanding. When the commanding general sends out foraging parties in an enemy's country the general will of course give special rules of action dependent on the policy of his Government, as instructed by the War Department. Such duties make this officer the representative of this Department with the army and the general commanding, and he is guided by the rules approved by the Secretary of War, and is by no means on the staff of the general, and if he discharges these duties, he ought to be acceptable to him, and loyalty to the general is no part of his qualifications.

Very respectfully, &c.,

T. G. WILLIAMS,
Lieutenant-Colonel and Commissary of Subsistence.

[First indorsement.]

OFFICE COMMISSARY-GENERAL OF SUBSISTENCE,
March 21, 1864.

The inclosed copy of extract of letter is respectfully furnished Maj. W. E. Moore, chief commissary of subsistence, Army of Tennessee, which will show him that the chief commissary of subsistence of an army and the other unattached commissaries serving with the army are component parts (together with the State purchasing commissaries) of the general system of the commissariat, and harmonious action is the natural result of these rules and principles.

By order of the Commissary-General of Subsistence:

T. G. WILLIAMS,
Lieutenant-Colonel and Commissary of Subsistence.

[Second indorsement.]

OFFICE COMMISSARY-GENERAL OF SUBSISTENCE,
April 13, 1864.

Respectfully returned to Secretary of War.

This paper, sent to Major Moore and other chief commissaries, was an extract from a letter to General Cooper. The last sentence, to which General Johnston refers, was perfectly appropriate to the circumstances under which it was written; is expressive of one of the general principles of the theory on which the disbursing bureaus are organized, and was appropriate to the consideration of the position of the chief of subsistence of an army, under the only system adequate to the collection of the scanty resources of the country, for distribution to all the armies. When General Johnston specifies any reason why that sentence should not have been used to the chief-commissary of his army, I will respond to what he may set forth, or admit the justice of his objection. As General Bragg does not know my reasons, he cannot judge of the appropriateness of my remark. This, however, is unimportant with what follows. General Johnston substantially seems to say that he would advance but cannot, because, first, the country over which his limited authority extends can furnish neither draft animals nor food, and the officers of the quartermaster and subsistence departments, upon whom he depends for food and forage and the means of transporting them, receive their orders from Richmond. He must therefore depend on the chiefs of those two departments for the means of crossing the Tennessee and marching to a productive country. It is because of the present system, which General Johnston has assailed, that his army has been subsisted. In the fall of 1862, when all of East Tennessee was open to him, he had to call on the supplies of this Bureau, because the previous system could not suffice. If the Secretary of War concurs in the above reading, he owes it to his Department and to the officers under him to require of General Johnston to state how long it is since he wanted to advance and was prevented as aforesaid; second, in what way the fact that the operations of the officers who collect in other States and turn over the supplies to his army can be benefited by other than the existing arrangements; third, in what way can his army be subsisted and kept ready to march if the previous arrangements were reinstituted as they were before the present system, and if that change would enable him to advance?

I think it important that each of these questions should be fully answered. I accept the issue. General Johnston's army has been subsisted precisely because of the present system. He never could have subsisted it otherwise. He has not been unable to move for want of subsistence since an advance was practicable, for the same subsistence which has so long sustained his army stationary could have sufficed to feed it moving. I furnish copy of Major Cummings' letter of February 13, 1864:

OFFICE CHIEF DISTRICT COMMISSARY,
Atlanta, Ga., February 13, 1864—8 p. m.

Col. L. B. NORTHROP,
Commissary-General of Subsistence, Richmond, Va.:

COLONEL : Since writing to you this morning by Major Steele it has occurred to me that I have neglected for some days past to advise you of the promising condition of the commissariat. Major Moore, chief of subsistence for the Army of Tennessee, advises me that no complaints now reach him in reference to quality and quantity of rations. With the prospects now before me, none shall. I can assure you that an immense weight of care has been lifted from my shoulders. If no interference takes pl e in changing my sources of supplies and taking from me the efficient men of my organization, I can safely promise ample provisions for the Army of Tennessee for some time to come. They now have ten days' reserve at Dalton. I am meeting regularly the daily demand, and I have advised General Johnston that I can furnish him thirty days' supplies, should he at any time desire to make a movement.

Very respectfully,

J. F. CUMMINGS,
Major and Commissary of Subsistence.

HEADQUARTERS FORREST'S CAVALRY DEPARTMENT,
Jackson, Tenn., March 30, 1864.

Brig. Gen. JAMES R. CHALMERS, *Commanding Division:*

GENERAL : The major-general commanding directs me to say that he has been advised by Colonel McCulloch that you have been returned to your command, and orders that you will report to him its condition, &c. (by courier), at this place, as early as practicable.

He directs also that you will move your division into the neighborhood of Somerville, or somewhere between Somerville and Whitesville, and keep him fully posted of all movements of the enemy from the direction of Memphis and Fort Pillow. He has ordered Colonel Neely to send all prisoners he may have captured to Corinth, to meet the prisoners forwarded from here this morning, and to send all captured negroes to this place.

CHAS. W. ANDERSON,
Aide-de-Camp to Major-General Forrest.

GADSDEN, *March* 30, 1864.

Brigadier-General PILLOW, *Montgomery, Ala.:*

GENERAL : I arrived here last evening via Selma, Montevallo, Talladega, Blue Mountain, and Jacksonville. I found the horses of my command literally on the point of starvation ; they only had three ears each last night. The country east, west, and north of this point to the Tennessee River is about exhausted in the way of forage, and the impressments heretofore have reduced the supplies of many families to less than is absolutely necessary for their maintenance for the present year. Many other families have for months been dependent upon charity and chance.

I am informed that there are a number of islands in the Tennessee River upon which there is corn, and I leave with a portion of my command for Guntersville in a few minutes, where I shall have to fight for supplies for men and horses, as the Yankees occupy Larkin's Ferry—infantry, cavalry, and artillery—total, about 1,500 ; Decatur, about seven regiments and the place fortified ; also the north bank of the Tennessee from Bridgeport to Decatur, and scout daily from one point to the other and have boats with which they can cross the river. They now threaten a raid from Larkin's Ferry to Decatur, on the south bank of the river, and although my effective force with me will not exceed 250 men, yet I hope I shall be able to damage them some if they come. I will have with me in ten days, near Decatur, 500 men, and will, before I return to Elyton or Montevallo, post myself fully as to the situation, strength, and purposes of the enemy. Any companies intended for my brigade had best report at Montevallo until my return, as this country will not be able to forage or subsist them. When the Tennessee falls we can subsist in Middle Tennessee. Our own cavalry has been a great terror to our own people in North Alabama. Stealing, robbing, and murdering is quite common. I have arrested some cavalry thieves, and will parole the robbers when I get them.

I have written in great haste as I am hurried, which you must excuse. Please show this to Governor Watts.

Your obedient servant,

JAS. H. CLANTON,
Brigadier-General.

[First indorsement.]

HEADQUARTERS CAVALRY, &c.,
Montgomery, April 4, 1864.

Respectfully referred to His Excellency the Governor of Alabama, for information, in obedience to the request of Brigadier-General Clanton.

GID. J. PILLOW,
Brigadier-General.

[Second indorsement.]

EXECUTIVE DEPARTMENT OF ALABAMA.

Respectfully returned to General Pillow, with thanks for the courtesy.

T. H. WATTS,
Governor of Alabama.

HDQRS. DEPT. SOUTH CAROLINA, GEORGIA, AND FLORIDA,
Charleston, S. C., March 30, 1864.

Brig. Gen. GID. J. PILLOW,
Commanding, &c., Montgomery, Ala. :

GENERAL : Your application of the 24th instant for several companies of cavalry from Florida has been referred to Maj. Gen. Patton Anderson, commanding that district, for his remarks, but I think his answer will be that he has not enough cavalry or other troops for his present wants, for he is now confronting the enemy at Jacksonville and Palatka. I am unable to send him re-enforcements from the other districts of the department, as I have lately received an order to send several regiments of cavalry to Virginia, which will very much weaken me in South Carolina and Georgia.

I thank you for your compliments relating to our success in this department. I am compelled in self-defense to defeat the enemy, otherwise I would be ruined at home.

Wishing you success in your new sphere of operations, I remain, respectfully, your obedient servant,

G. T. BEAUREGARD.

[MARCH 30, 1864.—For Taylor (T. H.) to Lee, about affairs in East Louisiana, see Vol. XXXIV, Part II, p. 1098.]

SPECIAL ORDERS, }   ADJT. AND INSP. GENERAL'S OFFICE,
No. 75.   }   *Richmond, Va., March 30, 1864.*

*   *   *   *   *   *   *

II. Maj. Gen. Howell Cobb, Provisional Army Confederate States, is assigned to the command of the reserve force in Georgia, under General Orders, No. 33, current series. His headquarters will be at Macon, Ga.

*   *   *   *

By command of the Secretary of War :

JNO. WITHERS,
Assistant Adjutant-General.

Abstract from return of the Army of Tennessee, General Joseph E. Johnston, C. S. Army, commanding, March 31, 1864: headquarters Dalton, Ga.

Command.	Present for duty.		Effective total present.	Aggregate present.	Aggregate present and absent.	Pieces of artillery.
	Officers.	Men.				
General staff	15	....	....	15	15	......
Hardee's corps:						
Staff	13			13	14	......
Cheatham's division	562	4,127	3,971	5,457	8,489	......
Cleburne's division	476	5,204	5,061	6,646	9,785	......
Walker's division	389	4,657	4,572	6,039	9,262	......
Bate's division	38!	3,532	3,402	4,476	6,971	......
Total	1,821	17,520	17,006	22,631	34,521	......
Hood's corps:						
Staff	20			20	22	......
Hindman's division	521	5,824	5,680	7,190	12,032	......
Stevenson's division	496	6,229	6,075	7,677	10,990	......
Stewart's division	440	5,343	5,213	6,728	11,566	......
Total	1,477	17,396	16,968	21,615	34,610	......
Battalion engineer troops	17	400	397	466	603	......
1st Louisiana Infantry (Regulars)	8	107	105	128	256	......
Total infantry	3,338	35,423	34,476	44,855	70,005	......
Cavalry:						
Wheeler's cavalry corps	459	4,507	4,415	6,161	10,639	......
Escort army headquarters	6	161	161	179	241	....
Escorts Hardee's corps	16	231	229	286	394	....
Escorts Hood's corps	3	86	86	169	228	.. ..
Total cavalry	484	4,985	4,891	6,795	11,502	......
Artillery:						
Hardee's corps	52	1,026	1,005	1,253	1,657	45
Hood's corps	48	854	824	1,039	1,287	36
Wheeler's corps	9	192	189	234	279	10
Reserve regiment	49	771	740	937	1,223	36
Total artillery	158	2,843	2,758	3,463	4,446	127
Grand total Army of Tennessee *a*	3,980	43,251	42,125	55,113	85,953	127

a Major-General Martin's division has recently returned from East Tennessee. No report has yet been received from the division. The effective total as mounted men of the cavalry with the army is 4,036, less the regiment of Moreland, left by Roddey in North Alabama, and Grigsby's brigade, recruiting near Oxford, Ala.

BRISTOL, TENN.,
March 31, 1864.

General R. E. LEE,
  Orange Court-House:

The Ninth Army Corps is said to have left Knoxville, and gone via Cumberland Gap east. It is so reduced in numbers that its movements are scarcely worth reporting. I think it short 3,000.

J. LONGSTREET,
Lieutenant-General.

Abstract from return of the Department of East Tennessee, Lieut. Gen. James Longstreet, C. S. Army, commanding, March 31, 1864; headquarters Bristol, Tenn.

Command.	Present for duty.		Effective total present.	Aggregate present.	Aggregate present and absent.	Pieces of artillery.
	Officers.	Men.				
General staff	17			17	20	
Field's division	849	3,875	3,875	5,387	10,503	
McLaws' division	392	4,542	4,542	6,023	11,044	
Buckner's division	307	3,401	3,401	4,474	8 218	
Wharton's brigade	51	842	738	955	1,365	
Jackson's brigade	46	250	316	396	688	
Total infantry	1,162	12,910	12,972	17,252	31,928	
Cavalry:						
Staff	8			8	10	
Jones' division	187	1,916	1,916	2,337	5,166	
Vaughn's division	277	2,348	2,348	2,947	4,881	
Total cavalry	472	4,264	4,264	5,292	10,057	
Artillery:						
Staff	4			4	4	
King's battalion	15	353	353	412	581	16
Leyden's battalion	19	357	357	437	598	13
Huger's battalion	18	441	441	520	874	26
Total artillery	56	1,151	1,151	1,373	2,057	55
Grand total	1,690	18,325	18,387	23,917	44,042	55

Organization of troops in the Department of East Tennessee, commanded by Lieut. Gen. James Longstreet, C. S. Army, March, 31, 1864.

M'LAWS' DIVISION. *

Brig. Gen. JOSEPH B. KERSHAW.

Kershaw's Brigade.

Col. JOHN D. KENNEDY.

2d South Carolina, Lieut. Col. Franklin Gaillard.
3d South Carolina, Col. James D. Nance.
7th South Carolina, Capt. Benjamin Roper.
8th South Carolina, Lieut. Col. E. T. Stackhouse.
15th South Carolina, Col. John B. Davis.
3d South Carolina Battalion, Capt. B. M. Whitener.

Humphreys' Brigade.

Col. D. N. MOODY.

13th Mississippi, Capt. Hugh Cameron.
17th Mississippi, Capt. Jesse C. Cochran.
18th Mississippi, Capt. W. H. Lewis.
21st Mississippi, Lieut. Col. John Sims.

Wofford's Brigade.

Col. C. C. SANDERS.

16th Georgia, Maj. J. H. Skelton.
18th Georgia, Maj. W. G. Calahan.
24th Georgia, Capt. F. C. Smith.
Cobb's (Georgia) Legion, Capt. C. H. Sanders.
Phillips (Georgia) Legion, Lieut. Col. Joseph Hamilton.
3d Battalion Georgia Sharpshooters, Lieut. Col. N. L. Hutchins.

Bryan's Brigade.

Brig. Gen. GOODE BRYAN.

10th Georgia, Lieut. Col. Willis C. Holt.
50th Georgia, Col. Peter McGlashan.
51st Georgia, Col. Edward Ball.
53d Georgia, Col. James P. Simms.

* Commanders given as indicated by inspection reports April 5-7.

FIELD'S DIVISION.

Maj. Gen. SIMON B. BUCKNER.

Jenkins' Brigade.

1st South Carolina, Col. James R. Hagood.
2d South Carolina Rifles, Col. Thomas Thomson.
5th South Carolina, Col. A. Coward.
6th South Carolina, Col. John Bratton.
Palmetto Sharpshooters, Col. Joseph Walker.

Anderson's Brigade.

7th Georgia. Col. W. W. White.
8th Georgia, Col. John R. Towers.
9th Georgia, Col. Benjamin Beck.
11th Georgia, Col. Francis H. Little.
59th Georgia, Col. Jack Brown.

Benning's Brigade.

2d Georgia, Col. Edgar M. Butt.
15th Georgia, Col. Dudley M. Du Bose.
17th Georgia, Col. Wesley C. Hodges.
20th Georgia, Col. James. D. Waddell.

Gregg's Brigade.

3d Arkansas, Col. Van H. Manning.
1st Texas, Col. A. T. Rainey.
4th Texas, Col. J. C. G. Key.
5th Texas, Col. R. M. Powell.

BUCKNER'S DIVISION. *

Brig. Gen. BUSHROD R. JOHNSON.

Johnson's Brigade.

17th and 23d Tennessee, Col. R. H. Keeble.
25th and 44th Tennessee, Col. John S. Fulton.
63d Tennessee, Col. Abraham Fulkerson.

Gracie's Brigade.

41st Alabama. Col. Martin L. Stansel.
43d Alabama, Col. Young M. Moody.
59th Alabama, Col. Bolling Hall, jr.
60th Alabama, Col. John W. A. Sanford.
23d Battalion Alabama Sharpshooters, Maj. Nicholas Stallworth.

Law's Brigade.

4th Alabama, Col. Pinckney D. Bowles.
15th Alabama, Col. William C. Oates.
44th Alabama, Col. William F. Perry.
47th Alabama, Col. Michael J. Bulger.
48th Alabama, Col. James L. Sheffield.

CAVALRY CORPS.

Maj. Gen. ROBERT RANSOM, Jr.

JONES' DIVISION.

Brig. Gen. WILLIAM E. JONES.

Jones' Brigade.

8th Virginia, Col. James M. Corns.
21st Virginia, Col. William E. Peters.
34th Virginia Battalion, Lieut. Col. Vinson A. Witcher.
36th Virginia Battalion, Maj. James W. Sweeney.
37th Virginia Battalion, Maj. James R. Claiborne.

Hodge's Brigade.

6th Confederate Battalion, Lieut. Col. A. L. McAfee.
7th Confederate Battalion, Lieut. Col. Clarence J. Prentice.
1st Kentucky Battalion, Lieut. Col. Ezekiel F. Clay.
2d Kentucky Battalion, Lieut. Col. Thomas Johnson.
27th Virginia Battalion, Lieut. Col. Henry A. Edmundson.

---

* Composition of Wharton's and Jackson's brigades not given.

VAUGHN'S DIVISION.

Brig. Gen. JOHN C. VAUGHN.

Giltner's Brigade.

16th Georgia Battalion, Col. S. J. Winn.
4th Kentucky, Lieut. Col. M. T. Pryor.
10th Kentucky, Col. Andrew J. May.
10th Kentucky Battalion, Maj. J. T. Chenoweth.
1st Tennessee, Col. James E. Carter.
64th Virginia, Col. Campbell Slemp.

Vaughn's Brigade.

3d Tennessee (Provisional Army, mounted), Col. N. J. Lillard.
12th Tennessee Battalion, Maj. George W. Day.
16th Tennessee Battalion, Lieut. Col. John R. Neal.
31st [39th] Tennessee (mounted), Col. William M. Bradford.
43d Tennessee (mounted), Col. James W. Gillespie.
59th Tennessee (mounted), Col. W. L. Eakin.
Detachment Vaughn's old brigade, 60th, 61st, and 62d Tennessee, Lieut. Col. William Parker.

ARTILLERY RESERVE.

Brig. Gen. E. PORTER ALEXANDER.

King's Battalion.

Otey (Virginia) Battery, Capt. David N. Walker.
Davidson's (Virginia) battery, Capt. George S. Davidson.
Dickenson's (Virginia) battery, Capt. Crispin Dickenson.
Lowry's (Virginia) battery, Capt. William M. Lowry.

Huger's Battalion.

Fickling's (South Carolina) battery, Capt. William W. Fickling.
Jordan's (Virginia) battery, Capt. John D. Smith.
Moody's (Louisiana) battery, Capt. George V. Moody.
Parker's (Virginia) battery, Capt. William W. Parker.
Taylor's (Virginia) battery, Capt. Osmond B. Taylor.
Woolfolk's (Virginia) battery, Capt. Pichegru Woolfolk, jr.

Leyden's Battalion.

Battery A, Capt. William Barnes.
Battery B, Capt. John Isom.
Battery C, Capt. Andrew M. Wolihin.
Battery D, Capt. Tyler M. Peeples.
Battery E, Capt. Billington W. York.

HEADQUARTERS,
Demopolis, March 31, 1864.

Hon. J. A. SEDDON,
          Secretary of War:

I am in receipt of your letter of the 16th, in reply to mine of the 3d, on the subject of the operations of the Bureau of Conscription in this department. The point made in my letter was not that the system I found in existence on taking command was better than that which you say was improperly superseded by it and to which you desire to return, but that if the system in existence was that of the War Department it could be better administered by the department commander than by an authority so remote as one at Richmond. The plan proposed by you, as it appeals to the sense of obligation of the citizen to respect the country's claim of service upon him or thus influences him to come forward and enroll himself as one which makes the application of military force unnecessary, and so makes the presence of a military organization a useless part of the machinery of the Conscription Bureau, and as it is that proposed by the legislation of Congress, is of course the method to be employed. I have no objection to urge to it, and shall be glad to see it tried. Confined to that mode of proceeding, the seat of its administration may as well be in Richmond as anywhere else, but let it not undertake the duty of supervising and managing the military police of my department; that is a duty which properly belongs to the department commander, and is as binding on him as the duty of policing the camps or garrisons of his command in any particular locality and for accomplishing which he should be held responsible. It is that feature of the work which was being attempted by the Conscription Bureau in my department to which I objected ; and as the law organizing or regulating that bureau does not contemplate its being charged with military duties, but leaves them where they naturally and properly belong, in the hands of the department commander, my objections to the working of the organization of the system are removed.

I shall now feel myself bound to organize such a police force as shall check all disorders throughout my command effectually, and arrest and return to their commands all stragglers and deserters, to whomsoever they may belong, and this is a measure indispensable to the peace and quiet of my department, the security of the property and the lives of the citizens, as well as the good order and discipline of my army in the field. To effect this I have already appointed a chief of military police for the whole department, and cut up its surface into subdivisions ; to each of these I have assigned subordinate chiefs, composed of supernumerary officers, preferring, as far as possible, those disabled for field duty. What I now desire is authority in conformity with the provisions of the laws of Congress to raise companies of exempts, to report to these chiefs of military police to enable them to enforce my orders, and that authority I now respectfully ask.

In your communication you say, "I am reluctant to oppose any objection to the authority you ask for the re-enlistment of deserters and stragglers into new organizations." I beg leave to say that in this you have entirely mistaken me, as an examination of my letter will show you ; on the contrary, no officer in the service has opposed a sterner opposition in his habitual practice to such a policy than I have, though I am constantly pressed upon that point. My conviction is that it is utterly subversive of discipline and would disintegrate and break up our armies. We can better dispense with the services of such men than endure the damaging effect of overlooking their desertions and compounding with them for the highest of military crimes. I have asked for authority to raise commands within the enemy's lines, or so near them that the conscript officer could not enforce his conscription, but with no view of taking in deserters ; on the contrary, I have issued an order that any man found in any cavalry or other command belonging to another organization shall be promptly given up, and if it can be shown that the party receiving him knew him to be a deserter he shall be proceeded against under the provisions of the Article of War prohibiting it. There is a district running around the western and northern boundary of my department, within which persons of the description I have named are to be found. My application, which I now respectfully repeat, had reference to that strip of country and to conscripts within it which could not otherwise be reached.

Hoping I may have the pleasure of receiving your answer by the messenger who is the bearer of this,

I remain, very respectfully, your obedient servant,

L. POLK,
Lieutenant-General.

P. S.—The course of events has been such in this department as to allow of the uprising of a feeling of discontent and lawlessness in certain parts of it, which has become threatening. Of the unsound and rebellious condition of the pine-land counties in Eastern Mississippi you have been advised. The same state of things is growing up throughout the river counties in Mississippi, especially in the northwest. I have to-day also had a paymaster, sent out by the War Department to pay certain claims against the Government in the counties of North Alabama, call at my quarters to inform me that he found things in that part of the State such as to make it impossible for him with safety to perform the work assigned him. Similar information comes to me from several other parties extending through this country. Now one of two things has to be done: either I must distribute the force I have combined in the army in the field, or so much of it as may be necessary to maintain order throughout the department, or I must be authorized to raise a force for that purpose out of material exempted by law from field service and organize that for such a duty. Your authority alone is necessary to enable me to accomplish the latter, as there is plenty of material at hand to enable me to do it, and I beg leave to add that the existing pressure demands immediate decision in this connection. I beg leave to call your attention to an indorsement made on a paper sent the War Department by the Alabama delegation concerning the defense of North Alabama, which I send to the Adjutant-General by the messenger who takes this. The change of boundary thus suggested, or something approaching it, is indispensable to successful operations and administration in that region. I trust we shall have the Department to act on it as early as possible.

L. P.

[First indorsement.]

The officer who left this letter will see the honorable Secretary Monday morning (April 11), which he says General Polk directed, to make fuller verbal communication in explanation of the subjects mentioned within.

R. G. H. KEAN,
Chief of Bureau of War.

[Second indorsement.]

APRIL 11, 1864.

To the CONSCRIPTION BUREAU :

Will you consider the inclosed letter and let me have your views upon General Polk's request at your earliest convenience, that I may have the advantage of them in answering the general's application?

J. A. SEDDON,
Secretary.

[Third indorsement.]

BUREAU OF CONSCRIPTION, *Richmond, April* 12, 1864.

Respectfully returned to the Secretary of War.

If the exigencies of his department are as represented by General Polk, it may be proper to grant him authority to raise companies of exempts to be employed in maintaining the external police of his army and the quiet of his department. In granting this, however, it does not seem to be consistent with the policy of the law or the provisions of General Orders, No. 26, to allow men between the ages of eighteen and forty-five, or of the reserve classes, who are enrolled and organized, to be embraced in troops called for the special exigencies of a department. The service of all such is prescribed by law and also the terms of organization, and the assignment to other service under different organization would certainly be in conflict with the law and concedes the authority to raise armies. There is certainly no existing warrant for General Polk to organize a police force either from conscripts or reserves, and instances are frequent of great confusion in and detriment to the service arising from generals commanding assuming to raise and organize troops for any purpose without full warrant of law. The recent condition of things in Alabama and Mississippi, and which in a great measure causes General Polk's difficulties, is a prominent instance of this evil, and this bureau is at this moment ordered to receive into the general service eight disbanded companies, raised, organized, and assigned by a general commanding a department. If the conscript authorities have not force enough -to manage the external police of General Polk's army, and it is deemed best not to increase that force, the readiest mode of meeting General Polk's views will be to assign to his police such organized companies of reserves as may be selected for that purpose by the Secretary of War under proper limitations. I respectfully recommend that it be done.

I deem it due to use this and all proper occasions to reiterate my conviction that neither conscription nor the enrollment, organization, and disposition of the reserves should under any circumstances be placed under the control of generals commanding in the field.

Respectfully submitted.

JNO. S. PRESTON,
Colonel and Superintendent.

HEADQUARTERS, *Demopolis, March* 31, 1864.

Colonels JACKSON AND IVES, *Near Tuscumbia:*

Orders were sent you by telegraph to Okolona, thence by courier, instructing you to fall back from your present position to one more remote from the enemy. That order is hereby revoked. You will use your discretion in the selection of a point to locate your commands which in your judgment will be most favorable to the furtherance of the objects you have in view, keeping a vigilant watch upon the enemy all the time. You will at once establish a line of couriers from your headquarters to some point on the Mobile and Ohio Railroad where telegraphic communication can be had with these headquarters.

By command of Lieutenant-General Polk:

T. M. JACK,
Assistant Adjutant-General.

JACKSON, *March* 31, 1864.

Brig. Gen. J. R. CHALMERS:

GENERAL : The general commanding has just left with his escort company, going in the direction of Purdy, having received information that there are about 6,000 Federals at Purdy ; he will skirmish with the enemy and endeavor to hold them in check. He directs that you will move in the direction of Pocahontas, leaving one regiment in the vicinity of Somerville, for the purpose of watching the movements of the enemy. The general directs that in the event of the enemy moving after the Federal prisoners that he will rely on you for assistance. He has ordered everything to move from this place this morning (a few dismounted men and some 240 guns) to join you, crossing the river at or below Estenaula. You will please communicate with me informing me where to join you on the other side of the river, and if you think it necessary you can send the unarmed men after the guns, as we are scarce of transportation. If possible you will communicate with the general commanding in the direction of Purdy or on the road from Montezuma to Pocahontas, as [it] is uncertain which road he will take. He has ordered General Buford to concentrate his command at Trenton as speedily as possible. Colonel Bell's wagon train has been ordered north of Hatchie.

Respectfully,

J. P. STRANGE,
Assistant Adjutant-General.

OFFICE CONTROLLING QUARTERMASTER
TAX IN KIND FOR MISSISSIPPI AND EAST LOUISIANA,
Columbus, Miss., March 31, 1864.

Col. T. M. JACK,
Assistant Adjutant-General, Demopolis, Ala. :

COLONEL : Through you I would respectfully represent to the lieutenant-general commanding that I am officially informed, through Capt. W. J. Bryant, post quartermaster engaged in collecting and transferring the tax in kind in the Seventh District, that "the state of affairs in a portion of his district is very annoying." That "the deserters have overrun and taken possession of the country, in many cases exiling the good and loyal citizens or shooting them in cold blood on their own door-sills." That his "agent in Jones County was ordered by them to leave the county, since which time he has not been heard from." That his "agent in Covington County has been notified by them (the deserters) to desist from collecting the tithe and to distribute what he has to their families, and the agent continues his duties at the risk of his life and property." That "the deserters from Jones and Perry Counties made a raid upon Augusta, in Perry County, capturing a part of the small force there and destroying the public stores which we had collected there," &c.

You will perceive that under these circumstances we cannot discharge our duty, and that the public interests, no less than the public honor, demand that a check be put to these lawless and pernicious acts. I respectfully appeal to the lieutenant-general to take such measures as in his judgment the exigency demands.

I would also state that great injustice is done to producers by the loose and careless manner in which the tithe is often collected by officers attached to the army. Unauthorized parties, both officers and privates, often exercise this power. I would respectfully ask your attention to the fifth article of General Orders, No. 117, Adjutant and Inspector General's Office, 3d September last, as to who are authorized. I would respectfully ask that the lieutenant-general commanding issue and promulgate his order to the effect that no officer attached to the army is authorized to exercise this privilege but those meeting the terms of the order above named, ánd that parties so collecting the tithe shall leave with the producer duplicate receipts for the same, and shall afterwards furnish to the post quartermaster of the district engaged in the business receipts for the same, with a list of the names of the producers from whom the tax had been collected. This is necessary that the parties may be properly debited and credited, as our instructions require. You cannot realize what disservice has been done to the cause by such irregularities, alienating the affections of the people and destroying the means of subsisting the army. I confidently leave the remedy in the hands of the lieutenant-general. Will you do me the favor to send me, if convenient, a half dozen copies of General Johnston's order, No. 248 ?

Very respectfully, your obedient servant,

JAMES HAMILTON,
Major and Controlling Quartermaster Tax in Kind
for Mississippi and East Louisiana.

[First indorsement.]

QUARTERMASTER-GENERAL'S OFFICE,
May 4, 1864.

Respectfully submitted to honorable Secretary of War.

A. R. LAWTON.
Quartermaster-General.

[Second indorsement.]

MAY 6, 1864.

ADJUTANT-GENERAL :

Refer to Lieutenant-General Polk for consideration and to afford all the protection that can be given.

By order :

J. A. CAMPBELL,
Assistant Secretary of War.

[Third indorsement.]

ADJUTANT AND INSPECTOR GENERAL'S OFFICE,
May 17, 1864.

Respectfully referred to Maj. Gen. S. D. Lee.
Please see indorsement of the Secretary of War.
By order of Adjutant and Inspector General :

H. L. CLAY,
Assistant Adjutant-General.

[Fourth indorsement.]

HEADQUARTERS,
Meridian, Miss., June 3, 1864.

Respectfully returned, with the information that the state of affairs in Jones, Covington, and the adjoining counties has been entirely changed. Deserters and absentees have, by the energetic measures of Lieutenant-General Polk, almost entirely disappeared, and more than 1,000 have been returned to their commands.

For Major-General Lee :

P. ELLIS, JR.,
Assistant Adjutant-General.

Abstract from return of the Department of Alabama, Mississippi, and East Louisiana, Lieut. Gen. Leonidas Polk, C. S. Army, commanding, March 31, 1864.

Command.	Present for duty.		Effective total present.	Aggregate present.	Aggregate present and absent.	Pieces of artillery.
	Officers.	Men.				
General headquarters :						
Staff and escort....	14	45	45	70	106	.....
Engineer troops....................	16	101	101	135	179	.....
Total............................	30	146	146	205	285	.....
Loring's division :						
Infantry	347	3,975	3,927	4,977	9,355	.....
Artillery	23	460	444	544	865	18
Total..........................	370	4,436	4,371	5,521	10,220	18
French's division :						
Infantry	239	2,170	2,147	2,845	4,921	.....
Artillery	11	168	159	189	272	8
Total.......................	250	2,338	2,306	3,034	5,193	8
Cavalry (Lee's)	652	7,685	7,611	9,981	16,640	.....
Posts :						
Cahaba	37	254	254	351	501	.....
Demopolis.........................	25	155	155	189	241	.....
Selma.............................	22	174	174	216	262	.....
Total............................	84	583	583	756	1,004	.....
Paroled and exchanged prisoners....	32	213	207	268	588	.....
Grand total *a*	1,418	15,401	15,224	19,765	33,930	26

a Forrest's cavalry and Withers' command (Alabama reserves) not accounted for.

NAVAL COMMANDANT'S OFFICE,
Mobile, Ala., April 1, 1864.

Lieut. Gen. L. POLK, C. S. A.,
Headquarters, Demopolis, Ala. :

GENERAL : I have the honor to forward to you, by Acting Master J. W. McCarrick, C. S. Navy, the inclosed copies of communications from the honorable Secretaries of War and Navy.

I will be much indebted to you if you will afford Mr. McCarrick the necessary facilities for executing his orders from me, which he is directed to show you.

I am, general, very respectfully, your obedient servant,
FRANK'N BUCHANAN,
Admiral, &c.

[Inclosure No. 1.]

C. S. NAVY DEPARTMENT,
OFFICE OF ORDERS AND DETAILS,
Richmond, Va. March 26, 1864.

Admiral F. BUCHANAN, C. S. N.,
Commanding, &c., Mobile, Ala. :

SIR : Inclosed are copies of letters, dated 22d instant, from General Cooper, Adjutant and Inspector General, to Lieut. Gen. L. Polk and Maj. Gen. D. H. Maury, directing the former to transfer to C. S. Navy 55 men and the latter 55 men from the respective armies under their commands.*

You will be pleased to send with all possible dispatch one lieutenant to each army, or other suitable officers, and one medical officer, together with such additional officers as you may deem necessary, to the headquarters of the commanding generals of the two armies for the men referred to above.

The officers sent by you charged with this service will accept and ship for the Navy all volunteers who are, in their judgment, fit for the service, and who shall pass the required medical examination, and have them conveyed promptly to Mobile, Ala.

Blank shipping articles are sent herewith, and all men shipped are to be duly returned to this office and the First Auditor, as directed thereon, and you will be pleased to make return of all men whom you actually receive under this order from the Army. Special inquiry should be made for firemen and coal-heavers, if those ratings be needed in your command. The necessary expenses of officers employed in this recruiting service will be allowed. Application should be made to the commanding general for necessary guards to accompany the drafts of men who may be transferred to the Navy, which it is hoped they will be able to furnish. These men will be assigned to duty in the squadron under your command.

By command of the Secretary of the Navy.

I have the honor to be, very respectfully, your obedient servant,
JNO. K. MITCHELL,
Commander in Charge.

DEMOPOLIS, *April* 1, 1864.

His Excellency Governor CLARK,
Macon, Miss. :

I desire to co-operate with you in opening the way for the transfer of the State troops under the action of your Legislature. If it is necessary I will leave for Macon to-morrow. The public interest would be consulted by my leaving on Monday next. Please answer.
L. POLK,
Lieutenant-General.

---

* See Cooper to Johnston. March 22, p. 666.

Reports of the batteries of light artillery of the Army of Tennessee.

Command.	Effective.	Present and absent.	3-inch rifles.	10-pounder Parrott rifles.	3¼-inch Blakely rifles.	2¼-inch Blakely rifles.	12-pounder Napoleons.	12-pounder howitzers.	6-pounder guns.	Total guns.	Horses serviceable.	Horses unserviceable.	Horses required.
Reserve Corps:													
Robertson's battalion:													
Lumsden's (Alabama) battery	94	155	....	....	....	....	4	....	....	4	62	2	14
Barret's (Missouri) battery	97	127	....	....	....	....	....	4	....	4	54	5	7
Havis' (Georgia) battery	102	145	....	....	....	....	2	2	....	4	52	....	24
Anderson's (Georgia) battery	117	161	....	4	....	....	....	....	....	4	51	7	25
Williams' battalion:													
Jeffress' (Virginia) battery	69	103	....	4	....	....	....	....	....	4	50	9	26
Kolb's (Alabama) battery	96	151	....	....	....	....	....	2	2	4	49	11	27
Darden's (Mississippi) battery	55	85	....	....	....	....	4	....	....	4	58	20	18
Waddell's battalion:													
Emery's (Alabama) battery	62	110	....	4	....	....	....	....	....	4	66	....	10
Bellamy's (Alabama) battery	65	112	....	....	2	2	....	....	....	4	70	....	....
Total	757	1,149	....	12	2	2	10	8	2	36	512	54	151
Hardee's corps:													
Hotchkiss' battalion:													
Swett's (Mississippi) battery	90	125	....	....	....	....	3	....	....	3	69	1	7
Semple's (Alabama) battery	82	136	....	....	....	....	4	....	....	4	70	1	6
Key's (Arkansas) battery	51	78	....	....	....	4	....	....	....	4	56	2	5
Martin's battalion:													
Bledsoe's (Missouri) battery	67	105	....	....	....	....	4	....	....	4	63	....	18
Ferguson's (South Carolina) battery	81	185	....	....	....	....	2	2	....	4	63	....	6
Howell's (Georgia) battery	77	125	....	....	....	....	....	4	....	4	50	....	11
Hoxton' battalion:													
McCants' (Florida) battery	72	90	....	....	....	....	....	4	....	4	45	2	10
Turner's (Mississippi) battery	80	127	....	....	....	....	....	4	....	4	65	6	11
Fowler's (Alabama) battery	95	151	....	....	....	....	4	....	....	4	66	9	10
Palmer's battalion:													
Corput's (Georgia) battery	79	146	....	....	....	....	4	....	....	4	51	5	25
Rowan's (Georgia) battery	108	160	....	....	....	....	4	....	....	4	75	4	1
Marshall's (Tennessee) battery	83	143	....	....	....	....	4	....	....	4	61	....	15
Total	965	1,560	....	....	....	....	33	14	....	47	734	30	126
Hood's corps:													
Courtney's battalion:													
Douglas' (Texas) battery	85	97	....	....	....	....	....	4	....	4	49	11	12
Garrity's (Alabama) battery	95	120	2	2	....	....	....	....	....	4	48	10	28
Dent's (Alabama) battery	111	132	....	....	....	....	2	2	....	4	61	7	8
Eldridge's battalion:													
Stanford's (Mississippi) battery	72	125	....	....	....	....	4	....	....	4	64	10	12
Eufaula (Alabama) Battery	102	155	4	....	....	....	....	....	....	4	53	8	23
Fenner's (Louisiana) battery	110	184	....	....	....	....	....	4	....	4	54	11	7
Cobb's battalion:													
Cobb's (Kentucky) battery	92	137	....	....	....	....	4	....	....	4	48	16	28
Slocomb's (Louisiana) battery	116	176	....	....	....	....	4	....	....	4	48	12	28
Mebane's (Tennessee) battery	66	98	....	....	....	....	4	....	....	4	39	11	22
Total	849	1,224	6	2	....	....	14	14	....	36	464	96	168
Grand total:													
Reserve artillery	757	1,149	....	12	2	2	10	8	2	36	512	54	151
Hardee's corps	965	1,580	....	....	....	....	33	14	....	47	744	30	126
Hood's corps	849	1,224	6	2	....	....	14	14	....	36	464	96	168
Total	2,571	3,953	6	14	2	2	57	36	2	119	1,720	180	445

Respectfully submitted.

W. C. PRESTON,
Inspector Artillery.

DALTON, *April 1*, 1864.

*Report of the batteries of light artillery of Wheeler's cavalry corps, Capt. W. L.
Scott, chief of artillery, April 1, 1864.*

Command.	Stations.	Effective.	Present and absent.	3-inch rifles.	12-pounder howitzers.	6-pounder guns.	Total guns.	Horses serviceable.	Horses unserviceable.
Batteries of Fourth Cavalry Division, Kelly's division.	Near Oxford, Ala.........	62	95	2	2	....	4	26	9
Ferrell's battery, Roddey's division.	Near Tunnel Hill	129	158	2	2	2	6	98	12
Freeman's battery, Dibrell's division.	En route from East Tennessee.	......	......	...	...	....	....	......	......
Wiggins' battery, Martin's division.	One section only near Oxford, Ala.	44	52	...	...	....	....	6	3
Total	....	235	305	4	4	2	10	:30	24

Respectfully submitted.

W. C. PRESTON,
Inspector Artillery.

DALTON, *April* 1, 1864.

[APRIL 1, 1864.—For Hardesty to Polk, about affairs in East
Louisiana, see Vol. XXXIV, Part —, p. —.]

DEMOPOLIS, *April* 2, 1864.

General J. E. JOHNSTON,
        Dalton:

My scouts report from Oxford, 25th, Sherman's horses preparing to
move ; can't learn where. Hurlbut and staff went up river Saturday.
Rumored Sixteenth and Seventeenth Army Corps ordered to Army
of Potomac ; four regiments infantry at Decatur fortifying ; Dodge's
division at Athens ; Logan's at Huntsville ; enemy's cavalry raiding
out from Decatur. Very much in want of Roddey's force in that
region. Secret-service man from Cincinnati says troops furloughed
in Western army ordered, after expiration of furlough, to report to
the Army of the Potomac ; expedition, composed of Banks' and Sherman's troops, which went up Red River not yet returned. General
Maury reports twenty-five vessels belonging to Navy and ten transports at Pensacola. Few troops at New Orleans, Baton Rouge, or
Port Hudson. Dispatch from Forrest reports capture of Union City
with 450 prisoners, 200 horses, and 500 small-arms ; captured Paducah, held it ten hours, discovered it infested with small-pox and
left, taking with him 50 prisoners, many stores and horses, burned
dry-dock, &c. Colonel Thompson, Third Kentucky, killed ; lost in
all about 25 killed and wounded ; enemy's loss, killed and wounded,
in Paducah, 55.

L. POLK,
Lieutenant-General.

DEMOPOLIS, *April 2*, 1864.

Major-General LEE,
    Canton.

You will resume the movement which was ordered on the 14th and suspended on the 15th of March.

                  L. POLK,
                Lieutenant-General.

HEADQUARTERS,
Demopolis, Ala., April 2, 1864.

Major-General LORING :

GENERAL : The lieutenant-general commanding desires you to move with your division to-morrow morning in the direction of Montevallo, on the Selma and Jacksonville road. The line of march will be indicated to you. You will report your arrival at Montevallo to these headquarters.

    Most respectfully, your obedient servant,
                  [T. M. JACK,]
              Assistant Adjutant-General.

JACKSON, TENN.,
April 2, 1864.

Lieutenant-General POLK :

SIR : Six hundred Federal prisoners will arrive at Ripley, Miss., to-day en route for Demopolis.

Colonel Neely engaged Hurst on the 29th of March near Bolivar, capturing his entire wagon train, routing and driving him to Memphis, killing 30 and capturing 35 prisoners, killing 2 captains and capturing 1. I am moving McCulloch's brigade to Gibson County. Must rest my horses ten or fifteen days ; many broken down.

If General Lee was here with his command we could gather 5,000 men in ten days.

                N. B. FORREST,
                Major-General.

CANTON, *April 2*, 1864.

Lieutenant-General POLK :

Your dispatch relative to resuming movement ordered on the 14th received, and will be attended to at once. Will send you cipher dispatch to-night.

                S. D. LEE,
                Major-General.

HEADQUARTERS CAVALRY, &c.,
Montgomery, April 2, 1864.

Lieut. Col. THOMAS M. JACK,
    Assistant Adjutant-General:

I inclose herewith an important letter from Senator Walker, of this State. Its information of the position, strength, and purposes of the enemy ought to be known to Lieutenant-General Polk. I am doing all that is possible to organize the small force placed at my disposal. The organization of Hatch's regiment is deferred for the present by the orders of the general sending it north. My own opinion is that unless some decisive steps are adopted by General Polk for the dislodgment of this force at Decatur sooner or later the great interests of Central Alabama, his own department, will be greatly endangered, if not destroyed. I am aware that Decatur is in General Johnston's department, and that General Polk ought not to be expected to do more than protect such interests as are confided to his care, but in this case these interests are necessarily involved in the proper defense of General Johnston's department.

It is certainly due to General Polk's own reputation with the Government and the country that an energetic protest should be made against being held responsible for consequences which may, and most probably will, ensue from this condition of things.

If I am provided with an adequate force I am willing to be responsible to the lieutenant-general, the Government, and country for the safety of this portion of his department; otherwise it must be obvious that I can do nothing. I have kept him fully advised of the condition of things in the north. It will be my pleasure to carry out his wishes.

Major-General Withers is still absent from the city.

With great respect,

GID. J. PILLOW,
Brigadier-General, C. S. Army.

[Inclosure.]

TUSCALOOSA, *March* 26, 1864.

General PILLOW:

DEAR SIR: I have been truly gratified to learn that you have been assigned to the command of the cavalry in North Alabama, and feel confident that you will, if furnished by the Government with anything like adequate means, render most valuable service in this new field of duty. I know that I need make no apology for communicating to you the latest intelligence received here as to the condition of things in that part of the State, even if the same information has already reached you through other sources. Judge Gibson (probate judge of Lawrence County) reached here yesterday from Moulton, and Col. J. T. Abernathy, of Lawrence County, and Mr. Donnell, member of the Legislature from Limestone, reached here to-day from the neighborhood of Leighton. These gentlemen all concur in stating that a considerable force of the enemy has crossed the river at Decatur, which point they are busily fortifying. Detachments of cavalry have been sent out from Decatur to ravage the valley, carry off negroes, steal horses, &c., and extensive depredations have been committed by them. The force of cavalry sent on these raids does not appear to be large; not more, according to my informants, than 600 or 700.

As to the numbers of the enemy at Decatur no very reliable information seems to have been obtained, but the best information which had reached my informants led them to believe that there were in all four regiments of infantry (two of which are composed of negroes) and one of cavalry. The pontoon bridge at Decatur has been completed, and the enemy has some artillery in that place. We have now in the valley (near Moulton) two battalions of cavalry

(Moreland's and Williams'), numbering, as I learn, about 500 effective men. Colonel Nixon, of Lawrenceburg, said to be a good officer, also has a new battalion, numbering about 150 or 200 men, somewhere in the valley, at what point I have not been able to learn. In addition to these, I learn that there are three companies of Johnson's regiment (Roddey's cavalry) still in the valley near Tuscumbia. It is safe to say, I presume, that the cavalry now in the valley, if concentrated, would number at least 700 effectives, perhaps more. Besides the cavalry there are now at Moulton two regiments of infantry, the Twenty-seventh and Thirty-fifth Alabama, sent up to recruit. They are small regiments (numbering about 250 each), but are first-rate troops. In addition to the forces above mentioned, Major Hatch's cavalry battalion (150 strong) left here yesterday under orders from General Polk on a scouting expedition to that part of the State. They expected to be gone several weeks. The gentlemen whom I have already mentioned are satisfied from all they could learn in North Alabama, and such is my own opinion, that it is the purpose of the enemy to hold Decatur permanently, fortify it thoroughly as they did Corinth and make it the point from which they will send out raiding columns to every part of Central and Northern Alabama where they can strike an effective blow. Now, it is easy to see that if they are permitted to carry out this plan the destruction at no distant day of the very extensive manufacturing establishment in this place, and of the far more valuable iron-works in Shelby and Bibb Counties, to say nothing of other injuries to the Government and the people, may be pretty confidently looked for. Of the importance to the Confederacy of the establishments alluded to I am sure you are fully advised. The destruction of the iron-works especially would be an irreparable loss to the Government, and would cripple most seriously our military operations. Can nothing be done, will nothing be attempted, to prevent the enemy from securing himself in his position at Decatur ? If all the troops now in the valley, with those on the way there, could be concentrated and turned over to you, and 1,000 effective cavalry, with one or two good batteries added to them, I believe you could succeed in driving the enemy from Decatur. At all events you could protect from further depredations the people of the valley who have already suffered so severely and who have the right to expect that some effort for their relief will be made, and you could save the important works in Central Alabama, the destruction of which is no doubt contemplated by the enemy. If you think there is any merit in my suggestions I feel sure that Governor Watts will most cheerfully aid you by all the means in his power to obtain command of the necessary forces.

Earnestly trusting that you will be able to take some speedy and efficient action in the premises, I am, with great respect, your obedient servant,

R. W. WALKER.

——

MONTGOMERY, *April* 2, 1864.

Lieutenant-General POLK :

The enemy's forces at Decatur are fortifying their position and with their cavalry raiding over the country, inflicting great injury upon the country.

Special couriers and urgent appeals are constantly arriving here from the regiments for a force to meet the enemy. It is certain that the forces will work [their] way south and destroy the valuable works in Central Alabama unless an adequate force is sent to that section. Can nothing be done? Enemy have six regiments at Decatur.

T. H. WATTS,
Governor of Alabama.

OKOLONA, *April 2,* 1864.

Col. T. M. JACK:

I left General Forrest at Jackson on 29th ultimo. Colonel Neely, with Richardson's brigade, was at Bolivar. Left General Buford, with one brigade, at Mayfield, Ky.; Colonel Bell, with brigade, between Trenton and Dresden; Colonel Wisdom, with regiment, at Hook's Bend, east of Purdy.

I do not know of other dispositions of his forces. The prisoners captured at Union City were at Jackson. Small force of enemy at Purdy as I passed.

FRANK C. WHITTHORNE,
Telegraph Operator, Forrest's Cavalry.

MOBILE, *April 2,* 1864.

Lieut. Col. T. M. JACK:

Forty-second,* 169 effective; 244 aggregate present and absent. Forty-sixth and Fifty-fifth* consolidated, 262 effective; 363 aggregate present and absent. Forty-ninth,* 183 effective; 268 aggregate present and absent. Fifty-third,* 222 effective; 339 aggregate present and absent. Artillery regiment at Shubuta has about 250 effective.

D. H. MAURY,
Major-General.

CIRCULAR.]   HDQRS. DEPT. OF ALA., MISS., AND E. LA.,
Demopolis, Ala., April 2, 1864.

I. Light batteries will hereafter be known by the names of the captains commanding them, and in no case be otherwise designated.

II. The use of private horses by non-commissioned officers of batteries is forbidden, and will be discontinued forthwith.

By command of Lieutenant-General Polk:

THOS. M. JACK,
Assistant Adjutant-General.

HEADQUARTERS,
Orange Court-House, April 2, 1864.

His Excellency JEFFERSON DAVIS,
President Confederate States:

Mr. PRESIDENT: I had a conversation with General Pendleton last evening, who gave me the result of his observations during his late visit to the Army of Tennessee. His report of the condition of that army, the buoyant spirit of the men, and above all the confidence reposed in their leader, gave me unalloyed pleasure. I regret the difficulties in the projected combination and movement of Gen-

---

* Tennessee regiments.

erals Johnston and Longstreet. Those arising from the scarcity of supplies I can realize. Those arising from the features of the country, the strength or position of the enemy, I cannot properly estimate. They should be examined and judged by the commanders who are to execute the movement. As far as I can judge, the contemplated expedition offers the fairest prospects of valuable results within the limits of the Confederacy, and its success would be attended with the greatest relief. I hope the obstacles to its execution, on being closely scanned, may not prove insurmountable, or may be removed by a modification of the plan. In the mean time provisions might be accumulated at some suitable point, and if drawn from the country south or west of that point they would always be convenient for the armies north of it. Other preparations might also be made, but if, after a full consideration of the subject by General Johnston, there should not be, in his opinion, reasonable grounds for expecting success I would not recommend its execution. He can better compare the difficulties existing to a forward movement with the disadvantages of remaining quiet, and decide between them.

I am, with great respect, your obedient servant,

R. E. LEE,
General.

HEADQUARTERS, *Bristol, April 2,* 1864.

General R. E. LEE, *Comdg. Army of Northern Virginia:*

MY DEAR GENERAL : Your favor of the 25th ultimo is just received. I very much regret the failure to get the horse equipments, but am not certain that they would have been so useful to me as I had expected. It was my intention to use them by mounting some of my infantry to drive out beef-cattle from Kentucky. We have been in such distress for want of forage for the last two weeks that our mules are hardly in condition for such a trip. I sent you by telegram yesterday that the Ninth Corps had left Knoxville via Cumberland Gap for the East. The Fourth, Seventh, Fourteenth, and Twenty-third Corps are now reported at Knoxville. The Fourth and Seventh I think are consolidated. I regret that I am in no condition now for any kind of operations. We are living on very short rations, particularly of forage.

If Grant goes to Virginia I hope that you may be able to destroy him. I do not think that he is any better than Pope. They won their successes in the same field. If you will outgeneral him you will surely destroy him. His chief strength is in his prestige.

I have recommended General Kershaw for General McLaws' division. If it meets your approval please send a recommendation for his promotion. He will be in Richmond in a few days to look after his interests. He is prompt, and gallant, and intelligent, and is the senior brigadier of the division and of the corps proper.

I fear that we shall not be able to set on foot any campaign in the West in time to make any interruption in the enemy's movements against Richmond, if he intends any; but I am of the opinion that a strong move here would break up his plans in the East if we could start it by the middle of April.

I remain, very respectfully and truly, your most obedient servant,

J. LONGSTREET,
Lieutenant-General.

HEADQUARTERS,
Bristol, April 2, 1864.

His Excellency President DAVIS :

SIR : I have the honor to acknowledge your favor of the 25th ultimo.

I shall be ready to undertake the move that you propose through Maryville as soon as we have accumulated enough provisions to start upon. With this view I have preserved the railroad bridges between this place and Greeneville.

I remain, sir, with great respect, your most obedient servant,

J. LONGSTREET,
Lieutenant-General, Commanding.

RICHMOND, VA., *April 2, 1864.*

Lieut. Gen. JAMES LONGSTREET,
Comdg. Department East Tennessee, Greeneville, Tenn. :

GENERAL : Your letter of the 20th ultimo, in regard to the appointment and assignment of Major-General Field, has been submitted to the President.

The advice you have asked as to "the distinguished services rendered by this officer and the high recommendations of his commanding generals which have induced the Government to make this unusual promotion and assignment" (I quote your own words) is considered highly insubordinate and demands rebuke. It is also a reflection upon a gallant and meritorious officer, who has been severely wounded in battle in the cause of the Confederate States, and is deemed unbecoming the high position and dignity of the officer who thus makes the reflection. The regulations of the Army, with which you should be familiar, prescribes that appointments of general officers are made by selection—selection by whom ? Of course by the Executive, by whom appointments are made under the Constitution.

The regulations referred to do not require the recommendation of general officers for the procurement of such appointments, and your inquiry is a direct reflection upon the Executive.

Very respectfully, your obedient servant,

S. COOPER,
Adjutant and Inspector General.

RICHMOND, VA., *April 2, 1864.*

General J. E. JOHNSTON,
Dalton, Ga. :

Special orders of this date direct General Roddey with his command to resume his former position and to report to Lieutenant-General Polk. General Clanton in same order is directed with his command to replace that of General Roddey and to report to you.*

S. COOPER,
Adjutant and Inspector General.

----

* On July 15, 1864, General Johnston, upon inquiry from War Department, reported that Clanton's brigade had never reached his army.

DALTON, GA., *April 2, 1864.*

General S. COOPER :

I beg that other troops than General Clanton's may replace General Roddey. Great discontent has been known to exist among them, which made it imprudent to mix with other Alabama troops. I recommend that they go to the Atlantic coast.

J. E. JOHNSTON,
General, Commanding.

DALTON, *April 2, 1864.*

General BRAGG :

GENERAL : I have just been informed by General Cooper by telegraph that orders just issued send Brigadier-General Roddey to his former position and Brigadier-General Clanton to replace him here. I have suggested, in reply by telegraph, that the latter be sent with his troops to the Atlantic coast. I recommend some locality where Alabama troops will not be encountered. You are aware of the discovery, early in the winter, of a secret society in that brigade.[*] It is unlikely that it was entirely suppressed, especially as it is well known to exist in the part of Alabama in which General Clanton has been stationed recently. Escaped prisoners report that the signs of this society are known in the "Army of the Cumberland." I think it dangerous to this army, therefore, to bring into it troops which I regard as so infected. Let me urge, therefore, most respectfully, that General Roddey's brigade be replaced by other troops.

I ordered Brigadier-General Roddey's brigade to the army because our cavalry with it was far too weak to resist that of the enemy. Of the eight brigades which you had more than five, as Major-General Wheeler informs me, were detached with Lieutenant-General Longstreet. The horses of the remaining force were in such condition from hard service in a barren country that it has been necessary to keep about one-third of it in the rear to recruit, the brigades alternating. This leaves us, exclusive of General Roddey's brigade, about 1,600 effective cavalry.

Major-General Martin's division amounts to but 1,500 men, according to his report, instead of 3,000, as you supposed, two-fifths being unarmed. From the verbal reports of General Wheeler and himself, it will be five or six weeks before his horses are fit for service. General Wheeler thinks that he has good information that the horses of the main Federal cavalry force were sent to Kentucky to winter.

In a letter to the President, dated about the end of February, Lieutenant-General Polk estimates his cavalry force for a movement into Middle Tennessee at 15,000. Brigadier-General Roddey's, including the regiment left at Tuscumbia, is 2,000. The enemy has not a strong force in Alabama, Mississippi, and West Tennessee. The transfer in question leaves me about 1,600 effective cavalry, with a powerful army in my front, a very long front to watch, and communications to guard which the enemy may reach by several lateral routes.

Most respectfully, your obedient servant,

J. E. JOHNSTON,
General.

* See Vol. XXVI, Part II, p. 548.

RICHMOND, *April 2*, 1864.

General J. E. JOHNSTON :

The act approved April 17 authorizes the employment of free negroes. General Orders, No. 32, in which it is published, directs the Bureau of Conscription to enroll and assign them to duty on fortifications, as teamsters, &c., in the field.

S. COOPER,
Adjutant and Inspector General.

ATLANTA, GA.,
April 2, 1864.

Brig. Gen. M. J. WRIGHT,
Commanding Post :

GENERAL : In compliance with your instructions of the 29th March, 1864, I have the honor to submit the following report of the local troops under my command. At the remuster of these troops in February last nearly one-third of them failed to be remustered, thereby rendering the organization much less effective than before. They are now composed exclusively of detailed soldiers and exempts, all those liable to conscription having been turned over to the enrolling officer under General Orders, No. 35, paragraph VIII, Adjutant and Inspector General's Office, Richmond, Va., current series, for assignments to commands in the field. The following statement shows the number and character of the local organizations, and exhibits the strength of each as per muster-rolls, and also the effective strength which can be relied upon at all times :

Command.	Effective strength.	Muster-roll.
Arsenal battalion, Maj. J. K. McCall	150	176
Capt. J. H. Hudson's company, artillery	99	105
Capt. T. C. Jackson's company, infantry	12	16
Capt. G. G. Hull's company, infantry	20	55
Capt. J. H. Porter's company, infantry	20	50
Capt. H. H. Witt's company, infantry	20	32
Capt. J. F. Alexander's company, cavalry	33	40
Capt. A. J. Baird's company, infantry	100	......
C. S. Naval Works company, infantry	80	......
Total	534	474

Captain Baird's and the C. S. Naval Works companies have never been mustered as the other local troops, but are organized and can be relied upon for the numbers represented, Captain Baird's company being composed of detailed men employed with Maj. G. W. Cunningham, quartermaster, and the C. S. Naval Works company of detailed men employed with Lieut. J. P. McCorkle, C. S. Navy. The Arsenal battalion and Captain Hudson's company of artillery are composed of detailed men and employés in the Atlanta arsenal. Captains Hull, Porter, and Witt's companies are composed of employés on Atlanta and West Point Railroad, Georgia Railroad, and in the Southern Express Company, respectively. Captains Jackson and Alexander's companies are composed exclusively of exempt citizens on account of disability, over and under age, &c. These troops are drilled once a week, and their movements are very creditable; their discipline is good. The officers are competent and efficient, and are zealous in the discharge of all duties.

I am, general, very respectfully, your obedient servant,

M. H. WRIGHT,
Colonel, Commanding.

HDQRS. DISTRICT OF WESTERN NORTH CAROLINA,
April 2, 1864.

General S. COOPER, *Adjutant and Inspector General:*

GENERAL: The recent change in the position of Lieutenant-General Longstreet's forces exposes the western frontier of my district for a distance of nearly 175 miles, and I have been ordered to Richmond by my department commander to report the condition of my district, and to seek to have augmented the forces for its protection. It is now practicable for the enemy to pass directly from East Tennessee to the neighboring sections of North and South Carolina, and an enterprising enemy could without much difficulty reach, by a cavalry raid, our railroad communications through the States referred to.

If, however, an adequate force is stationed here such raids would be rendered difficult, if not impossible. Many deserters and stragglers who, as soon as our armies begin to move, will seek to find shelter in these mountains could be promptly returned to their commands in the field, the enlistment by the enemy of tories and deserters prevented (an entire regiment was last year collected by the enemy within our borders, and recruiting officers had but a few days since again commenced their operations, but have been driven off), the gap leading to East Tennessee be guarded, and the movements of the enemy watched, and the country kept open for any movement on our part into East Tennessee or Northern Georgia.

Attention is respectfully directed to the fact that there are four railroad approaches from the east, to within 30 to 40 miles of the district.

My last field return exhibits an effective force of 475 Confederate troops (part Indians), 243 State troops, and a supporting force of home guards placed at my disposal by the Governor of North Carolina. These home guards are, however, undisciplined, and, besides, the season has arrived when citizens of this non-slaveholding region must be permitted to attend to their agricultural pursuits or serious evils will ensue.

I had until lately a section of artillery, under Lieutenant Collins, claimed by Col. Peter Mallet, commandant of conscripts for North Carolina, who has ordered it up to Raleigh, where it now is. I have other guns, but no men to work them. The enemy have recently been in the district with three pieces of artillery. It is evident that I have not an adequate force for the protection of the country under my command.

I am fully aware of the pressure for troops in other localities, and therefore respectfully make the following suggestions:

That as soon as possible a sufficient force, say 2,000, of those in North Carolina made liable to service within the State by the recent military law be assembled in camps of instruction, in this district, and placed under the control of the commanding officer of the district, and that a similar force of, say, 400 men be collected in South

Carolina stationed adjacent to the gaps leading from that State, in order that they may co-operate in case of emergency with the forces of this district. I beg to state that this plan has received the approval in writing of Lieutenant-General Longstreet, and also of Governor Bonham, of South Carolina.

If the foregoing suggestions cannot be carried out. I would suggest that at least a force of not less than 700 mounted men may be furnished in lieu thereof. With an adequate cavalry force to operate through the gap, the enemy could be prevented from running cars on the East Tennessee Railroad.

I likewise respectfully request that, if consistent with the public interest, Lieutenant Collins' section of artillery be ordered back to this district, with an additional detail of men to fill up his detachments and to work two other guns. This request is based upon the presumption that the section could be of more service in the field than in the conscript service.

In this connection I desire to state that there is in the district a battalion of conscripts between the ages of eighteen and forty-five, under Maj. J. C. McRae, belonging to the Bureau of Conscripts. Would it not be well to transfer this battalion from conscript to field service, in order that it might be available for general operations in this district?

In closing I desire, with great deference, but with equal earnestness, to state that, in my opinion, unless some additional protection is afforded this country it will before long be overrun with tories and deserters, organized and furnished with arms and ammunition by the Federal authorities, and in all probability, sooner or later, serious and most destructive raids will be made into North and South Carolina.

Very respectfully, your obedient servant,

JOHN B. PALMER,
Colonel, Commanding District of Western North Carolina.

GENERAL ORDERS, }   HDQRS. ARMY OF TENNESSEE,
No. 29.   }   *Dalton, Ga., April 3, 1864.*

I. Brig. Gen. F. A. Shoup, assigned by the President, will take command of the artillery of the army.

II. The organization by battalions will be retained.

III. The following battalions will be temporarily attached to the corps :

1. To Hardee's : Hoxton's, Hotchkiss', Martin's, and Cobb's, senior officer commanding.

2. To Hood's : Courtney's, Eldridge's, and Johnston's, Col. R. F. Beckham commanding.

3. To Wheeler's cavalry : Captains Huwald's, Ferrell's, and Wiggins' batteries, Maj. F. H. Robertson commanding.

The battalion of reserve will be commanded by Lieutenant-Colonel Hallonquist.

IV. The general of artillery is charged with the instruction, drill, and administration of the artillery, whether detached or with the reserve.

V. On the field the reserve will be under the immediate command of the general of artillery.

By command of General Johnston :

A. P. MASON,
Assistant Adjutant-General

GENERAL ORDERS, }   HDQRS. ARMY OF TENNESSEE,
   No. 30.   }   *Dalton, Ga., April 3, 1864.*

I. General Orders, Nos. 14 and 15, from these headquarters, and their modifications, which granted furloughs to the re-enlisted men in the proportion of 1 to 10, are suspended until the season of active operations is over.

II. General Orders, No. 227, from these headquarters. dated December 22, 1863, is continued in force and will apply both to the re-enlisted and non-re-enlisted troops. Applications will conform to the order and its different modifications.

By command of General Johnston :

KINLOCH FALCONER,
Assistant Adjutant-General.

CANTON, *April 3, 1864.*

Lieutenant-General POLK :

From many sources, without positive information, I am convinced that the enemy are concentrating a formidable expedition against Richmond under Grant. The veteran regiments on furlough from the Western army are going to Washington to re-enforce Grant. They think we will not attempt to hold Richmond. This I get from the observation of intelligent officers recently returned from Big Black on flag of truce, and from citizens coming out of their lines, and from the open talk of their officers, and am sure the attempt will be made as early as practicable.

S. D. LEE.

DEMOPOLIS, *April 3, 1864.*

General S. D. LEE,
      Canton :

Move immediately with Jackson's division into the Western District to aid Forrest. Order Ferguson to Macon, where Waties' battery will meet him. Leave Ross on the river. The Thirty-eighth Mississippi, Major McCay, mounted, now below Jackson, ordered to report to Ross for duty.

L. POLK,
Lieutenant-General.

EXECUTIVE OFFICE, C. S. A.,
Richmond, Va., April 4, 1864.

Lieut. Gen. L. POLK,
      Demopolis, Ala. :

GENERAL : The President desires me to thank you for your letter of February 22,* giving an account of the movements of the enemy in your department and the unsuccessful termination of his campaign.

A reply has been delayed longer than was anticipated in order to obtain the views of the Quartermaster and Commissary Generals

---

*See Part I, p. 333.

and the acting chief of the Engineer Bureau upon the points presented in your letter, which refer to the departments respectively of which they have charge.

The remarks of these officers are herewith transmitted in full, that you may have the most accurate information as to their views upon the subjects to which you refer, and may give to them the consideration they deserve.

Having the honor to express to you His Excellency's best wishes, I am, very respectfully, your obedient servant.

G. W. C. LEE,
Colonel and Aide-de-Camp.

[Probable inclosures.]

QUARTERMASTER-GENERAL'S OFFICE,
Richmond, March 9, 1864.

Respectfully returned, through the Commissary-General of Subsistence, to His Excellency the President.

The system of purchase and supply proposed by Lieutenant-General Polk is at variance with that which has always prevailed, and with the very existence of organized departments, if introduced generally. If every commander is to control the resources of his military department, what field of operation is left for the various bureaus supposed to be essential to efficiency of the service?

This plan involves, too, the necessity of each separate military department being self-sustaining, as there would be no controlling authority to direct the transfer of a surplus in one district of country to another, or in any way equalize the distribution of the scanty stores at our command. Vicious as this plan is regarded, still if General Polk will undertake to make his department self-sustaining further objections might be waived.

A. R. LAWTON,
Quartermaster-General.

OFFICE COMMISSARY-GENERAL OF SUBSISTENCE.
March 12, 1864.

Respectfully returned to His Excellency the President.

So far as the inclosed letter relates to this department, it shows that Lieutenant-General Polk does not comprehend the system of obtaining supplies now in operation. The evils complained of by him do not attach to this system, but experience shows them to be abundantly consequent upon the one he proposes to substitute.

This bureau knows of no order making it necessary for a requisition to be approved at Richmond before it is filled. On the contrary, officers acting under orders from this bureau are instructed to fill requisitions made upon them as far as possible.

The present system contemplates a hearty co-operation between the purchasing agents of the bureau and officers attached to armies in the field, and provides an ample sphere for the exercise of the functions of the latter without the slightest conflict. Under the plan proposed by General Polk, the agents and officers of an army in a country whose resources are expended must invade the territory of others; hence conflict of authority and competition of purchasers in the same interest without possible remedy, instead of the settled arrangement for co-operation provided by the present system.

It is believed that the practice of generals sending out agents to purchase for their commands in sections of country not occupied by their armies has had much to do with the present state of prices in the country.

Under the plan of General Polk, the army of one department might fare more plentifully, but those of many others starve. It is perhaps natural, and certainly usual, for a department commander to exhibit a desire to take charge of the subsistence of his army while in a country filled with supplies and but recently become the theater of war, and it is equally so for the same commander, when in a department desolated and destitute, to demand that the supplies collected by officers of the bureau in distant portions of the country be appropriated to his use. General Johnston while in Mississippi opposed the present system, but, transferred to Tennessee, declared that his army could not there be supported, and demanded help from abroad.

To make any military department self-sustaining is, in the opinion of this bureau, impossible, and it is respectfully submitted that it is in consequence of the present system, the most perfect for gleaning the whole country that can be devised, that the armies of Northern Virginia and of Tennessee are enabled to keep the field.

L. B. NORTHROP,
Commissary-General.

ENGINEER BUREAU, *March* 28, 1864.

Special authority was obtained more than a month since to construct the bridge over the Tombigbee River, near Demopolis, and Maj. Minor Meriwether placed in charge. Major M.'s reputation for skill and efficiency induces me to believe that everything will be done that can be to secure the prompt completion of the bridge.

Owing to the size of the river and the character of the freshets, however, the undertaking is one of such magnitude that in the present limited mechanical resources of the Confederacy it can scarcely be accomplished before midsummer.

A. L. RIVES,
Lieutenant-Colonel, &c.

CANTON, *April* 4, 1864.

Lieutenant-General POLK, *Demopolis:*

The expedition from Red River reported to have returned to Vicksburg on the 1st instant. Brigadier-General Parker [?], with command, left Vicksburg on 1st instant for up river to look after Forrest in Kentucky.

S. D. LEE,
Major-General.

OFFICE CHIEF PROVOST-MARSHAL, 2D DIST. ALA.,
Tuscaloosa, Ala., April 4, 1864.

Maj. J. C. DENIS, *Provost-Marshal-General:*

MAJOR: Inclosed please find letter from Capt. D. P. Walston, commanding rendezvous at Fayetteville, which will explain itself. The prisoner alluded to will reach this place to-night. I will keep him here until I see how his wound terminates.

Surgeon Westbrook informs me that he dressed the man's wounds a few nights ago, and that there is little or no chance of his recovery. Surgeon Westbrook and Lieut. W. C. Neill are both just from Fayetteville, and give a deplorable account from that quarter.

Five men were last week found dead tied up to trees, shot through the head. A Drury McMinn, Lieutenant Coudray (of what command I do not know), and two others, whose names were not furnished me, were found in one place, and the fifth one a few miles off, all the work of deserters and tories. I have here a prisoner, one L. Burnett, sent me as a hostage for McMinn. Inclosed you will please find copy of letter which accompanied Burnett. He has sworn out a writ of habeas corpus, and I have been ordered by circuit judge to have him at Fayette Court-House in two weeks from yesterday. Please instruct me at once in his case.

I renew my application for one or two companies of good cavalry.

I am, major, very respectfully,

T. H. BAKER,
Lieut. Col., Chief Provost-Marshal Second District.

[Indorsement.]

OFFICE PROVOST-MARSHAL-GENERAL,
Demopolis, April 9, 1864.

Respectfully forwarded to Lieut. Col. T. M. Jack, assistant adjutant-general, for his information.

J. C. DENIS,
Provost-Marshal-General.

[Inclosure No. 1.]

HDQRS. VOLUNTEER AND CONSCRIPT RENDEZVOUS,
Fayetteville, Ala., April 2, 1864.

Lieut. Col. T. H. BAKER,
Provost-Marshal-General, 2d Cong. Dist., &c., Tuscaloosa:

SIR: I send to you for safe custody James Mayfield, a citizen of Marion County, Ala., and a deserter from a company (Acres') of Patterson's Alabama regiment cavalry, who was wounded on Thursday night, the 24th ultimo, in an attack which he, together with a party of some 15 other bandits, made upon the house and family of one Mark Russell, a good and loyal citizen of this county, with the purpose of pillaging and robbing, and perhaps murdering him.

As a reason for moving him in his present weak and precarious condition, I need only state that it is known that an effort will be made by his confederates in crime to rescue him from the hands of the authorities and the penalties of the law if he remains here, and we have not sufficient force to prevent their success. Accompanying this I send you a list* of charges preferred against him, all of which can be sustained by ample proof.

I would most earnestly, sir, call your attention to the following report of the state and condition of things in Marion, Walker, and North Fayette Counties: These counties are almost, if not wholly, abandoned by any military force, and are filled up by deserters and disloyal men who are avoiding the service. They have, a large number of them, banded themselves together in a sort of banditti asso-

---

* Not found.

ciation for the double purpose of opposition to the·Government and resistance to the laws, and for harassing, robbing, and sometimes murdering the good and loyal citizens.

They make weekly, in fact almost daily, incursions from their headquarters, above Pikeville, Marion County, into the adjacent counties, and rob all good citizens in their course of their horses, arms, money, provisions, clothing, bed-clothing, and all else that can be of any use to them, and not unfrequently carry off as captives the males of the families. They never fail to do this if they find a man who has been prominent in the support of the Government and in aiding to send to the army deserters and others who are of our service. They are taken off ruthlessly from the bosom of their families, and are never heard of afterward, and there is little doubt that they are cruelly and brutally murdered. They are organized and their numbers daily increasing, and they growing more bold and extending their incursions farther and farther. They have within this week committed robberies and carried off one of the best citizens in this district, within 12 or 14 miles of this place.

The most of the good citizens of Marion County have either been robbed and driven from their homes or murdered, and the same scenes are beginning to be enacted in the northern portion of this county. They frequently hang a man by the neck till he is almost lifeless to make him tell where his money and valuables are. They are organized under the leadership of one John Stout, a desperate and bad though bold and not unskillful man.

The state of the county is indeed, sir, desperate, and must, unless some force can be sent to put down this organization, become totally ruined. I think, from the best informatian I can get, that they cannot muster at once more than 60 to 100 men, and perhaps regularly not more than 30 to 50. Lieutenant Neill, who will hand you this, can give you a fuller and more minute account of the state of things than it is possible for me to write.

I think, sir, and so does he, that if you can give him a detail of 50 good men, with plenty of ammunition, that with the volunteer citizens we can get we will be able to capture a large proportion of them and disperse the rest, and thus rid the county of such a dangerous enemy and sore pest; and I cannot omit to urge that whatever can be done be done immediately, or, at any rate, as early as possible.

In the above statement there is no particle of exaggeration; all the circumstances stated and much more of the same character can be amply proven.

Very respectfully, sir, your obedient servant,
D. P. WALSTON,
Captain, Commanding Rendezvous.

[Inclosure No. 2.]

FAYETTEVILLE, ALA.,
March 28, 1864.

COMMANDER POST,
Tuscaloosa, Ala. :

DEAR SIR : I beg leave to report that the tories on Wednesday night last made a raid into Marion County and captured and carried off with them Drury McMinn, a citizen of that county and a loyal man to the South. It is feared that they intend to deal foully with him, perhaps murder him, and therefore a respectable body of the citizens of the county have determined to seize and hold Lemuel Burnett, a citizen of Marion County, who is known to be a disloyal man and an aider and abettor of the tories, as a hostage for the safety and release of McMinn. The tories also took McMinn's horse, and we will take Burnett's [until] his is returned.

For safe-keeping we send Burnett and his horse to you, hoping that you may approve our action and thus aid us in our endeavor to rescue a good and loyal citizen from a vile captivity and perhaps horrible death. Sufficient evidence can be furnished of the disloyalty of said Burnett and of his complicity with the tories.

Very respectfully, &c.,

A. J. STEWART,
Captain Cavalry.

HEADQUARTERS ARMIES CONFEDERATE STATES,
Richmond. April 4, 1864.
General JOSEPH E. JOHNSTON,
Dalton, Ga. :

GENERAL : Your letter of 29th ultimo is received. I regret to learn from it the bad condition of the horses of that part of Major-General Martin's command which had reached you. That command had been reported by Lieutenant-General Longstreet as in fine condition, especially the horses. You say that Major-General Martin reports his effective force at 1,500 instead of 3,000 as supposed. Only half Martin's command was sent by Longstreet on the first order. Upon a renewal of the order the other half has moved ; the whole reported before marching to be 3,300 effective men.

The proposal of General Longstreet referred to, for a further division of our forces, has not and will not be entertained. Grant is very active in Virginia. visiting and inspecting all the commands. The Army of the Potomac has been entirely reorganized since his arrival, and an order has been published assembling at Annapolis the Ninth Army Corps (Burnside's) from Knoxville.

I remain, general, very respectfully,

BRAXTON BRAGG,
General.

HEADQUARTERS ARMY OF TENNESSEE,
Dalton, Ga., April 4, 1864.
Major-General WHEELER,
Commanding Cavalry :

GENERAL : General Johnston directs that you order Patterson's brigade, of Roddey's command, to proceed to North Alabama to operate against the enemy in that section.

I am, general. very respectfully, your obedient servant,

KINLOCH FALCONER,
Assistant Adjutant-General.

GENERAL ORDERS, }   HEADQUARTERS ARMY OF TENNESSEE,
    No. 31.   {   *Dalton, Ga., April* 4, 1864.

The President of the Confederate States having by proclamation called upon the people of the States to set apart Friday, the 8th day of April, as a day of humiliation, fasting, and prayer, it is ordered that all military duty be suspended on that day, that all may have an opportunity, as invited by the President, "to repair to their several places of public worship and beseech Almighty God to preside over our public counsels, and so inspire our armies and leaders with wisdom, courage, and perseverance, and so to manifest Himself in the greatness of His goodness and in the majesty of His power, that we may secure the blessings of an honorable peace and of free government, and that we as a people may ascribe all to the honor and glory of His name."

By command of General Johnston:

A. P. MASON,
Assistant Adjutant-General.

BRISTOL, *April* 5, 1864.

General S. COOPER,
Adjutant and Inspector General:

Our animals are dying for want of forage.

J. LONGSTREET,
Lieutenant-General, Commanding.

BRISTOL, *April* 5, 1864.

General S. COOPER:

The Ninth and Twenty-third Corps are reported to have gone to Kentucky. The Ninth is supposed to be en route for the East.

J. LONGSTREET,
Lieutenant-General, Commanding.

DUBLIN, VA., *April* 5, 1864.

Lieutenant-General LONGSTREET,
Bristol:

Am very sorry I can't forage your horses; this department is stripped. My artillery and cavalry horses are scattered to get forage, and at least 400 broken-down horses from your command are now in this department.

JNO. C. BRECKINRIDGE,
Major-General.

COLUMBUS, *April* 5, 1864.

Lieutenant-General POLK:

Yours with reference to Jackson's division received. The division is near Carthage, and is not moving in this direction. I send orders at once as directed. Will be in Demopolis by first train. My horses are here.

S. D. LEE,
Major-General.

HEADQUARTERS LEE'S CAVALRY DEPARTMENT,
Canton, Miss., April 5, 1864.
Lieut. Col. THOMAS M. JACK,
Assistant Adjutant-General:

COLONEL : I have the honor to report that in obedience to the orders of the lieutenant-general commanding Ferguson's brigade left yesterday for Macon, and that Jackson's division is now on the march for Grenada, to which place I will also go to-morrow by rail. I am inclined to think and sincerely hope that this move on my part will be a permanent one, and without knowing the exact object of it trust that matters may be so arranged that Ferguson's brigade may soon be united to the remainder of the force under my immediate command, and that I may be ordered to some other field of operations. With this view I have placed General Adams in command of this line, including General Taylor's district, with orders to report any important movement directly to you as well as to me. One brigade will be left here with him, and it is my settled conviction that this force will be amply sufficient for all purposes on this line, the principal and, in fact, very nearly the only duties being those of picketing and breaking up the illegal trade between citizens and the enemy. I hope that the lieutenant-general commanding agrees with me in this view of the case, and that dispositions may be made accordingly.

I have directed General Adams not to permit any cotton to pass out of our lines upon any contracts for the supply of our army until the equivalent in goods has been actually delivered, and request that you will give him special instructions to that effect.

He has orders also to break up the private trading with the enemy and to prevent by all means in his power any intercourse with them.

I am, general, very respectfully,

S. D. LEE,
Major-General.

MACON, *April 5, 1864.*
General LEE :

The following dispatch received from Colonel Jackson at Russellville, Ala. :

I have just learned that the enemy have landed five transports with 7,000 troops at Waterloo, also are moving up the river : they have also crossed a large cavalry force 6 miles above Savannah, which force is moving in the direction of Memphis—their cavalry force supposed to be 5,000.

L. POLK,
Lieutenant-General.

WHITESBURG, *April 5, 1864.*
Governor T. H. WATTS :

DEAR GOVERNOR : The enemy are shelling me at this place from across the river, but without effect thus far, as my pickets are protected by rifle-pits. I send you a Nashville paper, in which the "arch traitor" Jere. Clemens figures ; also that crazy man known as Humphreys. The people of Guntersville, this place, and all along this river of good sense and any respectability before the war are true.

Forage is very scarce. If I had my brigade all together here I could accomplish something handsome by crossing the river, but I

have only 500 men.   I will leave for Decatur in search of the Blue
Bellies this evening.   Would that I had a trumpet tongue to tell
every man and woman in Alabama the outrages of the Yankees on
the other side of the river.   They spare neither age, sex, nor condition.   Some time since they cursed and abused Governor Chapman's
little son, four years old, within the hearing of his aged mother, for
(child-like) wandering back to his native home, out of which the
family had just been turned to make way for a negro regiment.
They threatened to strip Mrs. Robert Patton, of Florence, in search
of money, and commenced to do so in the presence of her husband,
but she drew from her bosom a purse with $2,000 and gave them.
God assist us !
Your friend,

JAS. H. CLANTON.

MACON, April 5, 1864.

General LEE, Canton :

Forrest will be at Jackson as long as he is permitted to remain
there ; his object is to raise troops.

L. POLK,
Lieutenant-General.

HEADQUARTERS FORREST'S CAVALRY,
Jackson, April 5, 1864.

Brigadier-General CHALMERS, Commanding Division :

GENERAL : The general commanding directs me to say that it is
of the utmost importance that the bridge across Hatchie, at or near
Brownsville, should be built without delay, and you will use every
effort to complete it as soon as possible ; also the bridge across
Forked Deer, near Cherryville.   Capt. John G. Mann has been
ordered to superintend the work, and you will afford him every
facility to push the work forward with dispatch.

The general commanding directs that you will order Colonel
Neely with his command (if he is still on the south side of the river)
to go in the direction of Memphis as far as Raleigh, for the purpose of making a demonstration against the enemy, and to ascertain
their movements and force.

The general commanding directs that should you ascertain that the
enemy are moving in the direction of Mississippi as reported, that
you will immediately order Colonel McCulloch's brigade to follow
and fall in their rear, and keep between them and Memphis until
other forces can be ordered to their assistance.

Respectfully,

J. P. STRANGE,
Assistant Adjutant-General.

SPECIAL ORDERS, }   ADJT. AND INSP. GENERAL'S OFFICE,
   No. 81.   }   Richmond, April 6, 1864.

  *   *   *   *   *   *

XV. Brig. Gen. H. R. Jackson, Provisional Army, C. S., is hereby
assigned to duty with Maj. Gen. Howell Cobb, to whom he will report for orders.

  *   *   *   *

XXIV. Paragraph XXII, Special Orders, No. 136, Adjutant and Inspector General's Office, June 8, 1863, is hereby revoked, to take effect August 12, 1863. Mobile and its defenses, under the command of Maj. Gen. D. H. Maury, is hereby designated as the District of the Gulf, in the Department of Alabama, Mississippi, and East Louisiana.

*   *   *   *

By command of the Secretary of War :

JNO. WITHERS,
Assistant Adjutant-General.

NEW LEXINGTON, ALA.,
April 6, 1864.

Lieutenant-General POLK :

SIR : Two of my most reliable officers have just returned from Tennessee ; they left Eastport, Miss., Sunday morning, the 3d instant. They report that about 4,000 (at least calculation) of the enemy's cavalry crossed the Tennessee River from Middle Tennessee to West Tennessee on last Thursday, the 31st ultimo, at Crump's Landing, 4 miles above Savannah, Tenn. They went in the direction of Purdy ; it is believed their aim is to cut off General Forrest.

On Sunday morning, the 3d instant, five transports and two gunboats loaded with troops (Sherman's) came up Tennessee River to Eastport and landed on the north bank of Tennessee River opposite Eastport ; this force is estimated at from 4,000 to 5,000 infantry. It is believed they will march up the Huntsville road on the north side of Tennessee River, in the direction of Chattanooga, and it is feared they will cross at Decatur.

General Dodge's headquarters are still at Athens. He has about 2,500 troops in Decatur ; they are fortifying and have nine pieces of artillery. It is reported that General Dodge has ordered nearly all the citizens out of Decatur, and those who remain are drawing rations. They are raiding out but little.

The Twenty-seventh and Thirty-fifth Alabama are near Mount Hope. All of our cavalry are between Mount Hope and Decatur.

I leave for Mount Hope in the morning and will write you again as soon as I arrive there.

The tories are still very troublesome in the mountains. I will pay due respects to them as soon as I can collect force sufficient.

Very respectfully, your most obedient servant,

JNO. W. ESTES,
Lieut. Col. and Chief Provost-Marshal, First District.

DALTON, *April 6, 1864.*

Lieutenant-General POLK :

General Roddey is informed by Major Stewart, in whom he has confidence, who obtained his information from Mr. Sloss, president Central Railroad, that Grierson and Smith are concentrating their force at Decatur to move on Selma by Blue Mountain and Jones' Valley.

J. E. JOHNSTON.

RICHMOND, *April* 6, 1864.

General J. E. JOHNSTON :

Slaves not under my control. Have ordered the commandant of Georgia to forward you free negroes as rapidly as possible.

JNO. S. PRESTON.

HEADQUARTERS DEPARTMENT OF EAST TENNESSEE,
Bristol, April 6, 1864.

General S. COOPER,
Adjt. and Insp. Gen., C. S. Army, Richmond, Va.:

GENERAL : I have the honor to acknowledge the receipt of your letter of the 2d instant. I must beg a second reading for my letter of the 20th ultimo, as its purpose has been misconstrued.

I remain, general, very respectfully, your obedient servant,

J. LONGSTREET,
Lieutenant-General, Commanding.

OFFICE CHIEF INSP. OF FIELD TRANS., 2D DISTRICT,
Augusta, Ga., April 6, 1864.

Lieut. Col. A. H. COLE,
Insp. Gen. Field Transportation, Dalton, Ga.:

COLONEL : I have only time to write a few lines to-night to prevent General Johnston from expecting what I have no idea he will get. I really do not believe that in sixty days 1,000 mules can be obtained from all sources in this district. I have various things to write you about, but will leave them until the next mail.

Very respectfully, your obedient servant,

NORMAN W. SMITH,
Major and Chief Inspector.

DALTON, *April* 7, 1864.

Lieutenant-General POLK :

Colonel Patterson has moved with about 900 effective cavalry of Roddey's brigade to the district it formerly occupied.

J. E. JOHNSTON.

DALTON, *April* 7, 1864.

Lieutenant-General POLK :

Brigadier-General Roddey has just received the following dispatch from Major Stewart at Somerville :

I have reliable information that 5,000 troops landed at Eastport last Saturday and one brigade at Chickasaw, on the Tennessee side. General Sherman is at Decatur. Wagons arriving at Decatur in large numbers.

J. E. JOHNSTON.

SPECIAL ORDERS, ⎰ HDQRS. 1ST DIV., FORREST'S CAV. DEPT.,
No. —. ⎱ *Brownsville, Tenn., April 7, 1864.*

Col. W. L. Duckworth will assume command of all the troops near Brownsville, and will take vigorous measures to assemble his regiment as speedily as possible at that point, except the companies of Captains Russell, Alexander, and Lawler. They will be assembled by Lieutenant-Colonel Taylor near Mason's Depot. Ten days' rations will be collected, and two days' cooked rations will be kept constantly on hand. Scouts will be kept out in the direction of Fort Pillow, and a picket at the railroad bridge, who will prevent all crossing without proper authority, and will keep the water well pumped out of the boat in the pontoon bridge. In case the enemy should move on us or into Mississippi, five days' rations will be prepared at once, and everything be ready to move at a moment's notice.

By order of Brigadier-General Chalmers:
L. T. LINDSAY,
Acting Assistant Adjutant-General.

———

DALTON, *April 7, 1864.*

General BRAGG,
Richmond:

Scouts report 15,000 troops expected soon at Chattanooga. Hooker still in Lookout Valley. Buell is to take command in Knoxville. A large cavalry raid toward Selma preparing at Decatur.
J. E. JOHNSTON.

———

MACON, MISS., *April 7, 1864.*

Lieut. Col. T. M. JACK, *Demopolis:*

I leave for Columbus this morning; will be there few days.
L. POLK,
Lieutenant-General.

———

HEADQUARTERS FORREST'S CAVALRY DEPARTMENT,
Jackson, Tenn., April 7, 1864.

Brig. Gen. JAMES R. CHALMERS,
Commanding Division:

GENERAL: The major-general commanding directs that you will order Colonel Neely to move on Sunday morning next with his entire brigade with five days' cooked rations. He will proceed to Raleigh and make a demonstration of attempting to construct boats and bridges on which to cross Wolf River. He will also send a portion of his command, or a heavy scout, on the Big Creek and on the Macon roads, as if designing to cross a force there also. After maneuvering there for two or three days you will instruct him to fall back in the direction of Brownsville. He also directs that you order Colonel McCulloch to have five days' cooked rations and be ready to move on Monday next (11th instant), at 7 o'clock a. m. Further orders will be sent you as to his destination, &c.

By command of Major-General Forrest:
CHAS. W. ANDERSON,
Aide-de-Camp.

[First indorsement.]

HEADQUARTERS,
Jackson, Tenn., April 7, 1864.

Brigadier-General CHALMERS,
Commanding Division:

Order Colonel Neely when he falls back to bring with him every man between the ages of eighteen and forty-five ; also to take all the horses and mules suitable for artillery and cavalry, leaving the people stock sufficient to raise their crops, giving receipts for same. He will also arrest all officers and men absent without leave (except those furloughed). You will order your command to have 60 rounds of ammunition to the man, 40 rounds in cartridge-boxes, and 20 to be carried outside.

By order of Major-General Forrest :

CHAS. W. ANDERSON,
Aide-de-Camp.

[Second indorsement.]

Receipts for stock impressed to be made in duplicate, one to be given to the parties, and the duplicate to be forwarded to chief quartermaster of the department.

CHAS. W. ANDERSON,
Aide-de-Camp.

MISSISSIPPI CITY, *April 7,* 1864.

Maj. J. C. DENIS,
Provost-Marshal-General, Demopolis, Ala.:

MAJOR: In accordance with your orders I have to report that a band of deserters still continue prowling about the country, doing considerable damage to the farmers and molesting travelers. Though dispersed from Perry and Jones Counties, they appear in other parts. Large numbers of these from Jones County have gone down Pearl River to and near Honey Island, where they exist in some force and hold the country in awe, openly boasting of their being in communication with the Yankees.

In fact, it is dangerous to travel in that part of Louisiana. In Marion County, Miss., and the upper part of Washington Parish, La., they are banded together in large numbers, bid defiance to the authorities, and claim to have a government of their own in opposition to the Confederate Government.

Your obedient servant,

DANL. P. LOGAN.

SPECIAL ORDERS, }   ADJT. AND INSP. GENERAL'S OFFICE,
No. 82.   }   *Richmond, April 7,* 1864.
*   *   *   *   *   *   *

XX. Brig. Gen. W. N. Pendleton, Provisional Army, C. S., will proceed without delay to the headquarters of General Joseph E. Johnston, commanding Army of Tennessee, on inspection duty.

By command of Secretary of War :

JNO. WITHERS,
Assistant Adjutant-General.

SPECIAL ORDERS, }   HDQRS. DEPARTMENT OF TENNESSEE,
      No. 50.   }   *Dalton, Ga., April 7, 1864.*

I. Maj. Gen. Howell Cobb, Provisional Army, C. S., is relieved from duty in this department, and will proceed to the command assigned him by the Secretary of War.

*   *   *   *

By command of General Johnston :
            KINLOCH FALCONER,
            Assistant Adjutant-General.

RICHMOND, VA., *April 7, 1864.*

General J. LONGSTREET, *Bristol, Tenn. :*

GENERAL : The President directs that you move with that part of your corps proper now in the Department of East Tennessee (that is, McLaws' and Field's divisions, and one battalion of artillery, that lately commanded by Colonel Alexander) to Charlottesville, Va. Arrived there, you will report to General R. E. Lee. The infantry should first move by rail. If the means of transportation will permit, the artillery, its carriages, harness, &c., will go in the same manner ; otherwise, it will march. Should the artillery go by rail, the artillery horses will be sent the dirt road. Only such field transportation will be taken as is allowed for a campaign in the Army of Northern Virginia. Please see General Lee's special orders, indorsed. The excess in the Department of East Tennessee above that amount will be promptly put in motion for the gap in the Piedmont Railroad, between Danville, Va., and Greensborough, N. C., to assist in pr d ng necessary subsistence supplies for both your own corps and the troops who remain with General Buckner in the Department of East Tennessee.

Very respectfully, general, your obedient servant,
            S. COOPER,
            Adjutant and Inspector General.

DUBLIN, *April 7, 1864.*

Lieutenant-General LONGSTREET,
            Bristol, Tenn.:

There is no grass, but it is impossible to resist you. Send the horses. Can't you send back one of my brigades now with you ?
            JNO. C. BRECKINRIDGE,
            Major-General.

HEADQUARTERS DEPARTMENT OF EAST TENNESSEE,
            Bristol, April 7, 1864.

Brig. Gen. JOHN S. WILLIAMS
      (*Care Major-General Breckinridge*), *Dublin, Va. :*

The following dispatch is just received :

Brig. Gen. John S. Williams, Provisional Army, C. S., is relieved from duty with Department of East Tennessee, and will proceed to Georgia and report to General J. E. Johnston, commanding, &c., for assignment to the brigade of Kentucky cavalry commanded by Col. J. W. Grigsby, of the Sixth Kentucky Cavalry.
            S. COOPER,
            Adjutant and Inspector General.

            S. B. BUCKNER,
            Major-General.

HEADQUARTERS HARDEE'S CORPS,
Dalton, Ga., April 8, 1864.

Brigadier-General MACKALL,
Chief of Staff:

GENERAL : In the communication you sent me this morning from Major Locke to Colonel Northrop, the latter states on my authority that there were but 40.000 men of the Army of Tennessee present the other day with their standards. Major Locke is mistaken ; I gave him no such information. It is more than probable I told him that our effective strength did not exceed 40,000 men, but I did not state, nor did I intend to convey the impression, directly or indirectly, that there are only 40,000 men and officers present with this army, or that rations had been improperly drawn. There is a great difference, as every one acquainted with returns knows, between the effective total and the aggregate present in an army.

I will take occasion to add that Major Locke is a gentleman of high character, and a friend of mine, and I know he did not intentionally misrepresent me or the facts.

Very respectfully, your obedient servant,

W. J. HARDEE,
Lieutenant-General.

COLUMBUS, *April 8, 1864.*

Major-General FORREST,
Commanding, Jackson, Tenn., or elsewhere:

GENERAL : I am informed by General Johnston that Grierson and Smith are concentrating their forces at Decatur for a raid down through North Alabama via Elyton, Jones' Valley. This involves the necessity of my diverting General Lee's forces from any further co-operating with you, and seeing that by the time this communication reaches you you will have had the ten days you desired to get out troops, you will leave such force below Memphis as may be necessary to check the enemy in that direction, and any small detachment you may safely leave in the Western District to complete your recruiting ; you will then move with the rest of your force out of the Western District so as to unite with Lee in opposing the contemplated raid. Having indicated the point from whence that raid will start, and the line on which it is to move, I leave to your knowledge of the country the line of march best for you to pursue, remarking that it will be desirable for you to throw yourself as well up toward Decatur as you can, having reference to the supply of forage. If you have unorganized troops that you cannot take with you, send them to Columbus, Miss., where they may be organized and armed. I will give orders to your batteries and men who are here to be in readiness to join you at a moment's notice. You have been advised of a reported move of the enemy up Tennessee River to Waterloo in boats, with the design of making a forward movement from that point. They are reported to consist of 5,000 cavalry and 7,000 infantry. You will verify this movement, and keep your eye upon it. Loring's division is at Montevallo, on the railroad north of Selma, and General Johnston informs me that he has ordered Colonel Patterson with 900 of Roddey's command to move forward upon the left flank of the enemy's line of march, so as to be ready to strike it.

French's division is at Lauderdale, on Mobile and Ohio Railroad. Order any Alabama troops you may have to report to the post commandant of Tuscaloosa, and advise me which they are.

I am, general, with great respect, your obedient servant,

L. POLK,
Lieutenant-General.

COLUMBUS, MISS., *April* 8, 1864.

Maj. Gen. S. D. LEE, *In the Field:*

GENERAL : I am advised by General Johnston that Grierson and Smith are concentrating their troops for a raid down through North Alabama via Jones' Valley. This valley runs northeast and southwest and debouches at Tuscaloosa. Elyton is in that valley ; Loring's division is posted at Montevallo, on the railroad above Selma. I have ordered Ferguson to move rapidly to Tuscaloosa, with instructions to scout up the valley. I am informed by General Johnston this morning that he has ordered 900 men of Roddey's cavalry, under Colonel Patterson, to move forward and put himself in observation on the left of the enemy's contemplated movement. Supposing you to be on the Memphis and Charleston Railroad, I think your route will be via Ripley, crossing the river on a bridge at Smithville, thence via Fayette. You have already been informed of a reported movement up the Tennessee River in boats to Waterloo. Their force is reported to be 5,000 cavalry and 7,000 infantry ; its destination is not known. My opinion is that if the enemy are really intending a movement, they will strike at Tuscaloosa first, and then turn toward Selma, on the Mobile and Ohio Railroad. As information I mention that French's division is held at Lauderdale Station, on the Mobile and Ohio Railroad. Keep me advised at Columbus as you cross the Mobile and Ohio Railroad. You will doubtless find forage scarce, but I am informed that there is forage on the Tombigbee River, and you will have to pack it to Tuscaloosa. I am told that there is a good supply in Jones' Valley. It is desirable that you should reach the point indicated as soon as possible. Ensign Weisinger, of Starke's regiment, who takes this, carries dispatches also inclosed to you, for Major-General Forrest, which you will send forward at once by different routes by trusted couriers.

I am, general, with much respect, your obedient servant,

L. POLK,
Lieutenant-General.

CONFIDENTIAL.] HDQRS. FIRST DIV., FORREST'S CAV. DEPT.,
Jackson, Tenn,. April 8, 1864.

Col. J. J. NEELY, *Comdg. Brigade, near Whitesville, Tenn. :*

COLONEL: The brigadier-general commanding directs that you move on Sunday morning next with your entire brigade (excepting the Seventh Tennessee Cavalry) and Crews' battalion to the vicinity of Raleigh, and make every preparation as if to build a bridge across Wolf River at that place. You will also send a portion of your command on the Big Creek and Moscow road as if intending to cross the river at those places, the object being to impress the enemy with the belief that General Forrest is moving to attack Memphis. You will make no secret of your movement and pretended object. After maneuvering for two or three days you will fall back in the direction of Brownsville. Your command will move with five days' cooked rations.

Your movement is intended to co-operate with one to be made by General Forrest on Fort Pillow, and he desires that it should be made promptly and that the demonstration should be as heavy as possible. When you retire you will (if you are not followed by the enemy) deploy your command in every direction, with orders to arrest and bring to you at Brownsville all men between the ages of eighteen and forty-five years, and all officers and soldiers absent from their commands without proper authority. You will also send out proper officers to impress horses to mount your dismounted men, in accordance with the inclosed instructions* from General Forrest. A strong rear guard will be held together to protect your scattered men. If the enemy press you in force, you will keep together enough men to elude them.

Colonel Duckworth will be ordered to move to Randolph via Covington, and will return and meet you in Brownsville.

The brigadier-general commanding will go to Brownsville to-morrow; he will accompany the movement on Fort Pillow.

The contents of this letter, so far as it relates to the movements of General Forrest, are strictly confidential.

Respectfully, your obedient servant,
W. A. GOODMAN,
Assistant Adjutant-General.

CONFIDENTIAL.] HDQRS. FIRST DIV., FORREST'S CAV. DEPT.,
Jackson, Tenn., April 8, 1864.
Col. J. McGUIRK,
Comdg. Third Regt. Miss. State Cav., Holly Springs:

COLONEL : The brigadier-general commanding directs me to say to you, by instruction of Major-General Forrest, that you will move with your regiment on Sunday morning next, if possible, toward Memphis, and make a strong demonstration on that place. If it is not possible for you to move on Sunday, you will move on Monday morning. As this movement is intended to co-operate with one to be made by General Forrest, it is important that it should be made promptly. You will maneuver in front of Memphis, and in such a manner as to threaten that place, until Wednesday next, when you will withdraw your forces.

On your return you will bring with you all men between the ages of eighteen and forty-five years, and all officers and men absent from their commands without proper authority, and will deliver them to Col. T. W. White, chief of conscript bureau for that district. You will also collect and bring south of the Tallahatchie River all squads of men and unorganized and incomplete companies, especially those of Captains Rogers and Wimberley.

The First Regiment Mississippi Partisan Rangers, a part of which is at Abbeville and the remainder at Panola, will be ordered to co-operate with you in this movement and will be subject to your orders. They will be ordered to report to you at Como, unless you should direct them to some other point.

Respectfully, your obedient servant,
W. A. GOODMAN,
Assistant Adjutant-General.

---

* Not found.

MOBILE, *April* 8, 1864.

Admiral F. BUCHANAN,
   Comdg. Naval Dept. of the Gulf, Mobile, Ala.:

ADMIRAL : In the interview that took place between us yesterday in your office respecting my launch and her destination, you were pleased to infer that you had no idea of her destination or the character of the expedition that I had proposed to the Government, for which I have so often called upon you for your approval in conformity with the letter which I have from the honorable Secretary of the Navy.

I now respectfully inform you that I have completed her outfit and that she is ready for service, and only wait your permission to enroll my crew, under the rules and regulations of the naval service, to operate against the enemy at the mouths of the Mississippi River, and on the lakes, where there are many valuable captures to be made.

My first point of attack will be at the Head of the Passes, and capture one or two of the enemy's tow-boats. There are four of them, namely, Leviathan, Henry J. Tyler, Illinois, and Eliza ; three of these boats are propellers, the other is a side-wheel steamer. My armament will be composed of two armed launches, one pulling fourteen oars and the other twelve, carrying each a full crew of 20 armed men, including the officers, which will be seen in the copy of my stock contract* accompanying this letter.

Second. Should I fail in the capture of the tow-boats, or should I have to send a prize crew off, I then intend to push for the Mississippi coast, near the mouth of Pearl River, and break up a lucrative commerce that is now carried on to some extent by the enemy in that section of our coast, by burning and destroying the vessels that fall into my hands, and should an opportunity offer, which I have no doubt of, I shall push through the Rigolets and enter Lake Pontchartrain, and there await an opportunity of entering the new basin, where the enemy have a small high-pressure stern-wheel steamer, mounting one gun, with a crew of 20 men, black and white. This steamer is an easy capture, as none of her officers stay on board at night. There are also many lake schooners which are used as transports by the enemy that can be easily destroyed.

Could I but for a few moments claim your personal attention on this subject I am satisfied that I would enjoy a little more favorable opinion on these points.

My original intention was to take three armed launches and the full amount of stock taken (some in Richmond), but the many obstacles that I have had to surmount have almost disheartened me, but as I have expended a large amount of money I cannot withdraw now. I would furthermore state that I am prepared with the best lake and river pilots, engineers, and navigators, and with the means to carry out the expedition at my own cost, and only want your approval to our enterprise, which Mr. Mallory has promised that I should have. If you would kindly grant me the requested interview I then could give you any explanation on the subject that you may require.

I have the honor of remaining, your most obedient servant,
                                        E. M. JEFFERSON.

---

* Not found.

[Inclosure.]

NAVY DEPARTMENT, C. S. A.,
Richmond, February 12, 1864.

Capt. E. M. JEFFERSON, *Richmond, Va. :*

SIR : In reply to your statement that you are about to organize upon your account, at Mobile, an enterprise in boats against the enemy in the waters of Mississippi and Louisiana, for the command of which you desire an appointment in the Navy, to secure to you and your party the treatment due prisoners of war if captured, you are informed that Admiral Buchanan is instructed to report the means with which you propose to operate and the character of your enterprise, and you are requested to confer with him, presenting this letter. Such an expedition is desirable and the admiral will extend to it all the aid in his power.

Upon his report of your readiness to undertake what you propose, the appointment will be transmitted to him for you.

I am, respectfully, your obedient servant,

S. R. MALLORY,
Secretary of the Navy.

___

HEADQUARTERS DEPARTMENT OF THE GULF,
Mobile, Ala., April 9, 1864.

Lieut. Col. T. M. JACK,
Assistant Adjutant-General, Demopolis, Ala. :

COLONEL : Please say to the lieutenant-general commanding that I have received his telegram inquiring whether I can receive and hold here 1,000 Federal prisoners.

It is my duty so far as practicable to hold Mobile in readiness for attack. The presence here of prisoners, whether military or civil, will interfere with this. Mobile, on account of the great number of disloyal people in and about it, its propinquity to the enemy, the great number of ordnance, quartermasters', and subsistence stores accumulated in it, is peculiarly unfitted for a place of impriso ment or detention of any persons whose allegiance to our cause is questionable.

I respectfully suggest Greenville, Ala., as the place within my command best suited for such uses, and will make every practicable arrangement to insure the proper custody there of any enemies of the Confederacy whom it may be desirable in the opinion of the lieutenant-general commanding to hold.

Very respectfully, colonel, your obedient servant,

DABNEY H. MAURY,
Major-General, Commanding.

P. S.—Since writing the above I have received the lieutenant-general's second dispatch of yesterday relative to the prisoners, and have ordered two large cotton warehouses to be prepared for them.

D. H. M.

___

HEADQUARTERS MISSISSIPPI STATE TROOPS,
Aberdeen, April 9, 1864.

Lieutenant-General POLK,
Commanding Department, &c. :

GENERAL : I am here with about 550 prisoners, captured by Major-General Forrest's forces at Union City and elsewhere, and was directed to deliver them to you. I was informed at Okolona on yesterday that a train would be furnished me at West Point on Monday next, to which place I shall proceed at once and should be pleased to receive from you instructions as to the point to which you may desire them carried.

I am, general, with high respect, your obedient servant,

S. J. GHOLSON,
Major-General, Commanding, &c.

HEADQUARTERS LORING'S DIVISION,
Montevallo, Ala., April 9, 1864.

Lieut. Col. THOMAS M. JACK,
Assistant Adjutant-General:

COLONEL : I have the honor to report the arrival of my entire command at this point. There is no forage to be had at this place or its vicinity, and I shall be compelled to rely on Selma and its surrounding country. I find upon arrival that there is no telegraph line between this place and Selma. If I can be furnished with wire I will have the poles cut and the line established.

With respect, your obedient servant,

W. W. LORING,
Major-General, Commanding.

EXECUTIVE DEPARTMENT OF ALABAMA,
Montgomery, April 9, 1864.

General GIDEON J. PILLOW,
Montgomery, Ala. :

GENERAL : Inclosed I send you a copy of a letter I have this day received from Col. M. W. Hannon, informing me of the concentration by the enemy of a heavy force at Decatur. I deem the information reliable, and send you this letter that you may be informed, and may take the necessary steps to meet this demonstration by the enemy.

Very respectfully, yours,

T. H. WATTS,
Governor of Alabama.

[Inclosure.]

HDQRS. HANNON'S CAV. BRIG., RODDEY'S DIVISION,
Camp near Dalton, Ga., April 7, 1864.

Governor T. H. WATTS :

DEAR SIR : Having learned through General Roddey that the enemy are concentrating a heavy force at Decatur, North Ala., for the purpose of making a raid on Selma, I deem it my duty, and have his consent, to apprise you of the fact. He says the information is reliable, and has come to him per courier-line in a remarkably short time, only three days having elapsed since the courier started. We have given the information to General Johnston, but I fear he will not feel the importance of immediate action as much as we do. The force of the enemy will be led by the celebrated Grierson, of Mississippi notoriety, and in my judgment it will require some such man as Forrest or Roddey to thwart him. A portion of General Roddey's command left yesterday, under Colonel Patterson, for North Alabama. This force, however, was mostly composed of raw recruits, and will not accomplish a great deal. General Roddey has gone to-day to see General Johnston for the purpose of getting an order for my brigade to be sent. He says if he succeeds in getting the order he will then go himself, and feels confident of being able to defeat Grierson. My command is in fine condition, and reported by the inspector-general of the Army of Tennessee as the best brigade of cavalry in this army according to numbers. He also gives us great credit for discipline, something entirely new in cavalry. We are just moving camp. I will try and write you more at length this evening.

Very respectfully and hastily, yours,

M. W. HANNON,
Colonel, Commanding Brigade.

EXECUTIVE DEPARTMENT OF ALABAMA,
Montgomery, April 9, 1864.

Lieut. Gen. L. POLK,
Demopolis, Ala.:

DEAR SIR : I have received from Talladega County, Ala., a petition, of which the inclosed is a copy. I beg leave to call your special attention to it. The meeting was composed of our best citizens, and I have no doubt the representations made in the petition are strictly true. My personal knowledge of that county enables me to say that if relief can be granted it ought to be done. At this season of the year the planting operations ought to be disturbed as little as possible, and especially ought this to be done where large numbers of soldiers' wives are dependent on the charities of the rich for support, whilst their husbands and sons are in the field fighting for our righteous cause.

I trust it may be in your power to suspend the call recently made on that county until such time as the necessities of the planters in that county are less pressing.

I have the honor to remain, with great regard, your obedient servant,

T. H. WATTS,
Governor of Alabama.

P. S.—Allow me to include herewith a letter from General Lawler and others, of Talladega County, gentlemen of the highest character.

T. H. W.,
Governor of Alabama.

[Inclosure No. 1.]

TALLADEGA, *April* 4, 1864.

At a public meeting, held at the court-house in the town of Talladega, on Monday, the 4th day of April, 1864, by the citizens of said county, Hon. John T. Heflin was called to the chair, and Capt. Joseph Hardie appointed secretary. Hon. Lewis E. Parsons explained the object of the meeting, and on his motion a committee of seven was appointed to draught a memorial to His Excellency Thomas H. Watts, Governor of the State of Alabama, on the subject of the late call for slave labor, or impressment of the negroes to work on the fortifications at Mobile.

The committee retired, and after consultation submitted the following memorial:

His Excellency THOMAS H. WATTS,
            Governor, &c. :

The committee appointed at a meeting of the citizens of the county of Talladega and said State beg leave to call the attention of Your Excellency to the following facts:

First. This county has furnished twenty-seven companies of volunteers for the war. These were raised under a pledge, publicly given at a larger meeting of the citizens, that they would raise, if necessary, $20,000 a year while the war continued to aid in supporting the families of those who needed assistance.

Second. At that time, May, 1861, there was a white population in the county of 14,634 persons, and a slave population of about 8,865 persons, and there were only about 30 persons who needed and received aid from the county. Now there are 3,997.

This county is divided into what is called the "Valley" and the "Hills." A large proportion of these volunteers came from the "Hills." These twenty-seven companies are exclusive of those who have volunteered in other organizations, furnished substitutes, or been enrolled.

Third. In accordance with the above pledge, the people of the county have raised large sums each year, in addition to the fund raised by the State, to aid the wives and children of these soldiers. The slave population is mostly in the "Valley," and the men who have gone from the "Hills" have left at home, in most instances, none to plow a furrow or hoe a hill of corn, except their wives and little ones. They are therefore dependent, in a great degree, for support on the supplies raised in the "Valley."

During the year 1863, in addition to what the State furnished, the people of this county, under the pledge aforesaid, raised and placed in the hands of the judge of probate for distribution $7,276 in cash; 21,755 bushels of corn, at 50 cents per bushel; 2,570 bushels of corn, without any price, as a gift; 928 bushels of wheat, at $2 per bushel; 102 bushels of wheat, without any price and as a gift; 23 sacks of salt, at $20 per sack, and 16 sacks of salt without any price and as a gift.

It is proper to state that the average price of wheat, corn, and salt is much above these prices; the average price of wheat has been about $10, of corn about $3, of salt about $80 per sack.

Fourth. We would also state that these supplies are managed by the probate judge of this county, the Hon. W. H. Thornton, under a careful system of agencies for each beat or district in the county, and they are furnished to none but those who actually need assistance. Of course, this is entirely separate from the aid which every one is called on to render by individual calls on him for assistance.

Fifth. In view of this condition of things the undersigned beg leave to state that they will be unable to raise a sufficient crop this season to meet the just claims, the absolute necessities of these families, unless they are permitted to employ their slave labor for that purpose.

In this connection they would further respectfully call the attention of Your Excellency to the following facts, viz: On the 22d of December, 1862, there were impressed 90 negroes in this county. On the 29th of January, 1863, 120 negroes were impressed. On the 7th of March, 1863, 150 more and 5 wagons and teams. In the fall of 1863, 150 to 160 more. In February, 1864, 160 more, who are now at Mobile. In August, 1863, about —— wagons and teams were impressed and sent to Montevallo to haul coal and iron. In August, 1863, under an order, it was said, from General Wheeler, about 175 horses were impressed. Within a few days past, Captain Graham, under an order from Lieutenant-General Polk, it is said, has been here and impressed about —— horses and about —— mules, claiming and exercising the right to take every seventh mule, whether the same was actually necessary "to carry on the agricultural employments of the owner" or not. Moreover, a large proportion of the work oxen in this county have been obtained for the use of the Government by persons who informed the owners they were empowered by it to buy, and if they would not sell at such prices as they offered to give them they would impress them.

Large bodies of cavalry are now recruiting their horses at various points in this county, and thus consuming the tax in kind, which but for this might be purchased for the consumption of these poor people. These bodies of cavalry have been here for some time past. The season thus far has been very backward, and what corn has been planted will probably have to be planted over again.

As before stated, 160 of these negroes are now in Mobile at work on the public defenses, and on the 2d instant a new order arrived calling on the impressing agent for this county to impress 160 more, and have them ready to leave by the 17th of this month.

The premises considered, the undersigned respectfully request Your Excellency to aid them in procuring an order from Lieutenant-General Polk exempting this county from further impressment this season, if possible, or at least from this recent order.

L. E. PARSONS,
Chairman.
ALEX. WHITE.
TAUL BRADFORD.
W. R. STONE.
C. G. CUNNINGHAM.
I. L. ELSTON.
JNO. SAWYER.

On motion by Mr. White, Capt. Joseph Hardie was appointed special messenger to convey the within proceedings to His Excellency Governor Watts and, if necessary, to Lieutenant-General Polk.

On motion by Mr. Stone, the chairman and secretary were requested to sign a copy of the proceedings of this meeting to be conveyed to Governor Watts, and that the newspapers of the county be requested to publish the same.

JOHN T. HEFLIN,
Chairman.
JOS. HARDIE,
Secretary.

[Inclosure No. 2.]

ALPINE, TALLADEGA COUNTY,
April 6, 1864.

His Excellency T. H. WATTS,
Governor of Alabama:

SIR: The undersigned have been informed that another requisition for negroes has been made upon this county by General Maury, commanding at Mobile. We therefore beg leave to submit to you a statement of facts which will enable you the better to judge of the propriety of your official interposition to prevent any further drain upon the labor of this part of the State.

A large portion of the county is settled by persons owning no slaves. White laborers under forty-five are generally in the Army. Their families are dependent for subsistence upon the slave labor of the valley. Moreover, this county is environed by territory occupied almost exclusively by people of limited means, many of them, indeed, very poor. They come to this valley for corn from Coosa, Tallapoosa, Randolph, and part of Calhoun. We have refugees from North Alabama, which has been desolated by the enemy. All the country between this and North Alabama is sterile and destitute of labor. No refuge can therefore be found until they reach the Talladega Valley. Several thousand cavalry and artillery horses and mules are now in the county and have been for months. The consequence is that notwithstanding the large yield of grain last year there is barely enough now on hand to subsist the inhabitants of the county.

Under such circumstances it would be suicidal for the Government to take our labor from us now when we are planting our crops and doing all we can to raise provisions. It must inevitably result in great suffering, and deprive us of the means of supporting the families of the gallant men who are periling their lives in defense of liberty. This county has been a great thoroughfare for soldiers, being on the route from Johnston's to Polk's army.

Looking, then, alone to the public good and oblivious of our own personal interests, we respectfully request that you will use your influence to prevent any further impressment of labor in this county before next autumn. Very soon harvest will be upon us. Our corn crops are just being planted, and if labor be abstracted at this time the wheat must remain in the field or the corn go uncultivated. It seems to us to be far better to impress slaves in those counties where the poor are less numerous, labor more abundant, and the lands less productive of small grain.

Your Excellency is aware that the planters of Talladega have acted liberally in providing for the families of soldiers, having furnished corn at 50 cents per bushel. We mention this as an evidence of the true purpose of this request and to acquit us of suspicion of selfish designs.

Very respectfully,

LEVI W. LAWLER.	WILLIAM WISON.
WM. MALLORY.	MARTHA WILSON.
ABNER WYNN.	MARTH. T. POPE.
B. A. SMOOT.	MARY C. WILSON.
SAML. W. SMOOT.	JOS. D. HEACOCK.
SIMON MORRISS.	GEO. RISER.
N. WELCH.	M. J. CLIETT.
O. WELCH.	F. ALSTON BUTT.
JAMES MALLORY.	H. COLEMAN.
SARAH TUNDERLUNG.	WALTER REYNOLDS.
T. L. POPE.	A. D. BELL.
NAT. COOK.	THOS. H. REYNOLDS.
JAMES B. WELCH.	C. STAUFF,

DALTON, *April* 9, 1864.

General COOPER :

GENERAL : The last mail brought me paragraphs XIII and XIV, Special Orders, No. 78.*

About one-fourth of Brigadier-General Roddey's troops was left in the "former position." I sent back about half in consequence of your telegram of the 2d instant, and am retaining the other fourth until the arrival of the Kentucky brigade, which was sent to the rear to put its horses in condition for service.

The necessity of an efficient cavalry as part of this army justifies me in desiring the honorable Secretary of War to consider how much that arm of service in it has been weakened since the last campaign, when it was inferior in strength to that opposed to it, and on the contrary how much that of Lieutenant-General Polk has been increased. It is needless to contrast the enemy's force in his front with that in mine.

On the 28th of February General Polk estimated the cavalry with which he could operate this spring at 15,000. Brigadier-General Roddey has more than 2,000 effectives. His transfer leaves an effective force in the Army of Tennessee (cavalry) of a little above 2,000, mounted on horses not in proper condition to commence a campaign. It is true that Major-General Martin's division has returned from East Tennessee, but he describes it reduced from about 3,000 effectives to 1,500, 1,120 of whom appear by his requisitions to have lost or thrown away their arms. From the condition of the horses of this division, as described by Major-Generals Wheeler and Martin, it cannot be ready for service before the middle of May. With such a force we must observe a front of near 80 miles and protect the railroad to Atlanta against a cavalry which is estimated by Major-General Wheeler at above 12,000.

Most respectfully, your obedient servant,

J. E. JOHNSTON,
General.

GENERAL ORDERS, }   HEADQUARTERS HOOD'S CORPS,
    No. 50.   }   *Dalton, Ga., April* 10, 1864.

Maj. J. P. Wilson is hereby relieved from duty with this corps, at the request of General T. C. Hindman, to whom he will report for duty.

Maj. J. W. Ratchford, assistant adjutant-general, is hereby assigned to duty as assistant adjutant-general of this corps, to whom all official communications for the lieutenant-general commanding will be addressed.

By command of Lieut. Gen. J. B. Hood, commanding :

[J. W. RATCHFORD,]
Assistant Adjutant-General.

---

* Cited on p. 738.

Abstract from return of the Army of Tennessee, General Joseph E. Johnston, C. S. Army, commanding, April 10, 1864 ; headquarters Dalton, Ga.

Command.	Present for duty.		Effective total present.	Aggregate present.	Aggregate present and absent.	Pieces of artillery.
	Officers.	Men.				
General headquarters..........................	21	160	160	189	253	......
Hardee's army corps:						
Headquarters.................................	29	224	223	300	413	......
Infantry.....................................	1,843	17,462	16,941	22,914	34,498	......
Artillery....	48	973	942	1,229	1,632	48
Total Hardee's corps	1,920	18,659	18,106	24,443	36,543	48
Hood's army corps:						
Headquarters...........	29	164	163	213	288	......
Infantry.....................................	1,495	17,493	17,067	21,792	34,562	......
Artillery	46	853	840	1,058	1,332	39
Total Hood's corps.........................	1,570	18,510	18,070	23,063	36,182	39
Cavalry:						
Wheeler's corps a........................	580	5,734	5,598	8,058	17,066	......
Artillery attached	12	284	275	344	460	18
Total cavalry	592	6,018	5,873	8,402	17,526	18
Reserve artillery	54	783	754	950	1,237	36
Engineer troops	17	408	401	456	601	......
1st Louisiana Infantry (Regulars)......	9	102	100	123	254	.... .
Total...	26	505	501	579	855	......
Grand total	4,183	44,635	43,464	57,626	92,596	141

a Martin's division joined by transfer (effective total, 1,716; total present, 2,328; aggregate present and absent, 6,477). Deducting effective total Martin's division (1,716) and Grigsby's brigade (747) in rear recruiting horses, and Roddey's brigade, transferred to Mississippi (1,050) equals 3,513, which, deducted from 5,598, shows the effective total of cavalry in the army to be 2,085.

Armament and ammunition report of the Army of Tennessee, commanded by General Joseph E. Johnston, for the week ending April 10, 1864.

	Corps.		Total.
	Hardee.	Hood.	
Regiments in command	80	54	134
Armament, small-arms:			
Caliber .54..............................	3,070	6,778	9,848
Caliber .58..	2,994	1,034	4,028
Caliber .577.............................	8,105	5,608	13,713
Caliber .69..	3,191	3,242	6,433
Caliber .70..	....	79	79
Total arms	17,360	16,741	34,101
Ammunition:			
Rounds in cartridge-boxes of men......	631,717	625,847	1,257,564
In reserve wagons:			
Caliber .54...	130,839	252,680	383,519
Caliber .577...	443,108	250,667	693,775

Armament and ammunition report of the Army of Tennessee—Continued.

	Corps.		Total.
	Hardee.	Hood.	
Ammunition—Continued.			
In reserve wagons—Continued.			
Caliber .58	17,181	....	17,181
Caliber .69	129,238	127,161	256,402
Caliber .70	....	4,360	4,360
Total rounds of ammunition	1,352,083	1,260,718	a2,612,801
Regimental ordnance wagons	66	60	126
Unarmed men	152	227	379
Effective men	17,006	16,968	33,974

a Giving 82⅓ rounds to each arm.

I certify that the above report is correct, being a copy from corps ordnance officers' reports.

H. OLADOWSKI,
Lieutenant-Colonel, Ordnance Duty.

HEADQUARTERS FORREST'S CAVALRY DEPARTMENT,
Jackson, Tenn., April 10, 1864.

Lieut. Col. THOMAS M. JACK,
Assistant Adjutant-General:

COLONEL: I have the honor to state that Captain Oliver has reported to these headquarters with orders to thoroughly inspect my command, and regret very much that the position and the duties of the troops render it totally impossible for him to do so. In order to watch the enemy in all directions the command is much scattered, and heavy scouting as well as frequent moves are rendered unavoidable by scarcity of forage, preventing concentration at any one point, and no report or inspection can take place until I can draw in the regiments on outpost duty and get returns also from that portion of my command stationed on the Tallahatchie and those with my wagon trains at Aberdeen.

I expect in the course of ten or twelve days to move back into North Mississippi and expect to take out with me at least 2,000 more troops, conscripts and deserters included; if not moved upon by the enemy in that time will probably get out with even a greater number. Will then have my command together and full reports and thorough will be made. I have four regiments in Southern Kentucky, with orders as they move back to bring with them every man they can get hold of between the ages of eighteen and forty-five. Governor Harris is at Paris with a detachment of men who are performing the same duty. Bell's brigade, of Buford's division, is posted from Bolivar around by Raleigh, with orders to take up and send to Jackson every one subject to military duty and all absentees from the army. Would be glad if the lieutenant-general commanding would give me instructions as to what disposition to make of them; only those will be received in the cavalry who are well mounted. Old commands will be, as far as practicable, filled up; the balance will be forwarded or held as you may direct.

The enrollment of men between the ages of seventeen and eighteen and forty-five and fifty years of age is in my opinion of doubtful policy (at least for the present) in this section, as, according to law, they are held to duty only in the State and could only be removed temporarily from the State. Will carry out, however, as far as practicable, any orders the lieutenant-general may give in regard to this or other measures deemed necessary to secure the enrollment or conscription in West Tennessee or North Mississippi.

I am, colonel, very respectfully, your obedient servant,

N. B. FORREST,
Major-General, Commanding.

HEADQUARTERS FORREST'S CAVALRY,
Jackson, Tenn., April 10, 1864.

Major-General LEE,
Commanding Cavalry:

GENERAL: Your dispatch of the 6th instant is this moment received. I have heard nothing from General Polk since leaving Columbus. I requested General Polk to allow you to move with your command to this place for the purpose of operating against the enemy and conscripting this portion of the State. I would advise that you move immediately from Holly Springs to Brownsville, as that portion of the country is more abundantly supplied with forage, and also because I have a pontoon bridge at Brownsville. I will order that rations be procured for your division at that point. I move to-morrow on Fort Pillow with two brigades, the force at that point being 300 whites and 600 negroes. Grierson is reported moving up the State line road from Memphis, and I would suggest that you look well to that quarter. Colonel Neely, commanding Richardson's brigade, is near Raleigh and east of Wolf River. I will return to this point by the 15th.

I am, general, with respect, your obedient servant.

N. B. FORREST,
Major-General, Commanding.

HEADQUARTERS,
Columbus, Miss., April 10, 1864.

Major-General Lee will move Jackson's division and Ferguson's brigade of his command into Alabama and take a position near Tuscaloosa. He will throw a part of his command up Jones' Valley, in the neighborhood of Elyton, and advance his scouts well up toward the Tennessee River so as to be informed of the enemy's situation, strength, and purposes. He will establish a line of couriers from his headquarters to some convenient point on the railroad, so as to keep department headquarters constantly informed, and will report frequently. He will constantly advise Major-General Loring of condition of things in his front. Major-General Lee will also organize expedition against the deserters and tories of North Alabama. He will arrest them and will deal with all such as may be banded together for resistance in the most summary manner.*

By command of Lieutenant-General Polk:

[T. M. JACK,]
Assistant Adjutant-General.

---

*Published also in Special Orders, No. 110, April 19.

RICHMOND, *April* 11, 1864.

Lieutenant-General POLK :

Numerous and, I fear, well-founded complaints reach me in relation to military affairs in Adams, Wilkinson, and Franklin. I have watched long for improvement and have been disappointed. I suggest that you send Brigadier-General Ferguson to collect, organize, and command your scattered forces in that region.

JEFFERSON DAVIS.

MOBILE, *April* 11, 1864.

Lieutenant-General POLK :

The following dispatch just received from Cooper's Station, date April 10, 1864 :

> Could not draw enemy out. Farragut arrived to-day in flag-ship Pensacola. Eleven steam-ships in bay, other supply ships, and mortar-boats. General Thomas there ; destination said to be Mobile. Other ships daily expected.
> HENRY MAURY,
> *Colonel.*

D. H. MAURY,
Major-General, Commanding.

HEADQUARTERS DEPARTMENT OF THE GULF,
Mobile, Ala., April 11, 1864.

Lieut. Gen. L. POLK,
Demopolis, Ala .:

GENERAL : I have just received reports by an intelligent agent from New Orleans, Baton Rouge, and Port Hudson, which confirm the statements of Banks' defeat. They repeat the statements of great reductions of the garrisons along the Mississippi River. In Pensacola an increase of the shipping has been observed recently. The land forces there are not considerable. I am much in need of reliable cavalry to replace the pickets about the Perdido.

I am just now in receipt of a dispatch which informs me that Farragut is at Pensacola with twelve ships of war. General Thomas also is there. More war ships are expected ; the destination is Mobile. If Thomas is in Pensacola, some important movement is probably contemplated.

I sent you to Selma all of the Mississippi troops except Holland's (Thirty-seventh) regiment, detached in West Florida. Holland having been recommended to command the Mississippi brigade, and another having been appointed its brigadier, together with the attendant facts, have caused so much feeling amongst the officers that it would be best for the service, I think, that he should not return to the brigade. Colonel Coleman, the former acting brigadier of the Arkansas brigade, stands somewhat in the same position. I think it will be advisable to transfer Coleman's (North Carolina) regiment to Sears' brigade, and to put Holland's regiment into the Arkansas brigade.

I am much embarrassed by the arrangements of the quartermaster's department here. I can get nothing from the depot until the requisition on the depot quartermaster goes to Richmond and is approved by the Quartermaster-General. To-day I sent you a report on the subject made by me to the War Department; please enforce it as far as you consider proper.

On learning that 550 prisoners would be here to-day, the quartermaster made requisitions on Major Barnewall for cooking utensils for them. He will not issue them, I believe. If he refuses I shall have to take them, as I cannot otherwise procure them.

I hope the Quartermaster-General will relieve Major Barnewall from duty here, and intrust all of his affairs to one of the other officers of the Department who have been sent to report to me. I think it would be better for him to use Major McGivern, my chief quartermaster, and to repose some amount of discretion in him; any other course will be inevitably attended by embarrassments and inharmony. I do not believe it possible for any commander to conduct his affairs satisfactorily to himself or the country unless he can control the officers on whom he must call daily to supply his troops.

Very respectfully, general, your obedient servant,

DABNEY H. MAURY,
Major-General, Commanding.

HEADQUARTERS DEPARTMENT OF EAST TENNESSEE,
Bristol, April 11, 1864.

Maj. Gen. C. W. FIELD,
Commanding Division:

The commanding general desires that you will make your preparations to move your division by rail to Charlottesville, Va. Your transportation should be started for that point as soon as possible by the dirt road, under charge of a competent and reliable officer. Your heaviest baggage will be taken by rail, and for this purpose it ought to be deposited near the railroad, to permit its shipment without unnecessary hauling.

Arrangements will be made to enable your troops to take the cars at the point most accessible and convenient to your present camp. The transportation of the troops and stores is intrusted to Maj. E. Taylor, chief quartermaster, to whom your quartermaster should refer for information as to when the transportation will be ready for your division.

I am, general, very respectfully, your obedient servant,

G. M. SORREL,
Lieutenant-Colonel and Assistant Adjutant-General.

DALTON, GA., *April 11, 1864.*

Major GIBBONS,
Chief Inspector-General Transportation, Richmond, Va.:

MAJOR: Your letters and telegrams from 28th March down to 9th instant just received, for which accept my thanks.

This army to move, owing to the distance it will have to travel before reaching a country furnishing supplies, will have to start with twenty days' supplies. This will involve extra supply reserve trains, over and above that now on hand, 900 wagons and teams, and for which the chief quartermaster has never estimated; all he has called on Major Smith for is 600 artillery horses and wagons and teams for a pontoon train consisting of 135 wagons and teams—540 mules.

On my arrival here I found that no one in this army knew what transportation was on hand, nor what was needed for a campaign. I had therefore to go to work and inspect and ferret out everything in order to arrive at some calculation as to the deficiency. I have been here now ten days, and by hard labor night and day am prepared to show General Johnston what he has, what he requires, and what we may possibly be able to do for him.

Owing to either inefficiency, improper appropriation, or some other cause, I fear nothing is to be obtained from Paxton's district for this army. I strongly suspect he has not used proper exertion in procuring animals. Smith, on the contrary, has done wonders, and has his department in first-rate order. I shall be compelled to send officers into Paxton's district, and for that purpose obtained to-day a detail from this army of 7 first-class officers ; if we had the funds they could start to-morrow, and, funds or not, they must go as soon as Smith can furnish them instructions. I propose with them to cover all the ground in Alabama and Georgia and get everything not needed for the plow. If Johnston wants help I can send one or two of these officers to him. We must get some aid from North Carolina for this army, if it is the policy of the Government for it to move. Instead of taking horses I am now counting those as plow teams and taking good mules instead, as we are much better off on the horse question than we are on the mule. Paxton says, in a telegram received to-night, that he has had to impress in Mississippi for Gorgas' infernal ordnance train for the trans-Mississippi, for Lee's artillery (hence another nuisance) in Western Mississippi, and in Alabama for Polk's artillery, and mules for his transportation, besides horses in part for Buford's brigade, now in Western Tennessee.

Unless General Bragg will issue the order recommended by me fixing the allowance of transportation, we cannot stand it, and the system of allowing chief quartermasters to issue, sell, and trade, and otherwise assign or dispose of animals, unless checked, will destroy the Government.

Of the 400 or 500 fine horses impressed by Smith and sent here, I find 100 at least used by officers, wagon-masters, clerks, &c. The truth is, unless all such property is put under the control of our own officers, in or out of the armies, the public service must suffer.

I shall leave here in a few days and will meet Paxton at Montgomery, and may have to go to Mississippi to adjust General Polk's transportation, but before going there some order making the allowance uniform ought to be published. If it is done telegraph me. If I find General Polk in excess I shall insist on taking some from him, as we must do with Generals Beauregard, Whiting, Pickett, and others—that is, if the Government intends keeping this and General Lee's army efficient. I am now taking everything from post, substituting broken-down stock instead, but of course meet with violent opposition from all quarters. You must do the same thing in Virginia if you find it necessary to equip General Lee.

Whilst we are laboring to equip the two large armies, we can afford to neglect the smaller ones, or, in other words, tell them to wait. The neglect of Colonel McMicken to turn over to Smith the broken-down stock of this army has resulted in the death and loss of nearly 2,500 animals since January last. This accident is bad.

I find General Johnston most reasonable and entirely willing to yield everything I ask or even suggest. I shall be able to get him to make large deductions from his present allowance, but in order to do so, nave to remain here and make myself entirely acquainted with his whole status. I find every day I am furnishing him information concerning his transportation he never had before.

I return General Alexander's letter. He is a good fellow and I like him, but have very little confidence in his judgment about horses, and see nothing in his suggestions to justify the carrying out of his propositions, though I have not read it carefully and really have not the time. I wish you would look into it and act as you think best; say I am absent and will not be back for some time, if you think proper, but at any rate dispose of the matter.

I can't now see when I can get off from these quarters, as I cannot well leave here unless this army is fixed up. I shall leave for Montgomery in about ten days, but will return here after seeing Paxton. Whenever I am wanted let me know, as I shall remain out this way as long as I feel I am doing good.

General Bragg had better get out the forage order as suggested by me, as all these armies allow great abuse of forage in feeding officers' horses. Send word by all means to General Longstreet. You have no idea how much good our officers are with these armies.

Remember me to all friends and accept for yourself my kindest regards.

A. H. COLE.

They give me a grand review of all the transportation in the army to-morrow. The quartermasters here I find generally practical, good officers. Smith ought to have a million of new issue this month, and Paxton same; we cannot equip armies without it. Urge Green's promotion. He has well earned it. No better officer to be found.

A. H. C.

BRANDON, *April* 11, 1864.

Col. A. H. COLE
    (*Care of General Johnston*):

Impressing mules for Trans-Mississippi ordnance train, horses for Lee's artillery in West Mississippi, in Alabama for General Polk's artillery and mules for his transportation. Some small horses, 20 to 50, were issued to order General Polk's chief quartermaster, which were used in mounting Buford's (Kentucky) brigade, now in West Tennessee. All other issues were made upon requisition of same officer. Always prepare to show all official transactions, and that of General Polk's army as far as it has been possible to obtain it. Much embarrassment for want of new currency.

. A. M. PAXTON,
Major, &c.

GENERAL ORDERS, }   HDQRS. DEPT. OF EAST TENNESSEE,
    No. 1.   }   *Bristol, Va., April* 12, 1864.

In consequence of the withdrawal of Lieutenant-General Longstreet from this department, the undersigned hereby assumes command.

S. B. BUCKNER,
Major-General.

GENERAL ORDERS, }   HDQRS. DEPT. OF EAST TENNESSEE,
No. 3.   }   *Bristol, April* 12, 1864.

The following officers are announced on the staff of the major-general commanding; they will be obeyed and respected accordingly:

Maj. W. F. Mastin, assistant inspector-general.
Lieut. H. S. Foote, jr., acting assistant inspector-general.
Capt. Isaac Shelby, jr., chief commissary of subsistence.
Lieut. C. F. Johnson, aide-de-camp.
Lieut. S. F. Chipley, aide-de-camp.
Maj. A. C. Gibson, chief of ordnance for the field.
Maj. S. K. Hays, chief quartermaster.
Surg. W. Jennings, medical director for the field.
Lieut. Col. Thomas Claiborne will continue as heretofore on duty as assistant inspector-general of cavalry.

By command of Major-General Buckner:

J. N. GALLEHER,
Assistant Adjutant-General.

TUNNEL HILL, *April* 12, 1864—8 p. m.
General W. W. MACKALL,
            Chief of Staff:

Scouts report that two regiments of Yankee infantry, 800 or 1,000 strong, entered La Fayette at 7 a. m. to-day and camped half mile from the town, on the Dug Gap road.

J. H. KELLY,
Brigadier-General, Commanding,

HEADQUARTERS,
Savannah, April 12, 1864.
Lieut. Gen. L. POLK,
    Comdg. Dept. of East La., Miss., and Ala.:

GENERAL: A letter has been received by me from Lieut. Col. A. L. Rives, acting chief Engineer Bureau, in which he regrets to say that in consequence of many difficulties Lieutenant-Colonel Lockett has not been so successful in the organization of the engineer troops in the Department of East Louisiana, Mississippi, and Alabama as it was hoped he would be, or as other officers have been in other parts of the country.

Feeling how important to the service these troops are in the rapid construction and repair of roads, bridges, and works, special recommendations were made to Congress for the enactment of the present laws authorizing their organization, and believing that you acknowledge entirely the usefulness of this class of troops, I write to ask your countenance and aid in the difficult task of building up this valuable auxiliary to the army in your department.

The engineer troops in Tennessee and Virginia and the Trans-Mississippi Department have, after great efforts, been successfully organized, and the companies at Savannah, Mobile, and Wilmington are accomplishing all that could be expected from them, and give great encouragement to the Engineer Bureau to continue with vigor its labors in this direction.

So much depends, as you well know, upon the co-operation of

commanding officers that unless they will regard with favor our attempts they will rarely meet with success; and as one much interested in the engineer troops, and feeling confident that when organized they will be of the greatest assistance to you, I would ask your support and aid for the officers who are engaged in the formation of these troops in the Department of East Louisiana, Mississippi, and Alabama.

I am, general, very respectfully, your obedient servant,
                                        J. F. GILMER,
                        Major-General and Chief Engineer Bureau.

SPECIAL ORDERS, }   HEADQUARTERS,
   No. 103.   }   *Demopolis, Ala., April 12, 1864.*
      *   *   *   *   *   *

X. Col. John S. Scott, commanding First Louisiana Cavalry, will proceed with his regiment to the District of South Mississippi and East Louisiana and relieve Col. Thomas H. Taylor of the command of that district, and will report for purposes of organization and administration to these headquarters.

XI. Col. Thomas H. Taylor, when relieved by Colonel Scott, will report in person to these headquarters for orders.
      *   *   *   *   *

By command of Lieutenant-General Polk:
                                        T. M. JACK,
                                Assistant Adjutant-General.

                            HEADQUARTERS, &C.,
                        Montevallo, April 13, 1864.
Lieut. Col. T. M. JACK,
   Assistant Adjutant-General:

COLONEL: I have the honor to state that a courier from a scouting party of General Ferguson's from Elyton, Ala., reached my headquarters to-day. When this party left the general the 9th instant he was 25 or 30 miles the other side of Macon, Miss., and marching in the direction of Jones' Valley, some 80 miles in advance of him and about 30 miles above this. He will probably reach there about the 15th or 16th. I have directed the officer in command of the party of the scouts to send parties in the direction of Decatur, and any other point he may learn of the approach of an enemy, and keeping me advised.

I have directed a competent officer to go in that direction to examine the country and map it; also to take steps to furnish information in anticipation of the arrival of the cavalry.

With respect, your obedient servant,
                                        W. W. LORING,
                                        Major-General.

                    HEADQUARTERS SEARS' BRIGADE,
                        Selma, April 13, 1864.
Lieut. Col. T. M. JACK,
   Assistant Adjutant-General:

COLONEL: I had the honor of reporting this morning by telegraph my arrival at this point. I received marching orders last Sunday at Pollard for a portion of my brigade, the Thirty-seventh Mississippi Regiment having been retained, as it was on detached service. Through a fault in the transportation agent ordering transportation for only 1,200 when we had an aggregate of 1,800, we have been a good deal delayed in reaching this point. Upwards of 600 will arrive to-morrow morning with our baggage and field transportation. We have about twelve wagons and six ambulances. We await instructions as to sending wagons and ambulances by land.

I find the Forty-third Mississippi Regiment (Colonel Harrison) at this point under orders to report to Brigadier-General Featherston. The Forty-third is supposed to belong to my brigade, and I have to request that it be returned to my command. Am assured that such is the very general wish of its officers.

The absence of the Thirty-seventh and Thirty-eighth Mississippi Regiments and the number yet remaining under parole makes my command small, much smaller than General Featherston's.

Am awaiting orders from you as to my further movements.

I am, very respectfully, your obedient servant,

C. W. SEARS,
Brigadier-General, Commanding.

HEADQUARTERS FORREST'S CAVALRY,
In the Field, April 13, 1864.

Brigadier-General CHALMERS,
Commanding, &c. :

GENERAL : I am directed by the major-general commanding to say that he will move to Brownsville to-day and on to Jackson to-morrow. He directs that you order a regiment to report to him at Jackson to-morrow evening ; will send Wisdom on to McNairy County. It is reported that the enemy are preparing to move from Middle Tennessee and from Memphis, also, after us, and it is therefore important to be prepared and concentrate as early as practicable in order to meet them.

He directs that you send out and impress ox teams, and haul all the artillery, &c., as far as Brownsville, at which place you will send forward and have other ox teams gotten up to carry them on to Jackson. The general says have the salt rolled out so that it will be safe, and then burn up all the houses at the fort, except the one used as a hospital ; leave the Federal sergeant and such of the wounded as cannot travel or be moved and parole them : also parole and leave with them a nurse or two of slightly wounded men, sufficient to wait on them, sending forward all other prisoners and negroes to Jackson immediately. No negroes will be delivered to their owners on the march ; they must all go to Jackson.

Leave with the wounded five or six days' supply of provisions and any medicines they may need; the balance of provisions issue to your command.

The major-general directs that you have brought out all ammunition and all other supplies that you can get transportation for ; if you can haul them, bring also a few best tents ; destroy the balance with every building at Fort Pillow ; also destroy and tear the works to pieces as much as you can and move back with your entire command between the Hatchie and Forked Deer, so as to sweep the country, bringing in every man between the ages of eighteen and forty-five to Jackson. Order your officers to take no excuse, neither allow conscripts to go home for clothes or anything else; their friends can send them to Jackson. When you reach Brownsville send a courier on to let the general know what time you will reach that place. He also directs that you will endeavor to get teams beyond Brownsville and have forage hauled for your command to the neighborhood of Jackson, camping your command south of the Forked Deer River. If you find you cannot bring them off burn the light artillery, preserving and bringing out all the ammunition and accouterments belonging to them.

Very respectfully, your obedient servant,

CHAS. W. ANDERSON,
Aide-de-Camp.

DURHAMVILLE, TENN.,
April 13, 1864.

Brig. Gen. J. R. CHALMERS:

GENERAL: I am directed by Lieutenant-General Polk to move with my command to Alabama, to join General Lee to meet a Federal raid upon that State. You will collect McCulloch's and Bell's brigades together as rapidly as possible, and move to Brownsville and prepare to move to Tupelo with these two brigades, the artillery, wagons, and prisoners. I have ordered Lieutenant-Colonel Forrest, with all of Bell's men at Trenton, to join you at Brownsville. I wish you to come on to Brownsville at once to see me before I go to Jackson. Bring Colonel Bell with you if no damage threatens your command. I will remain at Brownsville until 12 m. to-morrow.

Respectfully,

N. B. FORREST,
Major-General, Commanding.

MOBILE, ALA.,
April 13, 1864.

General S. COOPER,
Adjutant and Inspector General:

GENERAL: I have the honor to report that, in obedience to orders from the Adjutant and Inspector General, bearing date March 17, 1864, I have inspected the District of Mobile, Maj. Gen. Dabney H. Maury commanding, and lay before the Department the following remarks, as the result of my observations:

TROOPS.

The troops in this district number ———, organized into five brigades. The active available force which composes the garrison, and is located in the vicinity of Mobile, is 9,334.

I found them well equipped and clad, and evincing in the precision of their drill and maneuvers a marked and most creditable efficiency. Their arms were in good, indeed excellent, condition, and indicated conclusively the attentive care of battalion and company officers. The entire force compares favorably with any of similar numbers I have seen in the armies of the Confederacy.

THE FIELD ARTILLERY

is admirable. Guns of superior manufacture, and the horses and harness in unexceptionable condition.

THE FORTIFICATIONS

consist, as the Department has no doubt been previously informed, in addition to the forts at the mouth of the Bay of Mobile and those at the debouchure of the river into the harbor, of three lines. The outer line consists of new rifle-pits, very far out, and now abandoned as a line of serious defense. The inner line, more elaborate and extensive, was for a time the main reliance of the garrison, and although well engineered and constructed, is commanded by elevations immediately beyond, and was so near the suburbs as to have rendered necessary in the event of an attack a vast destruction of property, both without and within the line. The third or middle line of defense is now in process of construction, and consists of a line of ten heavy redoubts, armed with 8-inch columbiads, 42, 32, and 24 pounders principally, and connected by curtains.

They evince a scientific proficiency in engineering unsurpassed, if equaled, by anything on this continent, and are themselves the most eloquent evidence of the educated skill of the engineer in charge, Lieut. Col. Von Sheliha.

A portion of this defense extends across the mouth of the river. Batteries Gladden and McIntosh, both of which are now far advanced to a state of completion and properly defended, will prove sufficient to protect Mobile against a very formidable advance.

Below are Forts Morgan, Gaines, and Powell, the latter in process of being greatly strengthened since the last attack of the enemy upon it. It is, however, much to be regretted that the laboring force at the disposal of the chief engineer is greatly inadequate and daily diminishing. The impressed labor is being hourly returned to the planters, and no sufficient means has yet been provided to supply it.

The prices authorized to be paid by the Department have and will undoubtedly continue to fail in procuring it, while every consideration of prudence and economy suggest the employment of an effective force of laborers, who in six months might make Mobile impregnable.

From personal observation, as well as consultation with the major-general commanding and the chief engineer, I feel constrained earnestly to call the attention of the Department to this most important subject.

THE COMMISSARIAT

I found consisting of supplies adequate to the subsistence of the troops in the district for six months; they were well stored and of excellent quality. I append a schedule returned by the chief commissary.*

The supplies of the quartermaster, as exhibited to me, consisted only of corn in sacks and a small amount of damaged clothing. The report of the quartermaster was to the effect that he had, under or-

---

* Omitted.

ders from the War Department, turned over to Major Barnewall, assistant quartermaster-general, all supplies. As Major Barnewall informed me he reported direct to the Quartermaster-General at Richmond. I did not deem it within the scope of my instructions to inspect his stores or accounts. It would seem to be a most anomalous condition of affairs herein that, although abundant supplies may be in Mobile, a requisition for the most trifling supplies must pass through official form in this district, be forwarded to the Quartermaster-General at Richmond. and from him be returned to be filled by the assistant quartermaster-general within 100 yards of the point the requisition emanated from, after performing a journey of nearly 2,000 miles; and in addition is the erection of a department of supply within a military command, yet over which the responsible commander has no control. As the most conclusive elucidation of the practical operation of the system, I inclose a requisition with the various indorsements thereon,* this being handed me by Major-General Maury. I deem it my duty only to state the facts, for the information of the Department.

The general commanding has efficiently organized a laboring force, composed of persons sentenced by courts-martial to hard labor, and in so doing has not only provided a valuable available laboring force, but by organizing them into companies has given employment to a number of meritorious officers whose original commands had been expended in service. The system works well and is highly creditable in its details to Major Harris, the senior officer in charge. I append a report of the force.†

All which I saw afforded gratifying evidence of the wisdom which had committed the interests of the Confederacy in this district to the charge of the distinguished soldier in command. To him, Lieutenant-Colonel Sheliha, chief engineer, to Major Flowerree, assistant adjutant-general, and the officers of his staff, I am greatly indebted for the promptness and zeal with which they facilitated and aided my efforts in the inspection. I append a consolidated report of the forces here, with a roster of field and staff officers for each battalion, and various exhibits, affording in small compass information desired by the Adjutant and Inspector General.* I shall proceed from here immediately to the headquarters of Lieutenant-General Polk, and commence the inspection of his department and army.

I am, general, with high respect, your obedient servant,

GEORGE B. HODGE,
Colonel and Assistant Inspector-General.

SPECIAL ORDERS, ⎱ ADJT. AND INSP. GENERAL'S OFFICE,
No. 86. ⎰ *Richmond, April 13, 1864.*

* * * * * * *

XXVII. Maj. Gen. S. D. Lee is restored to the command of the whole cavalry force under the control of Lieutenant-General Polk.

By command of Secretary of War:

JNO. WITHERS,
Assistant Adjutant-General.

------

* Not found. † Omitted.

PRIVATE.]   DALTON, GA., *April* 13, 1864.
General BRAXTON BRAGG,
      Commanding Armies of the Confederate States:

MY DEAR GENERAL: I received your letter, and am sorry to inform you that I have done all in my power to induce General Johnston to accept the proposition you made to move forward. He will not consent, as he desires the troops to be sent here and it is left to him as to what use should be made of them.

I regret this exceedingly, as my heart was fixed upon our going to the front and regaining Tennessee and Kentucky. I have also had a long talk with General Hardee. Whilst he finds many difficulties in the way of our advancing, he is at the same time ready and willing to do anything that is thought best for our general good. He has written a long letter to the President, which will explain his views, &c.

When we are to be in a better condition to drive the enemy from our country I am not able to comprehend. To regain Tennessee would be of more value to us than a half dozen victories in Virginia.

I received a letter from General R. E. Lee on yesterday, and he says, "You can assist me by giving me more troops, or driving the enemy in your front to the Ohio River. If the latter is to be done, it should be executed at once." I still hope we shall yet go forward; it is for the President and yourself to decide. I well know you have to grapple with many difficulties, as the President has done from the beginning of this war. He has directed us thus far, and in him I have unbounded confidence. Should we, from the many impediments in the way, fail to move forward from this position we must not allow ourselves to be deceived as to where the enemy will make his main effort. So soon as that is discovered we should concentrate and beat them decidedly.

Since McPherson's corps has moved up from the Lower Mississippi to join the Army of the Potomac or that of the Cumberland, would it not be well for General Polk's troops to unite with this army, as we should then be in a condition to re-enforce General Lee in case it should be necessary?

Please present my kindest regards to the President.
      Yours, truly,

                                             J. B. HOOD.

                                    DALTON, *April* 14, 1864.
Col. B. S. EWELL,
      Richmond:

Assuming offensive must depend on relative forces. I shall be ready to do it whenever they warrant it. It will be a month or six weeks before we can expect the necessary transportation. I cannot foresee what force the enemy may then have. I do not think our present strength sufficient for defensive since Longstreet's withdrawal. No one is more anxious than I for offensive operations by this army. Ask General Bragg enemy's force at Missionary Ridge and his present estimate. See to my application for Manning, vice Washington.

                                             J. E. JOHNSTON.

COLUMBUS, *April* 14, 1864.

General FORREST,
    At Jackson, or elsewhere:

I have been disappointed in not being frequently advised of your movements, and am therefore at a loss as to the orders proper to give you. I have not heard from you in two weeks. It is indispensable that I should be kept constantly informed of your situation and of all your operations. You have been ordered to move your unorganized troops out of West Tennessee to Columbus for organization, to leave a force below Memphis, and to move with the rest of your troops to Tuscaloosa, Ala. These orders are hereby revoked and other orders will be issued you in a day or two; in the mean season use your discretion as to movements proper for you at the present moment, remembering that your command will be required against the movements of Sherman on North Alabama and Georgia so soon as they shall have commenced. You are hereby ordered to send two companies under an efficient and determined captain into the Mississippi bottom, about Austin, for the arrest of one Captain Reasons and Lieutenant Edwards, deserters from the Fifteenth Mississippi, who, with their company, have deserted and are marauding upon the people. They must be captured at all hazards. You will order the company of Captain King, of McNairy County, formerly of Polk's battery, to report to Major Morphis, of the same county, for duty in Tennessee and North Mississippi at Tupelo. You will also order all Alabama companies, battalions, or regiments to report for duty to the commandant of the post at Tuscaloosa.

L. POLK.

CHIEF PROVOST-MARSHAL'S OFFICE, FIRST DIST. ALA.,
        Mount Hope, Ala., April 14, 1864.

[Maj. J. C. DENIS:]

MAJOR: I arrived here on the 11th and found everything comparatively quiet in the district. The tory raids in the mountains are becoming less frequent, and it is very evident that their main object in these raids is plunder, not caring a cent whom they rob. I thin I can break up the whole clan as soon as I can organize 100 goodmen.

The five boat-loads of Yankees that came up the Tennessee River and landed opposite Eastport on Sunday, the 3d instant, marched up the Huntsville road; are encamped between Athens and Decatur. They are said to be a part of Beacher's [Veatch's] and Tuttle's divisions, and number between 3,000 and 5,000.

I have a reliable scout just in from within 2 miles of Decatur. He represents the Yankees at Decatur about 2,500 strong, and intrenched (not re-enforced), but that there are about 5,000 encamped a few miles north of Decatur. They have a pontoon bridge at Decatur. Their whole force in and around Decatur and Athens will not reach 10,000. General Dodge's headquarters are at Athens, and small squads of Yankees are encamped from Florence to Athens, say from 50 to 150 in a squad.

I will have arrangements in a few days to get early and reliable information of the strength and all movements of the enemy in and around Decatur and Athens.

So far as can be judged from the movements of the enemy, their object is to create a diversion of our troops toward Decatur, and to protect the line of the railroad from Nashville via Columbia, Athens, Huntsville, and to Stevenson, so as to enable them to repair the Nashville and Chattanooga Railroad, and thereby secure two lines of railroad instead of one to Chattanooga, and further to prevent our forces from making raids from this valley into Middle Tennessee. They may, however, intend a move south (as some suppose), still I cannot believe this to be their intention. If they should move south they will doubtless go in the direction of Gadsden via Somerville and Blountsville.

General Clanton is at Danville, 14 miles east of Moulton ; Colonel Nixon is at Moulton, Colonel Johnson at Courtland, and Major Bradford between Moulton and Decatur.

The Twenty-seventh and Thirty-fifth Alabama Infantry Regiments are near this place. The enemy believe our forces in the valley to be nearly equal to theirs. They stay closely in Decatur ; there are no fears felt of a raid in this direction.

Colonels Jackson and Ives, with 100 men each, crossed the Tennessee River on the night of the 12th, a few miles below Florence, and surrounded a camp of 48 Yankee cavalry, killed 4 and captured 42, a whole company, and all their officers, only 2 escaping. They also captured and brought to this side of the river about 65 good horses, saddles. and all the arms of the company. Colonel Jackson lost 1 man killed, none wounded.

The company belonged to the Ninth Ohio Cavalry, and was on detail duty gathering up beef-cattle. They had collected about 250 head, all of which were turned out and scattered. The expedition was somewhat hazardous, but was very successful.

There is no other post or provost-marshal office in this district. I do not think it expedient to establish any other for the present. If the enemy leaves Decatur there should be another office in the east and one in the west end of the district. Time will soon develop what is best to do in this respect.

I expect to enroll the names of every man in the district between the ages of sixteen and fifty, with a view of organizing all who are allowed to volunteer into companies for local defense. The names of those who will not volunteer I will turn over to proper conscript officers. By this means I expect to ascertain the names and localities of all deserters and tories, and will better enable me to catch them.

Very respectfully, major, your obedient servant,
JOHN W. ESTES,
Lieut. Col. and Chief Provost-Marshal, First District Ala.

N. B.—I have just received information that I believe to be reliable that the Yankees have sent several trains loaded with troops from near Decatur and Athens in the direction of Nashville within the last few days.

[Indorsement.]

OFFICE PROVOST-MARSHAL-GENERAL,
Demopolis, Ala., April 19, 1864.

Respectfully forwarded to Lieut. Col. T. M. Jack, assistant adjutant-general, for his information.

J. C. DENIS,
Provost-Marshal-General.

HEADQUARTERS MISSISSIPPI STATE TROOPS,
Tupelo, Miss., April 14, 1864.

Lieut. Gen. L. POLK,
    Commanding Department of Mississippi, &c.:

GENERAL: Your dispatch of 11th instant, inquiring when and where the State troops can be inspected, &c., was brought to these headquarters during my absence, or it would have received an earlier reply. At this time my command is so scattered under orders that it cannot be collected without special orders from the Governor before 26th instant, at which time all my troops are to be at this place.

I am, general, very respectfully, your obedient servant,
                                     S. J. GHOLSON,
                                         Major-General, &c.

GRENADA, *April 14, 1864.*

Lieutenant-General POLK:

Expedition to Sunflower a failure, owing to recent orders issued by commandant of post at Helena prohibiting any merchandise passing below that point. Troops continue to pass up river.

Very truly, your obedient servant,
                                     C. S. REDDELL,
                                         C. S. Army.

HEADQUARTERS FORREST'S CAVALRY,
Jackson, April 15, 1864.

Brigadier-General CHALMERS,
    Commanding Division:

GENERAL: The general commanding directs me to say that he has ordered Colonel Neely to move with his brigade to La Grange and report to you, with the exception of Colonel Duckworth and Lieutenant-Colonel Crews, who will move to this place, as previously ordered, so as to arrive here by Monday next if possible. The general commanding has also ordered about 200 men of Colonel Wilson's regiment, now here, to move and join you at La Grange; and should you find either commands or squads moving in this direction you will take them with you, except those mentioned (Duckworth and Crews).

The general directs that you will move to Okolona, and on your arrival report to Lieutenant-General Polk for further instructions.

Respectfully,

                                     J. P. STRANGE,
                                         Assistant Adjutant-General.

P. S.—Since writing the above the general commanding has directed Colonel Neely to carry out your orders, "to concentrate all his command, &c., at Somerville," except Colonel Duckworth and Lieutenant-Colonel Crews.

Respectfully,

                                     J. P. STRANGE,
                                         Assistant Adjutant-General.

SPECIAL ORDERS, }   COLUMBUS, *April* 15, 1864.
No. —.   }

Major-General Lee will move Jackson's division and Ferguson's brigade of his command into Alabama and take a position near Tuscaloosa. He will throw a part of his command up Jones' Valley, in the neighborhood of Elyton, and advance his scouts well up toward the Tennessee River, so as to be informed of the enemy's situation, strength, and purposes. He will establish a line of couriers from his headquarters to some convenient point on the railroad, so as to keep department headquarters constantly informed, and will report frequently. He will constantly advise Major-General Loring of the condition of things in his front.

Major-General Lee will also organize expeditions against the deserters and tories of North Alabama. He will arrest them, and will deal with all such as may be banded together for resistance in the most summary manner.

By order of Lieutenant-General Polk:

DOUGLAS WEST,
Acting Assistant Adjutant-General.

A PROCLAMATION.

HEADQUARTERS,
Demopolis, April 16, 1864.

To all soldiers in this department absent from their commands without leave:

The lieutenant-general commanding has had presented to him a petition signed by the senate and house of representatives of the Legislature of Mississippi, setting forth that a large number of the men now absent from their commands in this department, who in a moment of weakness were induced to abandon their duty and desert their colors, have seen reason bitterly to regret their want of fidelity and are anxious to return.

They set forth also that many of these men, by reason of the absence of mail facilities, never saw the act of pardon offered by His Excellency the President; that they would now gladly return but for fear of the punishment due their offenses, and ask that such an offer of pardon be again tendered them.

The lieutenant-general commanding is free to say that the experience of the past in this and other armies of the Confederacy is not favorable to the expediency of the measures proposed. He is nevertheless willing, in deference to the wishes of so large a body of influential citizens, to add one more effort to the list of those already made to recover these misguided men and restore them to the service of their country.

The lieutenant-general commanding therefore by this proclamation offers pardon to all soldiers of this department absent from their commands (including exchanged and paroled prisoners) who shall, within ten days after having knowledge of this proclamation, report for duty to their respective commands, or to the commanding officer of the post at Meridian, Miss.; provided, however, that this offer of amnesty shall not extend to any person who fails to report by the 20th of May next; provided also, that it shall not extend to any person who may have joined the enemy, and provided that it shall not include any commissioned officers who may have deserted.

The lieutenant-general commanding desires to add the expression of the hope that this last opportunity now presented for wiping out the disgrace which attaches to the characters of these men, and must follow and brand their posterity after them, will be availed of by them, and that he will thus be relieved from the painful duty of making examples of those who, in contempt of the claims of their country upon their services, and in defiance of all law, have not only deserted their standards, but by banding themselves together have rendered the property and lives of peaceable citizens insecure and reduced society to the condition of lawlessness and violence.

The offer of pardon hereby tendered is not confined to soldiers from Mississippi, but is extended to those of other States within this department; and if there be soldiers of other armies absent from their commands within this department who desire to avail themselves of an act of amnesty, the lieutenant-general commanding informs them that upon reporting to Meridian he will intercede with their commanders in their behalf.

By command of Lieutenant-General Polk:

THOS. M. JACK,
Lieutenant-Colonel and Assistant Adjutant-General.

☞ Circulate this.

RICHMOND, *April* 16, 1864.
Lieut. Gen. L. POLK,
    Demopolis:
Please inform me by telegraph where your infantry force is now located, or if moving, in what direction.

BRAXTON BRAGG,
General.

OKOLONA, *April* 16, 1864.
Lieutenant-General POLK :
On the 10th instant there were two divisions of infantry and four regiments of cavalry at Decatur, one division infantry at Athens and on their [way] to Nashville, and one division at Huntsville, all under command of Logan, and preparing for a movement in two columns down Jones' Valley in direction of Tuscaloosa and Coosa Valley toward Selma. The commands number about 20,000. Logan's headquarters at Huntsville. I will come to Demopolis.

JAS. M. BURTON.

JACKSON, TENN., [*April ?*] 16, 1864.
(Received 21st.)
Lieutenant-General POLK,
    Demopolis:
Yours of 11th instant with General Johnston's dispatch just received. Lieutenant-Colonel Kelley, of my old regiment, arrived yesterday from Tuscumbia. He states there are only two regiments

at Decatur. No enemy west of Tennessee River from Decatur down. Have also just received dispatch from Colonel Wisdom, dated Purdy, 15th instant, as follows :

> No enemy in this vicinity, and my information induces me to believe that all is quiet in the direction of Eastport. I dispatched you yesterday stating that Brigadier-General Chalmers, commanding McCulloch's and Bell's brigades, were ordered to Okolona by way of Abbeville, and Colonel Neely's brigade was ordered to follow without delay, to report to you on their arrival, 22d instant. No enemy this side of Decatur as far as I can learn. A force came to Tennessee River, opposite Waterloo: burned all the corn in that region and returned to Athens. If forage and rations can be sent to Tupelo, would, on account of position and water, prefer to stop there. Orders will reach me at Tupelo or General Chalmers at Okolona.

N. B. FORREST,
Major-General.

HEADQUARTERS,
Montevallo, Ala., April 16, 1864.

Lieut. Col. T. M. JACK,
    Assistant Adjutant-General :

COLONEL : I have the honor to state that I received a communication from Brigadier-General Ferguson, commanding brigade of cavalry, of date the 14th instant, informing me that he had arrived at Tuscaloosa, Ala., with his command, and that he would guard the approaches by way of Jasper and Elyton. He would in a day or two, "move toward either Elyton, in Jones' Valley, or toward Jasper, in Walker County, as the movements of the enemy may necessitate."

He sends no information of any enemy, nor have I received word from any other source. I have not had time to hear from those I have sent to the front for the purpose.

With respect, your obedient servant,

W. W. LORING,
Major-General.

HEADQUARTERS DISTRICT OF THE GULF,
Mobile, Ala., April 16, 1864.

Col. T. M. JACK,
    Assistant Adjutant-General, Demopolis :

COLONEL: Please say to General Polk that in consequence of the want of labor many important defenses here are still incomplete. I desire to hire negroes by the year; the chief engineer will pay $360 per annum and feed and clothe the slaves. Can General Polk aid me in procuring them from Mississippi? If any negroes should be captured from the enemy I hope the general will send them here to work.

I recommend that this place be not made a place of imprisonment for any other Federal prisoners. If there be reasons why they cannot be held at Cahaba, I will have a prison built at Greenville for those now here. Shall I return the medical officer to the enemy's lines who is a prisoner with this party?

There are several deserters from our army amongst them, who, having been recognized, will be tried by court-martial. There was an officer brought down in irons; no charges against him have reached me and I am still ignorant of the reasons for so confining him. If possible, 3,000 negroes should be kept at work here; I shall not be able to get any more from Alabama until after harvest. Farragut is in Pensacola still with a large fleet.

Respectfully, colonel, your obedient servant,

DABNEY H. MAURY,
Major-General, Commanding.

[APRIL 16, 1864.—For Taylor (T. H.) to Polk, about affairs in East Louisiana, see Vol. XXXIV, Part III.]

SPECIAL ORDERS, }   ADJT. AND INSP. GENERAL'S OFFICE,
No. 89.   }   *Richmond, April* 16, 1864.

*   *   *   *   *   *   *

XXXIX. Brig. Gen. John S. Williams, Provisional Army, C. S., is relieved from duty in the Department of East Tennessee, and will proceed to Dalton, Ga., and report to General Joseph E. Johnston, commanding, &c., for assignment to the brigade of Kentucky cavalry now commanded by Col. J. W. Grigsby, of Sixth Regiment Kentucky Cavalry.

XL. The First,* Fifty-fourth, and Fifty-seventh Regiments Georgia Volunteers will proceed by railroad, under the command of Brig. Gen. H. W. Mercer, to Dalton, Ga., and report to General Joseph E. Johnston, commanding, &c., to relieve the Fifth, Forty-seventh, and Fifty-fifth Regiments Georgia Volunteers.

The last-named regiments, under the command of Brig. Gen. J. K. Jackson, will proceed by railroad to Savannah, Ga., as they are successively relieved.

*   *   *   *

By command of the Secretary of War :

JNO. WITHERS,
Assistant Adjutant-General.

ORDNANCE OFFICE,
Dalton, April 16, 1864.

Brig. Gen. W. W. MACKALL,
Chief of Staff, Army of Tennessee, Dalton, Ga. :

GENERAL : The requisition for supplies of ordnance and ordnance stores from corps commanded by Lieutenant-General Hardee, transmitted through headquarters Army of Tennessee, is received. I have the honor to report :

Total arms in the corps, as per report of 16th instant	17,643
Effective strength of the corps per last report	16,941
Surplus of arms in corps	702
Required as per requisition	457
Excess of arms over effective men	1,159
Total number rounds of ammunition in the corps is	1,323,455
Required as per requisition	77,000
Total	1,400,455

*So much of order as relates to First Georgia Volunteers was revoked April 28, 1864.

Giving to one effective man 83⅓ rounds. By monthly consolidated statement of ordnance stores in the corps is reported 19,417 sets of infantry accouterments, 12,610 knapsacks, 18,001 haversacks, 16,888 canteens. By issuing the amount required there would be in the corps surplus 2,784 accouterments, 761 knapsacks, 3,144 haversacks, and 1,388 canteens.

From the above number can be seen that the requisition submitted for approval of lieutenant-general commanding corps or the reports forwarded to this office is erroneous.

The last requisition from the corps was approved on the 30th ultimo. The articles, except 138 rifles and 680 bayonets for smooth-bore muskets, were issued. To issue more arms than effective strength is only to lose them. Before the engagement on 25th February last, 356 arms were collected, besides those turned in by brigade officers of ordnance.

The stores required in the requisition can be supplied immediately, excepting knapsacks, bayonets, small-arms implements, navy-pistol cartridges, spurs, harness leather, and those articles with time can be obtained, being under fabrication. The leather is supplied by the quartermaster's department.

As to the certificate upon requisition "to supply the place of arms regularly condemned," I have to report that no certificate of board of survey was transmitted to this office.

I have sixty pistols at Calhoun, and if permitted to issue them to other commands than General Wheeler's I will order them.

The requisition is herewith returned for your approval.

I am, general, very respectfully, your obedient servant,

H. OLADOWSKI,
On Ordnance Duty.

CIRCULAR.]   HEADQUARTERS ARMY OF TENNESSEE,
Dalton, Ga., April 16, 1864.

I. In obedience to instructions from the honorable Secretary of War, Lieut. William W. Carnes, C. S. Navy, is authorized to select 170 men of this army to be transferred to the naval service. Commanding officers are hereby directed to afford him the necessary aid for the discharge of this duty. In making these selections no organization must be destroyed, and as far as practicable seamen will be taken.

II. Lieutenant Carnes will furnish this office with a return of the men selected, when orders for their discharge from the army will be given.

By command of General Johnston:

KINLOCH FALCONER,
Assistant Adjutant-General.

DALTON, *April 17, 1864.*

General BRAXTON BRAGG,
Richmond:

Scouts from Middle Tennessee report that on the 10th part of McPherson's corps, under Major-General Veatch, landed at Waterloo, on Tennessee River, and marched to Huntsville. More expected to follow. Mcpherson has been at Huntsville some time. General Maury is willing to send 3,000 infantry and two batteries from Pollard. Can it be done immediately?

J. E. JOHNSTON.

———

DEMOPOLIS, *April* 17, 1864.

General COOPER :

Scouts report from Vicksburg and Memphis a continued movement of enemy's troops up the Mississippi ; also arrival of troops at Waterloo from below, by way of Tennessee River. They march thence around the shoals on north side to Decatur, where they are concentrating. There are few troops on the Mississippi. Following just received :

On the 10th there were two divisions of infantry and four regiments of cavalry at Decatur, one division of infantry at Athens, one on the way from Nashville, and one division at Huntsville, all under command of Logan, and preparing for a movement in two columns down Jones' Valley, direction of Tuscaloosa and Coosa Valley toward Selma. The command numbers about 20,000.

L. POLK,
Lieutenant-General.

———

DEMOPOLIS, *April* 17, 1864.

General BRAGG,
Richmond :

Loring's division is at Montevallo, on railroad, 50 miles above Selma ; French's division at Lauderdale Springs, near Meridian ; Sears' brigade at Selma ; Cantey's at Pollard ; the rest in Mobile. Three of Lee's brigades of cavalry near Tuscaloosa ; two in front of Baton Rouge and Vicksburg ; one of Forrest's above Grenada, the rest in West Tennessee. Gholson's Mississippi brigade at Tupelo. I refer you to a dispatch of to-day to General Cooper.

L. POLK,
Lieutenant-General.

———

MOBILE, *April* 17, 1864.

Lieutenant-General POLK :

The fleet, with exception of six vessels, has left Pensacola.

D. H. MAURY,
Major-General.

———

HEADQUARTERS,
Demopolis, April 18, 1864.

His Excellency President DAVIS,
Richmond, Va. :

From dispatches sent to the War Department you will have seen that it is the purpose of the enemy to move in force down through the northern part of this State upon the iron and coal region, and upon Selma and Montgomery.

You are aware that the infantry force at my command is very small, consisting, aside from the Mobile garrison, of less than 8,000, a force entirely inadequate to resist a column of at least 20,000, the command preparing for the proposed movement. I hope I shall not again be subjected to the trial of feeling caused by having to deal with such a disparity of force; and I write respectfully to repeat the application I have already made to have my old division, now commanded by Major-General Cheatham, ordered to report to me. They are very anxious to come and I to have them. They consist now of about 4,000 effectives, and I am confident if I had them I could in a short time run up their number to near double their present strength by getting out of West Tennessee a large amount of the absentees who until now have not been within reach.

General Hood has three divisions and General Hardee has four. Cheatham's is one of those commanded by General Hardee. If I had that I would be content and would feel that I had a share at least of the troops available for the defense of this part of the general field, and some assurance of offering successful resistance to the proposed invasion of a State that has a claim to share in the common protection. Will you, Mr. President, allow me to press this upon your attention and ask you earnestly to let me have those troops? I am satisfied that, besides the direct movement on this department indicated above, there will be a heavy flank movement upon General Johnston via Decatur and Rome.

With the additional force asked for I could place myself in a position to strike the enemy in flank in turn. An amount of force equal to that asked for, it will be remembered, was taken from this department and assigned to General Johnston's Army of Tennessee when this department was not pressed. The existing condition of things should warrant their return. Besides it could be more useful to General Johnston from my point of attack than from his. I hope it may be sent me.

I remain, very truly and respectfully, your obedient servant,

L. POLK,
Lieutenant-General.

[Indorsements.]

APRIL 26, 1864.

Received and referred to General Bragg for perusal and remarks.

J. D.

I cannot concur in the general's apprehensions. The enemy cannot afford to dissipate his means in such an expedition. The transfer of the division to that locality would soon see another large portion of them on stolen horses marauding over the country.

BRAXTON BRAGG.

———

DEMOPOLIS, *April* 18, 1864.

Maj. Gen. S. G. FRENCH,
Lauderdale:

General Polk desires you to move with your command from Lauderdale via Gainesville to Tuscaloosa, and there await orders.

THOS. M. JACK,
Assistant Adjutant-General.

HEADQUARTERS, &c.,
Montevallo, Ala., April 18, 1864.

Lieut. Col. T. M. JACK,
   Assistant Adjutant-General:

COLONEL: A communication received to-day from General Lee tells me he has arrived at Tuscaloosa; that General Ferguson has been ordered to Jones' Valley, taking position at Elyton; that General Jackson would reach Tuscaloosa on the 18th and take position near that place till more definite information is obtained relative to the enemy, and will scout on all roads leading to the Tennessee River. He says he would move nearer the Tennessee River, but is informed that it will be impossible to subsist his command; says he is of opinion, from information in the last few days, that the movement from Decatur is exaggerated.

A soldier of this command, of good reputation, has reached here to-day from the Tennessee River, near Larkin's Ferry, leaving there a week ago; he was absent upon leave, but came back before his time expired. He says the enemy, about 5,000 strong, had crossed the ferry before he left, and this was the occasion of his returning. His father, who resides there and is an intelligent man, tells him that the tories are informed that the Yankees intend moving a force of about 12,000 in the direction of Rome, Ga.

I have not had time to receive anything from the officers sent to the front.

With respect, I have the honor to be, your obedient servant,
W. W. LORING,
Major-General.

SPECIAL ORDERS, }   HDQRS. DEPT. OF ALA., MISS., AND E. LA.,
   No. 109.   }   *Demopolis, Ala., April 18, 1864.*

*   ·   *   *   *   *   *   *

XX. Brig. Gen. P. D. Roddey will report with his command to Maj. Gen. S. D. Lee, Tuscaloosa, Ala.

*   *   *   *   *

By command of Lieutenant-General Polk:
DOUGLAS WEST,
   Assistant Adjutant-General.

HDQRS. ARMIES OF THE CONFEDERATE STATES,
Richmond, April 18, 1864.

General SAMUEL COOPER,
   Adjutant and Inspector General, Richmond:

GENERAL: General Bragg requests that you cause the following order to be issued, viz: To General Maury, at Mobile, to send 2,000 infantry (an organized brigade) to report to General Johnston at Dalton. Let First South Carolina [Regulars], Colonel Butler, and Twentieth South Carolina, Colonel Keitt, be sent from Charleston, S. C., to General Johnston, at Dalton, Ga., to be replaced (after they reach Dalton) by the Tenth and Nineteenth South Carolina, now in Army of Tennessee.

Please let the orders be sent by telegraph in cipher.

I am, general, very respectfully, your obedient servant,
JNO. B. SALE,
Colonel and Military Secretary.

HDQRS. ARMIES OF THE CONFEDERATE STATES,
Richmond, April 18, 1864.
General S. COOPER :

GENERAL : I learn by a note from General Lee that Longstreet has transferred Law's brigade to Buckner, and left it at Bristol. This should be corrected by telegraph. As the charges against General Law are not sustained by the Department he should be restored to his command. Allow me to suggest early action on McLaws' case. He should be with his division. Allow me to suggest General Holmes for the duty of organizing and commanding the reserves in North Carolina. General Lee suggests the movement of Beauregard's surplus forces this way, to be ready to relieve Pickett, who should go to him. As the re-enforcements to the enemy in Florida seem really to have been the removal of the enemy from there, ought not our troops to come on to North Carolina, instead of again being buried in the district system in Georgia and South Carolina ?

BRAXTON BRAGG.

———

RICHMOND, VA.,
April 18, 1864.
Maj. Gen. S. B. BUCKNER,
Bristol, Tenn. :

Send Law's brigade to Charlottesville to report to General Field. General Law will be relieved from arrest and put in command of it. The charges against him will not be further entertained.

S. COOPER,
Adjutant and Inspector General.

———

RICHMOND, VA.,
April 18, 1864.
General G. T. BEAUREGARD,
Charleston, S. C.:

Send First South Carolina [Regulars], Colonel Butler, and Twentieth South Carolina, Colonel Keitt, to General Johnston, at Dalton. Upon their arrival at Dalton, the Tenth and Nineteenth South Carolina Regiments, now in Army of Tennessee, will be sent to Charleston.

S. COOPER,
Adjutant and Inspector General.

———

CIRCULAR.]   HEADQUARTERS ARMY OF TENNESSEE,
Dalton, Ga., April 18, 1864.

General Johnston deems it advisable to suspend for the present the granting of furloughs.

By command of General Johnston :

KINLOCH FALCONER,
Assistant Adjutant-General.

———

QUARTERMASTER-GENERAL'S OFFICE,
April 19, 1864.

The letter of General Johnston, with inclosures, is respectfully returned to the Secretary of War, whose attention is invited to the report of Major Gibbons, inspector field transportation, herewith sent. The frequent calls for horses from that army, varying in number at different times, induced me to send Col. A. H. Cole, chief inspector of field transportation, directly to General Johnston, that every possible assistance might be given in supplying his wants, and he is still there. I am informed that officers have been dispatched to all the sources of supply within reach to add to the large number already furnished General Johnston, as shown by Major Gibbons' report. All reports from General Johnston's army show that they have been better supplied with forage during the past winter than any other portion of our forces in the field, and the stock ought, therefore, to be in better condition.

Respectfully submitted.

A. R. LAWTON,
Quartermaster-General.

[Inclosure.]

OFFICE INSPECTOR-GENERAL FIELD TRANSPORTATION,
Richmond, Va., April 18, 1864.

General A. R. LAWTON,
Quartermaster-General:

SIR : In obedience to your call of 15th instant for a "report of the number of animals that have been called for by General Johnston's chief quartermaster, and the number furnished," I respectfully submit the following statement :

On 1st February, 1864, the transportation of the army had been filled up and was thought complete, and Major Smith turned his attention to supplying General Beauregard. On 13th February Lieutenant-Colonel McMicken called for 500 artillery horses, and on the 14th March 700 mules for a pontoon train. February 25, Major Smith commenced to fill these requisitions, and has furnished 525 artillery horses and 125 mules.

The entire number shown by actual report to have been furnished the Army of Tennessee since November 1, 1863, is as follows :

	Mules.
Taken by General Hardee from Mississippi on his return to the Army of Tennessee	740
Taken by Brigadier-General Baldwin to the Army of Tennessee from Mobile, and not brought back	120
Taken by Brigadier-General Quarles to the Army of Tennessee from Mobile, and not brought back	180
Sent by chief inspector field transportation in Mississippi to the Army of Tennessee	600
Supplied by Major Smith from his inspection district	306
	1,945
Furnished to the army 755 horses	755
	2,701

Very respectfully,

WM. H. GIBBONS,
Major and Acting Inspector-General Field Transportation.

DALTON, *April 19, 1864.*

General BRAXTON BRAGG, *Richmond:*

On January 25 our chief commissary, authorized by Maj. J. J. Walker, sent a party into Northeastern Alabama to procure beef.

The party was sent back by Lieutenant-General Polk. The agent reports that their cattle were taken from them. I ask that Lieutenant-General Polk be required to permit this army to draw food from his department.

J. E. JOHNSTON.

HEADQUARTERS,
Dalton, Ga., April 19, 1864.
Major-General WHEELER,
Commanding Cavalry, Tunnel Hill:
GENERAL : General Johnston directs that you bring Martin's command as near Rome as possible, having due regard to obtaining forage.

By direction of General Johnston, a telegram was sent this morning to meet the officer commanding the cavalry arriving from East Tennessee, directing that that command should take post at Resaca. I have already sent you this information by telegraph.

Very respectfully, your obedient servant,
A. P. MASON,
Major and Assistant Adjutant-General.

DALTON, GA.,
April 19, 1864.
Major-General WHEELER,
Commanding Cavalry, Tunnel Hill:
General Johnston has directed that the cavalry arriving from East Tennessee * take post at Resaca. A dispatch to that effect has been sent to meet the commanding officer.

A. P. MASON,
Assistant Adjutant-General.

BRISTOL, *April* 19, 1864.
General JOHNSTON,
Dalton:
Southern men of intelligence and Confederate officers from Knoxville, as we learn through flag of truce, credit a current report that three army corps are moving from Nashville to Chattanooga, and it is positively stated that the Federals have the key to the signal in use in the Confederate signal corps. The key was obtained from a deserter.

B. R. JOHNSON,
Brigadier-General, Commanding Department.

HEADQUARTERS LEE'S CAVALRY,
Tuscaloosa, Ala., April 19, 1864.
Lieut. Col. T. M. JACK,
Assistant Adjutant-General, Demopolis, Ala. :
COLONEL : I have the honor to state, for the information of the lieutenant-general commanding, that Ferguson's brigade left this

* Under command of Col. G. G. Dibrell.

point yesterday for Jones' Valley. Jackson's division is in this vicinity. Ferguson has been directed to establish a line of couriers to Montevallo, sending duplicates of his reports to me to Major-General Loring, at Montevallo. Jackson starts several regiments to-day to the infected counties above.

From what Colonel Baker tells me it will be a difficult matter to find the haunts of the tories, as they go in small parties and can only be caught by dogs ; however, every effort will be made in the matter. I can hear nothing definite from Decatur, except that the enemy are there about 2,000 strong (common report). Roddey and Clanton are there and were expected to attack the place. I expect reliable information soon from the scouts I have sent above. Colonel Jackson sent 42 prisoners here yesterday ; he captured them near Florence. The major who came down with the prisoners said Colonel Jackson had been ordered by General Clanton to Moulton. I think the importance of the occupation of Decatur has been overestimated as to its importance.

I heard this morning that the force which landed on the Tennessee near Eastport and marched towards Decatur passed that point and continued up the river. I should have stated that Ferguson had also been instructed to operate against disloyal parties. Should I find a larger force can be used I will send it. Have a line of couriers to Montevallo.

I am, colonel, yours, respectfully,

S. D. LEE,
Major-General.

CONFIDENTIAL.]   HEADQUARTERS CAVALRY DEPARTMENT,
Canton, Miss., April 19, 1864.
Lieut. Col. THOMAS M. JACK,
Assistant Adjutant-General:

COLONEL : Ascertaining several days since that the enemy was making active preparations at Vicksburg for an extensive raid through Yazoo and Holmes Counties, the force to consist of cavalry and mounted infantry, and having here at the time but 500 men with which to meet him, I determined to use a little finesse to delay his movements until I could, if possible, obtain additional forces. The arrangement made by General Ross to procure supplies of clothing for his command presented the opportunity I desired. The parties in the Yankee lines revealed to me the fact that bribery had to be used extensively to procure the passage of the goods and cotton through Vicksburg, and that the highest Federal officials there had been secured by this corrupt means.

Ascertaining thus that General McArthur, in command at Vicksburg, was an interested party, I therefore informed the contractors that in order to secure the prompt delivery and removal of their cotton and the goods that there must be no expedition by gun-boats up the Yazoo and no raids against the Central Railroad ; that if either was permitted I should at once annul the contract, and that General McArthur might be so informed. These contractors reached Vicksburg two days since.

There were 1,000 cavalry and three regiments of mounted infantry in readiness to move, and it was publicly announced that they would start this morning. Information from Confederates in their lines was positive, and I accordingly made the best disposition of my limited force and prepared to meet them, as telegraphed you last night. I sent a staff officer to General Dennis' quarters at Big Black to-day, ostensibly on other business, but chiefly to obtain information regarding this movement and the Federal account of the recent battle on Red River. He telegraphs me to-day that the expedition has been deferred two weeks. The intelligence from Red River has doubtless reached you by telegraph.

My force is quite inadequate to properly protect the line of Big Black and the Yazoo, and I should be glad to have an additional regiment if it can be spared from the northern or eastern portion of the department. I have collected about 100 hands for repairs of railroad, and the work is being pushed forward vigorously.

I have thoroughly scoured the county of Yazoo for deserters and conscripts, and have forwarded them, and shall at the earliest moment the force can be spared take in hand the counties of Madison, Hinds, and Copiah.

I am, colonel, very respectfully, your obedient servant,

WIRT ADAMS,
Brigadier-General.

BRANDON, *April* 19, 1864.
Lieut. Gen. L. POLK:

Shall I destroy boats on Pearl River trading with the enemy?

A. B. WATTS,
Brigadier-General.

CHARLESTON, S. C., *April* 19, 1864.
(Received 19th.)
General S. COOPER:

Telegram of 18th instant received. Order for movement will be issued, but I beg earnestly to call attention of War Department to the fact that First South Carolina [Regulars] and eight companies of Twentieth South Carolina are essential as artillerists for defense of batteries on Sullivan's Island. Shall order be carried out? Please answer.

G. T. BEAUREGARD,
General, Commanding.

[Indorsement.]

Suspend order for the First Regiment only; another will be substituted.

BRAXTON BRAGG.

OKOLONA, *April* 20, 1864.
Lieut. Col. T. M. JACK,
Assistant Adjutant-General:

I arrived at this place this evening with 250 prisoners from Fort Pillow. Please send guard after them. Let me know when they will get here. General Gholson wishes to retain negroes captured to work on railroad. Will guard and be responsible for their safety.

JOHN GOODWIN,
Provost-Marshal, Forrest's Cavalry.

HEADQUARTERS FORREST'S CAVALRY COMMAND,
Jackson, Tenn., April 20, 1864.
Col. T. M. JACK,
Assistant Adjutant-General:

COLONEL: Governor Harris leaves for department headquarters this morning, and can give the lieutenant-general commanding a statement of affairs as they exist in West Tennessee.

I shall leave here with General Buford as soon as he arrives from Kentucky. A few days' delay have unavoidably occurred, as he had detachments out conscripting and recruiting when he received orders to move southward, and it was necessary to gather all up before leaving. I expect to leave here on 22d, day after to-morrow, as I think his Kentucky brigade will reach here to-morrow evening.

General Chalmers with three brigades will be at Okolona before this reaches you. Would be glad if the lieutenant-general commanding would send me orders to Tupelo, and designate the point at which he desires I should hold my command until a move is necessary. My scouts report no enemy west of Decatur, and if a move is made into Alabama I am of opinion it will be from Decatur, or between that and Guntersville.

Have ordered my chief quartermaster and commissary to move to Aberdeen, provided they do not receive orders to the contrary from the lieutenant-general commanding, which he will please give should he deem it proper for them to remain at Columbus. I have ordered Major Rambaut, acting commissary of subsistence, to get up some rations for the command at Okolona, as they can be used there or transported by rail to other points. My scouts have just returned from Florence, and report no enemy between that place and Clifton. The force which came to Waterloo has returned to Athens. There are a few scattering companies of tories on the east side of Tennessee River.

I am, very respectfully, your obedient servant,
N. B. FORREST,
Major-General.

HEADQUARTERS FORREST'S CAVALRY,
Jackson, Tenn., April 20, 1864.
Lieut. Col. THOMAS M. JACK,
Assistant Adjutant-General:

COLONEL: I wrote you on yesterday morning, per Governor Harris, giving you the movements of my command. After his departure, I received through General Chalmers a dispatch countermanding or revoking the orders to move south; as General Chalmers received the orders before they reached me, he sent back Bell's and Richardson's brigades, and orders were immediately sent then to Colonel Neely, commanding Richardson's brigade, to move down toward Memphis and drive the country back to this place, gathering all conscripts and absentees, and Colonel Bell was ordered to Cherryville to begin close to the Mississippi River, and moving back to this place, to perform the same service. General Buford, then moving south, was ordered to spread out his Kentucky brigade and sweep the country.

Consequently, with the necessary detachments requisite to be sent out in all directions to protect me against any movement of the enemy, my command is much scattered, and it will take time to get them together.

This morning I received a letter from the lieutenant-general commanding, in which he expresses disappointment at not hearing from me oftener; also indicating requirements of my command against the forces of General Sherman.

I have written and forwarded by couriers letters to the lieutenant-general commanding as frequently as I was able to do so; also sent telegraphic dispatches to Tupelo to be forwarded, and am at a loss to know why they have not reached department headquarters. It is true that for more than a week at a time, during my trips to Union City, Paducah, and Fort Pillow, it was impossible to write or dispatch you, being in the saddle myself and commanding my troops in person; results, however, of all my operations as soon as they had transpired have been promptly forwarded.

It will require until the 1st of May to get all my troops together and move out, and my orders to brigade commanders sent out this morning direct that all be gathered up and concentrated at this place on that day, and expect to reach Tupelo with my entire command by the 5th of May, with all conscripts and deserters we catch. Have also ordered Brigadier-General Chalmers to leave one regiment of McCulloch's brigade on the Tallahatchie and to move back with the balance within the lines of my department and gather up all squads, detached companies, and conscripts found in the country and meet me at Tupelo on the 5th proximo, with his entire wagon and ordnance train.

I have also directed all my wagons and artillery to be moved up to Tupelo; have also ordered my commissary to get up 20,000 rations for my troops and all the forage possible by the 5th, using my teams to haul it to the depots and get the trains, if possible, to bring it up to Tupelo or this side of there, provided it meets with the approval of the lieutenant-general commanding.

I would like to have everything there in order to fully organize the command and shoe up the horses, most of which are in bad condition for want of shoes.

I would be glad also, if the lieutenant-general commanding could spare the time, that he would come up on the train and meet me at Tupelo on the 6th or 7th proximo. His presence would facilitate me in disposing of conscripts and organizing commands. As preparatory to the move indicated in his letter, it will require me to be all the time with my command.

I am, colonel, very respectfully, your obedient servant,

N. B. FORREST,
Major-General.

———

HEADQUARTERS FORREST'S CAVALRY,
Jackson, April 20, 1864.

Brigadier-General CHALMERS,
Commanding Division:

GENERAL : The general commanding directs me to say that you will leave one regiment, the wagon train belonging to the same, and 60 rounds of ammunition to the man, to scout from Waterford to Memphis, and watch the movements of the enemy.

The general directs that you will order two companies to proceed to the Mississippi River bottom, arrest and dismount one Captain Reasons and Lieutenant Edwards, and the men in company with them, and all others found absent from their commands without proper authority, and subject to conscription, and take them to Tupelo. The general also directs that you will order your ordnance and wagon train to Tupelo, and with the balance of your command will sweep the department of the major-general commanding from the Mississippi River and the southern boundary (Tallahatchie River), arresting all officers and men found absent from their commands without legal authority, and all men subject to conscription, and will arrive with your command at Tupelo by the 4th or 5th of May. You will send forward your quartermaster for the purpose of assisting in collecting forage at Tupelo for your command. The general also directs that you order Captains Rogers and Wimberly's and all other unattached companies to report to him at Tupelo by the 4th or 5th of May.

You will order Capt. W. H. Forrest to report to the general commanding at Tupelo, and will send and have the men with him arrested and taken to Tupelo. The prisoners and artillery will be sent to Columbus, where the artillery will remain until filled up.

Respectfully,

J. P. STRANGE,
Assistant Adjutant-General.

CONFIDENTIAL.]   HEADQUARTERS LEE'S CAVALRY,
                                 Tuscaloosa, Ala., April 20, 1864.

Lieut. Col. T. M. JACK,
     Assistant Adjutant-General, Demopolis, Ala.:

COLONEL : I have received no reply as yet to my communication with reference to removing my headquarters and the expedition proposed into Middle Tennessee and Kentucky, but hope to hear to-day. I urge that the Memphis and Charleston Railroad be at once completed to Corinth to facilitate furnishing supplies near the Tennessee River in case any movement is contemplated in that direction ; it is the only way forage, &c., can be furnished, as the Tennessee Valley is exhausted.

The railroad from Corinth to Barton Station, 28 miles west of Tuscumbia, on the Memphis and Charleston Railroad, is but little out of order and can be easily repaired. This I consider all-important, looking to future operations.

The move indicated I consider important, as it will divert a large force to garrison the railroad and to follow after the expeditions and so weaken the force at Chattanooga as to enable General Johnston to beat it. If the enemy do not garrison the railroad heavily it can be destroyed.

I do not think there is any move contemplated in Mississippi by the enemy, and that their entire strength will be brought to bear in Virginia and Georgia, and that the two battles there will materially affect the grand result, whereas any small expedition in Mississippi or Alabama will be subservient to those in Virginia and Georgia. A flank move from this department will disarrange all their plans. I also ask that direction be given to furnish wagons, &c., for the pontoon train now being built by Captain Wintter, near Gainesville, to be used by my command or by the infantry command as in the opinion of the commanding general may be expedient. I ask this as most of the pontoons are now constructed.

I am, colonel, yours, respectfully,

S. D. LEE,
Major-General.

GENERAL ORDERS, ⎰　　　HEADQUARTERS HOOD'S CORPS,
　No. 54.　　⎱　　　Dalton, Ga., April 20, 1864.

I. The regiments of this corps will have their battle-flags plainly marked with their numbers and the State to which they belong. This is done that in the event of the loss of colors no misunderstanding may arise as to who lost them.

II. But one stand of colors will be used by any regiment in time of battle.

By command of Lieut. Gen. J. B. Hood, commanding:

J. W. RATCHFORD,
Assistant Adjutant-General.

Abstract from return of the Army of Tennessee, General Joseph E. Johnston, C. S. Army, commanding, April 20, 1864 ; headquarters Dalton, Ga.

Command.	Present for duty.		Effective total present.	Aggregate present.	Aggregate present and absent.	Pieces of artillery.
	Officers.	Men.				
General headquarters	19	171	171	200	252	
Hardee's army corps :						
Headquarters	30	233	232	304	416	
Infantry	1,906	18,125	17,604	23,615	34,940	
Artillery	48	980	946	1,243	1,628	48
Total Hardee's corps	1,984	19,338	18,782	25,162	36,984	48
Hood's army corps :						
Headquarters	25	162	161	210	288	
Infantry	1,507	18,080	17,633	22,367	34,802	
Artillery	44	885	861	1,078	1,333	36
Total Hood's corps	1,576	19,127	18,655	23,645	36,423	36
Cavalry corps :						
Headquarters	9			9	9	
Martin's division	169	1,757		2,538	6,477	
Kelly's division	170	1,495	1,070	2,303	4,305	
Humes' brigade	122	1,228	1,072	1,553	3,012	
Roddey's brigade (two regiments)	44	562	471	742	1,038	
Artillery	17	354	27	420	587	22
Total cavalry a	540	5,396	2,640	7,565	15,458	22
Artillery reserve	50	822	792	1,016	1,247	36
Engineer troops	17	412	400	460	601	
Grand total	4,186	45,266	41,449	58,048	90,965	142

a Roddey's brigade transferred to General Polk's department, and has left the army, with the exception of the Fifty-third Alabama Regiment and Twenty-fourth Alabama Battalion, which are on picket in our immediate front and number 471 effectives. Morgan's and Iverson's brigades (Martin's division) are in rear recruiting their horses, and are not included in the effective total of the army. The entire artillery of Wheeler's cavalry corps, with the exception of one section of Ferrell's battery (effective total 27), is in rear recruiting horses.

*Organization of Buckner's Division, Brig. Gen. Bushrod R. Johnson, C. S. Army, commanding, April 20, 1864.**

Johnson's Brigade.	*Gracie's Brigade.*
Col. JOHN S. FULTON.	Brig. Gen. ARCHIBALD GRACIE, Jr.

17th Tennessee, } Col. R. H. Keeble.
23d Tennessee, }
25th Tennessee, } Lieut. Col. John L. Mc-
44th Tennessee, } Ewen, jr.
63d Tennessee, Col. Abraham Fulkerson.
Detachments,† Capt. Nathan Dodd.

41st Alabama, Col. Martin L. Stansel.
43d Alabama, Lieut. Col. John J. Jolly.
59th Alabama, Col. Bolling Hall, jr.
60th Alabama, Maj. Hatch Cook.
23d Alabama Battalion Sharpshooters, Maj. Nicholas Stallworth.

Jackson's Brigade.

Brig. Gen. ALFRED E. JACKSON.

Thomas' regiment,‡ Lieut. Col. James R. Love.
Walker's battalion,‡ Lieut. Col. James A. McKamy.
Levi's (Virginia) battery.
Burroughs' (Tennessee) battery. §
McClung's (Tennessee) battery. §

DALTON. *April 21, 1864.*

General BRAXTON BRAGG,
        Richmond:

In my dispatch of 19th great injustice was done to Lieutenant-General Polk. Papers just received from him show that he did not interfere with procuring supplies for this army, but put a stop to criminal proceedings.

J. E. JOHNSTON.

BRISTOL, *April 21, 1864.*

General J. E. JOHNSTON,
        Dalton:

Enemy's cavalry, under Stoneman, are making strong demonstrations in this direction from Kentucky. I report this, as it may be a part of a general movement.

S. B. BUCKNER.

CIRCULAR.]   HEADQUARTERS HARDEE'S CORPS,
                Dalton, Ga., April 21, 1864.

The battle-flags of this corps. known as "the Virginia battle-flag," will have inscribed on them the number of the regiment and the State to which it belongs ; the number in the upper angle formed by the cross and the name of the State in the lower angle.

By command of Lieutenant-General Hardee :

T. B. ROY,
Assistant Adjutant-General.

---

*As shown by inspection reports of Lieut. Col. Archer Anderson, assistant adjutant-general. Jackson's brigade at Carter's Depot, the others near Zollicoffer.
† From the Sixteenth Georgia Battalion and the Third, Thirty-first, Forty-third, Sixtieth, Sixty-first, and Sixty-second Tennessee Regiments.
‡ Otherwise known as the Thomas (North Carolina) Legion.
§ Detached at Saltville, Va,

HEADQUARTERS DEPARTMENT OF EAST TENNESSEE,
Bristol, April 21, 1864.
General S. COOPER,
Adjutant and Inspector General, Richmond, Va.:

GENERAL : It is proper that on assuming command of this department I should briefly state its condition.

It is almost entirely exhausted of supplies beyond the actual wants of citizens. After General Longstreet's troops shall have gone, including Brigadier-General Law's brigade, which will leave for Charlottesville to-morrow, there will be left in this department the following troops:

Johnson's and Gracie's brigades of infantry, of my proper division, and the greater part of Wharton's infantry brigade, formerly belonging to General Samuel Jones' department; in all, about 3,500 effective infantry ; in addition to this a few bridge guards.

Cavalry: Jones', Vaughn's, Giltner's, and Morgan's brigades ; perhaps near 4,000 effectives. Their condition is lamentable. The horses are so much reduced as to be unfit for any hard service. It is impossible to forage them in this vicinity, and for that reason their late commander, Major-General Ransom, was compelled, under authority received from my predecessor in command, to disperse them over a wide extent of country, from the Big Sandy, in Kentucky, to near Asheville, N. C. They are much exposed, and can contribute little in their present positions in the defense of this section of country. The spring is unusually backward, affording as yet no grass that can be relied on to sustain the animals for any work. It is only by constantly changing their localities that they can be kept alive.

I respectfully make the following suggestions : Saltville is the vital point of this section of the country ; that point and the line of the railway are exposed to raids from Kentucky, through Pound Gap and up the Louisa (or Levisa) Fork of the Sandy, especially by the latter road. Rapid movements of cavalry are essential to an effective defense. They cannot be made unless I am furnished with corn. Discipline cannot be restored or maintained if the commands are under the necessity of straggling for supplies. Small supplies of corn are beginning to arrive, but as yet not enough to bring about any decided amelioration in the condition of the cavalry and their animals.

The horses of one entire battalion of artillery are in North Carolina. I cannot recall them until I can feed them. The battalion, as a result, is disabled.

If my command is adequately supplied I am confident that, though small, it will render the Government effective service. You may rely upon every exertion being made here to collect all that the country can spare for the troops. But this department will not maintain either the troops or the animals that belong to it.

Let me ask, in order that I may be enabled to render efficient services to the Government, that you will divert, for the use of these troops, such supplies as can possibly be spared from other points.

In this connection I will also state that the troops of this department proper and part of those formerly belonging to the Department of Western Virginia have been mixed together to some extent during their service in this department in the same organization. Am I to regard the troops which I find serving in this department as belonging to it, or am I to consider the troops now with me and formerly comprising part of the command of General Jones as belonging properly to General Breckinridge? If the latter, what disposition must I make of these troops? They consist of Wharton's brigade of infantry, and the greater part of Jones' brigade of cavalry, and part of King's battalion of artillery. While there can be no want of harmonious co-operation between General Breckinridge and myself, whether this department remains separate or not, it is very desirable that I should know what I am to rely upon as my appropriate command.

I am, general, respectfully, your obedient servant,

S. B. BUCKNER,
Major-General, Commanding.

DEMOPOLIS, *April 21, 1864.*

Brigadier-General CHALMERS,
Abbeville, en route for Okolona:

I have ordered General Forrest to send a brigade to Grenada, and fearing that Forrest may not be enabled to inform you in time, I desire that you will send a brigade at once, informing General Forrest. A movement is now being made from Vicksburg up Yazoo River, about 1,500 strong, infantry, 250 cavalry, and a few pieces of artillery. Adams' brigade is moving to oppose it. Move the brigade ordered to co-operate with Adams; send a battery with the brigade, or a section at least. Answer.

L. POLK,
Lieutenant-General.

CHIEF PROVOST-MARSHAL'S OFFICE, FIRST DIST. ALA.,
Mount Hope, Ala., April 21, 1864.

[Maj. J. C. DENIS:]

MAJOR: I beg leave through you to make the following statement to the lieutenant-general commanding:

In a word, this district is almost destitute of subsistence for man or beast. There is not corn enough in this valley to support the citizens if there were no troops here, and cannot support the troops which are now here over one month and not that length of time without causing extreme suffering to the people.

Many families are compelled to suffer or leave here if some means of transporting subsistence is not provided, for there are no teams to do it. This great scarcity was caused by Yankee raids carrying off a large portion of negroes and teams of nearly all the large farms, and the country being compelled to subsist a large number of our own cavalry who have been regularly stationed here. The enemy must be forced to fall back so we can get subsistence from the north side of the Tennessee, or this district will finally have to be given up if subsistence cannot be brought from some other place.

With a view to the relief of the citizens who are now subsisting the troops which are or may be sent here, and of finally forcing the enemy to give up North Alabama, I would respectfully suggest to the general commanding the great necessity, propriety, and practicability of speedily repairing the Mobile and Ohio Railroad to Corinth and the Memphis and Charleston Railroad from Corinth to Cherokee, in Franklin County, Ala., 36 miles east of Corinth and within 18 miles of Tuscumbia. and the cars be placed on the same at the earliest day. If this can be done it will enable the citizens to procure subsistence to enable them to raise a good crop this year, and will afford means of transportation sufficient to subsist all the troops that will be likely to be sent into this section of the country. Cherokee is the key of the valley in going from the valley to North Mississippi or West Tennessee; would be a good starting point for any movement into West Tennessee, Middle Tennessee, or to check any movement of the enemy south from Decatur or Huntsville. Cherokee is 61 miles from Decatur, dirt road in good condition; 11 miles from Iuka, and about 8 miles from nearest point on the river.

In summing up advantages that would arise from repairing the railroad to Cherokee, it will not be amiss to note some danger and disadvantages that would have to be overcome and guarded. ·

Corinth would have to be occupied, and the enemy could land a force at Eastport, 9 miles from Iuka, and cut the road at any time if not prevented, but this can be prevented by placing a few pieces of rifle cannon on the height below Eastport, which could sink any boat they have sent there for six months, as their gun-boats are wood.

By preventing these boats from running above Eastport it will check the extensive trade that is regularly transacted between the Yankees and people of North Alabama in cotton, &c.

In order to place the condition of the road and the amount of damage done to it before the lieutenant-general I have sent an officer to Corinth with instructions to minutely inspect the road from that place to Cherokee. He did so, and you will find his report herewith inclosed, which shows the road to be in much better condition than I supposed, and that it can be placed in order with but very little labor, compared with the inestimable benefits and conveniences which would result from its repair.

The road from Cherokee to Tuscumbia, a distance of 18 miles, the track is at least one-half torn up and a great many of the ties burnt; from Tuscumbia to Courtland, 23 miles, is badly damaged, nearly all of the rails torn up and burnt and the ties burnt; from Courtland to Decatur, 22 miles, the road is but very little damaged.

I hope that the general will give this matter due consideration, and will pardon me for intruding my suggestions upon his consideration.

Very respectfully, your obedient servant,

JNO. W. ESTES,
Lieut. Col. and Chief Provost-Marshal First Dist. Ala.

[First indorsement.]

OFFICE PROVOST-MARSHAL-GENERAL,
Demopolis, April 28, 1864.

Respectfully forwarded to Lieut. Col. T. M. Jack, assistant adjutant-general.

J. C. DENIS,
Provost-Marshal-General.

[Second indorsement.]

HEADQUARTERS,
Demopolis, Ala., April 29, 1864.

Respectfully referred to Major Peters, chief quartermaster, for his information and recommendation in the premises.

By command of Lieutenant-General Polk:

THOS. M. JACK,
Assistant Adjutant-General.

[Third indorsement.]

OFFICE CHIEF QUARTERMASTER,
Demopolis, April 30, 1864.

I recommend that the suggestions of Lieutenant-Colonel Estes be adopted and the road promptly and speedily repaired, for the reasons stated by him.

Respectfully, &c.,

THOS. PETERS,
Quartermaster, &c.

[Inclosure.]

MOUNT HOPE, ALA., *April* 18, 1864.

Lieut. Col. JOHN W. ESTES,
Chief Provost-Marshal, District of North Alabama:

COLONEL: In compliance with Special Orders, No. 1, office chief provost-marshal First District North Alabama, I proceeded to Corinth, Miss., and inspected the Memphis and Charleston Railroad from that point to Cherokee Station.

The road from Corinth to Burnsville, a distance of 15 miles, is in good repair. The bridge over Yellow Creek, 1 mile east of Burnsville, has been burnt; one-half of the timbers destroyed. Said bridge is about 80 feet in length and 10 feet high; could be repaired easily, as good green timber could be procured within 200 yards of the place. Three and one-half miles east of Burnsville there is a bridge 60 feet in length and 10 feet high, which has the trestle on one side cut; the remainder in good repair. One mile east of this place a bridge of some length; two trestles and 6 cross-ties burnt. Two miles west of Iuka, a bridge has been slightly damaged by fire; could be repaired in two hours. Three miles east of Iuka, the timbers of a cattle-pit, 6 feet in length, have been burnt. From Iuka to Bear Creek, a distance of 7 miles, the damage to the road consists of a trestle 6 feet high and 30 feet long, totally burnt; bridge over Clear Creek, 40 feet long, 20 feet high, partially destroyed; 19 crossties burnt and 3 rails torn up. Road in good order from that point to Buzzard Roost Creek, 1 mile east of Dickson; said bridge is supported by three trestles, one of which is gone; remaining timbers good. From Buzzard Roost to Cherokee the road is in good repair. Timber adequate to repair the damage above mentioned is contiguous to the road. A large number of cross-ties ready for use are at different points on the road. An adequate supply of water-tanks, in good repair, are on the road. General Sherman, in October last, repaired the road to Cherokee, since which time no damage has been done to the road except the bridges and trestles mentioned. The rails and cross-ties generally are in good condition. The citizens have repaired the road for hand-cars to Iuka.

Respectfully submitted.

F. L. B. GOODWIN,
Captain.

MOUNT HOPE, ALA., *April* 21, 1864.

Lieut. Col. THOMAS M. JACK,
Assistant Adjutant-General:

COLONEL: I have just received the order from you, through Major Jones, to forward a report at once, and that you had not received a report from me since I left Demopolis. I have reported every week by courier-line established from this point to Tupelo, Miss.

The enemy still occupy Decatur with a strong force on the opposite side of the river. General Roddey has invested the place with his cavalry force. In the present condition of affairs I do not feel safe in scattering my force, and therefore keep them together so as to be able to retreat if necessary. This affair will be settled in a few days, when I can attend to my duties here.

I have the honor to request that with my command and the assistance of the citizens, which will be cheerfully given, I be permitted to build the Memphis and Charleston Railroad from Corinth to Cherokee, Ala., which I think, in a military point of view, to be highly essential to the army in Mississippi, and it would be an act of humanity to the citizens in the Tennessee Valley, who are almost on the point of starvation, and many of them have not nor can they procure subsistence for their families to supply them until wheat harvest; among them, general, some of your own relatives and friends.

The following is a letter to me inclosing the report of Captain Goodwin, sent by Colonel Estes to examine the road from Corinth to Cherokee:

> MOUNT HOPE, ALA.,
> *April 20, 1864.*
>
> Colonel JACKSON:
>
> Colonel Estes ordered me to send a copy of my report* in regard to the Memphis and Charleston Railroad to you, and request that you would write to General Polk on the subject, urging the necessity of having the road repaired immediately.
>
> The opinion of the citizens on the road is that it could be repaired in thirty days with a small force. The Mobile and Ohio Railway will be repaired to Corinth in a month, so some of the hands report. Colonel Estes thinks it very essential in a military point of view, as well as for the benefit of the citizens, that the road should be repaired.
>
> Respectfully,
> F. L. B. GOODWIN.

Very respectfully, colonel,

JAMES JACKSON.
Colonel, Commanding 27th Alabama Regiment Volunteers.

HEADQUARTERS FORREST'S CAVALRY,
Jackson, Tenn., April 21, 1864.

(Via Holly Springs, April 23, 1864; via Meridian, April 25, 1864. Received Demopolis, April 25, 1864.)

Col. THOMAS M. JACK,
Assistant Adjutant-General:

Your dispatch of the 19th is just received. McCulloch's brigade from Holly Springs has been ordered to move to Grenada, but owing to long and rapid marches will be compelled to advance slowly. Twelve transports loaded with infantry have passed up the Mississippi River; destination not known. All quiet in this section and on Tennessee River.

N. B. FORREST,
Major-General.

---

*See p. 806.

OKOLONA, *April* 21, 1864.

Lieutenant-General POLK :

Dispatch received. Will send as directed. There are 37 negroes.

J. GOODWIN,
Captain and Provost-Marshal.

HEADQUARTERS LEE'S CAVALRY,
Tuscaloosa, Ala., April 21, 1864.

Lieut. Col. T. M. JACK,
Assistant Adjutant-General, Demopolis, Ala.:

COLONEL : I received the orders relative to General Roddey's command this morning. Have sent instructions for as large a portion of this command to remain in the Tennessee Valley as can be subsisted ; rest to come to this point.

The last reports represent the enemy as 4,000 strong at Decatur, fortifying.

Have received no reports as yet from my own scouts. Ferguson reports he cannot stay in Jones' Valley, and I have ordered him to the railroad to get supplies, keeping his scouts, &c., well up Jones' Valley. Ferguson reports from above Elyton. Have directed that the supplies should not be exhausted in the valley.

There is nothing further of interest to report.

I am, colonel, yours, respectfully,

S. D. LEE,
Major-General.

HEADQUARTERS DEPARTMENT OF EAST TENNESSEE,
Bristol, April 21, 1864.

Brig. Gen. A. E. JACKSON :

GENERAL : I am directed by the major-general commanding to inform you that a raid is threatened in the direction of Saltville. He will go up in that direction to-morrow, and wishes you to assume command for the present of the cavalry in your front. If the raid should be an extensive one, it may descend the railroad, coming from direction of Pound Gap. In case it takes place, you should have scouts on this side as well as on the other side of your position. If the raid should occur, the bridges must be destroyed by all means, rather than to permit the enemy to hold them. The general will keep you advised as well as possible of the progress of the raid. You should communicate with General Vaughn, Ashe County, N. C., advising him of what is transpiring, and in case of necessity co-operate with him.

Very respectfully,

S. F. CHIPLEY,
Aide-de-Camp.

DEMOPOLIS, *April* 22, 1864.

General CHALMERS,
Panola, Miss. :

I telegraphed you yesterday to move one brigade down to unite with General Adams in opposing a movement of the enemy up Yazoo from Vicksburg. I now order you to add another brigade to that sent. You will take command of the division yourself. If the battery captured is in condition to be used, take it with you. I will send another * from Aberdeen. Communicate this to General Forrest and move rapidly. Answer.

L. POLK,
Lieutenant-General.

Mr. HART : Send this dispatch to Okolona also, and instruct the commander of the post to send it forward to General Chalmers, who may be coming that way from the direction of Abbeville. Send it also to General Forrest.

L. POLK,
Lieutenant-General.

JACKSON, TENN.,
April 22, 1864.
Lieut. Col. T. M. JACK,
Assistant Adjutant-General:

COLONEL : I respectfully acknowledge receipt of orders last night which places McCulloch's brigade at Grenada to co-operate in protecting the country east of Yazoo River, &c., which orders have been promptly given to Brigadier-General Chalmers. I had hoped, however, to collect my entire command at Tupelo (except one regiment), and before it moved again to have it thoroughly inspected, organized, and full and satisfactory reports made as to its numbers, condition, &c. ; and if at all consistent with the good of the service I trust the lieutenant-general commanding will order back McCulloch's brigade, except the regiment deemed absolutely necessary to remain on the Tallahatchie, to report at Tupelo for the purposes above stated, and place on duty at Grenada some command whose duties have not been so arduous, and whose animals are in suitable condition for service.

A review of the operations of my command since December last will, I think, justify me in saying that time and opportunity should, if possible, be given me to shoe up and rest my horses, and place my troops in the best possible condition for future service, and to render to the department proper field returns and inspection reports, and to thoroughly organize it at the earliest moment practicable.

I am making arrangements to have all my troops, conscripts, and deserters at Tupelo by the 5th or 6th proximo, and to prepare them for any service required.

There has been no movement of the enemy of any importance since I last wrote you.

Grierson came out with about —— men as far as Mount Pleasant and within 12 miles of Holly Springs, but has returned. He dare not venture across the Wolf or Tallahatchie, consequently his scouts are confined to the State Line road and the country between those rivers.

I am, colonel, very respectfully, yours, &c.,
N. B. FORREST,
Major-General.

---

* Morton's battery was designated to join Chalmers.

HEADQUARTERS LEE'S CAVALRY,
Tuscaloosa, Ala., April 22, 1864.
Lieut. Col. T. M. JACK,
   Assistant Adjutant-General, Demopolis, Ala.:
COLONEL: I have the honor to invite the attention of the lieutenant-general to the dismounted men in my command. Many of them
are unable to mount themselves, and they are of no use to my command or to the service as they are; it is impossible for them to
keep up on marches, and many of the depredations committed are
by those men in rear of the column. I recommend that such of them
as cannot mount themselves and the Government will not mount
be transferred to the infantry, and an equal number be transferred
from the infantry who can mount themselves. I prefer the dismounted men being transferred without an equivalent rather than
they should remain as they are.
   I am, colonel, yours, respectfully,

S. D. LEE,
Major-General.

ENGINEER OFFICE, *Mobile, April 22, 1864.*
Capt. L. J. FREMAUX,
   Engineer in Charge Lower Bay Line, Fort Gaines:
CAPTAIN: The Natchez, having been thoroughly overhauled,
leaves here at 4 o'clock this evening with orders to report to you for
the placing of the main ship-channel obstructions.
   Please inform Captain Gallimard that I fully coincide with his
views regarding Sughee Point as the key position to the western
part of the lower bay line. Unfortunately want of hands and
transportation will render it necessary to abandon that work for the
present, and turn our attention to more important points. The redoubt east of Fort Morgan once finished we may reassume operations
at Sughee Point. Fort Gaines does not require our attention for the
present. Please stop all operations at that point until the completion of the new redoubts at Fort Morgan, Fort Powell, and Sughee
Point justify us in reassuming operations there.
   Very respectfully, your obedient servant,
V. SHELIHA,
Lieut. Col. and Chief of Engineers, Dept. of the Gulf.

DALTON, *April 22, 1864.*
Major-General WHEELER:
   GENERAL: Information of the enemy's position near Ringgold and
Graysville would be valuable; I mean as to whether they have forti-
fied there, and, if so, where and in what manner. If you can get
such information please do so; if not, be so good as to inform me.
   Very respectfully, &c.,

J. E. JOHNSTON.

DALTON, *April 22, 1864.*
Major-General WHEELER:
   General Johnston has examined your letter giving your picket-
line as proposed.
   He says cavalry posted as close to us as Varnell's Station could

not give any timely notice of the advance of an enemy. He thinks your pickets should keep well up to the enemy's line, and cover our front, the bending of the line around our right flank does not, in his opinion, give as good security as its extension to the east in a direct line, and makes your line as long if not longer.

A scouting party was this morning captured by a regiment of the enemy's cavalry at Spring Place. This we hear from citizens. He calls your attention to this.

Respectfully, your obedient servant,

W. W. MACKALL,
Chief of Staff.

RICHMOND, VA.,
April 23, 1864.

Lieut. Gen. L. POLK,
Demopolis, Ala.:

Arms for the Trans-Mississippi Department must not be stopped. You will furnish such escort as may be required.

S. COOPER,
Adjutant and Inspector General.

RESACA, GA., *April 23, 1864.*

General MACKALL,
Chief of Staff, Dalton:

My division of cavalry has just arrived here. Camped one brigade upon each side of river.

G. G. DIBRELL,
Colonel, Commanding.

SPECIAL ORDERS,   ADJT. AND INSP. GENERAL'S OFFICE,
No. 95.   . *Richmond, April 23, 1864.*

*   *   *   *   *   *   *

XXXIV. The telegraphic order of April 5, 1864, from Lieut. Gen. L. Polk, commanding Department of Alabama, Mississippi, and East Louisiana, directing Brig. Gen. D. Ruggles and staff to proceed to Richmond, Va., and report to the War Department, is hereby revoked.

General Ruggles and staff will proceed to Demopolis, Ala., and report to Lieut. Gen. L. Polk, commanding, &c., for assignment to duty.

*   *   *   *   --

By command of the Secretary of War:

JNO. WITHERS,
Assistant Adjutant-General.

HEADQUARTERS ARMY CONFEDERATE STATES,
Richmond, April 23, 1864.

Lieutenant-General POLK,
Demopolis:

If Loring's division is not essential for immediate operations in your department, order it to join Johnston at Dalton. It should move direct to Rome, by Blue Mountain railroad, marching over the unfinished part, taking its transportation with it. Answer by telegraph.

B. BRAGG.

HEADQUARTERS CAVALRY BRIGADE,
Near Elyton, Ala., April 23, 1864.
Maj. Gen. S. D. LEE,
Commanding Cavalry:
GENERAL : The inclosed memorandum from Captain Thomas was received yesterday evening ; that officer represents the enemy as concentrating at Decatur. and says they have moved all their force from Huntsville to that place. His account, and that of one of Henderson's scouts, sent you yesterday, do not agree exactly. I hope to hear from Coffey by night.

I will remain, if practicable, in this valley to-morrow, and start for the railroad on the day following, by which time I hope forage may be in readiness.

I have not been able to learn of the existence of any body of tories and deserters large enough to warrant an expedition anywhere within my reach, and as the movement would be so very severe on my horses, have not sent out on the chance of coming upon any straggling ones.

While writing this the inclosed letter from Coffey and note from General Roddey have been received and are respectfully forwarded.*

Respectfully, your obedient servant,
S. W. FERGUSON,
Brigadier-General.

[Inclosure No. 1.]

APRIL 22.

Memorandum of information given by Captain Thomas, of General Loring's staff, who returned this evening from scout to vicinity of Decatur. He left the Tennessee Valley yesterday morning :

Enemy's force at and around Decatur estimated between 10,000 and 15,000 of infantry ; cavalry, two regiments. Thought that a raid is intended in direction of Rome, or its vicinity. General Roddey returned several days ago. General Clanton is ordered by General Bragg to report to General Johnston, at Dalton. General Clanton's force, 360 men, moved out with his command Thursday morning to attack the enemy ; I think at Decatur.

S. W. FERGUSON,
Brigadier-General.

[Inclosure No. 2.]

DANVILLE, *April* 21, 1864.
Brig. Gen. FERGUSON,
Commanding Brigade Cavalry:
GENERAL : I learn from Generals Clanton and Roddey that the enemy at Decatur are thought to be the advance guard of a large army of 30,000 men intended to operate on Johnston's flank or against

─────────────────

* Roddey's note not found.

Selma. They are not prepared to move at present, but have large reserves at the different depots on the railroad to Nashville and are said to be collecting and forwarding extensive supplies of commissary and quartermaster's stores ; there is also a force at Florence with numerous flat-boats, though General Clanton thinks this is to prevent our own forces from crossing.

There are but two cavalry regiments at Decatur, but others are said to be on the way from Nashville. Both the generals here express the opinion that another brigade in this vicinity would, in the present situation of affairs, be useless, and it could not be subsisted without the greatest difficulty and leaving the people entirely destitute, but that a reserve force at Tuscaloosa and Elyton could be brought up at any time soon enough to meet the enemy in the mountains. Clanton is leaving this morning with his brigade to report to General Wheeler. Patterson's brigade, of Roddey's command, takes his place.

The tories in the mountains are very quiet ; I saw none of them. I will camp in this neighborhood and rest my horses while awaiting your orders, unless something unexpected turns up, in which event I will advise you.

I am, general, with great respect, your obedient servant,

A. B. COFFEY,
Lieutenant, Commanding Scouts.

P. S.—General Roddey thinks if there is no rain the river will be forded in two days, and that a force of cavalry then thrown into the country west of Pulaski could do effective service.
Respectfully,

A. B. C.

HEADQUARTERS LEE'S CAVALRY,
Tuscaloosa, April 23, 1864.
Lieut. Col. T. M. JACK,
Assistant Adjutant-General, Demopolis :

COLONEL : I have the honor to inclose a scout report from vicinity of Decatur ; it is the only reliable information received since my last. Every one speaks of the country above this as exhausted, and I fear all the cavalry in the Tennessee Valley will have to be moved to this vicinity. Have ordered Jackson's division about 12 miles below this point, to be convenient for forage. Ferguson is ordered to the railroad within 25 miles of Montevallo, as the forage will not support him in Jones' Valley ; he keeps his scouts well up the valley.

I am, colonel, yours, respectfully,

S. D. LEE,
Major-General.

[Inclosure.]

APRIL 20, 1864.
General LEE :

SIR : The force at Decatur and vicinity, including Athens and Huntsville, is between 6,000 and 8,000. At Decatur and railroad junction opposite Decatur are three brigades of infantry and two regiments of cavalry; artillery train not large, but wagon train is

very large. They have Decatur strongly fortified and a good pontoon bridge across the river. The railroad is used at present to supply their army at Chattanooga, and General Dodge's army is supplied chiefly by wagons. They have no hard bread on hand, or but very little.

VOORHEES.

The bearer of this informs me that Roddey with all his force is at Hillsborough, 9 miles from Decatur, and Clanton at Danville.

S. W. FERGUSON,
Brigadier-General.

DEMOPOLIS, April 24, 1864.

Officer commanding troops of General Forrest at Okolona:

I have ordered General Chalmers, with the brigade he has with him, to the Yazoo River to co-operate with General Wirt Adams against a movement of the enemy going up that river. Order Chalmers' other brigade to move so as to join him, passing by Lexington ; instruct its commander to send forward a courier to find out where General Chalmers' command may be joined. Morton's battery has been ordered to join General Chalmers. Let the movement be made promptly. Answer.

L. POLK,
Lieutenant-General.

HEADQUARTERS LEE'S CAVALRY,
Tuscaloosa, April 24, 1864.

Lieut. Col. T. M. JACK,
Assistant Adjutant-General, Demopolis:

COLONEL: I have the honor to inclose a copy of a letter * from one of my staff, Major Jones, from near Decatur.

The major knows every one in the Tennessee Valley, and I consider his report reliable. From all the information I can gather, it is my opinion that the occupation of Decatur is merely to secure the use of the two railroads from Nashville to enable the enemy to throw supplies into Chattanooga, and also to give them a threatening point to prevent your sending re-enforcements to Johnston. I do not think any move is intended now, as the enemy are quite deliberate in their occupation of the country north of the Tennessee River. It will, however, be necessary to keep a force in this vicinity, as the enemy could readily cross at Decatur and move with their cavalry on Selma. They do not seem to be accumulating stores in the vicinity of Decatur, their object being to guard well the railroads leading from Nashville to Chattanooga. I think, colonel, the enemy can be anticipated by a cavalry raid into Middle Tennessee from this department. The fords on the Tennessee River will soon be practicable in the vicinity of Muscle Shoals, and from all I can learn they do not watch the Tennessee River lower than Florence, so with a pontoon train a force could be readily thrown across opposite Corinth. The enemy seem quite nervous about the fords. A force of 30,000 is reported in the vicinity of Nashville, apparently waiting the opening of the campaign. I will have the fords examined and hope to be able to

---

* Not found.

send a more satisfactory report as to the enemy across the river and toward Nashville soon. The valley of the Tennessee is said to be nearly exhausted. I send several other reports.

I am, colonel, yours, respectfully,

S. D. LEE,
Major-General.

HEADQUARTERS LORING'S DIVISION,
Montevallo, Ala., April 24, 1864.

Lieut. Col. THOMAS M. JACK,
Assistant Adjutant-General:

COLONEL: I sent Captain Thomas, an officer of my staff, into Northern Alabama soon after my arrival here; he returned yesterday. After traveling the road by way of Blountsville to Danville or Houston, the headquarters of Roddey and Clanton, he went as near Decatur as was possible, and came back by the way of Day's Gap and Elyton.

The only enemy he could hear of was that at Decatur, on both sides of the Tennessee River, estimated from the best information he could obtain about 10,000.

He does not think it possible for a force, however small, to support itself between this and the Tennessee on any of the roads leading here: the country is barren and desolate, and the people suffering for supplies. It was difficult to subsist himself and horse. Along the valley of the Tennessee there are some supplies. The opinion up there seems to be that the enemy intend taking that way in a raid upon Rome. If our forces are expected to operate against a raid in that direction, would it not be advisable to throw some supplies to Talladega or some other place on the railroad above here, as there is none to be had for either man or horse? Their moving to Decatur instead of Whitesburg, which is 10 miles by a good turnpike from Huntsville and 20 by land from Decatur, or to Guntersville, 30 miles from Huntsville and 50 from Decatur, both places on the river and on the line of march to Rome, would make it appear that it was not their intention to go there.

Respectfully, your obedient servant,

W. W. LORING,
Major-General.

HEADQUARTERS FORREST'S CAVALRY,
Jackson, April 24, 1864.

Brigadier-General CHALMERS,
Commanding Division:

GENERAL: The general commanding directs me to say you will find inclosed copy of dispatch received from Colonel Neely, giving movements of the enemy. The general commanding directs that you will order Colonel McCulloch's brigade, with the exception of the one regiment ordered to be left to scout between Waterford and Memphis, to proceed to Grenada with his ordnance and wagon trains, provided the enemy are not moving on you from Memphis.

The general commanding directs that you will obtain a field re-

port of Colonel McCulloch's brigade before leaving, as he desires you to have a complete report made of your command on your arrival at Tupelo.
Respectfully,

J. P. STRANGE,
Assistant Adjutant-General.

[Inclosure.]

HDQRS. FIRST BRIG., FIRST DIV., FORREST'S CAVALRY,
Near Whiteville, April 20, 1864—midnight.
Major-General FORREST :
GENERAL : My scouts report Grierson, with about 1,200 men, without artillery or wagons, crossed to-night at Lenman's shop, near the Marshall Institute. This shop is on the Memphis and Holly Springs road, 6 miles southeast of Collierville and about 9 miles from La Fayette. Two hundred men in La Fayette to-day; they were inquiring for the Macon bridge, and it was thought by citizens they were going to La Grange. I have sent a courier to Colonel Bell, at Dancyville, to-night.
Very respectfully, your obedient servant,

J. J. NEELY,
Colonel, Commanding Brigade.

ROME, GA., *April* 24, 1864.
General W. W. MACKALL,
Chief of Staff :
I am here with 1,300 men. Cantey's brigade was directed to this point by General Wright, awaiting orders.

J. F. CONOLEY,
Colonel Twenty-ninth Alabama, Commanding.

DALTON, *April* 24, 1864.
COMMANDING OFFICER, C. S. ARMY,
Rome :
Complete the defenses as quickly as possible. Use the labor of the troops. Let the engineers get negroes also if practicable.

J. E. J.

DEMOPOLIS, ALA.,
April 25, 1864.
General BRAXTON BRAGG :
GENERAL : I inclose you a roster of officers serving in staff departments at Montgomery.* I am sorry to say that it is not perfect, as some names are omitted, viz, Maj. A. M. Barbour, assistant quartermaster, and Captain Gonzales, acting as quartermaster under orders from General Johnston. There are too many officers at Montgomery, especially in the quartermaster's department. Several per-

---
* Not found.

sons acting in official capacity at that post were found to be without commissions. The enrolling officer and quartermaster were duly notified of the fact. Their names will be found on the inclosed roster. On reaching here I find the following to be the distribution of the forces of Lieutenant-General Polk : Loring's division at Montevallo, French's division at Tuscaloosa, Sears' brigade at Selma, Lee's cavalry division at Tuscaloosa, Wirt Adams' brigade on Yazoo River, Chalmers' brigade at Panola. Forrest's division is yet in Tennessee, but is expected at Tupelo toward the end of the week.

There is no complete roster of the staff departments at the headquarters of General Polk. The returns are but partial, although every effort has been made by the chiefs of the different departments to effect a full return. I hope that it will be perfected before I get through. The roster of quartermasters, incomplete as it is, shows that there are 173 quartermasters in the department, exclusive of cavalry. Many quartermasters and commissaries have never been bonded, and I have instructed that the names of such be handed over to the conscript officers, and that quartermasters will not pay their accounts. General Polk has organized a provost-marshal system for his department as follows : He has divided it into nine districts and eighteen sub-districts. There is a captain in each sub-district and a lieutenant-colonel in each district, the whole under the control of a provost-marshal-general at headquarters. These officers are selected from those who have been wounded or become supernumerary. The object of the organization is to arrest absentees and deserters, and break up the bands of marauders and robbers which now infest the department. It is at present sustained by detachments made from the army, but it is the design of General Polk to use the companies organized for local defense for this purpose.

Colonel Walter this day received his orders to proceed to Georgia, and will leave this evening. I shall go to Columbus, Miss., to-morrow.

I am, general, very respectfully, your obedient servant,

GEORGE WM. BRENT,
Colonel and Assistant Adjutant-General.

DEMOPOLIS, *April 25, 1864.*

General BRAGG :

I refer you to my dispatch of 17th instant to General Cooper. I have no reason to believe it the enemy's intention to abandon the movement therein indicated, and in view of the important interests at stake I think it not prudent to remove that division from my front for the present.

L. POLK,
Lieutenant-General.

OFFICE ASSISTANT CHIEF QUARTERMASTER,
Demopolis, April 25, 1864.

Maj. G. W. JONES.

Controlling Quartermaster Tax in Kind, Marion, Ala.:

MAJOR : It is very important that forage be furnished to the troops at Tuscaloosa and Montevallo. Will you please give your subordi-

nate tax-in-kind quartermasters and agents orders to ship all corn on the Warrior River, for two-thirds of the distance from Tuscaloosa to the mouth, to Tuscaloosa, also all corn on the river above Tuscaloosa, to that place, and to ship all corn on the Tombigbee above here to this place? Will you also direct all fodder at Marion and other convenient points to be baled and shipped to Montevallo? It has become necessary to supply corn from this department to the Army of Tennessee. You will therefore please see that no shelled sack corn is used in any case where the ear corn can be substituted. The orders from General Polk on this point are imperative.

Respectfully, your obedient servant,

J. W. YOUNG,
Major and Assistant Quartermaster.

DEMOPOLIS, *April 25,* 1864.

Brigadier-General CHALMERS:

Morton's battery was ordered on the 22d to move from Aberdeen so as to intercept you at Lexington. Send a courier so as to meet him with orders. Report to me your movements every six hours. A brigade has been ordered from Okolona to join you. I hope to intercept the enemy and cut off his retreat from Vicksburg. Keep in communication with General Adams.

L. POLK,
Lieutenant-General.

DEMOPOLIS, *April 25,* 1864.

Brigadier-General CHALMERS :

The order for you to move to the assistance of Adams is revoked. Make the disposition of your troops ordered by General Forrest, and move yourself with the rest to Tupelo with expedition. An officer from General Bragg will be there to inspect Forrest's command.

L. POLK,
Lieutenant-General.

DEMOPOLIS, *April 25,* 1864.

Brig. Gen. WIRT ADAMS,
Yazoo City (via Canton):

The order to General Chalmers in regard to co-operation with you is revoked.

L. POLK,
Lieutenant-General.

DEMOPOLIS, *April 25,* 1864.

F. C. WHITTHORNE,
Telegraph Operator, Forrest's Cavalry, Okolona:

The order to General Forrest is hereby revoked.

L. POLK,
Lieutenant-General.

DEMOPOLIS, *April 25, 1864.*
General FORREST,
Jackson, Tenn. (via Holly Springs):
Enemy returned to Vicksburg. Chalmers ordered to leave one regiment at Waterford and move with the rest of his command to Tupelo. Brigade ordered to join Chalmers from Tupelo ordered back to Tupelo, also battery of Morton ordered to return to Aberdeen. An officer from Richmond here on his way to Tupelo to inspect your command; you will leave such of it as you may desire in Tennessee and Kentucky and proceed yourself immediately to Tupelo to meet him.

L. POLK,
Lieutenant-General.

HEADQUARTERS,
Demopolis, Ala., April 25, 1864.
Colonel DUMONTEIL,
Commanding Fourteenth Confederate Cavalry:
COLONEL: You will order the companies of Gonzales and Mills, of your regiment, to report to Col. John S. Scott for temporary duty, and will order the rest of your regiment promptly to Pearl River and picket all the crossings from the head of Honey Island past Fordsville, Columbia, and Monticello, and as much farther as your command will allow. The object of this movement is to prevent all persons between the ages of seventeen and fifty from passing across the river from West to East Louisiana until further orders. You will also, after posting your command, report to Col. John S. Scott for orders. You are expected to require of your command the utmost fidelity and vigilance in the performance of the duty assigned them.
Very respectfully, colonel, your obedient servant,

THOS. M. JACK,
Assistant Adjutant-General.

HEADQUARTERS,
Demopolis, Ala., April 25, 1864.
Col. J. S. SCOTT:
COLONEL: The lieutenant-general commanding instructs me you will find inclosed in a copy of a letter instructions to Colonel Lowry for the Sixth Mississippi Infantry, indicating a campaign with which you are expected and hereby directed to co-operate against deserters and conscripts. Colonel Dumonteil will be posted by orders direct from these headquarters as indicated, and will be instructed to report to you for this temporary service. You will order three picked companies of the Ninth Louisiana Battalion, under a suitable officer, to be posted as indicated to cross Pearl River; also the companies of Mills, Gonzales, and Bryan, and the company from the Third Louisiana, to take position as indicated under Lieutenant-Colonel Hill. Order Colonel Powers to take position with his regiment on the line indicated. You will then post your own regiment upon Powers' left, extending to river below Bayou Sara. If there be other troops in East Louisiana or Mississippi, south of

the railroad, you will take charge of them and employ them as you may think most serviceable to the campaign. Captain Roberts will be found in Mississippi getting up a battalion. You will avail of all the information within your reach to ferret out the skulkers, and you will see that such young men as have good social positions and have hitherto evaded service be not spared. Orders upon this point are imperative. You will see that all who are liable to military service under existing laws, between the ages of seventeen and fifty, are enrolled and required to repair under orders, with an accompanying military force, to Jackson, Miss., where they will be held until organized and distributed. What has been said to Colonel Lowry is repeated to you, that in the prosecution of this campaign you are allowed to exercise a sound discretion in the execution of its details. You will nevertheless bear in mind that the country which is the theater of this campaign has been sadly demoralized and none other than the most vigorous and decisive measures will serve to impress its inhabitants with a sense of their duties to their Government and to bring it back to a sound and healthful moral condition. You will keep a list of all captures, and if in the execution of your orders you are resisted by force of arms you will not hesitate to punish the offender with death upon the spot. It is of the utmost importance that this movement should be made without a day's delay. You will therefore proceed to its execution immediately upon the receipt of these orders. You will keep yourself in immediate and constant communication with Colonel Lowry, so that co-operation shall be understood. You will keep me advised of the progress of the movement every day by telegraph, and by written communication more fully every three days. You will keep an accurate account of all arrests you make.

Very respectfully, colonel, your obedient servant,

THOS. M. JACK,
Assistant Adjutant-General.

[Inclosure.]

HEADQUARTERS,
Demopolis, Ala., April 25, 1864.

Colonel LOWRY :

COLONEL : The lieutenant-general commanding directs me to say that he has received your several reports of your operations with great satisfaction, and conveys to you and your command his thanks for the prompt, efficient, and vigorous manner in which you have conducted your campaign. The impression made by it has been felt, not only in the army but by the whole department, and must tell most favorably upon the success of our cause. I am instructed by him to say that he desires you to push your operations down Pearl River toward its mouth ; to deploy your troops so as to move upon Honey Island and clear it out, driving such men as may have sought refuge there over into Louisiana. You will enter upon a new campaign against all absentees and conscripts found in East Louisiana and Southwestern Mississippi. In this campaign you will have the co-operation of all the cavalry force under the command of Col. John S. Scott, commanding that district, and the desire of the lieutenant-general is that you make such thorough work in your operations as not to require them to be repeated. The lieutenant-general's orders to Colonel Scott are that he direct Colonel Dumonteil, commanding cavalry regiment, now in Copiah, to move eastward to Pearl River and to deploy it down that river so as to cover all the crossings as low down as the head of Honey Island, which will be about the point at which your right will rest after crossing that river. He will thus be in a position to prevent their recrossing above that point. He will, at the same time, post three companies of the Ninth Louisiana Cavalry Battalion, under Captain Amacker, near the mouth of the river, extending across it from Shieldsborough to Mandeville. These companies will prevent escape to Fort Pike on the lake shore. From Mandeville he will order four other cavalry companies, under the command of Lieutenant-Colonel Hill, to picket along the lake shore extending westward from the mouth of the Amite. From this point the regiment of Colonel Powers will be posted up the Amite, so as to picket it above Port Hudson. This line will run generally parallel with the Mississippi and within 7 miles of the river at Baton Rouge. Upon Colonel Powers' extreme left Colonel Scott's regiment will be posted so as to extend to the river below Bayou Sara. A cordon of pickets will thus be established down Pearl River to its mouth ; thence along the lake shore to within a short distance of the Mississippi River ; thence northward of that river to the Homo Chitto. This cordon will prevent the escape either to New Orleans or west of the Mississippi. After crossing the Pearl River with your command you will deploy your troops so as, in conjunction with the cavalry which will close in and co-operate with you, to drive the men you are pursuing northward and make their escape impossible. You will give instructions to arrest every man capable of bearing arms from seventeen to fifty, and to concentrate them at Jackson for organization and distribution. As you pass on up the river you will keep well on to the Mississippi, so as to clear out the bottoms and as far as possible the villages along its banks. In the prosecution of this campaign you are allowed to exercise a sound discretion in the execution of its details. You will nevertheless bear in mind that the country into which you are now sent has been sadly demoralized, and none other than a vigorous and decisive measure will serve to bring it back to a sound and healthful moral condition. It is of the utmost importance that the movement should be made without a day's delay. You will therefore proceed to its execution immediately upon the receipt of these orders. You will keep yourself in immediate and constant communication with Colonel Scott, so that the co-operation shall be understood. You will keep me advised of the progress every day by telegraph, and by written communication by courier more fully every three days. You will also keep an accurate account of all arrests you make.

Very respectfully, your obedient servant,
THOS. M. JACK,
Assistant Adjutant-General.

HEADQUARTERS FORREST'S CAVALRY,
Jackson, April 25, 1864.
Lieut. Col. THOMAS M. JACK,
Assistant Adjutant-General :

COLONEL : Everything quiet in this section. One brigade of infantry and fourteen pieces of artillery have been landed at Memphis. They came up the river. My entire command is engaged conscripting and arresting deserters. They are scattered in all directions, but are moving toward this place ; will have all concentrated here by the 30th, and will reach Tupelo by the 5th or 6th proximo. I shall move myself via Bolivar and Ripley, and any dispatches for me will meet me on the road.

I would be glad if the cars would run as far above Tupelo as possible, as I have about 80,000 pounds of bacon which I shall carry in wagons to Corinth, and send it down for my command on hand-cars until it meets a train.

I am, colonel, very respectfully, yours, &c.,
                                     N. B. FORREST,
                                         Major-General.

HEADQUARTERS FORREST'S CAVALRY,
                        Jackson, April 25, 1864.

Lieutenant-General POLK,
    Commanding Department:

GENERAL : A reliable man named Griswell, who used to be a scout of mine in Middle Tennessee, has just arrived. He reports that the enemy are evacuating the Northwestern Railroad, and that they are moving everything to the front by the Nashville and Chattanooga and Tennessee and Alabama Railroads to Chattanooga, and I am satisfied that the enemy's move will be on Dalton. He represents everything as being moved in that direction.

Much having been said in the Northern press in regard to the massacre at Fort Pillow, I shall forward you by next courier copies of all the correspondence in regard to the demand for surrender and a statement of all material facts ; an extra copy of same will also be sent you, with a request to forward to the President. Captain Young, the provost-marshal at Fort Pillow, now a prisoner, can corroborate all the facts, as he was the bearer of the enemy's flag of truce, and it would be well to have him taken care of on that account.

I am, general, very respectfully, yours, &c.,
                                     N. B. FORREST,
                                         Major-General.

HEADQUARTERS LEE'S CAVALRY,
                    Tuscaloosa, Ala., April 25, 1864.

Lieut. Col. T. M. JACK,
    Assistant Adjutant-General, Demopolis:

COLONEL : I received to-day the order from Richmond restoring me to the command of all the cavalry in General Polk's department. I have not yet assumed the command, as I desire the views of the lieutenant-general. So soon as I hear from him I propose establishing my headquarters at Columbus, Miss., as the most central point. If the command is to be a permanent one I shall relinquish the immediate command of my division, and a major-general should be appointed in my place. The command is large enough for two major-generals if I am to have all the cavalry, as is contemplated by the order. Brigadier-General Jackson was recommended for promotion by General J. E. Johnston and myself. This promotion will still meet my views.

Should the Department not deem it proper to promote General Jackson, I would suggest the names of Brig. Gen. F. C. Armstrong and J. R. Chalmers as competent ones for the position. I would like the command divided into two divisions, under two major-generals, and styled "Cavalry Corps, Department Mississippi, Alabama, East Louisiana, and Southwest Tennessee," or "Cavalry Corps, Lieutenant-General Polk's Department." I will take this occasion to state that I am not aware as to what influences were brought to bear to cause the order to be issued.

My desire is for active service in the field ; this I prefer with a smaller command rather than I should not be actively employed, which I fear will be the case with a command so scattered as the one to which I have been assigned. I ask if it is consistent with the views of the lieutenant-general that my recommendation for a move into Middle Tennessee and Kentucky (made while at Starkville) be again considered. I think a cavalry force of 8,000 or 10,000 sent into the country indicated on the opening of the campaign will be a powerful diversion for our armies, both in Virginia and Georgia, and will weaken the force of the enemy in Georgia to such an extent that our arms will certainly be successful there. I propose moving Jackson's division to the vicinity of Columbus, leaving Ferguson in Alabama. I do not think all the force now here is needed.

I ask the views of the lieutenant-general on the above points if he deems it proper to give them. I will soon have a large pontoon train ready except the wagons.

I am, colonel, yours, respectfully,

S. D. LEE,
Major-General.

SPECIAL ORDERS, }   HEADQUARTERS,
 No. 116. }   *Demopolis, Ala., April 25, 1864.*

*   *   *   *   *   *

XIII. Brig. Gen. G. J. Pillow will report to Maj. Gen. S. D. Lee for assignment.

*   *   *   *   *

By command of Lieutenant-General Polk :

THOS. M. JACK,
Assistant Adjutant-General.

HOUSE OF REPRESENTATIVES, CLERK'S OFFICE,
Richmond, April 25, 1864.

His Excellency the PRESIDENT :

I inclose herewith a letter just received from the Hon. R. W. Walker, C. S. Senator from Alabama. As the letter contains some important statements relative to movements of the enemy's troops, I have thought it proper to place it at your disposal for what it may be worth.

Very respectfully,

D. LOUIS DALTON,
Assistant Clerk, House Representatives.

[Inclosure.]

TUSCALOOSA, *April* 14, 1864.

D. L. DALTON, Esq.:

MY DEAR SIR: I leave here to-day for Montgomery, and will be glad if you will write to me to that place, care of W. B. Bell, whether you have succeeded in securing boarding quarters for me. I hope very much that you will be able to locate me at Mr. Sands'.

Mrs. Walker and other persons just out from Florence bring most deplorable accounts of the condition of things in Lauderdale County. The town is constantly infested either by Yankees or tories. It is hardly an exaggeration to say that every good horse in the county has been taken off, and a very large proportion of the slaves. The communication between Nashville and Florence is uninterrupted, and a good many citizens of Florence have recently been to Nashville. They all concur in the statement that very heavy re-enforcements have been passing through Nashville daily for three weeks for the army at Chattanooga.

Seven thousand Yankee infantry, just from Vicksburg, landed at Waterloo last week, and passed through Lauderdale County on their way to Chattanooga or Huntsville. One brigade passed through Florence the day before Mrs. Walker left home; the remainder of the force took the upper road. Either the Yankees mean to make two simultaneous campaigns—one in Virginia and one in Georgia—or they are intending one grand campaign in the latter State. I believe that the latter is their intention, and that their real movement will be against Atlanta, not Richmond.

I have read with interest and instruction your Mexico articles in the Enquirer. I hardly think you have exhausted the subject.

In haste, yours, truly,

R. W. WALKER.

DEMOPOLIS, *April* 26, 1864.

Colonel BAKER,
    Tuscaloosa:

I send you a number of copies of my proclamation* to absentees and deserters, and desire you to take immediate steps to have them distributed throughout your provost districts. You will send them into all parts of the following counties, viz: Tuscaloosa, Pickens, Fayette, Walker, Jefferson, and Bibb. Send twenty copies to each senator and representative in the Legislature from those counties, and to every sheriff, and in the margin you will write at the bottom of the page of one of the copies of these packages of twenty as follows: "You are requested respectfully to take prompt and active measures to bring the knowledge of the proclamation home to every one of your constituents who may be absent from his command."

L. POLK,
Lieutenant-General.

DEMOPOLIS, *April* 26, 1864.

Major-General FRENCH,
    Tuscaloosa:

GENERAL: I find it indispensable to clear my department of deserters and absentees, &c., by detachments from my army in the

* See p. 785

field. I find also that the best results are following upon the vigorous campaigns I am prosecuting in different parts of it. I have moved out already from their hiding places about 1,000 men, and the ranks of all commands raised in this department are being swelled by companies, both infantry and cavalry. I have a work to do in North Alabama, and I want you to make a detachment to do it. General Roddey has been ordered to picket the whole front from the Mississippi State line across the State, and along the Tennessee River, to prevent these tories and deserters from escaping to the enemy. I find infantry much more effective than cavalry for this work, and while General Ferguson's brigade has been ordered to move upon these men in the counties lying north of his position, I desire you to send General Cockrell's brigade forward upon that work also. Let him deploy his force right and left on a line running through Tuscaloosa, and take the country from the Mississippi line across toward the railroad, and sweep it all before him up to where he will meet Roddey's pickets, and order him to make thorough work of it. Let him arrest all tories, conscripts, and deserters, and if he shall find any in arms offering resistance let him punish them with death upon the spot. Order him to concentrate all he captures at Tuscaloosa, and hold them subject to my order.

Put yourself in communication with General Lee on the subject of this movement, so as to be informed of the instructions from General Ferguson; also send for Lieutenant-Colonel Baker, commanding post at Tuscaloosa, and get from him such intelligence as he may give to guide your movement. He is acquainted with the country and is a highly intelligent officer. He will indicate where officers in the service of the Government in North Alabama are to be found who may aid your troops in their work. Let the movement be made promptly. I have ordered the brigade of Brigadier-General Sears, now at Selma, to report to you as soon as practicable. You will find it a fine brigade of about 2,500 strong.

I am, general, respectfully, your obedient servant,

L. POLK,
Lieutenant-General.

P. S.—When General Cockrell shall have gone through this campaign he will report where you shall be found with your headquarters.

DEMOPOLIS, *April* 26, 1864.

Major-General LEE,
    Commanding, &c.:

GENERAL: You will have received before this reaches you the order of the War Department, "restoring you to the command of all the cavalry" of this department, from which it would appear that the wish you were understood by me to have expressed to be relieved of so much as was placed under command of General Forrest has not met with the approbation of the War Department.

I have ordered General Pillow to report to you for duty in the cavalry service. He has had assigned to him certain regiments, to constitute a brigade, and will report in a few days. I concur with you in thinking that he merits a division, and shall be pleased to see him placed in command of one. Should there not be troops enough in the brigade he is forming, Roddey, I hear, has four regiments and four battalions. I note what you say of sending Ferguson's brigade in pursuit of stragglers and deserters. I have ordered Major-General French to send an infantry command through all the counties of North Alabama to co-operate with General Ferguson, and I now desire you to give orders to General Roddey to deploy enough of his command along the line of the Tennessee River, as near as he may think proper, to intercept such tories and deserters as may attempt to escape into the enemy's lines that way. The movement of Ferguson and the infantry will drive such of them on to Roddey's troops as are not caught. I desire these movements should be made with vigor, and that they should cover the infected districts thoroughly.

The best results are following upon like operations in the southern counties of Mississippi, and under other commands at work under Forrest, &c., in the north, west, and east of that State. Over 1,000 men have been moved out.

Since writing the above your dispatch, asking that dismounted men should be assigned to the infantry, has been received. You will receive orders to that effect. I hope this assignment will be temporary, and these men may be informed that they shall be remounted so soon as horses can be had for them—that is, such as are good soldiers. I note, also, what is said in Jones' report as to the movements of the enemy.

Respectfully, general, your obedient servant,

L. POLK,
Lieutenant-General.

P. S.—You have no doubt heard of the success of Colonel Griffith in the brilliant affair of the gun-boat on the Yazoo. He captured it with a fine armament of eight 24-pounders, dismantled it, saving the guns, then burnt it. The Yankee movement of about 3.000 men then retreated and returned to Vicksburg.

P. S.—Your quartermaster, under the authority from Paxton, should act promptly in pressing horses for your artillery, as orders are out to make impressments for General Johnston's army.

L. P.

HDQRS. DEPT. OF ALABAMA, MISSISSIPPI, AND EAST LA.,
Demopolis, Ala., April 26, 1864.

Maj. Gen. S. D. LEE,
Commanding, &c.:

GENERAL: The lieutenant-general commanding directs me to say to you that he approves the suggestion contained in your favor of the 22d instant, and authorizes the transfer to infantry commands of the dismounted men of your command. As far as practicable they should be transferred to commands of their respective States, Mississippians to Mississippi troops, Alabamians to Alabama troops, &c. Let the transfer be made as soon as may be, and with proper precautions to avoid desertion. Send forward to these headquarters lists of the names of the men and their commands; also the command to which each is transferred, in order that formal orders may issue in the premises.

Most respectfully, general, your obedient servant,

THOS. M. JACK,
Assistant Adjutant-General.

DEMOPOLIS, *April 26*, 1864.

Col. J. S. SCOTT :

COLONEL : I have explained my views of the manner in which the orders with regard to the campaign against deserters and conscripts should be executed to Surgeon Hill. In all cases where there is a doubt as to exemptions of any party, let that party have the benefit of the doubt, and note the case for future examination. You will, while you are courteous, take good care to be firm and unyielding, having the same mode of proceeding for all parties, high and low. The time at which the privilege accorded to persons from seventeen to eighteen and from forty-five to fifty to enroll themselves expires on the 1st of May ; they must then be required by force to come to the aid of their country in its trial.

Respectfully, your obedient servant,

L. POLK,
Lieutenant-General.

EXECUTIVE OFFICE,
Macon, Miss., April 26, 1864.

Lieutenant-General POLK,
Commanding Department, Demopolis, Ala. :

GENERAL : In obedience to the mandate of the Legislature, I herewith transmit to you a series of resolutions adopted by that body in relation to the troops of Mississippi. Be pleased to communicate them to the Mississippi troops in your command in such manner as may best accomplish the object of the Legislature.

I have the honor to be, general, with high respect, your obedient servant,

CHAS. CLARK,
Governor of Mississippi.

[Inclosure.]

Resolved, That the thanks of this Legislature are due, and are hereby tendered, to the officers and soldiers of the Mississippi regiments in the several departments of the Confederate Army for their noble and patriotic conduct in re-enlisting for the war.

Resolved, That nothing has occurred since the commencement of this war which has so thrilled our hearts with pleasure as the news that has reached us that our brave soldiers, after having endured all the hardships and privations of a war of three years, have again determined that they will fight to the last, and gain our liberties or perish in the attempt, and we hereby renew the pledge which has been made before, that so long as we have any means to prevent it, the families of our brave soldiers shall never suffer in their absence.

Resolved, That the Governor be requested to transmit a copy of these resolutions to Generals Lee, Longstreet, Johnston, and Polk, with a request that they cause them to be read to each regiment of Mississippi troops in their departments.

Approved April 5, 1864.

HEADQUARTERS FRENCH'S DIVISION,
Tuscaloosa, Ala,. April 26, 1864.
Lieut. Col. THOMAS M. JACK,
Assistant Adjutant-General:
SIR: I arrived here this morning with my command and am encamped on the river above the town on the left bank. All well.
Yours, very respectfully,
S. G. FRENCH,
Major-General, Commanding.

HEADQUARTERS LEE'S CAVALRY,
Tuscaloosa, April 26, 1864.
Lieut. Col. T. M. JACK,
Assistant Adjutant-General, Demopolis, Ala.:
COLONEL: I have the honor to inclose a copy of the scout report* of Lieutenant Coffey, of Ferguson's brigade; I regard the report as reliable. The Nashville and Chattanooga Railroad, as is known to the general, has been almost impracticable for over a year from being in bad repair.

From all information I can gather the forces of the enemy have not been increased in North Alabama, Dodge's division having occupied that country since the evacuation of Corinth.

The enemy are carefully watching all the crossings in the vicinity of Muscle Shoals. I directed General Roddey to interfere with the railroads by sending small parties to destroy bridges, &c. I have not received a report since the one I sent you from General Roddey.

I would suggest that a part of the cavalry now here be sent to the prairie country near Columbus, where they are in good position for a move and forage. I think Ferguson and Roddey will be sufficient here, unless it is the intention of the general to move into North Alabama. The supplies on the Tennessee are represented as nearly exhausted.

I am, colonel, yours, respectfully,
S. D. LEE,
Major-General.

HEADQUARTERS RODDEY'S CAVALRY DIVISION,
Near Hillsborough, Ala., April 26, 1864.
Maj. Gen. S. D. LEE:
GENERAL: Your letter of the 22d instant, with accompanying orders, are at hand, in relation to subsisting my command, foraging, &c. Forage is scarce, but by grazing and reducing corn rations I think it can be made to do; a larger force here I think is not necessary, and in fact could not be subsisted.

I inclose herewith the latest report we have of the forces of the enemy on the north side of the Tennessee River and west side of Elk River. The river is strongly picketed and actively patrolled from above Decatur to Eastport, and for some distance below. From the latest reports the enemy have four regiments of infantry and one regiment of cavalry at Athens, Ala. Three brigades reported at

---

* Not found.

Decatur and vicinity coming from the direction of Athens. Whatever force was at Huntsville has been removed to the vicinity of Decatur also.

My forces are stationed on the river above to the river below Decatur, scouting daily to within a short distance of that place and keeping the enemy well closed in. I also picket the river as far down as Florence. I will keep you advised of all reports and movements of the enemy.

I would suggest, in consideration of the fact of the scarcity of forage and subsistence, that all scouting parties from your command be withdrawn from this section, as I think that I can impart all the information that they could obtain, and for another reason, that it is impossible for me to know and determine who are true and accredited and who are not. To guard against imposition I would suggest that all scouting parties and secret-service men sent to this section be ordered to report to these headquarters, and that they also be accredited, through the proper channels of communication (say by courier-line), with description and also with the signatures of the parties sent inclosed. I think this precaution very important—as an instance, a party of Federals just before the last raid into this section, dressed as Confederates and purporting to be from Forrest's command, passed unmolested and unsuspected through the country and gathered all the information they desired. The same party returned afterward with the raiders.

Prior to my return to Northern Alabama, parties having what seemed to be genuine orders from Wheeler, Forrest, and yourself, as scouts, passed our lines and were afterward known to boast in Huntsville, Athens, and other places that they had been to General Polk's and other headquarters. In view of all these facts I have issued orders that no one not having my authority shall be permitted to pass my lines.

Much complaint is made of a Lieutenant Harvey, commanding a party of 50 or 60 men, purporting to be sent here by General Armstrong. From all the information in my possession, he has authorized the illegal seizure of private horses for his command, stating that the horses of his men had broken down and died on the road, a very good proof to my mind that the worst-mounted men of his command were brought for the purpose of mounting them anew. He has defied authority in one instance, and refused to return horses taken from citizens who were nearly broken up by the enemy during the last raid, saying that he reported to no one, and was responsible to no one but General Armstrong, and what he had done he would do again if necessary, if he was cashiered for it.

As all the citizens have been nearly stripped of all their stock, and as they are willingly and cheerfully doing all in their power to support an army by raising produce, and as it is impossible for an army to be supported if their stock is taken from them, and as there is nothing in the impressment act that can be so construed as to allow the seizure of private property for the private uses of his men, I have, in view of all the circumstances, ordered the arrest of Lieutenant Harvey and his command wherever found, they and their horses to be held until the property so unwarrantably and illegally seized shall be returned to its proper owners. The conduct of Lieutenant Harvey I consider to be prejudicial to the good of the service and unbecoming an officer and a gentleman. To some parties he gave informal receipts for horses and to others none.

The courier-line indicated by you is not the nearest route, but as I am not familiar with the character of the country by the nearest route, and do not know the chances of foraging, I will, until something more definite is ascertained, connect with your line at Blountsville.

I forward to you, in charge of couriers, Philip Henson, who has been represented to me for the last twelve months as a spy for the Federals. My authorities are the most reliable men who were in my service, and who never failed to give me correct information—who are undoubted. They have reported to me constantly during that time that valuable information has been given by Henson to the Federals. He has papers, but I do not deem them sufficiently satisfactory to permit him to pass through my lines. This is another instance that justifies the suggestions I have above made in relation to accrediting scouts, &c. I believe firmly that the said Henson is a spy, and has been in the service of and the pay of the Federals all that time, and that all his sympathies are with them.

My information all summed up induces the belief that no attempt will be made by the enemy to raid south from Decatur with the force in sight. I will keep myself thoroughly advised as to their movements, and forward the information to you rapidly.

I have the honor to be, general, very respectfully, your obedient servant,

P. D. RODDEY,
Brigadier-General.

P. S.—I would suggest that you send this or a copy to General Polk.

[Inclosure.]

APRIL 25, 1864.

Brigadier-General RODDEY :

Two regiments now in Lauderdale County, viz, Ninth Ohio and Seventh Illinois. The Ninth Ohio has one company at mouth of Elk River, one company at Ben. Taylor's, and one at David Williams', and one at Bainbridge; the remainder of the regiment is at Cheatham's Ferry. The Seventh Illinois has two or three companies at Bailey's Springs; report says this evening that they are moving to Wright and Rice's and Florence ; one company at Waterloo, remainder in lower part of the county. General Sweeny's brigade is at Pulaski. The mound in northeast part of town fortified with one piece of artillery. My scout has just arrived and brings the foregoing, which may be relied on.

Respectfully,

JAMES JACKSON,
Colonel Twenty-seventh Alabama Regiment.

HEADQUARTERS DEPARTMENT OF EAST TENNESSEE,
Abingdon, April 26, 1864.

Maj. Gen. J. C. BRECKINRIDGE,
Comdg. Department of Western Virginia, Dublin, Va.:

GENERAL : I have received your note transmitting that of Col. W. P. Johnston. I have received accurate information from Central Kentucky to-day. Nearly all of the Federal cavalry recently near

Lexington has gone southward ; but a small force is now in front of us. A single brigade moved up against Colonel Clay and afterward retreated. Giltner is now covering Saltville. Jones' brigade is also near that place. I cannot throw them out far, as yet, for want of forage. General Jones is now at Saltville, and will be directed to give you such information as he may receive. The enemy were pressing my advance at Carter's Depot, on the Watauga, yesterday. They retired this morning, perhaps only temporarily.

I am sending my strongest brigade (Gracie's) to Richmond.

Respectfully and truly,

S. B. BUCKNER,
Major-General.

P. S.—I submitted the question the other day for decision, whether I was to regard Wharton, Jones, and King as belonging to this department or to yours.

S. B. B.

ABINGDON, *April* 26, 1864.

General S. COOPER ·

Most of the Federal cavalry recently near Lexington, Ky., have gone southward , their demonstration in this direction has retired. The Federals are sending a great deal of artillery southward through Lexington ; the enemy, apparently a strong reconnaissance, were skirmishing with General Jackson at Carter's Depot yesterday evening. Gracie's brigade is moving in obedience to your order ; part of it may be expected in Lynchburg to-night.

S. B. BUCKNER,
Major-General.

HEADQUARTERS DEPARTMENT OF EAST TENNESSEE,
April 26, 1864.

Colonel GILTNER, *Commanding Brigade :*

COLONEL : The major-general commanding directs that you move your command toward Saltville at daylight to-morrow, crossing to the south side of the Holston, moving up Rich Valley, and camping 6 or 8 miles from Saltville to-morrow night. You will order up the regiments which went forward to-day so that they will be very near you to-morrow night. The major-general commanding desires that you recognize the importance of having your brigade well in hand, as it may be needed for quick and hard service in a very few days.

As soon as you shall determine your camps you will report the location of your troops and your own headquarters. Hereafter report any changes your troops may make. Take measures at once to have a supply of corn to-morrow night.

Your obedient servant,

J. N. GALLEHER,
Assistant Adjutant-General.

HEADQUARTERS, &C., *Abingdon, April* 26, 1864.

Brigadier-General JOHNSON, *Zollicoffer :*

It is not expedient to meet the enemy on the Watauga. If he advances in force and it shall become necessary, let Jackson fall back on you at Zollicoffer. Of this you will be the judge. The cavalry has been ordered from above to move on Blountsville. Cannot reach there before the day after to-morrow. Will order one or more batteries to join you to-morrow. If you are satisfied the enemy is advancing in force, and you think it necessary, will send you another brigade.

S. B. BUCKNER,
Major-General.

HEADQUARTERS DEPARTMENT OF EAST TENNESSEE,
Abingdon, April 26, 1864.

Brigadier-General JONES, *Saltville, Va. :*

Move your brigade to this place, leaving pickets sufficient to observe the salt-works. Start to-night and come as far on the way as you conveniently can. To save time orders have been sent to Giltner to move at daylight to-morrow toward Blountsville. Send him the order also yourself to assure its reaching him.

S. B. BUCKNER,
Major-General.

GENERAL ORDERS, }   HEADQUARTERS ARMY OF TENNESSEE,
    No. 10.   }   *Dalton, Ga., April* 26, 1864.

Lieut. Richard J. Manning is appointed aide-de-camp to General Johnston, vice Lieut. J. B. Washington, transferred, and will be obeyed and respected accordingly.

By command of General Johnston :

A. P. MASON,
Major and Assistant Adjutant-General.

DEMOPOLIS, *April* 27, 1864.

His Excellency President DAVIS, *Richmond :*

I have been applied to by a large number of officers, who are supernumeraries, to be permitted to resign and form themselves into cavalry regiments. The number of such officers I have no means of knowing accurately, but am satisfied I can find enough to make up two or three full regiments in my department. I do not know a better disposition to make of them. A large number of them are out of service by no fault of theirs, and from their fidelity have won a claim on the consideration of the Government. I respectfully ask permission for the officers to be gratified in their wish. If the permission is granted, will you please, to save time, answer by telegraph.

I have just seen Governor Harris, who is direct from West Tennessee. He gives a very favorable account of things there, and is himself highly gratified with the state of feeling among the people. He was with General Forrest during the greater part of his campaign, and was in every county in the district except three. The necessity of placing Forrest's command at a point in Northern Mississippi within supporting distance of the rest of my command in Northeast Alabama interfered somewhat with his completing the work of clearing out all the military material within its borders. He leaves a detachment, nevertheless, to accomplish this. General Forrest is in Tupelo at present. I am pressing the completion of the

Mobile and Ohio Railroad up to Corinth, and so soon as that is completed will move Forrest's headquarters up there, take possession of the fort, will arm it and establish a post there. It will give me a point from which to afford protection to the Western District, to threaten Memphis and Paducah, and from whence to move on the Tennessee Valley, and so on the flank of any movement from Decatur southward or eastward. I find, too, it can be availed of as a point at which to receive from the Tennessee River, via the military road built by Halleck from Pittsburg Landing, 18 miles, commissary and quartermaster's stores in exchange for cotton under existing contracts. Under the authority of the War Department I am about completing an arrangement with an entirely reliable party, a contract for such supplies to be brought in by that route, the cotton in all cases not to be delivered until the goods are first received and in hand.

The receipts under the J. J. Pollard contract, via the Yazoo and Mississippi Rivers, have begun and promise to be what we could desire. I am pr   ng the completion of the Central and Great Northern Railroad upsto Holly Springs, and the connection across Pearl River with the Southern Railroad. In about ten days hope to be able to transport the stores delivered by rail from any point on that road via Jackson eastward. I shall have the railroad southward to the lake shore completed by the working parties now upon it about the same time. This will greatly facilitate the transportation of arms to the Trans-Mississippi Department, as the best point of crossing the river is about Tunica, as also to receive stores through that route should it be expedient. Great difficulty has been experienced, under existing orders from the War Department, in procuring the necessary labor to complete the works for the defense of Mobile, planters being extremely averse to having their hands impressed and being unwilling to hire. I think I have fallen upon a plan, which I am now putting into execution, for obviating the reluctance of planters, and hope soon to have the force necessary. I have found myself compelled to adopt stringent measures for reducing the disorders which I found more or less developed in the department when I took charge of it, and which have been ripened into outbreaks. The suppression of these seem to have been intrusted to the Conscript Bureau, which was charged with the arrest and restoration of deserters. Finding its action too feeble and the evil growing rapidly, I have been obliged to take it in hand, and the measures pursued have had the most salutary effect ; large numbers of absentees have returned and are still returning to their commands ; of this I will write more fully in a few days.

I have the honor to be, respectfully, your obedient servant,
L. POLK,
Lieutenant-General, Commanding.

DEMOPOLIS, ALA., *April 27*, 1864.

His Excellency President DAVIS, *Richmond, Va.:*

The condition of affairs along the western front of my department, originating in the intercourse of our people with the enemy, and developed by illicit trade, exhibiting itself in absenteeism, murder, and robbery, has given me great concern, and has been the subject of much reflection. I am fully convinced that the cause which operates more than all others to induce this state of things is the cotton in the hands of citizens along the border. This cotton should be got rid of, *i. e.*, out of the hands of the present owners, before we can reasonably expect much improvement in the condition of things. As long as the cotton remains in the hands of planters or citizens, just so long will they be resorting to all sorts of measures to push it into the enemy's lines, and either sell or exchange it for money or supplies, and to prevent this by guarding the lines of communication would require the united force of all arms in my department.

So general has this become, as I am informed, that all classes, more or less, in certain districts are engaged in the traffic, and the infection has extended itself in most instances to the soldiers guarding the roads, who connive at the trade by the inducement of a bribe in money or other valuables. In view of this condition of affairs, I beg leave respectfully to submit the following suggestions for your consideration :

Let the Government become the owner of all the cotton included within a belt of country extending from the lake shore to the Tennessee line and from the Mississippi River bank to the Central Railroad, either by purchase or impressment, as in the case of all other property. Let competent agents be employed, under the direction of the department commander, to thoroughly canvass this district and purchase or impress all the cotton found within its limits and have it all removed east of Pearl River, except so much as may be needed for purposes of exchange, and stored, subject to future orders of the Government, through its agents. It is my purpose to have the great lines of railroad communication through the entire length of Mississippi and Alabama completed, from near the lake shore to the line of the Memphis and Charleston Railroad. This will facilitate the transmission of the cotton whenever it may be required. I entertain but little doubt, if some such plan was adopted and placed in the hands of the department commander for execution, it would go very far toward enabling him to restore the infected districts to a healthful moral and military condition.

If any doubts should arise as to the propriety of impressing cotton, it may be said that if the Government has the right, upon the soundest principles of public policy, to impress corn and hay and meat and horses, and even men, for its defense in times of great national danger, there surely could be no doubt of its having the right to impress the cotton of private citizens, paying them for it a fair consideration.

The good order, and even the loyalty, of the region indicated demands that this cotton should be either seized or burned, and prompt action is required.

I remain, respectfully, your obedient servant,

L. POLK,
Lieutenant-General, Commanding.

———

TUPELO, [*April*] 27, 1864.

Lieutenant-General POLK :

Negroes captured at Fort Pillow by General Forrest all say they are escaped slaves.

S. J. GHOLSON,
Major-General, Commanding.

HEADQUARTERS, &C.,
Abingdon, April 27, 1864.
General J. C. BRECKINRIDGE, *Dublin, Va.:*

A movement of the enemy from East Tennessee has required me to withdraw my cavalry from Saltville. I will probably have 600 cavalry at Seven-Mile Ford to-morrow. If I have a fight below can you lend me any infantry for a few days? Please reply to-day.

S. B. BUCKNER,
Major-General.

HEADQUARTERS, &C.,
Abingdon, April 27, 1864.
Major-General BRECKINRIDGE, *Dublin, Va.:*

Averell with 2,500 cavalry was certainly at Point Pleasant on the 20th. My information is positive. He meditated a raid on the railway in a few days. As soon as I can manage matters below I will again concentrate near Saltville. Keep me advised in time to assist you. That point will probably be his object. How long would it require him to make the march?

S. B. BUCKNER,
Major-General.

HDQRS. DEPARTMENT OF WESTERN VIRGINIA,
April 27, 1864.
General S. B. BUCKNER,
Abingdon, Va.:

My only infantry within 70 miles are two regiments and a battalion at Narrows of New River and Princeton, and enemy reported active up the Kanawha and on my other front. Should enemy advance in force and press you toward Abingdon I will try to help you, if not urgently threatened elsewhere. Let me know if you think the infantry at Saltville could safely go to you.

JNO. C. BRECKINRIDGE,
Major-General.

HEADQUARTERS DEPARTMENT OF EAST TENNESSEE,
Abingdon, April 27, 1864.
Brig. Gen. B. R. JOHNSON, *Zollicoffer:*

I send Wharton to-night. Cavalry marching to-day, but cannot be at Bristol before to-morrow afternoon. Having reference to these movements, hold Carter's Depot if you think it advisable. My apprehension is that if the river is low it can be turned on our right, and the position taken in reverse. As you are on the ground I leave it to your judgment. Act as you deem best under all the circumstances until I come down. The artillery is marching to-day. If your position at Carter's is easily turned you had better evacuate it, if you are not sure of holding it until my cavalry gets up; when that arrives it can cover your flank. Send scouts to the enemy's rear. Keep me advised.

S. B. BUCKNER,
Major-General.

ABINGDON, *April* 28, 1864.
General B. R. JOHNSON,
    Zollicoffer:
    Send Wharton's brigade to Glade Springs by rail as soon as practicable. Morgan's dismounted men will return to the same place. Notify us when they will move.
                                        J. N. GALLEHER,
                                Assistant Adjutant-General.

HEADQUARTERS DEPARTMENT OF EAST TENNESSEE,
                                            April 28, 1864.
General B. R. JOHNSON,
    Zollicoffer, Tenn.:
    If the enemy are still in retreat, send Morgan's dismounted men back to Saltville on the same train on which they went down this morning. Information renders it advisable to cover the salt-works.
                                        S. B. BUCKNER,
                                            Major-General.

HEADQUARTERS DEPARTMENT OF EAST TENNESSEE,
                                Abingdon, April 28, 1864.
Brigadier-General JONES,
    Commanding Cavalry:
    GENERAL: The major-general commanding directs that you move your brigade back to Saltville. Move at daylight to-morrow. As soon as you shall determine your camp you will please•report the location of your troops, your own headquarters, and hereafter report any changes of position you may make. Take measures to obtain a supply of corn at your camp to-morrow night.
    I am, general, your obedient servant,
                                        J. N. GALLEHER,
                                Assistant Adjutant-General.

DALTON, *April* 28, 1864.
General BRAGG,
    Richmond:
    Scouts report infantry of Twenty-third Corps come to Cleveland from Knoxville.
                                        J. E. JOHNSTON.

HEADQUARTERS,
                                Demopolis, April 28, 1864.
Brigadier-General HODGE,
    Selma:
    DEAR GENERAL: I send you reports of General Forrest of his operations in West Tennessee, and also copies of reports of Colonels Maury and Lowry of their operations against the tories and de-

serters in Mississippi. I desire to call your attention to them and to ask that you, in your correspondence, call attention of the President to them, with a request from me that he will read them. I shall continue my operations in the same style until I shall have swept over the whole department and cleared it of absentees of all sorts. I am re-establishing the ascendency of the civil power in its courts, &c., as I go, and am, through the agency of commands for local defense, which I am organizing everywhere, providing the means of maintaining its ascendency in the future. These commands will also make it impossible for deserters to return and remain away from the army hereafter. You will find inclosed a letter* from a correspondent of the President, asking my attention and remarks. Please see that my indorsement is forwarded. The reports of my officers transmitted are my reply. May I ask you to see that the President receives my letter.

I hope to see you before you leave, and shall write the President more fully of such operations as those of Maury and Lowry and send him a copy of the map I have had made of the department with its sub-divisions into military districts. I think Colonel Lowry, whom I have long known, is one of the most gallant men in the army and one of the best officers; has entitled himself to the thanks of the Government, and should be promoted. I should find him of eminent service to me if he were made brigadier-general and ordered to report to me for special duty. I wish him to take charge of all such work as that pertaining to order in the department, and could work him into the command of the force raising for local defense.

Respectfully, general, your obedient servant,

L. POLK,
Lieutenant-General.

HEADQUARTERS FORREST'S CAVALRY,
Jackson, April 28, 1864.

Lieutenant-General POLK,
Meridian :

Dispatch of 25th received. Will be at Tupelo on 4th May. My command will be there on the 6th. Desire it thoroughly inspected. Dispatch General Gholson to detain officer from Richmond until I arrive. Hope to meet you there also before organizing my command. All quiet.

N. B. FORREST,
Major-General.

SPECIAL ORDERS, } HDQRS. DEPT. OF ALA., MISS., AND E. LA.,
No. 119. } *Demopolis, April 28, 1864.*

I. Brigadier-General Sears will move with his command across the country to Tuscaloosa, Ala., reporting on his arrival to Major-General French.

By command of Lieutenant-General Polk :

P. ELLIS, JR.,
Assistant Adjutant-General.

---

* Not found.

SPECIAL ORDERS, }   ADJT. AND INSP. GENERAL'S OFFICE,
No. 99.   }   *Richmond, Va., April* 28, 1864.
*   *   *   *   *   *   *

VIII. The Fifty-fourth Regiment Alabama Volunteers is relieved from duty at Montgomery, Ala., and will proceed by railroad to Dalton, Ga., and report to General Joseph E. Johnston, commanding, &c., for assignment to Brigadier-General Baker's Alabama brigade.

IX. Paragraph XLII, Special Orders, No. 89, current series, is hereby revoked, and Col. George A. Gordon, with his regiment (the Sixty-third Georgia Volunteers), will proceed by railroad to head-quarters Army of Tennessee, Dalton, Ga., and report to General J. E. Johnston, commanding, &c.

*   *   *   *   *   *   *

XIV. Maj. Gen. S. B. Buckner is assigned to duty in the Trans-Mississippi Department. He will proceed with the least delay practicable to the headquarters of that department, and report to General E. K. Smith, commanding, &c.

*   *   *   *

By command of Secretary of War:

JNO. WITHERS,
Assistant Adjutant-General.

MOBILE, *April* 29, 1864.

Hon. SECRETARY OF THE NAVY:

SIR: In reply to your communication of the 19th instant, I would respectfully desire to have all my papers and documents now on file in your office transferred, as you suggest, to the War Department, and there be placed on file, as all my future applications must be with that officer.

Cut short as I have been, as you are pleased to infer, by a late act of Congress, my boats and crews lying idle, after the very heavy expense and almost insurmountable obstacles that I have had to overcome in collecting together such material for my expedition—thus cut short, when I expected to be busily engaged against the enemy, nevertheless I do not yet relinquish the hope of shortly being among them, doing my country good service.

Hoping that you will be p   a   to give the transition of my papers from your Department all necessary attention, and soliciting your kind consideration and favorable opinion in my behalf,

I have the honor to remain, your obedient servant,

E. M. JEFFERSON.

DALTON, GA.,
April 29, 1864.

General WHEELER:

The enemy are advancing. Come up as soon as possible.

W. W. MACKALL,
Chief of Staff.

HEADQUARTERS HOOD'S CORPS,
Dalton, Ga., April 29, 1864.
Generals HINDMAN and STEVENSON :

GENERALS: You will place your command under arms at once. General Stewart is forming line of battle in Mill Creek Gap. By command of Lieut. Gen. J. B. Hood, commanding :
J. W. RATCHFORD,
Assistant Adjutant-General.

HEADQUARTERS HARDEE'S CORPS,
Dalton, Ga., April 29, 1864—8.30 a. m.
Major-General BATE,
Commanding Division :

GENERAL: Lieutenant-General Hardee directs me to communicate the following note to you, just received from the chief of staff :

The enemy are pressing the cavalry on the Ringgold road with infantry, artillery, and cavalry. General Johnston directs you to hold your corps in readiness for action.

Very respectfully, your obedient servant,
T. B. ROY,
Assistant Adjutant-General.

DALTON, *April 29, 1864.*
General JOSEPH E. JOHNSTON :

GENERAL: In compliance with your special instructions, April 8, to "proceed without delay to Richmond and explain to the Commander-in-Chief the matters orally committed to you" (me), I started on the journey immediately and arrived in Richmond on Tuesday, the 12th.

The subject-matter of my instructions is comprised under the following heads :

First. To make it appear that you had not in your correspondence with the Government declined to make an advance ; on the contrary, it was and had been your purpose to assume the offensive as soon as your preparations were completed and the promised re-enforcements received ; that objections were urged against a specified plan, and were intended to apply to no other ; and, further, that you thought it expedient to defer the arrangement of details and the marking of routes until ready to move, because of the varying position and force of the enemy.

Second. That you had been actively engaged in making preparations ; that those over which you had control were in a state of forwardness, but that in the essential element of transportation, your need of which had several times been communicated to the Government and which you had no means of collecting, nothing whatever had been done, 1,000 wagons at least being required before the army, increased as promised, would be able to move ; and that your request for artillery horses, as urgent, had not been complied with, though promises had been made that they would soon be furnished.

Third. That the surest means of securing a forward movement was to send the re-enforcements, or a large portion of them, at once, so that should the enemy assume the initiative we might be able promptly to defeat him on this side of the Tennessee River, where the results of a victory would be so much more favorable to us and those of defeat so much less disastrous than if the battle were fought north of the river.

Fourth. That the strength of the enemy in your front was supposed, from the best information, to be not less than that which he fought the battle of Missionary Ridge (about 80,000), and in addition McPherson's corps (15,000) ; that General Polk's infantry and artillery not being immediately needed in his department, might, as well as the larger portion of the garrison of Mobile, be employed in aiding you to hold your position.

Fifth. That the cavalry force under your command was much weaker and more inefficient than was represented.

. Understanding that General Bragg was the proper medium of communicating with the President, I immediately informed him on Wednesday, the 13th, why I had been sent to Richmond, and requested him to secure an interview. The general gave me every aid in his power. Before seeing the President I had a full and free conversation with him. He manifested every disposition to have your army properly re-enforced, and you otherwise put in a condition to move ; the choice of routes being, as I understood to be, left entirely to your discretion. At the same time he frankly declared his apprehension that in consequence of Longstreet's movements, the junction of his army with yours being thereby rendered impracticable, and of the pressure in Virginia and North Carolina, caused by the reported concentration and movements of the enemy, that little could be done, although he was anxious to do all he could. He further stated that he was desirous to have the matter settled, and with this feeling asked a categorical answer to the proposition of your assuming the offensive with an increase of 15,000 infantry and artillery from the departments of South Carolina and Mississippi to your present force, and that it was important that this answer be given in my interview with the President next day.

Unwilling without further instructions to assume the grave responsibility of answering this question, I at once sent a telegraphic message to you on this subject, but received no reply before seeing the President. After a careful consideration of my instructions, I gave to this proposition a decided affirmative answer as well to General Bragg as to the President.

The President received me courteously and listened with apparent interest to the different statements I made, entering into details in respect to the cavalry force, transportation, and artillery horses. He expressed his regrets that offensive movements in your army had not been made in time to have prevented the reported preparations for a formidable attack in Virginia and North Carolina, having for its object the capture of Richmond, stating that to have prevented this was one of the important objects for threatening movements by your army, and that though the primary object had failed, yet it was still very important that offensive operations be assumed, and that all possible re-enforcements should be at once sent, though it was thought inexpedient to divest General Polk's department, containing so much provision, of all means of defense, and that he feared General Lee would require all the aid to be derived for the present from Beauregard's army.

In my reply I entered into detailed statements (to the satisfaction, as I thought, of the President) concerning the transportation and the artillery, showing that even if re-enforcements had been sent a movement would have been impracticable, because of still existing deficiencies in these respects.

The President, as General Bragg had done before, informed me that no definite answer could be given for several days, but that every attempt would be made by the Department to re-enforce you. In the course of the conversation the President stated that it was not thought expedient to force a plan of campaign upon any general commanding an army, as without the hearty co-operation of the general its successful execution would be almost impossible. I observed that that was true, but as it was eminently proper for a general to state his objections whenever a plan is proposed to him, that these might be met or overruled, if the authorities so decided, to which he assented.

The day after the interview I went to Orange Court-House, and remained till the following Monday, the 18th. The next day, the 19th, General Bragg informed me that, as he had anticipated, the pressure at Richmond was too great to effectually aid you for the present; that when circumstances warranted troops should be ordered to you; and, further, that in the mean time a brigade had been sent from Mobile, and five large regiments ordered from General Beauregard's army in exchange for five small ones, by which he hoped your army would receive an immediate accession of about 4,000 men.

I thought it best before leaving Richmond to address the following communication to General Bragg, accompanied by the request that it be laid before the President and the Secretary of War:

RICHMOND, *April* 20, 1864.

GENERAL: To prevent misunderstanding and to test the fact of my having properly carried out my instructions, permit me to make a recapitulation, asking to be allowed to supply deficiencies before leaving Richmond (which I expect to do this evening), if in the verbal communication I had the honor to make to the President in your presence I was not sufficiently full and explicit. My object was to explain to His Excellency:

First, that General Johnston had no intention in his correspondence with the War Department or the Government of expressing a disinclination to begin offensive operations when prepared and re-enforced; on the contrary, he was anxious to advance, being fully satisfied of its expediency and necessity, and was and had been, since assuming command of the Army of Tennessee, willing to execute with vigor and zeal, and to the best of his ability, any plan, whether his own or that of the Government; that his objections were intended to apply only to the route proposed; that he thought the selection of the plan of advance had better be deferred till everything was ready for the move; that he designed taking the initiative unless anticipated by the enemy intending to force a battle on this side of the Tennessee River, or in case he could not advance.

Second. That as a condition-precedent to his advance, an increase of transportation was absolutely necessary. Commissary supplies for a march of 130 miles through a mountainous and barren region must be carried; that after reducing the transportation of the baggage to a minimum nearly 1,000 additional wagons, which he had no means of procuring, would be required to subsist the army re-enforced as proposed; that for this he had to depend on the Quartermaster's Department; that he had, soon after reaching Georgia, made this want known, and as yet had received nothing, and that a like want existed as to artillery horses, 1,000 having been promised but not yet delivered.

Third. That to secure an advance it was advisable and essential to send the troops intended to re-enforce the army at once, not only to save time by perfecting the organization but also to defeat the enemy should he take the offensive.

Fourth. That the strength of the army at Chattanooga, estimated at 80,000 last fall, is not now less. It is believed, upon the best available information, that by the return of wounded and accession of recruits the enemy is now as strong, and that McPherson with his troops (15,000) is en route for Chattanooga.

Fifth. That the infantry in Mississippi and the garrison at Mobile do not seem to be needed there at present, and might be advantageously employed in re-enforcing the Army of Tennessee.

Very respectfully, your obedient servant,

BENJ. S. EWELL,
Assistant Adjutant-General.

To this letter I received no reply. I left Richmond the evening of the day on which I delivered it, and neither saw nor heard from General Bragg again on the subject with which I was charged.

While with the Army of Northern Virginia I saw General Lee for a short time; explained to him briefly the condition of affairs in Georgia. He said he had no doubt but that the Eleventh and Twelfth, consolidated into a single army corps, and the Ninth Army Corps, from the Army of the West, had reached Annapolis and were intended to constitute Burnside's command, to move into the northern part of North Carolina on the coast, or the Suffolk line, or on the Peninsula co-operating with Meade in the advance on Richmond; that Meade's army had been largely re-enforced to 75,000 or 100,000 men by the withdrawal of the garrisons along the coast and the line of the Potomac, their places being supplied by negro troops.

He concurred with me in the opinion I expressed to him that there was not much probability of your obtaining re-enforcements, at least until the plans of the enemy were fully developed.

Very respectfully, your obedient servant,

BENJ. S. EWELL,
Colonel and Assistant Adjutant-General.

CIRCULAR.]   HEADQUARTERS HOOD'S CORPS,
Dalton, Ga., April 29, 1864.

Division commanders will send all their heavy baggage at once to Dalton, to be sent to the rear on the cars. One disabled officer and 3 disabled men from each brigade will be sent with it.

By command of Lieut. Gen. J. B. Hood, commanding

J. W. RATCHFORD,
Assistant Adjutant-General.

CONFIDENTIAL.]   BRISTOL, *April 29, 1864.*

General BRAXTON BRAGG,
Richmond:

GENERAL: In transmitting my report upon so much of the cavalry of this department as I have seen, I beg leave to inclose to you confidentially some rough notes handed me by Major-General Ransom. They will perhaps convey a better idea of the condition of these people than anything I could say.

I have the honor to be, very respectfully, your obedient servant,

ARCHER ANDERSON,
Lieutenant-Colonel, Assistant Adjutant-General.

Report of inspection of cavalry.

The cavalry of this army consists of Jones', Giltner's, and Vaughn's brigades, and a small number of mounted men belonging to General Morgan's force. Vaughn's brigade and Morgan's mounted men are in North Carolina recruiting their horses, and were not inspected.

Jones' brigade (April 24), Lieutenant-Colonel Cook commanding, composed of Eighth Virginia Regiment, Captain Sheffey commanding; Twenty-first Virginia Regiment, Lieutenant-Colonel Edmundson; Thirty-sixth Virginia Battalion, Captain Kirtley; Thirty-seventh Virginia Battalion, Major Claiborne; Twenty-seventh Battalion, Thirty-fourth Battalion, Sixty-fourth Regiment: The last three commands being on distant service, scattered about at wide intervals, were not inspected. Present at inspection, 66 officers, 887 men. Three regimental or battalion commanders in arrest. There is an examining board for the brigade to inquire into the competency of officers, but none have been examined. With the exception of the Eighth Virginia, there are no schools of tactics in the regiments. Company and battalion drills very rare. Some companies have not drilled for six months; others only once in four weeks. Officers and men seem unfamiliar with tactics. One hundred and sixty-nine men absent without leave, who went off on furlough.

Clothing not good; pantaloons particularly needed. Fifty-nine men entirely without shoes, 64 entirely without a blanket, 197 dismounted men. Subsistence as in the infantry. Horses of good bone, but in low order. They need three weeks' rest and good feeding on grass and corn before they will be fit for a campaign. Saddles, mixed; McClellan, Texan, citizen, &c. All good except about six Jenifer saddles in each company, of Government manufacture, which were invariably reported to hurt the horses' backs. I believe this would be the report of every cavalry officer in service, and if not already done the manufacture of this saddle ought to be stopped.

Forage is purchased by regimental quartermasters and drawn from the depots.

Average issue per private animal, last quarter: Eighth Regiment, 8 pounds corn, one-half allowance hay; Twenty-first Regiment, 8 pounds corn, 7 pounds hay; Thirty-sixth Battalion, 10 pounds corn, 12 pounds hay; Thirty-seventh Battalion, 8 pounds corn, 7 pounds hay.

Average issue present quarter: Eighth Regiment, 8 pounds corn, one-half allowance hay; Twenty-first Regiment, 6 pounds corn, 7 pounds hay; Thirty-sixth Battalion, 5 pounds corn, 6 pounds hay; Thirty-seventh Battalion, 6 pounds corn, 7 pounds hay.

Average issue last quarter to public animals: Eighth Regiment, Twenty-first Regiment, Thirty-sixth Regiment, and Thirty-seventh Regiment, full allowance corn and hay.

Transportation (of the four commands inspected) consists of 36 serviceable and 6 unserviceable wagons; 36 horses (2 unserviceable), and 128 mules (5 unserviceable); 5 ambulances and 1 forge. Wagons and harness in good condition. Animals much reduced, though able to march. Arms, principally rifles, long and short, and of all sizes. (The armament report of the ordnance officer has been mislaid, and hence particulars cannot be given.) A few companies only are armed with sabers. The guns were all rusty; three hundred are needed. No regular company books are kept. At regimental headquarters there are files of orders and morning-report books. The men have not been regularly charged with lost or damaged arms, except perhaps in the Eighth. Commanders report that damages to private property have always been settled for. The Articles of War have not been read on parade within six months. General sanitary condition good. The brigade was bivouacked 7 miles north of the salt-works. Bearing (except in the Eighth Virginia) unmilitary.

Giltner's brigade (April 26), Colonel Giltner, Fourth Kentucky Regiment, commanding: Composed nominally of the Fourth and Tenth Kentucky Regiments, First, Second, and Tenth Kentucky Battalions, and Sixth and Seventh Confederate Battalions; but that part which formed Hodge's brigade has never joined the other regiments, and no report of the whole as a brigade has ever been made up. After much riding I was only able to see the Fourth Kentucky Regiment, which I was informed was in better condition than the rest.

Fourth Kentucky Regiment Cavalry, Lieutenant-Colonel Pryor commanding: Only seven companies present; three on picket. Present at inspection, 22 officers, 277 men. Company and battalion drills rare; officers apparently not well acquainted with tactics. No school of tactics in the regiment. No enlisted men, who went off on furlough, remain absent without leave. Clothing bad, especially the pantaloons. Only 3 men without shoes; none without blankets. Nineteen men dismounted. Horses in low order; not able to make a campaign; at least three weeks' recruiting with good forage is needed: 19 disabled. Saddles, 58 bad, principally Jenifer; the rest generally McClellan. Forage, average issue per animal last quarter, 8 pounds corn, 4 pounds hay. Since 1st April 6 pounds of corn and little or no hay. Arms, Enfield, Springfield, and short Richmond rifles, rusty; one company with sabers.

Report as to other subjects the same as for Jones' brigade. The regiment was bivouacked 16 miles west of the salt-works, in Russell County.

ARCHER ANDERSON,
Lieut. Col., Asst. Adj. Gen., on Inspection Duty.

[Indorsement.]

HDQRS. ARMIES OF THE CONFEDERATE STATES,
May 6, 1864.

By direction of General Bragg, respectfully submitted to Adjutant-General, calling his attention to bad condition of Vaughn's command. It should be dismounted, and he be sent to some disciplinarian or left out of assignment.

JNO. B. SALE,
Colonel and Military Secretary.

[Inclosure No. 1.]

Giltner's brigade—Fourth and Tenth Regiments Kentucky, First and Second Kentucky Battalions, Sixth and Seventh Confederate Battalions, Tenth Kentucky Battalion. Of the battalion commanders I know nothing, except Major Chenoweth, Tenth Battalion, who is a fair officer. Giltner is efficient. His regiment (Fourth) is good. Consolidation of small commands necessary, and been recommended. Horses, so far as I have seen, are fully fair; many of them fine, but going down for want of forage. Arms pretty good. Clothing and accouterments poor. Horse equipments only tolerable. The Jenifer saddle is worse than worthless, as it is impossible to use it with any horse without ruining the back. There is great want of military information among all the officers; some in all the brigades. One squadron left on Holston. The First and Second Kentucky, the Sixth and Seventh Confederate Battalions in Kentucky. The rest going to Tazewell County, Va.

Brigadier-General Vaughn's brigade (formerly infantry)—First Tennessee Cavalry, Third [Provisional Army], Thirty-ninth, Forty-third, and Fifty-ninth Regiments Tennessee Mounted Infantry, Twelfth and Sixteenth Tennessee Battalions, Sixteenth Georgia Battalion, detachment of Sixtieth, Sixty-first, and Sixty-second Tennessee Infantry. Find strength from Adjutant-General's office. This brigade is in deplorable condition; only about 1,200 effective men. Something will have to be done or the command will be lost. General V. has no idea of discipline. (Find my letter to Adjutant and Inspector General.) Some of the commands are good; from what I can ascertain, the great fault is with the commander of the brigade. Another officer should be put in command of the mounted men, and General V. be made to take the dismounted and be assigned to some infantry division, under a strict officer. Thus far it has been impossible to get a correct report from this brigade. Recently changes have been made, throwing the troops from the same States into the same brigades. (See order in office.) Insist upon my suggestions being acted upon. Now the command is almost a band of marauders. The arms, equipments, and clothing are all poor. The animals of First Tennessee Cavalry and Twelfth and Sixteenth Tennessee Battalions and Sixteenth Georgia Battalion are fair; the others very indifferent, half of which have been stolen. Three squadrons on the Holston; the others in Ashe and Watauga Counties, N. C. Third, Thirty-ninth, Forty-third, and Fifty-ninth Tennessee, formerly Reynolds' brigade, Sixtieth, Sixty-first, and Sixty-second Tennessee, Vaughn's old brigade, paroled at Vicksburg.

Brig. Gen. W. E. Jones' brigade—Eighth Virginia Regiment, Twenty-first Virginia Regiment, Sixty-fourth Virginia Regiment, Twenty-seventh Virginia Battalion, Thirty-fourth Virginia Battalion, Thirty-sixth Virginia Battalion, Thirty-seventh Virginia Battalion. Not a fair commander among the officers. Colonel of Eighth a drinking blackguard; Twenty-first, a gentleman, but ignorant of military duty; the rest no account. There should be a consolidation of small commands. Jones is trying to get rid of incompetent officers. From the office you will get strength. The chief part of brigade is moving back to Wythe County, Twenty-seventh Battalion in Kentucky, Sixty-fourth Regiment in Lee County, Va. Horses better than you would suppose. The work during the winter has been constant and hard. Jones ought to be promoted; notwithstanding all his grumbling, he is a fine officer. Arms, half good; others indifferent. Accouterments and clothing poor.

[Inclosure No. 2.]

	Aggregate present.
Jones' brigade:	
8th Virginia	225
21st Virginia	317
64th Virginia	268
27th Virginia Battalion	240
34th Virginia Battalion	222
36th Virginia Battalion	184
37th Virginia Battalion	300
Vaughn's brigade:	
43d Tennessee Infantry (mounted)	215
31st [39th] Tennessee Infantry (mounted)	272
3d Tennessee Infantry (Provisional Army) (mounted)	199
59th Tennessee Infantry (mounted)	241

Aggregate
present.

Vaughn's brigade—Continued.
1st Tennessee 248
16th Tennessee Battalion 147
12th Tennessee Battalion... 234
16th Georgia Battalion Cavalry..................................... 334
Detachments of Vaughn's old brigade, Sixtieth, Sixty-first, and Sixty-
second Tennessee Regiments.. 48
Giltner's brigade :
4th Kentucky... 494
10th Kentucky.. 168
10th Kentucky Battalion... 67
1st and 2d Kentucky Battalions. (No report.)
6th and 7th Confederate Battalions. (No report.)

[Inclosure No. 3.]

Field returns of cavalry arms in East Tennessee, commanded by Maj. Gen. R.
Ransom, jr., for April 16, 1864.

Command.	Effective total.	Total.	Aggregate.	Horses.	
				Serviceable.	Unserviceable.
Jones' brigade a.......	1,492	1,540	1,673	1,146	319
Vaughn's brigade..	1,445	1,726	1,938	1,295	327
Giltner's brigade b.....	620	659	737	....	....
Total..	3,557	3,925	4,348	2,441	646

a Twenty-seventh Virginia Battalion and Sixty-fourth Virginia not reported.
b First and Second Kentucky and Sixth and Seventh Confederate Battalions not reported.

[Inclosure No. 4.]

Jones' Brigade.

Brig. Gen. W. E. JONES.

8th Virginia Regiment, Col. J. M.
Corns.
21st Virginia Regiment, Col. W. E.
Peters.
64th Virginia Regiment, Col. C. Slemp.
27th Virginia Battalion, Lieut. Col. H. A.
Edmundson.
34th Virginia Battalion, Lieut. Col. V. A.
Witcher.
36th Virginia Battalion, Maj. J. W.
Sweeney.
37th Virginia Battalion, Maj. J. R. Claiborne.

Giltner's Brigade.

Col. H. L. GILTNER.

4th Kentucky Regiment, Lieut. Col. M.
T. Pryor.
10th Kentucky Regiment, Col. A. J. May.
1st Kentucky Battalion, Lieut. Col. E.
F. Clay.
2d Kentucky Battalion, Lieut. Col.
Thomas Johnson.
10th Kentucky Battalion, Maj. J. T.
Chenoweth.
6th Confederate Battalion, Maj. A. L.
McAfee.
7th Confederate Battalion, Lieut. Col.
C. J. Prentice.

Vaughn's Brigade.

Brig. Gen. J. C. VAUGHN.

1st Tennessee Regiment Cavalry, Col. J. E. Carter.
3d Tennessee (Provisional Army) Infantry (mounted), Col. N. J. Lillard.
31st [39th] Tennessee Regiment, Col. W. M. Bradford.
43d Tennessee Regiment, Col. J. W. Gillespie.
59th Tennessee Regiment, Col. W. L. Eakin.
12th Tennessee Battalion Cavalry, Maj. G. W. Day.
16th Tennessee Battalion, Lieut. Col. J. R. Neal.
16th Georgia Battalion, Lieut. Col. S. J. Winn.
Detachment of Vaughn's old brigade, 60th, 61st, and 62d Regiments Tennessee Infantry, Lieut. Col. William Parker.

BRISTOL, TENN., *April* 29, 1864.
Col. GEO. W. BRENT, *A. A. G., Hdqrs. Armies of the C. S.:*

COLONEL: From the investigation I have been able to make, I have to report that the complaints of the citizens of Sullivan County, Tenn., contained in the memorial referred to me, are well founded. I am satisfied that the limitations of the impressment law have not been uniformly observed. Supplies needed for the support of the household have been taken; disputed questions have not been referred to the board of arbitrators required by law. Agricultural operations have been interfered with, and in a great number of cases payment has not been made on the spot, but receipts of the most informal character have been left, signed by forage-masters, commissary sergeants, officers of the line, and sometimes without any indication of the command for which, the supplies were taken. In addition to these abuses, robberies by soldiers in small parties have been frequent. In October last, it is stated, a regiment of cavalry (Peters' Twenty-first Virginia) was mounted in East Tennessee by the indiscriminate license granted by General Williams to seize horses wherever they could be found. No receipts were given, no money paid, and no form of law observed. General A. E. Jackson assured me that he had himself taken from men of this regiment more than 100 horses thus seized, which he recognized as belonging to perfectly loyal Southern men. General William E. Jones, in March, directed his purveying officers to leave three bushels of corn or two and a half of wheat for each member of a family, but his quartermaster informed me that he was satisfied this limitation had not been respected. I have received assurances from General A. E. Jackson, from the chief quartermaster and chief commissary of the department, from the quartermaster of Jones' brigade, and from numerous citizens that the country contains a large number of informal receipts of the kind above described. A good many of these I have myself seen. Mr. Wyndham Robertson declared to me that he knew of numerous cases in which all the safeguards of the impressment law were disregarded. The accompanying documents, marked A and B, will illustrate the various kinds of depredations to which the people have been subjected. Most of these are now beyond remedy, but something may be done toward paying the debts represented by informal vouchers. I would suggest that as full powers as the law will allow be conferred upon Major Glover, chief quartermaster for the State of Tennessee, or such subordinate as he shall designate, for the liquidation of claims of this character in his department in this quarter, and that similar powers be conferred upon Captain Shelby, chief commissary at General Buckner's headquarters. It would seem that cavalry officers might devise some plan of foraging their detachments without subjecting the citizens to the enormous hardship of collecting his money upon irregular vouchers. Their quartermasters might at least be required to follow and take up immediately all such paper. At present the quartermaster of this department is making no impressments. The commissary has impressing agents out, who are provided with money or blank forms receipted and with copies of the impressment law and the orders thereon, which they are instructed strictly to respect.

I have the honor to be, colonel, very respectfully, your obedient servant,
ARCHER ANDERSON,
Lieut. Col., Asst. Adjt. Gen., on Inspection Duty.

[First indorsement.]

HEADQUARTERS ARMIES CONFEDERATE STATES,
May 6, 1864.

Respectfully submitted to His Excellency the President. A copy of this report will be sent to Brig. Gen. William E. Jones, commanding department, that a rigid scrutiny may be made and all offenders brought to justice. It is confidently hoped he will not allow a continuance of the lawless and disgraceful transactions.

BRAXTON BRAGG,
General.

[Second indorsement.]

MAY 6, 1864.

It is painful to know that such outrages as those described have been committed by any portion of our Army, the justice and humanity of which has generally been scarcely less conspicuous than their gallantry. It is due to the citizen, to the good soldier, and the fair fame of the Government that these abuses should be visited with such correction as will serve for future warning to evildoers.

JEFFERSON DAVIS.

[Third indorsement.]

MAY 23, 1864.

Respectfully referred to the Adjutant-General.

BRAXTON BRAGG.

[Fourth indorsement.]

All that is requisite seems to have been done at General Bragg's headquarters.

CLAY.

[Inclosures.]

A.

Memorandum of affidavits in the possession of J. R. Anderson, of Bristol :

Conrad Shirrett declares that 4 milch cows belonging to him were impressed, against his consent and in violation of law, by Maj. John Hockenhull, commissary of subsistence. In an indorsement on the papers appears an order from Major Latrobe, of General Longstreet's staff, to return the cows, but they were never returned.

On the night of April 1, 5 soldiers forcibly took from James Torbit 125 pounds of bacon, 12 pounds of flour, and 6 gallons of molasses. From the same man 2 bay mares were taken by soldiers of Peters' regiment of cavalry (Twenty-first Virginia) on the 18th October, 1863.

On the 11th April, 1864, Lieut. C. T. Whitehead, Company G, Sixteenth Georgia Battalion of Cavalry, took 12 bushels of corn from James Morton (all he had), during his absence and against his family's cries and protestations, leaving the following receipt : "Rec'd April 11, 1864, of James Morton, 12 bushels of corn for the use of public animals, Co. G, 16th Ga. Batt'n Cavalry.—Lt. C. T. Whitehead, comdg. Co. G, 16th Ga. Batt'n Cav'y."

November 8, 2 men, giving their names first as Ross and Roller and then as Thomas Rolliff and James Watmore, and as belonging to the Sixteenth Georgia Battalion Cavalry, forcibly took from Abram Baker 1 gray mare and 1 bay horse. He had but 1 other work animal. Neither money nor receipt was given.

Isaac C. Anderson, sr., declares in a letter that on the 7th April some men from Vaughn's brigade took from him his last ear of corn, by impressment, it is supposed. Men from the same brigade stole from him a black mare. Longstreet's men impressed his bull, the only breeding stock he had.

W. H. Litheal makes affidavit that 600 pounds of hay needed for his own stock were impressed by an agent of Capt. H. Kenneworth, Buckner's division. No citizen seems to have been called on.

Mrs. Hannah Thomas makes affid.vit that several wagon loads of forage necessary for her own stock were impressed without her consent.

Mr. J. R. Anderson states (not on affidavit) that on Monday, 25th April, two men, calling themselves of Ashby's regiment of cavalry, which had just passed, forcibly took from Isaac Sells 1 roan mare and from Andrew Cowan 1 horse. He further states that Benning's brigade, Field's division, encamped on his farm, near Zollicoffer, went off without settling for 10 acres of timber which they had consumed, though they knew they were to move a week before they started.

ARCHER ANDERSON,
Lieut. Col., Asst. Adjt. Gen., on Inspection Duty.

———

B.

HEADQUARTERS,
Near Kingsport, April 18, 1864.
Maj. T. ROWLAND,
Assistant Adjutant-General:

MAJOR : Three nights ago the house of a highly respectable woman living near Dixon's Ford, above here, was entered and robbed in her presence. The drawers were rifled, her jewelry was taken before her eyes, and she was compelled to give to the thieves her finger-rings. Hearing of it, I ordered and commenced an immediate search and investigation. Very soon I had reason to suspect that Lieutenant Kidd, Fifty-ninth Tennessee Cavalry (who was left here in arrest by General Vaughn and against whom other charges were already pending), was implicated. So soon as he discovered that the investigation would lead to his exposure, he cautiously slipped out to where his horse was, and in a few moments was not to be found. He has deserted and gone. I would have placed him in close arrest before the hour of his escape, but the evidence against him was too uncertain and rather vague to authorize it without further investigation. Two others, however, members of Company G, Fifty-ninth Tennessee Cavalry, who were accomplices in the theft, I have in close arrest and dismounted. One of them, if not both, I am persuaded is an experienced scoundrel, and therefore advise that they be sent at once to prison, or at least to some more secure point than this. Please advise Major Toole what to do with them. We have use for their horses here and I will hold them, with your permission, subject to

General Ransom's order. I communicated with General Vaughn fully as to Kidd's breach of arrest and escape. I also sent two men in pursuit of him, but I have little thought of capturing him very soon. He rode an uncommonly fine horse, and is a very shrewd villain.

Very respectfully, your obedient servant,

JAS. W. HUMES,
Lieutenant-Colonel, Comdg. Detachment Second Brigade.

[Indorsement.]

MAY 7, 1864.

This officer should be dropped from rolls as a deserter.

BRAXTON BRAGG,
General.

COUNTY COURT, *April Term,* 1864.

On motion, the chairman of court appointed L. M. King, F. W. Earnest, and Joseph R. Anderson a committee to memorialize Lieutenant-General Longstreet, through this court, to grant relief to the citizens of this county from depredations from soldiers, and report immediately to this court.

BLOUNTSVILLE, *April* 4, 1864.

STATE OF TENNESSEE,
  Sullivan County:

Lieutenant-General LONGSTREET,
  Commanding Army East Tennessee:

SIR : We, the undersigned citizens of said county, being a committee appointed by the worshipful county court of this county to draft a suitable memorial to you in behalf of the citizens of the county, do most respectfully submit the following :

This county has furnished in all about 2,000 troops for the defense of the South and Southern institutions, a large number of whom have left poor families dependent upon the citizens for support, and owing to the present system of impressments and the daily violations of the laws governing the impressment of supplies we are utterly unable to render the relief their wants require. We look to you as the great conservator of our rights, and in the name of humanity and the cause of Southern independence we appeal to you for protection and relief. Families are being daily robbed of the supplies absolutely necessary for their support, by officers of the army, claiming to be authorized by you, while a well-organized system of robbery is carried on all over the country day and night, the only authority claimed for which is the terror of the bayonet. If this state of things continues it will not only demoralize and ruin the army, but will force good men to quit the ranks and return to their homes to defend their families against the excesses and outrages of unprincipled men and stragglers from our own army. The county is full of private soldiers, who plunder and rob with impunity when we are already reduced to a bare subsistence. Many of the impressments, we think, made by officers are in positive violation of the law of Congress and the orders of General Cooper on the subject. We are willing, as we ever have been, to contribute to the utmost of our ability to a cause so vital to our social and political existence. In considera-

tion of these things we therefore most respectfully ask you to protect us against further aggressions of the kind, and prevent the further impressment of supplies so necessary to the support of families of soldiers in the field. The exigencies of our situation, should we fail to get that relief which we pray at your hands, will compel us to appeal to the authorities at Richmond.
All of which is respectfully submitted.

L. M. KING,
F. W. EARNEST,
JOS. R. ANDERSON,
Committee.

The foregoing resolutions or memorials being submitted by the committee to the court, the same was unanimously adopted by the court, and it is ordered by the court that David S. Lyon, L. M. King, Joel L. Barker, esq., and Joseph R. Anderson and L. F. Johnson be appointed a committee to present this memorial to Lieutenant-General Longstreet and await his answer, and report the same to the court instanter, together with these proceedings.

A true copy of the proceedings of the court, this 4th day of April, 1864.
Attest: JOHN C. RUTLEDGE,
Clerk.

TUESDAY, *April 5, 1864.*

The court had the following proceedings on the report of Lieutenant-General Longstreet:

Returned into court the report of the committee, whereupon the court refers this matter to His Excellency Jefferson Davis, President of the Confederate States of America, and appoints L. M. King and F. W. Earnest, gentlemen and citizens of Sullivan County, to bear these proceedings to Richmond, that His Excellency may grant such relief as the exigencies of the case demand.

STATE OF TENNESSEE,
Sullivan County:

I, John C. Rutledge, clerk of the county court for said county, hereby certify the foregoing to be a true copy of the record as will appear in my office.

Given under my hand and private seal (having no office seal) at office in Blountsville, this 5th day of April, 1864.

[SEAL.]   JOHN C. RUTLEDGE,
Clerk.

[First indorsement.]

HEADQUARTERS,
April 5, 1864.

Respectfully forwarded.
The orders in this department require the strictest enforcement of the impressment authority. This is rendered absolutely necessary in order that our troops and animals may be partially fed. If we cannot get supplies from the East we must soon be forced to take more than the law allows to avoid starvation.

J. LONGSTREET,
Lieutenant-General, Commanding.

852   KY., SW. VA., TENN., MISS., ALA., AND N. GA.   [CHAP. XLIV.

[Second indorsement.]

General Bragg, for attention.
The indorsement of General Longstreet does not touch the complaint of the citizens against illegal seizures, robbery, &c.
J. D.

BLOUNTSVILLE, TENN.,
April 6, 1864.

The committee to whom the worshipful court referred the foregoing memorial would state further (without any intention of boasting) that the citizens of this county on the whole are as loyal as any within the Southern Confederacy, and as such have a right to claim and expect protection from wanton abuses on the part of our own army. They have contributed all their surplus to the use of the C. S. Army, even to a deprivation of their common pursuits in agricultural interests. This county has already paid into the C. S. Treasury as war tax upward of $100,000, as will appear from the files in said office. Notwithstanding all this, and much more that could be said in our behalf, the citizens of this county are willing to abide the acts of Congress and General Cooper's instructions on impressments; yet when within the last few days the whole county has been stripped by forage and commissary wagons (in many cases without even a receipt being given), one universal wail of lamentation has to be borne with this memorial in behalf of many families to you for relief. They are to-day dependent upon the C. S. Government for supplies, and it is believed and hoped you will grant them. This county has to-day quartered upon it the whole of General Longstreet's army from its length and breadth, which will of necessity make it a dependency upon the Government before any relief can reach us for the supplies of soldiers and other families. We trust you will not turn a deaf ear to the complaints of a people who still struggle to maintain their loyalty to the C. S. Government.
F. W. EARNEST,
JOS. R. ANDERSON.
L. M. KING.

ABINGDON, *April 29, 1864.*
Brigadier-General JOHNSON, *Zollicoffer:*
You will move with your infantry and the battery of artillery now with you, by easy marches, back to this place. You will leave with General Jackson the cavalry which now reports to you, and give to that officer such general instructions as you may think fit. Start to-day or to-morrow, as you wish.
J. N. GALLEHER,
Assistant Adjutant-General.

ABINGDON, *April 29, 1864.*
General BRECKINRIDGE:
Wharton's brigade, by written orders from Adjutant-General's Office, is ordered to report to you at Dublin Depot. I am to-day sending it to Glade Spring. Shall I direct it to continue its march by rail to Dublin? Please answer at once.
S. B. BUCKNER,
Major-General.

HDQRS. DETACHMENT GEN. ARMSTRONG'S BRIGADE,
April 29, 1864.
[Capt. T. B. SYKES,
Assistant Adjutant and Inspector General:]

CAPTAIN : I have the honor to submit the following report, to wit : In obedience to orders, through Brigadier-General Armstrong, from General Jackson, commanding division, I left Tuscaloosa on the morning of the 19th April, with a detachment from Ballentine's regiment, commanded by Captain Blackwell, and one from the Twenty-eighth Mississippi, commanded by Captain Woods, in all about 250 men. I proceeded, in accordance with instructions, to operate in Walker and Winston Counties, Ala., against the tories, who were reported to be depredating upon the property of loyal citizens. On the evening of the 20th of April I encamped in the edge of Fayette County, and had to scatter my command on account of the scarcity of forage. A young man from the Twenty-eighth Mississippi, who was in advance of the detachment some 200 or 300 yards, was halted by 2 men, who were armed ; he refused to halt, put spurs to his horse, and rode rapidly back to his command, procured re-enforcements and pursued them through the hills, where it became impossible to continue the pursuit farther.

On the evening of the 22d I arrived at Jasper, the county seat of Walker, where I found Lieutenant-Colonel McCaskill, who had been sent to Walker and Winston Counties, by order of General J. E. Johnston, with a detachment of 80 men. Colonel McCaskill had made some 40 arrests prior to my arrival, 30 of whom were in the jail at Jasper. I assisted him in guarding the prisoners, as fears were entertained that their friends would endeavor to rescue them. Colonel McCaskill left with the prisoners on the 27th for Dalton, Ga. I made seven or eight arrests, two of whom were sent to Dalton, Ga. The remainder were brought to this place and turned over to the commandant of the post.

The rumors of those counties are greatly exaggerated. I was informed by reliable men that Walker County never voted at any election more than 1,400 votes, and yet she has nineteen full companies in the Confederate service.

The scarcity of forage in these counties is a great drawback to cavalry operations, together with the unevenness of the ground. There are many places where it is impossible for a cavalryman to approach, cliffs so abrupt that nothing save a mountain goat or a deer would attempt to scale them. These fastnesses are the places sought for by deserters.

There is no scarcity of provision in these counties, and I would suggest that one or two infantry companies be sent there. It would be an easy matter to subsist them ; let them build stockades in various portions of those counties contiguous to the tories, and send out small scouting parties every day and drive the woods as though they were in pursuit of game. They would afford permanent protection. An infantry force scattered about in those counties, particularly if they were furnished with a pack of dogs, would be able to protect the country and drive out the last tory or deserter.

I am, captain, very respectfully,

W. L. MAXWELL,
Lieutenant-Colonel, Commanding Detachment.

APRIL 29, 1864.

Lieut. Gen. L. POLK,
  Commanding Department of Mississippi:
  MY DEAR GENERAL: I have finished inspecting Loring, French, and Lee, and am not only pleased greatly with the appearance of the troops, who in discipline and drill are superb, but am glad to find that all the subordinate general officers cordially approve the plan of the campaign. I will be glad to have Major West join me at Montgomery on the 5th May, and hope as I pass to see you.
  I am, general, with high respect, your friend and obedient servant,

GEO. B. HODGE.

JACKSON, TENN., *April* 29, 1864.

Lieutenant-General POLK:
  Enemy reported pressing horses and shops to prepare for a move against me from Memphis. Have the regiment on Tallahatchie left by General Chalmers, and will send Colonel Duckworth, of Seventh Tennessee Cavalry, to watch their movements; also will keep you advised.

N. B. FORREST,
Major-General.

ABINGDON, *April* 30, 1864.

General S. COOPER,
  Adjutant and Inspector General:
  General Johnson has just informed me that he has received instructions from General Bragg to throw his cavalry forward. This cannot be done at present, because the cavalry destined for that part of my line has not yet returned from North Carolina, and all the rest of my cavalry is concentrating at different points for a necessary purpose. I will explain more fully by mail.
  Please inform General Bragg that his orders, if given direct to me instead of to my subordinates, will be executed with the utmost promptness whenever practicable.

S. B. BUCKNER,
Major-General.

[Indorsements.]

Respectfully submitted to General B. Bragg.
JOHN W. RIELY,
Assistant Adjutant-General.

HEADQUARTERS ARMY OF CONFEDERATE STATES,
May 2, 1864.

Respectfully submitted to Adjutant and Inspector General.
Please inform General Buckner he had been relieved of his command and it had devolved on General Johnson before General Bragg's order was given.

BRAXTON BRAGG.

MAY 2, 1864.

See telegram to General Buckner.

J. W. R.

HEADQUARTERS DEPARTMENT OF EAST TENNESSEE,
Abingdon, April 30, 1864.

Brig. Gen. J. H. MORGAN,
Commanding Cavalry, Saltville:

GENERAL : I am directed by the major-general commanding to say that he wishes that portion of Giltner's brigade which lately formed Hodge's command to remain in the vicinity of Heyter's Gap, if he has not yet already moved. If it has moved, let the battalions be concentrated near the railroad, where corn can be furnished, and also in a locality which will afford pasturage. The officer in charge will notify these headquarters and Colonel Giltner of the position they may take.

The major-general commanding also directs me to say that, while he is anxious to mobilize your entire command as early as possible, yet the expedition he spoke with you of cannot be undertaken while threatened by a raid from the enemy, or at least while a portion of his cavalry is still absent.

Please issue the necessary orders to insure the concentration of Giltner's battalions, so that they can be paid and equipped. An officer goes to Richmond to-night to secure the articles needed.

I am, general, your obedient servant,
J. N. GALLEHER,
Assistant Adjutant-General.

ABINGDON, April 30, 1864.
(Received Dublin, April 30.)

General BRECKINRIDGE :

I have plenty of artillery at Saltville. I suggest that you take the section which you have there and send with Wharton. As soon as my horses come up I can give you a battery in addition. I wrote to-day.

S. B. BUCKNER.

HEADQUARTERS DEPARTMENT OF EAST TENNESSEE,
Abingdon, April 30, 1864.

Brigadier-General JACKSON, Carter's Depot:

General Vaughn's command has been ordered back to cover your line.

J. N. GALLEHER,
Assistant Adjutant-General.

HEADQUARTERS DEPARTMENT OF EAST TENNESSEE,
Abingdon, April 30, 1864.

Lieut. D. N. MONTGOMERY, Zollicoffer:

General Vaughn has been ordered back to the front of Bristol.

J. N. GALLEHER,
Assistant Adjutant-General.

DEMOPOLIS, April 30, 1864.

His Excellency President DAVIS, Richmond:

I wrote to you on the 27th, by Colonel Duncan. Among other things I adverted to the measures I had taken to recover this department from the evils to which it was subjected in consequence of the presence of a very large number of deserters from all the armies of the Confederacy, in which there were commands raised from it. These measures became indispensable from the extent to which these evils had reached. Formidable bands were being organized in different parts of this department and hostility to the Government began to be openly proclaimed. It became necessary to silence these discontents and to crush these incipient rebellions at once, and I took such measures as effectually to accomplish it. I inaugurated campaigns against all absentees all over the department by sending out detachments from my forces in the field. These have been very active and their operations have been very successful; many of the ringleaders found in arms and offering resistance were summarily disposed of, and such an impression thereby made upon their followers that they have either given themselves up or gone to their commands. I have reason to believe that over 1,000 of these men have been sent from the woods to their commands and others are daily returning. My operations still continue and will be kept up until I clear the department of them and they are forced back to their duty. To aid in accomplishing this I have been induced, after the measures I had been pursuing had demonstrated to the absentees that they could not escape, in reply to a petition from the senate and house of representatives of Mississippi, to issue a proclamation offering pardon to all who would return. The effect of this has proved very salutary, and while I have not relaxed my operations in ferreting them out they are moved by it to abandon their haunts and to return to duty.

To prevent their return to their hiding-places, and to complete more effectually the work of driving them out of their retreats, as well as to give protection to the civil power, which I am restoring where it has been driven out, I have cut up my department into military districts of a size to be easily managed. To the command of these I have assigned such officers of my command as have been disabled by the casualties of battle, or otherwise, to whom companies raised for local defense, composed of the material set apart by Congress for that purpose, and exempts have been ordered to report. By the acts of these I hope soon to bring the department into a satisfactory condition and to keep it so. These companies and all those making up the reserve I presume the Government will wish grouped into regiments, brigades, and divisions as soon as practicable, and they will be at its disposal when called for.

I send by the messenger who takes this a copy of a map of my department, with the sub-divisions into military police districts, for your information.

I remain, very truly and respectfully, your obedient servant,

L. POLK,
Lieutenant-General.

————

DEMOPOLIS, *April* 30, 1864.

Hon. J. A. SEDDON,
    Secretary of War, Richmond:

I have suspended, until I could hear from you, the orders given by the War Department to Lieutenants Johnston and Blackburn to operate on the Mississippi River against gun-boats and transports. This I did because I saw there was great danger of detached parties of this sort marring a plan I am maturing and hope shortly to put in operation for assailing those boats on an extended scale, with the prospect of accomplishing a result too valuable to be put in jeopardy by the action, though successful, of a single detachment; and I now respectfully ask that these young officers with their detachments, and all others to whom such commissions may have been given, be ordered to report to me. to be worked into the organization of which I speak. The object proposed, the capture or destruction of the boats, is the same. The results they may produce single-handed must be partial; in the combination I am completing they may be of the most extended character.

My plan, which I have carefully matured, is as follows: From Manchac to Cairo there are seven degrees of latitude; in each of these degrees I am placing on the river a battalion of four companies of mounted rifles, and to each battalion I assign a field battery of four guns. These battalions are made up of the material set aside by law for the reserves and for the local defense. This force, more or less of which is in position, will be charged with the duty of defending the localities to which the several commands are assigned against the enemy from without and the enemy from within. It will be instructed to break up the navigation of the river, to destroy the commerce on the border, and to prevent all efforts at agriculture from being successful. It will be at the same time charged with the military police of the district to which it is assigned; it will prevent the river border being used as a hiding-place for deserters and marauders of all sorts, and will give protection to our planters who desire to return to their plantations to cultivate. It will thus restore order to a region that has suffered the want of protection, and will enable the courts to do their functions and enforce the laws. These result, should they be attained, and I cannot see how they can fail, will be enough to warrant the organization, but I think it will prepare the way for attempting more, to wit, the capture of more or less of the gun-boats employed on the river. The battalions stationed along the river border from Cairo down will give me the command of all the men I require at the places I should require them. I propose, then, to place the movement under the command of a competent officer, who will, with a force of 500 picked men, captains, mates, pilots, and engineers, with other river men, take a position about Fort Pillow and will ship on a transport well known in the river, which I could easily arrange to purchase. Once on the river the party would "round to" as usual, to deliver the mails alongside of the first gun-boat encountered going down and capture it. After removing the crew, they would ship on the prize as much force as was necessary to manage it and proceed down stream until they encountered the next, which would be captured in turn, and so on as long as success attended the enterprise or there were boats to be captured. The force necessary from whence to draw for a constant supply to man the captured boats would be found in the battalions distributed along the river by appointment at places agreed upon. The principal difficulty would be in the first capture, after which it would not be easy to say how far the work might not proceed. As I have remarked, I am getting the battalions into position as fast as they can be organized, and feel confident at least of being able to prevent the enemy's navigation, break up his commerce, and prevent his agriculture, as well as clear out the deserters and robbers and establish order in the bottom; for the rest it will turn on tact and skill and energy and courage, and I believe we shall have no difficulty in getting up the proper combination. The funds to secure the transport will, of course, be needed. If the Department, therefore, is giving commissions to parties to raise commands to attack the enemy's boats on the river, to operate in my department, I respectfully ask that they may be directed to report to me and be placed under my orders.

I remain, respectfully, your obedient servant,

L. POLK,
Lieutenant-General.

P. S.—I find upon the examination of the resources of the department that I have very nearly field guns enough to equip the battalions with the batteries proposed, and shall get a large number of the mules and horses required for them from the plantations on the river in the hands of the enemy. I ask funds necessary to procure the transport, which I can manage through the use of cotton.

HEADQUARTERS LEE'S CAVALRY,
Tuscaloosa, Ala., April 30, 1864.

Brig. Gen. GIDEON J. PILLOW,
Commanding Brigade Cavalry:

GENERAL: In reply to your letter from Demopolis, General Lee directs me to say that he wishes you to return to Montgomery and to complete as rapidly as possible the organization of the brigade which you are now forming.

As soon as the organization is completed the general requests that you will notify him of the fact, and that you will also report as soon as possible its present condition and prospects.

I am, general, very respectfully, your obedient servant,

WILLIAM ELLIOTT,
Assistant Adjutant and Inspector General.

HEADQUARTERS LEE'S CAVALRY,
Tuscaloosa, Ala., April 30, 1864.

Lieut. Col. T. M. JACK,
Assistant Adjutant-General, Demopolis, Ala.:

COLONEL: I have nothing special to report as regards the enemy in North Alabama, not having received any reliable reports for several days. I am still of opinion no offensive move is intended against Middle Alabama, and that Decatur is re-enforced, as it is threatened, by Roddey. Roddey and Clanton have arranged to cross a large part of their commands, and before this I should have had the result of their operations and more definite information as to the intentions of the enemy.

Jackson's division is about Carthage, and Ferguson near the railroad opposite Centreville. While in Jones' Valley he had to move daily and exhausted the supplies where he went. He was compelled to move to his present position to get supplies by rail and draw a small supply from the country. The railroad (branch) northeast of Montevallo could not supply him, and owing to deficiency of transportation on the railroad he says now that he will not be able to get long forage for his horses. His horses are in bad condition and should be recruited if the exigencies of the service permit, and nothing can be obtained in the country near where he is at present. Have ordered General Pillow to complete the organization of his brigade as speedily as possible, when I propose increasing his command, probably giving him command of Roddey in addition to his brigade. Colonel Foster, Member of Congress from North Alabama, reports that Roddey will have nearly 3,000 men. Ferguson did not send out an expedition northeast of Elyton, as he was directed, stating that from all he could learn the deserters, tories, &c., were not in squads, but scattered through the woods in hiding-places almost inaccessible to cavalry and where there was no forage. I send him an order to-day to send 300 men in small squads over the country northeast of Elyton to move on a line with General French, who is organizing an expedition under your orders. I will furnish General French with several squadrons to aid him. It is almost impossible for cavalry to operate in the country above this, owing to want of forage, there being none in the country.

I sent orders recalling the detachments sent from this point so soon as your proclamation appeared in the papers, believing it to be your policy from the conversation we had at Columbus, where you stated you wished me to act before the proclamation was published. The last of the parties came in to-day, with the following results: The main detachments were sent to Pikeville and Jasper, and operated from these two points. Colonel Jones, at Pikeville, captured about 60 deserters and brought them in. They were delivered to Colonel Baker to send all of Roddey's men to him for trial, as most of them belonged to new organizations being raised under orders from Colonel Patterson, of Roddey's command.

The officers concerned are here now and will be tried by my courts, now in session. Colonel Jones reports affairs much exaggerated as to forces. He says there are a good many deserters, but not banded together, who are lying out in the mountains, and it is almost impossible to find them, owing to the rough country. He could get no forage for his animals, and reports that it is almost impracticable for cavalry to remain or operate in the country.

Will investigate thoroughly the conduct of the officers concerned in raising new organizations. Colonel Baker is preparing the charges.

Lieutenant-Colonel Maxwell and Major Perry report in substance the same as Colonel Jones. They report that infantry can operate better than cavalry. I send the reports for your perusal.* To accomplish anything against the deserters and tories it must be done by a command which can remain in the country some time and find their hiding-places from the people in the country. Expeditions for short periods can accomplish nothing, as they are easily avoided in this rugged country.

I doubt the propriety of sending the expedition now, as the proclamations are being distributed through the country. Colonel Baker, however, thinks that few will come in under the proclamation, and advantage had better be taken of the presence of the troops here now and new expeditions will be started in a few days.

I am, colonel, yours, respectfully,

S. D. LEE,
Major-General.

---

*For Maxwell's report, see p. 853.

[Inclosure.]

HDQRS. DETACH. FIRST AND SECOND MISS. CAV.,
En route Tuscaloosa, April 30, 1864.

Capt. T. B. SYKES,
    Assistant Adjutant and Inspector General:

CAPTAIN: The undersigned officer, detailed with a portion of the First and Second Mississippi Cavalry and assigned to Fayetteville Fayette County, Ala., begs leave to submit the following report:

Pursuant to orders, one company of detachment was left at Wyndham Springs four days; the others sent by companies to all parts of the county. None of the parties found or heard of any armed bands of tories or deserters. There are, from a summary, between 250 and 300 deserters in the county, the majority of them lying in the woods in small squads near their homes.

There were 7 captured by the detachment and turned over to the commandant of post at this place, the time not being sufficient to pursue them to their hiding-places; also 6 horses and 2 mules found belonging to deserters in the woods.

The citizens of that county, in the opinion of the undersigned, are generally loyal, but are not aiding the Confederacy, on account of inability.

The soil is poor and the people generally have nothing more than will subsist their families. A force of cavalry of any size cannot be subsisted there for any length of time without impoverishing the county. Corn is being hauled now from the prairies to make their crops and maintain the families of soldiers.

Respectfully submitted.

J. J. PERRY,
Major, Commanding Detachment.

Abstract from return of the Army in the District of the Gulf, Maj. Gen. Dabney H. Maury, C. S. Army, commanding, for the month of April, 1864; headquarters Mobile, Ala.

Command.	Present for duty.		Effective total present.	Aggregate present.	Aggregate present and absent.	Pieces of field artillery.
	Officers.	Men.				
General headquarters	12			12	13	
Page's brigade:						
Artillery	104	1,582	1,758	1,968	2,572	
Cavalry	11	231	244	265	336	
Quarles' brigade (infantry)	132	857	984	1,141	1,819	
Reynolds' brigade:						
Infantry	116	694	812	1,024	1,048	
Cavalry	38	551	660	758	1,336	
Artillery	5	145	146	160	239	8
Artillery brigade	110	1,210	1,284	1,510	2,442	
Detached commands:						
Bay batteries	16	209	293	323	471	
Cavalry	7	180	188	223	345	
Local defense companies	45	461	498	605	829	
Engineer troops	3	74	74	82	101	
Grand total	590	6,284	6,886	8,151	12,451	8

Troops in the District of the Gulf, Maj. Gen. Dabney H. Maury, C. S. Army, commanding, April 30, 1864.

Page's Brigade.

Brig. Gen. RICHARD L. PAGE.

1st Alabama Infantry (serving as artillery). Maj. Samuel L. Knox.
1st Alabama Artillery Battalion, Lieut. Col. Robert C. Forsyth.
7th Alabama Cavalry (four companies), Maj. Turner Clanton, jr.
21st Alabama, Col. C. D. Anderson.
30th Louisiana. Lieut. Col. Thomas Shields.
1st Tennessee Heavy Artillery, Lieut. Col. Robert Sterling.

Quarles' Brigade.

Brig. Gen. WILLIAM A. QUARLES.

4th Louisiana, Col. S. E. Hunter.
42d Tennessee, Col. Isaac N. Hulme.
46th and 55th Tennessee, Col. Robert A. Owens.
48th Tennessee, Col. William M. Voorhies.
49th Tennessee, Col. William F. Young.
53d Tennessee, Col. John R. White.

Reynolds' Brigade.

Brig. Gen. DANIEL H. REYNOLDS.*

7th Alabama Cavalry (detachment), Col. Joseph Hodgson.
1st Arkansas Mounted Rifles (dismounted), Lieut. Col. George W. Wells.
2d Arkansas Mounted Rifles (dismounted), Col. James A. Williamson.
4th Arkansas, Col. H. G. Bunn.
25th Arkansas, Maj. L. L. Noles.
15th Confederate Cavalry, Col. Henry Maury.
39th North Carolina, Col. David Coleman.
Alabama Battery, Capt. Edward Tarrant.
Tennessee Battery, Capt. Thomas F. Tobin.

Artillery Brigade.†

Col. CHARLES A. FULLER.

Alabama State Artillery. Company C, Capt. John B. Todd.
Alabama State Artillery, Company D, Capt. William H. Homer.
1st Louisiana Artillery, Lieut. Col. Daniel Beltzhoover.
22d Louisiana, Lieut. Col. J. O. Landry.
1st Mississippi Light Artillery, Capt. Edward L. Bower.
Alabama Battery, Capt. John J. Ward.

Unattached.

Engineer troops, Capt. L. Hutchinson.
Bay Batteries, Col. W. E. Burnet.
1st Mobile Regiment, Col. A. W. Lampkin.
Fire Battalion, Maj. W. S. Moreland.
Pelham Cadets, Capt. Price Williams, jr.

---

*Assigned April 1 by General Polk.
†Trueheart's battalion not accounted for.   On April 17 it was reported as consisting of Culpeper's South Carolina, Lowe's Missouri, Ward's Alabama, and Yates' Mississippi batteries.

Abstract from return of the Army, Department of Alabama, Mississippi, and East Louisiana, Lieut. Gen. Leonidas Polk, C. S. Army, commanding, for the month of April, 1864; headquarters Demopolis, Ala.

Command.	Present for duty.		Effective total present.	Aggregate present.	Aggregate present and absent.	Pieces of field artillery.
	Officers.	Men.				
General staff.	10			10	11	
Loring's division	393	4,322	4,259	5,405	10,273	
French's division	248	2,072	2,048	2,655	4,870	
Sears' brigade a	120	1,713	1,694	2,110	3,915	...
Post of Cahaba, Ala	37	254	254	351	501	
Post of Demopolis, Ala	25	287	284	350	799	
Post of Selma, Ala	22	174	174	216	262	
Engineer troops	16	111	111	143	184	
Paroled and exchanged prisoners	41	278	267	348	697	
Post of Columbus, Miss.	15	151	150	179	587	
Total b	917	9 362	9,241	11,757	22,088	
Lee's cavalry command c	652	7,685	7,611	9,981	16,640	...
Escort	4	49	49	60	95	
Total	656	7,734	7,660	10,041	16,735	
Artillery, Loring's division	18	393	380	453	862	18
Artillery, French's division	11	161	151	185	274	6
Artillery, Sears' brigade	4	84	82	96	105	
Total	33	638	613	734	1,241	24
Grand total	1,616	17,734	17,514	22,542	40,075	24

a Sears' brigade transferred from District of the Gulf.
b No report has ever been received from Major-General Withers.
c This report is taken from Major-General Lee's last report, January 20, 1864, which includes Chalmers' division. No report has ever been received from Major-General Forrest.

Troops in the Department of Alabama, Mississippi, and East Louisiana, Lieut. Gen. Leonidas Polk, C. S. Army, commanding, April 30, 1864.

GENERAL HEADQUARTERS.

Escort (Louisiana) Company, Capt. Leeds Greenleaf.

LORING'S DIVISION.

Maj. Gen. WILLIAM W. LORING.

Featherston's Brigade.

Brig. Gen. WINFIELD S. FEATHERSTON.

3d Mississippi, Col. T. A. Mellon.
22d Mississippi, Col. Frank Schaller.
31st Mississippi, Col. M. D. L. Stephens.
33d Mississippi, Col. J. L. Drake.
40th Mississippi, Col. W. Bruce Colbert.
43d Mississippi, Col. Richard Harrison.
1st Mississippi Battalion Sharpshooters, Maj. J. M. Stigler.

Scott's Brigade.

Col. THOMAS M. SCOTT.

55th Alabama, Maj. Joseph H. Jones.
57th Alabama, Lieut. Col. W. C. Bethune.
9th Arkansas, Col. Isaac L. Dunlop.
12th Louisiana, Lieut. Col. N. L. Nelson.

Adams' Brigade.

Brig. Gen. JOHN ADAMS.

6th Mississippi, Col. Robert Lowry.
14th Mississippi, Maj. R. J. Lawrence.
15th Mississippi, Col. M. Farrell.
20th Mississippi, Col. William N. Brown.
23d Mississippi, Col. Joseph M. Wells.

*Artillery.**

Alabama Battery, Capt. Stephen Charpentier.
Lookout (Tennessee) Artillery, Capt. Robert L. Barry.
Mississippi Battery, Capt. James J. Cowan.
Mississippi Battery, Capt. William T. Ratliff.
Pointe Coupée (Louisiana) Artillery, Capt. Alcide Bouanchaud.

FRENCH'S DIVISION.

Maj. Gen. SAMUEL G. FRENCH.

First Brigade.

Brig. Gen. MATTHEW D. ECTOR.

29th North Carolina. Col. William B. Creasman.
9th Texas, Col. William H. Young.
10th Texas Cavalry,† Col. C. R. Earp.
14th Texas Cavalry,† Col. John L. Camp.
32d Texas Cavalry,† Col. Julius. A. Andrews.

Second Brigade.

Brig. Gen. FRANCIS M. COCKRELL.

1st and 4th Missouri, Col. A. C. Riley.
2d and 6th Missouri, Col. P. C. Flournoy.
3d and 5th Missouri, Col. James McCown.
1st and 3d Missouri Cavalry,† Col. Elijah Gates.

SEARS' BRIGADE.‡

Brig. Gen. CLAUDIUS W. SEARS.

4th Mississippi, Col. T. N. Adaire.
35th Mississippi, Col. William S. Barry.
36th Mississippi, Lieut. Col. Edward Brown.
39th Mississippi, Lieut. Col. W. E. Ross.
46th Mississippi, Lieut. Col. W. H. Clark.
7th Mississippi Battalion, Lieut. Col. Lucien B. Pardue.
Tennessee Battery, Capt. William C. Winston.

Artillery.

Brookhaven (Mississippi) Artillery, Capt. James A. Hoskins.
Missouri Battery, Capt. Henry Guibor.

---

* Reported April 24 as Myrick's battalion, Stevenson's division.
† Dismounted.
‡ Transferred from Department of the Gulf and encamped near Selma, Ala. On
June 10 it appears as Third Brigade of French's division. Brigadier-General Sears
assigned to command by General Polk, April 1.

CAVALRY CORPS.*

Maj. Gen. STEPHEN D. LEE.

JACKSON'S DIVISION.

First Brigade.

Col. PETER B. STARKE.

1st Mississippi, Lieut. Col. F. A. Montgomery.
28th Mississippi, Maj. J. T. McBee.
Ballentine's (Mississippi) Regiment, Lieut. Col. William L. Maxwell.
Clark (Missouri) Artillery, Capt. Houston King.

Second Brigade.

Brig. Gen. LAWRENCE S. ROSS.

1st Texas Legion, Col. E. R. Hawkins.
3d Texas, Col. Hinchie P. Mabry.
6th Texas, Maj. Peter F. Ross.
9th Texas, Col. Dud. W. Jones.
Escort (Tennessee) Company, Capt. J. W. Sneed.
Columbus (Georgia) Light Artillery, Capt. Edward Croft.

Third Brigade.

Brig. Gen. SAMUEL W. FERGUSON.

2d Alabama, Col. R. G. Earle.
56th Alabama, Col. William Boyles.
12th Mississippi Battalion, Col. W. M. Inge.
9th Mississippi, Col. Horace H. Miller.
Arkansas Battery, Capt. James A. Owens.

Adams' Brigade.

Brig. Gen. WIRT ADAMS.

11th and 17th Arkansas Infantry (mounted), Maj. B. P. Jett.
2d Mississippi, Capt. William A. Rogers.
4th Mississippi, Lieut. Col. C. McLaurin.
Moorman's (Mississippi) Battalion, Maj. Calvit Roberts.
Wood's (Mississippi) Regiment, Lieut. Col. Thomas Lewers.

SCOTT'S BRIGADE.†

Col. JOHN S. SCOTT.

14th Confederate (one company), Capt. Louis S. Greenlee.
9th Louisiana Battalion, Capt. William Turner.
Miles' (Louisiana) Legion, Maj. James T. Coleman.
38th Mississippi (Company D), Capt. James H. Jones.
Powers' (Mississippi) Regiment, Col. Frank P. Powers.

FORREST'S COMMAND.‡

Maj. Gen. NATHAN B. FORREST.

FIRST DIVISION.

Brig. Gen. JAMES R. CHALMERS.

First Brigade.

Col. WILLIAM L. DUCKWORTH.

7th Tennessee, Col. William L. Duckworth.
12th Tennessee, Col. John U. Green.
13th Tennessee, Col. James J. Neely.
14th Tennessee, Col. Francis M. Stewart.

Second Brigade.

Col. ROBERT McCULLOCH.

1st Mississippi Partisan Rangers, Maj. J. M. Park.
5th Mississippi Battalion.
18th Mississippi Battalion, Lieut. Col. Alexander H. Chalmers.
19th Mississippi Battalion, Lieut. Col. William L. Duff.
2d Missouri, Lieut. Col. R. A. McCulloch.
McDonald's (Tennessee) Battalion, Lieut. Col. J. M. Crews.
Texas Battalion, Lieut. Col. Leonidas Willis.

---

*The actual date represented is uncertain. A note on original return, in connection with strength reported, states that Major-General Lee's report of January 20, 1864, was the last received.
†Formerly commanded by Col. Edward Dillon.
‡Date actually represented by original return not shown. Note in connection with strength reported, "No report has ever been received from Major-General Forrest." Artillery not accounted for.

SECOND DIVISION.

Brig. Gen. ABRAHAM BUFORD.

Third Brigade.

Col. A. P. THOMPSON.

3d Kentucky Infantry (mounted), Lieut. Col. G. A. C. Holt.
7th Kentucky Infantry (mounted), Col. Ed. Crossland.
8th Kentucky Infantry (mounted), Lieut. Col. A. R. Shacklett.
12th Kentucky Cavalry, Col. W. W. Faulkner.
Forrest's (Alabama) Regiment, Lieut. Col. D. M. Wisdom.

Fourth Brigade.

Col. TYREE H. BELL.

2d Tennessee, Col. C. R. Barteau.
15th Tennessee, Col. R. M. Russell.
16th Tennessee, Col. A. N. Wilson.

Abstract from return of the District of Western North Carolina, Col. John B. Palmer, C. S. Army, commanding, for the month of April, 1864; headquarters Asheville, N. C.

Command.	Present for duty.		Aggregate present.	Aggregate present and absent.
	Officers.	Men.		
District staff	5	....	5	5
Asheville, N. C., Capt. Augustus B. Cowan, commanding Sixty-second North Carolina Regiment.*a*	8	74	85	178
Marshall, N. C., Capt. B. T. Morris, commanding Sixty-fourth North Carolina Regiment.*a*	5	41	50	118
Mouth of Ivy, N. C., Lieut. Col. James L. Henry, commanding Fourteenth North Carolina Battalion (cavalry).	17	185	221	510
Mouth of Tuckaseegee, Col. William H. Thomas, commanding Thomas' Legion.*b*	7	196	206	383
Asheville, N. C., Lieut. R. Murdoch, commanding Fifty-eighth North Carolina Volunteers.	1	22	24	28
Grand total	38	518	591	1,122

a The Sixty-second and Sixty-fourth North Carolina Regiments were surrendered at Cumberland Gap. The report made here represents those who were not present, and have been collected together and placed on duty here.

b The larger portion of Thomas' Legion is in Brigadier-General Jackson's brigade in East Tennessee. The three companies reported here are composed of Indians principally.

Abstract from return of the Army of Tennessee, General Joseph E. Johnston, C. S. Army, commanding, for the month of April, 1864; headquarters Dalton, Ga.

Command.	Present for duty.		Effective total present.	Aggregate present.	Aggregate present and absent.	Pieces of artillery.
	Officers.	Men.				
General headquarters:						
Staff and escort	20	174	174	208	254	....
Hardee's army corps:						
Staff and escort	30	241	240	324	481	.....
Cheatham's division	580	4,332	4,167	5,696	8,459	.....
Cleburne's division	540	5,361	5,218	6,909	9,757	.....

Abstract from return of the Army of Tennessee, &c.—Continued.

Command.	Present for duty.		Effective total present.	Aggregate present.	Aggregate present and absent.	Pieces of artillery.
	Officers.	Men.				
Hardee's army corps—Continued.						
Walker's.division	449	5,304	5,200	6,916	9,793	
Bate's division	417	3,637	3,511	4,675	6,934	
Artillery	50	1,006	975	1,272	1,623	48
Total Hardee's corps	2,066	19,881	19,311	25,792	37,001	48
Hood's army corps:						
Staff and escort	28	169	168	209	280	
Hindman's division	547	6,213	6,057	7,614	12,018	
Stevenson's division	539	6,486	6,328	8,060	11,087	
Stewart's division	472	5,915	5,781	7,373	11,697	
Artillery	47	894	872	1,113	1,342	36
Total Hood's corps	1,633	19,677	19,201	24,369	36,424	36
Cantey's brigade: *a*						
Infantry	62	1,426	1,395	1,699	2,330	
Artillery	3	152	148	161	210	6
Total Cantey's brigade	65	1,578	1,543	1,860	2,540	6
Engineer troops	17	425	422	477	605	
Cavalry corps:						
Staff	9			9	9	
Martin's division	169	1,757		2,538	6,477	
Kelly's division	206	1,927	602	2,749	4,411	
Humes' division	189	2,047	907	2,618	4,538	
Grigsby's brigade	107	779	401	1,115	1,873	
Hannon's brigade	44	576	392	734	1,098	
Artillery	11	241	27	295	444	18
Total cavalry *b*	735	7,327	2,419	10,058	18,785	18
Artillery reserve	53	849	817	1,048	1,254	36
Grand total	4,589	49,911	43,887	63,807	96,863	144

a Joined from District of the Gulf and encamped at Rome. Report includes only the Seventeenth and Twenty-ninth Alabama Regiments and a battalion of sharpshooters. The effective total of the Thirty-seventh Mississippi, en route, estimated at about 400.

b Since last report Dibrell's and Harrison's brigades have joined from Department of East Tennessee. Being "in the rear recruiting horses," they are not reported in the effective total.

Organization of the Army of Tennessee, commanded by General Joseph E. Johnston, C. S. Army, April 30, 1864.

HARDEE'S CORPS.

Lieut. Gen. WILLIAM J. HARDEE.

CHEATHAM'S DIVISION.

Maj. Gen. BENJAMIN F. CHEATHAM.

Maney's Brigade.*

Col. GEORGE C. PORTER.

1st and 27th Tennessee, Col. Hume R. Feild.
4th Tennessee (Confederate), Lieut. Col. Oliver A. Bradshaw.
6th and 9th Tennessee, Lieut. Col. J. W. Buford.
41st Tennessee, Lieut. Col. James D. Tillman.
50th Tennessee, Col. Stephen H. Colms.
24th Tennessee Battalion, Lieut. Col. Oliver A. Bradshaw.

*Formerly of Walker's division; transfer reported on return for February 20.

Strahl's Brigade. *

Brig. Gen. OTHO F. STRAHL.

4th and 5th Tennessee, Col. Jonathan J. Lamb.
19th Tennessee, Col. Francis M. Walker.
24th Tennessee, Lieut. Col. Samuel E. Shannon.
31st and 33d Tennessee, Lieut. Col. F. E. P. Stafford.

Wright's Brigade. ˙

Col. JOHN C. CARTER.

8th Tennessee, Col. John H. Anderson.
16th Tennessee, Capt. Benjamin Randals.
28th Tennessee, Col. Sidney S. Stanton.
38th Tennessee, Lieut. Col. Andrew D. Gwynne.
51st and 52d Tennessee, Lieut. Col. John G. Hall.

Vaughan's Brigade.†

Brig. Gen. ALFRED J. VAUGHAN, Jr.

11th Tennessee, Col. George W. Gordon.
12th and 47th Tennessee, Col. William M. Watkins.
29th Tennessee, Col. Horace Rice.
13th and 154th Tennessee, Col. Michael Magevney, jr.

CLEBURNE'S DIVISION.

Maj. Gen. PATRICK R. CLEBURNE.

Polk's Brigade.	*Lowrey's Brigade.*
Brig. Gen. LUCIUS E. POLK.	Brig. Gen. MARK P. LOWREY.
1st and 15th Arkansas, Lieut. Col. W. H. Martin.	16th Alabama, Lieut. Col. Frederick A. Ashford.
5th Confederate, Capt. W. A. Brown.	33d Alabama, Col. Samuel Adams.
2d Tennessee, Col. William D. Robison.	45th Alabama, Col. H. D. Lampley.
35th Tennessee,‡ Col. Benjamin J. Hill.	32d Mississippi, Col. W. H. H. Tison.
48th Tennessee (Nixon's regiment), Capt. Henry G. Evans.	45th Mississippi, Col. A. B. Hardcastle.
Govan's Brigade.	*Granbury's Brigade.*§
Brig. Gen. DANIEL C. GOVAN.	Brig. Gen. HIRAM B. GRANBURY.
2d and 24th Arkansas, Col. E. Warfield.	6th Texas Infantry and 15th Texas Cavalry (dismounted), Capt. Rhoads Fisher.
5th and 13th Arkansas, Col. John E. Murray.	7th Texas, Capt. J. H. Collett.
6th and 7th Arkansas, Col. Samuel G. Smith.	10th Texas, Col. Roger Q. Mills.
8th and 19th Arkansas, Col. George F. Baucum.	17th and 18th Texas (dismounted cavalry), Capt. George D. Manion.
3d Confederate, Capt. M. H. Dixon.	24th and 25th Texas (dismounted cavalry), Col. F. C. Wilkes.

---

* Formerly of Stewart's division ; transfer reported on return for February 20.
† Formerly of Hindman's division ; transfer reported on return for February 20.
‡ Detached and ordered to report to Colonel Hill, provost-marshal-general.
§ Formerly Smith's.

WALKER'S DIVISION.

Maj. Gen. WILLIAM H. T. WALKER.

Jackson's Brigade. *

Brig. Gen. JOHN K. JACKSON.

1st Georgia (Confederate), Col. George A. Smith.
5th Georgia, Col. Charles P. Daniel.
47th Georgia, Col. A. C. Edwards.
65th Georgia, Capt. William G. Foster.
5th Mississippi, Col. John Weir.
8th Mississippi, Col. John C. Wilkinson.
2d Georgia Battalion Sharpshooters, Maj. Richard H. Whiteley.

Gist's Brigade.

Brig. Gen. STATES R. GIST.

8th Georgia Battalion, Lieut. Col. Z. L. Watters.
46th Georgia, Maj. S. J. C. Dunlop.
16th South Carolina, Col. James McCullough.
24th South Carolina, Col. Ellison Capers.

Stevens' Brigade. †

Brig. Gen. CLEMENT H. STEVENS.

25th Georgia, Col. W. J. Winn.
29th Georgia, Licut. Col. W. D. Mitchell.
30th Georgia, Maj. Henry Hendrick.
66th Georgia, Col. J. Cooper Nisbet.
1st Georgia Battalion Sharpshooters, Maj. Arthur Shaaff.
26th Georgia Battalion, Maj. J. W. Nisbet.

BATE'S DIVISION.

Maj. Gen. WILLIAM B. BATE.

Lewis' Brigade. ‡

2d Kentucky, Col. James W. Moss.
4th Kentucky, Lieut. Col. Thomas W. Thompson.
5th Kentucky, Lieut. Col. Hiram Hawkins.
6th Kentucky, Maj. George W. Maxson.
9th Kentucky, Col. John W. Caldwell.

Bate's [Tyler's] Brigade. ‡

37th Georgia, Lieut. Col. Joseph T. Smith.
10th Tennessee, Maj. John O'Neill.
15th and 37th Tennessee, Maj. J. M. Wall.
20th Tennessee, Lieut. Col. W. M. Shy.
30th Tennessee, Lieut. Col. James J. Turner.
4th Georgia Battalion Sharpshooters, Capt. W. M. Carter.

Finley's Brigade. ‡

1st Florida Cavalry (dismounted) and 3d Florida, Maj. Glover A. Ball.
1st and 4th Florida, Lieut. Col. Edward Badger.
6th Florida, Col. Angus D. McLean.
7th Florida, Lieut. Col. Tillman Ingram.

---

* Formerly of Cheatham's division ; transfer reported on return for February 20.
† Formerly Wilson's brigade.
‡ Formerly of Breckinridge's division ; reported on return for February 20 as transferred from Hood's corps. Actual brigade commander not indicated on original return.

HOOD'S CORPS.

Lieut. Gen. JOHN B. HOOD.

HINDMAN'S DIVISION.

Maj. Gen. THOMAS C. HINDMAN.

Deas' Brigade.

Brig. Gen. ZACH. C. DEAS.

19th Alabama, Col. Samuel K. McSpadden.
22d Alabama, Col. Benjamin R. Hart.
25th Alabama, Col. George D. Johnston.
39th Alabama, Lieut. Col. William C. Clifton.
50th Alabama, Col. John G. Coltart.
17th Alabama Battalion Sharpshooters, Capt. James F. Nabers.

Tucker's Brigade.*

Brig. Gen. W. F. TUCKER.

7th Mississippi, Lieut. Col. B. F. Johns.
9th Mississippi, Capt. S. S. Calhoon.
10th Mississippi, Capt. Robert A. Bell.
41st Mississippi, Col. J. Byrd Williams.
44th Mississippi, Lieut. Col. R. G. Kelsey.
9th Mississippi Battalion Sharpshooters, Maj. W. C. Richards.

Manigault's Brigade.†

Brig. Gen. ARTHUR M. MANIGAULT.

24th Alabama, Col. N. N. Davis.
28th Alabama, Lieut. Col. W. L. Butler.
34th Alabama, Col. J. C. B. Mitchell.
10th South Carolina, Col. James F. Pressley.
19th South Carolina, Lieut. Col. Thomas P. Shaw.

Walthall's Brigade.†

Brig. Gen. EDWARD C. WALTHALL.

24th and 27th Mississippi, Col. Samuel Benton.
29th, 30th, and 34th Mississippi, Col. W. F. Brantly.

STEVENSON'S DIVISION.‡

Maj. Gen. CARTER L. STEVENSON.

Brown's Brigade.

Brig. Gen. JOHN C. BROWN.

3d Tennessee, Lieut. Col. Calvin J. Clack.
18th Tennessee, Lieut. Col. William R. Butler.
26th Tennessee, Capt. Abijah F. Boggess.
32d Tennessee, Maj. John P. McGuire.
45th Tennessee and 23d Battalion, Col. Anderson Searcy.

Reynolds' Brigade.

Brig. Gen. ALEXANDER W. REYNOLDS.

58th North Carolina, Maj. Thomas J. Dula.
60th North Carolina, Lieut. Col. James T. Weaver.
54th Virginia, Col. Robert C. Trigg.
63d Virginia, Capt. Connally H. Lynch.

Cumming's Brigade.

Brig. Gen. ALFRED CUMMING.

34th Georgia, Maj. John M. Jackson.
36th Georgia, Maj. Charles E. Broyles.
39th Georgia, Lieut. Col. J. F. B. Jackson.
56th Georgia, Col. E. P. Watkins.

Pettus' Brigade.

Brig. Gen. EDMUND W. PETTUS.

20th Alabama, Col. J. M. Dedman.
23d Alabama, Lieut. Col. J. B. Bibb.
30th Alabama, Col. Charles M. Shelley.
31st Alabama, Col. D. R. Hundley.
46th Alabama, Capt. George E. Brewer.

---

*Formerly Anderson's.
†Formerly of Cheatham's division ; transfer reported on return for February 20.
‡Transfer from Hardee's corps reported on return for February 20.

STEWART'S DIVISION.

Maj. Gen. ALEXANDER P. STEWART.

Stovall's Brigade.

Brig. Gen. MARCELLUS A. STOVALL.

40th Georgia, Col. Abda Johnson.
41st Georgia, Maj. M. S. Nall.
42d Georgia, Col. R. J. Henderson.
43d Georgia, Maj. William C. Lester.
52d Georgia, Capt. Rufus R. Asbury.

Clayton's Brigade.

Brig. Gen. HENRY D. CLAYTON.

18th Alabama, Col. J. T. Holtzclaw.
32d and 58th Alabama, Col. Bushrod Jones.
36th Alabama, Lieut. Col. Thomas H. Herndon.
38th Alabama, Col. A. R. Lankford.

Gibson's Brigade.*

Brig. Gen. RANDALL L. GIBSON.

1st Louisiana (Regulars), Maj. S. S. Batchelor.
13th Louisiana, Lieut. Col. F. L. Campbell.
16th and 25th Louisiana, Col. J. C. Lewis.
19th Louisiana, Lieut. Col. Hyder A. Kennedy.
20th Louisiana, Maj. S. L. Bishop.
4th Louisiana Battalion, Maj. Duncan Buie.
14th Louisiana Battalion Sharpshooters, Maj. J. E. Austin.

Baker's Brigade.†

Brig. Gen. ALPHEUS BAKER.

37th Alabama, Lieut. Col. Alexander A. Greene.
40th Alabama, Capt. Elbert D. Willett.
42d Alabama, Lieut. Col. Thomas C. Lanier.

CAVALRY CORPS.‡

Maj. Gen. JOSEPH WHEELER.

MARTIN'S DIVISION.

Maj. Gen. W. T. MARTIN.

Morgan's Brigade.

Brig. Gen. JOHN T. MORGAN.

1st Alabama, Maj. A. H. Johnson.
3d Alabama, Col. T. H. Mauldin.
4th Alabama, Col. A. A. Russell.
— Alabama, Col. James C. Malone, jr.
51st Alabama, Lieut. Col. M. L. Kirkpatrick.

Iverson's Brigade.

Brig. Gen. ALFRED IVERSON.

1st Georgia, Col. S. W. Davitte.
2d Georgia, Col. C. C. Crews.
3d Georgia, Col. R. Thompson.
4th Georgia, Col. Isaac W. Avery.
6th Georgia, Col. John R. Hart.

---

* Formerly Adams' brigade.
† Formerly Moore's ; Baker assigned March 19.   Transfer from Cheatham's division reported on return for February 20.
‡ Roddey's brigade transferred to Department of Alabama, Mississippi, and East Louisiana.

KELLY'S DIVISION.

Brig. Gen. JOHN H. KELLY.

Allen's Brigade.

Brig. Gen. WILLIAM W. ALLEN.

3d Confederate, Col. P. H. Rice.
8th Confederate, Lieut. Col. John S. Prather.
10th Confederate, Capt. T. G. Holt.
12th Confederate, Capt. Charles H. Conner.

*Dibrell's Brigade.**

Col. GEORGE G. DIBRELL.

4th Tennessee, Col. William S. McLemore.
8th Tennessee, Capt. Jefferson Leftwich.
9th Tennessee, Col. Jacob B. Biffle.
10th Tennessee, Col. William E. De Moss.
11th Tennessee, Col. Daniel W. Holman.

HUMES' DIVISION.

Brig. Gen. WILLIAM Y. C. HUMES.

Humes' Brigade.

Col. JAMES T. WHEELER.

1st [6th] Tennessee, Maj. Joseph J. Dobbins.
2d Tennessee, Capt. John H. Kuhn.
4th Tennessee, Lieut. Col. Paul F. Anderson.
5th Tennessee, Col. George W. McKenzie.
9th Tennessee Battalion, Maj. James H. Akin.

Grigsby's Brigade.

Col. J. WARREN GRIGSBY.

1st [3d] Kentucky, Col. J. R. Butler.
2d Kentucky (Woodward's regiment), Maj. Thomas W. Lewis.
9th Kentucky, Lieut. Col. Robert G. Stone.
Allison's (Tennessee) Squadron, Capt. John H. Allison.
Dortch's (Kentucky) Battalion, Capt. John B. Dortch.
Hamilton's (Tennessee) Battalion, Maj. Jo. Shaw.

*Harrison's Brigade.**

Col. THOMAS HARRISON.

3d Arkansas, Col. A. W. Hobson.
8th Texas, Lieut. Col. Gustave Cook.
11th Texas, Col. G. R. Reeves.

Hannon's Brigade.

Col. M. W. HANNON.

53d Alabama, Lieut. Col. J. F. Gaines.
24th Alabama Battalion, Maj. Robert B. Snodgrass.

ARTILLERY.

Brig. Gen. FRANCIS A. SHOUP, Chief.

HARDEE'S CORPS.†

Col. MELANCTHON SMITH, Chief.

Hoxton's Battalion.

Alabama Battery, Capt. John Phelan.
Marion (Florida) Light Artillery, Lieut. Thomas J. Perry.
Mississippi Battery, Capt. William B. Turner.

Hotchkiss' Battalion.

Arkansas Battery, Capt. Thomas J. Key.
Semple's (Alabama) battery, Lieut. Richard W. Goldthwaite.
Warren (Mississippi) Light Artillery, Lieut. H. Shannon.

Martin's Battalion.

Bledsoe's (Missouri) battery, Lieut. Charles W. Higgins.
Ferguson's (South Carolina) battery, Lieut. R. T. Beauregard.
Howell's (Georgia) battery, Lieut. W. G. Robson.

Cobb's Battalion.‡

Cobb's (Kentucky) battery, Lieut. R. B. Matthews.
Johnston (Tennessee) Artillery, Capt. John W. Mebane.
Washington (Louisiana) Light Artillery (5th company), Lieut. W. C. D. Vaught.

---

* Joined from Department of East Tennessee.
† Actual commanders are not indicated on original return.
‡ Transfer from Hood's corps reported on return for April 10.

HOOD'S CORPS.*

Col. ROBERT F. BECKHAM, Chief.

Courtney's Battalion.

Alabama Battery, Capt. James Garrity.
Alabama Battery, Capt. S. H. Dent.
Douglas' (Texas) battery, Lieut. John H. Bingham.

Eldridge's Battalion.

Eufaula (Alabama) Artillery, Capt. McD. Oliver.
Louisiana Battery, Capt. Charles E. Fenner.
Mississippi Battery, Capt. Thomas J. Stanford.

Johnston's Battalion.†

Cherokee (Georgia) Artillery, Capt. Max. Van Den Corput.
Stephens' (Georgia) Light Artillery,‡ Capt. John B. Rowan.
Tennessee Battery, Capt. L. G. Marshall.

CAVALRY CORPS.

Lieut. Col. FELIX H. ROBERTSON, Chief.

Ferrell's (Georgia) battery.§
Huwald's (Tennessee) battery, Lieut. D. Breck. Ramsey.
Tennessee Battery, Capt. B. F. White. jr.
Wiggins' (Arkansas) battery, Lieut. J. P. Bryant.

ARTILLERY RESERVE.

Lieut. Col. JAMES H. HALLONQUIST.

Palmer's Battalion.

Alabama Battery, Capt. Charles L. Lumsden.
Georgia Battery, Capt. R. W. Anderson.
Georgia Battery, Capt. M. W. Havis.

Waddell's Battalion.

Alabama Battery, Capt. Winslow D. Emery.
Bellamy's (Alabama) battery, Lieut. Francis A. O'Neal.
Missouri Battery. Capt. Overton W. Barret.

Williams' Battalion.

Barbour (Alabama) Artillery, Capt. Reuben F. Kolb.
Jefferson (Mississippi) Artillery, Capt. Put. Darden.
Nottoway (Virginia) Artillery, Capt. William C. Jeffress.

DETACHMENTS.

CANTEY'S BRIGADE.‖

Brig. Gen. JAMES CANTEY.

17th Alabama, Col. Virgil S. Murphey.
29th Alabama, Col. John F. Conoley.
37th Mississippi, —— ——.
Battalion Alabama Sharpshooters, Maj. J. S. Moreland.

* Actual commanders are not indicated on original return.
† Transfer from Hardee's corps reported on return for April 10.
‡ Prior to November, 1863, known as Third Maryland Battery.
§ Only one section present ; remainder transferred, with Roddey's brigade, to Department of Alabama, Mississippi, and East Louisiana.
‖ Joined from Department of the Gulf and encamped at Rome, Ga.

ENGINEER TROOPS [THIRD REGIMENT].

Maj. S. W. PRESSTMAN.

Company A, Capt. R. C. McCalla.
Company B, Capt. H. N. Pharr, Cheatham's division.
Company C. Capt. A. W. Gloster, Stewart's division.
Company D, Capt. Edward Winston.
Company F, Capt. W. A. Ramsey, Cleburne's division.
Company G, Lieut. Robert L. Cobb, Hindman's division.
Sappers and Miners, Capt. A. W. Clarkson.

ESCORTS.

Army headquarters : Guy Dreux's Company Louisiana Cavalry, Lieut. O. De Buys, and Holloway's Company Alabama Cavalry (Crocheron Light Dragoons), Capt. E. M. Holloway.

Hardee's corps : Raum's Company Mississippi Cavalry, Capt. W. C. Raum.

Cheatham's division : Merritt's company (G, 2d Georgia Cavalry), Capt. T. M. Merritt.

Cleburne's division : Sanders' Company Tennessee Cavalry (Buckner Guards), Capt. C. F. Sanders.

Bate's division : Foules' Company Mississippi Cavalry, Capt. H. L. Foules.

Walker's division : Mastin's company (G, 53d Alabama Volunteers, Partisan Rangers), Capt. P. B. Mastin, jr.

Hood's corps : [Not reported].

Hindman's division : Lenoir's Independent Company Alabama Cavalry, Capt. T. M. Lenoir.

Stevenson's division : [Not reported].

Stewart division : McKleroy's company (A, 10th Confederate Cavalry), Capt. John M. McKleroy.

APPENDIX.

Embracing documents received too late for insertion in proper sequence.

CONFEDERATE CORRESPONDENCE, ETC.

GENERAL ORDERS, } HDQRS. ROSS' BRIG., JACKSON'S CAV. DIV.,
No. 4. } Benton, Miss., March 1, 1864.

I. For conspicuous gallantry in the engagement with the enemy at Moscow, Tenn., December 3, 1863, and on other occasions, Private Henry Brocke, Company E, First Regiment Texas Cavalry, is hereby promoted to be fifth sergeant in his company.

II. For gallant and conspicuous conduct in the affair with the enemy near Benton, Miss., February 28, 1864, Private Henry King, Company E, Third Regiment Texas Cavalry, is promoted to fifth sergeant in his company.

III. Private John Derritt, Company A, Sixth Regiment Texas Cavalry, for his courage and daring, deserves the thanks of his officers. Although but a boy in years, he has proven himself a man in gallant deeds. Doubtless there are many others in the command eminently entitled to similar notices, but as their names had not been made known to the brigadier-general he can only thank them in general terms. His gratitude is due and hereby acknowledged to the gallant men and officers of his command, who are ever prompt in the discharge of duty, brave and courageous in battle, and firm and unflinching amid the privations and sufferings to which we are all subjected during this period of our country's peril.

By order of Brigadier-General Ross:

D. R. GURLEY,
Assistant Adjutant-General.

GENERAL ORDERS, } HDQRS. ROSS' BRIG., JACKSON'S CAV. DIV.,
No. 5. } Benton, Miss., March 7, 1864.

Hereafter if a citizen shall claim any horse or mule in this command and can prove the property his it will at once be delivered up, and the man in whose possession it is found will be punished for stealing, unless he has the certificate of the person of whom he procured the horse showing that he obtained it honestly.

By order of Brigadier-General Ross:

D. R. GURLEY,
Assistant Adjutant-General.

(875)

SPECIAL ORDERS, }   HDQRS. DEPT. OF EAST TENNESSEE,
No. 61.   }   ·   *Greeneville, March 9, 1864.*

*   *   *   *   *   *   *

Maj. W. M. Owen, artillery, Provisional Army Confederate States, is assigned to duty with King's battalion, and will report to Lieut. Col. J. Floyd King.

*   *   *   *   *   *

By command of Lieutenant-General Longstreet:

G. M. SORREL,
Assistant Adjutant-General.

HDQRS. TEXAS BRIG., JACKSON'S CAVALRY DIVISION,
Benton, Miss., March 15, 1864.

Captain MOORMAN,
Assistant Adjutant-General:

CAPTAIN : Lieutenant Taylor, commanding scouts of this brigade, reports the enemy's cavalry (three regiments) came out from Vicksburg yesterday and camped at their old position on Clear Creek. My scouts have been within 3 miles of Vicksburg, and from the best information they could learn General Sherman's army left on the 10th. Seventeen transports went up the river. The Yazoo expedition made no stop at Vicksburg, but continued on down the river. They admit a loss of 80 whites and 300 blacks at Yazoo City. The enemy is trying to form on the ball ground, Prairie Place. Have about 100 men there armed, some whites. There is also a force of negro troops at Haynes' Bluff, 2 miles distant. I have no report from my scouts on the Mississippi River of any boats passing up. If the above is true about the seventeen transports leaving Vicksburg on the 10th going up the river, they have not yet had time to report it.

I am, captain, very respectfully, your obedient servant,

L. S. ROSS,
Brigadier-General.

GENERAL ORDERS, }   HDQRS. ROSS' BRIG., JACKSON'S CAV. DIV.,
No. 6.   }   *Benton, Miss., March 18, 1864·*

I. No officer nor soldier of this command is authorized to appropriate any species of captured property whatever without permission from these headquarters, and if any one shall be known to sell or otherwise dispose of such property, or shall fail to make prompt reports of any and all captures he may make, he will be arrested and tried for embezzling public property. Mules and horses captured, under whatever circumstances, belong to the Government, and the brigadier-general claims the right to say when such property shall be given to the parties who captured it, as a reward for their services.

II. All officers and men of this command are earnestly enjoined and requested to arrest and bring or send to these headquarters all stragglers, deserters, paroled prisoners, and conscripts with whom they may meet. It is expected that each officer and soldier will make it his special duty to question every man he sees, whose age appears to be within the limits prescribed by the conscript act; to find out his reasons for not being in the ranks, and if his case is not sufficient to entitle him to exemption under the law, or if he can show no *

*   *   *   *   *   *   *

---

* Rest of order missing.

HDQRS. TEXAS BRIG., JACKSON'S CAVALRY DIVISION,
Benton, Miss., March 22, 1864.
General W. H. JACKSON,
Commanding, &c. :

GENERAL : When you first came to my headquarters I gave you a full and fair statement of what had occurred with Colonel Wharton and his regiment, and expressed a perfect willingness to see the whole command broken up rather than establish the dangerous precedent. You could suggest no remedy, and did not imply that my conduct could be censured. I am willing to do my duty still. You direct me to cause the arrest of all officers and men engaged. Colonel Wharton does not know who they were, with one exception. He thinks Captain Rosamond was using some effort to suppress the trouble and quiet the excitement. It will afford me pleasure to arrest those whom I can prove to be guilty.

I desire to impress the fact, very respectfully, upon the minds of yourself and my superior officers generally, that I have had but little encouragement or assistance in resorting to military law or courts-martial in punishing offenders in this brigade. I have many officers now in arrest with charges hanging over them, and some of them have been in arrest more than one year without trial, or if tried, without having the findings of the court published. Officers of this brigade, in trying to curb the rebellious spirit of their commands, have appealed in vain for assistance ; have asked for courts to be organized and prompt and speedy action taken to bring to trial and punishment these unruly spirits, that others might be deterred. I have arrested and released, after long confinement, these men and officers and returned them to duty so often, without trial, that military law has become obsolete, and I may as well write what I think. My command, influence, or authority over them does not depend on their respect for or fear of military law or authority, but simply their love for me as an individual. To whom does blame attach here ? You require me to make some very serious charges against Colonel Wharton, and I would respectfully ask that the matter be deferred until it is understood clearly. I am unwilling to inflict so deep and lasting a disgrace upon him unnecessarily or without it is clearly my duty to do so. I would rather suffer than be the cause of irreparable injustice to him. If it is my duty, I will act conscientiously.

Very respectfully, your obedient servant,

L. S. ROSS,
Brigadier-General.

HDQRS. TEXAS BRIG., JACKSON'S CAVALRY DIVISION,
March 22, 1864.
Brigadier-General JACKSON :

GENERAL : Your note, demanding the reason why your order of 12th instant in reference to Colonel Wharton was not carried out, has just been received. I have the honor to inform you that I at once upon its reception ordered Colonel Wharton to assume command of his regiment in obedience thereto, and assured him that if he met with opposition I would support and sustain him. While on the way to visit the regiment, a short time subsequently, was informed that Colonel Wharton did not take command of the

regiment, but had been intimidated by demonstrations from the men of his command and had left camp and gone to a private house to spend the first night, and left for my headquarters the next morning. When I arrived at camp I inquired of Major Ross the truth of the matter. He could give me no information, further than that soon after Colonel Wharton arrived a note was handed him (Colonel Wharton), and afterward he and Captain Rosamond, of Company D, had several private conferences. Neither the contents of the note nor the matter of discussion between Colonel Wharton and Captain Rosamond was known, I think, to Major Ross, but he was satisfied that it related to the opposition in the command to Colonel Wharton. Colonel Wharton then went to a private house, spent the night; came back next morning, and I think asked Major Ross for advice and what demonstrations had been made by the men. He was informed by Major Ross that about 150 men came after dark to Colonel Wharton's headquarters and inquired for him. Being informed that Colonel Wharton was not there, they retired. Colonel Wharton then came to my headquarters, and when I met him he said he could not remain in the regiment. I again told him he might rely upon my assistance, but he was of the impression that his life would certainly be taken if he attempted to establish himself, even for a short time, in command of the regiment. I then advised him to resign.
Very respectfully, your obedient servant,

L. S. ROSS.

P. S.—It would not be improper to state that Colonel Wharton will do Major Ross the justice to say that he was willing to discharge his duty by sustaining his superior officer, without fear or favor.

L. S. ROSS,
Brigadier-General.

GENERAL ORDERS, } HDQRS. ROSS' BRIG., JACKSON'S CAV. DIV.,
No. 8.   } *Pritchett's Cross-Roads, Miss.,* Mar. 27, 1864.

The brigadier-general is aware that there exists among the men and officers of this command an erroneous idea that by mutinous conduct and threats of desertion they can establish their ideas of military discipline and rid themselves of officers with whom they happen to be displeased, and save themselves from deserved punishment by threats of breaking up the regiment by cowardly sneaking to their homes or other fields, bearing with them the lasting stigma of deserters. Such a cowardly course only injures themselves and causes no regrets to their officers or loss to their country. Before such an unmilitary and demoralizing precedent should be allowed in the brigade it would be far better to our cause that such men were out of the service. They do their country service only when they make good soldiers, and when they cease to be such and disregard military law and discipline it is the determination of their officers to enforce it or break up the command in the attempt. The disgraceful and unmilitary conduct of some members of the Sixth Regiment Texas Cavalry has brought upon the command a lasting disgrace and a stain that will forever darken the heretofore fair fame of this truly noble and gallant regiment. No one can regret the fact more than the general commanding the brigade, as his reputation and feelings are so closely and strongly identified with them. But it [is] his determination to sacrifice personal interest and attachments in the enforcement of discipline and crush this mutinous and rebellious spirit that has manifested itself in the brigade. Company officers are remiss in the discharge of duty and stand quietly by and suffer those whom it is their duty to command to ignore military authority without an effort to advise or check them, though it is as much their duty to lose their lives, if necessary, in upholding military authority and discipline in their commands as it is upon the battle-field. The Texans have won a name for glorious achievements, gallant deeds, and soldierly qualities unequaled by any troops in this department. Yet this unruly spirit is known to exist among them and greatly detracts from their reputation, and the major-general commanding has been forced to confess that notwithstanding the enviable reputation this brigade enjoys he regards them as being very uncertain on account of this spirit. This was extremely mortifying to the brigade commander to hear this reproach cast upon a command in which he has ever felt the greatest pride, and he hopes that the brigade may henceforth merit the unqualified approbation and entire confidence of its superior officers by their soldierly deportment as well as gallantry on the field of action.

By order of Brigadier-General Ross:

[D. R. GURLEY,]
Assistant Adjutant-General.

SPECIAL ORDERS, } HDQRS. ARTILLERY, ARMY OF E. TENN.,
No. 10.   }   *Bristol, April* 12, 1864.

I. Lieut. Col. J. Floyd King will report with his battalion to Major-General Buckner, commanding division.

II. Maj. A. Leyden will report with his battalion to Major-General Buckner, commanding division.

III. Maj. W. M. Owen is hereby relieved from duty with King's battalion, and assigned to duty with the Washington Artillery, Petersburg, Va.

By command of Brigadier-General Alexander:

JAS. C. HASKELL,
Captain and Assistant Adjutant-General.

SPECIAL ORDERS, } HDQRS. ROSS' BRIG., JACKSON'S CAV. DIV.,
No. 5.   }   *Five-Mile Creek, Ala., April* 25, 1864.

The organization known as Evans' Scouts is hereby dissolved, and the officers and men composing it will at once return to duty with their respective companies.

By order of Brig. Gen. L. S. Ross:

D. R. GURLEY,
Assistant Adjutant-General.

ALTERNATE DESIGNATIONS

OF

ORGANIZATIONS MENTIONED IN THIS VOLUME.*

Abert's (George W.) **Infantry.** See *Mississippi Troops, Confederate,* 14th *Regiment.*
Adaire's (T. N.) **Infantry.** See *Mississippi Troops, Confederate,* 4th *Regiment.*
Adams' (Robert N.) **Infantry.** See *Ohio Troops,* 81st *Regiment.*
Adams' (Samuel) **Infantry.** See *Alabama Troops, Confederate,* 33d *Regiment.*
Adams' (Silas) **Cavalry.** See *Kentucky Troops, Union,* 1st *Regiment.*
Adams' (Wirt) **Cavalry.** See *Mississippi Troops, Confederate.*
Akin's (James H.) **Cavalry.** See *Tennessee Troops, Confederate,* 9th *Battalion.*
Alabama First Infantry, A. D. See *Union Troops, Colored,* 55th *Regiment.*
Alabama First Siege Artillery, A. D. See *Union Troops, Colored,* 6th (7th) *Regiment, Heavy.*
Alabama Third Infantry, A. D. See *Union Troops, Colored,* 111th *Regiment.*
Alabama Fourth Infantry, A. D. See *Union Troops, Colored,* 106th *Regiment.*
Alabama State Artillery. See *Alabama Troops, Confederate.*
Aldrich's (Simeon C.) **Infantry.** See *Indiana Troops,* 44th *Regiment.*
Aleshire's (Charles C.) **Artillery.** See *Ohio Troops,* 18th *Battery.*
Alexander's (Francis N.) **Infantry.** See *Kentucky Troops, Union,* 30th *Regiment.*
Alexander's (J. F.) **Cavalry.** See *Georgia Troops, Local Defense.*
Allison's (John H.) **Cavalry.** See *Tennessee Troops, Confederate.*
Amacker's (O. P.) **Cavalry.** See *Louisiana Troops,* 9th *Battalion.*
Anderson's (C. D.) **Infantry.** See *Alabama Troops, Confederate,* 21st *Regiment.*
Anderson's (John H.) **Infantry.** See *Tennessee Troops, Confederate,* 8th *Regiment.*
Anderson's (Nicholas L.) **Infantry.** See *Ohio Troops,* 6th *Regiment.*
Anderson's (Paul F.) **Cavalry.** See *Baxter Smith's Cavalry, post.*
Anderson's (R. W.) **Artillery.** See *Georgia Troops.*
Anderson's (William B.) **Infantry.** See *Illinois Troops,* 60th *Regiment.*
Andrew's (William W.) **Artillery.** See *Indiana Troops,* 21st *Battery.*
Andrews' (Julius A.) **Cavalry.** See *Texas Troops,* 32d *Regiment.*
Angel's (Charles A.) **Infantry.** See *New Jersey Troops,* 35th *Regiment.*
Arkansas First Infantry, A. D. See *Union Troops, Colored,* 46th *Regiment.*
Arkansas Second Infantry, A. D. See *Union Troops, Colored,* 54th *Regiment.*
Arkansas Third Infantry, A. D. See *Union Troops, Colored,* 56th *Regiment.*
Arkansas Fourth Infantry, A. D. See *Union Troops, Colored,* 57th *Regiment.*
Armstrong's (Charles) **Infantry.** See *Union Troops, Veteran Reserve Corps,* 2d *Battalion,* 56th *Company.*
Armstrong's (Etheldred W.) **Cavalry.** See *Tennessee Troops, Union,* 9th *Regiment.*
Armstrong's (George F.) **Artillery.** See *Indiana Troops,* 20th *Battery.*
Armstrong's Pioneers. (Official designation not of record.) See *Captain Armstrong.*
Arndt's (Albert F. R.) **Artillery.** See *Michigan Troops,* 1st *Regiment, Battery B.*
Arsenal Battalion, Infantry. See *Georgia Troops, Local Defense.*
Asbury's (Rufus R.) **Infantry.** See *Georgia Troops,* 52d *Regiment.*

---

*References, unless otherwise indicated, are to index following.

Ashby's (H. M.) Cavalry. See *Tennessee Troops, Confederate.*
Ashford's (Frederick A.) Infantry. See *Alabama Troops, Confederate,* 16*th Regiment.*
Ashland Artillery. See *Virginia Troops.*
Atkins' (Smith D.) Infantry. See *Illinois Troops,* 92*d Regiment.* ·
Atlanta Arsenal Artillery. See *Georgia Troops, Local Defense.*
Austin's (J. E.) Sharpshooters. See *Louisiana Troops,* 14*th Battalion.*
Avery's (Isaac W.) Cavalry. See *Georgia Troops,* 4*th Regiment.*
Ayres' (Oliver H.) Artillery. See *Ohio Troops,* 6*th Battery.*
Babcock's (Walter S.) Heavy Artillery. See *Wisconsin Troops,* 1*st Regiment, Battery B.*
Backus' (William) Artillery. See *Ohio Troops,* 20*th Battery.*
Badger's (Edward) Infantry. See *Florida Troops,* 1*st and* 4*th Regiments.*
Bailey's (Chesley D.) Infantry. See *Kentucky Troops, Union,* 9*th Regiment.*
Bainbridge's (Edmund C.) Artillery. See *Union Troops, Regulars,* 5*th Regiment, Battery M.*
Baird's (A. J.) Infantry. See *Georgia Troops, Local Defense.*
Baird's (John P.) Infantry. See *Indiana Troops,* 85*th Regiment.*
Baker's (Myron) Infantry. See *Indiana Troops,* 74*th Regiment.*
Baldwin's (Norman A.) Artillery. See *Ohio Troops,* 1*st Regiment, Battery B.*
Baldwin's (Oliver L.) Cavalry. See *Kentucky Troops, Union,* 5*th Regiment.*
Ball's (Edward) Infantry. See *Georgia Troops,* 51*st Regiment.*
Ball's (Glover A.) Cavalry. See *Florida Troops,* 1*st Regiment;* also 3*d Florida Infantry.*
Ballentine's (John G.) Cavalry. See *Mississippi Troops, Confederate.*
Banbury's (Jabez) Infantry. See *Iowa Troops,* 5*th Regiment.*
Bancroft's (Eugene A.) Artillery. See *Union Troops, Regulars,* 4*th Regiment, Battery G.*
Banning's (Henry B.) Infantry. See *Ohio Troops,* 121*st Regiment.*
Barber's (Gershom M.) Sharpshooters. See *Ohio Troops,* 1*st Battalion.*
Barbour Artillery. See *Alabama Troops, Confederate.*
Barentzen's (Lauritz) Infantry. See *Ohio Troops,* 106*th Regiment.*
Barner's (Horatio G.) Cavalry. See *Iowa Troops,* 8*th Regiment.*
Barnes' (George F.) Cavalry. See *Kentucky Troops, Union,* 16*th Regiment.*
Barnes' (Thomas H.) Infantry. See *Kentucky Troops, Union,* 47*th Regiment.*
Barnes' (William) Artillery. See *Georgia Troops,* 9*th Battalion, Battery A.*
Barnett's (Charles M.) Artillery. See *Illinois Troops,* 2*d Regiment, Battery I.*
Barnhill's (Rigdon S) Infantry. See *Illinois Troops,* 40*th Regiment.*
Barnum's (William L.) Infantry. See *Missouri Troops, Union,* 11*th Regiment.*
Barret's (Overton W.) Artillery. See *Missouri Troops, Confederate.*
Barry's (Robert L.) Artillery. See *Lookout Artillery, post.*
Barry's (Robert P.) Infantry. See *Union Troops, Regulars,* 16*th Regiment,* 1*st Battalion.*
Barry's (William S.) Infantry. See *Mississippi Troops, Confederate,* 35*th Regiment.*
Barteau's (C. R.) Cavalry. See *Tennessee Troops, Confederate.*
Bassett's (Isaac C.) Infantry. See *Pennsylvania Troops,* 82*d Regiment.*
Batchelor's (S. S.) Infantry. See *Louisiana Troops, Regulars,* 1*st Regiment.*
Baucum's (George F.) Infantry. See *Arkansas Troops,* 8*th and* 19*th Regiments.*
Beach's (Albert F.) Artillery. See *Tennessee Troops, Union,* 1*st Battalion, Battery A.*
Beauregard's (R. T.) Artillery. See *Thomas B. Ferguson's Artillery, post.* ·
Becht's (John C.) Infantry. See *Minnesota Troops,* 5*th Regiment.*
Beck's (Arnold) Infantry. See *Missouri Troops, Union,* 2*d Regiment.*
Beck's (Benjamin) Infantry. See *Georgia Troops,* 9*th Regiment.*
Bedford Artillery. See *Virginia Troops.*
Beebe's (William O.) Artillery. See *Tennessee Troops, Union,* 1*st Battalion, Battery B.*
Beebe's (Yates V.) Artillery. See *Wisconsin Troops,* 10*th Battery.*

Bell's (Leroy S.) **Infantry.** See *Ohio Troops, 3d Regiment.*
Bell's (Robert A.) **Infantry.** See *Mississippi Troops, Confederate,* 10th Regiment.
Bellamy's (Richard H.) **Artillery.** See *Alabama Troops, Confederate,* 20th Battalion, *Battery B.*
Beltzhoover's (Daniel) **Heavy Artillery.** See *Louisiana Troops,* 1st Regiment.
Benjamin's (Samuel N.) **Artillery.** See *Union Troops, Regulars,* 2d Regiment, Battery E.
Bennett's (John E.) **Infantry.** See *Illinois Troops,* 75th Regiment.
Bentley's (Robert H.) **Cavalry.** See *Ohio Troops,* 12th Regiment.
Benton's (Samuel) **Infantry.** See *Mississippi Troops, Confederate,* 24th and 27th Regiments.
Berry's (William W.) **Infantry.** See *Kentucky Troops, Union,* 5th Regiment.
Bethune's (W. C.) **Infantry.** See *Alabama Troops, Confederate,* 57th Regiment.
Bibb's Cavalry. (Official designation not of record.) See *Captain Bibb.*
Bibb's (J. B.) **Infantry.** See *Alabama Troops, Confederate,* 23d Regiment.
Biffle's (Jacob B.) **Cavalry.** See *Tennessee Troops, Confederate.*
Biggs' (Jonathan) **Infantry.** See *Illinois Troops,* 123d Regiment.
Bingham's (John H.) **Artillery.** See *James P. Douglas' Artillery, post.*
Bishop's (Loomis K.) **Infantry.** See *Michigan Troops,* 21st Regiment.
Bishop's (S. L.) **Infantry.** See *Louisiana Troops,* 20th Regiment.
Bivin's (Felix C.) **Infantry.** See *Indiana Troops,* 66th Regiment.
Blake's (John W.) **Infantry.** See *Indiana Troops,* 40th Regiment.
Bland's (Charles C.) **Infantry.** See *Missouri Troops, Union,* 32d Regiment.
Bledsoe's (Hiram M.) **Artillery.** See *Missouri Troops, Confederate.*
Blessingh's (Louis von) **Infantry.** See *Ohio Troops,* 37th Regiment.
Boggess' (Abijah F.) **Infantry.** See *Tennessee Troops, Confederate,* 26th Regiment.
Bolton's (William H.) **Artillery.** See *Illinois Troops,* 2d Regiment, Battery L.
Bond's (John R.) **Infantry.** See *Ohio Troops,* 111th Regiment.
Booth's (Lionel F.) **Heavy Artillery.** See *Union Troops, Colored,* 6th (7th) Regiment.
Bouanchaud's (Alcide) **Artillery.** See *Pointe Coupée Artillery, post, Battery A.*
Boughton's (Horace) **Infantry.** See *New York Troops,* 143d Regiment.
Bowen's (Edwin A.) **Infantry.** See *Illinois Troops,* 52d Regiment.
Bower's (Edward L.) **Artillery.** See *Mississippi Troops, Confederate,* 1st Regiment, *Battery I.*
Bowles' (Pinckney D.) **Infantry.** See *Alabama Troops, Confederate,* 4th Regiment.
Bowman's (Daniel) **Infantry.** See *Ohio Troops,* 93d Regiment.
Boyd's (William S.) **Infantry.** See *Illinois Troops,* 66th Regiment.
Boyles' (William) **Infantry.** See *Alabama Troops, Confederate,* 56th Regiment.
Bradford's (William M.) **Infantry.** See *Tennessee Troops, Confederate,* 39th Regiment.
Bradley's (Cullen) **Artillery.** See *Ohio Troops,* 6th Battery.
Bradley's (Daniel) **Infantry.** See *Illinois Troops,* 20th Regiment.
Bradley's (Luther P.) **Infantry.** See *Illinois Troops,* 51st Regiment.
Bradshaw's (Oliver A.) **Infantry.** See *Tennessee Troops, Confederate,* 4th Regiment, *P. A.,* and 24th Battalion Sharpshooters.
Brantly's (W. F.) **Infantry.** See *Mississippi Troops,* 29th, 30th, and 34th Regiments.
Bratton's (John) **Infantry.** See *South Carolina Troops,* 6th Regiment.
Brewer's (George E.) **Infantry.** See *Alabama Troops, Confederate,* 46th Regiment.
Briant's (Cyrus E.) **Infantry.** See *Indiana Troops,* 88th Regiment.
Bridges' (George W.) **Cavalry.** See *Tennessee Troops, Union,* 10th Regiment.
Bridges' (Lyman) **Artillery.** See *Illinois Troops.*
Brigham's (Joseph H.) **Infantry.** See *Ohio Troops,* 69th Regiment.
Brockway's (Solomon P.) **Cavalry.** See *Michigan Troops,* 9th Regiment.
Brookhaven Artillery. See *Mississippi Troops, Confederate.*

Brooks Artillery. See *South Carolina Troops.*
Brown's (Charles E.) **Infantry.** See *Ohio Troops, 63d Regiment.*
Brown's (Edward) **Infantry.** See *Mississippi Troops, Confederate, 36th Regiment.*
Brown's (George R.) **Artillery.** See *Indiana Troops, 9th Battery.*
Brown's (Jack) **Infantry.** See *Georgia Troops, 59th Regiment.*
Brown's (John M.) **Infantry.** See *Kentucky Troops, Union, 45th Regiment.*
Brown's (Orlando, jr.) **Infantry.** See *Kentucky Troops, Union, 14th Regiment.*
Brown's (Simeon B.) **Cavalry.** See *Michigan Troops, 11th Regiment.*
Brown's (W. A.) **Infantry.** See *Confederate Troops, Regulars, 5th Regiment.*
Brown's (William N.) **Infantry.** See *Mississippi Troops, Confederate, 20th Regiment*
Browne's (William H.) **Infantry.** See *Virginia Troops, 45th Regiment.*
Brownlow's (James P.) **Cavalry.** See *Tennessee Troops, Union, 1st Regiment.*
Broyles' (Charles E.) **Infantry.** See *Georgia Troops, 36th Regiment.*
Brumback's (Jefferson) **Infantry.** See *Ohio Troops, 95th Regiment.*
Brunner's (John F.) **Artillery.** See *Missouri Troops, Union, 1st Regiment, Battery I.*
Bryan's (B. F.) **Cavalry.** See *W. R. Miles' Legion, post.*
Bryant's (George E.) **Infantry.** See *Wisconsin Troops, 12th Regiment.*
Bryant's (J. P.) **Artillery.** See *J. H. Wiggins' Artillery, post.*
Bryant's (Julian E.) **Infantry.** See *Union Troops, Colored, 51st Regiment.*
Buckner Artillery. See *Mississippi Troops, Confederate.*
Buckner's (Allen) **Infantry.** See *Illinois Troops, 79th Regiment.*
Buckner Guards, Cavalry. See *Tennessee Troops, Confederate.*
Budd's (Joseph L.) **Infantry.** See *Ohio Troops, 35th Regiment.*
Buell's (George P.) **Infantry.** See *Indiana Troops, 58th Regiment.*
Buford's (J. W.) **Infantry.** See *Tennessee Troops, Confederate, 6th and 9th Regiments.*
Buie's (Duncan) **Infantry.** See *Louisiana Troops, 4th Battalion.*
Bulger's (Michael J.) **Infantry.** See *Alabama Troops, Confederate, 47th Regiment.*
Bunn's (H. G.) **Infantry.** See *Arkansas Troops, 4th Regiment.*
Burdick's (James) **Artillery.** See *Ohio Troops, 15th Battery.*
Burge's (Hartwell T.) **Infantry.** See *Kentucky Troops, Union, 48th Regiment.*
Burgess' (James) **Infantry.** See *Indiana Troops, 124th Regiment.*
Burke's (Joseph W.) **Infantry.** See *Ohio Troops, 10th Regiment.*
Burroughs' (William H.) **Artillery.** See *Rhett Artillery, post.*
Burrows' (Jerome B.) **Artillery.** See *Ohio Troops, 4th Battery.*
Burton's (Josiah H.) **Artillery.** See *Illinois Troops, 1st Regiment, Battery F.*
Buswell's (Nicholas C.) **Infantry.** See *Illinois Troops, 93d Regiment.*
Butler's (J. R.) **Cavalry.** See *Kentucky Troops, Confederate, 3d Regiment.*
Butler's (Thomas H.) **Cavalry.** See *Indiana Troops, 5th Regiment.*
Butler's (William) **Heavy Artillery.** See *South Carolina Troops, 3d Regiment.*
Butler's (William R.) **Infantry.** See *Tennessee Troops, Confederate, 18th Regiment.*
Butler's (W. L.) **Infantry.** See *Alabama Troops, Confederate, 28th Regiment.*
Butt's (Edgar M.) **Infantry.** See *Georgia Troops, 2d Regiment.*
Byrne's (Edward P.) **Artillery.** See *Kentucky Troops, Confederate.*
Calahan's (W. G.) **Infantry.** See *Georgia Troops, 18th Regiment.*
Caldwell's (John W.) **Infantry.** See *Kentucky Troops, Confederate, 9th Regiment.*
Calhoon's (S. S.) **Infantry.** See *Mississippi Troops, Confederate, 9th Regiment.*
Callicott's (John A.) **Infantry.** See *Illinois Troops, 29th Regiment.*
Calloway's (James E.) **Infantry.** See *Illinois Troops, 21st Regiment.*
Cameron's (Daniel) **Infantry.** See *Illinois Troops, 65th Regiment.*
Cameron's (Hugh) **Infantry.** See *Mississippi Troops, Confederate, 13th Regiment.*
Camp's (John L.) **Cavalry.** See *Texas Troops, 14th Regiment.*
Campbell's (Calvin D.) **Infantry.** See *Indiana Troops, 6th Regiment.*
Campbell's (F. L.) **Infantry.** See *Louisiana Troops, 13th Regiment.*
Canby's (Samuel) **Artillery.** See *Union Troops, Regulars, 4th Regiment, Battery M.*
Capers' (Ellison) **Infantry.** See *South Carolina Troops, 24th Regiment.*

Capron's (Horace) Cavalry. See *Illinois Troops, 14th Regiment.*
Carey's (Oliver H. P.) Infantry. See *Indiana Troops, 36th Regiment.*
Carlin's (James W.) Infantry. See *Ohio Troops, 71st Regiment.*
Carman's (Ezra A.) Infantry. See *New Jersey Troops, 13th Regiment.*
Carson's (James M.) Infantry. See *Indiana Troops, 91st Regiment.*
Carter's (James E.) Cavalry. See *Tennessee Troops, Confederate.*
Carter's (James P. T.) Infantry. See *Tennessee Troops, Union, 2d Regiment.*
Carter's (W. M.) Sharpshooters. See *Georgia Troops, 4th Battalion.*
Case's (Charles) Infantry. See *Indiana Troops, 129th Regiment.*
Case's (Henry) Infantry. See *Illinois Troops, 129th Regiment.*
Catterson's (Robert F.) Infantry. See *Indiana Troops, 97th Regiment.*
Chalmers' (Alexander H.) Cavalry. See *Mississippi Troops, Confederate, 18th Battalion.*
Champion's (Thomas E.) Infantry. See *Illinois Troops, 96th Regiment.*
Chandler's (George W.) Infantry. See *Illinois Troops, 88th Regiment.*
Chandler's (William P.) Infantry. See *Illinois Troops, 35th Regiment.*
Chapman's (Fletcher H.) Artillery. See *Illinois Troops, 2d Regiment, Battery B.*
Charpentier's (Stephen) Artillery. See *Alabama Troops, Confederate.*
Chase's (Charles W.) Infantry. See *Union Troops, Veteran Reserve Corps, 23d Regiment.*
Cheney's (Samuel F.) Infantry. See *Ohio Troops, 21st Regiment.*
Chenoweth's (J. T.) Infantry. See *Kentucky Troops, Confederate, 11th Regiment.*
Cherokee Artillery. See *Georgia Troops.*
Chicago Board of Trade Artillery. See *Illinois Troops.*
Choate's (William A.) Infantry. See *Ohio Troops, 38th Regiment.*
Churchill's (Mendal) Infantry. See *Ohio Troops, 27th Regiment.*
Clack's (Calvin J.) Infantry. See *Tennessee Troops, Confederate, 3d Regiment.*
Claiborne's (James R.) Cavalry. See *Virginia Troops, 37th Battalion.*
Clancy's (Charles W.) Infantry. See *Ohio Troops, 52d Regiment.*
Clanton's (Turner, jr.) Cavalry. See *Alabama Troops, Confederate, 7th Regiment.*
Clark Artillery. See *Missouri Troops, Confederate.*
Clark's (Alonzo W.) Infantry. See *Illinois Troops, 44th Regiment.*
Clark's (Lewis M.) Infantry. See *Kentucky Troops, Union, 45th Regiment.*
Clark's (Samuel F.) Artillery. See *Wisconsin Troops, 6th Battery.*
Clark's (W. H.) Infantry. See *Mississippi Troops, Confederate, 46th Regiment.*
Clarke's (George R.) Infantry. See *Illinois Troops, 113th Regiment.*
Clarkson's (A. W.) Sappers and Miners. See *Confederate Troops, Regulars, 3d Regiment, Engineers.*
Clay's (Ezekiel F.) Cavalry. See *Kentucky Troops, Confederate, 3d Battalion, Rifles.*
Clayton's (William Z.) Artillery. See *Minnesota Troops, 1st Battery.*
Clift's (William J.) Cavalry. See *Tennessee Troops, Union, 5th Regiment.*
Clifton's (William C.) Infantry. See *Alabama Troops, Confederate, 39th Regiment.*
Cobb's (Robert) Artillery. See *Kentucky Troops, Confederate.*
Cobb's (Robert L.) Engineers. See *Confederate Troops, Regulars, 3d Regiment.*
Cobb's Legion. See *Georgia Troops.*
Cochran's (Jesse C.) Infantry. See *Mississippi Troops, Confederate, 17th Regiment.*
Cockefair's (James M.) Artillery. See *Indiana Troops, 3d Battery.*
Cockerill's (Armstead T. M.) Infantry. See *Ohio Troops, 24th Regiment.*
Cockerill's (Daniel T.) Artillery. See *Ohio Troops, 1st Regiment, Battery F.*
Cockerill's (Giles J.) Artillery. See *Ohio Troops, 1st Regiment, Battery D.*
Coe's (Alonzo W.) Artillery. See *Illinois Troops, 2d Regiment, Battery I.*
Cogswell's (Jesse W.) Infantry. See *New Jersey Troops, 34th Regiment.*
Cogswell's (William) Infantry. See *Massachusetts Troops, 2d Regiment.*
Colbert's (W. Bruce) Infantry. See *Mississippi Troops, Confederate, 40th Regiment.*
Coleman's (David) Infantry. See *North Carolina Troops, Confederate, 39th Regiment.*

Coleman's (David C.) Infantry. See *Missouri Troops, Union, 8th Regiment.*
Coleman's (James T.) Cavalry. See *W. R. Miles' Legion, post.*
Colgrove's (Silas) Infantry. See *Indiana Troops, 27th Regiment.*
Collett's (J. H.) Infantry. See *Texas Troops, 7th Regiment.*
Collins' (James A.) Artillery. See *North Carolina Troops, Confederate, 13th Battalion, Battery F.*
Collins' (William B.) Infantry. See *Missouri Troops, Union, 7th Regiment.*
Colms' (Stephen H.) Infantry. See *Tennessee Troops, Confederate, 50th Regiment.*
Coltart's (John G.) Infantry. See *Alabama Troops, Confederate, 50th Regiment.*
Columbus Artillery. See *Georgia Troops.*
Colvin's (John H.) Artillery. See *Illinois Troops.*
Comparet's (John M.) Infantry.* See *Indiana Troops, 51st Regiment.*
Conner's (Charles H.) Cavalry. See *Confederate Troops, Regulars, 12th Regiment.*
Conoley's (John F.) Infantry. See *Alabama Troops, Confederate, 29th Regiment.*
Conrad's (Joseph) Infantry. See *Missouri Troops, Union, 15th Regiment.*
Cook's (Gustave) Cavalry. See *Texas Troops, 8th Regiment.*
Cook's (Hatch) Infantry. See *Alabama Troops, Confederate, 60th Regiment.*
Cooper's (Wickliffe) Cavalry. See *Kentucky Troops, Union, 4th Regiment.*
Corbin's (Henry B.) Artillery. See *Michigan Troops, 1st Regiment, Battery D.*
Corbin's (Henry C.) Infantry. See *Union Troops, Colored, 14th Regiment.*
Cornell's (Peter) Artillery. See *Ohio Troops, 22d Battery.*
Corns' (James M.) Cavalry. See *Virginia Troops, 8th Regiment.*
Corput's (Max Van Den) Artillery. See *Cherokee Artillery, ante.*
Cowan's (Augustus B.) Infantry. See *North Carolina Troops, Confederate, 62d Regiment.*
Cowan's (James J.) Artillery. See *Mississippi Troops, Confederate, 1st Regiment, Battery G.*
Coward's (A.) Infantry. See *South Carolina Troops, 5th Regiment.*
Cowden's (Robert) Infantry. See *Union Troops, Colored, 59th Regiment.*
Cox's (Nicholas N.) Cavalry. See *Tennessee Troops, Confederate.*
Craddock's (William B.) Infantry. See *Kentucky Troops, Union, 30th Regiment.*
Cramer's (John F.) Infantry. See *Missouri Troops, Union, 17th Regiment.*
Crandal's (Frederick M.) Infantry. See *Union Troops, Colored, 48th Regiment.*
Crandall's (John R.) Cavalry. See *Missouri Troops, Union, Mississippi Marine Brigade, post, 1st Battalion.*
Crane's (Nirom M.) Infantry. See *New York Troops, 107th Regiment.*
Creasman's (William B.) Infantry. See *North Carolina Troops, Confederate, 29th Regiment.*
Crews' (C. C.) Cavalry. See *Georgia Troops, 2d Regiment.*
Crews' (J. M.) Cavalry. See *Charles McDonald's Cavalry, post.*
Crittenden's (Eugene W.) Cavalry. See *Kentucky Troops, Union, 12th Regiment.*
Crocheron Light Dragoons. See *Alabama Troops, Confederate.*
Croft's (Edward) Artillery. See *Columbus Artillery, ante.*
Cross' (Nelson) Infantry. See *New York Troops, 67th Regiment.*
Cross' (William) Infantry. See *Tennessee Troops, Union, 3d Regiment.*
Crossland's (Ed.) Infantry. See *Kentucky Troops, Confederate, 7th Regiment.*
Croxton's (John T.) Infantry. See *Kentucky Troops, Union, 4th Regiment.*
Cullen's (William A.) Infantry. See *Indiana Troops, 123d Regiment.*
Culpeper's (James F.) Artillery. See *Palmetto Battalion Artillery, post, Battery C.*
Culver's (Joshua B.) Infantry. See *Michigan Troops, 13th Regiment.*
Cumberland Artillery. See *Kentucky Troops, Confederate.*
Cummins' (John E.) Infantry. See *Ohio Troops, 99th Regiment.*
Cunningham's (C. J. L.) Infantry. See *Alabama Troops, Confederate, 57th Regiment.*
Cunningham's (George P.) Artillery. See *Illinois Troops, 1st Regiment, Battery D.*

---

* Temporarily commanding.

Cunningham's (Richard D.) **Heavy Artillery.** See *Union Troops, Colored, 8th Regiment.*

Curly's (Thomas) **Infantry.** See *Missouri Troops, Union, 27th Regiment.*

Currie's (George E.) **Infantry.** See *Missouri Troops, Union, Mississippi Marine Brigade, 1st Regiment.*

Curtiss' (Frank S.) **Infantry.** See *Illinois Troops, 127th Regiment.*

Cushing's (Harry C.) **Artillery.** See *Union Troops, Regulars, 4th Regiment, Battery H.*

Dammert's (William) **Artillery.** See *Ohio Troops, 1st Regiment, Battery I.*

Daniel's (Charles P.) **Infantry.** See *Georgia Troops, 5th Regiment.*

Darden's (Putnam) **Artillery.** See *Jefferson Artillery, post.*

Davenport's (William) **Home Guards.** See *Georgia Troops.*

Davidson's (George S.) **Artillery.** See *Virginia Troops.*

Davies' (John R.) **Heavy Artillery.** See *Wisconsin Troops, 1st Regiment, Battery C.*

Davis' (John B.) **Infantry.** See *South Carolina Troops, 15th Regiment.*

Davis' (Joseph H.) **Infantry.** See *Union Troops, Veteran Reserve Corps, 2d Battalion, 77th Company.*

Davis' (N. N.) **Infantry.** See *Alabama Troops, Confederate, 24th Regiment.*

Davis' (Reuben A.) **Cavalry.** See *Tennessee Troops, Union, 11th Regiment.*

Davitte's (S. W.) **Cavalry.** See *Georgia Troops, 1st Regiment.*

Dawley's (Richard L.) **Artillery.** See *Minnesota Troops, 2d Battery.*

Dawson's (William) **Infantry.** See *Indiana Troops, 30th Regiment.*

Day's (George W.) **Cavalry.** See *Tennessee Troops, Confederate, 12th Battalion.*

Dayton's (James H.) **Infantry.** See *West Virginia Troops, 4th Regiment.*

Dean's (Benjamin D.) **Infantry.** See *Missouri Troops, Union, 26th Regiment.*

Dean's (Henry S.) **Infantry.** See *Michigan Troops, 22d Regiment.*

De Buy's (O.) **Cavalry.** See *Guy Dreux's Cavalry, post.*

Dedman's (J. M.) **Infantry.** See *Alabama Troops, Confederate, 20th Regiment.*

De Gress' (Francis) **Artillery.** See *Illinois Troops, 1st Regiment, Battery H.*

De Groat's (Charles H.) **Infantry.** See *Wisconsin Troops, 32d Regiment.*

De Hart's (Richard P.) **Infantry.** See *Indiana Troops, 128th Regiment.*

Deimling's (Francis C.) **Infantry.** See *Missouri Troops, Union, 10th Regiment.*

De Moss' (William E.) **Cavalry.** See *Nicholas N. Cox's Cavalry, ante.*

Denning's (Benjamin F.) **Artillery.** See *Indiana Troops, 22d Battery.*

Dent's (S. H.) **Artillery.** See *Alabama Troops, Confederate.*

De Vries' (Peter) **Artillery.** See *Michigan Troops, 1st Regiment, Battery E.*

Dibrell's (George G.) **Cavalry.** See *Tennessee Troops, Confederate.*

Dick's (George F.) **Infantry.** See *Indiana Troops, 86th Regiment.*

Dickenson's (Crispin) **Artillery.** See *Ringgold Artillery, post.*

Dilger's (Hubert) **Artillery.** See *Ohio Troops, 1st Regiment, Battery I.*

Dillard's (William Y.) **Infantry.** See *Kentucky Troops, Union, 34th Regiment.*

Dilworth's (Caleb J.) **Infantry.** See *Illinois Troops, 85th Regiment.*

Dixon's (M. H.) **Infantry.** See *Confederate Troops, Regulars, 3d Regiment.*

Doan's (Thomas) **Infantry.** See *Indiana Troops, 101st Regiment.*

Dobbins' (Joseph J.) **Cavalry.** See *James T. Wheeler's Cavalry, post.*

Dobke's (Adolphus) **Infantry.** See *New York Troops, 45th Regiment.*

Doerflinger's (Charles) **Cavalry.** See *Wisconsin Troops, 2d Regiment.*

Doolittle's (Charles C.) **Infantry.** See *Michigan Troops, 18th Regiment.*

Dortch's (John B.) **Cavalry.** See *Kentucky Troops, Confederate.*

Doss' (W. L.) **Infantry.** See *Mississippi Troops, Confederate, 14th Regiment.*

Doughty's (George W.) **Cavalry.** See *Tennessee Troops, Union, 13th Regiment.*

Douglas' (James P.) **Artillery.** See *Texas Troops.*

Downey's (Thomas J.) **Infantry.** See *Union Troops, Colored, 15th Regiment.*

Drake's (J. L.) **Infantry.** See *Mississippi Troops, Confederate, 33d Regiment.*

888   KY., SW. VA., TENN., MISS., ALA., AND N. GA.   [CHAP. XLIV.

Dresser's (George W.) Artillery. See *Union Troops, Regulars, 4th Regiment, Battery M.*
Dreux's (Guy) Cavalry. See *Louisiana Troops.*
Driscoll's (Daniel) Infantry. See *Missouri Troops, Union, 24th Regiment.*
Drish's (James F.) Infantry. See *Illinois Troops, 122d Regiment.*
Drury's (Lucius H.) Artillery. See *Wisconsin Troops, 3d Battery.*
Du Bose's (Dudley M.) Infantry. See *Georgia Troops, 15th Regiment.*
Duckworth's (William L.) Cavalry. See *Tennessee Troops, Confederate.*
Duer's (John O.) Infantry. See *Illinois Troops, 45th Regiment.*
Duff's (William L.) Cavalry. See *Mississippi Troops, Confederate, 19th Battalion.*
Dufficy's (John P.) Infantry. See *Indiana Troops, 35th Regiment.*
Dula's (Thomas J.) Infantry. See *North Carolina Troops, Confederate, 58th Regiment.*
Dumonteil's (F.) Cavalry. See *Confederate Troops, Regulars, 14th Regiment.*
Duncan's (William) Cavalry. See *Illinois Troops, 15th Regiment.*
Dunlap's (Henry C.) Infantry. See *Kentucky Troops, Union, 3d Regiment.*
Dunlop's (Isaac L.) Infantry. See *Arkansas Troops, 9th Regiment.*
Dunlop's (S. J. C.) Infantry. See *Georgia Troops, 46th Regiment.*
Dunn's (David M.) Infantry. See *Indiana Troops, 29th Regiment.*
Dunwoody's (James A.) Artillery. See *Indiana Troops, 12th Battery.*
Dustin's (Daniel) Infantry. See *Illinois Troops, 105th Regiment.*
Dwight's (Augustus W.) Infantry. See *New York Troops, 122d Regiment.*
Dwyer's (Patrick) Infantry. See *Union Troops, Veteran Reserve Corps, 2d Battalion, 40th Company.*
Eakin's (W. L.) Infantry. See *Tennessee Troops, Confederate, 59th Regiment.*
Earle's (R. G.) Cavalry. See *Alabama Troops, Confederate, 2d Regiment.*
Earp's (C. R.) Cavalry. See *Texas Troops, 10th Regiment.*
Eaton's (Charles G.) Infantry. See *Ohio Troops, 72d Regiment.*
Edgarton's (Warren P.) Artillery. See *Ohio Troops, 1st Regiment, Batteries B and E.*
Edie's (John R.) Infantry. See *Union Troops, Regulars, 15th Regiment, 2d Battalion.*
Edmundson's (David) Cavalry. See *Virginia Troops, 21st Regiment.*
Edmundson's (Henry A.) Cavalry. See *Virginia Troops, 27th Battalion.*
Edwards' (A. C.) Infantry. See *Georgia Troops, 47th Regiment.*
Eggleston's (Beroth B.) Cavalry. See *Ohio Troops, 1st Regiment.*
Elgin Artillery. See *Illinois Troops.*
Elkin's (Rush L.) Cavalry. See *Texas Troops, 27th Regiment.*
Ellis' (John) Infantry. See *Tennessee Troops, Union, 1st Regiment.*
Elstner's (George R.) Infantry. See *Ohio Troops, 50th Regiment.*
Ely's (John J.) Artillery. See *Michigan Troops, 1st Regiment, Battery E.*
Emery's (Augustus H.) Artillery. See *Michigan Troops, 1st Regiment, Battery M.*
Emery's (Winslow D.) Artillery. See *Alabama Troops, Confederate, 20th Battalion, Battery A.*
Enyart's (David A.) Infantry. See *Kentucky Troops, Union, 1st Regiment.*
Erdelmeyer's (Frank) Infantry. See *Indiana Troops, 32d Regiment.*
Esembaux's (Michael) Infantry. See *New York Troops, 58th Regiment.*
Espy's (Harvey J.) Infantry. See *Indiana Troops, 6th Regiment.*
Estabrook's (George H.) Infantry. See *Illinois Troops, 7th Regiment.*
Estelle's (William M.) Infantry. See *Mississippi Troops, Confederate, 38th Regiment.*
Estep's (George) Artillery. See *Indiana Troops, 8th Battery.*
Eufaula Artillery. See *Alabama Troops, Confederate.*
Evans' (Henry G.) Infantry. See *Tennessee Troops, Confederate, 48th Regiment (Nixon's).*
Ewing's (Martin B.) Heavy Artillery. See *Ohio Troops, 2d Regiment.*
Fahnestock's (Allen L.) Infantry. See *Illinois Troops, 86th Regiment.*
Farrar's (Bernard G.) Heavy Artillery. See *Union Troops, Colored, 5th (6th) Regiment.*
Farrell's (M.) Infantry. See *Mississippi Troops, Confederate, 15th Regiment.*

Faulkner's (Lester B.) Infantry. See *New York Troops*, 136*th Regiment.*
Faulkner's (W. W.) Cavalry. See *Kentucky Troops, Confederate*, 12*th Regiment.*
Fearing's (Benjamin D.) Infantry. See *Ohio Troops*, *92d Regiment.*
Feild's (Hume R.) Infantry. See *Tennessee Troops, Confederate*, 1*st and* 27*th Regiments.*
Fenner's (Charles E.) Artillery. See *Louisiana Troops.*
Ferguson's (Thomas B.) Artillery. See *South Carolina Troops.*
Ferrell's (C. B.) Artillery. See *Georgia Troops.*
Fetterman's (William J.) Infantry. See *Union Troops, Regulars*, 18*th Regiment*, 2*d Battalion.*
Fickling's (William W.) Artillery. See *Brooks Artillery, ante.*
Fidler's (William H.) Cavalry. See *Kentucky Troops, Union*, 6*th Regiment.*
Fisher's (Rhoads) Infantry. See *Texas Troops*, 6*th Regiment;* also 15*th Texas Cavalry.*
Fitch's (John A.) Artillery. See *Illinois Troops*, 1*st Regiment, Battery E.*
Fitch's (William T.) Infantry. See *Ohio Troops*, 29*th Regiment.*
Flad's (Henry) Engineers. See *Missouri Troops, Union*, 1*st Regiment.*
Fletcher's (Thomas C.) Infantry. See *Missouri Troops, Union*, 31*st Regiment.*
Flood's (James P.) Artillery. See *Illinois Troops*, 2*d Regiment, Battery C.*
Flournoy's (P. C.) Infantry. See *Missouri Troops, Confederate*, 2*d and* 6*th Regiments.*
Flynn's (John) Infantry. See *Pennsylvania Troops*, 28*th Regiment.*
Flynn's (Patrick) Infantry. See *Illinois Troops*, 90*th Regiment.*
Foote's (Thaddeus) Cavalry. See *Michigan Troops*, 10*th Regiment.*
Forrest's (Jeffrey E.) Cavalry. See *Alabama Troops, Confederate.*
Forrest's (Nathan B.) Cavalry. See *Tennessee Troops, Confederate.*
Forney's (George H.) Infantry. See *Confederate Troops, Regulars*, 1*st Battalion.*
Forsyth's (Robert C.) Artillery. See *Alabama Troops, Confederate*, 1*st Battalion.*
Foster's (John S.) Cavalry. See *Ohio Troops*, 4*th Company.*
Foster's (William G.) Infantry. See *Georgia Troops*, 65*th Regiment.*
Foules' (H. L.) Cavalry. See *Mississippi Troops, Confederate.*
Fourat's (Enos) Infantry. See *New Jersey Troops*, 33*d Regiment.*
Fowler's (Alexander) Infantry. See *Indiana Troops*, 99*th Regiment.*
Fowler's (William H.) Artillery. See *Alabama Troops, Confederate.*
Foy's (James C.) Infantry. See *Kentucky Troops, Union*, 23*d Regiment.*
Frambes' (Granville A.) Infantry. See *Ohio Troops*, 59*th Regiment.*
Freeman's (Samuel L.) Artillery. See *Tennessee Troops, Confederate.*
Froehlich's (George) Artillery. See *Ohio Troops*, 4*th Battery.*
Frohock's (William T.) Infantry. See *Union Troops, Colored*, 66*th Regiment.*
Froman's (Anderson) Infantry. See *Illinois Troops*, 116*th Regiment.*
Fry's (John C.) Infantry. See *Ohio Troops*, 20*th Regiment.*
Fulkerson's (Abraham) Infantry. See *Tennessee Troops, Confederate*, 63*d Regiment.*
Fulton's (John S.) Infantry. See *Tennessee Troops, Confederate*, 25*th and* 44*th Regiments.*
Fulton's (Robert A.) Infantry. See *Ohio Troops*, 53*d Regiment.*
Fyan's (Robert W.) Infantry. See *Missouri Troops, Union*, 24*th Regiment.*
Gage's (Joseph S.) Infantry. See *Missouri Troops, Union*, 29*th Regiment.*
Gaillard's (Franklin) Infantry. See *South Carolina Troops*, 2*d Regiment.*
Gaines' (J. F.) Cavalry. See *Alabama Troops, Confederate*, 53*d Regiment.*
Gallagher's (Thomas) Artillery. See *Michigan Troops*, 1*st Regiment, Battery L.*
Gambee's (Charles B.) Infantry. See *Ohio Troops*, 55*th Regiment.*
Gardner's (George Q.) Artillery. See *Wisconsin Troops*, 5*th Battery.*
Garrity's (James) Artillery. See *Alabama Troops, Confederate.*
Gary's (Marco B.) Artillery. See *Ohio Troops*, 1*st Regiment, Battery C.*
Gary's (M. W.) Cavalry. See *Hampton Legion, post.*
Gates' (Elijah) Cavalry. See *Missouri Troops, Confederate*, 1*st and* 3*d Regiments.*

Gauen's (Jacob E.) Infantry. See *Illinois Troops*, 49th *Regiment*.
Gaw's (William B.) Infantry. See *Union Troops, Colored*, 16th *Regiment*.
Gay's (William H.) Artillery. See *Iowa Troops, 1st Battery*.
Geddes' (James L.) Infantry. See *Iowa Troops*, 8th *Regiment*.
George's (James) Infantry. See *Minnesota Troops*, 2d *Regiment*.
George's (James Z.) Cavalry. See *Mississippi Troops, Confederate*, 5th *Regiment*.
Giesy's (Henry H.) Infantry. See *Ohio Troops*, 46th *Regiment*.
Gilbert's (Henry C.) Infantry. See *Michigan Troops*, 19th *Regiment*.
Gilbert's (James I.) Infantry. See *Iowa Troops*, 27th *Regiment*.
Gilchrist's (Charles A.) Infantry. See *Union Troops, Colored*, 50th *Regiment*.
Gillespie's (James W.) Infantry. See *Tennessee Troops, Confederate*, 43d *Regiment*.
Giltner's (H. L.) Cavalry. See *Kentucky Troops, Confederate*, 4th *Regiment*.
Given's (Josiah) Infantry. See *Ohio Troops*, 74th *Regiment*.
Given's (William) Infantry. See *Ohio Troops*, 102d *Regiment*.
Gleason's (Newell) Infantry. See *Indiana Troops*, 87th *Regiment*.
Glenn's (John F.) Infantry. See *Pennsylvania Troops*, 23d *Regiment*.
Gloster's (A. W.) Engineers. See *Confederate Troops, Regulars*, 3d *Regiment*.
Godard's (Abel) Infantry. See *New York Troops*, 60th *Regiment*.
Godfrey's (George L.) Cavalry. See *Alabama Troops, Union*, 1st *Regiment*.
Golden's (Stephen) Infantry. See *Kentucky Troops, Union*, 49th *Regiment*.
Goldthwaite's (Richard W.) Artillery. See *Henry C. Semple's Artillery, post*.
Gonzales' (Joseph) Cavalry. See *Confederate Troops, Regulars*, 14th *Regiment*.
Good's (Joseph) Infantry. See *Ohio Troops*, 108th *Regiment*.
Goodnow's (James) Infantry. See *Indiana Troops*, 12th *Regiment*.
Goodspeed's (Wilbur F.) Artillery. See *Ohio Troops*, 1st *Regiment, Battery A*.
Gordon's (George A.) Infantry. See *Georgia Troops*, 63d *Regiment*.
Gordon's (George W.) Infantry. See *Tennessee Troops, Confederate*, 11th *Regiment*.
Gracey's (Frank P.) Artillery. See *Robert Cobb's Artillery, ante*.
Graves' (Rice E.) Artillery. See *Mississippi Troops, Confederate*.
Gray's (Samuel F.) Infantry. See *Ohio Troops*, 49th *Regiment*.
Greathouse's (Lucien) Infantry. See *Illinois Troops*, 48th *Regiment*.
Green's (Henry D.) Artillery. See *Cumberland Artillery, ante*.
Green's (John H.) Cavalry. See *Robert V. Richardson's Cavalry, post*.
Green's (Solomon L.) Cavalry. See *Ohio Troops*, 7th *Regiment*.
Green's (Thomas H.) Infantry. See *Wisconsin Troops, 1st Regiment*.
Greene's (Alexander A.) Infantry. See *Alabama Troops, Confederate*, 37th *Regiment*.
Greenleaf's (Leeds) Cavalry. See *Orleans Light Horse, post*.
Greenlee's (Louis S.) Cavalry. See *Confederate Troops, Regulars*, 14th *Regiment*.
Gregory's (James M.) Cavalry. See *Illinois Troops*, 11th *Regiment*.
Grider's (John H.) Infantry. See *Kentucky Troops, Union*, 52d *Regiment*.
Griffith's (John) Infantry. See *Arkansas Troops*, 11th *Regiment*.
Grobler's (Augustus W.) Infantry. See *New Jersey Troops*, 34th *Regiment*.
Grosvenor's (Charles H.) Infantry. See *Ohio Troops*, 18th *Regiment*.
Grower's (William T. C.) Infantry. See *New York Troops*, 17th *Regiment*.
Guenther's (Francis L.) Artillery. See *Union Troops, Regulars*, 5th *Regiment, Battery H*.
Guibor's (Henry) Artillery. See *Missouri Troops, Confederate*.
Guthrie's (James V.) Infantry. See *Illinois Troops*, 19th *Regiment*.
Gwynne's (Andrew D.) Infantry. See *Tennessee Troops, Confederate*, 38th *Regiment*.
Hagood's (James R.) Infantry. See *South Carolina Troops*, 1st *Regiment* (*Volunteers*).
Hale's (Francis E.) Artillery. See *Michigan Troops*, 1st *Regiment, Battery A*.
Hall's Cavalry. (Official designation not of record.) See ―― *Hall*.
Hall's (Bolling, jr.) Infantry. See *Alabama Troops, Confederate*, 59th *Regiment*.
Hall's (John G.) Infantry. See *Tennessee Troops, Confederate*, 51st and 52d *Regiments*.
Hall's (John P.) Infantry. See *Illinois Troops*, 56th *Regiment*.

Halpin's (William G.) Infantry. See *Kentucky Troops, Union, 15th Regiment.*
Ham's (T. W.) Cavalry. See *Mississippi Troops, Confederate.*
Hamblin's (Joseph E.) Infantry. See *New York Troops, 65th Regiment.*
Hambright's (Henry A.) Infantry. See *Pennsylvania Troops, 79th Regiment.*
Hamilton's (Joseph) Infantry. See *Phillips Legion, post.*
Hamilton's (O. P.) Cavalry. See *Tennessee Troops, Confederate*
Hammerstein's (Herbert von) Infantry. See *New York Troops, 78th Regiment.*
Hammond's (Charles M.) Infantry. See *Illinois Troops, 100th Regiment.*
Hampton Legion. See *South Carolina Troops.*
Hamrick's (John G.) Infantry. See *Illinois Troops, 83d Regiment.*
Hanna's (William) Infantry. See *Illinois Troops, 50th Regiment.*
Hanson's (Charles S.) Infantry. See *Kentucky Troops, Union, 37th Regiment.*
Hapeman's (Douglas) Infantry. See *Illinois Troops, 104th Regiment.*
Hardcastle's (A. B.) Infantry. See *Mississippi Troops, Confederate, 45th Regiment.*
Harmon's (Oscar F.) Infantry. See *Illinois Troops, 125th Regiment.*
Harper's (James P.) Heavy Artillery. See *Union Troops, Colored, 2d (3d) Regiment.*
Harris' (J. L.) Cavalry. See *Mississippi Troops, Confederate, 2d Regiment.*
Harris' (John B.) Infantry. See *Illinois Troops, 26th Regiment.*
Harris' (Samuel J.) Artillery. See *Indiana Troops, 19th Battery.*
Harris' (T. W.) Cavalry. See *Mississippi Troops, Confederate.*
Harris' (William C.) Infantry. See *Illinois Troops, 38th Regiment.*
Harrison's (Benjamin) Infantry. See *Indiana Troops, 70th Regiment.*
Harrison's (Richard) Infantry. See *Mississippi Troops, Confederate, 43d Regiment.*
Harrison's (Thomas J.) Cavalry. See *Indiana Troops, 8th Regiment.*
Hart's (Benjamin R.) Infantry. See *Alabama Troops, Confederate, 22d Regiment.*
Hart's (John R.) Cavalry. See *Georgia Troops, 6th Regiment.*
Hart's (William) Artillery. See *Arkansas Troops.*
Harvey's (Alonzo D.) Artillery. See *Indiana Troops, 15th Battery.*
Hatch's (Lemuel D.) Cavalry. See *Alabama Troops, Confederate, 8th Regiment.*
Havis' (M. W.) Artillery. See *Georgia Troops.*
Hawkins' (E. R.) Cavalry. See *Texas Troops, 27th Regiment.*
Hawkins' (Hiram) Infantry. See *Kentucky Troops, Confederate, 5th Regiment.*
Hawkins' (Isaac R.) Cavalry. See *Tennessee Troops, Union, 7th Regiment.*
Hawley's (Chauncey G.) Heavy Artillery. See *Ohio Troops, 1st Regiment.*
Hawley's (William) Infantry. See *Wisconsin Troops, 3d Regiment.*
Hay's (Henry S.) Infantry. See *Union Troops, Colored, 63d Regiment.*
Hayes' (Philip C.) Infantry. See *Ohio Troops, 103d Regiment.*
Hays' (William H.) Infantry. See *Kentucky Troops, Union, 10th Regiment.*
Heath's (Albert) Infantry. See *Indiana Troops, 100th Regiment.*
Heath's (Thomas T.) Cavalry. See *Ohio Troops, 5th Regiment.*
Heckman's (Lewis) Artillery. See *Ohio Troops, 1st Regiment, Battery K.*
Heinrich's (Gustav) Cavalry. See *Missouri Troops, Union, 4th Regiment.*
Helena Artillery. See *Arkansas Troops.*
Henderson's (Paris P.) Infantry. See *Iowa Troops, 10th Regiment.*
Henderson's (R. J.) Infantry. See *Georgia Troops, 42d Regiment.*
Hendrick's (Henry) Infantry. See *Georgia Troops, 30th Regiment.*
Henry's (James L.) Cavalry. See *North Carolina Troops, Confederate, 14th Battalion.*
Henshaw's (Edward C.) Artillery. See *Illinois Troops.*
Herndon's (Thomas H.) Infantry. See *Alabama Troops, Confederate, 36th Regiment.*
Herriott's (George F.) Cavalry. See *Indiana Troops, 3d Regiment.*
Hess' (Joseph C.) Cavalry. See *Pennsylvania Troops, 19th Regiment.*
Hester's (William W.) Infantry. See *Kentucky Troops, Union, 48th Regiment.*
Hewett's (John M.) Artillery. See *Kentucky Troops, Union, Battery B.*
Higgins' (Charles W.) Artillery. See *Hiram M. Bledsoe's Artillery, ante.*
Higgins' (John P.) Infantry. See *Illinois Troops, 84th Regiment.*

Hill's (Benjamin J.) Infantry. See *Tennessee Troops, Confederate, 35th Regiment.*
Hill's (Charles W.) Infantry. See *Ohio Troops, 128th Regiment.*
Hobart's (Harrison C.) Infantry. See *Wisconsin Troops, 21st Regiment.*
Hobson's (A. W.) Cavalry. See *Arkansas Troops, 3d Regiment.*
Hobson's (William E.) Infantry. See *Kentucky Troops, Union, 13th Regiment.*
Hockman's (Joseph) Artillery. See *Illinois Troops, 2d Regiment, Battery D.*
Hodges' (Wesley C.) Infantry. See *Georgia Troops, 17th Regiment.*
Hodgson's (Joseph) Cavalry. See *Alabama Troops, Confederate, 7th Regiment.*
Hoffman's (Daniel W.) Heavy Artillery. See *Ohio Troops, 2d Regiment.*
Holeman's (Alexander W.) Cavalry. See *Kentucky Troops, Union, 11th Regiment.*
Holland's (Orlando S.) Infantry. See *Mississippi Troops, Confederate, 37th Regiment.*
Holloway's (E. M.) Cavalry. See *Crocheron Light Dragoons, ante.*
Holman's (Daniel W.) Cavalry. See *Tennessee Troops, Confederate.*
Holt's (G. A. C.) Infantry. See *Kentucky Troops, Confederate, 3d Regiment.*
Holt's (H. C.) Artillery. See *Buckner Artillery, ante.*
Holt's (T. G.) Cavalry. See *Confederate Troops, Regulars, 10th Regiment.*
Holt's (Willis C.) Infantry. See *Georgia Troops, 10th Regiment.*
Holtzclaw's (James T.) Infantry. See *Alabama Troops, Confederate, 18th Regiment.*
Homer's (William H.) Artillery. See *Alabama State Artillery, ante, Battery D.*
Hoskins' (James A.) Artillery. See *Brookhaven Artillery, ante.*
Hotchkiss' (Charles T.) Infantry. See *Illinois Troops, 89th Regiment.*
Hotchkiss' (William A.) Artillery. See *Minnesota Troops, 2d Battery.*
Hottenstein's (John A.) Infantry. See *Union Troops, Colored, 13th Regiment.*
Houghton's (Luther S.) Artillery. See *Indiana Troops, 23d Battery.*
Houston's (Samuel) Infantry. See *Illinois Troops, 25th Regiment.*
Hovis' (L. B.) Cavalry. See *Mississippi Troops, Confederate, 1st Regiment, Partisan Rangers.*
Howard's (Noel B.) Infantry. See *Iowa Troops, 2d Regiment.*
Howe's (John H.) Infantry. See *Illinois Troops, 124th Regiment.*
Howell's (Evan P.) Artillery. See *Georgia Troops.*
Howland's (Horace N.) Cavalry. See *Ohio Troops, 3d Regiment.*
Hubbard's (Hiram P.) Artillery. See *Wisconsin Troops, 3d Battery.*
Hudson's (John H.) Artillery. See *Atlanta Arsenal Artillery, ante.*
Hugunin's (James R.) Infantry. See *Illinois Troops, 12th Regiment.*
Hull's (G. G.) Infantry. See *Georgia Troops, Local Defense.*
Hulme's (Isaac N.) Infantry. See *Tennessee Troops, Confederate, 42d Regiment.*
Humphrey's (Thomas W.) Infantry. See *Illinois Troops, 95th Regiment.*
Hundley's (D. R.) Infantry. See *Alabama Troops, Confederate, 31st Regiment.*
Hunter's (Morton C.) Infantry. See *Indiana Troops, 82d Regiment.*
Hunter's (S. E.) Infantry. See *Louisiana Troops, 4th Regiment.*
Hurd's (John R.) Infantry. See *Kentucky Troops, Union, 2d Regiment.*
Hurlbut's (Frederick J.) Infantry. See *Illinois Troops, 57th Regiment.*
Hurst's (Fielding) Cavalry. See *Tennessee Troops, Union, 6th Regiment.*
Hurst's (John S.) Infantry. See *Kentucky Troops, Union, 24th Regiment.*
Hutchins' (N. L.) Sharpshooters. See *Georgia Troops, 3d Battalion.*
Hutchins' (Rue P.) Infantry. See *Ohio Troops, 94th Regiment.*
Hutchinson's (L.) Engineers. See *Confederate Troops, Regulars, 3d Regiment.*
Hutchinson's (William W.) Infantry. See *Ohio Troops, 103d Regiment.*
Huwald's (Gustave A.) Artillery. See *Tennessee Troops, Confederate.*
Immell's (Lorenzo D.) Artillery. See *Missouri Troops, Union, 1st Regiment, Battery G.*
Inge's (W. M.) Cavalry. See *Mississippi Troops, Confederate, 12th Regiment.*
Ingersoll's (Ezekiel J.) Infantry. See *Illinois Troops, 73d Regiment.*
Ingram's (Tillman) Infantry. See *Florida Troops, 7th Regiment.*
Innes' (William P.) Engineers. See *Michigan Troops, 1st Regiment.*
Iowa First Infantry, A. D. See *Union Troops, Colored, 60th Regiment.*

Irvin's (James M.) Infantry. See *Union Troops, Colored*, 55*th Regiment*.
Isom's (John) Artillery. See *Georgia Troops*, 9*th Battalion, Battery B*.
Ives' (Samuel S.) Infantry. See *Alabama Troops, Confederate*, 35*th Regiment*.
Jackson's (Allan H.) Infantry. See *New York Troops*, 134*th Regiment*.
Jackson's (Charles H.) Infantry. See *Wisconsin Troops*, 18*th Regiment*.
Jackson's (Ezra P.) Infantry. See *Ohio Troops*, 58*th Regiment*.
Jackson's (James) Infantry. See *Alabama Troops, Confederate*, 27*th Regiment*.
Jackson's (J. F. B.) Infantry. See *Georgia Troops*, 39*th Regiment*.
Jackson's (John M.) Infantry. See *Georgia Troops*, 34*th Regiment*.
Jackson's (T. C.) Infantry. See *Georgia Troops, Local Defense*.
Jarvis' (Dwight, jr.) Infantry. See *Ohio Troops*, 13*th Regiment*.
Jeff. Davis Legion, Cavalry. See *Mississippi Troops, Confederate*.
Jefferson Artillery. See *Mississippi Troops, Confederate*.
Jefferson's (John W.) Infantry. See *Wisconsin Troops*, 8*th Regiment*.
Jeffress' (William C.) Artillery. See *Nottoway Artillery, post*.
Jenkins' (David P.) Cavalry. See *Illinois Troops*, 14*th Regiment*.
Jennison's (Samuel P.) Infantry. See *Minnesota Troops*, 10*th Regiment*.
Jessup's (Alexander S.) Cavalry. See *Illinois Troops*, 5*th Regiment*.
Jett's (B. P.) Infantry. See *Arkansas Troops*, 11*th and* 17*th Regiments*.
John's (B. F.) Infantry. See *Mississippi Troops, Confederate*, 7*th Regiment*.
Johnson's (Aaron C.) Artillery. See *Ohio Troops*, 12*th Battery*.
Johnson's (Abda) Infantry. See *Georgia Troops*, 40*th Regiment*.
Johnson's (A. H.) Cavalry. See *Alabama Troops, Confederate*, 1*st Regiment*.
Johnson's (Thomas) Cavalry. See *Kentucky Troops, Confederate*, 2*d Battalion, Rifles*.
Johnson's (Thomas) Infantry. See *Indiana Troops*, 65*th Regiment*.
Johnson's (William A.) Cavalry. See *Alabama Troops, Confederate*, 4*th Regiment* (*Roddey's*).
Johnston Artillery. See *John W. Mebane's Artillery, post*.
Johnston's (George D.) Infantry. See *Alabama Troops, Confederate*, 25*th Regiment*.
Jolly's (John H.) Infantry. See *Ohio Troops*, 89*th Regiment*.
Jolly's (John J.) Infantry. See *Alabama Troops, Confederate*, 43*d Regiment*.
Jones' (Bushrod) Infantry. See *Alabama Troops, Confederate*, 32*d and* 58*th Regiments*.
Jones' (Charles C.) Infantry. See *Illinois Troops*, 76*th Regiment*.
Jones' (Dudley W.) Cavalry. See *Texas Troops*, 9*th Regiment*.
Jones' (James H.) Infantry. See *Mississippi Troops, Confederate*, 38*th Regiment*.
Jones' (John J.) Infantry. See *Illinois Troops*, 46*th Regiment*.
Jones' (Joseph H.) Infantry. See *Alabama Troops, Confederate*, 55*th Regiment*.
Jones' (Patrick H.) Infantry. See *New York Troops*, 154*th Regiment*.
Jones' (Theodore) Infantry. See *Ohio Troops*, 30*th Regiment*.
Jones' (Warren C.) Infantry. See *Iowa Troops*, 14*th Regiment*.
Jones' (William) Infantry. See *Indiana Troops*, 53*d Regiment*.
Jordan's (Henry) Infantry. See *Indiana Troops*, 17*th Regiment*.
Jordan's (Thomas J.) Cavalry. See *Pennsylvania Troops*, 9*th Regiment*.
Jordan's (Tyler C.) Artillery. See *Bedford Artillery, ante*.
Justin's (William) Artillery. See *Michigan Troops*, 1*st Regiment, Battery H*.
Kaercher's (Jacob) Infantry. See *Missouri Troops, Union*, 12*th Regiment*.
Kammerling's (Gustave) Infantry. See *Ohio Troops*, 9*th Regiment*.
Kappner's (Ignatz G.) Heavy Artillery. See *Union Troops, Colored*, 2*d* (3*d*) *Regiment*.
Keeble's (R. H.) Infantry. See *Tennessee Troops, Confederate*, 17*th and* 23*d Regiments*.
Keegan's (Patrick H.) Infantry. See *Michigan Troops*, 11*th Regiment*.
Keeler's (William B.) Infantry. See *Iowa Troops*, 35*th Regiment*.
Keitt's (Lawrence M.) Infantry. See *South Carolina Troops*, 20*th Regiment*.
Kelly's (Henry C.) Artillery. See *Tennessee Troops, Union*, 1*st Battalion, Battery G*.
Kelsey's (R. G.) Infantry. See *Mississippi Troops, Confederate*, 44*th Regiment*.

Kemper's (Milton) **Pioneers.** See *Union Troops, Pioneer Brigade, 1st Battalion.*
Kendrick's (Frank A.) **Infantry.** See *Union Troops, Colored, 61st Regiment.*
Kennedy's (Hyder A.) **Infantry.** See *Louisiana Troops, 19th Regiment.*
Kennett's (Henry G.) **Infantry.** See *Ohio Troops, 79th Regiment.*
Kentucky First Heavy Artillery, A. D. See *Union Troops, Colored, 8th Regiment.*
Kenzie's (David H.) **Artillery.** See *Union Troops, Regulars, 5th Regiment, Battery K.*
Kern's (Louis) **Artillery.** See *Indiana Troops, 6th Battery.*
Ketcham's (John H.) **Infantry.** See *New York Troops, 150th Regiment.*
Ketchum's (William H.) **Artillery.** See *James Garrity's Artillery, ante.*
Key's (J. C. G.) **Infantry.** See *Texas Troops, 4th Regiment.*
Key's (Thomas J.) **Artillery.** See *Helena Artillery, ante.*
Kilgour's (William M.) **Infantry.*** See *Illinois Troops, 80th Regiment.*
Kimberly's (Robert L.) **Infantry.** See *Ohio Troops, 41st Regiment.*
King's Artillery. (Official designation not of record.) See *Captain King.*
King's (Houston) **Artillery.** See *Clark Artillery, ante.*
King's (John F.) **Infantry.** See *Illinois Troops, 114th Regiment.*
Kinney's (Thomas J.) **Infantry.** See *Illinois Troops, 119th Regiment.*
Kirby's (Isaac M.) **Infantry.** See *Ohio Troops, 101st Regiment.*
Kirkpatrick's (M. L.) **Cavalry.** See *Alabama Troops, Confederate, 51st Regiment.*
Kirtley's (Morris) **Cavalry.** See *Virginia Troops, 36th Battalion.*
Kirwan's (John S.) **Cavalry.** See *Tennessee Troops, Union, 12th Regiment.*
Kitchell's (Edward) **Infantry.** See *Illinois Troops, 98th Regiment.*
Klein's (Robert) **Cavalry.** See *Indiana Troops, 3d Regiment.*
Knefler's (Frederick) **Infantry.** See *Indiana Troops, 79th Regiment.*
Knox's (Samuel L.) **Infantry.** See *Alabama Troops, Confederate, 1st Regiment.*
Kolb's (Reuben F.) **Artillery.** See *Barbour Artillery, ante.*   *
Kuhn's (John H.) **Cavalry.** See *H. M. Ashby's Cavalry, ante.*
Kuhn's (John H.) **Infantry.** See *Illinois Troops, 9th Regiment.*
Lackland's (William R.) **Infantry.** See *Illinois Troops, 108th Regiment.*
Lamb's (Jonathan J.) **Infantry.** See *Tennessee Troops, Confederate, 4th and 5th Regiments.*
Lamberg's (Carl A.) **Artillery.** See *Union Troops, Colored, 2d Regiment, Battery D (F).*
Lampkin's (A. W.) **Infantry.** See *Mobile Infantry, post.*
Lampley's (H. D.) **Infantry.** See *Alabama Troops, Confederate, 45th Regiment.*
Lamson's (Horace P.) **Cavalry.** See *Indiana Troops, 4th Regiment.*
Landry's (J. O.) **Infantry.** See *Louisiana Troops, 22d Regiment.*
Lane's (James C.) **Infantry.** See *New York Troops, 102d Regiment.*
Lane's (John Q.) **Infantry.** See *Ohio Troops, 97th Regiment.*
Lanier's (Thomas C.) **Infantry.** See *Alabama Troops, Confederate, 42d Regiment.*
Lankford's (A. R.) **Infantry.** See *Alabama Troops, Confederate, 38th Regiment.*
Laurance's (Uriah M.) **Infantry.** See *Illinois Troops, 107th Regiment.*
Lawrence's (R. J.) **Infantry.** See *Mississippi Troops, Confederate, 14th Regiment.*
Lawson's (Joseph J.) **Infantry.** See *Pennsylvania Troops, 77th Regiment.*
Lee's (Henry S.) **Artillery.** See *Wisconsin Troops, 7th Battery.*
Leftwich's (Jefferson) **Cavalry.** See *George G. Dibrell's Cavalry, ante.*
Leonard's (George W.) **Infantry.** See *Indiana Troops, 57th Regiment.*
Lenoir's (T. M.) **Cavalry.** See *Alabama Troops, Confederate.*
Le Sage's (John B.) **Infantry.** See *Illinois Troops, 101st Regiment.*
Lester's (William C.) **Infantry.** See *Georgia Troops, 43d Regiment.*
Levi's (John T.) **Artillery.** See *Virginia Troops.*
Lewers' (Thomas) **Cavalry.** See *Wirt Adams' Cavalry, ante.*
Lewis' Cavalry. (Official designation not of record.) See *Captain Lewis.*
Lewis' (J. C.) **Infantry.** See *Louisiana Troops, 16th and 25th Regiments.*

---

* Temporarily commanding.

Lewis' (Thomas W.) **Cavalry.** See *Kentucky Troops, Confederate,* 2d *Regiment* (*Woodward's*).
Lewis' (W. H.) **Infantry.** See *Mississippi Troops, Confederate,* 18th *Regiment.*
Lieb's (Herman) **Heavy Artillery.** See *Union Troops, Colored,* 4th (5th) *Regiment.*
Lillard's (N. J.) **Infantry.** See *Tennessee Troops, Confederate,* 3d *Regiment, P. A.*
Lilly's (Eli) **Artillery.** See *Indiana Troops,* 18th *Battery.*
Little's (Francis H.) **Infantry.** See *Georgia Troops,* 11th *Regiment.*
Lockman's (Isaac P.) **Infantry.** See *New York Troops,* 119th *Regiment.*
Logan's (John) **Infantry.** See *Illinois Troops,* 32d *Regiment.*
Logie's (William K.) **Infantry.** See *New York Troops,* 141st *Regiment.*
Long's (Richard) **Infantry.** See *Ohio Troops,* 73d *Regiment.*
Lookout Artillery. See *Tennessee Troops, Confederate.*
Loudon's (De Witt C.) **Infantry.** See *Ohio Troops,* 70th *Regiment.*
Louisiana First Artillery, A. D. See *Union Troops, Colored,* 2d *Regiment, Battery A (C).*
Louisiana Second Artillery, A. D. See *Union Troops, Colored,* 2d *Regiment, Battery B (D).*
Louisiana Third Artillery, A. D. See *Union Troops, Colored,* 2d *Regiment, Battery C (E).*
Louisiana Seventh Infantry, A. D. See *Union Troops, Colored,* 64th *Regiment.*
Louisiana Eighth Infantry, A. D. See *Union Troops, Colored,* 47th *Regiment.*
Louisiana Ninth Infantry, A. D. See *Union Troops, Colored,* 63d *Regiment.*
Louisiana Tenth Infantry, A. D. See *Union Troops, Colored,* 48th *Regiment.*
Louisiana Eleventh Infantry, A. D. See *Union Troops, Colored,* 49th *Regiment.*
Louisiana Twelfth Infantry, A. D. See *Union Troops, Colored,* 50th *Regiment.*
Love's (James R.).**Infantry.** See *William H. Thomas' Legion, post.*
Lowe's (Schuyler) **Artillery.** See *Missouri Troops, Confederate.*
Lowell's (John W.) **Artillery.** See *Illinois Troops,* 2d *Regiment, Battery G.*
Lowry's (Robert) **Infantry.** See *Mississippi Troops, Confederate,* 6th *Regiment.*
Lowry's (William M.) **Artillery.** See *Virginia Troops.*
Lowry's (W. L.) **Cavalry.** See *Mississippi Troops, Confederate,* 2d *Regiment* (*State*).
Lucy's (Jackson A.) **Infantry.** See *Ohio Troops,* 115th *Regiment.*
Lum's (Charles M.) **Infantry.** See *Michigan Troops,* 10th *Regiment.*
Lumsden's (Charles L.) **Artillery.** See *Alabama Troops, Confederate.*
Lynch's (Connally H.) **Infantry.** See *Virginia Troops,* 63d *Regiment.*
Lyon's (William P.) **Infantry.** See *Wisconsin Troops,* 13th *Regiment.*
Mabry's (Hinchie P.) **Cavalry.** See *Texas Troops,* 3d *Regiment.*
McAfee's (A. L.) **Cavalry.** See *Confederate Troops, Regulars,* 6th *Battalion.*
McBee's (J. T.) **Cavalry.** See *Mississippi Troops, Confederate,* 28th *Regiment.*
McCall's (J. K.) **Infantry.** See *Arsenal Battalion, ante.*
McCalla's (R. C.) **Engineers.** See *Confederate Troops, Regulars,* 3d *Regiment.*
McCants' (Robert P.) **Artillery.** See *Marion Artillery, post.*
McCay's (R. C.) **Infantry.** See *Mississippi Troops, Confederate,* 38th *Regiment.*
McClanahan's (John W.) **Infantry.** See *Illinois Troops,* 53d *Regiment.*
McClelland's (Samuel) **Infantry.** See *Ohio Troops,* 7th *Regiment.*
McClung's (Hugh L. W.) **Artillery.** See *Tennessee Troops, Confederate.*
McClure's (John D.) **Infantry.** See *Illinois Troops,* 47th *Regiment.*
McCook's (Anson G.) **Infantry.** See *Ohio Troops,* 2d *Regiment.*
McCown's (James) **Infantry.** See *Missouri Troops, Confederate,* 3d and 5th *Regiments.*
McCown's (Joseph B.) **Infantry.** See *Illinois Troops,* 63d *Regiment.*
McCulloch's (R. A.) **Cavalry.** See *Missouri Troops, Confederate,* 2d *Regiment.*
McCullough's (James) **Infantry.** See *South Carolina Troops,* 16th *Regiment.*
McDonald's (Charles) **Cavalry.** See *Tennessee Troops, Confederate.*
McDougall's (Archibald L.) **Infantry.** See *New York Troops,* 123d *Regiment.*

McDowell's (Samuel M.) Artillery. See *Pennsylvania Troops, Battery B.*
McEwen's (John L., jr.) Infantry. See *Tennessee Troops, Confederate, 25th and 44th Regiments.*
McGill's (James D.) Artillery. See *Pennsylvania Troops, Battery E.*
McGlashan's (Peter) Infantry. See *Georgia Troops, 50th Regiment.*
McGowan's (John E.) Heavy Artillery. See *Union Troops, Colored, 1st Regiment.*
McGroarty's (Stephen J.) Infantry. See *Ohio Troops, 61st Regiment.*
McGuire's (John P.) Infantry. See *Tennessee Troops, Confederate, 32d Regiment.*
McGuirk's (John) Cavalry. See *Mississippi Troops, Confederate, 3d Regiment (State).*
McIlvain's (Alexander) Infantry. See *Ohio Troops, 64th Regiment.*
McIntire's (William T. B.) Infantry. See *Indiana Troops, 42d Regiment.*
McIntyre's (James B.) Cavalry. See *Union Troops, Regulars, 4th Regiment.*
McKamy's (James A.) Infantry. See *William H. Thomas' Legion, post.*
McKeaig's (George W.) Infantry. See *Illinois Troops, 120th Regiment.*
McKee's (George C.) Infantry. See *Illinois Troops, 11th Regiment.*
McKenzie's (George W.) Cavalry. See *Tennessee Troops, Confederate.*
McKleroy's (John M.) Cavalry. See *Confederate Troops, Regulars, 10th Regiment.*
McLaurin's (C.) Cavalry. See *Mississippi Troops, 4th Regiment (Wilbourn's).*
McLean's (Angus D.) Infantry. See *Florida Troops, 6th Regiment.*
McLemore's (William S.) Cavalry. See *Tennessee Troops, Confederate.*
McLendon's (J. M.) Artillery. See *Mississippi Troops, Confederate, 14th Battalion, Battery C.*
McNaughton's (Harlow P.) Artillery. See *Ohio Troops, 7th Battery.*
McNeely's (Charles C.) Cavalry. See *Kentucky Troops, Union, 7th Regiment.*
McReynolds' (J. H.) Infantry. See *Texas Troops, 9th Regiment.*
McSpadden's (Samuel K.) Infantry. See *Alabama Troops, Confederate, 19th Regiment.*
McSweeney's (Paul) Infantry. See *Iowa Troops, 9th Regiment.*
Madison Artillery. See *Louisiana Troops.*
Magevney's (Michael, jr.) Infantry. See *Tennessee Troops, Confederate, 13th and 154th Regiments.*
Malmborg's (Oscar) Infantry. See *Illinois Troops, 55th Regiment.*
Malone's (James C., jr.) Cavalry. See *Alabama Troops, Confederate.*
Manderson's (Charles F.) Infantry. See *Ohio Troops, 19th Regiment.*
Manion's (George D.) Cavalry. See *Texas Troops, 17th and 18th Regiments.*
Manning's (Van H.) Infantry. See *Arkansas Troops, 3d Regiment.*
Mannon's (James M.) Infantry. See *Illinois Troops, 102d Regiment.*
Marion Artillery. See *Florida Troops.*
Marsh's (Jason) Infantry. See *Illinois Troops, 74th Regiment.*
Marshall's (Alexander) Artillery. See *Ohio Troops, 1st Regiment, Battery G.*
Marshall's (L. G.) Artillery. See *Tennessee Troops, Confederate.*
Marshall's (William R.) Infantry. See *Minnesota Troops, 7th Regiment.*
Martin's (James S.) Infantry. See *Illinois Troops, 111th Regiment.*
Martin's (John A.) Infantry. See *Kansas Troops, 8th Regiment.*
Martin's (Samuel) Infantry. See *Kentucky Troops, Union, 37th Regiment.*
Martin's (W. H.) Infantry. See *Arkansas Troops, 1st and 15th Regiments.*
Mastin's (P. B., jr.) Cavalry. See *Alabama Troops, Confederate, 53d Regiment.*
Matson's (Courtland C.) Cavalry. See *Indiana Troops, 6th Regiment.*
Matthaei's (John L.) Artillery. See *Missouri Troops, Union, 1st Regiment, Battery C.*
Matthews' (R. B.) Artillery. See *Robert Cobb's Artillery, ante.*
Matzdorff's (Alvin V.) Infantry. See *Pennsylvania Troops, 75th Regiment.*
Mauff's (August) Infantry. See *Illinois Troops, 24th Regiment.*
Mauldin's (T. H.) Cavalry. See *Alabama Troops, Confederate, 3d Regiment.*
Maury's (Henry) Cavalry. See *Confederate Troops, Regulars, 15th Regiment.*
Maxson's (George W.) Infantry. See *Kentucky Troops, Confederate, 6th Regiment.*

Maxwell's (William L.) **Cavalry.** See *John G. Ballentine's Cavalry, ante.*
May's (Andrew J.) **Cavalry.** See *Kentucky Troops, Confederate, 10th Regiment* (*May's*).
Maynard's (Edward) **Infantry.** See *Tennessee Troops, Union, 6th Regiment.*
Mead's (Lemuel G.) **Guerrillas.** (Official designation not of record.) See *Lemuel G. Mead.*
Mebane's (John W.) **Artillery.** See *Tennessee Troops, Confederate.*
Mellon's (T. A.) **Infantry.** See *Mississippi Troops, Confederate, 3d Regiment.*
Memphis Light Artillery, A. D. See *Union Troops, Colored, 2d Regiment, Battery D (F).*
Merkle's (Christopher F.) **Artillery.** See *Union Troops, Regulars, 4th Regiment, Battery G.*
Merriam's (Jonathan) **Infantry.** See *Illinois Troops, 117th Regiment.*
Merritt's (T. M.) **Cavalry.** See *Georgia Troops, 2d Regiment.*
Metham's (Pren) **Infantry.** See *Ohio Troops, 80th Regiment.*
Meumann's (Theodore) **Infantry.** See *Missouri Troops, Union, 3d Regiment.*
Miles' (W. R.) **Legion.** See *Louisiana Troops.*
Miller's (Abram O.) **Infantry.** See *Indiana Troops, 72d Regiment.*
Miller's (Alexander J.) **Infantry.** See *Iowa Troops, 6th Regiment.*
Miller's (Horace H.) **Cavalry.** See *Mississippi Troops, Confederate.*
Miller's (Silas) **Infantry.** See *Illinois Troops, 36th Regiment.*
Mills' (Gilbert C.) **Cavalry.** See *Confederate Troops, Regulars, 14th Regiment.*
Mills' (Roger Q.) **Infantry.** See *Texas Troops, 10th Regiment.*
Milward's (Hubbard K.) **Infantry.** See *Kentucky Troops, Union, 18th Regiment.*
Mims' (David A.) **Infantry.** See *Kentucky Troops, Union, 39th Regiment.*
Minnis' (John B.) **Cavalry.** See *Tennessee Troops, Union, 3d Regiment.*
Mississippi First Cavalry, A. D. See *Union Troops, Colored, 3d Regiment.*
Mississippi First Heavy Artillery, A. D. See *Union Troops, Colored, 4th (5th) Regiment.*
Mississippi First Infantry, A. D. See *Union Troops, Colored, 51st Regiment.*
Mississippi Second Heavy Artillery, A. D. See *Union Troops, Colored, 5th (6th) Regiment.*
Mississippi Second Infantry, A. D. See *Union Troops, Colored, 52d Regiment.*
Mississippi Third Infantry, A. D. See *Union Troops, Colored, 53d Regiment.*
Mississippi Fourth Infantry, A. D. See *Union Troops, Colored, 66th Regiment.*
Mississippi Sixth Infantry, A. D. See *Union Troops, Colored, 58th Regiment.*
Mississippi Marine Brigade. See *Missouri Troops, Union; also Alfred W. Ellet.*
Missouri First Infantry, A. D. See *Union Troops, Colored, 62d Regiment.*
Missouri Second Infantry, A. D. See *Union Troops, Colored, 65th Regiment.*
Missouri Third Infantry, A. D. See *Union Troops, Colored, 67th Regiment.*
Missouri Fourth Infantry, A. D. See *Union Troops, Colored, 68th Regiment.*
Mitchell's (J. C. B.) **Infantry.** See *Alabama Troops, Confederate, 34th Regiment.*
Mitchell's (W. D.) **Infantry.** See *Georgia Troops, 29th Regiment.*
Mix's (Elisha) **Cavalry.** See *Michigan Troops, 8th Regiment.*
Mizner's (Henry R.) **Infantry.** See *Michigan Troops, 14th Regiment.*
Mobile Infantry. See *Alabama Troops, Confederate.*
Mobile Fire Battalion, Infantry. See *Alabama Troops, Confederate.*
Mong's (William J.) **Artillery.** See *Ohio Troops, 10th Battery.*
Montgomery's (F. A.) **Cavalry.** See *Mississippi Troops, Confederate, 1st Regiment.*
Montgomery's (James H. M.) **Infantry.** See *Ohio Troops, 33d Regiment.*
Montgomery's (Milton) **Infantry.** See *Wisconsin Troops, 25th Regiment.*
Moody's (George V.) **Artillery.** See *Madison Artillery, ante.*
Moody's (Young M.) **Infantry.** See *Alabama Troops, Confederate, 43d Regiment.*
Mooney's (James) **Infantry.** See *Union Troops, Regulars, 19th Regiment, 1st Battalion.*

57 R R—VOL XXXII, PT III

Moore's (Edwin) **Infantry.** See *Missouri Troops, Union,* 21st *Regiment.*
Moore's (Jesse H.) **Infantry.** See *Illinois Troops,* 115th *Regiment.*
Moore's (Jonathan B.) **Infantry.** See *Wisconsin Troops,* 33d *Regiment.*
Moore's (Joseph) **Infantry.** See *Indiana Troops,* 58th *Regiment.*
Moore's (Timothy C.) **Infantry.** See *New Jersey Troops,* 34th *Regiment.*
Moorman's (George) **Cavalry.** See *Mississippi Troops, Confederate.*
Moreland's (J. S.) **Sharpshooters.** See *Alabama Troops, Confederate.*
Moreland's (M. D.) **Cavalry.** See *Alabama Troops, Confederate.*
Moreland's (W. S.) **Infantry.** See *Mobile Fire Battalion, ante.*
Morgan's (Otho H.) **Artillery.** See *Indiana Troops,* 7th *Battery.*
Morgan's (Thomas J.) **Infantry.** See *Union Troops, Colored,* 14th *Regiment.*
Morgan's (William H.) **Infantry.** See *Indiana Troops,* 25th *Regiment.*
Morrill's (John) **Infantry.** See *Illinois Troops,* 64th *Regiment.*
Morris' (B. T.) **Infantry.** See *North Carolina Troops, Confederate,* 64th *Regiment.*
Morris' (John I.) **Artillery.** See *Indiana Troops,* 20th *Battery.*
Morrison's (Alfred) **Artillery.** See *Indiana Troops,* 5th *Battery.*
Morse's (Francis W.) **Artillery.** See *Indiana Troops,* 14th *Battery.*
Morton's (George H.) **Cavalry.** See *C. R. Barteau's Cavalry, ante.*
Morton's (John W., jr.) **Artillery.** See *Tennessee Troops, Confederate.*
Moss' (James W.) **Infantry.** See *Kentucky Troops, Confederate,* 2d *Regiment.*
Mueller's (Alexander) **Cavalry.** See *Missouri Troops, Union,* 4th *Regiment.*
Muhlenberg's (Edward D.) **Artillery.** See *Union Troops, Regulars,* 4th *Regiment,* Battery F.
Mullins' (Mathew) **Infantry.** See *Kentucky Troops, Union,* 40th *Regiment.*
Murdoch's (R.) **Infantry.** See *North Carolina Troops, Confederate,* 58th *Regiment.*
Murphey's (Virgil S.) **Infantry.** See *Alabama Troops, Confederate,* 17th *Regiment.*
Murray's (Albert M.) **Artillery.** See *Union Troops, Regulars,* 2d *Regiment, Battery F.*
Murray's (Charles D.) **Infantry.** See *Indiana Troops,* 89th *Regiment.*
Murray's (John E.) **Infantry.** See *Arkansas Troops,* 5th and 13th *Regiments.*
Myers' (James H.) **Artillery.** See *Indiana Troops,* 23d *Battery.*
Nabers' (James F.) **Sharpshooters.** See *Alabama Troops, Confederate,* 17th *Battalion.*
Nale's (John H.) **Infantry.** See *Illinois Troops,* 41st *Regiment.*
Nall's (M. S.) **Infantry.** See *Georgia Troops,* 41st *Regiment.*
Nance's (James D.) **Infantry.** See *South Carolina Troops,* 3d *Regiment.*
Naval Works Infantry. See *Georgia Troops, Local Defense.*
Naylor's (William A.) **Artillery.** See *Indiana Troops,* 10th *Battery.*
Neal's (John R.) **Cavalry.** See *Tennessee Troops, Confederate,* 16th *Battalion.*
Neely's (James J.) **Cavalry.** See *Tennessee Troops, Confederate.*
Neff's (Andrew J.) **Infantry.** See *Indiana Troops,* 84th *Regiment.*
Neff's (Francis L.) **Infantry.** See *Indiana Troops,* 31st *Regiment.*
Nell's (George W.) **Artillery.** See *Kentucky Troops, Union, Battery B.*
Nelson's (N. L.) **Infantry.** See *Louisiana Troops,* 12th *Regiment.*
Nelson's (T. M.) **Cavalry.** See *Georgia Troops.*
Newlan's (Thomas) **Infantry.** See *Illinois Troops,* 58th *Regiment.*
Nicklin's (Benjamin S.) **Artillery.** See *Indiana Troops,* 13th *Battery.*
Nisbet's (J. Cooper) **Infantry.** See *Georgia Troops,* 66th *Regiment.*
Nisbet's (J. W.) **Infantry.** See *Georgia Troops,* 26th *Battalion.*
Nitschelm's (Charles F.) **Artillery.** See *Ohio Troops,* 20th *Battery.*
Nixon's (George H.) **Cavalry.** See *Tennessee Troops, Confederate;* also 48th *Regiment, Infantry.*
Noles' (L. L.) **Infantry.** See *Arkansas Troops,* 25th *Regiment.*
Nottoway Artillery. See *Virginia Troops.*
Noyes' (Edward F.) **Infantry.** See *Ohio Troops,* 39th *Regiment.*
Oates' (William C.) **Infantry.** See *Alabama Troops, Confederate,* 15th *Regiment.*
O'Brien's (William) **Infantry.** See *Indiana Troops,* 75th *Regiment.*

O'Connell's (Patrick) Pioneers. See *Union Troops, Pioneer Brigade, Pontoon Battalion.*

O'Hara's (Thomas) Cavalry. See *Illinois Troops,* 11*th Regiment.*

Oliver's (John M.) Infantry. See *Michigan Troops,* 15*th Regiment.*

Oliver's (McDonald) Artillery. See *Eufaula Artillery, ante.*

O'Neal's (Francis A.) Artillery. See *Alabama Troops, Confederate,* 20*th Battalion, Battery B.*

O'Neill's (John) Infantry. See *Tennessee Troops, Confederate,* 10*th Regiment.*

Opdycke's (Emerson) Infantry. See *Ohio Troops,* 125*th Regiment.*

Orcutt's (Benjamin F.) Infantry. See *Michigan Troops,* 25*th Regiment.*

Orleans Light Horse Cavalry. See *Louisiana Troops.*

Orr's (J. A.) Infantry. See *Mississippi Troops, Confederate,* 31*st Regiment.*

Osband's (Embury D.) Cavalry. See *Union Troops, Colored,* 3*d Regiment.*

Osborne's (Richard) Artillery. See *Illinois Troops,* 2*d Regiment, Battery F.*

Otey Artillery. See *Virginia Troops.*

Owen's (Alfred D.) Infantry. See *Indiana Troops,* 80*th Regiment.*

Owens' (James A.) Artillery. See *Arkansas Troops.*

Owens' (Robert A.) Infantry. See *Tennessee Troops, Confederate,* 46*th and* 55*th Regiments.*

Packer's (Warren W.) Infantry. See *Connecticut Troops,* 5*th Regiment.*

Paddock's (Byron D.) Artillery. See *Michigan Troops,* 1*st Regiment, Battery F.*

Palmer's (William J.) Cavalry. See *Pennsylvania Troops,* 15*th Regiment.*

Palmetto Battalion, Artillery. See *South Carolina Troops.*

Palmetto Sharpshooters, Infantry. See *South Carolina Troops.*

Pardee's (Ario, jr.) Infantry. See *Pennsylvania Troops,* 147*th Regiment.*

Pardue's (Lucien B.) Infantry. See *Mississippi Troops, Confederate,* 7*th Battalion.*

Park's (J. M.) Cavalry. See *Mississippi Troops, Confederate,* 1*st Regiment, Partisan Rangers.*

Park's (Josiah B.) Cavalry. See *Michigan Troops,* 4*th Regiment.*

Parker's (William) Infantry. See *Tennessee Troops, Confederate,* 60*th,* 61*st, and* 62*d Regiments.*

Parker's (William W.) Artillery. See *Virginia Troops.*

Parrish's (Charles S.) Infantry. See *Indiana Troops,* 130*th Regiment.*

Parrott's (James C.) Infantry. See *Iowa Troops,* 7*th Regiment.*

Parry's (Agustus C.) Infantry. See *Ohio Troops,* 47*th Regiment.*

Partenheimer's (Frederick) Infantry. See *Missouri Troops, Union,* 18*th Regiment.*

Patrick's (John H.) Infantry. See *Ohio Troops,* 5*th Regiment.*

Patrick's (Matthewson T.) Cavalry. See *Iowa Troops,* 5*th Regiment.*

Patterson's (Michael L.) Infantry. See *Tennessee Troops, Union,* 4*th Regiment.*

Patton's (Samuel K. N.) Cavalry. See *Tennessee Troops, Union,* 8*th Regiment.*

Pearce's (John S.) Infantry. See *Ohio Troops,* 98*th Regiment.*

Pearson's (Robert N.) Infantry. See *Illinois Troops,* 31*st Regiment.*

Peat's (Frank F.) Infantry. See *Illinois Troops,* 17*th Regiment.*

Peeples' (Tyler M.) Artillery. See *Georgia Troops,* 9*th Battalion, Battery D.*

Pelham Cadets, Infantry. See *Alabama Troops, Confederate.*

Perkins' (George T.) Infantry. See *Ohio Troops,* 105*th Regiment.*

Perry's (Thomas J.) Artillery. See *Marion Artillery, ante.*

Perry's (William F.) Infantry. See *Alabama Troops, Confederate,* 44*th Regiment.*

Peters' (John H.) Cavalry. See *Iowa Troops,* 4*th Regiment.*

Peters' (William E.) Cavalry, See *Virginia Troops,* 21*st Regiment.*

Pharr's (H. N.) Engineers. See *Confederate Troops, Regulars,* 3*d Regiment.*

Phelan's (John) Artillery. See *William H. Fowler's Artillery, ante.*

Phillips Legion. See *Georgia Troops.*

Pickands' (James) Infantry. See *Ohio Troops,* 124*th Regiment.*

Ping's (Thomas) Infantry. See *Iowa Troops,* 17*th Regiment.*

Pinson's (R. A.) Cavalry. See *Mississippi Troops, Confederate, 1st Regiment.*
Pointe Coupée Artillery. See *Louisiana Troops.*
Porter's (J. H.) Infantry. See *Georgia Troops, Local Defense.*
Post's (P. Sidney) Infantry. See *Illinois Troops, 59th Regiment.*
Pott's (Benjamin F.) Infantry. See *Ohio Troops, 32d Regiment.*
Powell's (Eugene) Infantry. See *Ohio Troops, 66th Regiment.*
Powell's (R. M.) Infantry. See *Texas Troops, 5th Regiment.*
Powers' (Frank P.) Cavalry. See *Louisiana Troops.*
Prather's (Allen W.) Infantry. See *Indiana Troops, 120th Regiment.*
Prather's (John S.) Cavalry. See *Confederate Troops, Regulars, 8th Regiment.*
Pratt's (William M.) Artillery. See *Union Troops, Colored, 2d Regiment, Battery B (D)*
Prentice's (Clarence J.) Cavalry. See *Confederate Troops, Regulars, 7th Battalion.*
Prescott's (Mark H.) Artillery. See *Illinois Troops, 1st Regiment, Battery C.*
Pressley's (James F.) Infantry. See *South Carolina Troops, 10th Regiment.*
Presstman's (S. W.) Engineers. See *Confederate Troops, Regulars, 3d Regiment.*
Preston's (Simon M.) Infantry. See *Union Troops, Colored, 58th Regiment.*
Price's (Samuel W.) Infantry. See *Kentucky Troops, Union, 21st Regiment.*
Proffitt's (Bacchus S.) Infantry. See *North Carolina Troops, Confederate, 29th Regiment.*
Prosser's (William F.) Cavalry. See *Tennessee Troops, Union, 2d Regiment.*
Pryor's (M. T.) Cavalry. See *Kentucky Troops, Confederate, 4th Regiment.*
Putnam's (Azro C.) Artillery. See *Edward C. Henshaw's Artillery, ante.*
Putnam's (James F.) Artillery. See *Ohio Troops, 8th Battery.*
Quin's (Josephus R.) Cavalry. See *Confederate Troops, Regulars, 14th Regiment.*
Rainey's (A. T.) Infantry. See *Texas Troops, 1st Regiment.*
Ramsey's (D. Breck.) Artillery. See *Gustave A. Huwald's Artillery, ante.*
Ramsey's (W. A.) Engineers. See *Confederate Troops, Regulars, 3d Regiment.*
Randall's (Charles B.) Infantry. See *New York Troops, 149th Regiment.*
Randals' (Benjamin) Infantry. See *Tennessee Troops, Confederate, 16th Regiment.*
Ranney's (Robert) Artillery. See *Union Troops, Colored, 2d Regiment, Battery A (C).*
Ransom's (Albert G.) Artillery. See *Ohio Troops, 1st Regiment, Battery E.*
Ratliff's (William T.) Artillery. See *Mississippi Troops, Confederate, 1st Regiment, Battery A.*
Raum's (W. C.) Cavalry. See *Mississippi Troops, Confederate.*
Redfield's (James) Infantry. See *Iowa Troops, 39th Regiment.*
Reed's (Joseph R.) Artillery. See *Iowa Troops, 2d Battery.*
Reeve's (Felix A.) Infantry. See *Tennessee Troops, Union, 8th Regiment.*
Reeves' (G. R.) Cavalry. See *Texas Troops, 11th Regiment.*
Reynolds' (Arthur E.) Infantry. See *Mississippi Troops, Confederate, 26th Regiment.*
Rheinlander's (John) Infantry. See *Indiana Troops, 25th Regiment.*
Rhett Artillery. See *Tennessee Troops, Confederate.*
Rhodes' (Hinman) Infantry. See *Illinois Troops, 28th Regiment.*
Rice's (Americus V.) Infantry. See *Ohio Troops, 57th Regiment.*
Rice's (Elliott W.) Infantry. See *Iowa Troops, 7th Regiment.*
Rice's (Horace) Infantry. See *Tennessee Troops, Confederate, 29th Regiment.*
Rice's (P. H.) Cavalry. See *Confederate Troops, Regulars, 3d Regiment.*
Rice's (T. W.) Heavy Artillery. See *Tennessee Troops, Confederate.*
Richards' (W. C.) Sharpshooters. See *Mississippi Troops, Confederate, 9th Battalion.*
Richards' (William, jr.) Infantry. See *Pennsylvania Troops, 29th Regiment.*
Richardson's (Robert V.) Cavalry. See *Tennessee Troops, Confederate.*
Rider's (Godfrey, jr.) Infantry. See *Massachusetts Troops, 33d Regiment.*
Riedt's (August) Infantry. See *Pennsylvania Troops, 27th Regiment.*
Riley's (A. C.) Infantry. See *Missouri Troops, Confederate, 1st and 4th Regiments.*
Ringgold Artillery. See *Virginia Troops.*

Rippetoe's (William B.) **Artillery.** See *Indiana Troops, 18th Battery.*
Risdon's (Orlando C.) **Infantry.** See *Union Troops, Colored, 53d Regiment.*
Roberts' (Aurelius) **Infantry.** See *Iowa Troops, 30th Regiment.*
Roberts' (Calvit) **Artillery.** See *Seven Stars Artillery, post.*
Roberts' (Calvit) **Cavalry.** See *George Moorman's Cavalry, ante.*
Robertson's (Jesse) **Artillery.** See *Illinois Troops, 2d Regiment, Battery C.*
Robie's (Oliver P.) **Cavalry.** See *Ohio Troops, 4th Regiment.*
Robinson's (George) **Artillery.** See *Michigan Troops, 1st Regiment, Battery C.*
Robinson's (George J.) **Artillery.** See *Chicago Board of Trade Artillery, ante.*
Robinson's (James S.) **Infantry.** See *Ohio Troops, 82d Regiment.*
Robinson's (Solomon S.) **Infantry.** See *Union Troops, Regulars, 16th Regiment, 2d Battalion.*
Robinson's (William P.) **Infantry.** See *Missouri Troops, Union, 23d Regiment.*
Robison's (William D.) **Infantry.** See *Tennessee Troops, Confederate, 2d Regiment, P. A.*
Robson's (W. G.) **Artillery.** See *Evan P. Howell's Artillery, ante.*
Roby's (Jacob W.) **Infantry.** See *Wisconsin Troops, 10th Regiment.*
Rodgers' (Benjamin F.) **Artillery.** See *Illinois Troops, 2d Regiment, Battery K.*
Rodney's (George B.) **Artillery.** See *Union Troops, Regulars, 4th Regiment, Battery H.*
Rogers' **Cavalry.** (Official designation not of record.) See *Captain Rogers.*
Rogers' (Andrew W.) **Infantry.** See *Illinois Troops, 81st Regiment.*
Rogers' (William A.) **Cavalry.** See *Mississippi Troops, Confederate, 2d Regiment.*
Rolshausen's (Ferdinand H.) **Infantry.** See *Illinois Troops, 82d Regiment.*
Rombauer's (Raphael G.) **Artillery.** See *Illinois Troops, 1st Regiment, Battery G.*
Roper's (Benjamin) **Infantry.** See *South Carolina Troops, 7th Regiment.*
Ross' (Peter F.) **Cavalry.** See *Texas Troops, 6th Regiment.*
Ross' (Samuel) **Infantry.** See *Connecticut Troops, 20th Regiment.*
Ross' (W. E.) **Infantry.** See *Mississippi Troops, Confederate, 39th Regiment.*
Rousseau's (Laurence H.) **Infantry.** See *Kentucky Troops, Union, 12th Regiment.*
Rowan's (John B.) **Artillery.** See *Stephens Light Artillery, post.*
Rowett's (Richard) **Infantry.** See *Illinois Troops, 7th Regiment.*
Rucker's (E. W.) **Cavalry Legion.** See *Tennessee Troops, Confederate, 12th and 16th Battalions.*
Rumsey's (Israel P.) **Artillery.** See *Illinois Troops, 1st Regiment, Battery B.*
Russell's (A. A.) **Cavalry.** See *Alabama Troops, Confederate, 4th Regiment.*
Russell's (R. M.) **Cavalry.** See *Tennessee Troops, Confederate.*
Samuels' (D. Todd) **Cavalry.** See *Missouri Troops, Confederate, 1st and 3d Regiments.*
Sanders' (C. F.) **Cavalry.** See *Buckner Guards, ante.*
Sanders' (C. H.) **Infantry.** See *Cobb's Legion, ante.*
Sanderson's (Thomas W.) **Cavalry.** See *Ohio Troops, 10th Regiment.*
Sanderson's (William L.) **Infantry.** See *Indiana Troops, 23d Regiment.*
Sanford's (John W. A.) **Infantry.** See *Alabama Troops, Confederate, 60th Regiment.*
Savage's (Edward G.) **Cavalry.** See *Pennsylvania Troops, 9th Regiment.*
Schaller's (Frank) **Infantry.** See *Mississippi Troops, Confederate, 22d Regiment.*
Schmitt's (William A.) **Infantry.** See *Illinois Troops, 27th Regiment.*
Schuetz's (John C.) **Artillery.** See *Michigan Troops, 1st Regiment, Battery K.*
Schultz's (Frederick) **Artillery.** See *Ohio Troops, 1st Regiment, Battery M.*
Scott's (E. A.) **Cavalry.** See *Louisiana Troops. 9th Battalion.*
Scott's (Jefferson K.) **Infantry.** See *Indiana Troops, 59th Regiment.*
Scott's (John) **Infantry.** See *Iowa Troops, 32d Regiment.*
Scott's (John S.) **Cavalry.** See *Louisiana Troops, 1st Regiment.*
Scranton's (Leonidas S.) **Cavalry.** See *Michigan Troops, 2d Regiment.*
Scribner's (Benjamin F.) **Infantry.** See *Indiana Troops, 38th Regiment.*
Scully's (James W.) **Infantry.** See *Tennessee Troops, Union, 10th Regiment.*

Seaman's (Francis) **Artillery.** See *Ohio Troops,* 10th *Battery.*
Searoy's (Anderson) **Infantry.** See *Tennessee Troops, Confederate,* 45th *Regiment;* also 23d *Battalion.*
Segebarth's (Pennsylvania) **Artillery.** See *Daniel P.' Walling's Artillery, post.*
Selfridge's (James L.) **Infantry.** See *Pennsylvania Troops,* 46th *Regiment.*
Semple's (Henry C.) **Artillery.** See *Alabama Troops, Confederate.*
Seven Stars Artillery. See *Mississippi Troops.*
Shaaff's (Arthur) **Sharpshooters.** See *Georgia Troops,* 1st *Battalion.*
Shacklett's (A. R.) **Infantry.** See *Kentucky Troops, Confederate,* 8th *Regiment.*
Shafer's (Henry W.) **Artillery.** See *Indiana Troops,* 24th *Battery.*
Shafter's (William R.) **Infantry.** See *Union Troops, Colored,* 17th *Regiment.*
Shanks' (John P. C.) **Cavalry.** See *Indiana Troops,* 7th *Regiment.*
Shannon's (H.) **Artillery.** See *Warren Light Artillery, post.*
Shannon's (Samuel E.) **Infantry.** See *Tennessee Troops, Confederate,* 24th *Regiment.*
Shaw's (Jo.) **Cavalry.** See *O. P. Hamilton's Cavalry, ante.*
Shaw's (Thomas P.) **Infantry.** See *South Carolina Troops,* 19th *Regiment.*
Sheffey's (John P.) **Cavalry.** See *Virginia Troops,* 8th *Regiment.*
Sheffield's (James L.) **Infantry.** See *Alabama Troops, Confederate,* 48th *Regiment.*
Shelley's (Charles M.) **Infantry.** See *Alabama Troops, Confederate,* 30th *Regiment.*
Shelley's (James T.) **Infantry.** See *Tennessee Troops, Union,* 5th *Regiment.*
Shields' (Joseph C.) **Artillery.** See *Ohio Troops,* 19th *Battery.*
Shields' (Thomas) **Infantry.** See *Louisiana Troops,* 30th *Regiment.*
Shy's (W. M.) **Infantry.** See *Tennessee Troops, Confederate,* 20th *Regiment.*
Simms' (James P.) **Infantry.** See *Georgia Troops,* 53d *Regiment.*
Simonson's (Peter) **Artillery.** See *Indiana Troops,* 5th *Battery.*
Sims' (John) **Infantry.** See *Mississippi Troops, Confederate,* 21st *Regiment.*
Sipes' (William B.) **Cavalry.** See *Pennsylvania Troops,* 7th *Regiment.*
Sirwell's (William) **Infantry.** See *Pennsylvania Troops,* 78th *Regiment.*
Skelton's (J. H.) **Infantry.** See *Georgia Troops,* 16th *Regiment.*
Slack's (James R.) **Infantry.** See *Indiana Troops,* 47th *Regiment.*
Slemons' (W. F.) **Cavalry.** See *Arkansas Troops,* 2d *Regiment.*
Slemp's (Campbell) **Infantry.** See *Virginia Troops,* 64th *Regiment.*
Slevin's (Patrick S.) **Infantry.** See *Ohio Troops,* 100th *Regiment.*
Slocomb's (C. H.) **Artillery.** See *Washington Artillery, post,* 5th *Battery.*
Smith's (Baxter) **Cavalry.** See *Tennessee Troops, Confederate.*
Smith's (F. C.) **Infantry.** See *Georgia Troops,* 24th *Regiment.*
Smith's (Frank G.) **Artillery.** See *Union Troops, Regulars,* 4th *Regiment, Battery I.*
Smith's (George A.) **Infantry.** See *Confederate Troops, Regulars,* 1st *Regiment.*
Smith's (George W.) **Infantry.** See *Union Troops, Regulars,* 18th *Regiment,* 1st *Battalion.*
Smith's (J. Albert) **Infantry.** See *North Carolina Troops, Union,* 2d *Regiment (mounted).*
Smith's (John D.) **Artillery.** See *Bedford Artillery, ante.*
Smith's (Joseph T.) **Infantry.** See *Georgia Troops,* 37th *Regiment.*
Smith's (Luther R.) **Artillery.** See *Michigan Troops,* 1st *Regiment, Battery I.*
Smith's (Milo) **Infantry.** See *Iowa Troops,* 26th *Regiment.*
Smith's (Orlow) **Infantry.** See *Ohio Troops,* 65th *Regiment.*
Smith's (Robert F.) **Infantry.** See *Illinois Troops,* 16th *Regiment.*
Smith's (Samuel G.) **Infantry.** See *Arkansas Troops,* 6th and 7th *Regiments.*
Smyth's (William) **Infantry.** See *Iowa Troops,* 31st *Regiment.*
Sneed's (J. W.) **Cavalry.** See *William L. Duckworth's Cavalry, ante.*
Snodgrass' (John) **Infantry.** See *Alabama Troops, Confederate,* 55th *Regiment.*
Snodgrass' (Robert B.) **Cavalry.** See *Alabama Troops, Confederate,* 24th *Battalion.*
Snyder's (Joshua M.) **Infantry.** See *Illinois Troops,* 83d *Regiment.*
Spaulding's (Oliver L.) **Infantry.** See *Michigan Troops,* 23d *Regiment.*
Spencer's (George E.) **Cavalry.** See *Alabama Troops, Union,* 1st *Regiment.*

Spencer's (George W.) **Artillery.** See *Illinois Troops, 1st Regiment, Battery M.*

Spicer's (Newell W.) **Infantry.** See *Kansas Troops, 1st Regiment.*

Spooner's (Benjamin J.) **Infantry.** See *Indiana Troops, 83d Regiment.*

Squires' (William H.) **Infantry.** See *Ohio Troops, 26th Regiment.*

Stackhouse's (E. T.) **Infantry.** See *South Carolina Troops, 8th Regiment.*

Stackhouse's (William P.) **Artillery.** See *Indiana Troops, 19th Battery.*

Stafford's (F. E. P.) **Infantry.** See *Tennessee Troops, Confederate, 31st and 33d Regiments.*

Stafford's (Joab A.) **Infantry.** See *Ohio Troops, 1st Regiment.*

Stallworth's (Nicholas) **Sharpshooters.** See *Alabama Troops, Confederate, 23d Battalion.*

Stambaugh's (Joseph W. R.) **Pioneers.** See *Union Troops, Pioneer Brigade, 2d Battalion.*

Stanford's (Thomas J.) **Artillery.** See *Mississippi Troops, Confederate.*

Stansel's (Martin L.) **Infantry.** See *Alabama Troops, Confederate, 41st Regiment.*

Stanton's (Sidney S.) **Infantry.** See *Tennessee Troops, Confederate, 28th Regiment.*

Starke's (Peter B.) **Cavalry.** See *Mississippi Troops, Confederate, 28th Regiment.*

Starling's (Edmund A.) **Infantry.** See *Kentucky Troops, Union, 35th Regiment.*

Steinhausen's (Albert von) **Infantry.** See *New York Troops, 68th Regiment.*

Stephens Light Artillery. See *Georgia Troops.*

Stephens' (M. D. L.) **Infantry.** See *Mississippi Troops, Confederate, 31st Regiment.*

Stephens' (Thomas) **Cavalry.** See *Wisconsin Troops, 2d Regiment.*

Stephenson's (Robert B.) **Infantry.** See *Wisconsin Troops, 31st Regiment.*

Sterl's (Oscar W.) **Infantry.** See *Ohio Troops, 104th Regiment.*

Sterling's (Robert) **Heavy Artillery.** See *Tennessee Troops, Confederate, 1st Regiment.*

Stewart's Battalion. (Official designation not of record.) See —— *Stewart.*

Stewart's (Francis M.) **Cavalry.** See *Tennessee Troops, Confederate.*

Stewart's (James W.) **Cavalry.** See *Indiana Troops, 2d Regiment.*

Stibbs' (John H.) **Infantry.** See *Iowa Troops, 12th Regiment.*

Stigler's (J. M.) **Sharpshooters.** See *Mississippi Troops, Confederate, 1st Battalion.*

Stiles' (Henry E.) **Artillery.** See *Wisconsin Troops, 8th Battery.*

Stiles' (Israel N.) **Infantry.** See *Indiana Troops, 63d Regiment.*

Stock's (Christian) **Artillery.** See *New York Troops, 1st Regiment, Battery I.*

Stockdale's (Thomas R.) **Cavalry.** See *Mississippi Troops, Confederate, 4th Regiment* (*Wilbourn's*).

Stockton's (Joseph) **Infantry.** See *Illinois Troops, 72d Regiment.*

Stokes' (William B.) **Cavalry.** See *Tennessee Troops, Union, 5th Regiment.*

Stone's (George A.) **Infantry.** See *Iowa Troops, 25th Regiment.*

Stone's (Robert G.) **Cavalry.** See *Kentucky Troops, Confederate, 9th Regiment.*

Stout's (Alexander M.) **Infantry.** See *Kentucky Troops, Union, 17th Regiment.*

Stratton's (Philos) **Infantry.** See *Kentucky Troops, Union, 49th Regiment.*

Street's (Ogden) **Infantry.** See *Ohio Troops, 11th Regiment.*

Strombaugh's (Solomon) **Artillery.** See *Tennessee Troops, Union, 1st Battalion, Battery D.*

Sudsburg's (Joseph M.) **Infantry.** See *Maryland Troops, 3d Regiment.*

Sullivan's (John) **Artillery.** See *Ohio Troops, 3d Battery.*

Suman's (Isaac C. B.) **Infantry.** See *Indiana Troops, 9th Regiment.*

Sutermeister's (Arnold) **Artillery.** See *Indiana Troops, 11th Battery.*

Swain's (Edgar D.) **Infantry.** See *Illinois Troops, 42d Regiment.*

Swanwick's (Francis) **Infantry.** See *Illinois Troops, 22d Regiment.*

Swayne's (Wager) **Infantry.** See *Ohio Troops, 43d Regiment.*

Sweeney's (James W.) **Cavalry.** See *Virginia Troops, 36th Battalion.*

Swett's (Charles) **Artillery.** See *Warren Light Artillery, post.*

Tarrant's (Edward) **Artillery.** See *Alabama Troops, Confederate.*

Taylor's (Jacob E.) **Infantry.** See *Ohio Troops, 40th Regiment.*

Taylor's (Marsh B.) Infantry.   See *Indiana Troops*, 10*th Regiment*.
Taylor's (Osmond B.) Artillery.   See *Virginia Troops*.
Tennessee First Heavy Artillery, A. D.   See *Union Troops, Colored*, 2*d* (3*d*) *Regiment*.
Tennessee Second Heavy Artillery, A. D.   See *Union Troops, Colored*, 3*d* (4*th*) *Regiment*.
Tennessee (Confederate) First Cavalry.   See *James E. Carter's Cavalry, ante·*
Tennessee (Confederate) First [Sixth] Cavalry.   See *James T. Wheeler's Cavalry, post*.
Tennessee (Confederate) First [Seventh] Cavalry.   See *William L. Duckworth's Cavalry, ante*.
Tennessee (Confederate) Second Cavalry.*   See *C. R. Barteau's Cavalry, ante*.
Tennessee (Confederate) Second Cavalry.†   See *H. M. Ashby's Cavalry, ante*.
Tennessee (Confederate) Fourth Cavalry.   See *William S. McLemore's Cavalry, ante*.
Tennessee (Confederate) Fourth [Eighth] Cavalry.   See *Baxter Smith's Cavalry, ante*.
Tennessee (Confederate) Fifth Cavalry.   See *George W. McKenzie's Cavalry, ante*.
Tennessee (Confederate) Eighth [Thirteenth] Cavalry.   See *George G. Dibrell's Cavalry, ante*.
Tennessee (Confederate) Ninth [Nineteenth] Cavalry.   See *Jacob B. Biffle's Cavalry, ante*.
Tennessee (Confederate) Tenth Cavalry.   See *Nicholas N. Cox's Cavalry, ante*.
Tennessee (Confederate) Eleventh Cavalry.   See *Daniel W. Holman's Cavalry, ante*.
Tennessee (Confederate) Twelfth Cavalry.   See *Robert V. Richardson's Cavalry, ante*.
Tennessee (Confederate) Thirteenth [Fourteenth] Cavalry.   See *James J. Neely's Cavalry, ante*.
Tennessee (Confederate) Fourteenth [Fifteenth] Cavalry.   See *Francis M. Stewart's Cavalry, ante*.
Tennessee (Confederate) Fifteenth [Twentieth] Cavalry.   See *R. M. Russell's Cavalry, ante*.
Tennessee (Confederate) Sixteenth Cavalry.   See *A. N. Wilson's Cavalry, post*.
Tennessee (West) First Infantry, A. D.   See *Union Troops, Colored*, 59*th Regiment*.
Tennessee (West) Second Infantry, A. D.   See *Union Troops, Colored*, 61*st Regiment*.
Tenney's (Marcus D.) Artillery.   See *Kansas Troops*, 1*st Battery*.
Thielemann's (Christian) Cavalry.   See *Illinois Troops*, 16*th Regiment*.
Thomas' (De Witt C.) Infantry.   See *Indiana Troops*, 93*d Regiment*.
Thomas' (William H.) Legion.   See *North Carolina Troops, Confederate*.
Thomasson's (Theodore S.) Artillery.   See *Kentucky Troops, Union, Battery A*.
Thompson's (Charles R.) Infantry.   See *Union Troops, Colored*, 12*th Regiment*.
Thompson's (R.) Cavalry.   See *Georgia Troops*, 3*d Regiment*.
Thompson's (Thomas W.) Infantry.   See *Kentucky Troops, Confederate*, 4*th Regiment*.
Thomson's (Thomas) Infantry.   See *South Carolina Troops*, 2*d Regiment, Rifles*.
Thornburgh's (Jacob M.) Cavalry.   See *Tennessee Troops, Union*, 4*th Regiment*.
Tiemeyer's (John H.) Artillery.   See *Missouri Troops, Union*, 1*st Regiment, Battery M*.
Tillman's (James D.) Infantry.   See *Tennessee Troops, Confederate*, 41*st Regiment*.
Tillson's (John) Infantry.   See *Illinois Troops*, 10*th Regiment*.
Tison's (W. H. H.) Infantry.   See *Mississippi Troops, Confederate*, 32*d Regiment*.
Tobin's (Thomas F.) Artillery.   See *Tennessee Troops, Confederate*.
Todd's (John B.) Artillery.   See *Alabama State Artillery, ante, Battery C*.
Topping's (E. Hibbard) Infantry.   See *Illinois Troops*, 110*th Regiment*.
Torrey's (William H.) Cavalry.   See *Wisconsin Troops*, 1*s. Regiment*.

---

* With Forrest's command.
† With Wheeler's command.

Tourtellotte's (John E.) Infantry. See *Minnesota Troops, 4th Regiment.*
Towers' (John R.) Infantry. See *Georgia Troops, 8th Regiment.*
Tracy's (Albert) Infantry. See *Union Troops, Regulars, 15th Regiment, 1st Battalion.*
Trigg's (Robert C.) Infantry. See *Virginia Troops, 54th Regiment.*
True's (Clinton J.) Infantry. See *Kentucky Troops, Union, 40th Regiment.*
Trumbull Guards, Infantry. See *Ohio Troops.*
Tullis' (James) Infantry. See *Iowa Troops, 3d Regiment.*
Turner's (James J.) Infantry. See *Tennessee Troops, Confederate, 30th Regiment.*
Turner's (William) Cavalry. See *Louisiana Troops, 9th Battalion.*
Turner's (William B.) Artillery. See *Mississippi Troops, Confederate.*
Turner's (William D.) **Heavy Artillery.** See *Union Troops, Colored, 6th (7th) Regiment.*
Utley's (William L.) Infantry. See *Wisconsin Troops, 22d Regiment.*
Van Beek's (George W.) Infantry. See *Missouri Troops, Union, 33d Regiment.*
Van Deusen's (Delos) Infantry. See *Missouri Troops, Union, 6th Regiment.*
Van Tassell's (Oscar) Infantry. See *Illinois Troops, 34th Regiment.*
Van Vleck's (Carter) Infantry. See *Illinois Troops, 78th Regiment.*
Van Voorhis' (Koert S.) Infantry. See *New York Troops, 137th Regiment.*
Vaught's (W. C. D.) Artillery. See *Washington Artillery, post, 5th Battery.*
Voelkner's (Louis) Artillery. See *Missouri Troops, Union, 2d Regiment, Battery F.*
Voorhies' (William M.) Infantry. See *Tennessee Troops, Confederate, 48th Regiment (Voorhies').*
Waddell's (James D.) Infantry. See *Georgia Troops, 20th Regiment.*
Wade's (Alfred B.) Infantry. See *Indiana Troops, 73d Regiment.*
Walker's (David N.) Artillery. See *Otey Artillery, ante.*
Walker's (Francis M.) Infantry. See *Tennessee Troops, Confederate, 19th Regiment.*
Walker's (Joseph) Infantry. See *Palmetto Sharpshooters, ante.*
Walker's (Moses B.) Infantry. See *Ohio Troops, 31st Regiment.*
Walker's (Thomas M.) Infantry. See *Pennsylvania Troops, 111th Regiment.*
Walker's (W. C.) Infantry. See *William H. Thomas' Legion, ante.*
Wall's (J. M.) Infantry. See *Tennessee Troops, Confederate, 15th and 37th Regiments.*
Wallace's (Martin M. R.) Cavalry. See *Illinois Troops, 4th Regiment.*
Wallace's (William) Infantry. See *Ohio Troops, 15th Regiment.*
Waller's (Thomas B.) Infantry. See *Kentucky Troops, Union, 20th Regiment.*
Walley's (James H.) Artillery. See *Ohio Troops, 21st Battery.*
Walling's (Daniel P.) Artillery. See *Missouri Troops, Union.*
Ward's (Durbin) Infantry. See *Ohio Troops, 17th Regiment.*
Ward's (John H.) Infantry. See *Kentucky Troops, Union, 27th Regiment.*
Ward's (John J.) Artillery. See *Alabama Troops, Confederate.*
Ward's (Lyman M.) Infantry. See *Wisconsin Troops, 14th Regiment.*
Ward's (William D.) Infantry. See *Indiana Troops, 37th Regiment.*
Warfield's (E.) Infantry. See *Arkansas Troops, 2d and 24th Regiments.*
Warner's (Darius B.) Infantry. See *Ohio Troops, 113th Regiment.*
Warner's (Lewis D.) Infantry.* See *Pennsylvania Troops, 73d Regiment.*
Warren Light Artillery. See *Mississippi Troops, Confederate.*
Warren's (William H.) Cavalry. See *Alabama Troops, Confederate.*
Washington Artillery. See *Louisiana Troops.*
Waters' (David D.) Artillery. See *Alabama Troops, Confederate.*
Waties' (John) Artillery. See *Palmetto Battalion Artillery, ante, Battery B.*
Watkins' (E. P.) Infantry. See *Georgia Troops, 56th Regiment.*
Watkins' (William M.) Infantry. See *Tennessee Troops, Confederate, 12th and 47th Regiments.*
Watters' (Z. L.) Infantry. See *Georgia Troops, 8th Battalion.*
Watts' (Elijah S.) Cavalry. See *Kentucky Troops, Union, 2d Regiment.*

---

* Temporarily commanding.

Waul's (T. N.) Legion. See *Texas Troops*.
Weatherford's (James W.) Cavalry. See *Kentucky Troops, Union, 13th Regiment*.
Weaver's (James A.) Cavalry. See *Texas Troops, 32d Regiment*.
Weaver's (James T.) Infantry. See *North Carolina Troops, Confederate, 60th Regiment*.
Webb's (Junius Y.) Cavalry. See *Louisiana Troops*.
Webber's (A. Watson) Infantry. See *Union Troops, Colored, 51st Regiment*.
Wehler's (Edward) Infantry. See *New York Troops, 178th Regiment*.
Weir's (John) Infantry. See *Mississippi Troops, Confederate, 5th Regiment*.
Welker's (Frederick) Artillery. See *Missouri Troops, Union, 1st Regiment, Battery H*.
Welles' (George E.) Infantry. See *Ohio Troops, 68th Regiment*.
Wells' (George W.) Mounted Rifles. See *Arkansas Troops, 1st Regiment, Rifles*.
Wells' (Joseph M.) Infantry. See *Mississippi Troops, Confederate, 23d Regiment*.
West's (Francis H.) Infantry. See *Wisconsin Troops, 31st Regiment*.
West's (Theodore S.) Infantry. See *Wisconsin Troops, 24th Regiment*.
Wharton's (Jack) Cavalry. See *Texas Troops, 6th Regiment*.
Wheeler's (James T.) Cavalry. See *Tennessee Troops, Confederate*.
Wheeler's (William) Artillery. See *New York Troops, 13th Battery*.
Wheeler's (William C.) Infantry. See *Indiana Troops, 81st Regiment*.
Whitaker's (Richard T.) Infantry. See *Kentucky Troops, Union, 6th Regiment*.
White's (B. F., jr.) Artillery. See *Tennessee Troops, Confederate*.
White's (John R.) Infantry. See *Tennessee Troops, Confederate, 53d Regiment*.
White's (John S.) Artillery. See *Wilder Artillery, post*.
White's (W. W.) Infantry. See *Georgia Troops, 7th Regiment*.
Whiteley's (Richard H.) Sharpshooters. See *Georgia Troops, 2d Battalion*.
Whitener's (B. M.) Infantry. See *South Carolina Troops, 3d Battalion*.
Whittemore's (Henry C.) Artillery. See *Illinois Troops, 2d Regiment, Battery H*.
Wiedrich's (Michael) Artillery. See *New York Troops, 1st Regiment, Battery I*.
Wiggins' (J. H.) Artillery. See *Arkansas Troops*.
Wilder Artillery. See *Indiana Troops*.
Wilder's (John T.) Infantry. See *Indiana Troops, 17th Regiment*.
Wiles' (Greenberry F.) Infantry. See *Ohio Troops, 78th Regiment*.
Wiles' (William M.) Infantry. See *Indiana Troops, 22d Regiment*.
Wilkes' (F. C.) Cavalry. See *Texas Troops, 24th and 25th Regiments*.
Wilkinson's (John C.) Infantry. See *Mississippi Troops, Confederate, 8th Regiment*.
Wilkinson's (William) Infantry. See *Michigan Troops, 9th Regiment*.
Wilkinson's (William T.) Infantry. See *Missouri Troops, Union, 30th Regiment*.
Willett's (Elbert D.) Infantry. See *Alabama Troops, Confederate, 40th Regiment*.
Williams' (J. Byrd) Infantry. See *Mississippi Troops, Confederate, 41st Regiment*.
Williams' (J. T.) Cavalry. See *Alabama Troops, Confederate*.
Williams' (Price, jr.) Infantry. See *Pelham Cadets, ante*.
Williams' (Robert, jr.) Infantry. See *Ohio Troops, 54th Regiment*.
Williamson's (James A.) Infantry. See *Iowa Troops, 4th Regiment*.
Williamson's (James A.) Mounted Rifles. See *Arkansas Troops, 2d Regiment, Rifles*.
Willis' (Leonidas) Cavalry. See *T. N. Waul's Legion, ante*.
Willison's (Asias) Infantry. See *Illinois Troops, 103d Regiment*.
Willits' (Henry J.) Artillery. See *Indiana Troops, 4th Battery*.
Wilson's (A. N.) Cavalry. See *Tennessee Troops, Confederate*.
Wilson's (Cyrus J.) Infantry. See *Kentucky Troops, Union, 26th Regiment*.
Wilson's (De Witt C.) Infantry. See *Union Troops, Colored, 47th Regiment*.
Wilson's (George) Infantry. See *Wisconsin Troops, 15th Regiment*.
Wilson's (John) Infantry. See *Kentucky Troops, Union, 8th Regiment*.
Wilson's (John W.) Infantry. See *Ohio Troops, 14th Regiment*.
Wimberly's (A. T.) Cavalry. (Official designation not of record.) See *A. T. Wimberly*.

Winkler's (Frederick C.) **Infantry.** See *Wisconsin Troops, 26th Regiment.*
Winn's (S. J.) **Cavalry.** See *Georgia Troops, 16th Battalion.*
Winn's (W. J.) **Infantry.** See *Georgia Troops, 25th Regiment.*
Winston's (Edward) **Engineers.** See *Confederate Troops, Regulars, 3d Regiment.*
Winston's (William C.) **Artillery.** See *Tennessee Troops, Confederate.*
Wisdom's (D. M.) **Cavalry.** See *Jeffrey E. Forrest's Cavalry, ante.*
Witcher's (Vinson A.) **Cavalry.** See *Virginia Troops, 34th Battalion.*
Withers' (William T.) **Artillery.** See *Mississippi Troops, Confederate, 1st Regiment.*
Witt's (H. H.) **Infantry.** See *Georgia Troops, Local Defense.*
Wolfe's (Edward H.) **Infantry.** See *Indiana Troops, 52d Regiment.*
Wolfley's (Lewis) **Cavalry.** See *Kentucky Troops, Union, 3d Regiment.*
Wolihin's (Andrew M.) **Artillery.** See *Georgia Troops, 9th Battalion, Battery C.*
Wood's (Andrew M.) **Artillery.** See *Elgin Artillery, ante.*
Wood's (Charles H.) **Infantry.** See *Ohio Troops, 51st Regiment.*
Wood's (Edward J.) **Infantry.** See *Indiana Troops, 48th Regiment.*
Wood's (Gustavus A.) **Infantry.** See *Indiana Troops, 15th Regiment.*
Wood's (Peter P.) **Artillery.** See *Illinois Troops, 1st Regiment, Battery A.*
Wood's (Robert C., jr.) **Cavalry.** See *Wirt Adams' Cavalry, ante.*
Wood's (William F.) **Infantry.** See *Union Troops, Colored, 46th Regiment.*
Woodbury's (John D.) **Artillery.** See *New York Troops, 1st Regiment, Battery M.*
Woods' (William B.) **Infantry.** See *Ohio Troops, 76th Regiment.*
Woodward's (Thomas G.) **Cavalry.** See *Kentucky Troops, Confederate, 2d Regiment.*
Woolfolk's (Pichegru, jr.) **Artillery.** See *Ashland Artillery, ante.*
Yates' (J. H.) **Artillery.** See *Mississippi Troops, Confederate, 1st Regiment, Battery B.*
Yeoman's (Samuel N.) **Infantry.** See *Ohio Troops, 90th Regiment.*
York's (Billington W.) **Artillery.** See *Georgia Troops, 9th Battalion, Battery E.*
York's (Harrison B.) **Artillery.** See *Ohio Troops, 9th Battery.*
Yorke's (P. Jones) **Cavalry.** See *New Jersey Troops, 2d Regiment.*
Yost's (Theobold D.) **Artillery.** See *Ohio Troops, 26th Battery.*
Young's (David R.) **Artillery.** See *Tennessee Troops, Union, 1st Battalion, Battery D.*
Young's (Jeremiah F.) **Cavalry.** See *Missouri Troops, Union, 10th Regiment.*
Young's (Thomas L.) **Infantry.** See *Ohio Troops, 118th Regiment.*
Young's (Vau E.) **Infantry.** See *Union Troops, Colored, 49th Regiment.*
Young's (William F.) **Infantry.** See *Tennessee Troops, Confederate, 49th Regiment.*
Young's (William H.) **Infantry.** See *Texas Troops, 9th Regiment.*
Zickerick's (William) **Artillery.** See *Wisconsin Troops, 12th Battery.*
Ziegler's (George M.) **Infantry.** See *Union Troops, Colored, 52d Regiment.*

INDEX.

Brigades, Divisions, Corps, Armies, and improvised organizations are "Mentioned" under name of commanding officer; State and other organizations under their official designation. (See Alternate Designations, pp. 881-907.)

* Formerly Ketchum's; also known as Battery A, Alabama State Artillery.
† Sometimes called 7th Regiment.

Page.

922 INDEX.

Page.

Dumonteil, F. .

Correspondence with Leonidas Polk -- 819

Mentioned -- 819, 820

Duncan, ——. Mentioned --- 36

Duncan, Captain. Mentioned --- 487

Duncan, E. A. Mentioned -- 509

Duncan, James R. Mentioned --- 705, 707

Duncan, John. Mentioned -- 625

Duncan, R. R. Mentioned -- 855

Duncan, William. Mentioned --- 555

Dunlap, Henry C. Mentioned --- 552

Dunlop, Isaac L. Mentioned --- 604, 659, 862

Dunlop, S. J. C. Mentioned --- 868

Dunn, David M. Mentioned --- 559

Dunwoody, James A. Mentioned --- 212, 560

Dustan, Charles W. For correspondence as A. A. G., see *Ralph P. Buckland.*

Duston, Daniel. Mentioned -- 556

Duxbury, W. C. Mentioned --- 576

Dwight, Augustus W. Mentioned --- 218

Dwight, Jarvis, jr. Mentioned -- 552

Dwyer, Patrick. Mentioned -- 572

Eakin, W. L. Mentioned --- 723, 846

Earle, R. G. Mentioned --- 605, 660, 864

Earnest, F. W.

Correspondence with James Longstreet ------------------------------------ 850

Mentioned --- 850, 851

Earp, C. R. Mentioned -- 604, 659, 863

Eastef, Joanna. Mentioned -- 149

Eastern Kentucky. Operations in, March 28–April 16, 1864. Communications from

Gallup, George W. --- 302, 353

Hobson, Edward H. --- 357–360, 393

True, Clinton J. -- 358

East Louisiana, District of. See *South Mississippi and East Louisiana, District of.*

Eastman, Harry E. Correspondence with James B. McPherson ------------- 59

Easton, Langdon C.

Correspondence with George H. Thomas ----------------------------------- 424

Mentioned --- 424, 548

East Tennessee.

Campaign in. Communications from James Longstreet ---------------------- 637

Relief of citizens of. Communication from War Department, U. S. -------- 8

East Tennessee, Army of. (Confederate.)

Orders, Circular, series 1864: **March 8**, 597.

Orders, General, series 1864—*Buckner:* **No. 1**, 774 ; **No. 3**, 775.

Orders, Special, series 1864—*Longstreet:* **No. 61**, 876. *Alexander:* **No. 10**, 879.

Organization, strength, etc.

March 31, 1864 -- 721–723

April 16, 1864 -- 845, 846

April 20, 1864 -- 802

April 30, 1864 -- 865

Proposed movement of. Communications from

Lee, Robert E --- 736

Longstreet, James --- 586–588, 590, 637, 641, 679, 798

Page.

Georgia.

Cobb, Howell, assigned to command of reserve troops in 719
Jackson, H. R., assigned to duty in 751
Georgia Troops. Mentioned.

Artillery, Light—*Battalions:* 9th (*Batteries*), A, B, C, D, E, 723. *Batteries:* Anderson's, 687, 708, 709, 731, 872; Cherokee, 687, 692, 693, 695, 731, 872; Columbus, 605, 660, 864; Ferrell's, 732, 742, 801, 872; Havis', 687, 708, 709, 731, 872; Howell's, 687, 693–695, 731, 871; Stephens Light, 687, 692, 693, 695, 731, 872.

Cavalry—*Battalions:* 16th, 149, 723, 802, 845, 846. *Companies:* Nelson's, 605. *Regiments:* 1st, 870; 2d, 870, 873; 3d, 870; 4th (*Avery's*), 870; 6th, 282, 870.

Infantry—*Battalions:* 1st Sharpshooters, 868; 2d Sharpshooters, 868; 3d Sharpshooters, 721; 4th Sharpshooters, 868; 8th, 26th, 868. *Regiments:* 1st (*State*), 282; 1st (*Volunteers*), 788; 2d, 722; 5th, 788, 868; 7th, 106, 722; 8th, 9th, 722; 10th, 721; 11th, 15th, 722; 16th, 721; 17th, 722; 18th, 721; 20th, 722; 24th, 721; 25th, 29th, 30th, 868; 34th, 36th, 869; 37th, 868; 39th, 869; 40th, 41st, 42d, 43d, 870; 46th, 868; 47th, 788, 868; 50th, 51st, 721; 52d, 870; 53d, 721; 54th, 55th, 788; 56th, 869; 57th, 788; 59th, 722; 63d, 838; 65th, 66th, 868.

Local Defense.

Artillery, Light—*Batteries:* Atlanta Arsenal, 629, 740.
Cavalry—*Companies:* Alexander's, 629, 740.
Infantry—*Battalions:* Arsenal, 629, 740. *Companies:* Baird's, 629, 740; Hull's, 629, 740; Jackson's, 629, 740; Naval Works, 629, 630, 740; Porter's, 629, 740; Witt's, 629, 740.
Miscellaneous—Cobb's Legion, 721; Phillips Legion, 721; Davenport's Home Guards, 324.

Gholson, Samuel J.
Correspondence with
Mississippi, Governor of 652
Polk, Leonidas 761, 784, 834
Mentioned 617, 650, 651, 790, 797, 837
Gibbons, William H.
Correspondence with
Cole, A. H 772
Quartermaster-General's Office, C. S. A 794
Mentioned 794
Gibson, A. C. Mentioned 120, 775
Gibson, Charles. Mentioned 734
Gibson, Horatio G.
Correspondence with Stephen G. Burbridge..................... 186
Mentioned 209, 573
Gibson, Randall L. Mentioned 870
Gibson, R. T. Mentioned 690, 692
Gibson, William H. Mentioned 552
Giesy, Henry H. Mentioned 563
Gifford, Ira R. Mentioned 236
Gilbert, Henry C. Mentioned 556
Gilbert, James I. Mentioned 565
Gilbreth, Frederick W. For correspondence as A. A. D. C., see *Oliver O. Howard.*
Gilchrist, Charles A. Mentioned 565
Gile, David H. Mentioned 509

Page.

Hurlbut, Stephen A.—Continued.

Mentioned 35, 40, 50, 56, 57, 63, 67, 71,
 72, 103–105, 166, 167, 189, 195, 203, 210, 221, 227, 228, 230, 231, 233, 244, 245,
 248, 250, 252–254, 273, 275–278, 285, 288, 297, 298, 300, 304, 305, 309, 310, 316,
 317, 322. 323, 325, 328, 335, 362, 366, 367, 378, 382, 387, 395, 397, 402–406, 415,
 417, 419, 420, 422, 428, 431, 432, 437–440, 442, 443, 448–450, 452, 453, 462, 468,
 478, 482, 485, 501, 502, 517–519, 534, 546, 547, 561, 564, 577, 630, 631, 650, 732

Relieved from command of District of West Tennessee 397

Request of, for court of inquiry in relation to Forrest's expedition into
 West Tennessee 405

Hurst, Fielding.

Correspondence with Benjamin H. Grierson 116, 145, 235

Demand for surrender of. Communications from Nathan B. Forrest..... 117, 119

Mentioned 116–119, 132, 169, 196, 205, 566, 609, 663–665, 733

Hurt, John S. Mentioned 436, 571

Hutchins, N. L. Mentioned 721

Hutchins, Rue P. Mentioned 553

Hutchinson, L. Mentioned 661

Hutchinson, William W. Mentioned....................................... 436

Illinois, Steamer. Mentioned... 760

Illinois, Governor of. Correspondence with James B. McPherson 65

Illinois Troops. Mentioned.

 Artillery, Light—*Batteries:* Bridges', 211, 552; Chicago Board of Trade,
 213, 238, 557; Colvin's, 571; Elgin, 571; Henshaw's, 89, 321, 572. *Regiments:* 1st (*Batteries*), **A, B,** 562; **C,** 211, 553; **D,** 260, 568; **E,** 36, 565; **F,**
 563; **G,** 566; **H,** 562; **M,** 211, 552; 2d (*Batteries*), **B,** 565; **C,** 212, 560; **D,**
 564; **F,** 569; **G,** 566; **H,** 212, 560; **I,** 211, 554; **K,** 568; **L,** 260, 567.

 Cavalry—*Regiments:* **1st,** 529; **2d,** 205; **3d,** 204, 205, 528; **4th,** 568; **5th,**
 239, 567; **6th, 7th,** 204, 528; **9th,** 528, 529; **11th,** 567, 569; **13th,** 396;
 14th, 17, 303, 321, 572; **15th,** 555; **16th,** 303, 573.

 Infantry—*Regiments:* **7th,** 103, 125, 126, 141, 266, 309, 349, 389, 390, 442, 525,
 526, 535, 564, 830; **9th,** 356, 357, 459, 525, 526, 564; **10th,** 553; **11th,** 65, 260,
 567; **12th,** 123, 124, 564; **13th,** 524; **14th,** 260, 487; **15th,** 260; **16th,**
 553; **17th,** 259, 394, 567; **19th,** 553; **20th,** 65, 516, 568; **21st,** 551; **22d,**
 552; **24th,** 553; **25th,** 552; **26th,** 563; **27th,** 552; **28th, 29th,** 65, 568;
 30th, 65, 478, 487; **31st,** 65, 516, 568; **32d,** 65, 569; **34th,** 553; **35th,** 45,
 75, 552; **36th,** 551; **37th,** 216; **38th,** 551; **40th,** 189, 563; **41st,** 236, 260,
 569; **42d,** 552; **44th,** 551; **45th,** 65, 516, 568; **46th,** 65, 260, 567; **47th,**
 565; **48th,** 563; **49th,** 565; **50th,** 192, 312, 564; **51st,** 552; **52d,** 116, 123,
 564; **53d,** 65, 569; **54th,** 178, 190, 236; **55th,** 562; **56th,** 563; **57th,** 564;
 58th, 565; **59th,** 551; **60th,** 553; **63d,** 563; **64th,** 564; **65th,** 109, 121, 136,
 137, 139, 321, 436; **66th,** 564; **72d,** 191, 260, 567; **73d,** 551; **74th, 75th,** 551;
 76th, 260, 567; **78th,** 553; **79th,** 562; **80th,** 551; **81st,** 260, 516, 567; **82d,**
 365, 555; **83d,** 365, 458, 472, 560; **84th,** 551; **85th, 86th,** 554; **88th,** 551;
 89th, 552; **90th,** 563; **92d,** 238, 256, 558; **93d,** 563; **95th,** 260, 516, 567;
 96th, 551; **98th,** 238, 256, 557, 560; **100th,** 551; **101st,** 365, 555; **102d,**
 364, 556; **103d,** 485, 563; **104th,** 553; **105th,** 364, 556; **107th,** 320, 571;
 108th, 566; **110th,** 554; **111th,** 562; **112th,** 293, 321, 338, 350, 436; **113th,**
 566; **114th,** 565; **115th,** 551; **116th,** 562; **117th, 119th,** 565; **120th,**
 122d, 566; **123d,** 238, 256, 557; **124th,** 260, 567; **125th,** 554; **127th,** 562;
 129th, 364, 556.

Immell, Lorenzo D. Mentioned 211, 559

---

* Formerly 39th Indiana Infantry.

* Sometimes called 1st Battalion.

---

*Also called 10th Mounted Rifles; finally 13th Kentucky Cavalry.

---

* Composed of Louisiana and Mississippi troops.

Page.

* Also called 12th Battalion.

Page.

Negroes.

62 R R—VOL XXXII, PT III

Page.

Page.

Page.

*Also called 1st Regular Infantry.

---

* Formerly Starnes'.

---

* Also called 1st Texas Legion.

* Final designation 11th U. S. C. T. (new). † Consolidated. ‡ Department of the Cumberland.

○